NINTH EDITION

WRIGHTSMAN'S
PSYCHOLOGY
AND THE LEGAL SYSTEM

EDIE GREENE
University of Colorado Colorado Springs

KIRK HEILBRUN
Drexel University

 CENGAGE

Australia • Brazil • Mexico • Singapore • United Kingdom • United States

Wrightsman's Psychology and The Legal System, Ninth Edition

Edie Greene and Kirk Heilbrun

Product Director: Marta Lee-Perriard

Product Team Manager: Star M. Burruto

Product Manager: Erin Schnair

Content Developer: Tangelique Williams-Grayer

Product Assistant: Leah Jenson

Marketing Manager: Adrienne McCrory

Content Project Manager: Jim Zayicek

Production Service/Composition: Lumina Datamatics Inc.

Senior. Art Director: Vernon Boes

Text and Cover Designer: Liz Harasymczuk

Cover Image: stockdevil/iStock/Getty Images

For product information and technology assistance, contact us at **Cengage Customer & Sales Support, 1-800-354-9706.**

For permission to use material from this text or product, submit all requests online at **www.cengage.com/permissions**. Further permissions questions can be e-mailed to **permissionrequest@cengage.com.**

Library of Congress Control Number: 2017963506

ISBN: 978-1-337-57087-9

Cengage
20 Channel Center Street
Boston, MA 02210
USA

Cengage is a leading provider of customized learning solutions with employees residing in nearly 40 different countries and sales in more than 125 countries around the world. Find your local representative at **www.cengage.com**.

Cengage products are represented in Canada by Nelson Education, Ltd.

To learn more about Cengage platforms and services, visit **www.cengage.com**. To register or access your online learning solution or purchase materials for your course, visit **www.cengagebrain.com**.

Printed in the United States of America
Print Number: 01   Print Year: 2018

Dedications
To my siblings
Richard, Nancy, and Jim
How fortunate we are
-EG

To Olivia Marian Catizone
Long may you run
-KH

Brief Contents

Contents

Preface

This is the 9th edition of *Psychology and the Legal System*. Its longevity is a testament to the incisive, rigorous, and accessible presentation of various aspects of psychology and law originally provided by Lawrence Wrightsman in the 1st edition, published more than 30 years ago. Professor Wrightsman's name is included in the title to honor his many contributions to this book and to the field of psychology and law. As with two previous editions, we—Edie Greene and Kirk Heilbrun—are the sole authors.

We continue to believe that the law is inherently psychological. It is made by people with varying desires and ambitions, interpreted by individuals with different (sometimes contradictory) perspectives, and experienced—either directly or indirectly—by all of us. Both psychology and the law are about motivation and behavior. Indeed, for centuries the legal system has been a powerful influence on people's everyday activities. From the Supreme Court's 1954 school desegregation decision to its 2014 case concerning application of the death penalty to people with intellectual disabilities, both of which are described in this book, the courts have had considerable impact on individual lives.

As we move toward the third decade of the 21st century, we find it ever more useful to describe the law from the perspective of psychology, a behavioral science that also has a significant applied component. We are not alone. In fact, matters of law and psychology are often cited in the media. Whether they involve concerns about excessive use of force by police, partisanship in judicial elections, the impact of trauma on human behavior, or the role of extremist ideology and beliefs in fostering violence, headlines and lead stories are often about some aspect of psychology and law. Although this attention appears to cater to an almost insatiable curiosity about crime and other types of legal disputes, it also promotes some ambivalence about the law. Many citizens are suspicious of the police, but police are still the first responders in a crisis. Juries are sometimes criticized for their decisions, but most litigants would prefer to have their cases decided by juries rather than judges. Citizens value their constitutionally protected rights, but also demand security in a post-9/11 era. This 9th edition explores these tensions as well as many other captivating and controversial issues that arise at the crossroads of psychology and the law.

The primary audiences for *Psychology and the Legal System* are students taking a course in psychology and the law, forensic psychology, or the criminal justice system, and others who seek to learn more about the legally relevant science and practice of psychology. This book (and its individual chapters) may also be used as a supplement in psychology courses that emphasize applied psychology, social issues, or policy analysis. In addition, it covers a number of topics relevant to law school courses that introduce law students to social science research findings and applications.

We have attempted to find the right mix of psychology and legal analysis in the text. The book's emphasis remains on psychological science and practice, but we also summarize the legal history of many key topics and present the current status of relevant legal theories and court decisions. Specific recent topics that are covered in some detail in this edition include assessing the risk of terrorist acts based on ideologies and affiliations, the uptick in mass shootings, sexual harassment in the workplace, the toll of legal education on students' well-being, and how psychology has contributed to criminal profiling.

We continue to focus on the psychological dimensions of several topics that remain important in contemporary society, just as they were important when previous editions of this text were written. These include how attributions about the causes of behavior affect judgments of offenders and victims, lawyers' and judges' use of intuitive cognitive mechanisms to evaluate cases and make decisions, the association between beliefs about procedural fairness and people's willingness to obey the law, clinicians' assessments of competence in various domains, and racial influences on police, jury, and judicial decision-making. As in previous editions, we have updated each of these topics using the best available scientific evidence published since our most recent edition went to press.

NEW FEATURES AND REVISIONS

We have made the following major changes from the last edition:

- We strived to make *Psychology and the Legal System* more user friendly by providing current examples to illustrate the material in a straightforward and accessible way.
- We added new material on important alternatives to traditional prosecutions, namely, problem-solving courts that enable drug abusers, people suffering from mental illnesses, and veterans involved in the criminal justice system to receive structured treatments to address the underlying source of dysfunction.
- We provided several new real-world examples in boxes ("The Case of…"). These summaries describe scenarios and cases that illustrate or explain an important legal concept or psychological principle covered in the chapter. Readers will be familiar with many recent examples including clashes between white supremacists and others at the Unite the Right rally in Charlottesville, the shooting deaths of nine parishioners in Charleston, the false guilty plea that upended the career of football star Brian Banks, and the sexual assault trial of Bill Cosby. We also feature the historic cases of Ernest Miranda, Clarence Gideon, John Hinckley, Ted Bundy, and others. A few cases are either fictional (such as Dexter Morgan from the popular television series *Dexter*) or composites, but still highly applicable to the chapter material.
- We updated examples of the themes, introduced in Chapter 1, that pervade a psychological analysis of the law. These include the rights of individuals versus the common good; equality versus discretion as ideals that can guide the legal system; discovering the truth or resolving conflicts as the goals that the legal system strives to accomplish; and science versus the law as a source of legal decisions. Elsewhere (Greene & Heilbrun, 2016), we have noted that these themes continue to unify many of the research findings, policy choices, and judicial decisions detailed in the book and we return to them at several points in the text.
- This edition includes a thorough, authoritative revision of every chapter in light of research and professional literature published since the last edition. Highlights include the following:
- Chapter 1 provides an overview of the field and details the many roles that psychologists can play in the legal system.
- Chapter 2 includes new data on the well-being of law students and the professional satisfaction of practicing lawyers.
- Chapter 4, on the psychology of police, includes new material on the excessive use of force in police encounters with minority citizens, attempts to improve police-community relations, and recommendations from President Obama's Task Force on the Future of Policing in the 21st Century. They include practices that reduce crime, build public trust, and ensure officer wellness and safety.
- Chapter 5 updates the reforms to lineup procedures in cases involving eyewitness identification based on recent scientific data on eyewitness memory.
- Chapter 6 covers the psychology of victims of crime and violence. It updates research on the relationship between trauma, adverse experiences, and crime, as well as rape-supportive attitudes that include acceptance of rape myths, adversarial sexual beliefs, and hostile attitudes toward women. It notes that rape is a severe trauma that can lead to PTSD symptoms.
- Chapter 7, on the evaluation of criminal suspects, includes discussion of new techniques for detecting deception based on principles of cognitive psychology. It also describes how interrogation procedures are being reformed in light of psychological research on social influence factors.
- Chapter 8 provides new data on the effectiveness of various high-tech tools used during trials, including videoconferencing, animations, and virtual reality.
- Chapter 10 describes updates on forensic assessment in criminal cases, and Chapter 11 does the same for civil cases.
- Chapter 12 describes the complexity of jury selection in a location saturated with publicity about the crime. The case of Boston Marathon bomber, Dzhokhar Tsarnaev, serves as an example.
- Chapter 13 expands the discussion of juries in the previous chapter to cover their decision-making. We reorganized it to focus on jurors' reliance on relevant evidence, evaluated through the lens of their emotions. It includes updated information on their ability to understand and apply judicial instructions and on jury deliberations.
- Chapter 14 describes recent data on death-qualification in capital trials, a process whereby those with scruples against the death penalty are eliminated from the jury. The new research raises concerns about representativeness of the juries that decide capital cases.

MindTap for Greene and Heilbrun's *Wrightsman's Psychology and the Legal System*

MindTap is a personalized teaching experience with relevant assignments that guide students to analyze, apply, and improve thinking, allowing you to measure skills and outcomes with ease.

- Guide Students: A unique learning path of relevant readings, media, and activities that moves students up the learning taxonomy from basic knowledge and comprehension to analysis and application.
- Personalized Teaching: Becomes yours with a Learning Path that is built with key student objectives. Control what students see and when they see it. Use it as-is or match to your syllabus exactly—hide, rearrange, add, and create your own content.
- Promote Better Outcomes: Empower instructors and motivate students with analytics and reports that provide a snapshot of class progress, time in course, engagement, and completion rates.

In addition to the benefits of the platform, MindTap for *Wrightsman's Psychology and the Legal System* provides helpful assignments and activities, including section quizzes and chapter tests, as well as appendices— the Ethical Principles of Psychologists and Code of Conduct and the Specialty Guidelines for Forensic Psychology, both of which provide ethical guidance for practice and research in forensic psychology, as well as the Bill of Rights, which describes the amendments to the U.S. Constitution.

Acknowledgments

For assistance in preparing this edition, we thank the Cengage staff: Erin Schnair, Product Manager; Leah Jenson, Product Assistant; Star Burruto, Product Team Manager; Tangelique Williams-Grayer, Content Developer; and James Zayicek, Project Manager. Each was extremely helpful in writing the 9th edition of *Psychology and the Legal System*.

Supplements

Instructor Resource Center. Everything you need for your course in one place! This collection of book-specific lecture and class tools is available online via www.cengage.com/login. Access and download PowerPoint presentations, images, instructor's manual, and more.

Cognero. Cengage Learning Testing Powered by Cognero is a flexible, online system that allows you to author, edit, and manage test bank content from multiple Cengage Learning solutions, create multiple test versions in an instant, and deliver tests from your LMS, your classroom, or wherever you want.

Instructor's Manual. The Online Instructor's Manual contains chapter outlines and summaries, discussion questions, suggested videos, readings, websites, and YouTube videos, and class activities.

PowerPoint. The Online PowerPoints feature lecture outlines and important images from *Wrightsman's Psychology and the Legal System,* 9th edition.

Rebecca Siegel

Edie Greene is currently professor at Department of Psychology, University of Colorado Colorado Springs, where she also serves as director of the graduate concentration in psychology and law and director of the undergraduate honors program. She earned her Ph.D. in cognitive psychology and law at the University of Washington in 1983 and served there as postdoctoral research associate between 1983 and 1986. From 1994 to 1995, Greene was a fellow in Law and Psychology at Harvard Law School. She has received several federally funded grants to support her research on legal decision-making, eyewitness memory, and psycholegal aspects of aging. Greene received a college-wide award for Outstanding Research and Creative Works in 1999, a university-wide award for Excellence in Research in 2001, and the Chancellor's Award for Distinguished Faculty in 2009. She has been invited to lecture at the National Judicial College and at continuing legal education programs nationwide. She consults with lawyers on various trial-related issues including jury selection, trial strategies, and jury decisions, and has, on numerous occasions, testified as an expert witness on jury behavior and eyewitness memory. In addition to serving as coauthor of the 5th to 8th editions of *Psychology and the Legal System*, Greene is the author of a number of articles, columns, and book chapters, and cosigner on several *amicus* briefs presented to the U.S. Supreme Court. She also coauthored *The Adversary System* (with Frank Strier, 1990), *Determining Damages: The Psychology of Jury Awards* (with Brian Bornstein, 2003), and *The Jury under Fire: Myth, Controversy, and Reform* (with Brian Bornstein, 2017). She has served as President of the American Psychology-Law Society/APA Division 41 and, in 2008, received the Award for Outstanding Teaching and Mentoring from that Society.

Anna Heilbrun

Kirk Heilbrun is currently professor at Department of Psychology, Drexel University. He received his doctorate in clinical psychology in 1980 from the University of Texas at Austin, and completed postdoctoral fellowship training from 1981 to 1982 in psychology and criminal justice at Florida State University. His current research focuses on juvenile and adult offenders, legal decision-making, and forensic evaluation associated with such decision-making, as well as reentry and the diversion of individuals with behavioral health problems from standard prosecution. He is the author of a number of articles on forensic assessment, violence risk assessment and risk communication, and the diversion and treatment of mentally disordered offenders. In addition to serving as coauthor for the 6th to 8th editions of *Psychology and the Legal System*, he has published 10 other books on topics including forensic mental health assessment, juvenile delinquency, violence risk assessment, the Sequential Intercept Model, evaluating juvenile transfer, and forensic ethics. His practice interests also center around forensic assessment, and he directs a clinic within the department in this area, as well as a reentry project for the assessment and treatment of individuals returning to the community from federal prison. He is board certified in clinical psychology and in forensic psychology by the American Board of Professional Psychology, and has previously served as president of both the American Psychology-Law Psychology/ APA Division 41, and the American Board of Forensic Psychology. He received the 2004 Distinguished Contributions to Forensic Psychology award and the 2008 Beth Clark Distinguished Service award from the American Academy of Forensic Psychology, and the 2016 Distinguished Contributions to Psychology and Law award from the American Psychology-Law Society.

1 Psychology and the Law: Choices and Roles

ORIENTING QUESTIONS

1. Why do we have laws, and what is the psychological approach to studying law?

2. What choices are reflected in the psychological approach to the law?

3. How do laws reflect the contrast between due process and crime control in the criminal justice system?

4. What are five roles that psychologists may play in the legal system and what does each entail?

Consider the following stories, all of which were prominently featured in the news:

■ In a case that elevated debate about police shootings of African American citizens, a Minnesota jury had to decide whether Officer Jeronimo Yanez reasonably believed that Philando Castile was reaching for a gun when he was pulled over while driving. Among the rash of police shootings and indictments of police officers in recent years, this case was remarkable because Castile's girlfriend live-streamed and narrated the bloody scene as it unfolded. Yet the outcome was familiar: Like many other officers charged with shooting Black citizens, Yanez was acquitted.

■ A Denver radio host sued Taylor Swift for $3 million after she accused him of groping her during a routine meet-and-greet. But the pop star turned the tables by countersuing for $1, which removed any suspicion of personal gain and provided an opportunity, as she said, to be an example to other women who have endured similar humiliating acts. The jury's verdict? $1 to Taylor Swift.

■ A drunken driver who killed a 10-year-old boy in suburban Dallas was sentenced to spend 180 days in jail over the next 10 years, including every Christmas Day, New Year's Day, and June 8, the child's birthday. The judge said he wanted to remind the defendant of the family's loss on these important family holidays.

These stories illustrate a few of the psycho-legal topics that we consider in this book: police–community relations and discrimination, the motivations of offenders and victims, discretion in judges' sentencing decisions, and public perceptions of security and law enforcement officials. They show the real flesh and blood of some of the psychological issues that arise in the law. ●

The Importance of Laws

These examples also illustrate the pervasiveness of the law in our society. But how does the law work? This book will help you understand how the legal system operates by applying psychological concepts, theories, findings, and methods to its study.

Laws as Human Creations

Laws are everywhere. They affect everything from birth to death. Laws regulate our private lives and our public actions. Laws dictate how long we must stay in school, how fast we can drive, when (and, to some extent, whom) we can marry, and whether we are allowed to play our car stereos at full blast or let our boisterous dog romp through the neighbors' yards and gardens. Given that the body of laws has such a widespread impact, we might expect that the law is a part of nature, that it was originally discovered by a set of archaeologists or explorers. Perhaps we think of Moses carrying the Ten Commandments down from the mountain.

But our laws are not chiseled in stone. Rather, laws are human creations that evolve out of the needs for order and consistency. To be responsive to a constantly changing society, our laws must also change. As some become outdated, others take their place. For example, before there were shootings on school grounds, no laws forbade the presence of weapons in schools. But after a series of deadly incidents, laws that banned weapons from school property were widely established. On occasion, the reach of these zero-tolerance policies has been excessive, as Zachary Christie, a Delaware first grader learned. Zachary was suspended and ordered to enroll in an alternative program for troubled youths because he took to school a Cub Scout utensil that included a small, folding knife. When this sort of overreaching occurs, the public reacts, and the policies are revised again.

Laws Help Resolve Conflict and Protect the Public

Many standards of acceptable behavior—not purposely touching strangers on elevators, for example—seem universally supported. But in some situations, people have differences of opinion about what is considered appropriate, and disagreements result. When this occurs, society must have mechanisms to resolve the disagreements. Thus, societies develop laws and regulations to function as conflict resolution mechanisms. Customs and rules of conduct evolve partly to deal with the conflict between one person's impulses and desires and other people's rights. Similarly, laws are developed to manage and resolve those conflicts that cannot be prevented.

Public safety is always an important consideration in a civilized society. In earlier times, before laws were established to deter and punish unacceptable behavior, people "took the law" into their own hands, acting as vigilantes to secure the peace and impose punishment on offenders. Now, at least in the United States and most other nations, all governmental entities—federal, state, county, borough, municipality, and even some neighborhoods— have enacted laws to protect the public.

The Changing of Laws

The basic raw material for the construction and the revision of laws is human experience. As our experiences and opportunities change, laws must be developed, interpreted, reinterpreted, and modified to keep up with these rapid changes in our lives. As George Will put it, "Fitting the law to a technologically dynamic society often is like fitting trousers to a 10-year-old: Adjustments are constantly needed" (1984, p. 6).

The framers of the U.S. Constitution, and even legislators of 30 years ago, never anticipated how laws have changed and will continue to change. They probably never contemplated the possibility that advances in neuroscience, for example, would affect how police investigate cases, attorneys represent their clients, and juries and judges make decisions. But brain imaging technology is now used to detect brain injuries and assess pain in those involved in accidents, determine mental state and capacity for rational thought in justice-involved individuals, and detect lies and deception in those under interrogation. Although the correspondence between brain activity and behavior is far from clear at this point, neuroimaging will

undoubtedly raise thorny questions for the legal system. New rules, policies, and laws will have to be created to address them.

Similarly, no one could have anticipated the ways that DNA testing would change laws involving criminal investigations. Legislatures have passed statutes that mandate the collection of DNA samples from millions of Americans, including those who have simply been arrested and are awaiting trial. Some of these individuals have objected to having their DNA collected and catalogued. But law enforcement officials claim that widespread testing will help them solve more crimes and exonerate people who were wrongly convicted. (We describe the role of DNA analysis in the exoneration of convicted criminals in Chapter 5.)

Legislators must now consider what, if any, restrictions should be placed on online activities. (Cyber-law, virtually unheard of 30 years ago, has become an important subfield in the law.) For example, individuals have been convicted of sexually abusing minors after they sexted nude and seminude pictures, and drivers have been ticketed for sneaking a peek at their phones when stopped at red lights, thereby violating their states' hands-free requirements. Should laws regulate these activities? Many people believe that these laws protect the dignity and safety of the public, yet others claim that they interfere with constitutionally protected speech and privacy rights. But most people would agree that vast changes in society have necessitated far-reaching adjustments in the law.

The invention of the automobile produced several new adversaries, including pedestrians versus drivers, and hence new laws. Car accidents—even minor ones—cause conflicts over basic rights. Consider a driver whose car strikes and injures a pedestrian. Does this driver have a legal responsibility to report the incident to the police? Yes. But doesn't this requirement violate the Fifth Amendment to the U.S. Constitution, which safeguards each of us against self-incrimination, against being a witness in conflict with our own best interests?

Shortly after automobiles became popular in the first two decades of the 20th century, a man named Edward Rosenheimer was charged with violating the newly implemented reporting laws. He did not contest the charge that he had caused an accident that injured another person, but he claimed that the law requiring him to report it to the police was unconstitutional because it forced him to incriminate himself. Therefore, he argued that this particular law should be removed from the books, and he should be freed of the charge of leaving the scene of an accident. Surprisingly, a New York judge agreed and released him from custody.

But authorities in New York were unhappy with a decision that permitted a person who had caused an injury to avoid being apprehended, so they appealed the decision to a higher court, the New York Court of Appeals. This court, recognizing that the Constitution and the recent law clashed with each other, ruled in favor of the state and overturned the previous decision. This appeals court concluded that rights to "constitutional privilege"—that is, to avoid self-incrimination—must give way to the competing principle of the right of injured persons to seek redress for their sufferings (Post, 1963).

These examples illustrate that the law is an evolving human creation, designed to arbitrate between values in opposition to each other. Before the advent of automobiles, hit-and-run accidents seldom occurred. Before the invention of smartphones, texting at stoplights (or worse, while driving) never occurred. However, once cars and smartphones became a part of society, new laws were enacted to regulate their use, and courts have determined that most of these new laws are constitutional. The advent of Google Glasses and driverless vehicles will raise new questions about rights and responsibilities with which the law will have to grapple. Psychological research can be relevant to these questions by assessing, for example, whether navigating with Google Glasses while driving is more or less distracting than glancing at a GPS unit or phone.

The Psychological Study of Law

Laws and legal systems are studied by several traditional disciplines other than psychology. For example, anthropologists compare laws (and mechanisms for instituting and altering laws) in different societies and relate them to other characteristics of these societies. They may be interested in how frequently women are raped in different types of societies and in the relationship between rape and other factors, such as the extent of separation of the sexes during childhood or the degree to which males dominate females.

Sociologists, in contrast, usually study a specific society and examine its institutions (e.g., the family, the church, or the subculture) to determine their role in developing adherence to the law. The sociologist might study the role that social class plays in criminal behavior. This approach tries to predict and explain social behavior by focusing on groups of people rather than on individuals.

A psychological approach to the law emphasizes its human determinants. The focus in the psychological approach is on the individual as the unit of analysis. Individuals are seen as responsible for their own conduct and as contributing to its causation. Psychology examines the thoughts and actions of individuals—drug abuser, petty thief, police officer, victim, juror, expert witness, corporate lawyer, judge, defendant, prison guard, and parole officer, for example—involved in the legal system. Psychology assumes that characteristics of these participants affect how the system operates, and it also recognizes that the law, in turn, can affect individuals' characteristics and behavior (Ogloff & Finkelman, 1999). By *characteristics*, we mean these persons' abilities, perspectives, values, and experiences—all the factors that influence their behavior. These characteristics affect whether a defendant and his or her attorney will accept a plea bargain or go to trial. They influence whether a Hispanic juror will be more sympathetic toward a Hispanic defendant than toward a non-Hispanic defendant. They help determine whether a juvenile offender will fare better in a residential treatment facility or a correctional institution. And sometimes they can explain why people commit crimes. So after Stephen Paddock fired on a crowd of 22,000 people attending a country music festival in Las Vegas in 2017—the deadliest mass shooting in modern U.S. history—authorities tried very hard to understand his motivations.

But the behavior of participants in the legal system is not just a result of their personal qualities. The setting in which they operate matters as well. Kurt Lewin, a founder of social psychology, proposed the equation $B = f(p, e)$: behavior is a function of the person and the environment. Qualities of the external environment and pressures from the situation affect an individual's behavior. A prosecuting attorney may recommend a harsher sentence for a convicted felon if the case has been highly publicized, the community is outraged over the crime, and the prosecutor happens to be waging a reelection campaign. A juror holding out for a guilty verdict may yield if all the other jurors passionately proclaim the defendant's innocence. A juvenile offender may desist from criminal behavior if his or her gang affiliations are severed. The social environment affects legally relevant choices and conduct.

This book concentrates on the behavior of participants in the legal system. As the examples at the beginning of this chapter indicate, citizens are all active participants in the system, even if they do not work in occupations directly tied to the administration of justice. We all face daily choices that are affected by the law—whether to speed through a school zone because we are late to class, whether to report the person who removes someone else's laptop from a table at the library, or whether to vote in favor of or against a proposal to end capital punishment. Hence, this book will also devote some attention to the determinants of our conceptions of justice and the moral dilemmas we all face.

But this book will pay particular attention to the role of psychology in the criminal and civil justice systems and to the central participants in those settings: defendants and witnesses, civil and criminal lawyers, judges and juries, convicts and parole boards. It will also focus on the activities of **forensic psychologists** who generate and communicate information to answer specific legal questions or to help resolve legal disputes (Melton et al., 2017). Most forensic psychologists are trained as clinical psychologists, whose specialty involves the psychological evaluation and treatment of others. Forensic psychologists are often asked to evaluate a person and then prepare a report for a court, and sometimes provide expert testimony in a hearing or trial. For example, they may evaluate adult criminal defendants or children involved with the juvenile justice system and offer the court information relevant to determining whether the defendant has a mental disorder that prevents him from going to trial, what the defendant's mental state was at the time of the offense, or what treatment might be appropriate for a particular defendant. But psychologists can play many other roles in the legal system, as well. We describe these roles later in the chapter.

Basic Choices in the Psychological Study of the Law

Just as each of us has to make decisions about personal values, society must decide which values it wants its laws to reflect. Choices lead to conflict, and often the resulting dilemmas are difficult to resolve. Should the laws uphold the rights of specific individuals or protect society in general? Should each of us be able to impose our preferences on others, or must we be attentive to other people's needs? You may have pondered this question while stopped at a traffic light next to a car with a deafening subwoofer. One of Madonna's neighbors in a posh New York City apartment building certainly pondered this question. She filed a lawsuit against the pop icon, claiming that her music was so loud that the neighbor had to leave several times a day. Whose rights prevail? A commonly asked question that taps that dilemma is whether it is better for ten murderers to go free than for one innocent person to be sentenced to death. The law struggles with this fact: rights desirable for some individuals may be problematic for others.

Consider the simple question about whether to wear a seat belt. People who opt not to use seat belts in a car are making a seemingly personal choice. Perhaps they don't like the way the belt feels. Perhaps they like having freedom to move around the car. But that choice puts them at greater risk for death or serious injury in an accident, and accidents involve costs to society, including lost wages, higher insurance premiums, and disability payments to the injured person and that person's dependents. So the good of society can be adversely affected by the split-second decision of individuals as they step into their cars.

This tension between individual rights and the common good is one example of the basic choices that pervade the psychological study of the law. But there are others. In this chapter, we highlight four basic choices inherent in laws and that apply to each of us in the United States, Canada, and many other countries. Each choice creates a dilemma and has psychological implications. No decision about these choices will be completely satisfactory because no decision can simultaneously attain two incompatible goals—such as individual rights and societal rights—both of which we value. These four choices (and the tension inherent in their competing values) are so basic that they surface repeatedly throughout this book, as they did with different examples in earlier editions (see, e.g., Greene & Heilbrun, 2015). They unify many of the research findings, policy decisions, and judicial holdings that are discussed in subsequent chapters.

The First Choice: Rights of Individuals versus the Common Good

Consider the following:

- Smokers have long been restricted to smoky airport lounges and back sections of restaurants, and often huddle together outside of workplace doors. But now smokers are banned from lighting up in some public parks and beaches, and along shorelines and trails. When New York City enacted a ban on smoking in its 1,700 public parks in 2011, Lauren Johnston was ecstatic. She blogged about smokers polluting the air along her running loop. But Bill Saar saw it differently: "It's the most idiotic law they ever made. I've been a smoker for over 20 years. I'm not going to stop," said Saar as he puffed on a cigar while selling figurines in Union Square (Durkin, 2011). Should cities be able to limit smoking in parks shared by all? Whose rights prevail?

■ Gay and lesbian troops have served openly in the U.S. military since 2011, as have transgender troops since 2016. But in July 2017, President Trump tweeted that transgender people would be barred from enlisting and active-duty transgender personnel would be subject to expulsion. If this tweet becomes official White House policy, then opportunities for transgender individuals to serve in the military would be effectively eliminated. According to Trump, the military must be focused on winning and cannot be burdened with the "tremendous medical costs and disruption" of transgender service members. Transgender advocates quickly denounced this communication, claiming that it imposed one set of standards on transgender troops and another set on everyone else, and politicians from both parties stated that anyone who is willing to fight for their country should be welcomed into the military. Who is right?

■ In a less serious sort of dispute, a growing number of cities have made it a crime to wear "sagging pants" and some cases have actually gone to trial. Three defendants were charged with violating the "decency ordinance" in Riviera Beach, Florida. Their public defenders argued that the law violated principles of freedom of expression. But the town's mayor, Thomas Masters, said that voters "just got tired of having to look at people's behinds or their undergarments … I think society has the right to draw the line" (Newton, 2009).

Values in Conflict. The preceding vignettes share a common theme. On the one hand, individuals possess rights, and one function of the law is

to ensure that these rights are protected. The United States is perhaps the most individualistic society in the world. People can deviate from the norm, or make their own choices, to a greater degree in the United States than virtually anywhere else. Freedom and personal autonomy are two of our most deeply desired values; "the right to liberty" is a key phrase in the U.S. Constitution.

On the other hand, our society also has expectations. People need to feel secure. They need to believe that potential lawbreakers are discouraged from breaking laws because they know they will be punished. All of us have rights to a peaceful, safe existence. Likewise, society claims a vested interest in restricting those who take risks that may injure themselves and others, or who demand excessive resources, because these actions can create burdens on individuals and on society. The tension between individual rights and the collective good is illustrated in the situation we describe in Box 1.1.

It is clear that two sets of rights and two goals for the law are often in conflict. The tension between the rights of the individual and the constraints that may be placed on the individual for the collective good is always present. It has factored prominently into various U.S. Supreme Court decisions since the 1960s with respect to the rights of criminal suspects and defendants versus the rights of crime victims and the power of the police.

A gay couple celebrates their recent marriage.

BOX 1.1

The "Unite the Right" Rally in Charlottesville and the Speech Rights of White Supremacists

The First Amendment to the U.S. Constitution protects the freedom of speech so long as it does not include obscenities, fighting words, perjury, and a few other types of speech. Even racially offensive speech is protected, as the Supreme Court noted in *Matal v. Tam* (2017). According to Justice Samuel Alito, who wrote the opinion in the case, "Speech that demeans on the basis of race, ethnicity, gender, religion, age, disability, or any other similar ground is hateful; but the proudest boast of our free speech jurisprudence is that we protect the freedom to express 'the thought that we hate'."

Those protections came into sharp relief in 2017 after White nationalists held a rally in Charlottesville, Virginia that turned deadly. Charlottesville officials initially denied organizers' request for a permit to protest the removal of a statue of Confederate General Robert E. Lee from a city park. But after a lawsuit was filed by the American Civil Liberties Union (ACLU)—an organization whose work has included defending the speech rights of neo-Nazis—and a federal judge ruled against the city, rally organizers received their permit. The protest escalated into a brawl as White nationalists, some carrying clubs and assault weapons, clashed with counter-protestors, and a car attack injured 19 and killed one of the counter-protestors.

The ACLU has long maintained that its advocacy of free speech for White supremacists serves to protect the First Amendment rights of all Americans by confronting vile and detestable ideas head-on, rather than by suppressing them (Goldstein, 2017). But the freedom of speech does not extend to speech that is "directed to inciting imminent lawless action and is likely to incite or produce such action" (*Brandenburg v. Ohio*, 1969) and some contend that support from the ACLU actually encourages such actions. (The ACLU has vowed to review closely requests from White

Evelyn Hockstein/The Washington Post/Getty Images

White nationalists clash with counter-protesters at the Unite the Right rally in Charlottesville, VA.

supremacist groups to assess the potential for violence and has stated that it will refuse to represent groups who protest with guns.)

This incident raises difficult questions for the future: Will local officials be tempted to thwart extremist groups who wish to hold rallies and protests in their communities? Will doing so further embolden White nationalists who have risen in prominence in recent years? Is openly carrying a gun, allowed in 45 states, a form of free speech? (This discussion shows that it may be impossible, in open carry states, to disentangle First Amendment free speech rights and the Second Amendment right to keep and bear arms.) Even more fundamentally, how does one strike a balance between the right to free expression of speech—including hate-filled speech intended to intimidate and threaten—and the right of the community to be protected from speech that promotes "lawless action"?

CRITICAL THOUGHT QUESTION

What two values are in conflict in this incident?

In the 1960s, the Supreme Court established a number of principles that provided or expanded explicit rights for those suspected of breaking the law. The *Miranda* rule guaranteeing the right to remain silent (detailed in Chapter 7) was established

in 1966. About the same time, the courts required that criminal defendants, in all cases in which incarceration was possible, have the right to an attorney, even if they cannot afford to pay for one. These and other rights were established in an effort to redress a perceived imbalance between a lowly defendant and a powerful government.

But many of these rights were trimmed in subsequent years when courts frequently ruled in favor of the police. For example, in 1996, the Supreme Court ruled that the police can properly stop a motorist whom they believe has violated traffic laws even if their ulterior motive is to investigate the possibility of illegal drug dealing (*Whren v. United States*, 1996). In 2012, the Court ruled that jail officials can strip search petty offenders even if there is no suspicion they are concealing weapons or contraband (*Florence v. Board of Chosen Freeholders*, 2012).

Two Models of the Criminal Justice System.

The conflict between the rights of individuals and the rights of society is related to a distinction between two models of the criminal justice system. This distinction is between the due process model and the crime control model (Packer, 1964). The values underlying each of these models are legitimate, and the goal of our society is to achieve a balance between them. But because different priorities are important to each model, there is constant tension between them.

The **due process model**, favored in the 1960s, places primary value on the protection of citizens, including criminal suspects, from possible abuses by the police and the law enforcement system generally. It assumes the innocence of suspects and requires that they be treated fairly (receive "due process") by the criminal justice system. It subscribes to the maxim that "it is better that ten guilty persons shall go free than that one innocent person should suffer." Thus the due process model emphasizes the rights of individuals, especially those suspected of crimes, over the temptation by society to assume suspects are guilty even before a trial.

In contrast, the **crime control model**, favored in the 1990s, seeks the apprehension and punishment of lawbreakers. It emphasizes the efficient detection of suspects and the effective prosecution of defendants, to help ensure that criminal activity is being contained or reduced. The crime control model is exemplified by a statement by former Attorney General of the United States, William P. Barr, with respect to career criminals. He noted that the goal is "incapacitation through incarceration" (Barr, 1992)—that is, removing them permanently from circulation.

When the crime control model is dominant in society, laws are passed that in other times would be seen as unacceptable violations of individual rights. A 2017 Texas law known as a "show me your papers law" prohibits local authorities from limiting the ability of law enforcement or court personnel to demand proof of a person's immigration status and report it to federal officials. Texas Governor Greg Abbot claimed that the law protects public safety. But opponents contend that it erodes public trust and actually makes communities and neighborhoods less safe. Laws like this raise complicated questions about the rights of individuals to be free from police scrutiny and the obligation of the government to provide safety and security to its citizens.

Despite the drop in crime rates in recent years, vestiges of the crime control model still linger in the United States, more than in Canada, Europe, or Australia. As we point out in Chapter 14, the United States incarcerates a higher percentage of its citizens than any other country. The United States has only 4% of the world's population but 22% of its prisoners.

But the Great Recession of 2007–2009 changed societal options for dealing with crime. As federal and state budgets tightened, legislators and law enforcement officials reevaluated many "tough-on-crime" policies. Those strategies boosted spending on prisons but did little to prevent repeat offending by released inmates (Dvoskin, Skeem, Novaco, & Douglas, 2011). Because of reduced resources, officials tried to find cheaper and more effective alternatives for controlling crime and ensuring public safety. Some new programs were effective in reducing repeat offending. Crime rates in Texas dropped after it began investing in treatment programs for parolees. The prison population in Mississippi was reduced by 22% after it allowed inmates to earn time off their sentences by participating in educational and re-entry programs. Other proven alternatives included providing employment counseling and substance abuse and mental health treatment for inmates, and diverting offenders from the criminal justice system and into community-based treatment programs. We describe many of these alternatives in Chapter 9.

The Second Choice: Equality versus Discretion

Kenneth Peacock was a long-distance trucker who was caught in an ice storm and came home at the wrong time. He walked in the door to find his wife Sandra in bed with another man. Peacock chased the man away and some four hours later, in the heat of an argument, shot his wife in the head with a hunting rifle. Peacock pled guilty to voluntary manslaughter and was sentenced to 18 months in prison. At the sentencing, Baltimore County Circuit Court Judge Robert E. Cahill said he wished he did not have to send Peacock to prison at all but knew that he must to "keep the system honest" (Lewin, 1994). He continued, "I seriously wonder how many men … would have the strength to walk away without inflicting some corporal punishment."

Move the clock ahead one day. A female defendant pleads guilty to voluntary manslaughter in a different Baltimore courtroom. She killed her husband after 11 years of abuse and was given a 3-year sentence—three times longer than that sought by prosecutors (Lewin, 1994). Some people find no inconsistency in the severity of these punishments, believing that each case should be judged on its own merits. However, psychology analyzes these decisions as examples of a choice between the goals of equality and discretion.

What should be the underlying principle guiding the response to persons accused of violating the law? Again, we see that two equally desirable values—equality and discretion—are often incompatible and hence create conflict. The principle of **equality** means that all people who commit the same crime or misdeed should receive the same consequences. But blind adherence to equality can lead to unfairness in situations in which the particular characteristics of offender, victim, or offense matter. For example, most people would think differently about punishing someone who killed randomly, ruthlessly, and without remorse, and someone else who killed a loved one suffering from a painful and terminal illness. In this example, discretion is called for. **Discretion** in the legal system involves considering the circumstances of certain offenders and offenses to determine the appropriate consequences for wrongdoing. Psychology provides concepts through which this conflict can be studied and better understood.

The Principle of Equality.
Fundamental to our legal system is the assumption advanced by the founders of the American republic that "all men are created equal." In fact, the "equal protection clause" of the Fourteenth Amendment states that no state shall "deny to any person within its jurisdiction the equal protection of the laws." This statement is frequently interpreted to mean that all people should be treated equally and that

no one should receive special treatment by the courts simply because he or she is rich, influential, or otherwise advantaged. We cherish the belief that in the United States, politically powerful or affluent people are brought before the courts and, if guilty, convicted and punished just like anyone else who commits similar offenses. Consider the example of flamboyant hedge fund manager and pharmaceutical executive Martin Shkreli, who was convicted in 2017 of defrauding his investors to cover up massive stock losses and then jailed after a Facebook post offering $5,000 for a strand of Hillary Clinton's hair. Shkreli became infamous for raising the price of the drug Daraprim, used to treat newborn babies and HIV patients, from $13.50 to $750 per pill.

But the value of equality before the law is not always implemented. In the last three decades, Americans have witnessed a series of incidents that—at least on the surface—seemed to indicate unequal treatment of citizens by the legal system. A common practice among police and state patrols in the United States is *profiling*—viewing certain characteristics as indicators of criminal behavior. African American and Latino motorists have filed numerous lawsuits over the practice of profiling, alleging that the police, in an effort to seize illegal drugs and weapons or to find undocumented immigrants, apply a "race-based profile" to stop and search them more frequently than White drivers. Said Michigan Congressman John Conyers, Jr., "There are virtually no African-American males—including Congressmen, actors, athletes and office workers—who have not been

Martin Shkreli, a well-do-to CEO who was convicted of defrauding his investors.

stopped at one time or another for … driving while black" (Barovick, 1998).

The issue is not limited to driving. It affects people when they shop, eat in restaurants, travel in trains and airplanes, hail a cab, and walk through their neighborhoods. New York City police officers stopped approximately four million people between 2004 and 2012, questioning all, and frisking and arresting some. But police department statistics show that the stops were not race-neutral. African Americans accounted for 52% of the stops, and Latinos for 31%, despite constituting 23% and 29% of the city's population, respectively. According to columnist Bob Herbert, "[T]he people getting stopped and frisked are mostly young, and most of them are black or brown and poor…If the police officers were treating white middle-class or wealthy individuals this way, the movers and shakers in this town would be apoplectic" (Herbert, 2010). Moreover, New York City police were less likely to find weapons or contraband on African American and Latino suspects than on White suspects (Gelman, Fagan, & Kiss, 2007).

Since police agencies have started gathering statistics on the racial makeup of people targeted for traffic stops, border inspections, and other routine searches, and these disparities have come to light, some courts have ruled that a person's appearance may not be the basis for such stops. Psychologists also have a role to play on this issue, gathering data on the psychological consequences to victims of racial profiling, improving police training so that cultural and racial awareness is enhanced, and examining how decision makers form implicit judgments of others on the basis of race.

In keeping with the laudable goal of equality under the law, the U.S. Supreme Court has occasionally applied a **principle of proportionality** to its analysis of cases involving criminal sentencing. This principle means that the punishment should be consistently related to the magnitude of the offense. More serious wrongdoing should earn more severe penalties. If a relatively minor crime leads to a harsh punishment, then the fundamental value of proportionality and hence, equality, has been violated.

The principle of proportionality has influenced the way that juvenile offenders are sentenced. Recognizing that impulsiveness and psychosocial immaturity render juveniles less culpable *and* more likely to be rehabilitated than adult offenders, the U.S. Supreme Court has, in the quest for equality, overturned harsh sentences for juvenile offenders. Individuals who

commit murder before the age of 18 cannot be subjected to the death penalty (*Roper v. Simmons*, 2005) nor automatically sentenced to life without the possibility of parole (*Miller v. Alabama*, 2012). The Court has determined that because juveniles sentenced to life in prison would spend more years and a larger percentage of their lives behind bars, that sentence is disproportionately harsh and not equal to a life sentence received by adults. We describe the case that led to that ruling in Box 1.2.

The *Miller* ruling was expanded in a 2016 decision in which the Court said that *Miller* should be applied retroactively (*Montgomery v. Louisiana*, 2016). This means that those sentenced to mandatory life sentences as teenagers will now have a chance to be resentenced or paroled. But the prospect of resentencing thousands of people serving life sentences poses challenging questions for psychology and the courts. Whereas psychological research ably provided to the Court information about normative development (i.e., that adolescence is distinguished by immaturity and thus, lessened culpability), different sources of data will be necessary when deciding, on a case-by-case basis, how a given inmate should be resentenced. Courts may need to find information on the developmental status of individuals as they were at the original sentencing (in the case of Henry Montgomery which led to the ruling, more than 50 years earlier!) and decide how to interpret such retrospective data. Courts will also need to decide whether information about the individual's current rehabilitation status, including mental health issues, is relevant. Psychologists will play an important role in assisting the courts to incorporate relevant developmental and clinical data on the individuals considered for resentencing (Grisso & Kavanaugh, 2016).

The Value of Discretion. Although equality often remains an overriding principle, society also believes that in certain circumstances, discretion is appropriate. Discretion refers to judgments about the circumstances of certain offenses that lead to appropriate *variations* in how the system responds to these offenses. It acknowledges that rigid application of the law can lead to injustices.

Many professionals in the legal system have the opportunity to exercise discretion, and most do so regularly. Police officers show discretion when they decide not to arrest someone who has technically broken the law. They show discretion when they calculate the level of fines for speeding. (Incidentally,

The Case of Evan Miller: Life Sentences for Juvenile Offenders Are Excessive Punishment

BOX 1.2

On July 15, 2003, 52-year-old Cole Cannon knocked on the door of his neighbor's trailer in the small town of Speake, Alabama, asking for some food. That trailer belonged to the family of 14-year-old Evan Miller, an active drug user being raised in an extremely abusive family and suffering from mental health problems. After Cannon had eaten, Miller and a friend accompanied him back to his trailer, intending to get him drunk and rob him. The three played drinking games and smoked marijuana, and when Cannon passed out, Miller began hitting him, first with his fists and then with a baseball bat. The friend then set fire to Cannon's trailer, where he died of smoke inhalation.

Miller was charged with murder in the course of arson and was tried as an adult, subject to all the penalties of adult felons. After he was convicted, the judge imposed a mandatory sentence of life without parole. Miller's appeal focused on his immature judgment and lack of moral sense. His attorneys argued that such a severe sentence was a form of cruel and unusual punishment, banned by the Eighth Amendment.

The case was eventually decided by the U.S. Supreme Court. Among the documents that justices considered was a brief submitted by the American Psychological Association summarizing research relevant to adolescent development. It concluded that (a) adolescents are less mature than adults in ways that make them less culpable and (b) it is not possible to predict with any reliability whether a particular juvenile offender is likely to reoffend violently (APA, 2012). In her majority decision, Justice Elena Kagan acknowledged that youths are different than adults, given their "diminished culpability and heightened capacity for change." She concluded that laws which mandate life sentences, when applied to juvenile offenders, are unconstitutional. Miller's case was referred back to the courts in Alabama for reconsideration of his life sentence.

CRITICAL THOUGHT QUESTION

According to the Supreme Court, why does a sentence of life without parole constitute cruel and unusual punishment when applied to a juvenile offender?

saying "I'm sorry" actually results in lower fines [Day & Ross, 2011]!) Prosecutors exercise discretion when they decide which of many arrestees to charge and for what particular crime. Juries exercise discretion in not convicting defendants who killed under circumstances that may have justified their actions (e.g., self-defense or heat of passion; the jury in the case of Officer Yanez, described at the beginning of the chapter, is an example). Prison officials have discretion to award "good behavior," grant furloughs and move prisoners to more and less confining conditions. Probation officers and parole boards make discretionary recommendations based on the circumstances and characteristics of individual offenders.

Parole boards also have the opportunity to exercise discretion when they decide whether to commute a death sentence to life imprisonment (a process called granting clemency) or to allow an execution to proceed as planned. The Georgia Board of Pardons and Parole faced that stark choice in 2011 when it had to decide whether death row inmate Troy Davis, who had been

convicted for murdering a police officer, should be executed by lethal injection or allowed to live. This case, described in Box 1.3, raises interesting questions about both discretion and the possibility of error in the criminal justice system.

Discretion may be most obvious in the sentences administered by judges to convicted criminals. In many cases, judges are able to consider the particular circumstances of the defendant and of the crime itself when they determine the sentence. It would seem that this use of discretion is good. Yet as we describe in Chapter 14, it can also lead to **sentencing disparity**, the tendency for judges to administer a variety of penalties for the same crime. The contrasting sentences handed out by judges in the Baltimore cases we described earlier provide one example of sentencing disparity. Other examples stem from the fact that state laws typically determine sentencing options, so offenders sentenced in one state may receive different sanctions than offenders who commit the same offense in another state.

The Case of Troy Davis and a Parole Board's Discretion

Former President Jimmy Carter, Pope Benedict XVI, the Indigo Girls, Nobel Laureate Desmond Tutu, former FBI Director William Sessions, Amnesty International, and former Georgia Supreme Court justices may not agree on much. But in 2011 they all called for a stop to the pending execution of Georgia death row inmate Troy Davis, who they claimed was an innocent man. Davis was convicted of murder in the 1989 shooting death of off-duty Savannah police officer Mark MacPhail and sentenced to death. Over the course of 20 years, Davis maintained his innocence, and his claim was bolstered by the possible confession of another person and by the recantation of seven eyewitnesses who said they lied during Davis' trial because they were threatened by another suspect. Some jurors who convicted Davis signed affidavits declaring that they doubted his guilt.

In Georgia, the authority to commute a death sentence into a less severe sentence rests with the Georgia Board of Pardons and Paroles. (In some states, governors have this discretion.) That board had declined to commute Davis' sentence once before. With an execution date pending and all other options exhausted, Davis' attorneys appealed one last time to the five-member board, which conducted a hearing in which they heard from Davis' attorneys and supporters, and from

Supporters of Troy Davis.

prosecutors and MacPhail's relatives. Despite doubts about Davis' guilt, his surprising assortment of supporters, and petitions, rallies, and vigils held around the world on his behalf, the board denied Davis' request. He was executed in 2011.

CRITICAL THOUGHT QUESTION

Explain why the Georgia Board of Pardons and Paroles may not have been willing to grant clemency to Troy Davis.

Sentencing disparity is also apparent in the penalties given to African Americans and members of other minority groups. African Americans are imprisoned at rates five to seven times higher than those of White Americans partly due to disparities in arrests for drug crimes. Police concentrate more attention on drugs that racial minorities use, resulting in a far greater likelihood of jail time for drug use (Davis, 2011). Sentencing disparities can also be seen for Hispanics: One in six Hispanic males and one in 45 Hispanic females can expect to be imprisoned in his or her lifetime, more than double the rates of those who are not Hispanic (Mauer & King, 2007).

A simple explanation for this disparity is **racial bias**, whereby police officers, prosecutors, jurors, and judges use an individual's race as a basis for judging his or her behavior. Race-based stereotypes affect beliefs about offenders' culpability and dangerousness, as well as

perceptions of the likelihood of reoffending (Spohn, 2015). Sometimes bias and stereotyping is explicit and intentional, and other times it is implicit and unintentional. **Implicit bias** is especially concerning, since people are unaware that they are being influenced by race; for example, they may get a "bad feeling" from a Latino defendant (Hunt, 2015). But once these biases occur, they can act as a filter for interpreting and using other information about the offender and the circumstances. Fortunately, some studies have shown that once decision makers are made aware of the potential for racial bias, they can largely avoid it (Pearson, Dovidio, & Gaertner, 2009).

A subtler, more insidious form of race-based judgments may be prevalent in the justice system, however. Social psychological research has shown that individuals of the same race may be stereotyped and discriminated against to different degrees, depending how "typical" of their group they appear. Individuals receive longer sentences when they have more Afrocentric facial features (Blair, Judd, & Chapleau, 2004) and darker skin tones (Viglione, Hannon, & DeFina, 2011). Even more troubling, in death penalty cases involving White victims, the likelihood of a Black defendant being sentenced to death is influenced by whether he or she has a stereotypically Black appearance (Eberhardt, Davies, Purdie-Vaughns, & Johnson, 2006).

To counteract sentencing disparity, many states implemented what is known as **determinate sentencing**: the offense determines the sentence, and judges and parole commissions have little discretion. But judges were frustrated by the severe limitations on their discretion imposed by determinate sentencing. One federal judge who resigned his appointment in protest said, "It's an unfair system that has been dehumanized. There are rarely two cases that are identical. Judges should always have discretion. That's why we're judges. But now we're being made to be robots."

The pendulum has now swung away from determinate sentencing and toward allowing judges more discretion. Permitting judges more leeway to consider factors such as the defendant's background, motivations for committing the crime, and any psychological disorders may strike a balance between the uniformity that determinate sentencing imposed and the judicial discretion that many judges prefer.

The Third Choice: To Discover the Truth or to Resolve Conflicts

What is the purpose of a court hearing or a trial? Your first reaction may be "To find out the truth, of course!" Determining the truth means learning the facts of a dispute, including events, intentions, actions, and outcomes. All this assumes that "what really happened" between two parties can be determined.

Finding out the truth is a desirable goal, but it may also be lofty and sometimes downright impossible. The truth often lies somewhere between competing versions of an event. Because it is difficult for even well-meaning people to ascertain the true facts in certain cases, some observers have proposed that the real purpose of a hearing or trial is to provide social stability by resolving conflict. Supreme Court Justice Louis Brandeis once wrote that "it is more important that the applicable rule of law be settled than [that] it be settled right" (*Burnet v. Coronado Oil and Gas Co.,*

1932). This is a shift away from viewing the legal system's purpose as doing justice toward viewing its goal as "creating a sense that justice is being done" (Miller & Boster, 1977, p. 34).

Because truth is elusive, the most important priority of a hearing or a trial may be to provide a setting in which all interested parties have their "day in court." Justice replaces truth as the predominant goal. In fact, attorneys representing the opposing parties in a case do not necessarily seek "the truth." Nor do they represent themselves as "objective." They reflect a different value—the importance of giving their side the best representation possible, within the limits of the law. (The Code of Ethics of the American Bar Association even instructs attorneys to defend their clients "zealously.") Because lawyers believe the purpose of a hearing or trial is to win disputes, they present arguments supporting their client's perspective and back up their arguments with the best available evidence.

One argument in favor of the adversary system, in which a different attorney represents each party, is that it encourages the attorneys to discover and introduce all evidence that might induce the judge or jury to react favorably to their client's case. When both sides believe that they have had the chance to voice their case fully and their witnesses have revealed all the relevant facts, participants are more likely to feel they have been treated fairly by the system, and the system is more likely to be considered an effective one. This is an important part of a theory known as **procedural justice**, a concept presented in Chapter 2.

"Conflict resolution" and "truth," as goals, are not always incompatible. When all participants in a legal dispute are able to raise concerns and provide supporting documentation, the goal of learning the truth becomes more attainable. But frequently there is tension between these goals, and in some instances, the satisfactory resolution of a conflict may be socially and morally preferable to discovering an objectively established truth. Yet resolving conflict in a hurried or haphazard manner can have a downside, as illustrated by the experience of Richard Jewell.

Jewell was a security guard at the 1996 Summer Olympics in Atlanta. Shortly after a bombing that disrupted the Games, the Federal Bureau of Investigation (FBI) began to question Jewell, who discovered the bomb. Although at first the FBI denied that he was a suspect, they treated him like one, and his name and photograph were widely publicized. The pressure to find the person responsible for this terrifying act—and the desire

Eric Rudolph, a North Carolina fugitive, pled guilty in 2005 to a bombing at the 1996 Olympics in Atlanta.

to give people a sense that no more bombings would occur because the perpetrator had been caught—doubtless influenced the premature focus on Richard Jewell. Despite relentless FBI investigation, no charges were brought against Jewell, and in 2005, Eric Rudolph, a fugitive who lived in the hills of North Carolina for years after the bombing, pleaded guilty of the offense.

Truth versus Conflict Resolution in Plea Bargaining and Settlement Negotiations.

The legal system is a massive bureaucracy, and in every bureaucracy, there is a temptation to value pragmatic efficiency rather than correct or just outcomes. The heavy reliance on plea bargaining is often criticized because it appears to give priority to conflict resolution over truth seeking. As we describe in Chapter 8, between 90% and 95% of defendants never go to trial; they accept the offer of the prosecutor and plead guilty to a lesser charge. Even some innocent persons plea-bargain after being convinced that the evidence against them is overwhelming. Indeed, plea bargaining is an integral part of the criminal justice system.

The state benefits by avoiding the expense and trouble of a trial and the possibility of an acquittal, and sometimes, by obtaining the testimony of the accused person against others involved in the crime. The defendant benefits by receiving some kind of reduction in the penalty imposed. In addition to these pragmatic benefits, justice is furthered by a system that rewards a show of remorse (which usually accompanies a guilty plea) and enables the prosecutor and defense counsel, together with the judge, to negotiate a resolution appropriate to the degree of wrongdoing (Kamisar, LaFave, & Israel, 1999). Nonetheless, plea bargaining reveals that the goal of maintaining stability and efficiency in the system is achieved at some cost. That cost is the public's opportunity to determine the complete truth.

The civil justice system uses a procedure similar to plea bargaining to resolve about 90% of the conflicts between a plaintiff and a defendant. **Settlement negotiation** involves a sometimes lengthy pretrial process of give-and-take, offer-and-demand that ends when a plaintiff agrees to accept what a defendant is willing to offer (typically, money) to end their legal disagreement. It also favors the goal of conflict resolution at the expense of determining what *really* happened.

For example, in 2013, settlement negotiations led to an agreement between the National Football League (NFL) and thousands of former players who suffered concussive injuries on the gridiron. Players alleged that the NFL was responsible for the rules and regulations of the game and that it concealed information on the potential consequences of repetitive head injuries. They settled for $765 million, including $75 million for baseline medical exams for nearly 20,000 former players. The negotiated settlement avoided lengthy and expensive litigation, enabled many players to seek the medical attention they needed, and, according to one football commentator, "saved the game" (Spencer, 2013).

New Thoughts on Conflict Resolution.

Despite the traditional prominence of adversarial procedures to resolve disputes, many legal problems are actually handled in a nonadversarial manner. Throughout the book we present situations in which people work together in a cooperative way to settle their differences and reach a resolution that is acceptable to all.

Many divorcing couples opt to collaborate rather than contend with each other as they end their marriage. In situations where parents have failed to nurture their children, family court judges temporarily remove children from their homes and provide

Erik S. Lesser/Getty Images News/Getty Images

extensive counseling, education, and other social service interventions to parents, hoping eventually to restore the family unit. In some jurisdictions, people arrested for drug-related crimes are given the opportunity to have their cases resolved in drug courts that focus on treating the underlying problem of addiction, rather than simply punishing the offender. In lawsuits in which plaintiffs are injured due to defendants' negligence and the parties attempt to negotiate a settlement rather than go to trial, these negotiations offer an opportunity for defendants to apologize to plaintiffs. Research shows that apologies advance settlement negotiations (Robbennolt, 2013) and reduce plaintiffs' inclinations to sue (Greene, 2008). They also affect the bottom line: In medical malpractice cases, apologies reduce the average payout by $32,000 (Ho & Liu, 2011).

What these situations have in common is that they do not operate in a zero-sum fashion in which one party wins and another loses. Rather, they attempt to maximize positive outcomes for all concerned, with the objective of keeping the dispute from escalating further and involving more formal adjudication proceedings.

The idea that the law is a social force with consequences for people's well-being, an approach termed therapeutic jurisprudence, is discussed further in Chapter 2. Reform-minded lawyers, jurists, and legal scholars advocate for legal procedures and institutions that facilitate therapeutic ends. They ask how the law can be applied or reformed to enhance individuals' welfare. Therapeutic jurisprudence has been applied in nearly all areas of the law including criminal law, family law, employment law, probate, health care, workers' compensation, and labor arbitration.

The Fourth Choice: Science versus the Law as a Source of Decisions

When one discipline (in our case, psychology) seeks to understand another (the law), a dilemma is likely to arise because each approaches knowledge in a different way. When asked, "How do you know whether that decision is the right one?" each relies on different methods, even though both share the goal of understanding human experience.

As you read this book you will learn that in many cases the U.S. Supreme Court and other courts have considered data and conclusions presented by psychologists and other social scientists. In several of these, the

The justices of the U.S. Supreme Court.

Alex Wong/Getty Images News/Getty Images

American Psychological Association (APA) prepared a written document, called an **amicus curiae brief** ("friend of the court" brief), for consideration by an appellate court. Such *amicus curiae* briefs provide the courts with information from psychological science and practice relevant to the issues in a particular case. In many of its decisions (including *Miller v. Alabama*, presented earlier in this chapter), the Supreme Court incorporated input from the *amicus curiae* brief, although in other cases, it disregarded the social science data altogether. This inconsistency reflects the fact that the justices sometimes use different procedures and concepts from those of social science in forming their judicial opinions (Grisso & Saks, 1991).

In addition to employing different procedures, each profession may use idiosyncratic or unique concepts to describe the same phenomenon. An attorney and a social scientist will see the same event from different perspectives. Neither is necessarily more accurate than the other and their differences are the result of exposure to and training in different points of view. The following subsections illustrate such differences in more detail (see also Ogloff & Finkelman, 1999; Robbennolt & Davidson, 2011).

Law Relies on Precedents; Psychology Relies on Scientific Methods. In contrast to the law, psychology is generally committed to the idea that there is an objective world of experience that can be understood by adherence to the rules of science—systematic testing of hypotheses by observation and experimental methodology. As a scientist, the psychologist should be committed to a public, impersonal, objective pursuit of truth, relying on methods that can be repeated by others and interpreting results by using predetermined standards. Although this traditional view of psychology's approach to truth is sometimes challenged as naive and simplistic because it ignores the importance of the personal, political, and historical biases that affect scientists as much as nonscientists (Gergen, 1994), it still represents the values and methods in which most psychologists are trained. (It also represents the authors' beliefs that the scientific method and the research skills of psychologists are the most essential and reliable tools available for examining the many important legal questions we address throughout the book.)

By contrast, when they establish new laws, legal experts rely heavily on **precedents**—rulings in previous cases (as well as the Constitution and the statutes) for guidance. **Case law**—the law made by judges ruling in individual cases—is very influential; statutes and constitutional safeguards do not apply to every new situation, so past cases often serve as precedents for deciding current ones. The principle of *stare decisis* ("let the decision stand," reflecting the importance of abiding by previous decisions) is also important in this process. Judges typically are reluctant to make decisions that contradict earlier ones, as the history of the Supreme Court's school desegregation cases indicates.

When the U.S. Supreme Court decided unanimously in 1954, in *Brown v. Board of Education*, that public school segregation was contrary to the notion of equality for all, many reports claimed that it "supplanted" or even "overturned" a ruling in the 1896 case of *Plessy v. Ferguson*. But intermediate decisions by the Court permitted this seemingly abrupt change to evolve gradually. A brief history of rulings that led up to the *Brown v. Board of Education* decision illustrates this phenomenon, and the way that the law proceeds from case to case.

We begin with the state of Louisiana's dispute with Homer Plessy. During a train trip in Louisiana in the 1890s, Plessy sat down in a railroad car labeled "Whites Only." Plessy's ancestry was mostly Caucasian, but he had one Negro great-grandparent. Therefore, according to the laws of Louisiana at that time, Plessy was considered Black (or *colored*, the term used then). Plessy refused to move to a car designated for "colored" passengers, as a recently passed state law required. He took his claim to court, but a New Orleans judge ruled that, contrary to Plessy's argument, the statute that segregated railroad cars by race did not violate the Fourteenth Amendment to the Constitution. In other words, it did not fail to

give Plessy "equal protection under the law." Plessy persisted in his appeal, and eventually, in 1896, the U.S. Supreme Court upheld the decision of the judge and the lower courts. Judge Henry Billings Brown, speaking for the majority faction of the Supreme Court, declared that laws that had established separate facilities for the races did not necessarily imply that one race was inferior to the other.

Although this opinion was a far cry from the 1954 *Brown* decision, which highlighted the detrimental effects of segregation on the personality development of Black children, cases decided between *Plessy* and *Brown* would foreshadow the Court's eventual leanings. One case was brought by George McLaurin, the first Black student admitted to the University of Oklahoma's Graduate School of Education. Although McLaurin was allowed to enroll, he was segregated from all his classmates. His desk was separated from all the others by a rail, to which the sign "Reserved for Colored" was attached. He was given a separate desk at the library and was required to eat by himself in the cafeteria. In the 1950 case of *McLaurin v. Oklahoma State Regents*, the U.S. Supreme Court ruled unanimously that these procedures denied McLaurin the right to equal protection of the law. The Court concluded that such restrictions would "impair and inhibit his ability to study, to engage in discussion and exchange of views with other students." But the Court did not strike down *Plessy v. Ferguson* in this decision.

With a more liberal Court in the 1950s, however, there was enough momentum to reverse *Plessy v. Ferguson*. Chief Justice Earl Warren, who liked to ask, "What is fair?" spearheaded the unanimous decision that finally overturned the idea that separate facilities can be "equal." He wrote that separating Black children "from others of similar age and qualifications solely because of their race generates a feeling of inferiority as to their status in the community that may affect their hearts and minds in a way unlikely to ever be undone" (*Brown v. Board of Education*, 1954).

The school desegregation cases show that lawyers have historically reasoned from case to case. They locate cases that are similar to the one at hand and then base their arguments on the rulings from these legal precedents. Psychologists, on the other hand, value the scientific method, rely on experimental and evaluation studies, and prefer to gather data that describe large numbers of people.

Some commentators have recently suggested that society would be better served by a legal profession that was less resistant to objective, rigorous, and scientific evidence, however (Greiner & Matthews, 2016). They extol the virtues of using **randomized controlled trials (RCT)** to accumulate knowledge about what works in the legal system and what does not, but have discovered very few examples of such studies in law. One exception was a study of the effectiveness of mandatory domestic violence counseling that compared re-arrest rates after either one year of probation (the control condition) or a year of probation plus six months of counseling (the treatment condition). (There were no statistical differences; Feder & Dugan, 2002). Calling attention to the paucity of RCT studies in the law may spur legal research to become somewhat more evidence-based—and in that way, somewhat more like psychology—in the future.

Law Deals with Absolutes; Psychology Deals with Probabilities.

Legal questions often require an "either–or" response: A person is either fit or unfit to be a parent; a person was either insane or not insane when he or she committed a particular act (Ellsworth & Mauro, 1998). Psychologists are not comfortable reasoning in absolutes. They prefer to think in terms of probabilities (e.g., that a defendant's delusional thinking *could* indicate a psychiatric disorder, that a White eyewitness to a crime is *more likely to* misidentify a Black perpetrator than a White perpetrator). Although the law looks to psychologists for "either–or" answers (e.g., "Is the defendant competent to stand trial?" and "Was the defendant insane at the time of the crime?"), psychologists usually prefer to answer in terms of likelihoods or quantified "maybes." Lawyers may have difficulty with such inconclusive responses because they need a final resolution to a dispute.

Law Supports Contrasting Views of Reality; Psychology Seeks One Refined View of Reality.

As indicated earlier, judges and jurors must decide which of two conceptions of the truth is more acceptable in light of conflicting facts. Attorneys assemble all the facts that support their side and argue forcefully that their version of the facts is the correct one. Although this procedure is similar to some scientific activities (a psychologist may do a study that compares predictions from two theories), the psychologist is trained to be objective and open to all perspectives and types of data. The psychologist's ultimate goal is to integrate or assimilate conflicting findings into one refined view of the truth, rather than choosing between alternative views.

Some observers have likened this difference between psychology and law to the difference between scaling a mountain and fighting in a boxing match. As psychologists gain a clearer understanding of a topic (e.g., the causes of elder abuse), they scale a figurative mountain, at the top of which lies true and complete understanding. Although they may never actually reach this pinnacle of knowledge, psychologists highly value the accumulation of data, the development of psychological theory, and the quest for "truth." By contrast, lawyers are less interested in ascertaining the objective truth about a topic and are more concerned with winning against their adversary, resolving a dispute, or, more recently, enhancing the laws' effect on all parties.

Such distinctions only scratch the surface of the differences between law and psychology. In Chapter 2 we consider differing notions of justice in the two fields, and in subsequent chapters, we discuss the implications of these differences. As with the previous choices, selecting one domain over the other does not always yield a satisfactory resolution. The use of both perspectives moves us closer to an adequate understanding than does relying only on one. For example, using a psychological principle such as attribution of responsibility—a judgment of who is responsible for a particular outcome in a particular situation—can explain why some people decide to sue and others opt not to (Robbennolt & Hans, 2016). Both psychologists and lawyers should remain aware of the limits of their own perspective and realize that both viewpoints are essential for a fuller understanding of complex behavioral issues in the law.

But the contrast in knowledge-generating procedures does raise difficult procedural questions. What roles should the psychologist play in the legal system? What ethical concerns are associated with psychologists' involvement in the legal system? These and other basic questions are among the areas discussed in this book.

Psychologists' Roles in the Law

Most courses in psychology portray only two roles for psychologists: those of the scientist who conducts basic research about the causes and consequences of behavior and the applied psychologist (usually a clinical psychologist) who tries to understand and assist individuals or groups in addressing behavioral issues. The possibilities are more elaborate, however, when the psychologist is involved in the legal system. We describe five distinct

The Case of Tatiana Tarasoff: The Duty to Protect

BOX 1.4

Few legal decisions have had as much impact on the practice of psychotherapy as the now-famous case of *Tarasoff v. Regents of the University of California*. The decision focuses on the duties required of psychotherapists whose clients threaten violence to identifiable others.

Prosenjit Poddar was a graduate student at the University of California who became infatuated with Tatiana Tarasoff. Poddar was inexperienced in romantic relationships and was confused about Tatiana's on-again–off-again behavior; she was friendly toward him one day but avoided him completely the next night. After Poddar became a client of a psychologist at the university counseling center, he confided that he intended to kill a girl who had rebuffed him. The psychologist told his supervisor of this threat and then called the campus police, requesting that they detain Poddar. They did so but soon released him, believing his promise that he would stay away from Tatiana, who was out of the country at the time. Poddar didn't keep his promise. Two months later, he went to Tatiana's home and stabbed her to death. He was eventually convicted of murder.

Tatiana Tarasoff's parents sued the university, the psychologists, and the campus police for failing to warn them or their daughter about Poddar's threats.

The California Supreme Court ruled in the parents' favor by deciding that the university had been negligent. The first *Tarasoff* decision (1974) established a duty on psychotherapists to warn the victims of therapy patients when the therapist "knows or should have known" that the patient presented a threat to that victim. The court established a standard that therapists have a duty to use "reasonable care" to protect identifiable potential victims from clients in psychotherapy who threaten violence. A second *Tarasoff* decision in 1976 broadened this duty to include the protection of third parties from patient violence. Courts in several other states have extended this duty to the protection of property and the protection of all foreseeable victims, not just identifiable ones.

The *Tarasoff* case still governs psychologists' conduct in multiple states. Many psychologists feel caught in a no-win situation: They can be held responsible for their clients' violence if they do not warn potential victims, but they can also be held responsible for breaching their clients' confidentiality if they do.

CRITICAL THOUGHT QUESTION

Why is it necessary to specify explicitly what psychologists must do if they hear a client threaten to harm a person or property?

---

roles for psychologists in the legal system: basic scientist, applied scientist, policy evaluator, forensic evaluator, and consultant. The work inherent in these roles ranges from isolated academic research in psychology that may be relevant to law, on one end, to active collaboration with people who work in the legal system, on the other end.

As you will see, the five roles vary in several respects. But whatever the role, it includes standards about what is acceptable and unacceptable behavior. Professionals often develop explicit statements of ethical standards of behavior. For psychologists, those principles and standards (called the *Ethical Principles of Psychologists and Code of Conduct*) have been published by the American Psychological Association (2017). They describe a series of broad principles followed by a more specific set of standards. Adherence to the standards is mandatory

for psychologists. Among the many topics they cover is when psychologists should terminate treatment and how to do so.

Making the right ethical choice can be complicated. Sometimes, certain standards (e.g., confidentiality in therapy) may conflict with other obligations (e.g., the legal obligation to prevent harm to third parties inflicted by therapy patients). This conflict was apparent in the controversial *Tarasoff* decision by the Supreme Court of California, described in Box 1.4.

In the following sections, we describe the various roles that psychologists assume in relation to the legal system and the ethical issues that arise in each context. A footnote on psychologists' relationship to the law: Students often wonder how they can become involved in this field as basic scientists, applied scientists, policy evaluators, forensic evaluators, or consultants.

What career paths should one pursue, and what professional opportunities exist at the ends of those trails? How might a developmental psychologist, a cognitive neuropsychologist, or a clinician (for example) interact with the legal system? The website of the American Psychology-Law Society (a division of the APA) has practical and career-related advice for practitioners, educators, researchers, and students (www.ap-ls.org). Those undertaking careers in psychology and law should also familiarize themselves with the ethical requirements pertaining to their professions.

The Psychologist as a Basic Scientist of the Law

A **basic scientist** pursues knowledge for its own sake. Basic scientists study a phenomenon for the satisfaction of understanding it and contributing to scientific advances in the area. They do not necessarily seek to apply their research findings; many have no concern with whether the knowledge they generate will be used to resolve real-world problems. Yet often their results can address important practical issues, including some that arise in the law. For example, though not specifically conducted for use in the courtroom, laboratory research on visual perception can help us understand the accuracy of eyewitness testimony about a crime or accident. Psychologists who test different theories of memory promote a better understanding of whether repression can cause long-term forgetting of traumatic events. Basic research on the relationship between social attitudes and behavior can clarify why people obey or disobey the law. Research in personality psychology can help to show what kind of person will become a follower in a terrorist group and what kind of person will be a leader. Studies of adolescents' brain development may be relevant to their decisions about whether to commit crimes. Finally, research can assess whether forensic psychologists' attitudes about the causes of crime affect their professional evaluations of criminal defendants.

The Ethics of the Basic Scientist.

Like all scientists, psychologists who do basic research must adhere to standards of conduct in how they undertake and report their studies. In practical terms, this means that they cannot fabricate or forge data, plagiarize, or present a skewed selection of the data to hide observations that do not fit their conclusions. They must treat research participants in an ethical manner. (All institutions that receive federal research funding have review boards that evaluate the way scientists treat human and animal subjects.) Basic researchers sometimes have a conflict of interest when faced with competing concerns such as honestly reporting their research findings versus making a profit or "getting published." In these situations, they should learn to recognize and be honest about potential conflicts of interest and communicate them to interested parties before undertaking the research.

The Psychologist as an Applied Scientist in the Law

An **applied scientist** is dedicated to applying knowledge to solve real-life problems. Most of the public's awareness of a psychologist's work reflects this role, whether this awareness comes from viewing TV's Dr. Phil or watching a psychologist testify as an expert on cybercrime on the television show CSI. Indeed, an important role for psychologists who are interested in applying the findings of their profession involves serving as an expert witness in a legislative hearing or in a courtroom.

Juries, judges, and legislators cannot be well versed in every topic from abscesses to zinfandel wine. An **expert witness** is someone who possesses specialized knowledge about a subject, knowledge that the average person does not have. Psychologists may testify as expert witnesses during a trial based on their knowledge, experience, and training regarding psychological issues. The expert's task is to assist jurors and judges by providing an opinion based on this specialized knowledge.

Either side, as part of its presentation of the evidence, may ask the judge to allow expert witnesses to testify. The judge must be convinced that the testimony is of a kind that requires specialized knowledge, skill, or experience and that it will help promote better legal decision making. (When psychologists testify concerning a particular individual based on the results of a forensic evaluation, they take on a different role, one we describe later in this chapter.)

The psychological topics that call for scientific expertise are almost limitless. As expert witnesses, psychologists have been called on to testify in many types of cases. For example, expert testimony may be useful in understanding:

- Employee discrimination through selection and promotion procedures
- The effects of posting warning signs or safety instructions on potentially dangerous equipment
- The factors that may cause a suspect to make a false confession
- The effects of suggestive questions on children's memory of alleged abuse

The Ethics of the Applied Scientist/Expert Witness. The psychologist as expert witness represents a profession that stands for objectivity and accuracy in its procedures. Even though expert witnesses are usually hired and paid by one side, they are responsible for reporting all their conclusions, regardless of whether these favor the side paying them. It violates the ethical standards of both psychologists and lawyers for expert witnesses to accept payment that is contingent on the outcome of the case.

But achieving objectivity is not easy. When testifying as experts, psychologists have an ethical responsibility to be honest and open with the court about their opinions. Yet they may be tempted to sympathize with the side that has employed them. Is it possible to increase experts' objectivity? One commentator has proposed using "blinded" experts selected by an intermediary and hired to review the case without knowing which side has requested an opinion (Robertson, 2010). When blinded experts were pitted against traditional experts in a study examining mock jurors' decisions, the former were perceived as more credible and persuasive than the latter (Robertson & Yokum, 2011).

Another ethical dilemma arises whenever the adversary system forces an expert to make absolute "either–or" judgments. Has the pretrial publicity caused potential jurors to be biased against the defendant? In a custody case stemming from a divorce, which parent would be better for the child to live with? Does the evaluation of a defendant indicate that she is mentally ill? In all of these situations, the law requires the psychologist to reach a firm conclusion on the witness stand, regardless of ambiguity in the evidence (Sales & Shuman, 1993). This is an example of the absolute versus probabilistic judgment differences we described earlier in the chapter.

Admissibility of Expert Testimony. In order to maximize the likelihood that expert testimony is based on legitimate scientific knowledge and to exclude "junk science," lawmakers have developed criteria for judges to use when determining whether to allow an "expert" to testify. Each state and the federal government have their own criteria for determining admissibility.

In federal courts and over half of the states, these criteria are informed by a two-prong test developed by the U.S. Supreme Court in a highly influential case, *Daubert v. Merrell Dow Pharmaceuticals,*

Inc. (1993). First, the trial judge must determine whether the testimony is relevant and if relevant, whether it is based on reliable and valid science. In essence, judges function as "gatekeepers" who must evaluate potential expert testimony by the standards of science.

Judges have disallowed expert psychological testimony as irrelevant. Consider the case of unlucky Pedro Gil. On a night of wild abandon in the fall of 1993, Gil hoisted a bucket of plaster over the wall of a Manhattan rooftop. It dropped seven stories to the ground and hit and killed a police officer standing on the street below. Gil claimed that he expected the bucket to drop unceremoniously onto an unoccupied street directly below him, rather than to continue forward as it fell and land on the street where the police officer was positioned. To support his naive belief that objects drop straight down, Gil's attorneys attempted to introduce the testimony of a cognitive psychologist with expertise in intuitive physics. The expert planned to testify that people commonly misunderstand physical laws but the trial judge did not let him testify, claiming that intuitive physics was irrelevant to the issues under contention. The jury convicted Gil of second-degree manslaughter.

Judges have also disallowed expert testimony as unreliable. Richard Coons, a Texas psychiatrist, testified in death penalty trials that he developed his own methodology to determine whether a defendant poses a risk of future dangerousness. (Prior to sentencing a defendant to death, juries in Texas must agree that there is a probability that he or she poses a continuing threat to society.) Coons considers an offender's criminal history, attitudes toward violence, and conscience, yet he could not show that these factors have been validated by any research or that his predictions are accurate. After an appellate court deemed Coons' testimony unreliable, over-ruling a trial court judge who had admitted the expert testimony, a defense attorney quipped, "It's overdue."

One clear implication of the *Daubert* decision is that judges must become savvy consumers of science if they are to decide which opinions qualify as "scientific." Since the *Daubert* case, the admissibility of expert evidence has become an important pretrial issue and judges need to scrutinize the reasoning and methodology underlying experts' opinions (Chlistunoff, 2016). They have the option to appoint neutral experts to help them decide whether to admit disputed scientific evidence (Domitrovich, 2016).

The Psychologist as a Policy Evaluator in the Law

In addition to their knowledge of substantive problems, psychologists have methodological skills that they use in assessing or evaluating how well an intervention has worked. Psychologists and other social scientists have been asked so frequently in the last several decades to conduct evaluation studies that a separate subfield called policy evaluation, or evaluation research, has emerged. The **policy evaluator** provides data to answer questions such as "I have instituted a policy; how do I know whether it was effective?" Or, more laudably, "I want to make a change in our organization's procedures, but before I do, how do I design it so I will be able to determine later whether it worked?"

Psychologists working as policy evaluators might be asked whether changing the laws for teen drivers by restricting the number of passengers they can carry will reduce traffic accidents, whether the chemical castration of released rapists will reduce the rate of sexual violence, or whether changing from automobile patrols to foot patrols will improve relations between police and the community. The methodological skills of a psychologist as policy evaluator are essential in assessing existing programs and policies and designing innovations so that their effects can be tested.

As an example, psychologists have been involved in evaluating policies and programs intended to help children prepare to testify in court. In one program, nearly two hundred 4- to 17-year-olds attended Kids' Court School in Las Vegas a week or two before their scheduled testimony. Psychologists measured their court-related anxiety before and after an intervention that consisted of education about legal proceedings, stress inoculation, and a mock trial. As predicted, anticipatory anxiety decreased from pretest to posttest, suggesting that the program can serve as a model for reducing court-related stress in child witnesses (Nathanson & Saywitz, 2015).

The Ethics of the Policy Evaluator.

The psychologist who evaluates the impact of proposed or existing legislation and court or correctional procedures faces ethical responsibilities similar to those of the expert witness. The standard rules of scientific procedure apply, but because of the source of employment and payment, there are pressures to interpret results of evaluation studies in a certain way.

Consider, for example, a large state correctional system that wants to improve its parole process. Correctional officials know that when released into society, heavy drug users are likely to commit further crimes to maintain their drug habit, and are therefore likely to return to prison. Accordingly, the system seeks to introduce and evaluate an innovative halfway house program for parolees with a history of narcotics addiction. It hires a policy evaluator to design a study and evaluate the effects of this innovation. The correctional system provides funding to carry out the study, and officials are sincerely committed to its goals. Assume the psychologist concludes that the halfway house does not significantly reduce drug use by parolees. The authorities are disappointed and may even challenge the integrity of the policy evaluator. Yet, as scientists, program evaluators must "call 'em like they see 'em," regardless of the desirability of the outcome.

Even if the program is successful, the policy evaluator faces other ethical dilemmas. To assess such an innovative program, the researcher might conduct a randomized controlled trial that entails denying some parolees access to the program by placing them in a "no treatment" control group. The ethical dilemma becomes more critical when some potentially lifesaving innovation is being evaluated. But often it is only through such research methods that a potentially helpful new program can be convincingly demonstrated to be effective.

The Psychologist as a Forensic Evaluator in Litigation

In addition to evaluating policies and programs, psychologists may be asked to evaluate individuals involved in civil and criminal cases to report their findings to a judge, and on occasion, to testify about the results in court. Forensic evaluators assess matters such as:

- The competence of a defendant to proceed with adjudication of charges (often called "competence to stand trial," although most criminal charges are adjudicated through plea bargaining rather than trial)
- The mental state of a defendant at the time of an alleged offense (often called "sanity at the time of the offense")
- The degree of emotional or brain damage suffered by a victim in an accident
- The effects on a child of alternative custody arrangements after divorce
- The risk of future violent or otherwise criminal behavior
- The prospects for a convicted defendant's rehabilitation in prison or on probation

There are two ways that mental health professionals become involved in litigation as **forensic evaluators**: they are either court-appointed or hired by one of the parties involved in the litigation (defense, prosecution, or plaintiff). Serving in the court-appointed role involves receiving an order from the judge authorizing the mental health professional to evaluate a given individual for a specific purpose. The judge may also specify additional considerations such as how the results are to be communicated. There is typically an expectation that the resulting forensic evaluation will be considered by the judge without being introduced by either side.

Forensic evaluators for one of the parties involved in the litigation have a different expectation: That particular party may control when (and whether) the forensic assessment findings are actually introduced as evidence in the case. Some referrals for forensic assessment come from attorneys who authorize the evaluations without resorting to any kind of court authority. (This kind of right is usually reserved for the defense in a criminal prosecution; the prosecutor cannot request a **forensic mental health assessment** unless it is approved by the court—and therefore known to the defense.) These tasks will be discussed in much more detail in Chapters 10 and 11 of this book. They are also described in detail elsewhere (e.g., Heilbrun, Grisso, & Goldstein, 2009; Melton et al., 2017).

The Ethics of the Forensic Evaluator.
The ethical considerations associated with the role of forensic evaluator are fairly formal and specifically described in several documents. In addition to the ethical principles disseminated by the APA, two other sets of ethical guidelines affect the practice of forensic evaluators. Neither is "enforceable" in the sense that the APA *Ethical Principles of Psychologists and Code of Conduct* is. Nonetheless, both serve as important sources of authority and may affect the judgments of courts regarding the admissibility and weight of forensic assessment evidence. These two documents are the *Specialty Guidelines for Forensic Psychologists* (APA, 2013) and the *Guidelines for Child Custody Evaluations in Family Law Proceedings* (APA, 2010).

Across these three documents, there is substantial emphasis on providing evaluations that (1) are clear in their purpose; (2) are conducted by individuals who are competent by virtue of their education, training, and experience; (3) are respectful of appropriate relationships (and avoid multiple relationships, such as both forensic evaluator and therapist, in the same case);

(4) provide the appropriate level of confidentiality consistent with circumstances and the applicable legal privilege; (5) use methods and procedures that are accurate, current, and consistent with science and standards of practice; and (6) communicated appropriately.

Like other expert witnesses, forensic evaluators have an obligation to be objective in their assessments and reporting, yet may be tempted to favor the side that has retained them. This concern is illustrated by a study of how pairs of independent forensic psychologists, retained by opposing attorneys, evaluated a common individual. Despite using a standardized diagnostic test for psychopathy, the psychologists tended to rate the individual in a manner favorable to the side that retained them (Murrie, Boccaccini, Guarnera, & Rufino, 2013). This sympathy may not even be conscious; instead, the psychologist may simply reach conclusions that are motivated by subtle partisan allegiance to the client. For this reason, adherence to relevant ethical standards is of paramount importance.

The Psychologist as a Consultant in Litigation

The final role for psychologists in the law is that of consultant. The field of **trial consulting** provides one example of this role for psychologists working in the legal arena. Social scientists who began this work in the 1970s used so-called scientific jury selection procedures (further described in Chapter 12) to assist defense lawyers in highly politicized trials resulting from antiwar activities in the United States. Since then, these techniques have been refined and expanded. The national media devoted extensive coverage to the use of trial consultants in the celebrity-status trials of Martha Stewart and O. J. Simpson, and research on community attitudes was influential in the 2001 conviction of a former Ku Klux Klansman for the 1963 bombing of a Birmingham, Alabama church. (We describe this case in more detail in Chapter 13.)

Today the field of trial consulting is a booming business and involves far more than jury selection. Trial consultants also conduct community attitude surveys to document extensive pretrial publicity or to introduce findings as evidence in trials involving discrimination or trademark violation claims (Posey, 2015). They test the effectiveness of demonstrative evidence (Richter & Humke, 2011), provide guidance to attorneys seeking damage awards (Bornstein & Greene,

2011a), and prepare witnesses to testify (Stinson & Cutler, 2011).

There is no expectation of impartiality in any of these roles as there would be for psychologists acting as basic scientists, applied scientists, policy evaluators, or forensic evaluators. Nor is there an expectation that the consultant must present information in a balanced way. However, the psychologist must still provide the attorney with good information in order to promote more effective performance in litigation. How the attorney decides to use such information is within that attorney's discretion.

Critics have argued that these techniques essentially rig the jury (Kressel & Kressel, 2002) and create a perception that psychologists can manipulate the trial process (Strier, 2011). But at least in the realm of jury selection, it is difficult to determine whether scientific jury selection is more effective than traditional jury selection. Cases that employ scientific jury selection techniques differ in many ways from cases that do not, and "success" is hard to define (Lieberman, 2011). (Does a low-damage award or conviction on a less serious charge connote success? Perhaps.) Consultants suggest that they are simply borrowing techniques commonly used in politics and advertising and bringing them into the courtroom. Politicians hire people to help them project a better image, and advertisers try to enhance the ways that retailers connect with consumers. Shouldn't lawyers be able to do the same? Consultants also argue that in an adversarial system, attorneys should be able to use every tool available to them.

The Ethics of the Consultant in Litigation. As we noted earlier, when the psychologist becomes a consultant for one side in the selection of jurors, there may be ethical questions. Just how far should the selection procedures go? Should jurors have to answer consultants' intrusive questions about their private lives? Should consultants be able to sculpt the jury to their clients' advantage? Do these techniques simply constitute the latest tools in the attorney's arsenal of trial tactics? Or do they bias the proceedings and jeopardize the willingness of citizens to participate in the process? These questions deal with fairness, and scientific jury selection may conflict with the way some people interpret the intent of the law.

Returning to the advertising analogy, are psychologists who work for an advertising agency unethical when they use professional knowledge to encourage consumers to buy one brand of dog food rather than another? Many of us would say no; the free-enterprise system permits any such procedures that do not falsify claims. This example is analogous to jury selection because rival attorneys—whether they employ trial consultants or not—always try to select jurors who will sympathize with their version of the facts. Since the adversarial system permits attorneys from each side to eliminate some prospective jurors, it does not seem unethical for psychologists to assist these attorneys, as long as their advocacy is consistent with the law and the administration of justice. The same can be said about consultants retained by attorneys to provide information to enhance the presentation of a case.

When psychologists become trial consultants, they also subscribe to the ethical code of the attorneys, who, after all, are in charge of the trial preparation (Stolle & Studebaker, 2011). Trial consultants who are members of the American Society of Trial Consultants must adhere to the Code of Ethical Principles, Professional Standards, and Practice Guidelines developed by that organization (ASTC, 2017).

Summary

1. ***Why do we have laws and what is the psychological approach to studying law?*** Laws are human creations whose major purposes are the resolution of conflict and the protection of society. As society has changed, new conflicts surfaced, leading to expansion and revision of the legal system. A psychological approach focuses on individuals as agents within a legal system, asking how their internal qualities (personality, values, abilities, and experiences) and their environments, including the law itself, affect their behavior.

2. ***What choices are reflected in the psychological approach to the law?*** Several basic choices must be made between pairs of options in the psychological study of the law. These options are often irreconcilable because each is attractive, but both usually cannot be attained at the same time. The choices are (1) whether the goal of law is achieving personal freedom or ensuring the common good, (2) whether equality or discretion should be the standard for our legal policies, (3) whether the purpose of a legal inquiry is to discover the truth or to provide a means of conflict resolution, and (4) whether it is better to apply the methods of law or those of science for making decisions.

3. ***How do laws reflect the contrast between the due process model and the crime control model of the criminal justice system?*** The decade of the 1960s represented an era in which due process concerns were paramount and court decisions tended to favor rights of the individuals, particularly those suspected of crimes, over the power of the police and law enforcement. Since then, the crime control model, which seeks to contain or reduce criminal activity, has been favored by many. But some of the harsh policies and penalties consistent with

this perspective have resulted in large increases in prison populations and little reduction in rates of reoffending. The 2007–2009 recession caused legislators and judges to consider community-based alternatives that control crime more effectively.

4. ***What are five roles that psychologists may play in the legal system and what does each entail?*** Five possible roles are identified in this chapter: the psychologist as (1) a basic scientist, interested in knowledge related to psychology and law for its own sake; (2) an applied scientist who seeks to apply basic research knowledge to a particular problem in the legal system; a psychologist serving as an expert witness on a scientific question is an applied scientist in the law; (3) a policy evaluator who capitalizes on methodological skills to design and conduct research that assesses the effects of policies and program changes in the legal system; (4) a forensic evaluator who is either appointed by the court or retained at the request of one of the parties in the litigation to perform a psychological evaluation of an individual related to a legal question; and (5) a consultant who works on behalf of a party or position in litigation. Each role entails its own set of ethical dilemmas.

Key Terms

amicus curiae brief	due process model	implicit bias	randomized controlled trials
applied scientist	equality	policy evaluator	sentencing disparity
basic scientist	expert witness	precedents	settlement negotiation
case law	forensic evaluator	principle of proportionality	*stare decisis*
crime control model	forensic mental health assessment	procedural justice	trial consulting
determinate sentencing	forensic psychologists	racial bias	
discretion			

2 The Legal System: Issues, Structure, and Players

ORIENTING QUESTIONS

1. What is the difference between the adversarial and inquisitorial systems of justice?

2. How do notions of morality and legality differ?

3. How do different models of justice explain people's level of satisfaction with the legal system?

4. What is commonsense justice?

5. How are judges selected, and how do their demographic characteristics and attitudes influence their decisions?

6. How does the experience of law school affect its students?

7. What is known about lawyers' professional satisfaction?

8. What factors explain lawyers' overconfidence, and how can it be remedied?

To understand how and why psychologists interact with the law, one needs a basic understanding of how the legal system operates. Accordingly, in this chapter, we focus on the legal system itself. We describe the nature of the adversary system and psychological aspects of legality, morality, and justice. We discuss courts and examine the roles played by the major players in the legal system—judges and lawyers. An understanding of the workings of the legal system will help make clear why psychologists are interested in studying and assisting judges, lawyers, and ordinary citizens involved in the law. ●

The Adversarial System

In both criminal cases that concern conduct prohibited by law and civil cases that concern disputes between private parties, American legal procedures involve an **adversarial system** of justice. Exhibits, evidence, and witnesses are assembled by representatives of one side or the other to convince the fact finder (i.e., judge or jury) that their side's viewpoint is the correct one. During a trial, the choice of what evidence to present is within the discretion of those involved in the litigation and their attorneys. Judges rarely call witnesses or introduce evidence on their own.

The adversarial system is derived from English common law. This approach contrasts with the **inquisitorial system** used in Europe (but not in Great Britain), in which the judge has more control over the proceedings. Lind (1982) described the procedure in France as follows: "The questioning of witnesses is conducted almost exclusively by the presiding judge. The judge interrogates the disputing parties and witnesses,

referring frequently to a dossier that has been prepared by a court official who investigated the case. Although the parties probably have partisan attorneys present at the trial, it is evident that control over the presentation of evidence and arguments is firmly in the hands of the judge" (p. 14). In the inquisitorial system, the two sides do not have separate witnesses; the witnesses testify for the court, and the opposing parties are not allowed to prepare the witnesses before the trial.

The adversarial model has been criticized for promoting a competitive atmosphere that can distort the truth. During a trial, jurors may have to choose between two versions of the truth, neither of which is completely accurate, because witnesses often shade their testimony to favor their "side." In addition, skillful lawyers can effectively impugn the credibility of hostile witnesses, and criminal defendants rarely testify, despite being the most important source of information about the events in question (Slobogin, 2014).

Research on these contrasting approaches reveals several benefits of the adversarial model, however. A research team led by a social psychologist, John Thibaut, and a law professor, Laurens Walker (Thibaut & Walker, 1975; Walker, La Tour, Lind, & Thibaut, 1974) conducted programmatic research and concluded that the adversarial system led to less-biased decisions that were more likely to be seen as fair by the parties in dispute. One explanation for this more favorable evaluation of the adversarial system is that it is the system with which Americans are most familiar. But people who live in countries with nonadversarial systems (France and West Germany) have also rated the adversary procedure as fairer (Lind, Erickson, Friedland, & Dickenberger, 1978), perhaps because the adversarial system allows attorneys and their clients to control the arguments and strategies.

Because the adversarial system permits the litigants to "call the shots," it seems optimized to produce fair and just outcomes. But are they also the *correct* outcomes, given the facts of the case? Maybe not, according to Thibaut and Walker (1978). They noted that inquisitorial procedures seem optimized to produce truthful outcomes because they involve a neutral third party who gathers the relevant evidence without influence from the parties who have a stake in the dispute.

People's perceptions of justice and truth apparently do depend on the legal procedures to which they are exposed. In one study that demonstrated that point, participants read the evidence about an allergic reaction in a dog-bite case. The evidence was presented in either an adversarial manner where the litigants found their own scientific experts and worked with them prior to trial, or an inquisitorial manner where the judge appointed an expert witness who worked independently of the litigants. People exposed to adversarial procedures thought they produced verdicts that were just but not necessarily accurate, whereas those exposed to inquisitorial procedures thought the reverse: the verdicts were accurate but not necessarily just (Sevier, 2014). Stated simply, adversarial systems seem to provide more justice and inquisitorial systems seem to provide more truth. But in addition to justice and truth, one should also consider the tensions between what is legal (or illegal) and what is moral (or immoral).

Legality versus Morality

Laws are designed to regulate the behavior of individuals—to specify precisely what conduct is illegal. But do these laws always correspond to people's sense of right and wrong?

Consider the case of Lester Zygmanik. Lester was charged with murdering his own brother, George, because George had demanded that Lester kill him. A motorcycle accident a few days earlier had left George, age 26, paralyzed from the neck down. He saw a future with nothing but pain, suffering, and invalidism; as he lay in agony, he insisted that his younger brother Lester, age 23, swear he would not let him continue in such a desperate state. (Other family members later verified that this had been George's wish.) So, on the night of June 20, 1973, Lester slipped into his brother's hospital room and shot him in the head with a 20-gauge shotgun. Dropping the gun by the bed, he turned himself in moments later. There was no question about the cause of death; later, on the witness stand during his murder trial, Lester told the jury that he had done it as an act

of love for his brother. Because New Jersey had no laws regarding mercy killing, the prosecution thought a case could be made for charging Lester with first-degree murder.

The state believed it had a good case against Lester. His actions met every one of the elements that the law required for his guilt to be proved. First, there was premeditation, or a plan to kill. Second, there was deliberation (as defined in the New Jersey criminal code—"the weighing of the 'pros' and 'cons' of that plan"). Third, there was willfulness ("the intentional carrying out of that plan"). Lester had even sawed off the shotgun before hiding it under his coat, and he had packed the bullets with candle wax, which compacted the explosion and made it more deadly. Lester forthrightly admitted to his lawyer: "I gave it a lot of thought. You don't know how much thinking I did on it. I had to do something I knew that would definitely put him away" (Mitchell, 1976, p. vii). At his trial, Lester took the stand and described his motivations, explaining that he did what his brother wanted.

If you had been a juror in this trial, how would you have voted? College students usually split just about evenly between verdicts of "guilty of first-degree murder" and "not guilty." Those who vote guilty often hope that the sentence will be a humanitarian one, but they believe it is their duty to consider the evidence and apply the law. Certainly, this was an act of murder, they say, regardless of Lester's good intentions. But those who vote not guilty often feel that it is appropriate, on occasion, to disregard the law when mitigating circumstances are present or when community standards argue for forgiveness.

Both reactions are reasonable, and they illustrate the dilemma between treating similar offenders equally and showing discretion if circumstances warrant. They also demonstrate important differences between judgments based on **black-letter law** and those based on one's conscience or personal sentiments about a given situation. By "black-letter law" (sometimes referred to as the *law on the books*), we mean the law as set down by our founding fathers in the Constitution, as written by legislators, and as interpreted by judges. According to the black-letter law, Lester Zygmanik was guilty. But there is another way to judge his actions—by focusing on his altruistic motives and his desire to help his brother, rather than to harm him.

As Lester Zygmanik's trial began, the prosecutor was confident that he would be found guilty. The jury, composed of seven men and five women, was tough, conservative, and blue-collar. The judge had even ruled that the term *mercy killing* could not be used in the trial. But after deliberating for fewer than three hours, the jury found Lester Zygmanik not guilty. The jurors focused, apparently, on the relationship between Lester and his brother, and they concluded that Lester had been overcome by grief, love, and selflessness. Their decision implicitly acknowledged that moral considerations such as the commitment to care for others were more important to their decision than the strict guidelines of the law.

Obviously, the Lester Zygmanik trial is not the only one in which a defendant claimed his act was a mercy killing. Helping terminally ill patients to commit suicide (so-called assisted suicide) is usually justified by the "offender" as an act of compassion or mercy, ending the "victim's" pain and suffering. In fact, in five states—Oregon, Washington, California, Montana, and Vermont—it is legal for a physician, under narrowly defined circumstances, to help a person to die. In the United States, public support for this practice ranges from 47% to 69% (Emanuel, Onwuteaka-Phillipsen, Urwin, & Cohen, 2016). Many people would be loath to call the "perpetrators" of these acts criminals, and proponents of assisted suicide often hail them as heroes.

Mercy killings and assisted suicides are examples of **euthanasia**, the act of killing an individual for reasons that are considered merciful. They illustrate the often-tragic differences between what an individual feels is the morally right or just thing to do and what the law describes as an illegal act to avoid. Should someone who voluntarily, willfully, and with premeditation assists in killing another human *always* be punished? Or should that person, in some circumstances, be treated with compassion and forgiveness? Many people can imagine exceptional circumstances in which individuals who have technically broken the law should be excused. Often, these circumstances involve a lack of intention to harm another person and the desire to help a person who is suffering. The topic of euthanasia highlights the tension between legality and people's perceptions of what is moral, ethical, and just.

Citizens' Sense of Legality and Morality

We might assume at first that what is defined as "legal" and what is judged to be "morally right" would be synonymous. But in the Zygmanik case, what the jury considered to be a moral action and what the justice system considered the proper legal resolution were inconsistent. Legislators and scholars have argued for centuries about whether the law should be consistent with citizens' sense of morality. In fact, inconsistencies abound. For example, prostitution is universally condemned as immoral, yet it is legal in parts of Nevada and in many European and South American countries as well as in Australia and New Zealand. Acts of civil disobedience, whether performed six decades ago in racially segregated buses in Montgomery, Alabama, or, more recently, to protest President Trump's travel ban or treatment of women are applauded by those who consider some laws and policies to be morally indefensible.

Psychologists have now conducted a number of studies that illustrate the differences between citizens' sense of morality and justice, on the one hand, and the legal system's set of formal rules and laws, on the other. At first glance, it may seem nearly impossible to study people's views about the legitimacy of formal laws because there are so many variations in laws and so many different penalties for violating those laws. (Criminal penalties are decided on a state-by-state basis in the United States, so there could be 50 different penalties for the same crime.) Fortunately, though, a large majority of states base their criminal laws on the Model Penal Code drafted by the influential American Law Institute in the 1960s. Thus we can ask whether the principles embodied in the Model Penal Code are compatible with citizens' intuitions about justice and legality. Do people tend to agree with the Model Penal Code or does their sense of right and wrong diverge from this black-letter law? One set of relevant studies has examined the category of attempted crimes and the important role that intention plays in these cases.

Attempted Crimes and the Concept of Intention in Law and Psychology.   Consider the following fundamental question of criminal law: How should attempted (but not completed) crimes be punished? An attempt may be unsuccessful because the perpetrator tries to commit a crime but fails (e.g., he shoots but misses) or because the attempt is interrupted or abandoned (e.g., robbers are about to enter a bank with guns drawn when they see a police officer inside).

The Model Penal Code says that attempts should be punished in the same way as completed crimes. If the offender's conduct strongly corroborates his criminal **intention**—showing that he not merely thought about the crime but actually tried to accomplish it—the Model Penal Code decrees that he should be punished to the same degree as the successful offender. Focusing on the central role of intent, the Model Penal Code assigns the same penalty to attempted crimes as

The Case of a Duped Would-Be Offender

BOX 2.1

In March, 1987, George Taylor forced his way into a woman's apartment in New York City and made sexual advances while threatening her with a knife. Fearful of the knife, the victim tried to convince Taylor that he could be her boyfriend, that he didn't need to impose himself in this way, and that he could come to her house anytime. Taylor relented, walked into an adjacent room, and took off the surgical gloves he had been wearing, saying he was not going to need these anymore. The victim then persuaded Taylor to accompany her to a liquor store to buy a bottle to celebrate getting to know each other. But as they were leaving the apartment she ducked back inside, locked the door, and called the police.

Despite arguing that he voluntarily and completely abandoned any intention of carrying out a crime, Taylor was convicted of attempted rape. The appellate court pointed out that in a parallel situation, if a person shoots at an intended victim and misses, he has no defense to the charge of attempted murder because his poor aim, rather than his lack of criminal intent, allowed the victim to live. Following that logic, the court ruled that it was the victim's escape, rather than Taylor abandoning his criminal intention, that prevented the rape.

CRITICAL THOUGHT QUESTION

Did the jury that convicted Taylor and the appellate court that upheld his conviction follow the rule of the Model Penal Code? Do you think jurors should be asked to peer into an offenders' minds and guess what they were thinking at the time of an attempted but incomplete act? How far along in executing a crime must offenders go in order to be guilty of a crime that they did not complete?

completed crimes. Thus, the pickpocket who thrusts his hand into another person's pocket, only to find it empty, is just as guilty (and just as deserving of punishment) as the pickpocket who makes off with a fat wallet. Regardless of the outcome of this act, the pickpocket tried to steal—and so, by definition, a crime was committed. A similar situation arose in the interesting case of (*People v. Taylor*, 1992), described in Box 2.1.

According to the Model Penal Code, an offender who tries but fails is just as culpable as an offender who tries and succeeds. But do ordinary people think about intent and attempted crimes this way? Do they think that *trying* to break into a store is as serious as *actually* breaking into the store?

Psychologist John Darley and his colleagues asked respondents to read short scenarios that described people who had taken one or more steps toward committing either robbery or murder and to assign punishment to those people (Darley, Sanderson, & LaMantia, 1996). They found that people's intuitions differed in predictable ways from the position of the Model Penal Code. In situations where the person depicted in the scenario had taken only preliminary action (e.g., examining the store he planned to burgle or telling a friend about his plan), few people thought he was guilty, and those who did assigned mild punishments. Yet, according to the Model Penal Code, this person

is just as guilty as one who actually completed the burglary. When the scenario described a person who had reached the point of "dangerous proximity" to the crime, punishments increased, but they still were only half as severe as those assigned to the person who actually completed the crime. Apparently people do not accept the view that intent to commit an act is the moral equivalent of actually doing it. Their notions about criminality and the need for punishment are more nuanced, less "black and white" than what the Model Penal Code prescribed.

Psychology's focus on mental states also reflects more differentiations and less clear-cut distinctions than those of black-letter law. Psychology considers a spectrum of behavior, motivated by a variety of influences and ranging from accidents to behavior influenced by stress, peer pressure, or immature judgment, to actions that are deliberate and carefully planned.

Even this continuum may oversimplify variations in intention because it minimizes the importance of environmental and cultural influences that affect people differently. The social context in which behavior occurs can strongly influence a person's intention to behave in certain ways. In some contexts, it can be very hard for an individual to conceive of behavioral options. Therefore, one person's ability to intend a given behavior might be much more limited than that of another person who has more behavioral alternatives.

Psychologists have also studied how people assign causes, including intentions, to the behavior of others. A well-established theory in social psychology, **attribution theory**, focuses on how people explain others' intentions. According to the theory, attributions tend to vary along three dimensions: *internality*—whether we explain the cause of an event as due to something internal to a person or to something that exists in the environment; *stability*—whether we see the cause of a behavior as enduring or merely temporary; and *globalness*—whether we see the cause as specific to a limited situation or applicable to all situations. An individual who makes internal, stable, global attributions about an act of misconduct ("He is so evil that he doesn't care what anyone thinks or feels about him") will see an offender as more culpable and more deserving of punishment than a person who offers external, unstable, specific explanations for the same act ("As a result of hanging out with a rough crowd, she was in the wrong place at the wrong time").

When making inferences about what caused another person's behavior—especially behavior that has negative consequences—we tend to attribute the cause to stable factors that are internal to the person. That is, we are inclined to believe that others are predisposed to act the way they do. But when our own actions lead to negative outcomes, we are more likely to blame the external environment for the outcome, suggesting an unstable cause for our behavior that will probably change in the future.

Consequences of Citizen–Code Disagreements.

What difference does it make if laws do not comport with people's sense of right and wrong? Can people simply ignore laws they believe to be immoral? Indeed, we can find many examples of situations in which people opt not to obey laws and legal authority. When parents fail to make child support payments or when people violate restraining orders, it is often because they do not accept the legitimacy of a judge's decision. When people use illegal drugs or cheat on their income tax returns, it is often because they do not believe that the laws regulating these behaviors are just or morally right. During the era of prohibition in the United States, when alcohol consumption was outlawed, honest citizens became "criminals," entire illicit industries were created, and gang membership and gang-related violence increased significantly.

But there may be more significant and more general consequences of discrepancies between citizens' sense of

morality and the legal system's sense of legality. For the law to have any authority, it must be consistent with people's shared sense of morality. When that consistency is lacking, citizens may feel alienated from authority and become less likely to comply with laws they perceive as illegitimate (Carlsmith & Darley, 2008). Initial disagreement with one law can lead to contempt for the legal system as a whole, including the police who enforce laws and the judges who punish wrongdoers. If the law criminalizes behaviors that people do not think are immoral, it begins to lose its legitimacy. In the words of Oliver Wendell Holmes, "[The] first requirement of a sound body of law is that it should correspond with the actual feelings and demands of the community" (1881, pp. 41–42).

What Is Justice?

More than 2,000 years ago, at the beginning of the *Republic*, Socrates posed this question and we continue to ponder it today. Definitions of justice have changed throughout history. In the Old Testament and in Homer's *The Iliad*, justice meant something like revenge. By the time of the Golden Age of Athens in the fifth century B.C.E., the concept of justice came to be less about vengeance and more about achievement of the well-being of individuals (Solomon, 1990). The development of Christianity and Islam accentuated a conception of justice within religious traditions of morality. As a result, people began to see matters of social injustice (e.g., the suffering of the poor and the oppressed) as issues of concern, along with offenses against one's person or one's family (Solomon, 1990).

Distributive and Procedural Justice

Our discussion so far has assessed perceptions of legitimacy in the *outcomes* of legal disputes, such as whether the would-be pickpocket who came up empty-handed should be punished as severely as the one who got the loot. This focus on the fairness of the outcome in a legal dispute is the main concern of **distributive justice** models. According to the principles of distributive justice, a person will be more accepting of decisions and more likely to believe that disputes have been resolved appropriately if the outcomes seem just (or if the outcomes—in the same sense as salaries or promotions—seem distributed equitably, hence the term *distributive justice*).

A series of classic studies in psychology and law showed that although distributive justice theories were correct, there was clearly more to the story. This work, conducted by a psychologist and a law professor, suggests that disputants' perceptions of the fairness of the *procedures* are vitally important to the sense that "justice" was done (Thibaut & Walker, 1975). Such an orientation leads us to think of justice not only as punishment for wrongdoing but also as a process by which people receive what they deserve or are due. **Procedural justice** models suggest that if individuals view the procedures of dispute resolution or decision-making as fair, then they will view the outcome as just, regardless of whether it favors them or not. According to this perspective, important issues in a contested divorce include the means by which each person was wronged and whether the marriage can be dissolved in a manner satisfactory to both. In a dispute with an insurance company over an accident claim, one might ask whether the injured party was treated fairly or unfairly.

Generally, individuals perceive a decision-making process as fair to the extent that they believe they have a voice in how the process unfolds, are treated with dignity and respect during the process, and trust the authorities in charge of the process to be motivated by concerns about fairness (Sydeman, Cascardi, Poythress, & Ritterband, 1997). A full opportunity to state one's viewpoint and to participate actively and personally in the decision makes a strong contribution to an assessment of fairness, probably because it allows people to feel that they retain some control over their affairs (Ebreo, Linn, & Vining, 1996).

Procedural fairness is an important consideration in the resolution of child custody and child support disputes, for example. To the extent that family court judges use fair procedures, they are more successful in creating post-divorce situations in which both fathers and mothers are involved in their children's lives and take responsibility for financial and emotional support (Bryan, 2005). This is true regardless of the outcome. Thus, fathers, who often lose child custody hearings, are more likely to maintain contact with their children into the future if they believe that the hearing was fair.

These findings also apply in the real-world interactions that occur in police stations and courtrooms. Police officers and judges are not likely to generate warm feelings in the community when they give people less than what those people feel they deserved, or when they limit people's abilities to act as they wish. Do citizens have a better view of police officers and judges (and, by extension, of the entire legal system) if they perceive that they are being treated fairly? Will this

make it more likely that they will cooperate with legal authorities and comply with the law?

To answer these questions, Tyler and Huo (2002) interviewed individuals in Oakland and Los Angeles who had a recent experience with a police officer or a judge. The researchers asked about the fairness of the outcomes of those encounters with authorities, and about the fairness of the procedures that were used to achieve the outcomes. They also measured people's trust in the motives of a particular authority figure by asking participants whether they felt that their views had been considered and whether the authority cared about their concerns.

As one might expect, the favorability of the outcomes shaped participants' responses to this encounter. We feel better about situations and people when we get what we want from those situations and from those individuals. But importantly, the willingness to accept the decision of a police officer or judge was strongly influenced by perceptions of procedural fairness and trustworthiness: When people perceived that police officers and judges were treating them fairly and when they trusted the motives of these officials, they were more likely to accept their decisions and directives.

Procedural fairness also has long-term effects on people's willingness to obey the law. Tyler and Jackson (2014) surveyed 1,600 people who mirrored the demographics of the American population in their views of the police, courts, and the law, and in their public behaviors. They found, unsurprisingly, that the risk of being caught and punished affected compliance with the law, but so did people's views about the legitimacy of the police and the courts. If people thought these authorities were legitimate—a crucial component of procedural justice—they were more willing to obey laws regarding both minor crimes like speeding and littering and serious crimes like theft. The police themselves are affected by perceptions of procedural fairness: those who believe their departments have fair procedures and decision-making are likely to obey their supervisors, are psychologically and emotionally grounded, and trust the communities they police (Trinkner, Tyler, & Goff, 2016).

The principles and consequences of procedural fairness extend well beyond the confines of a police station or courthouse. How adults, particularly parents, resolve conflicts that inevitably arise in a family influences the behavior of children. One team of researchers asked middle-school students to describe how a recent conflict or disagreement with their parents was resolved: "Did your parents treat you with respect? Were they equally

fstop123/E+/Getty Images

Citizens are more likely to obey laws when they think that police use fair procedures.

fair to everyone involved?" The students also described mild forms of aggressive behavior—bullying—they had directed at other students. Analyzing these two sets of responses, the researchers determined that higher perceived levels of procedural fairness in the family were associated with lower frequencies of bullying behavior at school (Brubacher et al., 2009).

Commonsense Justice: Everyday Intuitions about Fairness

Another approach to the study of justice—one closely aligned with the analysis of citizens' agreement with the criminal code—is to learn about the intuitions that average people hold about culpability, fairness, and justice. Psychologist Norman Finkel examined the relationship between the black-letter law and what he called **commonsense justice**—ordinary citizens' basic notions of what is just and fair. Finkel's work has much to say about inconsistencies between the law and public sentiment in the types of cases we have examined in this chapter—assisted suicide and euthanasia—as well as in cases involving self-defense, the insanity defense, the

death penalty, and felony murder (Finkel, 1995). Commonsense justice is also reflected in cases in which a jury refuses to convict a defendant who is legally guilty of the crime charged—the phenomenon known as jury nullification.

According to Finkel and others who have pondered commonsense justice (e.g., Miller, Blumenthal, & Chamberlain, 2015), there is evidence that the black-letter law on the books may be at odds with community sentiment. This work is an important contribution to the field of law because it explains *how* people's sentiments depart from legal concepts and procedures. There are three identifiable discrepancies.

1. *The commonsense context is typically wider than the law's.* Ordinary people tend to consider the big picture: Their assessment of the event in question extends backward and forward in time (including, for example, a defendant's conduct prior to the incident and behavior after the crime), whereas the law allows consideration of a more limited set of circumstances. For example, in a date rape case or other case in which the victim and defendant knew each other, jurors would be likely to consider

the history of the individuals, both together and apart. Is the incident one in a series of troublesome encounters in a tumultuous relationship? Have these events been alleged by other partners?

Although people contemplate the wider context of the story, the law freezes the frame at the time of a wrongful act and then zooms in on that relatively finite moment. Reasoning that this narrower perspective will result in a cleaner and more precise judgment, the law determines culpability on the basis of actions and intentions within this narrow window. But people would often rather learn about the big picture; for many, viewing only the last act does little to reveal the entire drama (Finkel & Groscup, 1997).

2. *Commonsense perspectives on the actions of a defendant and victim are more subjective than the law allows.* In disputes that involve people with a prior history, for example, observers construct a story about what happened and why. They do this by stepping into the shoes of the disputants and viewing the events through their eyes. The stories they construct typically describe hidden motives and desires gleaned from past conduct. But this perspective can result in judgments based on changing and inconsistent sentiments rather than discernible and objective facts.

3. *Observers take a proportional approach to punishment, whereas the law asks them to consider the defendant in isolation.* Imagine a situation in which an armed robber enters a convenience store while his female accomplice watches guard outside the store. Further imagine that things go awry—the robber ends up shooting the cashier, and the cashier dies. The robber has certainly committed a crime, but what about the accomplice? According to the felony-murder doctrine (which applies in about half the states), the accomplice is as culpable as the triggerman. Yet this egalitarian approach seems to contradict the notion of proportional justice, in which a defendant's actions and intentions are assessed in comparison to others and more culpable defendants are dealt with more severely. People easily make distinctions among types of crimes and criminals, and they usually want more severe punishment for those they find most blameworthy.

It is now understood that community sentiments affect laws and policies in many aspects of our everyday lives, including same-sex marriage and divorce (Barth & Huffman, 2015), campus-related violence and safety (Campbell, 2015), the use of social media (Kwiatkowski & Miller, 2015) and child custody (Sigillo, 2015). In each instance, there are legitimate debates about the extent to which commonly held beliefs—community sentiments—*should* influence the laws and policies that govern our behavior.

Courts

We now turn our attention to the reality of resolving legal disputes and the structures our society has enacted to do so. Disputes that reach the legal system are often, though not always, resolved in court. New community-based alternatives to standard prosecutions are increasingly used. **Diversion** to an alternative system may occur upon one's first encounter with a police officer, or when the case is referred to any of several "problem-solving courts" (also called specialty courts). Rather than focusing on punishment for wrongdoing, as traditional courts tend to do, problem-solving courts deal with the underlying reasons that individuals commit crimes in the first place. Such problem-solving courts include drug court, mental health court, and veterans' court (addressing issues of drug abuse, mental illness, and exposure to trauma, respectively), among others. Chapter 9 describes community-based alternatives, including specialty courts, in detail.

Different kinds of courts have been created to handle specific legal issues. Because we cover various court cases relevant to psychology throughout this book, an understanding of the structure of both the traditional and alternative court system will be helpful. In the next section we describe the traditional court system.

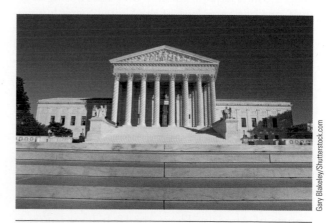

U.S. Supreme Court building.

State Courts

Although there are 50 different state court systems in the United States, they all typically include "lower" courts, trial courts, and appellate courts. Lower courts have jurisdiction over specific matters such as probate of wills (proving that a will was properly signed), administration of estates (supervising the payment of a deceased person's debts and the distribution of his or her assets), small claims, and traffic offenses. Family courts handle cases involving divorce, child custody, and child dependency. Juvenile courts deal with legal questions concerning delinquency and juvenile offenders. Both family courts and juvenile courts tend to focus on helping people rather than punishing them. In fact, juvenile courts have functioned for many years to protect children from the rough-and-tumble world of adult criminal courts and to resolve cases in a supportive, nonadversarial way.

Trial courts typically decide any case that concerns a violation of state laws. Most criminal cases (e.g., those involving drunken driving, armed robbery, and sexual assault) are tried in state trial courts. Prominent examples of trial courts in action come from the recent spate of prosecutions of police officers for assaulting or killing black citizens.

State court systems also include one or more courts of appeal, similar to the federal appellate courts, and a state supreme court. Like the U.S. Supreme Court, state supreme courts review only those cases deemed to be especially important or controversial. Published opinions are found in bound volumes called Reporters, and all opinions are accessible online.

Federal Courts

Federal courts have jurisdiction over cases arising under the Constitution or laws of the United States but typically do not have jurisdiction over cases arising under state law, unless the plaintiff and defendant in a civil case are from different states. Federal courts include trial courts, appellate courts, and the U.S. Supreme Court. When Congress passes a law regarding federal crime (e.g., the statute making identity theft a federal crime), the effect is to increase the caseload of the federal courts.

Federal trial courts are called U.S. District Courts. There is at least one district in every state; some states (California, for example) have several districts.

The federal appellate courts are called the U.S. Courts of Appeals. There are 13 federal courts of appeals, divided into geographical "circuits." In population, the largest circuit is the Ninth Circuit, which includes California, and the smallest is the First Circuit, which includes only a few New England states. Appeals are assigned to three-judge panels. The three judges examine the record (documents that the lawyers believe the judges need in order to decide the case), read the briefs (the lawyers' written arguments), and listen to the oral argument (the lawyers' debate about the case) before voting. The panel decides the case by majority vote and one of the judges writes an opinion explaining why the court decided as it did. Like state court opinions, these opinions are published in bound volumes called Reporters, which can be accessed online, including through the Westlaw and Lexis computerized legal research services.

The U.S. Supreme Court

Nine justices make up the U.S. Supreme Court, which has the authority to review all cases decided by the federal appellate courts. But the Supreme Court reexamines only a small percentage of the cases it is asked to consider—cases that the justices view as most significant. The Supreme Court also has the authority to review state court decisions that involve constitutional or federal law issues. Judges and lawyers refer to the latter as *raising a federal question*. A case involving the sale of violent video games to minors was both legally and psychologically significant, and illustrates how a state case raises a federal question. We describe it in Box 2.2.

Justices of the Supreme Court, like other federal judges, are appointed by the president and confirmed by the Senate. They are granted a lifelong tenure to allow them to be impartial, not influenced by the whims of political or legislative interests. In theory, their nomination is also expected to be above the fray of partisanship. But we saw a great deal of politicking surrounding the recent appointment of a replacement for Justice Antonin Scalia, who died in 2016. President Obama nominated Merrick Garland, the chief judge of the Court of Appeals for the District of Columbia, to replace Scalia. But Garland's confirmation was blocked by Republican lawmakers who argued that the appointment should fall to the President who would be elected later that year, rather than to the lame-duck Obama. So despite Garland's impressive credentials (Lyall, 2017), the vote on his confirmation never occurred and President Trump nominated Neil Gorsuch, also a federal appeals court judge, who was confirmed by the Republican-led

The Case of Violent Video Games and Minors' Free Speech Rights

BOX 2.2

Spurred by the efforts of state senator and child psychologist Leland Yee, the California legislature passed a law in 2005 that banned the sale or rental to minors of violent video games that portrayed "killing, maiming, dismembering, or sexually assaulting an image of a human being." Violators could be fined up to $1,000. But violent video games such as Grand Theft Auto and Call of Duty are big sellers, so video game makers immediately challenged the law in the U.S. District Court for Northern California, arguing that it restricted free speech rights guaranteed by the First Amendment. The district court judge ruled in their favor, as did the Ninth Circuit Court of Appeals. The U.S. Supreme Court, in a 7–2 ruling, agreed (*Brown v. Entertainment Merchants Association*, 2011), holding that the California law was an unconstitutional infringement on free speech.

Social science played a prominent and controversial role in this case, as both sides enlisted psychologists to comment on the connection between exposure to violent video games and harmful effects on children (Sacks, Bushman, & Anderson, 2011). Despite strong empirical evidence of increased aggressive behaviors, desensitization to violence, nightmares, and fear of being harmed that result from exposure to media violence (American Academy of Pediatrics, 2009), the Court accepted the video game makers' claim that the relationship is correlational and not causal; in other words, that the studies cannot prove that violent video games actually *cause* minors to act aggressively. They also agreed with the game makers that the law restricted the expression of free speech. But in a forceful dissenting opinion, Justice Stephen Breyer listed dozens of peer-reviewed scholarly articles on this topic and concluded that the bulk of the evidence supported the claim that violent video games do cause psychological harm to children.

CRITICAL THOUGHT QUESTION

Given that this case involved a California law, why was it tried in federal court rather than state court? What federal question did it raise?

Senate. This situation, apparently unprecedented in Supreme Court history (Kar & Mazzone, 2016; but see Whelan, 2016), raises serious questions about the nature of judicial appointments and whether appellate justices can rise above partisan politics and "call 'em as they see them."

Players in the Legal System: Judges

Most of us can easily conjure the image of a black-robed judge presiding over a hushed courtroom, approving plea bargains, determining what evidence will be admitted into a trial, and sentencing offenders to lengthy prison terms. To litigants—plaintiffs, defendants, prosecutors, and defense attorneys—indeed, even to the general public, the proclamations of a judge demand deference and, in most instances, respect. His or her words are often the "last words" in a legal dispute. Until recently, we knew relatively little about how judges make decisions, the extent to which their judgments are influenced by personality, attitudes, or past experiences, and how those decisions are constrained by various rules and roles. But psychologists have expressed increasing interest in judicial decision making (Vidmar, 2011). Thus, we are gradually beginning to understand how these robe-cloaked jurists think and how various structural features of the justice system influence their thoughts. One such feature is the means by which judges are selected to serve.

How Are Judges Selected?

We discussed judicial independence—the insulation of judges from the court of public opinion—in the context of the recent Supreme Court appointment. In theory, all U.S. federal judges, who are appointed by the president and serve for life, are shielded from the sometimes-fickle inclinations of politicians and the public. They can be removed from office only if impeached for "high crimes and misdemeanors."

The majority of state court judges face elections. Typically, the governor makes an initial appointment and the judge is then retained (or not) in a popular election. If retained, the judge serves a number of years, after which he or she again runs for retention. Supporters claim that this system makes judges accountable to the public and that a judge who makes unpopular decisions can be removed from the bench.

But like other elections, some judicial races have been hotly contested in recent years, with special interest groups and political parties pouring millions of dollars into advertising to elect judges of a certain persuasion. Alabama leads the nation in this regard: Between 2000 and 2009, appellate judges alone took in $206 million in campaign contributions, some from lawyers whose cases they would later decide. Furthermore, lower court judges in Alabama are able to contribute to the campaigns of appellate justices who may be in position to uphold their decisions (Sample, Skaggs, Blitzer, & Casey, 2010). The Alabama State Bar Association considers none of this unethical. But it raises the specter of "politicians in robes," a term coined by former Supreme Court Justice Sandra Day O'Connor.

Although the due process clause of the Fourteenth Amendment requires judges to avoid even the appearance of bias, campaign contributions from political parties and interest groups increase the chances that judges will favor litigants who align with those interests (Kang & Shepherd, 2011). Campaign contributions even affect judges' decisions by increasing their bias against criminal defendants. In analyzing the results of more than 3,000 criminal appeals in 32 states and merging them with data on the number of judicial election TV ads aired in the same period, Shepherd and Kang (2014) found that as spending on judicial elections increased, judges became less inclined to vote in favor of criminal defendants. This is concerning because criminal cases typically involve questions about rights guaranteed to all Americans.

Standing for election can also influence trial judges' sentencing decisions. According to one study, judges become more punitive as elections near. Using sentencing data from more than 22,000 criminal cases in the 1990s, Huber and Gordon (2004) found that judges added more than 2,700 years of additional prison time in aggravated assault, rape, and robbery cases when they were standing for election.

The politicization of judicial elections is unfortunate. What is a virtue in a legislative office—keeping a campaign promise—is a vice in a judicial office. Judges who promise in a campaign not to probate offenders either break their promise to the voters by probating an offender who deserves probation or violate their obligation as judge by denying probation. No judicial candidate should state or imply that he or she would favor one side over the other or decide an issue on anything other than the facts and the law.

There is no easy resolution to the issue of judicial selection. Perhaps the balance between public accountability and judicial independence can be achieved by a system that combines merit appointments with retention elections. In more than a dozen states, nonpartisan commissions provide voters with evaluations of judges' entire tenure in office, including feedback from attorneys and the public.

Influences on Judicial Judgments

There are at least two schools of thought about whether judges' rulings are influenced solely by the facts of a case and the applicable laws, or whether **extralegal factors** play a role. **Legal formalism** is the perspective that judges apply legal rulings to the facts of a case in a careful, rational, mechanical way and pay little heed to political or social influences on, or implications of, their judgments. In contrast, **legal realism** holds that judges' decisions are influenced by a variety of psychological, social, and political factors, and that judges indeed are concerned about the real-world ramifications of their decisions.

One caricature of legal realism is that judges are influenced by very personal matters, such as when they last ate. In fact, there is some empirical support of this idea: In their study of successive parole decisions by experienced judges, Danziger, Levav, and Avnaim-Pesso (2011) found that the percentage of favorable rulings dropped from approximately 65% to nearly zero as a morning or afternoon courtroom session wore on, but that the percentage of favorable rulings rose again to about 65% after the judge had taken a food break!

Food matters aside, much evidence suggests that trial judges, as human beings, reflect on their own experiences, assumptions, and biases when reaching decisions from the bench, especially when the choice involves some leeway (e.g., deciding whether to allow evidence to be presented in a trial or deciding on the length of a prison sentence). They may have biases for or against certain groups— gay or lesbian persons, racial minorities, and older adults—that affect the way they process evidence and make decisions. Judges who have been prosecutors may maintain their sympathy with the government's evidence in criminal trials; conversely, judges who were once defense attorneys may be biased in favor of defendants.

One commentator has compared judges to baseball umpires, proposing that although judges' decisions are constrained by procedural rules and precedents, there is still opportunity for personal discretion (Quinn, 1996). This would suggest that the life experiences of judges who are female or members of racial or sexual minorities might predispose them to make decisions that differ from those of their White, male, heterosexual counterparts, particularly in cases related to gender, race, and sexual preference (e.g., sexual offenses, harassment, and discrimination). Interestingly though, judges who have daughters, regardless of their gender, tend to be more liberal on gender issues than judges who do not have daughters (Glynn & Sen, 2015).

Although women make up more than half of the U.S. populace, until recently federal judges were almost exclusively male. Racial minorities and openly gay individuals are also vastly underrepresented on the bench. In fact, not until 2011 was an openly gay man appointed as a federal judge. One reason for the lack of diversity is the life tenure of federal judges, meaning that new judges are appointed only when current judges retire, resign, or die. This imbalance began to change during the presidencies of Jimmy Carter and Bill Clinton and for the first time ever, as of 2010, three women serve as justices of the U.S. Supreme Court.

Do judges' decisions tend to reflect their experiences and personal characteristics? Although there is limited evidence that judges show **in-group bias** (the tendency to favor one's own group) (e.g., Gazal-Ayal & Sulitzeanu-Kenan, 2010), their decisions generally cannot be predicted from their gender or race alone (e.g., Kulik, Perry, & Pepper, 2003) with the exception, apparently, of whether they have daughters! The powerful forces associated with years of legal education and practice usually trump the influence of personal characteristics. Legal socialization broadens attorneys' and judges' knowledge base and increases their respect for precedents and legal compliance. Because judges have typically practiced law for many years before assuming the bench, they understand that personal inclinations cannot dominate their decision making but rather that they must rule consistently with prior decisions and statutory guidelines (Vidmar, 2011). If they deviate radically from previous decisions, their rulings will be overturned on appeal.

As we explained, appellate judges perform different tasks than trial judges and thus may be influenced in different ways by case facts, relevant laws, and extralegal factors. Rather than assessing the credibility of certain witnesses and rendering a verdict, their job is to determine if the law has been correctly applied in previous decisions by trial judges and juries. Although the focus of their work differs from that of trial judges, their decisions can still be analyzed within the perspectives of legal formalism and legal realism. The legal formalism perspective is exemplified by Supreme Court Justice Clarence Thomas's assertion that "There are right and wrong answers to legal questions" (Thomas, 1996). It suggests that judges dispassionately consider the relevant laws, precedents, and constitutional principles, and that judicial bias has no part in decision making. Yet Supreme Court justices tend to vote in predictable ways on cases that reflect ideology-driven issues such as free speech and civil liberties, and decisions by conservative justices are more predictable than those of moderate or liberal justices (Wrightsman, 2006). Moreover, decisions by federal judges appointed by Democratic presidents differ from those of judges appointed by Republican presidents (Tiede, Carp, & Manning, 2010). Thus, judges' attitudes and predispositions *do* influence their decisions, at least in some kinds of cases. Indeed, most social scientists now reject the legal formalism model and instead favor the legal realism perspective, in which judges view the facts of the case "in light of [their] ideological attitudes and values" (Segal & Spaeth, 1993, p. 32).

How Do Judges Decide?

Psychologists have a ready explanation for why judges' attitudes and values affect their decisions: When people, including judges, have opinions about desired outcomes, those goals direct how they seek out and weigh empirical evidence. Information congruent with a particular goal is disproportionately attended to and valued, while incongruent evidence is dismissed. This process, called **motivated reasoning**, is typically outside of a person's awareness, but functions as a powerful determinant of how people evaluate information and reach conclusions about the law (Kahan, Hoffman, Braman, Evans, & Rachlinski, 2012; Kunda, 1990).

Also relevant to judges' decision making, cognitive psychologists have proposed various two-process models of human judgment. Though the details vary, all the models distinguish between **intuitive processes** that occur spontaneously, often without careful thought or effort, and **deliberative processes** that involve mental effort, concentration, motivation, and the application of learned rules. The former is sometimes referred to as System 1 and the latter, System 2 (Kahneman, 2011). Motivated reasoning is implicated in both because end goals can unconsciously steer both intuitive and deliberative evaluations of evidence.

A team of law professors has used a two-process model to explain trial judges' decision making and, in particular, to assess how emotions can influence their judgments (Wistrich, Rachlinski, & Guthrie, 2015). They claim that although judges try to make decisions by relying on facts, evidence, and legal rules rather than personal biases or emotions, because they are ordinary people (who happen to wear robes), judges tend, like all of us, to favor intuitive reactions over careful deliberate responses. And though quick judgments can be overridden by complex, deliberative thoughts, judges must expend the effort to do so.

To demonstrate the effect of emotions on judicial decisions, the researchers exposed 500 judges to a hypothetical case involving illegal immigration, among the most contentious social issues of our time. Judges were told they were deciding the case of a Peruvian citizen who had purchased a forged U.S. entry visa and pasted it into his genuine passport. The question was whether doing so constituted forgery of an identification document. If they answered yes, the defendant would almost certainly be convicted of a crime and sentenced to prison prior to deportation. If they answered no, he would be immediately deported. There were two versions: half the judges learned that the defendant was hired by a drug cartel to sneak into the United States illegally to kill someone stealing their profits, and the other half learned that he was a father trying to earn money to pay for a liver transplant for his critically ill nine-year-old daughter. Despite deciding a pure question of law ("does pasting a forged visa into a genuine document constitute forging an identification card?") about defendants who performed identical acts, judges' sympathies intervened and they responded differently to the two defendants. Only 44% who read about the father ruled that he had committed forgery, compared with 60% who read about the drug cartel's assassin.

The same team of law professors has shown that judges use intuitive and emotional decision processes to respond to suggested damage awards, descriptions of litigants' conduct, and inadmissible evidence (Guthrie, Rachlinski, & Wistrich, 2001; Wistrich, Guthrie, & Rachlinski, 2005). They have even shown that administrative judges, who handle massive numbers of disputes related to environmental safety, labor relations, civil rights violations, and regulatory compliance, and who have vast subject matter expertise, fall victim to the same snap judgments informed by intuitions and emotions (Guthrie, Rachlinski, & Wistrich, 2009). So despite Supreme Court Justice Elena Kagan's assertion, during her confirmation hearing, that judges' emotions play no role in determining the law (she stated "it's law all the way down"), these findings show that judges do not make decisions based entirely on the law alone.

Players in the Legal System: Lawyers

Lawyers are plentiful in the United States. The American Bar Association (ABA) reported that in 2015 there were more than 1,300,000 attorneys in the United States, or roughly one per every 265 citizens. This means that "every weekday morning [more than a million] chairs throughout the nation await indentation behind a lawyer's desk" (Kiser, 2010, p. 13).

Lawyers' Work Settings

The legal field permeates the American economy. In 2005, expenditures for legal services were more than twice what the federal government spent on research and development (National Science Board, 2008). The work of lawyers influences everything from "automobile design to pharmaceutical research, from kindergarten field trip waivers to Fortune 500 companies' earnings guidance" (Kiser, 2010, pp. 11–12). Given this vast array of legal services, it is not surprising that lawyers work in a wide variety of settings.

The most likely place to find a lawyer is in private practice. In 2005, 75% of licensed lawyers worked in that setting, most often in solo offices (American Bar Association, 2015). Lawyers who work in law firms attend to the needs of the firm's clients. Some of them specialize (e.g., in labor law or intellectual property), and others are generalists, trying to handle most of their clients' legal matters. Some lawyers work for corporations and have only one client—their corporate employer.

Many lawyers work for the government on the federal, state, or local level. Like attorneys for corporations, government lawyers have only one client: the governmental unit for which they work. Prosecutors are government lawyers responsible for prosecuting individuals charged with crimes. Federal prosecutors (called U.S.

Attorneys) are appointed by the president and prosecute people for violating federal laws. The head prosecutors for cities and counties, typically called States' Attorneys or district attorneys, are elected, often in partisan elections. They prosecute individuals who have allegedly broken city, county, or state laws.

Because many people accused of crime cannot afford to hire a lawyer, most criminal defendants are represented by public defenders who are also government employees. The history of public defenders dates from the 1963 case of *Gideon v. Wainwright*, in which the Supreme Court held that the State of Florida was obligated to pay for a lawyer for Clarence Earl Gideon, a small-town thief who lived on the fringes of society. His story is detailed in Box 2.3.

States responded to the Gideon case by appointing and paying lawyers to represent indigent defendants on a case-by-case basis and by establishing public defender

---

BOX 2.3

The Case of Clarence Gideon, His Famous Pauper's Plea, and the Right to an Attorney

At age 51, Clarence Earl Gideon was tried for breaking into a pool hall and stealing money from a cigarette machine and a jukebox. At his trial, Gideon asked the judge to appoint an attorney to defend him because he had no money to pay for one. The judge, following the laws in Florida, refused.

Gideon did not have a lawyer during his trial. Though no stranger to a courtroom, having been convicted on four previous occasions, he lost this case as

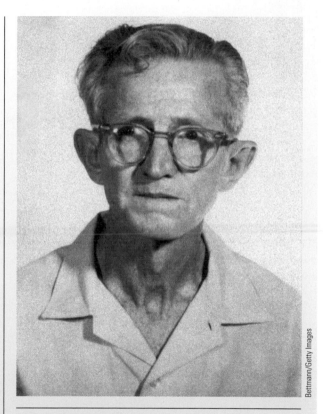

Clarence Earl Gideon

Source: Florida Supreme Court case files, S. 49, Box 2780, Case 31116. Petition for Writ of Habeas Corpus, Page 1.

well. Eventually, from his prison cell, Gideon filed a pauper's appeal to the U.S. Supreme Court. His contention, laboriously written in pencil and misspelled, was that the U.S. Constitution guaranteed the right of every defendant in a criminal trial to have the services of a lawyer. Gideon's effort was a long shot; well over 1,500 paupers' appeals are filed each term, and the Supreme Court agrees to consider only about 3% of them.

(Continued)

Furthermore, 20 years earlier, in the case of *Betts v. Brady* (1942), the Supreme Court had rejected the very proposition that Gideon was making by holding that poor defendants had a right to free counsel only under "special circumstances" (e.g., if the defendant was very young, illiterate, or mentally ill). Yet, ever since its adoption, the doctrine of *Betts v. Brady* had been criticized as inconsistent and unjust. The folly of requiring a poor person to represent himself is exemplified by Gideon's cross-examination of the most important witness for the prosecution:

Q. Do you know positively I was carrying a pint of wine?
A. Yes.
Q. How do you know that?
A. Because I seen it in your hand. (Lewis, 1964)

When Gideon's case was argued before the Supreme Court in January 1963, he was represented by Abe Fortas, a Washington attorney later appointed to the Supreme Court. Fortas argued that it was impossible for defendants to have a fair trial unless they were represented by a lawyer. He also observed that the "special circumstances" rule was very hard to apply fairly.

In 1963, the Supreme Court ruled unanimously that Gideon had the right to be represented by an attorney, even if he could not afford one. As Justice Hugo Black put it, "[that] the government hires lawyers to prosecute and [that] defendants who have the money hire lawyers to defend are the strongest indications of the widespread belief that lawyers in criminal cases are necessities, not luxuries" (*Gideon v. Wainwright*, 1963, p. 344). Nearly two years after he was sentenced, Clarence Gideon was given a new trial. With the help of a free court-appointed attorney, he was acquitted. The simple handwritten petition of a modest man had forever changed the procedures of criminal trials.

CRITICAL THOUGHT QUESTION
(1) What are some important functions performed by a defense attorney that a defendant such as Clarence Gideon could not provide in his own case? (2) How might this change if Mr. Gideon had been middle class and college educated? (3) What if Mr. Gideon had been a criminal attorney himself? (Why is there an old saying among lawyers that "the attorney who represents himself has a fool for a client?")?

programs, with lawyers hired by the state to represent those who cannot afford to hire them. Public defenders know the law, the system, and the other players in the system (the judge, the prosecutor, the probation officer), and though they have large caseloads, they often obtain excellent results for their clients.

Occasionally one reads of a public defender or appointed attorney who goes far beyond what can reasonably be expected of someone who is overworked and underpaid. Abbe Smith, now a law professor at Georgetown University, has written a book about her experience in representing Patsy Kelly Jarrett over a span of 25 years (Smith, 2008). Smith first met Jarrett in 1980, three years after Jarrett, driver of a getaway car, was convicted of felony murder and was sentenced to life imprisonment in New York. Convinced that Jarrett (whose conviction was based on eyewitness testimony) was innocent, Smith agreed to represent her and became a tireless advocate over the next 25 years, trying to secure Jarrett's freedom. Jarrett's conviction was eventually overturned.

Law Schools and Legal Education

American lawyers of the 18th and 19th centuries typically learned to practice law through the apprentice method: An enterprising young man (the first female lawyer graduated in 1869) would attach himself to an attorney for a period of time, until both he and the lawyer were satisfied that he was ready to be "admitted to the bar." He would then be questioned, often superficially, by a judge or lawyer and pronounced fit to practice (Stevens, 1983).

Powerful forces shaped legal education as we know it today. States began to require those aspiring to be lawyers to pass meaningful examinations. Influenced by the ABA, the states also gradually increased the educational requirements for taking these exams, first requiring some college, then some law school, and finally graduation from an accredited law school.

Legal education focuses on fostering analytic skills and deepening one's knowledge of the law, and although it is largely successful in this regard, it may take a toll on students' well-being. Recent studies show that attending law school tends to undermine students' values, motivation, and mental health. Researchers examined behavioral health issues in a sample of approximately 100 students at a Midwestern law school who completed various questionnaires regarding their psychological functioning and alcohol use (Reed, Bornstein, Jeon, & Wylie, 2016). Overall, students showed relatively high levels of psychological distress: 13% had scores that placed them above "normal" for anxiety, as did 11% on measures of stress and 10% on measures of depression. Levels of reported drinking were high: over half of the sample reported binge drinking in the previous month. First year students showed the most distress, consistent with the adage that "the first year will scare you to death, the second year will work you to death, and the third year will bore you to death."

These symptoms have been attributed to law schools' excessive workload, intimidating teaching practices, competitive grading systems, status-seeking job placement services, and the lack of concern about personal feelings, values, or subjective well-being (Reed & Bornstein, 2013). Researchers Sheldon (2004) and Krieger (2007) suggest that changes in motivation that occur over the course of one's law school career explain some of the dysfunction (perhaps especially among "bored to death" third-year students!). They focus on the **self-determination theory of optimal motivation** (Deci & Ryan, 2000), which describes situational and personality factors that cause positive and negative motivation and, eventually, changes in subjective well-being. Sheldon and Krieger (2004) found that the increase in mental health symptoms in the first year of law school was correlated with a decrease in **intrinsic motivation** (engaging in an activity because it is interesting and enjoyable). Over the course of that year, students moved from pursuing their professional goals for reasons of interest and enjoyment (i.e., because of their intrinsic motivation) to pursuing goals that would please and impress others (i.e., for reasons of **extrinsic motivation**). In other words, they felt less self-determined at the end of the year than they had at the beginning. Importantly, students who perceived that faculty supported their autonomy showed fewer declines in psychological well-being in the first year of law school and had higher grades in the third year (Sheldon & Krieger, 2007).

Professional Satisfaction among Lawyers

The psychological dysfunction that manifests in law school tends to subside within a few years of law school graduation but practicing lawyers still report significant levels of personal distress and job dissatisfaction (Reed & Bornstein, 2013). So although 81% of lawyers questioned in an American Bar Association–commissioned survey said their work was intellectually stimulating, only about half the respondents voiced satisfaction with their careers, and only 40% would recommend that others pursue law as a career (Ward, 2007). Nonwhite lawyers, whose numbers have been increasing steadily since the mid-1960s, tend to be less satisfied than their white counterparts, although they would still recommend a legal career to others and tend to regard the law as a promising opportunity for personal and professional growth.

There are multiple factors associated with job dissatisfaction that operate simultaneously (Reed & Bornstein, 2013). People with certain predispositions that are more susceptible to distress (e.g., achievement orientation, perfectionism) may self-select to pursue the law and thereby subject themselves to the stressors associated with attending law school, passing the bar exam, and establishing a law practice. Once they become practicing lawyers, they experience various environmental stressors such as work overload, time pressures, and competition, along with role conflicts and ethical dilemmas, all while operating in a milieu that has traditionally valued adversarial interactions—though the latter may be changing, slowly. (Given these features, it is impressive how many young people still aspire to become lawyers!)

Lawyers who do not possess typical "lawyer traits" may be most discontented by the practice of law. A particular constellation of characteristics distinguishes lawyers from the general adult population: a preference for dominance, competitiveness, the need for achievement, and interpersonal insensitivity (Daicoff, 1999). According to law professor Susan Daicoff, these traits fit well with traditional forms of legal practice that value winning, analytical reasoning, and the elevation of concerns about clients' legal rights (Daicoff, 1999). Certainly not all lawyers possess these traits and not all legal issues require an adversarial "I win–you lose" mentality. But attorneys who are not highly competitive, achievement-oriented, or motivated by dominance may experience the legal profession as a harsh and inhospitable place to work.

Fortunately, some legal institutions (including specialty courts and juvenile diversion programs) have begun to integrate principles of **therapeutic jurisprudence**, the notion that the law can serve therapeutic purposes, with traditional legal structures and procedures. Therapeutic jurisprudence identifies emotional consequences of legal matters and asks whether the law can be interpreted, applied, or enforced in ways that maximize its therapeutic, or healing, effects. Therapeutic use of the law to enhance people's well-being may promise a less adversarial future for lawyers and the practice of law.

How Do Lawyers Make Professional Decisions?

Although there is little systematic information about how lawyers undertake and perform their work, we are beginning to have a clearer picture of how they make decisions, particularly when the decisions are related to litigation (e.g., whether to pursue a case on behalf of a client who is eager to sue, or to settle a case or go to trial). The decision to settle a lawsuit by agreeing on a resolution prior to trial is especially important because delays and unnecessary trials can consume time and resources of the litigants, court officials, and lawyers themselves. On the other hand, premature settlement may compromise the quality of the agreement.

Andrew Wistrich and Jeffrey Rachlinski, researchers whose studies of judges' decisions we described earlier, have also evaluated how lawyers make decisions, including how they think about settlements (Wistrich & Rachlinski, 2013). They claim that, like the racket's sweet shot for hitting a tennis ball, there is a temporal sweet spot for settling a lawsuit. And they ask whether lawyers can find that sweet spot, and if not, why not.

To assess the quality of lawyers' reasoning, they presented short vignettes and asked lawyers to assume various roles. In one study, lawyers learned that a plaintiff would recover $200,000 if successful in a lawsuit that had a 50% chance of success. The incentive for settling was to avoid $50,000 in litigation expenses each side would incur if the case did not settle. Half of the lawyers were assigned to represent the plaintiff and the other half to represent the defendant and each received a "take it or leave it" offer. The question for the lawyers was whether to advise their client to accept the offer.

Using this methodology, Wistrich and Rachlinski (2013) determined that, like judges, lawyers often rely on intuitive cognitive mechanisms rather than deliberative processes to evaluate cases. As a result, they take chances on trials that are not worth taking, seek information that supports their misguided choices and avoid information that would be useful—the so-called **confirmation bias**, and continue to invest resources even when it would be advantageous to cut their losses. Taken together, these intuitive reasoning processes lead to significant wasteful litigation.

But there's more. Lawyers are also overly confident of their abilities, including their ability to predict and produce successful case outcomes (Goodman-Delahunty, Granhag, Hartwig, & Loftus, 2010). Whether lawyers are deciding whether to take on a new client or settle a case, they have to make predictions about case outcomes months and years in advance of those outcomes. These are **probabilistic estimates**, in the sense that the correct answer is not yet known. Like all of us, lawyers make more optimistic predictions about events in the distant future than in the near future (Gilovich, Kerr, & Medvec, 1993) and over time—including hours of strategizing, preparing arguments and locating witnesses—they become increasingly confident that their predicted outcomes are attainable (Trope & Liberman, 2003). Lawyers who are more confident than is warranted by the outcomes of their cases have demonstrated the **overconfidence bias**.

How can lawyers improve their ability to assess the likelihood of future outcomes? A seemingly simple way to gain insight is to discuss the case with peers—other lawyers—who are less invested in the outcome (Jacobson, Dobbs-Marsh, Liberman, & Minson, 2011). In a variety of situations that involve probabilistic estimates, both novices and experts benefit from the opinion of just one other person, even though they continue to give more weight to their own opinions than to the opinions of others.

Summary

1. *What is the difference between the adversarial and inquisitorial models of trials?* The trial process in the United States and several other countries is called the adversarial model because all the witnesses, evidence, and exhibits are presented by one side or the other. In contrast, in the inquisitorial model used in much of Europe, the judge does nearly all questioning of witnesses. Although the adversarial model has been criticized for instigating undesirable competition between sides and distorting the presentation of evidence, in empirical studies it has been judged to be fairer and to lead to less-biased decisions.

2. *How do notions of morality and legality differ?* What is considered moral is not always what is ruled legal, and vice versa. When determining right and wrong, some people rely on the law almost entirely, but many people have internalized principles of morality that may be inconsistent with the laws.

3. *How do different models of justice explain people's level of satisfaction with the legal system?* According to the distributive justice model, people's acceptance of a legal decision is related to whether they think the outcome, or decision, is fair. According to the procedural justice model, fairness in the procedures is a more important determinant of satisfaction. When people think they have been treated fairly, they are more accepting of legal outcomes.

4. *What is commonsense justice?* Commonsense justice reflects the basic notions of everyday citizens about what is just and fair. In contrast to black-letter law, commonsense justice emphasizes the overall context in which an act occurs, the subjective intent of the person committing the act, and a desire to make the legal consequences of the act proportionate to the perceived culpability of the actor.

5. *How are judges selected and how do their demographic characteristics and attitudes influence their decisions?* Federal judges are appointed for life. Many state court judges are appointed and then run on their records in retention elections. Judges' demographic characteristics tend not to influence their decisions, probably because the experiences of law school and years of work as a lawyer are powerful socializing forces. On the other hand, judges' biases and predispositions do tend to influence their judgments.

6. *How does the experience of law school affect its students?* Attending law school tends to undermine students' values, motivation, and psychological health because it reduces their intrinsic motivation and sense of self-determination.

7. *What is known about lawyers' professional satisfaction?* Although most lawyers think their work is stimulating, fewer would recommend that others pursue a career in the law. Lawyers who do not have typical "lawyer traits" of competitiveness and achievement orientation are less satisfied than those who do.

8. *What factors explain lawyers' overconfidence and how can it be remedied?* Lawyers, particularly trial lawyers, are overconfident about their chances of future success because they rarely get useful feedback about their decisions and often assume that they can control case outcomes. Discussing a case with just one other attorney can lead to more accurate predictions about future results.

Key Terms

adversarial system
attribution theory
black-letter law
commonsense justice
confirmation bias
deliberative processes
distributive justice

diversion
euthanasia
extralegal factors
extrinsic motivation
in-group bias
inquisitorial system
intention

intrinsic motivation
intuitive processes
legal formalism
legal realism
motivated reasoning
overconfidence bias
probabilistic estimates

procedural justice
self-determination theory
    of optimal motivation
therapeutic jurisprudence

3   Psychology of Crime

Offending in the United States

Crime is a serious problem in our society. How often are crimes committed? What are the important influences to consider in understanding such offending? Questions about the causes of crime are the concern of **criminology**, which is the study of crime and criminal behavior. The patterns of thinking and behavior associated with criminal offending are also the focus of **forensic psychology** and **correctional psychology**. In addition, there are sociological and biological theories of crime. In this chapter, we summarize these major theories of crime, beginning with a review of the historical predecessors of 21st-century criminology. We offer examples of particularly serious and troubling offenses, and discuss why they occur.

Serious Offending

Rates of serious crime have been steadily declining in the United States. This decrease is confirmed by both victimization studies and official police statistics. According to the National Crime Victimization Survey (Bureau of Justice Statistics, 2016), the rate of violent crime dropped sharply between 1993 and 2001, and has decreased (but more slowly, with year-to-year variations) since 2002, with these variations including slight rises in recent years.

Despite this downturn in crime rates, many Americans continue to list crime and the fear of crime as one of their most serious concerns. If the rate of crime is declining, why do so many individuals continue to perceive crime as a major threat in their lives? One reason is that the rate of violent crime is still relatively high despite recent decreases: 16 out of every 1,000 males (the highest risk group for violent victimization) experienced violent crime in 2015. Rates of violent and

property crime were both higher in urban areas. In the western United States, a property crime was reported in nearly 15% of households in 2015 (Bureau of Justice Statistics, 2016). People's fear of crime is also heightened by the highly publicized crimes of a few individuals that evoke images of an epidemic of random violence beyond the control of a civilized society. The media, particularly cable networks, provide extensive coverage of heinous crimes, contributing to a heightened state of public fear. Awareness of specific crimes is increased by the rapid, widespread access facilitated by the Internet. Crime coverage invokes people's fascination and fear: "if it bleeds, it leads."

Consider these examples:

- In June 2016, 29-year-old Omar Mateen shot and killed 50 people and injured another 53 at Pulse, a popular gay nightclub in Orlando, Florida.
- In September 2013, a former Navy contractor and enlisted man named Aaron Alexis killed 12 people and wounded 3 more, engaging in a gun battle with responding authorities at the Washington, D.C. Navy Yard before being shot and killed himself in the process.

The involvement of youthful offenders in serious violent crime remains troubling. However, offending trends for this group have shown encouraging decreases. The number of serious violent offenses committed by persons ages 12–17 declined by 61% from 1993 to 2005, and arrests for violent offenses 2006–2012 continued to drop (except for minor increases between 2006 and 2008) (OJJDP, 2017a). Arrests of juveniles for serious violent offenses, as a proportion of all arrests, has moved from 16% (2006–2008) to 12% (2012), declining steadily along the way (OJJDP, 2017b).

What about homicide, the most serious crime? In 2002, juveniles were involved in approximately 8% of all homicides, a percentage that did not change in 2010 (Sickmund & Puzzanchera, 2014). Although the number of murders involving juveniles sharply decreased between 1994 and 2000, it remained stable (with some fluctuations) between 2001 and 2010, and continued to decrease between 2011 and 2014 (OJJDP, 2015).

Nonetheless, public perception, fueled by the high visibility and rapid dissemination facilitated by social media, remains affected by high-profile fatal events in schools:

- In April 1999, two students at Columbine High School in Littleton, Colorado, shot 12 of their classmates and a teacher before killing themselves.
- In February 2009, an eighth grader named Lawrence King was shot in the head in his classroom in Oxnard, California, while classmates looked on horrified. Police allege that the shooter, 14-year-old Brandon McInerney, and some other boys had previously taunted King because he was gay. At the time of this death, King was living in a shelter for abused and troubled children.
- In October 2015, a 15-year-old high school freshman at Marysville Pilchuck High in Marysville, Washington, shot five students in the school cafeteria before committing suicide. Four of the students were fatally wounded.

School Violence

The public becomes especially fearful about crime when they perceive it is occurring in traditionally safe environments. In the past three decades, crime in the workplace and violence in our schools have caused great national concern. In some respects, this concern is misplaced. Student deaths from homicide or suicide rarely occur in school. In 2012–2013, for example, there were 1,186 homicide deaths of school-aged children—but only 31 happened at school. There were even more suicides (about 1,590) involving youth of this age, but only six occurred at school (Zhang, Musu-Gillette, & Oudekerk, 2016). However, the *perception* that school shootings make our schools unsafe has been growing, very likely fueled by immediate and extensive coverage (enhanced by social media and the immediacy of the Internet) of horrific events in Newtown, Connecticut; DeKalb, Illinois; Blacksburg, Virginia; Red Lake, Minnesota; and Littleton, Colorado—in each of these

communities, school students were killed or wounded by fellow students or former students. Even though the number of youth deaths in school showed no overall increase between 1992 and 2012 (Zhang et al., 2016), this perception of danger to children is troubling to parents, schools, and communities. There are also other kinds of harm to schools and students where a shooting has occurred, including decreased enrollments and lower standardized test scores among remaining students (Beland & Kim, 2016).

High-profile shootings occur both in high schools and on college campuses. Seung-Hui Cho was a child of South Korean immigrants who moved to the United States in 1992. In his earlier school days, he was often so uncommunicative that he would not even respond when his teacher took the roll. He enrolled at Virginia Tech. On April 16, 2007, at 7:15 A.M., Cho shot and killed two students in a campus dormitory. Later that morning, he took the two handguns and ammunition he had obtained off campus and went from room to room in Norris Hall, a building on campus. Police responded quickly to an emergency call placed at 9:43 A.M., but by the time they were able to break into the building eight minutes later (Cho had chained several doors shut), Cho and 30 students and faculty members were dead.

The school shooting fatalities had experts, parents, teachers, and youngsters themselves trying to understand what motivates school shootings and what can be done to prevent them. Are school environments to blame? Is the ready availability of guns one explanation?

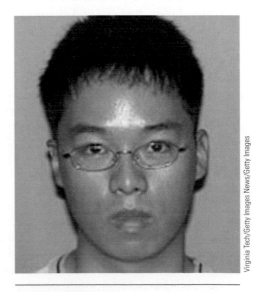

Seung-Hui Cho

Virginia Tech/Getty Images News/Getty Images

Were the killers mentally ill or severely emotionally disturbed? Were they driven by violent music and gory video games? Did their parents fail to support and supervise them adequately?

Statistics about school violence, and the case histories of those who have murdered their classmates at school, provide some possible answers. First, nonfatal victimization in schools is decreasing (from 181 per 1,000 students in 1992 to 33 per 1,000 students in 2014). Second, serious violent victimization against students ages 12–18 was lower in school than elsewhere in most years between 1992 and 2008, and about the same during 2009–2014. Third, deaths from homicide when the victim was at school were very rare (1–2% of the overall homicide deaths in this age group) (National Center for Education Statistics, 2016).

Although homicides at school remain very rare, they attract a great deal of speculation about the motives of the shooters when they do occur (Cornell, 2006). Based on the small sample of cases, a few common characteristics have been cited in the backgrounds of the boys responsible for school killings (Cloud, 1998; Verlinden, Hersen, & Thomas, 2000). Such boys tend to be more experienced with guns, socially isolated, preoccupied with violence (media, music, Internet, video games), teased due to physical appearance, angry brooders, and have developed a plan for their aggression and often communicated it to others prior to the event.

But such descriptions are difficult to develop with accuracy. The number of school shooters is small, and there is a range of characteristics and circumstances in this small group. The U.S. Secret Service and the U.S. Department of Education collaborated in the Safe School Initiative by investigating what we can learn about school shootings (Vossekuil, Fein, Reddy, Borum, & Modzeleski, 2004). The report cautions that there is no "profile" of the school shooter, as there was variability in the 41 attackers involved in 37 incidents of serious school violence (Vossekuil et al., 2004).

Considering the nature and limits of this kind of information, it is evident why school shootings cannot be "profiled" and predicted. Taking the most distinctive aspects of school shooters identified in these studies, we might identify being bullied, having an interest in violent themes, and experiencing difficulty in coping with significant loss as important risk factors. But such a profile would target an extremely high percentage of school-aged adolescents who would never go on to commit a school shooting.

So how can we make schools safer without unnecessarily targeting those who would not seriously threaten their classmates? A number of reforms and programs have been attempted: requiring school uniforms, beefing up security measures, passing tougher gun laws, offering violence prevention programs, and restricting access to violent movies, among others. Another promising approach involves reducing the influences that are commonly seen in school shootings—particularly bullying—while being attentive to particular interest in violent themes and the experience of loss and **trauma** among students. Providing a school environment that greatly reduces bullying while offering safe and effective help for students experiencing loss would facilitate assistance for many students rather than identifying (often mistakenly) the potential school shooter.

There are two other steps that have the potential for reducing the risk of school shootings. The first is communication. Better communication between students and school administrators is important in identifying the planning surrounding school violence and weapons (Mulvey & Cauffman, 2001). A second step involves a careful **threat assessment** using a multidisciplinary team. This team would respond to any identified threat by carefully considering the nature of the threat, the risk posed by the individual, and the needed response to reduce the risk of harmful action (Cornell & Sheras, 2006). This allows a graduated response depending upon the seriousness of the harm and the likelihood that the threat will be carried out, with the most serious threats treated proportionally. Threat assessment has been refined by organizations such as the U.S. Secret Service in their work with threats of targeted violence toward those they protect (such as the U.S. president and vice president and their families), and modified for use in other settings such as schools and colleges.

Additional research on secondary school and campus shootings (Cornell, 2003, 2006; Flynn & Heitzmann, 2008; Heilbrun, Dvoskin, & Heilbrun, 2009; Reddy et al., 2001) underscores several important points:

- The most prevalent problem with aggression in education settings is not shootings. In school contexts, it is bullying; on college campuses, it is more likely to be date rape and hazing. Much of this aggression is unreported and hence underestimated by official records.
- Most of those who make implied or direct threats will not go on to commit serious violence. Threatening communications are made for a variety of reasons, including angry disputes, fear, jealousy, and ideology.

■ "Zero tolerance" policies are ineffective and have the potential to stigmatize and harm a variety of mistakenly identified individuals.

A related approach, termed threat assessment, involves carefully considering the nature of the threat, the risk posed by the individual, and the needed response to reduce the risk of harmful action. Threat assessment has been refined by organizations such as the U.S. Secret Service in their work with threats of targeted violence toward those they protect (such as the U.S. president and vice president and their families). It has also been modified for use in other settings such as schools and colleges.

Mass Killings in Public Places

It sometimes seems that mass killings (defined as the killing or attempted killing of four or more individuals) in public places (rather than private homes), excluding drug- and gang-related activity, are increasingly frequent. Is this an illusion created by social media—or is it supported by evidence?

One interesting way to consider this question involves tracking the time between such events. Using such a methodology, scholars (Cohen, Azrael, & Miller, 2014) compared the average time between public mass killings from 1982 to 2011 with the time elapsed between such events between 2011 and 2013. They found that the frequency of such shootings had increased substantially. The average time between events from 1982 to September 2011 was 172 days. This dropped to an average of 64 days between mass killing events between September 2011 and 2013, a nearly three-fold increase.

A second study using some of the same events, involving mass killings or attempted killings between 2000 and 2013, reached a similar conclusion about the recent increase in such events (Federal Bureau of Investigation, 2013). In particular, an average of 6.4 incidents occurred in 2000–2006, increasing to an average of 16.4 in the 2007–2013 time period (a total of 160 events comprised the study). Most of these events (70%) occurred in either a commerce/business or educational setting. Limited information was cited regarding those who perpetrated these crimes. All but two involved a single shooter; most were male (in at least 6 of the 160 events, a female shooter was involved). At least nine of the events involved shooting and killing a family member in a residence before moving to a more

public location. Finally, in 64 of the events (40%), the perpetrators committed suicide—most at the scene of the crime.

For several reasons, it is difficult to learn about the characteristics, motivation, and influences on individuals who commit mass killings. Although they may be increasing, they are still very rare events. Those perpetrating them often commit suicide or are killed by responding law enforcement officers. It may be that some of the same influences that affect violent crime generally—substance use, weapon availability, family dysfunction, unemployment, emotional volatility—exert some influence on such individuals. It may also be that wanting to die, wishing to become famous, seeking revenge for real or perceived slights, and other more distinctive influences are also at work. For reasons we discussed in the previous section on school shootings, it will probably never be feasible to "profile" such individuals or predict such events with accuracy. But as we learn more about such rare but highly destructive tragedies, it may be possible to better prepare for them.

Highly publicized acts of violence at school or in the workplace threaten fundamental assumptions about personal security and the safety of our children and have a major effect on how individuals feel about their quality of life. For these reasons, policymakers and social scientists must pay particular attention to workplace and school violence, although neighborhood violence also continues to be a concern.

Why Does Crime Happen?

Behavioral scientists argue that to ease the crime problem, we must first understand its causes. Why does crime happen? What motivates people to commit illegal acts? Bad genes? Inadequate parents? Failed schooling? Twisted impulses? Harsh environments? Delinquent friends? Social disadvantage? Drug addiction? Easy access to weapons? Some combination of these factors? Can crime be predicted from knowing about a person's early life? Or are many people capable of crime under the wrong circumstances—an unfortunate mix of intoxication, anger, and accessible victims, which come together, in the words of novelist Daniel Woodrell (1996), "like car wrecks that you knew would happen … almost nightly, at the same old crossroads of Hormones and Liquor" (p. 27)? Are some crimes, like those of Dexter Morgan (see Box 3.1), so extreme that they defy scientific explanation, or can behavioral scientists make sense of them?

The Case of Dexter Morgan: A Fictional Psychopath?

BOX 3.1

Dexter Morgan is playful, handsome, and has a wonderfully ironic sense of humor. He is the fictional star of novels (*Dearly Devoted Dexter, Darkly Dreaming Dexter, Dexter in the Dark*) and a television series (*Dexter*). To his coworkers and fiancée, he is the blood-splatter analyst for the Miami Police Department. Privately, however, he is a selective serial killer who is guided by an internal companion whom he calls "the Dark Passenger." Dexter's adoptive father, a Miami cop, taught him to present himself as "normal"—and to kill only those who deserve it, according to a strict set of rules designed to avoid detection.

Can a fictional character such as Dexter tell us anything about reality? Are there real-life, nonfictional Dexter Morgans out there? Perhaps not, but reading about and watching Dexter can illustrate genuine phenomena. Engaging in a heinous act, such as the killing of neighborhood pets, and needing to be taught to act "as if" one feels certain emotions are associated with the personality disorder known as **psychopathy**. Dexter's character might meet some of the criteria for this disorder, but does he qualify as a psychopath? Would a real measure of this disorder (the Hare Psychopathy Checklist-Revised, or PCL-R; Hare, 2003) classify the fictional Dexter as a psychopath? Let's consider how some of the PCL-R items might apply.

In some respects, the fictional Dexter Morgan (Phillips, 2006) is quite similar to those who have the personality disorder of psychopathy. These similarities

Michael Hall plays Dexter Morgan.

are most apparent in his superficial emotions and lack of the capacity for deep emotional attachments. But Dexter does not possess some of the other characteristics and much of the history that are core elements of psychopathy. We might conclude that Dexter Morgan is a charming fictional character who can portray what it's like to have difficulty feeling deep emotions—but it's not clear whether he would be classified as a psychopath.

CRITICAL THOUGHT QUESTIONS

Dexter Morgan is obviously very disturbed. Why would he not be classified as a psychopath?

PCL-R ITEM	DEXTER
Glibness/superficial charm	• Flirts with women to keep up appearances. • Talks his way out of difficult situations easily.
Pathological lying	• Lies often, but presumably for self-preservation rather than without any understandable motivation.
Conning/manipulative	• Able to obtain files from clerks with flirting and donuts. • Plans his killings carefully, using ruses and cons to capture and subdue his victims.
Lack of remorse or guilt	• Does not describe feeling these things for his victims. • Also does not feel remorse or guilt for anything he does with coworkers or his wife or her children, although he feigns these emotions to fit in.

PCL-R ITEM	DEXTER
Callous/lack of empathy	• Shows no empathy for his victims.
Promiscuous sexual behavior	• No. He describes himself as disinterested in all aspects of sexuality, including both physical and emotional intimacy.
Need for stimulation/proneness to boredom	• Describes this as a hunger for killing, which he must satisfy periodically. • Has a professional position involving the inspection of highly stimulating phenomena (homicide crime scenes). • In other respects, however, he is not a great stimulation seeker, nor does he portray himself as easily bored.
Parasitic lifestyle	• No. He has a steady job and does not rely on others for assistance.
Poor behavioral controls	• No. He is careful and calculating, the antithesis of an impulsive offender.
Irresponsibility	• No. He is gainfully employed and does his job well. • He is committed to his wife and her family, although not attracted to the intimacy. • He uses both his job and his relationships as a cover for his self-designated role as the protector of society from serial killers.
Early behavior problems	• Showed behavior that could have resulted in arrest (e.g., killing neighborhood pets, taping up and threatening a classmate).
Criminal versatility	• No. He is a "specialist" whose offending is limited to abducting and killing his victims

Theories of Crime as Explanations of Criminal Behavior

Theories of crime are as old as crime itself. Aristotle claimed that "poverty is the parent of revolution and crime." But most ancient explanations of crime took a religious tone; crime was either equivalent to or due to sin, a view that was popular throughout the Middle Ages and lives on today in many religious belief systems.

In the 17th century, Sir Francis Bacon argued that "opportunity makes a thief." During the 1700s, philosophers and social critics such as Voltaire and Rousseau emphasized concepts such as free will, hedonism, and flaws in the social contract to explain criminal conduct. These principles ultimately grew into the **classical school of criminology**.

The two leading proponents of classical criminology were the Italian intellectual Cesare Beccaria and the British philosopher Jeremy Bentham, who believed that lawbreaking occurred when people freely chose to behave wrongly when faced with a choice between right and wrong. People chose crime when they believed that the gains from crime outweighed the losses it entailed. Classical theorists were interested in reforming the harsh administration of justice in post-Renaissance Europe, and they believed that punishment of criminals should be commensurate with the crimes committed—that punishment should fit the crime. (This is seen in contemporary thinking about **proportionality** in sentencing.)

Classical theory influenced several principles of justice in Western societies (e.g., the U.S. Constitution's Eighth Amendment ban against "cruel and unusual punishment"). It still exerts an important effect on modern correctional philosophy.

Modern theories of crime developed from the **positivist school of criminology**. Rather than focusing on individuals' free will, positivists emphasized factors that they believed determined criminal behavior.

They sought to understand crime through the scientific method and the analysis of empirical data. Some stressed sociological factors, whereas others preferred biological, psychological, or environmental explanations.

An early positivist was Adolphe Quetelet, a Belgian statistician who studied crime data and concluded that crime occurred more often in certain geographic areas and under specific social conditions. Lombroso (1876) and Garofalo (1914), other theorists who relied on scientific data, emphasized the physical characteristics of criminals and proposed a strong biological predisposition to crime. Although the early positivists considered themselves scientists, their methods were crude by current standards and led to conclusions that are not taken seriously today. Positivists believed that punishment should fit the criminal rather than the crime. This position foreshadowed rehabilitation as a correctional priority and the indeterminate sentence—from 6 to 10 years, for example—as a means for achieving it.

Most modern theories of criminal behavior—including those of biology, genetics, psychology, sociology, economics, anthropology, and religion—are a legacy of the positivist tradition. The validity of these theories varies greatly. Most can account reasonably well for certain types of crime, but none explains all forms of criminality—and some explain very few. Empirical data, rational analyses, moral values, and political ideologies all play a role in shaping preferences for the leading theories in criminology.

For the most part, criminologists have concentrated on those crimes that frighten the average citizen—violent acts (e.g., robbery, rape, assault, and murder) or aggressive behavior against property (e.g., burglary, theft, and arson). But many other kinds of legally prohibited conduct—environmental plunder, price fixing, and business fraud, for example—can cause great damage to individuals and society. (Consider the securities fraud perpetrated by Bernard Madoff, the hedge-fund trader and former chairman of the Nasdaq stock market, who may have plundered up to $50 billion of his clients' money.) However, the major focus of criminologists is on violent and property crime. These are also what the public thinks of first when it debates the "crime problem."

Most theories of crime have focused on men. This may be reasonable, given that about three-quarters of all those arrested are male, and that almost 85% of violent crimes are committed by men. However, the factors that influence female criminality deserve attention, at least in part because crime by females has increased greatly in recent years. The rate of growth in the female inmate population has been substantial in the last four decades; between 1980 and 2014, the number of women in jails, and in state and federal prisons nationwide, increased by 700% (The Sentencing Project, 2016). These numbers grew from 1980 (26,378) to 1990 (81,023) to 2000 (164,221), with additional substantial growth in 2010 (205,190) and a slight leveling off in 2014 (215,332). In 2014, there were 1.2 million women under correctional supervision. The vast majority of these women were on probation (966,029) (The Sentencing Project, 2016). Despite increases in violent criminal behavior, women are still most often arrested for larceny and theft. Such arrests often involve collaborating with a male partner. One implication of this pattern is that explanations of female crime need to carefully consider the role of coercion, especially as it is exerted in close relationships.

There are four contemporary theories that attempt to explain criminal offending. We group these theories as sociological, biological, psychological, and social–psychological. There are important distinctions among them.

Crime may appear to result from an individual's experience with his or her environment. This belief is explained through **sociological theories**, which maintain that crime results from social or cultural forces that are external to any specific individual; exist prior to any criminal act; and emerge from social class, political, ecological, or physical structures affecting large groups of people (Nettler, 1974).

Alternatively, criminal behavior may appear to result from an individual's biological characteristics. **Biological theories of crime** stress genetic influences, neuropsychological abnormalities, and biochemical irregularities. But as we shall see, there is little empirical evidence that either sociological or biological theories independently predict criminal behavior. Instead, current theories of crime incorporate a combination of environmental and biological factors to understand the causes of offending behaviors.

Some **psychological theories** emphasize that crime results from personality attributes that are uniquely possessed, or possessed to a special degree, by the potential criminal. For example, some psychological approaches have focused on patterns of thinking—particularly with respect to recognized risk factors such as pro-criminal attitudes or certain kinds of personality disorders. Others focus on intellectual functioning or cognitive and social development (Moore, 2011).

Social–psychological theories (Arrigo, 2006) bridge the gap between the environmentalism of sociology and the individualism of psychological or biological theories. Social–psychological theories propose that crime is learned, but they differ from sociological and psychological theories in about *what* is learned and *how* it is learned.

Sociological Theories of Crime

Sociological theories may be divided into **structural** and **subcultural explanations**. Structural theories emphasize that dysfunctional social arrangements (e.g., inadequate schooling, economic adversity, or community disorganization) thwart people's efforts toward legitimate attainments and result in their breaking the law. Subcultural theories hold that crime originates when various groups of people endorse cultural values that clash with the dominant, conventional rules of society. In this view, crime is the product of a subculture's deviation from the accepted norms that underlie the criminal law.

Structural Explanations.   A key concept of structural approaches is that certain groups of people suffer fundamental inequalities in opportunities to achieve the goals valued by society. Differential opportunity, proposed by Cloward and Ohlin (1960) in their book *Delinquency and Opportunity*, is one example of a structural explanation of crime. This theory can be traced to Émile Durkheim's ideas about the need to maintain moral bonds between individuals in society. Durkheim thought that life without moral or social obligations becomes intolerable and results in **anomie**, a feeling of normlessness that often precedes suicide and crime. One implication of anomie theory was that unlimited aspirations pressure individuals to deviate from social norms.

According to Cloward and Ohlin (1960), people in lower socioeconomic subcultures usually want to succeed through legal means, but society denies them legitimate opportunities to do so. For example, consider a person from Nicaragua who immigrates to the United States because of a sincere desire to make a better life for his family. This person faces cultural and language differences, financial hardships, and limited access to the resources that are crucial for upward mobility. It remains more difficult for poor people to obtain an advanced education, despite advances in the practice of need-blind admissions and tuition adjustments based on need that are now offered by some U.S. universities. In addition, crowding in large cities makes class distinctions more apparent.

This theory maintains that when legal means of goal achievement are blocked, intense frustration results—and crime is more likely to ensue. Youthful crime, especially in gangs, is one consequence of this sequence. The theory of differential opportunity assumes that people who grow up in crowded, impoverished, deteriorating neighborhoods endorse conventional, middle-class goals (e.g., owning a home). Thus, crime is an illicit means to gain an understandable end.

Consistent with this theory of differential opportunity, Gottfredson (1986) and Gordon (1986) have attempted to explain the higher crime rate of lower-class Black youth in terms of their poorer academic performance. Denied legitimate job opportunities because of low aptitude scores or grades, lack of required skills, or a scarcity of positions, these youth discovered that they can make several hundred dollars weekly dealing crack cocaine (and, more recently, drugs like oxycodone, heroin, and marijuana as well).

The theory of differential opportunity has several limitations (Lilly, Cullen, & Ball, 1989). First, a great deal of research indicates that seriously delinquent youth display many differences from their law-abiding counterparts other than differing educational opportunities, and they tend to show these differences as early as the beginning of elementary school. Second, the assumption that lower-class juveniles typically aspire to membership in the middle class is also unproven. Furthermore, the major terms in the theory, such as *aspiration*, *frustration*, and *opportunity*, are defined too vaguely; the theory does not explicitly explain what determines adaptation to blocked opportunities (Sheley, 1985). Last and most apparent, some crimes are committed by people who have never been denied opportunities; in fact, they may have basked in an abundance of good fortune. Think of Subway spokesman Jared Fogle's guilty plea in 2015 to having sex with minors and obtaining child pornography. Many other examples come to mind: the head of a local charity who pockets donations for personal enrichment; the pharmacist who deals drugs under the counter; and the attorney general of Pennsylvania, Kathleen Kane, who resigned her office following a conviction for perjury and criminal conspiracy. Indeed, think of many white-collar offenses, motivated not by lack of opportunity but by the desire to expand substantial opportunities and resources even further.

Subcultural Explanations.   The subcultural version of the sociological theory maintains that a conflict between norms held by different groups causes criminal behavior. This conflict arises when various groups endorse subcultural norms, pressuring their members to deviate from the norms underlying the criminal law (Nietzel, 1979). Gangs, for example, enforce behavioral norms about how to behave. For many youths, a gang replaces the young person's parents as the main source of norms, even when parents attempt to instill their own values.

Like structural theories of crime, subcultural explanations have not demonstrated a strong theoretical or empirical basis. Questions remain: How do cultural standards originate? How are they transmitted from one generation to the next? How do they control the behavior of any one individual? The most troublesome concept is the main one—subculture. Some critics reject the assumption that different socioeconomic groups embrace radically different values.

Biological Theories of Crime

Biological theories of crime search for genetic vulnerabilities, neuropsychological abnormalities, or biochemical irregularities that predispose people to criminal behavior. These dispositions, biological theorists believe, are then translated into specific criminal behavior through environments and social interactions. Research on biological theories commonly focuses on twin and adoption studies to distinguish genetic from environmental factors.

In twin studies, the researcher compares the **concordance rate** (the percentage of pairs of twins sharing the behavior of interest) for **monozygotic twins** (identical twins) and **dizygotic twins** (commonly called fraternal twins). If the monozygotic concordance rate is significantly higher, the investigator concludes that the behavior in question is genetically influenced, because monozygotic twins are genetically identical, whereas dizygotic pairs share, on average, only 50% of their genetic material.

In a major Swedish study using twin (N = 36,877 pairs), adoptee-parent (N = 5,068 pairs), adoptee-sibling (N = 10,610 pairs), and sibling designs (N = 1,521,066 pairs), the heritability ratings (the extent to which genes are responsible for variations between individuals, ranging between 0 and 1.0) for violent offending were .40 to .50 (Frisell, Pawitan, Langstrom, & Lichtenstein, 2012). Such evidence suggests that inherited tendencies may play a crucial role in causing crime. However, studies that distinguish between crimes against property and violent crimes against persons have found that although heredity and environment play important roles in both types of crime, the influence of heredity is higher for aggressive types of antisocial behavior (e.g., assaults, robberies, and sexual offenses) than for nonaggressive crimes such as drug taking, shoplifting, and truancy (Eley, 1997).

Other adoption studies also support the contention that genetic factors play some role in the development of criminality. Cloninger, Sigvardsson, Bohman, and von Knorring (1982) studied the arrest records of adult males who had been adopted as children. They found that men whose biological parents had a criminal record were four times more likely to be criminal themselves (a prevalence rate of 12.1%) than adoptees who had no criminal background (2.9%) and twice as likely to be criminal as adoptees whose adoptive parents had a criminal history. Other researchers conducted a review of several twin and adoption studies in this area and found similar results (Tehrani & Mednick, 2000).

The larger pattern of results in this area was considered in a meta-analysis of 51 twin and adoption studies addressing the genetic and environmental influences on antisocial behavior. The investigators (Rhee & Waldman, 2002) described moderate proportions of variance due to shared genetic influences and somewhat larger effects of environmental influences.

An interesting possibility regarding a biological contributor to offending was first raised by a 1993 study (Brunner, Nelen, Breakefield, Ropers, & van Oost, 1993). Studying individuals who had committed offenses, the investigators noted five participants who showed both borderline intellectual deficiency and impaired control of impulsive aggression. These individuals each showed a complete absence of activity of a certain enzyme (monoamine oxidase type A, or MAO-A, which affects important neurotransmitters). This absence resulted from a mutation on the X chromosome in the gene coding for MAO-A.

The MAO-A mutation was dubbed the "warrior gene" in a 2004 review in the journal *Science*, and that name continues to be used (with the unfortunate consequence of possibly exaggerating the influence of the mutation). The MAO-A allele occurs in apes, monkeys, and humans; some have suggested that it had a common ancestor 25 million years ago and was favored by natural selection (Horgan, 2011).

Without replication, the initial finding—involving a small number of affected individuals—would not have had implications for the broader scientific and legal fields (Appelbaum, 2005). But a second study with a large cohort (1,037 individuals followed since birth in Dunedin, New Zealand) replicated and extended these findings (Caspi et al., 2002). The investigators considered both the levels of MAO-A and the history of maltreatment between the ages of 3 and 11. Using multiple measures of antisocial behavior, they reported that the 12% of their participants who had both low MAO-A and maltreatment accounted for 44% of the total convictions for violent offenses, with 85% of individuals with both low MAO-A and maltreatment later showing some form of antisocial behavior.

What is the current status of this controversy? In a detailed review, Buades-Rotger and Gallardo-Pujol (2014) describe the evidence and its limitations. They conclude that there is converging evidence indicating that the low MAO-A mutation contributes to antisocial behavior when combined with a history of childhood abuse. They describe several implications of this conclusion: (1) incorporating genetic data into current violence risk assessment procedures could make them more accurate; (2) considering these genetic data could be useful to detect individuals at a greater risk of having the mutation; and (3) using genetic data could also help in comparing the impact of specific treatments, including psychological and pharmacological.

Certainly there are cautionary notes to be sounded. Using a term such as "warrior gene" suggests an influence on violent behavior that is not supported by the research. By no means should one conclude that having this genetic mutation (combined with childhood abuse) means that one will behave violently. Nor should one conclude that not having the mutation-abuse constellation means that one will not. Rather, it appears to be a risk factor that exerts some influence—but violence is a behavior that has multiple causes and influences, and this may be one—and only one. Also, this condition may be seen with different frequency across different racial and ethnic groups. When investigators (e.g., Lea & Chambers, 2007) identify rates of MAO-A mutation as occurring in Maori men (56%), Caucasians (34%), Hispanics (29%), Africans (59%), and Chinese (77%), then it raises the question of whether some would use race or culture as a proxy for violence risk. This would be wrong for at least two reasons. First, risk should be an individualized determination rather than one that relies only on influences such as one's racial or ethnic group—and it is objectionable to use race on the grounds of fairness and equal protection as well. Second, the empirical data do not indicate that any single risk factor—including the MAO-A mutation—has a compelling influence on violence risk. The picture is more complex and multidetermined than that.

Genetic and Biological Influences on Crime: Promising Possibilities.

If genetic or biological factors do influence crime, the important question has always been: what influences what? There is a lengthy list of likely candidates (Brennan & Raine, 1997), but five possibilities are emphasized:

1. *Low MAO-A in combination with a history of maltreatment.* As we just mentioned, current evidence may help to explain how a combination of an adverse experience (child maltreatment) and a biological risk factor (low MAO-A) could affect impulsivity and propensity to antisocial behavior.

2. *Neuropsychological abnormalities.* High rates of abnormal electroencephalogram (EEG) patterns have been reported in prison populations and in violent juvenile delinquents. These EEG irregularities may indicate neurological deficits that result in poor impulse control and impaired judgment. Studies of violent offenders have shown slow-wave EEG patterns indicating underarousal (Milstein, 1988). Although a high percentage of persons in the general population also have EEG abnormalities, rates of EEG abnormalities are somewhat higher in delinquent youth (Raine, Venables, & Williams, 1989) and impulsive adult offenders (Zukov, Ptacek, & Fischer, 2008).

More promising results have been reported concerning abnormalities in four subcortical regions of the brain—the amygdala, hippocampus, thalamus, and midbrain—specifically in the right hemisphere of the brain, which has been linked to the experience of negative emotions. In one study (Raine, Meloy, & Buchshaum, 1998), brain scans of a group of homicide offenders showed that, compared with normal controls, the offenders experienced excessive activity in the four subcortical structures. Excessive subcortical activity may underlie a more aggressive temperament that could, in turn, predispose an individual to violent behavior.

A review of the neuropsychological literature supports a relationship between deficits in the prefrontal cortex, a region of the brain responsible for planning, monitoring, and controlling behavior, and antisocial behavior (see Raine, 2002). Damage to the prefrontal cortex may predispose individuals to criminal behavior in one of several ways. Patients with impairment in this region of the brain have decreased reasoning abilities that may lead to impulsive decision-making in risky situations (Bechara, Damasio, Tranel, & Damasio, 1997). In addition, prefrontal impairment is associated with decreased levels of arousal, and individuals may engage in stimulation-seeking and antisocial behaviors to compensate for these arousal deficits (Raine, Lencz, Bihrle, Lacasse, & Colletti, 2000). A review of 17 neuroimaging studies (Bufkin& Luttrell, 2005) identified the prefrontal cortex and medial temporal regions as areas associated with aggressive and/or violent behavior histories, particularly when this behavior is impulsive. Problems in regulating negative emotions are associated with impairments in these brain regions. Impairments in the prefrontal cortex may help to explain why offenders, on average, have about an 8- to 10-point lower IQ (intelligence quotient) than nonoffenders and are less able to (1) postpone impulsive actions, (2) use effective problem-solving strategies (Lynam, Moffitt, & Stouthamer-Loeber, 1993), and (3) achieve academic success in schools as a route to socially approved attainments (Binder, 1988).

In one longitudinal study of 411 London boys, a low IQ at ages 8–10 was linked to persistent criminality and more convictions for violent crimes up to age 32 (Farrington, 1995). Low IQ is among the most stable of risk factors for conduct disorder and delinquency (Murray & Farrington, 2010). In a comparison of intelligence of juvenile offenders within different racial/ethnic groups (Black, Hispanic, and White; Trivedi, 2011), White violent offenders had lower Performance IQ scores than White nonviolent offenders. Overall, however, gender, ethnicity, and lower IQ scores also seem to be related in a complex way, indicating the need for further investigation.

1. *Autonomic nervous system differences.* The autonomic nervous system (ANS) carries information between the brain and all organs of the body. Because of these connections, emotions are associated with changes in the ANS. In fact, we can "see" the effects of emotional arousal on such ANS responses as heart rate, skin conductance, respiration, and blood pressure. Some offenders—particularly those whose offending is most chronic—are thought to differ from noncriminals in that they show chronically low levels of autonomic arousal and weaker physiological reactions to stimulation (see Patrick, 2008, discussed in detail in the next section). These differences, which might also involve hormonal irregularities (see the next section), could cause this group of offenders to have (1) difficulty learning how to inhibit behavior likely to lead to punishment and (2) a high need for extra stimulation that they gratify through aggressive thrill seeking. These difficulties are also considered an important predisposing

factor by some social–psychological theorists, discussed later.

2. *Physiological differences.* A number of physiological factors might lead to increased aggressiveness and delinquency (Berman, 1997). Among the variables receiving continuing attention are (1) abnormally high levels of testosterone, (2) increased secretion of insulin, and (3) lower levels of serotonin (Booij et al., 2010).

One study using animal models provides further support for the role of these physiological variables in aggressive behavior. Researchers found that rats with increased production of testosterone and lower levels of serotonin exhibited more aggressive behaviors; these rats displayed an increased number of attacks and inflicted a greater number of wounds on other rats compared to rats with lower testosterone and higher serotonin levels (Toot, Dunphy, Turner, & Ely, 2004). Such findings may be helpful in understanding the biological contributions to human aggression as well. Low levels of serotonin might be linked to aggressiveness and criminal conduct in any of several ways—for example, through greater impulsivity and irritability, impaired ability to regulate negative moods, excessive alcohol consumption, or hypersensitivity to provocative and threatening environmental cues (Berman, Tracy, & Coccaro, 1997).

A major review of psychophysiological studies of aggression and violence (Patrick, 2008) encompassed research using autonomic, electrocortical, and neuroimaging measures. Physiological correlates of persistent aggressive behavior were identified as (1) low baseline heart rate, (2) greater autonomic reactivity to stressful or aversive stimuli, (3) enhanced EEG slow-wave activity, (4) reduced brain potential response, and (5) dysfunction in frontocortical and limbic brain regions that influence emotional regulation. One of the proposed explanations for these findings was impairments in emotional regulation circuits in the brain that would otherwise inhibit impulsive aggression.

3. *Personality and temperament differences.* Some dimensions of personality are highly heritable, and thus can be discussed within the scope of genetic influence on behavior. Some heritable dimensions are further related to antisocial behavior. Individuals with personalities marked by undercontrol, unfriendliness, irritability, low empathy, callous unemotionality, and a tendency to become easily frustrated are at greater risk for antisocial conduct

(McLoughlin, Rucklidge, Grace, & McLean, 2010). We discuss some of these characteristics more fully in the next section on psychological theories of crime.

Psychological Theories of Crime

Psychological explanations of crime emphasize individual differences in the way people think or feel about their behavior. These differences, which can take the form of subtle variations or more extreme personality disturbances, might make some people more prone to criminal conduct by increasing their anger, weakening their attachments to others, or fueling their desire to take risks and seek thrills.

Criminal Thinking Patterns. A systematic and scientifically validated approach to investigating the role of offender thinking has been undertaken by Glenn Walters, who for many years served as a psychologist with the Federal Bureau of Prisons. He developed the Psychological Inventory of Criminal Thinking Styles (PICTS), an 80-item, self-report inventory that measures cognitive patterns that are supportive of offending. Data from both male and female offenders, as well as meta-analyses, indicate that the PICTS is reliable, correlated with previous offending, and modestly predictive of future adjustment and release outcome (Walters, 2002). A similar measure (the Measure of Offending Thinking Styles–Revised) was developed as well, also focusing on offender thinking styles, and following a comparable pattern of appropriate scientific development and validation (Mandracchia & Morgan, 2011). This general approach, involving the appraisal of thinking styles and cognitive "errors" among offenders, has added significantly to our current ability to assess offender risk and rehabilitation needs.

Personality-Based Explanations. Most of the influence of personality-based explanations for criminal offending in the last three decades has been provided by the construct of psychopathy, which we discuss in this section. Historically, however, there have been a number of theories of personality that have been offered to help understand offending. These include Eysenck's PEN theory (**psychoticism, extroversion**, and **neuroticism**; Eysenck & Gudjonsson, 1989); Costa and McCrae's five-factor model (Neuroticism, Extraversion, Openness to Experience, Agreeableness, and Conscientiousness; McCrae & Costa, 1990); and Cloninger's seven-factor temperament and character model (Novelty Seeking, Harm Avoidance, Reward

Dependence, Persistence, Self-directedness, Cooperativeness, and Self-transcendence; Cloninger, Dragan, & Przybeck, 1993). In some respects, these theories describe overlapping constructs. But which of those are important in understanding antisocial behavior?

A meta-analytic review (Miller & Lynam, 2001) addresses precisely that question. Those who were low on Agreeableness or low on Conscientiousness were more likely to be involved in antisocial behavior. The other dimensions were less important—so it seems best to conclude that general personality theory has identified two domains (agreeableness and conscientiousness) that are important to understanding criminal offending. More recent research on these dimensions (Wilcox, Sullivan, Jones, & van Gelder, 2014) considered how agreeableness and conscientiousness interacted with opportunity to commit crime in affecting adolescent offending (N = 2,200), with opportunity less likely to lead to offending when individuals were agreeable and conscientious.

Psychopathy. Many individuals attribute crime to personality defects, typically in the form of theories that focus on the criminal's basic antisocial or psychopathic nature. The concept of *psychopathy* has a long history. This term refers to individuals who engage in frequent, repetitive antisocial activity for which they feel little or no remorse. Such persons appear chronically deceitful and manipulative; they seem to have a nearly total lack of conscience that propels them into repeated conflict with society, often from a very early age. They are superficial, arrogant, and do not seem to learn from experience; they lack empathy and loyalty to individuals, groups, or society (Hare & Neumann, 2008). Psychopaths are selfish, callous, and irresponsible; they tend to blame others or to offer plausible rationalizations for their behavior.

The closest diagnosis within the Diagnostic and Statistical Manual-5 (American Psychiatric Association, 2013) is **antisocial personality disorder**. The two disorders are similar in their emphasis on chronic antisocial behavior, but they differ in the role of personal characteristics, which are important in psychopathy but are not among the diagnostic criteria for antisocial personality disorder. About 80% of psychopaths are men, and their acts sometimes are well publicized (see Box 3.2).

Are psychopathy and antisocial personality really different disorders? One answer to that question is "no"—the different names and somewhat different diagnostic criteria represent the attempts of different constituencies (psychology and psychiatry) and functions (researchers

The Case of Ted Bundy: A Real-Life Psychopath

BOX 3.2

Born in 1946, Theodore Robert Bundy seemed destined for a charmed life; he was intelligent, attractive, and articulate (Holmes & DeBurger, 1988). A Boy Scout as a youth and then an honor student and psychology major at the University of Washington, he was at one time a work-study student at the Seattle Crisis Clinic. Later he became assistant to the chairman of the Washington State Republican Party. It is probably around this time that he claimed his first victim, a college-age woman who was viciously attacked while sleeping, left alive but brain damaged.

From 1974 through 1978, Bundy stalked, attacked, killed, and then sexually assaulted as many as 36 victims in Washington, Oregon, Utah, Colorado, and Florida. Apparently, some of the women were taken off guard when the good-looking, casual Bundy approached, seeming helpless: walking with crutches, or having an apparent broken arm. He usually choked them to death and then sexually abused and mutilated them before disposing of their bodies in remote areas (Nordheimer, 1989).

Maintaining a charming façade is characteristic of many people with psychopathy; acquaintances often describe them (as they did Bundy) as "fascinating," "charismatic," and "compassionate." Beneath his superficial charm, though, Bundy was deceitful and dangerous. Embarrassed because he was an illegitimate child and his mother was poor, he constantly sought, as a youth, to give the impression of being an upper-class kid. He wore fake mustaches and used makeup to change his appearance. He faked a British accent and stole cars in high school to help maintain his image. He constantly sought out the company of attractive women, not because he was genuinely interested in them but because he wanted people to notice and admire him.

At his trial for the murder of two Chi Omega sorority sisters in their bedrooms at Florida State University, he served as his own attorney. (Bundy had attended two law schools, although he did not graduate from either.) He was convicted; he was also found guilty of the kidnapping, murder, and mutilation of a Lake City, Florida, girl who was 12 years old. Bundy was sentenced to death.

Shortly before he was executed on January 24, 1989, Bundy gave a television interview to evangelist James Dobson in which he blamed his problems on pornography. He said, "Those of us who are … so much influenced by violence in the media, in particular pornographic violence, are not some kind of inherent monsters. We are your husbands, and we grew up in regular families" (quoted by Lamar, 1989, p. 34).

Bettmann/Getty Images

Serial killer Ted Bundy

Bundy claimed that he spent his formative years with a grandfather who had an insatiable craving for pornography. He told Dr. Dobson, "People will accuse me of being self-serving but I am just telling you how I feel. Through God's help, I have been able to come to the point where I, much too late, but better late than never, feel the hurt and the pain that I am responsible for" (quoted by Kleinberg, 1989, p. 5A).

The tape of Bundy's last interview, produced by Dobson and titled "Fatal Addiction," has been widely disseminated, especially by those who seek to eliminate all pornography. But Bundy's claim that pornography was the "fuel for his fantasies" should be viewed skeptically. It may merely have been one last manipulative ploy to buy more time. In none of his previous interviews, including extensive conversations in 1986 with Dorothy Lewis, a psychiatrist he had come to trust, did he ever cite "a pornographic preamble to his grotesqueries" (Nobile, 1989, p. 41).

CRITICAL THOUGHT QUESTIONS

How would Dexter Morgan, a "fictional psychopath," compare with Ted Bundy, who was apparently the real thing?

and clinicians) to describe something that is basically the same disorder, but in a somewhat different way. Another answer is "not really," with antisocial personality disorder representing a milder version of the more serious personality disorder psychopathy. Although they are often discussed as though they were different, there is a great deal of overlap between the two. They are certainly not entirely separate disorders—and they may be the same. As long as they have different names and somewhat different diagnostic criteria, we continue to emphasize their differences. But readers should be aware that their similarities greatly outweigh their differences.

Psychopathy, as measured by the Hare Psychopathy Check List (Hare, 2003), has been well established as a risk factor for offending and for violent offending. Perhaps the best demonstration of this relationship comes from a meta-analysis on this topic (Leistico, Salekin, DeCoster, & Rogers, 2008). The authors integrated 95 nonoverlapping studies (N = 15,826 participants) to summarize the relation between the Hare Psychopathy Checklists and antisocial conduct. Their results indicated that higher PCL total scores and the scores on Factor 1 (describing interpersonal characteristics) and Factor 2 (describing chronic antisocial behavior) were moderately associated with increased antisocial conduct. These results depended on the setting from which the participants were drawn. PCL scores were more strongly associated with offending in the community than with serious misconduct in correctional facilities and secure hospitals.

There are a multitude of theories about what causes psychopathic behavior. One view is that psychopathic people suffer a cortical immaturity that makes it difficult for them to inhibit behavior. Hare himself has proposed that psychopaths may have a deficiency in the left hemisphere of their brains that impairs **executive function**, the ability to plan and regulate behavior carefully (Moffitt & Lynam, 1994). Considerable research supports a strong relationship between antisocial behavior and impaired executive functioning (Morgan & Lilienfeld, 2000).

Compared to normal controls, psychopaths experience less anxiety subsequent to aversive stimulation and are relatively underaroused in the resting state as well. This low autonomic arousal generates a high need for stimulation. Consequently, the psychopath prefers novel situations and tends to pay less attention to many stimuli, thereby being less influenced by them.

Quay (1965) advanced the **stimulation-seeking theory**, which claims that the thrill seeking and disruptive behavior of the psychopath serve to increase sensory input and arousal to a more tolerable level. As a result of such thrill seeking, the psychopathic person seems "immune" to many social cues that govern behavior. Eysenck (1964) proposed a theory that emphasizes the slower rate of classical conditioning for persons classified as psychopaths. He argued that the development of a conscience depends on acquisition of classically conditioned fear and avoidance responses, and that psychopathic individuals' conditioning deficiencies may account for their difficulties in normal socialization.

Another popular explanation for psychopathy involves being raised in a dysfunctional family (Loeber & Stouthamer-Loeber, 1986). Buss (1966) identified two parental patterns that might foster psychopathy. The first is having parents who are cold and distant. The child who imitates these parents develops an unfeeling, detached interpersonal style that conveys a superficial appearance of social involvement but lacks the empathy required for stable, satisfying relationships. The second pattern involves having parents who are inconsistent in their use of rewards and punishments, making it difficult for the child to imitate a stable role model and develop a consistent self-identity. A child in this situation learns to avoid blame and punishment but fails to learn the finer differences between appropriate and less appropriate behavior. Children with callous-unemotional traits (a central aspect of the adult disorder of psychopathy) were significantly worse compared to those lower on this dimension on stress management, frequency of criminal convictions among parents, and dysfunctional parenting, according to a review (McLoughlin, Rucklidge, Grace, & McLean, 2010).

Limitations of Psychopathy in Explaining Offending. The major drawback of psychopathy as an explanation for crime is that it describes only a small percentage of offenders. It might be tempting to classify most offenders as psychopaths and explain their offending with that classification. But most offenders are not psychopathic. One study found that only about 25% of a correctional sample could be classified as psychopathic, and this percentage was even smaller for women than for men (Salekin, Trobst, & Krioukova, 2001). This is generally consistent with other estimates in the literature.

In addition, there is controversy about using the PCL and revised versions of the instrument as diagnostic tools on which legal decisions are based. Although the PCL-R has an excellent inter-rater reliability when carried out in accordance with instructions (indicating that two raters using the PCL-R would tend to reach the same conclusion), a lack of training and possible biases on the part of the clinician may contribute to disparities in scores. Slight differences in scores may account for differences in courts' dispositions of these cases.

For these reasons, expert testimony invoking psychopathy may be problematic. Expert testimony about an offender's psychopathy or *psychopathic traits* (the preferred term for adolescents showing features of psychopathy) is associated with an increase in severity of the court's disposition (Zinger & Forth, 1998). Potential jurors were influenced in their decisions regarding juveniles by descriptions of antisocial behavior, psychopathic traits, and the colloquial use of the term *psychopath* (Boccaccini, Murrie, Clark, & Cornell, 2008). Research with juveniles suggests that the "antisocial behavior" label has a stronger effect than "psychopathic traits" on the judgments of juvenile probation officers, however (Murrie, Cornell, & McCoy, 2005).

Furthermore, because the PCL depends partly on self-report, the information obtained may be inaccurate. As a safeguard against potentially erroneous information, the administrator must have access to collateral information to compare with information obtained from the examinee. Because the number of judicial decisions that rely on the PCL-R is considerable, the ongoing training efforts for this measure are particularly important.

Yet another criticism of the use of these psychopathy assessment instruments in criminal proceedings revolves around their use in cases involving adolescent and female offenders. Although some evidence suggests that these instruments can be successfully used with female offenders (Nicholls, Ogloff, Brink, & Spidel, 2005; Vitale & Newman, 2001) and male adolescents (Corrado, Vincent, Hart, & Cohen, 2004; Marsee, Silverthorn, & Frick, 2005), other evidence is more mixed. For example, one component of psychopathy (deficient affective experience) was related to aggression in female juveniles, but when victimization experience was taken into account, such deficient affect no longer showed an impact. PCL-Youth Version scores in this study were not predictive of future offending, while victimization experiences significantly increased the odds of re-offending (Odgers, Reppucci, & Moretti, 2005). It appears presently that while psychopathy may have some applications with women (Kreis & Cooke, 2012) and adolescents, there are important gender and developmental differences, respectively, that must be considered—and the application of psychopathy to these groups is not straightforward. While it is fair to say that these psychopathy assessment tools offer a valuable way of assessing personal characteristics and history that are related to criminal offending by some offenders, there are other contributors as well. These include social influences, to which we now turn.

Social–Psychological Theories of Crime

Social–psychological explanations view crime as being learned through social interaction. Sometimes called social-process theories in order to draw attention to the processes by which an individual becomes a criminal, social–psychological theories fall into two subcategories: control theories and direct learning theories. **Control theory** assumes that people will behave antisocially unless they learn, through a combination of inner controls and external constraints on behavior, not to offend. **Learning theory** stresses how individuals directly acquire specific criminal behaviors through different forms of learning.

Control Theories. Control theories assume that people will behave antisocially unless they are trained not to by others (Conger, 1980). Young people are bonded to society at several levels. They differ in (1) the degree to which they are affected by the opinions and expectations of others, (2) the payoffs they receive for conventional behavior, and (3) the extent to which they subscribe to the prevailing norms. Some people never form emotional bonds with significant others, so they never internalize necessary controls over antisocial behavior.

Reckless's (1967) **containment theory** is an example of a control theory. Reckless proposed that it is largely external containment (i.e., social pressure and institutionalized rules) that controls crime. If a society is well integrated, has well-defined limits on behavior, encourages family discipline and supervision, and provides reinforcers for positive accomplishments, crime will be contained. But if these external controls weaken, control of crime must depend on internal restraints, mainly an individual's conscience. Thus, a positive self-concept becomes a protective factor against delinquency. Strong inner containment involves the ability to tolerate frustration, be motivated by long-term goals, resist distractions, and find substitute satisfactions (Reckless, 1967).

Containment theory is an "in-between" view, neither rigidly environmental nor entirely disposition-based. Containment accounts for the law-abiding individual in a high-crime environment. But this theory explains only a part of criminal behavior. It does not apply to crimes within groups that are organized around their commitment to deviant behavior.

The British psychologist Eysenck (1964) proposed a related version of containment theory in which "heredity plays an important, and possibly a vital, part in predisposing a given individual to crime" (p. 55). Socialization practices then translate these innate tendencies into criminal acts. Socialization depends on two kinds of learning. First, **operant learning** explains how behavior is acquired and maintained by its consequences: Responses that are followed by rewards are strengthened, whereas responses followed by aversive events are weakened. Immediate consequences are more influential than delayed consequences. However, according to Eysenck (1964), in the real world the effects of punishment are usually "long delayed and uncertain [whereas] the acquisition of the desired object is immediate; therefore, although the acquisition and the pleasure derived from it may, on the whole, be less than the pain derived from the incarceration which ultimately follows, the time element very much favors the acquisition as compared with the deterrent effects of the incarceration" (p. 101).

Because of punishment's ineffectiveness, the restraint of antisocial behavior ultimately depends on a strong conscience, which develops through **classical conditioning**. Eysenck believed that conscience is conditioned through repeated, close pairings of a child's undesirable behaviors with the prompt punishment of these behaviors. Conscience becomes an inner control that deters wrongdoing through the emotions of anxiety and guilt.

Learning Theories. Learning theory focuses on how criminal behavior is learned. For example, Sutherland and Cressey (1974) proposed various explanations of criminal behavior, including the following:

1. Criminal behavior is learned through interaction with other persons in a process of communication.
2. When criminal behavior is learned, the learning includes (a) techniques of committing the crime, which are sometimes very complicated but at other times simple and (b) the specific direction of motives, drives, rationalizations, and attitudes.
3. A person becomes delinquent because there are more examples favorable to violating the law than unfavorable to violating the law.

Sutherland's theory has been translated into the language of operant learning theory as developed by B. F. Skinner. According to **differential association reinforcement theory** (Akers, Krohn, Lanz-Kaduce, & Radosevich, 1996), criminal behavior is acquired through operant conditioning and modeling. A person behaves criminally when reinforcement for such behavior is more frequent than punishment. Families, peer groups, and schools control most sources of reinforcement and punishment and expose people to many behavioral models (Akers et al., 1996).

Such theory attempts to explain crime in places where it would not necessarily be expected (e.g., among lawbreakers who grew up in affluent settings). But it has difficulty explaining impulsive violence, and it does not explain why certain individuals, even in the same family, have the different associations they do. Why are some people more likely than others to form criminal associations?

Social Learning Theory/Social Cognitive Theory. One answer comes from **social learning theory**. (The name of this theory was subsequently changed to "social cognitive theory" to reflect the enhanced emphasis on thinking.) **Social cognitive theory** acknowledges the importance of differential reinforcement for developing new behaviors, but it assigns more importance to cognitive factors and to observational or **vicarious learning**. Its chief proponent, Bandura (1986), observed that "most human behavior is learned by observation through modeling" (p. 47). Learning through modeling is more efficient than learning through differential reinforcement. Complex behaviors such as speech and driving a car require models from which to learn. In all likelihood, so does crime. Observational learning depends on (1) *attention* to the important features of modeled behavior; (2) *retention* of these features in memory to guide later performance; (3) *reproduction* of the observed behaviors; and (4) *reinforcement* of performed behaviors, which determines whether they will be performed again.

The most prominent attempt to apply social learning theory to criminal behavior was made by Bandura (1973, 1986). The theory emphasizes modeling of aggression in three social contexts.

1. *Familial influences.* Familial aggression assumes many forms, from child abuse at one extreme to aggressive parental attitudes and language at the other. It is in the arena of discipline, however, where children are exposed most often to vivid examples of coercion and aggression as a preferred style for resolving conflicts and asserting desires.
2. *Subcultural influences.* Some environments and subcultures provide context that supports aggression and an abundance of rewards for their most

combative members. "The highest rates of aggressive behavior are found in environments where aggressive models abound and where aggressiveness is regarded as a highly valued attribute" (Bandura, 1976, p. 207).

3. *Symbolic models.* The influence of symbolic models on aggression has been attributed to the mass media, particularly Internet and television. A large number of studies have investigated the effects of televised violence on viewers, especially children.

A longitudinal study, conducted over a 15-year period, suggests that there are significant long-term effects from watching violent television in childhood (Huesmann, Moise-Titus, Podolski, & Eron, 2003). Results from this study revealed a significant relationship between watching violence on television as children and aggressive behavior in adulthood. This pattern held for male and female participants, although the types of aggressive behavior differed. Males engaged in more overt aggression (e.g., domestic violence, physical fights), whereas women engaged in more indirect aggression (e.g., traffic violations). Women who watched violent television as children were also four times more likely than other women to be victims of domestic violence. Furthermore, the study found that early exposure to violence on television significantly predicted aggression in adulthood regardless of the level of aggression the individual displayed in childhood.

Researchers also hypothesized that viewing television violence in childhood can lead to other potentially harmful effects. For instance, children may become desensitized to the effects of violence (e.g., may care less about others' feelings) or experience a heightened fear of victimization. Children younger than eight years old may be especially vulnerable to the effects of viewing violence because of their cognitive limitations in distinguishing fantasy and cartoon violence from reality. Of more recent interest is the question of whether movies and video games, which often feature much more graphic depictions of violence than those allowed on TV, exert stronger modeling effects on aggression. We describe a relevant case in Box 3.3.

A recent review by a task force of the American Psychological Association on violent media (2015) drew a number of conclusions from the existing scientific evidence:

- There is a consistent relationship between the use of violent video games, increases in aggression (behavior, thinking, and emotion), and decreases in prosocial behavior and empathy.

- These are more than temporary effects. They occur in short-term laboratory studies and longer-term longitudinal observations.
- These effects remain when other influences are statistically controlled, but thus far only a small number of studies has been conducted on this question.
- Higher amounts of gaming experience are associated with higher levels of aggression and other problematic outcomes.
- Most of the research has been conducted on individuals between age 14 and young adulthood. Also, limited research is available on gender, race, ethnicity, or culture as influences—so conclusions are limited on the question of how these factors influence the relationship between violent video game exposure and adverse outcomes.

Social cognitive theory also points to several environmental cues that increase antisocial behavior. These "instigators" signal when it might be rewarding to behave antisocially (rather than risky to do so). One instigator is *models*: observing others and modeling their behavior can influence some, particularly when they have been frustrated or see the aggression as justified. A second (related) instigator is *prior aversive treatment*. People often treat others the way they have been treated. A third is *incentive inducements*, which includes the anticipated rewards of misbehavior. Habitual offenders often overestimate their chances of succeeding in criminal acts and ignore the consequences of failing. A fourth is *instructions*, particularly from one in authority. Milgram's (1963) famous study demonstrating widespread willingness to follow orders to inflict "pain" on another person is a good illustration. Although not a common feature of offending, this kind of influence may play a role in some hate crimes, in which the perpetrator believes he or she is doing the will of a religious or patriotic fanatic. A fifth is *delusions and hallucinations*: individuals occasionally respond aggressively to false beliefs or hallucinated commands that stem from severe mental illness. Finally, there is a strong, positive association between crime and *alcohol or drug use*, especially for violent crime (Parker, 2004; Richardson & Budd, 2003). By depressing a person's responsiveness to other cues that could inhibit impulsive or aggressive behavior, alcohol often leads to an increase in antisocial behavior even though it is not a stimulant. Drug use, by virtue of its cost and deviant status, also acts as a catalyst to or amplifier of criminality, especially property crime.

According to social learning theorists, people also regulate their behavior through self-reinforcement.

The Case of "Teenage Amusement," a Murder, and a Video Game

BOX 3.3

A 2006 report from the National Coalition for the Homeless noted a disturbing trend: there were 122 attacks and 20 murders of homeless people in 2005, several of them by teenage perpetrators. According to the Coalition's executive director Michael Stoops, "It's disturbing to know that young people would literally kick someone when they're already down on their luck. We recognize that this isn't every teenager, but for some this passes as amusement."

Three teenage perpetrators from Milwaukee—16-year-old Luis Oyola, 17-year-old Andrew Ihrcke, and 15-year-old Nathan Moore—claimed that killing Rex Baum was never part of their plan. But the trio, who had been drinking with Baum at his campsite, suddenly began punching and kicking the 49-year-old man and then hurled anything they could find—rocks, bricks, even a barbeque grill, at the hapless victim. After smearing him with feces, cutting him, and bragging about their actions, they were arrested. One of the teens told police that killing "the bum" reminded him of playing the violent video game "Bumfights," which depicts homeless people pummeling each other to make a few bucks.

CRITICAL THOUGHT QUESTIONS

What are your hypotheses about the influences on the three adolescents who viciously attacked and killed Rex Baum?

Individuals who derive pleasure, pride, revenge, or self-worth from an ability to harm or "con" others enjoy an almost sensual pleasure in the way criminal behavior "feels" (Katz, 1988). Conversely, people will discontinue conduct that results in self-criticism and self-contempt.

People can also learn to exempt themselves from their own conscience after behaving antisocially. These tactics of "self-exoneration" assume many forms: minimizing the seriousness of one's acts by pointing to more serious offenses by others, justifying aggression by appealing to higher values, displacing the responsibility for misbehavior onto a higher authority, blaming victims for their misfortune, diffusing responsibility for wrongdoing, dehumanizing victims so that they are stripped of sympathetic qualities, and underestimating the damage inflicted by one's actions.

The major strength of social learning theory is that it explains how specific patterns of criminal offending are developed by individuals. A second strength is that the theory applies to a wide range of crimes. The major limitation of social learning theory is that little empirical evidence indicates that real-life crime is learned according to behavioral principles. Most of the data come from laboratory research where the experimental setting nullifies all the legal and social sanctions that actual offenders must risk incurring. A second problem is that the theory does not explain why some people fall prey to "bad" learning experiences and others resist them. Learning might be a necessary ingredient for criminality, but probably not a sufficient one. Individual differences in the way people respond to reinforcement need to be considered. The theory we review next does so.

Multiple-Component Learning Theory. Some theorists have integrated several learning processes into comprehensive, learning-based explanations of criminality (e.g., Feldman, 1977). The most influential and controversial multiple-component learning theory is Wilson and Herrnstein's (1985) book *Crime and Human Nature.* Wilson and Herrnstein begin by observing that criminal and noncriminal behavior have both gains and losses. Gains from committing crime include revenge, excitement, and peer approval. Gains associated with not committing crime include avoiding punishment and having a clear conscience. Whether a crime is committed depends, in part, on the net ratio of gains and losses for criminal and noncriminal behavior. If the ratio for committing a crime exceeds the ratio for not committing it, the likelihood of the crime being committed increases.

Wilson and Herrnstein argued that several individual differences influence these ratios and determine whether an individual is likely to commit a crime. Like Eysenck, they proposed that individuals differ in the ease with which they learn to associate, through classical conditioning, negative emotions with misbehaviors and positive emotions with proper behaviors. These conditioned responses are the building blocks of a strong conscience that enhances the gains of not offending and the losses associated with crime.

Another important factor is what Wilson and Herrnstein called *time discounting.* All reinforcers lose strength as they become more removed from a behavior, but people differ in their ability to delay gratification and obtain reinforcement from potential long-term gains. More impulsive persons have greater difficulty deriving benefits from distant reinforcers. Time discounting is important for understanding crime because the gains associated with crime (e.g., revenge, money) accrue immediately, whereas the losses from such behavior (e.g., punishment) occur later, if at all. Thus, for impulsive persons, the ratio of gains to losses shifts in a direction that favors criminal behavior.

Another major component in Wilson and Herrnstein's theory is a set of constitutional factors, including gender, intelligence, variations in physiological arousal, and impulsivity, all of which combine to make some persons more attracted to wrongdoing and less deterred by the potential aversive consequences of crime.

Of several social factors linked to criminal behavior, Wilson and Herrnstein believe that family influences and early school experiences are the most important. Families that foster (1) *attachment* of children to their parents; (2) *longer time horizons*, where children consider the distant consequences of their behavior; and (3) *strong consciences* about misbehavior will go far in counteracting criminal predispositions.

Research on parenting practices and the quality of the parent–child relationship underscores the relevance of familial interaction to childhood delinquency. Findings from a qualitative study with juvenile offenders and their parents revealed that their family interactions featured poor communication and high levels of conflict between children and parents. These interactions were associated with children's perceptions of lack of parental concern and warmth (Madden-Derdich, Leonard, & Gunnell, 2002). In addition, an intergenerational study examining the effect of parenting styles on antisocial behavioral patterns across generations suggests that familial interactions have far-reaching implications: parental conflict and highly demanding, unresponsive parents were related to childhood behavioral problems in two successive generations (Smith & Farrington, 2004).

The remedies to these harmful patterns involve warm supportiveness combined with consistent enforcement of clear rules for proper behavior. Unfortunately, individuals whose parents were demanding, unresponsive, and high in conflict are not likely to become parents who are warm, supportive, and consistent in their enforcement of rules. Therefore, many at-risk children face the double whammy of problematic predispositions coupled with inadequate parental control and support.

Biological factors interact with family problems and early school experiences to further increase the risks of poorly controlled behavior. Not only are impulsive, poorly socialized children of lower intelligence more directly at risk for criminality, but their interactions with cold, indifferent schools that do not facilitate educational success can further discourage them from embracing traditional social conformity. Consistent with this part of the theory is a long line of research studies showing that children officially diagnosed with early conduct problems and/or attention deficit/hyperactivity disorder face a heightened likelihood of becoming adult offenders (Slobogin & Fondacoro, 2011).

Because they took hereditary and biological factors seriously, Wilson and Herrnstein have come under heavy fire from critics who portray their theory as purely genetic. It is not. Instead, it is a theory that restores psychological factors (some heritable, some not) and family interaction variables to a place of importance in criminology, which for decades was dominated by sociological concepts.

Social Labeling Theory. The most extreme version of a social–psychological theory of crime is the social labeling perspective. Its emergence as an explanation reflects frustration about the inability of prior approaches to provide comprehensive explanations and a shift in emphasis from why people commit crimes to why some people are labeled "criminals" (Sheley, 1985).

The basic assumption of social labeling theory is that that society assigns labels to certain acts, which leads to the perception of deviance. Deviance is not simply based on the quality of the act; rather, it stems also from an act's consequences in the form of society's official reactions to it. Social labeling theory makes a distinction between **primary deviance**, or the criminal's actual behavior, and **secondary deviance**, or society's reaction to the offensive conduct (Lemert, 1951, 1972). With regard to primary deviance, offenders often rationalize their behavior as a temporary mistake, or they see it as part of a socially acceptable role (Lilly et al., 1989). Whether or not that self-assessment is accurate, secondary deviance serves to brand them with a more permanent "criminal" stigma.

One illustration of social labeling is the allegation that police use **racial profiling** as a basis for making a disproportionate number of traffic stops of minority motorists, particularly African Americans. Police officials have sometimes justified such practice as a tool for catching drug traffickers, but arresting motorists for "driving while black" as a pretext for additional criminal investigations clearly raises the risk of harmful and inappropriate labeling, to say nothing of its discriminatory impact. The outcry over racial profiling has resulted in a call for federal legislation that would prohibit the practice and has led to litigation. This is also the kind of behavior that leads Black citizens to perceive that they are being singled out unfairly, with sometimes fatal consequences, leading to protests such as "Black Lives Matter" and eroding the trust between citizens and police that is so important for citizens to feel safe and police to perceive that they can do their jobs effectively. The main point of the **social labeling theory** is that the stigma of being branded a deviant can create a self-fulfilling prophecy (Merton, 1968). Even those former inmates who seek an honest life in a law-abiding society are spurned by prospective employers and by their families and are labeled "ex-cons." Frustrated in their efforts to make good, they may adopt this label and "live up to" its negative connotations by engaging in further lawbreaking (Irwin, 1970). According to this perspective, the criminal justice system produces much of the deviance it is intended to correct.

The social labeling approach raises our awareness about the difficulties offenders face in returning to society. It reminds us that some lawbreakers (e.g., those who live in crime-ridden neighborhoods where the police patrol often) are more likely to be caught and "criminalized" than are others. But the social labeling approach does not explain most criminal behavior. Nor is it favored as a serious explanation for criminal offending in the 21st century. Primary deviance (i.e., a law violation in the first place) usually has to occur before secondary deviance takes its toll, and many lawbreakers develop a life of crime before ever being apprehended. Behavioral differences between people exist and persist, whatever we call them.

Integration of Theories of Crime

Where do all these theories leave us? Do any of them offer a convincing explanation of crime? Do they suggest how we should intervene to prevent or reduce crime? Although many commentators decry the lack of a convincing theory of crime, knowledge about the causes of serious crime has accumulated and now provides certain well-supported explanations for how

repeated, violent criminality develops. Many serious offenders are extraordinarily versatile, with careers that include violent behavior, property offenses, vandalism, and substance abuse.

One implication of the discussion in this section is that individuals travel several causal pathways to different brands of criminality. No single variable causes all crime, just as no one agent causes all fevers or all upset stomachs. However, several causal factors are associated reliably with many types of criminality. Any one of these factors may sometimes be a sufficient explanation for some type of criminal behavior, but more often they act in concert to produce criminality. Our attempt to integrate these various factors (see Figure 3.1) emphasizes four contributors to crime that occur in a developmental sequence.

Our model emphasizes what we believe are the variables best supported by criminological research as causal factors in crime:

1. *Antecedent conditions.* Chances of repeated offending are increased by biological, psychological, and environmental antecedents that make it easier for certain individuals to learn to behave criminally and easier for this learning to occur in specific settings. The leading candidates for biological risk are genetic inheritance, neurochemical abnormalities, brain dysfunction, and autonomic nervous system irregularities.

   Psychological variables enhancing risk of offending include poor social skills; lower verbal intelligence; personality traits of irritability, impulsiveness, callousness, and low empathy; and deficiencies in inner restraint (or conscience) leave some people with attitudes, thinking, and motivations that encourage antisocial behavior—and also render them relatively immune to negative consequences for misconduct. These psychological factors may accompany biological risks or may convey their own independent vulnerability to crime.

   Finally, certain environments are rife with opportunities and temptations for crime and help translate biological or psychological predispositions toward criminal behavior into ever-stronger antisocial tendencies. Such environments function this way because of social impoverishment and disorganization, fundamental economic inequalities, a tradition of tolerating (or even encouraging) crime, social dissension and strife, and an abundance of inviting targets and easy victims of crime. Such environments promote offending in those who have a propensity toward crime (Wikstrom, Ceccato, Hardie, & Treiber, 2010).

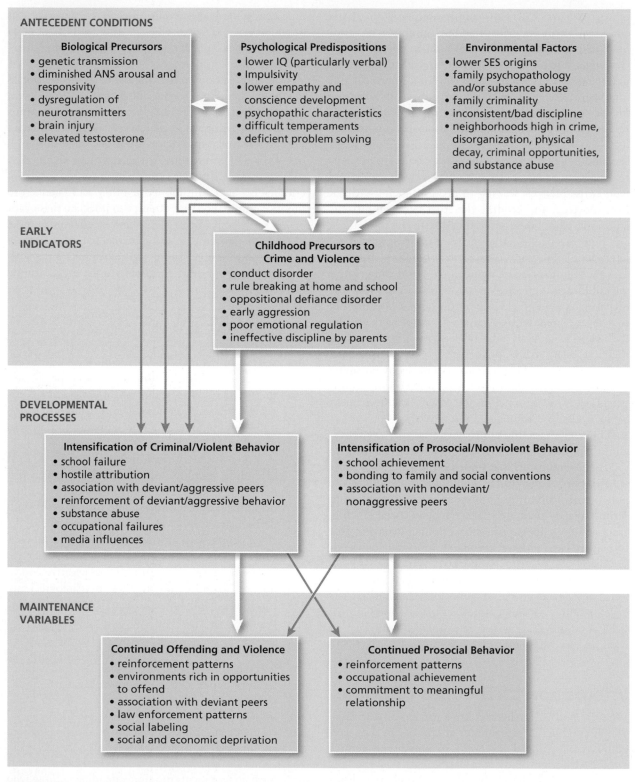

FIGURE 3.1   An Integrated model for explaining repeated crime

Note: Thick arrows indicate probable paths; thin arrows indicate less likely paths.

Within family environments, high levels of mental disorders, criminality, parental absenteeism, and substance abuse also lead to more violence. These links may be forged through any of several factors: genetic influence, modeling, increased hostility against a constant backdrop of harsh living conditions, disturbed attachments with parents, or lax or overly punitive discipline that does not teach youngsters how to control behavior. Research suggests that early exposure to harsh family living conditions can aggravate some of the biological factors that contribute to aggression, such as a child's physical and emotional reactions to threat (Barnow, Lucht, & Freyberger, 2001; Gallagher, 1996; Zelechoski, 2016).

2. *Early indicators.* Repetitive antisocial conduct can be stable over time. Aggressive children often grow up to be aggressive adults, and the precedents for adult violence and substance abuse are often manifested as aggression in pre-school and elementary school children (Asendorpf, Denissen, & van Aken, 2008; Temcheff et al., 2008). Although there are tests that can identify youth who are at elevated risk for behavioral problems, it remains difficult to predict whether these individuals will commit serious, violent acts later in life (Sprague & Walker, 2000). Relatively few at-risk youth commit serious, violent offenses, but many display major long-term adjustment problems. For instance, youth identified as "at risk" in childhood may experience drug and alcohol abuse, domestic and child abuse, divorce or multiple relationships, employment problems, mental health problems, dependence on social services, and involvement in less-serious crimes (Obiakor, Merhing, & Schwenn, 1997).

Although not all chronic offenders were violent children, many repetitively aggressive adults began to exhibit that pattern early. In fact, most psychologists who study aggression believe that severe antisocial behavior in adulthood is nearly always preceded by antisocial behavior in childhood. These early indicators include officially diagnosed conduct disorder, oppositional defiant disorder, and attention deficit/hyperactivity disorder (Goldstein, Grant, Ruan, Smith, & Saha, 2006; Temcheff et al., 2008). Developmental models have enhanced our understanding of the onset and maintenance of antisocial behavior. For instance, one model suggests two subtypes of adolescent offenders: those who display behavioral problems later in

adolescence and desist in early adulthood, and the relatively smaller group who display conduct-disordered behaviors earlier in adolescence that persist into adulthood. Adolescent offenders in the latter group are more likely to develop antisocial personality disorder than those in the former group.

Another model suggests that early emergence of conduct-disordered behavior that is displayed across multiple and diverse settings may predict the development of antisocial personality disorder in adulthood. One study found that early indicators of a diagnosis of antisocial personality disorder included a formal diagnosis of conduct disorder by age 10, participation in frequent and varied conduct-disordered behavior at an early age, and significant drug use in childhood or early adolescence (Myers, Stewart, & Brown, 1998). Recent reviews show that most children and adolescents who are involved in offending stop sometime in their teenage years or early 20s, but some persist into adulthood (Russell & Odgers, 2016; Woolard & Fountain, 2016). These are the individuals who are much more likely to be diagnosed with antisocial personality disorder, and who continue to be at risk for criminal offending well into their adulthood.

The "Pathways to Desistance" study followed 1,354 serious juvenile offenders over a seven-year period following their enrollment in the study between 2000 and 2003. It featured multiple sources of information (self-report, family and friends' collateral report, and official records) and follow-up at regular interviews. Among their important findings are: (1) about 9% of youth continued in serious offending; 15% reduced their level of offending but continued, and the remainder desisted; (2) substance abuse is a strong risk factor, even for nondrug offending; (3) quality services reduce rearrest rate; (4) initial offense is a poor predictor of reoffending risk; (5) increasing the duration of community-based supervision reduces risk, while harsh punishment increases it; and (6) fair, respectful contact with police reduces risk (Mulvey, 2011).

Long-term longitudinal studies have demonstrated that aggression in childhood predicts violence in adulthood—particularly in the subgroup of individuals who persist in aggression and offending throughout the lifespan. Huesmann, Eron, and Yarmel (1987) measured aggression in childhood and tracked the boys and girls for 22 years. They found that aggression began to crystallize around the age of eight and remained stable into adulthood (Eron, 1990; Huesmann, Eron, Lefkowitz, & Walder, 1984). Aggressive boys turned into men who were more likely to commit serious crimes, abuse their spouses, and drive while intoxicated. Aggressive girls turned into women who were more likely to punish their children harshly. Another 19-year longitudinal study (Asendorpf, Denissen, & van Aken, 2008) followed inhibited and aggressive preschool children into young adulthood. As adults, inhibited boys and girls were delayed in establishing a first stable partnership and finding a first full-time job. However, only the most inhibited children (upper 8%) showed internalizing problems such as self-rated inhibition. Aggressive boys showed more conduct problems, were educational and occupational underachievers, and showed a higher delinquency rate than those rated as nonaggressive as children, even after controlling for gender and socioeconomic status. In a New Zealand cohort followed from birth, 11% of males followed a trajectory of persistent aggression between the ages of 7 and 15 (Odgers et al., 2008). Among high-risk and all-offender samples, highly stable subgroups composed of those who persist in offending have been identified (Connell, Klostermann, & Dishion, 2012; Miller, Malone, & Dodge, 2010).

3. *Developmental processes.* Whether early indicators of criminal offending harden into patterns of repeated adult crime or soften into prosocial nonviolent conduct depends on several developmental processes. These processes occur in families, schools, peer groups, and the media—and in the thinking of the youth themselves.

Delinquency is often associated with poor school achievement. Grades in school begin to predict delinquency around age 15. As adolescent youth fall further and further behind in school, they have fewer and fewer opportunities or reasons to stay bonded to school and to strive for academic success (Hoge, 2016). School failure seems to narrow the options for prosocial behavior because it decreases the chances of employability and job success. Modeling and peer pressure also promote criminality. Crime increases when peers support it, as is sometimes the case in the criminal justice system itself when, by virtue of its official processing of offenders, "beginning" criminals are thrown together with more serious offenders. Furthermore, the more delinquent friends a youth has, the more likely he or she is to behave criminally—at least until age 20 (Monahan, Steinberg, & Cauffman, 2009).

Other research suggests that the association between delinquency and negative peer influences may be even more complex than previously thought. One study found that poor parental monitoring and supervision, as well as increased social stress and poor social skills, affected the relationship between adolescents' delinquent behavior and negative peer affiliation (Kimonis, Frick, & Barry, 2004). On the basis of these findings, the authors concluded that intervening with training in parenting skills and social skills, specifically encouraging more parental involvement and monitoring of their child's behavior, may be especially important in reducing negative peer affiliation and decreasing delinquency.

Modeling influences can also be mediated through the media. One investigator (Murray, 2008) noted that 50 years of research strongly suggested a relationship between TV violence and the increase in aggressive attitudes, values, and behaviors among children. A more recent Task Force report (APA, 2015) suggests a similar relationship between violent video games and aggression. These changes may be mediated by neurological changes in children who view frequent TV violence or engage in frequent violent gaming. It is, of course, difficult to know whether there is a causal relationship between such TV, gaming, and other media violence and aggressive behavior. What makes this even more difficult is that most of the studies in this area are surveys, rather than controlled experiments. But other investigators (Glymour, Glymour, & Glymour, 2008) considered these difficulties and concluded, in light of the existing evidence, that there is likely (but not certainly) a causal relationship between exposure to TV violence and subsequent adult aggression, consistent with the conclusions about violent gaming and subsequent aggressive attitudes and behavior (APA, 2015). Despite the growing evidence of this linkage, it is not clear that U.S. courts will intervene to reduce the violence on television or in gaming. For instance, the U.S. Supreme Court overturned a California law banning the sale of violent video games to children on First Amendment grounds, protecting the free speech rights of video game makers (*Brown v. Entertainment Merchants Association*, 2011).

Another intensifier of aggression is alcohol and substance abuse (Snyder & Sickmund, 2006). Numerous mechanisms could account for the tendency for substance abuse to lead to more crime. Alcohol is a depressant, so it might suppress the ability of certain areas of the brain to inhibit behavior effectively. The more time a youth spends abusing drugs and alcohol, the less time he or she has for prosocial, academic activities. Substance abuse typically results in more associations with deviant peers, thereby increasing the opportunities for antisocial behavior to be reinforced. Repeated substance abuse during adolescence serves as one more "trap" that shuts off many youngsters' options for prosocial behavior. These limits, in turn, increase the reinforcing potential of antisocial conduct.

Unfortunately, these developmental processes tend to compound one another. The impulsive, low-IQ child is more likely to fail at school. School dropouts increasingly associate with antisocial peers. Parents who fail to monitor and sanction their children when they misbehave tend not to show as much concern about what movies their children watch or what video games they play. Finally, early conduct and academic problems are strongly related to later substance abuse. When it comes to crime, at-risk youth have multiple influences that can interact to push them toward offending.

4. *Maintenance factors.* Violent offending can become an entrenched way of life when one or more of the following maintenance factors are in place: The short-run positive payoffs for offending are stronger and more probable than the long-term risks of apprehension and punishment. The person lives in environments that are rich in opportunities for offending and low in the chances of being detected. As a result of the inevitable arrests and incarcerations that repeat offenders experience, their associations with aggressive peers increase, just as contacts with law-abiding citizens decrease. As the long-run consequence of many earlier estrangements from conventional norms and values, delinquents begin to feel growing resentment and indifference for social rules. These maintenance factors do not cause crime so much as solidify it. Once they start to work their influence, the battle is often already lost, because criminal conduct has become a part of a person's identity.

An implication of our integrative model is that preventing crime might be a better way of fighting the "crime problem" than rehabilitating criminals. Certainly, with the help of treatment programs that strengthen their social skills, build better cognitive controls, model prosocial behavior, and reinforce law-abiding conduct, some people can "turn around" a life of violent offending (Andrews & Bonta, 2006). But however promising the rates of "success" in correctional rehabilitation might eventually become, it is still likely that some who are arrested and incarcerated will continue to offend throughout their lives.

This should not be surprising. After a protracted history of learning antisocial behavior, rejecting prosocial behavior, and facing closed doors to legitimate opportunity, repeat offenders will not yield easily to attempts to suppress criminal conduct. That is why prevention becomes so important. If most at-risk youth can be reliably identified, we can then intervene in multiple areas—with individuals, families, schools, peer groups, and neighborhoods—to interrupt those processes that eventually ensnare youth into antisocial lifestyles. Brought about by adverse environments and the decisions of youth themselves, these processes include experimenting with alcohol and drugs, learning from violent media and subcultures, dropping out of school, failing at legitimate employment, and associating with others who break the law. These are the pathways to deviance that must be blocked early—before they become too well traveled—for meaningful change to occur.

Summary

1. ***Theories of crime can be grouped into four categories. What are they?*** The most common theories can be classified into four groups: sociological, biological, psychological, and social–psychological.

2. ***Among sociological explanations of crime, how does the subcultural explanation differ from the structural explanation?*** The structural explanation for crime emphasizes chronic barriers to conventional success that certain people face; these barriers include cultural and language differences, financial hardships, and limited access to those resources crucial to upward mobility. In contrast, the subcultural explanation proposes that certain groups, such as gangs, adhere to norms that conflict with the values of others in society and encourage criminal conduct.

3. ***What is emphasized in biological theories of crime?*** Both genetic and physiological factors are emphasized in biological explanations of criminal behavior. Hereditary factors influence criminal behavior, but the mechanisms through which this influence is exerted are unclear. The most likely candidates involve neurotransmitters, such as serotonin, and certain subcortical and cortical brain structures, particularly the prefrontal cortex, which is responsible for monitoring behavioral inhibition, planning, and decision-making. A more specific prospect involves a mutation on the X chromosome in the gene coding for MAO-A, in combination with maltreatment as a child.

4. ***What psychological factors have been advanced to explain crime?*** Psychological theories of criminal behavior emphasize criminal thinking patterns or a personality disorder such as psychopathy.

5. ***How do social–psychological theories view crime?*** Social–psychological theories view criminal behavior as a learned response resulting from classical conditioning, reinforcement, observation or modeling, and social labeling.

Key Terms

anomie

antisocial personality disorder

biological theories of crime

classical conditioning

classical school of criminology

concordance rate

containment theory

control theory

correctional psychology

criminology

differential association reinforcement theory

dizygotic twins

executive function

extroversion

forensic psychology

learning theory

monozygotic twins

neuroticism

operant learning

positivist school of criminology

primary deviance

proportionality

proportionality

psychological theories (of crime)

psychopathy

psychoticism

racial profiling

secondary deviance

social cognitive theory

social labeling theory

social learning theory

social–psychological theory (of crime)

sociological theories (of crime)

stimulation-seeking theory

structural explanations

subcultural explanations

threat assessment

trauma

vicarious learning

4 Psychology of Police

ORIENTING QUESTIONS

1. What is the role of the police in our society?
2. What procedures are used to select police?
3. How has the training of police officers expanded into new areas?
4. Describe the different activities of the police. Is law enforcement central?

5. What stressors do the police face?
6. What is the relationship between the police and the communities they serve?
7. What is the future of policing in the United States in the 21st century?

In any survey of public concerns, "crime" is usually near the top. This ranking stems from the nature of crime in our country, as well as from the fear that crime typically instills. It is true, of course, that crime in the United States has been decreasing for the last two decades. The rates of criminal offending in the United States for violent crime (crimes involving direct contact with people, such as homicide, assault, sexual assault, and robbery) and property crime (crimes involving many kinds of theft, but without direct contact with people, such as burglary and motor vehicle theft) have been dropping consistently and strongly over the last 20 years. In 2015, the rate of violent crime was 58% of its level in 1996 and the rate of property crime was 56% of its 1996 rate. During this 20-year period, there were only four years in which the rate of violent crime did not decrease from its previous year's rate, and two years in which the property crime rate did not go down (FBI, 2015). The trend toward a lower crime rate is certainly encouraging (and at odds with the frequently cited view that crime in the United States is increasing). Despite such progress, however, the annual economic impact of crime (whether measured in lost cash, damaged property, medical expenses, emotional trauma, or lost income due to injuries) amounts to billions of dollars.

The road from reporting a crime to convicting and punishing an offender can be long and tortuous, but in most cases, the police are the officials in the criminal justice system with whom citizens have the most contact. The police must confront criminal activities face to face, and we expect them to keep our streets safe and our homes secure. They are the "thin blue line" that stands between the law-abiding citizen and public disorder. The visibility of the police is heightened by the uniforms they wear, the weapons they carry, and the special powers they are given. This visibility makes the police convenient targets for the public's frustrations with the criminal justice system. At the same time, many people place enormous trust in the police, and police are the first people whom most citizens call in emergencies. Consequently, there are conflicting attitudes held by many within our society about the police. Some seek protection at all costs; others resist police intrusion and seek to avoid the police; most strike some kind of balance.

Police are responsible for a complex set of tasks in the criminal justice system. To succeed at their jobs, street officers must combine physical prowess, perceptual acuity, interpersonal sensitivity, and careful discretion. They need to make quick judgments about all sorts of human behavior, often under very stressful conditions. They should be well versed in the law and should have at least some familiarity with the social sciences. Despite the complexity of these demands, police are often overworked and underappreciated. These factors, along with the job pressures they face, the criminal offenders they encounter, and the isolated conditions in which they often work, can make officers susceptible to bribery, corruption, and abuses of power.

When we consider the police from a psychological perspective, we encounter various dilemmas. Law enforcement in a democratic society must strike a balance: protecting citizens through crime prevention and investigation while simultaneously respecting constitutional rights. Police officers investigate crime, but they must also make arrests and maintain an image of stability in society. Operating within this balance can be very difficult, particularly when domestic terrorism, cybercrime, and other relatively recent challenges are added to the traditional kinds of criminal offending.

But when this balance is not achieved, either effective crime control or civil liberties/criminal rights can suffer. When police are perceived as treating citizens of racial, ethnic, or cultural minority status unfairly, then public trust is eroded—making it more difficult for both citizens and police to achieve that balance in which rights are respected but crime is prevented and offenders apprehended.

Another conflict arises when social scientists question the validity of techniques that the police often use, such as lineup identifications and lie detector tests. Last, but of great importance to the police, is the dilemma of equality versus discretion. Related to the issue of trust and fairness, this dilemma raises important questions. When should an arrest be made, and when should only a warning be issued? How much force can legitimately be used in an arrest? Should all suspects be treated the same way? ●

Selection of Police Officers

One purpose of this chapter is to examine the police officer from a psychological perspective. How are police officers selected? Do the selection criteria work? Do police officers share certain personality characteristics?

How are the police trained, and does training improve their performance on the job? Can the police officer's image in the community be improved?

These questions have taken on a special urgency since the 1990s as a result of highly publicized cases in which police officers had brutally beaten suspects in their custody, or used lethal force in encountering a suspect. Many of these cases involved White officers attacking Black citizens, raising the possibility that racial bias was a motive.

Beginning with the prosecution of the Los Angeles police officers who were videotaped beating Rodney King (described in Box 4.1), which was followed by other, similar incidents, concerns have grown over police behavior. For instance, in June 2004, videotapes showed Stanley Miller, a suspect in an auto theft, apparently trying to surrender while Los Angeles officers tackled him and began kicking and repeatedly hitting him in the head (CNN, 2004).

Similar incidents were reported in several cities throughout the country, including Detroit, New York, Louisville, Pittsburgh, and Miami. There was heated national debate over the relationship between minorities and the police in the wake of the assault against Abner Louima, the Haitian immigrant who was beaten and

---

The Case of Rodney King: Videotaped Police Brutality?   BOX 4.1

In March 1991, police chased a Black motorist who they alleged was speeding through a Los Angeles suburb in his 1988 Hyundai. As the unarmed man emerged from his car, a police officer felled him with a blast from a 50,000-volt stun gun, and three patrolmen proceeded to beat and kick him while a police helicopter hovered overhead. As a result of this attack, which was witnessed by at least 11 other police onlookers, Rodney King—a 25-year-old man who, it was later learned, was on parole—lay seriously injured with multiple skull fractures, a broken ankle, a cracked cheekbone, and several internal injuries.

One special feature of this attack was that a nearby citizen captured the entire episode on his video camera; within hours, the tape of this terrifying beating was played across the country on network news programs. Soon thereafter, local, state, and federal agencies

launched investigations into the beating and into the entire Los Angeles Police Department. Three of the four officers who were charged with beating King were initially acquitted of all criminal charges, an outcome that shocked millions of Americans. But in a second trial, brought in federal court, two of the officers were found guilty of depriving King of his civil rights and were sentenced to prison. King was awarded $3.8 million in a civil case and used part of this money to start a record label. He was arrested and imprisoned several times after that and died in 2012.

CRITICAL THOUGHT QUESTION

What are the advantages and disadvantages of using physical force in apprehending offenders?

sodomized with a bathroom plunger by New York City police officer Justin Volpe as a second officer, Charles Schwarz, held Louima down. After Volpe pled guilty, a federal jury convicted Schwarz of conspiracy to sodomize and of violating Louima's civil rights, but it acquitted three other officers who had also been charged in the beating.

Other highly publicized deaths of African American men in the course of police encounters have fueled the perception that minorities are disproportionately targeted by police. Alton Sterling in Baton Rouge, Philando Castile in Minnesota, Freddie Gray in Baltimore, and Eric Garner in New York all died in the course of police encounters. Is there strong evidence that minority citizens are disproportionately targeted by police and much more often the victims of lethal violence?

Apparently this is not a simple question. For example, according to the *Washington Post*, 50% of the fatal police shootings in 2014 involved White victims and 26% involved Black victims. Roland Fryer, a Harvard economist, conducted a study of 1,000 police shootings from 10 large police departments in California, Florida, and Texas. He also studied police

Abner Louima was brutally assaulted in 1997 by several New York City police officers. Eventually, they were convicted on federal criminal charges.

Stan Honda/AFP/Getty Images

use of nonlethal force and considered racial differences in both. Blacks and Hispanics were more than 50% more likely to experience some form of nonlethal force in interactions with police, a difference that could not be fully accounted for by controls for context and civilian behavior. For officer-involved shootings, however, Fryer reported no racial differences (either in the raw data or when contextual factors were considered). He concluded that some police officers have a "preference for discrimination," but this does not extend to disproportionate officer shootings of minority citizens.

What does this mean? Are police encounters with minorities consistently carried out without discrimination? (No.) Are most of the citizens killed in police-involved shootings minorities? (No.) Is there discrimination by police that increases the number of nonlethal force events in their encounters with minority citizens? (This is supported by Fryer's data, although the most meaningful comparison would be the percentage of legitimate criminal suspects who are stopped for good cause, rather than the percentage of the general population of a certain minority group.)

Certainly there is much evidence, both from scientific studies and the accounts of individuals, that racial discrimination continues to be a very real problem in the United States. Police officers, as the public face of law enforcement, must pursue the challenging combination of keeping the public's trust while preventing crime and apprehending offenders. Are certain police officers more inclined to use unnecessary force? If so, can they be identified in advance and screened out of police work?

Psychological evaluation of police personnel began in 1916 when Lewis Terman, the Stanford University psychologist who revised Alfred Binet's intelligence scales to produce the Stanford-Binet intelligence test, tested the intelligence of 30 applicants for police and firefighter jobs in San Jose, California. Terman (1917) found that the average IQ among these applicants was 84 and recommended that no one with an IQ below 80 be accepted for these jobs. A few years later, L. L. Thurstone tested the intelligence of 358 Detroit policemen, using the Army Alpha Intelligence Examination. Like Terman, he reported below-average IQ scores, and he also found that police of higher ranks scored lower than entry-level patrolmen.

Throughout the years, psychologists continued to assess police candidates, although in a way that was often unsystematic and poorly evaluated. As late as 1955, only 14 American cities with populations greater than 100,000 formally tested police candidates; by 1965, 27% of local police agencies reported some psychological evaluation of applicants (Ostrov, 1986). In the 1960s and 1970s, the period when police psychology became an established specialty, several national commissions recommended formal psychological assessment of police personnel in all departments. By the mid-1980s, 11 states required psychological screening of police candidates, and more than 50% of the country's departments psychologically screened beginning police officers (Benner, 1986). By the 1990s, formal assessment of police candidates had become routine, due in part to attempts by municipal governments to prevent or defeat lawsuits claiming that they were liable for dangerous or improper conduct by their police employees. This has continued into the 2000s (Weiss, Hitchcock, Weiss, Rostow, & Davis, 2008).

Psychological evaluation of police applicants can focus on selecting candidates who appear most psychologically fit—or on eliminating individuals who appear least suited for police work. Most selection methods are developed to screen out disturbed candidates, because it is very difficult to agree on the "ideal" police profile. Despite concerns about the validity of psychological evaluations in police selection, a number of experts (Arrigo & Claussen, 2003; Bartol & Bartol, 2006) believe that psychological screening is useful in the selection process and should be included. However, the current standards for screening may not be sufficient. Psychological tests are currently used to assess levels of psychopathology that may interfere with officers' abilities to perform their duties rather than focusing on specific skills or capacities that are directly relevant to police work (see Detrick & Chibnall, 2008; Detrick, Chibnall, & Rosso, 2001).

In general, the courts have upheld the legality of psychological screening of police candidates as long as the evaluation and testing involved do not violate the provisions of various civil rights acts or the Americans with Disabilities Act and are in compliance with federal guidelines.

If it were your task to select police officers from a pool of applicants, what psychological qualities would you look for? Your answers would probably reflect your values, as well as your impression of what police officers do. Among the psychological characteristics usually cited in such a list are the following:

- *Incorruptible*: A police officer should be of high moral character. Reports of officers taking bribes or framing innocent suspects are especially disturbing, because the police officer must treat all citizens fairly within the rules of law.
- *Well adjusted*: A police officer should be able to carry out the stressful duties of the job without becoming seriously and continuously affected by the stress. Officers are always in the public view. They need to be thick-skinned enough to operate without defensiveness, yet they must be attentive to the needs of others. They also need to cope with the dangers of their jobs, including the constant awareness that injury or death could occur at any time. In 2015, a total of 42 officers were killed in the line of duty, an increase of 4% from the number killed in 2014—but a substantial decrease from the number of officers killed in 2009 (117) and 2010 (160).
- *People oriented*: A police officer's major duty is service to others. An officer needs to have a genuine interest in people and compassion for them. At a commencement program of the New York City Police Academy, new officers were told, "There is one thing we cannot teach you and that is about people. The bottom line is to treat people as people and you'll get by" (quoted by Nix, 1987, p. 15).
- *Free of overly emotional reactions*: Although a degree of caution and suspiciousness may be desirable for the job, the police officer should be free of impulsive, overly aggressive reactions and other responses in which emotions overcome the discipline imposed by training. Restraint is essential because officers are trained to take an active stance in crime detection and are even encouraged by their superiors to be wary of what is happening around them (Barber, Grawitch, & Trares, 2009).
- *Dedicated*: Officers should be committed to their jobs, and not be inclined toward frequent lateness or absenteeism or have personal problems that interfere with this commitment in an ongoing way.
- *Disciplined*: Police officers should be team players, able to function effectively within a chain of command. This includes the ability to give orders to supervisees and accept orders from superior officers.

■ *Logical*: Police officers should be able to examine a crime scene and develop hypotheses about what happened and what characteristics might be present in the lawbreaker.

Keep these characteristics in mind as we discuss particular approaches to evaluating police candidates. To what extent can each of these characteristics be accurately assessed? There are several reported purposes for evaluating police candidates, including screening out those who are (1) chronically late or absent; (2) disciplinary problems; (3) at risk for inflicting needless harm on citizens; and (4) otherwise reckless or irresponsible (Shusman, Inwald, & Landa, 1984). Psychological evaluation is not likely to identify "ideal" candidates—but it can be used to screen out those with specific problems that would interfere with their effective functioning as police officers.

The selection of police officer candidates can involve up to 10 steps: (1) application/prescreening, (2) entrance exam (focusing on reading, writing, problem-solving, judgment, and memory), (3) simulated scenario and verbal response, (4) physical fitness, (5) background investigation, (6) drug testing, (7) psychological testing, (8) polygraph, (9) oral interview, and (10) medical exam (International Association of Chiefs of Police, 2016). Consulting psychologists can provide parts of the entrance exam, simulated scenario, psychological testing, and oral interview. More specifically, psychologists may conduct or participate in an interview, observe candidates' responses to simulated scenarios, and provide testing. How much emphasis different psychologists place on these procedures depends on several factors, including their professional background and training, the resources available for the evaluation, and the focus of the assessment (e.g., different strategies will be used for assessing mental disorders than for predicting what type of person will do best in which kind of position; various police departments will use somewhat different approaches to personnel selection).

A national survey of municipal police departments sought to identify selection and psychological assessment practices for police officers (Cochrane, Tett, & Vandecreek, 2003). Of the 355 police agencies surveyed, a total of 155 (43%) responded. The majority of police departments used selection measures that included a background investigation, medical exam, interview with applicant, drug test, physical fitness exam, and polygraph test. More than 90% required some kind of psychological evaluation of applicants.

The Interview

Personal interviews are the most widely employed tool, despite evidence that interviews are subject to distortion, low reliability, and questionable validity. The extent to which an interview yields the same information on different occasions or with different interviewers (*reliability*) and the degree to which that information is accurately related to important job performance criteria (*validity*) have not been clearly established for most police selection interviews.

However, there is good evidence that reliability, at least, is increased by the use of **structured interviews**—those in which the wording, order, and content of the interview are standardized (Rogers, 2001). One semi-structured interview for the psychological screening of law enforcement candidates, the Law Enforcement Candidate Interview, uses content from other measures for screening law enforcement personnel and for assessing personality. Modest inter-rater reliability and prediction of performance in the police academy was achieved (Varela, Scogin, & Vipperman, 1999). It is also possible for a police department to construct their own structured interview for personnel selection purposes, using established guidelines (U.S. Office of Personnel Management, 2008), to more effectively use the advantages of structured interviewing.

Interviews are a necessary part of an evaluation, according to guidelines recommended by police psychologists (Dantzker, 2010). They are also valuable as a rapport-building introduction to the evaluation process. They increase applicants' cooperation while reducing their apprehension. Interviews are also popular because they can be flexible and economical. However, because they are subject to distortions and impression management by candidates, interviews are still more useful for orienting candidates to the evaluation than for predicting subsequent performance.

Situational Tests

Situational tests incorporate tasks that are similar to those that will actually be undertaken by officers on the job. They are designed to predict performance in the training academy and in the field. At one time, this approach was a widely discussed aspect of police selection, involving tasks such as observing patrols, analyzing clues, and discussing cases (see Mills, McDevitt, & Tonkin, 1966). The situational testing approach appears to be less favored than it once was, judging from the dearth of research or even discussion following the Mills et al. (1966) article. Situational *components*, such as simulations and candidate responses, are still incorporated (IACP, 2016). But one reason that broader situational testing has become less-frequently employed is its time intensiveness and cost. Accordingly, current situational aspects of screening are more focused, involving tasks such as report writing that are common aspects of police work. (For one part of the National Police Officer Selection Test (POST), see http://www.kacp.cc/misc/post.pdf)

Psychological Tests

Many standardized psychological tests have good reliability and can be objectively scored and administered to large groups of participants at the same time. Consequently, they are important in police screening. Two types of tests are included in most selection batteries: tests of cognitive or intellectual ability and tests of personality traits, integrity, or emotional stability.

Police officers tend to score in the average to above-average range on intelligence tests (Brewster & Stoloff, 2003), and intelligence tends to correlate fairly strongly with the performance of police recruits in their training programs. However, intelligence scores are only weakly related to actual police performance in the field (Bartol, 1983; Brewster & Stoloff, 2003). These results point to the issue of predicting performance, both in the training academy and on the job, an important consideration that we discuss in the next section.

The Minnesota Multiphasic Personality Inventory (MMPI; the 1989 revision of this test is called the MMPI-2 and a 2008 revision is the MMPI-2-RF) is the test of personality most often used in police screening; other psychological tests often used in police selection are the California Psychological Inventory (CPI) and the Sixteen Personality Factor Questionnaire (16PF). Evidence for the validity of these tests in screening out candidates unsuitable for police work is mixed. There is research supporting the validity of the MMPI (Bartol, 1991), the MMPI-2 (Weiss, Davis, Rostow, & Kinsman, 2003), and the CPI (Ho, 2001), although others (e.g., Hogg & Wilson, 1995) have questioned the general value of psychological testing of police recruits.

One personality test developed in 1979 specifically to identify psychologically unsuitable law enforcement candidates is the Inwald Personality Inventory (IPI; Detrick & Chibnall, 2002; Inwald, 1992; Inwald, Knatz, & Shusman, 1983). It is a behaviorally based personality measure designed and validated specifically for the use in high-risk occupations, such as law enforcement. Consisting of 26 scales that tap past and present behaviors presumed to have special relevance for law enforcement applicants (Lack of Assertiveness, Trouble with Law and Society, Undue Suspiciousness, and Driving Violations, for example), it can predict poor job performance better than traditional tests of personality and psychopathology such as the MMPI and its revisions (Inwald, 2008). Inwald has also developed other measures, including a predictor of positive work-related characteristics (the Hilson Personnel Profile/Success Quotient; Inwald, 1988) and the Inwald Survey-5 Revised (Inwald, 1992), which focuses on areas such as integrity, anger, frustration tolerance, attitudes about antisocial behavior, problems getting along with people, work ethic, job performance, and domestic violence. The development of these measures reflects a trend in the field toward designing and implementing more specialized tests, rather than depending on more general measures of personality and psychopathology.

Another written tool developed for the selection of entry-level police officers is the POST, noted earlier as having a job situational component. In addition to incident report writing, the POST measures arithmetic and reading comprehension. It has demonstrated adequate reliability and validity in some research (Henry & Rafilson, 1997; Rafilson & Sison, 1996). It has also been mandated as a statewide screening measure in several states and adopted by the police chiefs' associations in some jurisdictions.

The Validity of Police Screening

Although experts disagree on the usefulness of psychological screening of police, they all agree that good empirical research on this topic is difficult to conduct (Bartol, 1996; Gaines & Falkenberg, 1998; Inwald, 2008). Studying **predictive validity** using actual police performance in the field as the outcome is time-consuming and expensive, so most departments do not do this. Instead, they employ research that examines the relationship between screening results and performance by police recruits in police academies or training schools. This relationship is usually positive, but success or failure in the training academy is of less interest than actual performance as a police officer. One fairly inexpensive form of assessment involves gathering peer ratings from trainees as they progress through their training classes together; these ratings have been shown to correlate with job retention of police officers, but not with most other measures of job performance or with supervisor ratings (Gardner, Scogin, Vipperman, & Varela, 1998).

Another problem with studies of validity is that the police candidates who do poorly on screening evaluations are eliminated from the pool of trainees and potential employees. Although this decision is reasonable, it makes it impossible to study whether predictions of poor performance by these individuals were valid.

In addition, applicants for police work, like applicants for most jobs, are likely to try to present an unrealistically positive image of themselves. They may deny or underreport symptoms of mental illness, answer questions to convey a socially desirable impression, and respond as they believe a psychologically healthy individual generally would. If evaluators fail to detect such "fake good" test-taking strategies, they may mistakenly identify some candidates with significant behavioral health problems as well-adjusted. For these reasons, tests such as the MMPI-2 and the IPI include various **validity scales** intended to detect test takers who are trying to "fake good" (Baer, Wetter, Nichols, Greene, & Berry, 1995; Inwald, 2008). Research on these scales has shown that they are useful in detecting defensiveness and deception by some candidates for police positions (Detrick & Chibnall, 2008; Weiss et al., 2003).

Finally, selecting adequate criteria to measure effective police performance is notoriously difficult. Supervisor ratings are often inflated or biased by factors that are irrelevant to actual achievements or problems. In some departments, especially smaller ones, individual police officers are expected to perform so many diverse functions that it becomes unreasonable to expect specific cognitive abilities or psychological traits to be related in the same way to various aspects of performance. In addition, if we are interested in predicting which officers will act in risky or inappropriate ways, our predictions will be complicated by the fact that such behaviors occur only rarely in any group of people. As a consequence, these assessments, if offering such predictions, will yield many "false positives"—erroneous predictions in which predicted events do not actually occur.

Fitness-for-Duty Evaluations

Another type of psychological assessment of police officers is the **fitness-for-duty evaluation**. As a result of stress, injuries, a life-threatening incident, a series of problems, or other indicators that an officer may be psychologically impaired, police administrators can order an officer to undergo an evaluation of fitness to continue performing his or her duties.

Such evaluations pose difficulties for everyone involved. Administrators must balance the need to protect the public from a potentially impaired officer against the legal right of the officer to privacy and fair employment. Clinicians must navigate a narrow path between a department's need to know the results of such an evaluation and the officer's expectation that the results will be kept confidential. Finally, the officers themselves face a dilemma: They can be honest and reveal problems that could disqualify them from service, or they can distort their responses to protect their jobs and consequently miss the opportunity for potentially beneficial treatment.

Two different models of fitness-for-duty evaluations have been used. In the first, a department uses the same psychologist to perform the evaluation and to provide whatever treatment is necessary for the officer. In the other, the psychologist who evaluates the officer does not provide any treatment; this avoids an ethical conflict between keeping the therapy confidential (as part of duty to the patient) and disclosing an officer's psychological functioning to supervisors (as part of duty to the department). The second approach is endorsed in the "Guidelines for Fitness for Duty Evaluations" distributed by the Police Psychological Services Section of the International Association for Chiefs of Police (IACP, 2013).

Training of Police Officers

Once police candidates have been selected, they participate in a course of police training that usually lasts several months. Many major American cities require 24 weeks of training, with 40 hours of training per week. Smaller jurisdictions have training programs averaging 14–16 weeks. A growing number of departments are now requiring that police officers complete at least some college education.

Two types of criticism of police training programs are common. One is that after rigorous selection procedures, few trainees fail the training. In a sample of 93 cadets who began training in 2003, only about 10% either dropped out or failed mandatory academic or physical endurance exercises (Phillips, 2004). Advocates count this rate of success as an indication that the initial selection procedures were valid, but critics complain that graduation is too easy, especially given the burnout rate of on-the-job police officers. The rate of police officers leaving the job during the first 16 months was nearly 25% in one study (Haarr, 2005), a considerably higher rate than the 10% of cadet training dropouts noted in the prior study.

A second criticism is that there is insufficient training in the field, as well as a lack of close supervision of trainees during the time they spend on patrol. The limited time that trainees spend with veteran training officers on patrol may give them a false sense of security and deprive them of opportunities to learn different ways of responding to citizens from various cultural backgrounds or resolving disputes other than through arrests.

However, it is also possible that there are limits to the benefits of extensive supervision by senior officers. It is possible that such contacts teach new officers to be cynical about law enforcement, to "cut corners" in their duties, and, above all, to identify almost exclusively with the norms of police organizations rather than with the values of the larger and more diverse society (Tuohy, Wrennall, McQueen, & Stradling, 1993).

Training in Crisis Intervention

The police are often asked to maintain public order and defuse volatile situations involving persons who are mentally ill, intoxicated, angry, or motivated by politically extreme views. Because of the instability of the participants in such disputes, they pose great risks to the police as well as to bystanders. In this section, we examine three types of crisis situations to which police are often called: incidents involving mentally ill citizens, family disturbances, and the taking of hostages. Psychologists have made important contributions to each of these areas by conducting research, designing interventions, and training the police in crisis intervention skills.

Interactions with Mentally Ill Citizens

For the past four decades, several influences have forced mentally ill persons from residential mental health facilities, where they formerly lived, into a variety of noninstitutional settings, including halfway houses, community mental health centers, hospital emergency rooms, detoxification facilities, "flophouses," the streets, and local jails. Deinstitutionalization itself is an admirable goal; spending much of one's life in an institution breeds dependency, despair, and hopelessness. People with mental illness should receive treatment in the least restrictive environment possible, allowing them to function in and contribute to their local communities. (Indeed, the contemporary focus is on the recovery of as many aspects of life as possible, rather than simply the

During this police Crisis Intervention Training, one officer role-plays a potentially violent person in crisis. The officers learned how to work with people showing signs of mental illness and get them into treatment, rather than jail.

control of symptoms and the maintenance of stability, for people with mental illness.) However, the evidence on how people with such illness have fared suggests that deinstitutionalization in the United States has not achieved its lofty goals. The problems stem from two fundamental difficulties.

First, despite important advances in medication and nonmedical interventions, severe mental illness can be difficult to treat effectively. The impairments associated with disorders such as schizophrenia and serious mood disorders can be profound, and relapses are common. For example, less than a third of nonhospitalized persons with schizophrenia are employed at any given time. Second, sufficient funding for alternative, noninstitutional care has not been provided in the United States. As a result, community-based treatment of severely mentally ill persons seldom takes place under proper circumstances, despite the fact that the economic costs of severe mental disorders rival those of diseases such as cancer and heart disease and could be reduced considerably if proper care were provided.

One consequence of deinstitutionalization is that supervising people with mental illness has become a primary responsibility for the police. A recent review (Reuland, Schwarzfeld, & Draper, 2009) indicated that

- The majority of law enforcement encounters with people with mental illness are for low-level charges, or for simply being a nuisance.
- The majority of such encounters are resolved by talking, rather than taking the individual into custody or to treatment.

- Possible suicide or self-harm is one of the reasons for encounters with police in an estimated 10–30% of cases.
- There is a small subset of individuals who have repeated encounters with police.

In addition, such encounters with individuals who may have behavioral health problems form a substantial part of police responsibilities. One survey found that 33% of all calls made to a police district in a one-year period were for mental health-related situations (Steadman, Deane, Borum, & Morrissey, 2000).

At one time, the presence of mental illness was shown to increase the probability of arrest. A large study (Teplin, 1984) observed and coded the interactions of police officers with citizens over a 14-month period in two precincts in a large U.S. city. Using a symptom checklist and a global rating of mental disorder to assess mental illness, investigators studied 884 nontraffic encounters involving a total of 1,798 citizens, of whom 506 were considered suspects for arrest by the police. Arrest was relatively infrequent, occurring in only 12.4% of the encounters and 27.9% of the individuals. For the small number of individuals who were considered mentally ill, however, the arrest rate was 46.7%. Mentally ill suspects were more likely to be arrested regardless of the type or seriousness of the incident involved. Teplin (1984, 2000) concluded that the mentally ill were being "criminalized" and that this outcome was the result not only of the provocative nature of their psychological symptoms but also of the inadequacies of the mental health system in treating them, and the lack of training in mental illness for some police officers.

Whether this remains accurate nearly four decades after this study is not clear. But we will discuss some of the subsequent influences that may affect the risk of arrest for individuals with mental illness. In certain respects, the criminal justice system has become a "default option" for individuals for whom appropriate community-based or hospital treatment is not available. The rate of severe mental disorders in jail populations, often combined with diagnoses of substance abuse and personality disorder in the same individuals, is alarmingly high. One of the best estimates of the prevalence of individuals with severe mental illness in jails, obtained by administering a structured clinical interview to 822 inmates in Maryland and New York jails, is 14.5% for male inmates and 31% for female inmates (Steadman, Osher, Robbins, Case, & Samuels, 2009).

Another study examined police responses to incidents involving individuals with mental illness in three jurisdictions differing in the level of mental health training that police received. Findings suggested that the jurisdictions with specialized mental health training were especially effective in crisis intervention and made fewer arrests. However, the officers' decisions about how to handle the situation depended on the overall resources available; jurisdictions with mobile crisis units were able to transport mentally ill individuals to treatment locations to ensure that they obtained treatment, while those without crisis units could only refer individuals for treatment (Steadman et al., 2000).

The Memphis Police Department started the Memphis **Crisis Intervention Team (CIT)** program, which has now has become known as the "Memphis Model" for crisis intervention (CIT National Advisory Board, 2006). This program was designed to increase officer and consumer safety while attempting to redirect those with mental illness from the judicial system to the mental health system. Along with these broad goals, the program provides law enforcement officers with the tools and skills necessary for dealing with mentally ill persons. Many police departments around the country have started their own CIT programs, some based on this "Memphis Model." A pilot program for police crisis intervention was started in Philadelphia; it made the news because two officers, recently trained in CIT, were able to use their newly acquired skills in communicating with people with mental disorders. Encountering a man who was very depressed and had climbed up on a bridge, these officers talked to him—and convinced him to come down, preventing a possible suicide. Not surprisingly, this pilot program became a full-scale attempt to train as many police officers as possible in CIT. As of late 2016, more than 2,500 Philadelphia officers had received this training.

One study (Skeem & Bibeau, 2008) addressed the question of whether CIT intervention decreases the risk of violence. The investigators reviewed police reports ($N = 655$) for CIT events that occurred between March 2003 and May 2005. They were able to classify 45% of these events as reflecting a danger to self, and another 26% as situations in which the individual involved was dangerous to others. The research showed that officers were more likely to use force when the individual was perceived as threatening to others. However, consistent with CIT training, the officers were inclined to use low-lethality force—even when encountering individuals presenting a high risk for violence. Some 74% of these events resulted in hospitalization, while only 4% were concluded by arrest. These results are consistent with the potential for CIT to result in safe and treatment-oriented resolution of high-risk situations involving individuals with mental disorder.

A review of the existing studies on CIT (Compton, Bahara, Watson, & Oliva, 2008) yielded several conclusions. First, this research provided support for the notion that CIT may be an effective way to link individuals with mental illnesses with indicated mental health treatment. Second, the training component of CIT may have a favorable impact on officers' attitudes, beliefs, and knowledge about these interactions; CIT-trained officers report feeling better prepared for their encounters with individuals with mental illnesses. Finally, CIT may have a lower arrest rate and lower associated criminal justice costs than other diversionary approaches. This review was updated in 2012 (Heilbrun, DeMatteo, Yasuhara, Brooks-Holliday, Shah, King, Bingham, Hamilton, & LaDuke), with most studies indicating that diversion from prosecution upon first encounter with police (facilitated by CIT) is associated with greater time in the community, fewer subsequent arrests, less homelessness, greater treatment participation, and fewer community hospital days.

The importance of evaluating how police interact with individuals with mental illness is underscored by the prevalence of mentally ill offenders in prisons and jails. Using a broader definition of mental health problem than that used by Steadman et al. (2009), the Bureau of Justice Statistics (2006) estimated that 56% of state prisoners, 45% of federal inmates, and 64% of those incarcerated in jails had a mental health problem. (As of 2016, this BJS report remains the most current estimate of behavioral health problems of those who are incarcerated.) Whether one uses the narrow definition (Steadman et al., 2009, of "serious mental illness") or the broader BJS (2006) definition of "mental health problem," the proportion of those incarcerated who have this kind of difficulty is substantial.

The jailing of mentally ill persons does not reflect improper behavior by the police as much as a failure of public policy regarding the treatment and protection of people with serious mental illness. More and better training of police officers in the recognition and short-term management of mentally ill persons is necessary, but an adequate resolution to this problem requires better organization and funding of special services for those with serious mental illness (Griffin, Heilbrun, Mulvey, DeMatteo, & Schubert, 2015).

One possibility is to increase the use of **jail diversion programs** through the use of community-based alternatives for justice-involved individuals with severe mental illness. The first contact between mentally ill individuals in the justice system is most often the police; to the extent that police are trained to use options other than arrest as a result of such encounters, the number of justice-involved mentally ill individuals may decrease (Munetz & Griffin, 2006). A growing body of research indicates that such diversion, or other community-based services, can be effective in providing needed services to individuals with severe mental illness without a commensurate increase in their risk of reoffending (Heilbrun et al., 2012).

Domestic Disturbances

When violence erupts in a family or between a couple, the police are often the first people called to the scene. What will they encounter when they arrive? Are the participants armed? Are they intoxicated or high? Do they experience behavioral health problems? How much violence has already taken place? What is certain is that responding to family disturbances is one of the most dangerous activities that police perform. The level of danger involved when intervening in a domestic dispute is not surprising, considering that strangers (not known to the victim) perpetrated 41% of violent victimizations in 2005, 39% in 2010, 34% in 2013, and 40% in 2014—with the remaining violence perpetrated by family members, neighbors, and others known to the victim (Bureau of Justice Statistics, 2010, 2015a).

Police spend a great deal of time investigating domestic disturbances, and these are high-risk situations for officers (Ellis, Choi, & Blaus, 1993). A large-scale study investigating the circumstances of 1,550 assaults on police in Baltimore County, Maryland, between 1984 and 1986 (Uchida & Brooks, 1988) indicated that about 25% of these assaults occurred during the investigation of a domestic disturbance. Perpetrators were more likely to use blunt objects than guns or knives. The risk to officers of injury in responding to domestic disturbances include (1) answering the call alone, (2) effort to make an arrest, (3) verbal abuse or physical threat made to officers, (4) intoxication of the disputants, and (5) victim physical injury (Ellis et al., 1993). Some evidence suggests that female officers are at greater risk of assault in such domestic calls (Rabe-Hemp & Schuck, 2007).

Empirical research has contributed to our understanding of domestic violence. We are now better able to recognize the false beliefs about family violence, which are relevant to how such offenses are investigated and prosecuted.

Myth 1: Family Violence Is Perpetrated Only by Men. A review of over 200 studies with data on domestic violence by both men and women (Straus, 2011) observed comparable rates for both genders, supporting the "gender symmetry" of violence in the home. This is an area fraught with debate; some have suggested that this gender symmetry applies to less serious aggression (e.g., slapping, shoving) but not more severe violence (e.g., choking, punching, use of a weapon). In light of all the research reviewed, however, the author drew two conclusions: (1) domestic violence prevention could be enhanced by addressing interventions to girls and women as well as boys and men and (2) the effectiveness of offender treatment could be enhanced by changing treatment programs to address assaults by both partners when applicable.

Myth 2: Family Violence Is Confined to People with Behavioral Health Disorders. When we hear or read that a woman has plunged her two-year-old son into a tub of boiling water or that a man has had sexual intercourse with his six-year-old daughter, our first reaction might be, "That person is terribly sick!" The portrayal of family violence in the mass media often suggests that "normal people" do not harm family members. In reality, however, family violence is too widespread to be adequately explained by mental illness, although perpetrators of serious domestic violence often experience depression or personality disorder (Andrews, Foster, Capaldi, & Hops, 2000).

Myth 3: Family Violence Is Confined to Poor People. Violence and abuse are more common among families of lower socioeconomic status, but they are by no means limited to such families. There are risk factors associated with poverty (e.g., unemployment, limited education, and sparse social support) that increase the risk for family violence (Barnett, Miller-Perrin, & Perrin, 2005; Magdol et al., 1997).

Myth 4: Battered Women Like Being Hit; Otherwise, They Would Leave. This belief combines two myths. We noted earlier that family violence is perpetrated by both males and females, although violence by men against women tends to produce more serious injuries. But faced with the fact that many female victims of partner violence do not leave even the most serious of abusers, people seek some rational explanation.

A common belief is that women who remain in violent relationships must somehow provoke or even enjoy the violence. This form of "blaming the victim" is not a useful explanation. The concept of **learned helplessness** is much more useful in explaining why so many women endure such extreme violence for so long (Walker, 1979). Psychologist Lenore Walker observed that women who suffer continued physical violence at the hands of their partners have a more negative self-concept than women whose relationships are free from violence. She proposed that the repeated beatings leave these women feeling that they won't be able to protect themselves from further assaults and that they are incapable of controlling the events that go on around them. Under such circumstances, they develop the belief that there is nothing they can do to change their circumstances and that any effort at starting a new life not only will be futile but also will lead to even more violence against them.

Myth 5: Alcohol and Drug Abuse Are the Real Causes of Violence in the Home. "He beat up his children because he was drunk" is another popular explanation of domestic violence, and most studies do find a considerable relationship between drinking and violence (Gerber, Ganz, Lichter, Williams, & McCloskey, 2005; Magdol et al., 1997), especially among male perpetrators. An estimated 42% of those committing domestic violence had been using drugs or alcohol, which is comparable to the rates seen for violence against a boyfriend or girlfriend (37%) or a friend or acquaintance (40%), but much higher than the estimated percentage of stranger perpetrators of violence (17%) (Bureau of Justice Statistics, 2005a).

So higher rates of drug or alcohol use are associated with domestic violence. In a longitudinal study considering the relationships among drinking, alcohol-related problems, and recurring incidents of partner violence over a five-year period (Caetano, McGrath, Ramisetty-Mikler, & Field, 2005), investigators found that the rate of domestic violence among men who drink more than four drinks at a time at least once per month was three times higher than that among men who abstain or drink less often and less frequently. This pattern also held for women. But does the substance cause the violence? Some assume that since alcohol is a disinhibitor of behavior, it therefore facilitates the expression of violence. Although there is certainly some truth to this, those who have been drinking may also tend to place more blame on their condition than is justified ("I was drunk and didn't know what I was doing"). Furthermore, those who have trouble controlling their aggressive behavior while drinking can certainly anticipate this and take steps to manage their risk (e.g., drinking in moderation or not at all).

Because of their danger and frequency, family disturbances pose a difficult challenge for the police. Can these encounters be handled in a manner that protects potential victims, reduces repeat offenses, and limits the risk of injury to responding officers?

The first project on crisis intervention with domestic disputes was developed by Morton Bard, a psychologist in New York City. Bard (1969; Bard & Berkowitz, 1967) trained a special group of New York City police officers (nine Black and nine White volunteers) in family disturbance intervention skills for a project located in West Harlem. The month-long training program focused on teaching officers how to intervene in family disputes without making arrests. The training emphasized the psychology of family conflict and sensitivity to cross-racial differences. Role-playing was used to acquaint officers with techniques for calming antagonists, lowering tensions, reducing hostilities, and preventing physical violence.

For two years after the training, all family crisis calls in the experimental precinct were answered by the specially trained officers. They performed 1,375 interventions with 962 families. Evaluation of the project concentrated on six desired outcomes: (1) a decrease in family disturbance calls, (2) a drop in repeat calls from the same families, (3) a reduction of homicides in the precinct, (4) a decline in homicides among family members, (5) a reduction of assaults in the precinct, and (6) a decrease in injuries to police officers. But results indicated that the intervention affected only two of these outcomes. Fewer assaults occurred in the precinct, and none of the trained officers was injured (compared with three police officers who were not part of the program but were injured while responding to family disturbances).

Much of the specialized police training during the last decade has been associated with the Crisis Intervention Team approach. (Although work in the 1960s was termed "crisis intervention," the CIT approach of the 2000s is more formal and widespread.) CIT officers are trained to use techniques that facilitate nonviolent resolutions and fewer arrests when individuals have behavioral health problems. Such problems are frequently seen in the course of domestic disturbances.

This approach is not consistent with policies begun by many police departments in the 1970s that call for the arrest and prosecution of serious domestic batterers. Is arrest a better alternative than crisis intervention or counseling for those who commit domestic violence?

The first well-controlled evaluation of the effects of arresting domestic batterers was the Minneapolis Domestic Violence Experiment (Sherman & Berk, 1984). In this experiment, police officers' responses to domestic violence were randomly assigned to (1) arresting the suspected batterer, (2) ordering one of the parties to leave the residence, or (3) giving the couple immediate advice on reducing their violence. Judging from official police records and interviews with victims, subsequent offending was reduced by almost 50% when the suspect was arrested, a significantly better outcome than that achieved by the two nonarrest alternatives. These findings quickly changed public and expert opinion about the value of arresting domestic batterers, and soon many cities had replaced informal counseling with immediate arrest as their response to domestic violence cases.

Since the initial Minneapolis Experiment, at least five other jurisdictions—Charlotte, Colorado Springs, Miami, Omaha, and Milwaukee—have conducted studies designed to test whether arresting batterers is the best deterrent to repeated domestic violence. The results of these projects, collectively known as the Spouse Assault Replication Program, have shown that across all five sites, arresting the violent partner significantly reduced future victimization, independent of other criminal justice sanctions or individual factors (Maxwell, Garner, & Fagan, 2002).

What conclusion should we reach about the value of arrest as a deterrent to future spouse abuse? At this point, the evidence points to the effectiveness of arrest as a deterrent—but such effectiveness is not so powerful as to justify the enthusiastic claims that are sometimes made for arrest programs.

Questions about how best to quell domestic violence illustrate an interesting phenomenon often encountered with social reforms. Social problems and well-intentioned efforts to modify them tend to revolve in cycles rather than moving in a straight line toward progress and increased sophistication. A reform in vogue today, aimed at correcting some social wrong, often fosters its own difficulties or inequities and ultimately becomes itself a problem in need of reformation.

Crisis intervention was originally preferred over arrest as a more psychologically sophisticated response by police to family disturbances; however, this intervention fell out of favor and was criticized as an inadequate response to serious domestic violence. Official arrest was then championed as the most effective intervention, but as additional data are gathered about its effectiveness, new questions are raised about whether arrest and prosecution are the best answers for domestic violence. The other important point, however, is that we cannot judge what is effective without gathering outcome data in a systematic way. Anecdotal impressions and highly publicized single cases, as much as they may resonate with the general public, do not provide a well-informed basis for decisions involving publicly funded social policies. It may also be that treatment-oriented resolutions such as those used in CIT are more appropriate in some cases (e.g., a seriously mentally ill individual who has discontinued prescribed medication) but not in others (e.g., a spouse with a history of battering his partner, and who inflicts fairly serious injury in the course of a violent episode).

Hostage Negotiation and Terrorism

Although hostage incidents are at least as old as the description in Genesis of the abduction and rescue of Abraham's nephew Lot, most experts agree that the massacre of 11 Israeli athletes taken hostage and murdered by Palestinian terrorists at the 1972 Munich Olympic Games spurred the creation of new law enforcement techniques for resolving hostage incidents. Developed through extensive collaboration among military, law enforcement, and behavioral science experts, these hostage negotiation techniques are still being refined as more is learned about the conditions that lead to effective negotiations.

One study of 120 hostage-related incidents found that the perpetrator used a barricade to separate himself and his hostage from police in over half of the incidents (55.8%) (Feldmann, 2001), creating a complicated situation for negotiation strategies because police could not be fully aware of the perpetrator's activities and intentions. Soskis and Van Zandt (1986) have identified four

As part of hostage negotiation training, police officers learn how to minimize violence and end the incident by talking to the hostage-takers.

types of hostage incidents that differ in their psychological dynamics and techniques for resolution (see also Hatcher, Mohandie, Turner, & Gelles, 1998).

The first type, describing more than half of hostage incidents, involves *persons suffering a mental disorder* or experiencing serious personal or family problems (Feldmann, 2001). In these situations, the hostage takers often have a history of depression, schizophrenia, or other serious mental illness, or they harbor feelings of chronic powerlessness, anger, or despondency that compel a desperate act. Disturbed hostage takers pose a high risk of suicide, which they sometimes accomplish by killing their hostage(s) and then themselves. In other situations, they try to force the police to kill them; such victim-precipitated deaths are termed **suicide by cop**. This underscores the importance of incorporating mental health consultants' expertise into the effort to peacefully negotiate and resolve these hostage situations.

A second common type of hostage situation involves the *trapped criminal*. Here, a person who is trapped by the police while committing a crime takes any hostage who is available and then uses the hostage to bargain for freedom. Because these incidents are unplanned and driven by panic, they tend to be very dangerous to the victims and the police, especially in their early stages.

The third type of hostage situation, also involving criminals, is the *takeover of prisons* by inmates who capture prison guards or take other inmates as hostages. In these incidents, the passage of time tends to work against nonviolent resolution because the hostage takers, working as an undisciplined group with volatile leadership, have a high potential for violence.

Consider the following comment, on the relationship between psychology and hostage negotiation, by police psychologist Laurence Miller:

Hostage negotiation is all about psychology, and successful crisis negotiators are among the most skilled practical psychologists I've ever met. Think about it: In the typical hostage scenario, lives are at imminent risk of violent death at the hands of a depressed, suicidal, homicidal, delusional, drug-fueled, or cold-blooded hostage-taker, often in the midst of a chaotic and uncontrolled workplace or family environment. Resolution of hostage crises may take hours or even days of incredibly focused and intense negotiation, and require the use of virtually every type of skilled communication strategy in the crisis intervention skillbox (2007, http://www.policeone. com/standoff/articles/1247470-Hostage-negotiations-Psychological-strategies-for-resolving-crises/).

This kind of hostage negotiation and skill application is most relevant to the three kinds of hostage situations just identified: an individual with a behavioral health disorder, an offender who is trapped, and a takeover of a correctional facility.

The fourth type of hostage taking, and the one that is most widely publicized, is **terrorism**. Terrorists use violence or the threat of violence "to achieve a social, political, or religious aim in a way that does not obey the traditional rules of war" (Soskis & Van Zandt, 1986, p. 424; see also Lake, 2002). Terrorists usually make careful plans for the kidnapping of hostages or the taking of property, and they are typically motivated by extremist political or religious goals. These goals may require their own deaths as a necessary but "honorable" sacrifice for a higher cause. For this reason, terrorists are less responsive to negotiation techniques that appeal to rational themes of self-preservation. Therefore, new ways of responding to this type of terrorism must be sought.

One terrorism specialist suggested that a country has three options in responding. At the lowest level of response, it may increase its internal security to prevent further attacks, as anyone who has flown in an airplane the last 15 years knows only too well. A more proactive response may be to attempt to capture or eliminate the terrorists in a limited operation targeting the leaders of the terrorist organizations. Lastly, a country may implement a military retaliation with the aims of eradicating the terrorists and their organizations and deterring future attacks from other groups (Lake, 2002).

Another approach would involve identifying those at greater risk for engaging in terroristic activities. One review (Monahan, 2012) effectively described the challenges to assessing an individual's risk for terrorist activity in the same way that the field has assessed the risk of criminal violence for nearly 30 years: the idea that some "at risk" individuals will be released and observed to see if they are involved in terrorist activities is a necessary part of research validation of a risk assessment measure, but obviously unacceptable from a public safety standpoint. Even retrospective validation, such as assessing individuals incarcerated for terrorist acts and comparing them with a control sample of individuals who had not committed such acts— would be enormously challenging from a practical perspective. Monahan is careful to point out that there are different kinds of "terrorist" activities that could be considered in a risk assessment, so specifying the target of the assessment (e.g., specific types of terrorism, specific phases in the process of becoming a terrorist, specific roles in terrorist activity) is important. He adds that we know little about individual risk factors for becoming radicalized, but points to ideologies, affiliations, grievances, and "moral" emotions as promising possibilities.

The 21st century has brought additional forms of terrorism that redefine what it means to be "taken hostage." For example, **bioterrorism**, in which biological "weapons" such as viruses and bacteria are released or threatened, could hold far larger populations hostage than conventional guns or bombs. One study examined public distress following the anthrax-related incidents that occurred shortly after the September 11, 2001 attacks. Findings suggested that even for individuals not actually exposed to the anthrax, initial media exposure to the anthrax attacks was a significant predictor of distress. Levels of distress were especially high when the attacks were first detected (Dougall, Hayward, & Baum, 2005).

It has been suggested that cyberterrorism has not developed into a widespread weapon because of the absence of technical skill necessary to make it effective. This may be changing, however. The 2017 WannaCry ransomware attack, involving control of about 300,000 computers in more than 150 countries with the demand for bitcoin ransom, may provide a model for terrorist groups such as ISIS and Al-Qaeda. Such attacks can inflict damage that includes lost data, damaged equipment, chaos, and panic (Acharya & Acharya, 2017). In some respects, such widespread cyberattacks are more harmful that a physical attack in one specific location. Effective countermeasures to such threats require new collaborations among law enforcement officials, public health experts, and behavioral scientists.

Hostage Negotiation. Successful hostage negotiation requires an understanding of the dynamics of hostage incidents so that these dynamics can be applied by the negotiator to contain and ultimately end the incident with a minimum of violence (Vecchi, Van Hasselt, & Romano, 2005). For example, in many hostage situations, a strong sense of psychological togetherness and mutual dependency develops between the hostages and their kidnappers. These feelings emerge from (1) the close, constant contact between the participants, (2) their shared feelings of fear and danger, and (3) the strong feelings of powerlessness induced by prolonged captivity. This relationship, dubbed the **Stockholm syndrome**, involves mutually positive feelings between the hostages and their kidnappers. This term derives from a 1973 event in which hostages held in a Swedish bank developed a close emotional attachment to their captors (Eckholm, 1985). Hostages may come to sympathize with the lawbreakers and even adopt, at least temporarily, their captors' ideological views. The behavior of Patricia Hearst, a newspaper heiress who was kidnapped in 1974 and later helped her captors rob a bank, has been explained through this syndrome. It was also seen in 1985, when 39 passengers from Trans World Airlines (TWA) Flight 847 were detained as hostages for 17 days by hijackers in Beirut. Allyn Conwell, the spokesperson for the hostages in the hijacking, was criticized for his statements expressing "profound sympathy" for his captors' Shiite position, but he explicitly denied that he was influenced by the Stockholm syndrome (Eckholm, 1985).

Hostage negotiators try to take advantage of this dynamic by becoming a part of it themselves. First attempting to become a psychological member of the hostage group who nevertheless maintains important ties to the outside world, negotiators will then try to use their outside contacts to persuade hostage-takers to bring the crisis to a peaceful end. Successful negotiators make contact with hostage takers in as nonthreatening a manner as possible and then maintain communication with them for as long as necessary. Generally, the negotiator attempts to isolate the hostage takers from any "outside" communication in order to foster their dependency on the negotiator as the crucial link with other people. Once communication is established, the negotiator tries to reduce the hostage takers' fear and tension so that they will be more willing to agree to a reasonable solution. Negotiators structure the situation in ways that maximize predictability and calm. For example, they may offer help with any medical needs the hostage group has, thereby fostering positive feelings associated with the Stockholm syndrome. Finally, through gradual prompting and reinforcement, the negotiator tries to encourage behaviors that promote negotiation progress (e.g., more conversation, less violence and threats as part of such conversation, and the passage of time without violence).

Increasingly, police departments have developed special crisis/hostage negotiation teams that usually include a psychologist as a consultant or adviser (Bartol & Bartol, 2006). In this capacity, the psychologist helps select officers for the team, provides on-the-scene advice during hostage incidents, profiles the hostage taker's personality, and assesses the behavior of the hostages themselves.

Do psychologist-consultants make a difference? In the one study evaluating the effects of psychological consultation in hostage incidents, Butler, Leitenberg, and Fuselier (1993) found that using a psychologist resulted in fewer injuries and deaths to hostages and more peaceful surrenders by hostage takers. Empirical evidence regarding the effectiveness of specific negotiation techniques has yet to be gathered (Vecchi et al., 2005), although psychologists have been involved in using "crisis communication" in the course of critical incidents such as hostage situations, kidnappings, suicide threats, and violence in school and workplace (Vecchi, 2009).

The Police Officer's Job

In the eyes of most citizens, the job of the police officer is to catch criminals and enforce the law, just as the officers on the various police shows do weekly on TV. But the police are responsible for more functions than these. The major duties of the police are divided into three general areas:

- *Enforcing the law,* which includes investigating complaints, arresting suspects, and attempting to prevent crime. Although most citizens perceive law enforcement to be the most important function of the police, it accounts for only about 10% of police activity.
- *Maintaining order,* which includes intervening in family and neighborhood disputes and keeping traffic moving, noise levels down, rowdy persons off the streets, and disturbances to a minimum. It is estimated that 3 out of every 10 requests for police officers involve this type of activity.
- *Providing services,* such as giving assistance in medical and psychological emergencies, finding missing persons, helping stranded motorists, escorting funerals, and rescuing cats from trees.

Much police work is focused on the third category. Should the police spend so much time on community services? The major objections to community services are that they waste police resources and distract the police from the crucial roles of law enforcement and public protection for which they are specially trained. In the 1990s, special initiatives were taken to increase the time police commit to crime-fighting activities. Federal legislation providing funds for cities to hire thousands of new police officers was justified with the promise that additional police would lead to more arrests of criminals. Urban police forces have found that concentrating more police officers in high-crime areas and instructing them to arrest all lawbreakers (even for relatively minor offenses such as loitering and public drunkenness) have resulted in lowered crime rates. This **zero-tolerance** policy requires that police officers concentrate more time on apprehension and arrest activities. Although it was credited with bringing about reductions in crime, the zero-tolerance policy has also been linked to increases in citizen complaints and lawsuits against the police (Greene, 1999). This policy now appears to have yielded to the provision of more specialized interventions (such as when officers are trained specifically to interact more effectively with citizens with behavioral health problems) and other interventions short of arrest.

There are two advantages to the police continuing to provide an array of social services. First, short of spending massive amounts of money to train and employ a new cadre of community service workers, there is no feasible alternative to using the police in this capacity. Second, by providing these services, the police create a positive identity in the community that carries goodwill, respect, and cooperation over to their crime-fighting tasks.

These "side effects" serve as a buffer that gives the police opportunities to interact with people who are not behaving criminally, thereby reducing the tendency of police to develop cynical, suspicious attitudes toward others. They also may encourage citizens to perceive the police in a less threatening and less hostile manner.

Stress and the Police

Not only is the police officer's job composed of multiple duties, but the requirements of these duties may lead to feelings of stress, to personal conflicts, and eventually to psychological problems. Scores of books, technical reports, and journal articles have been written on the causes and treatment of police stress (e.g., Harpold & Feemster, 2002; Hille, 2010).

Certainly no one would suggest that a police officer's job is easy. Certain factors make the occupation particularly difficult. One problem that comes with being a police officer is the "life in a fishbowl" phenomenon. Officers are constantly on public view, and they realize that their every act is being evaluated. This perception can be even more acute with the recent trend toward having police wear body cameras, and with the constant presence of smartphones that can be used to video police encounters with citizens and then post those videos immediately on a social media site. When police perform their job differently than the public wants, they are likely to hear an outcry of protest. Police

are sensitive to public criticism, and this criticism also leads their spouses and children to feel isolated and segregated.

Some have divided the stress of police work into different categories according to the sources of the stress or the type of problem involved. Project Shield, a large-scale study conducted by the National Institute of Justice, asked police officers to respond to a series of questions about the negative effects of stress in several different categories, including psychological, physical, behavioral, and organizational public health (Harpold & Feemster, 2002).

Results from the surveys showed that officers reported an increased vulnerability to alcohol abuse and heightened levels of anxiety within the first five years of employment. In addition, approximately 1% of officers in the study reported having contemplated suicide at some point. Compared to the general population, officers reported more experiences of physical and medical problems over their lifetime, including cancer, heart disease, hypertension, acute migraine headaches, reproductive problems, chronic back problems, foot problems, and insomnia. They also reported increased behavioral problems in their personal lives, such as physical abuse of their spouses and children, as a result of job-related stress. Officers reported the highest levels of organizational, or job-related, stress when faced with making split-second decisions with serious consequences, when hearing media reports of police wrongdoing, when working with administrators who did not support the officers, and when not having enough time for personal or family responsibilities.

According to questionnaire studies of police stress, the following sources of stress are common for police:

1. *Physical and psychological threats.* Included here are events related to the unique demands of police work, such as using force, being physically attacked, confronting aggressive people or grisly crime scenes, and engaging in high-speed chases. A total of 56 law enforcement officers were feloniously killed in the line of duty in 2010 (another 72 officers died in accidents while performing their duties, and 53,469 officers were assaulted in the line of duty) (FBI, 2011a). There were 51 officers feloniously killed in 2014 in the line of duty (FBI, 2015) and another 41 killed in 2015 (FBI, 2016). Danger can emerge from even apparently routine tasks. In 2009, a man wearing a bullet-proof vest opened fire on police officers responding to a domestic disturbance call in Pittsburgh.

BOX 4.2

Body Armor, Automatic Weapons, and the North Hollywood Shootout

The North Hollywood shootout (or "Battle of North Hollywood") involved two heavily armed and body armored individuals who had robbed a bank and the police in the North Hollywood district of Los Angeles. Nearly 2,000 rounds of ammunition were fired before the two bank robbers were killed by police.

On February 28, 1997, Larry Phillips and Emil Mătăsăreanu robbed a bank in North Hollywood. As they left the bank that morning, they encountered police officers and a massive shootout ensued. Phillips ran and Mătăsăreanu drove their getaway car, each continuing to shoot as they fled. But they had prepared for the robbery with illegally modified weapons (a fully automatic AK-47 variant assault rifle, a Bushmaster XM15 Dissipator, and aHK-91 rifle with high capacity-drum magazines as well as a Beretta 92FS pistol). They also wore homemade body armor that protected them from handguns and shotguns fired by the first officers who responded. Police at that time were equipped with .38 Special revolvers or 9 mm pistols, and some police vehicles carried shotguns. But until the SWAT team arrived, responding officers were literally outgunned by Phillips and Mătăsăreanu. This remains one of the longest and bloodiest confrontations in the history of American policing, with about 1,100 rounds fired by the suspects and 650 by the police.

CRITICAL THOUGHT QUESTION

Under what circumstances is deadly force justified for protection of the public and apprehension of criminal suspects?

Three officers were killed and two more injured before the shooter could be arrested. Pittsburgh had not had an officer killed in the line of duty in the previous 18 years. In 1997, in a pitched battle between two men who had robbed a bank wearing body armor and with fully automatic weapons and extensive ammunition and police—the so-called "Battle of North Hollywood"—the impact of such body armor and weaponry was clear. Thankfully such events are very rare, but they remain in the "possible" realm for police officers (see Box 4.2)

2. *Evaluation systems.* These stressors include the ineffectiveness of the judicial system, court leniency with criminals, negative press accounts of the police, the public's rejection of the police, and disrespect and mistreatment of police officers in the courts.

3. *Organizational problems and lack of support.* Examples of these stressors include bureaucracies, inadequate leadership by police administrators, weak support and confused feedback from supervisors, lack of clarity about job responsibilities, and poor job performance by fellow officers. In some studies (Stinchcomb, 2004; Violanti & Aron, 1994), organizational problems proved to be one of the most important sources of stress—more influential even than physical danger, bloody crime scenes, and public scrutiny. A certain degree of stress is inevitable, given the demands placed on the police. Yet police officers often find it hard to acknowledge that the stressful nature of their job is affecting them. There is a stigma about admitting a need for professional help. Too often, police officers believe that if they acknowledge personal problems or ask for assistance, they will be judged to be unprofessional or inadequate.

These concerns are understandable. Officers found to have psychological problems are sometimes belittled by other officers or are relieved of their weapons and badges and assigned to limited-duty tasks. Fear of these consequences induces some officers to hide the fact that they are suffering from job-related stress.

Stressful working conditions also lead to **burnout**, which is "a syndrome of emotional exhaustion, depersonalization, and reduced personal accomplishment that can occur among individuals who work with people in some capacity" (Maslach & Jackson, 1984, p. 134). Emotional exhaustion reflects feelings of being emotionally overextended and "drained" by one's contact with other people. Both emotional exhaustion and depersonalization (callous or insensitive responding to people, particularly crime victims and others needing assistance) have been related to police burnout (Hawkins, 2001). Research on police officers in South

Africa (Storm & Rothman, 2003) validated a measure of officer burnout in a random sample of 2,396 officers. Three factors—exhaustion, cynicism, and professional efficacy—were identified; all three applied well to officers of different races. This suggests that burnout in police officers can be more specifically described on these three dimensions, which are remarkably consistent with the earlier studies on police burnout.

In the United States, many more police officers die as a result of suicide than of homicide. For instance, in 2010, there were 145 police suicides in the United States, a slight increase over 2009, during which there were 143 suicides (Badge of Life, 2010); this decreased to 126 in 2012 (Badge of Life, 2015). By comparison, as noted earlier in this section, 56 law enforcement officers were feloniously killed while on duty in 2010 (FBI, 2011a), 51 were killed in the line of duty in 2014 (FBI, 2015), and another 41 killed in 2015 (FBI, 2016).

A recent review of the current literature on managing police burnout (Portland State University, 2014) made recommendations in nine areas:

- Decrease officer stress by incorporating exercise and stress reduction techniques, enhancing job meaningfulness, clarifying criteria for promotion, and employing 10-hour shifts (rather than 8 or 12) when possible.
- Develop policies describing reasonable use of force, and provide feedback on behavior in this area.
- Use peer support and counseling effectively.
- Monitor negative workplace conditions (perhaps by using organizational psychologists).
- Make officer partner assignments between officers who are as compatible as possible in personality and policing orientation (e.g., service orientation vs. crime-fighting style; Terpstra & Schaap, 2013), and promote better working relationships between officers and their supervisors (Hassell & Brandl, 2009; Scott, 2004).
- Encourage continuing formal education, and provide enhanced training in areas such as CIT and diversity (Dowler, 2005), in part by strengthening training academies.
- Emphasize characteristics such as conscientiousness, stability, resilience, and coping in officer selection (Pienaar et al., 2007).

Implementing these recommendations would, one hopes, reduce the acute and chronic stress experienced by police officers to more manageable levels. That, in turn, should have a favorable impact on reducing police burnout.

Two other strategies for decreasing burnout among police are the use of **team policing** and **counseling**. Team policing involves a partial shift of decision making from a centralized authority to front-line officers and their immediate supervisors, who share the responsibility of setting policing priorities and making management decisions. Teams are often organized around neighborhoods, where they focus their efforts for extended periods of time. Within a neighborhood team, members perform several different functions so that they come to realize how important each team member is to the overall success of the group. In addition, because the team stays in the neighborhood, citizens should come to know the officers more closely and develop a better understanding of them.

In addition to team policing, many police agencies have developed their own stress management programs or referred their officers to other agencies for counseling to reduce burnout. These programs emphasize the prevention of stress through various techniques, including relaxation training, stress inoculation, detection of the early signs of stress, and effective problem solving. As useful as these types of techniques may be, the stigma associated with obtaining mental health treatment may be strong enough to discourage some officers from participating.

But despite attempts to prevent stress and to change organizations in positive ways, some officers will experience stress-related problems that require counseling. Psychological treatment of police officers is complicated because police officers are often reluctant to become involved in therapy or counseling, for several reasons. First, they tend to believe that capable officers should be able to withstand hardships—and failure to do so shows a lack of professionalism or emotional control. Second, police fear that counseling will brand them with the stigma of mental disorder and thus diminish their peer officers' respect for them. Finally, officers are justifiably concerned that the department's need to know their psychological status related to fitness for duty will override their rights of confidentiality and lead to embarrassing disclosures of personal information.

Police departments have developed several alternatives for providing psychological counseling to their officers. Each addresses some of the obstacles that arise in police counseling programs. Peer counseling, involving the delivery of services by police officers, has the potential to overcome the stigma of being involved in treatment with a psychiatrist or psychologist. This approach offers better access to individuals who would otherwise avoid any kind of therapy or counseling; it has contributed to an increase in mental health referrals and a decrease in sick days, poor work performance, and job-related suicide (Levenson & Dwyer, 2003).

A second method is to provide counseling targeted at problems specific to police officers. The most noteworthy example of these focused interventions is with officers who have been involved in the use of deadly force (Blau, 1986). The emotional aftermath of shooting incidents is among the most traumatic experiences the police encounter and can often lead to symptoms of posttraumatic stress disorder. Providing post-incident counseling is a common service of police psychologists; in many departments, counseling for officers involved in shooting incidents is mandatory (Hatch, 2002). The goals of this counseling, which often also relies on peer support, are to reassure officers that their emotional reactions to incidents are normal, to give them a safe place to express these emotions, to help them reduce stress, and to promote a timely return to duty. Many departments also try to make counseling services available to family members of officers who have been involved in traumatic incidents.

There are several ethical considerations involved in psychological counseling for police officers (D'Agostino, 1986), and some of the most difficult concern confidentiality. Police counseling services are usually offered in one of two ways: by an in-house psychologist who is a full-time employee of the police department or by an outside psychologist who consults with the department on a part-time basis. In-house professionals are more readily available and more knowledgeable about police issues. Outside consultants, because of their independence from the department, may be better able to protect the confidentiality of their clients' disclosures.

Police–Community Relations

Police officers are justified in feeling that they live in a "fishbowl." Their performance is constantly being reviewed by the courts and evaluated by the public. Several amendments to the U.S. Constitution impose limits on law enforcement officers; such limits are part of the first 10 amendments, known as the Bill of Rights. The Fourth Amendment protects citizens against unreasonable search and seizure of persons or property. The Fifth Amendment provides guarantees for persons accused of a crime. For example, no person "shall be compelled in any criminal case to be a witness against himself, nor be deprived of life, liberty, or property, without due process of law." Limits on police activities are frequently reevaluated on the basis of current court interpretations of these amendments.

These amendments also have implications for police procedures. Protection against "cruel and unusual punishment" is provided under the Eighth Amendment, and the Fourteenth Amendment guarantees all citizens "due process." These amendments also govern and constrain several police activities.

Historically, the interrogation practices used by the police to elicit confessions from suspects have been a major focus of concern. A review of the risk factors for inducing inaccurate confessions has been provided using a summary of the available literature (Kassin, Drizin, Grisso, Gudjonsson, Leo, & Redlich, 2009). Such risk factors include physical custody and isolation, the presentation of false evidence, offense minimization and "unspoken promises," developmental immaturity, cognitive and intellectual disabilities, and certain kinds of personality and psychopathology. To the extent that such situational and dispositional factors are often present in police interrogations, there is a greater likelihood of false confessions—and the conviction of innocent defendants.

A second police technique that has caused widespread concern is racial profiling—the practice of making traffic or pedestrian stops involving a larger percentage of minority than nonminority individuals. Although some law enforcement officials have defended this procedure as a reasonable crime control tool, the public outcry over its potential for abuse has led several states to abandon it. Termed "driving while black," or "stop-and-frisk" (or, outside of New York City, the Terry stop), the phenomenon of police being more likely to stop African Americans is highly problematic, and creates major concerns regarding equal protection under the law for citizens of all races and ethnic groups. There is some evidence that the traffic stop phenomenon is stronger in local communities than state highway patrols (Warren, Tomaskovic-Devey, Smith, Zingraff, & Mason, 2006).

In New York City, extensive data have been gathered under stop-and-frisk policies. Police are required to submit a form with basic information about who was stopped and what was found. Between 2002 and 2015, there were a total of 5,150,122 stops of citizens, about half of whom were between ages 14 and 24 and about 90% of whom were Black or Hispanic. The percentage of these stops in which there was no arrest or further action was close to 90% across all years (New York ACLU, 2016). The debate between public safety (over 500,000 of these stops resulted in the discovery of contraband and possibly arrest) versus individual rights (nearly 90% of these stops did not yield anything problematic, yet youth and minorities were clearly disproportionately subjected to stop-and-frisk) is clear in this example. But even for those who are convinced that the benefit to public safety outweighs the cost of millions of stops that yielded nothing illegal, it is easy to see how members of minority communities would perceive this policy as discriminatory—and trust the police less as a consequence.

Another major concern of some community groups is excessive force or brutality by the police (Holmes & Smith, 2008). This is seen currently in the Black Lives Matter movement, which was influenced in its development by the perception that African American men were disproportionately victimized by lethal force in police encounters. (We discussed this early in this chapter, showing that minority citizens are disproportionately the subject of force in police encounters—but not lethal force.) For example, the spotlight shone on five New Orleans police officers who, in the aftermath of Hurricane Katrina, were captured on film beating a Black man in the French Quarter. They were convicted of criminal charges in this beating. Another particularly vivid case—also involving police brutality filmed by a bystander (before smartphones were everywhere)—involved Rodney King and a 1991 case in Los Angeles (see Box 4.1). The U.S. Supreme Court has restricted the use of deadly force by police (see Box 4.3).

In 2000, the U.S. Civil Rights Commission, an independent, bipartisan agency established by Congress, reviewed the findings of its 1981 report on police practices and concluded that many of its 1981 findings still applied in alleged police brutality, harassment, and misconduct toward people of color, women, and the poor. How can we explain incidents in which officers have used excessive force? One popular explanation is that police excesses stem from the personality problems of a "few bad apples." In this view, brutality reflects extreme aggressiveness and toughness of an authoritarian personality. A contrasting explanation is that brutality is the unfortunate price occasionally paid for situations in which rising numbers of violent, even deadly, criminals demand forceful responses from the police. A third explanation is that police brutality reflects a fundamental sociological pathology—that the deep strains of racism are still apparent in society.

Police use of excessive force is another example of a problem for which psychology seeks explanations in the interactions between persons and the situations in which they function, rather than simply in the individual's characteristics or the situational influences.

BOX 4.3

The Case of Edward Garner and Limits on the Use of Deadly Force

In the 1985 case of *Tennessee v. Garner*, the U.S. Supreme Court struck down a Tennessee law that allowed police to shoot to kill, even when an unarmed suspect fleeing a crime scene posed no apparent threat. In October 1974, Edward Garner, then 15, fled when the police arrived just after he had broken the window of an unoccupied house. He was pursued by Officer Elton Hymon. As Garner scaled a 6-foot fence at the back of the property, Officer Hymon yelled, "Police—halt!" Garner didn't halt, and Officer Hymon, knowing that he was in no shape to catch the fleeing youth, shot and killed him with a bullet to the back of the head.

Garner's father sued public officials and the city of Memphis, alleging that the police had violated his son's civil rights by the use of excessive force. The city defended itself on the basis of a state statute giving police officers the right to use deadly force if necessary to stop a fleeing felon. The lower courts agreed with the city, but 11 years later the U.S. Supreme Court struck down the statute in a 6–3 decision (*Tennessee v. Garner*, 1985).

The majority held that shooting a person, even one suspected of a felony, violates that person's Fourth Amendment right to be free from unreasonable searches and seizures. The majority opinion added, however, that deadly force would be justified if the officer had reason to believe that the suspect posed an immediate threat to him or others.

CRITICAL THOUGHT QUESTION
Should facilitating capture of a suspect be justification for using deadly force?

From this perspective, we begin with police officers who typically are strongly committed to maintaining the conventional order and to protecting society. We repeatedly put them into potentially dangerous situations, we arm them well, we urge them to be "tough on crime," and we train and authorize them to use appropriate force. The result of mixing this type of person with these types of situations is not surprising: In some encounters, the police will use excessive force against citizens who are suspected of wrongdoing that threatens public safety. In addition, police justifications for extreme force can be motivated by stereotypes, mistaken information, and the mutual mistrust that can develop between individuals from different cultural and ethnic backgrounds.

In recent decades, a number of attempts have been made to improve police relations with people in the community, especially in neighborhoods with large numbers of ethnic minorities. Over the years, the Los Angeles Police Department has changed from what African Americans referred to as an "occupation force of hardliners" into an organization that actively courts and wins support from its African American and Latino populations. (This transformation is described in attorney Connie Rice's 2012 book, *Power Concedes Nothing: One Woman's Quest for Social Justice in America.*)

But there remains a powerful emotional component to the perception by many minority citizens that they cannot trust the police. There is also a strong emotional component to the perceptions of police that they are asked to prevent crime and apprehend offenders, but blamed and mistrusted when they try to do that. Is there anything that would ease the historical tension between minority citizens and police, something that would promote greater legitimate trust in the police but still retain their effectiveness in preventing crime and apprehending offenders?

This is an urgent question. Psychology and other behavioral sciences can offer some steps that might help, judging from some of the earlier discussion in this chapter. First, it is clear that policing is a stressful and sometimes dangerous job, associated with the risk of suicide, death, or injury at higher rates than most other jobs. To the extent that communities can provide police officers with better training, and more effective tools for managing stress and doing their jobs, it is likely that cynicism and burnout among officers will decrease—and have less impact on their encounters with citizens.

Second, the improved documentation of police–citizen interactions using tools such as body cameras, can protect both citizens from being subjected to excessive force and officers from being subjected to unwarranted complaints. Such documentation, and associated monitoring of whether officers are consistent with applicable use of force policies,

are needed for another reason: with the near-constant availability of camera-enabled smartphones, the filming and posting of parts of such encounters on social media sites are likely to increase. Having documentary evidence of the entire encounter will facilitate a fairer and more accurate consideration of complaints and investigation of events in which injury or death result.

Third, we must improve the communication between police and the citizenry. This applies to the individual encounter between a police officer and an individual, to groups representing citizen interests, and to police leaders. Mutual respect and acknowledgment of the other's positions are a necessary precursor to sufficient trust for a good working relationship. These strategies, and others, are discussed in the next section that covers a presidential task force report on the future of U.S. policing in the 21st century.

Before that, we turn to one promising approach to improving this communication that has been implemented over the last four decades. This innovation in police work is **community-based policing**. In this approach, police officers develop a proactive, problem-solving approach with active collaboration from local citizens who support the police in the effort to combat crime, promote safety, and enhance the overall quality of neighborhoods. This type of policing was designed to enhance the working relationship between the police and the public (Zhao, Lovrich, & Thurman, 1999).

Community policing is a philosophy designed to increase the amount and quality of specific police officers' contact with citizens and to involve police more in crime prevention and community maintenance activities.

Melanie Stetson Freeman/The Christian Science Monitor /Getty Images

In most versions of community policing, there are more foot patrols by officers who stay in the same neighborhoods. As a result, community-based policing seeks to humanize police and citizens in one another's eyes and to broaden the roles that police play in a community. For example, Chicago's version of community policing contained six basic features (Lurigio & Skogan, 1994):

1. *A neighborhood orientation*, in which officers forge friendships with individual residents in a community, identify the "hot spots" for crime, and develop partnerships with community organizations for fighting crime.

2. *Increased geographic responsibility*, which means that officers regularly walk a given neighborhood "beat" and become highly visible, well-known experts about problems in that area.

3. *A structured response to calls for police service*, in which emergency calls are handled by a special-response team, thereby permitting beat officers to stay available for routine calls and maintain a high-profile presence.

4. *A proactive, problem-oriented approach*, whereby more effort is devoted to crime prevention (e.g., closing down drug houses, breaking up groups of loitering youth) than to responding to discrete disturbances or criminal activities.

5. *Brokering more community resources for crime prevention*, as police enlist the help of other city agencies to identify and respond to local community problems.

6. *Analysis of crime problems*, which enables officers to focus their attention on the highest risk areas by using computer technology to keep accurate track of crime patterns.

Unfortunately, the effectiveness of community-based policing in Chicago was considerably diminished by 2016. An evaluation of the first 10 years of its functioning indicated that both African American and White citizens reported a decrease in crime problems and fear of crime, although Latinos did not. African Americans in particular perceived a decrease in social disorder and physical decay in their neighborhoods, and all groups described increased policy favorability ratings (Chicago Community Policing Evaluation Consortium, 2004). But after the early 2000s, Chicago invested fewer resources in community policing, took a harder line on crime following an increase in homicides (that followed six consecutive years of decreases), moved officers from community-based policing to street patrol, and held fewer meetings. The once-vibrant program now appears to be a shadow of itself (Rhee, 2016).

There are important lessons in the rise and fall of community-based policing in Chicago. First, when properly funded and staffed, this program appeared to have a favorable impact on relations between police and the community and may have decreased both criminal activity and the fear of crime. Second, there will be challenges to maintaining such a program. When there is an increase in crime, a change in political leadership, or a crisis, there is a temptation to shift resources from a program like this into harder-line crime control. This is often a short-term solution to a long-term problem; maintaining favorable relations between police and citizens will be important over a period of decades, even if it appears to be a lower priority in a crime-driven crisis. Third, if communities succumb to the temptation to shift funding and other resources away from community policing, there will be a commensurate decrease in the program's vitality and effectiveness.

The experience with community-oriented policing in Chicago is a microcosm of the broader approach within the United States: development and rapid growth in the 1990s, continued support up to around 2008, and diminishing resources after that. For example, the Community-Oriented Policing Services, a division of the U.S. Department of Justice, received $148 million in 1994 funding, which grew rapidly to $1.42 billion in 1997. Its budget began shrinking in the mid-2000s, dropping from $495 million (2011) to $208 million (2015) (United States Department of Justice, 2016).

Should this be considered a failed experiment, or does community policing have the potential to improve many of our current problems involving relationships between citizens and police? What is the evidence for its effectiveness? The results have been mixed. Some cities that have introduced community-policing initiatives report large improvements in the public's attitude toward their police departments (Adams, Rohe, & Arcury, 2005; Peak, Bradshaw, & Glensor, 1992) and sizable reductions in rates of serious crimes.

There are several important considerations in whether community-based policing is effective, according to one review (Portland State University, 2011). It must be supported by funding and staffing—and a plan that includes accountability, decentralization, collaboration, and problem-solving (Connell, Miggans, & McGloin, 2008). It should also include training of officers and administrators in community policing practices, incentives to officers for implementation, and encouragement to management to incorporate the philosophy of community policing (Chappell, 2008).

Technology should be used as effectively as possible. Community crime mapping can help police to identify and address problems (Hickman & Reaves, 2001). Data sharing partnerships can be facilitated by the gathering of such crime mapping and other data amenable to combination in a single database. Written agreements can help such data sharing collaborations to work more smoothly (Boba, Weisburd, & Meeker, 2009). The use of communications technology such as social media, websites, e-mail, and texting can ease the strain of communication through more traditional approaches such as 911 operators and police dispatchers. Such approaches are already in use as police convey information using websites (77% of agencies surveyed) and communicate using e-mail (40% of surveyed agencies) (Rosenbaum, Graziano, Stephens, & Schuck, 2011).

Stakeholders must be considered in effective partnerships between police and the community. Participants should include businesses, schools, churches, city agencies, and individual community members, particularly consumers of justice-involved services (Payne & Button, 2009). Those forming and operating these partnerships should also ensure that there is appropriate representation from underrepresented minority communities and that the program is publicized through various media and in different languages (Skogan, Steiner, DuBois, Gudell, & Fagan, 2002).

The Future of Policing in the United States in the 21st Century: The President's Task Force Report

Much of the most recent evidence and thinking about contemporary policing was captured in a recent task force report (**President's Task Force on 21st Century Policing**, 2015). In December 2014, President Barack Obama signed an executive order commissioning a task force to identify best practices in policing and make recommendations on how policing practices can both promote effective crime reduction and build public trust. Through seven meetings in January and February 2015, the Task Force's 11 members met with over 100 individuals from law enforcement and the community—with civic leaders, advocates, researchers, scholars, and others—and reviewed other information (including written testimony). They produced a final report (President's Task Force on 21st Century Policing, 2015) that may serve as an important guide for changes in police work over the coming decades. We describe this report in some detail, both for its scholarly and practical value, and because it offers a valuable perspective on the stability of the trends and evidence discussed in this chapter.

There were two overarching recommendations. First, the Task Force recommended that the President support the creation of another task force (the National Crime and Justice Task Force) to consider criminal justice reforms in the wake of the report. Second, members recommended support for programs that are community-based, addressing important issues such as poverty, education, health, and safety. In this respect, the Task Force clearly placed policing in the broader context of our communities and criminal justice system, identifying risk factors for crime and seeking to reduce them.

The report also made more specific recommendations in six topic areas: Building Trust and Legitimacy, Policy and Oversight, Technology and Social Media, Community Policing and Crime Reduction, Officer Training and Education, and Officer Safety and Wellness. We describe each of these and discuss them in the context of other material in this chapter.

Building Trust and Legitimacy

The Task Force clearly adopted a **procedural justice** perspective (Tyler, 1990) regarding the police: people are more likely to behave lawfully when they perceive those enforcing laws are acting on legitimate authority. Such authority is more likely to be seen as legitimate if police act in procedurally just ways (treating people with dignity and respect, giving people "voice," being neutral and transparent in making decisions, and communicating motives that are trustworthy).

As part of using procedural justice as a guiding structure, the Task Force recommended that law enforcement adopt a "guardian" rather than a "warrior" mindset. Establishing transparency and accountability was seen as very important in establishing and acting upon policies consistent with procedural justice. Promoting trust through positive, nonenforcement-based activities (similar to those described in the community policing section earlier in this chapter) was also recommended. Actually measuring "trust of police" by the community through regular surveys was cited, as it is difficult and often misleading to use anecdotal accounts and single cases to gauge broader trust levels. Finally, the Task Force recommended having police officers as a group reflect the diversity of race, gender, culture, language, and life experience that is part of the community that the police serve.

Policy and Oversight

Police policies should be developed and modified in collaboration with civilian representatives from the community, according to the Task Force. (Again, note the influence of community policing.) Policies on the use of force in particular should include training on alternatives such as de-escalation (see the discussion of CIT earlier in this chapter). Other policies and aggregate data—in areas such as mass demonstrations, consent before searches, gender identification, and racial profiling—should be made publicly available. Routine review of such policies should be conducted, including nonpunitive peer review of critical incidents. To assist law enforcement and the community to succeed in this area, the Task Force recommended technical assistance, incentive funding, interagency collaboration, and other assistance and cooperation using the U.S. Department of Justice and relevant professional organizations.

Technology and Social Media

Given the rapid and significant advances in this area, the Task Force's recommendations in this section of the report are particularly timely. It is often unclear how new technology and applications can assist law enforcement in their effectiveness and efficiency without violating individual rights. Accordingly, the Task Force recommended that the Department of Justice should collaborate with law enforcement to establish standards relevant to research and development of new technologies; these would include auditory, visual, and biometic data, "less than lethal" technologies. Such standards would also include compatibility and operation of social media for law enforcement purposes, again considered using the dual criteria of effectiveness/efficiency and respect for citizens' rights. It can be very difficult for a federal agency to develop standards that are subsequently imposed on local jurisdictions, however. Often a preferable strategy involves the development of model standards, implemented through demonstration projects and publicized widely on both a national and a local level.

Community Policing and Crime Reduction

The community policing approach is built on the assumption that positive, nonenforcement-related interactions between citizens and police have favorable consequences that include the enhancement of the procedural justice components described earlier. In addition to increasing trust of the police and perception of their legitimacy, this approach is also assumed to increase the effectiveness of crime prevention and investigation through better collaboration between police and citizens. Yet the problems with community policing, described earlier using Chicago as a particular example, involve the temptation to divert community policing resources to equipment and crime investigation when there are changes in leadership or an increase in offending. There has been a noteworthy diminishing of the use of community policing in the last decade.

It is very interesting, therefore, to see that the Task Force has made community policing a central pillar of their recommendations. Community policing is identified as a foundational philosophy for both law enforcement and the community in the 21st century. This assumes that community policing can be revived, supported, and expanded. Among the recommendations in this area are the protection and promotion of dignity for citizens—particularly vulnerable children and youth—by avoiding stigmatizing them and minimizing the role of police in public schools. Youth are recognized as important in (a) contributing to community decision-making, (b) participating in research and problem-solving, and (c) developing leadership and life skills. All of these, according to Task Force recommendations, should be facilitated through positive interactions between police and youth (such as the Police Athletic League).

Training and Education

As the scope of law enforcement duties has expanded, so has the importance of training in areas such as mental health, cultural competence, technology, immigration, and terrorism. The Task Force recommends greater use of community experts in providing relevant training to law enforcement personnel throughout their careers. This could be facilitated, according to the report, by the establishment of training innovation hubs involving universities and police academies. A national center for training senior police executives would provide valuable knowledge to senior leaders. The inclusion of CIT as a mandatory aspect of training, perhaps in police academies, would help future generations of police officers move from "CIT training optional" status (where it often is currently) to including CIT skills among the mandatory competencies for police officers.

Officer Wellness and Safety

There is general recognition in the report that officer safety *and* wellness are both important. Training in tactical first aid and the use of seat belts and bulletproof vests are examples of recommendations that would enhance officer safety. Better attention to shift length, exercise, sleep, behavioral health, and medical health are all considerations that would improve the general health of police officers, which could improve performance in both routine encounters and crisis situations. The Task Force makes recommendations that rely on the collection and analysis of data, in areas such as shift length, officer injuries, and "near misses." It is very interesting to see the foundational similarity between the Task Force's assumption that empirical data and specific expertise are valuable to their mission, and the assumption in this book that psychology can contribute to the law in similar ways.

Summary

1. ***What is the role of the police in our society?***
   Policing is necessary in any society concerned with maintaining public order, even though in a democratic society, we must balance public safety with civil liberties and criminal rights. Police officers daily face the dilemma of equality versus discretion: whether to treat all suspects or lawbreakers equally or to provide an effective response that varies somewhat according to the circumstances.

2. ***What procedures are used to select police?***
   Selection of police officers is usually informed by psychological tests and an interview. Another assessment device is the use of some version of a situational test, in which the candidate responds to real-life challenges that would face a police officer, such as intervening in a dispute between a wife and her husband or writing an incident report. Responses to these situational tasks can be valuable additions to psychological testing and interviewing, but they can also be costly and time-consuming.

3. ***How has the training of police officers expanded into new areas?*** Training of police officers usually involves a variety of activities, including criminal law, human relations training, self-defense, and the use of firearms. Most training programs last at least six months. Police officers are now frequently trained in crisis intervention, including handling situations involving individuals with mentally illness, resolving family disputes, and responding to hostage-taking situations.

4. ***Describe the different activities of the police. Is law enforcement central?*** The police officer's job is multifaceted. Law enforcement (including investigation of complaints, arrest and prosecution of suspects, and efforts at crime prevention) accounts for only about 10% of police activity. Maintaining order (intervening in family and neighborhood disputes, keeping traffic moving, responding to disturbances of the peace) accounts for about 30% of police activity. Providing social services to the community is even more time-consuming. These proportions may vary if officers are involved in the approach known as community policing.

5. ***What stressors do the police face?*** Three problems are especially significant: the "life in a fish-bowl" phenomenon, job-related stress, and burnout. Job duties, perceptions of police work, and specific responses can be modified to reduce burnout and help officers manage chronic and acute stress.

6. ***What is the relationship between the police and the communities they serve?*** Some community groups have been critical of police behavior, focusing on unequal and disproportionate use of police force against the poor and racial minorities. Efforts to improve police–community relations include team policing, crisis intervention training, reorganization of the police department that restructures the traditional chain of command, community-based policing, and greater use of communications technology. These interventions have had some success, although

funding for community-based policing has decreased during the last decade.

7. *What is the future of policing in the United States in the 21st century?* According to the President's Task Force on 21st Century Policing (2015), there are six major areas in which recommendations for police work can be prioritized in the coming decades: building trust and legitimacy, policy and oversight, technology and social media, community policing and crime reduction, training and education, and officer wellness and safety. The Task Force used procedural justice as a guiding framework for making recommendations, and cited the importance of empirical evidence, specialized experts, and community-based policing in their implementation.

Key Terms

bioterrorism

burnout

community-based policing

counseling

Crisis Intervention Team

fitness-for-duty evaluation

jail diversion programs

learned helplessness

predictive validity

President's Task Force on 21st Century Policing

procedural justice

Stockholm syndrome

structured interviews

suicide by cop

team policing

terrorism

validity scales

zero-tolerance

5 Eyewitnesses to Crimes and Accidents

ORIENTING QUESTIONS

1. What psychological factors contribute to the risk of mistaken identifications in the legal system?

2. What are the defining features of estimator, system, and postdiction variables in the study of eyewitness memory?

3. How do jurors evaluate the testimony of eyewitnesses, and how can psychological research help jurors understand the potential problems of eyewitness testimony?

4. Can children accurately report on their experiences of victimization? What factors affect the accuracy of their reports? Are they likely to disclose abuse?

5. Can memories for trauma be repressed, and if so, can these memories be recovered accurately?

The police investigate crimes and accumulate evidence so that suspects can be identified and arrested. At the early stages of an investigation, eyewitnesses to those crimes provide important information to police, sometimes the only solid leads. Eyewitnesses also play a vital role in later stages of a prosecution. According to defense attorney David Feige, "It's hard to overstate the power of eyewitness testimony in criminal cases. In thousands of cases every year, testimony of a single eyewitness, uncorroborated by forensic or any other evidence, is used to sustain serious felony charges, including robbery and murder" (Feige, 2006). In 1999, the National Institute of Justice estimated that approximately 75,000 defendants are implicated by eyewitnesses in the United States every year (Department of Justice, 1999).

But in their attempts to solve crimes—and especially in their reliance on eyewitness observers—police and prosecutors face a number of challenges. Although many eyewitnesses provide accurate reports, some make mistakes. The recollections of eyewitnesses can lead the police down blind alleys or cause them to arrest the wrong suspect. As we will show, the investigative actions of the police sometimes compound those problems. Various studies of actual eyewitness identifications provide a startling statistic: approximately one in five eyewitnesses who feel they are capable of recognizing a perpetrator selects an innocent person during an identification procedure (Steblay, 2015). The result is wrongful convictions by judges and juries, an all-too-familiar scenario by now. And while the innocent person languishes behind bars, the guilty perpetrator remains on the streets, possibly committing other offenses.

It is now apparent that eyewitness errors create real problems for the justice system (and for the people mistakenly identified!). DNA procedures developed in the 1980s made it possible to take a new look at evidence left at a crime scene. Unfortunately, only a small fraction of crimes—most notably sexual assaults—have DNA-rich evidence, although even when DNA is present, it is often not tested or is destroyed. In 2009, the Supreme Court ruled that states are not required to make DNA evidence available to convicted offenders (*District Attorney's Office for Third Judicial District v. Osborne*, 2009). As a result, many wrongly convicted people have no way to prove their innocence.

But when DNA testing *is* conducted, it sometimes reveals that the person convicted of a crime and incarcerated—sometimes for decades—was not the actual perpetrator. Further analysis of the evidence in these cases often shows that eyewitness errors are to blame. They are a leading cause of wrongful convictions, particularly in sexual assaults and robberies. According to the Innocence Project, the largest and most prominent organization devoted to proving wrongful convictions, mistaken identifications account for 72% of wrongful convictions revealed by DNA tests; more than false confessions, problems with snitches, and defective or fraudulent science combined (Innocence Project, 2015).

Concern about eyewitnesses' accuracy is not restricted to criminal cases or to the identification of persons. The results of civil lawsuits are also often affected by the reports of eyewitnesses (Terrell & Weaver, 2008), and law enforcement officials know that eyewitness descriptions of unusual events cannot always be trusted. Consider the reports from eyewitnesses to the assassination of President Abraham Lincoln, as documented by historian Bruce Catton. All witnesses agreed that John Wilkes Booth pulled the trigger and then leaped from the presidential box where Lincoln was seated and onto the stage. But their descriptions of Booth's actions from that point vary widely:

...he made a 15-foot leap, ran swiftly off-stage, and vanished ... he slid down a flagpole (which did not actually exist), and more or less crept away ... [he limped] painfully across the stage moaning incoherently ... [he stalked] off calmly, dropping his "Sic semper tyrannis" as a good actor might ... [he ran] furiously, saying nothing at all ... he went off-stage on his hands and knees, making noises ... (Catton, 1965, p. 105) ●

Examples of Mistaken Eyewitness Identification

Cases of wrongful convictions based on faulty eyewitness testimony abound. The ordeal of Calvin C. Johnson, Jr., is a good example. Johnson, a college graduate with a job at Delta Airlines, spent 16 years behind bars for a rape he did not commit. He is not alone. In fact, Johnson was the 61st person in the United States to be exonerated through the use of DNA testing. Such testing in Johnson's case indicated that he was not the man who raped and sodomized a College Park, Georgia, woman in 1983. Yet the victim picked Johnson out of a photographic lineup and identified him as the rapist at trial. The all-White jury convicted Johnson, who is Black, despite the fact that forensic tests excluded him as the source of a pubic hair recovered from the victim's bed. The jury also apparently chose to disregard the testimony of four alibi witnesses who claimed that Johnson was home asleep at the time. One of the jurors stated that the victim's eyewitness testimony had been the most compelling evidence in the case.

One reason why mistakes are so common is that when eyewitnesses make a tentative identification, police often stop investigating other leads and instead look for further evidence that implicates the chosen suspect. This is an example of **confirmation bias**, whereby people look for, interpret, and create information that verifies an existing belief. In terms of eyewitness identification, the goal of finding the truth is neglected, often unintentionally, in a rush to solve the crime. In Johnson's case, police pushed ahead with the case even after the victim picked someone else at a live lineup (conducted after the photographic lineup). She testified at trial that she had picked the wrong person at the live lineup because looking at Johnson was too much for her: "I just pushed my eyes away and picked someone else," she reported (Boyer, 2000).

You might think that people like Calvin Johnson would have some recourse—that they could get something back for the time they lost in prison. But only 32 states have laws that compensate the wrongly imprisoned. Furthermore, such financial compensation is generally small, and social service assistance is rare. Johnson received nothing because Georgia did not have a law providing compensation for people who were wrongly convicted. Unfortunately, many exonorees leave prison with "next to nothing" (Clow, Leach, & Ricciardelli, 2012, p. 330). One commentator has suggested that the new crime is how little some of these lost lives are worth (Higgins, 1999).

How Mistaken Eyewitness Identifications Occur

Mistakes in the process of identification can occur the moment the crime is committed. It may be too dark, events may move too swiftly, or the encounter may be too brief for the victim to perceive the incident accurately. These conditions diminish memory strength. Yet, when questioned by police, victims are asked to give specific details about criminals' height, hair color, voice, and other identifying features. When such descriptions are inaccurate, they hinder the investigation. On the other hand, *accurate* descriptions can lead to correct identifications (Meissner, Sporer, & Susa, 2008).

Mistakes can also occur during the investigation of a crime. Police often ask eyewitnesses to examine a series of photos (called a **photographic lineup** or **photospread**) or a video lineup of suspects and decide whether the perpetrator is present. At this point, eyewitnesses want to help the police solve the crime; they may feel implicit pressure to identify someone, and are likely to assume that the perpetrator is in the lineup. Although accurate identifications are more likely than inaccurate identifications, we know that innocent people are sometimes selected and guilty people are sometimes overlooked.

During trial, jurors may watch an eyewitness confidently identify the defendant as the perpetrator. In DNA exoneration cases, the mistaken eyewitnesses were uniformly confident that their memories were correct, even though some had been uncertain about their initial identifications (Garrett, 2011). Juries are impressed by confident eyewitnesses (Semmler, Brewer, & Douglass, 2012). But by relying on confidence as an indication of accuracy, they fail to recognize the many problems

Sketches based on eyewitnesses' recollections.

that can undermine an eyewitness's report. We describe several such problems in this chapter.

The study of eyewitness identification grew out of our understanding of the basic principles involved in perception and memory. We all are prone to making errors in perceiving and remembering events that we experience. But eyewitnesses must remember experiences that are typically brief, complicated, and sometimes very frightening. So they are especially prone to error. To illustrate these errors, we consider the steps involved in acquiring and recalling information from the outside world—steps an eyewitness must take to record a memory.

Basic Information Processing

We all have had the experience of greeting someone we recognize, only to realize that we were wrong—that the person is actually a stranger. Similar mistakes can be made when crimes are observed. To process information about a crime, we must first perceive a stimulus and then retain it in our minds at least momentarily. But failures and errors can emerge along the way.

Perception

Although our perceptual abilities are impressive (Penrod, Loftus, & Winkler, 1982), we do make errors. We tend to overestimate the height of criminals. We overestimate the duration of brief events and underestimate the duration of prolonged incidents. When watching a short film, we notice more about the actions than about the persons doing the acting. In short, we get the basic gist of events and people but we fail to notice specific details (Migueles, Garcia-Bajos, & Aizpurua, 2016).

Consider a situation in which a weapon is present when a crime is committed. Eyewitnesses may devote more attention to the weapon than to the facial features or other physical aspects of the person who has the weapon. This **weapon focus effect** appears to be caused by **selective attention**: because we have limited attentional capacity and cannot process all of the stimuli available at a given time, we unconsciously select what information to attend to. The threatening aspect of a weapon draws witnesses' attention (Hope & Wright, 2007). This limits the amount of attention they can pay to other aspects of the situation and reduces their ability to recognize and describe the perpetrator (Fawcett, Peace, & Greve, 2016).

The presence of a weapon can also affect the processing of auditory information. Professor Kerri Pickel and her colleagues showed a film of a man holding either a weapon (e.g., a gun, a switchblade knife) or a neutral object (e.g., a soda pop bottle, a ballpoint pen) and speaking to a woman in such a way that his words were either easy or difficult to understand (Pickel, French, & Betts, 2003). Witnesses had difficulty understanding the man's speech in the latter condition, and the presence of a weapon further impaired their comprehension. A reasonable explanation is that their focus on the weapon and their attempt at language comprehension competed for limited processing time. They had a hard time doing both things at once. In general, when people must divide their attention between two or more stimuli, they are more suggestible (Lane, 2006).

Memory

Cognitive psychologists subdivide the building of a memory into three processes: encoding, storage, and retrieval. We describe the memory of eyewitnesses in each of these three stages.

Encoding. **Encoding** refers to the acquisition of information. Many aspects of a stimulus can affect how it is encoded; stimuli that are only briefly seen or heard cannot be encoded fully, of course. The complexity of a stimulus also affects its encoding. As the complexity of an event increases (consider an earthquake, explosion, or hurricane), some aspects of the event probably will be misremembered, while others will be accurately recalled.

Contrary to what many people believe about a stressful event being "etched into memory forever," heightened arousal does not enhance the encoding of events.

The stress of being victimized causes a defensive "fight or flight" reaction that interferes with the encoding of precise details. So although mild stress or arousal may indeed increase alertness and interest in a task, extreme stress usually causes the person to encode the information incompletely or inaccurately (Deffenbacher, Bornstein, Penrod, & McGorty, 2004). Performance on many tasks is best when the level of arousal is sufficient to ensure adequate attention but not so high as to disrupt accuracy.

A study of the accuracy of eyewitness memory in highly stressful military survival school interrogations provides good evidence of the effects of stress on memory (Morgan et al., 2004). Survival school interrogations are one of the greatest training challenges experienced by active duty military personnel. (These interrogations are intended to test one's ability to withstand exploitation by the enemy, and to train people to hold up under the physical and mental stresses of capture.) Participants in this study were 500 soldiers, sailors, and pilots who were placed in mock prisoner of war (POW) camps and deprived of food and sleep for approximately 48 hours prior to interrogation. During 40 minutes of intense questioning, half of them were physically threatened and all participants were tricked into giving away information. One day later, they were asked to identify their interrogators from an eight-picture photographic lineup (chance accuracy is therefore 1/8, or 12.5%). The results were startling. Among those who experienced moderate stress without the threat of physical injury, 76% were correct in identifying the target. But only 34% of participants who experienced the high stress of a physically threatening situation were correct.

Characteristics of the witness also affect encoding in a variety of ways. The effects of stress are felt more acutely by those higher in anxiety and neuroticism (Reisberg & Heuer, 2007). We all differ in visual acuity and hearing ability. When we have prior experience perceiving a stimulus we usually notice its details better than when we perceive something new. This is why experienced judges notice flaws in a gymnast's performance that the rest of us can detect only in a slow-motion replay. Different expectancies about upcoming events also influence how they are encoded; in general, we have a tendency to see what we expect to see.

Storage. The second step in building a memory is the **storage** of stimulus information. How well do we retain what we encode? Many years ago, psychologist Hermann Ebbinghaus showed that memory loss is rapid.

This is important for eyewitness accuracy because it is likely that some time will pass between the commission of a crime and police questioning of eyewitnesses. In one study, eyewitnesses attempted to recall details of a video either one, three, or five weeks after viewing it. Eyewitnesses who recalled the video for the first time five weeks after seeing it were significantly less accurate than eyewitnesses who attempted recall after one or three weeks, supporting the notion that memory fades as the **retention interval**, the period of time between viewing an event and being questioned about it, increases (Odinot & Wolters, 2006). Meta-analyses of 53 studies showed that the longer the retention interval, the more memory loss for previously seen faces (Deffenbacher, Bornstein, McGorty, & Penrod, 2008).

A second phenomenon—both surprising and concerning—also occurs during the storage phase. Activities that eyewitnesses carry out or information they learn after they observe an event, termed **post-event information**, can alter their memory of the event. For example, simply talking to other witnesses can introduce new (not always accurate) details into one's memory. A study of actual eyewitnesses at an identification unit in the United Kingdom showed that 88% of cases involved multiple eyewitnesses (Skagerberg & Wright, 2008), suggesting that an exchange of information during the retention interval is a real possibility. We know that most witnesses *do* share information about serious events such as crimes. A survey of Australian undergraduates who witnessed actual assaults or robberies revealed that 86% discussed the event with co-witnesses (Paterson & Kemp, 2006).

The now-classic studies of Professor Elizabeth Loftus (1975, 1979) showed how exposure to post-event information can affect memory. In one study, participants viewed a film of an automobile accident and were asked questions about it. The first question asked either how fast the car was going "when it ran the stop sign" or how fast it was going "when it turned right." Then all participants were asked whether they had seen a stop sign in the film. In the first group, which had been asked about the speed of the car "when it ran the stop sign," 53% said they had seen a stop sign, whereas only 35% of the second group said they had seen the sign. The effect of the initial question was to "prompt" a memory for the sign. In a second study, Loftus included a misleading follow-up question that mentioned a nonexistent barn. When questioned one week later, 17% of the participants reported seeing the barn in the original film. In essence, the new information conveyed as part of a question was added to

The Case of Larry Fuller and the Victim Who "Never Wavered"

Six o'clock on a foggy April morning in 1981, 45 minutes before sunrise in Dallas, a woman awakens to find a man with a knife atop her. The only light in the room comes from a digital alarm clock. The intruder cuts her and rapes her. Shortly afterwards, hospital personnel collect sperm in a rape kit. Two days later, the victim looks at photographs of possible suspects; Larry Fuller's picture is among them. Because she cannot make an identification, the investigating officer recommends that the investigation be suspended. But other detectives persist, showing the victim a second photospread several days later. Importantly, Fuller's picture is the only one in the second photospread that was also in the first. At this point, the victim positively identifies him and he is arrested. Subsequent to a trial during which the prosecution claimed that the victim "never wavered," Fuller is convicted and sentenced to 50 years in prison.

Larry Fuller was 32 years old at the time, raising two young children. He had served two tours of duty in Vietnam where he was shot down several times. After being honorably discharged, he pursued a degree in the arts while working several jobs. From prison he petitioned the Innocence Project to take his case, but the Dallas District Attorney's Office opposed requests for DNA testing, as it had done many times before. (That district attorney has since been replaced.) After a judge ordered testing—that excluded Fuller as the

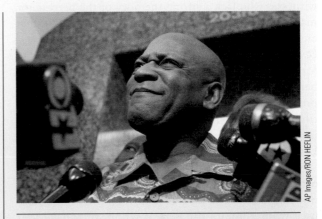

Larry Fuller

perpetrator, he became the 186th person exonerated through DNA analysis. Fortunately, the Texas legislature passed a generous compensation law in 2009, and the new Dallas district attorney has vowed to cooperate with defense attorneys requesting DNA testing in cases involving other inmates.

CRITICAL THOUGHT QUESTION

Why would post-event exposure to Fuller's photograph increase the likelihood that the victim would identify him?

---

the memory of the original stimulus. Not surprisingly, post-event information that conforms to one's beliefs is more likely to be integrated into memory (Luna & Migueles, 2008).

Viewing photographs of suspects after witnessing a crime can also impair an eyewitness's ability to recognize the perpetrator's face in a lineup. Exposure to photographs reduces both correct identifications (identifying the actual perpetrator when he is present in the lineup) and correct rejections (rejecting the choices in a lineup when the perpetrator is absent) and increases false alarms (identifying someone who is not the perpetrator) (Deffenbacher, Bornstein, & Penrod, 2006). The case of Larry Fuller, described in Box 5.1, provides an example of the effects of post-event exposure to photographs.

Retrieval. The third and final step in establishing memory is the **retrieval** of information. When eyewitnesses are asked whether they recognize the culprit from a lineup or a show-up (the presentation of a single suspect), they sometimes respond with an immediate positive identification. This suggests an **ecphoric experience**, a subjective sense of recognition based on a good memory and a good likeness of the perpetrator (or better yet, the *actual* perpetrator) in the lineup (Charman & Wells, 2012).

But other times, the eyewitness's response is not automatic. Instead, it entails more effortful and deliberative thinking, during which various aspects of the situation (for example, the way questions are worded) can affect retrieval (Charman & Wells, 2006). Consider the question "What was the man with the mustache doing with the young boy?" Assume that the man in question had no mustache. This form of the question may influence memory of the man's appearance. Later, if asked to describe the man, eyewitnesses who lack a strong memory of the perpetrator may incorporate the detail (in this case, the mustache) embedded in the question (Leippe, Eisenstadt, Rauch, & Stambush, 2006). Repeated retrieval procedures—for example, searching through a series of mug shots before viewing a lineup or seeing a suspect at various pretrial hearings—can increase an eyewitness's susceptibility to suggestion (Chan & LaPaglia, 2011) and inflate a witness's confidence (Odinot, Wolters, & Lavender, 2009).

In recalling information from our memory, we often generate memories that are accurate but are not relevant to the task at hand. Victims sometimes pick from a lineup the person whom they have seen before but who is not the actual criminal. For example, a clerk at a convenience store who is the victim of a late-night robbery may mistakenly identify an innocent shopper who frequents the store. In an actual case, a Los Angeles judge who was kidnapped and attacked while jogging picked a suspect's picture from a photographic lineup. She later stated that she had forgotten that the suspect appeared before her in court for similar offenses four years earlier, and that she had sentenced him to unsupervised probation (Associated Press, 1988). This phenomenon is called **unconscious transference** (not to be confused with the psychoanalytic notion of transference in a therapeutic context). It is one reason that innocent persons are sometimes charged with a crime and eventually convicted.

Weaving together these strands of perception and memory, prominent researcher Nancy Steblay has written:

Consider the ideal eyewitness: All sensory systems operate optimally (including required eyewear and absence of the ubiquitous ear-buds), in an attentive, calm, and nonintoxicated witness, within a situation that provides an unobstructed, well illuminated view at a distance and for a duration of time that allows a reasonable study of the culprit and circumstances. The ideal witness will attend to and perceive all that transpires; encode this information completely, meaningfully, and accurately into memory; retain the information across time; and then retrieve and report it faithfully and fully when requested by investigators…alas, this ideal witness does not exist (2015, p. 191).

How Psychologists Study Eyewitness Identification

We have already described studies of various influences on eyewitness memory. We now expand on three techniques that psychologists use to study eyewitness issues and describe their advantages and disadvantages. Knowing how the studies are conducted can help you to understand what we can justifiably conclude from them.

Experimental methodology, in which a researcher stages a crime or shows a filmed crime to unsuspecting participant witnesses, is the primary research method. In an experiment, the researcher manipulates some variable (e.g., the presence or absence of an instruction to witnesses, prior to viewing a lineup, that the perpetrator "may or may not be in the lineup") and measures its effects (e.g., the likelihood of choosing someone from the lineup). The value of an experiment is that the researcher knows exactly what the witnesses experienced (termed **ground truth**) and can measure, fairly precisely, how the manipulated variable affected what the witnesses remember. In other words, an experiment can establish cause-and-effect relations. But any individual experiment may lack **ecological validity**, meaning that the study may not approximate the real-world conditions under which eyewitnesses observe crimes and police interact with eyewitnesses. Still, if a number of experiments conducted under varying conditions and with different populations tend to reach the same conclusion, we can be fairly certain that the result would apply to the "real world."

A second way to study eyewitness identification is via **archival analysis** that involves after-the-fact examination of actual cases. Archival analyses typically begin with proven wrongful convictions and examine features of the cases that could have led to the mistaken verdicts. A study of the first 200 exonerations based on DNA testing analyzed the evidence that apparently supported the convictions (e.g., eyewitness testimony, forensic evidence) (Garrett, 2008). Archival analyses have confirmed inaccurate identifications that occur when eyewitnesses choose a filler from a lineup (Pezdek, 2012) and other variables associated with lineup outcomes, for example, exposure duration and viewing distance (Horry, Halford, Brewer, Milne, & Bull, 2014). The value of archival analysis is that it uses real-life situations as the backdrop; the disadvantage is that it can only document what happened in those cases and it cannot explain why.

Field studies combine the rigorous control of an experiment with the real-world setting of archival analyses. Field studies of eyewitness identification examine the procedures used by the police in actual cases. We describe a field study of lineup procedures later in this chapter. A field study may have more ecological validity than an experiment, but it also has a downside. Because we cannot be certain whether a suspect is really guilty, we cannot distinguish correct identifications of the guilty from incorrect identifications of the innocent.

The Variables That Affect Eyewitness Accuracy

Building on the research on basic information processing and using these methodologies, psychologists have identified several other variables that can influence the validity of identifications. Professor Gary Wells, a prolific researcher in the area of eyewitness identification, introduced a useful taxonomy to categorize these variables (Wells, 1978). He coined the term **system variable** to refer to those factors that are under the control of the criminal justice system (e.g., the instructions given to eyewitnesses when they consider a lineup and the composition of that lineup). The term **estimator variable** refers to factors that are beyond the control of the justice system and whose impact on the reliability of the eyewitness can only be estimated (e.g., the lighting conditions at the time of the crime and whether the culprit was wearing a disguise). A third variable—a **postdiction variable**—does not directly affect the reliability of an identification, but is a measure of some process that correlates with reliability (Wells, Memon, & Penrod, 2006). The confidence that a witness feels about an identification is an example of a postdiction variable.

Because system variables hold more promise for preventing errors in eyewitness identification (they are, after all, controllable), many psychologists have focused their research efforts on those variables. But research on estimator variables is important because it can help us understand situations in which eyewitnesses experience problems in perception and memory, and studies of postdiction variables allow an after-the-fact assessment of eyewitness accuracy. The next sections review these kinds of variables, all relevant in different ways to our understanding of the psychology of eyewitness identification.

Assessing the Impact of Estimator Variables

We have already described two estimator variables—the witness's stress level at the time of the crime and the presence of a weapon. Other factors also come into play.

Race of the Eyewitness. Eyewitnesses are usually better at recognizing and identifying members of their own race or ethnic group than members of another race or ethnic group. The chances of a mistaken identification have been estimated to be 1.56 times greater when the witness and suspect are of different races than when they are of the same race (Meissner & Brigham, 2001). This phenomenon, termed the **other-race effect**, has been examined extensively in experimental studies involving a variety of racial groups, and archival analysis of DNA exoneration cases shows that it is also a significant problem in actual cases.

Understanding the reasons for the other-race effect has vexed psychologists for some time. Racial attitudes are apparently not related to this phenomenon (people with prejudicial attitudes are not more likely to experience the other-race effect than are people with unbiased attitudes). Recent explanations of the other-race effect have tended to involve both cognitive and social processes.

Cognitive interpretations hold that there are differences between faces of one race and faces of another race in terms of the variability in features, something called **physiognomic variability**. Faces of one race differ from faces of another race in terms of the *type* of physiognomic variability. For example, White faces show more variability in hair color, and Black faces show more variability in skin tone. For eyewitnesses to correctly identify members of other races, they must focus on the characteristics that distinguish that person from other people of the same race. Thus, Black eyewitnesses would be better off noticing and encoding a White perpetrator's hair color than her or his skin tone, whereas White eyewitnesses could more profitably pay attention to a Black assailant's skin tone. But most of us have more experience with members of our own race, so our natural inclination is to focus on the features that distinguish members of *our own group*. We have less practice distinguishing one member of another race from other people of that race.

These ideas are supported by studies involving sophisticated eye-movement monitoring technology to assess the encoding processes people adopt when viewing own-race and other-race faces. One study showed that we fixate on more, and more distinctive, features when viewing own-race faces than when viewing other-race faces (Goldinger, He, & Papesh, 2009).

Social psychologists have also tried to explain the other-race effect. One reasonable hypothesis is based on social perception and **in-group/out-group differences** (Sporer, 2001). When we encounter the face of a person from another race or ethnic group (the out-group), our first job is to categorize the face as a member of that group (e.g., "That person is Asian"). Attentional resources that are directed toward categorization come at the expense of attention to facial features that would distinguish that person from other members of the out-group. But when we encounter the face of a person from our in-group, the categorization step is eliminated, so we can immediately devote attention to distinguishing that person from other members of the in-group. Because identifying people of other races involves both a cognitive and a social process, both explanations may be right.

Age and Gender of the Eyewitness.

Do males make better eyewitnesses than females and do young people make better eyewitnesses than older people? The age and gender of an eyewitness are also estimator variables; we can't control their influence but we can estimate them.

The evidence for gender effects is not overwhelming but tends to indicate an own-gender bias, at least for women. Women are better at recognizing female faces than male faces, whereas men recognize female and male faces equally well (Palmer, Brewer, & Horry, 2013). Women apparently pay more attention at encoding to female faces than male faces.

There is some evidence that the age of the eyewitness matters: Older eyewitnesses make more errors than younger and middle-aged adults, regardless of whether they are identifying perpetrators or rejecting lineups in which perpetrators are absent (Erickson, Lampinen, & Moore, 2016). One explanation is that older adults base judgments more on gist information (central aspects) than on recollection of precise details. Because lineup fillers look like the perpetrator, at least to some extent, they activate gist-like memory traces (Gomes, Cohen, Desai, Brainerd, & Reyna, 2014). We describe the issues associated with children as witnesses later in the chapter.

Controlling the Impact of System Variables

System variables are those factors in an identification over which the justice system has some control. In general, system variables tend to come into play after the crime, usually during the investigation. They are associated with how a witness is questioned and how a lineup is constructed and shown to the eyewitness. We have already described two system variables: the influence of post-event information and the effects of questions posed to eyewitnesses. Other system variables are also important.

Research on these variables can suggest changes to procedures that investigators use with eyewitnesses.

To explain why system variables and procedures are so important, it may be helpful to draw an analogy to the steps used by researchers doing an experiment (Wells & Luus, 1990). Like scientists, crime investigators begin with a hypothesis (that the suspect actually committed the crime), test the hypothesis (by placing the suspect in a lineup), observe and record the eyewitness's decision, and draw conclusions from the results (that the suspect was the assailant).

There are certain principles that are essential to good experimental design (e.g., that observers should be unbiased), and violation of those principles affects the usefulness of the experiment's findings. In similar fashion, violating the principles of good criminal investigation affects the results of the investigation. For example, if the suspect appears to be different from the other people in the lineup in some obvious way, or if the person conducting the lineup conveys his or her suspicions to the eyewitness, then the results of that identification procedure can be erroneous. Applying the analogy of an experiment to criminal investigations enables us to evaluate critically the steps involved in these investigations.

Reforming Identification Procedures

One important aspect of a system variable is that because it is controllable, it can be modified. Because the police want to catch the real culprits and avoid mistakes, they have begun to incorporate procedures recommended by psychologists and other researchers for interviewing eyewitnesses and constructing and presenting lineups. For example, research findings suggest ways to increase the likelihood that a guilty perpetrator, rather than an innocent filler, is selected from a lineup. This concept, termed a lineup's **diagnosticity**, has informed the way that police conduct lineups.

In fact, since the publication of an important article that outlined research-based recommendations for collecting and preserving eyewitness evidence (Wells et al., 1998), the pace of reform has quickened (Wells & Quigley-McBride, 2016). In 1999, the U.S. Department of Justice (DOJ) recommended procedures for collecting eyewitness evidence based on psychological research studies and distributed guidelines to more than 16,000 law enforcement agencies in the U.S. The National Research Council validated these and other recommendations from eyewitness research (National

Research Council, 2014). Several state courts have imposed requirements for eyewitness evidence by relying on social science findings (e.g., *State v. Henderson*, 2011; *State v. Lawson*, 2012). And many jurisdictions have voluntarily reformed their identification procedures in light of relevant research.

In the sections that follow, we describe some of the scientific findings on system variables that led to these policy changes. You will notice that the reforms (e.g., warning an eyewitness that the suspect may or may not be in the lineup) may come with a trade-off: although they reduce the likelihood of mistaken identifications, they also reduce the likelihood of correct identifications. How people value this trade-off will depend on whether they are primarily concerned about due process rights of criminal defendants or about crime control and the conviction of guilty offenders, as well as other complicated policy issues (Clark, 2012).

Interviewing Eyewitnesses

The police often want more information from eyewitnesses than those witnesses can provide (Kebbell & Milne, 1998). So psychologists have devised ways to enhance information gathering. The **cognitive interview** is an interviewing protocol based on various concepts of memory retrieval and social communication (Fisher & Geiselman, 1992; Geiselman, Fisher, MacKinnon, & Holland, 1985). Before describing the cognitive interview, we describe a standard police interview so you can understand why a new method was needed.

A "standard" police interview relies on a predetermined set of questions with little opportunity for follow-up, an expectation that the witness will be willing and able to answer all of the questions, repeated interruptions, and time constraints. By contrast, in a cognitive interview, the interviewer first engages the witness in order to develop rapport, then asks the witness to provide a narrative account of the event, and finally, probes for details with specific questions. The interviewer allows the witness to direct the subject matter and flow of the questioning, interrupts infrequently, and listens actively to the witness's responses.

Perhaps the most distinctive element of a cognitive interview (and the reason for its name) is its reliance on a set of cues developed from research on memory retrieval. Cognitive psychologists have observed that reinstating the context in which a witness encoded an event provides retrieval cues and thereby increases accessibility of information stored in memory. With this objective in mind, the interviewer may cue a witness to mentally reconstruct the physical and emotional experiences that existed at the time of the crime. The interviewer may direct the witness to form an image of the situation, recollect sights, sounds, smells, and physical conditions (e.g., heat, cold, darkness) and recall any emotional reactions experienced at the time. When the witness has mentally reconstructed the event, the interviewer asks for a detailed narrative and then uses follow-up questions to probe for specific information. Witnesses are sometimes asked to recall events in different temporal orders (e.g., describing the event from the end to the beginning), from different perspectives, or from the point of view of different people. A cognitive interview allowed British police to solve a kidnapping that gripped the nation for eight days in 1992. We describe the case in Box 5.2.

A meta-analysis of 65 experiments gauged the effectiveness of the cognitive interview. It showed that compared to the traditional interview method, the cognitive interview can generate substantial increases in correct recall, though it can also produce a small increase in incorrect details (Memon, Meissner, & Fraser, 2010). The cognitive interview is especially effective for older adults, who rely more on external cues to retrieve information from memory. Personnel from organizations including the FBI, Department of Homeland Security, National Transportation Safety Board, and some state and local police departments have been trained on cognitive interviewing procedures. However, agencies have been slow to adopt them, perhaps because the cognitive interview is a more demanding interview protocol.

Lineup Instructions

There is ample evidence that when conducting a lineup, an investigator should instruct the witness that the offender may or may not be present (Malpass & Devine, 1981). Without this admonition, eyewitnesses may assume that their task is to pick someone, so they choose the person who looks most like the perpetrator. Evaluating experimental studies on the "might or might not be present" admonition, Professor Nancy Steblay determined that this instruction reduced the rate of mistaken identifications (i.e., saying that the offender was present in the lineup when he was not) from 70% to 43% (Steblay, 2013). The rate of accurate identifications is also slightly reduced by the instruction, but that decline is much smaller than the decline in mistaken identifications.

The Case of Wooden-Legged Michael Sams and His Victim's Cognitive Interview

On January 22, 1992, real estate agent Stephanie Slater arranged to show property to a prospective client in Birmingham, England. But Michael Sams was no client. At the rundown house, he put a knife to Slater's throat, forced her into his car, and drove her to a remote warehouse where he held her, handcuffed, blindfolded, and gagged for eight days. Though Sams had killed before, this time he released his victim after receiving ransom money from Slater's manager.

Now the police had a single eyewitness to the crime—the victim—and needed to find her kidnapper. Through careful questioning that included context reinstatement, Slater was able to recall that during captivity she heard nearby trains and an old telephone ring. She described the smell of the kidnapper's clothes. And she recalled the feel of walking across cobblestones. Sparse though these details were, they allowed police to piece together a physical description of her attacker and trace the place of her confinement. After releasing this information to the public they received hundreds of tips, including one that led to Michael Sams, a wooden-legged criminal who had kidnapped and murdered a sex worker the previous year. This case

Michael Sams

was a landmark application of the principles of cognitive interviewing.

CRITICAL THOUGHT QUESTION

For what reasons would Slater have been able to remember more when questioned via the cognitive interview than a standard police interview?

The vast majority of police officers report that they give eyewitnesses the option of not making a selection from the lineup (Wogalter, Malpass, & McQuiston, 2004). Unfortunately, some detectives also give a pre-admonition suggestion to the eyewitness that the perpetrator is in the lineup ("Surely, you can pick the perpetrator"). When they do so, the beneficial effects of the subsequent admonition ("The suspect might or might not be present") are reduced and the likelihood of a false identification increases (Quinlivan et al., 2012).

Lineup Presentation Method

In a traditional lineup, all lineup members are shown to the witness at once. This procedure is termed **simultaneous presentation**. An alternative procedure, used with increasing frequency, is to show lineup members sequentially, one at a time, in a procedure called **sequential presentation**. The witness makes a decision about each lineup member before seeing the next one.

The manner in which a lineup is presented can affect the accuracy of identification. In a field study that compared simultaneous and sequential lineup procedures used by police in four sites across the country, psychologists found that the rates of identifying the suspect did not differ between the two techniques. Importantly though, simultaneous procedures yielded more mistaken identifications of fillers (18%) than did sequential procedures (11%) (Wells, Steblay, & Dysart, 2015).

These results are consistent with a meta-analysis that compared simultaneous and sequential presentations in lab studies involving more than 13,000 participant-witnesses (Steblay, Dysart, & Wells, 2011). The chance of mistaken identification was reduced by 22% when presentations were sequential rather than simultaneous. However, there was a trade-off: correct identifications were also reduced (by 8%) when lineups were shown sequentially. In general, sequential lineups result in fewer identification attempts, so both mistaken and accurate identifications are reduced (Meissner, Tredoux, Parker, & MacLin, 2005).

A deputy sheriff is showing a simultaneous photographic lineup to an eyewitness.

The beneficial effects of sequential lineup presentation may depend on how the lineup is constructed and presented (Steblay, 2015). Sequential presentation is advantageous in situations in which there is a single suspect with at least four (usually five) fillers, cautionary instructions that the perpetrator may or may not be in the lineup, and only one attempt at identification.

Why are there more mistaken identifications in a simultaneous lineup? In the simultaneous presentation of individuals in a lineup, eyewitnesses tend to identify the person who, in their opinion, looks most like the culprit

relative to other members of the group. In other words, they make a **relative judgment**. As long as the perpetrator is in the lineup, the relative-judgment process works well. But what happens when the actual culprit is not shown? The relative-judgment process may still yield a positive identification, because someone in the group will always look *most* like the culprit (Wells et al., 1998).

Contrast this situation with a lineup in which the members are presented sequentially, one at a time. Here, the eyewitness compares each member in turn to his or her memory of the perpetrator and, on that basis, decides whether any person in the lineup is the individual who committed the crime. In other words, they make an **absolute judgment**. The value of sequential presentation is that it decreases the likelihood that an eyewitness will make a relative judgment in choosing someone from the lineup.

Professor Gary Wells cleverly demonstrated the use of relative-judgment processes in his "removal without replacement" study (Wells, 1993). In this procedure, all eyewitnesses watched a staged crime. Some were shown a photographic lineup that included the actual culprit and five fillers. Another group saw the same photographic lineup with one exception: The culprit's photo was removed and was not replaced with another photo. If identifications of the culprit by the culprit-present group are based solely on their recognition of him, then the percentage of people in that group who identified him *plus* the percentage who said "not there" should be exactly the same as the percentage in the culprit-absent group who said "not there." Wells tested this idea by showing 200 eyewitnesses to a staged crime either a culprit-present lineup or a lineup in which the culprit was absent but was not replaced by anyone else (see Table 5.1). When the culprit was present in the lineup, 54% of eyewitnesses selected him, and 21% said "not there." Did 75% of eyewitnesses in the "target-absent" lineup say "not there"? Unfortunately, no. The "not there" response was given by only 32% of people in that group. The others all mistakenly identified someone else

TABLE 5.1   **Rates of choosing lineup members when a culprit (#3) is present versus removed without replacement**

| | LINEUP MEMBER | | | | | | |
	1	2	3	4	5	6	No Choice
Culprit present	3%	13%	54%	3%	3%	3%	21%
Culprit removed (without replacement)	6%	38%	—	12%	7%	5%	32%

Source: "What do we know from witness identification?" from G. Wells. (1993). *American Psychologist, 48,* 553–571.

from the lineup, even though they had been warned that the offender might not be in the lineup. Why? Through a process of relative judgment, eyewitnesses apparently select whoever looks most like the perpetrator. The weaker one's memory, the more likely one is to use a relative judgment in this situation (Clark & Davey, 2005).

The Influence of Feedback

Recall our analogy between a criminal investigation and a scientific experiment. One of the cardinal rules of a good experiment is that the person conducting the experiment should not influence the results, a problem referred to as **experimenter bias**. To avoid such bias, experimenters should know little about the study's hypotheses and less about the experimental condition in which any participant is placed. Nearly all clinical drug trials adhere to these rules—neither the patient taking the pills nor the doctor assessing the patient's health know whether the pills are actually a new drug or a placebo. These so-called **double-blind testing procedures**, commonplace in medicine and other scientific fields, should also be used in police investigations with eyewitnesses. Not only should the witness be blind to the identity of the suspect, but the lineup administrator should be as well.

When lineups are conducted by detectives who selected the fillers and know which person is the suspect, their knowledge can affect the eyewitness in various ways. First, it can increase the likelihood that an eyewitness will choose someone from the lineup (Phillips, McAuliff, Kovera, & Cutler, 1999). This is more likely to occur when the administrator has failed to provide instructions that the suspect may or may not be in the lineup, in which case the eyewitness may presume that the suspect is present and looks to the administrator for cues (Greathouse & Kovera, 2009). Furthermore, eyewitnesses who have frequent contact with the administrator— either because they are in close physical contact or because they have extensive interactions—are likely to make decisions consistent with the administrator's expectations (Haw & Fisher, 2004). Perhaps most concerning, neither the eyewitness nor the administrator is typically aware of this influence (Garrioch & Brimacombe, 2001). An obvious solution to this situation is to have the lineup administered by someone who does not know which person in the lineup is the suspect. Experimental studies now document that double-blind procedures reduce both false identifications and confidence in those mistaken identifications (Charman & Quiroz, 2016).

Eyewitnesses can express increased certainty in their identifications due to events that occur after they choose someone from a lineup. For example, feedback from a lineup administrator suggesting that an identification is accurate or mistaken distorts eyewitnesses' certainty in that identification compared with eyewitnesses who receive no such feedback. Remarkably, feedback that confirms an identification also leads eyewitnesses to report that they had a better view of, and paid more attention to the perpetrator and that it was easier for them to identify that person. It increases their sense that they have good memory for strangers and willingness to testify about their eyewitness experience at a trial (Steblay, Wells, & Douglass, 2014). In the words of one observer, "This dramatic effect is produced by a simple, casual, even seemingly helpful, comment from the lineup administrator" (Steblay, 2015, p. 205).

Even *without* confirming feedback, eyewitnesses infer from the facts of an ongoing investigation and eventual prosecution that they must have picked the suspect from the lineup. Hence, their confidence increases. This enhanced confidence is troubling because of the repeated finding that the confidence expressed by eyewitnesses during their trial testimony is one of the most compelling reasons why jurors believe such identifications are accurate (Brewer & Burke, 2002). We would expect that the rape victim described in Box 5.1 was more confident of her identification of Larry Fuller at his trial than she was when viewing his photograph. Is there a remedy to this problem of ever-increasing certainty? A blind administrator should take a video-recorded statement of the eyewitness's confidence at the time of the lineup, before any feedback can occur.

Eyewitness Confidence

A question that has vexed psychologists for many years is whether there is an association between witnesses' confidence and their accuracy. How likely is it that witnesses who are confident about their identifications are accurate, and conversely, that those who lack confidence are mistaken? The answer may depend on several things, including whether confidence in the identification is expressed in the courtroom or at the police station and whether procedures used to obtain an identification were free from bias. Researchers generally agree that statements of confidence made from the witness stand during a trial are generally uninformative because in that setting, there are many factors other than witnesses' accuracy that can boost confidence. But confidence statements made immediately after a positive identification from a lineup, assuming the lineup was conducted properly, can provide useful information about accuracy (Brewer & Wells, 2006).

Whether witnesses' statements of confidence at the lineup are indicative of accuracy depends on how that identification was secured and reported. What does a properly conducted lineup look like? The suspect does not stand out from the fillers, the lineup administrator provides unbiased ("may or may not be present") instructions and avoids giving post-identification feedback, and confidence is measured precisely and immediately after an identification. Unfortunately, these conditions often don't occur in the real world, despite being supported by empirical research (Police Executive Research Forum, 2013). This can explain why eyewitnesses in hundreds of DNA exoneration cases were confident, but wrong (Smalarz & Wells, 2015). And it suggests that criminal justice personnel should review their eyewitness identification practices in order to bring them in line with "best practices." Only then can eyewitness confidence tell us something about eyewitness accuracy (Wixted & Wells, 2017).

As investigators "clean up" their identification procedures, they must be attentive to other ways that they can affect eyewitnesses' confidence statements. An interesting aspect of witness confidence is its apparent malleability: After making an identification from a lineup, witnesses who were told that another witness identified the same person became more confident of their identifications (Charman, Carlucci, Vallano, & Gregory, 2010). In another study, witnesses' rated confidence depended on whether they might be contradicted by another witness. Confidence increased when there was no chance of contradiction and decreased when there was (Shaw, Appio, Zerr, & Pontoski, 2007). These findings show that multiple factors can affect the certainty of an eyewitness's identification.

The Eyewitness in the Courtroom

Despite limitations on the reliability of eyewitness identifications, jurors put a great deal of weight on testimony from an eyewitness. In a study showing this influence, Loftus (1974) gave subjects a description of an armed robbery that resulted in two deaths. Of mock jurors who heard a version of the case that contained only circumstantial evidence against the defendant, 18% convicted him. But when an eyewitness's identification of the defendant was presented as well, 72% of the mock jurors convicted him. It is hard to overstate the power of confident eyewitnesses to convince a jury of the correctness of their testimony.

Why do jurors have difficulty inferring the accuracy of an eyewitness's memory? In particular, why do they overestimate accuracy? One reason is that, as we

mentioned, jurors rely on witness confidence as an indicator of accuracy and by the time eyewitnesses get to trial, most are quite confident. Jurors themselves believe that when they are sure of something, they are likely to be correct, so why not eyewitnesses, too (Bornstein & Greene, 2017)? As a result, jurors tend to trust both overt statements of confidence such as "I'm sure that's the guy" and subtler indications of confidence such as voice pitch, intonation, and speed.

There are other explanations for jurors' over-reliance on eyewitness testimony (see, e.g., Semmler et al., 2012):

- Jurors cannot verify an eyewitness's version of an event against some objective record of what occurred. Instead, they may rely on a positive stereotype about memory credibility, suggesting an insensitivity to the impact of estimator variables.
- Jurors assume that eyewitnesses' testimony is a reflection of their memory quality, and not the way they were questioned or interacted with the lineup administrator. This suggests an insensitivity to the role of system variables in shaping a witness's recollection. More broadly, it is an example of the fundamental attribution error: the tendency to assume that the causes of behavior are internal to a person rather than the result of external factors such as the role of a lineup administrator and the nature of the lineup.

Safeguards against Mistaken Identification

Scientists have focused more attention on assessing the effects of various identification procedures than on trial processes that could reduce the rates of wrongful convictions (Semmler et al., 2012). But some studies examine ways to counter jurors' overreliance on eyewitness identification.

One possibility is to inform jurors about whether investigators followed DOJ guidelines for conducting lineups. This would allow jurors to gauge whether the procedures and outcome warrant their trust. A mock jury study tested this idea (Lampinen, Judges, Odegard, & Hamilton, 2005). Some jurors were informed that detectives violated DOJ guidelines and others were not so informed. Those who learned about guideline violations thought the prosecution's case was weaker and were less likely to convict the defendant, suggesting that failure to adhere to DOJ guidelines could discredit the prosecution.

Until the guidelines are consistently applied or reforms adopted more broadly, other mechanisms should be available to educate jurors and judges about the problems inherent in eyewitness reports. We discuss three ways to do this. One proposal limits the testimony of eyewitnesses in particular ways. Another remedy allows psychologists who are knowledgeable about the relevant research on perception and memory to testify as expert witnesses on eyewitness reliability. Finally, judges could instruct juries about the potential weaknesses of eyewitness identifications and suggest how to interpret this testimony.

Limiting Eyewitness Testimony

Suppose that an eyewitness to a convenience store robbery made a tentative identification of a suspect from a lineup, and after being shown a second lineup in which the suspect was the only person repeated, made a more confident identification. A judge could rule that the eyewitness can testify about the initial, tentative identification, but not about the second identification. A prosecutor faced with the exclusion of powerful testimony is likely to pressure the police to use less suggestive procedures in the future (Wells & Quinlivan, 2009).

Expert Testimony

In all but two states, experts may testify about research on eyewitness identification; typically, they do so on behalf of the defendant. Their testimony focuses on factors that influence eyewitness accuracy. Such testimony might indicate that (1) extreme stress tends to inhibit encoding, (2) feedback from a lineup administrator can increase an eyewitness's confidence, and (3) differences in the way lineups are constructed and presented to witnesses affect eyewitness accuracy. Note that the expert witness does not tell the jury what to believe about a particular eyewitness or whether the eyewitness is accurate. Rather, the expert's task is to provide the jury with a scientifically based frame of reference within which to evaluate the eyewitness's evidence.

To be most helpful, expert testimony should aid jurors in discriminating between circumstances that enhance eyewitness memory (e.g., double-blind lineup administration) and those that impair it (e.g., weapon focus). The data are mixed on whether this happens. Some studies show that experts can sensitize jurors to questionable viewing conditions or suggestive police procedures (e.g., Devenport, Stinson, Cutler, & Kravitz, 2002; Laub, Kimbrough, & Bornstein, 2016). But other studies show that expert testimony makes

jurors skeptical of eyewitness memory and less likely to convict, regardless of the quality of the witnessing conditions and identification procedures (e.g., Jones, Bergold, Dillon, & Penrod, 2017; Martire & Kemp, 2011). Variations in the level of detail in the testimony and its match to evidence in the case may explain these discrepancies. But because jurors tend to overvalue eyewitness testimony, especially when it is highly confident, simply reducing their reliance a bit may be a useful outcome (Bornstein & Greene, 2017).

A report of one actual crime lends anecdotal support to the conclusion that the testimony of an expert witness has some impact. Loftus (1984) described the trial of two Arizona brothers charged with the torture of three Mexicans. Two juries were in the courtroom at the same time, one deciding the verdict for Patrick Hanigan, the other deciding the fate of his brother, Thomas. Most of the evidence was from eyewitnesses, and was virtually identical for the two defendants. However, expert testimony about the inaccuracy of eyewitnesses was introduced only in Thomas's trial. (The jury hearing Patrick's case waited in the jury room while this evidence was presented.) Patrick Hanigan was convicted by one jury; his brother was acquitted by the other. This is as close to a "natural experiment" as the legal system has offered for assessing the influence of a psychologist in the courtroom. Unfortunately, even when allowed, expert testimony is an expensive safeguard that is available in only a small fraction of the cases that come to trial each year (Wells et al., 1998). Are there other more affordable and readily available remedies?

Jury Instructions

Another option for alerting jurors to the limitations of eyewitnesses is a jury instruction delivered by the judge at the end of a trial. The defense typically requests that such an instruction be given, and the judge decides whether to grant the request.

What effects do cautionary instructions have on jurors' beliefs about eyewitness accuracy? Research testing the impact of a frequently used instruction on eyewitness reliability, the so-called *Telfaire* instruction (*United States v. Telfaire*, 1972), found that it reduced mock jurors' sensitivity to eyewitness evidence, probably because it gives little indication how jurors *should* evaluate the evidence (Greene, 1988). However, an instruction that incorporated information likely to be delivered by an expert preserved jurors' sensitivity to the factors that influence eyewitness reliability (Ramirez, Zemba, & Geiselman, 1996).

These findings suggest that instructions that are issue-specific, tailored to the facts present in a particular case, and based on scientific research findings might be most effective. Rather than providing only general directives about eyewitness evidence (e.g., "consider the conditions under which the identification was made"), they instruct jurors about scientific findings on relevant estimator and system variables and inform them how to incorporate this information into their decision-making. But one study that incorporated these sorts of instructions into a mock sexual assault trial found little evidence of a sensitization effect. Why? Surprisingly, jurors were sensitive to the quality of the identification evidence on their own, convicting in conditions where the identification conditions were good and acquitting when they were poor (Jones et al., 2017). Perhaps awareness of the problems of mistaken identifications has seeped into public consciousness in recent years.

Children as Witnesses

Sometimes a child is the only witness to a crime—or its only victim. A number of questions arise in cases where children are witnesses. Can they remember the precise details of these incidents? Can suggestive interviewing techniques distort their reports? Do repeated interviews increase errors? Is it appropriate for children to testify in a courtroom? Society's desire to prosecute and punish offenders may require that children testify about their victimization, but defendants should not be convicted on the basis of inaccurate testimony. In this section, we focus on the accuracy of children as witnesses and on concerns about children testifying in court.

Children as Eyewitnesses to Crimes

Like adults, children are sometimes asked to identify strangers or to describe what they witnessed regarding crimes. In kidnappings and assaults, the child may be the only witness to a crime committed by a stranger. To test children's eyewitness capabilities, researchers create situations that closely match real-life events. In these studies, children typically interact with an unknown adult (the "target") for some period of time in a school classroom or a doctor's office. They are later questioned about what they experienced and what the target person looked like, and they may attempt to make an identification from a lineup.

Two general findings emerge from these studies. First, children ages five and older can make reasonably reliable identifications from lineups (Pozzulo, Dempsey, Crescini, & Lemieux, 2009). Second, children are generally less accurate than adults when making an identification from a lineup in which the suspect is absent. In these situations, children tend to select someone from the lineup, thereby making a false-positive error (Fitzgerald & Price, 2015). Such mistakes are troubling to the police because they thwart the ongoing investigation.

Psychologists have attempted to devise identification procedures for children that maintain identification accuracy when the suspect is in the lineup but reduce false-positive choices when the suspect is absent. Presenting lineup members in a face-off procedure that breaks the task into a series of binary decisions, rather than showing all lineup members together, decreased guessing and the incidence of false identifications from target-absent lineups (Price & Fitzgerald, 2016).

Children as Victims of Maltreatment

The most likely reason that a child becomes involved with the legal system is that he or she has been maltreated. Here the issue is not who committed the crime. Rather, it is what happened to the child. Psychologists have been particularly interested in the effects—socioemotional, neurobiological, mental health, *and* cognitive—of maltreatment. In this chapter, we focus on the cognitive effects, particularly the implications for memory, of child abuse, including child sexual abuse (CSA).

Most CSA cases rest solely on the words of the victim because these cases typically lack any physical evidence. (The most frequent forms of sexual abuse perpetrated on children are fondling, exhibitionism, and oral copulation.) Yet anyone who has spent time with young children knows that their descriptions of situations can sometimes mix fact and fantasy. There are concerns about whether preschoolers and even older children can be trusted to provide accurate details and to disclose experiences of abuse. There are also concerns about the accuracy of memory on the part of adolescents and adults who previously experienced maltreatment. Developmental psychologists have investigated these issues over the past several decades. We focus on studies that assess the effects of interviewing techniques on children's memory of events they experienced and that examine patterns of disclosure of maltreatment and the accuracy of memory for abuse.

Investigative Interviews

One feature of CSA cases is crucial to the accuracy of child witnesses: the nature of the investigative interview. Some interviewers now use a structured questioning protocol that first builds rapport between interviewer and child, and then encourages children to provide details in their own words ("Tell me everything that happened from the beginning to the end as best you can remember"). The protocol discourages the use of **suggestive questions** (questions that assume information not disclosed by the child or suggest the expected answer, such as "He touched you, didn't he?").

In research studies, investigative interviewers trained in this protocol have questioned preschool-aged children who were suspected victims of child abuse. Five-year-olds were able to provide forensically important information in response to **open-ended questions**, and even three-year-olds were able to share information when invited to elaborate on an earlier response (Hershkowitz, Lamb, Orbach, Katz, & Horowitz, 2012). These findings suggest that central details (the "gist") of victimization experiences can be remembered well when they are elicited by nonsuggestive questioning.

After a child has recounted an experience in his or her own words and in response to open-ended questions, investigators may ask specific questions about the event. For example, if a child said that she was touched, a follow-up question might be "Where were you touched?" Although children tend to provide more detail in response to specific questions than to open-ended questions, the use of specific questions comes at a cost: Children are less accurate in answering specific questions. This difficulty is not restricted to very young children. After seeing a stranger in their classroom handing out candy the previous week, two groups of children (four- to five-year-olds and seven- to eight-year-olds) were asked specific, misleading questions (e.g., "He took your clothes off, didn't he?"). Older children were just as likely as younger children to assent to these suggestions (Finnila, Mahlberga, Santtilaa, Sandnabbaa, & Niemib, 2003), though suggestibility typically declines with age (e.g., Paz-Alonso & Goodman, 2016). Of course, most interviewers would never intentionally mislead a child, but they may have misinformation or suspicions that could color the nature of the questions they pose.

Children are less accurate in answering specific questions than more general queries

because specific questions demand precise memories of events that the child may never have encoded or may have forgotten (Poole, Brubacher, & Dickinson, 2015). Additionally, the child may answer a question that she or he does not fully understand in order to appear to be cooperative (Waterman, Blades, & Spencer, 2001). Finally, the more specific the question, the more likely it is that the interviewer will accidentally include information that the child has not stated. Specific questions can easily become suggestive.

A sizeable number of children experience multiple incidents of sexual abuse, and although the central features of the experiences may be constant, peripheral details may change. But before prosecutors can file multiple charges, they must provide evidence that reflects the critical details of each separate incident. In other words, the child has to "particularize" his or her report by providing precise details about each specific allegation. Can a child do this? Studies that examine children's recall of repeated events typically expose them to a series of similar incidents with certain constant features and some details that vary across episodes. Although source monitoring (identifying the source of a memory) improves with age (Quas & Schaaf, 2002), children often recall information from one event as having occurred in another (Brubacher, Glisic, Roberts, & Powell, 2011). In fact, exposure to recurring events is a double-edged sword: Repeated events enhance memory for aspects of the incident that are held constant but impair the ability to recall details that vary with each recurrence (Dickinson, Poole, & Laimon, 2005).

Investigative interviews are an essential part of child sexual abuse cases.

If they experience multiple incidents of maltreatment, children may be subjected to repeated interviews. One line of research has shown negative effects of repeated interviews on children's memory and suggestibility. In these studies, experimenters describe to children true and false events (e.g., in one famous study, children were told that their hand had been caught in a mousetrap), imply that the children experienced all of them, and tell the children that their parents or friends said the events had occurred. After repeated questioning, approximately one-third to one-half of pre-school-aged children provided additional details of the false events (e.g., Bruck, Ceci, & Hembrooke, 2002). A separate line of research has documented beneficial effects of repeated interviews, however. These studies found that children exposed to repeated interviews were not prone to errors. In fact, their memory improved with repeated interviews (e.g., Waterhouse, Ridley, Bull, La Rooy, & Wilcock, 2016).

What accounts for these conflicting findings? One hint comes from a study that varied the number of interviews and the nature of the questions asked (Quas et al., 2007). In this study, children played alone in a laboratory setting and were questioned either once or three times about what happened while they played. The questions were either biased (implying that the child played with a man) or unbiased. Children interviewed only once by the biased interviewer were most likely to claim they played with a man, and children interviewed on multiple occasions (regardless of the type of question asked) were less likely to do so. This suggests that biased interview questions can lead to false reports in a single interview (Goodman & Quas, 2008). Stated in another way, "When and how children are interviewed is at least as important for their accuracy as is how many times they are interviewed" (Goodman & Quas, 2008, p. 386). It also suggests that forensic interviewers must question children in developmentally appropriate ways, using evidence-based techniques, and more than once if possible. Unfortunately, widespread training has had only limited impact on the quality of interviews (Lamb, 2016).

A robust finding in cognitive psychology, termed the **reminiscence effect**, can explain why multiple interviews might be useful. When people attempt to remember pictures or events they viewed previously, they often report (reminisce) new information on each recall attempt, suggesting that recollection may be incomplete on the first telling but unrecalled information can be produced in later interviews. Reminiscence effects are facilitated by the use of open-ended questions that allow interviewees to provide information in their own words.

Repeated interviewing is necessary when an alleged victim is too distressed to provide useful information initially, when victims fail to disclose abuse that is subsequently documented by medical examinations or suspects' confessions, or when new evidence comes to light (La Rooy, Katz, Malloy, & Lamb, 2010). A reminiscence effect occurred when a victim of CSA, described in Box 5.3, was interviewed on multiple occasions.

Disclosure of Child Maltreatment

Children are often reluctant to disclose abusive experiences and may even deny them when asked. One study involved interviews of approximately 4,300 high school students, 45% of whom reported experiences of unwanted sexual abuse. Of these, only 65% of females and 23% of males had disclosed that abuse (Priebe & Svedin, 2008). Not surprisingly, disclosure of extra-familial abuse is more likely than disclosure of abuse within the family (London, Bruck, Wright, & Ceci, 2008). These data suggest that large numbers of children fail to disclose maltreatment when they are young and, therefore, that reported cases of CSA are the tip of a large iceberg (Ceci, Kulkofsky, Klemfuss, Sweeney, & Bruck, 2007). Disclosure is facilitated by supportive relationships and by other people's willingness to detect and report the abuse (Jones, Stalker, & Franklin, 2017).

Some studies have focused on what individuals remember about being maltreated. In fact, children can remember significant details of abuse experiences and, if asked directly, can describe them quite accurately. One team of developmental psychologists contacted approximately 200 adolescents and young adults who, during the 1980s, had been involved in a study of the effects of criminal prosecutions on victims of CSA (Alexander et al., 2005). Participants had been 3–17 years old at the time of the original data collection. All of them had been sexually abused. Upon renewing contact years later, psychologists provided a list of traumatic events (including CSA) and asked respondents to indicate which events happened to them and, among those events, which was the most traumatic. Respondents who designated CSA as their most traumatic experience were remarkably accurate in reporting details of their experiences. These data suggest that memory for emotional, even traumatic, victimization experiences can be retained quite well even decades after the events occurred.

The Case of the 14-Year-Old Sexual Assault Victim Interviewed Twice

BOX 5.3

A 14-year-old girl, whose identity cannot be disclosed for privacy reasons, reported to her mother that the mother's former partner had sexually assaulted her. Independent, external evidence supported her allegation. When prompted by the investigative interviewer who said, "My job is to talk to people about things that might have happened to them. It's important that you explain to me why you are here today," the victim recounted three different episodes of abuse, disclosing many details in response to open-ended questions. After that interview, the victim told her mother that she had forgotten to mention another abusive experience, so on the next day she was interviewed again, also in an open-ended question format.

Here is an excerpt of what she reported during the initial interview (in regular type) and what she reported for the first time during the second interview (**in bold type**):

It started when I was about eleven, going on twelve. **He was downstairs with my mum and then he came up to tuck us in like he usually does.** He was in my room. My sister fell asleep and then he took me into a different room. It started from there. He started feeling me. He touched my fanny (vagina) with his hands. He got his finger and rubbed it round my fanny. It was under my clothes. **He had clothes on...**

My mum had gone out. I was upstairs in my room. I think he told me to "get on the bed," so I did and then he started touching me again, and he tried to put his willy inside me, but he couldn't. He touched me with his hands and his willy. He put his hands on my fanny and in my fanny. He put his fingers inside me...

It was downstairs. I was doing my homework or something. He made me watch a video. He sat with me and we watched the video. It had people on it showing sex and things like that. **They had their clothes off. The willy was going in the fanny...**

One day he brought a video camera home. It was upstairs in the bedroom that was my mum's. He switched the video camera on. He told me to take my clothes off so I did. He said to "get on the bed," so I did. He had no clothes on either. He told me to pull his willy up and down. He tried to put his willy inside me again. It hurt. He was on top of me (adapted from La Rooy et al., 2010).

Notice that during the second interview, the girl provided information relevant to an entirely different episode of abuse and that she was able to give additional details about the incidents she had described previously.

CRITICAL THOUGHT QUESTION

What features of these interviews were crucial in allowing the victim to recall what had happened to her?

Still, a subgroup of abuse victims either forgets the abuse or remembers it poorly. Why do some maltreated people have full access to memories of those experiences and others have none? Processes that people use to regulate their emotions—in particular, their coping strategies—may be implicated (Harris et al., 2016). People who cope with maltreatment by trying to suppress, inhibit, or ignore their thoughts about it may weaken or even eliminate memories of those experiences over time. As a result, they may have memory deficits for these traumatic events.

The Child Witness in the Courtroom

Though most child maltreatment cases end in admissions of guilt or plea bargains, tens of thousands of children, often preschoolers, must testify in abuse trials each year. In one study, although only 18% of all CSA cases involved children five years old or younger, 41% of the cases that went to trial involved children of this age (Gray, 1993). Two questions arise: What is the effect on the child of having to discuss these issues in court and how do jurors weigh the testimony of a child witness?

Talking about victimization in a public setting may increase the trauma for many children. Sexual abuse victims are especially fearful of confronting the alleged offender in criminal court (Hobbs et al., 2014). Professor Gail Goodman and her colleagues examined the short- and long-term outcomes for children who testified in CSA cases, initially interviewing a group of 218 CSA victims when their cases were referred for prosecution (Goodman et al., 1992) and reinterviewing many of them 12 years later (Quas et al., 2005). The experience of testifying was quite traumatic for some children. They had nightmares, vomited on the day of their appearance in court, and were relieved that the defendant had not tried to kill them (Goodman et al., 1992). Twelve years later, when compared to a group of individuals with no CSA history, CSA victims who had been involved in criminal cases showed some long-term negative consequences. Most affected psychologically were those who were young when the case started, testified repeatedly, and opted not to testify when the perpetrator received a light sentence.

How do jurors perceive child witnesses? Do they tend to doubt the truthfulness of children's testimony, reasoning that children often make things up and leave things out? Or do they tend to believe children in this setting? In mock jury studies, child eyewitnesses are generally viewed as less credible than adult eyewitnesses (e.g., Pozzulo & Dempsey, 2009). But something quite different happens in CSA cases. Here, younger victims are viewed as *more* credible than adolescents because they are deemed more trustworthy and honest. In fact, laypeople believe that the "ideal" witness in a child sexual abuse case would be an 8-year-old and the least ideal would be a 12-year-old (Nunez, Kehn, & Wright, 2011). Jurors can recognize the effects of suggestive questioning; mock jurors who read a transcript of a highly suggestive forensic interview tended to discount the child's testimony (Castelli, Goodman, & Ghetti, 2005).

Procedural Modifications When Children Are Witnesses

Judges allow various courtroom modifications to protect children from the potential stress of testifying. One innovation is the placement of a screen in front of the defendant so the child witness cannot see him or her while testifying. This arrangement was used in the trial of John Avery Coy, who was convicted of sexually assaulting two 13-year-old girls. Coy appealed his conviction on the grounds that the screen deprived him of the opportunity to confront the girls face-to-face, a reference to the **confrontation clause** of the Sixth Amendment that guarantees defendants the right to confront their accusers. The right to confrontation is based on the assumption that the witness will find it more difficult to lie in the presence of the defendant. In a 1988 decision, the Supreme Court agreed with Coy, saying that his right to confront his accusers face-to-face

was not outweighed "by the necessity of protecting the victims of sexual abuse" (*Coy v. Iowa*, 1988).

But just two years later, in the case of *Maryland v. Craig* (1990), the Court upheld a law permitting a child to give testimony in a different part of the courthouse and have the testimony transmitted to the courtroom via close-circuit TV (CCTV). The law applied to cases where the child was likely to suffer significant emotional distress by being in the presence of the defendant. *Craig* thus modified the rule of the *Coy* case.

Proponents of CCTV claim that in addition to reducing the trauma experienced by a child, this technology will also provide more complete and accurate reports. Opponents claim that the use of CCTV violates the defendant's right to face-to-face confrontation of witnesses. Several studies have assessed the veracity of children who testify in and out of courtrooms and whether observers perceive differences in their credibility. A common finding is that children give more detailed statements when allowed to testify on CCTV (Goodman et al., 1998). Children also feel less nervous when allowed to testify outside of the courtroom (Landstrom & Granhag, 2010). On this basis, one might argue for its use in every case in which a child feels anxious about testifying. But things aren't quite so simple. Children who testify via CCTV or in pre-recorded videos are viewed less positively than children who testify in open court (Antrobus, McKimmie, & Newcombe, 2016). It seems that jurors want to see children in person in order to assess the truthfulness of their reports. Clearly, the impact of CCTV on jurors' decisions in CSA cases is complex. Perhaps it should be reserved for cases in which the prospect of testifying is so terrifying to children that they would otherwise become inept witnesses—or would not testify at all.

Judges make other accommodations when children must testify. In cases involving CSA, physical abuse, or adult domestic violence, a support person—typically a parent, guardian, or victim assistant—is almost always present with the child to decrease stress and ideally to increase accuracy and completeness. The effect may not be what the victim intended, however, as mock jurors deem child victims less accurate and trustworthy when a support person is present (McAuliff, Lapin, & Michel, 2015). A growing and controversial trend is to allow children to nuzzle with trained therapy dogs during testimony (Galberson, 2011).

Finally, we should note that although testifying has the potential to inflict further trauma on the child, it can be a therapeutic experience for some children (Quas & Goodman, 2012). It can engender a sense of control over events, and if the defendant is convicted, provide some satisfaction to the child. One 15-year-old girl said, "If I, as a young person, were a victim of a sexual abuse or rape case, I would *want* to testify before a full court. I might be scared at first or a little embarrassed, but I'd want to be present to make my assailant look like a complete fool. I'd want to see him convicted— with my own eyes. It would make me stronger" (quoted in Gunter, 1985, p. 12A).

Repressed and Recovered Memories

Retrieving memories over short time periods, as eyewitnesses must do, is a complex task. Yet it pales in comparison with retrieving memories that have been stored, and in some cases, forgotten, over lengthy intervals. Two basic processes need to be distinguished in understanding long-lost memories. The first is natural forgetting, which tends to occur when people simply do not think about events that happened years earlier. Just as you might have trouble remembering the name of your fourth-grade teacher, witnesses to crimes, accidents, and business transactions are likely to forget the details of these events, if not the entire event, after the passage of months or years. Such forgetting or misremembering is even more likely when the event is confused with prior or subsequent experiences that bear some resemblance to it. No one disputes the reality of natural forgetting.

Much more controversial is a second type of lost "memory"—the memories that are presumed to have been repressed over long time periods. This process involves events that are thought to be so traumatizing that individuals bury them deeply in their unconscious mind through a process of emotionally motivated forgetting called **repression**. For example, soldiers exposed to the brutal horrors of combat and individuals who experienced a natural disaster such as an earthquake are sometimes unable to remember the traumas they obviously suffered. In such cases, repression is thought to serve a protective function by sparing the individual from having to remember and relive horrifying scenes. These repressed memories sometimes stay unconscious, and hence forgotten, unless and until they are spontaneously recalled or retriggered by exposure to some aspect of the original experience. (The smell of gasoline might remind a soldier of the battlefield, or the sight of an unusual cloud formation might remind an

earthquake victim of the sky's appearance on the day of the disaster.) But the notion of repression is highly controversial; some suggest that repression has never been scientifically established, and that the inability to remember traumatic effects can be explained by ordinary forgetting.

A related unconscious process is **dissociation**, in which victims of abuse or other traumas are thought to escape the full impact of an experience by psychologically detaching themselves from it (Dalenberg et al., 2012). This process is believed to be particularly strong in children, who, because they are still forming integrated personalities, find it easier to escape from the pain of abuse by fantasizing about made-up individuals and imagining that the abuse is happening to those others. Many clinical psychologists believe that such early episodes of dissociation, involving unique ideas, feelings, and behavior, form the beginning of the altered personalities that are found in dissociative identity disorder.

Repressed Memories of Child Sexual Abuse

Most of the reports of repressed and recovered memories involve claims of CSA. The theory is that individuals (1) suffered sexual or physical abuse as children, often at the hands of parents or other trusted adults; (2) repressed or dissociated any memory of these horrors for many years as a form of unconscious protection; and (3) recovered their long-lost memories of the abuse when it was psychologically safe to do so.

A widely cited study suggests that it may be possible for people to forget horrible events that happened to them in childhood. Williams (1994) interviewed 129 women who had experienced well-documented cases of CSA. She asked detailed questions about the abuse experiences, which had occurred an average of 17 years earlier. More than one-third of the women did not report the abuse they had experienced in childhood. Of course, this does not prove that the forgetting was due to repression. It is possible that when the abuse occurred, the women were too young to be fully aware of it. Perhaps they were unwilling to report sexual abuse to an interviewer, who was a relative stranger, even if they did remember it. Yet reports of recovered memories accompanied by corroboration continue to surface (e.g., Colangelo, 2009), supporting therapists' claims about the veracity of these memories.

Repressed memories are sometimes recovered after a person has participated in "memory-focused" psychotherapy that applies techniques such as hypnosis, psychopharmacology, pressures to recall, and guided imagery, all in an attempt to help clients remember past abuse. Some therapists suspect clients of harboring repressed memories of abuse and ask the clients highly suggestive questions, such as "You show many of the signs of childhood sexual abuse; can you tell me some of the things you think might have happened to you when you were a very young child?" Interestingly, people who are likely to seek psychotherapy are also likely to believe that they experienced childhood trauma and abuse they cannot remember (Rubin & Boals, 2010). This finding suggests that some psychotherapy clients may be only too eager to have their suspicions confirmed. But many therapists will vouch for the veracity of recovered memories (Magnussen & Melinder, 2012), despite the fact that, as some maintain, "the belief that hidden memories can be 'recovered' in therapy should have been exorcised years ago" (Cara, 2014, p. 1).

Indeed, researchers and other clinicians question the validity of memories that resurface years after the alleged incidents, particularly after the individual has been in therapy (Patihis, Ho, Tingen, Lilienfeld, & Loftus, 2014). (These professionals are not denying the reality of CSA, of course. Not only does it occur, it is a very serious problem throughout the world, and children who were abused are at increased risk to suffer mental health disorders in adulthood.) They point out that most people who suffer severe trauma do not forget the event; in fact, some of them suffer intrusive recollections of it for years afterward. Skepticism is fueled by the fact that some alleged victims claim to have recalled traumas that happened when they were less than one year old. Nearly all research on childhood memory and amnesia shows this is not possible, for reasons related to neurological development.

The real question is whether allegations of child abuse that surfaced only after searching for them in therapy are trustworthy. In a clever study designed to compare memories of abuse recovered in therapy to memories recovered outside of therapy and memories never forgotten, Professor Elke Geraerts and her colleagues sought independent corroboration of the abuse from other people who were abused by the same perpetrator, individuals who learned of the abuse soon after it occurred, or from perpetrators themselves. They were able to corroborate 45% of the abuse memories that had never been forgotten, 37% of the memories that were recalled out of therapy, but 0% of the memories that were recalled in therapy (Geraerts et al., 2007).

Scientists now believe that there are at least two kinds of recovered memories of CSA: those that are gradually recovered in the context of suggestive therapy and those that spring up spontaneously without prompting or attempts to reconstruct the past. Memories recovered spontaneously can be more easily corroborated, suggesting that they are more likely to be genuine (Geraerts, 2012).

Importantly, there are also differences in the cognitive profiles of people who have these varying experiences (Geraerts et al., 2009). People who recover memories through therapy tend to have heightened susceptibility to constructing false memories, whereas those who recover abuse memories spontaneously are prone to forget previous incidents of remembering the abuse.

So what should we make of the recollection of past abuse events that a person claims to have repressed for years? Can we be sure that alleged abuses took place? Answers to these questions are vitally important to the criminal justice system where issues related to recovered memories can be contentious. Among the issues are the admissibility of recovered memory evidence, delayed disclosure of abuse, exaggeration of CSA-related symptoms, and the impact on juries of recovered memories.

Clearly, it is possible that given the right circumstances, people can spontaneously recall thoughts they had suppressed, and perhaps even whole experiences they had repressed, for many years. And just as clearly, it is possible that some recovered memories, especially those that appear to have been repressed for years and then recovered through aggressive "memory work" therapy are imagined or made up. Later, we examine other ways that false memories can be created.

Recovered Memories in Court

Legal cases based on recovered "memories" have typically involved claims of personal injury against wrongdoers—for example, adult daughters suing their fathers for alleged child sexual abuse and adults suing the Catholic Church, claiming they were abused by priests (Milchman, 2012). (The latter issue was depicted in the 2015 film, *Spotlight*.) These are civil lawsuits in which complainants must prove their case by a preponderance of evidence. Prosecutors rarely file criminal charges based on claims of recovered memories because they must prove the case beyond a reasonable doubt.

These cases can be quite contentious because the "victim" often has a close tie to the "defendant" and other family members may be forced to take sides, causing strain and animosity within a family. They can also be controversial because they concern events that were alleged to have happened in the distant past. For example, when Connolly and Read (2006) analyzed 2,000 claims of "historic" CSA—which they defined as two years or more between the end of the offense and the trial—they found that the mean age of the complainant at the time of the alleged abuse was 12.39, but the mean age at trial was 26.09, a difference of nearly 14 years. Jurors tend to be rather skeptical of recovered memory claims at trial (Bornstein & Muller, 2001), despite the fact that laypeople tend to believe traumatic memories can be repressed and then retrieved accurately in therapy (Patihis et al., 2014).

Jurisdictions have varying processes in place to deal with these issues. In some states, the statutes of limitations—the period during which a lawsuit can be pursued—have been extended for victims who claim they had forgotten the experiences or did not understand that they caused harm. Some states require corroboration of the abuse. In some jurisdictions, experts are allowed to testify about traumatic amnesia and recovered memories. So in many respects, the legal system's response to concerns about the validity of recovered memories mirrors the scientist-practitioner divide. Suffice to say, there are differences of opinion.

Creating False Memories

Before Bill O'Reilly—at one time, the highest rated host on Cable TV—was dismissed by Fox News for sexual harassment, he got himself into hot water of a different sort. He often said that he had been in a war zone or a combat situation during the Falklands War and that many people died. In actuality, he was at a violent protest, not on the Falkland Islands, and no one died. Was this an intentional fabrication to bolster his image of toughness and grit? Or was it a genuinely false memory? In recent years, many psychologists have used laboratory research and real-life cases to document how false memories can be created. There is now general agreement that given the right set of circumstances, people can create memories of incidents that never occurred.

One way that psychologists have been able to implant false memories is by enlisting the help of family members, who suggest to adult research participants that these relatives recall a fabricated event. In a now-classic study, Loftus and Pickrell (1995), with help from participants' relatives, constructed a false story that the participant had been lost during a shopping trip at the age of five, was found crying by an elderly person, and was eventually reunited with family members. After reading this story, participants wrote what they remembered about the event. Nearly 30% of participants either partially or fully remembered the made-up event, and 25% claimed in subsequent interviews that they remembered the fictitious situation.

Suggestive techniques leading to false memories can affect people in a variety of ways. They can change people's beliefs about themselves and others; inspire new, healthier habits; and affect daily behaviors. Falsely suggesting to people that they became sick, years before, after eating a particular food actually influenced their food choices. The suggestion deterred them from eating that food when it was offered (Geraerts et al., 2008). Scientists have now shown that people can be induced, via suggestion, to create false memories of committing serious crimes (theft, assault, and assault with a weapon) as adolescents. As Shaw and Porter (2015) noted, "imagined memory elements regarding what something *could* have been like can turn into elements of what it *would* have been like, which can become elements of what it *was* like" (p. 298). Some of the false memories were highly descriptive and multi-sensory (Shaw & Porter, 2015), supporting the contention that innocent people can be convicted because they confess to crimes they only *believe* they committed.

Psychologists have used other experimental procedures to examine the malleable nature of **autobiographical memory** (memory for one's past experiences). These include asking participants to imagine events that never occurred (Mazzoni & Memon, 2003) and doctoring family photographs by inserting childhood portraits to portray events such as hot-air balloon rides that never took place (Wade, Garry, Read, & Lindsay, 2002). Merely imagining or viewing a photo associated with a fabricated event can dramatically increase the rate of false memories. In one study, researchers provided false suggestions to adults about various school-related pranks (e.g., putting Slime on a teacher's desk in Grade 1 or 2). Some participants viewed group class photos from that time and others did not. The rate of false memory reports was substantially higher among participants who viewed the photographs (Lindsay, Hagen, Read, Wade, & Garry, 2004). This is concerning because some memory-focused therapists recommend that adults who think they have been abused should view family photo albums to cue long-forgotten memories of abuse.

Simply imagining an event from one's past can also affect the belief that it actually occurred, even when the event is completely implausible—for example, proposing marriage to a Pepsi machine (Seamon, Philbin, & Harrison, 2006) or shaking hands with Bugs Bunny at a Disney theme park (Braun, Ellis, & Loftus, 2002). (The Bugs Bunny character was created by Warner Brothers, not Disney.)

In studies using memory implantation or imagination inflation techniques, scientists have measured various aspects of autobiographical memories. These include the extent to which people say they "remember" the suggested experiences, agree that those experiences occurred, embellish them, and create a coherent story to explain them. When the results of several studies and more than 400 memory reports were analyzed together in a "mega-analysis," researchers determined that 30.5% of these reports met the definition of a false memory and another 23% involved accepting the suggested event as true to some degree. Thus, more than half the participants in these studies came to believe that they experienced a suggested, fabricated event (Scoboria et al., 2017).

How can we account for this? One possibility is **source confusion**. The act of imagining may make the suggested event seem more familiar, but that familiarity is mistakenly related to childhood memories rather than to the act of imagination itself. The creation of false memories is most likely to occur when people who are having trouble remembering are explicitly encouraged to imagine events and discouraged from thinking about whether their constructions are real.

Keep in mind that although false childhood memories can be implanted in some people, the memories that result from suggestions are not always false. Unfortunately, without corroboration, it is very hard to know whether someone is recalling an event from their past or reporting reconstructions that originated from other sources of information. These concerns led Scoboria et al. (2017) to write, "Even under highly controlled laboratory conditions, memory researchers struggle to define and observe memory." Problematically for our purposes, they continue, "How, then, can we expect therapists, forensic investigators…or jurists to be any better at this task?" (p. 159).

Summary

1. ***What psychological factors contribute to the risk of mistaken identifications in the legal system?*** Evidence produced by eyewitnesses often makes the difference between an unsolved crime and a conviction. In the early stages of a crime investigation, eyewitness accounts can provide important clues and permit suspects to be identified. But witnesses often make mistakes, and mistaken identifications have led to the conviction of numerous innocent people. Errors can occur at the moment the crime is committed or at any of the three phases of the memory process: encoding, storage, and retrieval. Furthermore, subsequent questioning and new experiences can alter what is remembered from the past.

2. ***What are the defining features of estimator, system, and postdiction variables in the study of eyewitness memory?*** In describing the factors that affect the reliability of eyewitness memory, psychologists distinguish (1) estimator variables whose impact on an identification can only be estimated and not controlled, (2) system variables that are under the control of the justice system, and (3) postdiction variables that correlate with the accuracy of an identification. Much recent research has focused on a particular set of system variables related to the way lineups are conducted.

3. ***How do jurors evaluate the testimony of eyewitnesses, and how can psychological research help jurors understand the potential problems of eyewitness testimony?*** Jurors are heavily influenced by the testimony of eyewitnesses, and they tend to overestimate the accuracy of such witnesses, relying to a great extent on the confidence of the eyewitness. To alert jurors to these problems, two types of remediation have been described (in addition to limiting eyewitness evidence when it was gleaned through suggestive procedures). In some

cases, psychologists testify as expert witnesses about the problems inherent in eyewitness memory. Laboratory evaluations of mock juries are mixed on whether such testimony properly sensitizes jurors to factors that affect an eyewitness's reliability. The other intervention involves the judge giving a "cautionary instruction," sensitizing jurors to aspects of the testimony of eyewitnesses they should consider. Data are mixed on its effectiveness.

4. *Can children accurately report on their experiences of victimization? What factors affect the accuracy of their reports? Are they likely to disclose abuse?* When children are questioned in a nonsuggestive manner and are asked open-ended questions, the resulting report will be more accurate than when suggestive interrogation procedures are used. Children are less accurate in answering specific question than more general questions, and sometimes recall information from one event as having occurred in another. Multiple interviews can facilitate memory recall under some circumstances. Most children are able to remember details of their maltreatment and describe them accurately, though victims who suppressed their thoughts about it may have memory deficits.

5. *Can memories of trauma be repressed, and if so, can these memories be recovered accurately?* Sometimes, memories of trauma are apparently forgotten and later recovered. When spontaneously recalled, such memories tend to be accurate. But when the recollections occur in the context of therapies that use suggestive memory retrieval techniques, their accuracy is suspect. Recent research shows that people can "remember" events that never happened, sometimes simply by imagining them. Litigation involving the recovery of repressed memories involves lawsuits brought by victims claiming that they were abused in the past.

Key Terms

absolute judgment	ecphoric experience	open-ended questions	retrieval
archival analysis	ecological validity	other-race effect	selective attention
autobiographical memory	encoding	photographic lineup	sequential presentation
cognitive interview	estimator variable	photospread	simultaneous presentation
confirmation bias	experimental methodology	physiognomic variability	source confusion
confrontation clause	experimenter bias	postdiction variable	storage
diagnosticity	field studies	post-event information	suggestive questions
dissociation	ground truth	relative judgment	system variable
double-blind testing procedures	in-group/out-group differences	reminiscence effect	unconscious transference
		repression	weapon focus effect
		retention interval	

6 Psychology of Victims of Crime and Violence

ORIENTING QUESTIONS

1. What is the frequency of crime victimization?

2. What types of research have psychologists conducted on victimization?

3. What factors predict the development of PTSD after being a crime victim?

4. What are the components of the battered woman syndrome?

5. What are the three major strategies that have been used to prevent sexual assault?

6. What are two types of sexual harassment recognized by the courts?

Perception of Those Who Experience Crime and/or Violence

One element of almost every crime is the presence of at least one victim. Even so-called victimless crimes—crimes such as prostitution, ticket scalping, and gambling—have victims, even if they do not immediately recognize it or would not describe themselves that way. The social burdens and psychological costs of these offenses—the squandering of a person's income as a consequence of the inevitable losses from habitual gambling or the physical abuse and underworld crimes that surround prostitution—are often delayed. Ultimately, however, society and individuals are victimized by these crimes.

Society has different reactions toward victims. While most individuals feel sympathy toward them, we also tend to question why they became victims, and sometimes we even blame them for their plight. One reason for this is the need to believe in a "just world." The thought of becoming victims ourselves is so threatening that we feel compelled to find an explanation for why other people are victimized (Lerner, 1980). These justifications often take the form of singling out victims as the primary cause of their own plight.

Such judgments are predicted by the perspective known as attribution theory, which originated with the work of Heider (1958). Heider stated that people operate as "naive psychologists"; they reach conclusions about what caused a given behavior by considering both personal and environmental factors. Generally, when considering someone else's actions, we use **dispositional attributions** that focus on the person's ability level, personality, or even temporary states (such as fatigue or luck) as explanations for the conduct in question. To explain a person's misfortune as the consequence of his

or her physical disabilities, lack of effort, or moral values reflects a kind of defensive attribution that places the responsibility for bad outcomes on the person rather than on the environment. Such reactions help shape our responses to victims. The norms of our society demand that we help others if they deserve our help, but if people are responsible for their own suffering, we feel less obligated to help them (Mulford, Lee, & Sapp, 1996).

The phrase *blaming the victim* was first popularized by Ryan (1970). He observed that people on welfare were often seen as lazy or shiftless and hence responsible for their fate. An extreme example of blaming the victim was offered by trial attorney Robert Baker, who represented O. J. Simpson in his civil trial for the wrongful deaths of Nicole Brown and Ronald Goldman. His opening statement for the defense included a scorching attack on Nicole Brown, whom he portrayed as a heavy-drinking party girl whose dangerous lifestyle often included companions who were prostitutes and drug dealers. Sometimes by implication and sometimes by direct comment, he communicated that she had many boyfriends and had had at least one abortion. As a trial observer noted, "it was as close to calling her a slut [as one could come] without using the word" (quoted by Reibstein & Foote, 1996, p. 64). Baker demeaned the victim for a reason, of course; he wanted to imply that a sordid lifestyle had led to her becoming involved with someone other than O. J. Simpson and that this supposed individual had killed her (Toobin, 1996). Simpson himself has echoed this claim, stating that he was angry at Nicole because, he felt, her careless lifestyle contributed to her being murdered.

A different example of "blaming the victim" may be seen in the wake of the worldwide economic recession of 2008 and the sluggish recovery of the U.S. economy with respect to reemploying many of those who had lost jobs in the recession. Losing a job is a traumatic life event that many would prefer to think could not happen to them. One way to perpetuate this belief is to conclude that those who lost jobs somehow "deserved" it, because they were less capable, industrious, or motivated. This actually combines two beliefs discussed in this book—belief in a just world and a tendency to blame the victim—that may be held to protect individuals from the frightening realization that they are also at risk of losing a job. Some would even extend this to believing that newly graduated college students or law students in 2015—many of whom did not have the benefit of pre-recession employment opportunities— were less deserving of being offered a job.

Types of Victims

There is no shortage of victims in our society. Estimates of the numbers of children who are sexually abused, adults who are battered by their partners, and women and men who are assaulted, robbed, or raped run into the millions each year.

The primary source of information on crime victims in the United States is the Bureau of Justice Statistics' National Crime Victimization Survey, which can be found at www.ojp.usdoj.gov/bjs/. Each year, data are collected from a national sample of households and individuals on the frequency and consequences of criminal victimization in the form of rape and other sexual assaults, robbery, theft, assault, household burglary, car theft, and so on. From these figures, one can calculate the rate of victimization nationwide. For example, it is estimated that in 2015, approximately 10 million households experienced at least one property crime, and 2.7 million individuals were victimized by crimes of violence. The overall rate of violent victimization has decreased substantially between 1993 and 2015, from a rate of over 75 per 1,000 to under 25 per 1,000 citizens (most of this decrease occurred between 1993 and 2000). Moreover, the majority of criminal victimizations are not reported to the police. In 2015, a total of 47% of those victimized by any violent crime (involving direct contact with persons) reported the offense to the police; this rose to 55% when the violent crime was more serious (e.g., robbery, aggravated assault, sexual assault). But even within these offenses, there was discrepancy in reporting to police: robbery and aggravated assault (62%), rape or sexual assault (32%), simple assault (42%). By comparison, 35% of those victimized by property crimes reported the

offense to police authorities. Based on these figures, we can conclude that there is good news (reported crime has dropped substantially in the last 20 years) and bad news (the majority of crimes are not reported by victims, making them difficult or impossible to investigate). Additional statistics on the frequency, consequences, and prevention of criminal victimization can be found at the National Center for Victims of Crime website (www.ncvc.org).

For other offenses, it is difficult to assess the frequency of victimization, but what we do know is that they happen all too often. Included here, for example, are acts of racial or religious discrimination in which the recipient is denied rights that are accorded to others. Homophobic attitudes, teasing, and bullying are frequently reported (Harris Interactive and GLSEN, 2005), and verbal and physical victimization based on sexual orientation has been related to posttraumatic stress symptoms (Dragowski, Halkitis, Grossman, & D'Augelli, 2011). We describe the story of three victims of apparent religious bias in Box 6.1.

The Harris survey (Harris Interactive and GLSEN, 2005) involved a nationally representative sample of 3,450 students ages 13–18 and a nationally representative sample of secondary school teachers. There were several major findings relevant to Lesbian/Gay/Bisexual/ Transgender (LGBT) students. Verbal or physical harassment was reported to be a common problem, with 65% of students indicating that they had been harassed during the last year because of appearance, sexual orientation, race/ethnicity, disability, or religion. A total of 39% reported such harassment due to their appearance, and 33% said they were harassed because of their actual or perceived sexual orientation. LGBT students were three times as likely to report feeling unsafe at school (22% vs. 7% of non-LGBT students), and 1.5 times as likely to have been harassed (90% vs. 62%). More teachers (53%) than students (36%) reported that they considered bullying or harassment to be a "serious problem" at their school.

In an even larger study of high school youth (Espelage, Aragon, & Birkett, 2008), investigators surveyed 13,921 high school youth from a Midwestern U.S. school district, identifying three groups: heterosexual, those questioning their sexual identity, and those identifying as lesbian, gay, or bisexual (LGB). They found that LGB youth were more likely to report high levels of depression or suicidal feeling and high levels of alcohol or marijuana use. But the questioning students actually reported the highest rates of teasing, drug use, and depression-suicidal feeling across all three groups. Positive school climate

BOX 6.1

The Murder of Muslim Students in Chapel Hill: A Hate Crime?

In the summer of 2013, Leah Barakat and his roommate, Imad Ahmad, were moving into a condominium complex in Chapel Hill, North Carolina, when Craig Hicks, another complex resident, stopped by to talk about parking rules: each resident received one space, with one more for a guest. Hicks, a gun collector in an open carry state, was known in the complex as fanatic about parking and noise, often talking to other residents about these matters.

A Muslim demonstrator holds up a poster with photos of Leah Barakat, his wife, Yusor Mohammad Abu-Salha, and her sister, Razan Mohammad Abu-Salha.

Barakat was scheduled to begin dental school at the University of North Carolina that fall. He was engaged to Yusor Abu-Salha, an undergraduate at North Carolina State. Both had grown up in observant Muslim families. Fine-boned and slender with wide-set eyes, Abu-Salha wore the hijab. Barakat's parents were immigrants from Syria; Abu-Salha's parents were Palestinians who had lived in Kuwait and Jordan. But both considered themselves to be integrated into U.S. culture in the Chapel Hill area.

Barakat tried to handle Hicks' complaints with reason. When Hicks came by to complain about parking, once while carrying a holstered gun, Barakat did not escalate the conflict. Instead, he obtained a parking lot map, marked the spaces that were permitted for parking, and gave this to his family and others who would visit him. Ahmad worried about Hicks, but Barakat would tell him that Hicks was "smart enough" not to do anything serious. Barakat and Abu-Salha were married in 2015 and moved into a new apartment together in the same complex.

Hicks had lost a job as an auto-parts salesman, worked at a deli, and subsequently took classes at a local community college in the hope of becoming a paralegal. He was not "on his way up," as were many of the graduate student residents of the complex. He was on his third marriage, estranged from his 20-year-old daughter from the first marriage, and presented himself on Facebook as a libertarian gun enthusiast who wanted all religions to "go away." Although people saw him as an angry bully, it came as a huge shock when he shot and killed Barakat, Abu-Salha, and her sister Razan on February 10, 2015.

Was this about parking? Was it an argument about noise and territory gone tragically wrong? Were Hicks' motivations fueled by cultural and religious bias, or was that most of the story? While this may not have been as simple as Craig Hicks hating Muslims, there is strong evidence that this played an important part in his violent rampage.

CRITICAL THOUGHT QUESTION

Why should an offense be considered worse because it is directed toward a member of a minority group?

and parental support protected the LGB and questioning youth against depression and drug use (Espelage et al., 2008).

Technological advancements and cultural changes have brought new forms of victimization to the fore. Identity theft, in which information about an individual's personal and financial life is stolen by computer hackers and then used fraudulently, has become a major fear of people in the 21st century. Cyberstalking is a technique favored by some sexual predators as a way to target victims. Dissemination of sexually explicit images without a person's consent has proliferated with the widespread use of cellphone cameras. Cyberbullying can occur through blogs, Facebook, and other social networking sites. The first-ever cyberbullying trial involved a Missouri woman, Lori Drew, who perpetrated a "mean-spirited Internet hoax" (Risling, 2008). Drew created a fictitious 16-year-old boy on MySpace and sent flirtatious messages to her 13-year-old neighbor, Megan Meier, who had apparently been mean to Drew's daughter. But after the "boy" dumped Meier, saying, "The world would be a better place without you," Meier hanged herself in her bedroom closet. Drew was convicted on three misdemeanor charges.

In addition to cyberbullying, psychologists have identified four other subtypes of bullying: physical, verbal, social exclusion, and spreading rumors (Wang, Iannotti, Luk, & Nansel, 2010). Males were more likely to be victims of all types of bullying.

This chapter concentrates on four types of victims and the effects of victimization on them: people who experience adversity and trauma in childhood, targets of sexual harassment, battered spouses, and victims of violent crime—particularly rape, the violent crime that has been studied most often. For each of these, the field of psychology has generated theory and research relevant to the laws and court decisions instituted to protect such victims.

Source: United States Postal Service

Identity theft warning.

The responses of the legal system reflect conflicting views in our society about the nature of victims, especially victims of sex-related offenses. For example, how extreme does a situation need to be before we conclude that sexual harassment exists, and how distressed does the response of the victim need to be? In the case of a battered woman who kills her batterer, will a jury accept a claim of self-defense? Why do as many as two-thirds of rape victims never report the attack to the police?

Adversity and Trauma in Childhood

There are two kinds of adverse experiences that are particularly important to consider in the course of human development. The first involves experiences that are emotionally painful and overwhelming for the individual's capacity to cope effectively. Examples include the abuse of children of various kinds (e.g., sexual abuse, physical abuse, severe neglect). The second refers to the kind of chronic adversity that results from influences such as poverty, racism, and other such longstanding, less acute but more pervasive aspects of the lives of some children. Although adversity may be accompanied by the development of coping strategies, it has a cumulative impact that can affect an individual's development and adult functioning in various problematic ways.

The relationship between traumatic childhood experiences and physical and emotional health outcomes in adult life is at the core of the landmark Adverse Childhood Experiences (ACE) Study. The ACE Study involved the cooperation of over 17,000 middle-aged (average age was 57), middle-class Americans who agreed to help researchers study the following nine categories of childhood abuse and household dysfunction: recurrent physical abuse; recurrent emotional abuse; contact sexual abuse; an alcohol and/or drug abuser in the household; an incarcerated household member; a household member who is chronically depressed, mentally ill, institutionalized, or suicidal; a mother who is treated violently; one or no parents; and emotional or physical neglect. Each participant received an ACE score in the range of 0–9 reflecting the number of such experiences he or she reported (Felitti et al., 1998).

The study has two major findings. First, adverse childhood experiences are much more common than anticipated or recognized—even in the middle-class population that participated in the study, all of whom were receiving health care via a large health maintenance organization (HMO). It is reasonable to assume that the prevalence of ACEs is significantly higher among young African American and Latino males—many of whom live with chronic stress and do not have a regular source of health care.

The study's second major finding is that adverse childhood experiences have a strong relationship to health outcomes later in life. As the ACE score increases, so does the risk of an array of social and health problems such as social, emotional, and cognitive impairment; presence of health-risk behaviors; disease, disability, and social problems; and early death. ACEs are strongly correlated with adolescent health, teen pregnancy, smoking, substance abuse, sexual behavior, the risk of revictimization, performance in the workforce, and the stability of relationships, among other health determinants. The higher the ACE score, the greater the risk of heart disease, lung disease, liver disease, suicide, HIV and STDs, and other risks for the leading causes of death (Felitti et al., 1998).

Consequences of Early Victimization

One might wonder whether early victimization experiences increase the likelihood of adolescent and adult criminality. Widom (1989, 1992) used court records to identify a group of 908 children in a Midwestern American city who had suffered abuse (i.e., sexual abuse or physical assault leading to injury) or severe neglect (i.e., inadequate food, clothing, shelter, or medical care) between 1967 and 1971. This "abuse/neglect" group was matched to a group of 667 children who had not been exposed to abuse or neglect but who were similar in gender, age, ethnicity, and family socioeconomic status. Matching the abused and nonabused groups on these variables was important because it enabled Widom to conclude that any differences between the groups in violent behavior in adolescence or adulthood were not due to differences in demographic characteristics.

Widom's analysis of police and court records showed that, as earlier research had suggested, abused or neglected children were significantly more likely than the comparison group to have been arrested for violent crimes as juveniles or as adults. In addition, the abused or neglected individuals were, on average, a year younger than comparison subjects at the time of their first arrest and had committed twice as many total offenses over the 15- to 20-year period studied. These differences were seen in boys and girls and in European Americans and African Americans; however, the relationship between abuse and violence was particularly strong among African Americans.

Follow-up data on this sample were collected 22–26 years after the abuse or neglect (Maxfield & Widom, 1996). The researchers found that by age 32, almost half of the abused/neglected group (49%) had been arrested for a nontraffic offense. This percentage was considerably greater than for the matched control sample (38%). Furthermore, victims of abuse and neglect were more likely than members of the control group to have been arrested for violent crimes, even after controlling for age, race, and gender.

Widom and her colleagues next examined the impact of sexual abuse, physical abuse, and neglect in childhood on adult mental health outcomes (Horwitz, Widom, McLaughlin, & White, 2001). Findings suggested that both men and women with histories of childhood abuse and neglect displayed increased levels of mood disorders and antisocial personality characteristics when compared with matched controls. The abused and neglected women also reported more alcohol problems than both the men and the matched groups. Although this line of research has suggested a strong association between childhood experiences of abuse and neglect and elevated levels of mental health problems in adulthood, these differences decreased after controlling for other stressful life events.

Widom and colleagues (Widom, Schuck, & White, 2006) next conducted a follow-up study with these data focusing on potential pathways between childhood victimization and violent criminal behavior, focusing on early aggressive behavior and problematic drinking. They found different pathways for men and women. For men, child maltreatment is related to later aggression toward others as well as later problematic alcohol use. In women, early victimization was directly related to later alcohol problems, which in turn were related to later violence toward others.

More recently, Kaplow and Widom (2007) identified documented cases of children who were physically and sexually abused and neglected prior to age 12 (N=496), and followed them into adulthood. Earlier onset of maltreatment predicted more symptoms of anxiety and depression in adulthood, even when controlling for gender, race, current age, and other abuse reports. Later onset of maltreatment was associated with more behavioral problems in adulthood.

A review of the empirical literature on the relationship between trauma, adverse experience, and crime (Zelechoski, 2016) concluded that it is not clear that trauma causes increased offense risk—but this is probably the result of not having the right kind of research to allow us to draw such a conclusion. (For obvious reasons, it would be unethical to deliberately expose children to trauma or adverse experience, and then follow up to determine whether the exposed children were more often involved in crime.) But Zelechoski also observed that there is very likely a relationship between trauma exposure and juvenile offending, and we are getting closer to understanding the precise nature of that relationship.

Some of the Widom studies may actually *underestimate* the risks created by childhood abuse. Only offenses that resulted in arrest or trial were included in the research linking early victimization to later criminality. Members of the abused/neglected group may have committed undetected or unreported crimes. These findings highlight the importance of considering early child abuse and neglect as part of a broader constellation of life stressors rather than isolating them as independent predictors of adult outcomes.

Violence, Crime, and Posttraumatic Stress Disorder

The dilemmas confronted throughout this book, especially the attempt to preserve both the rights of suspects and the rights of victims, come into sharp focus when we consider the victims of crime, particularly victims of violent crimes such as rape. Historically, society had not paid as much attention to crime victims as it should have. Their trial testimony was necessary to obtain convictions, but most of the legal rights formally protected in the adversarial system are extended to defendants, not victims. As a result, the needs and rights of crime victims have often been ignored.

This imbalance began to change in the late 1970s and early 1980s as victim advocacy groups, mental health professionals, police, and court officials all began to acknowledge the need to better recognize and serve crime victims. Several developments reflect the growing stature and influence of the victims' rights movement:

- The emergence of the interdisciplinary field of **victimology**, which concentrates on studying the process and consequences of victimization experiences and how victims (or *survivors*, which is the term preferred by many) recover
- The increasing availability of services to crime victims, including compensation and restitution programs, victim assistance programs in the courts, self-help programs, and formal mental health services
- The expanded opportunity for victims to participate in the trials of their victimizers through mechanisms such as victim impact statements

- The heightened focus on victims brought about by the establishment of professional journals (e.g., *Victimology*; *Violence and Victims*); organizations such as the National Organization for Victim Assistance; and commissions such as the American Psychological Association's Task Force on the Victims of Crime and Violence

For their part, psychologists have conducted research on and delivered clinical services to a diverse array of crime victims. Three areas have received special attention: the consequences of physical/sexual abuse on child victims; the role of violent victimization as a cause of psychological disorders, particularly posttraumatic stress disorder (PTSD); and the psychology of rape. We have discussed the consequences of child abuse earlier in this chapter; we now turn to the latter two topics.

Posttraumatic Stress Disorder

Individuals who suffer a severe trauma and, weeks or months later, continue to experience intense, fear-related reactions when reminded of the trauma, may be experiencing **posttraumatic stress disorder** (PTSD). By definition, such trauma must involve a threat of serious injury or death. We have seen vivid and disturbing examples of PTSD in soldiers returning from the wars in Vietnam, Iraq, and Afghanistan. As well, most instances of violent crime qualify as trauma severe enough to trigger PTSD in at least some victims.

The symptoms of PTSD fall into four broad classes under DSM-5. These symptoms must last longer than one month to qualify as PTSD:

1. Intrusion symptoms—the trauma is persistently re-experienced in at least one way that includes recurrent memories, nightmares, dissociative reactions, distress following trauma reminders, and physical reactions after trauma reminders;
2. Avoidance—persistent effort to avoid trauma-related stimuli after the event;
3. Negative alterations in cognitions and mood that began or worsened after the traumatic event in areas such as difficulty recalling the trauma, persistent negative beliefs, distorted blame, trauma-related emotions, diminished interest in activities, feelings of alienation, and constricted emotion; and
4. Alterations in arousal and reactivity in areas such as irritability, recklessness, hypervigilance, exaggerated startle reaction, and problems in concentration and sleep.

The case of Joe (Box 6.2) reveals how these diagnostic criteria apply to a real-life case. After being sexually abused by parents and older boys, Joe suffered a series of extremely traumatic events and other adverse experiences throughout his childhood and adolescence. Among the symptoms he experienced were difficulty sleeping, avoidance of people and human relationships, hypervigilance, and nightmares. The correct diagnosis and appropriate treatment resulted in some improvement, but Joe's life was still very difficult.

How common is PTSD? The National Comorbidity Survey Replication (NCS-R) involved interviews of a nationally representative sample of 9,282 Americans who were at least 18 years old. Using criteria from the American Psychiatric Association's DSM-IV-TR (2000), PTSD was assessed among 5,692 participants. The NCS-R estimated the lifetime prevalence of PTSD among adult Americans to be 6.8% (Kessler et al., 2005), with 3.6% prevalence for men and 9.7% for women.

Do military veterans experience PTSD more commonly than individuals in the general population? Using the figures described in the previous paragraph for comparison, the answer is yes. The National Center for PTSD (Department of Veterans Affairs, 2012) provides information about the rates of PTSD experienced by various population subgroups. Among military veterans, the lifetime prevalence rates for Vietnam veterans at the time of the National Vietnam Veterans Readjustment Study (1986–1988) were 30.9% for men and 26.9% for women, and the rates of PTSD experienced at the time of the study were 15.2% for men and 8.2% for women (Kulka et al., 1990). The time-of-study (1995–1997) PTSD prevalence rate for Gulf War veterans was estimated at 12.1% (Kang, Natelson, Mahan, Lee, & Murphy, 2003) and the time-of-study (2008) PTSD prevalence for veterans of Operation Enduring Freedom/Operation Iraqi Freedom at 13.8% (Tanielian & Jaycox, 2008).

About half of the women in the United States experience one or more traumatic events over the course of their lives, according to the findings from a sample of 10,000 participants (the National Comorbidity Survey Replication; Alegria, Jackson, Kessler, & Takeuchi, 2015). Such traumas include sexual assault and childhood sexual abuse, which women experience at higher rates than

The Case of Joe: Adverse Experience, Multiple Traumas, and Posttraumatic Stress Disorder

BOX 6.2

Joe's life of adverse experience and trauma began in his childhood. He reported that both of his parents sexually abused him. He added that his father once "split my skull … because I was in his way." Joe was a ward of the state and sent to an orphanage as a young child. When he was moved to a wing housing older boys, he said, "I was raped the first night. The rapes continued as long as I stayed at the home."

Today Joe is in his 50s. But the effects of his childhood are still with him. He suffers from posttraumatic stress disorder, which includes intense anxiety, nightmares, constant fear for one's safety, and always being on guard.

Joe attempted suicide for the first time when he was 12, and his adolescence included three more attempts. He ended up leaving the orphanage and hitchhiking around, but says that he still lived in fear, could never relax, and tended to sabotage himself. He tried working so much that he became "sort of a workaholic"; he tried relationships (including a marriage) that didn't work out, and always assumed that other people didn't want to be around him. He was on workplace disability, seeing one therapist after another (most frequent diagnosis: chronic depression), when eventually he came in contact with a psychiatrist who spent enough time with Joe and asked the right questions to diagnose Joe with PTSD. He improved a good deal, although he still experiences chronic insomnia. He works with male survivors of abuse online and an in-person support group.

Many think of PTSD as a disorder associated with war. Joe's case demonstrates that it can be associated with adverse experience and trauma at other stages of life as well (Kopfinger, 2007).

CRITICAL THOUGHT QUESTION

Does everyone exposed to life-threatening trauma develop PTSD? If not, why not?

SOURCE: Courtesy of Sunday News, Lancaster, PA.

do men (Tolin & Foa, 2006). Although men apparently experience serious trauma at a higher rate overall than women (Norris, Foster, & Weishaar, 2002), the diagnosis of PTSD occurs more often for women (an estimated 9.7%) than for men (3.6%) (Alegria et al., 2015). This is particularly important because PTSD has been related to suicidal ideation and suicidal attempts (Cougle, Resnick, & Kilpatrick, 2009).

The nature of one's trauma is an important consideration. Military service is a risk factor for PTSD, as may be seen by the elevated "current prevalence" rates cited earlier. The extent of physical injury during trauma also predicts whether PTSD symptoms will develop. Women who were physically injured by a trauma are more likely to develop PTSD symptoms than those who were not. Victims' perceptions of trauma are also important in determining the likelihood of PTSD. The victim's belief that his or her life is in danger and that he or she has no control over the trauma increases risk for PTSD (Tolin & Foa, 2006). One study suggests that cognitive processing during the trauma (such as persistent dissociation) and beliefs after the trauma (such as negative interpretations of trauma memories) predict PTSD symptoms to a greater degree than objective and subjective measures of the severity of the trauma (Halligan, Michael, Clark, & Ehlers, 2003).

Although traumas are unfortunate aspects of life, there is a reason to believe that PTSD—in some trauma victims, at least—can be prevented. For one thing, although many persons who experience severe trauma may develop **acute stress disorder** (trauma-related symptoms that last less than one month), most do not go on to develop PTSD. One reason may be that those experiencing trauma, but not PTSD, tend to receive high levels of social support from family, friends, or counselors immediately following the event (Grills-Taquechel, Littleton, & Axsom, 2011). Thus, providing immediate social support for trauma victims may prevent their experiences from progressing into PTSD.

Two other characteristics distinguish people who develop PTSD from those who do not. Individuals who suffer PTSD often perceive the world as a dangerous place from which they must retreat, and they come to view themselves as helpless to deal with stressors. If these two misconceptions could be eliminated, full-blown cases of PTSD might be prevented in many victims. Edna Foa (well known for her use of exposure therapy in treating PTSD, involving gradually "exposing" individuals to milder forms of the trauma and thereby reducing the associated anxiety) has developed a four-session prevention course designed to change these two misconceptions in women who have been raped or assaulted. Foa includes the following elements in her PTSD prevention course:

1. Education about the common psychological reactions to assault in order to help victims realize that their responses are normal
2. Training in skills such as relaxation so that the women are better prepared to cope with stress
3. Emotionally reliving the trauma through imagery-based exposure methods to allow victims to defuse their lingering fears of the trauma
4. Cognitive restructuring to help the women replace negative beliefs about their competence and adequacy with more realistic appraisals

Foa and her colleagues evaluated these procedures on 10 women who had recently been raped or assaulted and who completed the four-week course. Victims' PTSD symptoms were compared with those of 10 other women who had also been assaulted or raped but who did not take part in the course. At the times of two follow-up assessments (2 months and 5.5 months, respectively, after the assaults) victims who had completed the prevention course had fewer PTSD symptoms than control subjects who had not received treatment. Two months after their trauma, 70% of the untreated women, but only 10% of the treated women, met the criteria for PTSD (Foa, Hearst-Ikeda, & Perry, 1995). These results suggest that a brief program that facilitates emotionally re-experiencing trauma *and* correcting beliefs about personal inadequacy can reduce the incidence of PTSD.

Regardless of whether they result in PTSD, the frequency and consequences of traumatic and other adverse events may be greater than many have thought. As discussed earlier, the Adverse Childhood Experience (ACE) Study (Felitti et al., 1998) found a graded relationship between the number of categories of childhood exposure and each of the adult health risk behaviors and diseases that were studied (including alcoholism, drug abuse, depression, suicide attempts, smoking, poor health, multiple sexual partners and sexually transmitted disease, and severe obesity). Such adverse experiences have been linked to increased risk of PTSD (Breslau et al., 1998; Breslau, Chilcoat, Kessler, & Davis, 1999; Perkonigg, Kessler, Storz, & Wittchen, 2000; Roberts, Gillman, Breslau, Breslau, & Koenen, 2011) as well as anxiety disorders and lower intellectual functioning (Breslau, Lucia, & Alvarado, 2006).

The question of how such traumatic events affect the risk of antisocial behavior toward others, in the form of juvenile delinquency and criminal offending, is a complex one. First, as described earlier in the Widom research and Zelechoski summary, there is evidence of a relationship between trauma and posttraumatic symptoms in younger cohorts. When adolescents are studied, the evidence suggests that this relationship is similar to the adverse outcomes experienced by adults (Breslau et al., 2006; Cuffe et al., 1998; Giaconia et al., 1995), although adolescents may be particularly vulnerable because the context in which the trauma occurs (often the family) is where the individual continues to live in many instances. Second, such traumatic events are risk factors for antisocial behavior in youth, who have often been abused or neglected (Swahn et al., 2006). Consistent with this finding, Abram et al. (2004, 2007) have conducted large-scale studies of incarcerated youth and described a substantially elevated risk for traumatic history and psychiatric comorbidity (multiple diagnoses) among such youth. This suggests that early victimization experiences may be related to multiple psychiatric diagnoses and criminal conduct among adolescents.

Findings from the National Child Traumatic Stress Network Core Data Set (Dierkhising, Ko, Woods-Jaeger, Briggs, Lee, & Pynoos, 2013) documented various forms of trauma and adverse experience among youths (N=658) referred for trauma-focused treatment and recently involved with the juvenile justice system. These youth had experienced an average of 4.9 different types of trauma, including loss (61.2%), caregiver impairment (51.7%), domestic violence (51.6%), emotional abuse (49.4%), physical abuse or maltreatment (38.6%), and community violence (34%). These findings are noteworthy, in that adverse experience does not have to be life-threatening to function as a risk factor for juvenile delinquency (Maschi, Bradley, & Morgen, 2008).

Battered Spouses

Prevalence Rates

The extent of physical abuse directed toward spouses and romantic partners in American society is difficult to estimate, but many observe that it is extensive. It was once estimated that some form of physical aggression occurs in one-fourth to one-third of all couples (Straus & Gelles, 1988). More recent estimates suggest that 33% of men and 25% of women have been involved in a physically aggressive altercation, with the most severe episodes occurring in or near a bar for the men and in the home for the women (Leonard, Quigley, & Collins, 2002). One-year prevalence estimates for

violence against women in the United States have been described as 0.3–4% for severe violence and 8–17% for total violence. The prevalence of lifetime domestic violence ranges from 1.9% in Washington State to 70% in Hispanic women in the Southeastern United States (Alhabib, Nur, & Jones, 2010).

According to the National Intimate Partner and Sexual Violence Survey conducted by the Centers for Disease Control and Prevention (Black et al., 2011):

- 35.6% of women and 28.5% of men in the United States have experienced rape, physical violence, and/or stalking by an intimate partner in their lifetime.
- 24.3% of women and 13.8% of men have experienced serious physical violence by an intimate partner (e.g., hit with a fist or something hard, beaten, slammed against something) in their lifetime.
- 48.4% of women and 48.8% of men in the United States have experienced psychological aggression by an intimate partner in their lifetime.
- Most victims of rape, physical violence, and/or stalking by an intimate partner (69% of female victims; 53% of male victims) experienced some form of intimate partner violence for the first time before 25 years of age.
- Nearly 3 in 10 women and 1 in 10 men in the United States have experienced rape, physical violence, and/or stalking by an intimate partner and reported at least one adverse outcome from experiencing these or other forms of violent behavior in the relationship (e.g., being fearful or concerned for safety; experiencing PTSD symptoms or injury; needing health care, housing services, victim's advocate services, or legal services; contacting a crisis hotline; or missing at least one day of work or school).
- The majority of both female and male victims reported experiencing violence from one perpetrator.
- The majority of female victims reported that their perpetrators were male.
- Men and women who experienced rape or stalking by any perpetrator or physical violence by an intimate partner in their lifetime were more likely to report adverse consequences such as frequent headaches, chronic pain, difficulty with sleeping, activity limitations, poor physical health and poor mental health than men and women who did not experience these forms of violence. Women who had experienced these forms of violence were also more likely to report having asthma, irritable bowel syndrome, and diabetes than women who did not experience these forms of violence.

Although relationship aggression by women against men is as frequent as male-to-female aggression (Magdol et al., 1997), male aggression toward women is significantly more likely to result in serious injuries (Tanha, Beck, Figueredo, & Raghavan, 2010; Tjaden & Thoennes, 2000). In 2008, 40% of the women murdered in the United States were killed by their intimate partners, most of whom were male (Bureau of Justice Statistics, 2011). For this reason, most of the research on relationship aggression has concentrated on male aggression against female partners. This is also our focus in this chapter—although we note that *any* violence by one partner against another in an intimate relationship is very problematic.

Despite these disturbing statistics and the continuing research on relationship aggression, myths about battered women still abound. The mass media often pay little attention to this kind of violence (except in highly publicized cases). As a result of mistaken beliefs about battering, some professionals, such as physicians and police, fail to ask appropriate questions when a woman reports an attack by her intimate partner; arrest and prosecution of perpetrators of partner violence remain unpredictable; and protective restraining orders against batterers are often not consistently enforced.

Beliefs about Domestic Violence

Many misconceptions in this area were widely held at one time. For example, Follingstad (1994) pointed to misplaced ideas that those who are victimized by domestic violence are masochists, provoke such violence, are very rare, and are limited to specific socioeconomic and racial groups. This has changed some in recent decades. A survey regarding attitudes and beliefs shows that most respondents think of domestic violence as stemming from individual problems, relationships, and families, but not from the nature of our society. Not many think that women cause their own abuse—but about 25% believe that some women want to be abused, and most believe that women can end abusive relationships (Worden & Carlson, 2005).

Research conducted in some other countries has yielded results consistent with changing attitudes regarding domestic violence. For instance, a national study conducted in Singapore found that the overwhelming majority of the 510 participants disapproved of battery, and only about 6% agreed that under some circumstances, it is acceptable for a husband to use physical force against his partner (Choi & Edleson, 1996). Another study conducted with Israeli husbands found that the majority of participants (58%) agreed that "there is no excuse for a man to beat his wife" (p. 199). However, investigators also found that nearly one-third believed that wife beating is justified on certain occasions (e.g., unfaithful sexual behavior, disrespect of relatives) (Haj-Yahia, 2003). The attitudes of this latter group are consistent with the belief that women provoke domestic assaults and are treated in the way they deserve.

Misconceptions in this area have obscured several truths about the plight of battered women. Battered women face many real obstacles that make it difficult for them to leave their abusers, and when they do attempt to leave abusive relationships—as many women do—they often suffer further threats, recriminations, and attacks.

The Causes of Battering

What are the main risk factors for battering? Researchers who have studied the causes of battering have focused on the characteristics of the battering victim, the nature of violent intimate relationships, and the psychological makeup of those who batter.

We focus our coverage on individuals who batter. One review points to several risk factors in the lives of batterers as important (Rosenbaum & Gearan, 1999). Although such individuals come from all socioeconomic and ethnic backgrounds, they are more likely than nonbatterers to be unemployed, less well educated, members of minority groups, and of lower socioeconomic status. Individuals who batter tend to have been raised in families in which they either suffered physical abuse as children or observed an abusive relationship between their parents. Adolescents who later become batterers have experienced a higher rate of conduct problems and are more likely to have engaged in early substance abuse; early experiences with coercive or aggressive behavior may set the stage for similar strategies in adult relationships (Magdol, Moffitt, Caspi, & Silva, 1998). In addition, batterers usually have poor self-concepts, are not very good problem solvers, and often have limited verbal skills. They are prone to extreme jealousy and fear of being abandoned by their partners. As a result, they monitor their partners' activities closely and exert excessive control over their partners' whereabouts and activities. They overreact to signs of rejection and alternate between rage and desperation.

Although research suggests that batterers have many characteristics in common, not all batterers share a common profile. For instance, one comprehensive study revealed three distinct types of batterers: generally violent, psychopathological, and family-only (Waltz, Babcock, Jacobson, & Gottman, 2000). These groups were distinguished by the degree of violence within the relationship and the degree of general violence reported, as well as by personality characteristics. For instance, generally violent batterers displayed the highest levels of aggressive-sadistic behavior, psychopathological batterers exhibited more passive-aggressive/dependent characteristics, and family-only batterers displayed violent behaviors but generally did not hold violence-supportive beliefs and attitudes.

Findings from this study further indicated that differences in life experiences accounted for some of the variations in each of the group's behavior. For instance, when the generally violent batterers and the family-only batterers were compared, both groups were found to have experienced physical abuse as children, but significant differences existed in the frequency and severity of interparental violence witnessed; the generally violent batterers had witnessed more frequent and severe parental violence. These findings suggest that understanding the risk factors associated with batterers may be quite complex.

A number of specialized measures have been developed to assess the likelihood that an individual will commit violence toward an intimate partner and to identify intervention strategies to reduce this risk. One such measure was developed in the 1990s (the Spousal Assault Risk Assessment Guide, or SARA; Kropp, Hart, Webster, & Eaves, 1994, 1999). Subsequent specialized measures include the Domestic Violence Screening Instrument (Williams & Houghton, 2004) and the Ontario Domestic Assault Risk Assessment (Hilton et al., 2004). Using these measures helps mental health professionals understand the risk factors for domestic violence. For example, the SARA has four broad areas: *Criminal History* (e.g., past assault of family members, strangers or acquaintances), *Psychosocial Adjustment* (recent relationship or employment problems, substance abuse, suicidal or homicidal thoughts, psychotic symptoms, and personality disorders), *Spousal Assault History* (past sexual assault/sexual jealousy/use of weapons and/or credible death threats, recent escalation in frequency or severity of assault, extreme minimization or denial of spousal assault history), and *Alleged Current Offense Variables* (severe and/or sexual assault, use of weapons and/or credible threats of death, and violation of "no contact" orders). Using a structured professional

judgment measure like the SARA allows a clinician to make a well-informed judgment about the risk of future domestic violence. As may be seen, this probability depends upon a number of considerations; generally, the more extensive the individuals' history of criminal offending and domestic violence, the poorer their psychosocial adjustment, and the more serious the current alleged violence—the greater the risk of future violence toward an intimate partner.

The Cycle of Violence

Batterers are sometimes described as displaying a **cycle of violence** involving a Jekyll-and-Hyde pattern of emotional and behavioral instability that makes their victims all the more fearful of the battering they believe is inevitable. For example, a man may be loving and attentive to a woman's needs early in their relationship as he cultivates her affection and relies on her to satisfy his dependency needs; however, when disappointments or disagreements occur in the relationship, as they invariably do, a *tension-building phase* begins, characterized by increased criticism of the partner and perhaps even minor physical assaults.

This phase leads to a second stage in the cycle, an *acute battering incident*. By the time, this more serious form of aggression occurs, the woman has become too dependent on the man to break off the relationship easily. He has succeeded in controlling her behavior and curtailing her contact with friends who might have possibly helped extract her from her plight. The woman also tends to believe that if only she can find the right way to mollify the man's anger and reassure him of her faithfulness and obedience, he will change his behavior.

Following a battering, a third stage (called the *contrite phase*) occurs, in which the batterer apologizes for his attack, promises never to do it again, and persuades the woman that he is a changed man. Often this is an empty pledge. Indeed, sometimes the humiliation that the man feels over having apologized so profusely to his partner simply fuels more intense anger and violence, and the cycle repeats itself.

How pervasive is the cycle of violence? Even though Walker (1979) portrays it as a significant dynamic faced by battered women, she identified it in only about two-thirds of the 400 women she studied. What the *cycle of violence* may actually be describing is an underlying personality disorder that typifies a certain category of batterer.

According to Dutton (1995, 2000), a psychologist at the University of British Columbia, as many as 40% of batterers have the features of **borderline personality disorder**, a severe disturbance that is characterized by unstable moods and behavior. People with borderline personality disorder are drawn into intense relationships in which they are particularly unable to tolerate and modulate certain emotions. They are demandingly dependent, which causes them to feel easily slighted, which then leads to jealousy, rage, aggression, and subsequently, guilt. These emotional cycles repeat themselves, providing the underlying motivation for the cycle of violence. In addition to emotional instability, batterers are also prone to believing the worst about others; for example, they are quick to attribute hostile intentions to their partners (Eckhardt, Barbour, & Davison, 1998). Dutton traces the origin of this personality disorder to insecure attachments that batterers experienced with their parents, which later cause them to feel intense anger toward partners whenever things go awry in a relationship.

Responses to Victims of Battering

Although societal attitudes regarding domestic violence have changed, many still hold. The prevalence of many myths about battered women reflects the negative feelings toward crime victims described earlier in this chapter. A deep uneasiness, even hostility, exists toward some victims of battering (Plumm & Terrance, 2009; Russell & Melio, 2006; Walker, 2009). They may be seen as pathological "doormats" or delusional alarmists "crying wolf" over minor disagreements. When victims retaliate against their abusers—for example, when battered women kill their batterers—they may receive a greater punishment than men who commit acts with similar outcomes. But the question of whether women receive harsher sentences than men for domestic homicide is actually difficult to answer because the circumstances may be quite different.

Ewing (1987) surveyed the cases of 100 women who had killed their batterers. All were charged with murder, manslaughter, or some form of criminal homicide. Most (85) went to trial, and the majority of those who went to trial (65) were convicted. However, the great majority of those convicted (48) received prison sentences of 10 years or less. In addition, the homicide convictions of battered women are apparently reversed by appellate courts at a higher rate than other kinds of homicide convictions, with one review citing a 40% reversal rate in 239 appellate decisions involving battered women's homicide convictions, compared to the national average of under 10% for appellate reversals of homicide convictions (Maguigan, 1991).

Battering as a Legal Defense. Few battered women kill their attackers, but those who do receive a great deal of public scrutiny, usually in connection with their trial for murder. When they go to trial, battered women may use either insanity or self-defense as a defense.

At one time the experience of domestic violence was described as leading to **battered woman syndrome** (Walker, 2009) in many cases. This particular syndrome was hypothesized to contain several elements: learned helplessness about escaping the violence; social isolation and economic dependence on the abuser; increasing fearfulness about sustaining serious harm or being killed in the future; diminished self-esteem, guilt, and shame; and hypervigilance about signs of imminent violence. While these remain useful descriptive aspects of this particular form of trauma, legal proceedings call for a broader framework that is better supported empirically. This could be accomplished by an evaluation to determine whether the victim meets the criteria for PTSD under DSM-5.

How have claims of battered woman fared in court? Does making claims of self-defense advance the cause of victims who feel they are forced to retaliate after years of abuse? A battered woman's claim of self-defense often faces both legal hurdles and the skepticism of jurors (Russell & Melio, 2006; Schuller, McKimmie, & Janz, 2004). These obstacles might account for the fact that the majority of battered women charged with murdering their abusive partner are convicted.

Historically, a claim of **self-defense** has applied to homicides in which, at the time of the killing, the individual reasonably believed that he or she was in imminent danger of death or great bodily harm from an attacker. The defense was usually invoked in cases in which a specific attack or fight put defendants in fear for their lives; however, the typical case in which a battered woman relies on a theory of self-defense to clear her of charges of murdering her partner is much different. The violence does not involve a specific episode; rather, it is ongoing. The woman's response may seem disproportionate to what a "reasonable" person believes was necessary; often she kills her abuser while he is unarmed or sleeping.

Some mock jury research has explored the effect of expert testimony in a criminal homicide case in which the defendant was a battered woman (Schuller et al., 2004). Participants were more inclined to accept the woman's claim of self-defense when they heard from an expert testifying for the defense. In addition, compared to the no-expert control condition, those exposed to expert testimony on battered woman syndrome believed that the defendant's options were far more limited.

But any use of battered woman syndrome in legal proceedings provides a good example of how this (as well as other) mental health syndromes and diagnoses must be carefully considered for their relevance and accuracy in court. One particular critique of the battered woman syndrome notes that (a) there is no single profile of a battered woman; (b) there is no single profile of the effects of battering; (c) the name of the syndrome itself is vague, without a clearly defined set of criteria to operationalize it; (d) battered woman syndrome (or any other syndrome or diagnosis) is not uniquely relevant to understanding domestic violence; (e) the relevant information needed in such cases extends beyond the psychological impact of battering, to include the dynamics of violence, the victim's responses, the short- and long-term outcomes of these efforts, and the context of the abuse; and (f) the term creates an image of pathology (Dutton, 2014). Even a syndrome that appears directly relevant to the facts of certain kinds of cases, therefore, should be considered with healthy skepticism to avoid relying more than is justified on the presence of a syndrome.

No single set of reactions or characteristics can describe all victims of battering. Although battered women share the experience of being victimized by a violent partner, their reaction to this aggression and how they cope with it takes many different forms. This variation has implications for developing the most effective types of intervention for these women. Rather than assuming that they need traditional services such as psychotherapy or couples counseling, it would be more effective to provide battered women with special advocates who would support these survivors and help them find the resources they need to improve their lives. Just such an intervention has proved very effective in helping bring about changes that allowed battered women to become violence-free (Sullivan & Bybee, 1999). After providing battered women with a personal advocate who helped them gain access to the resources they needed to reduce their risk of partner abuse, Sullivan and Bybee found that the women who received advocacy services were twice as likely, during the two-year outcome period, to be free of any battering than were women without such a service.

The Psychology of Rape

Historically, rape victims have often been misunderstood, harassed, and neglected. For example, if a rape victim did not resist her attacker, people might incorrectly assume that she wanted to be raped. In contrast, people never raise the question of whether victims wanted to be robbed, or struck by a hit-and-run driver, or have their identity stolen. Furthermore, society struggles over how to deal with convicted rapists. Is rape a sexual crime or an act of violence? Is it the act of a disordered mind or a result of extraordinary circumstances?

Among serious crimes, rape is one of the most appropriate for psychological analysis (Allison & Wrightsman, 1993). Myths abound about the nature of rapists and their relationship to their victims. Rape is a crime in which the interaction between the criminal and his victim is crucial to addressing responsibility and blame (Stormo, Lang, & Stritzke, 1997). Since the 1970s, there has been a good deal of psychological research directed toward understanding sexual assaults (Beech, Fisher, & Thornton, 2003; Ellis, 1991; Hall & Hirschman, 1991; Jones, Wynn, Kroeze, Dunnuck, & Rossman, 2004; Marshall, Fernandez, & Cortoni, 1999). For these reasons, we devote special attention to the crime of rape and its victims. We focus on female rape victims, although the fact that men are also raped should not be overlooked.

Misleading Stereotypes about Rape

Various misleading stereotypes about rape, rapists, and rape victims may incorporate the inaccurate perceptions that victims cannot be raped against their will—or that reports of rape are often exaggerated or even faked. These mistaken perceptions contribute to creating a climate hostile to rape victims, often portraying them as willing participants in or even instigators of sexual encounters. In fact, these attitudes often function as self-serving rationalizations and excuses for blaming the victim.

Rape means different things to different people, and these differing attitudes and perceptions affect behaviors toward both offenders and their victims. Some respondents feel more empathy toward rape victims than others do. Empathy varies according to an individual's experience as a victim (or a perpetrator); women with victimization experience showed greatest empathy with female victims, while men with perpetration histories showed more empathy for a male perpetrator in one study (Osman, 2011). Thus, the measurement of attitudes about rape can clarify what different people believe about this crime, its victims, and its perpetrators.

What Accounts for Misleading Stereotypes about Rape?

Individuals who are unsympathetic to victims and tolerant of rapists also tend to endorse some of the misleading stereotypes about rape described earlier. According to a study involving 598 Minnesota adults (Burt, 1980), there are three factors that distinguish those who endorse such stereotypes about rape from those who do not:

1. *Adversarial sexual beliefs.* This refers to the belief that sexual relationships are fundamentally exploitive—that participants in them are manipulative, unfaithful, and not to be trusted. To a person holding this ideology, "rape might seem the extreme on a continuum of exploitation, but not an unexpected or horrifying occurrence, or one justifying sympathy or support" (Burt, 1980, p. 218).
2. *Acceptance of interpersonal violence.* This involves the belief that force and coercion are legitimate behaviors in sexual relationships, approving of men dominating women and overpowering passive partners with violence and control.
3. *Sex-role stereotyping.* This involves the extent to which an individual holds beliefs associated with traditional gender roles.

It is useful to consider how well this study, which was conducted nearly 40 years ago, continues to describe individuals who are more supportive of the act of rape. To what extent have societal attitudes changed over four decades? One review of more than 70 studies that employed a variety of measures of attitudes about rape supports Burt's conclusions (Anderson, Cooper, & Okamura, 1997). Those people who are more tolerant of rape are more likely to have traditional beliefs about gender roles, more adversarial

sexual beliefs, greater needs for power and dominance, and heightened expressions of aggressiveness and anger. This appears to be true for both men and women, although participants in one study did differ by gender on rape myth acceptance (women were lower), attribution of fault to society (women were higher), and feelings of anger and fear in response to rape (women were higher) (Earnshaw, Pitpitan, & Chaudoir, 2011). Other reviews are also consistent with the importance of rape supportive attitudes in the specific context of campus sexual assault (Lonsway, Cortina, & Magley, 1998; Suarez & Gadalla, 2010). Rape supportive attitudes in this context include the acceptance of rape myths, adversarial sexual beliefs, and hostile attitudes toward women (Widman & Olson, 2013). It would appear, therefore, that such attitudes have been a stable risk factor as part of sexual offending over a period of decades. They can also explain how some people perceive those who are raped and those who commit rape.

Facts about Rape

As we have seen, mistaken beliefs about rape are related to general attitudes toward law and crime. Still, what are the facts about rape? The United States has one of the highest rates of forcible rape among the world's industrialized countries, although there has been some decrease in the last decade. The FBI estimates that there were 79,770 forcible rapes reported to U.S. law enforcement in 2013. This figure is 6% lower than the 2010 estimate, and considerably lower than the figures for 2006 and 2001 as well (FBI, 2014).

A major study of rape, published in 2000, provided valuable data on women's reactions to this crime. The National Women's Study was organized and funded by several governmental agencies and crime victim organizations. A nationwide, stratified sample of 8,000 adult women and 8,005 adult men were interviewed over the telephone about their experiences as victims of sexual aggression. Since children and adolescents were excluded from the sample, the figures underestimate the total number of rapes, but they do give us an idea of the lifetime magnitude of the problem with adults. Among the study's findings are the following:

1. In the sample surveyed, 17.6% of all women said they had been the victim of rape or attempted rape sometime in their lifetime, and 21.6% of these

women reported that they were younger than 12 years old at the time of their first rape.

2. Among rape victims, 31.5% reported being physically injured during their most recent rape.

According to the National Violence Against Women Survey, almost 18 million women (and almost 3 million men) in the United States have been raped. Women who reported being raped as minors were twice as likely to report being raped as adults (Tjaden & Thoennes, 2006).

Women of all ages, social classes, and ethnic groups are vulnerable to rape. According to the 2010 National Criminal Victimization Survey, the high-risk age groups are children and adolescents for most offenses (sexual as well as nonsexual), as well as women ages 18–24 for rape (National Archive of Criminal Justice Data, 2010). According to the National Violence against Women Study, however, only 19% of the women and 13% of the men who were raped after age 18 said their rape was reported to the police (Tjaden & Thoennes, 2006). Several factors account for the low report rates (Feldman-Summers & Ashworth, 1981): Victims may be convinced that reporting won't help, that they would suffer further embarrassment as a result of reporting, and/or that law enforcement officers would not believe them. Many victims are afraid that the attacker will retaliate if charges are made, and these fears are sometimes justified. According to FBI figures, only about half of reported rapes result in an arrest, and if a male suspect is charged and the female victim is a witness at a trial, the defense attorney may challenge her testimony and attack her character.

Motivations and Characteristics of Rapists

Rape involves diverse combinations of aggressive and sexual motivation and deviant lifestyles for different offenders (Barbaree & Marshall, 1991). Experts have developed typologies of rapists, some proposing as many as nine types (Prentky & Knight, 1991), others as few as two or three (Groth, 1979) (see Robertiello & Terry, 2007 for a review of typologies described over the last 30 years). Most typologies have emphasized four factors that distinguish different types of rapists: (1) the amount and type of aggression the rapist used; (2) when the level of aggression was high, whether it heightened sexual arousal in a sadistic manner; (3) whether the

offender showed evidence of psychopathy or antisocial personality disorder; and (4) whether the offender relied on deviant sexual fantasies to produce sexual arousal. Theories of sexual aggression combine several causal factors into an integrated scheme that accounts for the different types of rapists (Sorenson & White, 1992).

From a somewhat different perspective, Ellis (1989) identified three theories of rape: the *feminist theory*, emphasizing rape as a pseudosexual act of male domination and exploitation of women (Donat & D'Emilio, 1992; White & Sorenson, 1992); the *social-learning approach*, suggesting that sexual aggression is learned through observation and imitation; and the *evolutionary theory*, holding that natural selection favors men who use forced sexual behavior (Buss & Malamuth, 1996).

These different approaches illustrate that rape cannot be easily explained by any one theory, and yet every one of these classification systems fails to capture the full spectrum of behaviors and motivations that typify rapists. Some of these systems are also limited by the fact that they are based on studies of convicted rapists who have been sentenced to prison. The majority of those who commit rape are never imprisoned for their offenses; fewer than 10% of rapes result in convictions or prison sentences (Frazier & Haney, 1996).

Box 6.3 describes allegations against Bill Cosby that he drugged and then sexually assaulted a number of women when they could not consent. How might the typologies discussed in this section apply to Mr. Cosby?

Acquaintance Rape and "Date Rape"

The 2000 National Women's Study reported that only 14.6% of rapes were committed by a stranger to the victim; 16.4% were committed by a nonrelative acquaintance; 6.4% by a relative; and 64% by an intimate partner. As of 2008, the estimate for sexual assault committed by a "known" individual was about 70% (Bureau of Justice Statistics, 2011). Among women 18–24 years old, whether enrolled in college or not, the percentage of sexual assaults in which the perpetrator knew the victim was approximately 80% (Bureau of Justice Statistics, 2014).

The closer the relationship between the female victim and the offender, in general, the greater the likelihood that the police were not told about the assault. When the offender was a current or former husband or

The Case of Bill Cosby: Prominence and the Accusation of Sexual Assault

BOX 6.3

Bill Cosby was an American icon. An early African American star of a television show (*I Spy*), the guiding force and star of one of the most popular television shows about a family (*The Cosby Show*), a talented and durable comedian—he was simply one of the most admired and influential individuals in the entertainment industry. So it came as a shock to many when Cosby was accused of drugging and sexually assaulting Andrea Constand in 2004 after inviting her over to his home. Constand was a Temple University employee; Cosby received his undergraduate degree from Temple and served for a number of years on Temple's board.

The shock grew as a number of women with similar stories came forward. These stories involved being drugged and sexually assaulted by Mr. Cosby. How accurate were they? Why had the women not reported

Bill Cosby

these encounters to the police? How is it possible that so many sexual victimizations had reportedly occurred without criminal prosecution?

Some answers to these questions may emerge in the wake of a second trial following the June 2017 mistrial in Montgomery County, Pennsylvania. Mr. Cosby is criminally charged in the Constand case. Prosecutors and Cosby's defense attorneys have sparred over whether the testimony of women other than Constand should be admitted at trial. One prosecutor described Cosby as showing a "lifetime of sexual assault on young women" and sought to introduce the testimony of these women to show a pattern of behavior. Defense attorneys questioned the memories and motives of these possible witnesses.

Because Cosby was a trusted and admired figure in American culture, and because this behavior (if described accurately) was so abusive and destructive, there has been a great deal of media coverage in this case. Because he is also an individual of considerable wealth, he can afford a vigorous defense that involves questioning the memories and motives of his accusers. This played out in the media over a period of years, and it was not clear until 2016 that these accusations would ever lead to criminal prosecution. Now that they have, the importance of the questions of prior behavior and possible patterns has become very clear.

CRITICAL THOUGHT QUESTION

What are the advantages and disadvantages of admitting evidence concerning the history of previous allegations of sexual assault by the alleged perpetrator? Of admitting previous allegations of sexual assault made by the alleged victim?

boyfriend, about three-fourths of all victimizations were not reported to police. When it was a friend or acquaintance, most sexual crimes (61% of completed rapes, 71% of attempted rapes, and 82% of sexual assaults) went unreported. But when the offender was a stranger, a different pattern emerged. A total of 54% of completed rapes, 44% of attempted rapes, and 34% of sexual assaults were not reported to the police—meaning that the majority of all forms of sexual assault *were* reported (Bureau of Justice Statistics, 2002).

In general, date rapes differ from sexual assaults by a stranger in several ways. They tend to occur on weekends, between 10:00 P.M. and 1:00 A.M., and they usually take place at the assailant's home or apartment. Date rapes tend to involve situations in which both the attacker and the victim have been using alcohol or drugs but they are less likely to involve the use of weapons; instead, the date rapist employs verbal threats and physical strength.

Consequences of Being Raped

Rape victims suffer physical injuries, emotional pain and humiliation, and sometimes-severe psychological aftereffects. Recovery from the trauma of rape can be very slow, and victims often describe a sense that they will never be the same again. Providing psychological assistance to rape victims is of utmost importance.

The consequences of being raped have received increased attention through a number of highly publicized cases in which women have come forward to report their experiences. As these cases have unfolded in the public eye, sexual aggression has become a topic of increased discussion among men and women. Highly publicized reports such as the accusations of multiple women that comedian and actor Bill Cosby drugged and sexually assaulted them (see Box 6.3) have helped to focus this nation's attention on matters of sexual conduct and on the plight of the victims of sexual aggression.

One part of this discussion has been a debate about whether the names of victims of sexual assault should be made public. The tradition in this country has been to protect the identity of rape victims by not using their names in media coverage. Still, in some cases, both television and online reporting break with this tradition and publish the name of the accuser. Defenders of this practice argue that not naming rape victims perpetuates the stigma of having been raped, making it more difficult in the long run for victims to come forward and confront their attackers. Critics claim that publishing the victim's name invades the individual's privacy and perhaps adversely affects her future. According to the National Women's Study, most rape victims prefer not to have their names published; over three-quarters of the respondents said they would be less likely to report a rape if they knew their names would be made public.

How Do Victims React to Being Raped?

Rape is a form of severe trauma that can lead to the experience of PTSD (American Psychiatric Association, 2013). Those with PTSD have been exposed to at least one serious traumatic event (actual or threatened death, serious injury, or sexual violence). They experience at least one of the following "intrusion symptoms:"

- Recurrent, involuntary, and distressing memories of the traumatic event
- Recurrent distressing dreams about the event
- Reactions in which the individual feels or acts as if the event were recurring
- Intense or prolonged psychological distress at exposure to cues that symbolize the event
- Physiological reactions to cues that symbolize the event.

Those with PTSD also experience persistent avoidance of stimuli (e.g., memories, thoughts, or feelings; people, places, or activities) associated with the traumatic event. There are two or more of the following symptoms of altered mood:

- Inability to remember an important aspect of the event
- Persistent and exaggerated negative belief (e.g., "nobody can be trusted," "I am bad")
- Persistent negative emotional state (e.g., fear, anger, guilt)
- Markedly diminished interest or participation in significant activities
- Feelings of detachment or estrangement from others
- Persistent inability to experience positive emotions

Finally, as evidenced by two or more of the following, those with PTSD show changes in arousal and reactivity associated with the traumatic event:

- Irritable behavior or angry outbursts with little provocation
- Reckless or self-destructive behavior
- Hypervigilance
- Exaggerated startle response
- Problems with concentration
- Sleep disturbance

But not all those who are victimized by sexual assault develop PTSD. There is a range of responses in terms of severity. Although these responses may not combine to justify a full diagnosis of PTSD, there are a number of commonly experienced emotions (e.g., guilt, embarrassment, fear, distrust, sadness, vulnerability, anger, lack of control, numbness, confusion, shock) and symptoms (e.g., nightmares, flashbacks, depression, concentration problems, anxiety, disturbance in eating and sleeping, substance use) on the part of those victimized by sexual assault (National Sexual Violence Resource Center, 2010).

There was once an attempt to describe trauma symptoms experienced by rape victims in terms of emotional responses, disturbances in functioning, and changes in lifestyle (Burgess & Holstrom, 1974). This specific description was termed **rape trauma syndrome**. Contemporary thinking would probably avoid such specific classification for some of the same reasons that battered woman syndrome (discussed earlier) is problematic. We know that those who experience multiple traumas are more likely to have various kinds of adverse reactions. Women who have been sexually assaulted in the past or who were sexually abused as children are two to three times more likely to suffer a subsequent sexual attack than women without prior sexual victimizations (Nishith, Mechanic, & Resick, 2000; Wasco, 2004). Although the reasons for the heightened risk are not clear, one possibility is that some women who have been victimized before are slower to recognize when they are at risk and therefore are more likely to remain in situations where they are vulnerable (Wilson, Calhoun, & Bernat, 1999). Women with more than one sexual victimization across their childhood and adult years are more likely to report unplanned and aborted pregnancies (Wyatt, Guthrie, & Notgrass, 1992).

But unless responses are in the area of sexual functioning, it is hard to know whether they were caused (or worsened) by the sexual assault, or by other influences such as other nonsexual traumatic events. Some responses are directly related to sexual functioning, however, so the link is clearer. In one study, women (N=175) who were sexually abused in adulthood were more sexually dissatisfied and nonsensual than women with no history of sexual abuse. Additionally, women with a history of sexual abuse as a child or as an adult were less satisfied with their most recent sexual relationship than women with no history of abuse. These women also tended to have a higher number of unsafe sexual partners (Bartoi & Kinder, 1998). Another

study of women who had been sexually assaulted (Wolf, 2009) included adult women (N=64) who were six months post-assault, and found that following a sexual assault, women commonly find themselves struggling with posttraumatic stress symptoms and experience difficulty in coping with normal daily activities. Those with strongly supportive relationships had less severe posttraumatic stress symptoms and were able to function better in daily activities. Unfortunately, however, many women did not receive this kind of support.

The impact of rape has been described sequentially (Ellison & Buckhout, 1981) as beginning with the attack and lasting a few hours or a day. During this acute phase, the primary needs of the victim are to understand what is happening, regain control over her life, predict what will happen next, and communicate her feelings to someone who will listen without passing judgment. At this point, police officers investigating the crime can either help or hinder the victim, as can medical personnel. For example, a pelvic examination and the collection of any semen samples are necessary at this point because it is unlikely that the suspect can be prosecuted in the absence of such evidence. But the examination may cause a resurgence of the initial feelings of disruption, helplessness, hostility, and violation—a reaction known as **secondary victimization**. In fact, negative experiences with legal and medical authorities have been shown to increase rape victims' symptoms of PTSD (Campbell et al., 1999).

Within a few hours or days of the attack, many victims slip into a period of false recovery. Denial occurs: "I'm OK; everything is the same as before." Then a secondary crisis occurs, in which some of the earlier symptoms such as phobias and disturbances in eating and sleeping are again experienced. Because of increased public awareness of the needs of rape victims, rape crisis centers have been established in many cities. These centers provide crisis counseling to victims. Most follow up with at least one further interview (usually by phone), and a third of their clients have from two to six follow-up interviews. The crisis center also checks for pregnancy and sexually transmitted disease.

Whether individuals acknowledge a previous sexual assault makes a difference; unacknowledged victims were nearly twice as likely to report having experienced an attempted rape during the six-month follow-up period (in part because they also reported more risk factors, such as hazardous alcohol use and continuing in their relationship with the assailant) (Littleton, Axsom, & Grills-Taquechel, 2009).

The long-term consequences of rape are also concerning. Although specific counseling for sexual assault is available, there is strong evidence for the effectiveness of certain kinds of more general interventions for trauma. There are various theories regarding how PTSD develops, including cognitive (Ehlers & Clark, 2000), schema (Horowitz, 1986), and multiple representation (Dalgleish, 2004). But one of the best-researched approaches to effective trauma treatment has been termed prolonged exposure (Foa & Kozak, 1986). In its current version, this approach includes *in vivo exposure* (real-life confrontation with feared stimuli, undertaken with low risk of harm—for example, post-assault fear of leaving home might be addressed with the goal of taking regular walks), *imaginal exposure* (imaging the feared stimuli), and *processing* (immediately following the imaginal exposure, discussing the experience of revisiting the trauma memory—but focusing on new learning and changed beliefs). There have been 25 randomized controlled trial studies supporting the effectiveness of prolonged exposure in reducing trauma symptoms, both acute and chronic, with rapid change and large effects still maintained at one-year follow-up (McLean & Foa, 2011). An optimal treatment strategy, therefore, might involve both counseling on the sexual assault itself and prolonged exposure to treat the trauma symptoms.

Providing social support is another helpful intervention. The therapeutic power of social support may derive in part from the fact that women, in particular, tend to react to stress by seeking opportunities for attachment and caregiving—or what psychologist Shelley Taylor has termed the *tend-and-befriend* response (Taylor et al., 2000). (Men, on the other hand, are more likely to respond to stress with the well-known "fight-or-flight" strategy.) Therefore, it might be especially useful to female crime victims to have ample opportunities for social support so that their preference to be with others in times of need can be fully addressed.

Rape Trauma in Court. Psychologists, along with psychiatrists and other physicians, testify as expert witnesses in rape trials, especially about the nature and consequences of rape trauma (Melton et al., 2007). This testimony is best-supported when presented as an example of PTSD if the individual meets PTSD criteria, similar to that experienced by veterans of combat, survivors of natural disasters, and victims of other violent crimes. The expert can be of special use to the prosecution in those trials in which the defendant admits that sexual intercourse took place but claims that the woman was a willing participant; evidence of rape trauma can be consistent with the complainant's version of the facts. In addition, jurors are often not familiar with the reactions that rape victims frequently experience (Borgida & Brekke, 1985), so psychological experts can educate the jury. Courts around the country are divided, however, on the admissibility of such testimony, and the resulting controversy has generated considerable debate.

The main argument against admitting expert testimony on a disorder as specific as rape trauma syndrome is as follows: The psychological responses of rape victims are not unique to rape and are not uniform, so it is impossible to say with certainty that a woman exhibiting any given set of responses has been raped. Therefore, a psychologist should not be allowed to testify that a woman is suffering from rape trauma syndrome because to do so is tantamount to telling the jury that she has been raped, which should remain a matter for the jury to decide. Many courts also reject expert testimony on rape trauma syndrome on the ground that the reliability of the syndrome has not been established.

Preventing Rape

As we learn more about the frequency and consequences of rape, a primary goal of concerned citizens, law enforcement officials, and social scientists has been to develop effective interventions for preventing rape. Three basic strategies have been emphasized: (1) training potential victims how best to protect themselves against rape, (2) designing effective treatment for offenders so that they do not repeat their crimes, and (3) emphasizing the collective responsibility of both men and women to communicate more openly, seek affirmative consent for sexual behavior, identify high risk situations, and intervene to deter behavior that might be sexually coercive. We observe that the third strategy is increasingly advocated on contemporary college campuses, where the first strategy is perceived as unfairly making women (more often victimized by sexual assault) responsible for their safety, and using the second strategy is generally

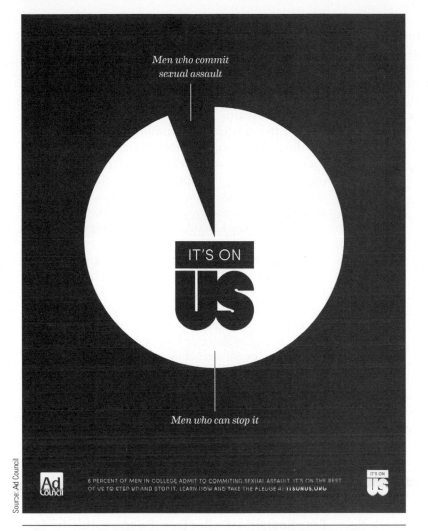

Source: Ad Council

It's On Us, a public service campaign, aims to reduce sexual violence against women on college campuses.

Kelley, 1985) found that women who did not resist a rape attack were twice as likely to suffer a completed rape as women who tried to protect themselves. But though fighting back was more likely to result in rape avoidance, it was also associated with increased physical injury when a weapon was present. Screaming and fleeing when confronted with a weapon was associated with less severe sexual abuse than were pleading, crying, or reasoning.

As we have already seen, national surveys suggest that the majority of college women who have been sexually assaulted were acquainted with their assailants before the assault. Research has also uncovered several risk factors associated with sexual assault, including using alcohol and drugs. Several colleges and universities have incorporated this information about risk factors into rape prevention programs aimed at changing attitudes about sexuality, challenging rape myths and sex-role stereotypes, and improving women's coping responses in potentially dangerous situations.

In the typical rape prevention program, participants discuss several facts and myths about rape, recognize the risks associated with heavy use of alcohol, practice resisting pressure for unwanted sexual activity, and role-play other strategies for protecting themselves. The programs try to help women change behaviors and to dispel the notion that victims cause sexual assault. They also strive to minimize the blaming of women that can occur following sexual victimization. One study (Orchowski, Gidycz, & Raffle, 2008) investigated the impact of a sexual assault risk reduction program with a self-defense component for 300 college women. Using a placebo-control group, the study indicated that this program was effective in increasing levels of self-protective behaviors, self-efficacy in resisting against potential attackers, and use of assertive sexual communication over a four-month period, as well as reducing the incidence of rape among participants over the two-month follow-up. Another study of 500 college

not indicated because of the small number of college students who have previously been convicted of sexual assault. Each will be discussed.

Training Potential Victims to Reduce the Risk of Rape. If a woman finds herself in a situation in which a man begins to sexually assault her, what should she do? Should she scream? Should she fight back? Should she try to reason with him? Or should she submit to the attack, especially if the assailant has a weapon? There is no uniformly correct response, just as there is no one type of rapist. However, on the issue of passive compliance, a Justice Department survey of over a million attacks (quoted in Meddis &

women who received a comparable sexual assault risk-reduction program also found an increase in self-protective behavior displayed by program participants during the six months following completion. In this study, however, there were no significant differences between participants and controls in rates of sexual victimization, assertive communication, or feelings of self-efficacy (Gidycz, Rich, Orchowski, King, & Miller, 2006).

Designing Effective Treatments for Individuals Who Rape.

Society is rightfully concerned about the likelihood of sex offenders repeating their crimes. In some states, men convicted of sex crimes are required to complete a sex-offender treatment program before being considered for parole. In such programs, the offender must acknowledge responsibility for his actions and participate in special treatment programs (Glamser, 1997).

The treatment of rapists can involve psychological, physical, and medical procedures; in many treatment programs, different interventions are often combined. In programs outside the United States, neurosurgery and surgical castration have been used, but their effectiveness is unclear. Because of the ethical controversies that surround these procedures, few experts advocate their use in the United States (Marshall, Jones, Ward, Johnston, & Barbaree, 1991).

In the United States, it is not uncommon for antiandrogen drugs to be prescribed to sex offenders in order to reduce their sex drive, a procedure sometimes referred to as **chemical castration**. The most common treatment involves giving offenders a synthetic female hormone, MPA, which has the trade name of Depo-Provera. MPA decreases the level of testosterone in the body, thereby decreasing sexual arousal in most men; however, the drug has also been associated with a number of negative side effects, including weight gain, hair loss, feminization of the body, and gall bladder problems.

Anti-androgen treatments have problems other than negative side effects. The rate of men dropping out of such treatment prematurely is very high, and failure to complete treatment is one of the strongest predictors of recidivism for sex offenders (Larochelle, Diguer, Laverdiere, & Greenman, 2011). In addition, the treatment does not always reduce sexual arousal and sexual offenses. In some men, arousal is not dependent on their level of testosterone, so the drugs have little effect on their sexual behavior. This is related to the fact that rape is often an act of violence,

not of inappropriate sexual arousal; consequently, drugs aimed at reducing sexual desire may be pointing at the wrong target. Even if the drugs inhibit sexual appetites, they may not control violent behavior. Hence, they would not meaningfully control these offenders.

Another major approach to treating aggressive sexual offenders involves combining several behavior therapy techniques into an integrated treatment package designed to increase offenders' self-control, improve their social skills, modify their sexual preferences, and teach them how to prevent relapses of their offenses. These programs are usually situated in prisons, but they have also been implemented in the community.

These integrated programs employ a wide range of treatment techniques. Sex education and training in social skills are common ingredients because of the widespread belief that sex offenders are often socially incompetent. Biofeedback and aversive conditioning are often used to decrease inappropriate sexual arousal and replace it with arousal to nonaggressive sexual cues. Existing programs appear to be able to produce short-term decreases in recidivism, but long-term improvements have been difficult to achieve. As a result, relapse prevention techniques (which have proved useful in the treatment of drug addictions and cigarette smoking) are incorporated into many programs. Programs with a cognitive-behavioral orientation have shown effectiveness in reducing subsequent sexual offending against children (Beggs & Grace, 2011).

Emphasizing Collective Responsibility for Preventing Sexual Assault.

The third major strategy for preventing sexual assault has been implemented primarily on college campuses over the last decade. In certain respects, this strategy may be seen as an extension of changing views on sexual assault. There is far less tolerance for sexual misconduct generally, as we discuss in the next section. Consent is no longer assumed from the absence of "no"—many colleges have implemented policies requiring clear consent by both parties at each stage of a sexual encounter. Making women (who are more likely to be victimized by sexual assault on a college campuses) primarily responsible for their own safety, it has been suggested, is not only ineffective but insulting.

Certainly there are some major challenges to developing university policies that minimize the risk of sexual assault while respecting the privacy of those involved in sexual behavior. For example:

- Investigating sexual assault would typically fall under the jurisdiction of local police, with defendants prosecuted within the criminal justice system. But many universities have taken on the responsibility of investigating and adjudicating reports of sexual misconduct—meaning that campus police, offices of student life, and committees that may be composed of faculty members and administrators are tasked with doing what seasoned police investigators and prosecutors do in the criminal justice system. Such university officials have far less experience in these areas.
- Many college undergraduates are between the ages of 18 and 22, legally adults but often dependent on their families for financial support. Students who are accused of sexual assault may contact their families; parents, in turn, contact college leaders, who feel pressure to support those reportedly victimized *and* be fair to those who are accused.
- Younger college students who are experiencing less supervision having left home, have easier access to drugs and alcohol, and are actively exploring their own sexuality may become involved in situations in which they consent to sex but later regret it, other situations in which they are uncertain (and subsequently believe they did not consent to sex), and yet others in which they clearly did not consent (e.g., they were coerced) or could not consent (e.g., they were unconscious).

Some of these are complex, while others seem straightforward. (Unconscious or extremely inebriated individuals obviously cannot give consent.) How have universities, using this "collective responsibility" strategy, attempted to minimize the risk of sexual assault while respecting the privacy of their students?

In a large study of campus sexual assault funded by the National Institute of Justice, several investigators (e.g., Krebs, Lindquist, Warner, Fisher, & Martin, 2007) conducted the Campus Sexual Assault (CSA) Study, which gathered data on different kinds of sexual assault experienced by university students, with the primary goal of informing the development of intervention strategies. Investigators surveyed over 6,800 undergraduate students (5,466 women and 1,375 men). They reported that 13.7% of undergraduate women had experienced at least one completed sexual assault since entering college, with 4.7% the victims of physically forced sexual assault, 7.8% sexually assaulted when they were incapacitated after voluntarily consuming drugs and/or alcohol, and 0.6% sexually assaulted when they were incapacitated after having been given a drug without their knowledge. Self-reported rates of sexual assault victimization and perpetration among males were very low. There were several implications of this study for the "collective responsibility" strategy. The first involves the role of voluntarily consumed drugs or alcohol, which were implicated in the majority of the reported sexual assault. Considering this, it should be the responsibility of the entire college community—men and women; students, administrators, and faculty—to strive to ensure that alcohol is used responsibly, that individuals do not drink to the point of disabling intoxication, and that there are multiple mechanisms for intervening should this occur (e.g., the person is accompanied home by friends, escorted by campus police). Second, the low rate of endorsement of any kind of sexual assault by men may indicate that some men view sexual behavior differently—and might be more likely to assume that the absence of protest, even from an individual who was very intoxicated or unconscious—would nonetheless serve as agreement to have sex. If this is true, then education programs focusing on the importance of affirmative consent, the influences that can preclude it, and the potential consequences for assuming consent when it has not been given should be part of student orientations, websites that are important to read, and public service messages.

The U.S. Congress passed the Campus Sexual Violence Elimination Act ("Campus SaVE Act") in 2013. This legislation is intended to address the needs of victims of sexual assault on university campuses by mandating certain protections for students (e.g., increased reporting of crime statistics). Universities are required to create a plan to prevent sexual violence, to detail the procedures taken after a sexual assault is reported, and to inform reported victims of their rights and resources (Schroeder, 2014). Hopefully the combination of changing values, relevant law, and campus action under the collective responsibility strategy will substantially reduce the rate of campus sexual assault in the coming years.

Sexual Harassment

Even though *sexual harassment* has been a significant problem in educational and work environments for many years, the term itself was not coined until 1974. At that time, a group of women at Cornell University, after becoming aware that several of their female colleagues had been forced to quit because of unwanted advances from their supervisors, began to speak out against such harassment (Brownmiller & Alexander, 1992). Also in the early 1970s, the U.S. Equal Employment Opportunity Commission (EEOC) emerged as a major tool for redressing sexual harassment by employers.

Defining Sexual Harassment

U.S. federal law defines harassment as follows: Unwelcome sexual advances, requests for sexual favors, and other verbal or physical conduct of a sexual nature constitute sexual harassment when (1) submission to such conduct is made either explicitly or implicitly a term or condition of an individual's employment, (2) submission to or rejection of such conduct by an individual is used as the basis for employment decisions affecting such individual, or (3) such conduct has the purpose or effect of unreasonably interfering with an individual's work performance or creating an intimidating, hostile, or offensive working environment (16 Code of Federal Regulations Section 1604.11).

Some of the studies described in this section use the term *sexual harassment* to mean unwanted sexual attention. But sexual harassment also has a specific meaning under the law, as we see in the previous paragraph. Title VII of the Civil Rights Act of 1964 prohibits discrimination in the workplace because of a person's gender. It therefore provides the legal basis for banning sexual harassment, although there is continued confusion about the nature of sexual harassment. Such questions can be clearly answered with the kind of workplace harassment training described by the U. S. EEOC (2016).

In educational settings, sexual harassment is subject to Title IX of the Education Amendments of 1972 (Title IX) regarding sexual harassment. Revised guidance issued by the U.S. Department of Education (2001) reaffirms that a school should recognize and effectively respond to sexual harassment of students as a condition of receiving federal financial assistance. This is based on the legal authority indicating that sexual harassment of students can be a form of sex discrimination under Title IX. The U.S. Supreme Court has held (in *Gebser v. Lago Vista Independent School District*, 1998) that an educational institution in which an instructor sexually harasses a student may be liable for monetary damages, and further (in *Davis v. Monroe County Board of Education*, 1999) that such monetary damages may apply if one

student sexually harasses another student. The liability set forth in the *Gebser* and *Davis* decisions is limited to private action for monetary damages. However, *Gebser* also gives federal agencies like the Department of Education the authority to enforce Title IX even when such monetary damages would not be justified.

There are certain differences between men and women in how sexual harassment is perceived. For instance, according to a meta-analysis on this topic (Rotundo, Nguyen, & Sackett, 2001), the female–male difference was larger for behaviors that involve hostile work environment harassment, derogatory attitudes toward women, dating pressure, or physical sexual contact (areas in which there were gender differences about what constitutes harassment) than sexual propositions or sexual coercion (topics upon which both men and women seem to agree as they relate to sexual harassment).

One problem with the federal definition of sexual harassment is that it leaves key terms such as *unwelcome* and *unreasonably interfering* open to varying interpretations. When men and women differ in their evaluations of potentially harassing interactions, women are more likely than men to classify a specific act as harassment (Rotundo et al., 2001). Who, then, determines when an act is harassing—the alleged victim, the alleged perpetrator, or an outside, "neutral" observer?

A large-scale survey of men and women serving in the U.S. military (1,764 men; 4,540 women; Settles, Buchanan, Yap, & Harrell, 2014) addressed the issues of perpetrator characteristics (sex and rank) and outcomes (psychological distress, role limitations, and work satisfaction). Results indicated that whether women who were harassed found this conduct distressing depended upon whether it was frightening—but men who were harassed found it distressing regardless of whether it was frightening. Having a perpetrator who was male or higher status was more likely to make the behavior frightening to women. But the relationship between frightening appraisals and more psychological distress, more role limitations, and less work satisfaction was stronger for men than women. The investigators considered these results in terms of sexual harassment as a form of dominance, concluding that serious and more frightening harassment was distressing to both genders—but less serious harassment was more frightening and otherwise consequential to men. This is consistent with the results of an earlier meta-analysis (Blumenthal, 1998), reporting that both men and women were more likely to perceive behavior directed by someone of higher status at someone of equal or lesser rank in the workplace as harassment than if such behavior occurred between peers.

When psychologists study the way individuals define sexual harassment, they usually do this by presenting participants with a set of facts and asking them whether they believe those facts indicate that sexual harassment occurred. In some studies, the subjects read a summary of the facts; in others they watch or listen to a taped description of the events. For example, Wiener and his colleagues conducted a complex experiment that simultaneously assessed the impact of observers' gender and sexist attitudes on perceptions of allegedly harassing behavior in two workplace situations (Wiener, Hurt, Russell, Mannen, & Gasper, 1997). They classified participants as being either high or low in *hostile sexism* and *benevolent sexism*. Hostile sexism involves antipathy toward women, reflecting a belief that males are superior to women and should be dominant over them. Benevolent sexism is an attitude of protection toward women; it reflects a belief that as the "weaker sex," women need to be shielded from the world's harshness.

In addition to finding that females were more likely than males to find that sexual harassment had occurred in these two situations, Wiener et al. (1997) examined the impact of participants' attitudes on their perceptions of sexual harassment. They predicted that those high in hostile sexism would be less inclined to conclude that sexual harassment had occurred. The results supported their prediction. Participants high in hostile sexism were less likely than those who scored low on this dimension to find that the defendant's behavior constituted sexual harassment.

The courts, following federal guidelines, have recognized two types of sexual harassment. The *quid pro quo* type involves sexual demands that are made in exchange for employment benefits; it is essentially sexual coercion. **Quid pro quo harassment** is seen in an implicit or explicit bargain in which the harasser promises a reward or threatens punishment, depending on the victim's response (Hotelling, 1991). When a teacher says to a student, "Sleep with me or you fail this course," it qualifies as *quid pro quo* sexual harassment (McCandless & Sullivan, 1991).

The second, more common type of harassment, usually referred to as **hostile workplace harassment**, involves demeaning comments, acts of touching or attempted intimacy, or the display of provocative photographs or artwork. Under Title VII, it is illegal for employers to create or tolerate "an intimidating, hostile, or offensive working environment." In the 1986 case of *Meritor Savings Bank v. Vinson*, the U.S. Supreme Court recognized for the first time that sexual harassment creating a hostile work environment violates Title VII. Although evidence of repeated offensive behavior or behavior of a severe nature is usually required for the plaintiff to prevail, the effects of such harassment need not "seriously affect [an employee's] psychological well being" or lead the plaintiff to "suffer injury" to constitute *hostile workplace* harassment (*Harris v. Forklift Systems, Inc.*, 1993; see Box 6.4).

Prevalence Rates

Several cases involving sensational charges of sexual harassment have received widespread attention and focused awareness on the problem of sexual harassment. A well-known case involved the four-year legal battle in which Paula Jones, a former Arkansas state employee, charged that then-governor Bill Clinton pressured her to perform oral sex in a Little Rock hotel room. Although he admitted no wrongdoing and refused to apologize to Jones, President Clinton eventually paid her $850,000 to drop the lawsuit. The consequences of the case went well beyond this, however, in that Clinton's apparently deceitful testimony in the Paula Jones case was a primary impetus for his eventual impeachment.

Talk show host Bill O'Reilly was accused of subjecting the former producer of his television show, Andrea Mackris, to "unwanted sexual conduct" and "a hostile work environment" by detailing his sexual fantasies during multiple phone calls (Spilbor, 2004). About two weeks after the suit was filed and without acknowledging culpability, O'Reilly agreed to pay Mackris approximately $2 million to settle the case (Kurtz, 2004). In April 2017, O'Reilly was dismissed from his position at Fox after a *New York Times* article reported that Fox had paid over $13 million to settle cases with other women employed by Fox who had also accused him of sexual harassment. In a similar vein, former Fox talk show host Gretchen Carlson filed suit against Roger Ailes, the head of Fox News, claiming that her June 2016 firing came after Mr. Ailes reduced her role on shows and paid her less because she refused a sexual relationship or sexual banter with him. Mr. Ailes subsequently resigned from Fox News, followed less than a year later by Mr. O'Reilly.

The Case of Teresa Harris: Sexual Harassment on the Job

BOX 6.4

Teresa Harris was the rentals manager at Forklift Systems in Nashville. Her boss (the company president) made a number of suggestive and demeaning comments to her. At first she tried to ignore him, and then she confronted him. He promised to stop, but a month later, in public, he asked whether she had slept with a client to get his account. This was the last straw; after working there for two years, Harris quit. She sought relief from the EEOC and the courts, claiming that her boss's behavior had created a hostile workplace. She asked for back wages as part of the litigation.

When she did not receive satisfaction from the lower courts, she brought her appeal to the U.S. Supreme Court, which agreed to hear the case because different circuit courts had been inconsistent in their decisions in such cases. Some courts had adopted a subjective approach, focusing on the impact of the alleged harassment on the plaintiff. Others, taking a more objective approach, had asked whether a reasonable person would have found the environment abusive. Another question involved the degree of impact. Was it sufficient that the environment interfered with the complainant's work performance, or was it necessary for "psychological injury" to have occurred? Sexual harassment can produce psychological damage—but should plaintiffs be forced to prove that they were psychologically harmed in order to persuade a jury that the sexual harassment has occurred?

The unanimous decision of the Court, announced by Justice Sandra Day O'Connor, was in favor of Harris and held that it was not necessary for plaintiffs to prove that they had suffered psychological injuries. The Supreme Court decision listed several criteria by which to decide whether an action constitutes sexual harassment, including the frequency and severity of the behavior, whether the behavior was physically threatening or humiliating, and whether it would unreasonably interfere with an employee's work performance.

Prior to this decision there was controversy about whether to assess potentially harassing behavior from the perspective of a "reasonable man," "reasonable person," or "reasonable victim" (Gutek & O'Connor, 1995; Wiener & Gutek, 1999). Justice O'Connor's opinion suggested that if conduct was not sufficiently severe and pervasive that it created an "objectively hostile" work environment as defined by a *reasonable person*, then it was not sexual harassment. The Court's decision reflected an intermediate position; harassment was no longer defined solely by the individual doing the harassing, or the individual who was receiving it.

CRITICAL THOUGHT QUESTION

If you had been Justice O'Connor trying to determine whether a workplace environment was "objectively hostile," would you have selected the perspective of "a reasonable man," "a reasonable victim," or "a reasonable person"?

How frequent is sexual harassment? Research has suggested that 50% of women will experience some form of sexual harassment in the workplace over the course of their working careers (Ilies, Hauserman, Schwochau, & Stibal, 2003) and 15% of men will also experience some form of workplace sexual harassment (U.S. Merit Systems Protection Board, 2016). In workplace environments that are predominantly male, the rates of such harassment have been estimated to be even higher, ranging from two-thirds or more of women and one-third of men (Antecol & Cobb-Clark, 2001; Department of Defense, 2004; Department of Defense Inspector General, 2005; Hansen, 2004).

A large meta-analysis (Ilies, Hauserman, Schwochau, & Stibal, 2003) used 86,000 respondents from 55 samples to estimate that 58% of women report having experienced potentially harassing behavior, and 24% report having experienced sexual harassment at work. A survey of 480 nursing students and faculty found that women were more likely than men to experience mild or moderate forms of sexual harassment (e.g., teasing, attempts to initiate romantic relationships). However, men were more likely to experience severe types of sexual harassment (e.g., intimate touch, forcing the respondent to touch someone else in an intimate way) (Bronner, Peretz, & Ehrenfeld, 2003).

Andrea Mackris accused Bill O'Reilly of sexual harassment; Talk show host Bill O'Reilly.

A recent broad survey of workplace harassment conducted by the U.S. Equal Employment Opportunity Commission (2016) yielded a number of relevant conclusions about the current status of this form of harassment:

Workplace Harassment Remains a Persistent Problem. Almost one-third of the approximately 90,000 charges received by EEOC in 2015 included an allegation of workplace harassment.

Workplace Harassment Too Often Goes Unreported. Common workplace-based responses by those who experience sex-based harassment are to avoid the harasser, deny or downplay the gravity of the situation, or attempt to ignore, forget, or endure the behavior. About three-fourths of those who experienced harassment never discussed it formally with anyone at work, citing fear of having their report disbelieved, their claim not acted upon, being blamed, or being the victim of social or professional retaliation.

There Is a Compelling Business Case for Stopping and Preventing Harassment. In 2015, the EEOC by itself recovered $164.5 million for workers alleging harassment. Those who experience workplace harassment can suffer mental, physical, and economic harm. The environment created by this behavior can also affect other workers, and decrease productivity, increase turnover, and harm reputations. Outcomes of such harassment include difficulties such as anxiety, depression, and post-traumatic stress symptoms (Willness, Steel, & Lee, 2007) that may persist beyond a year after the occurrence of the harassment (Munson et al., 2000). It may have negative consequences in the workplace: less commitment to and satisfaction with work, poorer productivity, and greater likelihood of leaving the job (Cogin & Fish, 2009; Langhout et al., 2005; Lapierre, Spector, & Leck, 2005).

Leadership and Accountability Are Critical. Workplace culture has the most influence on whether harassment is frequent or minimal. Such leadership includes providing effective harassment prevention and a workplace environment in which harassment is not tolerated.

Training Must Change. Much training over the last three decades has been delivered with the goal of avoiding legal liability. Effective training must be part of a broader culture that does not condone harassment, should be tailored to specific work staff and environment, and should include middle managers and immediate supervisors. Promising modified training approaches include "bystander intervention training" and "workplace civility training."

It's on Us. Workplace harassment may be reduced through this kind of campaign, which was originally devised to reduce sexual violence in campus settings. It incorporates the idea that students, faculty, and campus staff should all be part of the training and the campaign, distributing the responsibility far beyond those who are the immediate victims of sexual violence or harassment. This kind of campaign, consistent with the "collective responsibility" strategy described in the last section, has yet to be implemented with respect to sexual harassment in the workplace, but shows considerable promise.

Applying Psychological Knowledge to Detecting Harassment

Psychological approaches contribute to our understanding of sexual harassment in two other ways. First, some psychologists have attempted to predict when sexual harassment will occur. Other psychologists have tried to determine the likelihood of a favorable outcome in litigation when a person who alleges sexual harassment files a complaint. We consider these issues next.

When and in what environments is sexual harassment more likely to occur? Pryor, Giedd, and Williams (1995) proposed that certain individuals are inclined toward behavior that would be sexual harassment and that the norms in specific organizations function to encourage the expression of harassment. For example, a workplace that permits its employees to display highly sexualized material in their work areas may encourage harassment on the part of a worker who, in another environment, would not exhibit such behavior. Similarly, a company that provides sexually oriented entertainment at office parties or has work-related parties that exclude one gender is expressing a norm that gives tacit approval to at least some forms of harassment.

One study (Begany & Milburn, 2002) suggested that authoritarian personality characteristics (such as a belief in obeying authority above all else) predicted men's self-reported likelihood of engaging in sexual harassment; men who reported higher levels of authoritarian characteristics are more likely to engage in sexual harassment. Other personality characteristics have also been associated with a greater propensity for sexual harassment, including more traditional beliefs about women's roles, more negative attitudes toward women, and less concern with social desirability (Driscoll, Kelly, & Henderson, 1998). Men who are higher in hostility, particularly toward women, are more likely to engage in workplace sexual harassment under conditions of perceived unfairness on the job (Krings & Facchin, 2009).

To determine trends in workplace harassment claims upheld by the Equal Employment Opportunity Commission, a study of such claims from 1992 to 2006 was conducted (Cunningham & Benavides-Espinoza, 2008). Results show a sharp increase during the 1990s, followed by a decline in the 2000s. This observed trend followed the political climate, with more progressive social policies in the 1990s and a more conservative agenda in the 2000s. Particular claims were most likely to succeed when the alleged harassing behaviors were serious, the complainant had supporting witnesses, and the complainant had notified management prior to filing formal charges (Terpstra & Baker, 1988). These findings were consistent with a subsequent analysis of 133 court decisions between 1974 and 1989 (Terpstra & Baker, 1992). In addition to the three criteria distinguishing successful claims found in their prior (1988) study, they also noted that supporting documentation and management's failure to act following notification were important.

Offenders' Experience as Victims of Crime, Violence, and Trauma

When offenders are also victims, or report that they are victims, of crime, violence, or other kinds of trauma, then society's reaction becomes even more complex—and

decisions made by the legal system become even more controversial. Considering the association between victimization and offending using a measure of youth lifestyles, one study found a positive association between violent and nonviolent offending, and being a victim of violent and nonviolent crime (Deadman & MacDonald, 2004). Consistent with this, other investigators (e.g., Abram et al., 2004) have reviewed the relationship of various kinds of trauma (perceived impending harm to self or a family member, physical assault, sexual assault, threat with a weapon, serious accident, natural disaster, exposure to violence, and exposure to dead bodies) and offending in justice-involved youth. More than half of the youth (total sample = 898 arrested and newly detained adolescents) had experienced six or more such traumatic events, and over 90% had at been exposed to at least one. Findings using data from the National Child Traumatic Stress Network Core Data Set (Dierkhising et al., 2013) indicated that justice system-involved youth referred for trauma-focused treatment (N=658) experienced an average of about five different kinds of trauma, including loss and bereavement (61.2%), impaired caregiver (51.7%), domestic violence (51.6%), abuse or maltreatment (emotional: 49.4%; physical: 38.6%), and community violence (34%). Such findings led one recent scholar to conclude that there is clearly a relationship between trauma exposure and juvenile justice system involvement—although it may be a complex one (Zelechoski, 2016).

Consider the cases of Lyle and Erik Menendez, and Susan Polk. What do these trials have in common? In each case, the defendant or defendants, charged with serious crimes, claimed the role of victim and argued that they were retaliating against an unwanted act or trying to prevent a feared attack. At their trials, the Menendez brothers described episodes of physical and sexual abuse from their father, with their mother as a passive accomplice; fearing the worst, they said, they decided to kill their parents first. Susan Polk, charged with the murder of her 70-year-old wealthy husband, Frank (Felix) Polk, a prominent Berkeley psychologist, claimed that she had long been controlled, abused, and battered by her husband, and acted in self-defense when he flew into a rage and attacked her.

How did the juries react to these defenses? Jurors' reactions in the Menendez brothers' trials were complicated. In the first trials, the jurors could not agree, producing a hung jury. The jurors agreed that each brother was guilty of a crime, but they could not agree on whether each should be convicted of murder or manslaughter (Thornton, 1995). With each jury deadlocked over the appropriate charge for conviction, the result was a mistrial. At the second trial, both brothers were found guilty of murder and sentenced to life in prison. Susan Polk was convicted of second-degree murder, despite testimony that she suffered from PTSD as a battered woman.

In cases like those of Polk and the Menendez brothers, in which a defendant claims to be a victim, critics are concerned that jurors will be tempted to accept what has been called the **abuse excuse**—"the legal tactic by which criminal defendants claim a

history of abuse as an excuse for violent retaliation" (Dershowitz, 1994, p. 3). Although Dershowitz concluded that a number of defense lawyers use the abuse excuse and that juries are accepting it, this is probably a more complex question than is being presented. We now know that the experience of trauma and serious adversity inclines individuals toward criminal offending. Is this an inevitable result? No. Is it something that a legal decision maker should consider in trying to understand the motivation of a criminal offender? Probably—particularly when the consequences being considered are very serious.

Summary

1. ***What is the frequency of crime victimization?*** According to the National Crime Victimization Survey, it is estimated that in 2015 approximately 10 million households experienced at least one property crime, and 2.7 million individuals were victimized by crimes of violence. The overall rate of violent victimization has decreased substantially between 1993 and 2015, from a rate of over 75 per 1,000 to under 25 per 1,000 citizens (most of this decrease occurred between 1993 and 2000).

2. ***What types of research have psychologists conducted on victimization?*** Four areas of victimization have received special attention from psychologists: adverse childhood experience; violent victimization and PTSD, including the psychology of rape; domestic violence (particularly spousal battering); and sexual harassment.

3. ***What factors predict the development of PTSD after being a crime victim?*** The extent of injury suffered in the crime and the belief that the victim has no control over his or her life heighten the risk of developing PTSD. Cognitive-behavioral treatments that help restore a sense of control and that help victims re-experience the trauma so that its emotional power is drained are the most effective interventions for preventing and reducing PTSD after a criminal victimization.

4. ***What are the components of battered woman syndrome that make it more specific than Posttraumatic Stress Disorder?*** Battered woman syndrome consists of a collection of responses, which may be displayed by individuals who are repeatedly physically abused by their intimate partners. The most specific of these components are learned helplessness, social isolation, and economic dependence.

5. ***How can rape be prevented?*** Prevention of rape has taken three routes. One includes promoting shared responsibility for the safety of all. A second is strengthening the capacity for self-protection from sexual assault. The third is the use of effective treatments for convicted rapists. Anti-androgen drugs, which reduce sex drive, and a combination of various behavior therapy techniques have shown some effectiveness as treatment for convicted rapists.

6. ***What are two types of sexual harassment recognized by the courts?*** The first type of harassment, *quid pro quo* harassment, consists of sexual demands made in conjunction with offers of benefits in exchange for compliance or threats of punishment if the respondent does not comply. The second type is harassment that creates a hostile work environment; it often involves demeaning comments, acts of touching or attempted intimacy, or the display of provocative photographs or artwork.

Key Terms

abuse excuse

acute stress
   disorder

battered woman
   syndrome

borderline personality
   disorder

chemical castration

cycle of violence

dispositional attributions

hostile workplace
   harassment

posttraumatic stress
   disorder

quid pro quo harassment

rape trauma syndrome

secondary victimization

self-defense

victimology

7 Evaluating Criminal Suspects

ORIENTING QUESTIONS

1. What are some psychological investigative techniques used by the police?

2. What is criminal profiling?

3. Is the polygraph a valid instrument for lie detection? What are some problems associated with it?

4. What are the premises of cognitive-based methods to detect deception and how effective are those protocols?

5. What brain-based techniques are used to detect deception, and how well do they work?

6. How valid is confession evidence? What kinds of interrogation procedures can lead to false confessions?

7. What are some of the reforms proposed to prevent false confessions?

In this chapter, we discuss three additional activities that psychology can provide to assist law enforcement: profiling criminal suspects, assessing the truthfulness of suspects, and evaluating the validity of their confessions. The common thread that ties these topics together is the assumption that psychological theory and techniques can be used to improve police officers' evaluations of criminal suspects.

These contributions occur in a logical sequence. Psychological profiling is usually performed at the beginning of a criminal investigation when the police need help focusing on certain types of people who might be the most likely suspects.

Once suspects have been identified, law enforcement officials use other procedures to determine whether they should be charged. While questioning suspects, police rely on various visual and verbal cues to determine whether they are giving truthful responses. But as you will see, people are not especially adept at detecting deception by relying on these kinds of cues.

Suspects are sometimes given so-called lie detection (or polygraph) tests to provide more information about their guilt or innocence and, sometimes, to encourage them to confess. However, assumptions about the effectiveness of polygraph procedures conflict with some psychological findings about their accuracy. Many psychologists question the objectivity of the procedure as it is usually administered and, hence, the validity of its results.

Increasingly, law enforcement agents and industry personnel are using brain-based technologies, including neuroimaging and brain-wave measurements, to detect deception. Although promising, these techniques have not yet been subjected to the kind of rigorous, real-world testing that is required before they become commonplace investigatory tools.

The police interrogate suspects and encourage them to confess because confessions make it more likely that suspects will be successfully prosecuted and eventually convicted. But in the quest for conviction, confessions can be coerced. Courts have tried to clarify when a confession is truly voluntary, but psychological findings often conflict with the courts' evaluations of confessions.

Thus, a consistent theme throughout this chapter is the conflict between the legal system and psychological science regarding ways of gaining knowledge and evaluating truth. A related conflict involves the competing interests of determining the truth and resolving disputes.

Profiling of Criminal Suspects

Do criminals commit their crimes or choose their victims in distinctive ways that leave clues to their psychological makeup, much as fingerprints point to their physical identity or ballistics tests reveal the kind of gun they used? There is some evidence that psychological characteristics are linked to behavioral patterns and that these links can be detected by a psychological analysis of crime scenes. Behavioral scientists and police use **criminal profiling** to narrow criminal investigations to suspects who possess certain behavioral and personality features that were revealed by the way the crime was committed. (Another way to think about profiling is that it involves the attempt to "reverse engineer" a final product—the crime scene—in the attempt to gain leads about the individual[s] who created that final product.)

Profiling, which has also been called "criminal investigative analysis," does not identify a specific suspect. Instead, profilers offer a general psychological description of the most likely type of suspect, including personality and behavioral characteristics suggested by a thorough analysis of the crimes committed, so that police can concentrate their investigation of difficult cases in the most profitable directions. (Profiles also help investigators search for persons who fit descriptions known to characterize hijackers, drug couriers, and undocumented aliens; Monahan & Walker, 2014.) The results of a careful profile may provide specific information about suspects, including psychopathology, characteristics of their family history, educational and legal history, and habits and social interests (Woodworth & Porter, 2000). Although profiling can be used in diverse contexts, it is considered most helpful in crimes in which the offender has demonstrated some form of repetitive behavior with unusual aspects, such as sadistic torture, ritualistic or bizarre behavior, evisceration, or staging or acting out a fantasy (Woodworth & Porter, 2000).

A successful profiler should possess several key attributes, including both an understanding of human psychology and investigative experience (Hazelwood, Ressler, Depue, & Douglas, 1995). There is some controversy regarding who should be considered a successful profiler. Because of the importance of investigative experience in criminal profiling, some have suggested that mental health professionals may not be fully qualified to engage in profiling (Hazelwood & Michaud, 2001). Others maintain that clinical (forensic) psychologists possess a level of expertise that contributes to the effectiveness of criminal profiling (Copson, Badcock, Boon, & Britton, 1997; Gudjonsson & Copson, 1997). One survey (Torres, Boccaccini, & Miller, 2006) found that only 10% of the psychologists and psychiatrists surveyed reported any profiling experience, and 25% considered themselves knowledgeable about profiling. Although fewer than 25% believed that criminal profiling was scientifically reliable or valid, most felt it had some usefulness in criminal investigation. Certainly any professional who attempts to conduct profiling should be knowledgeable and experienced with offenders and the process of criminal investigation, which typically means that an individual must have experience as a criminal investigator.

Many famous fictional detectives have been portrayed as excellent profilers because they could interpret the meaning of a small detail or find a common theme among seemingly unrelated features of a crime. Lew Archer, the hero in Ross MacDonald's popular series of detective novels, frequently began his search for a missing person (usually a wayward wife or a troubled daughter) by looking at the person's bedroom, examining her reading material, and rummaging through her closet to discover where her lifestyle might have misdirected her. Lincoln Rhyme, the "criminalist" in Jeffrey Deaver's novels, focuses on learning everything humanly possible from painstaking scrutiny of the crime scene, and using that information to support (or disconfirm) possibilities about potential perpetrators. Profiling has now infiltrated popular culture through TV programs such as *Law and Order* and its offspring (*Criminal Intent* and *Special Victims Unit*), as well as *Criminal Minds and Mindhunter*.

One of the earliest cases of criminal profiling involved the 1957 arrest of George Metesky, otherwise known as the Mad Bomber of New York City. Over an eight-year period, police had tried to solve a series of more than 30 bombings in the New York area. They finally consulted Dr. James Brussel, a Greenwich Village psychiatrist, who, after examining pictures of the bomb scenes and analyzing letters that the bomber had sent, advised the police to look for a heavyset, middle-aged, Eastern European, Catholic man who was single and lived with a sibling or aunt in Connecticut. Brussel also concluded that the man was very neat and that, when found, he would be wearing a buttoned double-breasted suit. When the police finally arrested Metesky, this composite turned out to be largely accurate.

Not all early profiles were so useful, however. For example, the committee of experts charged with the task of profiling the Boston Strangler predicted that the killer was not one man but two, each of whom lived alone and worked as a schoolteacher. They also suggested that one of the men would be homosexual. When Albert DeSalvo ultimately confessed to these killings, police discovered that he was a heterosexual construction worker who lived with his wife and two sons (Porter, 1983).

Two important aspects to this kind of reconstructive activity have involved *crime scene analysis* (detecting physical evidence that would provide important investigatory and prosecution support) and inferences about offender characteristics (patterns of perpetrator thinking, feeling, and behavior deduced from evidence left at the crime scene). Disciplines such as biology and biochemistry have provided tools for advances in the former area, while psychology, psychiatry, and criminology have provided important contributions in the latter (see Turvey, 2012, for an extensive discussion).

A major source of research and development on criminal profiling has been the FBI's Behavioral Science

Unit (the BSU), which worked on criminal profiles between the 1970s and 2014, when it was disbanded. The BSU was one of the instructional components of the FBI's Training and Development Division, located at the FBI Academy in Quantico, Virginia. It provided training, conducted research, and offered consultation in the behavioral and social sciences. The BSU also coordinated with other FBI units, such as the National Center for the Analysis of Violent Crime (NCAVC), which continues to provide operational assistance to FBI field offices and law enforcement agencies. The NCAVC now has separate units that focus on crimes against adults, crimes against children, apprehension of violent criminals, and counterterrorism and threat assessment. Its mission combines investigative and operational support, research, and training (without charge), which it provides to federal, state, local, and foreign law enforcement agencies—particularly in the context of investigation of unusual or repetitive violent crimes. The NCAVC also provides support through expertise and consultation in nonviolent matters such as national security, corruption, and white-collar crime investigations.

Following September 11, 2001, the FBI placed a higher priority on counterterrorism (FBI Academy, 2002). Profiling terrorist suspects in the United States has proved challenging, and no reliable profile has been developed. There are a number of reasons for this, described succinctly in a review on the topic (Monahan, 2012). The author observes that individual risk factors for criminal behavior (e.g., age, gender, marital status, social class, past crime, major mental illness, and personality) do not serve as risk factors for terrorism. Indeed, while there are some advantages to considering "terrorism" broadly, Monahan describes the strategy of being more specific about types of terrorism, such as suicidal, homegrown, inside, jihadist/Salafist, and so on, as also potentially useful. Finally, he offers four categories of "promising" risk factors in this area: ideology, affiliation, trauma/loss, and disgust. Even focusing on these more promising strategies, however, would not allow the prospective validation of a risk assessment tool for terrorism. (Imagine "validating" such a tool by administering it to a large number of individuals and releasing some of them to observe how many carried out terrorist activity.) In addition, applying such risk factors in a population in which terrorists are rare, such as the United States, would risk violating Americans' civil liberties and producing an overwhelmingly large number of "false positives" (those who are predicted to present a threat but who actually do not).

Historically, much of the BSU's focus was on violent offenders, especially those who commit bizarre or repeated crimes (Jeffers, 1991). Particular attention was given to rapists (Ressler, Burgess, & Douglas, 1988), arsonists (Rider, 1980), sexual homicides (Hazelwood & Douglas, 1980), and mass and serial murderers (Porter, 1983). Interest in these topics continues, particularly in the area of serial and mass murder (Fox & Levin, 2005; Hickey, 2009; Morton & Hilts, 2008; Mullen, 2004). There is also continued interest in the topic of crime scene analysis and offender profiling (Ainsworth, 2001; Owen, 2004; Petherick, 2005). The focus of such work is on describing those who have committed a specific type of offense in order to learn how they select and approach their victims, how they react to their crimes, what demographic or family characteristics they share, and what personality features might predominate among them. For example, as part of its study of mass and serial killers, the FBI conducted detailed interviews with some of the United States' most notorious homicide offenders—among them Charles Manson, Richard Speck, and David Berkowitz—to determine the similarities among them.

Classifying Homicide Offenders: Mass and Serial Murderers

On the basis of this research, behavioral scientists have been able to classify mass murderers and add to the portrait of contemporary homicide offenders. Historically, most homicides have been committed by killers who were well acquainted with their victims, had a personal but rational motive, killed once, and were then arrested. In the past few decades, however, increased attention has been paid to patterns of homicide involving killers who attack multiple victims, sometimes with irrational or bizarre motives, and who are less likely to be apprehended than in former days because their victims are strangers. There is also a question of whether a given attack might have been motivated by religious ideology. For example, Omar Mateen, a 29-year-old security guard, killed 49 people and wounded 53 others in June 2016 at Pulse, a gay nightclub in Orlando, in the deadliest mass killing of LGBT individuals in U.S. history. Mateen attributed his actions to his allegiance to the Islamic State of Iraq and the Levant (ISIL), although there was no credible evidence that he was involved with this group. Mateen could not be questioned further, as he was killed by police after negotiations over three hours did not convince him to surrender.

The criminal trails of those who commit serial homicide may center on one locale and period of time, or cross through different locations and stretch over a longer period of time. This does not mean, of course, that the patterns of homicide offending have necessarily changed. It is quite likely that changes in mass communication technology have changed the *awareness* of homicide offending with multiple victims. (See http://www.shootingtracker.com/ for figures on mass killings between 2013 and 2016.) Indeed, mass murderers have been a favorite subject of lurid "true crime" books such as *The Only Living Witness* (about Ted Bundy), *The Co-Ed Killer* (Edmund Kemper), *Killer Clown* (John Gacy), and *Bind, Torture, Kill* (Dennis Rader), as well as of more scholarly comparative studies of multiple homicides (Fox & Levin, 1998; Meloy et al., 2004; Morton & Hilts, 2008).

Although experts differ on the precise number of victims to use in defining "multiple homicide," Fox and Levin's (1998) criterion of "the slaying of four or more victims, simultaneously or sequentially, by one or a few individuals" is probably the most widely accepted opinion. It is difficult to estimate how many double homicides are committed each year, but the consensus is that they are increasing, and this increase does not reflect merely greater media attention or police apprehension rates.

Mass murders are also increasing in frequency, though they remain relatively rare, which makes it virtually impossible to formulate predictive statistical models that are accurate. The particular problem with trying to predict such rare events is the "false positive" error rate: even approaches that have a good overall accuracy rate will identify a relatively large number of false positives (those who are predicted to be violent, but actually are not). As an alternative to prediction, current research has focused on identifying characteristics of these homicide offenders and examining patterns among individuals. One study comparing 30 adult with 34 adolescent mass murderers found striking similarities between the two groups (Meloy et al., 2004). Three-quarters of the entire sample were Caucasian (75%); the majority of both the adolescents (70%) and the adults (94%) were described as "loners"; almost half of the adolescent sample (48%) and almost two-thirds of the adult sample (63%) demonstrated a preoccupation with weapons and violence; and about 43% of both groups had a violent history.

Two types of multiple homicides have been identified: mass murders and serial murders. These types share some similarities but are marked by several differences (Meloy & Felthous, 2004). The **mass murderer** kills four or more victims in one location during a period of time that lasts anywhere from a few minutes to several hours. It is estimated that about two mass murders were committed every month in the United States in the 1990s, resulting in the deaths of 100 victims annually (Fox & Levin, 1998). A different approach considered the average time period between mass murders that took place in public in which the shooter and victims were generally unrelated and not known to one another. Since 1982, such a mass killing has occurred on average every 172 days—but between 2011 and 2014, these events occurred at about three times this frequency, suggesting an accelerated pace of mass killings in the United States involving assaults on strangers in public (Cohen, Azrael, & Miller, 2014). Although most mass murderers are not severely mentally ill, they do tend to harbor strong feelings of resentment and are often motivated by revenge against their victims.

But the majority of mass murderers do not attack strangers at random; in almost 80% of studied mass murders, the assailant was related to or well acquainted with the victims, and in many cases, the attack was a carefully planned assault rather than an impulsive rampage. For every Seung-Hui Cho, who killed 32 people and wounded 25 others in a mass shooting at Virginia Tech in 2007 or Stephen Paddock, who killed 58 people and wounded over 500 others at a music festival in Las Vegas in 2017, there are many more people like Bruce Pardo. Pardo, dressed as Santa Claus, opened fire at a Christmas party at the home of his former in-laws and killed nine people before killing himself. Most mass murders are solved by law enforcement; the typical assailant is killed at the location of the crime, commits suicide, or surrenders to police. **Spree killers**

Crime scene investigator speaks during a murder trial.

are a special form of mass murderers: attackers who kill victims at two or more different locations with no "cooling-off" interval between the murders. The killing constitutes a single event, but it can either last only a short time or go on for a day or more.

Serial murderers kill four or more victims, each on a separate occasion. Unlike mass murderers, **serial killers** usually select a certain type of victim who fulfills a role in the killer's fantasies. There are cooling-off periods between serial murders, which are usually better planned than mass or spree killings. Some serial killers (such as Angel Maturino Resendiz, called the Railway Killer because the murders he was charged with took place by railroad tracks) travel frequently and murder in several locations. Dr. Michael Swango, trained as a physician, is suspected by the FBI of killing up to 60 individuals, typically by poisoning them, between 1981 and 1997. He moved around a great deal, and is suspected of killings in Illinois, New York, Ohio, and South Dakota—as well as Zimbabwe. Others (such as Gary Ridgway, the so-called Green River Killer, who confessed to killing 48 women, mostly prostitutes, and dumping their bodies along the Green River in Washington) are geographically stable and kill within the same area. The Unabomber, who apparently remained in one place but chose victims who lived in different parts of the country to receive his carefully constructed mail bombs, reflected an unusual combination of serial killer characteristics.

Because they are clever in the way they plan their murders, are capable of presenting themselves as normal members of the community, kill for idiosyncratic reasons, and frequently wait months between killings, serial murderers are difficult to apprehend. It took 30 years for Wichita police to figure out that Dennis Rader, a Boy Scout leader and president of Christ Lutheran Church, was a brutal serial killer who used the moniker "BTK"—an acronym for "bind, torture, kill." He confessed to 10 counts of first-degree murder in 2005.

Social scientists have gained some knowledge about these criminals, who may number as many as 100 in the United States. One study compiled a list of characteristics from 157 serial offenders and found that most were White males in their early 30s (Kraemer, Lord, & Heilbrun, 2004). More than half of the offenders were employed at the time of the offense, and approximately one-third were married. The average offender had an 11th-grade education. Victims of these offenders were most often White females in their early to mid-30s who were strangers to their killers. More than half of the murders were sexually motivated. These characteristics

Dennis Rader, the "BTK Killer"

differ from those of single-homicide offenders, who often know their victims and kill for emotional reasons such as anger or sexual jealousy (Kraemer et al., 2004).

In another study that compared multiple homicide offenders (MHOs, N = 160) with single homicide offenders (SHOs, N = 494), investigators (DeLisi & Scherer, 2006) reported that almost 30% of MHOs were habitual offenders before their final homicide. Some distinguishing features between these two groups were prior rape convictions, misdemeanor convictions, more extensive prison histories, and current involvement in rape and burglary—all were seen more often in the MHO group. However, nearly 40% of MHOs had never been arrested prior to their current justice system involvement.

Serial killers tend to select vulnerable victims of some specific type who gratify their need to control people. Consistent with the motive of wanting to dominate people, they prefer to kill with "hands-on" methods such as strangulation and stabbing, rather than with guns, which are the preferred weapons of mass murderers. They are often preoccupied with sexualized or sadistic fantasies involving capture and control of their victims. Many serial killers use pornography and violent sexual fantasies intensively as "rehearsals" for and "replays" of their crimes, and they often keep souvenirs (sometimes in the form of body parts from victims) to commemorate their savage attacks. Despite the apparent "craziness" of their behavior, serial killers are not typically psychotic individuals. Most of them, however, have personality disorders and lack the ability to experience empathy and remorse. In fact, serial killers often revel in the publicity that their crimes receive.

Fox and Levin (2005) have provided examples of different motivations for serial and mass murder (including power, revenge, loyalty, profit, and terror), along with brief vignettes illustrating these motivations (see Table 7.1).

Similar examples of possible motivations for homicide, as well as additional information (e.g., signature aspects of violent crime, staging and undoing at crime scenes, and recommendations for interrogation) are contained in the *Crime Classification Manual* (Douglas, Burgess, Burgess, & Ressler, 2006). As you might suspect, the classification with respect to offender motivation can be complex. For example, was the Virginia Tech shooter Seung-Hui Cho motivated by power? What about revenge? Some evidence suggests that both may have influenced him. This example vividly illustrates the point that many influences and motivations may come together in the rare and tragic context of multiple homicide.

Steps Involved in Criminal Profiling

Douglas, Ressler, Burgess, and Hartman (1986) divided the FBI's profiling strategy into five stages, with a final, sixth stage being the arrest of the correct suspect. The six phases, as they evolve in a murder investigation, seem to apply reasonably well three decades later. They are as follows:

1. *Profiling inputs.* The first stage involves collecting all information available about the crime, including physical evidence, photographs of the crime scene, autopsy reports and pictures, complete background information on the victim, and police reports. The profiler does not want to be told about possible suspects at this stage, because such data might prejudice or prematurely direct the profile.

2. *Decision process models.* In this stage the profiler organizes the input into meaningful questions and patterns along several dimensions of criminal activity. What type of homicide has been committed? What is the primary impetus for the crime—sexual, financial, personal, or emotional disturbance? What level of risk did the victim experience, and what level of risk did the murderer take in killing the victim? What was the sequence of acts before and after the killing, and how long did these acts take to commit? Where was the crime committed? Was the body moved, or was it found where the murder was committed?

3. *Crime assessment.* On the basis of the findings in the previous phase, the profiler attempts to reconstruct the behavior of the offender and the victim. Was the murder *organized* (suggesting an

TABLE 7.1 Generic examples of motivations for multiple murder

| Motivations for multiple murder | TYPES OF MULTIPLE MURDER | |
	Serial murder	Mass murder
Power	Inspired by sadistic fantasies, a man tortures and kills a series of strangers to satisfy his need for control and dominance.	A pseudo-commando, dressed in battle fatigues and armed with a semiautomatic weapon, turns a shopping mall into a "war zone."
Revenge	Grossly mistreated as a child, a man avenges his past by slaying women who remind him of his mother.	After being fired from his job, a gunman returns to the work site and opens fire on his former boss and coworker.
Loyalty	A team of killers turns murder into a ritual for proving their dedication and commitment to one another.	A depressed husband/father kills his family and himself to spare them from a miserable existence and bring them a better life in the hereafter.
Profit	A woman poisons to death a series of husbands to collect on their life insurance policies.	A band of armed robbers executes the employees of a store to eliminate all witnesses to their crime.
Terror	A profoundly paranoid man commits a series of bombings to warn the world of impending doom.	A group of antigovernment extremists blows up a train to send a political message.

Source: From Fox and Levin (2005), p. 20.

intelligent offender who carefully selects victims against whom to act out a well-rehearsed fantasy) or *disorganized* (indicating an impulsive, less socially competent, possibly even psychotic offender)? Was the crime staged to mislead the police? Can details such as cause of death, location of wounds, and position of the body reveal anything about the killer's motivation? Criminal profilers are often guided by the following hypotheses:

- Brutal facial injuries point to killers who knew their victims.
- Murders committed with whatever weapon happens to be available are more impulsive than murders committed with a gun and may reveal a killer who lives fairly near the victim.
- Murders committed early in the morning seldom involve alcohol or drugs.

4. *Criminal profile.* In this stage, profilers formulate an initial description of the most likely suspects. This profile includes the perpetrator's race, sex, age, marital status, living arrangements, and employment history; psychological characteristics, beliefs, and values; probable reactions to the police; and past criminal record, including the possibility of similar offenses in the past. This stage also contains a feedback loop whereby profilers check their predictions against stage-2 information to make sure that the profile fits the original data.

5. *Investigation.* A written report is given to investigators, who concentrate on suspects matching the profile. If new evidence is discovered in this investigation, a second feedback process is initiated, and the profile can be revised.

6. *Apprehension.* The intended result of these procedures—the arrest of a suspect—allows profilers to evaluate the validity of their predictions. The key element in this validation is a thorough interview of the suspect to assess the influences of background and psychological variables.

The Validity of Criminal Profiles

What is the evidence for the validity of psychological profiling? Are profilers more accurate than other groups in their descriptions of suspects, or is this activity little more than a reading of forensic tea leaves? Do profilers use a different process in evaluating information than other investigators?

In a review of criminal profiling, Homant and Kennedy (1998) concluded that different kinds of crime scenes can be classified with reasonable reliability and that differences in these crimes do correlate with certain offender characteristics, such as murderers' prior relationships and interactions with victims (Salfati & Canter, 1999); organized versus disorganized approaches; and serial versus single offenders (e.g., Kraemer et al., 2004). At the same time, this research suggests several reasons for caution: (1) Inaccurate profiles are quite common, (2) many of the studies have been conducted in house by FBI profilers studying a fairly small number of offenders, and (3) the concepts and approaches actually used by profilers have often not been objectively and systematically defined. A majority of the psychologists and psychiatrists responding to one survey (Torres et al., 2006) did not view criminal profiling as scientifically reliable or valid (but nonetheless endorsed it as a potentially useful tool in criminal investigation).

One important study (Pinizzotto & Finkel, 1990) investigated the effectiveness of criminal profiling as practiced by real-life experts. In this investigation, four different groups of participants evaluated two criminal cases—a homicide and a sex offense—that had already been solved but were completely unknown to the subjects. The first group consisted of four experienced criminal profilers who had a total of 42 years of profiling experience and six police detectives who had recently been trained by the FBI to be profilers. The second group consisted of six police detectives with 57 years of total experience in criminal investigations but with no profiling experience or training. The third group was composed of six clinical psychologists who had no profiling or criminal investigation experience. The final group consisted of six undergraduates drawn from psychology classes.

All participants were given, for each case, an array of materials that profilers typically use, including crime scene photographs, crime scene descriptions by uniformed officers, autopsy and toxicology reports (in the murder case), and descriptions of the victims. Three tests of profiling quality were used: All subjects prepared a profile of a suspect in each case, answered 15 questions about the identity (e.g., gender, age, employment) of the suspects, and were asked to rank order a written "lineup" of five suspects, from most to least likely to have committed each of the crimes.

The results indicated that, compared with the other three groups, the profiler group wrote longer profiles that contained more specific predictions about suspects, included more accurate predictions, and were rated as more helpful by other police detectives. Profilers were more accurate than the other groups in answering specific questions about the sex offense suspect, though the groups did not differ in their accuracy about the homicide suspect. Similar results were found with the "lineup" identification: Profilers were the most accurate for the sex offense, whereas there were no differences for the homicide case.

This study suggests that profilers can produce more useful and valid criminal profiles, even when compared to experienced crime investigators. This advantage may be limited, however, to certain kinds of cases or to the types of information made available to investigators.

Another study (Canter, Alison, Alison, & Wentink, 2004) tested the "organized/disorganized" dichotomy by using specialized statistics to analyze aspects of serial killing derived from murders committed by 100 U.S. serial killers. There was no distinct subset of offense characteristics associated with organized versus disorganized killings. Researchers did find a subset of organized features (e.g., evidence of planning, bringing a weapon, use of a vehicle) that were characteristic of most serial killings, but disorganized features such as impulsivity, failure to use precautions that would limit evidence left at the scene, and related behaviors were far more unusual. The investigators suggested that these results cast doubt on whether killings can be reliably and validly classified using this dichotomy.

Based on the absence of empirical scientific data supporting the process of profiling, some (e.g., Risinger & Loop, 2002) have argued that profiling lacks the requisite scientific support to allow experts to testify to the findings in the course of litigation.

On this point, a review of evidence existing about 15 years ago led one investigator (Kocsis, 2003) to conclude that there is support for the view that professional profilers can produce a more accurate description of an unknown offender than can other groups. This conclusion has been strongly criticized by other investigators, however. One review criticized the methodology used to yield this conclusion, suggesting that greater scientific rigor would yield less support for profiling accuracy (Bennell, Jones, Taylor, & Snook, 2006, but see Kocsis, 2006, for a response). A subsequent pair of meta-analyses (Snook, Eastwood, Gendreau, Goggin, & Cullen, 2007) indicated that experienced profilers did not outperform comparison groups in describing offenders' cognitive processes, physical attributes, offense behaviors, or social habits and history, although they were somewhat better at describing overall offender characteristics. This led to the question of whether much of the thinking on

the validity of profiling is based upon illusory belief, influenced by anecdote and repeated messages that it does work (Snook, Cullen, Bennell, Taylor, & Gendreau, 2008).

Where does that leave us on the question of offender profiling validity? Some (Kocsis & Palermo, 2015) argue that because profilers are often "trait-based" (seeking to identify stable aspects of offenders' functioning) they are not as accurate as they could be—but still conclude that there is scientific support for profiling validity. Others (e.g., Chifflet, 2015) describe the current status of profiling as supported by uncertain theories and limited data.

A noteworthy different approach to profiling—using statistically derived behavioral profiles for burglary offenders—showed that burglary arrest rates for agencies receiving the statistical profile were significantly higher (Fox & Farrington, 2015). This approach may offer an interesting and potentially valuable alternative to the use of human profilers.

How do psychologists themselves view criminal profiling? In a survey of 152 police psychologists, 70% questioned the validity of crime scene profiling (Bartol, 1996). Nonetheless, despite such reservations, profiling continues to be used in law enforcement and is now practiced, in some form or other, in several countries (Woodworth & Porter, 2000).

Given the mixed reviews on the question of profiling validity, there does not appear to be an adequate scientific foundation for expert testimony in this area. Whether courts admit profiling evidence will probably continue to depend on the particular judge.

Becoming an FBI Profiler

Despite the mixed evidence about profiling validity, there is little doubt that it is used with some frequency and perceived as a helpful investigatory tool by many. One of the questions frequently asked by those considering a career in law enforcement is "How do I become an FBI profiler?" Of course, the FBI is not the only law enforcement agency that uses profiling—it may be used in other agencies at the federal, state, and community levels. But our discussion here considers the FBI as an example of an agency that has been prominently associated with this profiling, and has incorporated the contributions of psychology in a significant way.

So the question about "becoming a profiler" may be answered in different ways. Consider the advice offered by Mary Ellen O'Toole, PhD, a retired FBI agent and criminal profiler, to those with interest in FBI profiling:

■ Consult the website (www.fbi.gov) and review the current information on job requirements for becoming an FBI agent. FBI profilers are all agents. If you are interested, you can get further details from your local FBI office (applicant coordination).

■ To become an agent, you would need, at minimum, a four-year college degree (any major). You would spend about four months in rigorous training at the FBI Academy if accepted; such training includes psychology, interviewing, and legal issues as well as physical fitness and firearms use.

■ Following graduation from the Academy, you would be placed in a specific FBI field office, so you must be willing to relocate. You would work on a variety of investigations as part of this assignment.

■ Field experience as an FBI agent is important before applying to the Behavioral Analysis Unit or other FBI unit that provide profiling services. Most FBI profilers have 7–15 years of investigative experience before being accepted into such a unit.

■ Work as an FBI profiler includes analysis, interviewing, writing, public speaking, and assessing individual and group behavior. Coursework in psychology, sociology, philosophy, journalism, and public speaking might be particularly helpful. See http://maryellenotoole.com/meo/becominganfbiprofiler/.

One particularly important aspect of this advice is the emphasis on criminal profiling as only one aspect of law enforcement, improved by competence and experience in other aspects of criminal investigation.

Detecting Deception

In the short-lived television crime drama *Lie to Me*, actor Brendan Hines assisted law enforcement by investigating criminals and trying to ascertain their truthfulness. The twist was that he felt a moral imperative to tell the truth himself, to "shoot out the truth" without censoring himself. Unfortunately, such "radical honesty" is far more likely to appear on television than in reality.

People tell lies fairly often—on average, between once and twice a day, according to self-report studies (Hartwig, 2011). They do so for a variety of reasons: so that others will perceive them favorably, to avoid tension and conflict in social situations, and to minimize hurt feelings (Vrij, Granhag, & Porter, 2010). People also lie to conceal their wrongdoings, so successfully detecting these liars can have profound societal benefits. Consider the work of a customs official who intercepts a cache of weapons, a detective who doubts the veracity

of a suspected child molester, or an airport security officer who suspects that a passenger about to board a plane harbors ill intent. Consider the fact that each of the 19 terrorists who launched the September 11 attacks lied to authorities on at least three occasions, and that none of their lies was ever detected (Honts & Kircher, 2011).

Throughout history, many societies have assumed that criminals can be detected by the physical manifestations of their denials. Ever since King Solomon tried to discover which of two women who claimed to be the mother of an infant was lying by watching their emotions when he threatened to cut the baby in half and divide it between them, people have believed that the body will reveal when the mind is lying. People judge others' truthfulness by observing their behavior, often without conscious awareness of doing so. In late-night conversations, parents gauge the veracity of their teenagers' stories about where they had been and with whom. During job interviews, employers make quick judgments of the candor and honesty of prospective employees.

Police officers and other law enforcement officials know that deception is common, and their ability to detect lying has profound implications for the people who pass through the criminal justice system. Being deemed "truthful" can absolve guilty people of suspicion, allowing them to remain on the streets to commit more crimes. Being deemed "deceptive" can launch someone—perhaps an innocent person—into a criminal prosecution and toward eventual conviction and imprisonment. How well law enforcement officials can assess deception is vitally important to the fair and effective operation of the justice system. Fortunately, psychologists have provided tools to help them. In this section, we describe what psychologists have learned about people's ability to detect deception unaided, using only their eyes and ears and relying only on verbal and behavioral cues. This technique—simple observation—is actually the most common form of lie detection (Vrij et al., 2010).

It is difficult to be certain when people are fibbing and when they are telling the truth (at least as they believe it). It is also difficult to assess how people distinguish honesty from dishonesty in others. For this reason, psychological scientists have developed research protocols that mimic real-world lying and truth-telling.

In these studies, researchers instruct some participants to lie and others to tell the truth about a particular experience or intention—a film they saw or intend to see, the contents of their pockets, or what they plan to do that evening. Some studies have involved more forensically relevant situations such as asking participants to provide a true or false statement about their whereabouts during a certain timeframe on a particular day (e.g., Evans, Pimentel, Pena, & Michael, 2017). These stories—lies and truths alike—are videotaped and shown to observers who then judge the truthfulness of those statements. Scientists measure the ability to detect deception—that is, to realize that a truthful person is telling the truth and that a liar is lying—as the percentage of correct judgments. In a simple two-alternative forced choice, the chance level of an accurate decision is 50%.

How accurately can people detect deception? In a meta-analysis that evaluated the decisions of nearly 25,000 observers in hundreds of studies, Bond and DePaulo (2006) determined that people are correct only 54% of the time, hardly better than chance. The analysis revealed several other interesting clues to how people judge deception. For example, it uncovered a **truth bias**, meaning that people were biased toward judging statements as being truthful. People tend to take most assertions at face value, assuming that they are true unless their authenticity is called into question for some reason. (Think about asking someone what time it is.) As a result, subjects in the meta-analysis correctly classified 61% of truthful statements as nondeceptive but only 47% of lies as deceptive.

Many of the people involved in these deception studies were college students who had no expertise or specialized training (and perhaps little desire) to do the tasks well. In addition, there were few consequences for failing to convince observers of their honesty. Are people more accurate at detecting lies under more realistic circumstances, for example, in conditions that involve high emotions and strong motivations to be believed? This question was addressed in a meta-analysis of 144 samples involving more than 9,000 liars and truth-tellers, some of whom provided statements during criminal investigations or legal proceedings (Hartwig & Bond, 2014). The meta-analysis revealed that deception was equally detectable regardless of circumstances, meaning that the heightened motivations and emotions elicited in more realistic settings did little to help observers distinguish lies from truthful statements. It also revealed an accuracy rate for detecting lies of 67%, an improvement over the 54% noted in the Bond and DePaulo (2006) meta-analysis. Researchers attributed improved accuracy to the fact that more recent studies incorporated multiple behavioral cues to deception, rather than single cues. Even so, an accuracy rate of 67% means that one of every three judgments was incorrect.

Might people who have more experience judging deception be better at it? When playwright Tennessee Williams wrote that "mendacity is the system we live in," he may have been referring to people whose occupations expose them to multiple lies on a daily basis: police officers, judges, customs officials, border patrol officers, and the like. A classic study supports the idea that it helps to have experience with people who both lie and tell the truth. Ekman and O'Sullivan (1991) found that U.S. Secret Service agents (who frequently interview individuals who may present a threat to the president or vice president and their families) were the only participants—among participants from the CIA, FBI, National Security Agency, Drug Enforcement Agency, and California police and judges—who could detect deception at greater than chance levels. But more recent studies have found only very small individual differences in detecting deception (Bond & DePaulo, 2008).

These studies raise the question whether people can be trained to become better lie catchers. To some extent, yes, although trained observers are only *somewhat* better than untrained observers at distinguishing between truths and lies (Hauch, Sporer, Michael, & Meissner, 2016). And while training generally improves people's ability to tell that someone is lying, it has less effect on the ability to tell that someone is truthful. Still, training may be useful to police and parole officers who tend to be biased toward judging statements as lies, even when they are true, a phenomenon known as **lie bias** or investigator bias (Meissner & Kassin, 2002).

Methods of Detecting Deception

Arousal-Based Methods of Detecting Deception. Over the years, people suspected of wrongdoing have faced various tests of their veracity. The ancient Hindus forced suspects to chew rice and spit it out on a leaf from a sacred tree. If the rice was dry, the suspect was deemed guilty. Arabian Bedouins required conflicting witnesses to lick a hot iron; the one whose tongue was burned was thought to be lying (Kleinmuntz & Szucko, 1984). These procedures reflect activity of the sympathetic nervous system (under emotional stress, salivation usually decreases) and thus are crude measures of emotion.

In modern times, police investigators have developed interview protocols to help them garner insights into a person's truthfulness. These tools, which analyze both verbal and nonverbal behavior, are based on the premise that liars will be more nervous than truth-tellers and exhibit more nervous behaviors. The Behavior Analysis Interview (BAI; Inbau, Reid, Buckley, & Jayne, 2013) is an example. According to the firm that developed the protocol, more than 300,000 professionals have been trained in its use (Vrij, 2015). The BAI consists of a set of predetermined questions—both nonthreatening and behavior-provoking—designed to assess whether a suspect is likely to be guilty. Among other things, suspects are asked whether they committed the crime themselves and whether they know who committed the crime. Police investigators assume that guilty suspects are more likely than innocent people to display nervous behaviors such as crossing their legs, shifting their position, avoiding eye contact, and performing grooming behaviors. These suspects are then subjected to the Reid method of interrogation, which we describe later in the chapter.

Studies of the effectiveness of the BAI in detecting deceit yield rather disappointing results, however. In one field study, police officers judged the truthfulness of suspects who had either lied or told the truth during actual videotaped interviews. The officers were also asked which cues they used to make this decision. The more the officers attended to the BAI's cues to deception (e.g., fidgeting), the worse they performed (Mann, Vrij, & Bull, 2004).

For many years, a standard way to assess truthfulness was to measure signs of physiological arousal in combination with a specific questioning strategy. The **polygraph** (sometimes referred to as the *lie detector*) is a computer-based machine that measures blood pressure, electrodermal activity, and respiratory changes during questioning. Its use is also based on the premise that liars will exhibit a particular constellation of emotional responses that distinguish them from truth-tellers.

The **Control Question Test** (CQT, sometimes referred to as the *Comparison Question Test*) has become the most popular approach to polygraphic examinations (Meijer & Verschuere, 2010). The polygrapher asks a series of questions and focuses on responses to two kinds of questions. *Relevant questions* inquire about the crime under investigation (e.g., "Did you steal the law school's video monitor?"). *Comparison questions* are not directly concerned with the crime but are designed to induce an emotional reaction because they cover common misdeeds that nearly all of us have committed (e.g., "Prior to the age of 21, did you ever do anything that was dishonest or illegal?"). Most polygraphers consider a denial to be a "known lie." But subjects *will* deny, thereby providing a characteristic physiological response to a lie. Polygraphers expect that guilty subjects will be more aroused by the relevant questions (to which they must respond with a lie in order to maintain their innocence) whereas innocent subjects will be more aroused by the comparison

questions (because they will worry that admitting to a past misdeed might make them look more like a criminal). Therefore, this procedure works best when innocent subjects lie or show greater emotional arousal in response to the comparison questions, and guilty subjects lie and become more emotionally aroused in response to the relevant questions.

The level of accuracy has been of great concern in debates about the validity of the polygraph. Examiners are accurate when they expose liars and believe truthful suspects. They err when they believe that a liar is truthful (a *false negative*) or that a truthful subject is lying (a *false positive*). Advocates of polygraph procedures claim very high rates of accuracy, and in laboratory studies in which some participants are instructed to commit a minor crime, others are not, and then all are tested with a CQT, accuracy rates can be as high as 90% (Offe & Offe, 2007). Yet a panel of scientists who reviewed studies on the CQT concluded that it could discriminate lying from truth-telling at rates above chance, but far below perfection (National Research Council, 2003).

An alternative to the CQT is the **Concealed Information Test** (CIT). Both the procedure and the purposes of this method are fundamentally different from the control question approach. The goal is to detect the presence of concealed information in the suspect's mind, not to detect lying. The procedure relies on the accumulation of facts that are known only by the police, the criminal, and any surviving victims. The polygrapher creates a series of multiple-choice questions and presents them to the suspect. For example, the polygrapher may ask, "In what room was the victim's body found? What strange garment was the victim wearing? What was the victim clutching in his hand?" Each alternative would appear equally plausible to an innocent person. But the true criminal will, in theory, be revealed by heightened physiological reactions that accompany recognition of concealed information.

The CIT has several limitations. It can be used only when the details of the crime have been kept from the public. Even then, it is conceivable that the suspect is not the perpetrator but, rather, was told about the crime by the true criminal and therefore possesses concealed knowledge. It is possible that some guilty subjects are so distraught or pay so little attention to the details of their crimes that they actually lack the required information on which this method relies.

Arousal-based theories of deception detection all stem from the idea that because deceivers fear being caught in a lie, they will exhibit predictable behaviors that signal their stress. Over the years, people have come to associate deception with lack of eye contact, fidgety movements, and certain grooming behaviors, among other behavioral cues (e.g., Strömwall & Granhag, 2003). But the cues to deception are far less obvious and less reliable than many people believe (DePaulo et al., 2003). In fact, psychologists have found very few reliable cues to deception. Moreover, many verbal and nonverbal behaviors are influenced by cultural norms. Whereas it is expected for Caucasians to look into the eyes of their conversational partners, Japanese consider direct eye contact to be rude, and African Americans avert their gaze more often than European Americans (Johnson, 2006). Chinese speakers tend to use higher pitched voices when lying than when telling the truth; just the opposite is true among Hispanics (Matsumoto & Hwang, 2015). But most importantly, people who are telling the truth can experience the same emotions as liars, particularly when they are worried that they won't be believed. As Aldert Vrij, a psychologist at the University of Portsmouth, reminds us, there is nothing as obvious as Pinocchio's growing nose to alert us to a lie.

Cognitive Methods of Detecting Deception.
Given the difficulty of using behavioral cues to detect deception, a new paradigm for detecting deception has emerged in recent years. Cognitive methods of deception detection are based on the assumptions that lying is more mentally taxing than telling the truth, and that truth-tellers and liars use different strategies in responding to questions. These premises have led to the development of new questioning methods to detect deceit.

There are many reasons that lying is mentally taxing. Liars must first formulate their fabrications and then remember what they said earlier and to whom. They need to avoid providing any new information to interviewers. Because they know they are being deceitful, they may have to pay more attention to their own demeanor and to reactions from the interviewer to see if they are getting away with their lies. Finally, they have to suppress the truth. All of these activities require mental effort which, when compounded by the need to answer interviewers' questions, can confound and confuse deceitful subjects. One group of researchers summed it up simply: "lying takes time" (Suchotzki, Verschuere, Bockstaele, Ben-Shakhar, & Crombez, 2017).

Exploiting this fact, researchers have developed interview protocols that elicit and increase **cognitive load** more in liars, who are already preoccupied, than in truth-tellers. Among the techniques that effectively increase cognitive load is asking subjects to recall a series of events in reverse chronological order, and requiring them to perform a secondary task during the interview, such as determining whether a figure that reappears on a computer screen is similar to a target figure shown earlier. These interventions cause liars to show more **diagnostic cues** to deception. In other words, by making subjects think harder in an interview, investigators are better able to distinguish liars from truthful interviewees (Vrij et al., 2008).

Another cognitive approach to detecting deception exploits the fact the liars prepare themselves for anticipated questions by rehearsing—indeed, *overrehearsing*—their responses. But rehearsal only works when liars correctly anticipate the questions they will be asked. Although they may anticipate certain predictable questions (e.g., "What did you do in the restaurant?"), they typically do not anticipate spatial questions (e.g., "In relation to the front door and where you sat in the restaurant, where were the closest diners?"), temporal questions (e.g., "Who finished their food first, you or your friend?"), or requests to draw the scene. In one study, when observers viewed responses to anticipated questions, they could not distinguish truth-tellers from liars above chance level. But when they viewed responses to unanticipated questions, they correctly classified 80% of the truth-tellers and liars (Vrij et al., 2009). These findings suggest that asking unanticipated questions can be a surprisingly effective way to betray a liar.

Yet another cognitive method for detecting deceit relies on the premise that liars and truth-tellers use different strategies in investigative interviews. Whereas truth-tellers are generally forthcoming, liars tend to avoid certain topics and deny certain behaviors. This distinction allows investigators to be strategic about revealing evidence they possess about the suspect's actions. For example, withholding evidence until late in the interview leaves room for deceitful suspects to blatantly lie, denying any involvement in the crime. So when the interviewer eventually reveals incontrovertible evidence—a surveillance video, for example—suspects must scramble to explain away the lie, often by telling another lie. The strategic use of evidence also increases investigators' abilities to distinguish liars and truth-tellers (Hartwig, Granhag, & Luke, 2014).

How well do these cognitive methods of deception detection stack up against standard methods of questioning? According to a recent meta-analysis, cognitive lie detection approaches are effective, increasing accuracy rates from 56% using standard questioning procedures to 71% (Vrij, Fisher, & Blank, 2015). Should we be concerned that even these newer techniques yield correct classifications just 71% of the time? Absolutely; before lie detection procedures can be applied with confidence by police, border control agents, or others who assess people's truthfulness, they should be more accurate even than this. Might other methods work better?

Brain-Based Lie Detection. Rather than relying on measures of physiological arousal as the polygraph does, or verbal responses as cognitive approaches do, recent developments in detecting deception monitor changes in the brain's activity in response to stimuli. Two of the prominent brain-based methods of lie detection are neuroimaging and brain-wave analysis.

Neuroimaging in Deception Detection. Neuroimaging techniques such as **functional magnetic resonance imaging** (fMRI) use scanners fitted with powerful electromagnets to measure blood flow and oxygen utilization in selected parts of the brain. Increases in oxygen consumption and blood flow in a particular part of the brain indicate that that region of the brain is involved when a subject undertakes a certain task. The primary function of fMRI is to diagnose neurological disorders. But because it is highly sensitive to cognitive processes involved in memory (Binder, Desai, Graves, & Conant, 2009) and motivation (Hare, O'Doherty, Camerer, Schultz & Rangel, 2008), it holds promise as a way to monitor deception.

Early studies using fMRI to detect deception typically asked simple questions about one's past experiences or knowledge (e.g., "Who was your best friend in primary school?" "Does a bicycle have six wheels?"). Participants pressed buttons to answer "yes" or "no." Some were told to conceal information by lying in response to specific questions, whereas others were told to respond truthfully. Scientists then compared brain activity in response to truthful answers and lies.

At this point, you may wonder whether lying about the name of a best friend is comparable, in any way, to lying about criminal activity. In doing so, you are asking whether these studies have **external validity**. Many neuroscientists—particularly those who are skeptical that neuroimaging can identify deception—have wondered the same thing.

So scientists have now begun to use more realistic methods to simulate the processes of truth-telling and lying. For example, one team of researchers asked some research participants to fire a starter pistol with blank bullets in the testing room of a neuroimaging center. Prior to fMRI questioning, half of each group was instructed to tell the truth and the other

half was instructed to lie when asked, "Did you shoot that gun?" (Mohamed et al., 2006). Results showed that different patterns of brain activation were associated with truth-telling and lying. Several brain regions in the frontal, parietal, and anterior cingulate cortex responded more strongly during lies. These brain areas are associated with planning and other high-level executive functions, underscoring the fact that telling lies requires more cognitive effort than telling the truth.

Although fMRI holds some promise as a method of detecting deception, a number of issues have not yet been resolved. It is not clear whether fMRI technology can handle situations in which a subject's response cannot be neatly categorized as the truth or a lie. This occurs when a response is partly true and partly false, when people imagine that a fabricated memory is true, and when they consider the possibility of lying but ultimately decide to tell the truth (Appelbaum, 2007). Also, questions remain about the use of fMRI for detecting deception in people with medical or psychiatric disorders, youth, the elderly, and those who take medications or use **countermeasures**. Finally, there is only limited evidence of the accuracy of fMRI in lie detection, and it is not particularly encouraging: accuracy levels range from 76% to 90% but drop precipitously when countermeasures were employed (Langleben & Moriarty, 2013). Despite these lingering concerns, fMRI techniques are being marketed commercially and occasionally used in court. Joel Huizenga, who founded a company called No Lie MRI, asserts confidently, "Once you jump behind the skull, there's no hiding." Not all neuroscientists agree, but fMRI test results were used in the case we describe in Box 7.1.

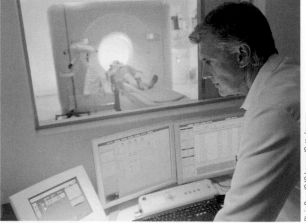

fMRI monitors changes in brain activity to detect deception.

BOX 7.1

The Case of Contested Poisoning: Munchausen's Syndrome By Proxy or Not? Can fMRI Tell the Difference?

Munchausen syndrome by proxy is a mental health disorder in which parents, guardians, or other caregivers deliberately inflict pain and injury on vulnerable children in order to attract attention to themselves. Perpetrators are overwhelmingly female, and often are mothers of the victims. The disease is difficult to diagnose because many of the child's symptoms could result from organic causes or undiagnosed illnesses. The question posed in a recent case in England was whether a child's poisoning had been carried out by the victim's mother. She was convicted of the charge and served four years in prison.

In a groundbreaking experiment, Professor Sean Spence, a pioneer of fMRI technology to detect deception, examined the woman's brain activity as she alternately repeated her protestations of innocence and her accusers' account of the poisoning (Spence, Kaylor-Hughes, Brook, Lankappa, & Wilkinson, 2008). The tests, repeated four times, showed that her prefrontal and anterior cingulate cortices were activated when she endorsed statements she believed to be false, namely her accusers' versions of the event. In short, the data suggested that she lied when she agreed with her accusers' statements. According to Professor Spence, "[A]t the present moment, this research doesn't prove that this woman is innocent. Instead, what it clearly demonstrates is that her brain responds as if she were innocent ... If proved to be accurate, and these findings replicated, this technology could be used alongside other factors to address questions of guilt versus innocence."

CRITICAL THOUGHT QUESTION

A question arises whenever new technology is introduced into legal proceedings: At what point is the technology sophisticated enough to merit its use in investigations and trials? In your opinion, should the answer be different depending on whether the new technology is used for investigative purposes (e.g., to assess suspects' truthfulness), or offered as evidence during a trial (e.g., to show that a witness had lied)?

Brain-Wave Analysis in Deception Detection. Imagine that a suspect denies that he or she was at the scene of a crime. Further imagine that he or she is confronted with pictures or verbal descriptions of the scene. Relatively new technology that measures brain-wave patterns that occur in response to familiar and unfamiliar images may eventually help investigators determine whether people are being deceptive when they claim, "I wasn't there." This technique, termed **brain fingerprinting**, was the "brainchild" of Lawrence Farwell. It uses an electroencephalogram (EEG) to record electrical activity on the surface of the scalp, reflecting spontaneous activity from the underlying cerebral cortex.

The premise of brain fingerprinting is that the brain houses information about experienced events and emits electrical signals in response to stimuli. A unique brain-wave pattern—the P300 wave—is elicited by a stimulus that is meaningful to the subject. It derives its name from its positive polarity and its occurrence approximately 300–900 milliseconds after the onset of a stimulus. Brain fingerprinting evaluates neural activity

to assess how a suspect responds to crime scene details known only to the perpetrator. For example, after showing a suspect a series of common images while measuring P300 waves, investigators might show critical images of the crime scene and compare activation patterns. A guilty person, but not an innocent subject, would react differently to the critical details because they are meaningful. (You can probably see that this protocol borrows heavily from the Concealed Information Test used with the polygraph.)

Researchers estimate the accuracy of brain fingerprinting by asking some participants to lie and others to tell the truth about a witnessed mock crime or autobiographical event when answering questions. They measure detection rates based on the resulting patterns of brain waves. Estimates range from 85% to 95% accuracy in distinguishing liars from truth-tellers under optimized laboratory conditions (Rosenfeld, Soskins, Bosh, & Ryan, 2004). Meta-analysis showed that the P300 component of the brain wave measured in conjunction with the Concealed Information Test reliably detects concealed information under laboratory conditions, though the technique is less accurate with realistic mock crime scenarios (Meijer, Selle, Elber, & Ben-Shakhar, 2014). The technique's originator, Lawrence Farwell, has patented, developed, and promoted a commercial version of the tool that he claims is 100% accurate (Farwell, 2011) despite limited empirical support (Rosenfeld, 2005).

Brain-Based Lie Detection in Court. Brain-based technologies could be used in at least two different ways in legal contexts. Defendants and witnesses could try to introduce the results of these tests to bolster their credibility. In one U.S. case, defendant Terry Harrington's murder conviction was reversed after Lawrence Farwell used brain fingerprinting to conclude that the record of the crime stored in Harrington's brain did not match the crime scene, but did match the alibi. When confronted with this information, a key prosecution witness recanted his testimony and admitted that he accused Harrington to avoid being prosecuted (*Harrington v. Iowa*, 2003).

Many people would agree that defendants and witnesses should be able to offer neuroscience evidence to support their version of the facts, so long as that evidence is based on valid and reliable scientific testing procedures. But many observers believe that the processes underlying these methods of deception detection are not sufficiently developed and understood to be routinely used in courts of law (e.g., Rusconi & Mitchener-Nissen, 2013). And when one ponders another use of this type of evidence—demanding that defendants and witnesses be screened for deception—even more people will balk.

A host of legal issues arise when brain-based techniques are conducted against the wishes of the subject being scanned. What happens if a person refuses to undergo an fMRI or brain-wave test? Can his or her credibility be questioned? Some have pondered whether these practices constitute a "search" of the brain that should be governed by the Fourth Amendment's prohibition against unreasonable search and seizure (Farah, Hutchinson, Phelps, & Wagner, 2014). A related question is whether brain-based tests conducted without the consent of the subject violate the protection against self-incrimination guaranteed by the Fifth Amendment. Alternatively, perhaps brain fingerprinting is just another form of physical evidence, similar to DNA or fingerprint evidence.

Although probing a person's brain to detect a lie may seem highly intrusive, the government's interests in crime control and public protection may offset these concerns. How far the law can extend into the realm of exposing (and protecting) private thoughts is

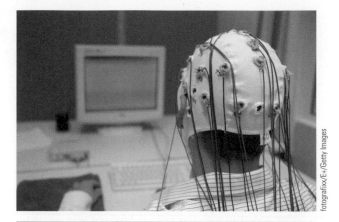

Brain fingerprinting, one method of detecting deception, uses electroencephalogram (EEG) – like the one shown here – to record electrical activity on the surface of the scalp, reflecting spontaneous activity from the underlying cerebral cortex.

unclear. Many commentators urge judges to resist the temptation to admit this evidence until more conclusive data are available (Aronson, 2010), and a team of legal scholars has proposed legislation that would prohibit the use of brain-based lie detection techniques until regulatory systems can be put in place to evaluate and monitor their safety and effectiveness (Greely & Illes, 2007). Perhaps the only certainty is that the controversy over brain-based lie detection systems will continue for some time.

Evaluating Confessions

When investigators have a hunch that a person is acting deceptively—due to a "failed" polygraph, neuroscientific test results, or simply through observation and interview—they may target that person for more formal interrogation, with the hope of extracting a confession. Throughout history, confessions have been accorded enormous importance. Many religions maintain that confession is the first step toward redemption and have evolved special rituals to encourage it. Interrogations and confessions also play a role in military and intelligence matters. People detained as terrorist threats in military jails in Afghanistan, Iraq, Guantanamo Bay, and elsewhere have been interrogated by harsh methods. These include both physical and psychological torture practices deemed illegal and condemned by the American Psychological Association. But tactics used in military and intelligence-gathering interrogations have been applied in criminal interrogations as well (Evans et al., 2010).

Confessions play a prominent role in the criminal justice system; many consider them to be the most powerful weapon at the state's disposal (Kassin & Gudjonsson, 2004). When the police capture suspects, one of their first acts is to encourage them to confess. A confession will, of course, permit a district attorney or grand jury to bring charges. Even if the suspect later denies the confession and pleads not guilty, the confession can be introduced into evidence at the trial.

Although disputed "confessions" by defendants occur surprisingly often and observers have documented many false confessions (see, e.g., Center for Wrongful Convictions), the number of false confessions is actually a matter of contention. Prosecutors observe that defendants can easily recant confessions by alleging that police coerced them, but defense attorneys say that false confessions happen more often than prosecutors acknowledge.

Historical Background and Current Legal Standing

Until the mid-20th century, many "confessions" came only after intense questioning by the police—questioning that involved promises, threats, harassment, and even brutality. Until 1966, the traditional test for admissibility of a confession in court was voluntariness. A voluntary confession is given without overt inducements, threats, promises, or physical harm. The trustworthiness of a confession was believed to be lost when it was obtained through one or more of those means (*Hopt v. Utah*, 1884).

But assessing the voluntariness of confessions proved difficult for many reasons. The task was highly subjective, and it resulted in countless "swearing contests" between police and suspects about what went on behind the closed door of interrogation rooms. Therefore, in *Miranda v. Arizona* (1966), the Supreme Court held that a confession resulting from in-custody interrogation was admissible in court only if, in addition to being voluntary, it had been obtained after the police had ensured the suspect's protection from self-incrimination by giving the so-called *Miranda* warnings (see Box 7.2). One year later, the Supreme Court extended those rights to juveniles (*In re Gault*, 1967). The *Miranda* warnings are intended to protect suspects from conditions that might give rise to unfounded confessions.

The *Miranda* case did not solve all problems associated with the validity of confessions. Although the

warnings add a new element to interrogations, intense and secretive interrogations continue to this day, with the interrogator intent upon persuading the suspect to confess. Furthermore, most suspects waive their *Miranda* rights, and after a suspect voluntarily enters the interrogation room, investigators can use any number of tactics to obtain a confession.

Why do suspects waive their rights? A primary reason is because they do not understand them. Psychologists have documented problematic vocabulary and terminology of some *Miranda* warnings (Rogers, Rogstad, Steadham, & Drogin, 2011), widely held misconceptions about the warnings (Rogers et al., 2010), and juveniles' difficulties understanding them (Rogers et al., 2016). The stress that comes from being accused of wrongdoing undermines comprehension of *Miranda* warnings, even in well-adjusted, intelligent adults (Scherr & Madon, 2012). As we will show, young and mentally impaired suspects waive their rights because they are vulnerable to the tactics of a skillful interrogator (Zelle, Romaine, & Goldstein, 2015).

Whittling Away at Miranda

Miranda v. Arizona (1966) was one of the most controversial decisions of the past century. The Chief Justice at the time, Earl Warren, was castigated in congressional committees and on the floor of Congress (Warren, 1977), and "Impeach Earl Warren" billboards were widely seen. Although the decision has survived for more than 50 years, it remains controversial to this day. It survived a major challenge in 2000 when the Supreme Court reaffirmed that *Miranda* was a constitutional ruling and that the warnings are part of the national culture (*Dickerson v. United States*, 2000). The *Dickerson* case is a good example of *stare decisis*—the court's preference for maintaining stability in the law through "abiding by settled principle" whenever possible. Given *Miranda*'s long-standing acceptance in the United States, the Court opted against changing the law of confessions.

The U.S. Supreme Court has weakened the *Miranda* requirements through a series of other decisions, however. Here are some of the changes:

1. *Confessions that violate* Miranda *may still be used at a trial.* Suppose a person confesses when arrested, and the confession is taken in violation of the *Miranda* warnings. If the defendant testifies to his or her innocence at trial, the prosecutor may use

The Case of Ernesto Miranda and the Right to Remain Silent: Changing Forever the Face of Police Work

BOX 7.2

One of the best-known U.S. Supreme Court cases decided during the last century, *Miranda v. Arizona* (1966) dealt with the problem of coerced confessions. Late on a Saturday in May of 1963, an 18-year-old woman left her job in downtown Phoenix. As she was walking home, a man grabbed her and dragged her to his car, tied her hands and laid her down in the back seat, then drove to the desert and raped her. As he waited for her to get dressed, he demanded money. She gave him the four $1 bills in her purse.

Ernesto Miranda

AP Images

A week after the rape, the victim's brother-in-law spotted a car like the one she had described. He remembered enough of the license plate for the police to trace the car to Ernesto Miranda. When police located the car, they saw a rope strung along the front seat, just as the victim had described. They put together a lineup, selecting three Mexican Americans to stand with Miranda. But he was the only person with eyeglasses and tattoos—features the victim remembered about her assailant. Still, she couldn't identify anyone.

Frustrated, the police then took Miranda to an interrogation room for what they thought was routine questioning. But the exchanges that occurred in that tiny chamber changed forever the way police interact with citizens. Miranda asked about the lineup: "How did I do?" "You flunked," a police officer replied, and began to question Miranda. No attorneys, witnesses, or tape recorders were present. The police later reported that Miranda voluntarily confessed. Miranda described the interrogation differently:

> Once they get you in a little room and they start badgering you one way or the other, "You better tell us … or we're going to throw the book at you. … And I haven't had any sleep since the day before. I'm tired. I just got off my work, and they have me and they are interrogating me. They mention first one crime, then another one; they are certain I am the person. … Knowing

what a penitentiary is like, a person has to be frightened, scared. And not knowing if he'll be able to get back up and go home." (Quoted in Baker, 1983, p. 13)

Whichever story one believes, Ernesto Miranda emerged from the questioning a confessed rapist. In June of 1963, he was convicted of rape and kidnapping and was sentenced to 20–30 years for each charge. He appealed his conviction to the U.S. Supreme Court, and the Court—by a 5–4 vote—concluded that his right against self-incrimination had been violated. Henceforth, they stated, the police must warn suspects of certain rights before starting a custodial interrogation. If these procedures are not followed, any damaging admissions made by suspects cannot be used by the prosecution in a trial.

Ironically, on the night of January 31, 1976, Miranda was playing poker in a flophouse section of Phoenix. A drunken fight broke out and Miranda was stabbed. He was dead on arrival at the hospital. Miranda's killer fled, but his accomplice was caught. Before taking him to police headquarters, a police officer read to him from a card:

> You have the right to remain silent. Anything you say can be used against you in a court of law. You have the right to the presence of an attorney to assist you prior to questioning and to be with you during questioning, if you so desire. If you cannot afford an attorney, you have the right to have an attorney appointed for you prior to questioning. Do you understand these rights? Will you voluntarily answer my questions?

CRITICAL THOUGHT QUESTION

What problems are the *Miranda* warnings intended to solve? What aspects of Miranda's case might have led Supreme Court justices to decide that his confession was not given freely?

the confession to show that the defendant should not be believed (*Harris v. New York*, 1971).

2. Miranda *does not apply unless the suspect is in the custody of the police*. The Supreme Court has interpreted *custody* in various ways. For example, the Court held that roadside questioning of a motorist stopped for drunk driving is not "custody," even though the motorist is not free to go (*Berkemer v. McCarty*, 1984). Warnings are not required in this circumstance. "Stop-and-frisk" questioning is also usually viewed as noncustodial because such questioning merely accompanies temporary detentions in public places.

3. Miranda *does not apply unless the defendant is being interrogated*. A volunteered confession is always admissible. Suppose the police arrest a robbery suspect and decide, for whatever reason, not to question him. On the way to the station, the accused person volunteers that he wouldn't have been caught if he'd kept his mask on. This confession is admissible because it was not in response to police questioning (*Rhode Island v. Innis*, 1980).

The Validity of Confession Evidence

In a perfect world, guilty people would always confess, and innocent people would never do so. Unfortunately, this is far from reality. Scientists know that two kinds of erroneous outcomes are possible: **false denials** (when guilty suspects proclaim their innocence and deny involvement in actual crimes) and **false confessions** (when innocent suspects confess to alleged crimes). False denials occur when crime perpetrators lie by saying "I didn't do it," and false confessions occur when innocent suspects say "I did it" and provide factually untrue descriptions of how and why the crime occurred.

Although false denials occur more often than false confessions, the latter have captured the attention of psychological scientists, lawyers, judges, and the public. Indeed, we focus a great deal of attention on the reasons for false confessions later in this chapter. But it is important to bear in mind that false denials are also critical errors for the criminal justice system and the public. Because they are more frequent than false confessions and can result in the release of guilty and potentially dangerous offenders back into the community, their costs should not be underestimated. As we discuss some of the reasons why false confessions occur, keep in mind that these influences promote confessions by the guilty—important in the investigation and conviction of criminal offending—as well as making false confessions more likely.

Relatively few studies have looked at how guilty suspects tend to lie to authorities, although one study involved questioning prison inmates about the strategies they used to tell lies during interrogations (Stromwall & Willen, 2011). It documented both verbal and nonverbal techniques of deception, including providing statements that are close to the truth (but not the *whole* truth), and not giving away any information. These strategies reveal a sophisticated understanding of how to manage impressions and information during an interrogation.

One might ask why so much attention has been devoted to uncovering false confessions and relatively little to understanding false denials. There are various answers to that question. It may reflect widespread philosophical agreement that it is "better for ten guilty persons to go free than one innocent person to be convicted," and it may reflect the interests of many psychology and law scholars in illuminating ways that the criminal justice system ensnares innocent people (Cutler, 2011; Garrett, 2011). But it is worth remembering that if society wants the police to refrain from using tactics that yield false confessions, there will be a corresponding reduction in the number of true confessions that lead to the convictions of guilty suspects. Consider, for a moment, the possibility that among those fewer convictions are people who are guilty of multiple counts of sexually abusing children over a period of many years. False denials, like false confessions, come at a cost to society.

Why Do Innocent Suspects Falsely Confess? Why would a truly innocent person falsely confess to a crime that he or she did not commit? How often does this really happen? What are the circumstances that would lead someone to confess falsely? Any attempt to quantify the problem is almost certainly an underestimation, because false confessions often are not revealed, and thus go unacknowledged by police and prosecutors and unreported by the media. But they are a global problem (Gudjonsson, 2010). In 2016, the Innocence Project reported that approximately 29% of cases in which DNA evidence led to exonerations involved false confession evidence. Interrogation-induced false confessions tend to occur in more serious cases like homicides and other high-stakes felonies when the police are under pressure to solve the crime, and thus use more psychologically coercive tactics to wear the suspect down (Gross et al., 2005). Lacking a victim or an eyewitness to describe the crime, the police may need a confession to secure a conviction.

Scientists understand some the circumstances that give rise to false confessions. But before we describe them, we ask how one can know for certain that a confession is false. Do we simply take suspects or defendants at their word when alleging that an admission of guilt was wrong? Alternatively, do we need some kind of evidence that proves, unequivocally, that they could not have committed the crime to which they confessed?

Proving That a Confession Is False. There are four reasons one can be certain that a disputed confession is false (Drizin & Leo, 2004). First, a suspect could confess to a crime that never happened. For example, three intellectually disabled defendants (including Victoria Banks) were convicted by an Alabama jury of killing Ms. Banks's newborn child. Only after the three had served time in prison was it determined that Ms. Banks was incapable of giving birth to a child because she had had a tubal ligation operation that prevented her from getting pregnant.

Confessions can be proved to be false in situations where it was physically impossible for a suspect to commit the crime, as, for example, when jail records show that the defendant was incarcerated at the time the crime was committed. Three men suspected of committing crimes in Chicago were actually in jail when those crimes were committed (Drizin & Leo, 2004).

A third way in which a disputed confession can be proved false is that the actual perpetrator is identified and guilt is objectively established. This happened in the case of Christopher Ochoa, a high school honor student, who confessed to robbing, raping, and murdering a woman in an Austin, Texas, Pizza Hut in 1988. Ochoa, who served 12 years in prison, claims that he confessed in order to avoid the possibility of a death sentence. He was released and exonerated only after the real perpetrator confessed to killing the woman and led authorities to the weapon and the bag in which he had placed the money (Drizin & Leo, 2004).

Finally, a confession is false when there is scientific evidence—most commonly DNA—that definitively establishes the defendant's innocence. For example, three teenagers (Michael Crowe, Joshua Treadway, and Aaron Houser) all falsely confessed to the 1998 murder of Michael's 12-year-old sister Stephanie in Escondido, California. Charges against the boys were dropped only after DNA testing proved that blood found on the sweatshirt of a mentally ill drifter who had been in the neighborhood on the night of the murder was Stephanie's (Drizin & Colgan, 2004).

Few cases involving disputed confessions come with independent evidence that the suspect is innocent, however (Leo, 2008). Rarely will the actual perpetrator come forward to claim responsibility and remove the blame from an innocent confessor, and in most cases there is no DNA evidence to compare to the confessor's DNA. As a result, few confessors can prove definitively that their confessions were false. Even when DNA evidence exonerates a false confessor, prosecutors sometimes refuse to concede innocence and juries sometimes convict. For example, in 1991, Jeffrey Deskovic was convicted of raping and murdering a high school classmate despite DNA testing that excluded him as a perpetrator. Why? Probably because in the course of a manipulative and grueling interrogation, the 16-year-old confessed. Since then, several other cases have come to light in which confessors were convicted despite unequivocal DNA evidence of their innocence (Drizin & Riley, 2014). In cases like these, prosecutors explain away inconsistencies between the confession and the DNA evidence by suggesting, for example, that the victim had prior consensual sex with another man (the so-called unindicted co-ejaculator) (Appleby & Kassin, 2016; McMurtrie, 2015).

Let's return to the question of why a person would confess to a crime he or she did not commit. One reason is to protect someone else. Another is to escape the pressures of a harsh interrogation. Yet another reason is that various tactics of psychological coercion induce suspects to confess, particularly when those suspects are young or have mental limitations. Brendan Dassey, who confessed to raping and murdering a woman with his uncle, Steven Avery, in the Netflix series, *Making a Murderer*, was both young and cognitively impaired. Before confessing, he endured hours of questioning without his lawyer present. Several years later, a judge overturned his conviction because investigators had falsely promised Dassey that he would not be prosecuted for his alleged crimes. In Box 7.3, we provide another example of the compounding effects of interrogators' coercive tactics and suspects' vulnerable state at the time of questioning.

Inside the Interrogation Room: Common Interrogation Techniques

Based on his own observations of more than 100 police interrogations and his review of recorded interrogations

The Case of Henry McCollum and Leon Brown: Young, Intellectually Disabled Half-Brothers Who Falsely Confessed

BOX 7.3

Red Springs, North Carolina; September, 1983. Eleven-year-old Sabrina Buie had been raped and suffocated by underwear stuffed down her throat. Nineteen-year-old Henry Lee McCollum and his 15-year-old half-brother Leon Brown were picked up after police received a tip from a local teenager, despite the absence of physical evidence tying them to the crime. Their interrogations went on for five hours with no lawyers present and with their mother weeping in the hallway, unable to join them. McCollum cracked first. He concocted a story about how he and three others attacked and killed the girl, and then asked, "Can I go home now?" (Years later, McCollum recounted that he had never before been under such pressure, with detectives "hollering at me and threatening me.") Armed with a confession from his half-brother, police worked on Brown next, threatening him with execution if he failed to cooperate. He also confessed and signed a statement prepared by police. Even though both men claimed their confessions were coerced, they were convicted, sentenced to death, and languished in prison for 30 years. But after decades of legal battles, their fortunes turned in 2014 when DNA evidence from a cigarette butt found near the victim's body implicated another man who lived only a block away. McCollum and Brown were freed later

Henry McCollum and Leon Brown

Chuck Liddy/Raleigh News & Observer/MCT/Getty Images

that year. But like other prosecutors who attempt to explain away contradictory DNA evidence by invoking the theory of an "unindicted co-ejaculator," the original prosecutor, Joe Freeman Britt, continues to believe in their guilt.

CRITICAL THOUGHT QUESTION

What police tactics may have led to McCollum and Brown's false confessions? How do you suspect those tactics influenced them?

in several hundred other cases, Professor Richard Leo noted a fundamental contradiction concerning the nature of interrogations: "On the one hand, police need incriminating statements and admissions to solve many crimes, especially serious ones; on the other hand, there is almost never a good reason for suspects to provide them. Police are under tremendous organizational and social pressure to obtain admissions and confessions. But it is rarely in a suspect's rational self-interest to say something that will likely lead to his prosecution and conviction" (Leo, 2008, pp. 5–6).

Because physical intimidation and "third-degree" tactics are virtually nonexistent today, interrogators now use psychologically oriented coercion to overcome the anticipated resistance of suspects and to yield legally admissible confessions (Kassin et al., 2010). Most of

these techniques are detailed in interrogation training manuals; the most popular are *Criminal Interrogation and Confessions*, commonly referred to as the Reid technique (Inbau et al., 2013) and *Practical Aspects of Interview and Interrogation* (Zulawski & Wicklander, 2001). For example, the Reid technique consists of nine steps that interrogators are instructed to use in order to obtain confessions. To understand why someone would falsely confess, one must be aware of the techniques of social influence recommended by these manuals and put into practice in interrogation rooms.

One can divide an interrogation into the pre-interrogation "softening up" stage and the interrogation itself. Throughout the encounter, police use well-crafted, deliberate strategies to secure incriminating evidence from suspects.

Pre-Interrogation—"Softening Up" the Suspect.

Would you prefer to be "interviewed" or "interrogated?" (Probably the former.) When the police arrange to question a suspect, they may "invite" him or her to the station house because they "just want to ask a few questions" to "clear up a little matter." They may explicitly tell the suspect that they do not consider him or her a suspect. This all sounds innocuous enough. But the police have actually misrepresented the nature and purpose of the "discussion" to disarm the suspect and reduce resistance (Leo, 2008).

When a suspect arrives at the police station for questioning, he or she is typically shuffled off to a small, soundproof room with armless, straight-backed chairs, thereby removing sensory stimulation and distractions. By physically and socially isolating the suspect, the police begin to subtly exert pressure on him or her to talk. The interrogator may then try to soften up the suspect by using flattery, ingratiation, and rapport building—asking benign questions and engaging in pleasant small talk. According to one detective, "I don't care whether it is rape, robbery or homicide … the first thing you need to do is build rapport with that person … I think from that point on you can get anybody to talk about anything" (Leo, 2008, p. 123). All the while, the detective is concealing the fact that he or she has already determined that the suspect is guilty of a crime and is intent on extracting incriminating evidence.

Although the police are required by law to give the *Miranda* warnings prior to questioning, there are various ways they can circumvent these warnings, such as trivializing the implications of a *Miranda* waiver for future outcomes for the suspect (Scherr & Madon, 2013). Leo observed a detective who stated, "Don't let this ruffle your feathers or anything like that, it's just a formality that we have to go through, okay. As I said this is a *Miranda* warning and what it says is …." The intent here is to get the suspect to waive his or her rights and begin to talk, thereby increasing the police's chances of hearing incriminating information. Recall that the warnings are required only when the suspect is being interrogated while in custody. By telling suspects that they are not under arrest and are free to go, there is no need to warn them that their statements may be used against them. On other occasions, police can persuade the suspect to talk in order to tell "his (or her) side of the story." Almost all suspects waive their *Miranda* rights and talk to interrogators (Leo, 2008).

The Interrogation Itself.

During the heart of the questioning, interrogators use a set of carefully orchestrated procedures with the goal to eventually overwhelm even the most reluctant suspect and get him or her to provide incriminating statements. These procedures can be reduced to a few basic strategies. One strategy is the use of **negative incentives** to break down a suspect's defenses, lower resistance, and instill feelings of fear, despair, and powerlessness. Negative incentives like accusations, attacks on denials, and evidence fabrications convey to the suspect that there is no choice but to confess. The police also use **positive inducements** to motivate the suspect to see that an admission is in his or her best interest. All interrogators try, implicitly or explicitly, to send the message that the suspect will receive some benefit in exchange for an admission of wrongdoing (Leo, 2008).

After the suspect has either implicitly or explicitly agreed to talk, the interrogation can become accusatorial, with the interrogator confronting the suspect with a statement indicating absolute belief in guilt. Accusations are one of the most basic tactics in interrogations; police use them routinely. One subtle effect of an accusation is shifting the burden of proof from the state to the suspect. In what may be one of the most "ingenious psychological aspects of American interrogation" (Leo, 2008, p. 135), the suspect must now work to convince the police of his or her innocence.

During questioning, interrogators also challenge denials that suspects make, often by simply cutting them off or expressing disbelief in their version of events (Kassin et al., 2010). They also introduce information, either intentionally or unintentionally, about details of

Police interrogators are specially trained to use various techniques, including psychologically oriented coercion to overcome suspect resistance.

the crime (Appleby, Hasel, & Kassin, 2013). The effect of these ploys is to undermine suspects' confidence in their memories, which may cause inconsistencies in later retellings of the truth, and eventually, false confessions consistent with interrogators' version of the facts.

The most powerful tool in the interrogator's arsenal is the opportunity to present **fabricated evidence**. Even if interrogators have no evidence of suspects' wrongdoing, they can make them believe that they do. They can point to "signs" of nonverbal behavior that indicate guilt, tell suspects that other people including eyewitnesses and accomplices have implicated them, and make up stories about the existence of fraudulent fingerprint and DNA evidence and surveillance videos that capture their images. On occasion, a suspect may take a polygraph examination, presented as an opportunity to prove innocence, when all along investigators plan to confront the suspect with evidence of a failed test and urge him or her to confess.

Finally, police use positive inducements to persuade suspects that they will benefit from complying with authorities and confessing. This can take the form of providing scenarios to explain or justify suspects' actions (e.g., suggesting that they were probably acting in self-defense or in the "heat of the moment"), or of promising some sort of a deal for confessing. Sometimes detectives simply imply that suspects can go home if they accept interrogators' demands. In another famous case involving false confessions—the Central Park jogger case, in which five young men confessed to brutally raping and beating a female jogger—each suspect confessed in a way that minimized his own involvement, and each thought that after confessing he could go home (Kassin, 2005).

A 2007 survey of more than 600 police investigators showed that they commonly practiced many of these ploys, including physically isolating suspects, establishing rapport, finding contradictions in their accounts, confronting them with evidence of their guilt, and appealing to their self-interest (Kassin et al., 2007). But one recent study hints that interrogation tactics may have changed somewhat over the intervening years, at least in one jurisdiction. By analyzing 29 recorded interrogations provided by the Robbery-Homicide Division of the Los Angeles Police Department, Kelly, Miller, and Redlich (2016) found that rapport-building was the favored tactic at the beginning of the interrogation, and that provoking emotions by offering rationalizations or appealing to one's conscience tended to increase as the interrogation progressed. But confrontational tactics such as accusations of guilt and implied threats for noncompliance were used relatively infrequently. Moreover, interrogations that ended in a confession contained fewer confrontations than those that ended in denial, suggesting that suspects are less likely to cooperate with detectives when questioned in an accusatory or threatening manner. Whether these findings hold up in a larger sample and these practices take place in other departments are questions for future research.

An Empirical Look at Interrogation Tactics. Psychological scientists have examined some of these interrogation tactics and now understand why innocent people waive their *Miranda* rights, how interrogators' presumption of guilt affects the nature of the questioning, which, in turn, affects the suspect's responses, and how false evidence ploys elicit confessions.

To test the possibility that innocent people are likely to waive their rights and submit to questioning, Kassin and Norwick (2004) conducted a study in which participants were instructed either to steal $100 from a drawer (guilty condition) or to open the drawer but not take any money (innocent condition). When questioned by a "detective" who sought a waiver of their *Miranda* rights, innocent participants were considerably more likely to grant the waiver than those who were guilty, by a margin of 81–36%. When asked to explain why, 72% of innocent people said that they waived their rights precisely because they were innocent. A typical comment: "I did not have anything to hide." Innocents may waive their rights and answer questions because they assume, naively, that their innocence will set them free. But ironically, "innocence may put innocents at risk" (Kassin, 2012, p. 433).

Recall that many interrogations begin with the detective issuing a statement of belief in the suspect's guilt. This presumption of guilt can apparently influence the way a detective conducts the questioning, causing the suspect to become defensive or confused, and increasing the chances of a false confession. This phenomenon—referred to as a self-fulfilling prophecy or **behavioral confirmation** (Meissner & Kassin, 2004)—has been demonstrated in a wide range of settings (McNatt, 2000; Rosenthal & Jacobson, 1968). After people form a particular belief (e.g., in the guilt of a suspect), they unwittingly seek out information that verifies that belief, overlook conflicting data, and behave in a manner that conforms to the belief. In turn, the target person (here, the suspect) behaves in ways that support the initial belief.

Psychologists have also examined the effects of an implicit assumption of guilt on the behavior of interrogators and suspects, and on judgments of the interrogation by neutral observers. The first section of a multipart study (Hill, Memon, & McGeorge, 2008) asked whether interviewers' assumption of guilt affected the kinds of questions they ask suspects. Prior to formulating their questions, some participant-interviewers were led to believe suspects were guilty of cheating on a test; others believed they were innocent. As expected, expectations of guilt resulted in more guilt-presumptive questions, indicating that confirmation bias led interviewers to seek information confirming their expectations.

In a follow-up study, independent observers listened to audiotaped interviews of "suspects" who had been questioned with either guilt-presumptive or neutral questions, and rated their behavior. Importantly, observers did not hear the questions asked, only the suspects' responses, and none of the responses contained a confession. Still, observers rated the suspects questioned in a guilt-presumptive manner as more nervous and defensive and less plausible than suspects questioned in a neutral manner, and judged the former to be guiltier than the latter.

The presumption of guilt apparently ushers in a process of behavioral confirmation by which the expectations of interrogators affect their questioning style, suspects' behavior, and, ultimately, judgments of the guilt of the suspect. These findings may actually *underestimate* the risks of behavioral confirmation in actual interrogations, where questioning can go on for hours rather than minutes and interrogators have years of experience in questioning suspects, as well as confidence in their ability to get a confession (Meissner & Kassin, 2004).

Finally, we consider the role of **evidence ploys** in eliciting confessions. As we mentioned, it is legal for interrogators to lie to suspects about the existence of evidence linking them to the crime. Researchers have now investigated how these ruses lead people to believe they committed acts they did not actually commit. In one study (Nash & Wade, 2009), participants were falsely accused of cheating on a computerized gambling task. Some were shown a doctored video that portrayed them doing so, and others were only told that their cheating was documented on video. Participants who saw the fake video were more likely to provide confabulated details and confess without resistance. Feeding false information to suspects can apparently cause them to doubt their memories and rely instead on external sources to infer what happened.

So far, we have considered the effects of interrogation tactics on adults accused of committing crimes. But a substantial number of juveniles are also interrogated by police who use the same strategies on them (Cleary & Warner, 2016). Hayley Cleary painted a particularly troubling picture of juvenile interrogations after observing 57 recorded interviews (Cleary, 2014). One account of those interrogations noted, "Even when police interrogators left the room, cameras kept recording the teenage suspects. Some paced. Several curled up and slept. One sobbed loudly, hitting his head against the wall, berating himself. Two boys, left alone together, discussed their offense, joking. What none did, however, was exercise his constitutional rights. It was not clear whether the youths even understood them. Therefore, none had a lawyer at his side. None left, though all were free to do so, and none remained silent. Some 37 percent made full confessions, and 31 percent made incriminating statements" (Hoffman, 2014).

False Confessions

Innocent people tend to waive their *Miranda* rights, police presume guilt, and interrogators use carefully scripted techniques to elicit confessions. Consequently, detectives draw out confessions from innocent people as well as from the guilty. Yet not all false confessions are alike; they occur for different reasons and can be explained by different situational and dispositional factors. Kassin and Wrightsman (1985) devised a taxonomy of false confessions. Although it has been refined over the years (Kassin & Gudjonsson, 2004), it still serves as a good framework for understanding why false confessions happen.

Some innocent people confess to criminal acts with little prodding. When Charles Lindbergh's baby was kidnapped in 1932, more than 200 people came forward and claimed responsibility. After the murder of child beauty-pageant contestant JonBenét Ramsey had gone unresolved for several years, prosecutors were eager to consider the confession of Mark Karr. But Karr's DNA did not match the sample found on the victim and he was never charged. These **voluntary false confessions** arise because people seek notoriety, desire to cleanse themselves of guilt feelings from previous wrongdoings, want to protect the real criminal, have difficulty distinguishing fact from fiction (McCann, 1998), or, as in one reported case, want to impress a girlfriend (Radelet, Bedau, & Putnam, 1992).

Sometimes suspects confess in order to escape or avoid ongoing aversive interrogations or to gain some sort of promised reward. Legal history is full of examples dating as far back as the Salem witch trials of 1692 during which approximately 50 women confessed to being witches, some after being "tyed … neck and heels till the blood was ready to come out of their noses" (Karlsen, 1989, p. 101, cited by Kassin & Gudjonsson, 2004). The false confessions in the Central Park jogger case were of this sort; each of the defendants said he confessed because he wanted to go home. These confessions are termed **compliant false confessions** because the suspect is induced to comply with the interrogator's demands to make an incriminating statement. They occur when suspects know that they are innocent but publicly acquiesce to the demand for a confession because the short-term benefit of confessing—such as being left alone or allowed to leave—outweighs the long-term costs—such as being charged with or convicted of a crime (Madon et al., 2011).

Some suspects confess because they actually come to believe that they have committed the crime. These so-called **internalized false confessions** can be directly related to the highly suggestive and manipulative techniques that interrogators sometimes use during questioning. An internalized false confession can result when, after hours of being questioned, badgered, and told stories about what "must have happened," suspects begin to develop a profound distrust of their own memory. Being vulnerable, they are easily influenced by external suggestions and come to believe that they "must have done it."

We previously described the case of 14-year-old Michael Crowe, who falsely confessed to killing his sister. Despite his initial vehement denials, Michael apparently came to believe, over the course of three grueling interrogations, that he had actually stabbed her: "I'm not sure how I did it. All I know is I did it" (Drizin & Colgan, 2004, p. 141). During the interrogations, detectives told Michael at least four lies: that his hair was found on his sister's body, that her blood was in his bedroom, that all of the doors to the house had been locked, and that he failed a lie detector test. With no memory of the killing but persuaded by these details, Michael was apparently convinced that he had dissociative identity disorder and that the killing was accomplished by the "bad Michael" while the "good Michael" blocked out the crime (Drizin & Colgan, 2004).

Inside the Courtroom: How Confession Evidence Is Evaluated

The first source of error involving confession evidence stems from what happens in the interrogation room. A second source of error occurs when prosecutors, defense attorneys, judges, and especially juries fail to understand why the suspect might have confessed and uncritically accept a false confession as valid. The false confession sets in motion a chain of events with adverse consequences for the suspect because attorneys, juries, and judges make decisions—about plea-bargaining, convicting, and sentencing—assuming that what the suspect said was true.

Many prosecutors assume that only guilty suspects confess. So when they secure a confession, they tend to treat suspects harshly, charging them with the highest number and types of offenses possible, requesting higher bail, and being reluctant to accept a plea bargain to a reduced charge (Drizin & Leo, 2004). The confession becomes, in essence, the crux of the prosecution's case. Even defense attorneys assume that people who confess are guilty, and urge them to accept plea bargains rather than risk their chances in a trial with confession evidence (Nardulli, Eisenstein, & Fleming, 1988).

Judges are also likely to treat confessors harshly. In cases of disputed confessions, they almost always decide that confessions are voluntary and thus admissible as evidence in a trial (Givelber, 2001). In some cases, defendants who confessed will nevertheless enter a plea of not guilty and go to trial. If the jury convicts, judges' sentences are likely to be harsh because they tend to punish offenders who claim innocence, waste resources in a trial, and fail to show remorse or apologize (Leo, 2008).

Confessions are an especially potent form of evidence to jurors, even more influential than eyewitness and character testimony (Kassin & Neumann, 1997). Juries are quite likely to convict defendants who confessed, even when confession are false. Archival analyses of actual cases in which false confessors pled not guilty and proceeded to trial show that conviction rates ranged from 73% (Leo & Ofshe, 1998) to 81% (Drizin & Leo, 2004).

For several reasons, jurors tend to accept confession evidence. They assume that suspects would not act against their own self-interests and confess to something they had not done (Kassin et al., 2010) and that interrogators are adept at identifying liars (Costanzo, Shaked-Schroer, & Vinson, 2010). They are persuaded by secondary confessions in which suspects confess to another person who provides information to the police, even when those informants are motivated to lie (Wetmore, Neuschatz, & Gronlund, 2014). Jurors are impressed by contextual details in confessions, particularly if the details include nonpublic information, but they fail to account for the fact that police could have scripted the confession in a manner consistent with their theory of the case. But jurors' awareness may be changing in subtle ways. One recent study showed that jurors can be made aware that situational pressures, rather than guilt, may have motivated defendants to confess (Woestehoff & Meissner, 2016).

In general though, when people, including jurors, explain the causes of others' behavior, they often commit the **fundamental attribution error**: They do not give sufficient weight to the external situation as a determinant of behavior; instead, they believe the behavior is caused by stable, internal factors unique to the actor. In many instances, jurors take a confession at face value, fail to adjust or correct for situational forces on behavior, and assume that if suspects confess, they must be guilty (Wrightsman & Kassin, 1993). So a jury trial will not provide much of a safeguard for defendants who falsely confess and then claim their confessions were coerced (Bornstein & Greene, 2017).

Psychologists sometimes participate in cases of disputed confessions, functioning as consultants to defense attorneys or testifying as expert witnesses in pretrial admissibility hearings and during trials. The objective is to educate jurors and judges about the nature of police interrogations and the dispositional and situational factors that lead to false confessions. Their testimony can successfully alert jurors to whether the confession is consistent with other trial evidence (Henderson & Levett, 2016). But might there be a more efficient way to prevent wrongful convictions based on false confessions? Wouldn't it be better to assess, early in the investigation of a case, whether a suspect's confession resulted from a coercive interrogation? Several commentators advocate reforming the system with this objective in mind.

Reforming the System to Prevent False Confessions

Recording all police interrogations can provide a complete, objective, and reviewable record of how the suspect was questioned. It can improve the quality of interrogations by deterring manipulative tactics by investigators and frivolous claims of coercion by defendants (Kassin, Kukucka, Lawson, & DeCarlo, 2014). It can also preserve an objective record of the entire session—an important benefit because police reports of interrogations frequently understate the use of confrontation, maximization, leniency, and false evidence (Kassin, Kukucka, Lawson, & DeCarlo, 2017). Several states and the federal government require video-recording, and hundreds of other jurisdictions voluntarily record interrogations.

How the interrogation is recorded is important. Daniel Lassiter and his colleagues have shown that when the camera is focused on the suspect, observers are more likely to judge the confession as voluntary, compared with the same confession recorded from a different camera perspective (e.g., focused equally on the suspect and the interrogator or solely on the interrogator) (Lassiter, Ware, Ratcliff, & Irvin, 2009). This is an example of **illusory causation**—the tendency to attribute causation to one stimulus because it is more conspicuous than others. When the recording shows both the suspect and the interrogator, observers are more attuned to situational pressures exerted by the interrogator.

A more radical reform would reconceptualize the fundamental nature of police interrogations. At present, American interrogation practices are confrontational and accusatorial, and police claim that these techniques are necessary to get reluctant suspects to confess. By contrast, police interviews in the United Kingdom are not coercive or overtly confrontational, and interviewers are not allowed to lie to suspects or present false evidence. The goal is to obtain useful information about a crime, rather than to extract a confession (Gudjonsson & Pearse, 2011). Data suggest that the nonconfrontational, U.K.-type interviews produce fewer false confessions and more true confessions than accusatory interrogations (Meissner et al., 2014), probably because they encourage suspects to say more (Evans, Michael, Meissner, & Brandon, 2013), which leads to more accurate credibility judgments (Vrij et al., 2015). One scholar, a prominent observer of the Supreme Court, advocates that judges take a stand against deception in police interrogations (Wrightsman, 2010).

Summary

1. *What are some psychological investigative techniques used by the police?* The police use a variety of techniques to increase the likelihood that suspects will be prosecuted and convicted. Among these are criminal profiling; unaided judgments of deception; the so-called lie detector (technically, the polygraph technique); brain-based techniques for gauging deception; and procedures to induce confessions.

2. *What is criminal profiling?* Criminal profiling is an attempt to use what is known about how a crime was committed to infer what type of person might have committed it. Evidence about profiling suggests that it may have some utility as a means of narrowing police investigations to the most likely suspects.

3. *Is the polygraph a valid instrument for lie detection? What are some problems associated with it?* No measure of physiological reactions can precisely distinguish between guilt and other negative emotions, such as fear, anger, or embarrassment. Although some studies show high rates of accuracy in distinguishing between subjects who are lying and those who are not, many scientists are skeptical of those claims.

4. *What are the premises of cognitive-based methods to detect deception and how effective are those protocols?* Cognitive methods of deception detection are based on the facts that lying is mentally taxing, and that truth-tellers and liars reveal information in different ways. Researchers have developed interviewing protocols that increase cognitive load on already-taxed liars and that reveal evidence strategically, forcing deceptive suspects to be caught in their lies.

5. *What brain-based techniques are used to detect deception, and how well do they work?* Two techniques, neuroimaging using fMRI and brain fingerprinting using electroencephalograms, record brain activity while people are either lying or telling the truth. Studies show that different patterns of brain activation are associated with truth-telling and lying. Advocates of these procedures promote their effectiveness in detecting deception, but a number of complicating issues have not been resolved.

6. *How valid is confession evidence? What kinds of interrogation procedures can lead to false confessions?* Two kinds of errors arise in the context of confessions: guilty suspects falsely proclaiming their innocence and innocent suspects falsely confessing. Among the interrogation techniques that can lead to false confessions are prolonged social isolation, confronting a suspect and expressing a belief in his or her guilt, exaggerating or fabricating evidence against the suspect, and offering psychological and moral justification for the offense.

7. *What are some of the reforms proposed to prevent false confessions?* Critics of police interrogations suggest that these interrogations should be recorded in order to improve the quality of questioning, deter police misconduct, and preserve a record that can be evaluated at a later time. A more radical approach would replace the accusatorial style of interrogations with nonconfrontational interviews such as are now being conducted in the United Kingdom.

Key Terms

behavioral confirmation

brain fingerprinting

cognitive load

compliant false confessions

Concealed Information Test

Control Question Test

countermeasures

criminal profiling

diagnostic cues

evidence ploys

external validity

fabricated evidence

false confession

false denial

functional magnetic resonance imaging

fundamental attribution error

illusory causation

internalized false confessions

lie bias

mass murderer

negative incentives

polygraph

positive inducements

serial killers

spree killers

truth bias

voluntary false confessions

8 Traditional Prosecutions: Arrest, Bail, Plea Bargain and Settlement, and Trial

ORIENTING QUESTIONS

1. What are the major legal proceedings between arrest and trial in the criminal justice system?

2. What is bail, and what factors influence the amount of bail set?

3. Why do defendants and prosecutors agree to plea bargain?

4. What are settlement negotiations, and why are most civil lawsuits resolved through settlement rather than trial?

5. What is the purpose of a trial?

6. What are the steps involved in a trial?

7. How has the introduction of emerging technologies changed the way that trials are conducted?

Between the time that the police make an arrest and a case is eventually resolved at sentencing, traditional prosecutions involve several steps with psychological implications. One feature of traditional prosecutions has obvious psychological overtones: a trial. The trial is the penultimate act in our adversary system of justice. (For criminal defendants who are found guilty to be guilty, sentencing and punishment come afterwards and for civil litigants, further wrangling sometimes ensues.) Trials are public battles waged by two combatants (prosecution versus defense in a criminal trial, plaintiff versus defendant in a civil trial), each vying for a favorable outcome. They can be fiercely contested; prosecutors desire convictions, criminal defendants seek their freedom through acquittals, civil plaintiffs want compensation for wrongs they have suffered, and civil defendants hope to be absolved of wrongdoing and not required to pay damages. Psychological issues abound.

Although the trial may be the most visible and dramatic ritual in our system, many other factors play larger—often decisive—roles in determining case outcomes. For example, in the weeks and months following arrest, many criminal cases are simply dismissed for lack of evidence or other difficulties that prosecutors perceive in the case. Of some 56,000 felony cases filed during May 2009 in the 75 most populous counties in the United States, 25% were dismissed prior to formal prosecution (Reaves, 2013).

For the vast majority of people charged with crimes and not fortunate enough to have the charges dropped, **plea bargains**, not trials, resolve their cases. Plea bargaining, described in more detail later in the chapter, is a process in which a defendant agrees to plead guilty in exchange for some concession from the prosecutor. Such concessions typically involve a reduction in the type of charge, the number of charges, or the recommended

sentence. By pleading guilty, defendants give up their right to a trial, allowing attorneys and judges to move on to other cases. The vast majority of civil cases are also resolved without a formal trial in a process termed *settlement negotiation*, described in more detail in this chapter.

If most cases are settled without a trial, why is our society (including psychologists who work in the legal arena) so fascinated by trials and trial procedures? Without a doubt, there are theatrical aspects to many trials, especially those featured in news media, films, and novels. Trials grab our attention because they vividly portray the raw emotions of sad, distraught, and angry people. Interest in trials is also related to their very public nature; most trials are conducted in open court for all to see. Some are televised or even available for online viewing.

In contrast, negotiations about plea bargains and settlements are largely hidden from public view. Prosecutors offer concessions to defense attorneys over the phone or in courthouse hallways. Defense attorneys convey these offers to their clients in offices or jail cells. Settlement negotiations in civil cases are also conducted in private. In fact, the eventual settlements in civil cases are often never made public.

You may notice that we expend many more pages of this book on psychological issues before and during trials than we do on plea bargains or settlement negotiations. This choice reflects the nature of the research findings available to us. Like the general public, psychologists have been intrigued by the interpersonal dramas and behavioral complexities involved in trials. Thus, psychologists have conducted a great deal of research on trials and have much to say about them. Just keep in mind that most cases are disposed of in different and less public ways—through plea bargains and settlement discussions that are core concepts of this chapter. In future editions of this book, we hope to be able to say more about the plea-bargaining process. But the scope of research in this area would have to broaden to include plea negotiations in order for that to happen.

In addition to plea bargains and settlements, this chapter examines other pretrial proceedings in criminal cases including pretrial motions and bail setting, and outlines the basic steps involved in a trial. All of these procedures raise important psychological questions that have been addressed through experimentation, observation, or empirical analysis. We preface those issues by describing the customary sequence of activities that occur after an arrest has been made in a criminal case.

Steps Between Arrest and Trial

If the police believe that a suspect committed a crime, they will probably arrest the suspect. However, being arrested for a crime and being charged with a crime are two different events, and a person may be arrested without being charged. For example, the police may arrest drunks to detain them and sober them up, but formal charges might never be filed. Charging implies a formal decision to continue with the prosecution, and that decision is made by the prosecuting attorney rather than the police. A few studies have focused on psychological factors associated with prosecutors' decision to pursue criminal charges. For example, by reviewing files in 400 child maltreatment cases in North Carolina, Eldred and colleagues determined that only 40% of individuals arrested for child maltreatment were charged, and that the presence of a concurrent nonchild maltreatment charge was associated with that decision (Eldred, Gifford, McCutchan, & Sloan, 2016).

The Initial Appearance

Following arrest, the **initial appearance** is a crucial step in the criminal process. The Fourth Amendment to the U.S. Constitution requires that any person arrested be brought before a judge within 48 hours of arrest. This is one of the most important protections of the Bill of Rights. In many countries the police arrest people (or "detain" them, a euphemism for arrest) and hold them without charge for extended periods—or indefinitely. In the United States, however, anyone who is arrested must be taken without delay before a judge, an essential protection against abuse of power by the police. The primary purpose of the initial appearance is for the judge to review the evidence summarized by the prosecutor and determine whether there is reason to believe that the suspect committed the crimes charged. In addition, the judge will inform defendants of the charges against them, remind them of their constitutional rights, review the issue of bail, and appoint attorneys for those that cannot afford to hire their own.

The Preliminary Hearing

The next step is the **preliminary hearing**. One of its purposes is to filter out cases in which the prosecution has insufficient evidence. At a preliminary hearing, the prosecution must offer some evidence on every element of the crime charged and the judge must decide whether the evidence is sufficient to pursue the case further. No jury is present and defendants rarely testify or offer any evidence of their own. The judge will sometimes send the case to a grand jury (described next) or reduce the charges, either because the judge believes the evidence does not support the level of crime charged by the prosecutor or because of a plea bargain between the prosecutor and the defense attorney.

The Grand Jury

Consisting of citizens drawn from the community, the **grand jury** meets in private with the prosecutor to investigate criminal activity and return **indictments**

Courtroom trial in session.

(complaints prepared and signed by the prosecutor describing the crime charged). The grand jury may call witnesses on its own initiative if it is dissatisfied with the witnesses presented by the prosecutor. In some states the defendant has a right to testify. In about one-third of the states, a criminal defendant cannot be prosecuted unless a grand jury has found grounds to do so. The remaining states permit the prosecutor to proceed either by grand jury indictment or by a preliminary hearing.

If the grand jury decides there is sufficient evidence to justify the defendant being tried, it issues an indictment. For example, six Baltimore police officers were indicted by a grand jury in relation to the 2015 death of Freddie Gray, a young black man who died while in police custody. None of the officers was convicted.

Arraignment

A grand jury gives its indictments to a judge, who summons those indicted to court for arraignment. At the **arraignment**, the judge makes sure that the defendant has an attorney and appoints one if necessary. The indictment is then read to the defendant, and the defendant is asked to plead guilty or not guilty. It is customary for defendants to plead not guilty at this time, even those who ultimately plead guilty. The reasons for a not-guilty plea at this stage involve providing opportunities for both plea bargaining and discovery (described next), so that the defendant's attorney can review some of the evidence against the defendant.

Discovery and Pretrial Motions

In criminal cases, defendants and their attorneys want to be aware of the evidence the prosecution will use to prove its case. In civil trials, each side is entitled to **discovery**— that is, each side has a right to depose (or question) the witnesses on the opposing side, and to review and copy documents that the other side might use at trial.

Just how much the prosecution must reveal to the defense varies widely. Some states require prosecutors to turn over to the defense all reports, statements by witnesses, and physical evidence. Most states require only that the prosecutor share certain evidence (e.g., laboratory reports) and evidence that is **exculpatory** (i.e., that tends to show the defendant is not guilty or suggests that prosecution witnesses are not credible). In part because prosecutors failed to share exculpatory evidence, a Colorado man spent eight and a half years in prison for a crime he didn't commit. We describe his case in Box 8.1.

Discovery is a two-way street. In general, states require the defense to turn over the same types of materials that the prosecution must turn over. If the prosecution is required to reveal laboratory reports, the defense will likewise be required to share such reports. In many states, the defense is required to notify the prosecution if it intends to rely on certain defenses, notably insanity and alibi defenses. The reason for requiring such pretrial notice is to give the state an opportunity to investigate the claim and avoid being surprised at trial.

During the discovery phase of the case, both sides file pretrial motions seeking favorable rulings on the admissibility of evidence. Motions commonly filed by the defense are the following:

1. *Motion for separate trials.* When two or more defendants are jointly indicted, one of them can be counted on to request a separate trial, claiming that to be tried together would be prejudicial. Such a motion was granted in the case of Timothy McVeigh and Terry Nichols, who were convicted in separate trials of bombing the federal building in Oklahoma City, killing 168 people. McVeigh was convicted of murder and sentenced to death, but Nichols was convicted of a lesser charge (conspiracy) and sentenced to life imprisonment.

2. *Motion to sever counts.* Suppose the indictment charges the defendant with robbing a convenience store on April 13 and burglarizing a house on April 15. The defendant may request separate trials on these offenses. A defendant may argue that it is prejudicial for the same jury to hear evidence about separate crimes because the jury will be tempted to combine the evidence introduced on the separate crimes to find the defendant guilty of each crime. There is good reason for defendants to be concerned about how a jury will react to multiple charges. Psychological research studies that simulate jury decision-making have shown that jurors are more likely to convict a defendant on any charge (e.g., robbery) when it is combined with another (e.g., burglary) than when it is tried alone (e.g., Greene & Loftus, 1985). A review of nearly 20,000 federal criminal trials over a five-year period reached a similar conclusion (Leipold & Abbasi, 2006).

3. *Motion for change of venue.* The defendant may request a **change of venue** (moving the proceedings to a different location) on the ground that community opinion, usually the product of prejudicial pretrial publicity, makes it impossible to seat

BOX 8.1

The Case of Tim Masters and Prosecutors' Failure to Disclose Evidence

Tim Masters

In late January, 2008, Tim Masters became perhaps the first person in Colorado to walk up to a counter at the Department of Motor Vehicles and, without first taking a number and waiting in line, get a drivers' license. The crowds of people waiting their turns were happy to give Masters a break; after all, he had been released from prison just a few days before when his murder conviction and life sentence were wiped out by DNA evidence that pointed to another suspect. The DNA testing was the final chapter in a long saga of misplaced hunches, shoddy procedures, and prosecutors' failure to disclose crucial evidence.

In 1987, Masters—then only 15 years old—lived with his father in a trailer outside of Fort Collins, Colorado. A woman's body was found in a field about 100 feet from his home; she had been stabbed and sexually mutilated. Detectives interrogated Masters, who admitted to walking past the body on his way to catch a school bus and failing to report it. They also searched his home, confiscating violent pictures he had drawn in his school notebooks. Over the next several years, prosecutors built a circumstantial case against Masters based on "psychological analysis" of his drawings, the fact that the murder coincided with the anniversary of his mother's death, and their suspicions. Masters was convicted of murder and sentenced to life imprisonment in 1999.

But several years later, a new team of investigators and attorneys began to glean clues that prosecutors knew more than they revealed in 1987. They learned that police had an alternate suspect back then, something not revealed to the defense. They learned that counter to the judge's orders, prosecutors had taken evidence from the case for their own examination. They alleged that prosecutors deliberately "stonewalled, delayed, and obstructed" in order to preserve the conviction. Eventually, DNA tests excluded Masters as a suspect. His conviction was set aside, he was released from prison, and he finally got the chance to drive.

CRITICAL THOUGHT QUESTION

What had the prosecutor in this case failed to do, and why was that mistake costly to Masters, and eventually, to the police department, prosecutor's office, and the community?

---

a fair-minded jury. Psychologists are sometimes involved in analyzing the extent and impact of the publicity on prospective jurors.

4. *Motion to suppress a confession or other statement by the defendant.* The Fifth Amendment protects against self-incrimination, and the Sixth Amendment forbids the use of a statement taken in violation of the right to counsel. One or both of these constitutional provisions may become relevant any time the prosecution offers a confession or other statement by a defendant as evidence of guilt. Typically, defense counsel files a motion alleging that the confession was obtained in violation of the defendant's constitutional rights, the prosecutor files a written response, and the court holds a hearing at which the defendant and police give their versions of the circumstances under which the confession was obtained. The judge decides the issue on the basis of what was said and the credibility of the witnesses. Questions of who is telling the truth are usually resolved in favor of the police. Criminal defendants who believe that their confessions were coerced or made involuntarily have good reason to try to suppress them, because juries tend to accept a defendant's confession without careful evaluation of the circumstances that led to the confession.

AP Images/RJ Sangosti

5. *Motions* in limine. Perhaps the most common pretrial motions are those that seek advance rulings on evidentiary issues that will arise at trial. A **motion** *in limine* is simply a request for a pretrial ruling. Suppose, for example, that the defendant was previously convicted of burglary. The judge must decide whether to allow the prosecution to introduce that conviction into evidence in order to discredit the defendant if he or she chooses to testify. The defendant obviously wants a pretrial ruling on this issue in order to plan the questioning of the jurors and to decide whether to testify. Similarly, the prosecutor may want a pretrial ruling on the admissibility of a certain piece of evidence in order to plan the opening statement.

The Decision to Set Bail

Judges must decide whether to keep criminal defendants in custody during the lengthy process between arrest and trial or whether to release them into the community with a promise to reappear for subsequent hearings. Judges have many options. In capital cases and cases in which the defendant poses a serious risk of fleeing or committing other crimes, they can deny bail altogether. Approximately half of all murder defendants are denied bail, compared with less than 10% of defendants charged with other crimes (Reaves, 2013).

Short of denying bail, judges can require that money (or a bail bondsman's pledge) be deposited with the court or that a third person agrees to be responsible for the defendant's future appearances and to forfeit money if the defendant does not appear. When bail is higher than defendants can afford, they have no choice but to remain in jail. In fact, nearly three-quarters of people awaiting trial in New York City jails are detained because they could not pay bail, yet fewer than 8% of them had committed a serious crime (Bellafante, 2017). Most defendants who promise to reappear do so. In the 75 most populous counties in the United States in 2009, only 17% of released defendants missed a court appearance and were issued a warrant for their arrest (Reaves, 2013). Whether bail bonds actually reduce the risk of nonappearance is not clear. Box 8.2 describes some techniques that bail-bond agents use to ensure that defendants who post bail will show up for court.

In addition to ensuring the defendant's return to court, bail has a secondary purpose: protecting public safety. In fact, bail evolved in the American legal system as an attempt to resolve the basic conflict between an individual's right to liberty on the one hand and societal rights to be protected from criminal behavior on the other. The Eighth Amendment to the U.S. Constitution says that excessive bail shall not be required, but the Supreme Court has ruled that this provision does not guarantee a right to bail; it simply requires that bail, if any, should not be excessive (*United States v. Salerno*, 1987). Although various laws govern the bail decision, they are typically vague and ill-defined, allowing judges considerable leeway in the factors they consider and the way they make the decision about bail.

What Considerations Affect the Decision to Set Bail?

Psychologists and other social scientists have examined how judges make bail-setting decisions (e.g., Beattey, Matsuura, & Jeglic, 2014). In particular, they have evaluated the factors that judges consider and the cognitive processes by which judges weigh and combine these factors.

Bail decisions are influenced by both legal and extralegal factors. **Legal factors** are related to the offense or the offender's legal history; research has shown that bail is likely to be denied or set very high when the offense was serious and when the offender has prior convictions (Williams, 2016). Even *perceptions* of crime seriousness matter: In one study, judges imposed higher bail on those charged with sexual offenses than on those charged with nonsexual offenses at the same statutory offense level (Beatty et al., 2014). Since there is not strong, consistent evidence that defendants charged with sexual offenses are at higher risk to reoffend (Beatty et al., 2014), they may be particularly disadvantaged in the bail-setting context. This suggests that judges may be considering even the legally relevant factor of crime seriousness in an unsystematic, stereotype-influenced way.

Because laws relevant to bail decisions are ill defined and there is little public scrutiny of this step in the criminal process, **extralegal factors** such as offenders' race and gender can affect judges' decisions as well. There is evidence that this occurs (e.g., Freiburger, Marcum, & Pierce, 2010; Kutateladze & Andiloro, 2014). For example, in cases prosecuted by the New York County District Attorney in 2010–2011, judges detained a higher percentage of Black felony defendants (61%) than Latinos (56%), Whites (43%), or Asians (28%).

BOX 8.2

The Case of Marcella Deann Gomez and the Cybersearch for Defendants on the Run

FBI TEN MOST WANTED FUGITIVE

Unlawful Flight to Avoid Prosecution - Criminal Homicide, Criminal Attempt to Commit Homicide in the First Degree, Criminal Homicide of a Law Enforcement Officer, Criminal Attempt to Commit Criminal Homicide of a Law Enforcement Officer

ERIC MATTHEW FREIN

Photograph
taken in
August of
2011

Aliases: Eric Frein, Eric M. Frein

DESCRIPTION

Date(s) of Birth Used:	May 3, 1983	**Hair:**	Brown
Place of Birth:	New Jersey	**Eyes:**	Blue
Height:	6'1"	**Sex:**	Male
Weight:	165 pounds	**Race:**	White
NCIC:	W011862497	**Nationality:**	American

Remarks: Frein is known to be a heavy smoker, a weapons enthusiast, and a survivalist. He claims to have fought with Serbians in Africa, and he has studied Russian and Serbian languages. He may have shaved his head on both sides and have long hair on top. He was last seen with no facial hair and was wearing a brown and gold windbreaker, khaki shorts, and sneakers. He was carrying a dark green backpack with black trim. Frein has ties to the mid-Atlantic region of the United States, including the states of Pennsylvania, New Jersey, and New York.

CAUTION

Eric Matthew Frein is wanted for his alleged involvement in the shooting death of one Pennsylvania State Police trooper and the wounding of another outside the Blooming Grove Barracks in Pike County, Pennsylvania, on September 12, 2014

REWARD

The FBI is offering a reward of up to $100,000 for information leading directly to the arrest of Eric Matthew Frein.

SHOULD BE CONSIDERED ARMED AND EXTREMELY DANGEROUS

If you have any information concerning this person, please contact your local FBI office or the nearest American Embassy or Consulate.

PASP/FBI/Splash News/Newscom

Bail bond agents like Duane Lee "Dog" Chapman (star of the reality television program *Dog the Bounty Hunter* that ran for eight seasons) are renowned for their diligence in tracking down defendants who have skipped bail and failed to return to court as required. Bonding agents stand to lose the value of the bond posted if the defendant cannot be located, so their financial incentive for locating and returning the defendant to custody is considerable.

Although bonding agents have been criticized in the past for strong-arm search-and-return tactics, increasingly they are turning to modern technology to catch offenders on the run. For instance, a Facebook page is devoted to Arkansas' Most Wanted Bail Bond Jumpers. One of the fugitives featured there at one point was Marcella Deann Gomez, described as a 41-year-old White woman with multiple warrants out in multiple states and accompanied with the advisement "bond at own risk."

CRITICAL THOUGHT QUESTION

What are the implications for most defendants, fugitive defendants like Marcella Deann Gomez, and the general public when suspects are released on bail prior to trial?

After controlling for charge seriousness and prior record, Blacks were still 10% more likely to be detained than Whites. What accounts for these results? Even if race *per se* does not influence bail-setting, factors correlated with race, such as a defendant's perceived probability of re-arrest, may guide judges' decisions (see, e.g., McIntyre & Baradaran, 2013). In other words, racial and gender disparities emerge because judges regard Black defendants as more likely to be re-arrested than Whites, and female defendants as less likely to be re-arrested than males.

Psychologists have assessed the cognitive processes that judges use in determining whether bail should be allowed. In some studies, judges respond to simulated cases presented as vignettes. In other studies, researchers observe judges dealing with real cases in the courtroom (Dhami, 2003; Dhami & Ayton, 2001). In both settings, judges tend to use a mental shortcut called the **matching heuristic**: They search through a subset of available case information and then make a decision on the basis of only a small number of factors (e.g., offense severity and prior record), often ignoring other seemingly relevant information. This is not especially surprising; judges' large caseloads force them to make fast decisions, and people often use shortcut reasoning strategies when forced to think quickly (Kahneman, 2011).

The opinions of police and prosecutors can also sway judges' decisions about bail. Dhami (2011) analyzed bail setting decisions in two London courts and found that prosecutors' requests and the position of the police strongly influenced judges' choices. Problematically, neither of these recommendations was related to important factors in the case, including an offender's risk of committing further crimes while out of jail. Finally, although judges were highly confident that they had made the appropriate decisions, there was significant disagreement among judges who responded to the same simulated fact patterns, raising troubling questions of fairness and equality.

Does Pretrial Release Affect Trial Outcome?

What if the defendant cannot provide bail and remains in jail until the time of trial? Does this pretrial detention affect the trial's outcome? Clearly, yes. Defendants who are detained in jail are more likely to plead guilty or be convicted and to receive longer sentences than those who can afford bail, even when the seriousness

of their offenses and the evidence against them are the same (Phillips, 2012). Some data suggest that prosecutors use pretrial detention as a "resource" to encourage (or coerce) guilty pleas. Pretrial detention is likely to cost defendants their jobs, making it harder for them to pay attorneys—so the threat of it may make them more likely to plead guilty. Among defendants who actually go to trial, an accused person who is free on bail finds it easier to gather witnesses and prepare a defense. A jailed defendant cannot go to his or her attorney's office for meetings, has less time working with the attorney to prepare for trial, and has less access to records and witnesses. Detention also corrodes family and community ties and affects job stability.

Can High-Risk Defendants Be Identified?

Around 1970, a push began for legislation that would increase the use of **preventive detention**—the detention of persons who pose a risk of flight or danger, including violent offenders, individuals with severe mental illness, and suspected terrorists. Civil libertarians oppose the preventive detention of individuals believed to be at high risk of re-offending because it conflicts with the fundamental assumption that a defendant is innocent until proven guilty (Cole, 2014; Margulies, 2011).

Preventive detention of so-called high-risk offenders also assumes that valid assessments of risk and accurate predictions of future dangerous conduct can be made. Kraemer and colleagues defined the assessment of risk as the "process of using risk factors to estimate the likelihood (i.e., probability) of an outcome occurring in a population" (Kraemer et al., 1997, p. 337). Mental health professionals now have the capacity to assess violence risk in some situations, particularly when using specialized tools (see, e.g., Otto & Douglas, 2010; Wilson, Desmarais, Nicholls, Hart, & Brink, 2013). But there remains a debate about how precise such estimates can be, with some authors identifying the limits of specialized tools and strategies (e.g., Ewing, 2011).

Thus, judges have difficulty knowing which defendants are high risk and which can be trusted. For example, in Shepherd, Texas, Patrick Dale Walker tried to kill his girlfriend by putting a gun to her head and pulling the trigger. The loaded gun failed to fire. Walker's original bail was set at $1 million, but after he had been in jail for four days, the presiding judge lowered his bail to $25,000. This permitted Walker to be released. Four months later, he fired three bullets at close range and killed the same woman. Afterward, the judge did not think he was wrong in lowering the bail, even though, since 1993, Texas has had a law that permits judges to consider the safety of the victim and of the community in determining the amount of bail. But Patrick Walker had no previous record, was valedictorian of his class, and was a college graduate. Would a psychologist have done any better in predicting Walker's behavior?

The preventive detention of suspected terrorists is an altogether different matter, though no less contentious. (Recall the outcry over President Trump's 2017 order banning citizens from seven predominately Muslin countries from entering the United States until a stricter vetting system could be developed to ensure they did not pose a national security risk.) Although many citizens approve of preventive detention of suspected terrorists, believing that society's need to be protected from possible future harm outweighs individual rights, our ability to identify future terrorists is in its infancy. Many risk factors for common forms of violence (e.g., domestic violence) are not relevant to violent terrorism based on ideologies, affiliations, and grievances (Monahan, 2012). Moreover, individual risk factors for being recruited into a terrorist network and actually carrying out a terrorist act are probably not the same, and the many varieties of terrorist acts may each reflect a different constellation of precursors.

Plea Bargaining in Criminal Cases

Most criminal cases—by some accounts, 95%—end prior to trial when the defendant pleads guilty to some charge, usually in exchange for a concession by the prosecutor. The extensive use of plea bargaining in the criminal justice system illustrates the dilemma between truth and conflict resolution as goals of our legal system.

Plea bargaining has been practiced in the United States since the middle of the 19th century, and lately it has threatened to put the trial system out of business. Of nearly 50,000 felonies adjudicated in the 75 largest counties in the United States during 2009, 96% were resolved via guilty pleas (Reaves, 2013). Interestingly, murder defendants were less likely to plead guilty than defendants charged with other violent felonies. Guilty pleas were offered by 97% of robbery suspects but by only 73% of murder suspects. The harsh sentences imposed on most convicted murderers—often life in prison without parole—make it worthwhile for murder

defendants to go to trial and hope for sympathetic judges or juries.

Both mundane and serious cases are resolved by plea bargains. In a routine case that would never have been publicized if the defendant had not been a judge, Roger Hurley, a judge from Darke County, Ohio, pled guilty in a domestic violence case. He was accused of grabbing his estranged wife by the neck during an argument and threatening her with a bread knife. According to Hurley, he accepted a plea bargain in order to get on with his life and end the hurt and friction that this incident caused to his family. In a more notorious case, James Earl Ray, the assassin of Martin Luther King, Jr., died in prison while serving a life sentence as a result of a plea bargain. That plea deal was not well received: many thought Ray had not acted alone, and the plea agreement meant that the facts would never be aired in a public forum. After Ray's death in 1998, the King family released a statement expressing regret that Ray had never had his day in court and the American people would never learn the truth about Dr. King's death.

The defendant's part of the plea bargain requires an admission of guilt. This admission relieves the prosecutor of any obligation to prove that the defendant committed the crimes charged. The prosecutor's part of the bargain may involve an agreement to reduce the number of charges or allow the defendant to plead guilty to a charge less serious than the evidence supports. For example, manslaughter is a lesser charge than murder, and many murder prosecutions are resolved by a plea of guilty to manslaughter.

In a common procedure known as **charge bargaining**, the prosecutor drops some charges in exchange for a guilty plea. But charge bargaining may lead prosecutors to charge the defendant with more crimes or with a more serious crime than could be proven at trial, as a strategy for enticing defendants to plead guilty. Indeed, until 2013, unless defendants were willing to enter a plea bargain at the first opportunity, federal prosecutors were required to charge defendants with the most serious crimes that could be proved (Rakoff, 2014). Laboratory research using role-playing procedures indicates that "overcharging" is effective: Research participants were more likely to accept a plea bargain when more charges were filed against them (Gregory, Mowen, & Linder, 1978). The defendants who engage in this type of bargaining may win only hollow victories. Cases in which prosecutors offer to drop charges are likely to be ones for which judges would have imposed concurrent sentences for the multiple convictions anyway.

Plea bargaining may also take the form of **sentence bargaining**, in which prosecutors recommend reduced or less restrictive sentences in return for guilty pleas. In role-playing research, adults (but not juveniles) were much less likely to accept a plea bargain when the offer included jail time than when it did not (Redlich & Shteynberg, 2016), suggesting that sentencing bargaining can be an effective tool, at least for adult defendants. As you can see, prosecutors have a great deal of control over the terms of a plea deal.

Sentencing is ultimately the judge's decision, and although judges vary in their willingness to follow prosecutors' recommendations, many simply rubber-stamp prosecutorial sentencing recommendations. In general, defendants can expect that judges will follow the sentences that have been recommended by a prosecutor, and prosecutors can earn the trust of judges by recommending sentences that are reasonable and fair.

Benefits of Plea Bargaining for Defendants and Attorneys

Why do defendants plead guilty? There are multiple reasons: because the evidence of guilt is strong and therefore, the likelihood of conviction is high, and because, if convicted, they would face lengthy sentences (Redlich & Shteynberg, 2016).

Some court observers suspect that tougher sentencing laws of the past few decades have allowed prosecutors to gain even greater leverage over criminal defendants, threatening them with mandatory or harsh sentences. So no matter how convinced defendants are of their innocence, they take a risk by turning down plea bargains and facing the possibility of additional charges or mandatory sentences (Oppel, 2011). So in essence, they choose a certain more lenient option over a potential more serious one (Helm & Reyna, 2017). We describe one such case in Box 8.3.

Although prosecutors have most of the power in plea bargaining, defendants have the final say in any decision. Before accepting a guilty plea, judges ask defendants if they made the decision freely and of their own accord. Defense attorneys can have an impact in this decision. Their recommendations interact with the defendant's wishes in complex ways to yield a decision. Defense attorneys gauge whether to recommend a plea offer based on the strength of the evidence against the defendant and the severity of the punishment (Brank & Scott, 2012). When the evidence points toward conviction and the defendant is facing a lengthy prison sentence, defense attorneys

---

BOX 8.3

The Case of Shane Guthrie and the Power of the Prosecution in Plea Bargaining

Shane Guthrie, age 24, was arrested in Gainesville, Florida in 2010 and charged with aggravated battery on a pregnant woman and false imprisonment. The charges stemmed from Guthrie allegedly beating his girlfriend and threatening her with a knife. The prosecutor initially offered Guthrie a plea deal of two years in prison and probation. Believing in his innocence, Guthrie rejected that offer, as well as a subsequent offer of five years in prison, despite apparently being warned that higher charges would be filed if he refused to accept the offer. But Guthrie's attorney maintained that there was no evidence the girlfriend was pregnant, that she started the fight by hitting Guthrie in the forehead with a pipe and changed her story several times, and that she had been arrested in 2009 for attacking Guthrie and telling police that he struck her.

The prosecutor's response to Guthrie's unwillingness to plead guilty? A year later, he filed more serious charges, including first-degree felony kidnapping, which would have meant life imprisonment if Guthrie, who had already spent time in prison, was convicted. "So what he could have resolved for a two-year term could keep him locked up for 50 years or more" (Oppel, 2011). This case illustrates the power that a prosecutor, who determines what charges to file, has over a defendant's destiny.

CRITICAL THOUGHT QUESTION

How do the prosecutor's actions in this case differ from the more typical ways that prosecutors handle plea bargains?

---

will recommend strongly that defendants accept plea offers.

At least in some circumstances, defense attorneys also take their clients' preferences into account. Kramer, Wolbransky, and Heilbrun (2007) had attorneys read vignettes that varied the strength of the evidence against a hypothetical defendant, the potential sentence if convicted, and the defendant's wishes. When the probability of conviction was high and the likely prison sentence was long, attorneys strongly recommended the plea offer, regardless of the defendant's desires. But when the probability of conviction was low and the prison sentence was short, attorneys were willing to consider the defendant's wish to proceed to trial.

Unfortunately, zealous representation by defense attorneys in plea negotiations may not apply to all defendants equally. When she asked defense attorneys from across the country to respond to scenarios that varied the race of the defendant, Edkins (2011) found that the plea deals attorneys felt they could secure for Caucasian clients contained shorter sentences than those they felt they could obtain for African American clients, even though they were slightly more likely to think that the Caucasian clients were guilty. Defense attorneys' own biases, or alternatively, their knowledge of judges' biases, may come into play when they advocate for their clients.

Defendants plead guilty in order to obtain less severe punishment than they would receive if they went to trial and were convicted. But why do prosecutors plea bargain? What advantages do they seek, given that they hold the more powerful position in this bargaining situation? Prosecutors are motivated to plea bargain for one or more of the following reasons: (1) to dispose of cases in which the evidence against the defendant is weak or the defense attorney is a formidable foe; (2) to ensure a "win" when their office keeps a record of the "wins" (convictions) and "losses" (acquittals) of each prosecuting attorney in the office; (3) to obtain the testimony of one defendant against a more culpable or infamous codefendant; and most importantly (4) to expedite the flow of cases for an overworked staff and a clogged court docket.

Plea bargaining serves the need of the defense attorney to appear to gain something for his or her client. In addition to the reasons we just enumerated, prosecutors also wish to appear fair and reasonable. Both prosecutors and defense attorneys believe they are making the "punishment fit the crime" by individualizing the law to fit the circumstances of the case, and both are comfortable with a system in which most cases are resolved without a clear winner or clear loser. Experienced prosecutors and defense attorneys teach plea bargaining to the rookies in their offices, and lawyers from both sides engage in a ritual of give and take, with changing facts and personalities but with the same posturing and rationalizations. In fact, plea-bargaining procedures are so well known that in some cases no formal bargaining even takes place. Rather, everyone involved—prosecutor, defense attorney, defendant, and judge—knows the prevailing "rate" for a given crime, and if the defendant pleads guilty to that crime, the rate is the price that will be paid.

Psychological Influences on the Plea-Bargaining Process

There are various psychological explanations of plea-bargaining behavior. One factor concerns **framing effects**. Psychologists who study decision making have learned that the way decision alternatives are presented (or framed)—as either *gains* or *losses*—can have a significant impact on a person's choice. Individuals are more willing to take chances when the decision alternatives are presented in terms of gains rather than losses. Imagine that two defendants have been charged with the same crime, each has a 50% chance of being convicted at trial, and, if convicted, each is likely to be sentenced to 20 years in prison. The prosecutor has offered both defendants a deal that would result in only 10 years imprisonment in exchange for a guilty plea. Now imagine that Defendant A's options are framed as a *gain* and Defendant B's options are framed as a *loss*. Defendant A is told that if he went to trial, there would be a 50% chance that he would be acquitted and *gain 10 years* outside of prison compared to the plea-bargain offer. Defendant B is told that if he went to trial, there would be a 50% chance that he would be convicted and *lose an additional 10 years* of life in prison compared to the plea-bargain offer. Although the two situations are identical except for the decision frame, Defendant A is more likely to take his chance at trial and Defendant B is more likely to take the plea bargain to avoid a loss.

The choice to plead guilty to reduced charges also implicates a phenomenon called **anchoring** whereby the initial charge serves as a reference point against which other offers are compared. If the initial charge is excessive (which is often the case), then anything less will be perceived by a defendant as a good deal, even if it is still more serious than what the evidence could prove at trial (Haby & Brank, 2013).

Other psychological factors affect and sometimes distort offenders' and attorneys' decisions concerning plea bargains. In general, people tend to be too optimistic about their chances of securing favorable outcomes and are therefore overconfident. The **overconfidence bias** suggests that because defendants and their attorneys believe (incorrectly) that they have a chance to win at trial, they might reject reasonable offers from prosecutors.

Overconfidence skews beliefs about the likelihood of acquittal. Denial mechanisms affect thoughts about one's guilt and the chances for successful plea-bargain arrangements. Offenders often have difficulty acknowledging guilt to their attorneys; some cannot even admit it to themselves (Bibas, 2004). Thinking about one's immoral or illegal actions is painful and depressing, and denial mechanisms allow people to avoid dealing with those thoughts. But denial results in minimizing the harm caused to others and an unwillingness to accept responsibility for wrongdoing. Defendants in denial are unlikely to take a plea bargain even when it is advantageous for them to do so.

Evaluations of Plea Bargaining

The U.S. Supreme Court has called plea bargaining "an essential component of the administration of justice" (*Santobello v. New York*, 1971), and has stated that defendants have a constitutional right to effective representation in plea negotiations, including competent advice and information about prosecutors' offers (*Lafler v. Cooper*, 2012). Still, plea bargaining remains a controversial and largely unregulated procedure (Blume & Helm, 2014). It has been defended as a necessary and useful part of the criminal justice system (American Bar Association, 1993), and condemned as a practice that should be abolished from our courts (Lynch, 2003). Advocates justify the procedure by pointing out that guilty pleas lessen the backlog of cases that would otherwise engulf the courts, facilitate the prosecution of other offenders, and reduce the involvement of criminal justice participants, including police officers who don't have to spend hours in court, and victims who are spared the trauma of a trial.

Critics urge the abolition, or at least, a revision, of plea-bargaining practices. They claim that (1) improper sentences—sometimes too harsh but more often too lenient—are likely; (2) plea bargaining encourages defendants to surrender their constitutional rights; (3) prosecutors exert too much power in negotiating guilty pleas; and (4) innocent defendants might feel pressure to plead guilty because they fear the more severe consequences of being convicted by a jury.

Data on these contentions are limited, but the available evidence suggests that plea bargaining works approximately as advertised. Defendants who are convicted at trial do indeed suffer more severe sanctions than those who accept plea bargains. In 2006, 89% of felons convicted during a trial were sentenced to jail or prison, compared with only 76% of those who committed the same crime and accepted plea bargains. In addition, judges imposed longer sentences on offenders who went to trial (an average sentence of 8 years and 4 months) than on those who pled guilty (an average sentence of 3 years and 11 months) (Rosenmerkel, Durose, & Farole, 2009).

There are some "dark sides" to plea bargaining, however. The large-scale study of all cases disposed of by the New York County District Attorney's Office in 2010–2011 revealed various racial disparities: In drug cases, Blacks were less likely than Whites to receive reduced charge offers, and more likely to receive offers that included incarceration rather than community service, probation or fines (Kutateladze & Andiloro, 2014). Other concerns focus on youthful offenders. Adolescents may be more likely than adults to accept guilty pleas (Grisso et al., 2003), in part, because they lack the comprehension skills necessary to intelligently weigh the trade-offs inherent in plea bargaining and to consider the long-term consequences of their decisions (Redlich & Shteynberg, 2016). Innocent adolescents are especially at risk, assuming—like adults—that the truth of their innocence eventually will be revealed.

Plea bargaining may also work against the long-range goal of achieving justice. First, it may prevent families of victims from seeing the defendants "get justice" or hearing them acknowledge full responsibility for their offenses, as exemplified by the King family's reaction to James Earl Ray's plea agreement.

Second, plea bargaining removes the opportunity for juries—ostensibly comprised of defendants' peers—to decide whether people should be punished and incarcerated for their actions. It also diminishes the chance for laypeople to act as a check on prosecutors, legislators, and judges. One commentator has suggested that allowing juries to hear information about any plea offer would remove the incentive that pushes criminal defendants to give up jury trials (Thomas, 2017).

Finally, the pressures to enter into a plea agreement may lead some defendants to plead guilty to crimes they never committed. Extensive interviews of defendants who pleaded guilty to felonies in New York City revealed that 27% of the youth and 19% of the adults claimed they were completely innocent of the charges (Zottoli, Daftary-Kapur, Winters, & Hogan, 2016). One estimate is that approximately 10% of legally acknowledged exonerations involve innocent defendants (Rakoff, 2014). We provide an example in Box 8.4.

Finally, it is troubling that cases are not always resolved in line with the gravity of the offense. When these "errors" are in the direction of sentencing leniency, they often are attributed to a perceived overload in the prosecutor's office or the courts. A defendant should not be able to plead to a greatly reduced charge simply because the criminal justice system lacks the resources to handle the case. However, the answer to problems of unwarranted leniency is not the abolition of plea bargaining; rather, adequate funding must be provided for the court system, as well as for the correctional system,

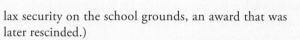

The Case of Brian Banks and Football Aspirations Derailed by a False Guilty Plea

BOX 8.4

Brian Banks, center, with mother and father.

Most exonerees—people convicted of crimes and later proven innocent—have no reasonable expectation of playing in the National Football League (NFL). But Brian Banks did. His performance as a star linebacker in high school attracted the attention of college coaches and recruiters, and he dreamed of playing in the big leagues. In fact, in 2002, he verbally committed to play for the University of Southern California. But that all unraveled when a high school acquaintance, Wanetta Gibson, accused Banks of rape and kidnapping after first claiming that the two had consensual sex on the school campus. (Years later, Gibson admitted she lied, but not before receiving $1.5 million from the Long Beach Unified School District for

lax security on the school grounds, an award that was later rescinded.)

Banks faced an excruciating choice: either fight the charges and face a sentence of 41 years to life or agree to a plea bargain that would land him in prison for just 5 years. He opted for the latter, though it meant curtailing his football aspirations and lifetime registration as a sex offender. In 2012, following Gibson's recantation, Banks' conviction was overturned, but by then he had served five years in prison and another five on probation as a registered sex offender. He did have a short stint in the NFL in 2013.

Federal judge Jed Rakoff, who served as both prosecutor and defender prior to assuming the bench, provides a succinct explanation for why false plea bargains occur: "The typical person accused of crime combines a troubled past with limited resources: he thus recognizes that, even if he is innocent, his chances of mounting an effective defense at trial may be modest at best. If his lawyer can obtain a plea bargain that will reduce his likely time in prison, he may find it 'rational' to take the plea" (Rakoff, 2014). Banks' trial attorney practically told him as much: that as a big black teenager, no jury would believe anything he said.

CRITICAL THOUGHT QUESTION

In addition to concerns about whether a jury would believe him, what other factors were working against Banks in the plea-bargaining context?

so that when severe penalties are necessary, severe penalties can be given. In the long run, if plea bargaining serves primarily as a method for managing the underfunded budgets of our courts and correctional systems, it will cease to be a bargain in the larger sense and will become, instead, too great a price for our society to pay.

Settlements in Civil Cases

Just as most criminal cases are resolved through plea-bargaining procedures prior to trial, the vast majority of civil disputes are also resolved (or settled) without a trial, typically in private negotiations between

attorneys representing the disputing parties. This process is known as **settlement negotiation**. (Attorneys also negotiate with insurers, regulators, and sometimes even with their own clients in an attempt to settle a dispute.) Most divorces, landlord–tenant disputes, claims of employment discrimination, and accident cases are resolved without a trial.

Large class-action lawsuits that may involve hundreds or thousands of plaintiffs are also typically resolved in settlement negotiations. In 2012, attorneys representing the oil giant BP and more than 100,000 Gulf Coast residents and businesses affected by the 2010 Deepwater Horizon oil spill reached a settlement

Attorneys often informally negotiate settlements in civil cases.

that eliminated the threat of a trial. One commentator suggested that as lawsuits go, "this was going to be the Super Bowl wrapped up in the World Series—only with much, much more money at stake" (Walsh, 2012).

Lawyers spend considerable time negotiating settlements because they would almost always prefer the certainty of a negotiated compromise to the uncertainty of a jury trial. Because their caseload (or docket) is so large, judges would always prefer that the participants in a civil dispute resolve their differences themselves, without using the considerable resources necessary for a trial.

Disputing parties obviously have different objectives in settlement negotiations. Hence, the attorneys representing these parties will have very different roles to play in the negotiation. In a personal injury case, a common type of civil dispute, plaintiffs' lawyers will try to extract every dollar that a defendant will pay, whereas defendants' lawyers will try to avoid paying all but the minimal cost necessary to settle the case. In the Deepwater Horizon case, plaintiffs' attorneys were motivated to avoid years of uncertain litigation and the possibility of obtaining less money for their clients than they would receive in the settlement. Defense attorneys representing BP opted to settle in order to avoid having the company's mistakes paraded in open court, particularly in light of ongoing litigation with federal, state, and local governments.

Some lawyers have become highly skilled at negotiating settlements. Consider, for example, the case of Valerie Lakey, who, at age five, was disemboweled by the suction power of a pool drain pump produced by Sta-Rite Industries. Valerie sat on an open pool drain after other children removed the protective cover that a swim club had failed to install properly. Despite 12 prior suits with similar claims, Sta-Rite continued to make and sell drain covers lacking installation warnings. Former North Carolina Senator and presidential hopeful John Edwards served as the attorney for plaintiffs Valerie Lakey and her family. After lengthy negotiations that continued "backstage" throughout the trial, Sta-Rite eventually settled and the Lakey family received $25 million—at the time, the largest personal injury award in North Carolina history.

What makes some lawyers skilled at negotiating and winning large damage awards? Do they have a knack for deciding whether a case is worth pursuing and an ability to assess accurately what it might be worth? Do they have a particular interpersonal style that facilitates compromise? Are they particularly skilled negotiators? In recent years, psychologists, economists, and game theorists (scientists who study behavior in strategic situations) have conducted studies of actual and simulated settlement negotiations to determine what factors predict settlement amounts.

Factors That Determine Settlement Amounts

The legal merits of the case matter most, of course. In an automobile accident case in which there is strong evidence of the defendant's reckless driving and in which there are obvious and severe injuries, a plaintiff

sirtravelalot/Shutterstock.com

will recover more money than will a plaintiff whose case is weak on liability or damages.

But other factors matter as well. Negotiation theory suggests that outcomes are also influenced by the negotiators' **reservation price**, or bottom line (Korobkin & Doherty, 2009). The defendant's reservation price is the *maximum* amount of money that he or she would be willing to pay to reach an agreement, whereas the plaintiff's reservation price is the *minimum* amount of money that he or she would accept to settle the claim. Let's assume that a plaintiff was injured when a piece of machinery malfunctioned, injuring him or her and resulting in medical and other costs of approximately $100,000. The defendant manufacturer may set a reservation price of $75,000, authorizing the defense attorney to negotiate a settlement that does not exceed that amount, while the plaintiff may set a reservation price of $25,000, meaning that he or she will accept nothing less. Though the parties are not initially aware of one another's reservation prices, they have a $50,000 "bargaining zone" in which to negotiate a compromise. If they fail to reach a compromise, negotiators walk away from the bargaining table and the case goes to trial. Various psychological factors influence reservation points, including perceptions of the likely outcome if the case goes to trial and negotiators' goals and views on the merits of the case.

In considering the merits of their case, plaintiffs, defendants, and attorneys alike are influenced by psychological biases, often referred to as **heuristics**, which affect their ability to gauge when it is in their best interest to settle the case prior to trial (Knutson, Gordon, & Greene, 2015). Because of these reasoning errors, both plaintiffs and defendants lose more by going to trial than by settling. In one study, 61% of plaintiffs who passed up a settlement offer and proceeded to trial were awarded less than had been offered, and 24% of defendants were forced to pay more than they had offered—specifically, an average $1,140,000 more in damages (Kiser, Asher, & McShane, 2008)!

One such heuristic, the **self-serving bias**, occurs when people interpret information or make decisions in ways that are consistent with their own interests, rather than in an objective fashion. When evaluating their cases, people often have difficulty seeing the merits of the other side, believing that the evidence favors their position and that the fairest resolution is one that rewards them. For example, even law students who were randomly assigned to represent one side or another in an appellate court case judged the evidence and moral value of their arguments as strongly

supporting their arbitrarily assigned roles (Eigen & Listoken, 2012). Self-serving biases can also lead to impasse because people who are unable to take the perspective of their negotiation opponents are less likely to reach a deal than those who are able to take their opponents' perspective (Galinsky, Maddux, Gilin, & White, 2008).

A heuristic that we mentioned in the context of plea bargaining—**anchoring**—occurs when negotiators are strongly influenced ("anchored") by an initial starting value and when, in subsequent discussion, they do not sufficiently adjust their judgments away from this starting point. This bias is quite pervasive, and even wildly extreme anchors can influence judgments. People provided higher estimates of the average temperature in San Francisco when first asked whether it was higher or lower than 558 degrees, a number that may have induced people to consider the (unlikely) possibility that San Francisco temperatures are high (cited by Guthrie, Rachlinski, & Wistrich, 2001). In the context of settlement negotiations, the first offer can serve to anchor the final negotiated compromise: the higher the offer, the higher the ultimate settlement (Korobkin & Doherty, 2009).

Many legal disputes involve intense emotions that can also influence the likelihood of resolution. Imagine, for example, the despair and anguish that Rachel Barton Pine must have experienced after being dragged 200 feet underneath a Chicago commuter train in 1995. The then-21-year-old classical violin prodigy had her left leg severed above the knee, lost part of her right foot, and badly injured her right knee as terrified passengers tried to alert the engineer to halt the train. Barton sued the train company for $30 million. After several years of negotiations and 25 operations, she received nearly that amount and gave a sizeable portion to charity.

Emotions on the part of plaintiffs, defendants, and their attorneys all play a role in negotiation. The emotion most closely associated with disputes may be anger; parties involved in settlement discussions often feel resentment, antagonism, and sometimes, outright fury. Presumably those expressions would harm the chances for concessions and compromise, and psychological data suggest that they do. Higher levels of anger in one party to a lawsuit are related to angry responses from the other party (Friedman et al., 2004), a greater likelihood of deception (Yip & Schweitzer, 2016), and a greater frequency of impasse (Hillebrandt & Barclay, 2017). Angry disputants have difficulty resolving their competing claims.

If anger tends to inhibit dispute resolution, do positive emotions tend to enhance it? The answer is yes; positive emotions such as happiness foster cooperation and concession making (Kopelman, Rosette, & Thompson, 2006), stimulate creative problem solving (deVries, Holland, Corneille, Rondeel, & Whitteman, 2012), increase the likelihood that parties will disclose personal information (Forgas, 2011), and positively influence negotiators' expectations (Carnevale, 2008). Experiencing positive emotions improves one's chances for successful settlement negotiations.

What Is the Purpose of a Trial?

Sometimes settlement negotiations fail and plea bargains prove to be elusive. In those situations, disputants have no choice but to have their case resolved in a trial, a topic to which we devote the remainder of this chapter. Every trial, civil or criminal, presents two contrasting versions of the truth. Both sides try to present the "facts" in question in such a way as to convince the judge or the jury that their claims are true. The judge or jury must render judgments on the probable truth or falsity of each side's statements and evidence.

The jury system evolved from an ancient ritual during which a defendant stood before a priest, surrounded by friends who swore that the defendant had not committed the crime. But the victim also brought friends who swore to just the opposite (Kadri, 2005). Because this arrangement was not especially satisfactory to anyone, the English monarchy began to have

After a witness testifies during a trial, the witness is then cross-examined by the opposing attorney, followed by redirect questioning by the original attorney, if needed.

defendants appear in front of a panel of citizens whose task was to swear to the innocence or guilt of the defendant.

If one is asked about the purpose of a modern trial, the first response might be "to determine the truth, of course." But is this really the prime function of a trial? In fact, trials also serve other purposes: They provide a sense of stability and a way to resolve conflicts so that the disputants can receive satisfaction. Many years ago, Miller and Boster (1977) identified three images of the trial that reflect these contrasting conceptions and that still hold true today.

The Trial as a Search for the Truth

Many people see a trial as a rule-governed event involving the parties' collective search for the truth (Miller & Boster, 1977). This view assumes that what really happened can be clearly ascertained—that witnesses are capable of knowing, remembering, and describing events completely and accurately. Although this image of the trial recognizes that the opposing attorneys present only those facts that buttress their positions, it assumes that the truth will emerge from the confrontation of conflicting facts. It also assumes that judges or jurors, in weighing these facts, can "lay aside their prejudices and preconceived views regarding the case and replace such biases with a dispassionate analysis of the arguments and evidence" (Miller & Boster, 1977, p. 25).

But this image of the trial as a rational, rule-governed event has been challenged on several grounds. Eyewitnesses are not always thorough and accurate reporters, as the legal system would like to believe. Interrogations can sometimes result in false confessions, and jurors are not particularly good at distinguishing false confessions from true confessions. Jurors may have difficulty setting aside their own experiences and prejudices. Although this image of the trial remains as an inspiring ideal, other images need to be considered as well.

The Trial as a Test of Credibility

A second conception—that the trial is a test of credibility—acknowledges that facts and evidence are always incomplete and biased. Hence the decision makers, whether judge or jury, must not only weigh the information and evidence but also evaluate the truthfulness of the opposing sources of evidence (Miller & Boster, 1977).

They must focus on the way evidence is presented, the qualifications of witnesses, and the inconsistencies between witnesses. Competence and trustworthiness of witnesses take on added importance in this image.

The image of the trial as a test of credibility also has problems. Both judges and jurors can make unwarranted inferences about witnesses and attorneys on the basis of race, gender, mannerisms, or style of speech. Judges' and jurors' judgments of credibility may be based more on stereotypes, folklore, or "commonsense intuition" than on the facts.

The Trial as a Conflict-Resolving Ritual

The first two images share the belief that the primary function of a trial is to produce the most nearly valid judgment about the guilt of a criminal defendant or the responsibility of a civil defendant. The third image shifts the function of the trial from determining the truth to providing a mechanism to resolve controversies. Miller and Boster (1977) express it this way: "At the risk of oversimplification we suggest that it removes primary attention from the concept of doing justice and transfers it to the psychological realm of *creating a sense that justice is being done*" (p. 34). Truth remains a goal, but participants in the trial process also need both the opportunity to have their "day in court" and the reassurance that, whatever the outcome, "justice was done." In other words, they need closure that only a trial can provide.

A trial conducted in Oklahoma in 2004 exemplified this desire for closure. Several years before, Oklahoma City bombing suspect Terry Nichols was convicted on federal charges and sentenced to life in prison, rather than to death (his codefendant, Timothy McVeigh, was executed in 2001). An Oklahoma prosecutor, responding to some victims' families who were eager to see Nichols also put to death, charged him in state court with 161 counts of first-degree murder (for the 160 people and 1 fetus who were killed in the blast) and requested the death penalty. But Nichols was again spared execution when this second jury, despite convicting him, deadlocked over his sentence. By law, Nichols was sentenced (again) to life in prison—161 consecutive life sentences, to be exact—and those families hoping for closure were disappointed (again).

The stabilizing function of a trial is worthless, of course, if the public doubts that justice was done in the process. That sense of closure is sometimes missing after a trial; the widespread dissatisfaction in some segments of our society with the outcome of O. J. Simpson's murder trial (Brigham & Wasserman, 1999) ensured continued media interest and public fascination with his actions and statements. (In 2016 alone, the public had two opportunities to relive the details: the TV series *The People v. O.J. Simpson: American Crime Story* and *O.J.: Made in America*.) The belief that "he got away with murder" even led to proposals to reform and restrict the jury system. Other segments of society were equally dissatisfied with the verdict in Simpson's civil trial, in which he was found liable for the deaths of his ex-wife and her friend Ronald Goldman. Perhaps together, the verdicts in the two trials converged on a reasonable outcome—Simpson probably was the killer, but this couldn't be proven beyond a reasonable doubt, the level of certainty required for a criminal conviction.

These three contrasting images remind us that truth in the legal system is elusive, and that truth seekers are subject to human error, even though the system seems to assume that they approach infallibility. The failure to achieve perfection in our decision making will become evident as we review the steps in the trial process.

Steps in the Trial Process

In the next section, we sketch out the usual steps in a trial in brief detail. Though some of these procedures are conducted out of the public eye, they all involve—either implicitly or explicitly—issues of interest to psychologists.

Preliminary Actions

Discovery is the pretrial process by which each side tries to gain vital information about the case that will be presented by the other side. This information includes statements by witnesses, police records, documents, material possessions, experts' opinions, and anything else relevant to the case.

The U.S. Constitution provides criminal defendants with the right to have the charges against them judged by a jury of their peers, though a defendant can decide instead to have the case decided by a judge. If the trial is before a jury, the selection of jurors involves a two-step process. The first step is to draw a panel of prospective jurors, called a *venire*, from a large list (usually based on lists of registered voters and licensed drivers). Once the venire for a particular trial has been selected—this may be anywhere from 30 to 200 people, depending on the customary practices of that jurisdiction and the nature of the trial—a process known as *voir dire* is employed to question and select the eventual jurors. Prospective jurors who reveal biases and are unable to be open-minded about the case are dismissed from service, so the task of jury selection is really one of elimination. Prospective jurors who appear free of these limitations are thus "selected." Voir dire can have important effects on the outcome of the trial.

The Trial

All trials—whether related to criminal law or to civil law—include similar procedural steps. At the beginning of the trial itself, lawyers for each side are permitted to make **opening statements**. These are not part of the evidence, but they serve as overviews of the evidence to be presented. The prosecution or plaintiff usually goes first, because this side is the one that brought charges and bears the burden of proving them. Attorneys for the defendant, in either a criminal or civil trial, can choose to present their opening statement immediately after the other side's opening statement or to wait until it is their turn to present evidence.

Some psychologists have wondered whether the timing of the opening statement matters. In other words, would it be preferable for the defense attorney (and more beneficial to the defendant) if the defense's opening statement immediately followed the prosecutor's opening statement or would it be better for the defense attorney to wait until all of the prosecution witnesses have testified? Their study, using a mock jury simulation, varied the timing of the defense opening statement in an auto theft case (Wells, Wrightsman, & Miene, 1985). The results were striking: When the defense opening statement was given earlier rather than later, verdicts were more favorable to the defense, and the perceived effectiveness of the defense attorney was enhanced. Defense attorneys who take their first opportunity to make an opening statement can apparently counter the story told by the prosecutor, or at least urge jurors to consider an alternative interpretation of the evidence.

After opening statements, the prosecution or plaintiff calls its witnesses. Each witness testifies under oath, with the threat of a charge of **perjury** if the witness fails to be truthful. That witness is then cross-examined by the opposing attorney, after which the original attorney has a chance for **redirect questioning**. Redirect questioning is likely if the original attorney feels the opposition has "impeached" his or her witness; **impeachment** in this context refers to a cross-examination that has effectively called into question the credibility (or reliability) of the witness.

The purpose of redirect examination is to "rehabilitate" the witness, or to salvage his or her original testimony. The defense, however, has one more chance to question the witness, a process called **recross** (short for "re-cross-examination"). After the prosecution or plaintiff's attorneys have presented all their witnesses, it is the defense's turn. The same procedure of direct examination, cross-examination, redirect, and recross is used. After both sides have presented their witnesses, one or both may decide to introduce additional evidence and witnesses and so ask the judge for permission to present **rebuttal evidence**, which attempts to counteract or disprove evidence given by an earlier witness.

Once all the evidence has been presented, each side is permitted to make a **closing argument**, also called a summation. Although jurisdictions vary, typically the prosecution or plaintiff gets the first summation, followed by the defense, after which the prosecution or plaintiff responds and has the final word.

The final step in the jury trial is for the judge to give instructions to the jury. (In some states, instructions precede the closing arguments.) The judge informs the jury of the relevant law. For example, a definition of the crime is given, as well as a statement of what elements must be present for it to have occurred—that is, whether the defendant had the motive and the opportunity to commit the crime. The judge also instructs jurors about the standard they should use to weigh the evidence.

With criminal charges, the jurors must be convinced beyond a reasonable doubt that the defendant is guilty before they vote to convict. Although the concept of "reasonable doubt" is difficult to interpret, generally it means that jurors should be strongly convinced (but not necessarily convinced beyond *all* doubt). Each of us interprets such an instruction differently, and this instruction is often a source of confusion and frustration among jurors.

In a civil trial, in which one party brings a claim against another, a different standard is used. A **preponderance of evidence** is all that is necessary for a finding in favor of one side. Usually, judges and attorneys translate this to mean "Even if you find the evidence favoring one side to be only slightly more convincing than the other side's, rule in favor of that side." Preponderance is sometimes interpreted as meaning at least 51% of the evidence, though it is difficult (and potentially misleading) to quantify a concept that is expressed verbally.

The jury is sometimes given instructions on how to deliberate, but these are usually sparse. Jurors are excused to the deliberation room, and no one—not even the bailiff or the judge—can be present during or eavesdrop on their deliberations. When the jury has reached its verdict, its foreperson informs the bailiff, who informs the judge, who in turn reconvenes the attorneys and defendants (and plaintiffs in a civil trial) for announcement of the verdict.

Now that we have detailed the steps involved in trials, we consider the advantages accorded by these procedures to the prosecution and the defense in criminal trials. You will notice that opposing sides have roughly offsetting advantages. For example, the prosecution gets the first and last chance to address the judge or jury, but it also has the burden of proving its case. The defense, on the other hand, is not given the opportunity to speak first or to speak last. But it has the advantage of not needing to prove anything to the judge or jury. If the prosecution is unable to meet its obligation to convince the judge or jury of the defendant's guilt, then the defendant prevails. What other advantages does each side have in a criminal case?

The prosecution, in its efforts to convict wrongdoers and seek justice, has several advantages, including these:

1. It has the full resources of the government at its disposal to carry out a prosecution. Detectives can locate witnesses and subpoena them. The prosecutor can request testimony from chemists, fingerprint examiners, medical examiners, psychiatrists, photographers, or other appropriate experts.

2. In the trial itself, the prosecution presents its evidence before the defense, getting "first crack" at the jury. At the end of the trial, when both sides are permitted closing arguments, the prosecution again gets to go first and also gets the chance to offer a final rebuttal to the defense attorney's closing argument. Therefore, the prosecution has the advantages of both *primacy* and *recency* in its attempts at jury persuasion, and research shows that information presented first (primacy) and last (recency) has more persuasive influence than information presented in the middle of a discussion.

Trial procedures also provide defendants with certain benefits, including the following:

1. The defense is entitled to "discovery"; the prosecution must turn over all exculpatory evidence (evidence that would tend to absolve the defendant),

but the defense does not have to turn over all incriminating evidence.

2. If a trial is before a jury, the defense may have more opportunities than the prosecution to remove potential jurors without giving a reason.

3. Defendants do not have to take the stand as witnesses on their own behalf. In fact, they do not have to put on any defense at all; the burden is on the prosecution to prove beyond a reasonable doubt that the defendant is guilty of the crime.

4. Defendants who are found not guilty can never be tried again for that specific crime. So for example, even if Baltimore police uncover new evidence against Caesar Goodson, the officer acquitted of murder in Freddie Gray's death, Goodson can never be retried on those charges.

Sentencing

If the defendant in a criminal trial is deemed guilty, a punishment must be decided. In the vast majority of jurisdictions, the trial judge decides punishment. In the past, judges have had wide discretion to impose sentences by taking into account all they knew about the defendant and his actions, regardless of whether those actions constituted a crime or were proven to a jury. But in a landmark 2004 decision, the U.S. Supreme Court ruled that judges may not increase defendants' sentences on the basis of what they perceive as aggravating factors (circumstances that seem to make the "crime" worse). In *Blakely v. Washington* (2004), the Court reserved those determinations for juries.

The ruling came from a case in which the defendant, Ralph Blakely, pled guilty to kidnapping his estranged wife, a crime that carried a penalty of 53 months. But the judge, after deciding that Blakely acted with "deliberate cruelty"—a circumstance that Blakely had not admitted and that no jury had decided—increased his sentence to 90 months. In overturning this sentence (and thereby striking down dozens of state sentencing laws and affecting thousands of cases), the Court said the imposition of additional time violated Mr. Blakely's right to a jury trial.

In a handful of states, sentencing is determined by a jury. After the verdict is rendered, the jury is reconvened, and attorneys present evidence relevant to the sentencing decision. The jury then deliberates until it agrees on a recommended punishment. In cases involving the death penalty, jurors, rather than judges, decide the sentence (*Ring v. Arizona*, 2002).

The Appellate Process

Involvement of guilty defendants within the legal system does not end when they are sentenced to a prison term or to probation. To protect their rights, defendants who claim they have been convicted unjustly can appeal to a higher level of court. (Defendants who plead guilty are often required to waive their appellate rights as a condition of the plea agreement.) Appeals are also possible in virtually every civil suit.

As in earlier steps in the legal process, a conflict of values occurs as appeals are pursued. One goal is equality before the law—that is, to administer justice consistently and fairly. But appellate courts also try to be sensitive to individual differences in what at first glance appear to be similar cases. Appellate courts recognize that judges and juries can make errors. The appellate process can correct mistakes that impair the fairness of trials; it also helps promote a level of consistency in trial procedures.

When a decision is appealed to a higher court, the appellate judges read the transcript of the trial proceedings, the motions and accompanying documents filed by the attorneys, and written arguments, called briefs, from both sides about the issues on appeal. They then decide whether to overturn the original trial decision or to let it stand. Appellate judges rarely reverse a verdict on the basis of the facts of the case or the apparent legitimacy of that verdict. When they do reverse a verdict, it is usually because they believe that the trial judge made a procedural error, such as allowing controversial evidence to be presented or failing to allow the jury to consider some evidence that should have been included.

If a verdict in a criminal trial is overturned or reversed, the appeals court will either order a retrial or order that the charges be thrown out. In reviewing the decision in a civil case, an appellate court can let the decision stand, reverse it (rule in favor of the side that lost rather than the side that won), or make some other changes in the decision and remand (return) the case to a lower court for reconsideration. One possible conclusion in either civil or criminal appeals is that certain evidence should not have been admitted or that certain instructions should not have been given; hence, a new trial may be ordered.

There is relatively little psychological research on the appellate court decision making process. Exceptions include an evaluation of small group dynamics in appellate court decisions (Miller & Curry, 2017) and books on the psychology of judicial decision making that touch on issues arising in appellate courts (Klein & Mitchell, 2010; Wrightsman, 1999; 2006).

Courtroom of the Future

With only minor variations, courtroom trials and appeals have followed these procedures for much of our nation's history. The trials of John Scopes (tried in 1925 for teaching the theory of evolution in a Tennessee public school science class), Julius and Ethel Rosenberg (tried in 1951 on espionage charges), and defendants facing charges across the United States today all follow essentially the same format.

But recently, the introduction of emerging technologies into the legal system has begun to change the look of trials. Today, juries and judges expect attorneys to use more than yellow legal pads and grainy videos. Many jurors, especially younger jurors and those who are more tech-savvy, now expect to see and hear multimedia approaches (Griffin, 2008), and some judges want all documents presented during a trial to be displayed electronically. People are already considering how, in 2030, a well-designed courtroom could enhance the delivery of forensic science evidence (Horan & Maine, 2014). In this hypothetical scenario, mathematical models are used to prepare visual crime scene animations; witnesses use high-quality holograms and 3D holographic displays; internationally acclaimed experts testify from remote locations over holographic link-ups; all evidence is retrieved instantaneously without interrupting the flow of proceedings; and each juror has a tablet with a video transcript in time- and word-searchable form and custom-designed questions to work through during deliberation.

Even today, technologies being used in courts extend far beyond surveillance videos which would have been novel only a few years ago. One noteworthy development is the proliferation of smartphone videos, particularly clips of encounters between citizens and police, which have dominated the news recently. Scores of websites dedicated to "cop-watching" now exist and various groups monitor high-crime areas for examples of hostile police–citizen interactions (Hoffberger, 2013). Federal courts have affirmed the right to film police in action, and police departments have responded by investing in wearable cameras ("body-cams") which film their actions automatically. In Box 8.5, we describe a case that turned heavily on a smartphone video.

The Case of Antonio Buehler and the Power of Visual Technology

BOX 8.5

Antonio Buehler, a Stanford and West Point graduate and Afghan war veteran, was arrested outside a 7-11 in Austin, Texas in the early hours of New Years Day, 2012 after an altercation with police. While stopped for gas, Buehler witnessed a drunk driving investigation in which police were pulling a woman from her car as she urged bystanders to "film this!" (Bock & Schneider, 2017). Buehler took some still shots while calling out to police that their tactics were overly aggressive. An officer then confronted him and arrested him for public intoxication, assault related to allegedly spitting on an officer, and refusing to obey a lawful order. The first two charges were dropped and Buehler opted to go trial on the last charge, claiming that the reason he was charged was because he filmed police activity.

At trial, jurors saw four videos: two dash-cam videos from the arresting officer's car, a clip from a surveillance camera at the convenience store, and a smartphone video shot by a bystander across the street that showed the entire scene. Crucially for Buehler, the bystander's video shown him being thrown to the ground while shouting "Why are you doing this?" This evidence bolstered Buehler's testimony that he thought the officer was the aggressor in the incident and seemed to contradict the officer's recollection that Buehler was verbally abusive and spat on him. In fact, dash-cam clips revealed that the arresting officer was loud and agitated throughout the incident. Much of the prosecution's case was an attempt to downplay the video evidence and explain to the jury why it is important for officers to control situations and defend themselves. But Buehler was acquitted, perhaps because jurors could witness the officer's demeanor for themselves from the vantage point of the bystander's smartphone. Those images may have revealed more than words could ever say.

CRITICAL THOUGHT QUESTION

In what ways might visual technologies such as smartphones and dashboard and body cameras transform the bail-setting, plea-bargaining, and trial stages of a case?

Technology has provided other tools for attorneys and judges to use during trials. These include

- videoconferencing that permits live, two-way video and audio communication between hearings and trials in courtrooms and remote sites—useful when witnesses and defendants are medically incapacitated or incarcerated, and to allow for the presence of interpreters in a courtroom
- electronic and digital evidence, such as digital recordings, documents, and photographs, that allows judges and jurors to easily observe the evidence themselves, rather than hear others' descriptions of it.
- computer animations and simulations that feature computer-generated depictions of complex physical events like accidents and crimes, often accompanied by voice-overs from participants in the event.
- virtual reality technologies that allow observers to experience a re-creation of an event as if they were actually present when it occurred. Virtual reality environments allow judges and jurors to immerse themselves in an artificially created world such as a crime scene, operating room, factory, or accident site to gauge for themselves what could be seen from different points of view and what likely happened given the circumstances.

Each of these high-tech methods raises interesting and complex questions that psychologists have begun to address. What effect does remote viewing have on a judge or juror's ability to determine whether a witness is credible and sincere? Are nuances of body language and verbal expression adequately captured in videoconferencing, or are they missing? Does the person testifying at a remote site—a setting that lacks the trappings and formality of a courtroom—feel less obligated to show respect and tell the truth? Answers are beginning to emerge and they suggest that, among other things, defendants may be disadvantaged by videoconferencing. It results in less favorable outcomes for defendants in bail hearings, perhaps because it tends to be brief (Diamond, Bowman, Wong, & Patton, 2010; describing videoconferencing as a "cattle call" approach to justice, p. 885). Remote video technologies result in more deportations in immigration cases than in-person hearings because detained persons on video are less engaged in the adversarial process (Eagly, 2015).

Other questions arise. Do computer animations, simulations, and virtual reality reenactments make difficult or technical concepts easier to visualize and, hence, to understand? Might they also serve to cement one version of a contested event in observers' minds, making it harder to construe alternative explanations? In other words, might observers assume that animations, simulations, and virtual realities represent true and uncontroversial facts, rather than just one party's theory of the case?

Lawyers and judges should be especially interested in the answers to these questions because according to the Federal Rules of Evidence (2009), evidence may not be introduced into a trial if its **probative value** (relevance to legal proof) is outweighed by any prejudicial effects on the opposing party or if it misleads or confuses the jury. Thus, it is imperative that judges have good information about the effects of high-tech evidence presentations on legal judgments.

Psychological research can now provide some relevant information. One study examined the effects of visual presentations on jurors' verdicts in a racial discrimination case involving statistical evidence (Park & Feigenson, 2013). In a simulated trial in which African American employees sued the railroad company they worked for, mock jurors saw different versions of the plaintiffs' and defendant's opening statements. Researchers varied whether attorneys' spoken statements were accompanied by visual presentations that illustrated the statistical evidence.

The results of these variations on liability determinations were most pronounced when one party used a visual presentation and the other party did not. So when the plaintiffs included a visual presentation and the defendant did not, jurors deemed the defendant most responsible. Apparently, even a relatively simple visual presentation by the plaintiffs helped participants understand the statistical evidence that supported their racial discrimination claim. But that pattern was reversed when only the defendant included a visual presentation, in which case jurors deemed the defendant least responsible. Presumably, more extensive or dramatic visual displays would have an even greater impact.

Why do visual displays persuade people in ways that words cannot? Basic psychological theorizing about the **vividness effect** suggests that information has a greater impact on judgments and decisions when it is vivid and attention grabbing than when it is pallid and bland. In the racial discrimination study we just described, recall of each party's evidence improved when that party presented visual displays, suggesting that information presented in a highly imaginable way is more memorable than simple verbal descriptions of the same material. By itself, vivid information is not necessarily prejudicial in a courtroom, but it rises to that level when the likelihood of prejudice exceeds the objective probative value of the evidence (Young, 2014).

Virtual reality environments have piqued psychologists' interests in the notion of **presence**, or the degree to which a user or observer has the impression of actually "being in another world" and present in the virtual environment. Because complete immersion of the senses—a sense of presence—is persuasive in ways that two-dimensional computer animations are not (Young, 2014), virtual environments also raise questions about whether observers will give this evidence more weight than it deserves; in short, whether its prejudicial effects outweigh its probative value.

Another concern about the use of virtual environments in court is that people who witness them may be so swept up in the experience and persuaded by the lifelike nature of these scenes that they have difficulty imagining or visualizing a different point of view. This notion, termed **experiential inflammatory bias**, suggests that virtual environment demonstrations may be prejudicial to the side that did not introduce them, and that both sides should have the opportunity to manipulate and alter any virtual environment introduced into evidence (Bailenson, Blascovich, Beall, & Noveck, 2006).

Although virtual environment technology is not yet routinely used in actual trials, that day may arrive soon. Indeed, proponents believe that the technology is already mature enough to warrant its use in court: "If a picture is worth a thousand words, then a … virtual reality simulation should be worth at least ten thousand" (Bailenson et al., 2006, p. 265). The day has already arrived for body- and dash-cam recordings, animations, simulations, remote videoconferencing, and other forms of digitally presented evidence. To what extent do they alter the way that trials are conducted? Psychologists, judges, and lawyers will grapple with this question for some time to come.

Summary

1. ***What are the major legal proceedings between arrest and trial in the criminal justice system?*** (1) An initial appearance, at which defendants are informed of the charges, of their constitutional rights, and of future proceedings; (2) a preliminary hearing, in which the judge determines whether there is enough evidence to hold the defendant for further processing; (3) action by the grand jury, which decides whether sufficient evidence exists for the defendant to be tried; (4) an arraignment, involving a formal statement of charges and an initial plea by the defendant to these charges; (5) a process of discovery, requiring that the prosecutor reveal to the defense certain evidence; and (6) pretrial motions, which are attempts by both sides to win favorable ground rules for the subsequent trial.

2. ***What is bail, and what factors influence the amount of bail set?*** Bail is the provision, by a defendant, of money or other assets that are forfeited if the defendant fails to appear at trial. In determining whether to release a defendant prior to trial, the judge should consider the risk that the defendant will not show up for his or her trial. Judges also consider the seriousness of the offense and the defendant's prior record as well as the defendant's race and gender.

3. ***Why do defendants and prosecutors agree to plea bargain?*** Plea bargaining is an excellent example of the dilemma between truth and conflict resolution as goals of our legal system. The vast majority of criminal cases conclude between arrest and trial with the defendant pleading guilty to some (often reduced) charges. Plea bargaining benefits both defendants and prosecutors. Defendants who plead guilty often receive reductions in the charges or in their sentences; prosecutors secure a "conviction" without expending their time at trial.

4. ***What are settlement negotiations, and why are most civil lawsuits resolved through settlement rather than trial?*** Settlement negotiations are private discussions held between the attorneys representing disputing parties in a civil lawsuit. The objective of the negotiations is to resolve the dispute in a manner agreeable to both sides. Settlement negotiations are often preferable to trials because (1) a negotiated compromise is more appealing to most litigants than the uncertainty of a jury trial and (2) judges have large caseloads (or dockets) and therefore prefer that participants in civil disputes resolve their differences themselves without using the considerable resources necessary to a trial.

5. ***What is the purpose of a trial?*** Every trial presents two contrasting views of the truth. Although at first glance, the purpose of a trial seems to be to determine truth, conflict resolution may be an equally valid purpose. This debate is exemplified by three contrasting images of a trial: (1) as a search for the truth, (2) as a test of credibility, and (3) as a conflict-resolving ritual.

6. ***What are the steps involved in a trial?*** Pretrial procedures include discovery, or the process of obtaining information about the case held by the other side. Once the jury is selected (through a process called *voir dire*), the following sequence of steps unfolds in the trial itself:
   a. Opening statements by attorneys for the two sides (prosecution or plaintiff goes first)
   b. Direct examination, cross-examination, and redirect and recross of witnesses, with prosecution witnesses first, then defense witnesses
   c. Presentation of rebuttal witnesses and evidence
   d. Closing statements, or summations, by the two sides, usually in the order of prosecution, then defense, then prosecution again
   e. Judge's instructions to the jury (in some jurisdictions, these come before the closing statements)
   f. Jury deliberations and announcement of a verdict
   g. If the verdict is guilty, determination of the punishment

7. ***How has the introduction of emerging technologies changed the way that trials are conducted?*** Over time, the emergence of more sophisticated technologies into the legal system has begun to change the look of courtroom trials and appeals.

As judges, lawyers, and jurors have become more tech-savvy, documentation and presentation methods of the past are being replaced by newer technologies such as computer animations and simulations, videoconferencing, virtual reality, and electronic and digital presentations of evidence. These high-tech methods have raised a number of interesting and complex psychological questions regarding the influence and effectiveness of technology in the courtroom.

Key Terms

anchoring

arraignment

change of venue

charge bargaining

closing argument

discovery

exculpatory

experiential inflammatory bias

extralegal factors

focal concerns perspective

framing effects

grand jury

heuristics

impeachment

indictments

initial appearance

legal factors

matching heuristic

motion in limine

opening statements

overconfidence bias

perjury

plea bargains

preliminary hearing

preponderance of evidence

presence

preventive detention

probative value

rebuttal evidence

recross

redirect questioning

reservation price

self-serving bias

sentence bargaining

settlement negotiation

vividness effect

9 Alternatives to Traditional Prosecution

ORIENTING QUESTIONS

1. What is alternative dispute resolution (ADR)? What are some types of ADR?

2. What is the Sequential Intercept Model?

3. What are the major stages (or intercepts) for community-based alternatives to standard prosecution?

4. What are the similarities and differences between community court and other kinds of problem-solving courts?

The previous chapter described the components of our legal system that have been in place for centuries. Valuing precedent as it does, the law is slow to change, but the last three decades have witnessed various innovations that are important and useful. These will be discussed in the present chapter. The first major area—alternative dispute resolution—has been applied in both criminal and civil contexts. The second major area of discussion is community alternatives to standard prosecution. Our discussion of this area is framed within the Sequential Intercept Model, which identifies different points at which certain groups of individuals can be diverted from standard prosecution into an approach that is more rehabilitation oriented. The discussion will include relevant research findings, which are very important in considering the effectiveness of interventions at these different stages. ●

Alternative Dispute Resolution

If you watch cable and online news and entertainment, you might get the impression that most lawsuits are resolved by a jury trial. In fact, most cases are resolved through negotiation or by alternative dispute resolution (ADR), and relatively few cases are settled in trials. In a 2001 study of courts in 46 randomly selected counties in 22 states, the National Center for State Courts found that the number of cases tried had decreased by 50% in 10 years (Post, 2004c).

The drop-off of trials in the federal courts—particularly civil trials—is even more dramatic. In 1962, 11.5% of federal civil cases were decided in a trial, compared with 6.1% in 1982, 1.8% in 2002, and only 1.2% in 2009 (Qualters, 2010). In 2016, the figure dropped to 0.7%. On the criminal side, trials also decreased, though not as sharply. In 1962, 15.4% of criminal cases went to trial; in 2002 only 4.7% involved

a trial (Galanter, 2004). These trends continued into the second decade of the 21st century (Galanter & Frozena, 2014).

These declines are attributable to several factors, including the perceived cost of litigation—the "transaction costs," in economists' language. Lawyers' fees to prepare for and try a case, as well as the fees paid to expert witnesses, often make a trial economically unfeasible. In addition, federal courts pressure litigants to settle or to plead guilty. The federal sentencing guidelines give criminal defendants an incentive to plead guilty because judges can decrease the length of a sentence on the basis of "acceptance of responsibility" (which normally requires a guilty plea) (Galanter, 2004). Finally, federal trials have decreased because it has been some time since Congress passed sweeping legislation that creates liability for certain actions and that brings lawsuits into the courts to determine the boundaries around that liability. Legislation such as the Americans with Disabilities Act of 1990 is an example (Qualters, 2010).

In civil cases, federal judges are required to attempt to resolve disputes through ADR, and in both state and federal courts, judges can require litigants to try to settle their cases without going to trial. Increasingly, American courts assume that cases will be settled, not tried, to the point where a trial is viewed "as a failure of the system" (Sanborn, 2002, p. 25). Edmund Ludwig, a judge with over 30 years of experience, describes it this way:

Litigation represents a breakdown in communication, which consists in the civil area of the inability of the parties to work out a problem for themselves and in the criminal area, of ineffectively inculcating society's rules and the consequences for violating them. Trials are the method we have ultimately used to deal with those breakdowns. However, the goal of our system is not to try cases. Rather, it is to achieve a fair, just, economical, and expeditious result by trial or otherwise (Ludwig, 2002, p. 217).

Many cases are settled by **negotiation**, without the assistance of a third party. Negotiation might be formal, as happens when management and union representatives negotiate a labor contract, or informal, as when attorneys go back and forth in a series of phone calls to settle a personal injury claim. Another informal mechanism involves collaborative divorce, in which lawyers and psychologists work with a divorcing couple to finalize all issues without going to court. Typically, there is a heightened sense of trust, openness, and disclosure in collaborative divorce (Degoldi, 2008). We describe one example in Box 9.1.

As in trials, procedural justice considerations are important in successful negotiations. People care about both the outcome of negotiations and the fairness of the process. In a study in which law students role-played attorneys in a simulated negotiation about a contract dispute, participants thought negotiations were fair when they believed that they had been listened to and treated with courtesy, and when they perceived the other party as trustworthy (Hollander-Blumoff & Tyler, 2008).

Arbitration

One form of ADR, binding **arbitration**, bears the closest resemblance to a trial. When the parties agree to binding arbitration, they agree to accept the decision of an arbitrator. Salary arbitration in major league baseball is a good example of binding arbitration. The contract between the owners and the players' union provides that players' salary disputes are settled by binding arbitration, and it further provides that the arbitrator must accept either the owner's offer or the union's offer but cannot split the difference. The parties have an incentive to make an offer as close as possible to the player's "value" (their estimate of the arbitrator's valuation of the player's worth). Although many cases require binding arbitration, other cases are resolved by nonbinding arbitration. If one of the parties is dissatisfied with the arbitrator's decision, that person may ask that the case be tried before a judge or jury.

Arbitration, whether binding or nonbinding, uses trial-like procedures. The parties present evidence and argue the case, and the arbitrator makes a decision. Though initially promoted as a way to avoid the contentiousness and expense of a trial, in recent years arbitration has been criticized for being overly formal and time consuming (Stipanowich, 2010). Other methods for resolving disputes, such as mediation (which we discuss later), are more streamlined.

Summary Jury Trial

The **summary jury trial** is an interesting variation on arbitration. The concept was created by Federal District Court Judge Thomas Lambros in the early 1980s as a result of his difficulty resolving two personal injury

---

The Case of Sarah Smith, David Boyle, and Their Swift Collaborative Divorce

BOX 9.1

Whereas a full-scale divorce litigated in a courtroom can cost more than $75,000 and a negotiated divorce involving adversarial lawyers can total more than $25,000, Sarah Smith and David Boyle spent roughly $5,000 for their collaborative divorce in 2005. Smith and Boyle, who live in neighboring suburbs of Boston, were mainly concerned about the welfare of their children, ages five and nine at the time. Together with their lawyers, Smith and Boyle worked out an arrangement by which the children spend time with each of them.

Lawyers are increasingly likely to embrace collaborative divorce. As of 2007, more than 20,000 had received training in collaborative law, which requires them to pledge to work together with their clients and other professionals to devise outcomes that are beneficial to all parties.

Children of a divorcing couple reap a secondary benefit from collaborative divorce. Psychologists have shown that an important factor in emotional well-being in children is the nature of the parents' post-divorce relationship (Baxter, Weston, & Qu, 2011). The extent of court involvement during the divorce (little, moderate, or high levels of litigation) is associated with children's coping ability: the higher the level of court involvement, the less successful the coping ability (Bing, Nelson, & Wesolowski, 2009).

CRITICAL THOUGHT QUESTION

What factors explain the increasing popularity of collaborative divorce as compared to traditional, adversarial methods of divorcing?

cases using other forms of ADR. The parties in these cases refused to settle, each assuming that it would get a more favorable verdict from a jury. Judge Lambros reasoned that chances for settlement would increase if the parties had a sense of what a jury would do. He instituted an abbreviated and expedited form of a jury trial that he suspected would be especially helpful in resolving relatively simple, lower-value cases.

A summary jury trial is much like a conventional jury trial, though shorter. A jury is empanelled, and the lawyers tell the jurors what the witnesses would say if they were present. The lawyers argue the case and try to answer the jurors' questions about the facts. The judge tells the jury what the law is and tries to answer jurors' questions about the law. The jurors then deliberate and decide the case. In the original conception of a summary jury trial, the "verdict" did not bind the parties, it was merely advisory. In recent years, verdicts have become binding and enforceable. Regardless of these variations, the intent is the same: the process educates the lawyers and clients on how a conventional jury might view the facts and the law. Once educated, the lawyers and their clients are more amenable to settling the case (National Center for State Courts, 2012).

The *American Bar Journal* has reported favorable comments from lawyers and judges who had availed themselves of this form of ADR (McDonough, 2004). Commenting on the summary jury trial, federal judge William Bertelsman said,

> I believe that substantial amounts of time can be saved by using summary jury trial in a few select cases. Also … the summary jury trial gives the parties a taste of the courtroom and satisfies their psychological need for a confrontation with each other. Any judge or attorney can tell you that emotional issues play a large part in some cases. When emotions are high, whether between attorneys or parties, cases may not settle even when a cost-benefit analysis says they should. A summary jury trial can provide a therapeutic release of this emotion at the expenditure of three days of the court's time instead of three weeks (McKay v. Ashland Oil Inc., 1988, p. 49).

Mediation

Another form of ADR, **mediation** involves a neutral person (the mediator) who works with the litigants and their lawyers to achieve a settlement of the controversy. The mediator does not have authority, as an arbitrator does, to decide the controversy. Rather, the mediator acts as a facilitator. Mediation often involves *shuttle diplomacy*, a term associated with former Secretary of State Henry Kissinger. Much as Kissinger would "shuttle" between the two sides in international diplomacy, the mediator goes back and forth between the parties, meeting first with one side, then with the other, in an attempt to broker an agreement between the two (Hoffman, 2011).

One thinks of lawyers as eager to do battle—to slay their opponents with rhetorical swords. Increasingly though, disputants prefer procedures in which a neutral third party helps them to craft a resolution of their own; in short, people prefer mediation (Shestowsky, 2014). Why? People are **risk averse**; they work to avoid taking risks. They prefer that controversies be settled *by them* rather than decided *for them*. A mediator can assist in facilitating a resolution, and people prefer the certainty of a settlement over the uncertainty of arbitration or trial.

Mediation also has a role in divorce proceedings. An alternative to collaborative divorce (in which both parties employ their own lawyers, who agree to cooperate), a mediated divorce involves a third party who helps the couple to dissolve their marriage. Psychologists have assessed whether a mediated divorce leads to more desirable outcomes than litigation. One remarkable study assessed parent–child contact and co-parenting in families whose custody disputes had been resolved 12 years earlier by either mediation or litigation (Emery, Laumann-Billings, Waldron, Sbarra, & Dillon, 2001). Families who mediated custody showed more cooperation and flexibility than families who litigated. In particular, nonresidential parents who mediated had more contact with their children and were more intimately involved in parenting, and fathers who mediated were much more satisfied with their custody arrangements. Compared to litigated divorces, mediation apparently encourages parents to comply with divorce agreements, remained involved in their children's lives, and renegotiate relationships in a more adaptive way

Mediators work with litigants to settle legal cases.

fizkes/Getty Images

Beliefs about Alternative Dispute Resolution

What form of ADR do people tend to favor? The answer to this question is important because ADR procedures will be accepted and used only if they are respected and considered legitimate. One study investigated the preferences for different dispute resolution features among people involved in actual disputes. They indicated their preferences for a particular process and set of rules. The most consistent finding was that participants favored options that offered them control (e.g., a neutral third party helping disputants to arrive at *their own* resolutions, and processes that allow disputants to control *their own* presentation of evidence) (Shestowsky, 2014).

Should courts force litigants to try ADR before setting a case for trial? The reports from courts that mandate ADR are mixed. Some attorneys like the process, believing that both the process and the outcomes are fair (Boersema, Hanson, & Keilitz, 1991; Wissler & Dauber, 2007). But some attorneys doubt that arbitration, for example, saves time or money and express concerns about whether arbitrators have adequate knowledge of the issues (Wissler & Dauber, 2007). Another counterargument is that litigants have a constitutional right to trial by judge or jury. Judges are paid to enforce that right and mandating ADR undermines it. According to Federal Judge G. Thomas Eisele (1991), mandatory ADR can lead to an unintended effect: some lawyers (he calls them "piranhas") file meritless claims, knowing that their claims will have "settlement value" in mediation.

Community Alternatives to Standard Prosecution

We now move from ADR, which is practiced in both civil and criminal law, to community alternatives to standard prosecution (criminal law only). Have you ever wondered whether there was a more effective way than conviction and incarceration for our society to respond to certain kinds of offenders? Drug abuse was once considered an indication of poor motivation and weak character; now it is treated as a disease. But what about the offender who continues to break the law by stealing, possessing substances that are illegal, and behaving under their influence? If such an individual were successfully treated for drug abuse and monitored to ensure that she did not continue to behave illegally, that would be a far better approach than incarceration. This is a description of the kind of offender who is well-suited for a drug court—a specialized kind of **problem-solving court**, developed to rehabilitate and monitor individuals in the community rather than incarcerate them. Problem-solving courts are discussed in this section.

There has been increasing attention over the last decade to community-based alternatives to conviction and imprisonment for certain individuals. As we will discuss, such community-based alternatives have developed because they are more humane, less expensive, and make our society safer (or at least do not increase the risk of crime). Typically they apply to members of a certain subgroup whose experience or behavioral health symptoms might account for a number of minor offenses committed by members of this group. For example, individuals with severe mental illness—schizophrenia, bipolar disorder, major depressive disorder, and other psychotic disorders—might have a greater likelihood of being arrested for domestic disturbances, encounters with police, and interactions with other citizens when the symptoms of such disorders are active. Individuals with serious drug problems may become involved in offenses such as theft, prostitution, and public intoxication for reasons related directly to the need to buy drugs and the consequences of taking them. Military veterans may become involved in offenses such as traffic violations, drug or weapon possession, or problematic interactions with police, fueled in part by posttraumatic stress disorder or traumatic brain injury. Each of these examples recognizes that some criminal behavior involves acting upon symptoms that could be contained with targeted treatment and rehabilitation.

This is the basic philosophy underlying the development of community alternatives to standard criminal arrest, prosecution, and incarceration. Three major justifications have been offered for the development and expansion of such community alternatives. The first is humanitarian. In the words of the U.S. Supreme Court, the Eighth Amendment (which states that "cruel and unusual punishments" may not be inflicted) must draw its meaning from the "evolving standards of decency" that characterize a "maturing society" (*Trop v. Dulles*, 1958). But *Trop v. Dulles* was a death penalty case. What about criminal offenses that are much less serious? When behavioral health disorders are associated with minor offending, this could be handled through standard criminal justice processing—but might also be addressed in a more humane and rehabilitative fashion through alternative approaches. Some offenders with severe mental illness are similar to general offenders in most of their rehabilitation needs (Skeem & Eno Louden, 2006). But those whose crimes involve influences that are specific to their disorders may be very good candidates for lower-intensity, briefer, community-based interventions—particularly when they present a low risk for criminal offending, and this risk is reduced even further by treating the disorder.

The second justification for community-based alternatives to standard prosecution is cost. Put simply, it is much less expensive to monitor and treat an offender in the community than it is to incarcerate that individual. California, for example, currently spends about $2 billion annually on health care for offenders who are incarcerated in prison. This is more than $11,000 for each inmate (Kiai & Stobo, 2010), and does not include the nonhealth care costs of operating prisons. Individuals who are provided with treatment and monitoring services in the community but do not need housing or board—and may be able to continue working—cost much less to rehabilitate.

The third justification involves the kind of specialized treatment services that can be provided in the community, as contrasted with services that can be delivered in a prison or jail. Correctional facilities house inmates who, as a group, have wide-ranging rehabilitation needs. More inmates need job training, housing assistance, or substance abuse rehabilitation, for example, than require the combination of medication, psychosocial skills intervention, co-occurring disorder treatment, and recovery focus that is optimal in working with inmates with severe mental illness. In addition, correctional facilities must prioritize security and rule compliance highly, which reduces the resources available for treatment and rehabilitation. When populations are more homogeneous (e.g., as in mental health or drug treatment settings), and security concerns are fewer, then specialized and intensive treatment is more feasible.

Community-Based Alternatives and the Sequential Intercept Model

One of the useful models describing community-based alternatives is the **Sequential Intercept Model** (Munetz & Griffin, 2006). It identifies five stages of the overall criminal justice process at which standard prosecution and incarceration could be interrupted and a community treatment alternative substituted. These stages are: (1) law enforcement and emergency services; (2) post-arrest: initial detention/initial hearing and pre-trial services; (3) post-initial hearings: jail/prison, courts, forensic evaluations, and commitments; (4) re-entry from jails, prisons, and forensic hospitalization; and (5) community corrections (including parole) and community support. This model is relatively new, but its impact has grown recently. A review

of the evidence for intervention effectiveness at each of these intercepts has been published (Heilbrun et al., 2012), as has a book describing its applications (Griffin, Heilbrun, Mulvey, DeMatteo, & Schubert, 2015). However, since this section focuses on community-based alternatives prior to incarceration, we will consider only the first three intercepts in this discussion.

Law Enforcement and Emergency Services (Intercept 1). When individuals with behavioral health disorders encounter police or other "first responders," it is the first step in the process that can result in arrest, criminal charges, conviction, and incarceration. Annual police encounters with citizens with mental health problems have been estimated at more than 300 encounters per 100,000 population across jurisdictions, with this rate increasing annually (Durbin, Lin, & Zaslavska, 2010). In some such encounters, arrest is unnecessary. What if police officers received specialized training in recognizing behavioral health symptoms and interacting with such individuals in a way that did not result in the escalation of conflict—but instead perhaps yielded the opportunity for needed treatment? This is the goal of **specialized police responding**. In particular, the approach known as **Crisis Intervention Team (CIT)** (Compton, Bahora, Watson, & Oliva, 2008) provides police and other first responders (e.g., fire fighters, emergency medical personnel) with enhanced knowledge and skills for use when they encounter individuals who may be experiencing a behavioral health crisis. CIT is intended to increase the number of treatment-oriented dispositions and decrease the number of minor arrests in such cases, as well as decreasing the number of incidents in which the individuals or the police officers are harmed. For instance, an individual with bipolar disorder, off medication and in the midst of a manic episode, might be taken by CIT-trained police to the local psychiatric emergency room rather than arrested for disturbing the peace and battery on an officer. We share a representative story in Box 9.2, provided by a CIT-trained officer in Florida, describing the difference that such CIT training can make in correctional facilities as well as in the community.

What is the evidence that CIT is effective in diverting such individuals, resulting in more treatment dispositions and fewer arrests? Research on this topic has been summarized (Heilbrun et al., 2012) on several points related to CIT: characteristics and knowledge of CIT-trained officers; characteristics of diverted individuals; and outcomes such as the number of diverted individuals, services delivered to them, and number of arrests following

Ron Bull/Toronto Star/ZUMA Press/Newscom

Police Crisis Intervention Teams are specially trained to help people in the midst of emotional crisis or psychiatric distress. These officers are part of a mobile CIT run jointly by a hospital and local police department.

police encounters. CIT-trained police officers reported better preparation for handling interactions with those experiencing a behavioral health crisis (Borum, Williams, Deans, Steadman, & Morrissey, 1998), were more likely to help individuals obtain mental health services (Compton et al., 2008), and were less likely to use physical force (Compton et al., 2008; Skeem & Bibeau, 2008). Jail days were fewer for such individuals, and costs were shifted from criminal justice to treatment sources; diverted participants were also more likely to utilize mental health treatment (comply with medication, use hospital stay and emergency room visits, participate in counseling) and less likely to be treated for substance abuse on a residential basis (Steadman & Naples, 2005). Following such diversions, those who were diverted did not differ from others in their number of arrests over the next year (Teller, Munetz, Gil, & Ritter, 2006; Watson et al., 2010).

Post-Arrest: Initial Detention/Initial Hearing and Pre-trial Services (Intercept 2).

If an individual is arrested upon first encounter with police or another first responder, the second intercept identifies the point at which that person is brought to "first appearance" before a judge. This occurs before the individual enters a plea or proceeds to trial. In some jurisdictions, there is a specialized team that works as part of the court system, identifying defendants who would be appropriate for behavioral health diversion. While some specialized problem-solving courts (e.g., drug court, mental health court, veterans' court, community court) function at this stage, it is more typical to have them take referrals at Intercept 3. Accordingly, Intercept 2 diversion is more likely to send individuals directly to treatment, or assign them to specialized probation.

A number of studies on Intercept 2 have used effectiveness criteria like those employed in studies on Intercept 1. Addressing outcomes for individuals who receive diversion following arrest, investigators have examined services use, mental health, substance use, offending, and quality of life (Broner, Lattimore, Cowell, & Schlenger, 2004; Broner, Mayrl, & Landsberg, 2005). They have also employed criteria such as whether the individual had housing (National GAINS Center, 2002).

Almost all the existing research identifies differences between diverted and nondiverted individuals at this stage. It is not necessarily accurate to conclude that such differences are *attributable* to the diversion; that would require the use of experimental designs (using random assignment to condition) that are virtually impossible to implement in a criminal justice context. (Judges and clinical administrators are understandably reluctant to allow random assignment of defendants to conditions, because an unfortunate outcome such as a serious offense committed by an individual in a no-treatment control group is hard to justify after the tragic event.) However, correlational designs, particularly when accompanied by a comparison group, can provide useful information on the strength (although not the causal direction) of the relationship between the diversion variable and the different outcomes. For example, the studies described later in this paragraph using a comparison group typically obtain their groups from (1) individuals who have been diverted, or (2) those in a standard condition such as probation, and consider how these two groups fare on certain relevant outcomes. This is sometimes called a quasi-experimental design because it does not have the genuine experimental attribute (random assignment to group) that allows the researcher to control all variables except the one of interest—diversion status—and hence draw conclusions about whether diversion causes differences in outcomes. For this intercept, several investigators reported that diverted individuals had more time in the community (Broner et al., 2005; Hoff, Baranosky, Buchanan, Zonana, & Rosenheck, 1999; Lamberti et al., 2001; Steadman & Naples, 2005), fewer hospital days in the community (Lamberti et al., 2001), fewer arrests (National GAINS Center, 2002; Shafer, Arthur, & Franczak, 2004), and less homelessness (National GAINS Center, 2002).

Post-Initial Hearings: Jail/Prison, Courts, Forensic Evaluations, and Commitments (Intercept 3).

The third intercept in the Sequential Intercept Model is the most widely recognized of the five. This is the stage at which problem-solving courts (also called specialty courts) such as drug courts, mental health

CIT for Police, First Responders and Correctional Officers

BOX 9.2

Please allow me to share this story with you. It is a little long, so be patient. The other day a 65-year-old transient female was arrested on two out-of-county misdemeanor warrants. It seems the woman was involved in a fight earlier in the day, which resulted in numerous cuts, bruises, and abrasions. Upon her arrest, she was initially transported to (a local medical facility) for medical clearance prior to being transported to the county jail. Unable to accurately detail the events leading to her arrest, she was subsequently treated and cleared from the hospital, then sent to directly to the county jail.

Upon arrival, the woman, who is elderly and petite in stature, now bruised and battered and obviously in some form of physical distress, is placed in a female dorm along with other offenders of various classifications. It always amazes me that most female offenders will come to the aid of the elderly and help them along with their personal needs. They help them shower, tend to personal needs, and even assist in changing their sheets and clothing. There seems to be an inmate code with the elderly and disabled. Well, as fate would have it, the woman begins to require additional needs, which cannot be met in a county jail, and this concern is finally brought to the attention of the supervisor by an attentive block officer.

Now here is where it starts to come together. The supervisor in this matter is CIT-trained and just knows in the pit of his stomach that something is wrong and just doesn't make sense. He immediately realizes that the woman needs supplementary care, medical attention, and proactive intervention. He instructs the officers to bring the female to booking, where she can be isolated from the general population. He then notifies the on-duty medic and initiates a 15-minute watch on her so she can be observed on a more regular basis. He instructs the female officers, with the assistance of some female inmates, to change her linen and clothing, which is soiled—and make her comfortable until the medic arrives. The woman appears to be resting comfortably on her bunk, but shortly after the supervisor notices she is extending her arm above her body as if to motion for assistance. The supervisor approaches the cell and realizes something is not right; he gets that gut feeling again. Her breath appears labored and she just had a look on her face that she was in need of some assistance, but was unable to ask. He summoned a female officer for additional aid and again notified the

on-duty medic. Weak, frail, and pathetic, she is unable to properly communicate her concerns.

While the medical responders are treating her, they learn that the woman is asthmatic, suffers from emphysema, requires immediate oxygen, and was in pulmonary distress. The woman was immediately sent to the hospital. After returning, one of the female deputies assigned to the woman noticed that when she was assisting the woman with her change of clothing, (there appeared to be some bruising on and about the woman's groin area. The Deputy then stated that "I think this woman was a victim of a sexual assault" and went on to say, "I wonder if they (hospital) did a rape kit on her?" After piecing various facts together, the supervisor, a trained CIT member, knew something was wrong. Shortly after, while officers were discussing what had happened, the classification officer mentioned that he had received a phone call from a victim in another matter, who stated something to the effect that the guy that assaulted her also tried to rape an elderly female the same night.

Now here is where it all finally comes together. The supervisor, aware of what might have happened to this woman, immediately contacted the Victim Services Advocate and the CID Detectives Bureau. After explaining the circumstances surrounding this matter, the detectives interviewed the woman in the safety of her hospital room. The victim's advocate immediately (pointed out that the perpetrator in this case) might very well be incarcerated in the very same jail on unrelated charges. Subsequently, the county, which issued the charges against the woman, rescinded the warrants, and she was released and transferred to another hospital for treatment. The woman ultimately suffered a stroke while in the hospital and is currently being treated for her injuries and current medical condition. Without the intervention of a trained Crisis Intervention Team member, perhaps this end result would have been much different. Doctors stated that the woman was operating with only 1% lung capacity, and if gone untreated she would not have made it through the night. The woman is alive today due to the actions of a CIT-trained individual.

CRITICAL THOUGHT QUESTION

How might CIT training, which is increasingly provided to correctional officers as well as police and first responders, have made a difference in this case?

courts, homeless courts, domestic violence courts, and community courts have been developed. There have also been courts developed for other groups, such as veterans and prostitutes, but these problem-solving courts are sufficiently new that there has not been research investigating how well they work. Specialized problem-solving courts are also discussed later in this book in Chapter 15.

Problem-Solving Courts

Certain offenders are summoned back to court and returned to prison repeatedly. For them, the criminal justice system has become all-too-familiar home (Wiener, Winick, Georges, & Castro, 2010). Fed up with this model of "revolving-door" justice, states and communities increasingly are creating problem-solving courts (also called specialty courts) that combine the traditional criminal justice system with specialized treatment-oriented principles to address underlying causes of antisocial behavior (Casey & Rottman, 2005).

The premise of specialty courts is that the legal system should help troubled individuals cope with the chronic problems that brought them into contact with the criminal justice system in the first place. This collaborative, nonadversarial nature of specialty courts, in which judges work side by side with mental health professionals, community agencies, and offenders themselves, focuses more on meeting the ongoing needs of participants than on punishing them.

This approach, in which the law is used as a vehicle to improve people's lives, is called **therapeutic jurisprudence**.

Examples include courts specialized to deal with problems involving drugs, mental health, homelessness, and domestic violence, as well as veterans' issues, and courts that integrate these problems, for example, by applying mental health court techniques in domestic violence cases (Winick, Wiener, Castro, Emmert, & Georges, 2010). Regardless of the problem, all specialty courts involve a few common elements, including immediate interventions such as drug or alcohol counseling, frequent court appearances in a non-adversarial context, an interdisciplinary team approach, and a set of clearly defined objectives (Watson, Hanrahan, Luchins, & Lurigio, 2001).

Working together with mental health providers, attorneys, and probation officers, judges in these courts become social workers and cheerleaders as much as jurists. Rather than impose punishment, they offer opportunities for people to deal with their addictions, anger, and disputes (Hartley, 2008). Those who comply with the judges' orders may have their sentences reduced or dismissed.

Although some aspects of these courts are traditional—for instance, judges wear robes—many characteristics of specialty courts are unconventional. For example, the people who appear in court are often called clients rather than defendants. These "clients" are able to speak directly to the judge, rather than communicating through their attorneys. Judges often have a great deal of information about clients, and may interact with them over a number of years. On occasion, a friendly relationship develops, as described in Box 9.3.

The Case of a "Client" of Justice Matthew D'Emic   BOX 9.3

An immigrant from Barbados in his early 20s arrived in the New York courtroom of Justice Matthew D'Emic in 2003, facing a serious charge of arson after starting a fire that damaged a small public housing complex (Eaton & Kaufman, 2005). The man was delusional, believing that he was the son of God; he had been hospitalized nine times in five years. In a traditional courtroom, the case would have been disposed of by a guilty plea or verdict, and the defendant would have been sent to prison. But in the mental health court over which Justice D'Emic presided, something very different happened. The judge decided that the young man could safely return to live with his mother, provided that he continued to take his medications. Later, when the man complained of stomach cramps and began to

miss appointments, the judge suggested that he change his medicine. The judge insisted that the man sign up for job training, allowing him to "graduate" from court with only a misdemeanor on his record. Most remarkably, Justice D'Emic gave the client his cell phone number and urged him to call if he got into a jam. The man said he used it just once, to ask the judge for advice about a woman he was considering marrying.

CRITICAL THOUGHT QUESTION

What are the pros and cons of resolving this dispute in a mental health court, rather than through the workings of the traditional criminal justice system?

Drug Courts. The most common kind of specialty court is drug court, created to deal with offenders whose crimes are related to addiction. Drug courts developed in response to an increase in antidrug law enforcement efforts and stiffer sanctions for drug offenders during the 1980s and 1990s. By the end of 2014, the National Institute of Justice estimated that there were more than 3,000 drug courts of various kinds operating throughout the 50 states (https://www.nij.gov/topics/courts/drug-courts/pages/welcome.aspx).

Drug courts were developed to address the abuse of alcohol and other drugs and criminal activity related to their abuse. Drug courts divert cases from the traditional criminal justice system and link drug-addicted offenders with treatment programs and extensive supervision. In exchange for successful completion of the program, the court may dismiss the original charge, reduce or set aside a sentence, assign some lesser penalty, or make a combination of these adjustments. The ultimate goal, in addition to improving the lives of drug-addicted individuals, is to reduce the number of drug offenders in prisons.

How successful are drug courts in reducing drug-related criminal activity? The findings are encouraging, though some drug courts work better than others. A **meta-analysis**—a statistical technique that combines the results of individual studies with similar research hypotheses—of 60 studies that compared a treatment condition to a control condition, and that included at least one measure of criminal behavior as an outcome measure, concluded that drug courts have a significant, though modest, effect on recidivism. Offenders assigned to drug court had a 45.5% recidivism rate, while the comparison group had a 54.5% recidivism

rate (Shaffer, 2011). The most successful programs were those that excluded violent offenders, worked with and treated offenders who had not yet entered a plea, and employed well-qualified and competent staff who ensured that the program was delivered as designed and who interacted positively with participants.

According to Seattle judge J. Wesley Saint Clair, "Drug courts work, and not because they're fuzzy—let me tell you, I can be a hard man to deal with." One offender to appear in Judge Saint Clair's courtroom was 36-year-old Jenifer Paris, who, after 22 years of heroin and cocaine use and stretches of prostitution and homelessness, was now clean. "You guys are the first people to believe in me … I'm full of gratitude for the opportunity and for you not kicking me out," she said, tearfully. Replied Judge Saint Clair with a hint of a smile, "We're not done yet" (Eckholm, 2008).

Problem-solving courts have particular appeal within communities, as judges often interact with treatment providers and advocacy groups in a way that is not usually seen in traditional courts. Judges like Wesley Saint Clair often play a much more active role, setting aside judicial restraint and impartiality in favor of more direct involvement in the interventions and responses of problem-solving court participants.

Mental Health Courts. The number of individuals hospitalized long term for mental illness has dropped significantly in the past four decades. But **deinstitutionalization**, the long-term trend of closing mental hospitals and transferring care to community-based mental health treatment facilities, has left many mentally ill individuals without services or medication. As a result, the mentally ill have experienced higher rates of homelessness, unemployment, alcohol and drug use, and physical and sexual abuse. They also experience high rates of incarceration: 17% of men and 34% of women in jails suffer from a serious mental illness or post-traumatic stress disorder (Steadman, Osher, Clark Robbins, Case, & Samuels, 2009). Unfortunately, most local jails lack treatment resources and are highly stressful environments, especially for people suffering severe mental illnesses.

According to the **criminalization hypothesis**, a subgroup of mentally ill offenders are arrested for offenses *caused* by their untreated symptoms of mental illness. Mental health courts were developed for offenders dealing with serious mental illness and seek to "decriminalize" this population. By 2016, there were over 300 mental health courts in the United States, according to the Council for State Governments (https://csgjusticecenter.org/mental-health-court-project).

Daniel Acker/Bloomberg/Getty Images

Drug courts, like this one in Illinois, are only address crimes related to drug and alcohol abuse.

As with the drug court model, the first decision in a mental health court is whether to divert the offender from the regular criminal courts to treatment programs associated with the mental health court. This decision, which usually requires the consent of both the offender and the victim, is made after an evaluation of the offender and by considering the nature of the offense. If the offender is diverted, the mental health team prepares a treatment plan for mental health care and reintegration into society. Close monitoring is essential. Defendants are often assigned to a probation officer who is trained in mental health and who carries a greatly reduced caseload in order to provide a more intensive level of supervision and expertise. The charges are typically dismissed if the offender follows the treatment plan (Lurigio, Watson, Luchins, & Hanrahan, 2001).

Evaluations of mental health courts suggest that they have been effective in reducing recidivism, though whether they provide therapeutic value to participants is less clear (Honegger, 2015). People who completed a treatment program associated with a rural North Carolina mental health court were 88% less likely to recidivate than people who did not complete treatment (Hiday & Ray, 2010). Although findings are limited, it appears that mental health courts are also cost effective, reducing the need for services such as psychiatric emergency room visits and other crisis interventions.

There are two broad concerns associated with mental health courts, however. First, participants may feel coerced into participating. In one study involving over 200 participants, investigators found that although most said they had agreed to participate, the majority were unaware that the program was voluntary and did not understand many of the nuances of the program. This led the researchers to question whether diversion to mental health courts is truly voluntary (Redlich, Hoover, Summers, & Steadman, 2010).

The second concern involves the selection of participants. Specialty courts, including mental health courts, admit only a fraction of the people who are eligible, and admission decisions typically involve multiple perspectives and parties (e.g., clients, treatment providers, judges, prosecutors, defense attorneys, and victims) (Wolff, Fabrikant, & Belenko, 2011). Recent studies suggest that gender and racial bias may influence the way that potential clients are identified, recruited, and eventually selected to participate. Specifically, Caucasian males are overrepresented in mental health courts. According to a meta-analysis of 18 studies (Sarteschi,

Vaughn, & Kim, 2011), the majority of participants in mental health courts are Caucasian males in their mid-30s, whereas African American males constituted the largest demographic group in prisons and jails in 2007 (Sabol & Couture, 2008) and mental health diagnoses are more prevalent among disadvantaged minority groups (Minsky, Vega, Miskimen, Gara, & Escobar, 2003).

A related concern is the possibility that the selection process, rather than the interventions provided, accounts for the modest positive outcomes associated with participating in mental health courts. This could happen if only those potential clients who accept their mental health disorder and who are amenable to treatment are invited to participate. After evaluating the selection procedures in six demographically diverse mental health courts, Wolff et al. (2011) concluded that client selection might explain findings on the effectiveness of mental health courts.

Homeless Courts. People living on the streets are frequently cited for public nuisance offenses such as public intoxication and loitering; they often fail to appear when summoned to court. As a result, they are unable to access vital services such as housing, employment opportunities, and public assistance.

Homeless courts were started in southern California in the late 1980s. They are designed to assist marginalized individuals, address the underlying problems that resulted in their homelessness, and reintegrate these people into society. Homeless "court" is typically held in shelters or agencies that serve this population. Rather than being fined or taken into custody, participants are given alternative sentences—including assignment to programs and activities such as employment training, counseling, Alcoholics Anonymous meetings, and volunteer work.

New York City has created a variant on this approach termed community courts (discussed in more detail later in this section) in Times Square and the Red Hook area of Brooklyn (Post, 2004a). Meeting in a refurbished Catholic school, the judges, prosecutors, and defenders in the Red Hook community court see their goal as improving the quality of life for citizens. They know the people of the community. They also make it a point to know the offenders and to make sure the offenders know them. "The clerk of court has been known to stop her car at street corners and tell defendants the judge has issued a warrant for them and they'd best get over to court" (Carter, 2004, p. 39). The result is a reduction in low-level crime, and decreased recidivism by those under the jurisdiction of this problem-solving court. Some community courts also aim to reduce homelessness by dealing with landlord–tenant problems, and addressing some of the underlying causes of homelessness—mental illness, poor job skills, and language barriers.

Domestic Violence Courts. Historically, legal responses to domestic violence cases have been fragmented, with different court divisions issuing restraining orders, prosecuting perpetrators, and protecting children. Victims have been considered merely "witnesses" and the needs of children have been largely ignored (Casey & Rottman, 2005). As this kind of problem-solving court has matured, however, there have been coordinated efforts to hold perpetrators accountable, enhance victim and child safety, and promote informed judicial decision-making. Domestic violence court personnel work with community-based agencies to strengthen the entire community's response to domestic violence (Sack, 2002). Estimates of the number of domestic violence courts in the United States range from 160 (Keilitz, 2004) to 208 (Labriola, Bradley, O'Sullivan, Rempel, & Moore, 2010), to more than 300 (Casey & Rottman, 2005). This discrepancy probably depends on whether the court has at least one specialized unit, process, or service for domestic violence cases—or handles these cases as part of a broader problem-solving court.

Like other specialty courts, domestic violence courts involve judges and staff specially trained in the relevant domain, coordination among community resources, and close monitoring of the perpetrator both before and after case disposition. But domestic violence courts differ from other specialty courts in important respects. They start from the premise that offenders' behavior is learned rather than rooted in a treatable addiction or illness. Therefore, court proceedings are primarily adversarial rather than therapeutic. They often involve both victim and offender attempting to reach agreement on protection orders. The needs of children are considered, and co-occurring child abuse and neglect are addressed.

Although few studies have evaluated the effectiveness of domestic violence courts, including their ability to reduce recidivism (Wiener et al., 2010), victims, perpetrators, advocates, and judges have generally reacted positively. Both victims and perpetrators express satisfaction with the court processes and outcomes. Compared with traditional courts, domestic violence courts process cases faster and have higher rates of guilty pleas. In addition, perpetrators are more likely to comply with court-ordered conditions (Casey & Rottman, 2005).

Community Courts. In contrast to drug courts and mental health courts, each of which is characterized by jurisdiction over a very specific group, a community court is neighborhood-focused and designed to address local problems such as vandalism, prostitution, shoplifting, vagrancy, and the like. Community courts use problem-solving and strive to create relationships with outside stakeholders such as residents, merchants, churches, and schools (Center for Court Innovation, 2012).

Community court participants generally like how they are treated in this kind of court. Participants see them as fairer than traditional courts (Frazer, 2006), and give them high marks in achieving goals such as working productively, assigning useful community service, and treating participants equally (Justice Education Center, 2002). Perhaps one reason for such favorable ratings has been the use of alternative sanctions by community courts; they are less likely to incarcerate individuals as part of disposition of charges (Hakuta et al., 2008). Although such courts are slightly more expensive when measured by cost per case, they are also associated with higher levels of compliance with sanctions and greater reduction of particular outcomes such as prostitution, illegal vending, and other problems particular to community courts (Kralstein, 2005). We provide one example of a community court in Box 9.4.

Veterans' Courts. The most recent version of specialty court—veterans' courts—was launched in 2008 to address the complicated psychological and legal problems of members of the U.S. military who have returned from war. There are now dozens of such courts across the country.

More than 2 million Americans have served in the wars in Iraq and Afghanistan, making these the largest deployments since the Vietnam War. Approximately one-third of them suffer from posttraumatic stress disorder (PTSD), traumatic brain injury, depression, or other mental illness, and one-fifth are addicted to drugs or alcohol (Marvasti, 2010). Sadly, only about half of the veterans with PTSD or depression have sought help, and of those, only about half received satisfactory care (Tanielian & Jayco, 2008). Given their training in the military to react immediately to any perceived threat, it is not surprising that thousands of returning veterans have reacted impulsively and

BOX 9.4

Seattle Community Court: Creative Solutions for High-Impact, Low-Level Crime

When a minor crime is committed over and over, is it still too small for concern? Judge Fred Bonner, who presides over the Seattle Community Court, says that people in survival mode commit acts of theft to survive, and these small crimes often indicate larger societal problems that are significant. Many of the low-level crimes, such as theft and prostitution, committed in Seattle were by individuals who were homeless or mentally ill. "Criminal trespass, theft, prostitution, alcohol and drug-related crime—those were the main kinds of crimes we were dealing with," said Assistant City Attorney Tuere Sala. "They are what we call quality-of-life crimes—and they are usually crimes that are committed more out of a need to survive than an intention to injure others."

Although the intention of such offenses may not be to injure any one individual, the cumulative effect of this kind of offending on a community can be very substantial. "Even if you think it's a faceless crime," said defense attorney Nancy Waldman, "somebody is violated. If a business feels that way, they're more inclined to move their business away from any given district. It has an effect on the whole city." Seattle City Attorney Peter S. Holmes said, "This is a non-partisan issue: Everyone wants to reduce crime and save money, and that's ultimately what community court is about."

In the search for an appropriate response to Seattle's low-level crime, the Seattle Community Court opened in 2005 to serve the downtown district. "We took those individuals who had no place to go, who had spent many days in jail over the years," said Judge Bonner, "and we designed our program to address those needs." Like most community courts across the United States, by combining punishment with help, the Seattle Court seeks to address the social needs associated with crime, repair the harm done, and help transform offenders into productive members of the community. The Seattle Community Court handles only defendants who

have committed low-level misdemeanors and do not present a public safety risk. Rather than paying a fine or spending time in jail, all defendants who agree to participate in community court are assessed for social service needs and then must contact each social service link, such as community service opportunities identified during assessment. It is common practice in community courts to use alternatives to detention, such as community service, as a sanction. Participants in the Seattle Court have completed over 50,000 hours of community service, but Judge Bonner stresses the importance of developing such programs to also educate people about the effects that quality-of-life crime has on the community.

Seattle continues to develop its programs and services to address the needs of offenders as those needs change. "We've just developed a theft awareness class and life-skills training, which would constitute community service," said Judge Bonner, who added that Seattle Community Court also recently launched three stand-alone sites that provide young prostitutes with housing and classes on avoiding sexually transmitted diseases. They can earn community service hours at these sites, as well as receive literacy training and counseling. Seattle Community Court also has new protocols that allow for community service alternatives for individuals with disabilities. The court already partners with 25 community service organizations, and coordinators from the Seattle Community Court have recently started to expand options for individuals not physically able to perform traditional community service. For example, individuals who are unable to pick up trash could be required to answer phones or do filing. "Offenders find that they feel proud of putting in a full day's work," said Karen Murray, of the Associated Counsel for the Accused. "Then we can link them to employment services. Landlords and employers can see people's capacity

violently in heated situations. Sometimes, as a result, they have been arrested and charged with serious criminal offenses, including child abuse, sexual assault, and homicide.

In a typical veterans' court, a district attorney may opt to defer prosecution or offer a plea bargain to a reduced charge if it is clear that the offense was related

to the veteran's disability and the veteran agrees to seek treatment. Veterans who plead guilty to a nonviolent felony or misdemeanor are teamed with volunteer veteran mentors who ensure that the offender adheres to a strict regimen of counseling, personalized rehabilitation programs, and court appearances. Judges may issue alternative sentences that require to change." Seattle Community Court is also evolving to address the different needs that veteran offenders have. "We have a marvelous caseworker from the veterans' hospital coming to our court, and we're trying to do a docket right now just for veterans," said Murray. "They never had criminal histories before and suddenly they're coming back and they're acting out. Do we actually expect people to get off the plane and come back into society as though nothing happened? That's another role for community court in our time."

Another defining element of our time is the strained economic climate experienced throughout the country, and community courts are not immune to this struggle. "We have been suffering some serious budget issues here," said Judge Bonner, "but one of the things that the city council has said is, 'We don't want to reduce or cut community court.' It has been recognized that not only does it save the city money, it also saves lives."

In 2009, the Justice Management Institute issued an independent evaluation of Seattle Community Court. The report stated that individuals involved in the community court committed 66% fewer offenses within 18 months of community court intervention, while those in the control group (undergoing traditional prosecution, and receiving probation if convicted) showed an increase of 50%, suggesting that the court is significantly more effective at reducing the frequency of recidivism than the traditional court process. "The study adds to the value of understanding these kinds of interventions; even though they seem at the surface to be cost-intensive, that may actually not be the case," said Elaine Nugent-Borakove, president of the Justice Management Institute and primary researcher on the evaluation. Furthermore, the Seattle Mayor's Office of Policy and Management estimates that through reduced recidivism and jail use the community court saved the city $1,513,209 during the court's first three years of operation. "We're still studying why crime is down nearly double digits percentage-wise in Seattle over the past 16 months," said City Attorney Holmes, "but I have

to think that community court is a factor." Holmes also discussed how community court may have helped alleviate the strain on funds. "When I was on the campaign trail in 2009, it was seen as inevitable that Seattle was going to break ground on a new jail with a price tag of 400 million dollars within the next five years. We have to give some credit to the community court diverting people from incarceration for the fact that Seattle is no longer seriously on the track to build a new jail."

For some who work in the court, the problem-solving approach is new. Craig Sims, chief of the Criminal Division, said, "When I came here in January 2010, I didn't know much about community court. I've been a prosecutor since the late nineties, working in the traditional mode of prosecution: Someone does something wrong, they go to court, they get prosecuted, they go to jail, and we move on to the next one. It was quite refreshing for me to collaborate with the court and the defense to figure out a different way to resolve lower-level crimes." "We're all partners in this," added Holmes, and the Seattle community can see the tangible benefits of this partnership. "We've had some wonderful public events," said Holmes. "Rather than spending time in jail, low-level offenders were out beautifying the community and giving back. Community murals have had unveiling events, heavily attended by local community groups and local media, and the community is able to feel less cynical about the criminal justice system."

"I like the fact that it's an opportunity court," said Sala. "You have an opportunity to make a difference, to change something. As a prosecutor, I would rather see that than the same offenders constantly coming back."

CRITICAL THOUGHT QUESTION

How is community court similar to other kinds of problem-solving courts, such as drug court, mental health court, and veterans' court? How is it different?

offenders to seek psychological treatment. By completing the required program, an individual may avoid going to prison. Whether these provisions should be made available to veterans charged with felonies is a matter of ongoing debate. There are yet very few studies of their effectiveness. The sparse data that exist suggest that offenders who are diverted to veterans'

court are less likely to reoffend than those whose cases go through the traditional criminal justice system (Mador, 2010). A recent study (Knudsen & Wingenfeld, 2016) included 86 veterans in an Ohio jail diversion and trauma recovery treatment court who were interviewed at baseline, and 6- and 12-months later to determine if the program led to improvements in

AP Images/Don Heupel

Veterans' courts, like this one, aim to address crimes perpetrated by members of the U.S. Military returning from war.

jail recidivism, psychiatric symptoms, quality of life, and recovery. Results suggested that participants experienced significant improvement in various outcomes relative to baseline (PTSD, depression, substance abuse, overall functioning, emotional well-being, relationships with others, recovery status, social connectedness, family functioning, and sleep). However, without a control or comparison group, we do not know whether this improvement was significantly better than other approaches to processing participants in the criminal justice system.

Criticisms of Problem-Solving Courts. Despite the apparent successes of problem-solving courts, they have also been criticized. One concern is that regardless of the type of specialty court, they are presided over by middle-class judges who inevitably reflect their own values and who may become inappropriately paternalistic in what they require of people (Eaton & Kaufman, 2005). Some have argued that problem-solving courts lack legitimacy because threatening punishment to coerce rehabilitation is unfair and because guilt or innocence is not determined by a trial (Casey, 2004). Prosecutors and public defenders have expressed concern over the "social worker" roles inherent in drug court philosophy; prosecutors feel pressured to favor rehabilitation of the offender over protection of society, and defenders feel pressured to plead their clients guilty and to inform the court of clients' failure to comply with the terms of probation (Feinblatt & Berman, 2001). Finally, social scientists worry about the lack of rigorous, empirical studies that assess *how* specialty courts influence (or fail

to influence) offenders' conduct and what impact they have on the underlying social and psychological problems of offenders (Wiener et al., 2010).

In spite of these criticisms, problem-solving courts have shown remarkable growth and the ability to address some of the influences on criminal offending that respond to interventions. As a result, they have the potential to reduce recidivism rates and to improve the lives of participants and their families. Problem-solving courts will probably continue to develop and evolve, focusing on the reasons why people are in court in the first place.

Research on Intercept 3 of the Sequential Intercept Model is the most mature and consistent of the evidence described thus far. Specialty courts of different kinds have been studied, with the general focus on the particular characteristics of participants, the perceptions of favorability on the part of such participants, and outcomes such as cost, the nature of appropriate services delivered, and change in justice-relevant outcomes such as rearrest and subsequent incarceration. The evidence on the delivery of appropriate services, the perception of favorability on the part of participants, and the reduction of the incidence of subsequent arrest and incarceration seems largely favorable for drug courts, community courts, and mental health courts.

The Sequential Intercept Model describes two other points at which specialized interventions can occur for offenders in the community: during the transition from incarceration back to the community (the reentry process) and while on parole following release from incarceration. These are both discussed in Chapter 15.

The Future of Community-Based Alternatives to Prosecution

The alternatives to traditional prosecution described in this chapter have grown substantially during the last two decades. Part of their appeal involves their bipartisan nature. For conservative legislators who focus on public safety and cost, there is growing evidence that alternative approaches such as specialized police responding and problem-solving courts reduce the risk of criminal offending, and also contain criminal justice costs (although they may shift costs to systems that deliver rehabilitation services). For progressive legislators who might be inclined to emphasize rehabilitation, there is more specific treatment and rehabilitation associated with such alternative approaches. But such approaches have grown partly because the original areas of rehabilitation need (e.g., substance abuse, mental health) have been expanded to include a number of other areas as well.

Will this trend continue? Will we see the development of "trauma courts" or other similar problem-solving courts? If so, we hope that research is used both in the development and the maintenance of these new courts, so our society has evidence that they work as intended. But it seems unlikely that the community alternatives approach will ever replace our traditional system of prosecution and incarceration, particularly for serious crime. Our society also values the importance of punishing criminal offending through incarceration.

Summary

1. ***What is alternative dispute resolution (ADR)? What are some types of ADR?*** Alternative dispute resolution (ADR) is an umbrella term for alternatives to the court and jury as a means of resolving legal disputes. The most common forms are arbitration, in which a third party decides the controversy after hearing from both sides, and mediation, in which a third party tries to facilitate agreement between the disputants. The summary jury trial is another ADR mechanism.

2. ***What is the Sequential Intercept Model?*** The Sequential Intercept Model is a model identifying the most relevant points of interception from the standard process of arrest, prosecution, conviction, and incarceration of criminal offenders.

3. ***What are the major stages (or intercepts) for community-based alternatives to standard prosecution?*** The intercepts that are relevant to community-based alternatives, diverting offenders from jail or prison into a rehabilitative community disposition, are (1) specialized law enforcement and emergency services responding; (2) post-arrest initial detention/hearing; and (3) jail/prison, courts, forensic evaluations, and commitments.

4. ***What are the similarities and differences between community court and other kinds of problem-solving courts?*** The underlying philosophy of all problem-solving courts reflects the view that identifying and rehabilitating a subset of criminal offenders can be accomplished less expensively, less restrictively, and more safely in the more rehabilitation-oriented problem-solving court than with the traditional criminal process. Most problem-solving courts accept a specific subgroup of offenders, based on their symptoms (e.g., mental health court, drug court) or experience (e.g., veterans' court), with the assumption that those in such groups have a specific constellation of rehabilitation needs which, if addressed, would make them less likely to reoffend. By contrast, community court is more heterogeneous, and may include a variety of groups of offender in need of rehabilitation for particular reasons that relate strongly to their risk for future offending.

Key Terms

arbitration

criminalization hypothesis

Crisis Intervention Team

deinstitutionalization

mediation

meta-analysis

negotiation

problem-solving court

risk averse

Sequential Intercept Model

specialized police responding

summary jury trial

therapeutic jurisprudence

10 Forensic Assessment in Juvenile and Criminal Cases

The Scope of Forensic Psychology

Forensic psychologists use knowledge and techniques from psychology, psychiatry, and other behavioral sciences to answer questions about individuals involved in legal proceedings. In most cases, forensic psychological assessment is conducted by clinical psychologists or clinical neuropsychologists, and the field of forensic psychology has prospered and matured considerably in the last 30 years (Heilbrun & Brooks, 2010; Heilbrun, Grisso, & Goldstein, 2009). For example:

- Forensic psychology is officially recognized as a specialty by the American Board of Professional Psychology and by the American Psychological Association.
- A revised version of specialty guidelines for the practice of forensic psychology has been approved (American Psychological Association, 2011), updating the original version (Committee on Ethical Guidelines for Forensic Psychologists, 1991).
- Forensic psychology predoctoral training concentrations and postdoctoral fellowships are available, providing formal training in the field.
- The research and clinical literature on forensic practice have increased dramatically.

It appears likely that growth in this field will continue. There are several reasons for this. First, mental health experts have expertise in a variety of areas relevant to litigation. As scientists learn more about human behavior, attorneys will find new ways to use this information in various legal proceedings. In this and the following chapters, we focus on several topics that mental health professionals are called on to assess for individuals involved in court proceedings.

Second, forensic psychology is flourishing because the law permits, and even encourages, the use of expert testimony in a host of areas, including psychology, anthropology, criminology, engineering, toxicology, genetics, and medicine (National Research Council, 2009). Expert testimony is used in all these areas, but psychological topics have enjoyed particular prominence.

Finally, expert testimony by forensic psychologists thrives because it can be very lucrative. With hourly rates between $200 and $800, forensic experts can earn thousands of dollars per case. If one party in a lawsuit or criminal trial hires an expert, the other side usually feels pressure to respond with their own expert. Consequently, the use of psychological experts promotes the further use of such experts, and it has become a significant source of income for many professionals.

In general, a qualified expert can testify about a topic if such testimony is relevant to an issue in dispute and if the usefulness of the testimony outweighs whatever prejudicial impact it might have. If these two conditions are satisfied—as they must be for any kind of testimony to be admitted—an expert will be permitted to give opinion testimony if the judge believes that "scientific, technical, or other specialized knowledge will assist the trier of fact to understand the evidence or to determine a fact in issue" (Federal Rule of Evidence 702). The U.S. Supreme Court ruled in the 1993 case of *Daubert v. Merrell Dow* that federal judges could decide whether expert testimony has a sufficiently relevant and reliable scientific foundation to be admitted into evidence. For opinions offered by behavioral scientists and mental health experts, the *Daubert* standard suggests that admissible expert testimony should be grounded in scientifically based methods and theory

(Melton, Petrila, Poythress, & Slobogin, 2007). In addition, the U.S. Supreme Court has held (in *Kumho Tire Co., Ltd v. Carmichael*, 1999) that this requirement also applies to expert opinions that are provided by those with technical or professional skills, such as clinicians.

Expert testimony plays a crucial role in the insanity defense, one of the most difficult and controversial issues faced by courts and forensic evaluators. Our discussion of the insanity defense begins in Box 10.1, describing the case of Andrea Yates.

The question of whether Andrea Yates—or any criminal defendant—was insane at the time of a criminal offense is one of the most challenging questions that

forensic psychologists and psychiatrists are asked to help courts decide. The question has generated a good deal of research by social scientists, although less in recent years. In this chapter, we discuss the construct of insanity—how it is defined, how claims of insanity are assessed by mental health professionals, and some of the implications of the insanity defense. Prior to that, we describe competence to stand trial, which is sometimes confused with insanity. We cover trial competence and insanity together in this chapter because these issues both occur in the criminal context, are raised together in some cases, and occur fairly close to one another within the sequence of criminal adjudication. We also discuss two other

---

The Case of Andrea Yates: Tragedy and Insanity   BOX 10.1

8708/Gamma-Rapho/Getty Images

Andrea Yates with her family

On the morning of June 20, 2001, Andrea Yates, a 37-year-old wife and mother of five, said goodbye to her husband as he left for work. Before her mother-in-law arrived to help care for the children, who ranged in age from six months to seven years old, Yates filled the bathtub of her Texas home with water. Beginning with her middle son, Paul, she drowned each of her children in turn. She laid the four youngest children on the bed, covering them with a sheet. Her oldest boy was left floating lifelessly in the bathtub. She then called the police and her husband to tell them what she had done.

Prior to the killing of her children, Yates had a long history of severe mental illness. She reportedly suffered numerous psychotic episodes and had been diagnosed with schizophrenia and postpartum depression. These episodes resulted in several hospitalizations, including one just a month prior to the killings, and required psychotropic medications to help stabilize her ("The Andrea Yates Case," 2005).

Yates pled not guilty by reason of insanity to drowning three of her children; she was not charged in the other two deaths. Her insanity plea was based on her claim that she had no choice but to kill them while they were still innocents, to prevent them from burning in hell (Wordsworth, 2005). No one disputed that Yates systematically killed each of her children, but the question remained: Was she so disturbed by the symptoms of her severe mental illness that she could not be held criminally responsible for the murders?

At the conclusion of her trial, Yates was found guilty and sentenced to life in prison. After she had served three years of her sentence, however, the court declared a mistrial and Yates's conviction was overturned. During the trial, one of the psychiatric experts testified that the television show "Law and Order" had aired an episode in which a defendant had been acquitted by reason of insanity after drowning her children in the bathtub. Although the expert himself did not link this observation to Ms. Yates's thinking or motivation, the prosecutor did so in closing arguments. In fact, there had never been an episode of "Law and Order" with this specific story line. Yates was subsequently found not guilty by reason of insanity in a retrial, and is now hospitalized in the Texas state forensic hospital system.

CRITICAL THOUGHT QUESTION

Why would it make a difference in the jury's consideration of the insanity defense for Andrea Yates if "Law and Order" had shown an episode in which an individual had drowned her children in a bathtub—and Ms. Yates had viewed this episode?

important issues that involve assessment by forensic psychologists: capital sentencing evaluations, and the transfer of juveniles from juvenile to criminal (adult) court. In Chapter 11, we explore several other forensic questions that clinicians assess, including questions that arise in civil litigation, divorce and child custody disputes, commitment hearings, and other types of legal proceedings.

Competence

In addition to the question of her sanity, the Andrea Yates case highlights the importance of evaluating a defendant's competence to stand trial. Did Yates understand the nature of her charges—murder involving drowning her children—and the possible consequences of those charges? This question is particularly salient in light of an interview with Yates's mother, who recalled that Andrea Yates (while in prison for these murders) asked her mother who would be watching them (Gibson, 2005). Questions were also raised about whether Yates was taking her antipsychotic medication at the time of the murders as well as during her trial.

What do we mean by competence to stand trial? How do clinicians assess this kind of legal competence? What legal standards should be applied? The question of a defendant's **competence** is the clinical-legal issue most frequently assessed in the criminal justice system. **Competence to stand trial** refers to a defendant's capacity to function meaningfully and knowingly in a legal proceeding. Defendants may be adjudicated (i.e., determined by a judge) to be incompetent if they are seriously deficient in one or more abilities, such as understanding the legal proceedings, communicating with their attorneys, appreciating their role in the proceedings, or making legally relevant decisions. Concerns about a defendant's competence are tied to one fundamental principle: Criminal proceedings should not continue against someone who cannot understand their nature and purpose, or cannot assist in defending against prosecution on these charges.

Competence is an important doctrine in our legal system, and the law requires defendants to be competent for several reasons (Melton et al., 2007). First, defendants must be able to understand the charges against them so that they can participate in the criminal justice system in a meaningful way, making it more likely that legal proceedings will arrive at accurate and just results. Second, punishment of convicted defendants is morally acceptable only if they understand the reasons why they are being punished. Finally, the perceived fairness and integrity of our adversary system of justice requires participation by defendants who have the capacity to defend themselves against the charges of the state.

The accepted national standard for competence to stand trial is a "sufficient present ability to consult with [one's] attorney with a reasonable degree of rational understanding, and … a rational, as well as factual, understanding of the proceedings against [one]" (*Dusky v. United States*, 1960). With minor differences across jurisdictions, this is the standard for competence to stand trial in all United States courts. It establishes the basic criteria for competence as the capacities for factual and rational understanding of the court proceedings and for consulting with one's attorney in a rational way. These criteria refer to *present* abilities rather than to the mental state of the defendant at the time of the alleged offense, which, as we will discuss later, is the focus of evaluations of a defendant's sanity. Given the U.S. Supreme Court's decision in *Dusky*, the requirement that a defendant be competent to stand trial has a Constitutional basis.

The *Dusky* standard does not specify how the evaluator assessing competence should judge the sufficiency of rational understanding, ability to consult, or factual understanding. However, to allow evaluators to provide courts with more detailed information in these areas, a number of courts and mental health groups have expanded on *Dusky* by listing more specific criteria related to competence. For example, evaluators may consider a number of relevant psycholegal abilities (Zapf & Roesch, 2009):

- Understanding

    - The roles of key participants within the legal process
    - The current charges faced by the defendant
    - The elements of an offense
    - The consequences of conviction
    - The rights waived in making a guilty plea

- Appreciating

    - The likelihood that he or she will be found guilty
    - The consequences for the defendant of being convicted
    - The available legal defenses and their likely outcomes
    - The ability of the defendant to make rational decisions regarding the specific case, including whether or not to testify

- Reasoning

    - Distinguishing more relevant from less relevant information
    - Seeking relevant information
    - Weighing and evaluating various legal options and their consequences
    - Making comparisons
    - Providing reality-based justification for making particular case-specific decisions or conclusions

- Assisting in one's defense

  - Consulting with his or her lawyer
  - Relating to the lawyer
  - Planning legal strategy
  - Engaging in his or her defense
  - Challenging witnesses
  - Testifying relevantly
  - Managing his or her courtroom behavior

- Decision-making abilities relevant to decisions likely to arise during the proceedings.

The issue of competence also arises when defendants plead guilty. By pleading guilty, defendants waive several constitutional rights: the right to a jury trial, the right to confront their accusers, the right to call favorable witnesses, and the right to remain silent. The Supreme Court has held that waiving such important rights must be done knowingly, intelligently, and voluntarily (*Johnson v. Zerbst*, 1938), and trial judges are required to question defendants about their pleas in order to establish clearly that they understand that they are waiving their constitutional rights by pleading guilty. A knowing, intelligent, and voluntary guilty plea also includes understanding the charges and the possible penalties that can be imposed, and requires the judge to examine any plea bargain to ensure that it is "voluntary" (i.e., that it represents a considered choice between constitutionally permissible alternatives). For example, prosecutors can offer lighter sentences to a defendant in exchange for a guilty plea, but they cannot offer the defendant money to encourage a guilty plea.

Logically, **competence to plead guilty** would require that defendants understand the alternatives they face and have the ability to make a reasoned choice among them. In some respects, this standard is more demanding than that for competence to stand trial. Defendants standing trial must be aware of the nature of the proceedings and be able to cooperate with counsel in presenting the defense, paying attention to the proceedings and controlling their behavior over the course of a trial. This creates a strong demand for *attention, concentration,* and *behavioral control*. Defendants pleading guilty, on the other hand, must understand the possible consequences of pleading guilty instead of going to trial and must be able to make a rational choice between the alternatives. This underscores the importance of the defendant's *cognitive awareness* and *reasoning*.

Adjudicative Competence

Despite this, the U.S. Supreme Court ruled that the standard for competence to stand trial would be applied in federal courts to other competence questions that arise in the criminal justice process (*Godinez v. Moran*, 1993). In so doing, it rejected the idea that competence to plead guilty involves a higher standard than competence to stand trial. As a result of this decision, the terms *competence to plead guilty* and *competence to stand trial* have become somewhat confusing. Some scholars have suggested that **adjudicative competence** is a clearer description of the various capacities that criminal defendants need in different legal contexts (Bonnie, 1993; Hoge et al., 1997). The term competence to stand trial is still used frequently, although it acquired a broader meaning after the *Godinez* decision. We discuss adjudicative competence with the understanding that it is synonymous with competence to stand trial, post-*Godinez*. We begin this discussion with the case of Jared Loughner, described in Box 10.2.

Raising the Issue of Competence

Competence to stand trial is the most frequently-raised issue in forensic mental health, with estimates ranging as high as 60,000 motions annually in the United States (Poythress, Bonnie, Monahan, Otto, & Hoge, 2002). The question of a defendant's competence can be raised at any point in the criminal process, and it can be raised by the prosecutor, the defense attorney, or the presiding judge. Once the question of incompetence is raised, the judge may order an evaluation of the defendant if a "bona fide doubt" exists that the defendant is competent. Judges consider the circumstances of each case and the behavior of each defendant when making this determination. However, if the question of competence is raised, an examination will usually be conducted. Because it is relatively easy to obtain such evaluations, attorneys often seek them for reasons other than a determination of competence. Competence evaluations are used for several tactical reasons: to obtain information about a possible insanity defense, to guarantee the temporary incarceration of a potentially dangerous person without going through the cumbersome procedures of involuntary civil commitment, to deny bail, and to delay the trial as one side tries to gain an advantage over the other (Winick, 1996). Defense attorneys have questions about their clients' competence in up to 15% of felony cases (approximately twice the rate for defendants charged with misdemeanors); in many of these cases, however, the attorney does not seek a formal evaluation (Hoge et al., 1997; Poythress, Bonnie, Hoge, Monahan, & Oberlander, 1994).

Evaluating Competence

After a judge orders a competence examination, arrangements are made for the defendant to be

The Case of Jared Loughner: Assessing Competence

Jared Loughner, following his arrest

Jared Loughner was arrested after being wrestled to the ground in a grocery store parking lot in Tucson, Arizona on January 8, 2011, after he walked up to United States Congresswoman Gabrielle Giffords, an Arizona Democrat, and shot her. Following that, Mr. Loughner turned his gun on others in the crowd. Those dying in the shooting included John Roll, a federal judge in Tucson; 9-year-old Christina-Taylor Green; and four other bystanders. Twelve other individuals in addition to the congresswoman were injured.

Mr. Loughner was a troubled young man with a history of classroom outbursts at Pima Community College, which had expelled him, and bizarre postings on the Internet. Before he could be tried for these offenses, however, the issue of Mr. Loughner's competence to stand trial was raised. Among the questions that the mental health experts were asked to address, and the court ultimately had to decide, were whether Mr. Loughner indeed had a mental illness—and, if so, how the symptoms of that illness affected his capacities to understand his legal circumstances, assist counsel in his own defense, and make rational decisions in the process.

Judge Larry A. Burns of the U.S. District Court considered the findings of two mental health experts

in the case: Christina Pietz, Ph.D., a psychologist appointed at the request of the prosecution, and Matthew Carroll, M.D., a psychiatrist appointed by the judge. Dr. Pietz reported that Mr. Loughner's thoughts were random and disorganized, that he experienced delusions, and that he responded to questions in an irrelevant fashion. Dr. Carroll also described delusions as well as bizarre thoughts and hallucinations. Both experts concluded that Mr. Loughner suffered from schizophrenia, a form of severe mental illness. They described these symptoms as seriously impairing Mr. Loughner's ability to understand his legal circumstances and assist counsel in his own defense. The judge adjudicated him incompetent to stand trial and committed him to the Federal Medical Center in Springfield, Missouri for treatment to improve his symptoms and restore these capacities.

Because of the horrific and widely publicized nature of these alleged offenses, there was (and will continue to be) a great deal of scrutiny of Mr. Loughner's case. The prosecution in such cases experiences pressure to consider the death penalty, and to bring the defendant to trial and convict. The defense may struggle in working with a severely mentally ill defendant, even one whose symptoms are in remission, because the defendant may continue to show irrational thinking and behavior that is not consistent with defense attorneys' strategic recommendations. A judge must balance the arguments of both prosecution and defense in a highly charged, widely scrutinized atmosphere. Such cases test the limits of our legal system in the pursuit of justice under very trying circumstances.

CRITICAL THOUGHT QUESTION

Why does the highly publicized nature of an alleged offense like Jared Loughner's affect the proceedings on a question like competence to stand trial?

evaluated by one or more mental health professionals. Although these evaluations were historically conducted in a special hospital or inpatient forensic facility, most evaluations since the 1980's have been conducted in the community on an outpatient (nonhospitalized) basis (Melton et al., 2007; Nicholson & Norwood, 2000). The transition from inpatient to outpatient

facilities occurred because inpatient exams are more costly and time-consuming, and local outpatient evaluations are usually sufficient for evaluative purposes (Winick, 1996).

Physicians, psychiatrists, psychologists, and social workers are authorized by most states to conduct competence examinations, but psychologists are the professional group responsible for the largest number of reports (Nicholson & Norwood, 2000). Some data suggest that nonmedical professionals with relevant forensic specialty knowledge prepare reports of trial competence evaluations that are comparable in quality to those prepared by forensic psychiatrists (Lander & Heilbrun, 2009; Sanschagrin, Stevens, Bove, & Heilbrun, 2006).

Under the *Dusky* standard, the presence of mental illness or mental retardation does not guarantee that a defendant will be found incompetent to stand trial. The crucial question is whether the disorder impairs a defendant's ability to participate knowingly and meaningfully in the proceedings and to work with the defense attorney. A psychotic defendant might be competent to stand trial in a relatively straightforward case but incompetent to participate in a complex trial that would demand more skill and understanding. Consider the case of John Salvi, who, despite having an apparent psychotic disorder, was found competent to stand trial and was convicted of murdering two people and wounding five others during a shooting spree at two Massachusetts medical clinics that performed abortions. Salvi later committed suicide in prison. Apparently his symptoms (unlike those of Jared Loughner) did not substantially compromise his ability to understand the charges against him and the basic nature of his trial. Thus, he was found competent to stand trial.

Trial competence evaluations focus on the defendant's present ability to function adequately in the legal process. This focus has been sharpened by the development of several structured tests or instruments specifically aimed at assessing the capacities relevant to competence to stand trial. Psychological testing remains a common ingredient in competence evaluations, and although clinicians have begun to use one or more of these specially designed competence assessment instruments in their practice, their use is not as widespread as it should be (Lander & Heilbrun, 2009; Skeem, Golding, Cohn, & Berge, 1998). There have been a number of such instruments historically. The most current and best supported empirically are described in the following paragraphs.

Interdisciplinary Fitness Interview (IFI). The IFI and its revision, the IFI-R (Golding, 1993), are versions of a semi-structured interview that evaluates a defendant's abilities in five specific legal areas. It also assesses 11 categories of psychopathological symptoms. Evaluators rate the weight they attached to each item in reaching their decision about competence. These weights vary depending on the nature of the defendant's case;

for example, hallucinations might impair a defendant's ability to participate in some trials, but they would have limited impact in others and would therefore be given less weight. Golding, Roesch, and Schreiber (1984) found that interviewers using the IFI agreed on final judgments of competence in 75 of 77 cases evaluated. These judgments agreed 76% of the time with independent decisions about competence made later at a state hospital.

Fitness Interview Test—Revised. The Fitness Interview Test—Revised (FIT-R) is a structured interview for assessing a person's competence to stand trial. Like the IFI-R, it uses a structured professional judgment approach to assessing competence capacities. Using this approach, various areas are considered but not "scored," and there is not a total score that is related to a category or level of impairment. It was originally designed for use in Canada, but has been updated for use in the United States and Great Britain as well. It includes 16 items in three broad domains (Factual Knowledge of Criminal Procedure, Appreciation of Personal Involvement In and Importance Of the Proceedings, and Ability to Participate in Defense). Research on the FIT-R (Roesch, Zapf, & Eaves, 2006; Zapf & Roesch, 1997) suggests that it is a promising screening tool.

The MacArthur Measures of Competence. Growing out of the concept of adjudicative competence, which describes several interrelated components that need to be considered in the evaluation of competence, the *MacArthur Structured Assessment of the Competence of Criminal Defendants* (MacSAC-CD; Hoge et al., 1997) is a highly regarded research instrument. Most of the 82 items in the MacSAC-CD rely on a hypothetical vignette about which the defendant is asked questions that tap foundational and decisional abilities. Defendants are asked the questions in a sequence. Open-ended questions come first. If there is a wrong answer, correct information is provided to the defendant. Defendants are then asked additional open-ended questions to determine whether they now have the necessary understanding based on this disclosure; a series of true–false questions concludes each area of assessment. This format has several advantages. It offers a more standardized evaluation across different defendants, and it makes it possible to assess separately defendants' preexisting abilities as well as their capacity to learn and apply new information.

One major disadvantage of the MacSAC-CD is that it was developed as a research instrument and takes about two hours to complete, far too long to be used in clinical practice. To overcome this limitation, a 22-item clinical version of this measure, called the *MacArthur Competence Assessment Tool—Criminal Adjudication* (MacCAT-CA) was developed (Poythress et al., 1999). This instrument begins with a hypothetical vignette about a crime, upon which the first 16 items are based. These items assess the defendant's general understanding of the legal system and adjudicative process and his or her reasoning abilities in legal situations. The remaining six items are specific to the defendant's own legal situation.

The Evaluation of Competence to Stand Trial–Revised.

The *Evaluation of Competence to Stand Trial–Revised* (ECST-R) (Rogers, Tillbrook, & Sewell, 2004) is a semi-structured interview that was developed using the *Dusky* criteria. Its three factors (factual understanding of proceedings, rational understanding of proceedings, and consultation with counsel) have been empirically tested using a statistical technique known as confirmatory factor analysis. It focuses on information that is specific to the case of the individual being evaluated (unlike the MacCAT-CA, which uses a general vignette involving two individuals who fight in a bar). It also addresses the question of whether the evaluee is trying to exaggerate or fake deficits that might make that person appear incompetent to stand trial. Both the case specificity and the built-in measure of possible exaggeration are useful features of the ECST-R, which appears well supported by the relevant research (Norton & Ryba, 2010; Rogers, Grandjean, Tillbrook, Vitacco, & Sewell, 2001).

Competence Assessment for Standing Trial for Defendants with Mental Retardation.

One specialized measure, the *Competence Assessment for Standing Trial for Defendants with Mental Retardation* (CAST-MR; Everington & Luckasson, 1992), was developed specifically for assessing defendants with mild to moderate intellectual disability (previously called mental retardation). Two validation studies have been conducted; although the number of participants has been small, the results have been somewhat encouraging (Grisso, 2003). In addition, the CAST-MR is the only specialized tool developed specifically for assessing trial competence with individuals with developmental disabilities.

One important issue being studied by researchers is the extent to which defendants can successfully fake incompetence on these tests. Some research suggests that although offenders can simulate incompetence, they often take such simulations to extremes, scoring much more poorly on specialized measures of competence capacities than their truly incompetent counterparts (Gothard, Rogers, & Sewell, 1995; Gothard, Viglione, Meloy, & Sherman, 1995). Therefore, very poor performance should make evaluators suspicious that a defendant might be exaggerating his or her deficiencies. As noted earlier, one specialized tool (the ECST-R) has a built-in measure to help the evaluator determine whether the defendant is exaggerating deficits. Research indicates that the ECST-R is sensitive to the exaggeration of both symptoms of mental illness and intellectual deficits (Vitacco, Rogers, & Gabel, 2009).

This issue has gained a great deal of attention because estimates of malingering (faking or grossly exaggerating) mental illness in competence evaluations have been estimated as nearly one in five (18%; Rogers, Salekin, Sewell, Goldstein, & Leonard, 1998). Therefore, screening tools have been developed to offer a more scientific method of detecting malingering in patients who are being evaluated for their competence to stand trial. One of these instruments is the Miller Forensic Assessment of Symptoms Test (M-FAST; Miller, 2001). The M-FAST is a brief, 25-item structured interview that can accurately identify individuals who are attempting to feign mental disorders (see Miller, 2004). Empirical evidence thus far supports the use of the M-FAST in detecting malingering (Jackson, Rogers, & Sewell, 2005), but it is a screening instrument and should be used in conjunction with a wider array of assessments to determine whether the defendant is actually malingering.

Consider the case of former pro wrestler Jimmy "Superfly" Snuka. Mr. Snuka was charged with the beating death of his girlfriend more than three decades after the crime, after a newspaper story in 2013 raised new questions about his culpability. When he appeared before a Pennsylvania judge in Lehigh County for a competence to stand trial hearing in 2016, his lawyer argued that he suffered from dementia after many years of head injuries in the ring. The prosecution, by contrast, suggested that Snuka (who was 73-years-old at the time of the hearing, and has since died) experienced only problems associated with normal aging, and was faking his symptoms of confusion when asked simple questions such as his age or the current year. The judge was not convinced that he was faking, however, describing him as "vacant" and not "smart enough" to malinger—and formally judged him to be incompetent to stand trial (Foxnews.com, 2016).

This is the kind of case in which a formal evaluation of symptoms of cognitive impairment would be helpful. Were Mr. Snuka's symptoms genuine? Did he more closely resemble defendants with real symptoms of dementia—or those who fake such symptoms? But in addition to a specialized measure of malingering, it would also be useful for the evaluator to obtain other sources of information. Had Mr. Snuka ever received medical treatment for dementia? Would collateral observers who saw him frequently (e.g., friends, caretakers, relatives) describe him as displaying such symptoms? Clearly there are multiple sources of information that could be useful in answering this question.

Following the collection of assessment data, evaluators communicate their findings to the judge. Often, they submit a written report that summarizes the evidence on competence to stand trial, as well as the likelihood that appropriate treatment will sufficiently improve competence-relevant deficits. In controversial or strongly contested cases, it is more likely that there will be a formal competence hearing where the evaluating experts testify and are questioned by attorneys from both sides.

In formal competence hearings, who bears the burden of proof? Must prosecutors prove that defendants are competent, or are defendants required to prove their incompetence? In the 1992 case of *Medina v. California*, the U.S. Supreme Court held that a state can require a criminal defendant to shoulder the burden of proving that he or she is incompetent. But how stringent should that burden be? Most states established the criterion to be a "preponderance of the evidence," meaning that the defendant had to show that it was more likely than not that he or she was incompetent. But four states—Oklahoma, Pennsylvania, Connecticut, and Rhode Island—required a higher standard of proof: evidence that was "clear and convincing." Yet in 1996, the Supreme Court held that this higher standard was too stringent (*Cooper v. Oklahoma*, 1996), so the standard remains "preponderance of the evidence."

Results of Competence Evaluations

About 70% of the defendants referred for evaluation are ultimately found competent to stand trial (Melton et al., 2007; Nicholson & Kugler, 1991); when very rigorous examinations are conducted, the rate of defendants found competent approaches 90%. Judges seldom disagree with clinicians' decisions about competence, and

opposing attorneys often will **stipulate** (agree without further examination) to clinicians' findings (Melton et al., 2007).

One study asked judges, prosecutors, and defense attorneys to rank in order of importance eight items typically offered by expert witnesses in competence evaluations (e.g., clinical diagnosis of the defendant, weighing different motives and explanations, providing an ultimate opinion on the legal issue) (Redding, Floyd, & Hawk, 2001). The results revealed that judges and prosecutors agreed that the expert's ultimate opinion on the legal issue was one of the three most important pieces of information the expert could provide.

Another study asked juvenile and criminal court judges (N = 166) about information they considered valuable in competence evaluations. Results showed that judges (1) consider clinicians' ultimate opinion to be an essential component of reports, (2) regard forensic and psychological testing as valuable, (3) seek similar but not identical characteristics in juvenile and adult competence evaluations, and (4) consider opinions about maturity to be an important component of competence evaluations in juvenile court (Viljoen, Wingrove, & Ryba, 2008). Depending upon how such "ultimate opinions" are used, this may suggest that mental health professionals exert great—perhaps excessive—influence on this legal decision.

What are the characteristics of those judged to be incompetent? Investigators report relatively high percentages of serious mental illness, lower intelligence, and more problems with certain aspects of memory among incompetent defendants (Cooper & Zapf, 2003; Zapf & Roesch, 1998), as well as co-occurring substance use disorder, unemployment, and homelessness (Schreiber, Green, Kunz, Belfi, & Pequeno, 2015). Hospitalized incompetent defendants were more likely to have been diagnosed with schizophrenia, and more likely to have a history of prior mental health treatment (Hoge et al., 1997), as well as be single, unemployed, poorly educated, and perform poorly on specific competence assessment instruments (Nicholson & Kugler, 1991).

If a defendant referred for a competence evaluation is adjudicated competent to stand trial, the legal process resumes, and the defendant again faces the possibility of trial or disposition of charges through plea bargaining. If the defendant is found IST, however, the picture becomes more complicated. For crimes that are not serious, the charges are occasionally dropped, sometimes in exchange for requiring the defendant to receive treatment. In other cases, however, the defendant is hospitalized to be treated for restoration of competence, which, if successful, will result in the defendant proceeding with disposition of charges.

Prior to the 1970s, defendants found incompetent were often confined in mental hospitals for excessive periods of time. (Sometimes such confinements were even longer than their sentences would have been had they stood trial and been convicted.) But the practice of providing long periods of hospitalization for defendants incompetent for trial was limited in 1972 when the U.S. Supreme Court decided the case of *Jackson v. Indiana*. This decision held that defendants who had been committed because they were incompetent to stand trial could not be held "more than a reasonable period of time necessary to determine whether there is a substantial probability that [they] will attain that capacity in the foreseeable future." As a result of this decision, the length of time an incompetent defendant can be confined is now limited, and many states have passed statutes that "limit" such hospitalization to a period not to exceed the maximum sentence that could have been imposed if the defendant were convicted of charges. In cases involving serious felony charges, such a period might well be 10 years or longer.

How successful are efforts to restore defendants' competence? One study evaluated an experimental group treatment administered to a sample of incompetent defendants sent to one of three Philadelphia facilities (Siegel & Elwork, 1990). In addition to receiving psychiatric medication, defendants assigned to these special treatment groups watched videotapes and received special instructions on courtroom procedures. They also discussed different ways of resolving problems that a defendant might face during a trial. A matched control group received treatment for their general psychiatric needs, but no specific treatment relevant to incompetence. Following their treatment, defendants participating in the special competence restoration group showed significant increases in their assessment scores compared to the controls. In addition, hospital staff judged 43% of the experimental subjects competent to stand trial after treatment compared to 15% of the control subjects. Other research, however, indicates that providing general legal information is about as effective as highly specialized programs focusing on individual deficits (Bertman et al., 2003). In general, most defendants have their adjudicative competence restored, usually with about six months of treatment (Melton et al., 2007;

Zapf & Roesch, 2011), and the most important intervention for most defendants is the administration of appropriate psychotropic medication (Zapf & Roesch, 2009).

The real dilemma for IST defendants occurs when treatment is not successful in restoring competence and holds little promise of success in the future. At this point, all options are problematic. Theoretically, the previously-described *Jackson* ruling bars the indefinite confinement of an individual adjudicated incompetent to stand trial. The law varies across states as to how long such involuntary hospitalization is allowed, but many states permit the defendant to be hospitalized for a period up to the maximum sentence that he or she could have received if convicted of the charges. Once such a defendant has been hospitalized for this period, however, he or she can be found "unrestorably incompetent." Research indicates that the major influences associated with unrestorable incompetence are (1) chronic severe mental illness associated with long-term hospitalization and poor response to medication, and (2) cognitive limitations (e.g., intellectual disability, dementia) (Morris & Parker, 2008; Mossman, 2007).

Typically, unrestorably incompetent defendants are committed to a hospital through involuntary civil commitment proceedings. Standards for this type of commitment are narrower than for being found IST, however. The state must show that the person is mentally ill and either imminently dangerous to self or others or so gravely disabled as to be unable to care for himself or herself.

Should an incompetent defendant not meet the criteria for involuntary hospitalization, what happens? Despite the ruling in the *Jackson* case, some states simply continue to confine incompetent defendants for indefinite periods. Although this "solution" might appease the public, we believe it jeopardizes defendants' due process rights and results in lengthy periods of punishment (disguised as treatment) without a conviction. Several alternative procedures have been proposed to resolve this problem, including abolishing the IST concept altogether (Burt & Morris, 1972), allowing defendants to seek trial continuances without going through an elaborate evaluation, or waiving their right to be competent under certain circumstances (Winick, 1996). To date, however, there has been no effectively-implemented alternative to the Constitutional requirement that a defendant be competent to stand trial in order to proceed—and regain competence if adjudicated IST.

Competent with Medication, Incompetent without

For most defendants found IST, psychoactive medication has been the treatment of choice, as it is considered the best intervention for restoring defendants to competence in a reasonable period of time. Can incompetent defendants refuse this treatment? If medicated, will defendants be found competent to stand trial even though the medication, because of its temporarily tranquilizing effects, might undercut a defense such as insanity? The U.S. Supreme Court case *Sell v. U.S.* (2003) concerns questions of competence and forced medication (Box 10.3).

Other Legal Competencies

Because questions about competence can be raised at any point in the criminal process, several other competences are at issue in deciding whether a defendant can participate knowingly in different functions. Competence for any legal function involves (1) determining what functional abilities are necessary, (2) assessing the context where these abilities must be demonstrated, (3) evaluating the implication of any deficiencies in the required abilities, and (4) deciding whether the deficiencies warrant a conclusion that the defendant is incompetent (Grisso, 1986).

BOX 10.3

The Case of Charles Sell: Involuntary Medication to Restore Competence?

Charles Sell, once a practicing dentist, had an extensive history of severe mental illness and was hospitalized several times. He was accused of fraud after he allegedly submitted fictitious insurance claims for payment. His competence to stand trial was evaluated, and he was found competent and released on bail. Subsequently, a grand jury indicted Sell on 13 additional counts of fraud and, later, attempted murder. During his bail revocation hearing, Sell's mental illness was markedly worse, and his behavior was "totally out of control," including "spitting in the judge's face" (2003, p 2 His competence was again evaluated, at which time he was adjudicated incompetent to stand trial He was hospitalized for treatment to help restore his competence Hospital staff recommended antipsychotic medication, which Sell declined to take The hospital administered these medications to him involuntarily Sell challenged this in court, arguing that involuntary medication violates the Fifth Amendment right to "liberty to reject medical treatment" p 10 The lower court found that Sell was a danger to himself and others, that medication was the only way to render him less dangerous, that the benefits to Sell outweighed the risks, and that the drugs were substantially likely to return Sell to competence The court further held that medication was the only viable hope of rendering Sell competent to stand trial and was necessary to serve the Government's interest in obtaining an adjudication on the issue of his guilt Sell appealed and this case was granted certiorari by the United States Supreme Court.

At the heart of this case is the question of whether it is a violation of a defendant's rights to be forcibly medicated in order to make that defendant competent to proceed to trial, with the associated possibility of conviction and incarceration in prison. But if the defendant cannot be restored to competence without medication, he or she may remain hospitalized, and thus also deprived of his or her liberty, for a lengthy period of time. In this decision, the Court weighed these considerations and outlined the conditions under which the government may forcibly administer psychotropic medication to render a mentally ill defendant competent to stand trial. The treatment must be (1) medically appropriate, (2) substantially unlikely to have side effects that may undermine the trial's fairness, and (3) necessary to significantly further important government trial-related interests.

CRITICAL THOUGHT QUESTION

Assume that a defendant is hospitalized as incompetent to stand trial with a severe mental illness, and assume further that he is actively psychotic and declines to take prescribed medication while in the hospital. Finally, assume that he does not present a threat of harm toward others or himself. Under those circumstances, what are the advantages and disadvantages of forcing him to take psychotropic medication?

Mental health professionals are sometimes asked to evaluate each of the following competencies (see also Melton et al., 2007).

Capacity to Waive *Miranda* Rights. The waiver of *Miranda* rights is required in order for defendants in police custody to make a legally-admissible confession—and the waiver of these *Miranda* rights (Fifth Amendment right to avoid self-incrimination and Sixth Amendment right to counsel and trial) must be made in a knowing, intelligent, and voluntary fashion. It is difficult to assess these abilities because, in most cases, the waiver and confession have occurred months before the professional's evaluation, requiring a reconstruction of the defendant's mental and emotional state at the time.

One aspect of a defendant's rights guaranteed by *Miranda* involves the Sixth Amendment right to be represented by counsel when in police custody. The same standard to waive this right—knowing, intelligent, and voluntary—is applied to the questions of waiving counsel and making a confession.

A slightly different twist on the right to be represented by counsel involves the question of whether defendants can decide that they do not want a lawyer to represent them at trial. The U.S. Supreme Court has held that defendants have a Constitutional right to waive counsel and represent themselves at trial, if they make this decision competently (*Faretta v. California*, 1975). In addition, the presiding judge must be convinced that the waiver of counsel is both voluntary and intelligent. Defendants do not have to convince the court that they possess a high level of legal knowledge, although some legal knowledge is probably important.

Competence to waive the right to counsel was at issue in the trial of Colin Ferguson, who was charged with murdering six passengers and wounding 19 more when he went on a killing rampage aboard a Long Island Rail Road train in December 1993. Ferguson insisted on serving as his own attorney, after rejecting the "black rage" defense suggested by his lawyers. At first, Ferguson proved effective enough to have several of his objections to prosecution evidence sustained. But then, giving new meaning to the old saying that a defendant who argues his own case has a fool for a client, Ferguson opened his case by claiming that "There were 93 counts to that indictment, 93 counts only because it matches the year 1993. If it had been 1925, it would be a 25-count indictment." This was a prelude to Ferguson's attempt at cross-examining a series of eyewitnesses, who, in response to his preposterous suggestion that someone else had been the murderer, answered time after time, "No, I saw the murderer clearly. It was you."

Competence to Refuse the Insanity Defense. In cases in which it is likely that the defendant was insane at the time of the offense, can the defendant refuse to plead insanity? If there is evidence that a defendant was not mentally responsible for criminal acts, do courts have a duty to require that the defendant plead insanity when the defendant does not want to do so? Courts are divided on this question. In some cases, they have suggested that society's stake in punishing only mentally responsible persons requires the imposition of an insanity plea even on unwilling defendants (*Whalen v. United States*, 1965). Other decisions (*Frendak v. United States*, 1979) use the framework of competence to answer this question—if the defendant understands the alternative pleas available and the consequences of those pleas, the defendant should be permitted to reject an insanity plea. This latter approach is followed in most courts.

This question was at the heart of the prosecution of Theodore Kaczynski, a reclusive mathematician who was dubbed the "Unabomber" for sending a series of mail bombs to universities and airlines between 1978 and 1995. Although the consensus of several experts was that Kaczynski suffered from paranoid schizophrenia, he adamantly refused to let his attorneys use an insanity defense, arguing that he did not want to be stigmatized, in his words, as "a sickie." Was Kaczynski competent to make this decision, or was Judge Garland E. Burrell, Jr. correct in ruling that Kaczynski's lawyers could control his defense, even over the defendant's persistent objections? It is doubtful that an insanity defense would have been successful—Kaczynski's own diary showed that he understood and intended to commit his crimes—but we will never know. Ultimately, to avoid the possibility of the death penalty, Kaczynski pled guilty to murder and was sentenced to life in prison.

Competence to Be Sentenced. For legal and humanitarian reasons, convicted defendants are not to be sentenced unless they are competent. In general, the standard for this competence is that defendants can understand the punishment and the reasons why it is being imposed, and can meaningfully execute their right to address the court at sentencing. Competence to be sentenced is often a more straightforward question for the clinician to evaluate than adjudicative competence, which involves issues of whether the accused can interact effectively with counsel and appreciate alternative courses of action.

Competence to Be Executed. A particularly controversial aspect of this area is determining whether a defendant is competent to be executed. The U.S. Supreme Court decided, in the case of *Ford v. Wainwright* (1986), that the Eighth Amendment ban against cruel and unusual punishments prohibits the execution of defendants while they are incompetent. Therefore, mental health professionals are at times called on to evaluate inmates waiting to be executed to determine whether they are competent to be executed. The practical problems and ethical dilemmas involved in these evaluations are enormous (Heilbrun, 1987; Heilbrun & McClaren, 1988; Mossman, 1987; Susman, 1992) and have led some psychologists to recommend that clinicians refrain from performing such evaluations. If they are to be conducted, however, it is preferable to observe guidelines and a structured approach (see, e.g., Zapf, Boccaccini, & Brodsky, 2003).

Juvenile Competence to Stand Trial

In a series of decisions about justice-involved adolescents, the U.S. Supreme Court held that developmental immaturity distinguishes adolescents in some important ways from adult defendants (*Graham v. Florida*, 2010; *JDB v. North Carolina*, 2011; *Miller v. Alabama*, 2012; *Roper v. Simmons*, 2005). This complicates the question of juvenile competence for trial, because adolescents may experience severe mental illness or intellectual disability (the two major reasons why adult defendants may be incompetent to stand trial)—but developmental immaturity is a third important influence.

Are juveniles competent to stand trial? Does it make a difference whether they are being processed in juvenile court or tried as adults? Do adolescents differ from adults in their abilities to participate in trials, and if so, what are these differences? These are questions posed by researchers (Grisso et al., 2003) when they studied a group of 927 adolescents in juvenile detention facilities and community settings. Participants were administered a specialized measure of competence for adults (the MacCAT-CA) as well as the MacArthur Judgment Evaluation (MacJen), which was designed to examine immaturity of judgment. Their research goal was to provide data on *competence to proceed* (comprehension of the purpose and nature of the trial process, ability to provide relevant information to counsel and to process information, and ability to apply information to oneself without distortion or irrationality) and *decisional competence* (ability to make important decisions about waiver of constitutional rights and maturity of judgment).

Juvenile courts bring together youth service departments, schools, social workers, probation officers and mental health providers to safely divert juveniles from adult criminal courts.

Results indicated that participants who were age 15 and younger were significantly impaired in ways that compromised their abilities to function as competent defendants in a criminal (adult) proceeding. More specifically, one-third of 11–13-year-olds and one-fifth of 14–15-year-olds were as impaired in their functional legal capacities as mentally ill adults who were incompetent to stand trial. Below-average intelligence was also associated with deficits in these functional legal capacities. Since a large proportion of adolescents in the juvenile justice system have below-average IQ, the risk for incompetence is further increased when adolescents in this system are transferred into criminal court (Grisso et al., 2003).

These findings have fewer implications for adolescents when they are in juvenile court, however. Since the expectations for competence in juvenile court are different—adolescents are being tried in a setting that is designed for juveniles—it is more likely that an adolescent with limited functional legal capacities would be adjudicated competent in juvenile court than if he or she were tried in adult criminal court. But it is still important for lawmakers to consider the evidence on adolescent maturity and other functioning related to competence to stand trial. Policy researchers have developed a guide to them with this task (see Larson & Grisso, 2011).

The Insanity Defense

Any society that respects the rights of individuals recognizes the possibility that some of its citizens cannot comprehend the consequences or the wrongfulness of their actions. Our legal system allows defendants who claim that they lack these abilities to invoke the insanity defense. Yet the evaluation of insanity defense claims is challenging. For example, it may be very difficult to accurately gauge a defendant's mental state at the time of the offense, as must be done when a defendant uses insanity as a defense. The jury or judge must answer the question "What was he experiencing when he fired the gun?" rather than "Did he fire the gun?" How can we determine whether a defendant is legally insane? Can we know what a person's state of mind was when they committed an antisocial act? This becomes even more difficult when the fact finders—juries and judges— must determine not whether the person is currently insane—but rather whether he or she was insane at the time of the crime, possibly months or years earlier.

This problem is further complicated by the reality that there are far fewer specialized tools specifically designed to assess insanity than there are to assess competence. One brief screening instrument—the Mental Status Examination at the Time of the Offense (Slobogin, Melton, & Showalter, 1984)—has been developed, but research on its reliability and validity is limited to one study. More research has been conducted on the Rogers Criminal Responsibility Scales (RCRAS; Rogers, 1986), a set of 25 scales that organize the many factors and points of decision that clinicians need to consider when assessing criminal responsibility. Although the RCRAS has clear limitations, it is the only formal instrument with some demonstrated reliability and validity for guiding clinicians' decision-making process in insanity evaluations (Nicholson, 1999).

Another reason why insanity questions are so difficult involves the conflict between law and behavioral sciences as alternative pathways to knowledge. Insanity is a legal concept, not a medical or psychological one. In many states, a defendant could be hallucinating, delusional, and diagnosed with schizophrenia, but if the individual knew the difference between right and wrong, he or she would be legally sane. Thus, psychiatrists and clinical psychologists are called upon as forensic experts to provide information regarding a decision that is ultimately outside the traditional diagnose-and-treat framework of these professions. (Of course, the same could be said about *any* legal question that is the focus of a forensic mental health evaluation—but evaluations with clear clinical-legal criteria and that are focused on present mental state and capacities are more straightforward.) The therapeutic goals of psychiatry and clinical psychology (diagnosis and assessment that are probabilistic and complex) do not fit well with the legal system's demand for a straightforward "yes-or-no" answer (Heilbrun, 2001). Furthermore, although mental health experts can offer diagnoses, any particular

diagnosis is less important than the specific symptoms and their impact on the functional legal demands associated with the insanity standard (whether the defendant "knew" the behavior was wrong; in some states, additionally, whether the defendant could conform his or her conduct to the requirements of the law).

Rationale for the Insanity Defense

Insanity refers to the defendant's mental state at the time the offense was committed (as contrasted with *competence to stand trial*, which refers exclusively to the defendant's relevant legal capacities at the time of the trial or plea bargain). Why do we have laws about insanity? Wouldn't it be simpler to do away with insanity in the legal system? Allowing a criminal defendant to plead not guilty by reason of insanity reflects a fundamental belief that a civilized society should not punish people who do not know what they are doing or are incapable of controlling their conduct. Thus, the state must occasionally tell the victim's friends and family that even though it abhors the defendant's acts, some offenders do not deserve punishment. Before it can do that, however, a judgment must be made about whether such persons were responsible for their actions.

What is the legal standard for insanity? There is no single answer. The following sections describe several definitions currently in use. The legal standards that define criminal responsibility vary from state to state, but in all states, the defendant is initially presumed to be responsible for his or her alleged offense. Therefore, if pleading insanity, defendants must present some evidence that would rebut the initial presumption of criminal responsibility in their case. A related legal issue is the assessment of **mens rea**, or the mental state of knowing the nature and quality of a forbidden act. To be a criminal offense, an act not only must be illegal but also must be accompanied by the necessary *mens rea*, or guilty mind.

Varying Insanity Defense Rules

The M'Naghten Rule: An Early Attempt to Define Insanity.   In 1843, an Englishman named Daniel M'Naghten shot and killed the private secretary of the British prime minister. Plagued by paranoid delusions, M'Naghten believed that the Prime Minister, Sir Robert Peel, was part of a conspiracy hatched by the Tory party against him. M'Naghten initially sought to escape his imagined tormentors by traveling through Europe. When that didn't work, he stalked the Prime Minister and, after waiting in front of his residence at No. 10 Downing Street, shot the man he mistakenly thought was Peel.

M'Naghten was charged with murder, and his defense was to plead not guilty by reason of insanity. Nine medical experts, including the American psychiatrist Isaac Ray, testified for two days about his mental state, and all agreed that he was insane. On instructions from the lord chief justice, the jury rendered a verdict of not guilty by reason of insanity without even leaving the jury box to deliberate. M'Naghten was committed to the Broadmoor Asylum for the Insane, where he remained for the rest of his life.

The public was infuriated, as was Queen Victoria, who had been the target of several attempts on her life. She demanded a tougher test of insanity. Subsequent debate in the House of Lords led to what has come to be called the **M'Naghten rule**, which was announced in 1843, long before psychiatry became a household word. The M'Naghten rule, which became the standard for defining insanity in Great Britain and the United States, "excuses" criminal conduct if defendants, as a result of a "disease of the mind," (1) did not know what they were doing (e.g., believed they were shooting an animal rather than a human), or (2) did not know that what they were doing was wrong (e.g., believed killing unarmed strangers was "right").

The M'Naghten rule (or a close variation) is used in 23 states and the federal jurisdiction (US Legal LawDigest, 2016), so it is the most frequently-employed legal standard for insanity in the United States. It has often been criticized on the basis that the cognitive focus ("knowing wrongfulness") is too limiting, and does not allow consideration of motivational and other influences affecting the control of behavior. There have been a number of alternative legal tests of insanity since the M'Naghten rule was first established, which are described in the sections that follow.

The Brawner Rule, Stemming from the Model Penal Code.

A committee of legal scholars in the American Law Institute developed the Model Penal Code, which led to what is now called the **Brawner rule**. This rule states that a defendant is not responsible for criminal conduct if he, "at the time of such conduct as a result of mental disease or defect, [lacks] substantial capacity either to appreciate the criminality [wrongfulness] of his conduct or to conform his conduct to the requirements of the law." This standard, or a variation, allows judges and juries to consider whether mentally ill defendants have the capacity to understand the nature of their acts or to behave in a lawful way. As of 2015, it was used in 19 states (US Legal LawDigest, 2016).

Federal courts have also adopted the Brawner rule in a drastically altered form (which we describe later).

The Brawner test differs from the M'Naghten rule in three substantial respects. First, by using the term *appreciate*, it incorporates the emotional as well as the cognitive influences on criminal behavior. Second, it does not require that offenders exhibit a total lack of appreciation for the nature of their conduct, but only a lack of "substantial capacity." Finally, it includes both a cognitive element and a volitional element, making defendants' inability to control their actions a sufficient criterion by itself for insanity.

The Insanity Defense Reform Act.

In the wake of the trial of John Hinckley, Jr., who attempted to assassinate President Ronald Reagan, the U.S. Congress enacted the Insanity Defense Reform Act (IDRA) in 1984. The law modified the existing insanity defense (eliminating the "volitional" prong and retaining the "cognitive" prong), with the expectation that fewer defendants would be able to use it successfully. This law did not abolish the insanity defense, but changed it substantially. In addition to eliminating the volitional prong, it also changed the insanity defense process as follows:

1. It prohibited experts from giving ultimate opinions about insanity (i.e., whether the defendant was insane at the time of the crime). Although this prohibition may have little effect on jurors, reformers believed it would prevent expert witnesses from having excessive influence over the jury's decision.
2. It placed on the defendant the burden to prove insanity, replacing the previous requirement that the prosecution must prove a defendant's sanity.

Empirical Research Relevant to Varying Insanity Defense Rules.

What little research has been conducted on the Insanity Defense Reform Act suggests that it does not accomplish either what its proponents envisioned or what its critics feared. At least in mock jury studies, verdicts do not significantly differ regardless of whether the jurors have heard IDRA instructions, Brawner instructions, or no instructions (Finkel, 1989). In addition, states with the broadest test of insanity (Brawner) do not show higher rates of insanity acquittals than states with the narrowest test (M'Naghten) (Melton et al., 2007).

In theory, varying rules for insanity should influence jurors' understanding of the defense, but psychologists have questioned whether the typical juror can comprehend the legal language of these definitions and then apply them as intended by the courts. Elwork, Sales, and Suggs (1981) found jurors only 51% correct on a series of questions testing their comprehension of instructions regarding the M'Naghten rule. Ogloff (1991) obtained similar results: Regardless of what insanity rule was used, college students showed very low rates of recall and comprehension of crucial components in various insanity definitions. It may be that jurors (or mock jurors) do not understand the differences between these different tests very well, consistent with the broader conclusion that jurors do not understand the nuances of a variety of legal instructions that are provided to them (Lieberman, 2009).

The limited empirical evidence indicates that different standards of insanity also make little difference in verdicts. Although instructions have some effect on jury decision making in insanity cases, they tell only part of the story—and perhaps a minor part at that (Finkel & Slobogin, 1995; Ogloff, 1991; Roberts & Golding, 1991).

A much greater influence may be exerted by preexisting attitudes toward the insanity defense (Eno Louden & Skeem, 2007). This decision process is an example of how jurors are prone to interpret "facts" in the context of a personal story or narrative that "makes the most sense" to each of them subjectively. Differences among jurors in the individual narratives they weave about the same set of trial "facts" may be related, in turn, to the different attitudes they hold about the morality of the insanity defense and the punishment of mentally ill offenders (Roberts & Golding, 1991). For instance, one study found that jurors conceptualized the prototypical insanity defendant in one of three ways: (1) severely mentally disordered (SMD), characterized by extreme, chronic, uncontrollable mental illness and/or intellectual disability that impair the defendant's ability to function in society; (2) morally insane (MI), typified by symptoms of psychosis and psychopathy, a categorization used to represent a malevolent, detached, and unpredictably violent offender; or (3) mental-state-centered (MSC), describing a defendant who suffered from varied, but clearly supported, impairments in his mental state at the time of his offense (Skeem & Golding, 2001). Jurors who held SMD- or MI-like prototypes made up the vast majority of the sample (79%), and they tended to believe that the insanity defense was frequently raised, was easily abused, and jeopardized public safety. By contrast, those jurors who held MSC-like prototypes (21%) were less likely to perceive the insanity defense as unjust and tended to believe that the constitutional rights ascribed to defendants were necessary components of the legal process.

Insanity and Terrorism. Terrorism is very much a part of contemporary life. This is true even in the United States, which experiences fewer acts of religious or ideological violence than many other countries. But is there a relationship between the insanity defense and terrorism? Would individuals who commit terrorist acts (if they survive them) be candidates for an insanity defense?

This is explored in Box 10.4, which describes the 2016 acts of a student at Ohio State University who drove a car on campus and deliberately struck other students, then jumped out and stabbed a number of them with a knife. We may never know what motivated Abdul Razak Ali Artan to do this, although we do know that he was Muslim and a Somali refugee who was a legal permanent resident of the United States, because he was shot and killed by a campus police officer.

When behavior is motivated by religious ideology and cultural belief, it would not be appropriate to describe it as a good fit with an insanity defense. As discussed earlier in this section, one foundational aspect of insanity is that the individual suffers from a mental disease or defect—which does not describe someone whose beliefs (however misguided) are shaped by their religion and their culture.

But what about individuals who do suffer from a mental disease or defect, *and* commit acts that are (for example) cited as jihad? To what extent might such an individual qualify for an insanity defense? This is a more complex question that must be considered in light of the nature of the insanity defense and our understanding of terrorist motivation and behavior.

Famous Trials and the Use of the Insanity Plea

Before reporting on the actual frequency and effectiveness of attempts to use the plea, we will review the results of several highly publicized trials that have molded public opinion about insanity pleas.

Trials in Which the Insanity Plea Failed. Among murder defendants who have pleaded insanity as a defense are Jack Ruby, whom millions of television viewers saw kill Lee Harvey Oswald, President John F. Kennedy's alleged assassin; Sirhan Sirhan, charged with the assassination of Robert F. Kennedy; John Wayne Gacy, who was convicted of killing 33 boys in Chicago; Andrew Goldstein, who threw Kendra Webdale to her death in front of a New York City subway train; Eddie Ray Routh, who shot former Navy

Is The Insanity Defense Relevant to Possible Terrorist Acts? The 2016 Ohio State Attack

BOX 10.4

On November 28, 2016, a young man who was a student at Ohio State University drove a car on campus and deliberately rammed students, and then jumped out and stabbed a number of them with a knife. The man was identified as Abdul Razak Ali Artan; he was a Somali refugee who was a legal permanent resident of the United States. He was quickly shot and killed by a nearby campus police officer. Ironically, Artan had been selected earlier that year, at random, for an interview for the campus paper, with the interview appearing in August. In the interview, Artan talked about his Muslim faith, and why it was important for him to have a quiet place to pray. He added that Ohio State seemed "huge" to him, and that he was "kind of scared" as a Muslim, considering how the media portrayed those of his faith. Early investigations following the attack could not definitively conclude that this was an act of terrorism—that kind of conclusion should be reached only after an intensive and detailed review—but authorities could not rule out terrorist motivation, despite the absence of an immediate indication that Abdul Artan was acting with such motivations.

(Instructor's Manual): For the answer to this question to be "yes" (or even possibly), several considerations would be relevant. First, unless a criminal court were to interpret radical Jihadist ideology as a "mental disease or defect" (without the defendant showing signs of having a severe mental illness or intellectual disability), then there would be no "threshold issue" on which to based the claim of insanity. But assuming that a defendant could make a convincing argument about having both symptoms of a severe mental illness *and* radical Jihadist beliefs, then the next question would be whether this combination kept the individual from understanding the nature, quality, or wrongfulness of terrorist acts—or conforming his conduct to the requirements of the law.

Perhaps we should not be surprised that terrorist acts and the insanity defense are rarely mentioned together. Our best evidence is that the strongest influences on the development of radical Jihadist ideology are cultural, religious, and political—not the result of mental illness. Even for individuals who might have a recognizable mental disorder and become radicalized, it would seem far more likely that they would remain committed to their radical beliefs than agree to a defense that excuses criminal conduct based on mental illness or intellectual disability.

CRITICAL THOUGH QUESTION

Is the insanity defense ever relevant to such acts?

SEAL sniper Chris Kyle; and James Holmes, who killed 10 people in an Aurora, Colorado theater during the midnight premiere of "The Dark Knight Rises." All these defendants were convicted of murder despite their pleas of insanity.

In the Jeffrey Dahmer case, jurors rejected a plea of insanity as a defense against murder charges. Dahmer admitted killing and dismembering 15 young men in Milwaukee over about a 10-year period, but his attorney, Gerald Boyle, argued that Dahmer was insane at the time—a sick man, not an evil one. Prosecutor Michael McCann disagreed, arguing that Dahmer knew that what he was doing was wrong. After listening to two weeks of evidence, including taped interviews in which Dahmer explained how he had dismembered his victims and expert testimony about Dahmer's mental condition, the jury ruled, by a 10–2 margin, that Jeffrey Dahmer was sane. He was subsequently sentenced to life in prison for his crimes, and was killed in prison by a fellow inmate.

Wisconsin defines insanity using the Brawner rule; consequently, to have found Dahmer insane, the jury would have had to conclude that he suffered a mental disorder or defect that made him unable either to appreciate the wrongfulness of his behavior or to control his conduct as required by the law. The jury rejected both conclusions, perhaps because of evidence that Dahmer was careful to kill his victims in a manner that minimized his chances of being caught. This cautiousness suggested that he appreciated the wrongfulness of his behavior *and* could control it when it was opportune to do so.

Several other famous defendants who might have attempted to escape conviction through use of the insanity plea did not do so. Among these are Son of Sam serial murderer David Berkowitz, cult leader Charles Manson, and Mark David Chapman, who killed John Lennon.

Trials in Which the Insanity Plea "Succeeded."

Occasionally, when a judge or jury concludes that the defendant is not guilty by reason of insanity, the defendant spends only a short period of time in a treatment program. After being acquitted on charges of malicious wounding (for cutting off her husband's penis), Lorena Bobbitt was released from the state psychiatric hospital following only several weeks of evaluation to determine whether she met criteria for involuntary hospitalization (she did not).

But sometimes when the insanity plea succeeds, the defendant spends more time in an institution than they would have spent in prison if found guilty. In fact, this outcome has led defense attorneys to request that judges be required to instruct jurors that if the defendant is found not guilty by reason of insanity, he or she will probably be committed to a secure psychiatric hospital (Whittemore & Ogloff, 1995). The Supreme Court, however, has refused to require such an instruction (*Shannon v. United States*, 1994).

The case of John W. Hinckley, Jr. has had the greatest influence of any of those discussed in this chapter, triggering much of the court reform and legislative revision regarding the insanity plea since 1982. It is summarized in Box 10.5.

Even though the Hinckley case is one in which the insanity defense was successful in the narrow sense of the word, that outcome was largely a result of a decision by the presiding judge regarding the burden of proof. Judge Barrington Parker instructed the jury in accordance with federal law at the time, which required the prosecution to prove the defendant sane beyond a reasonable doubt. After listening to two months of testimony, the Hinckley jury deliberated for four days before finding the defendant not guilty by reason of insanity. Afterward, several jurors said that, given the instruction that it was up to the government prosecutors to prove Hinckley sane, the evidence was too conflicting for them to agree. They thought his meandering travels raised a question about his sanity, and both sides' expert psychiatric witnesses had testified that he suffered from some form of mental disorder.

Facts about the Insanity Defense

When the Insanity Defense Is Used.

The insanity defense is most often used in cases in which the defendant is charged with a violent felony. In the largest study to date of insanity acquittees, data on NGRI acquittees from four states ($N = 1,099$) were obtained (Steadman et al., 1993). These investigators found that 22.5% of the insanity acquittees had been charged with murder and that 64% had been charged with crimes against persons (murder, rape, robbery, or aggravated assault).

Available research consistently suggests that the majority of defendants found not guilty by reason of insanity (NGRI) have been diagnosed as psychotic, suggesting severe and probably chronic mental impairments (Melton et al., 2007). Steadman and colleagues (1993) reported that 67.4% of the insanity acquittees described in their study were diagnosed with a schizophrenic disorder and that another 14.9% were diagnosed with another major mental illness.

In their large study, Steadman et al. (1993) observed that the decision to acquit by reason of insanity was most strongly influenced by clinical factors. They compared those who successfully employed the insanity defense with others who entered this plea but were nevertheless found guilty, and reported that 82% of the former group but only 38% of the latter group had been diagnosed with a major mental illness.

On the basis of research studies, we have learned more about defendants who are found not guilty by reason of insanity (NGRI). For instance,

1. Although most NGRI defendants have a record of prior arrests or convictions, this rate of previous criminality does not exceed that of other felons (Boehnert, 1989; Cohen, Spodak, Silver, & Williams, 1988).
2. Most NGRI defendants come from lower socioeconomic backgrounds (Nicholson, Norwood, & Enyart, 1991).
3. Most NGRI defendants have a prior history of psychiatric hospitalizations and have been diagnosed with serious forms of mental illness, usually psychoses (Nicholson et al., 1991; Steadman et al., 1993).

The Case of John W. Hinckley, Jr. and the Attempted Assassination of President Reagan

BOX 10.5

John W. Hinckley, Jr

Television replays show John Hinckley's March 30, 1981, attempt to kill President Ronald Reagan. When Hinckley came to trial 15 months later, his lawyers didn't dispute the evidence that he had planned the attack, bought special bullets, tracked the president, and fired from a shooter's crouch. But he couldn't help it, they claimed; he was only responding to the driving forces of a diseased mind. Dr. William Carpenter, one of the defense psychiatrists, testified that Hinckley did not "appreciate" what he was doing; he had lost the ability to control himself.

The defense in John Hinckley's trial made several other claims:

1. Hinckley's actions reflected his pathological obsession with the movie *Taxi Driver*, in which Jodie Foster starred as a 12-year-old prostitute. The title character, Travis Bickle, is a loner who is rejected by the character played by Cybill Shepherd and subsequently befriends Foster's character; he stalks a political candidate but eventually engages in a bloody shootout to rescue the Foster character. It was reported that Hinckley had seen the movie 15 times and that he so identified with the hero that he

had been driven to reenact the fictional events in his own life (Winslade & Ross, 1983).

2. Although there appeared to be planning on Hinckley's part, it was really the movie script that provided the planning force. The defense argued, "A mind that is so influenced by the outside world is a mind out of control and beyond responsibility" (Winslade & Ross, 1983, p. 188).

3. The defense tried to introduce the results of a CAT scan—an image of Hinckley's brain using computerized axial tomography—to support its contention that he had schizophrenia. The admissibility of this evidence created a controversy at the trial. The prosecution objected, claiming that all the apparent scientific rigor of this procedure—the physical evidence, the numerical responses—would cause the jury to place undue importance on it. The prosecution also contended that there were no grounds for concluding that the presence of abnormal brain tissue necessarily denoted schizophrenia. Initially, the judge rejected the request to admit this testimony, but he later reversed the decision on the ground that it might be relevant.

Mr. Hinckley was acquitted by reason of insanity and hospitalized at St. Elizabeths Hospital, a forensic facility in Washington, D.C., where he remained until he was fully released in September 2016 to live with his elderly mother.

CRITICAL THOUGHT QUESTION

The Hinckley defense argued that he was so influenced by the movie "Taxi Driver" that he was not in control of his actions and therefore (under the prevailing federal insanity standard at that time) not guilty by reason of insanity. If you had been a member of the jury, how much weight would you have placed on evidence that he had seen the movie many times and seemed to be reenacting parts of it in his own life?

4. Most NGRI defendants have previously been found incompetent to stand trial (Boehnert, 1989).
5. Although most studies have concentrated on males, one study on female defendants found NGRI in Florida described them as having similar

socioeconomic, psychiatric, and criminal backgrounds to their male NGRI counterparts (Heilbrun, Heilbrun, & Griffin, 1988), while studies in Colorado (Seig, Ball, & Menninger, 1995), Connecticut (Zonana, Bartel, Wells, Buchanan, &

Getz, 1990), and Oregon (Rogers, Sack, Bloom, & Manson, 1984) observed that women were charged with more serious offenses, were older than their male counterparts, and were hospitalized for a shorter period of time. On the question of female insanity acquittees, therefore, the existing studies do not provide us with consistent trends regarding offenses and characteristics. It may be that much of this variability is attributable to the particular state in which the study is done.

Can Insanity Be Faked? How often do criminal defendants being assessed for insanity try to fake a mental disorder? On the basis of his research, Rogers (1986, 1988; Rogers & Shuman, 2000) estimated that about one of four or five defendants being assessed for insanity engages in at least moderate malingering of mental disorders. This figure suggests that crafty conning is not rampant but is frequent enough to cause concern. As a result, psychologists have developed a number of assessment methods to detect persons who are trying to fake a mental disorder. These methods include special structured interviews, individual psychological tests, and specialized measures (Rogers, 2008). These techniques have shown promising results in distinguishing between subjects who were trying to simulate mental illness (to win monetary incentives for being the "best" fakers) and those who were reporting symptoms truthfully.

Public Perceptions of the Insanity Defense

The American public has repeatedly expressed its dissatisfaction with the insanity defense. Several surveys have concluded that most U.S. citizens view the insanity defense as a legal loophole through which many guilty people escape conviction (Skeem & Golding, 2001). After John Hinckley was found not guilty by reason of insanity (NGRI), a public opinion poll conducted by ABC News showed that 67% of Americans believed that justice had not been done in the case; 90% thought Hinckley should be confined for life, but 78% believed he would eventually be released back into society.

The public's disapproval of the insanity defense appears to be stimulated by trials such as Hinckley's that receive massive publicity. Melton et al. (2007) reported the following three beliefs to be prevalent among the public: (1) A large number of criminal defendants use

the insanity defense, (2) those defendants found NGRI are released back into society shortly after their NGRI acquittals, and (3) persons found insane are extremely dangerous.

How accurate are these views? Are they myths or realities? Given the interest and debate surrounding the insanity defense, it is surprising that so few empirical studies have been conducted to investigate its actual outcomes. But there are some data concerning each of these questions.

How Often Is the Plea Used, and How Often Is It Successful? The plea is used much less often than people assume. A survey of the use of the insanity defense in eight states between 1976 and 1985 found that although the public estimated that the insanity defense was used in 37% of the cases, the actual rate was only 0.9% (Silver, Cirincione, & Steadman, 1994). Consistent with these figures, the data reported from the states of California, Georgia, Montana, and New York (Steadman et al., 1993) indicate that defendants in those states, over a 10-year period, entered an insanity plea in 0.9% of felony cases and were successfully acquitted as NGRI in 22.7% of the cases in which this plea was entered. When New Jersey, Ohio, Washington, and Wisconsin are also considered within this group, the overall plea rate is .93% and 26.3% of those insanity pleas succeed (Callahan, Steadman, McGreevy, & Robbins, 1991).

Studies such as these are particularly valuable because few individual states keep complete records on the use of the insanity plea and its relative success. The findings reported in these studies suggest that of the nine insanity pleas raised in every 1,000 criminal felony cases, about two will be successful.

To answer the question of how many people are acquitted by reason of insanity each year, Cirincione and Jacobs (1999) contacted officials in all 50 states and asked for the number of insanity acquittals statewide between the years 1970 and 1995. After persistent attempts to collect these data from a variety of sources, they received at least partial data from 36 states. Few states could provide information for the entire 25-year period, but the results shown in Table 10.1 were obtained.

What Happens to Defendants Who Are Found NGRI? Many mistakenly assume that defendants who are found NGRI go free. Steadman and Braff (1983) found that defendants acquitted on the basis of the insanity plea in New York had an average hospital stay

TABLE 10.1   Insanity Acquittals per 100,000 People

- The median number of insanity acquittals per state per year was 17.7.

- California and Florida had the highest annual averages (134 and 111, respectively).

- New Mexico (0.0) and South Dakota (0.1) had the lowest annual averages.

- Most of the acquittals were for felonies rather than misdemeanors.

of three years in a secure hospital. Researchers also found a clear trend for longer detentions of defendants who had committed more serious offenses: the average length of involuntary hospitalization was greater for those who had been charged with violent offenses (34.1 months) than for individuals with other categories of offenses (Steadman et al., 1993). The average length of confinement for all NGRI individuals was 28.7 months. But this figure undoubtedly underestimates the "true" average period of confinement. Why? These data describe only individuals who were hospitalized and released—they cannot tell us about individuals who were hospitalized but not released. This points to one of the important differences between a criminal sentence, which often is determinate (of fixed length), and the hospital commitment following acquittal by reason of insanity, which is indeterminate (depending on the individual no longer meeting criteria for hospitalization).

Researchers have been particularly interested in learning whether defendants found not guilty by reason of insanity are confined for shorter periods than defendants who are found guilty of similar crimes. A survey of the use of the insanity defense across several states, covering nearly one million felony indictments between 1976 and 1985, sought answers to that question (Silver, 1995). On the basis of more than 8,000 defendants who pleaded insanity during this period, Silver (1995) found that compared to convicted defendants, insanity acquittees spent less time in confinement in four states and more time in confinement in three states. Those acquitted by reason of insanity on a charge of murder are hospitalized, on average, for a longer period than those acquitted of other charges (Dirks-Linhorst, 2012; Steadman et al., 1993).

Some states use a procedure known as *conditional release*, in which persons found NGRI are released to the community (following a period of hospital confinement) and are monitored and supervised by

mental health personnel. Conditional release is the mental health system's counterpart to parole; it functions like a form of outpatient commitment. According to one four-state follow-up of 529 persons found NGRI, about 60% of these individuals were conditionally released within five years of their confinement (Callahan & Silver, 1998). Of those released, the median period of hospital confinement was 3.6 years for violent offenders and 1.3 years for those charged with less serious offenses.

How Dangerous Are Defendants Found NGRI? Because most defendants who are found NGRI are quickly committed to a secure hospital following their acquittal, it is difficult to assess the risk they pose to public safety at that time. In addition, they are likely to receive treatment in the hospital to which they are committed, further complicating the question of their risk of reoffending without this treatment. The limited evidence available on this question suggests either no difference in recidivism rates between NGRI defendants and "regular" felons or slightly lower recidivism rates among the NGRI group (Cohen et al., 1988; Melton et al., 2007). For instance, in a year-long study examining rehospitalization and criminal recidivism in 43 NGRI acquittees, nearly half (47%) were rehospitalized, a minority of the patients (19%) were rearrested or had committed a new crime, and about a fourth of the patients (24%) were reintegrated into the community without difficulty (Kravitz & Kelly, 1999).

Thus, insanity acquittees continue to have legal and/or behavioral health problems. But but their overall rate of criminal recidivism falls in the range found for general offenders who have been convicted.

Current Criticisms of the Insanity Defense

Even if the insanity defense is not successful as often as presumed, legitimate concerns remain about its continued use. We will now evaluate several of these.

It Sends Criminals and Troublemakers to Hospitals and Then Frees Them. Those without mental illness but charged with a serious offense can try to capitalize on the insanity plea to escape prison and eventually get released from the hospital. How often this happens is unknown. Some data indicate that persons found NGRI are confined more frequently and

for longer periods than defendants convicted of similar crimes (Perlin, 1996). Other research finds that those acquitted by reason of insanity *and subsequently released* are confined for a shorter average time than those convicted of comparable offenses (Steadman et al., 1993). After confinement, acquittees also may undergo an additional period of conditional release. So we can conclude that some are released from the hospital sooner than they would have left prison, others stay as long (or longer) than they would have served in a prison sentence, and yet other insanity acquittees do not leave the hospital. This criticism has a grain of truth, therefore, but is largely inaccurate.

The biggest problem with such insanity acquittals is that they are sometimes highly publicized, contributing to the public's perception that they "happen all the time," and that the insanity defense is therefore a constant threat to justice. Such acquittals are relatively rare, in reality. Furthermore, if in the interest of protecting society all NGRI defendants were kept hospitalized until they no longer showed symptoms of mental illness, then society would have to be willing to violate the rights of many mentally ill persons to protect against the violence of a few.

It Is a Defense Only for the Rich.

The parents of John W. Hinckley, Jr. spent between $500,000 and $1,000,000 on psychiatric examinations and expert psychiatric testimony in their son's trial—an amount that contributes to the perception of the insanity defense as a prison dodge for the rich. Of all the criticisms leveled at the insanity defense, this one is perhaps the most clearly contradicted by the data. Numerous studies have failed to find socioeconomic or racial bias in the use or the success of the insanity defense (Boehnert, 1989; Howard & Clark, 1985; Nicholson et al., 1991; Steadman et al., 1993). In addition, this criticism is further weakened by the Supreme Court's 1985 ruling, in the case of *Ake v. Oklahoma*, that poor defendants who plead insanity as part of capital (death penalty) cases are entitled to psychiatric assistance at state expense in pursuing this defense. Many states and communities have extended this ruling by providing public funding for indigent defendants asserting an insanity defense.

Although defendants who can afford to hire their own experts might be more likely to benefit from raising the issue of insanity, this is not a problem unique to the insanity defense. Defendants who can afford ballistics experts, chemists, and their own private detectives also have an advantage over poor defendants, but no one suggests that a defense based on ballistics evidence, blood analyses, or mistaken identity should be prohibited because of the expense.

It Relies Too Much on Mental Health Experts.

Several issues are pertinent here. One criticism is that testifying about insanity forces psychiatrists and clinical psychologists to give opinions about things they are not competent or trained to do—for example, to express "reasonable certainty" rather than probability about a person's mental condition, and to claim greater knowledge about the relationship between psychological knowledge and legal questions than is justified.

Within the field of psychology, there is debate on these matters. The debate centers on two related questions: (1) Can clinicians reliably and validly assess mental illness, intellectual disability, neuropsychological disorders, and disorders occurring in childhood and adolescence? (2) Will this assessment permit the formulation of accurate opinions about a defendant's criminal responsibility for acts committed in the past? Researchers have found some support for the reliability and validity of psychologists' evaluations of criminal responsibility. Results from several studies revealed strong agreement (88% to 93%) between evaluators' recommendations and courts' decisions about defendants' criminal responsibility (see Viljoen, Roesch, Ogloff, & Zapf, 2003), which is important because courts' decisions are one kind of "outcome validation measure" in this kind of research.

Additionally, critics are concerned over the intrusion of psychology and psychiatry into the decision-making process. They want to reserve the decision for the judge or jury, the fact finder in the trial. This criticism is an example of the general concern over the use and willingness of experts to answer legal questions for which they possess limited scientific evidence and mental health data. One remedy proposed to solve this problem is to prevent experts from giving what is often called **ultimate opinion testimony**; that is, they could describe a defendant's mental condition and the effects it could have had on his or her thinking and behavioral control, but they could not state conclusions about whether the defendant was sane or insane. The federal courts, as part of their reforms of the insanity defense, now prohibit mental health experts from offering ultimate opinion testimony about a defendant's insanity. But does this prohibition solve any problems, or is it merely a "cosmetic fix" (Rogers & Ewing, 1989) that has few effects?

In a study of whether prohibiting ultimate opinion testimony affects jury decisions (Fulero & Finkel, 1991), subjects were randomly assigned to read one of 10 different versions of a trial, all of which involved a defendant charged with murdering his boss and pleading insanity as a defense. For our purposes, the comparisons among three different versions of the trial are of greatest interest. Some subjects read transcripts in which the mental health experts for both sides gave only *diagnostic testimony* (that the defendant suffered a mental disorder at the time of the offense); a second group read a version in which the experts gave a diagnosis and then also offered differing *penultimate opinions* about the effects this disorder had on the defendant's understanding of the wrongfulness of his act; a final group read a transcript in which the experts offered differing diagnoses, penultimate opinions, and *ultimate opinion testimony* about whether the defendant was sane or insane at the time of the killing. Did ultimate opinion testimony affect the subjects' verdicts? Not in this study; subjects' verdicts were not significantly different regardless of the type of testimony they read. The lack of difference could be interpreted as evidence that the prohibition of ultimate opinion testimony is unnecessary, or it could indicate that the ban streamlines the trial process without sacrificing any essential information.

Finally, there is the feeling that the process of assessing sanity in criminal defendants harms the reputation of the mental health professions. When the jury sees a parade of mental health experts representing one side and then the other, their confidence in the behavioral sciences is jeopardized; this is also true for the general public, when they read about this process involving a number of different experts (Slater & Hans, 1984). Further, some experts, in an effort to help the side that has retained them, offer explanations of such an untestable nature that their profession loses its credibility with jurors and the public. However, in many cases involving claims of insanity, the experts retained by each side basically agree on the question of insanity. These cases receive less publicity because they often end in a plea agreement.

Revisions and Reforms of the Insanity Defense

Several reforms in the rules and procedures for implementing the insanity defense have been introduced. Proposals have ranged from abolition of the insanity defense (as has already been done in four states), to provision of a "guilty but mentally ill" verdict, to reform of insanity statutes, to maintenance of the present procedures. We review three reforms in this section.

The Guilty but Mentally Ill (GBMI) Verdict.
Since 1976, about a quarter of the states have passed laws allowing juries to reach a verdict of guilty but mentally ill (GBMI) in cases in which a defendant

pleads insanity. These GBMI rules differ from state to state, but generally they give a jury the following verdict alternatives for a defendant who is pleading insanity: (1) guilty of the crime, (2) not guilty of the crime, (3) NGRI, or (4) GBMI. Typically, a judge will sentence a defendant found GBMI exactly as he or she would another defendant found guilty of the same offense. In some jurisdictions, the GBMI-convicted individual starts his or her term in a hospital and then is transferred to prison after treatment is completed. In others, the individual simply receives treatment (if needed) while serving a prison sentence.

Proponents of GBMI verdicts hoped that this compromise verdict would decrease the number of defendants found NGRI. However, actual GBMI statutes have not produced decreases in NGRI verdicts in South Carolina or Michigan. One possible explanation for the lack of change in NGRI verdicts in states with GBMI statutes is that jurors do not understand the differences between the verdicts. One study examined jurors' knowledge about the two verdicts and found that only 4% of potential jurors correctly identified meanings and outcomes of both NGRI and GBMI verdicts (Sloat & Frierson, 2005).

Other problems have led to a "second look" at the GBMI reform, leading to skepticism about its value (Borum & Fulero, 1999). If regular insanity instructions are confusing to jurors, the GBMI verdict only adds to the confusion by introducing the very difficult distinction for juries to make between mental illness that results in insanity and mental illness that does not. However, one mock jury study showed that the presence of a GBMI option makes it less likely that either a conviction or an NGRI acquittal will result (Poulson, Wuensch, & Brondino, 1998).

Also, the claim that the GBMI option will make it more likely that mentally ill offenders will receive treatment is largely a false promise. In one Michigan study, 75% of GBMI offenders went straight to prison with no treatment (Sales & Hafemeister, 1984). Overcrowding at hospitals in most states has impeded implementation of this part of the GBMI option. In Kentucky, in spite of a statute that appears to promise treatment to those found GBMI, the chair of the parole board filed an affidavit in 1991 stating that "from psychological evaluations and treatment summaries, the Board can detect no difference in treatment or outcome for inmates who have been adjudicated as 'Guilty But Mentally Ill,' from those who have been adjudicated as simply 'guilty'" (Runda, 1991).

The Defense of Diminished Capacity. Several states allow a defense of **diminished capacity**, which is a legal doctrine that applies to defendants who lack the ability to commit a crime purposely and knowingly. Like the insanity defense, diminished capacity often involves evidence that the defendant suffers a mental disorder. It differs from insanity in that it focuses on whether defendants had the state of mind to act with the purpose and the intent to commit a crime—that is, to consider the consequences of their contemplated actions—not on whether they knew the crime was wrong or whether they could control their behavior. Suppose M'Naghten knew that murder was wrong but, because of his mental condition, wasn't thinking clearly enough to intend to kill Peel's secretary. Under these conditions, he would not be insane, but he would lack the *mens rea* (the necessary specific intent) for first-degree murder, so he probably would have been convicted of second-degree murder or manslaughter.

The rationale for this defense is straightforward: Offenders should be convicted of the crime that matches their mental state, and expert testimony should be offered on the issue of their mental state. The majority of states permit expert testimony about a defendant's *mens rea*, thereby allowing clinicians to present testimony that could be used in support of a diminished-capacity defense (Melton et al., 2007). As long as proof of a defendant's *mens rea* is required, defendants are likely to put forward expert evidence about it, especially in those states that have abolished the insanity defense. Even when the diminished capacity defense "works," it still usually leads to a prison sentence.

Elimination of the Insanity Plea. Winslade and Ross (1983) reviewed seven trials (mostly for murder) in which the insanity defense was used and psychiatric testimony was introduced to justify it. Based on their analysis of the outcomes of these trials, Winslade and Ross recommend that the insanity defense be eliminated. They conclude that the possibility of an insanity defense often leads to injustice, for the following reasons:

1. Juries are asked to decide questions that predispose them to make arbitrary and emotional judgments because of either over-identification with or alienation from the defendant;
2. Mental health professionals are encouraged to offer opinions, guesses, and speculations under the banner of scientific expertise; and

3. Society's views about criminality and "craziness" are so intertwined that an insanity defense to a crime does not make much sense (p. 198).

Arguments against Eliminating the Plea. James Kunen (1983), a former public defender, challenged the proposal to eliminate the insanity defense, noting that "Anglo-American legal tradition ... has required that to convict someone of a crime, the prosecution must prove not only that he did a particular act—such as pulling a trigger—but that he did it with a particular state of mind" (p. 157). Kunen argued that we cannot talk about legal guilt without considering the person's state of mind. If a defendant slashes his victim's throat, thinking that he is slicing a cucumber, we say that he committed an act but not that he was guilty of the intent to commit a crime. This is why, even in those few states that have abolished the insanity defense, defendants may still introduce evidence that they lacked the mental state required for the crime.

We believe that the NGRI plea should be maintained as an option, modifications of the system should be restricted to those that clarify the rule, and defendants for whom the defense was successful should be evaluated. For example, the Insanity Defense Reform Act changed the law that required the prosecution to prove that John Hinckley was not insane. If an act similar to Hinckley's were committed today in a federal jurisdiction or in the vast majority of states, the defendant, not the prosecution, would bear the responsibility of proving the plea; otherwise, the defendant would be found guilty. States should carefully monitor people committed after NGRI verdicts to ensure that they are not released while still mentally ill and dangerous. All indications are that this precaution is being taken.

Capital Sentencing Evaluations

Although mental health professionals are involved in many aspects of the legal process, none has more implication for a defendant's life than capital sentencing evaluations, which have been described as literally "a life or death matter" (*Satterwhite v. Texas*, 1988, p. 1802). The U.S. Supreme Court, in *Eddings v. Oklahoma* (1982), held that a trial court must consider any potentially mitigating information—evidence that argues *against* a death sentence. Mitigating factors are defined as "... any aspect of a defendant's character or record, or any of the circumstances of the offense that the defendant proffered as a basis for a sentence less than death" (*Lockett v. Ohio*, 1978, p. 604). This leaves the forensic clinician with a very broad focus for the evaluation. Evaluators must consider information about a defendant's physical, cognitive, social, and developmental history. Understanding, judgment, impulsivity, and values are influenced by developmental, cognitive, neuropsychological, cultural, community, situational, and other life influences, and it is important to consider these dimensions as part of a capital sentencing evaluation.

Some jurisdictions also consider the question of a defendant's future risk to society, and forensic clinicians often evaluate and testify about these risks. Texas requires that the jury consider future risk in weighing a sentence of death (Cunningham, 2010). Oregon and Virginia also specify future dangerousness as a consideration in capital sentencing. Two other states (Oklahoma and Wyoming) list future dangerousness as a potential aggravating factor—evidence that argues *for* a death sentence, and four additional states (Colorado, Maryland, New Mexico, and Washington) note its absence as a potential mitigating factor (Bright, 2014).

In addition to considering factors encompassing mitigation and future violence risk, clinical evaluations must also address the question of eligibility for capital sentencing if the defendant may be intellectually disabled, which would exempt the defendant from the death penalty, consistent with the Supreme Court decision in *Atkins v. Virginia* (2002). It is also useful to consider the quality of such evaluations, given the enormous importance of the sentencing decision (DeMatteo, Murrie, Anumba, & Keesler, 2011).

Juvenile Transfer

During the 1980s and 1990s, there was substantial reform in the juvenile and criminal justice systems in the United States to allow more frequent prosecution of juveniles in criminal (adult) court. Such reform was motivated largely by the perception that juvenile crime had increased—and become more serious. A "get tough" approach was adopted in the attempt to decrease the rate of juvenile offending. One aspect of this "do the crime, do the time" philosophy involved expansion of ways in which adolescent (under 18 years old) offenders could be **transferred** (also called certified or waived) into criminal court.

A number of criteria are described in state laws on juvenile transfer. Two of the most important are public safety and **treatment needs and amenability**. Another criterion often used is **sophistication-maturity**. Those evaluating a juvenile for a possible transfer must focus on the risk of future offending, the interventions needed to reduce this risk, and the likelihood that the youth will respond favorably to such interventions. The extent to which a juvenile is mature—cognitively and psychosocially—and the degree to which he/she is "adult-like" in their criminal thinking and behavior can both affect their response to interventions. The risk/need/responsivity (RNR) model (Andrews & Bonta, 1990) is useful in this respect, as it prompts the evaluator to consider risk of reoffending and risk-relevant deficits (e.g., substance abuse, family problems, education/employment problems) carefully. This consideration can be facilitated by using an empirically supported specialized tool, such as the Structured Assessment of Violence Risk in Youth (SAVRY; Borum, Bartels, & Forth, 2005), the Youth Level of Service/Case Management Inventory (YLS/CMI; Hoge & Andrews, 2002), or the Risk-Sophistication-Treatment Inventory (Salekin, 2004).

Assessing a youth being considered for transfer is a forensic evaluation. It involves a legal question that will be answered by the judge, just as competence does. With juveniles, this means that evaluators must pay particular attention to school and family functioning, often by obtaining school records and conducting interviews of family members. They should also obtain information in other important areas. Peers, for example, can have an important influence on an adolescent's behavior. Was the offense committed alone, or was the youth with peers who may have encouraged one another to offend—or at least refused to back down? Substance abuse is another very important risk factor for offending; both using drugs and selling drugs are areas that should be targeted for intervention. Determining whether such intervention will be effective with a particular individual is difficult. Whether intervention will help a particular youth to desist from offending may be judged partly from the individual's expressed motivation, capacity to admire and respect authority figures, and responses to previous interventions (Grisso, 1998).

States vary in their specification of the age at which an adolescent is eligible for prosecution in the criminal system. Some states do not have any age limit; others have passed legislation decreasing the age of eligibility. Most still use the age of 14 or 15, however. There are several justifications for transferring an adolescent into the criminal system: (1) a charge of homicide; (2) a charge of other specific violent felonies (e.g., sexual assault, armed robbery, aggravated battery); or (3) a history of prior juvenile offending, suggesting a failure to respond to interventions provided by the juvenile system. In addition, some states have a policy involving "once an adult, always an adult," under which any adolescent convicted (or even tried) in criminal court will be charged in criminal court for future offenses, regardless of their nature or that individual's age. As of 2017, a total of 31 states plus the District of Columbia had this kind of statute (Teigen, 2017).

Juveniles can be transferred to criminal (adult) court in several different ways. The state legislature in a given jurisdiction can determine that certain offenses allegedly committed by an adolescent must be filed directly in adult court (Griffin, 2003). For example, a state legislature may pass a law dictating that certain serious felony charges (e.g., armed robbery, sexual battery) be prosecuted in criminal court if the defendant is over a certain age. This approach to transfer has been called **statutory exclusion**. As of 2017, 29 states had statutory exclusion for certain offenses (Teigen, 2017).

A second approach to transferring juveniles to criminal court has been termed **judicial waiver**. When this procedure is used, the juvenile court judge uses discretion to decide whether the youth should be transferred to criminal court (as of 2009, 44 states plus the District of Columbia had this kind of option; 13 states plus D.C. had presumptive transfer schemes in which certain circumstances create the assumption of transfer; and 15 states had mandatory transfer schemes for certain circumstances; Griffin, Addie, Adams, & Firestine, 2011). In exercising judicial discretion regarding transfer, the judge typically considers statutorily specified influences such as the youth's risk to public safety, amenability to treatment, and maturity (Brannen et al., 2006; Heilbrun, DeMatteo, King, & Filone, 2017). Such factors can be evaluated by mental health professionals, and the results described in the report and in expert testimony, to help inform the judge in making this decision. Generally, judicial discretion transfer laws authorize, but do not mandate, a move to adult court.

A third approach to juvenile transfer is called **prosecutorial discretion**, which requires prosecutors to decide whether cases are filed initially in juvenile or adult court. As of 2017, 14 states plus the District of Columbia had established the option of prosecutorial discretion for certain offenses (Teigen, 2017).

There are two other dispositional considerations for justice-involved youth. For those who are initially charged or transferred into criminal court, some states allow a motion to return to juvenile court. This is called **reverse waiver**, and was featured in 24 states as of 2009 (Griffin et al., 2011). Finally, the option of **blended sentencing** allows either a juvenile court to integrate criminal sentencing options into the disposition (14 states) or the criminal court to include juvenile placement in the disposition (18 states), as of 2009 (Griffin et al., 2011).

Is putting juveniles in the adult system effective in reducing reoffending? Common sense might suggest that adolescents would be less likely to offend if they knew that offending could result in more severe punishment. But research has not supported this. Research on general deterrent effects has reflected no decline in juvenile crime after these transfer laws came into effect. One study found no differences in the juvenile homicide/manslaughter rates in the states with prosecutorial discretion policies in the first five years after transfer laws were enacted (Steiner & Wright, 2006). Housing juveniles with adult criminals may also promote criminal attitudes and motivations (Forst, Fagan, & Vivona, 1989). Juveniles detained in New York's adult system were 89% more likely to be rearrested for a violent offense and 44% more likely to be rearrested for a property offense than juveniles in the New York metropolitan area who were detained within New Jersey's juvenile court system (Fagan, 1996). Higher rates of recidivism have also been observed in other studies with youth detained in the adult correctional system (Bishop, Frazier, Lanza-Kaduce, & Winner, 1996; Mason & Chang, 2001; Myers, 2001). Research also suggests that juveniles in adult facilities were more likely to be sexually assaulted and physically assaulted than were youth in the juvenile facilities (Beyer, 1997).

A summary of the available evidence made by the Centers for Disease Control (Task Force on Community Preventive Services, 2007) concluded that transfer to the adult system typically increases rates of violence among those who were transferred, although the evidence was not sufficient to gauge the impact of transfer on violent crime in the overall juvenile population. Based on this review, the Task Force recommended against the transfer of juveniles to the adult criminal justice system for the purpose of reducing violence.

Summary

1. ***What is the scope of forensic psychology?*** Forensic psychology is a specialty that involves the application of knowledge and techniques from the behavioral sciences to answer questions about individuals involved in legal proceedings. The range of topics about which psychological and psychiatric experts are asked to testify continues to grow, facilitated by the development of scientific research and specialized forensic assessment measures.

2. ***What is meant by competence in the criminal justice process?*** Adjudicative competence entails having a sufficient present ability to consult with one's attorney with a reasonable degree of rational understanding and with a rational, as well as factual, understanding of the proceedings. This same standard is applied to the questions of whether a defendant is competent to plead guilty and whether a defendant is competent to stand trial, so the phrase "competence to stand trial" is often used to refer to the entire process of disposition of charges, not merely the trial.

3. ***How do clinicians assess competence?*** When mental health professionals assess a defendant's competence, they should use one of several specialized instruments designed specifically for the purpose of evaluating how well a defendant understands the charges and potential proceedings. These specific tests and structured interviews have made competence assessments more reliable, valid, and useful. Competence evaluations are sometimes complicated by such factors as malingering, amnesia, and the problem of whether incompetent defendants can be treated against their will. Other competence issues (e.g., competence to refuse the insanity defense and competence to be sentenced) can arise at different points in the criminal process.

4. ***What are the consequences of being found incompetent to proceed in the criminal justice process?*** When defendants are found incompetent to stand trial, they can be committed for a period of treatment designed to restore their competence. If later found competent, they will stand trial or dispose of their charges through the plea-bargaining process. If treatment is not successful in restoring competence, the state will usually attempt to commit the person to a state psychiatric hospital for a period of time. The alternatives that have been proposed for dealing with the unrestorably incompetent criminal defendant include waiving the right to be found incompetent to proceed to trial and using a special form of commitment for incompetent defendants who are judged at a provisional trial to be guilty of the crimes with which they are charged.

5. ***What is the legal definition of insanity?*** Two major definitions of insanity are used currently. The M'Naghten rule defines insanity as not knowing the nature, quality, or wrongfulness of behavior because of mental disease or defect: "To establish a defense on the grounds of insanity it must be clearly proved that, at the time of committing the act, the accused was laboring under such a defect of reason, from disease of the mind, as not to know the nature and quality of the act he was doing, or, if he did know it, that he did not know what he was doing was wrong." A total of 21 states plus the federal jurisdiction use some version of the M'Naghten rule to define insanity, while another four states combine M'Naghten with the irresistible impulse test.

The Brawner rule states that a person is not responsible for a criminal act if, as a result of mental disease or defect, the person lacked "substantial capacity either to appreciate the criminality of his conduct or to conform his conduct to the requirements of the law." This rule or a variation of it is the standard in 18 states. Until 1984, it was also the federal standard, but the federal system now requires the defense to show that, as a result of a severe mental disease or defect, the defendant was unable to appreciate the nature and quality or the wrongfulness of his or her acts. Five states have outlawed insanity as a defense, although these states still allow the defendant to introduce evidence about his or her mental condition that is relevant to determining mens rea. Some highly publicized trials have led to "successful" use of the insanity defense. But many others who used this defense were found guilty.

6. *How frequently is the insanity defense used, and how successful is it?* The insanity plea is used much less frequently than people assume; it is attempted in fewer than 1% of cases, and it succeeds in only about 23% of these cases. When it does succeed, there is no guarantee that the defendant will be released from the hospital any sooner than he or she would have been paroled from prison.

7. *What are the major criticisms of the insanity defense, and what attempts have been made to reform it?* Some examples of early release of NGRI defendants have led to justified criticism of the procedure. Other criticisms are that insanity cannot be reliably and validly assessed and that the insanity defense relies too much on mental health expert testimony. Reforms include the Insanity Defense Reform Act and the adoption in several states of a "guilty but mentally ill" verdict, resulting (at least in theory) in the defendant's being treated in a state hospital until releasable and then serving the rest of the sentence in prison. A number of states also allow the diminished capacity plea, a partial defense based on mental condition.

8. *What are the important criteria in deciding on juvenile transfer?* One important consideration is public safety—the risk that a youth would commit further offenses subsequent to rehabilitation in the juvenile system. A second related consideration is the youth's needs and likely response to interventions reducing the risk of future offending, often called "treatment needs and amenability." Many jurisdictions also cite a youth's "sophistication-maturity," involving the extent to which the developmental level and the approach to offending are similar to those of adults.

Key Terms

adjudicative competence

Brawner rule

blended sentencing

competence

competence to plead guilty

competence to stand trial

diminished capacity

insanity

M'Naghten rule

mens rea

prosecutorial discretion

reverse waiver

sophistication-maturity

statutory exclusion

stipulate

transferred

treatment needs and amenability

ultimate opinion testimony

ORIENTING QUESTIONS

1. What problems are associated with expert testimony based on these evaluations? What reforms have been proposed?

2. Under what conditions can a plaintiff be compensated for psychological damages?

3. What is workers' compensation, and how do mental health professionals participate in such cases?

4. What capacities are involved in civil competence?

5. What criteria are used for decisions about disputes involving child custody or parental fitness?

6. What steps are taken in civil commitment? How well can clinicians assess the risk of dangerousness or violent behavior, a key criterion for civil commitment?

Whether a defendant is mentally competent to stand trial (often called *adjudicative competence*, because it refers to a defendant's capacities to dispose of charges either through a trial or via plea bargaining) and whether a defendant was insane at the time of an alleged criminal offense are perhaps the best-known legal questions that mental health professionals help courts decide. However, they are certainly not the only questions. Throughout earlier chapters, we examined other questions arising in the legal system that psychologists are often asked to consider. Is a given individual a good candidate to become a police officer? Will a person who is suffering from mental illness be violent in the future? How accurate is one's memory for, and testimony about, highly traumatic events likely to be? These questions—like those of competence and insanity—are often asked of forensic psychologists and psychiatrists, and they are usually answered through a combination of research knowledge and the results of individual assessments performed by forensic clinicians.

Different kinds of litigation are making use of scientific knowledge and expert opinion. Psychology and psychiatry are two fields in which the use of experts has proliferated. Melton, Petrila, Poythress, and Slobogin (2007) offer a comprehensive listing and description of the legal questions that are most often addressed in civil, juvenile/family, and criminal cases. In addition to the legal questions discussed in previous chapters, mental health experts are involved in hearings or trials in the areas of civil commitment; psychological damages in civil cases; psychological autopsies (i.e., determination of the extent to which psychological problems are attributable to a preexisting condition); negligence and product liability; trademark litigation; discrimination; guardianship and conservatorship (a guardianship-like arrangement for an individual's financial assets); child custody; adoption; termination of parental rights;

professional malpractice; and other social issues such as sexual harassment in the workplace. In certain jurisdictions, therefore, judges must now decide whether the expert testimony that an attorney seeks to introduce at trial meets the criteria that the U.S. Supreme Court has established in the federal courts as the standard for admitting scientific evidence and expert testimony.

In this chapter, we provide information about expert testimony in civil cases, and describe six areas of forensic assessment in which psychologists and psychiatrists are involved: (1) psychological damages to civil plaintiffs, (2) workers' compensation claims, (3) the assessment of civil competencies and capacities, (4) psychological autopsy, (5) child custody and parental fitness, and (6) civil commitment and risk assessment. Although these areas do not receive the publicity commanded by adjudicative competence or insanity at the time of the offense, they illustrate several ways in which psychological expertise can be applied to important legal questions. For each of the six areas, we

- discuss the basic psycholegal questions that experts are expected to address,
- describe the techniques typically used by forensic clinicians to evaluate these questions, and
- summarize the empirical evidence and legal status associated with the forensic activity. ●

Experts in the Adversarial System

In general, a qualified expert can testify about a topic if such testimony is relevant to an issue in dispute and if the usefulness of the testimony outweighs whatever prejudicial impact it might have. If these two conditions are met, an expert will be permitted to testify if the judge believes that the testimony is based on sufficiently relevant and reliable scientific evidence. In other words, under criteria established by the U.S. Supreme Court in *Daubert v. Merrell Dow Pharmaceuticals* (1993) and *Kumho Tire Co. v. Carmichael* (1999), the judge serves as a "gatekeeper" who must determine whether the theory, methodology, and analysis that are the basis of the expert's opinion measure up to scientific standards. If they meet this standard, the judge will probably admit relevant expert testimony; if they do not, the judge should not allow the testimony. The *Daubert* and *Kumho* decisions apply to all cases in federal court. In state court, the prevailing standard may also be *Daubert*—or it may stem from an earlier decision (*Frye v. United States*, 1923) holding that expert testimony must be based on techniques and process that are "generally accepted" in the field to which they belong. States have the discretion to decide which standard they will use by passing state legislation.

Judges generally do not perform the gatekeeper function well (Gatowski et al., 2001). Many judges lack the scientific training that *Daubert/Kumho* appears to require. Even for those with substantial scientific training, the range of expert topics about which judges need information is staggering. As a result, many critics, including experts and judges themselves, believe that the difficulty of distinguishing valid from invalid scientific evidence will result in jurors too often being exposed to "expert" testimony that is based on little more than "junk science" (Grove & Barden, 1999; see Box 11.1).

There are clear advantages to having mental health professionals provide expert testimony. Mental health professionals have specialized knowledge and training that can provide the court with valuable information in a variety of cases. For example, some psychologists are trained to administer tests to determine neuropsychological problems and symptom genuineness in workers' compensation cases, or are experienced in conducting interviews and obtaining other information from multiple sources in order to assess parental fitness.

However, judges, lawyers, and mental health professionals themselves have expressed great concern about the reliability, validity, propriety, and usefulness of expert testimony and the forensic assessment on which it is based. Former federal appellate judge David T. Bazelon (1974) once complained that "psychiatry ... is the ultimate wizardry ... in no case is it more difficult to elicit productive and reliable testimony than in cases that call on the knowledge and practice of psychiatry." This view was echoed by Warren Burger (1975), a former chief justice of the

U.S. Supreme Court, who chided experts for the "uncertainties of psychiatric diagnosis." Critiques of psychologists' expert testimony in this area has continued over the decades (see, e.g., Grisso, 2003; Tillbrook, Mumley, & Grisso, 2003).

What are the main problems with testimony by psychological or psychiatric experts? Over 25 years ago, Smith (1989) cited the following potential problems:

1. The scientific foundation for much of the testimony offered in court is often less than adequate, leading to unreliable information and therefore potentially incorrect verdicts.
2. Much of the testimony is of limited relevance, therefore wasting court time and burdening an already crowded docket.
3. Experts are too often permitted to testify about "ultimate issues" (Is the defendant insane? Was the plaintiff emotionally damaged?), which should be left to juries to decide.
4. Expert testimony is frequently used to introduce information that would otherwise be prohibited because it is hearsay. (Experts are permitted to share this information with juries if it is the kind of information they routinely rely on in reaching expert opinions.)
5. The adversarial system compromises experts' objectivity. Experts may have some bias toward the side that retained them.
6. Expert testimony is very expensive, and relying on experts gives an advantage to the side with more money.
7. Testing the reliability and validity of expert opinions through cross-examination is inadequate because

Expert witnesses often testify if their testimony is relevant to the case.

BOX 11.1

The Case of Columbine Shooter Eric Harris, Antidepressant Medication, and Violence: Expert Opinion or Junk Science?

In 2002, Mark Taylor, a survivor of the Columbine High School shooting, sued the pharmaceutical company that manufactures Luvox, the antidepressant drug that one of the shooters, Eric Harris, was taking at the time of the shooting. Is there scientific evidence that this drug caused Eric Harris to be violent? Peter Breggin, M.D., one of the experts involved in the litigation, thought so. Was his testimony impartial and based on good science? Or was it an example of expert bias, poor science, or both?

Breggin opined in a preliminary report filed with the U.S. District Court in Denver that Luvox triggered Harris's rampage. "Absent persistent exposure to Luvox, Eric Harris would probably not have committed violence and suicide," noted Breggin.

Breggin, a psychiatrist who was then based in Washington, D.C., described himself as a medical expert with 30 years of experience in product liability lawsuits involving psychiatric drugs. However, some of this history reflects the skepticism of legal fact finders about his impartiality. A Wisconsin judge in 1997 observed, "Dr. Breggin's observations are totally without credibility. I can almost declare him [to be a] fraud or at least approaching that. I cannot place any credence or credibility in what he has to recommend in this case." On the question of whether his opinion reflects good science, another court held in 1995 that "Dr. Breggin's opinions do not rise to the level of an opinion based on 'good science.' The motion to exclude his testimony as an expert witness should be granted." The question of Breggin's impartiality may be one reason that Taylor eventually dropped his lawsuit in exchange for a

Eric Harris and Dylan Klebold, Columbine High shooters, shown via school surveillance video.

contribution from the pharmaceutical company to the American Cancer Society.

CRITICAL THOUGHT QUESTIONS

1. **What are some of the characteristics you would expect from an expert whose testimony is grounded in science?**
2. **How might "litigation bias" influence an expert who was conducting the scientific research, as opposed to citing the research of others?**
3. **How might one court's critical language about an expert influence that expert's work on similar litigation matters in the future?**

attorneys are usually not well equipped to conduct such cross-examination, and juries often fail to understand the significance of the information that is uncovered during the cross-examination.

8. The spectacle of experts disagreeing with one another ultimately reduces the public's confidence in mental health professionals.

Grisso (2003) has discussed criticisms of forensic mental health assessment that he calls "the five I's": ignorance, irrelevance, intrusion, insufficiency, and incredibility. These refer to not knowing (or not using)

the proper legal standard; providing evidence that goes beyond what is relevant to the proceeding; offering conclusions that impinge upon the court's domain; providing limited supporting evidence for one's conclusions; and offering conclusions that are not justified by the evidence one does provide. These criticisms are similar in many respects to those described by Smith (1989) over 25 years ago. Although Smith was talking about expert testimony and Grisso was referring to forensic assessment more broadly, their overlap underscores an important point: good expert testimony is based on a good evaluation.

In response to these concerns, some of which are also supported by empirical research discussed later in this chapter, several reforms of expert testimony have been proposed. Most of these suggestions are aimed at reducing the undue influence or excessive partisanship that can adversely affect expert testimony. As a result, the federal courts do not permit testimony on the "ultimate issue" of insanity in forensic cases. This change was part of the overall reform of federal law concerning insanity that occurred in 1984. Still, there is little evidence that such limitation of expert testimony has much impact on the use or success of the insanity defense (Borum & Fulero, 1999), and it is even less likely to affect the kinds of cases we discuss in this chapter.

Most authors and sources of authority suggest that partisanship in expert witnesses should be reduced or eliminated entirely. But there are a few who do not. For instance, in his book entitled *Behind the Scenes with an Expert Witness*, Tanay (2010) describes his own experience as a psychiatric expert—particularly on the legal question of insanity—and argues that the expert should

be a strong advocate so that unjust jury verdicts are less likely. Reviewing this book, prominent psychologist Stan Brodsky (who has done a great deal of work on the topic of expert testimony) discusses the personal and idiosyncratic approach taken by Dr. Tanay to expert testimony. Such an approach, says Brodsky, makes for interesting reading—but it also involves more advocacy (and less impartiality) than is appropriate for the forensic expert.

Other suggestions have involved reducing the overly adversarial nature of expert testimony by limiting the number of experts on a given topic, requiring that the experts be chosen from an approved panel of individuals reputed to be objective and highly competent, and allowing testimony only from experts who have been appointed by a judge rather than hired by one of the opposing attorneys. Although these changes would appear to reduce the "hired gun" problem, it is not clear which experts would belong on an approved list, or whether being appointed by a judge ensures an expert's impartiality. Furthermore, some research suggests that jurors might already be inclined to discount the testimony of experts whom they perceive to be "hired guns" because of the high fees such experts are paid and their history of testifying frequently (Cooper & Neuhaus, 2000).

It may be that there are a few forensic psychologists and forensic psychiatrists who are motivated primarily by money and can be consistently relied upon to render opinions that are favorable to the attorney who retains them. In our view, however, this is a small number—and these individuals develop a certain reputation in forensic mental health and legal circles. The more common problem that may influence many experts, however, is what has been called "allegiance bias" or "retention bias." The question of whether experts can remain impartial and accurate without regard to which side has retained them has been explored recently through research. In a comprehensive review, Murrie and Boccaccini (2015) summarized the factors that can diminish impartiality and concluded that working at the request of one side in an adversarial proceeding can cause experts' opinions to "drift" toward the retaining party, even in scoring "objective" procedures. They suggest that this process is part of a larger influence on human decision-making, in which "cognitive biases" have an important influence on how human beings make decisions.

There are other kinds of bias that apply to human decision-making more broadly. The work of Daniel Kahneman and Amos Tversky (see, e.g., Kahneman, 2013; Lewis, 2017) identified a number of factors that affect how people make decisions under conditions of uncertainty, when there are no clear and objectively "right" answers. These influences can impair the impartiality and accuracy of evaluations and testimony presented by forensic clinicians, particularly in the context of an adversarial system. Such influences have been discussed as they apply to forensic assessment and testimony, identifying six that are particularly relevant:

- Representativeness—overemphasizing evidence that resembles a typical representation of a prototype (e.g., making attributions about an individual's motivation because that individual resembles a "drug addict" in many ways);
- Base rate neglect—judging the likelihood of an outcome without considering information about the actual probability of this outcome, as conveyed by base rates (e.g., predicting a serious act of violence by someone who shows predictors consistent with a group that rarely behaves this way);
- Availability—overemphasizing the probability of occurrence when similar instances are easy to recall (e.g., from a recent, highly publicized case);
- Confirmation bias—selectively gathering and interpreting evidence that confirms a hypothesis while ignoring evidence that might disconfirm it (e.g., as a result of using early impressions in an evaluation to shape the gathering of additional evidence);
- WYSIATI (what you see is all there is)—organizing activated information to derive the most coherent "story" while leaving out nonactivated information (e.g., by focusing on information that has been "activated," perhaps via confirmation bias, and consequently constructing an account that is excessively consistent because it excludes contradictory information); and
- Anchoring—information encountered first is the most influential.

Acknowledging the presence of such biases among forensic mental health professionals, and developing "debiasing" strategies, thus seem to have broad potential for improving both forensic mental health evaluation and the expert testimony that may result. One such debiasing strategy is to conduct forensic evaluations that are guided by foundational principles, and basing expert testimony on the results of such evaluations (Heilbrun, Grisso, & Goldstein, 2009). Another is to conduct training, and periodically review one's professional performance, by reviewing whether the biases described in the last paragraph are affecting performance. A third debiasing strategy, aimed more at the public perception of experts' impartiality and accuracy, is to avoid public comment regarding ongoing cases, particularly in social media formats (e.g., Twitter) in which the depth and nuance of the comment is severely limited.

Several scholars have suggested that courts not permit clinical opinion testimony unless it can be shown that it satisfies standards of scientific reliability. The standard required by the *Daubert/Kumho* decisions has made this recommendation more feasible (Imwinkelried, 1994). Such a requirement might reduce the frequency of testimony by forensic psychologists and psychiatrists, but unless lawyers and judges are educated more thoroughly about scientific methodology, it is unlikely that many of them will be able to correctly apply the concepts described in *Daubert* (e.g., falsifiability, error rate) toward making informed distinctions between "good" and "bad" science (Gatowski et al., 2001).

A more modest reform would involve simply banning any reference to witnesses as providing *expert* testimony, a term that suggests that jurors should give it extra credence. Instead, judges would always refer—in the presence of juries—to *opinion* testimony or witnesses.

In addition to deleting any mention of expert testimony, federal judge Charles Richey (1994) recommended that juries be read a special instruction before hearing any opinion testimony in order to reduce its possible prejudicial impact. Here is an example of his recommended instruction:

> *Ladies and Gentlemen, please note that the Rules of Evidence ordinarily do not permit witnesses to testify as to their opinions or conclusions. Two exceptions to this rule exist. The first exception allows an ordinary citizen to give his or her opinion as to matters that he or she observed or of which he or she has firsthand knowledge. The second exception allows witnesses who, by education, training and experience, have acquired a certain specialized knowledge in some art, science, profession or calling to state an opinion as to relevant and material matters. The purpose of opinion witness testimony is to assist you in understanding the evidence and deciding the facts in this case. You are not bound by this testimony and, in weighing it, you may consider his or her qualifications, opinions and reasons for testifying, as well as all other considerations that apply when you evaluate the credibility of any witness. In other words, you should give it such weight as you think it fairly deserves and consider it in light of all the evidence in this case.*

Psychological Damages to Civil Plaintiffs

When one party is injured by the actions of a second party, the injured individual can sue the second party to recover monetary damages as compensation for the injury. This action is covered by an area of civil law known as torts. A **tort** is a wrongful act that causes harm to an individual. The criminal law also exacts compensation for wrongful acts, but on behalf of society as a whole; by punishing an offender, the criminal law attempts to maintain society's overall sense of justice. Tort law, on the other hand, provides a mechanism to remedy the harms that individuals have suffered from wrongful acts by another party.

As illustrated by the O. J. Simpson case, both criminal punishment and civil remedies can be sought for the same act. Simpson was prosecuted by the state, under the criminal law, for murder; he was also sued for monetary damages by the surviving relatives of the victims, who alleged that he caused the wrongful deaths of Nicole Brown Simpson and Ronald Goldman.

Many kinds of behavior can constitute a tort. Slander and libel are torts, as are cases of professional malpractice, invasion of privacy, the manufacture of defective products that result in a personal injury, and intentional or negligent behavior producing harm to another person.

Four elements are involved in proving a tort in a court of law and all involve behavioral issues. First, torts occur in situations in which one individual owes a **duty**, or has an obligation, to another. For instance, a physician has a duty to treat patients in accordance with accepted professional standards, and individuals have a duty not to harm others physically or psychologically. Second, a tort typically requires proving that one party breached or violated a duty that was owed to other parties. The **breached duty** can be due to negligence or intentional wrongdoing. **Negligence** is behavior that falls below a standard for protecting others from unreasonable risks; it is often measured by asking whether a "reasonable person" would have acted as the civil defendant acted in similar circumstances. **Intentional behavior** is a conduct in which a person meant the outcome of a given act to occur. Third, the violation of the duty must have been the proximate cause of the harm suffered by a plaintiff. A **proximate cause** is one that constitutes an obvious or substantial reason why a given harm occurred. It is sometimes equated with producing an outcome that is "foreseeable." So if a given event would be expected to cause a given outcome, it is a proximate cause. Fourth, a **harm**, or loss, must occur, and the harm has to involve a legally protected right or interest for which the person can seek to recover damages that have been suffered. If it can be established that (1) there was a duty, (2) that was breached, (3) which proximately caused the (4) resulting harm, then a tort can be proven in a civil lawsuit.

The damages a person suffers from a tort can involve destruction of personal property, physical injuries, and/or emotional distress (sometimes called "pain and suffering"). Historically, the law has always sought to compensate victims who are physically hurt or sustain property losses, but it was reluctant to allow compensation for emotional distress, largely out of concern that such damages are too easy to fake and too difficult to measure. In cases in which recovery for emotional damages has been allowed, the courts have historically required that a physical injury has accompanied the psychological harm or that a plaintiff who was not physically injured was at least in a "zone of danger." (For example, even if the plaintiff was not injured by the attack of an escaped wild animal, the plaintiff was standing next to his or her children when the animal attacked them.) More recently, however, a growing number of states are abandoning the "zone of danger" restriction and allowing recovery for psychological harm suffered when the individual was not within the zone of danger (Buckley & Okrent, 2004).

One case that received extensive international coverage illustrates this historical approach to emotional damages. On the afternoon of March 22, 1990, the *Aleutian Enterprise*, a large fishing boat, capsized in the Bering Sea. Within 10 minutes, the boat sank, killing nine crew members. Twenty-two sailors survived the disaster; of these men, two returned to work in a short time, but the other twenty filed a lawsuit against the company that owned the ship. Of the 20 plaintiffs, 19 consulted a psychologist or psychiatrist, and every one of these 19 individuals was subsequently diagnosed with posttraumatic stress disorder (PTSD) by his evaluating mental health professional (Rosen, 1995). (The defendant company hired its own psychologist, who evaluated the plaintiffs and diagnosed PTSD in only five of them and some other post-incident disorder in three others.) The surviving sailors were entitled to recover for their psychological injuries because they had been in the "zone of danger."

In recent years, the courts have progressed to a view in which psychological symptoms and mental distress are more likely to be compensated regardless of whether the plaintiff suffered physical injuries. Two types of "purely" psychological injuries are now claimed in civil lawsuits: those arising from "negligent" behavior and those arising from "extreme and outrageous" conduct that is intended to cause distress. In the former type of case, plaintiffs are often allowed to sue for psychological damages if they are bystanders to an incident in which a loved one is injured (e.g., a parent sees her child crushed to death when a defective roller coaster—on which the child was riding—derails).

In the case of intentional torts causing psychological distress, a plaintiff must prove that a defendant intentionally or recklessly acted in an extreme and outrageous fashion (sometimes defined as "beyond all bounds of decency") to cause emotional distress. In addition, the plaintiff must prove that the distress is severe. In other words, the effects must be something more than merely annoying or temporarily upsetting (Merrick, 1985).

What kinds of behavior might qualify? Courts have found that a debt collector who was trying to locate a debtor acted outrageously when he posed as a hospital employee and told the debtor's mother that her grandchildren had been seriously injured in a wreck and that he needed to find the debtor to inform him of this fact (*Ford Motor Credit Co. v. Sheehan*, 1979).

In recent years, an increasing number of cases have dealt with psychological injuries resulting from the tort of sexual harassment, usually in the workplace. A plaintiff who claims to have been sexually harassed at work can sue the workers responsible for the harassment and can also sue the company itself, if the plaintiff can show that the company knew (or should have known) about the harassment and failed to stop it. These cases can be filed either in state courts or in federal courts, where Title VII of the federal Civil Rights Act of 1991 applies to companies with at least 15 employees. Plaintiffs can seek both **compensatory damages** (payment for injuries suffered) and **punitive damages** (punishment of the company for its failure to respond properly to the misconduct).

Of course, the tort of harassment is not always based on gender. It may incorporate other characteristics—including racial/ethnic group or religious beliefs, as we see in the case of antiterrorism officer "John Doe," described in Box 11.2.

Assessment of Psychological Damages

When a mental health professional assesses a plaintiff, the clinician will typically conduct an evaluation that, like most evaluations, includes a social history, a clinical interview, and a number of psychological tests and specialized forensic measures (Boccaccini & Brodsky, 1999; Melton et al., 2007). One major difference, however, between standard clinical evaluations and forensic assessments is the much greater use of third-party interviews and review of available records in forensic examinations. This practice is based on two basic considerations (Heilbrun, 2001; Melton et al., 2007). First, forensic experts must be sure that their opinions are based on accurate information, and self-reported information in the context of litigation is not necessarily accurate. Second, forensic experts are often asked to evaluate an individual's psychological condition at some specific time or in some particular situation in the past. Therefore, clinicians must use independent sources of information, when possible, to verify their descriptions and judgments about such matters.

The Case of Antiterrorism Officer "John Doe": Racial/Ethnic and Religious Discrimination in the Workplace

BOX 11.2

Discrimination in the workplace can occur for different reasons. Consider the case of "John Doe," an undercover police officer in the New York City Police Department (NYPD). Egyptian-born and Muslim, he was subjected to treatment that may have been discriminatory for ethnic and religious reasons. The NPYD has contained an undercover unit of investigators, most of whom are of Middle Eastern or Asian backgrounds, who use their language and cultural skills to investigate potential terrorist threats against New York City. But one Egyptian-born analyst in the unit filed a suit charging that he was subjected to hundreds of anti-Muslim and anti-Arab e-mail messages sent out by a city contractor over the course of three years. In an interview, "Mr. Doe" (who was not named because he is still in the unit) said he complained repeatedly to supervisors but that no one took action.

The lawsuit cites e-mail briefing messages sent out several times a day to members of the unit by Bruce Tefft, a former Central Intelligence Agency (CIA) official who has identified himself in the past as the Police Department's counterterrorism adviser. (The suit was filed against both the NYPD and Tefft.) The e-mail messages were sent to everyone in the division, according to the suit, which also alleges that the briefing messages were preceded by anti-Muslim and anti-Arab statements like, "Burning the hate-filled Koran should be viewed as a public service at the least" and "This is not a war against terrorism … it is against Islam and we are not winning." In one, he asked, "Has the U.S. threatened to vaporize Mecca?" and responded, "Excellent idea, if true." The lawsuit alleged that e-mails "ridiculed and disparaged the Muslim religion and Arab people, and stated that Muslim- and Arab-Americans

were untrustworthy and could not reliably serve in law enforcement positions or handle sensitive data."

According to a NYPD spokesman, the police commissioner was not aware of the "offensive commentary" until the complaint was made. "As soon as the Police Department became aware of a complaint about the content of e-mail sent by an individual not employed by the Police Department, we took immediate action to block his e-mails, followed by a cease and desist letter to the individual and his employer, a consulting firm," he wrote.

Reportedly the department's contract with this advisor ended in 2003, but Tefft continued to send the e-mail messages on his own, circumventing attempts by the department to block them. Mr. Doe's lawyer commented, "It's incredible in this day and age that hundreds of racist e-mails could be sent to hundreds of NYPD officials over three years, and not one person did a thing to stop it."

This unit was profiled on "60 Minutes" and in the *Wall Street Journal* and the New York *Daily News*. Mr. Doe said, "The NYPD was happy to introduce us to the press—'Here these guys are, the best of the best, they are doing a great job.' But then they failed to protect us under this smear, this constantly daily attack against my religion and against good Muslim Arab-Americans, and I will say good because the majority are good."

CRITICAL THOUGHT QUESTION

Can you apply a tort law framework in analyzing this lawsuit? What are the questions that a court will need to answer in deciding whether the lawsuit should be decided in favor of the plaintiff (the officer who filed the suit)?

Using data from these sources, the clinician arrives at an opinion about the psychological condition of the person in question. With the exception of greater reliance on third-party interviews and records, this part of the evaluation resembles a standard clinical evaluation of individuals assessed for diagnostic and treatment purposes. The more difficult question the clinician must answer in litigation, however, is whether the psychological problems were caused by the tort, aggravated by the

tort, or existed before the tort. In fact, given that some research suggests that psychological problems make people more prone to accidents, the clinician needs to consider whether certain psychological conditions might have contributed to the plaintiff being injured in the first place.

There is no established procedure for answering these questions, although most clinicians try to locate records and other sources of information that help them describe the development of any disorder that is diagnosed. In some situations, a plaintiff might allege that he or she was targeted for harassment precisely because the defendants knew of some prior difficulty that made the plaintiff vulnerable to a particular kind of harassment. In such cases, the clinician must consider this additional information before reaching a conclusion about the significance of the prior psychological problem.

Another complication may affect the evaluations of individuals who claim to have suffered psychological harm: Plaintiffs may be motivated to exaggerate their symptoms in order to improve their chances of winning large awards. Sometimes such symptom exaggeration or fabrication (called **malingering**) involves outright lying. In other cases, a genuine behavioral health disturbance is present, but the plaintiff exaggerates its seriousness.

A meta-analysis found that the possibility of receiving compensation for an injury was associated with more frequent reports of pain (Rohling, Binder, & Langhinrichsen-Rohling, 1995). Similar findings were observed in a second meta-analysis, focusing in particular on mild traumatic brain injury (Belanger, Curtiss, Demery, Lebowitz, & Vanderploeg, 2005). Of course, such findings do not necessarily show that litigation involvement causes exaggeration. It might work in the other direction as well—individuals with more intransigent pain might be more likely to litigate their claims. Or a third influence might affect both; for instance, lifestyle might influence both recovery from injury and propensity toward litigation. But it is certainly possible that litigation involvement increases both the experience of pain and the report of such pain resulting from injury (Greene, 2008).

In a review of the ethics of attorneys "coaching" their clients on how to "beat" psychological tests in civil litigation cases, Victor and Abeles (2004) argued that these techniques are well within the ethical boundaries of legal practice and that attorneys often view such coaching as an important part of advocating for their clients. Another study found that some attorneys believe it to be malpractice *not* to coach their clients on the malingering scales of psychological assessments (e.g., the Minnesota Multiphasic Personality Inventory-2 [MMPI-2], often used in civil litigation) (Youngjohn, 1995). These coaching strategies may be effective. One study revealed that the *F* scale on the MMPI-2 (one of the instrument's validity scales designed to detect possible malingering) was not as effective at identifying coached malingerers as at identifying noncoached malingerers (Storm & Graham, 2000). Of course, forensic evaluators who suspect that coaching has occurred are likely to compensate by gathering additional information from sources other than self-report.

Spurred by results like these and by estimates from experienced clinicians that malingering and self-serving presentations are not at all uncommon in forensic evaluations (Rogers, 2008), some have recommended that clinicians consistently consider response style in forensic evaluations. This refers to whether evaluees are responding as accurately as they can ("reliable"), exaggerating or fabricating symptoms ("malingering"), denying or minimizing symptoms ("defensive"), or failing to engage in the evaluation and respond meaningfully to questions ("uncooperative"). When response style appears anything other than reliable, then evaluators should take extra steps to evaluate it (Heilbrun, 2001; Williams, Lees-Haley, & Djanogly, 1999).

Workers' Compensation

When a worker is injured in the course of his or her job, the law provides for the worker to be compensated through a streamlined system that avoids the necessity of proving a tort. This system is known as *workers' compensation law*. All 50 states and the federal government have some type of workers' compensation system in place. Prior to workers' compensation, a person who was injured at work had to prove that the employer was responsible for a tort in order to receive compensation. This was difficult because employers had several possible defenses to the worker's claim. They often blamed the employee's negligence or the negligence of another worker for the injury. In other cases, employers said that a worker's injuries were simply the unavoidable risks of particular jobs and that the worker was well aware of these risks at the time of employment. As a result, until early in the 20th century, many seriously injured workers and their families were denied any compensation for their work-related injuries.

Workers' compensation systems were developed around the beginning of the 20th century to provide an alternative to the tort system. In workers' compensation systems, employers contribute to a large fund that insures workers who are injured at work, and employers also waive their right to blame the worker or some other individual for the injury. For their part, workers give up their right to pursue a tort case against their employers, and if they are compensated, the size of the award they receive is determined by (1) the type and duration of the injury and

(2) their salary at the time of the injury. Workers can seek compensation for

- physical and psychological injuries suffered at work
- the cost of whatever treatment is given
- lost wages
- the loss of future earning capacity

Determining how much impairment in future earning capacity a given mental disorder or psychological condition might produce is very difficult. Physicians can assess the degree of impairment from a ruptured disc or a paralyzed arm, but how can we measure the degree or permanence of a mental disability? To bring some uniformity to these assessments, many states require evaluators to use the American Medical Association's *Guides to the Evaluation of Permanent Impairment* (AMA, 2007). The *Guide* provides five categories of impairment, ranging from "no impairment" to "extreme impairment," that clinicians can use to organize their descriptions of a claimant. In general, however, ratings of psychological impairments are hard to quantify reliably.

Both employers and employees should benefit from a process in which workers' claims can be resolved fairly quickly, which is a major goal of the workers' compensation system. Formal trials are not held, and juries do not resolve these cases; they are heard and decided by a hearing officer or commissioner. (These decisions can be appealed.) In theory, workers' compensation cases should be handled expeditiously, but they often drag on for years as both sides go through a process of hiring one or more experts to examine the worker and give opinions about the injuries and any disability suffered.

How do mental health professionals become involved in workers' compensation claims? Because psychological injuries or mental disorders arising from employment can be compensated, clinicians are often asked to evaluate workers and render opinions about the existence, cause, and implications of any mental disorders (Piechowski, 2011).

Claims for mental disability usually arise in one of two ways, though there is a third (less likely) basis for a claim as well. First, a physical injury can lead to a mental disorder and psychological disability. A common pattern in these *physical–mental* cases is for a worker to sustain a serious physical injury (e.g., a broken back or severe burns) that leaves the worker suffering chronic pain. As the pain and the disability associated with it continue, the worker also experiences associated psychological problems, usually depression and anxiety. These problems can worsen until they become full-fledged mental disorders, resulting in further impairments of the worker's overall functioning.

The second work-related pathway to mental disability is for an individual either to suffer a traumatic incident at work or to undergo a long period of continuing stress that leads to substantial psychological difficulties. A night clerk at a convenience store who is the victim of an armed robbery and subsequently develops posttraumatic stress disorder is an example of such *mental–mental* cases. Another example is the clerical worker who, following years of overwork and pressure from a boss, experiences an anxiety disorder.

In a third kind of case, known as *mental–physical*, work-related stress leads to the onset of a physical condition such as high blood pressure. Many states have placed restrictions on these types of claims, and psychologists are seldom asked to evaluate them.

The number of psychological claims in workers' compensation litigation has increased dramatically in the last 25 years, and much of the increase can be attributed to a surge in mental–mental cases (Bonnie & Monahan, 1996; Melton et al., 2007). At least three explanations have been proposed to account for this increase in psychological claims. First, because more women have entered the workforce, and because women are more often diagnosed with anxiety and depressive disorders than men, the rise in psychological claims might be due to the increased percentage of female workers. A second possibility is that a shift in the job market from manufacturing and industrial jobs to service-oriented jobs has produced corresponding increases in job-related interpersonal stressors and decreases in physical injuries. A third possibility is that claims of psychological impairments are motivated primarily by financial incentives, generating a range of cases in which genuine impairments are mixed in with exaggerated or false claims of disability.

Assessment in Workers' Compensation Claims

Some empirical studies have been conducted on the assessment of psychological damages in workers' compensation cases. They usually focus on one of the following questions:

- How do workers' compensation claimants score on standard psychological tests such as the MMPI-2 and the MMPI-2-RF?

- Are certain injuries or stressors associated with a particular pattern of psychological test scores?
- Can psychological tests distinguish claimants who are suffering from a genuine disorder from those who are faking or exaggerating their problems?
- What factors threaten the impartiality of forensic evaluations in workers' compensation cases?

In a study relevant to the first bullet point, investigators analyzed archival MMPI-2s produced by 192 women and 14 men involved in litigation related to alleged workplace sexual harassment and discrimination. Among the women, 28% produced a profile that was within normal limits. The remaining profiles fell into four distinctive clusters representing different approaches to the test items (Long, Rouse, Nelsen, & Butcher, 2004). For example, the first cluster combined a defensive unwillingness to acknowledge problems with evidence of depression and physical complaints. The second cluster involved responding that was neither exaggerated nor defensive, and also featured evidence of depression and physical problems. Both the third and fourth clusters were marked by exaggeration of problems and reports of generalized psychopathology, although the fourth cluster featured very extreme exaggeration.

Regarding the association between injuries and test scores, the research does not suggest that particular injuries or claims are reliably linked with different patterns of test scores (Melton et al., 2007). One reason for the lack of distinguishing patterns might be that regardless of the injury or the stressor, most people manifest psychological distress through a mixture of physical complaints and negative emotions such as anxiety, depression, and feelings of isolation.

When injured at work, the worker's compensation law helps employees seek compensation from the employer.

We now turn to the question of whether psychological tests can distinguish between claimants with genuine disorders and those who are exaggerating. The MMPI-2 and MMPI-2-RF contain sets of items that are sometimes used to assess the test-taking attitudes of a respondent. These validity scales can be examined to determine whether respondents might have tried to fool the examiner by exaggerating or denying psychological problems. Other tests such as the Validity Indicator Profile (Frederick, 1997, 2000; Frederick & Crosby, 2000) and the Test of Memory Malingering (Tombaugh, 1997) have been developed to detect malingering on cognitive and neuropsychological measures.

The typical case of a person trying to exaggerate or fake mental disorder involves the individual answering many items in the "bad" direction, thereby attempting to look as disturbed as possible. However, the strategy might be more complicated in the case of a person who is faking or exaggerating a disorder in a workers' compensation case. These individuals usually want to appear honest, virtuous, and free of any psychological problems that might have existed prior to the injury, while at the same time endorsing many symptoms and complaints that would establish that they had been harmed by a work-related incident. In other words, their motivation involves a combination of faking good and faking bad. A special validity scale composed of MMPI-2 items that tap this simultaneous fake-good/fake-bad strategy has been developed and has had some success in distinguishing between genuine and faked psychological injury claims (Lees-Haley, 1991, 1992; Nelson, Sweet, & Demakis, 2006), although others (Butcher, Arbisi, Atlis, & McNulty, 2008) have argued that the scale is more likely to represent general maladjustment than malingering.

One study included a sample of MMPI-2s of worker's compensation and personal injury cases (N = 289) to consider the relationship of various indicators of exaggeration. The investigators concluded that malingering may take the form of inconsistent responding as well as symptom exaggeration, with patients evaluated at the request of plaintiff attorneys showing a seemingly greater degree of symptom exaggeration and inconsistent responding than did those referred by defense counsel (Fox, Gerson, & Lees-Haley, 1995).

The impartiality of psychological evaluations performed in workers' compensation cases can be threatened by several factors (Tsushima, Foote, Merrill, & Lehrke, 1996). Chief among these problems is that attorneys often retain the same expert to conduct evaluations of different cases. An expert who is repeatedly hired by the same attorney, whether a plaintiff's or defense attorney, may risk opining what the attorney wants rather than rendering impartial opinions about each case.

One study investigated this issue by examining whether psychological assessments of workers' compensation claimants were related to the side that had retained the expert. Hasemann (1997) collected and compared 385 reports that had been prepared by various mental health professionals. Of these reports, 194 had been conducted by defense-hired experts, 182 were completed by plaintiff-hired experts, and 9 evaluations could not be classified. Did plaintiff and defense experts differ in their opinions in these cases? Several results indicate that they did and that they might have been unduly influenced by the adversarial system.

Consider these three results:

- Plaintiff experts gave impairment ratings to claimants that were nearly four times larger than the impairment ratings assigned by defense experts.
- Defense experts concluded that MMPIs completed by claimants were invalid or malingered in 72% of their evaluations, whereas plaintiff experts reached this conclusion in 31% of their evaluations.
- Of the 19 experts who had conducted three or more evaluations, 17 tended to do so almost exclusively for one side. Ten experts conducted a total of 107 plaintiff evaluations and only 8 defense evaluations. Seven experts completed 147 assessments for the defense and only 36 for the plaintiffs.

Comparing the numbers of evaluations conducted for plaintiffs with the number conducted for defendants can be misleading however, because these numbers depend on the number of referrals from each side. A better measure of evaluator impartiality involves the proportion of "useful" opinions (i.e., opinions helpful to the referring attorney) relative to the overall number of referrals. For example, an evaluator who has conducted 90 evaluations for the defense and 10 for plaintiffs might appear less impartial than the evaluator who has done 50 for the defense and another 50 for plaintiffs. However, looking more closely at the "usefulness" proportion might reveal that the first evaluator has reached a conclusion favorable to the referring attorney in 50% of the defense cases and 45% of the plaintiff cases, whereas the second evaluator has favored the referring attorney in 98% and 100% of defense and plaintiff cases, respectively. Which evaluator appears less impartial?

Other influences can affect the apparent impartiality of forensic evaluations. Even if experts are reasonably impartial, attorneys may selectively introduce expert opinions depending on whether those opinions support their side. In order to consider this possibility, investigators would need to acquire the results of evaluations requested by attorneys but not subsequently presented as evidence. This is comparable to the "file drawer problem" encountered by investigators performing meta-analysis: Because research reporting nonsignificant differences is often not accepted for publication, such results tend to languish, unpublished, in a file drawer, which limits the accuracy of the investigator's ability to determine an overall "effect" of a research phenomenon based on all the evidence. (Circa 2017, perhaps this should be renamed the "hard drive problem.") Even if forensic evaluators can be reasonably impartial, they still conduct such evaluations in the context of an adversarial system, and decisions about whether to introduce such reports as evidence are often made by attorneys who are advocates for their clients.

It is these kinds of concerns that prompted the writing of a series of "best practice" books in forensic mental health assessment, published by Oxford University Press. These books describe several different kinds of civil questions relevant to this chapter. One (Piechowski, 2011) focuses on evaluation for workplace disability. The second such book (Goodman-Delahunty & Foote, 2011) addresses the topic of workplace discrimination and harassment. A third (Kane & Dvoskin, 2011) describes the process of conducting evaluations for personal injury claims more broadly. These books discuss the steps that potential evaluators can take to promote thorough, accurate, and balanced evaluations on this topic. They do not, of course, ensure that future evaluations will be conducted as recommended. But they do identify best practices, as well as steps to avoid, so evaluators who wish to do this work in a way that is consistent with the strongest approaches developed in the field have clear guidance in this effort.

Civil Competencies

The concept of legal competence extends to many kinds of decisions that individuals are called on to make throughout their lives. When we discussed competence to stand trial, we focused on the knowledge that criminal defendants must have and the decisions they are required to make. However, the question of mental competence is raised in several noncriminal contexts as well; we refer to these other situations with the general term **civil competencies**.

The question of civil competence focuses on whether an individual has the capacity to understand information that is relevant to decision-making in a given situation and then make an informed choice about what to do in that situation. Here are some questions that address issues of civil competence:

- Is a person competent to manage his or her financial affairs?
- Can an individual make competent decisions about his or her medical or psychiatric treatment?
- Is a person competent to execute a will and decide how to distribute property to heirs or other beneficiaries?
- Can a person make advance decisions about the kind of medical treatment he or she wants or does not want to receive if terminally ill or seriously injured?

Scholars who have studied this issue usually point to four abilities that contribute to competent decision-making (Appelbaum & Grisso, 1995; Grisso, 2003). A competent individual is expected to be able to (1) understand basic information that is relevant to making a decision; (2) apply that information to a specific situation in order to anticipate the consequences of various choices; (3) use logical—or rational—thinking to evaluate the pros and cons of various strategies and decisions; and (4) communicate a personal decision or choice about the matter under consideration.

The specific abilities associated with each of these general criteria depend on the decision that a person must make. Deciding whether to have risky surgery demands different information and thinking processes than deciding whether to leave property to children or to a charitable organization.

Decisions about medical treatment that one might receive in the future, including the desire to have life-sustaining medical treatments discontinued, involve a special level of planning that has been encouraged by a 1990 federal statute known as the Patient Self-Determination Act. Planning about future medical treatments is formalized through what are known as **advance medical directives**, in which patients indicate what kinds of treatment they want should they later become incapacitated and incompetent to make treatment decisions.

One of the most important of these advance directives is the "living will," in which a patient essentially asserts that he or she prefers to die rather than to be kept alive on a ventilator or feeding tubes. The ethical and practical issues involved in determining patients' competence to issue advance medical directives are substantial, but the trend, revealed in Supreme Court decisions such as *Cruzan v. Director, Missouri Department of Health* (1990), is to recognize that patients have great autonomy in accepting or rejecting a variety of treatments and health care provisions (Hanson & Doukas, 2009).

Advance medical directives seem like a simple and direct way to communicate end-of-life decisions. Investigators surveyed 405 outpatients of 30 primary care physicians and 102 members of the general public on the topic of advance directives, which were preferred by 93% of the outpatients and 89% of the general public. When people were asked to imagine themselves incompetent and with a poor prognosis, they decided against life-sustaining treatment about 70% of the time. Health, age, and other demographic features did not predict these choices, however (Emanuel, Barry, Stoeckly, Ettelson, & Emanuel, 1991).

But for living wills to be effective, individuals must be able to generate preferences that are stable over time and across changes in health. Unfortunately, individuals' predictions about what kind of care they might want in the future vary from one occasion to the next and are affected by the status of their present health. In studies that examined the stability of advance directives, participants were asked to record their preferences for various life-sustaining treatments (e.g., cardiopulmonary resuscitation [CPR]) in different medical scenarios, such as coma. After an interval ranging from one month to two years, these individuals recorded their preferences again. The average stability of preferences across all judgments was 71%, suggesting that over time periods as short as two years, there were substantial changes in stated treatment preferences (Ditto et al., 2003). Of course, a person could change his or her preferences for good reason—perhaps as a result of some relevant intervening life experience such as a health crisis or a relative's need for life-sustaining treatment. However most people are unaware that their preferences change; they mistakenly believe that the preferences they express at the second interview are identical to those they provided at the first interview (Gready et al., 2000).

Preferences are also dependent on the context in which they are made. For example, when patients recently discharged from hospitals are asked about their desire for life-sustaining treatment, they show a characteristic "hospital dip"; they report less desire for interventions than they did prior to hospitalization—and less than they do several months after their discharge (Ditto, Jacobson, Smucker, Danks, & Fagerlin, 2006). Apparently people do not have stable preferences for future medical care.

Assessing Competence to Make Treatment Decisions

The question of competence to consent to treatment usually arises when a patient refuses treatment that seems to be medically and psychologically justified. Under these circumstances, the first step might be to break down the explanation of the treatment decisions facing the patient into smaller bits of information. (Research results have shown that patients can better understand treatment information when it is presented to them one element at a time.) Using this kind of presentation might facilitate a patient's appreciation of whether a recommended treatment would be in his or her best interest. If there were still an impasse between the patient and treating professionals after such a presentation, it would be important to administer a clinical assessment instrument to determine whether a given patient lacks the necessary ability to reach a competent decision. Such an instrument—the MacArthur Competence Assessment Tool for Treatment Decisions (MacCAT-T)—is now commercially available (Grisso & Appelbaum, 1998a, 1998b).

The research for the MacCAT-T, conducted as part of a larger MacArthur Research Network on Mental Health and Law study on competencies, coercion, and risk assessment, focused on the capacities of individuals with severe mental disorders to make decisions and give informed consent about their own psychiatric treatment. Can persons with serious mental disorders make competent treatment decisions for themselves? Do their decision-making abilities differ from those of persons who do not suffer mental disorders?

Researchers in the MacArthur Treatment Competence Study developed a series of structured interview measures to assess the four basic abilities—understanding information, applying information, thinking rationally, and expressing a choice—involved in legal competence (Grisso, Appelbaum, Mulvey, & Fletcher, 1995). For example, here is an item that taps a person's ability to apply information to the question of whether he or she has a condition that could be effectively treated:

> *"Most people who have symptoms of a mental or emotional disorder like your doctor believes you have can be helped by treatment. The most common treatment is medication. Other treatments sometimes used for such disorders are having someone to talk to about problems, and participating in group therapy with other people with similar symptoms." "… [D]o you believe that you have the kind of condition for which some types of treatment might be helpful?" "All right, you believe that … (paraphrase of the patient's expressed opinion).*

Can you explain that to me? What makes you believe that … (again paraphrase as above)?" For a patient who believes that treatment will not work because he or she is "just too sick," the interviewer would ask: *"Imagine that a doctor tells you that there is a treatment that has been shown in research to help 90% of people with problems just as serious as yours. Do you think this treatment might be of more benefit to you than getting no treatment at all?" (Grisso et al., 1995, p. 133)*

Standardized interviews, using items of this type, were conducted with three groups of patients—those with schizophrenia, those with major depression, and those with heart disease—and with groups of people from the community who were *not* ill but were demographically matched to the patient groups (Grisso & Appelbaum, 1995). Only a minority of the persons in all the groups showed significant impairments in competent decision-making about various treatment options. However, the patients with schizophrenia and major depression tended to have a poorer understanding of treatment information and used less adequate reasoning in thinking about the consequences of treatment than did the heart patients or the members of the community sample. These impairments were more pronounced and consistent across different competence abilities for patients with schizophrenia than for patients with depression, and the more serious the symptoms of mental disorder (especially those involving disturbed thinking), the poorer the understanding.

These results obviously have implications for social policies involving persons with mental disorders. First, contrary to popular impressions, the majority of patients suffering from severe disorders such as schizophrenia and major depression appear to be capable of competent decision-making about their treatment. On the other hand, a significant number of patients—particularly those with schizophrenia—show impairments in their decision-making abilities.

Assessing Competence to Execute a Will

Clinicians may also be asked to evaluate whether a person (called a "testator") was competent to execute a will; such competence is a requirement for the provisions of the will to be valid. Typically, challenges to this capacity are raised when there is reason to think that the testator lacked the necessary mental capacity to execute a valid will (Frolik, 1999; Melton et al., 2007).

In one example, Ronald Eisaman challenged his aunt's will in a Pennsylvania probate court, arguing that his aunt, Harriet Schott, lacked **testamentary capacity**.

Schott executed a will in 1993, leaving the bulk of her estate to Eisaman. But she executed a second will in 1997, reducing his share to 50% and passing the remaining 50% to the corporation that owned the assisted-living facility where she resided prior to her death. The expert witnesses who testified about Schott's mental capacity were equivocal. Thus, the judge determined that Eisaman had not established that his aunt lacked testamentary capacity to change her will. The 1997 version was accepted, therefore.

According to one study, situations that may raise concern about capacity to execute a will include the following: There is a radical change from a previous will (seen in 72% of cases); undue influence is alleged (56% of cases); the testator has no biological children (52% of cases); the testator executed the will less than a year prior to death (48% of cases); and the testator suffered from comorbid conditions such as dementia (40% of cases), alcohol abuse (28% of cases), or other neurological/psychiatric conditions (28% of cases) (Shulman, Cohen, & Hull, 2004).

The legal standard for testators' competence to execute a will is derived from *Banks v. Goodfellow* (1870), in which the court held as follows:

1. Testators must know at the time of making their wills that they are making their wills.
2. They must know the nature and extent of their property.
3. They must know the "natural objects of [their] bounty."
4. They must know the manner in which the wills they are making distribute their property.

This type of competence has a lower threshold than other competencies because it requires only that persons making a will have a general understanding of the nature and extent of their property and of the effect of their will on members of their family or others who may naturally claim to benefit from the property cited in the will (Melton et al., 2007). A person cannot be deemed incompetent to execute a will simply on the basis of the presence of a mental illness, unless there is clear evidence that the mental illness specifically interfered with the individual's ability to meet the standard set at the time the will was written.

Assessment of this competence focuses on the individual's functional abilities at the time his or her will was written. Melton and colleagues (2007) outline some strategies used by mental health professionals in assessing competence to execute a will. First, they recommend

structuring the evaluation to conform to the associated legal elements. They suggest using the sources available (e.g., the testator, family, friends, records) to first determine the purpose of the will and why it was written at that time. Second, they recommend gathering information about the testator's property holdings, which may include asking questions about occupation and salary, tangible property, and intangibles (e.g., bank accounts, investments). Third, the clinician should determine the testator's "values and preferences" (p. 361) to better understand the family dynamics (e.g., with whom does the testator have a good relationship, with whom does he or she does not get along). This information can shed light on the testator's rationale for bequeathing his or her belongings to specific individuals. Finally, Melton and colleagues recommend that clinicians assess the general consequences of the dispositions outlined in the will.

One of the obvious difficulties in these types of evaluations is that the testator, the subject of the evaluation, is often deceased at the time the question of competence to execute the will arises. Thus, the sources of information will be different. If the testator is alive, he or she will be a primary informational source—but if he or she is deceased, the evaluator must gather information from family, friends, acquaintances, medical records, and other available sources without the testator's specific input.

Psychological Autopsies

Like most clinical assessments, the typical forensic assessment involves a clinician interviewing, observing, and testing a client to arrive at an understanding of the case. However, in a few unusual circumstances, clinicians may be called on to give an opinion about a deceased person's state of mind as it existed at a specific time before death. Obviously, in these cases, the clinician must conduct an evaluation without any participation by the individual whose prior condition is in question. These evaluations are termed **psychological autopsies** (Ogloff & Otto, 1993).

Psychological autopsies originated in the 1950s when a group of social scientists in the Los Angeles area began assisting the coroner's office in determining whether suicide, murder, or accident was the most likely mode of death in some equivocal cases. Their use has spread over the years, and now they are encountered most often in cases such as determining the cause of death in situations where an insurance company could deny death benefits if the policy holder committed suicide; assessing claims in workers' compensation cases that stressful working conditions or work trauma contributed to a worker's death or suicide; evaluating a deceased individual's mental capacity to execute or modify a will; and assessing the validity of an argument occasionally made by criminal defendants that a victim's mode of death was suicide rather than homicide.

Although there is no standard format for psychological autopsies, most of them rely on information from two sources: interviews with third parties who knew the decedent and prior records. General guidelines for what should be included in psychological autopsies have been published (La Fon, 2008). Some investigators concentrate on more recent data, generated close in time to the person's death. What was the person's mood? How was the person doing at work? Were there any pronounced changes in the person's behavior? Others—especially those who take a developmental perspective on behavior—look for clues early in the person's life. As a child, how did the person interact with his or her parents and siblings? What was the individual's approach to school? Peers? Hobbies and other activities?

As with any assessment technique, the first question to be considered is the reliability of the psychological autopsy. There are several reasons to suspect that the reliability of psychological autopsies is low. For starters, the person in question is not available to be interviewed or tested. Obviously, the decedent's "true" state of mind is unknown; if it *were* known, the autopsy would be unnecessary. Also, the persons who are interviewed might not remember the past accurately, or they might have reasons to distort their answers.

A review of research on psychological autopsy studies (Foster, 2011) revealed specific life events (particularly interpersonal conflict) as risk factors for suicide, with some evidence that the greater the conflict, the higher the risk. However, limitations of psychological autopsy studies suggest the need for complementary research into life events prior to serious suicide attempts. One study addressed the question of reliability of psychological autopsy indirectly, using information from the investigation of the U.S.S. *Iowa* explosion (see Box 11.3).

The Case of the U.S.S. *Iowa*: Gauging Reliability of the Psychological Autopsy

BOX 11.3

On April 19, 1989, 47 U.S. Navy sailors were killed when an explosion ripped through turret 2 of the U.S.S. *Iowa*. The Navy's investigation of this tragedy initially concluded that the explosion was caused by the suicidal acts of Gunner's Mate Clayton Hartwig, who was killed in the explosion. The major foundation for this conclusion was a psychological autopsy conducted by FBI agents working at the National Center for the Analysis of Violent Crime. The Navy's conclusions were later evaluated by a congressional committee, which commissioned its own panel of 14 psychological and psychiatric experts to review the FBI's analysis. Partly on the basis of this panel's input, the congressional committee rejected the FBI analysis as invalid. Ultimately, the U.S. Navy also concluded that the cause of the explosion could not be determined.

Forensic psychologist Randy Otto and his colleagues asked 24 psychologists and psychiatrists to rate the reports of the 14 experts who reviewed the FBI analysis of the U.S.S. *Iowa* explosion (Otto, Poythress, Starr, & Darkes, 1993). Three raters judged each of the 14 reports, and although they failed to show precise agreement in how they thought the reports should be interpreted, they did achieve a moderate amount of broad agreement in their

Thomas Jarrell/US Navy/DOD/The LIFE Picture Collection/Getty Images

The U.S.S. *Iowa*, damaged in an explosion

ratings. Note, however, that this agreement pertains only to how the raters interpreted the 14 panelists' reports, not to the contents or opinions in the reports themselves.

CRITICAL THOUGHT QUESTION

What are the major challenges in conducting a psychological autopsy—and what kind of forensic mental health assessments in particular include such challenges?

How has testimony about psychological autopsies fared in court? In cases involving workers' compensation claims and questions of whether insurance benefits should be paid, the courts have usually admitted psychological autopsy testimony; in criminal cases or in cases involving the question of whether a person had the mental capacity to execute a will, the courts have been more reluctant to permit the testimony (Ogloff & Otto, 1993). Judges are more hesitant to allow expert testimony in criminal cases than in civil ones, perhaps because the risks of prejudicial testimony are greater when one's liberties can be taken away. One reason for the courts' hesitancy in permitting psychological autopsy testimony in cases involving the validity of wills might be that, in such cases, the state of mind of the deceased is the critical question for the jury. Allowing expert testimony on this matter might therefore be viewed as invading the province of the jury, a perception that judges usually want to avoid.

Child Custody and Parental Fitness

The "Best Interests of the Child" in Custody Disputes

One of the growing areas of forensic psychology involves the evaluation of families for the purpose of recommending the particular custodial arrangement that is in the best interests of a child whose parents are divorcing or separating. The increase in these cases is attributable to two facts. First, about 40–50% of marriages in the United States now end in divorce. As of 2015, 26% of households with children in the United States were single-parent families. There are also a variety of other family arrangements, including children living with two married parents (62%, an all-time low), children living with remarried parents (15%), and those living with parents who are cohabiting (7%) (Pew Research Center, 2015). Therefore, the issue of custody is a practical concern for millions of families. Second, from the end of the 19th century to about the middle of the 20th century, the prevailing assumption was that awarding custody of young children (sometimes called children of "tender years") to their mothers was usually in their best interests. This preference for maternal custody has diminished at the beginning of the 21st century; now many courts want to know about the parenting abilities of each parent before making a decision about custody (Fuhrman & Zibbell, 2012).

Currently, the prevailing standard for custody decisions is the **future best interests of the child**. Although the child's "best interests" must be assessed on a case-by-case basis, the Uniform Marriage and Divorce Act indicates that courts should consider the following criteria: (1) the wishes of the child; (2) the wishes of the child's parents; (3) the relationships between the child and the parents, siblings, and significant others who interact with the child; (4) the child's adjustment at home and school and in the community; and (5) the physical and mental health of the parties involved.

Child custody evaluations usually arise in situations in which divorcing parents disagree about which of them can better meet the needs of their children and should therefore have custody. Most states permit two kinds of custodial arrangements—sole and joint custody, each with two aspects (physical and legal). *Physical custody* refers to the living arrangement, whereas *legal custody* concerns the responsibility for decision-making. In **sole custody**, the child will live only with one parent (although the other parent may be granted visitation rights), and/or all legal decision-making authority for that child will rest with one parent. In **joint custody**, both parents can retain parental rights concerning decisions about the child's general welfare, education, health care, and other matters (this is called joint legal custody), and the child can alternate living in the home of the mother and in the home of the father according to the schedule provided in the custody decision (this is called joint physical custody). Joint custody does not necessarily mean that the child spends equal time with each parent, however. Usually, one parent is designated the residential parent, and the child spends more time living at the home of that parent. In general, families that are functioning better at the time that custody is awarded are more likely to ask for joint custody than families that are experiencing ongoing difficulties (Gunnoe & Braver, 2001).

The three main differences between sole custody and joint custody are as follows:

1. Joint custody distributes the frequency of interaction more evenly between the children and each parent.
2. Joint custody requires more interactions between the divorced parents and generates more demands for cooperation concerning the children.
3. Joint custody results in more alterations in caregiving arrangements, along with more separations and reunions between children and parents (Clingempeel & Reppucci, 1982).

Psychologists have examined the effects of sole custody and joint custody on children and parents. Although the findings are not clear-cut, there appear to be several advantages to joint custody arrangements. In a meta-analysis of 21 studies, Bauserman (1997) concluded that children in joint custody fared better than children in sole custody on a number of measures related to adjustment and interpersonal relations. Fathers benefited from joint custody because they had more frequent contact with their children. Joint custody was advantageous for mothers because it afforded them greater opportunity for courtship; as a result, these mothers re-partnered more rapidly than mothers with sole responsibility for their children, a situation that may be economically beneficial for the children (Gunnoe & Braver, 2001).

Some research has also addressed the impact of having one or both parents who are gay or lesbian on the subsequent adjustment of children in custody following a divorce or other ending of the parental relationship. A review of the legal and empirical literature in this area (Haney-Caron & Heilbrun, 2014) summarized empirical findings on parenting ability, impact on children's sexual orientations, social stigma confronting children, and children's general adjustment. Research to date provides no evidence that lesbian and gay parents differ from heterosexual parents in these domains. The authors recommended that research-informed policy should reflect equitable decisions under the law regarding gay and lesbian parents in the area of child custody—particularly since some judges have expressed concerns about adverse impact on children as a basis for awarding custodial preference to the parent who is not gay or lesbian.

Other evidence on the effects of divorce on children comes from different kinds of research, including long-term longitudinal studies (Hetherington & Kelly, 2002; Wallerstein & Kelly, 1980), large-sample repeated surveys (Furstenberg, Peterson, & Nord, 1983; Zill, Morrison, & Coiro, 1993), smaller studies, retrospective perceptions of parents' separation or divorce (Braver, Ellman, & Fabricius, 2003; Marquardt, 2006), and meta-analyses (Amato, 2001; Amato & Keith, 1991; Bauserman, 2002). Researchers have also looked at the children of never-married parents (Insabella, Williams, & Pruett, 2003). Based on this evidence, it appears that the most significant effects of divorce on children occur in the first year or two. Temporary behavioral changes are frequent (Hetherington, Cox, & Cox, 1982; Wallerstein & Blakeslee, 2003), including problems in emotional regulation, disturbed sleep patterns, behavioral or academic problems, grief reactions, and loyalty conflicts (Wallerstein, Corbin, & Lewis, 1988). Most parents and children return to behavior that is more typical for them after this one- to two-year period (Laumann-Billings & Emery, 2000; Marquardt, 2006).

Both the well-being of the primary parent and the level of parental conflict are major factors influencing outcomes (Hetherington & Kelly, 2002). Children from families in which the parents had a great deal of conflict seem to do better following divorce than do children from low-conflict families (Amato, 2001; Amato, Loomis, & Booth, 1995). Importantly, around 75% of children whose parents divorce will not experience significant developmental challenges or long-term negative effects of the divorce (Kelly & Emery, 2003).

Recent research (Nielsen, 2017) has updated our knowledge about the impact of parental conflict on child custody outcomes. It now appears that parents with joint physical custody do not differ in their cooperativeness or conflict from parents with sole physical custody. Indeed, the quality of the relationship between parents and children are more strongly associated with outcomes than are conflict and poor parenting, except when the conflict is extreme. Accordingly, we should be particularly attentive to helping parents strengthen their relationships with their children as part of divorce and custody actions.

What makes it more or less likely that divorce will adversely affect the children involved? Risk and protective influences have been summarized (Fuhrmann & Zibbell, 2012) as follows.

Risk factors:

- stress of the initial separation (Kelly & Emery, 2003)
- diminished parenting (Hetherington et al., 1982)
- loss of significant relationships (including extended family, e.g., grandparents), and friends (Amato & Booth, 2001)
- multiple moves (including change of schools and loss of friends) (Braver, Ellman, & Fabricius, 2003; Hetherington & Kelly, 2002)
- financial problems (the stress of which can affect parenting style or quality) (Duncan & Hoffman, 1985)
- either parent becoming involved with a new partner (Hetherington & Kelly, 2002; Kelly & Emery, 2003)

Protective factors:

- The custodial parent is competent and well adjusted (Hetherington & Kelly, 2002; Wallerstein & Kelly, 1980).

- The noncustodial parent has regular and consistent contact and (particularly important) takes an active interest in the activities and school performance of the child (Amato & Gilbreth, 1999; Nord, Brimhall, & West, 1997).
- A good relationship between parent and child (Nielsen, 2017).
- The custodial parent has extended family support (Hetherington & Kelly, 2002).

Assessment in Custody Disputes

Many mental health professionals regard child custody cases to be the most ethically and clinically difficult forensic evaluations they perform. First, the emotional stakes are extremely high, and both parents are often willing to spare no expense or tactic in the battle over which of them will win custody. The children involved are usually forced to live—for months, if not years—in an emotional limbo in which they do not know in whose home they will be residing, where they will be going to school, or how often they will see each parent.

Second, a thorough custody evaluation requires that the clinician evaluate the children, both parents, and others who have interacted with the child, such as relatives, teachers, and family health care providers. Often, not all the parties agree to be evaluated or do so only under coercion, resulting in a lengthy and sometimes tense process. Such tension can be increased if the evaluation is requested by the attorney for one of the two divorcing spouses, which may lead the other spouse to perceive the evaluator as unfairly biased in favor of the spouse who retained this evaluator. An alternative arrangement—having the court order the evaluation and designate a neutral expert, with both parties agreeing to this appointment—can help to reduce this perception of bias.

Third, to render a valuable expert opinion, a clinician must be quite knowledgeable—about the children and parents under evaluation, but also about child development, bonding and attachment, family systems, the effects of divorce on children, adult and childhood mental disorders, and several different kinds of testing. Evaluators should also be knowledgeable about scientific evidence regarding the impact of any specific aspects of a particular evaluation, such as parents' sexual orientation (see Haney Caron & Heilbrun, 2014).

Finally, child custody evaluations are often highly adversarial, with each parent trying to expose all the faults of the other and each side vigorously challenging any procedures or opinion by an expert with which it disagrees. Clinicians who conduct custody evaluations must be prepared for challenges to their evaluation methods, scholarly competence, and professional ethics. Even evaluators who operate under court appointment may have their findings challenged in some cases.

There are three major approaches to appointing evaluators: (1) a judge can appoint one clinician to conduct a custody evaluation that is available to all the parties, (2) each side can retain its own expert to conduct independent evaluations, or (3) the litigants can agree to share the expenses of hiring an expert to conduct one evaluation (Fuhrmann & Zibbell, 2012). Historically, most evaluators have preferred either the first or the third option because of the pressures that result when separate experts are hired by each side (Keilin & Bloom, 1986). Attorneys tend to agree with this preference, believing that the second option leads to greater bias (LaFortune & Carpenter, 1998).

Specific guidelines for conducting custody evaluations have been developed by the American Psychological Association (2009), the Association of Family and Conciliation Courts (AFCC, 2006a, 2016), and the American Academy of Child and Adolescent Psychiatry (AACAP, 1997; Kraus, Thomas, & the CQI, 2011). Although the methods used in custody evaluations vary depending on the specific issues in each case, most evaluations include the following components: (1) clinical, social history, and mental status interviews of the parents and the children; (2) standardized testing of the parents and the children; (3) observation of interactions between each parent and the children, especially when the children are minors; (4) assessments or interviews with other people who have had opportunities to observe the family (adult children of the parents, grandparents, neighbors, the family physician, schoolteachers, and other observers); and (5) documents or records that might be relevant to the case (medical records of children and parents, report cards, and arrest records).

In any forensic psychological evaluation, it is useful to include a specialized tool that has been developed to measure capacities associated with the legal decision. In child custody evaluations, these include parenting skills and capacities (for the parents) and needs (for the children). Although specialized approaches are available for child custody evaluations, these tests are of questionable validity (see Melton et al., 2007, Otto & Edens, 2003), so it remains for the field to develop a specialized measure that is consistent with the principles of scientific test development.

Custody evaluations are time-consuming. In a national survey of mental health professionals who conducted child custody evaluations, Ackerman and Ackerman (1997) found that experts spent an average of about 30 hours on each evaluation, which, another study found, may even have increased (Brey, 2009). Much of this time was devoted to interviewing and observing the parties in various combinations. In fact, more than two-thirds of the respondents indicated that they conducted individual interviews with each parent and each child, observed each parent interacting (separately) with each child, and conducted formal psychological testing of the parents and the children.

Experts also reported how often they recommended different kinds of custodial arrangements (Keilin & Bloom, 1986). Joint legal custody (parents share the decision-making, but one parent maintains primary physical custody) was the most common recommendation (42.8%), and sole custody without visitation was the least often recommended alternative (4.6%). Sole custody with visitation (30.4%) and joint physical custody (21.7%) were among the other preferred recommendations. These findings were replicated and expanded in a subsequent study (Ackerman & Ackerman, 1997).

There have been a number of problems associated with child custody evaluations in terms of scientific support and relevance of measures. These have been summarized as follows: (a) inadequate scientific support for tests specifically developed to assess questions relevant to custody; (b) certain constructs ("parent alienation syndrome," for example) also having very poor scientific support; (c) limited relevance of most psychological tests to the main questions that are part of child custody litigation; and (d) little scientific data on other important questions, such as the impact of children's wishes or how very young children are affected by overnight visits (Emery, Otto, & O'Donohue, 2005). Clearly this is an area that is badly in need of further scientific study.

In recent years, divorced couples have sometimes returned to court to ask judges to resolve both ongoing and novel disputes. For example, Pamela Peck, a divorced mother, went to family court in Dallas to seek an injunction that would ban her ex-husband's girlfriend from spending the night at his house when his son was there. A Texas judge ruled in her favor, enjoining both parties from having overnight guests of the opposite sex when "in possession of" their nine-year-old son. One of the thorniest custody issues is whether a custodial parent can relocate. An example of a "move-away case" is described in Box 11.4.

Because divorce is a potent stressor for children and because protracted custody battles tend to leave a trail of emotionally battered family members in their wake, increasing attention is being given to helping parents and children cope with these transitions or to finding

---

The Case of *Ciesluk v. Ciesluk:* Can a Custodial Parent Move Away?

BOX 11.4

When Michelle and Christopher Ciesluk were divorced in 2002, they arranged to share joint legal custody of their son, Connor, who lived primarily with his mother. But when Michelle Ciesluk lost her job with Sprint in early 2003, and the company offered to rehire her, provided that she was willing to move from Colorado to Arizona, Christopher Ciesluk objected. He opposed the move, fearing he would lose any relationship with his son and would miss his son's school and athletic activities. Unfortunately for Ms. Ciesluk, neither the Colorado legislature nor the courts made it easy for her. In 2001, the legislature abolished a legal presumption that a custodial parent has the right to move away, and an appellate court ruled that a parent who wishes to move must demonstrate a *direct* beneficial effect on the child. (The more commonly used test requires the parent to show that the move would have

an *indirect* effect on the child, typically by enhancing the custodial parent's job opportunities.) Michelle Ciesluk was not able to meet that test, so she remained in Colorado with her son, working for $10 an hour as an administrative assistant and feeling that her "whole life is on hold" (Eaton, 2004). In 2005, the Colorado Supreme Court reversed the decision by the appellate court and sent the case back to the trial court (*Ciesluk v. Ciesluk*, 2005).

CRITICAL THOUGHT QUESTION

In the Ciesluk case, which of the risk factors for adverse childhood adjustment are increased by each of the alternatives (mother moving versus mother staying)? Which of the protective factors are increased by each alternative?

alternatives to custody fights (Grych & Fincham, 1992; Kelly, 1996; Silver & Silver, 2009). Many judges require divorcing couples to attempt to settle issues of custody, visitation, and support through mediation, a form of alternative dispute resolution that minimizes the adversarial quality of the typical custody dispute. If mediation fails, the couple can return to court and have the judge decide the issues. The benefits of custody mediation are that resolutions are reached more quickly, and with better compliance among the participants, than with adversarial procedures.

The Association of Family and Conciliation Courts (2000a) has developed model standards for the practice of family and divorce mediation, indicating that a mediator shall (among other things):

- Recognize that mediation is based on the principle of self-determination by the participants.
- Conduct the mediation process in an impartial manner; disclose all actual and potential grounds of bias and conflicts of interest reasonably known to the mediator; structure the mediation process so that participants make decisions based on sufficient information and knowledge.
- Assist participants in determining how to promote the best interests of children.
- Recognize a family situation involving child abuse or neglect or domestic violence and take appropriate steps to shape the mediation process accordingly.
- Suspend or terminate the mediation process when the mediator reasonably believes that a participant is unable to effectively participate or for other compelling reasons.

Research generally supports the favorable adjustment of those who go through mediation. Two reviews of a decade of research (Hahn & Kleist, 2000; Kelly, 1996) indicate that families that go through mediation to determine custody have better adjustment than those going through the more traditional child custody litigation process. A more recent meta-analysis (Shaw, 2010) showed that mediation is a beneficial alternative to litigation for couples who are divorcing. Outcomes considered in this meta-analysis include satisfaction with process and outcome, emotional satisfaction, spousal relationship, and understanding children's needs.

Assessing Fitness to Be a Parent

Evaluations of parental fitness involve different questions than those involved in the typical custody dispute (Condie, 2003). In every state in the United States, the agency responsible for the protection of children will intervene if it receives a credible report that a child is being abused or neglected. After an investigation, the agency might file a petition asking a court to remove the child from the home and arrange placement with a relative or in foster care. In such cases, the issue before the court is whether the child should be left with the parents or removed from the home because of parental unfitness.

The question for the evaluator is what arrangement protects the child's well-being, while properly respecting the rights of the parents. Although parental rights are important, the state must protect children from parents who cannot or will not provide adequate food, shelter, and supervision. The state must also protect children from parents who abuse them, physically or psychologically. A clinician might recommend that the child be placed temporarily in foster care and that the parents receive training in parenting skills as a condition of having the child returned to them. In extreme cases—those in which parents abandon a child or are clearly incapable of caring for a child—the state might seek to terminate parental rights. This is done most often when relatives or others wish to adopt the child (Heilbrun, DeMatteo, Brooks-Holliday, & LaDuke, 2014).

In an interesting twist on the usual circumstances of termination cases, 12-year-old Gregory Kingsley asked a Florida judge in 1992 to terminate his parents' right to function as parents on his behalf. Gregory had been removed from his home and placed in foster care, but when the state attempted to return him to his birth parents, Gregory objected and tried to sever his parents' ties to him. Courts had never before confronted the question of whether a 12-year-old can bring a termination petition, but both the trial judge and an appellate court ruled in Gregory's favor (Haugaard & Avery, 2002).

Civil Commitment and Risk Assessment

All 50 states and the District of Columbia have **civil commitment** laws that authorize the custody and restraint of persons who, as a result of mental illness, are a danger to themselves or others or who are so gravely disabled that they cannot care for themselves. This restraint is usually accomplished by compulsory commitment to a mental hospital. The courts also provide safeguards and rules for how these involuntary commitments are to be accomplished.

Many of these procedures were instituted in the 1970s, in response to a concern that in the 1950s and

1960s it was too easy to commit people to state psychiatric facilities. At that time, people who were mentally ill could be involuntarily committed whenever the state believed they needed treatment. Beginning around 1970, commitment proceedings began to be reformed, resulting in more legal rights for the mentally ill to resist compulsory commitment. A key case in this reform movement was *O'Connor v. Donaldson* (1975), in which the Supreme Court held that mental illness and a need for treatment were insufficient justifications for involuntarily committing mentally ill persons who were not dangerous.

Similar limits on involuntary hospitalizations were upheld by the Supreme Court in the 1990s (e.g., *Foucha v. Louisiana*, 1992). The standard for commitment changed from mental illness combined with a need for treatment, to mental illness that is associated with dangerousness or a grave lack of ability to care for oneself. This narrowing of the commitment standard, along with other societal influences during the last 40 years (e.g., the community mental health movement, deinstitutionalization), has resulted in fewer public hospital beds for mental health treatment, and shorter hospital stays.

Although the legislative changes of the 1970s were intended to protect the rights of the mentally ill, an exclusive concern with rights can sometimes leave patients without adequate care, housing, or the effective psychiatric treatment that can be provided in some hospitals (Turkheimer & Parry, 1992; Wexler, 1992). Resources in the community devoted to treatment and recovery for individuals with mental illness—focusing on such necessities as housing and employment as well as mental health care and case management—could have replaced the need for extended hospital care in most cases. Unfortunately, however, community-based resources for individuals with mental illness have not been increased substantially following the downsizing of public psychiatric hospitals, starting in the 1970s and continuing to the present. As a consequence, some individuals have not had access to adequate treatment in either hospitals or in the community during these decades (Leifman & Coffey, 2015).

Four Types of Commitment Procedures

The law permits four types of civil commitment: (1) emergency detention, (2) voluntary inpatient commitment, (3) involuntary inpatient commitment, and (4) outpatient commitment. Emergency detention is the means by which most individuals are initially admitted to hospitals.

A police officer, a mental health professional, or sometimes a private citizen can initiate involuntary detention of another person. Usually, the cause is actual or anticipated harmful behavior by the patient either against self (e.g., attempted suicide) or against others. An examination is performed by a physician or a qualified mental health professional. Patients committed on an emergency basis can be detained for only a specified length of time—usually two or three days—before a review takes place. At that time a preliminary hearing must be held before the patient can be confined any longer.

A person may volunteer to enter a psychiatric hospital, although he or she still must meet the criteria for hospitalization (typically some version of "mentally ill and in need of treatment"), but even those who are being hospitalized "voluntarily" may feel pressure from family, mental health personnel, or the legal system to enter the hospital. Individuals who have been provided with more information and given the chance to express their views report feeling less coercion, regardless of whether they are voluntarily or involuntarily hospitalized (Dennis & Monahan, 1996). While voluntarily hospitalized, the patient may find that the hospital has instigated commitment proceedings to challenge or delay release.

The third type of commitment—involuntary inpatient commitment—requires a court order. The criteria for obtaining an involuntary civil commitment vary from state to state; in general, however, the person must be mentally ill and must also be dangerous to self and others, or so gravely disabled as to be unable to provide for his or her own basic needs. Although the criterion of "dangerousness" is the most often discussed standard and therefore is deemed the most important for involuntary hospitalization, grave disability is the standard that determines most commitments (Turkheimer & Parry, 1992).

To obtain an involuntary commitment, the concerned persons must petition the court for a professional examination of the individual in question. A formal court hearing usually follows the examination. In most states, the hearing is mandatory, and persons whose commitment is sought can call witnesses and have their lawyer cross-examine witnesses who testify against them.

A fourth type of commitment procedure, known as outpatient commitment, is available in nearly all states and allows a patient to be mandated to receive treatment in an outpatient setting, such as a community mental health center, rather than in a hospital (Hiday & Goodman, 1982). Outpatient commitment often involves conditional release from a hospital. That is, formerly hospitalized patients are ordered to continue treatment in the community. It may also be used prior to hospitalization, as an alternative to inpatient commitment. This approach appears to have some promise. One study (Pollack, McFarland, Mahler, & Kovas, 2005) found that those released from involuntary hospitalization on outpatient commitment were more likely (relative to a group released without any kind of commitment) to use outpatient and residential mental health services and psychotropic medication. However, outpatient commitment should not simply be used as a mechanism for ensuring compliance with treatment if the individual does not meet the commitment criteria (which typically have a public safety component).

Dangerousness and Risk Assessment

Dangerousness is one of the central constructs of mental health law. Whether a person is now or could in the future be dangerous is an issue that underlies many decisions in our system of justice, including questions of civil commitment. Although the law often uses the terms *dangerous* and *dangerousness*, these terms are difficult to define. They actually merge three distinct constructs: (1) risk factors (variables associated with the probability that violence or aggression will occur), (2) harm (the nature and severity of predicted and actual aggression), and (3) risk level (the probability that harm will occur) (National Research Council, 1989). In some combination, these factors provide a major justification for involuntarily committing the mentally ill to hospitals.

The construct of dangerousness to others recurs throughout the law. Dangerousness is the basis for requiring therapists to protect third parties from possible acts of violence against them by the patients of these therapists. It is also a reason for denying bail to certain defendants and the justification for hospitalizing defendants after they have been found not guilty by reason of insanity. Some states also use future dangerousness as one factor a jury can consider when deciding whether to sentence a convicted murderer to life in prison or death by execution.

Difficulties in Assessing Dangerousness

Because dangerousness is hard to define, we prefer to use the term *violence risk* and will do so throughout the remainder of this chapter. Can mental health experts accurately assess a person's present violence risk and then predict whether that person will be violent in the future? Is mental illness a sign that a person is likely to be violent? Do certain types of mental illness make a person more prone to violent behavior? These questions have been examined extensively by researchers for more than three decades, and they are at the heart of many real-life cases. For example, should the mental health professionals who treated John Hinckley have predicted that he posed a danger to President Reagan? What about Jeffrey Dahmer, who killed a number of young men and had sex with the bodies? Was his brutal behavior predictable, given his early psychological problems?

Clinicians who attempt to answer these questions perform **risk assessments**; using the best available data and research, they try to predict which persons are and which are not likely to behave violently in certain circumstances, give some estimate of the risk for violence, and offer suggestions on how to reduce the risk (Heilbrun, 2009; Monahan & Steadman, 1994).

Many factors make such predictions difficult. For example, the base rate of violence in some groups is low, so clinicians are being asked to predict a phenomenon that rarely occurs. The clinical assessments of persons assessed for violence risk are often conducted in hospitals or prisons, whereas the environment where violence is being predicted is the community. The predictions have often been for long-term risk, which is harder to predict than violence risk over a shorter time frame.

The original consensus of researchers was that clinicians could not accurately predict future violence. Leading scholars such as John Monahan (1984) summarized the research this way: "In one study after another, the same conclusion emerges: For every correct prediction of violence, there are numerous incorrect predictions" (Pfohl, 1984). Another early summary of the research on clinicians' ability to predict violence was that their predictions were wrong in two of every three cases in which a "yes" prediction of future violence was made.

Subsequent research changed the early pessimism about clinicians' ability to predict violence, however. Researchers have learned that these predictions can sometimes reach moderate to good levels of accuracy under certain conditions (Borum, 1996; Otto & Douglas, 2010). Specifically, clinicians who consider factors that are empirically related to future violence can predict such violence considerably better than they could before 1990 (Heilbrun, 2009). Specifically, when clinicians have information about a range of historical, personal, and environmental variables related to violence, when they limit their predictions to specific kinds of violent behavior, and when they concentrate on appraising risks in certain settings rather than in all situations, they can assess violence risk with a fair degree of accuracy. Although they still make a large number of errors, they do significantly better than chance.

One of the most important advances in the area of risk assessment has involved the development and use of specialized risk assessment tools (Heilbrun, 2009). A number of specialized tools are now available (Otto & Douglas, 2010), some of which are actuarial. An actuarial tool (such as the Violence Risk Appraisal Guide; Harris, Rice, & Quinsey, 1993) uses specified risk factors that are rated and scored, with scores being combined into a final score that is then applied to the

prediction in a way that is specified by a formula (which in turn has been developed through empirical research). Other tools (such as the HCR-20^{V3}, which measures historical, clinical, and risk management variables [Douglas, Hart, Webster, & Belfrage, 2013]) employ "structured professional judgment." They do not combine scores on included variables to yield a total score. Rather, the evaluator is asked to make a judgment about risk in light of the status of these risk factors. Evidence indicates that good actuarial and structured professional judgment approaches to risk assessment are comparably accurate in predictions of violence (Heilbrun, Douglas, & Yasuhara, 2009).

Summary

1. **What problems are associated with expert testimony, and what reforms have been proposed?** The main objections to expert testimony are that it is too adversarial and thus not impartial, introduces irrelevant information, and is often founded on an insufficient scientific base that may also be influenced by cognitive biases that affect human decision-making more generally. Proposed reforms have focused on using greater structure by linking testimony to evaluation reports that are consistent with foundational principles. Following such principles reduces the potential influence of factors such as retention bias and more general cognitive bias, provides judges with more information about the scientific foundation of expert testimony, and limits the scope of expert testimony to the highly relevant aspects of the evaluation. Limiting such testimony's scope and having judges consider the scientific foundation more carefully are proposals that have been implemented.

2. **Under what conditions can a plaintiff be compensated for psychological damages?** Plaintiffs can seek damages in civil trials if they allege that they have been victimized by a tort, which is a wrongful act that must be proved to have caused them harm. Although the law has historically been skeptical of claims for psychological harm and emotional distress unless they are accompanied by physical injuries, the more recent trend has been to allow plaintiffs to be compensated for emotional

damages (without any physical injuries) resulting from intentionally outrageous or negligent conduct.

3. **What is workers' compensation, and how do mental health professionals participate in such cases?** Workers' compensation is a no-fault system now used by all states and in the federal system to provide a streamlined alternative for determining the compensation of workers who are injured in the course of their jobs. Formal trials are not held nor juries used in workers' compensation cases. Psychologists may testify in workers' compensation hearings about the extent, cause, and likely prognosis for psychological problems that have developed following a physical injury and/or work-related stress.

4. **What capacities are involved in civil competence?** Questions of civil competence focus on whether an individual has the mental capacity to understand information that is relevant to decision-making in a given situation and then make an informed choice about what to do. The issue of civil competence is raised when it is not clear that an individual is capable of meeting the demands of a given task specified under civil law. Examples of such tasks include giving informed consent to current or future medical treatments, and executing a will.

5. **What criteria are used for decisions about disputes involving child custody or parental fitness?** The best interest of the child is the main criterion

applied to disputes about which parent should have custody of a child following divorce. Evaluations of parental fitness address a different question: Should a parent's custody of a child be limited or terminated because of indications of parental unfitness? Many mental health professionals regard custody and parental fitness assessments as the most difficult evaluations they perform. For this reason, and in an attempt to reduce the stress of custody battles, custody mediation has been developed as a less adversarial means of resolving these disputes.

6. *What steps are taken in civil commitment, and how well can clinicians assess dangerousness or the risk of violent behavior, a key criterion for civil commitment?* People who are considered gravely disabled or dangerous to themselves or others may be committed to a state psychiatric hospital against their will, but they have the right to a hearing shortly thereafter to determine whether they should be retained. After (or instead of) being hospitalized, some patients may be placed on outpatient commitment. Long-term predictions of violent behavior are more difficult to make with accuracy, but there is a reliable association among historical, personal, and environmental factors and dangerous behavior that provides a basis for reasonably accurate short-term assessments of risk. The use of structured risk assessment, whether through the use of a specialized actuarial risk assessment measure or a tool using structured professional judgment, can increase predictive accuracy beyond what is possible with unstructured judgment.

Key Terms

advance medical directives

breached duty

civil commitment

civil competencies

compensatory damages

dangerousness

duty

future best interests of the child

harm

intentional behavior

joint custody

malingering

negligence

proximate cause

psychological autopsies

punitive damages

risk assessments

sole custody

testamentary capacity

tort

12 Preparing for Trials

ORIENTING QUESTIONS

1. How do juries' verdicts differ from those of judges?
2. What does the legal system seek in trial juries?
3. What stands in the way of jury representativeness?
4. What procedures are used in *voir dire*?
5. What personality and attitudinal characteristics of jurors, if any, are related to their verdicts?

How effective are lawyers at responding to these characteristics?

6. What role do trial consultants play in a trial?
7. In what ways does pre-trial publicity pose a danger to fair trials? How can these dangers be reduced?

Most disputes are resolved before they reach a courthouse because they are diverted from the criminal justice system, plea bargained, or settled through alternative dispute resolution mechanisms such as mediation and negotiation. But some civil and criminal cases are resolved through a trial; moreover, the trial is a foundational aspect of our legal system and Constitution. Before a trial commences, various issues must be resolved. We address three of these issues in this chapter: (1) whether the case should be decided by a jury or a judge; (2) if the choice is a jury, how a representative group of fair-minded citizens can be chosen to serve as jurors; and (3) what happens when those citizens are exposed to information about the case prior to setting foot in a courtroom. Each of these topics has been examined by psychological scientists. ●

Who Should Decide: Jury or Judge?

Before a trial begins, one choice looms large for all criminal defendants and most civil plaintiffs: should the case be heard by a judge or a jury? If the opposing party consents, defendants and plaintiffs can opt to have the verdict decided by a judge, in a proceeding called a **bench trial**. Edward Nero, a Baltimore police officer involved in the 2015 arrest of Freddie Gray, a 25-year-old Black man who died while in police custody, requested a bench trial. It is tempting to say that Nero gambled correctly, as he was acquitted of all charges by Judge Barry Williams. But did he? Might he have been equally (or even more) likely to have been acquitted by a jury? Later in this section we present data on the rates of conviction by juries versus judges that will help answer this question.

The preference for a bench trial or a jury trial obviously involves thoughts of who will issue the most favorable ruling (Bornstein & Greene, 2017). But it may be influenced by race and ethnicity as well. When researchers asked approximately 1,500 Texas residents whether they would favor a bench trial or a jury trial, African Americans and Hispanics showed less support for a jury trial than Whites, perhaps reflecting the belief that the majority group's views, including any prejudices and biases, might predominate during deliberations. Minority group members may doubt that a jury is composed of a cross-section of the community who would be able to grasp their situations and understand their perspectives. Thus, judges appear to be the less risky choice (Rose, Ellison, & Diamond, 2008).

How Judges and Juries Compare

In general, does it matter who decides? Do juries and judges generally agree with each other? When they disagree, can we say who made the better decision? Of course, jury verdicts are not systematically compared against some "correct," back-of-the-book answer—even if

In bench trials, a judge determines the verdict.

Alina555/E+/Getty Images

there were such a thing (which there is not!). Fortunately, we have some data that illustrate how frequently judges and jurors agree and why they might disagree.

The groundbreaking data were collected by Harry Kalven and Hans Zeisel (1966), professors at the University of Chicago, who carried out an extensive survey of the outcomes of jury trials. In a classic application of the methods of social science to understand legal decisions, Kalven and Zeisel asked each district court judge in the United States to provide information about recent jury trials over which he or she had presided. Of approximately 3,500 judges, only about 500 responded to a detailed questionnaire. But some judges provided information about a large number of trials, so the database consisted of approximately 3,500 trials.

Two questions are relevant to our discussion: (1) What was the jury's verdict? (2) Did the judge agree? In criminal trials, the judges reported that their verdict would have been the same as the jury's actual verdict in 75% of the cases (see Table 12.1 for detailed results). Thus, in three-fourths of the trials, two independent fact-finding agents would have brought forth the same result. Similar consistency was found for civil trials, as illustrated in Table 12.2. This level of agreement suggests that jurors are not deviating to a great extent from their mandate to follow the law and use only the judge's instructions plus the actual evidence to reach their verdict.

One might speculate on an optimal level of agreement between judge and jury. What if they agreed 100% of the time? Obviously, that outcome would reflect no difference whatsoever between judges' and juries' verdicts. But if judge and jury agreed only 50% of the time, given only two possible outcomes of guilty and not guilty (putting aside "hung" juries momentarily), it would reflect a level of agreement no better than chance. (Two independent agents, choosing yes or no at random, would agree 50% of the time by chance alone.)

TABLE 12.1   Agreement of judges' and juries' verdicts based on 3,576 criminal trials (in percentage of all trials). Jury verdicts shown in columns; judge verdicts shown in rows

Judge Verdict	Jury Verdict		
	Acquit	Convict	Hung
Acquit	**13.4**	2.2	1.1
Convict	16.9	**62.0**	4.4

Source: Adapted from Kalven and Zeisel (1966, p. 56). Figures in bold show cases in which judge and jury agreed on the verdict.

TABLE 12.2   Agreement of judges' and juries' decisions in civil trials (as percentage of all trials). Jury verdicts shown in columns; judge verdicts shown in rows

Judge Verdict	Jury Verdict	
	Plaintiff	Defendant
Plaintiff	**47**	10
Defendant	12	**31**

Source: Adapted from Kalven and Zeisel (1966, p. 63). Figures in bold show cases in which judge and jury agreed on the verdict.

Appropriately enough, the 75% level of agreement is halfway between chance and perfect agreement.

Among the 25% of the criminal cases in which there was disagreement, 5.5% resulted in hung juries; that is, the jury members could not agree on a verdict. Thus, it is more appropriate to say that in only 19.5% of the criminal cases did the jury return a guilty verdict where the judge would have ruled not guilty, or vice versa.

In most of these discrepant decisions, the jury was more lenient than the judge. The judge would have convicted the defendant in 83.3% of these cases, whereas the jury convicted in only 64.2% of them. For every trial in which the jury convicted and the judge would have acquitted, there were almost eight trials in which the reverse was true.

The level of agreement between the jury and the judge was also high in civil trials, as shown in Table 12.2. Judges reported that their verdict would have favored the side favored by the jury in 78% of the civil suits analyzed by Kalven and Zeisel. Also important is the nearly equal likelihood of finding for the plaintiff; the jury ruled for the plaintiff in 59% of the cases, whereas the judge did so in 57%.

These figures are a healthy data-based response to the stereotype that juries are swayed by sympathetic plaintiffs, particularly in cases involving defective products or negligent doctors (Bornstein & Greene, 2017). In fact, in certain kinds of cases, plaintiffs who go to trial before juries win infrequently.

Juries do occasionally make high awards to injured plaintiffs, sometimes higher than what judges would award (Hersch & Viscusi, 2004). What's more, media tend to report these uncharacteristically large damage awards (Kritzer & Drechsel, 2012). But in controlled studies, most juries make decisions—verdicts and awards—quite like those made by judges and experienced lawyers. There is little evidence that juries are especially pro-plaintiff, as several critics have claimed. In fact, some would argue that because the jury can apply its sense of community standards to a case, their award of damages in a civil case might actually be more fitting than a judge's award: "The appreciation of pain and suffering, and the likely impact on an individual's life and his or her ability to earn a living, are not matters which judges are any more qualified to assess than is a member of the public applying his or her life experience" (Watson, 1996, p. 457).

Determinants of Discrepancies

What accounts for the discrepancies between judge and jury? Are jurors less competent than judges and less able to apply the law in predictable ways? Or are there other, subtler factors at work? Kalven and Zeisel attempted to answer these questions by delving more deeply into the judges' reactions to the cases and comparing them to the juries' verdicts.

A few of the jury–judge discrepancies resulted from facts that one party knew but the other did not. For example, in several cases, the judge was aware of the defendant's prior arrest record (a matter not introduced into evidence) and would have found him guilty, but the jury acquitted him. The reverse situation can also occur. Especially in a small community, a member of the jury might share with fellow jurors some information about a witness or a defendant that was not part of evidence and was not known to the judge at the time.

A second, smaller source of judge/jury discrepancies was the relative effectiveness of the two attorneys. In some trials, the jury was apparently swayed by the superiority of one lawyer over the other and produced a verdict that was, at least in the judge's opinion, contrary to the weight of the evidence. But it is not surprising that some number of jury verdicts would be determined by this extralegal factor, because jurors spend considerable time attending to the preparedness and demeanor of the attorneys.

Perhaps the most important explanation of judge–jury differences, accounting for roughly half of the disagreements, involves what Kalven and Zeisel called **jury sentiments**. They used this term to cover situations in which, *in the judge's view*, the jury's verdict was detrimentally affected by factors beyond the evidence and the law. (There is an implicit assumption here that the judge's decision was free of sentiments—a dubious claim, given that judges are all too human and subject to the same predispositions as most jurors.)

Jurors' sentiments play a role in decision-making when jurors believe that the "crime" is just too trivial for any punishment or at least for the expected punishment, and find the defendant not guilty to ensure that he or she will not be punished. In one case included in the Kalven and Zeisel study, a man was brought to trial for stealing two hot dogs. Because this was his second crime, he would have been sentenced to prison. Whereas the judge would have found him guilty, the jury voted 10–2 for acquittal.

In other instances, jurors believe that the defendant has already been sufficiently sanctioned, and therefore punishment by the legal system is unnecessary. In a case of income tax evasion, the following series of misfortunes plagued the defendant between the crime and the trial: "His home burned, he was seriously injured, and his son was killed. Later he lost his leg, his wife became seriously ill, and several major operations were necessary … his wife gave birth to a child who was both blind and spastic" (Kalven & Zeisel, 1966, p. 305). The jury found the defendant not guilty of income tax evasion, apparently concluding that he had already suffered divine retribution. The judge would have found him guilty.

Jurors sometime acquit (when judges would have convicted) because they believe that a law is unfair. In trials for the sale of beer and liquor to minors who were in the military, juries concluded that there was minimal social harm. Apparently they felt that if a young man can be forced to die for his country, "he can buy and consume a bottle of beer" (Kalven & Zeisel, 1966, p. 273). Jury sentiments have surfaced in many cases involving "unpopular" crimes—for example, small misdemeanors such as traffic offenses and arguably victimless crimes such as prostitution. "Why waste our time over such minor affairs?" they might have been thinking.

So jury–judge discrepancies should probably not be attributed to a lack of competence on the part of juries. Such disagreements are more appropriately attributed to the jury's interest in fairness, or its consideration of a range of factors that are broader than those considered by an individual judge (Shuman & Champagne, 1997).

The study by Kalven and Zeisel was a massive undertaking. But the actual data were collected between 1954 and 1961, and in the intervening decades, the methodological limitations of the study have become increasingly apparent:

1. Judges were permitted to choose which trial or trials they reported. Did they tend to pick those cases in which they disagreed with the jury, thus causing the results to misrepresent the true extent of judge/jury disagreement?

2. Only approximately 500 judges out of 3,500 provided responses to the survey, leading us to question how well these results can be generalized to the entire population of judges and juries.

3. The membership of juries has changed; they are more heterogeneous today than in the past. This increased diversity might increase their rate *of disagreement* with the judge's position because their broader experiences and cultural differences might give them insights or perspectives on the trial evidence to which judges do not have access (Hans & Vidmar, 1986). For example, a jury of African Americans may be less likely than a White judge to believe a White police officer's testimony that a drug dealer "dropped" a bag of crack cocaine.

4. As for *causes* of discrepancies between verdicts by the judge and jury, we have only the judge's beliefs about the jurors' feelings and sentiments (Hans & Vidmar, 1991).

Newer Data on Judge/Jury Differences

Updating Criminal Case Comparisons A replication of this study was long overdue when researchers at the National Center for State Courts collected data from jurors, judges, and attorneys in more than 350 trials in four jurisdictions: Los Angeles, Phoenix, the Bronx (in New York City), and the District of Columbia (Eisenberg et al., 2005). They examined some of the same issues that Kalven and Zeisel had explored, including how often judges and juries agreed on verdicts in criminal trials.

Participants in felony trials completed questionnaires that asked about preferred verdicts and their evaluation of the evidence. There was a very high response rate (questionnaires were returned in 89% of cases), so we can be fairly certain that the data are representative of most trials. As before, judges stated, prior to hearing the juries' verdicts, whether they would acquit or convict and what they thought about the evidence. One obvious advantage of this study over its predecessor is that all groups (judges, attorneys, and jurors alike) gave their views of the evidence, thus reducing an important concern about Kalven and Zeisel's work—that all the information about a trial came from the judge.

The most striking finding was how closely the new results mirrored those of the earlier study. The rate of jury/judge agreement was 70% (compared to Kalven and Zeisel's 75%). When there was disagreement, it also mirrored the earlier asymmetry: Juries were more

lenient. They were more likely to acquit when judges opted to convict than they were to convict when judges would have acquitted (see Table 12.3).

Further scrutiny of the data collected by the National Center for State Courts revealed the circumstances in which jurors were more likely than judges to return "not guilty" verdicts (Givelber & Farrell, 2008). Jurors were more impressed than judges by the presence of a third-party defense witness (someone other than the defendant). Thus, when the defendant *and* another defense witness testified, jurors were 50% more likely than judges to acquit. Jurors were also impressed by the absence of a prior criminal record: when the defendant and another defense witness both testified *and* when the defendant had no prior record, jurors were 90% more likely to acquit!

Juries are also more lenient than judges in death penalty cases. Although the Supreme Court has ruled that only juries may impose a death sentence (*Ring v. Arizona*, 2002), this was not always so. Therefore, it is possible to compare sentencing outcomes from the era when judges made decisions and the period when juries did. Hans and her colleagues (2015) conducted a historical analysis of all 146 capital trial outcomes in Delaware from 1997 to 2007 and found that judges were significantly more likely than juries to impose a death sentence.

A reasonable explanation for these differences is that jurors and judges assume their roles differently. While jury duty is a unique experience for a juror, judges have probably heard it all (or most of it) before. So jurors may take more seriously their instruction to acquit unless the prosecution can prove the case beyond a reasonable doubt, may feel sympathy for someone in the defendant's situation, and may possess a common-sense understanding of what motivates people to act impulsively.

TABLE 12.3 Agreement of judges' and juries' verdicts based on 350 trials (National Center for State Court data, in percentage of all trials). Jury verdicts shown in columns; judge verdicts shown in rows

Judge Verdict	Jury Verdict		
	Acquit	**Convict**	**Hung**
Acquit	**11.6**	5.0	1.9
Convict	16.0	**58.5**	6.9

Source: Adapted from Eisenberg et al. (2005). Figures in bold show cases in which judge and jury agreed on the verdict.

Updating Civil Case Comparisons. There are also newer findings on how judges compare to juries in civil cases. One of the largest studies examined plaintiffs' win rates (the proportion of cases in which the verdict favored the plaintiff) in federal cases tried before either juries or judges from 1979 to 1989 (Clermont & Eisenberg, 1992). For many types of cases, including contracts, property damage, civil rights, and labor disputes, plaintiffs' win rates were equivalent regardless of who decided.

But differences emerged in two types of cases—products liability and medical malpractice—where plaintiffs had more success with judges (48% win rate) than with juries (28% win rate). Researchers attributed these differences to **selection effects** by which the selection of cases tried by juries differed in important ways from those tried by judges. Because defense lawyers expected juries to be biased in favor of plaintiffs, they tended to settle cases in which the plaintiff had a strong case. That meant that on average, juries were left to decide relatively weaker cases for the plaintiff and appeared to make different decisions than judges. The selection effect makes it rather difficult to compare judge verdicts and jury verdicts in different cases because features of the cases themselves, rather than the decision makers, could explain any discrepancies (Bornstein & Greene, 2017).

A related question is whether jury awards for punitive damages are different from awards assessed by judges, and whether the two groups differ on the reasons for those awards. Punitive damage awards are intended to punish and deter corporations that have engaged in serious wrongdoing. Some punitive damage awards have been very high, and the Supreme Court has ruled on several occasions about whether they were excessively high.

A comprehensive study of jury/judge agreement on punitive damages, conducted by Theodore Eisenberg and his colleagues (Eisenberg, LaFountain, Ostrom, Rottman, & Wells, 2002), analyzed data from more than 9,000 trials that ended in 1996 in 45 of the nation's largest trial courts. The primary finding was that judges and juries did not differ substantially in these cases. They awarded punitive damages at about the same rate (i.e., in only 4–5% of cases), although the range of the jury awards was somewhat greater than that of the judicial awards.

These results call into question the notion that juries are unable to set reasonable limits on punitive damages. In fact, jurors do about as well as judges in attending to the relevant evidence in these cases

and setting aside any sympathy for the plaintiff. They tend to focus on the factors that *should* matter to the determination of punitive damages, such as the actions of the defendant, rather than factors that *should not*, such as the extent of harm to the plaintiff (Robbennolt, 2002).

Returning to the question we posed earlier—whether jurors perform as well as judges when deciding damage awards—we find little evidence that jurors' reasoning is much different from that of judges. Some studies suggest that jurors render erratic and unpredictable awards, in part because their decision-making is influenced by various cognitive biases (see, e.g., Sunstein, Hastie, Payne, Schkade, & Viscusi, 2002). But judges are also human, and apparently are affected by the same cognitive illusions as juries (Wistrich, Rachlinski, & Guthrie, 2015). More generally, it is satisfying to know that Kalven and Zeisel's landmark study has withstood the test of time, even as the makeup of juries has changed in the intervening years.

When a lawsuit reaches the trial stage and the parties opt to have a jury, rather than judge, be the arbiter, specific procedures for selecting that jury come into play. We describe those procedures next, focusing on the psychological considerations and consequences of jury selection that begin not in the courtroom, but in the community.

Jury Selection Begins in the Community: Forming a Panel, or *Venire*

Jury selection begins before potential jurors arrive at the courthouse, as officials assemble a panel, or **venire**, of prospective jurors. Each state, as well as the federal government, has its own procedures for determining how the panel of prospective jurors will be chosen. But the general rule is the same: jury selection must neither systematically eliminate nor underrepresent any subgroups of the population.

To encourage representativeness, U.S. Supreme Court cases going back to 1880 (*Strauder v. West Virginia*) have forbidden systematic or intentional exclusion of religious, racial, and other **cognizable groups** (members of which, because of certain shared characteristics, might also hold unique perspectives on selected issues) from jury panels. But as recently as 50 years ago, the composition of most *venires* was homogeneous, with middle-aged, well-educated White men generally overrepresented (Beiser, 1973; Kairys, 1972).

Judicial and Legislative Reforms

In a series of decisions and lawmaking, the U.S. Supreme Court and the Congress established the requirement that the pool from which a jury is selected must be a representative cross-section of the community. These decisions were driven by two policy concerns, each of which includes psychological assumptions (Vidmar & Hans, 2007).

First, the government believed that if the pools from which juries were drawn represented a broad cross-section of the community, the resulting juries would be more heterogeneous. That is, they would be composed of people who were more diverse with respect to age, gender, ethnic background, occupation, and education. The courts assumed that this diversity would produce various benefits—for example, that minority group members might discourage majority group members from expressing prejudice. This assumption seems logical; casting a wider net will yield members of smaller religious and ethnic groups whose presence might reduce outright prejudicial remarks.

Another assumed benefit was that heterogeneous juries would be better fact finders and problem solvers. Extensive research on the dynamics of groups shows that, other things being equal, groups composed of people with differing abilities, personalities, and experiences are better problem solvers than groups made up of people who share the same background and perspectives (Antonio et al., 2004). Heterogeneous groups are more likely than homogeneous groups to evaluate facts from different points of view and to have richer discussions.

Does this also happen in juries? Apparently so. Samuel Sommers (2006) used actual jury pool members to examine the effects of racial heterogeneity on jury deliberations in a rape trial. He asked the jurors to take part in simulated (mock) trials in which he varied the racial mix of jurors and recorded their deliberations. Sommers found that mixed-race groups had several advantages over juries composed of only White jurors. First, the mixed-race groups had longer, more thorough deliberations and were more likely to discuss racially charged topics such as racial profiling. Second, White jurors on racially mixed juries mentioned more factual information and were more aware of racial concerns than were their counterparts on all-White juries. A follow-up study suggested that White jurors in diverse groups may actually process information differently than those in all-White groups (Sommers, Warp, & Mahoney, 2008). White jurors who expected to discuss

a race-relevant topic in diverse groups showed better comprehension of relevant background information than did White jurors in all-White juries. On the basis of these studies, we can conclude that representative and diverse *venires* do, indeed, result in juries who undertake better, more thorough and accurate fact-finding and discussion (Sommers, 2008).

The second policy reason for the Court and Congress's decisions on representativeness is related to the *appearance* of legitimacy, rather than to the jury's actual fact-finding and problem-solving skills (Vidmar & Hans, 2007). Juries should reflect the standards of the community. When certain components of the community are systematically excluded from jury service, the community is likely to reject both the legal process and its outcomes as invalid.

The racial composition of a jury *can* affect public perceptions of the fairness and legitimacy of a trial and of the resulting verdict. Participants in one survey study read a description of a shoplifting trial in which the racial makeup of the jury and the verdict was varied (Ellis & Diamond, 2003). Half of the respondents read that there were 12 Whites on the jury (racially homogeneous), and half read that there were 8 Whites and 4 African Americans (racially heterogeneous). In half of the descriptions, the jury's verdict was guilty and in the other half, not guilty. The researchers measured observers' perceptions of the fairness and legitimacy of the trial procedures. As shown in Figure 12.1, when the verdict was not guilty, racial composition of the jury had no effect on fairness ratings. But when the verdict was guilty, the racial composition of the jury *was* important. Observers considered a trial with a homogeneous

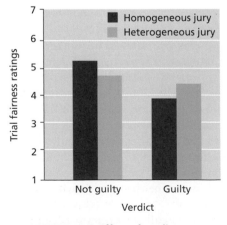

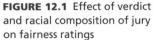

FIGURE 12.1 Effect of verdict and racial composition of jury on fairness ratings

jury less fair than a trial with a heterogeneous jury. Different elements of the community must see that they are well represented among those entrusted with doing justice—that they have a voice in the process of resolving disputes (Hans, 1992).

The historic 1992 riots in Los Angeles that erupted after four White police officers were acquitted of assault in the beating of Black motorist Rodney King illustrate this problem dramatically. The jury eventually selected for the trial contained no Black jurors. After the jury found the police officers not guilty, the Black community rejected the verdict as invalid and angrily challenged the legitimacy of the entire criminal justice system. Shaken by the surprising verdicts and shocked by the ensuing riots, many Americans, regardless of their race, questioned the fairness of the jury's decision, in part because of the absence of Black citizens from its membership.

Representativeness of jury pools that includes both demographic and attitudinal diversity is a worthwhile goal. But how should courts go about forming the *venire* in order to reach this goal? For many years, voter registration lists were used as the primary source for jury pool selection. However, such lists underrepresent certain segments of the community because smaller percentages of young people, the poor, Latinos, and other minorities register to vote. Recently, other sources such as lists of licensed drivers, persons receiving public assistance, and unemployed people have supplemented voter lists as a source of prospective jurors (Mize, Hannaford-Agor, & Waters, 2007).

From those persons who are eligible for jury service, members of the *venire* are randomly selected and summoned to appear at the courthouse for jury service. Unfortunately, many people never receive the summons and others simply opt to ignore it. A study in Washington state revealed that nearly half of all qualified jurors, and three-quarters of Latino and Asian American prospective jurors, ignored the jury summons, even though doing so constitutes a violation of law (Bloeser, McCurley, & Mondak, 2012). Cultural barriers contribute to low compliance rates among minorities; some people worry about language proficiency and others doubt their ability to serve or anticipate they would not be treated with respect by court personnel (Rose, Diamond, & Musick, 2012).

So several factors—underrepresentation of some groups in jury pool source lists, difficulty contacting certain prospective jurors, and cultural hurdles—threaten the representativeness requirement for jury pools. In fact, minorities are often underrepresented on criminal trial juries. In most locations in the United States, including those that are racially diverse, juries are majority White (Wilkenfeld, 2004). A study of the racial composition of juries from one jurisdiction in the southeastern United States revealed that in 2013 and 2014, Whites constituted roughly half of the adult population but nearly two-thirds of those called for jury selection. As a result, approximately two-thirds of criminal defendants were tried by juries in which minorities were absent or outnumbered (Gau, 2016).

Another concern is that people will often go to great length to avoid serving on a jury, and some have concocted creative ways to escape jury service. As Liz Lemon on "30 Rock," Tina Fey once dressed up as Princess Leia, complete with toga and ear buns, to avoid jury service. Vincent Homenick, the chief jury clerk of the courthouse in Manhattan, once received a summons that someone had returned with the word "deceased" written on it, along with a plastic bag supposedly containing the ashes of the prospective juror (Green, 2004)! Physical illnesses are another frequently used excuse. As Phoenix lawyer ha, former chairwoman of the American Jury Project, put it aptly: "Everyone likes jury duty—just not this week."

Prospective jurors sometimes avoid jury service by claiming personal hardship. Some judges are sympathetic to claims of ill health, business necessity, vacation plans, and the like. But many other judges are unwilling to dismiss individual jurors because of perceived "hardships." During the jury selection for the O. J. Simpson civil trial, Judge Hiroshi Fujisaki responded to one prospective juror who had requested dismissal because she suffered from claustrophobia, "How big is your living room? Is it as big as this courtroom?" She remained in the pool.

When prospective jurors are excused for reasons of hardship, the result is a further winnowing down of the pool. Thus, even before the formal jury selection begins in a courtroom—that is, before jurors are questioned by attorneys and the judge—some people have been removed from the panel of prospective jurors. These removals can distort the representativeness of juries.

Jury Selection Continues in the Courtroom: The *Voir Dire* Process

Once the panel of prospective jurors has been assembled and summoned to the courthouse, selection issues change. The focus shifts from concerns about the representativeness of prospective jurors to questions about a given juror's ability and willingness to be fair and impartial.

As part of the constitutional right to be tried by an "impartial" jury, a defendant is afforded the opportunity to screen prospective jurors to determine whether any of them are prejudiced. The forum in which the judge and/or the attorneys question prospective jurors is called **voir dire**, a French term that literally means "to see, to say." *Voir dire* is conducted in a variety of ways, depending on a jurisdiction's rules and a judge's preferences. Who asks the questions, what questions are asked and how they are phrased, how long the questioning goes on, and whether the questions are posed to individual jurors or to a group are all matters left to judges' discretion.

The most limited form of *voir dire* involves a small number of questions asked in yes-or-no format only by the judge and features group rather than individual questioning of prospective jurors. An example: "Do any of you have an opinion at this time as to the defendant's guilt or innocence?" Yes-or-no questions are effective in controlling the answers of witnesses and reducing the time spent in *voir dire*, but they offer little insight into jurors' beliefs and attitudes. Also note that this form of questioning requires jurors to self-identify any biases and report them to the judge. But **implicit biases**—beliefs borne of experiences and attitudes that predispose us to think in a certain way and of which we are unaware—make it difficult for jurors to accurately know their own predilections (Morrison, 2014).

Several studies show that limited *voir dire* has drawbacks as a means of identifying biased jurors. One of the most compelling demonstrations came from a project initiated by District of Columbia Superior Court Judge Gregory Mize (1999). Prior to this study, Judge Mize, like many judges, conducted limited *voir dire* during which he asked questions in open court to a group of prospective jurors. He and the attorneys would then pose follow-up questions to those who responded affirmatively to the initial question. Judge Mize revised his procedures for the study by interviewing all prospective jurors, regardless of whether they had responded affirmatively to the first question. In doing so, he determined that a number of jurors who were silent in response to a preliminary question actually had a great deal to say when prompted individually. Among the responses:

- "I was frightened to raise my hand. I have taken high blood pressure medications for twenty years. I am afraid I'll do what others tell me to do in the jury room."
- "My grandson was killed with a gun so the topic of guns makes my blood pressure go up."
- And remarkably, this one: "I'm the defendant's fiancée."

Why is limited *voir dire* so ineffective at uncovering juror bias? Obviously, some jurors will fail to disclose important information because of privacy concerns, embarrassment, or a failure to recognize implicit biases. But another important psychological dynamic, termed the **social desirability effect**, is also a factor at this stage. Most people want to present themselves in a positive, socially desirable way. This desire to appear favorably, especially in the presence of a high-status person such as a judge, shapes how people answer questions and influences what they disclose about themselves.

At the other extreme is extended *voir dire*, in which both the judge and attorneys ask open-ended questions that require elaboration, cover a wide range of topics, and question jurors individually. Extended *voir dire* has several advantages in uncovering biases. Open-ended questions (e.g., "What experiences have you had in your life that caused you to

During jury selection, jurors are questioned by both the judge and attorneys.

Michael Kelley/The Image Bank/Getty Imagese

believe that a person was being discriminated against because of the color of his skin?") encourage jurors to talk more about their feelings and experiences. Individual questioning can result in disclosures that jurors might not otherwise offer. But extended *voir dire* can take a long time, so most courts tend not to favor it. Typical *voir dire* procedures involve a compromise between the limited and extended versions; both the attorneys and the judge pose questions to a group of prospective jurors, and then they ask brief follow-up questions of selected individuals.

Challenges for Cause and Peremptory Challenges.

Technically, opposing attorneys do not select a jury; rather, the judge gives them the opportunity to exclude a number of potential jurors from the eventual jury. There are two mechanisms—challenges for cause and peremptory challenges—by which panelists are excluded from serving on a jury. We explain both in detail below. Here, we simply point out that after all the challenges have been made and ruled on, and some prospective jurors have been dismissed, the people who remain are sworn into service as the jury. Because attorneys strive to exclude those jurors who seem unfavorable to their client, the respective challenges tend to balance out and both extremes are eliminated, leaving a jury composed of people who are less biased and more open minded.

In any trial, each side can claim that particular jurors should be excluded because they are inflexibly biased or prejudiced or because they have a relationship to the parties or the issues that creates an appearance of bias. These exclusions are known as **challenges for cause**. For example, a relative or business associate of a defendant would be challenged, or excused, for cause. Additionally, the judge may excuse a panelist for cause without either attorney requesting it if the prospective juror is unfit to serve. In criminal cases, judges often inquire about whether prospective jurors have been crime victims and may excuse those who say that their own victimization experiences would affect their ability to be fair jurors. There is good reason to ask, because mock jurors who had been victims of the crime for which the defendant was being tried were more likely than non-victims to convict (Culhane, Hosch, & Weaver, 2004).

After a prospective juror has raised a concern about the ability to be fair and impartial (or after one of the attorneys has done so), the judge will typically ask the juror whether he or she can be impartial. Then, using the juror's assessment of those abilities and observing the juror's demeanor, the judge decides whether to dismiss that person for cause. But judges may have difficulty determining which jurors are truly impartial (Crocker & Kovera, 2010). In making that decision, judges may be overly reliant on the juror's expression of confidence. Small changes in the confidence that jurors express about their ability to be fair (e.g., "I would try" versus "Yes") can determine whether they will be excused for cause or remain on the jury. Unfortunately, jurors are not particularly insightful about their ability to be fair, and their confidence is not a reliable gauge of their bias (Rose & Diamond, 2008). So jurors who can be fair are sometimes dismissed, and those who cannot are sometimes retained—simply because of subtle variations in their responses to questions about impartiality.

In theory, each side has an unlimited number of challenges for cause. In reality, few prospective jurors are excused for reasons of bias. In a survey of New Mexico courts over a three-year period, only about 1 of every 20 jurors was dismissed for cause (Hans & Vidmar, 1986).

Each side may also exclude a designated number of prospective jurors "without a reason stated, without inquiry, and without being subject to the court's control" (*Swain v. Alabama*, 1965). This procedure is known as a **peremptory challenge**. The number of peremptory challenges allocated to each side varies from one jurisdiction to another and also by the type of case (civil or criminal) and seriousness of the charge.

Peremptory challenges have multiple purposes. First, they allow attorneys to challenge potential jurors whom they believe will be unsympathetic to their client, for whatever reason. The peremptory challenge has a second, largely symbolic function: When the parties in a lawsuit play a role in selecting the people who decide the outcome, they may be more satisfied with that outcome (Saks, 1997). The third function of peremptory challenges is to allow the attorney to begin to indoctrinate prospective jurors and influence those who ultimately will make up the jury. Attorney folklore in Texas is that an entire case can be tried during *voir dire* (Drummond, 2017). Consider the question "Do you agree with the rule of law that requires acquittal in the event there is reasonable doubt?" The real purpose of this question is to alert prospective jurors that reasonable doubt could exist in the case, and to make jurors aware of the rule so that they will look for reasonable doubt and then vote to acquit.

The Supreme Court has imposed more and more limits on the exercise of peremptory challenges. As a result, the overall status of this jury selection tool is in flux. Although opinions about the importance of the peremptory challenge remain divided—some experts favor its elimination altogether and others argue that it is crucial for fair trials—we now have useful data on the use of peremptory challenges in real trials. Among the questions researchers asked: Are peremptory challenges used to remove minority jurors or other specific groups? Do the prosecution and defense repeatedly dismiss different types of jurors?

Answers come from a study that tracked the fate of 764 prospective jurors questioned during jury selection in 28 cases (Clark, Boccaccini, Caillouet, & Chaplin, 2007). Of this total roughly equal numbers were dismissed by the prosecution and the defense. More importantly, jurors' race seemed to factor into the exercise of peremptory challenges. This finding was replicated in a study that tracked the fate of jurors in two racially diverse counties in the southeastern United States in 2013 and 2014 (Gau, 2016). The question was whether jurors' race was related to peremptory-challenge removals and the results were clear: prosecutors used their strikes disproportionately against Black venirepersons, and defense attorneys systematically dismissed White venirepersons. Several studies have found that prosecutors strike a high proportion (roughly, 80%) of African American jurors from venires (e.g., Equal Justice Initiative, 2010).

Peremptory Challenges: No Exclusion on Account of Race or Gender. The Supreme Court has ruled that peremptory challenges may not be based *solely* on a juror's race or gender. The decision regarding race was triggered by the case of James Batson, a Black man convicted of second-degree burglary by an all-White jury. During the *voir dire*, the prosecuting attorney used four of six peremptory challenges to dismiss all the Black persons from the *venire*. In *Batson v. Kentucky*, decided in 1986, the Court held that Batson was denied his Fourteenth Amendment right to equal protection by the prosecution's dismissal of Black members of the panel. In *Powers v. Ohio* (1991), the Court held that a White defendant could also complain about the exclusion of Blacks because the principle of representativeness was violated by the arbitrary exclusion of *any* racial group.

These decisions address the concern that attorneys will make unwarranted assumptions about minority jurors (assuming, for example, that they will acquit minority defendants) and then use peremptory challenges in a discriminatory way in order to keep them from serving on juries (Hunt, 2015). They also reflect the Court's stance that systematic efforts by attorneys to exclude members of cognizable groups violate the constitutional rights of members of those groups. Simply stated, all citizens—regardless of race, religion, or creed—have the right to serve on juries.

In the *Batson* case, the Supreme Court developed a procedure for determining whether a peremptory challenge was racially based. When a defense attorney believes that the prosecution's peremptory challenge was motivated by racial factors, he or she initiates a so-called *Batson* challenge, and the judge then asks the prosecutor for an explanation. The prosecutor typically advances a race-neutral explanation for the challenge—for example, that the prospective juror has a brother in prison or has filed a lawsuit against the police. The judge then determines whether the explanation is genuine, taking into account the other jurors who were not challenged by the attorney. For example, if a prosecutor stated that she dismissed a Black juror because he had been robbed, the judge would want to know why she had not dismissed a White juror who also had been robbed.

It might appear that creative prosecutors would be tempted to lie by citing "race-neutral" reasons for excluding minorities from the jury. In fact, this is not hard to do because their reasons do not have to be particularly compelling (*Purkett v. Elem*, 1995), and because people are quite adept at generating benign explanations to justify their biased judgments.

The ease of generating neutral-sounding explanations was shown in a study in which college students, law students, and practicing attorneys assumed the role of a prosecutor trying a Black defendant (Sommers & Norton, 2007). They were given profiles of two prospective jurors, one Black and the other White, and had to use one remaining peremptory challenge. When the first juror was Black, he was challenged 77% of the time but when the first juror was White, he was challenged only 53% of the time. More to the point, participants rarely cited race as a factor in their decision. It was relatively easy for them to generate an ostensibly neutral explanation, such as the prospective juror's skepticism of statistics, to justify their choice. This is an example of **casuistry**, defined as fallacious reasoning in order to justify questionable behavior.

Psychological research on **social judgments** can explain why we are adept at generating false but plausible explanations of unseemly behavior. People infrequently admit (even to themselves) that social category information such as race influences their decisions, often because they want to appear to be unprejudiced and to avoid the social consequences of showing racial bias (Axt, Ebersole, & Nosek, 2016). These findings

BOX 12.1

The Case of Timothy Foster and Racial Bias in Jury Selection

Thomas Foster

During jury selection in the 1987 murder trial of Timothy Foster, an African American charged with killing an elderly White woman in Georgia, prosecutors struck all four Black prospective jurors and an all-White jury convicted Foster and sentenced him to death. But in notes that surfaced decades later, prosecutors left tell-tale signs of their intentions to remove Black jurors from the panel, and in 2016, the U.S. Supreme Court deemed those peremptory strikes unconstitutional (*Foster v. Chatman*, 2016).

The notes included highlighting on names of all Black prospective jurors and circles drawn around the word "black" where jurors indicted their race on questionnaires. These prospective jurors were rank-ordered in the event that prosecutors had to pick one. Yet when questioned about their strikes, the prosecutors denied that race was a factor and instead, said that the stricken jurors seemed disrespectful, nervous, or hostile. In fact, the chief prosecutor offered 11 reasons for striking 34-year-old Marilyn Garrett, including the fact that she was too young and was divorced. But the Supreme Court found these reasons "pretextual," noting that the state declined to strike eight prospective White jurors who were under the age of 36, including one who was only 21, and three of the four prospective White jurors who were also divorced (Liptak, 2016). It concluded that the strikes of Black jurors were motivated "in substantial part by discriminatory intent." So the *Foster* case has turned out to be an exception to the largely "toothless and symbolic" Batson framework (Liptak, 2015).

CRITICAL THOUGHT QUESTION

In examining attorneys' peremptory challenges during the *voir dire* in Foster's trial, appellate justices read the trial transcript that provided a verbatim account of everything that was said in the courtroom. But it took the discovery of handwritten notes and highlighting to bring the discriminatory nature of those choices to light. Why would it have been difficult for justices to find evidence of racial bias in attorneys' explanations of which jurors they excused?

suggest that attorneys are unlikely to acknowledge considering the race of prospective jurors, even when race has been a factor in jury selection.

Recall that the judge, after hearing the prosecutor's explanation, must ultimately decide whether the attorney dismissed a prospective juror because of race. Easily concocted, plausible, and (above all) race-neutral justifications leave judges with little reason to reject them, and archival analyses of actual *voir dire* proceedings show that judges are unlikely to find that peremptory challenges violate the *Batson* rule (Melilli, 1996). But one high-profile case proved an exception to this rule. We describe it in Box 12.1.

Despite this exception, a number of legal scholars have now deemed the *Batson* framework largely ineffective at eliminating racial discrimination from jury selection (e.g., Marder, 2012; Morrison, 2014). Acknowledging that problems assembling jury pools also contribute to underrepresentation of African Americans on jury panels, Morrison (2014) claims that if *Batson* was genuinely addressing race-based peremptory challenges, we would have fewer cases like that of Darryl Batts, an African American who, in 2003, was convicted of robbery by an all-White jury in Kentucky. There had been 10 prospective Black jurors in the panel, but five were eliminated by random selection and

The Case of *J. E. B. v. Alabama ex rel. T. B.*: Whose Child Is This and Who Gets to Decide?

The facts of this case are relatively simple: Teresia Bible gave birth to a child in May 1989; she named the child Phillip Rhett Bowman Bible, claimed that James E. Bowman, Sr. was the father, and filed a paternity suit against him to obtain child support. Even though a blood test showed that there was a 99.92% probability that he was the father, Mr. Bowman refused to acknowledge paternity, so a trial was held.

The jury pool was composed of 24 women and 12 men. After three jurors were dismissed for cause, the plaintiff used 9 of her 10 peremptory challenges to remove males, the defendant used 10 of his 11 challenges to remove women, and the resulting jury was composed of 12 women. (Note that in this case, it was men who were systematically excluded from the jury.) The jury concluded that Mr. Bowman was the child's father and ordered him to pay child support of $415.71 per month.

Bowman appealed and the U.S. Supreme Court eventually ruled that peremptory challenges that were used to eliminate one gender were, like those used to exclude a race, unacceptable. The Court's decision acknowledged that peremptory strikes against women harken back to stereotypes about their competence and predispositions, traced from a long history of sex discrimination in the United States (Babcock, 1993).

CRITICAL THOUGHT QUESTION

Given what you know about how attorneys support their exclusions in "Batson challenges," how might creative attorneys justify excluding jurors of a particular gender?

the prosecutor struck the remaining five. Still, the judge ruled that the *Batson* requirement was not violated and sentenced Batts to 50 years imprisonment.

Given the ineffectiveness of peremptory challenges to address racial discrimination in jury selection, some observers are now advocating "race-related *voir dire*" to moderate the impact of racial attitudes. By talking about race during *voir dire*, judges could issue strongly worded messages to avoid bias, and attorneys and jurors alike may gain insight into their own implicit prejudices. Brayer (2015) claims that if such discussion is conducted in "an unhurried, relaxed, and non-judgmental environment," the impact of racial attitudes can be reduced (p. 3). Accordingly, the two most important factors in overcoming jurors' implicit racial biases may be race-relevant *voir dire* and the presence of African Americans in the jury pool—the latter suggestion consistent with psychological research on the effects of racial heterogeneity on deliberations (Sommers, 2008).

In 1994, the Supreme Court extended the logic of *Batson* to peremptory challenges based on another cognizable characteristic—gender. No longer could attorneys base their peremptory challenges solely on a jurors' gender. The leading case of *J. E. B. v. Alabama ex rel. T. B.* (1994) is described in Box 12.2.

How many different cognizable groups are there, and could limitations on peremptory challenges eventually be extended to cover all of them? In Houston, Texas, the attorney for accused murderer Jeffrey Leibengood asked to include only people less than five feet tall in the jury pool because his client's height was four feet six inches. The attorney told the judge, "We say a short person is subject to discrimination, and we hope to have two or three short people end up on the jury. *Batson* should be extended to include the little people" (quoted by Taylor, 1992, p. 43). The judge disagreed.

On a more serious note, courts are divided on the use of peremptory strikes based on prospective jurors' sexual orientation. Shortly after the Supreme Court ruled that same-sex couples could lawfully marry in the United States (*U.S. v. Windsor*, 2013), the Ninth Circuit deemed peremptory strikes on the basis of sexual orientation impermissible (*SmithKline Beecham Corp. v. Abbott Laboratories*, 2014). However, in most states it is still legal to base peremptory strikes on a prospective juror's sexual orientation or expression. So in general, attorneys' discretion in jury selection remains relatively unfettered, except that jurors cannot be challenged because of their race or their gender.

Lawyers' Theories: Stereotypes in Search of Success.

Do the jury selection strategies of attorneys conflict with the goal of having unbiased fact finders? Before we answer this question, we need to answer a more basic one: How do lawyers go about selecting or excluding jurors, and do their strategies work?

In everyday life, our impressions about others are governed largely by what psychologists have termed implicit personality theories. An **implicit personality theory** is a person's organized network of preconceptions about how certain attributes are related to one another and to behavior. Trial lawyers often apply their implicit personality theories to jury selection. For example, William J. Bryan (1971) advised prosecutors to "never accept a juror whose occupation begins with a P. This includes pimps, prostitutes, preachers, plumbers, procurers, psychologists, physicians, psychiatrists, printers, painters, philosophers, professors, phonies, parachutists, pipe-smokers, or part-time anythings" (p. 28). Another attorney vowed always to use a peremptory strike against any prospect who wore a hat indoors.

Implicit personality theories lead to stereotypes when a person believes that all members of a distinguishable group (e.g., a religious, racial, sexual, age, or occupational group) have the same attributes. They also produce assumptions that two personal characteristics are associated—for example, that slow-talking jurors are also unintelligent—when they actually may not be.

We tend to link characteristics together and form our own implicit personality theories. Sometimes these judgments are rationally based; we may have had sufficient experience to draw a valid conclusion about the linkage. Other theories, however, such as the examples just presented, are only intuitive or are based on limited experiences and purely coincidental associations and ignore within-group variability. But the emergence of implicit personality theories is almost inevitable when people form impressions of others and make interpersonal decisions. After all, human behavior is very complex and one must simplify it in some way. When attorneys have only limited information on which to judge a prospective juror, it is likely that implicit personality theories will influence their thoughts.

The jury selection decisions in the trial of *J. E. B. v. T. B.* reflect the use of implicit personality theories and stereotypes. Ms. Bible's attorney dismissed male jurors, assuming they would be sympathetic to the man alleged to be the baby's father, whereas the defense dismissed female jurors because of similar beliefs that women would be biased in favor of another woman. But the courts prohibit the use of such stereotypes. In his majority opinion in the *J. E. B.* case, Justice Harry Blackmun wrote, "Virtually no support [exists] for the conclusion that gender alone is an accurate predictor of [jurors'] attitudes," and if gender does not predict a juror's predisposition, then there is no legitimacy to dismissing jurors on this basis only (quoted by Greenhouse, 1994, p. A10).

Lawyers must choose which prospective jurors to challenge with their quota of peremptory challenges. Hence, their own implicit personality theories and stereotypes come into play. Richard "Racehorse" Haynes, a highly successful lawyer, once defended two White Houston police officers charged with beating a Black prisoner to death. Like all lawyers, Haynes had his ideas about the kind of juror who would be sympathetic to his police officer clients, but his candor was a surprise. After the trial was over, Haynes was quoted as saying, "I knew we had the case won when we seated the last bigot on the jury" (Phillips, 1979, p. 77).

Even if they are allowed to question prospective jurors individually, lawyers cannot be certain they are being told the truth. By necessity, they fall back on their own impressions. What attributes do lawyers find important? Textbooks and journal articles on trial advocacy provide a wealth of folklore about jurors' characteristics and their relation to beliefs. Not surprisingly, characteristics that are visible or easily determined—age, gender, race, religion, occupation, country of origin—receive special attention, and attorneys are naively "advised" about how jurors with certain attributes tend to think.

In addition to applying their own theories of personality to juror selection, some attorneys use their understanding of group structure. For example, they play hunches about which jurors will be the most dominant during the deliberations. Who will be selected as foreperson if, as in most jurisdictions, that choice is left up to the jury? Understanding group dynamics is more complicated than relying on simple stereotypes of individual jurors, so lawyers who try to forecast group behavior also make assumptions. Some lawyers maintain a simple "one-juror verdict" theory—that is, they believe that the final group decision is usually determined by the opinions of one strong-willed, verbal, and influential juror. Lawyers who adhere to this maxim look for one juror who is likely to be both sympathetic and influential and then, during the trial, concentrate their influence attempts on that individual. In pursuing this search for a "key juror," the typical attorney follows one basic rule of thumb: "In general, an individual's status and power within the jury group will mirror his status and power in the external world" (Christie, 1976, p. 270).

If jurors themselves are asked who among them was most influential during their deliberations, three characteristics tend to emerge: male gender, an extroverted personality style, and height greater than that of their fellow jurors (Marcus, Lyons, & Guyton, 2000). It should come as no surprise then that former Senator and Secretary of State John Kerry was elected to serve as foreperson in a 2005 trial in Suffolk County Massachusetts. Fellow jurors described him as a "natural leader."

Another common attorney strategy is based on the assumption that jurors who are demographically or socially similar to a litigant will be predisposed to favor that litigant, a belief known as the **similarity–leniency hypothesis**. Does this rule of thumb hold true? Are jurors more likely to favor litigants with whom they share certain characteristics? One could make the opposite prediction in some cases—that sharing similar qualities with another might make a juror more skeptical of that person's excuses or justifications for behavior that the juror dislikes. Here, the so-called **black sheep effect** may apply: Although people generally favor individuals who are part of their in-group, they may sometimes strongly sanction those fellow members who reflect negatively on and embarrass the in-group.

Although the strength of evidence against a defendant is the most powerful predictor of jurors' sentiments (Devine, Krouse, Cavanaugh, & Basora, 2016), similarity between jurors and defendants may also have an influence. But the nature of that influence depends on whether the defendant has a prior record. When the offender has committed previous wrongdoings, jurors render harsher judgments against members of their in-group than members of an out-group. This supports the black sheep effect: people distance themselves from others like them who are deviant in some way. But for offenders without prior wrongdoings, the similarity–leniency hypothesis seems more apt: jurors tend to view law-abiding members of their in-group more positively than members of an out-group (Gollwitzer & Keller, 2010).

Do Jurors' Demographic Characteristics Predict the Verdicts? Trial attorneys must make informed guesses about which prospective jurors will be more favorable to their side. To do so, they often rely on demographic features of jurors because many of these characteristics (e.g., age, race, gender, socioeconomic status [SES]) are easily observable (Kovera, Dickinson, & Cutler, 2002). Indeed, many attorneys actively select (or, rather, deselect) jurors on the basis of demographic information. When researchers (Olczak, Kaplan, & Penrod, 1991) gave attorneys mock juror profiles that varied along demographic lines (including gender, age, marital status, and nationality) and asked them to rate the extent to which each profiled juror would be biased toward the defense or prosecution, they found that attorneys could do this task easily, focusing on one or two characteristics to the exclusion of others.

But though demographic characteristics of jurors and juries are *sometimes* related to their verdicts, the correlations are weak and inconsistent from one type of trial to another (Devine & Caughlin, 2014). The relationships that emerge are usually small and offer no guarantee of success to the attorney who deals with only a few individuals and one trial at a time.

The relationship between demographic characteristics and verdicts also depends on the type of case. For example, in trials that involve issues such as sexual assault, domestic violence, and sexual harassment, women are more likely than men to convict (Golding, Bradshaw, Dunlap, & Hodell, 2007), but gender differences are not apparent in other kinds of cases (Devine & Caughlin, 2014). Nor is gender a reliable predictor of verdicts or punitive damages in high-stakes civil litigation (Vinson, Costanzo, & Berger, 2008). The most consistent gender difference involves social influence rather than content; men are generally perceived by other jurors as more influential than women (Marcus et al., 2000).

Although few studies have examined the relationship between jurors' SES and their verdicts, the general consensus is that wealthy jurors are somewhat more likely than poorer jurors to assume that criminal defendants are guilty, particularly in trials involving theft, burglary, and fraud. Well-to-do jurors may have a desire to protect the social order and become wary of those who take what is not rightfully theirs (Devine, 2012). Laboratory research has shown that high-SES mock jurors are less harsh than low-SES jurors on civil defendants (Bornstein & Rajki, 1994). Perhaps the most powerful effect of SES occurs at the deliberation table, where jurors of higher status are regarded as more influential because of what others believe about their competence (York & Cornwell, 2006).

Using jurors' race to predict their verdicts is complicated because as we described, the racial mix of the jury influences an individual juror's decision. Based on the existing data, we can tentatively conclude that Black jurors may be more lenient than Whites in the typical criminal case (Devine et al., 2016), but only if the defendant is also Black (Sommers & Ellsworth, 2000). The mix of races and genders on juries—that is, jury demographic diversity—may also be important, as individual jurors on juries with more race-gender subgroups (e.g., Latino females) are less likely to convict (Devine et al., 2016).

In general though, with regard to jurors' demographic features, there is little evidence that these characteristics can consistently predict verdicts in criminal cases (Devine et al., 2016) or damage awards in civil cases (Vinson et al., 2008). This is probably good news because verdicts should be based on the evidence presented during the trial and not on the personal features of the decision makers.

Jurors' Personality and Attitudinal Characteristics as Predictors of Verdicts. Given that demographic variables have only a weak relationship to verdicts, one might wonder whether jurors' personality and attitudinal characteristics are better predictors. Personality characteristics are relatively stable patterns of behavior that describe "how people act in general" (Funder, 2004, p. 109). Attitudinal characteristics are evaluative reactions toward someone or something that are exhibited in feelings, beliefs, and intended actions (Olson & Zanna, 1993).

A number of studies concluded that enduring aspects of one's personality and attitudes may influence courtroom decisions, though usually only to a modest degree. Using simulated and real juries, this research has indicated that certain personality attributes of mock jurors such as Authoritarianism, the Need for Cognition, and Trust in the Legal System may be related to jurors' verdicts. Personality and attitudinal variables are somewhat better predictors of verdict decisions than are demographic factors (Lieberman & Olson, 2009), though keep in mind that the relationships between personality and attitudinal factors on the one hand, and verdicts on the other hand, are, at best, only modest.

Authoritarianism is one personality characteristic of jurors that is modestly correlated with their verdicts in criminal cases. People with an authoritarian personality tend to adhere to traditional values, identify with and submit to powerful figures, place less emphasis on civil liberties, and tend to be punitive toward those who violate established norms. In terms of the legal system, authoritarian jurors are more likely to vote for conviction in mock criminal jury studies (Devine & Caughlin, 2014).

Authoritarian beliefs may be more powerful determinants of decisions in death penalty trials than in noncapital trials. In one study, prospective jurors reporting for jury duty in Florida read a condensed version of a capital case and recommended an appropriate sentence (life without parole or death). They also rated the extent to which various aggravating factors (those aspects of a crime that support a death sentence) and mitigating factors (aspects that support a life sentence) were present in the evidence (Butler & Moran, 2007). Jurors who scored high on a measure of Authoritarianism endorsed more aggravating factors and fewer mitigating factors, and were more likely to select a death sentence than their counterparts lower in Authoritarianism.

Interestingly, when highly authoritarian jurors encounter a defendant who symbolizes authority, their usual tendency to punish the defendant is reversed (Nietzel & Dillehay, 1986). In fact, about the only time that authoritarian mock jurors are not more conviction-prone than nonauthoritarians is in trials in which the defendant is a police officer. In such cases, the more authoritarian jurors tend to identify with the powerful and punitive image of the officer.

Another personality variable—the **Need for Cognition**—may influence how jurors evaluate evidence in a trial. The Need for Cognition refers to a person's inclination to engage in and enjoy effortful cognitive work (Cacioppo, Petty, Feinstein, & Jarvis, 1996). The Need for Cognition explains why some people are motivated to think hard and analyze arguments thoroughly, and others are disinclined to do so. This concept is assessed by whether people agree with statements such as "I only think as hard as I have to" and "The notion of thinking abstractly is appealing to me." In a courtroom, the Need for Cognition can distinguish those jurors who scrutinize the evidence carefully and examine its weaknesses from jurors who accept trial testimony at face value and have little desire to pore over the evidence (DeWitt, Richardson, & Warner, 1997). Jurors with low Need for Cognition may pay more attention to witnesses' credentials than to the essence of their testimony.

The Need for Cognition influences how jurors process evidence presented by an expert witness. This evidence is often complicated, technical, or scientific, and may require effortful thinking on the part of jurors. When mock jurors read a summary of a sexual harassment trial in which an expert witness presented research that varied in terms of scientific rigor and quality, jurors high in Need for Cognition were attentive to the validity of the research. They evaluated the expert evidence more favorably when the research was valid, and tended to support the side that presented that evidence. On the other hand, jurors low in Need for Cognition were not attentive to flaws in the expert evidence and were less likely to support the side that presented the valid study (McAuliff & Kovera, 2008). One study showed that jurors who are low in Need for Cognition can be helped by a detailed cross-examination of an expert who presented flawed research during direct examination. These jurors are unlikely to process the expert testimony thoroughly themselves (Salerno & McCauley, 2009).

Psychologists have also examined the relationship between jurors' verdicts and other attitudinal characteristics. For example, in their meta-analysis of 272 empirical studies of criminal jury trials, Devine and Caughlin (2014) observed that general Trust in the Legal System, as measured by the Juror Bias Scale (Kassin & Wrightsman, 1983), was positively associated with conviction rates. Jurors with higher levels of Trust in the Legal System were more likely to convict, probably because they had faith that the defendant was the actual perpetrator and that he or she had engaged in illegal conduct. This finding is consistent with the observation, based on verdict data and questionnaire responses from 2000 jurors who served in actual cases in four jurisdictions across the United States, that trust and confidence in the police increases the likelihood of conviction in criminal cases (Farrell, Pennington, & Cronin, 2013).

In general then, studies suggest that some personality and attitudinal variables may be modestly related to individual jurors' verdicts, at least in criminal cases. The relationships are less strong in civil cases and, in both contexts, probably depend upon the type of case (Vinson et al., 2008). But the trials used in these studies were "close calls." That is, the evidence for each side was manipulated to be about equally persuasive—in such cases, individual juror characteristics may have their greatest influence (Penrod, 1990). In the real world, trial evidence is often so conclusive for one side that the jurors' personality dispositions may have less impact. In any event, attitudes that are relevant to the evidence in a case—for example, beliefs about mental health and illness in a case involving the insanity defense, and attitudes toward the death penalty in a capital murder case—will provide better information about how a prospective juror might reason (Kovera & Austin, 2016).

Attorney Effectiveness in *Voir Dire*. Attorneys take pride in their skill in selecting a favorable jury. For example, a president of the Association of Trial Lawyers in America wrote, "Trial attorneys are acutely attuned to the nuances of human behavior, which enables them to detect the minutest traces of bias or inability to reach an appropriate decision" (Begam, 1977, p. 3). But psychologists and other observers of jury trials are less sanguine. They have noted that because attorneys rarely get extensive training or feedback on the wisdom of past choices, they may overvalue the role of obvious, identifiable demographic variables and undervalue the importance of attitudinal characteristics when making peremptory challenges. As psychologist Reid Hastie has suggested, "[a]n attorney's ability to predict appears limited by a very low ceiling of precision" (1991, p. 712).

There is good reason for social scientists to be skeptical of how much lawyers can accomplish in *voir dire*. In a study of attorney effectiveness, experienced trial attorneys used juror selection strategies that were not different from or better than those used by inexperienced college and law students who were asked to evaluate mock jurors (Olczak et al., 1991). Trial attorneys did not appear to think any more accurately when making personality judgments than did nonprofessionals. Even when asked to perform a more realistic task—rating jurors from the videotapes of a previous *voir dire*—attorneys did no better than chance in detecting jurors who were biased against them (Kerr, Kramer, Carroll, & Alfini, 1991). In short, "attorneys cannot read jurors like open books" (Devine, 2012).

Why are attorneys' judgments hampered in this way? One reason is that, like all of us, they are affected by their assumptions and expectations about other people. Kennard and colleagues demonstrated the powerful pull of expectations by recruiting practicing prosecutors and defense attorneys to conduct mock *voir dires* of community members (Kennard, Otis, Austin, Zimmerman, & Kovera, 2014). They manipulated attorneys' expectations of the pro-prosecution and pro-defense attitudes of 12 community members in a random fashion, meaning that the information researchers provided to attorneys was often at odds with what a community member *actually* thought. The attorneys then conducted a mock *voir dire* and indicated which six prospective jurors they would most want on the jury. Attorneys' expectations about a venireperson's verdict leanings persisted even after they had the chance to ask questions of these individuals and regardless of a person's actual inclinations. In other words, prosecutors struck more people whom they assumed to have pro-defense leanings and defense attorneys struck more people whom they assumed were pro-prosecution.

Interestingly, when community members then read a summary of a capital murder case and reached a verdict, venirepersons who were expected to be pro-prosecution rendered more guilty verdicts than venirepersons expected to favor the defense. This result is an example of **behavioral confirmation processes** that occur when someone's (e.g., an attorney's) perception of another person (e.g., a prospective juror) causes that person to behave in a manner consistent with the perceiver's expectation (Stukas & Snyder, 2002).

This relatively poor performance by attorneys during jury selection has been analogized to biased hypothesis testing in scientific endeavors (see, e.g., Kovera & Austin, 2016). In order to make effective choices—that is, in order to select jurors who will be favorably inclined toward one's position—attorneys must generate hypotheses about the relationship between jurors' traits, attitudes, and preferences, gather information during *voir dire* to test their hypotheses, and then make inferences about how those predilections will play out in their case. Each of these tasks—generating hypotheses, gathering information, and making inferences—is made more difficult by the cursory nature of jury selection in terms of time allotted and the depth of questioning. So it is not surprising that attorneys make inaccurate decisions about a venireperson's leanings.

Scientific Jury Selection: Does It Work Any Better?

For years, trial lawyers have been "picking" jurors on the basis of their own theories about how people behave. But some attorneys—convinced of the importance of jury selection yet skeptical of their ability to do it well, or limited in the time they can devote to it—hire social scientists as jury selection consultants. These consultants use empirically based procedures, such as focus groups, shadow juries, systematic ratings of prospective jurors, and surveys of the community, to identify desirable and undesirable jurors (Lieberman, 2011). This collection of techniques is known as **scientific jury selection**. These techniques were first used to aid defendants in several highly publicized "political" trials of the Vietnam War era, and are now practiced in high profile criminal and civil trials (Posey, 2016). The prime-time TV series *Bull*, loosely based on the experiences of Texas trial consultant Phil "Dr. Phil" McGraw, depicts aspects of scientific jury selection, though real-life consultants claims that it contains a fair amount of bull (Tedder-King & Marinakis, 2016). Trial consultant Jo-Ellan Dimitrius, who assisted O.J. Simpson's defense team, was also involved in selecting the jury for the 2014 sentencing trial of Jodi Arias, accused of murdering her ex-boyfriend. We describe that case in Box 12.3.

Scientific jury selection raises a number of complex issues and generates significant controversy. Some critics claim that it subverts the criminal justice system because it favors the wealthy over individuals of modest means (Strier, 1999) and creates a perception among the public that the system is rigged (Brown, 2003). Others claim that it is ineffective (Kressel & Kressel, 2002; Saks, 1997). Not surprisingly, consultants (and some attorneys) dispute these claims, pointing out that public defenders have benefitted from their services and touting the value of professional training and experience: "We've collected a lot of research and we can spot things a lawyer wouldn't normally be paying attention to.... Most attorneys do just one or two trials a year, if they're lucky. But a good consultant has studied hundreds of juries and knows which behaviors and characteristics to look out for" (quote by consultant Dan Wolfe, cited by McCann, 2004). Moreover, because the American system of justice remains fundamentally adversarial, litigants are expected to present their version of the case as zealously as possible. So they should be able to use any legal means available to convince the jury to reach a favorable decision.

How effective *are* trial consultants at selecting juries? When attorneys in criminal trials first began to rely on empirically grounded scientific jury selection, they were often successful. Although the procedure seemed to work, the success rate may have been inflated by the following factors: (1) Many of the more widely discussed cases involved weak or controversial evidence against defendants. (2) Attorneys who made the extra effort to enlist jury consultation resources may also have been more diligent and thorough in other areas of their case preparation.

To assess the impact of trial consultants, ideally one would conduct an experiment in which two identically composed juries would decide two identically tried cases, one that involved the services of a consultant and another that did not. By holding constant all aspects of the trial, including the nature of the evidence and the identities of the participants, and by varying only the involvement of a trial consultant, one might be able to reach some conclusion about that person's impact. Unfortunately, it is impossible to conduct such an experiment, so we may never know with any precision or certainty whether and to what extent trial consultants are changing the outcomes of trials.

In addition, the effectiveness of scientific jury selection depends on a number of variables over which the consultant has no control. These include how many peremptory challenges are allowed; the extent to which questions delve into matters beyond superficial demographic details of prospective panel members; whether

The Case of Jodi Arias, Her Two Sentencings, and Her Trial Consultant

BOX 12.3

Jodi Arias

The body of Travis Alexander, a salesman for a legal services company, was discovered in the shower of his home in Mesa, Arizona on June 9, 2008. He had been stabbed nearly 30 times, his throat had been cut, and he had been shot in the head. Exactly one month later, his ex-girlfriend, Jody Arias, was indicted on charges of first-degree murder and the prosecutor announced that he would seek the death penalty. Despite her claims of physical, emotional, and sexual abuse by Alexander (delivered over an "unprecedented" 18 days of

testimony) and her attorneys' arguments that the killing was in self-defense, Arias was found guilty in May, 2013. The sentencing phase ensued, but ended in a mistrial when jurors were unable to agree on a sentence.

By this point, the case had attracted widespread national attention due to gavel-to-gavel coverage on cable network HLN. So when prosecutors launched a second penalty phase with a new jury in 2014, 300 prospective jurors were summoned, and the defense team did some summoning of its own, enlisting trial consultant Jo-Ellan Dimitrius to help with jury selection. A primary concern was the possibility that a stealth juror—someone who had already made up his or her mind about punishment—would lie in order to be chosen. The second sentencing phase also ended in a hung jury, and Arias was eventually sentenced to life imprisonment without the possibility of parole.

CRITICAL THOUGHT QUESTION
Trial consultants often assist lawyers by formulating questions to ask during *voir dire*. What are some questions that Jo-Ellan Dimitrius might have suggested to defense attorneys that would have helped them to select favorable jurors?

attorneys act on the guidance of the consultant; and, perhaps most importantly, the extent to which jurors' attitudes and beliefs will determine the outcome of the case (Greene, 2002). The more freedom and flexibility inherent in the jury selection procedures and the more the case hinges on jurors' belief systems, the more room exists for consultants to ply their trade and the greater the chances they can succeed.

A few empirical studies have investigated the effectiveness of scientific jury selection, but their procedures were somewhat artificial. For example, Horowitz (1980) trained law students in either scientific jury selection or traditional selection methods and investigated their performance in four criminal cases. Traditional selection methods included relying on past experiences, interactions with similar jurors in prior trials, and conventional wisdom. Those trained

in scientific jury selection received pre-trial survey responses and profiles showing the desirability of prospective jurors. Horowitz determined that neither approach was superior for all four trials: traditional methods were superior in cases in which there were weak links between demographic, personality, and attitudinal factors (e.g., in a murder case), whereas scientific methods were superior when those associations were strong (e.g., in a drug sale case).

A study of scientific jury selection used in a series of actual capital murder trials provides somewhat more data on the effectiveness of trial consultants. Nietzel and Dillehay (1986) examined the outcomes of 31 capital trials, some involved a trial consultant and others did not. Juries recommended the death sentence in 61% of the trials in which consultants were not used by the defense but in only 33% of the trials in which they were used. Of course, these cases differed on many variables besides the use of consultants, so it is not possible to conclude that different outcomes were due to their presence alone. But the results are consistent with claims that trial consultants might be effective in cases in which jurors' attitudes are particularly important, as when the choice is between life and death. Clearly though, there is limited evidence of the effectiveness of scientific jury selection, and higher-quality contemporary studies are sorely needed.

Still, trial-watchers and social scientists of the jury agree that in most cases the evidence is more important than jurors' attitudes or demographic characteristics (Jonakait, 2003; Kressel & Kressel, 2002) and that scientific jury selection may be of limited value in cases where the evidence is unambiguous. Richard Seltzer, a political scientist and trial consultant himself, acknowledged this indirectly: "Jurors cannot be predicted with the type of accuracy associated with experiments in physics" (2006).

Recognizing that jurors' demographic and personality characteristics do not correlate strongly with verdicts in general, many trial consultants have shifted their focus from advising lawyers about jury selection to providing services in realms other than jury selection (Posey, 2016). These include developing case themes and testing those themes in pre-trial focus groups, preparing witnesses to testify in court, monitoring the effectiveness of evidence presentation during the trial, and interviewing jurors after the trial has ended. Consultants also assist attorneys during mediations.

Pre-Trial Publicity

Legal cases have always attracted media attention, and the judicial system has struggled for centuries with the fallout of publicity that occurs prior to a trial. With the development of 24-hour news networks, thousands of cable and satellite channels, online news sources, and social media, trial-related information is more accessible to the public than ever before. As a result, the judicial system is experiencing new and growing concerns about the impact of this information on prospective jurors, and the number of defendants who claim their case has been jeopardized by pre-trial publicity has more than doubled in the past 20 years (Daftary-Kapur, Dumas, & Penrod, 2010). The civil litigation system is also affected by publicity concerning product liability and medical malpractice claims, among others, and by the reporting of unusually large damage awards (Kritzer & Drechsel, 2012).

One recent example in criminal law involved the 2013 Boston marathon bombing in which three people were killed and approximately 280 people were injured. The defendant, Dzhokhar Tsarnaev, was charged with conspiring to use a weapon of mass destruction resulting in death. (Tsarnaev's brother, Tamerlan, who had allegedly become a follower of radical Islam, was also involved but was killed in the days following the bombing after being shot by police.) Prior to trial, Tsarnaev's attorneys argued on multiple occasions that because so many Bostonians had been affected by the bombing and exposed to publicity about victims' injuries and bystanders' heroism, the trial should be moved to a different location. But Judge George O'Toole denied their requests, noting that "the time tested method for determining whether a juror can actually set aside his beliefs and apply the presumption of innocence is voir dire" (Boeri & Sobel, 2015). Indeed, nearly all prospective jurors had heard details of the bombing and although many presumed that Tsarnaev was guilty, they were not automatically dismissed. Rather, Judge O'Toole reminded jurors that the law requires that they set aside their opinions, and then asked whether they could decide the case based solely on the evidence that would emerge during the trial and on his instructions. Many prospective jurors said they could. The jury that was eventually selected found Tsarnaev guilty and sentenced him to death. But this trial highlights some of the challenges to the legal system's goal of forming fair and impartial juries when the case has attracted a great deal of pre-trial publicity.

Conflicting Rights

Pre-trial publicity highlights tensions between two cherished rights protected by the U.S. Constitution: freedom of the press as guaranteed by the First Amendment, and the right to a speedy and public trial before an impartial jury, as guaranteed by the Sixth Amendment. In the majority of cases, the liberties ensured by the First and Sixth Amendments are compatible and even complementary. The press informs the public about criminal investigations and trials, and the public learns the outcomes of these proceedings and gains increased appreciation for both the justness and the foibles of our system of justice.

On occasion, however, the First and Sixth Amendments clash. The press publishes information that, when disseminated among the public, threatens a defendant's right to a trial by impartial jurors. This can occur in cases in which defendants and/or victims, because of their fame or infamous acts (like those of Tsarnaev), have gained national reputations. More commonly, it happens when local news media, online postings, and press releases disseminate information about a crime or the parties involved that is inflammatory, biased, emotion-laden, or factually erroneous. Examples of this information include details about a person's prior criminal record, a confession made by the accused, unfavorable statements regarding the defendant's character, and criticisms of the merits of pending cases.

The Supreme Court has considered several cases in which defendants claimed that their right to an impartial jury was impaired by inflammatory pre-trial publicity. In one case, Jon Yount's confession that he had killed a high school student was published in two local papers in 1966. Prior to trial, like Tsarnaev, Yount cited continuing publicity about the case and requested that the trial be moved to a different jurisdiction. The judge denied the motion despite the fact that 77% of prospective jurors admitted they had an opinion about Yount's guilt. Yount appealed his conviction, claiming that the publicity had made a fair trial impossible. The Supreme Court ruled against him, reasoning that a "presumption of correctness" should be given to the trial judge's opinion because, being present at the trial, the judge was in a better position to evaluate the demeanor, credibility, and, ultimately, the competence of prospective jurors (*Patton v. Yount*, 1984).

But in *Rideau v. Louisiana* (1963), the Court decided that dissemination of news that included information strongly pointing to the defendant's guilt violated his rights. On three occasions, a local TV station broadcast a 20-minute clip of Rideau, surrounded by law enforcement officials, confessing in detail to charges of robbery, kidnapping, and murder. Rideau's request for a change of venue was also denied, and Rideau was convicted and sentenced to death by a jury, of which at least three members had seen the televised confession. The Supreme Court reversed this decision, Rideau was granted a new trial, and he was eventually convicted of manslaughter, rather than murder. (In the 43 years he spent in prison prior to his 2005 release, Rideau transformed himself from an illiterate eighth-grade dropout to a national advocate for prison reform, a filmmaker, and an award-winning editor of Angola State Prison's renowned *Angolite* magazine. Perhaps most important, he acknowledged responsibility for his crime and apologized for the harm he caused [Green, 2005].)

Finally, in its most recent look at the potentially prejudicial effects of pre-trial publicity (*Mu'Min v. Virginia*, 1991), the Supreme Court held that if prospective jurors claim they can be impartial, defendants do not have a constitutional right to ask them about the specifics of their exposure to pre-trial publicity. According to the Court, such assurances are all that the Constitution requires.

Yet it is difficult to know how much trust to place in jurors' claims of impartiality. The problem is not that jurors lie about their beliefs, although some probably do. The issue is that people might not be aware of or admit the full measure of their prejudices in public. Prospective jurors would have to acknowledge that they received biasing information, know that they integrated those details with other pieces of information, and be able to reverse or control the biasing effects of this information—a very difficult cognitive task (Bornstein & Greene, 2017).

Even if completely aware of their biases, prospective jurors might not be willing to disclose them in an open courtroom before a judge who encourages them to be fair and open-minded. They might experience **evaluation apprehension**, whereby they provide the answers that they perceive the judge wants to hear, regardless of whether their responses are truthful. One wonders whether this occurred during *voir dire* in the Boston marathon bombing trial.

Effects of Pre-Trial Publicity

A large number of studies have measured the effects on jurors of various kinds of pre-trial publicity presented in different media. Both experimental and field studies have been conducted. In experimental studies, participants are first exposed (or not exposed, in the control group) to some form of publicity and then are asked to assume the role of jurors in a simulated trial. In field studies, community-respondents are surveyed to assess the effects of naturally occurring publicity about an actual case. Taken together, these studies point to the conclusion that jurors exposed to pre-trial publicity are more likely than those not so exposed to favor the prosecution and prejudge the defendant as guilty.

Experimental Studies of the Effects of Pre-Trial Publicity. Using experimental procedures, researchers manipulate the presence and type of pre-trial publicity and measure its impact on perceptions of witnesses and the defendant, evaluations of evidence, and the final verdict. Because all aspects of the trial except the publicity are held constant, scientists can assess whether variations in publicity cause differences in responses.

Many experimental studies have examined the effects of negative or anti-defendant information in pre-trial publicity on perceptions of the defendant. These studies generally show that pre-trial publicity affects jurors' evaluations of the defendant's character and criminality, the extent to which they like or sympathize with him, their pre-trial sentiments about his guilt, and their final verdicts (Steblay, Besirevic, Fulero, & Jiminez-Lorente, 1999). A few studies have explored the effects of positive or pro-defendant pre-trial publicity. In one (Ruva & McEvoy, 2008), mock jurors who were exposed to positive publicity were less likely to convict the defendant than were jurors exposed to negative or no publicity.

Still other studies have attempted to explain why these effects occur. Three explanations seem reasonable. First, pre-trial publicity may bias jurors' interpretations of the evidence to which they are exposed at trial. If pre-trial publicity about the defendant is negative, jurors evaluate trial testimony—even ambiguous testimony—in a manner adverse to the defendant yet consistent with the publicity (Ruva & Guenther, 2015). In short, the publicity affects jurors' ability to determine the true probative value of the evidence. Second, jurors exposed to publicity come to believe, wrongly, that the pre-trial information was actually presented as part of the evidence at trial. This is a **source monitoring** error: jurors are mistaken about the source of their information (Ruva, McEvoy, & Bryant, 2007). Finally, pre-trial publicity often elicits emotional responses that are associated with jurors' verdicts. In one study, jurors who were exposed to anti-defendant information pre-trial were angrier after the trial than jurors not exposed to this information, and as anger increased, so did guilt ratings (Ruva, Guenther, & Yarbrough, 2011).

An interesting question, given the pervasiveness of digital news sources and the declining readership of newspapers, is whether pre-trial information conveyed on a screen has a different impact than information conveyed in print. In an experiment designed to test this question, participants were randomly assigned to one of three conditions that varied the format by which pre-trial media information was presented about the Mount Cashel orphanage case, a highly publicized case in Canada concerning alleged sexual abuse by a group of Roman Catholic men who ran an orphanage in Newfoundland (Ogloff & Vidmar, 1994). The damaging pre-trial material was presented to participants through (1) television, (2) newspaper articles, or (3) both TV and newspapers. Presentation of publicity via television had a greater biasing impact than the same information presented in print, but the combined effects of TV and newspaper publicity had the greatest impact of all. Of additional interest, participants were generally unaware that their opinions had been biased by this material. An obvious next step in this line of research is to evaluate the impact of pre-trial information communicated via various online sources.

To this point, we have considered the effects of **specific pre-trial publicity**, showing that case-specific information made available prior to trial can affect the sentiments of jurors in that trial. But jurors can also be influenced by **generic prejudice**—that is, prejudice arising from media coverage of issues not specifically related to a particular case but thematically relevant to the issues at hand. Highly stigmatized conduct such as deviant sexual behavior can engender strong feelings among jurors that are unrelated to the facts of any particular case (Wiener, Arnot, Winter, & Redmond, 2006). In fact, the late Judge Abner Mikva of the Court of Appeals for the District of Columbia suggested that generic prejudice may be more problematic than specific pre-trial publicity:

> Pretrial publicity is not the big difficulty. It is generic prejudice. I do not think you can get a fair child abuse trial before a jury anywhere in the country … I do not care how sophisticated or how smart jurors are, when they hear that a child has been abused, a piece of their mind closes up, and this goes for the judge, the juror, and all of us (cited by Doppelt, 1991, p. 821).

Psychological research seems to support Judge Mikva's assertion. For example, Wiener et al. (2006) found evidence of generic prejudice among mock jurors, and the effects of prejudice were greater in cases of sexual assault than homicide. Kovera (2002) showed that media exposure and preexisting attitudes interact: exposure to a story about a rape case influenced participants' appraisals of the witnesses and verdicts in a different rape case, but preexisting attitudes also affected the impact of the media on mock jurors' judgments.

Generic prejudice probably works by transferring preexisting beliefs and stereotypes about categories of people to a particular defendant in a trial setting (Vidmar, 2002). As a result, the facts of the case and the personal characteristics of the defendant go relatively unheeded. Racial and ethnic stereotypes are the most common forms of generic prejudice; for example, some people believe that an African American defendant is more likely to be guilty of a crime than a White defendant, all other things being equal. Muslim Americans on trial in the United States these days may also experience some form of generic prejudice.

Field Studies of the Effects of Naturally Occurring Publicity. Serious crimes attract extensive news coverage, typically from the prosecutor's view of the case. Field studies, a research technique favored by trial consultants, can assess the saturation of a news story in a community by polling people about their knowledge of an actual crime. In some instances, polling occurs in the community where publicity is assumed to be widespread, as well as in jurisdictions farther from the crime, allowing for comparisons between respondents in two or more locales.

Whether surveying opinions about notorious crimes (Studebaker et al., 2002) or cases of only local interest (Vidmar, 2002), these studies consistently find that persons exposed to pre-trial publicity possess more knowledge about the events in question, are more likely to have prejudged the case, and are more knowledgeable of incriminating facts that would be inadmissible at the trial. On rare occasions, when a field study demonstrates that the volume of publicity has been overwhelming and when a crime has touched the lives of large numbers of local residents, a judge will have no option but to move the trial. The Oklahoma City bombing case described in Box 12.4 is a good example.

In field studies, participants are typically asked about their knowledge of the crime in question, their perceptions of the defendant's culpability, and their ability to be impartial in light of their knowledge. (As we noted, responses may be of questionable validity because of jurors' inability to detect their own biases.) Surveys have revealed both specific prejudice, which stems from media coverage of a particular case (as in the Oklahoma City bombing), and more generic prejudice, which derives from mass media reports of social and cultural issues. Moran and Cutler (1991) showed that media descriptions of drug crimes influenced attitudes toward particular defendants who were charged with drug distribution. Cases involving sexual abuse also engender strong sentiments, fed in part by media coverage. Furthermore, generic prejudices can be engendered by publicity about jury damage awards and the controversy over tort reform in civil cases (Kritzer & Drechsel, 2012). Nearly half of prospective jurors awaiting jury selection in Seattle said that their attitudes about tort reform were informed by the media and the more these individuals supported tort reform, the more negatively disposed they were to civil plaintiffs (Greene, Goodman, & Loftus, 1991). On the other hand, publicity about lawsuits that involve consumer safety issues such as contaminated food or dangerous products can

be very valuable because it enables people to avoid those things (Kritzer & Drechsel, 2012).

Field studies have several strengths. For example, they use large and representative samples of prospective jurors, and they rely on naturally occurring publicity about actual cases. They also have a weakness: the data are correlational in nature and cannot indicate the direction of any relationship between exposure to publicity and prejudice. For example, does exposure to publicity lead to prejudicial sentiments about the defendant, or, alternatively, do people with an anti-defendant bias voluntarily expose themselves to such publicity? Reasoning from Kovera's (2002) study on the interactive effects of the media and pre-existing attitudes in a rape case, we suspect that both alternatives are possible.

Some scholars (e.g., Carroll et al., 1986) have suggested another weakness in field surveys. They argue that courts should not conclude that pre-trial publicity biases jurors just because it affects their attitudes; to be truly prejudicial, it must also affect their verdicts. According to this logic, we need to know whether pre-trial publicity effects persist through the presentation of trial evidence. Some evidence suggests that anti-defendant biases held at the beginning of the trial persist through the presentation of evidence and may even influence the way the evidence is interpreted (Ruva & Guenther, 2015).

Using Multiple Methods to Assess Effects of Pre-Trial Publicity. Given the limitations of both experimental and field studies, a few researchers have opted to use multiple methods to understand effects of pre-trial publicity in an actual trial as it occurred. One study focused on the shooting death of Sean Bell by three New York City police officers on the morning of Bell's wedding. The incident generated a great deal of controversy about the actions of the officers and, more broadly, about the treatment of African Americans by the New York City police. The three-stage study involved analyzing news articles, experimentally exposing residents of Boston (where case familiarity was almost nonexistent) to pre-trial publicity, and measuring the impact of varying levels of naturally occurring exposure in New York City residents (Daftary-Kapur, Penrod, O'Connor, & Wallace, 2014).

Results showed that regardless of whether exposure was experimentally manipulated or naturally occurring, those who had read pro-prosecution articles were more familiar with the case and more likely than those who read pro-defense articles to judge the defendants guilty prior

BOX 12.4

The Case of Timothy McVeigh: Data on the Prejudicial Effects of Massive Pre-Trial Publicity

BOB DAEMMRICH/AFP/Getty Images

Timothy McVeigh

At 9:02 A.M. on April 19, 1995, a massive explosion destroyed the Murrah Federal Building in Oklahoma City. The bombing killed 163 people in the building (including 15 children in the building's day-care center, which was visible from the street) as well as 5 people outside. The explosion trapped hundreds of people in the rubble and spewed glass, chunks of concrete, and debris over several blocks of downtown Oklahoma City. It was the country's most deadly act of domestic terrorism.

Approximately 75 minutes after the blast, Timothy McVeigh was pulled over while driving north from Oklahoma City because his car lacked license tags. Two days later, the federal government filed a complaint against McVeigh on federal bombing charges. By August 1995, McVeigh and codefendant Terry Nichols had been charged with conspiracy, use of a weapon of mass destruction, destruction by explosives, and eight counts of first-degree murder in connection with the deaths of eight federal law enforcement officials who had been killed in the blast.

The bombing, the heroic actions of rescue workers, and the arrest of McVeigh all generated a tremendous amount of publicity. Millions of Americans saw images of McVeigh, wearing orange jail garb and a bullet-proof vest, being led through an angry crowd outside the Noble County Jail in Perry, Oklahoma. Predictably, McVeigh's defense team requested that the trial be moved from Oklahoma City to a more neutral (or at least a less emotionally charged) locale.

As part of their motion to move the trial, McVeigh's attorneys enlisted the help of a group of psychologists to provide information to the court about the extent and type of publicity in the Oklahoma City newspaper and in the papers from three other communities (Lawton, Oklahoma, a small town 90 miles from Oklahoma City; Tulsa; and Denver) (Studebaker & Penrod, 1997). Their media content analysis identified all articles pertaining to the bombing in these four papers between April 20, 1995, and January 8, 1996, and coded the content of the text, including positive characterizations of victims, negative characterizations of the defendant, reports of a confession, and emotionally laden publicity. They also measured the number of articles printed in each paper and the amount of space allotted to text and pictures (*United States v. McVeigh*, 1996).

The data were compelling: During the collection period, 939 articles about the bombing had appeared in the Oklahoma City newspaper and 174 in the *Denver Post*. By a whopping 6,312–558 margin, the *Daily Oklahoman* had printed more statements of an emotional nature (e.g., emotional suffering, goriness of the scene) than the *Denver Post* (Studebaker & Penrod, 1997). On the basis of this analysis and other evidence presented at the hearing, Judge Richard Matsch moved the trial to Denver. In June 1997, McVeigh was convicted on all 11 counts and sentenced to death. He was executed in June 2001.

Critics have long suggested that studies of pre-trial publicity lack usefulness because they do not measure the public's reactions to naturally occurring publicity. (As we pointed out, researchers often "expose" participants to news reports in the context of an experiment.) To address these concerns, Christina Studebaker and her colleagues conducted an online study to examine how differences in naturally occurring exposure to pre-trial publicity affected public attitudes, evidence evaluation, and verdict and sentencing preferences in the *McVeigh* case (Studebaker et al., 2002). They found, among other things, that the closer people were to the bombing site, the more they knew about it and the more they believed that McVeigh was guilty. This study employs a novel methodology to explore important real-world effects of pre-trial information.

CRITICAL THOUGHT QUESTION

Why would prospective jurors with more knowledge about the case also be more likely to convict Timothy McVeigh?

to trial. People exposed to greater quantities of publicity were more biased than those exposed to less publicity. Importantly, exposure occurred eight weeks before participants rendered verdicts, suggesting that the effects of pre-trial publicity may be long lived. The study also lends external validity to laboratory studies in which exposure to media accounts is manipulated by researchers.

Remedies for the Effects of Pre-Trial Publicity

Given that pre-trial publicity adversely affects jurors' impartiality, what can be done to restore the likelihood of a fair trial for the defendant? Four alternatives are available.

1. *Continuance.* The trial can be postponed until a later date, with the expectation that the passage of time will lessen the effects of the prejudicial material. This view remains in vogue with some judges. But although continuances may decrease jurors' reliance on factual pre-trial publicity, they do not dampen jurors' recall or use of emotionally biasing information (Kramer, Kerr, & Carroll, 1990). Futhermore, prejudicial effects of pre-trial publicity can linger for at least eight weeks post-exposure Daftary-Kapur et al. (2014).

2. *Expanded voir dire.* The most popular method for handling pre-trial prejudice involves conducting a thorough *voir dire* of potential jurors in order to identify and dismiss those with particularly strong biases. But expanded *voir dire* may be of limited usefulness. Jurors may not recognize their own biases, and can hide their true feelings from an examiner if they so choose. They may also be hesitant to self-disclose in a public courtroom. Finally, Freedman, Martin, and Mota (1998) found that the impact of pre-trial publicity actually increased, rather than decreased, when jurors were questioned about their exposure prior to trial.

3. *Judicial instructions.* A fairly simple remedy for the biasing effects of pre-trial publicity is an instruction from the judge telling jurors to ignore what they learned about the case prior to trial and admonishing them to base their decision on the evidence. But cautionary instructions may also be insufficient to reduce the biasing effects of exposure to pre-trial publicity. In one mock jury study, participants learned that a defendant was charged with killing his estranged wife and a neighbor (Fein, McCloskey, & Tomlinson, 1997). Before trial, half

of the jurors read articles about the murders and some also read an article in which the defense attorney complained about the negative publicity: "The coverage of this case serves as another fine example of how the media manipulates information to sell papers, and knowingly ignores acts which would point toward a defendant's innocence" (p. 1219). Despite judicial instructions to ignore this information, jurors' verdicts were significantly influenced by it, unless the defense attorney had made them suspicious of the media's motives. In other words, mock jurors could follow the instruction only when they were given some reason to suspect that the pre-trial information was biased.

On the basis of existing research, these three remedies appear to be largely ineffective. These methods probably fail as safeguards because of the way that people remember and use information to form impressions and make judgments (Ruva & Guenther, 2015). Unless they have some reason to discount or ignore pre-trial publicity when it is first encountered, most people will use it to help them interpret subsequent information and to make various pieces of information "fit" together in a coherent theme. Therefore, once the idea of a guilty perpetrator is established, it may become an organizing principle for the processing of additional information about the person. For these reasons, safeguards that attempt to remove an existing bias may never work as well as trying to find jurors who never had a bias to start with. For this reason, most social scientists prefer changes of venue.

4. *Change of venue.* A **change of venue**, the most extreme remedy for pre-trial prejudice, is typically requested by defense attorneys in cases that have generated a great deal of biased publicity (e.g., the Boston marathon bombing case). Changing venue means that the trial is held in a different geographic jurisdiction and that jurors for the trial may be drawn from this new jurisdiction. But venue changes are expensive, inconvenient, and time-consuming, so judges are reluctant to grant them, though some evidence suggests that they are more easily persuaded when defense attorneys provide media analyses documenting the extent of news coverage (Spano, Daftary-Kapur, & Penrod, 2011). Venue changes can result in significant variations in characteristics of the communities, and hence, the jurors, involved, as illustrated by the case of William Lozano, a Hispanic police officer who was convicted of killing an African American motorist

in Miami. After his conviction was reversed because of pre-trial publicity and he was granted a retrial, the case was first moved to Tallahassee (which has a much smaller Hispanic population than Miami) and eventually tried in Orlando (where the Hispanic population is more sizeable). The Florida appellate court reasoned that in cases in which race may be a factor and changes of venue are appropriate, trials should be moved to locations where the demographic characteristics are similar to those of the original location (*State v. Lozano*, 1993).

In some instances, judges have imported jurors from a nearby jurisdiction under the assumption that they are less likely to be influenced by local publicity. The judge in Bill Cosby's 2017 sexual assault trial undertook this plan when he agreed to bring in jurors from outside of suburban Philadelphia, where the trial was held. This solution reduces inconveniences for the judge, other court personnel, and attorneys, but obviously increases hardships on jurors.

Psychologists have been enlisted to support a lawyer's motion for one or more of these protections against pre-trial prejudices. When publicity is pervasive, a professionally conducted public opinion survey is the technique of choice for evaluating the degree of prejudice in a community. Public opinion surveys gauge how many people have read or heard about a case, what they have read or heard, whether they have formed opinions, what these opinions are, and how their opinions influence perceptions of the case.

Public opinion surveys are also time consuming, and often require more resources than the typical client can afford. However, they usually yield valuable information. Obtaining a change of venue for a highly publicized case is probably the most effective procedure available for improving the chances for a fair trial. Moreover, even if the venue is not changed, the results of the survey can often be used in jury selection. Because of the multiple purposes for which they can be used, public opinion surveys are a popular tool among trial consultants.

Summary

1. *How do juries' verdicts differ from those of judges'?* The question of whether juries' and judges' verdicts differ significantly was answered in a massive empirical study by Harry Kalven and Hans Zeisel. In actual trials, 75% of the time the jury came to the same verdict that the judge would have reached. In 19.5% of trials, the judge and jury disagreed. In the vast majority of these disagreements, the jury was more lenient than the judge. The major source of discrepancies was what Kalven and Zeisel called "jury sentiments," or factors beyond the evidence and the law. Recent replications of this classic study showed remarkably similar results: In criminal cases, the judge and jury agreed on a verdict in 70% of trials, and when there was disagreement, jurors were more likely than judges to acquit.

2. *What does the legal system seek in trial juries?* The legal system seeks representative and unbiased juries. Both are hard to achieve. The jury selection process can, in some instances, create an unrepresentative jury.

3. *What stands in the way of jury representativeness?* The lists from which jurors' names were selected—originally only voter registration lists—underrepresent certain segments of society such as youth, older adults, and minorities. Many people fail to respond to their jury summons. Others seek dismissal by claiming personal hardship. To make jury pools more representative, jurisdictions have broadened the sources of names of prospective jurors.

4. *What procedures are used in voir dire?* The goal of *voir dire* is an unbiased jury. Prospective jurors who have biases or conflicts of interest can be challenged for cause and discharged. Using peremptory challenges, each side may also dismiss a certain number of prospective jurors without giving any reason. Questioning of the prospective jurors is done at the discretion of the judge. In most trials, there is some combination of questions from the judge and the attorneys. When questioning jurors, most attorneys also try to sway them to

their viewpoint through various ingratiation and indoctrination techniques.

5. *What personality and attitudinal characteristics of jurors, if any, are related to their verdicts? How effective are lawyers at responding to these characteristics?* A few personality- and attitude-related characteristics of jurors—Authoritarianism, Need for Cognition, and Trust in the Legal System—are related to their verdicts. Attorneys tend not to focus on jurors' personality characteristics during jury selection, probably because they are difficult to identify. In choosing jurors, lawyers base decisions on their implicit personality theories and stereotypes.

6. *What role do trial consultants play in a trial?* Initially, practitioners of scientific jury selection tried to determine which demographic characteristics of jurors were related to sympathy for one side or the other in trials. More recently, consultants have broadened their work to include (1) pre-trial assessments of reactions to the evidence and (2) the development of themes that organize the evidence for specific jurors likely to be swayed by this approach. There is some evidence that science-oriented consultation may be useful in cases in which jurors' attitudes about the evidence are especially important.

7. *In what ways does pre-trial publicity pose a danger to fair trials? How can these dangers be reduced?* Freedom of the press and the right to a fair trial are usually complementary, but some trials generate so much publicity that the parties' right to an impartial jury is jeopardized. In addition, publicity about other cases or about social or cultural issues can create generic prejudice that can influence jurors' reasoning in a particular case. Psychologists have studied the effects of pre-trial publicity on potential fact-finders and have also evaluated various mechanisms for reducing the negative effects of pre-trial publicity. Change of venue, though the most costly remedy, may also be the most effective because it does not require jurors to disregard information to which they have been exposed.

Key Terms

Authoritarianism

behavioral confirmation processes

bench trial

black sheep effect

casuistry

challenges for cause

change of venue

cognizable groups

evaluation apprehension

generic prejudice

implicit biases

implicit personality theory

jury sentiments

Need for Cognition

peremptory challenges

scientific jury selection

selection effects

similarity–leniency hypothesis

social desirability effect

social judgments

source monitoring

specific pre-trial publicity

venire

voir dire

13 Jurors and Juries

ORIENTING QUESTIONS

1. Describe the issue of jury competence.

2. What evidence is most important to jurors when deciding guilt in criminal trials? When deciding liability and damages in civil trials?

3. How can jurors be helped to understand their instructions?

4. What is the impact of extralegal information on jurors?

5. Can jurors disregard inadmissible evidence?

6. What is meant by the statement "Bias is inevitable in jurors"?

7. What reforms of the jury system do psychologists suggest?

One out of three Americans will serve as a juror at some point in their lives. Other than voting, there is no more direct way that citizens can be involved in their government. Juries are a vital institution of a democratic society. A trial by jury is the only right to appear in both the main body of the U.S. Constitution (Article 3) and the Bill of Rights (Sixth Amendment for criminal cases and Seventh Amendment for civil cases). The U.S. Supreme Court underscored the importance of the jury by stating that "[t]he guarantees of jury trial in the state and federal constitutions reflect a profound judgment about the way in which the law should be enforced and justice administered" (*Duncan v. Louisiana*, 1968, p. 149). More recently, the Supreme Court acknowledged the preeminent role of juries in our legal system when it announced that nearly any contested fact that increases the penalty for a crime must be determined by a jury (*Blakely v. Washington*, 2004).

Trial by jury is an institution that routinely draws ordinary citizens into the apparatus of the justice system. Although the number of U.S. cases decided by juries has dropped recently as a result of rising litigation costs and alternative dispute resolution, many countries around the world are changing their legal systems to include laypeople as jurors (Hans, Fukurai, Ivkovic, & Park, 2017). In fact, jury trials have been reintroduced in Russia and Spain; instituted in Japan, South Korea, Venezuela, and Argentina; and form an integral part of the legal system in countries in Africa (e.g., Ghana, Malawi), Asia (e.g., Sri Lanka, Hong Kong), South America (e.g., Brazil), and Europe (e.g., England, Scotland, Ireland, Denmark). Jurors also decide many criminal cases in Canada, Australia, and New Zealand.

For many jurors, their participation demands sacrifices of income, time, and energy. In a massive class action lawsuit against the Ford Motor Corporation, one juror continued to attend the trial even after suffering injuries in a hit-and-run accident and in spite of requiring constant pain medication; another juror whose family moved out of the county opted to live in a hotel near the courthouse in order to continue hearing the case. On occasion, jury service can be extremely unpleasant: in 2009 a San Diego judge declared a mistrial in a kidnapping case after the defendant flung feces at the jury. Fortunately, he missed. Yet serving on a jury can also be educational and inspiring. Many jurors have a positive view of the court system after serving (Bornstein & Greene, 2017). Occasionally, jury service even brings great personal satisfaction, as it did for Erika Ozer and Jeremy Sperling, who married a few years after they met in a New York City jury box.

The American legal system relies on laypeople to serve as jurors in both criminal and civil trials, and in both federal and state courts. Although laws and procedures differ somewhat in the state and federal systems, the task for jurors is essentially the same: listen attentively to the evidence, decide what "facts" are true, and consider those facts in light of the relevant laws as explained by the judge to reach a verdict. Jurors in criminal trials have a different objective than those in civil trials, however. In criminal trials, the question is whether the government, by way of the prosecutor, has proven "beyond a reasonable doubt" that the defendant is guilty of the crime charged. In civil trials, juries typically make two decisions: first, whether the defendant (or, in some instances, the plaintiff) is **liable**, meaning responsible for the alleged harm, and second, whether the injured party (typically the plaintiff) should receive any money to compensate his or her losses, and if so, how much. These monies are called **damages**. For example, if a pedestrian is injured by a fast-moving bicyclist, jurors can be called on to decide whether the bicyclist was at fault and how much money the pedestrian should receive. Although the vast majority of civil cases are resolved outside the courtroom, often in settlement discussions between the opposing lawyers, thousands of civil cases are tried before juries each year.

The jury system casts its shadow well beyond the steps of the courthouse, because predictions about jury verdicts influence decisions to settle civil lawsuits and to accept plea bargains in criminal cases. Thus, the jury trial is an important and influential tradition; no other institution of government places power so directly in the hands of the people and allows average citizens the opportunity to judge the actions of their peers (Abramson, 1994).

Antecedents of the contemporary jury system may be seen in citizen juries used by the ancient Greeks and Romans, and formalized in English laws of 800 years ago. Despite this long history, the jury system has often been criticized. One commentator described the jury as, at best, 12 people of average ignorance. Another critic, Judge Jerome Frank, who served on the federal appeals court, complained that juries apply law they don't understand to facts they can't get straight. Even Mark Twain took a swing at the jury system. In *Roughing It*, he called the jury "the most ingenious and infallible agency for defeating justice that wisdom could contrive."

The civil jury, in particular, has been vilified. Among the criticisms: civil juries are incompetent, capricious, unreliable, biased, sympathy prone, confused, gullible, hostile to corporate defendants, and excessively generous to plaintiffs (Vidmar, 1998). We examine, and debunk, many of these claims later in this chapter.

Much of the public outcry focuses on the seemingly excessive nature of jury damage awards. For example, Marc Bluestone of Sherman Oaks, California, received a jury award of $39,000 after his mixed-breed Labrador retriever, valued at $10, died a few days after returning home from a two-month stay at a pet clinic. Explains Steven Wise, a lawyer and animal rights activist: "The courts are beginning to realize that the bond between humans and animals is very powerful" (Hamilton, 2004). Other large damage awards have come in cases against the tobacco industry for its role in smokers' illnesses and deaths (Box 13.1).

To be sure, the jury system also has its defenders. Many authors (e.g., Bornstein & Greene, 2017) point out that claims about juries are often based on anecdotes

---

BOX 13.1

The Case of Ex-Smoker Lucinda Naugle and Her $300 Million Jury Award

Lucinda Naugle started smoking Benson and Hedges cigarettes in 1968 when she was 20 years old, believing that it made her look older and more sophisticated. She quit at age 45, but by then it was too late; she had contracted severe emphysema. She sued the manufacturer of Benson and Hedges, Philip Morris USA, claiming that it had committed fraud by hiding knowledge that smoking was addictive and harmful to smokers' health. Remember that the public knew little about the health hazards of cigarette smoking in 1968, so the critical issues in these cases are what tobacco industry insiders knew, when they knew it, and what they shared with the public.

When her case was tried before a jury in 2009, Ms. Naugle's condition was serious: she testified that she could not walk without struggling for breath and that she had to carry a walkie-talkie to the bathroom in case she needed help. She required a lung transplant that she was unable to afford—until the jury determined that Philip Morris was 90% responsible for Naugle's condition and awarded her $56 million in compensatory damages and $244 million in punitive damages.

As the largest single damage award in an individual lawsuit against a tobacco company, the verdict generated significant publicity and controversy. Its size stunned even the judge, who said, "From the moment I read the verdict and took a deep breath, I have considered that verdict and what I should do." Judges can reduce jury awards they deem excessive, and Judge Jeffrey Steitfeld, who presided over the trial in Broward County, Florida, vowed to do so. He called the jury award "excessive and shocking" and suspected that jurors were upset and inflamed by Philip Morris' "blame the smoker" defense. He may also have considered that more than 9,000 former smokers have filed similar lawsuits against the tobacco industry in courts across Florida.

CRITICAL THOUGHT QUESTION

Why would the jury verdict in this case have generated significant controversy?

that are unrepresentative or fabricated and on studies that lack scientific validity. Most of us never hear about the hundreds of thousands of juries each year that toil out of the spotlight and, after careful deliberation, reach reasonable verdicts. In fact, as we point out in this chapter, the bulk of scientific evidence shows that juries generally do a commendable job (Bornstein & Greene, 2011b).

Proponents further argue that trial by jury epitomizes what is special about the justice system in that it ensures public participation in the process. Verdicts reached by representative juries can and often do increase the legitimacy of the process in the eyes of the public, particularly in controversial trials. Juries can serve as a check on the arbitrary or idiosyncratic nature of a judge. Because juries do not give a reason for their verdicts (as judges are required to do), they retain a flexibility that is denied to judges. Finally, participating on a jury can both educate jurors and enhance their regard for the justice system. Alexis de Tocqueville (1900), a 19th-century French statesman, wrote, "I do not know whether the jury is useful to those who are in litigation, but I am certain it is highly beneficial to those who decide the litigation; and I look upon it as one of the most efficacious means for the education of the people which society can employ" (p. 290). Tocqueville was right: engaging in meaningful deliberations reinforces jurors' confidence in fellow citizens and public institutions (Gastil, Black, Deess, & Leighter, 2008).

So, are juries capable of making fair and intelligent decisions, or are the criticisms justified? If the criticisms are fair, can the legal system do anything to improve the functioning of juries? Psychologists are in a good position to answer these questions because their studies of juror and jury decision-making have become so plentiful that they occupy a central place in psychology and law research. From their findings, psychologists have been able to obtain a better picture of how the jury system works.

How Jurors Think

Jurors are expected to evaluate and weigh the evidence presented by both sides in a trial in order to determine the "facts," that is, what actually happened sometime in the past. The evidence can come from laypeople who witnessed or have first-hand knowledge of the events and people involved. Evidence can also come from experts who, given their training or experiences, can offer professional opinions relevant to the issues in dispute. Jurors then consider those facts in light of the relevant law, as explained by the judge, and in terms of the standard of proof. In a criminal trial, they must ask themselves whether the prosecutor proved her case "beyond a reasonable doubt"

and in a civil trial, whether the plaintiff proved his claims "by a preponderance of evidence." Criminal juries decide whether the defendant is guilty of the crimes charged, and civil juries decide whether the defendant is liable for harm suffered by the plaintiff and if so, how much money is owed the plaintiff in compensation.

Over the past several decades, researchers have subjected the jury to careful scientific scrutiny by applying theories and principles of social psychology (e.g., stereotyping, attribution, social influence, conformity, and small-group behavior) and cognitive psychology (e.g., memory, reasoning, judgment, and decision-making). Later in the chapter, we consider psychological research on how jurors work together as members of a jury to reach their verdicts. In this section, we focus on how psychologists characterize the thought processes of individual jurors.

In the cognitive realm, **dual-process models** of information processing capture individual jurors' thought processes as they attend to and evaluate evidence presented during a trial. A number of dual-process models exist (including one espoused by Nobel-prize winning psychologist Daniel Kahneman in his 2011 book, *Thinking, Fast and Slow*), but they all propose two ways in which people process information—either by rationally and deliberately evaluating the content of the information or by reacting to it quickly and intuitively, without careful analysis. The former requires motivation, effort, and ability; the latter does not.

One dual-process model, termed cognitive–experiential self theory, is especially relevant to decisions that jurors make (Krauss, McCabe, & Lieberman, 2012). This theory suggests that when people rely on analysis and logical arguments, they are using a rationally based cognitive system that is active, deliberate, and effortful. On the other hand, when people rely on emotion, intuition, or stereotypical thinking from past events, they are using an experientially based system that is unconscious and effortless. The experiential mode is the default mode of processing, and jurors will shift to cognitive processing only if the importance of careful analysis is stressed to them. When they *do* think rationally about the evidence, they tend to become more lenient toward criminal suspects because they are alerted to possible reliability issues with the evidence (Rassin, 2016). But they will revert to experiential processing when they are emotionally aroused (Epstein, 2003) or have to decipher complicated evidence (Levett & Kovera, 2008).

The Story Model

Another influential model of individual jurors' decision-making is the **story model**, developed by psychologists

Reid Hastie and Nancy Pennington (see, generally, Pennington & Hastie, 1993). They chose the name story model because they suspected that the core cognitive process involved in juror decision-making was construction of a story or narrative summary of the events in dispute.

In many ways, the juror's task is like that of a mystery reader. The joy of reading a mystery comes from savoring each clue, combining it with prior clues, and evaluating its significance in the overall puzzle of who committed the crime. According to the story model, that is how most jurors operate. As they listen to the evidence, they form a **schema**, or mental structure that aids in the processing and interpretation of information. Just like mystery readers who remember clues that fit their hypothesis and forget clues that do not, jurors construct their own private stories about the evidence so that it makes sense to them; in the process, they pay inordinate attention to certain pieces of evidence while ignoring others. Good lawyers know this. In fact, really great lawyers know that an important task is to convince the jury that their story, and not their opponent's story, is the right one. Famed criminal defense attorney "Racehouse" Haynes once said, "The lawyer with the best story wins."

According to the model, jurors actively construct stories by considering three sources of information: the evidence presented during the trial, their personal experience in similar situations, and their broad knowledge of the elements of a story. After jurors learn about the verdict options in the case, they map their story onto the verdict options and determine which verdict fits best with their constructed story.

To illustrate the role of story construction in juror decision-making, Hastie and Pennington interpreted the dramatic differences between White Americans' and African Americans' reactions to the 1995 acquittal of O.J. Simpson on charges he murdered his wife and her friend. They suspected that because of life experiences and beliefs, African Americans could more easily construct a story about police misconduct and police brutality than could White Americans. Thus, African Americans were more likely than Whites to accept the "defense story" that a racist police detective planted incriminating evidence on Simpson's property (Hastie & Pennington, 1996). (According to a 2016 Washington Post-ABC News poll, the majority of both Black and White Americans now agree that Simpson was at least "probably guilty.")

In one of their early empirical studies, Pennington and Hastie (1986) interviewed mock jurors who had seen a filmed reenactment of a murder trial and who were asked to talk out loud while making a verdict decision. The evidence summaries constructed by jurors had a definite narrative story structure, and, importantly, jurors who reached different verdicts had constructed different stories.

In a later study, Pennington and Hastie (1988) assessed whether the order in which evidence is presented influences jurors' judgments. Apparently so. They found that stories were easy to construct when the evidence was presented in a temporal order that matched the occurrence of the original events ("story order") but harder to construct when the evidence was presented in an order that did not match the sequence of the original events ("witness order").

Prosecutors and defense attorneys would be wise to familiarize themselves with these findings, because the study has significant implications for the practice of actual trials. When Pennington and Hastie manipulated the order of evidence in a simulated trial, they affected the likelihood of a guilty verdict. For example, mock jurors were *most* likely to convict a criminal defendant when the prosecution evidence was presented in story order and the defense evidence in witness order. They were *least* likely to convict when the prosecution evidence was presented in witness order and the defense evidence in story order.

Is the story model a complete and accurate description of how jurors decide the verdict in a trial? No. For starters, it focuses only on *jurors* and does not address the complex nuances that come into focus when jurors deliberate as a jury. But as a framework for understanding the cognitive strategies employed by individuals to process trial information prior to deliberations, it is highly useful. Later in the chapter, we consider models that integrate pre-deliberation preferences of individual jurors and the collective experience of deliberating as a jury.

Are Jurors Competent?

In this section, we focus on a broad question about jurors: are they competent to execute their duties properly? Some commentators have suggested that jurors in criminal cases make more mistakes than the public should tolerate, in part because they are faced with tough cases—cases in which the evidence is neither flimsy enough to warrant dismissal nor compelling enough to induce a guilty plea (Arkes & Mellers, 2002). Reexamining the data on jury–judge comparisons first presented by Harry Kalven and Hans Zeisel (1966; described in Chapter 12), Professor Bruce Spencer estimates that jury verdicts are incorrect in at least one out of every eight cases (Spencer, 2007). He asks, "Can we be satisfied knowing that innocent people go to jail for many years for wrongful convictions?" (*Science Daily*, 2007).

Psychologists have examined the impact of specific kinds of evidence and other factors on the accuracy of jurors' verdicts. Some of their studies focus on whether jurors can listen attentively to expert testimony and use it appropriately, that is, without giving it undue weight. Other studies have asked whether, as the legal system assumes, jurors understand and correctly apply the judge's instructions on the law and have the necessary reasoning skills to understand protracted and complex cases. Researchers have tested the assumption that in reaching their verdicts, jurors rely only on the evidence and disregard information that is not evidence (e.g., preexisting beliefs; irrelevant facts about the defendant, victim, plaintiff, or witnesses; and any information that the judge asks them to disregard).

To address these issues, psychologists have used a variety of methodologies, including questioning jurors after trials, analyzing archival records of past verdicts, and conducting field studies and jury simulation studies. In simulation studies, the researcher introduces and experimentally manipulates some piece of information (e.g., the defendant's race or gender, the presence of an alibi witness) and measures the extent to which that information, as well as the actual evidence, influences jurors' reasoning and verdicts. Although simulation studies sometimes cast this information in a more prominent light than would be likely in real trials (e.g., a defendant's physical appearance might seem salient in an abbreviated and simulated trial but would lose its impact in a lengthy proceeding), they are nonetheless useful techniques for exploring how jurors reason and make decisions. They involve random assignment of research participants to conditions (the "gold standard" in experimental methodology) and allow researchers to control what the participants experience. As a result, researchers learn precisely what effects their manipulations have on resulting jury performance.

Jurors Rely on Relevant Evidence, Seen through the Lens of Their Emotions

On the basis of these studies, psychologists have learned something very important: jurors in both criminal and civil cases pay considerable attention to the strength of the evidence. In fact, **evidentiary strength** is the most important determinant of jurors' verdicts (Devine, Krouse, Cavanaugh, & Basora, 2016). Differences in strength of the evidence can have profound effects on jury verdicts: Some studies have shown a 70% increase in conviction rates as the evidence against the accused increases (Devine, Clayton, Dunford, Seying, & Pryce, 2001).

Professor Stephen Garvey and his colleagues (2004) analyzed the verdicts of 3,000 jurors in felony trials in four metropolitan areas to find out what explained jurors' first votes. They measured the strength of the evidence by asking the judge who presided in the case to estimate it. They then determined that the judge's assessment of the strength of the evidence was powerfully associated with the jurors' first votes: The stronger the evidence against the defendant, the more likely the juror was to convict.

Jurors' judgments in civil trials also tend to reflect the strength of the evidence, in particular, the severity of the plaintiff's injury. More seriously injured plaintiffs engender more sympathy and receive greater compensation than less seriously injured plaintiffs (Bright & Goodman-Delahunty, 2011; Greene & Bornstein, 2003). Awards specifically intended to compensate plaintiffs for pain and suffering are correlated with economic damage awards that compensate plaintiffs for medical expenses and lost wages (Hans & Reyna, 2011).

These findings are important because they speak to the question of whether jurors are competent to execute their duties as the law intends. One would hope that jurors in criminal trials would convict when the strength of the evidence against a defendant was strong, and acquit when it was weak. Apparently they do just that. And one would hope that jurors would assess damage awards by taking into account the extent of the plaintiff's losses. They do that, too. So there is reason for optimism about jurors' abilities to manage their assigned tasks.

Although the legal system expects jurors to evaluate guilt, liability, and losses objectively, jurors' emotional reactions can also influence assessment of the facts and evidence. Of particular concern are emotions that are integral to the case itself, that is, emotions that arise out of the contentious, graphic, or violent nature of the evidence, particularly in criminal trials. Until recently, psychologists had tended to overlook this important determinant of jurors' reasoning, probably because it was difficult to measure and to distinguish from jurors' moods and emotions that are incidental to the trial process. But recent research has shown powerful effects of jurors' emotion on their reasoning process. There can be large emotional swings over the course of a trial, in both positive emotions such as happiness and hope, and negative emotions such as anger, disgust, and frustration (Georges, Wiener, & Keller, 2013). The experience of one particular emotion—anger—has an especially powerful effect on judgments of culpability and responsibility. As you might expect, as anger increases, the motivation to be fair-minded and objective decreases, and jurors become more punitive (Georges et al., 2013; see also

Nunez, Myers, Wilkowski, & Schweitzer, 2017). Understandably, jurors also have strong emotional reactions to seeing gruesome photographs of victims of extreme violence. In those cases, convictions increase as jurors' sense of disgust increases (Salerno, 2017).

Jurors' Understanding of Expert Testimony

Another aspect of competent decision-making is appropriate attention to witness testimony, which can be problematic if the testimony entails complicated or technical information. As society has become increasingly specialized and knowledge has accumulated rapidly, the judicial system has come to rely on expert witnesses to inform jurors about these advances. Experts typically testify about scientific, technical, or other specialized topics with which most jurors are not familiar. In accident cases, they may describe the nature and causes of various claimed injuries. In commercial cases, they may detail complex financial transactions and contractual arrangements. In criminal cases, they may describe procedures used to gather and test forensic evidence such as blood, fingerprints, DNA, and ballistics.

In general terms, expert testimony exerts a small, reliable effect on jurors' decisions, particularly when the testimony is not overly technical and can be understood by jurors (Vidmar, 2005). In these sorts of trials, when prosecutors introduce expert testimony, convictions are more likely, and when the defense introduces expert testimony, convictions are less likely. In Box 13.2 we describe a case in which expert testimony appeared to exert appropriate influence.

BOX 13.2

The Case of Dharun Ravi: Expert Testimony from an I.T. Specialist

In a case that galvanized concerns about suicide by gay teens, Rutgers University student Dharun Ravi used a webcam to remotely spy on his roommate kissing another man, and sent Twitter and text messages to other dormitory residents, encouraging them to watch when the roommate, Tyler Clementi, invited the man back two nights later. After discovering Ravi's actions, Clementi committed suicide by jumping off the George Washington Bridge, a mere three weeks into his freshman year. Ravi then deleted his text messages.

Former Rutgers University student, Dharun Ravi, was convicted of using a webcam to spy on his roommate.

The controversy that swirled around this case for more than a year focused on whether this was a hate crime or simple boorish and childish behavior on Ravi's part. Eventually he was charged with 15 crimes.

One of the witnesses who testified for the prosecution at Ravi's 2012 trial was Douglas Rager, a former Rutgers University police detective and information technology expert. He established the trail of electronic evidence, including Twitter feeds, cell phone records, dining card swipes, and dormitory surveillance cameras, and provided a "net flow" analysis that described how the computers in the dormitory were connected. His testimony must have been useful to jurors, as they convicted Ravi on all 15 counts, including invasion of privacy, bias intimidation, lying to investigators, and tampering with evidence. Adding further controversy to an already-contentious case, the judge sentenced Ravi to a mere 30 days in jail. Said Judge Glenn Berman, "I do not believe he hated Tyler Clementi. I do believe he acted out of colossal insensitivity."

CRITICAL THOUGHT QUESTION

Given what you've learned about the ways that jurors use expert testimony, what do you suspect they focused on when discussing Detective Rager's testimony during deliberations?

One concerning issue is whether, because many jurors lack rigorous analytical skills, they resort to unsystematic or effortless (i.e., experiential) processing of expert testimony and attend to peripheral or superficial aspects of experts' testimony (their credentials, appearance, personality, or presentation style), rather than the content of the testimony. But analysis of 50 real jury deliberations in civil trials, recorded as part of the Arizona Jury Project, and results of other studies show that, in most cases, characteristics of the messenger (i.e., the expert) have minimal influence. In fact, jurors are affected by peripheral details only when they do not fully understand the content of the expert's testimony (Bornstein & Greene, 2017). Even then, jurors can rely on other members of the jury with more sophisticated knowledge or experience (Greene, 2009). So there is little reason to believe that jurors focus excessively on superficial aspects of expert testimony.

Nonetheless, there is one kind of expertise—complicated scientific and technical expertise—that challenges jurors. In fact, jurors tend to underutilize expert testimony when it involves scientific information such as DNA or other forensic science evidence (Bornstein, 2004; Koehler, Schweitzer, Saks, & McQuiston, 2016). As a result, they may have difficulty distinguishing between reliable scientific evidence and "junk science."

Jurors tend to be inattentive to the nuances of scientific methodology. In one study, mock jurors' guilt ratings were largely unaffected by the validity of the scientific tests about which the expert testified. So whether a fingerprint matching method had been scientifically validated was irrelevant to their judgments (Koehler et al., 2016). Jurors even have difficulty evaluating the validity of scientific research when sensitized to the flaws of the methodology by an opposing expert (Levett & Kovera, 2008). In these circumstances, they *do* tend to place undue weight on the experts' experience and qualifications (Koehler et al., 2016). How can jurors be made more attentive to the quality of scientific evidence? Koehler and his colleagues suggest that courts, legislatures, and rules committees promote policies and instructions that minimize an expert's background and emphasize the quality of the scientific methodology being used.

Jurors' Abilities to Understand Their Instructions

Jury instructions, provided by the judge to the jury near the end of a trial, play a crucial role in every case. They explain the laws that are applicable to the case and direct jurors to reach a verdict in accordance with those laws. Ironically, jurors are often treated like children during the evidence phase of the trial—expected to sit still and pay attention, and infrequently allowed to ask questions—but are treated like accomplished law students during the reading of the judge's instructions, when they are expected to understand the complicated legal terminology of the instructions. An appellate court acknowledged as much in granting a plaintiff a new trial in 2012. One judge called the jury instructions "a dreadful muddle" (Qualters, 2012).

Psychologists assess comprehension by providing instructions to jurors, typically in the context of a mock trial, and then testing them using true-false, multiple-choice, or open-ended questions. Findings from those studies have been supplemented by analyses of the jury deliberations in civil trials that constituted the Arizona Jury Project (Diamond, Murphy, & Rose, 2012).

According to the Arizona study, discussion about instructions constituted 17% of the comments made during deliberations, and not surprisingly, jurors focused more on case-specific instructions than on the general rules applicable in all cases. Importantly, jurors were quite accurate in how they discussed the instructions: only 19% of their comments were incorrect. But nonetheless, they averaged 52 errors per case. One source of confusion was the legal language itself. In general, jury instructions repeat statutory language and therefore contain legal terms that are unfamiliar to laypeople. (For example, in most civil cases, jurors are informed that the burden of proof is on the plaintiff to establish his or her case by a *preponderance* of the evidence, but the word *preponderance* appears 0.26 times per million words in the English language!).

Can this situation be rectified? Could the instructions be rewritten, or could their presentation be revised so that jurors have a better chance of understanding and implementing them properly? Yes. A large number of research studies have focused on improving comprehension by modifying the language of the instructions. These studies borrow principles from the field of **psycholinguistics** (the study of how people understand and use language), including minimizing or eliminating the use of abstract terms, negatively modified sentences, and passive voice, and reorganizing the instructions in a more logical manner. These simplified instructions are easier for jurors to understand and use (Lieberman, 2009).

Many states have revised portions of their jury instructions. California was the first state to finalize "plain-English" instructions for both civil and criminal trials (Post, 2004b). Consider these changes to the California civil jury instruction on "burden of proof":

> Old: *"Preponderance of the evidence means evidence that has more convincing force than that opposed to it. If the evidence is so evenly balanced that you are unable to say that the evidence on either side of an issue preponderates, your finding on that issue must be against the party who had the burden of proving it."*

> New: *"When I tell you that a party must prove something, I mean that the party must persuade you, by the evidence presented in court, that what he or she is trying to prove is more likely to be true than not true. This is sometimes referred to as 'the burden of proof.'"*

Not surprisingly, simplified instructions enhance jurors' comprehension of the law and result in far fewer questions to the judge about what the jury instructions mean (Post, 2004b).

But confusion about language was not the primary source of comprehension errors in the Arizona deliberations: only approximately 30% of the errors involved language misunderstanding and these were often corrected by other jurors. The more common errors stemmed from the piecemeal construction of jury instructions and the fact that they failed to address crucial topics. According to Diamond and her colleagues, the instructions are put together "like a patchwork quilt with pieces from the defense, pieces from the plaintiff, and pieces from the judge" (Diamond et al., 2012, p. 1598). This means that jurors themselves have to try to fit the pieces together without much advice or guidance from the judge. On the other hand, instructions about seemingly important topics like insurance and attorneys' fees are typically omitted altogether. As a result, jurors use their own knowledge and assumptions about these topics, which can result in unwarranted disparity in their decisions.

There is yet another way that instruction comprehension can be improved, namely, by providing instructions at the beginning of the trial, rather than waiting until the end. Instructions are typically given after the evidence has been presented and just before the jury retires to deliberate, though some states require judges to provide preliminary instructions before any of the evidence is presented, and many individual judges do so of their own accord (Dann & Hans, 2004).

Instructing the jury at the conclusion of the trial reflects a belief in the **recency effect**: that the judge's instructions will have a more powerful impact on a jury's decision when they are given late in the trial, after the presentation of evidence. The recency effect suggests that recent events are generally remembered better than more remote ones. Having just heard the judge's instructions, deliberating jurors would have them fresh in their minds and be more likely to use them.

Logical as it might seem, this idea has been questioned by a number of authorities who have raised concern that jurors have already made up their minds by the time they hear their instructions. Judge E. Barrett Prettyman's (1960) position reflects this concern:

> It makes no sense to have a juror listen to days of testimony only then to be told that he and his conferees are the sole judges of the facts, that the accused is presumed to be innocent, that the government must prove guilt beyond a reasonable doubt, etc. What manner of mind can go back over a stream of conflicting statements of alleged facts, recall the intonations, the demeanor, or even the existence of the witnesses, and retrospectively fit all these recollections into a pattern of evaluations and judgments given him for the first time after the events; the human mind cannot do so (p. 1066).

The obvious alternative is to give the instructions earlier in a trial. This idea reflects schema theory—that jurors should be instructed *before* the presentation of testimony because this gives them a mental framework to appreciate the relevance or irrelevance of testimony as it unfolds. This line of reasoning gains support from research in cognitive psychology showing (1) that people learn more effectively when they know in advance what the specific task is, and (2) that schematic frameworks facilitate comprehension and recall (Bartlett, 1932; Neisser, 1976).

The delivery of jury instructions at the beginning of the trial rests on the notion of a **primacy effect**—that instructions will have their most beneficial effect if they are presented first, because jurors can then compare the evidence they hear to the requirements of the law and apply the instructions to the evidence in order to reach a verdict. In this way, jurors know the rules of the trial and the requirements of the law before the trial commences. ForsterLee and Horowitz (2003) reported that mock jurors who received instructions at the beginning of the trial recalled and used more of the evidence than did jurors who were instructed after the evidence.

Preliminary instructions have other beneficial effects. In a study conducted in Los Angeles Superior Court, jurors who received pretrial instructions said that they were able to focus better during the trial (Judicial Council of California, 2004). Judges also believe that substantive preliminary instructions help jurors to follow the evidence (Dann & Hans, 2004).

We would argue that judicial pre-instructions are vastly underutilized. There is no reason why general instructions about the law (e.g., burden of proof, assessment of the credibility of witnesses) should not be given at both the beginning and the end of trials. Interim instructions can be given as needed to explain issues that come up during the trial, and instructions that depend on the specific evidence in a trial can be given at the end (Ellsworth & Reifman, 2000).

Finally, we believe that jurors should be allowed to ask questions about their instructions, rather than simply listen passively as the judge reads the instructions aloud, as is common practice now. Increasingly, jurors have the opportunity to ask questions of various witnesses who testify during the trial. Wouldn't it make sense for them to have the chance to inquire about any confusions or lack of clarity in the law itself?

Jurors' Willingness to Apply Their Instructions

Two questions arise pertaining to jurors' willingness to apply their instructions. First, must they follow the letter of the law if doing so violates their sense of justice and results in an unfair verdict? Second, how can judges insist, in the digital era, that jurors avoid online media during the trial, and once instructed, are jurors willing to obey those orders?

The first question concerns **jury nullification**, the implicit power to acquit defendants despite evidence and judicial instructions to the contrary. Throughout history, juries have occasionally ignored the law rather than enforced it, particularly when they believed the law was unjust. In the mid-1800s, juries acquitted abolitionists of helping slaves escape from the South even though the abolitionists' actions violated the fugitive slave law. But there are also cases of nullification where White southern juries refused to convict members of the Ku Klux Klan and others who terrorized Blacks during the early years of the civil rights movement. One case concerns Byron de la Beckwith and the murder of civil rights leader Medgar Evers (see Box 13.3).

The controversy about jury nullification resurfaced in the turbulent Vietnam War period when the government began to prosecute antiwar activists, usually on charges of conspiracy, and juries often acquitted. Jury nullification acknowledges that while the public trusts jurors to resolve the facts and apply the law in a given case, they also expect them to represent the conscience of the community (Abramson, 1994).

Jurors' Online Activities. You may know what this means:

imho def glty
jury dty cwot

You would be correct if you guessed, "In my humble opinion, the defendant is guilty. Jury duty is a complete waste of time." If you suspected that this message was texted from a courtroom during a trial, you would probably be correct. Jurors' use of smartphones, iPads™, and other devices to access blogs, Twitter, Facebook, and other websites—whether to tweet minute-to-minute coverage of a trial, conduct Google searches on defendants, victims, attorneys, and excluded evidence, or simply pass the time—has increased exponentially in the past few years. Nine of the twelve jurors in a high-profile federal drug trial in Florida admitted to doing online research in direct violation of the judge's orders. A prospective juror in West Virginia contacted a defendant via MySpace even *before* jury selection, telling him that "God has a plan for you and your life." At a minimum, these actions constitute willful disobedience of court rules. More likely, they involve outright misconduct. In some instances, the consequences have been cataclysmic: a Kentucky murder conviction was reversed because two jurors Facebook-friended the victim's mother during the trial and an Arkansas death row inmate's conviction was tossed because a juror had tweeted from the courtroom.

Web browsing and postings prior to, during, and after a trial raise concerns about whether a criminal defendant's Sixth Amendment right to a fair trial can be protected. When jurors rely on information that comes from unknown and unreliable sources and is not subjected to the adversarial context of a trial, has the integrity of the proceedings been threatened?

Judges have struggled with this problem. Some courts now prohibit jurors' use of electronic devices during trials and others monitor jurors' online activities. Jurors in California, for example, are told that they are prohibited from using "*any* electronic device or medium, *any* Internet service, *any* text or instant-messaging service, and *any* Internet chat room, blog, or website to exchange *any* information about the case until the panel is discharged" (California Civil Jury Instructions 100, 2011). For most jurors, such strongly worded instructions are sufficient; they abstain. But many jurors have deliberately disregarded the directive, and more than a few defendants have argued, in appealing their convictions, that jurors' access to the Internet prejudiced their verdicts.

The Case of Byron De La Beckwith: Jury Nullification and Race

BOX 13.3

Eager to see his children after a long day at work, civil rights leader Medgar Evers stepped out of his car in Jackson, Mississippi, on a hot June night in 1963 and was gunned down from behind by an assassin. The shooting ignited a firestorm of protest that ended in several more deaths and galvanized the civil rights movement.

The case against Byron de la Beckwith was strong but circumstantial. His rifle with his fingerprint was found at the scene, and a car similar to his was seen in the vicinity of Evers's home. But no one saw Beckwith pull the trigger, and his claim that he was 90 miles away at the time of the shooting was substantiated by two former police officers.

Beckwith was tried twice in 1964; both times the all-White, all-male jury deadlocked and failed to reach a verdict. This was an era of volatile race relations in which African Americans were excluded from jury service and in which attorneys for Ku Klux Klan members charged with killing civil rights leaders openly appealed to White jurors for racial solidarity. Beckwith's segregationist views were a common bond between himself and the juries that failed to convict him.

Byron De La Beckwith was convicted in the slaying of civil rights leader Medgar Evers.

But things were different when Beckwith was retried in 1994. Despite the obstacles presented by stale evidence, dead witnesses, and constitutional questions, prosecutors put Beckwith on trial for the third time. This time, Beckwith's racist ideology was a liability. Despite pleas from defense attorneys that jurors not focus on Beckwith's sensational beliefs, a jury of eight Blacks and four Whites convicted him of murder in 1994. He was immediately sentenced to life in prison. Darrell Evers, the slain civil rights leader's son, who was nine years old at the time of the shooting, said he attended the trial to confront Beckwith: "He never saw my father's face. All he saw was his back. I wanted him to see the face, to see the ghost of my father come back to haunt him."

CRITICAL THOUGHT QUESTION

Contrast jury nullification in trials that occurred in the mid-1800s, in the early years of the civil rights movement, and in Beckwith's retrial in 1994. What do these examples have in common? How are they different?

Though this issue has attracted scant scholarly attention, we can extrapolate from previous research to understand why it occurs and, perhaps, how to remedy it. Just as jurors chafe under instructions to disregard inadmissible evidence they deem pertinent (as we explain later in the chapter), they are also annoyed by restrictions on accessing information online. Such prohibitions may seem, especially for tech-savvy jurors, to impair their ability to glean information needed to deliver a just verdict. Being restricted from accessing information online may actually impel some jurors to do just that. In fact, acknowledging that jurors are active information processors who want to make the right decisions helps to explain why they seek out online information. It can provide clarity about a legal term, background and context information that jurors

lack, and insights about the parties and their situations. Jurors perceive that it will help them render more just decisions (Morrison, 2011). So when the judge says, "Don't use the Internet," jurors have difficulty believing that the judge *really* means, "No Internet use" (MacPherson & Bonora, 2010).

Previous research also suggests some remedies. Psychologists know that pretrial instructions are effective in giving jurors a roadmap for the evidence they will hear. It follows that judges should instruct jurors about restrictions on Internet access—including reasons for those restrictions and consequences for ignoring them—when jurors first enter the courtroom for jury selection and at designated times throughout the trial. We suggest that judges should acknowledge jurors' desire to conduct online research and to share their experiences on social media. Judges should explain clearly that doing so introduces inconsistencies and inaccuracies into the proceedings, and they should remind jurors that defendants have a constitutional right to a trial by an impartial jury. Discussing these issues with jurors during *voir dire* and seeking a commitment to abide by the rules is important. We suspect that treating jurors in this way may reduce some of the problems associated with this phenomenon. Others believe that more extreme measures are needed, such as informing jurors of the legal penalties they face for engaging in prohibited activities and then implementing those punishments (Zora, 2012).

Jurors' Abilities to Decide Complex Cases

Judge John V. Singleton looked up as his law clerk leaned against his office door as though to brace it closed. "You won't believe this," she said breathlessly, "but there are 225 lawyers out there in the courtroom!" (Singleton & Kass, 1986, p. 11). Judge Singleton believed it. He was about to preside over the first pretrial conference in *In re Corrugated Container Antitrust Litigation* (1980), at that time one of the largest and most complicated cases ever tried by a jury. The modern day equivalent is the case between Apple and Samsung over technology patents. In a 2012 trial (there have been several trials, held all across the globe), jurors received 109 pages of instructions and a 20-page verdict form with approximately 700 very detailed questions. Among the questions were per-device dollar amounts that Apple and Samsung might owe each other for violating various intellectual property rights. Apple won that round, as jurors determined that Samsung infringed on its patents for mobile devices and awarded Apple more than $1 billion in damages. But the U.S. Supreme Court set aside a portion of the award in 2016.

The case in Judge Singleton's court actually entailed three trials: a 15-week criminal trial that involved 4 corporations, 27 corporate officers, scores of witnesses, and hundreds of documents; a four-month-long trial with 113 witnesses and 5,000 exhibits; and a second trial involving plaintiffs who had opted out of the original lawsuit. Discovery and trials took five years. In the midst of this organizational nightmare, Judge Singleton worried about the "unsuspecting souls out there in the Southern District of Texas whose destiny was to weigh the facts under the complex antitrust law" (Singleton & Kass, 1986, p. 11).

The loudest and most vehement concerns about juror competence center on their abilities to decide complex cases. In product liability and medical malpractice cases, for example, there are difficult questions related to causation (i.e., who or what actually caused the claimed injuries), and in business cases there are intricate financial transactions that must be dissected and evaluated. These cases often require jurors to render decisions on causation, liability, and damages for multiple plaintiffs, multiple defendants, or both (Vidmar, 1998). In criminal cases, the use of forensic evidence contributes to case complexity (Heise, 2004).

Many arguments have been made against the use of juries in complex cases. Some prominent examples include (1) the evidence is too difficult for a layperson to understand; (2) the general information load on juries is excessive because of the large number of witnesses, particularly expert witnesses, who testify in these cases; and (3) because of *voir dire* procedures that result in the exclusion of jurors with some understanding of or interest in the case, less-capable jurors are left to decide.

Data about jurors in complex trials support some, but not all, of these concerns. Interview studies (e.g., Sanders, 1993) consistently point to a substantial range in the abilities of jurors to understand and summarize the evidence. Some jurors are willing and able to attend to the complicated nature of the testimony and the sometimes-arcane questions of law that they raise; others are overwhelmed from the beginning. Lempert (1993) systematically examined the reports of 12 complex trials. He concluded that in 2 of the 12 cases, the expert testimony was so complicated and esoteric that only professionals in the field could have understood it. On the other hand, Lempert found little evidence that jurors were befuddled—and concluded that their verdicts were largely defensible.

But jurors *can be* confounded by the presence of multiple parties and claims. When Reiber and Weinberg (2010) presented hypothetical cases of varying complexity to individuals summoned for jury duty, they found that comprehension worsened as the number of parties and claims increased. Mock jurors had difficulty deciding a breach of contract case that involved a claim, an affirmative defense, a permissive counterclaim, and a third-party claim (no surprises there!). They managed capably to decide an automobile negligence case that involved a single plaintiff and single defendant.

These findings point to the need for attention to how a complex case is presented to the jury. A judge has wide discretion to set the tone and pacing of the trial, to implement procedures to assist the jury, and, ultimately, to ensure equal justice under law. Jury aids such as written summary statements of expert testimony and interim summaries can enhance the quality of jurors' decision-making, as can other reforms discussed later in the chapter.

One would not expect a college student to pass a course without taking notes, asking questions to seek clarification, or discussing an interesting concept with a professor or fellow student. Yet all too often, jurors are handicapped by trial procedures that discourage or even forbid these simple steps toward better understanding. We suspect that jurors would have an easier time—and their verdicts would be more reasoned—if judges structured jurors' tasks to be more conducive to their learning (e.g., giving well-organized pre-instructions and simplifying the language of the instructions). Fortunately, as we point out later in the chapter, many judges now do so.

Effects of Extralegal Information

By now it should be clear that jurors do a reasonably good job in their role as legal decision makers: they put appropriate weight on the most important evidence presented during a trial, namely, the strength of the relevant evidence. They understand and utilize most expert testimony properly, and according to analyses of their deliberations, they understand most of their instructions. But jurors are also affected by irrelevant information such as the defendant's background or appearance, what they read in the newspaper or see online, and other sources of extraneous details, all of which constitute **extralegal factors**. As a very simple example, unattractive defendants are slightly more likely than attractive defendants to be convicted (Devine & Caughlin, 2014). In this section, we consider the myriad ways that jurors' decisions are affected by legally irrelevant information, including racial differences.

Jurors' decisions in criminal trials are influenced by a complicated interaction of defendant's race, jurors' race, and the type of crime charged. There is a general tendency, albeit weak, for jurors to be harsher toward defendants of different races than their own (Devine & Caughlin, 2014). In one study, Black jurors rated White defendants as more aggressive, violent, and guilty than Black defendants, and White jurors were harsher on Black defendants than on White defendants, but only when the crime was *not* racially charged (Sommers & Ellsworth, 2000). When the crime *was* racially charged, the defendant's race did not influence White jurors' verdicts. Professor Samuel Sommers (2007) interpreted

the race-based results in the context of **aversive racism**, a social-psychological concept that proposes that most White jurors are motivated to avoid showing racial bias and, when cued about racial considerations (e.g., when the crime was racially charged or when jurors were instructed to avoid prejudice), they tend to render color-blind decisions. But without those explicit reminders to be objective, subtle racial biases influence their decisions.

What accounts for the fact that although evidence strength is, in many cases, the primary influence on jurors' decisions, extralegal evidence still exerts an impact in other cases? According to the **liberation hypothesis** (Kalven & Zeisel, 1966), when the evidence in a case clearly favors one side or the other, juries will decide the case in favor of the side with the stronger evidence. But when the evidence is ambiguous (i.e., the prosecution and defense cases are evenly balanced), jurors are "liberated" and allowed to rely on their assumptions, sentiments, and biases. In this situation, extralegal evidence affects verdicts.

One can understand jurors' attention to extralegal information by applying the cognitive–experiential self theory we introduced earlier. When jurors deliberately focus on the arguments or evidence provided during a trial, they are relying on a rationally based system of information processing. That is likely to occur when the evidence is unambiguous and comprehensible. But when the evidence is contradictory or confusing, jurors may be more likely to rely on an experientially based system. In these circumstances, extralegal factors can assert their influence.

Support for these ideas comes from post-trial questionnaire data collected from jurors, judges, and attorneys in 179 criminal cases. Professor Dennis Devine and his colleagues determined that extralegal factors such as demographics of the foreperson and exposure to pretrial publicity were related to jury verdicts only when the prosecution's evidence was weak (Devine, Buddenbaum, Houp, Studebaker, & Stolle, 2009). In the face of ambiguity, jurors were more likely to use experiential processing, and extralegal information had an impact. But when the evidence was unambiguous— clearly favoring one side—they were likely to rely on the logic of the arguments and think rationally. As a result, extralegal factors had less effect. Consistent with these findings, people who tend to process information experientially are more likely than rational processors to acknowledge that extralegal factors would affect their verdicts (Gunnell & Ceci, 2010). Psychologists have now examined the impact of various kinds of extralegal information in both criminal and civil trials.

Impact of Extralegal Information in Criminal Trials

The Influence of Prior-Record Evidence. In 2009, church custodian Jose Feliciano was a fugitive on charges related to assault on a seven-year-old girl in 1999. When the parish priest, Edward Hinds, learned of these charges, he threatened to fire Feliciano. This led Feliciano to stab Hinds multiple times, according to Chatham, New Jersey prosecutors. Feliciano was charged with murder, and prosecutors moved to introduce the 1999 charges to show that he was motivated to kill Hinds.

Once jurors hear evidence about a defendant's prior criminal record or prior criminal charges, they may no longer be able to suspend judgment about that defendant and decide his or her fate solely on the basis of evidence introduced at trial. Therefore, the prosecution is often not permitted to introduce evidence of a defendant's criminal record, for fear that jurors will be prejudiced by it and judge the current offense in light of those past misdeeds. However, if defendants opt to testify, then prosecutors may be able to question them about certain types of prior criminal involvement in order to impeach their credibility as witnesses. In that circumstance, the judge may issue a **limiting instruction** to the effect that evidence of a defendant's prior record can be used for limited purposes only: to gauge the defendant's credibility but not to prove the defendant's propensity to commit the charged offense. Defense attorneys and even some judges are decidedly suspicious of jurors' ability to follow this rule, as well they should be; limiting instructions are rarely effective. Thus, defendants with prior criminal records have three bad choices: take a plea bargain regardless of actual guilt, go to trial but do not testify, or testify and risk the possibility that jurors will learn about a prior record and be more likely to convict (Rickert, 2010).

Some of these possibilities have been assessed empirically by researchers who studied more than 300 criminal trials in four jurisdictions across the country: Los Angeles, Phoenix, the Bronx (New York City), and the District of Columbia (Eisenberg & Hans, 2009). They determined that the existence of a prior record affected a defendant's decision to testify, as 60% of those without criminal records testified on their own behalf, compared to only 45% with criminal records. They also determined that in about half of the cases in which defendants with prior records opted to testify, the jury learned about that prior record. This rarely occurred when defendants did not testify. Finally and most importantly, juries apparently relied on their knowledge of the prior record to convict defendants when other evidence in the case against them was weak. This suggests that a prior record can lead to a conviction even when the evidence in a case normally would not support this verdict.

Why does evidence of a prior record increase the likelihood of conviction on a subsequent charge? For some jurors, the prior record, in combination with allegations related to the subsequent charge, may show a pattern of criminality; together they point to an individual who is prone to act in an illegal or felonious manner. Other jurors, upon hearing evidence of a prior conviction, may need less evidence to be convinced of the defendant's guilt beyond a reasonable doubt on the subsequent charge. Prior-record evidence may lead a juror to think that because the defendant already has a criminal record, an erroneous conviction would not be serious. This juror might therefore be satisfied with a slightly less compelling demonstration of guilt.

The Impact of Character and Propensity Evidence. Evidence about a defendant's character—for example, that he is a kind and gentle person—is generally not admissible on the issue of whether the defendant committed a crime. There are exceptions, however. Character evidence can be used to provide evidence on guilt when it is relevant to the defendant, the alleged victim, or a witness. Of course, character evidence can be either glowing or damning. When admitted in trials, these types of character evidence affect jurors differently. Professor Jennifer Hunt and colleagues have shown that although positive character evidence has little impact on jurors' judgments, evidence about negative character traits increases the likelihood of conviction (Hunt & Budensheim, 2004; Maeder & Hunt, 2011). This is consistent with social–psychological findings that judgments are more influenced by negative information than by positive information.

Evidence of other crimes or wrongdoing (so-called **propensity evidence**) is also typically inadmissible because of its potential for prejudice. Thus, prosecutors may not suggest that because a defendant had the propensity to act in a criminal manner, he or she is guilty of the crime charged. However, sex crimes are treated differently. In 1994, Congress passed a law making evidence of other sex offenses admissible to show a defendant's propensity to commit the charged sex offense. (The promulgation of this law reflects a belief that some people have a propensity toward aggressive and sexual impulses.) The California legislature enacted a similar law, and the California Supreme Court upheld the law in the case described in Box 13.4.

BOX 13.4

The Case of Charles Falsetta and His Propensity to Commit Sex Crimes

When Charles Falsetta was tried for rape and kidnapping in Alameda County Court, the prosecutor introduced evidence of two prior uncharged sexual assaults allegedly committed by Falsetta. In the first, the defendant was alleged to have begun jogging beside a woman, asked her where she was going, and then tackled and raped her. In the second incident, the defendant allegedly blocked the path of a woman as she walked to work and later jumped out from behind some bushes, grabbed her, threw her into the bushes, and sexually assaulted her. These incidents bore a striking resemblance to the Alameda County case in which the defendant was alleged to have stopped a 16-year-old girl as she was walking to her house from a convenience store. After initially refusing a ride, the girl eventually accepted and was driven to a darkened parking lot and raped. The defendant was convicted and appealed his conviction, contending that the admission of evidence of other uncharged rapes violated his rights.

In an appeal to the California Supreme Court, Richard Rochman, the deputy attorney general who argued the case on behalf of the State of California, stated that because victims of sex offenses often hesitate to speak out and because the alleged crimes occur in private, prosecutors are often faced with a "he said, she said" credibility problem. Allowing prosecutors to present propensity evidence in these cases would give jurors the full picture of the defendant's past sexual misconduct, reasoned Rochman. The California Supreme Court agreed (*People v. Falsetta*, 1999).

CRITICAL THOUGHT QUESTION

Why is propensity evidence *not* admissible in most cases, and why is it *admissible* in cases that involve sexual behavior?

Perhaps you considered the case of beloved comedian Bill Cosby and wondered why, since he faced numerous allegations of sexual assault, his 2017 trial involved only one incident with one woman. Those other alleged assaults were inadmissible as evidence because Pennsylvania, unlike California, bars the introduction of propensity evidence, even in sexual assaults (Colb, 2016).

What effect does propensity evidence have on jurors? In arguing in support of allowing propensity evidence in the *Falsetta* case, the California Attorney General assumed that jurors could properly use propensity evidence to gauge the defendant's disposition to commit sex crimes. Yet psychologists can point to a fundamental error in this assumption—the belief that this characteristic or trait is stable over time and that situational factors are irrelevant (Eads, Shuman, & DeLipsey, 2000). In short, making this assumption constitutes the fundamental attribution error.

Impact of Extralegal Information in Civil Trials.

In recent years psychologists have paid increased attention to the workings of civil juries. As a result, they are able to address the question of whether jurors are competent to decide civil cases fairly and rationally. Do jurors determine liability and assess damages in a rational way, relying on the legally appropriate sources of information? Or are they swayed by emotion and prejudice or overly attentive to extralegal factors?

The Impact of Injury Severity on Liability Judgments. An important decision that jurors must make in civil cases concerns the parties' respective responsibility for the harm that was suffered. When psychologists study juries' liability judgments, they are really asking how people assign responsibility for an injury. When a baby is stillborn, do jurors perceive the doctor to be at fault for not performing a caesarean section? Would the child have died anyway? When a smoker contracts lung cancer, do jurors blame the cigarette manufacturer for elevating the nicotine level in its product, or the smoker who knowingly exposed himself or herself to a dangerous product over the course of many years? Or do they blame both, as did the jurors described in Box 13.1?

Jurors should decide liability on the basis of the defendant's conduct. Were his or her actions reckless? Were they negligent? Were they malicious and evil? For the most part, jurors' liability decisions align with evidence regarding the defendant's conduct: defendants whose actions were clearly negligent or malicious are likely to be found liable. But jurors also consider the severity of an injury or accident, sometimes referred to as **outcome severity**, when judging a defendant's liability. Although outcome severity is legally relevant to decisions about the damage award, it is largely irrelevant to a judgment concerning liability or legal responsibility. The defendant should not be saddled with a liability judgment simply because the plaintiff was seriously injured. But in their simulation of an automobile negligence case, Greene and her colleagues found that the defendant was perceived to be more negligent when the plaintiff suffered more serious injuries (Greene, Johns, & Smith, 2001). These results are consistent with a meta-analysis (Robbennolt, 2000) showing that people attribute greater responsibility to a wrongdoer when the outcome of an incident is severe than when it is minor.

Why would people assign more responsibility to an individual as the consequences of his or her conduct become more serious? One explanation is **defensive attribution** (Fiske & Taylor, 1991), an explanation of behavior that defends us from feelings of vulnerability. As the consequences of one's actions become more severe and more unpleasant, we are likely to blame a person for their occurrence, because doing so makes the incident somehow more controllable and avoidable.

As in criminal cases, jurors' emotional state during a trial can affect their judgments in civil cases. For example, jurors who are angered by evidence of wrongdoing and harm to others feel more sympathy for a plaintiff (Feigenson, Park, & Salovey, 2001) and less sympathy for a defendant (Bornstein, 1994). These experienced emotions are likely to interact with jurors' preexisting emotional states, implying that the legal assumption of strict objectivity in how jurors evaluate evidence is probably inaccurate (Wiener, Bornstein, & Voss, 2006).

Irrelevant Considerations Related to Damages Assessments. Pity the poor man. Michael Brennan, a St. Paul, Minnesota, bank president, was simply responding to nature's call when he was sprayed with more than 200 gallons of raw sewage as he sat on the toilet in the bank's executive washroom. The geyser of water came "blasting up out of the toilet with such force that it stood him right up," leaving Brennan "immersed in human excrement." He sued a construction company working in the bank at the time, but the jury awarded Brennan nothing. Why, then, did a jury award $300,000 to a workman who slipped from a ladder and fell into a pile of manure (a story aired on CBS's *60 Minutes*)?

One of the most perplexing issues related to juries is how they assess damages (Greene & Bornstein, 2003; Vidmar & Wolfe, 2009). This complex decision seems especially subjective and unpredictable because people value money and injuries differently and because jurors are given scant guidance on how to award damages (Greene & Bornstein, 2000). The awards for punitive damages—intended to punish the defendant and deter future malicious conduct—are of special concern because the jury receives little instruction about how those awards should be determined. Consider the staggering $145 billion punitive damage award against the tobacco industry in a case brought by many state attorney generals in 2000. Even the judge in the case was amazed. "A lot of zeros," he observed dryly, after reading the verdict.

Social scientists have conducted research on this issue and have learned that few people get rich by suing for damages. In state court civil trials in 2005, the median damage award was $28,000 and only 4% of winning plaintiffs received more than $1 million (Langton & Cohen, 2008). Although the media are eager to tell us about multimillion-dollar damage awards, these colossal awards are very unusual. Also, the monies requested by the plaintiff—when grounded in quantitative evidence presented during the trial—serve as "anchor points" for jurors' damage awards. But when the requests are unsupported by the evidence, they are viewed as outrageous and are disregarded (Diamond, Rose, Murphy, & Meixner, 2011).

What factors do jurors consider in their decisions about damages? Data from interviews with actual jurors, simulation studies, and videotapes of actual jury deliberations show that, as in criminal cases, jurors put most weight on the evidence they hear in court. But according to professors Shari Diamond and Neil Vidmar (2001), discussions about insurance coverage and attorney's fees—issues that are theoretically irrelevant to decisions about the amount of damages—are also quite common in jury rooms. Reviewing the deliberations of juries in the landmark Arizona Jury Project, they found that conversations about insurance occurred in 85% of these cases and the topic of attorneys' fees came up in 83% of discussions. Other research has shown that, although jurors discuss these issues, the resulting awards are not directly influenced (Greene, Hayman, & Motyl, 2008).

Can Jurors Disregard Inadmissible Evidence?

Anyone who has ever watched television shows depicting courtroom drama is familiar with the attorney's statement, "I object!" If the judge sustains an objection, the opposing attorney's objectionable question or the witness's objectionable response will not be recorded, and the judge will instruct, or admonish, the jury to disregard the material. But are jurors able to do so?

Inadmissible evidence is evidence that is presented in court but is unrelated to the substance of the case. Research indicates that a judge's admonition to disregard inadmissible evidence is relatively ineffective (Steblay, Hosch, Culhane, & McWerthy, 2006). On occasion, instructions to ignore inadmissible evidence actually backfire and result in jurors being *more* likely to use the inadmissible evidence than if they had not been told to ignore it (Lieberman & Arndt, 2000). For example, Broeder (1959) presented a civil case in which mock jurors learned either that the defendant had insurance or that he did not. Half the subjects who were told that he had insurance were admonished by the judge to disregard that information. Juries who believed that the defendant lacked insurance awarded an average of $33,000 in damages. Juries who believed that he did have insurance awarded an average of $37,000. But those juries that were aware of the insurance but had been admonished to disregard it gave the highest average award, $46,000.

These findings imply that instructions to disregard certain testimony may heighten jurors' reliance on the inadmissible evidence. Psychologists have explained this phenomenon using **reactance theory** (Brehm & Brehm, 1981) which suggests that instructions to disregard evidence may threaten jurors' freedom to consider all available information. When this happens, jurors may respond by acting in ways that restore their sense of decision-making freedom. Interestingly, simply providing jurors with a reason for the inadmissibility ruling makes them more likely to comply with it.

Jurors' overreliance on evidence they are admonished not to use may also reflect a cognitive process described in **thought suppression** studies. In a now-classic study, Professor Daniel Wegner found that asking people "not to think of a white bear" increased the tendency to do just that. In fact, the harder people try to suppress a thought, the less likely they are to succeed (Wegner, 1994). Jurors may think more about inadmissible evidence as a direct consequence of their attempts to follow the judge's request to suppress thoughts of it (Clavet, 1996). An appellate court was aware of that possibility: "(the judge) could reasonably have believed that an instruction to the jurors to disregard what they had just heard … would have been just about as effective as a directive not to think about a pink elephant" (*Sowell v. Walker*, 2000, p. 448).

But what happens when individual jurors come together to deliberate? Will the process of discussing the case with others motivate jurors to follow the judge's instructions, or will the thoughts of white bears and pink elephants still prevail? As we describe later in this chapter, jury deliberations can indeed lessen the impact of inadmissible evidence (London & Nunez, 2000).

Jurors' decisions could also be influenced by many other irrelevant factors including pretrial publicity; the personal style and credibility of attorneys; the order of presentation of evidence; and the gender, race, age, physical appearance, and attractiveness of the litigants and other witnesses (Devine et al., 2009). Sometimes the extraneous information comes from jurors themselves, rather than from the trial. For example, explicit reference to a defendant's ethnicity during deliberations in a sexual assault trial in Colorado (i.e., "Mexican men are physically controlling of women because they have a sense of entitlement and think they can do whatever they want with women") resulted in a U.S. Supreme Court ruling that racial or ethnic bias in the deliberation room will not be tolerated. The decision creates an exception to the rule that jury deliberations must be kept secret (*Pena-Rodriguez v. Colorado*, 2017).

Judges implicitly assume that jurors are able to eliminate such irrelevant considerations from their decisions. But psychologists emphasize that, as active information processors, jurors desire to make a decision based on what they believe is just, not necessarily one based on legally relevant information. So, for example, when mock jurors were told to disregard certain evidence because of a legal technicality, they allowed that evidence to influence their verdicts when they thought that it enhanced the accuracy of their decisions (Sommers & Kassin, 2001). Psychologists understand that jurors have difficulty performing the mental gymnastics required to use evidence for a limited purpose or to ignore it altogether. But they have not yet developed effective strategies to combat those problems (Daftary-Kapur, Dumas, & Penrod, 2010).

Are Jurors Biased?
The Assumption of a Blank Slate

Another broad concern about jurors is whether, as courts assume, they can put aside any preconceptions about the guilt of a criminal defendant or the merits of civil plaintiffs when forming their judgments. In other words, is it appropriate to assume that jurors enter a trial as "blank slates," free of overwhelming biases? (In criminal cases, the "blank slates" should be tinted at the outset by a presumption that the defendant is innocent of the charges.) This concern has practical importance because if jurors cannot set aside their biases, they should be excused for cause.

The judge and the attorneys inquire about a prospective juror's biases during the jury selection process. A frequent question during *voir dire* takes the following form: "Do you believe that you, as a juror, can set aside any negative feelings you might have toward the defendant (because he is from the Middle East or a police officer or a used-car salesman—whatever the group membership is that possibly elicits prejudice) and make a judgment based on the law and the facts of this case?" If prospective jurors say yes, the judge usually believes them, and they are allowed to serve as jurors.

On occasion, prospective jurors have ties to the defendant that could influence their ability to be impartial. Consider the case against former Penn State assistant football coach Jerry Sandusky (see Box 13.5).

The courts assume that individual jurors can divest themselves of any improper "leaning" toward one side or the other, and that through jury selection procedures the ideal of open-minded jurors can be achieved. Courts also assume that attorneys can identify and dismiss prospective jurors whose preconceptions would affect their verdicts, so the trial can begin with a fair and unbiased jury. For various reasons, this optimism may be misguided. First, attorneys are motivated to select jurors who are favorable to their own side, rather than those who are neutral. Second, it is impossible for anyone to be entirely free of influence by past experiences and resulting prejudices.

Inevitability of Juror Bias

In a society that respects all persons, some biases (e.g., age, race, or gender bias) are clearly prejudicial and should be shunned. But many biases—including those based on expectations and experiences—may actually be inevitable. As we use the term here, **juror bias** is a juror's predisposition to interpret and understand information

---

The Case of Jerry Sandusky: The Search for Unbiased Jurors BOX 13.5

Former Penn State assistant football coach Jerry Sandusky being led out of courthouse after conviction on charges of child sexual abuse.

In a highly anticipated criminal trial, former Penn State football coach Jerry Sandusky faced accusations of sexually molesting boys and young men over several years. The trial was held in Bellefonte, Pennsylvania, approximately 12 miles from Penn State, where football is high profile and enormously profitable. Perhaps

it was no surprise, then, that many prospective jurors had affiliations with and allegiances to Penn State. It was somewhat more surprising that so many were selected to serve on the jury. The group of 12 jurors and 4 alternates included a woman whose family has had Penn State football season tickets since the 1970s, a Penn State junior who was working in the athletic office and whose cousin played on the football team, two professors—one on the faculty for 24 years and another who retired, two women employed by the university, and three graduates of Penn State, including one who heard Jerry Sandusky speak at her graduation ceremony. Of course, having personal ties with the university does not necessarily render these jurors incapable of delivering fair verdicts. One wonders whether it was easy for them to do so—but they did convict Mr. Sandusky on 45 felony charges.

CRITICAL THOUGHT QUESTION

Why might court observers be concerned about the ability of these jurors to be objective?

Patrick Smith/Getty Images News/Getty Images

based on past experience. When people are exposed to new events, they respond by relying on past experiences. When they view a traffic accident, for instance, they may make judgments that one car ran a red light or that another car was in the wrong lane. They may assume that an accident involving teenaged drivers was caused by excessive speed or texting while driving.

Bias in responses to the actions of others is inevitable because people must make assumptions about the causes of behavior. Why was Emily so abrupt when she spoke to me this morning? Why did Juan decide to buy a new car? Why did the defendant refuse to take a lie detector test? Individuals also make decisions on the basis of their assumptions. College admission officers decide who will be admitted on the basis of applicants' credentials and academic promise. Judges decide who should be paroled based on the belief that the parolee will not commit additional crimes. Criminal defense lawyers make recommendations to their clients on how to plead on the basis of their expectations about the reactions of prosecuting attorneys, judges, and jurors. Expectations about the outcomes of one's choices rest partly on one's biases.

People make assumptions about others to understand what happened in the past and to predict what will happen in the future. Virtually all descriptions of how a juror makes decisions in a criminal trial propose that verdicts reflect two judgments on the part of jurors. One judgment is an estimate of the probability of commission—that is, how likely it is that the defendant actually committed the crime. Most jurors base their estimates of this probability on the strength of the evidence, but as we have noted, extralegal factors and jurors' previous beliefs and experiences also have an impact on how they interpret the evidence (Finkel, 1995).

A second judgment by the criminal juror concerns reasonable doubt. Judges instruct jurors in criminal cases that they should deliver a not-guilty verdict if they have any reasonable doubt of the defendant's guilt. Because the legal system has difficulty defining reasonable doubt (a common, but not very informative, definition is that it is a doubt for which a person can give a reason), jurors apply their own standards for the threshold of certainty deemed necessary for conviction.

Because bias is inevitable, most jurors come to this task with either a pro-prosecution bias or a pro-defense bias. Jurors with a pro-prosecution bias view conflicting evidence in the case through the filter of their experiences and beliefs, which make them more likely to think that the defendant committed the crime. Persons

Juror decisions are influenced by relevant and irrelevant factors, including the evidence, prior experience and the attorney's personal style and presentation.

with pro-defense biases filter the same evidence in light of *their* experiences and reactions, which make them more sympathetic to the defense.

To determine how bias affects verdicts, Lecci and Myers (2009) asked jury-eligible adults to complete the Pretrial Juror Attitudes Questionnaire (PJAQ), which includes statements such as "Criminals should be caught and convicted by any means necessary" and "Defense lawyers are too willing to defend individuals they know are guilty." Later, mock jurors watched a videotaped armed robbery trial, gave individual verdicts, deliberated as a jury, and gave post-deliberation individual verdicts. Jurors who voted guilty prior to deliberating were compared with those voting not guilty to see whether their personal biases differed. Indeed they did: jurors who convicted were more likely to endorse pro-prosecution sentiments on the PJAQ than jurors who acquitted. Biases revealed by the PJAQ predicted post-deliberation verdicts as well, suggesting that the deliberation process did little to correct for individuals' bias. It appears that even when jurors all hear the same evidence during the trial, their personal beliefs and values can affect their verdicts.

Personal predispositions may also affect the way evidence is evaluated. Professor Jane Goodman-Delahunty and colleagues found that mock jurors' beliefs about the death penalty influenced their perceptions of evidence (Goodman-Delahunty, Greene, & Hsiao, 1998). Participants watched the videotaped murder of a convenience store clerk that was captured on film. When asked about the defendant's motive and intentions, jurors who favored the death penalty were more likely than those who opposed it to "read" criminal intent into the actions of the defendant. For example, they were more likely to infer that the defendant intended to murder the victim and that his specific actions indicated premeditation. These findings remind us of the common situation in which two people experience the same event—a movie or a play, for example—and interpret the actions in very different ways, partly because of the "mindset" with which they watched or experienced that event. These beliefs, or schemas, can apparently influence the way jurors make sense of the evidence in a trial.

Psychologists have learned something interesting about how those schemas affect jurors' verdicts. When jurors are exposed to a new piece of evidence, they evaluate the evidence in a manner consistent with their current verdict preferences rather than in an objective fashion. Assume that two jurors hear the same evidence that favors the prosecution. Also assume that, at that point in the trial, Juror A favors the prosecution and Juror B favors the defense. According to the notion of **predecisional distortion**, these jurors will distort their evaluation of the evidence in a direction that supports their verdict choice. Thus, Juror A would evaluate this evidence as favoring the prosecution, whereas Juror B might evaluate it as favoring neither party, distorting his or her interpretation of the evidence away from its objective value (i.e., in favor of the prosecution) and in the direction of the side favored (Blanchard, Carlson, & Meloy, 2014).

Do jurors' biases predispose them to favor one side over another in a civil case? It seems natural for people to have feelings of compassion for injured persons and for these feelings to translate into favorable verdicts and lavish damage awards for plaintiffs. When jurors awarded $181 million in damages in 2012 to three workers injured in the explosion of a grain elevator in southern Illinois, did sympathy influence their thinking?

Surprisingly, perhaps, a variety of studies using different methodologies suggest that sympathy plays only a minor role in civil jurors' judgments. In her study of claims by individuals against corporate defendants, Professor Valerie Hans (1996) interviewed jurors and ran experimental studies that manipulated variables related to this **sympathy hypothesis**. All the data pointed to the same conclusion: that the general public is "quite suspicious of, and sometimes downright hostile to, civil plaintiffs" (p. 244). A survey conducted by the consulting firm DecisionQuest yielded similar results: 84% of the 1,012 people polled agreed with the statement "When people are injured, they often try to blame others for their carelessness." According to the same survey,

potential jurors do not think highly of civil defendants, either. For example, more than 75% of respondents believe that corporate executives often try to cover up evidence of wrongdoing by their companies, and more respondents say that product warnings are intended to protect manufacturers than say they are intended to keep consumers safe.

How Juries Deliberate

Although many studies have assessed individual jurors' reasoning process, verdicts are not issued by twelve individual jurors in criminal cases or by some variable number of jurors in civil cases, depending on where the trial takes place. Rather, they come from a group, a jury. How do individual preferences, biases, and reactions to the evidence combine to result in an agreed-upon consensus? (A unanimous verdict is required in nearly all criminal trials in the United States, and at least a majority verdict is required in civil trials.) In the process of reaching agreement, how and why will some jurors change their minds to coalesce around the group's decision?

Deliberations are important to the final resolution of a trial. Jurors do not simply pool their individual pre-deliberation verdict preferences, engage in a bit of horse-trading, and call it a day. Even on the question of damages, when it might seem logical for jurors to average their individual judgments, their discussion of the evidence and individual verdict preferences is crucial. Indeed, what happens over the course of the group discussion has a significant impact on the final verdict (Hastie, Schkade, & Payne, 1998).

The deliberation process can also improve the quality of jury decisions. We've already shown that jurors correct each other's mistaken interpretations of the jury instructions during group discussion. Can deliberations also reduce jurors' inclinations to rely on inadmissible evidence? There is reason to suspect that it can. When jurors have to share their preferences publicly, they may evaluate their own sentiments more carefully and challenge the conclusions reached by others (Bornstein & Greene, 2011).

Psychologists have studied this issue by comparing the decisions of mock jurors who deliberate and those who do not, and by examining a single group of mock jurors prior to and after deliberating. The conclusion from these studies is that deliberation can serve to decrease reliance on irrelevant information. For example, London and Nunez (2000) assessed the impact of inadmissible evidence on jurors before and after deliberation. The defendant in their mock trial was charged with taking nude photographs of a child. This evidence was deemed admissible in one condition and inadmissible in another, and was not presented in a control condition. Prior to deliberations, jurors who were told that the photos were inadmissible were as likely to convict as jurors who were told the photos could be considered, demonstrating the powerful biasing effect of inadmissible evidence. But after deliberations, convictions dropped significantly in the inadmissible evidence condition and were comparable to the control condition. Group discussion reduced the influence of inadmissible evidence, probably because jurors reminded each other of the mandate not to consider that evidence. Other studies have shown that biasing effects of pretrial publicity are also reduced by deliberations (e.g., Ruva, McEvoy, & Bryant, 2007).

Deliberating juries do not *always* make better decisions than individual jurors do, however. Whether group deliberation reduces or amplifies bias may depend on the strength of the evidence (Kerr, Niedermeier, & Kaplan, 1999). When the evidence for one side in a trial is strong, deliberation seems to decrease bias in jurors' pre-deliberation sentiments. But when the evidence is ambiguous, deliberation seems to increase biases, probably because without hearing compelling evidence during the trial, jurors stick to their beliefs, values, and assumptions during the deliberations.

What do jurors actually talk about when they deliberate? Answers to that question come from recordings of mock juror deliberations and from the civil juries that constituted the Arizona Jury Project (Diamond & Vidmar, 2001; Diamond et al., 2012). Observers have identified three stages of jury deliberations: orientation, when jurors discuss general procedures, elect a foreperson, and begin discussion; open conflict in which jurors actively try to persuade others to see things their way; and reconciliation or resolution, when jurors strive to guarantee that the chosen verdict is acceptable to everyone. On occasion, juries have opted to "sleep on it," that is, to reach a verdict one day, but not announce it until the next day, giving members some time to decide if they are comfortable with the choice.

The open conflict portion of the deliberation is obviously the most contentious. During this period, jury members use various forms of persuasive influence spelled out in social psychological theories of group dynamics. Persuasion occurs through informational and normative social influence. **Informational social influence** occurs when some compelling information, data, or interpretation convinces a juror that her personal perspective was incorrect or incomplete, and that it makes sense to change her mind. In doing so, she can state publicly, and believe privately, that she has reached the correct decision. By contrast, **normative social influence** occurs when a juror simply goes along with the group's decision in order to be conciliatory. So whereas a juror might state publicly that he agrees with a certain verdict, privately he thinks otherwise (Kaplan & Miller, 1987). Which type of influence predominates during deliberation is determined by the question being debated. If the verdict choices require careful and deliberative analysis—determining the precise amount of money to award in compensatory damages, for example—informational social influence is more likely to occur. But if the choices are more subjective, then normative influences prevail.

The open conflict portion of deliberations has also been characterized as either verdict-driven or evidence-driven (Hastie, Penrod, & Pennington, 1983). In a **verdict-driven deliberation**, jurors take a straw poll very early in their discussion. This vote reveals the general sentiment of the group and establishes the factions that see things in different ways. From here on, the deliberations involve each faction attempting to gain support from members of other factions by arguing that their interpretation of the evidence is the appropriate one. By contrast, in an **evidence-driven deliberation**, jurors do not take an early vote. Instead, they review crucial pieces of evidence in order to reach an agreed-upon consensus about how to interpret that evidence. Only then do they try to match their interpretation to various verdict options. As you might suspect, evidence-driven deliberations last longer, but are ultimately more satisfying for jurors (Hastie et al., 1983).

In recent years, psychologists have begun to integrate models of juror and jury decision-making. One possibility is that during deliberations, the jury engages in narrative construction that mirrors what occurs in the minds of individual jurors (Hastie, 2009). The result is a group-derived story that provides a synthesis of the evidence. Another, somewhat more elaborate possibility is that jurors create narrative explanations of the evidence that they bring to the deliberating table. Then, by means of a process termed "story sampling" (Devine, 2012), individual jurors exert informational influence by sampling from their memory and sharing their perspectives, and factions exert normative and informational influence in proportion to their size and the cohesiveness of their arguments. After various iterations of this process, if all goes well, a large majority faction will emerge and eventually, the jury will agree on a compelling story that is consistent with the evidence.

Jury Reform

Jury trials are conducted under strict rules developed over the years by statutes, case law, and tradition. These imperatives stem from the belief that justice is best served by an adversarial system in which the evidence is vetted through a neutral judge and limited by rules of the court. Under these rules, jurors were prohibited from investigating the facts themselves and asking questions during the trial, and they were warned not to discuss the evidence with anyone until they reach a verdict.

This model treats jurors as passive recipients of information who, like digital recorders, take in a one-way stream of communication. Jurors were expected to process all incoming information impassively, without interpretation, until finally instructed by the judge to decide something. As we pointed out earlier, this conception of juror-as-blank-slate is largely wrong; jurors actively evaluate the evidence through the lens of their personal experiences and frames of reference, pose questions to themselves, and construct narratives or stories to help them understand the evidence and make a judgment about it.

Acknowledging that most jurors are active "thought processors," psychologists and other social scientists started suggesting reforms to the jury system in the 1970s. By the 1990s, judges were also beginning to question the traditional view of jurors as passive blank slates. Against this backdrop, creative court personnel and forward-thinking judges implemented changes in trial procedures that take advantage of jurors' natural inclinations and provide tools to encourage jurors' active involvement in the process. Many of these reforms have now been implemented in courts across the country.

Some reforms are uncontroversial and benign: providing notebooks that list the witnesses and summarize their testimony in long or complex cases; giving pre-instructions or interim instructions during the course of a lengthy trial; allowing jurors to take notes; designating alternate jurors only after the presentation of evidence is completed; providing a written copy of the judge's instructions to each juror; and allowing jurors to examine the demonstrative evidence during their deliberations. Some proposed reforms are downright radical.

This includes the possibility of having opposing experts testify together in a process called a hot tub (though it does not involve a physical hot tub!), explaining to the judge or jury what they agree about and why they disagree. There could be many advantages to such a system. Theoretically, it could reduce the adversarial nature of expert testimony and enable jurors to make better comparisons between opposing viewpoints (Greene & Gordon, 2016). The hot tub has been used in administrative hearings in some countries, but rarely in the United States, and never in a jury trial.

Two reforms are only moderately controversial: allowing jurors to pose questions to witnesses (questions are screened by the judge, who decides whether they are appropriate) and to discuss the evidence in the midst of trial. These reforms have also been implemented in many jurisdictions, and research studies have charted their effectiveness. Through such studies, psychologists have learned that these new practices contribute in beneficial ways to fair and accurate decisions.

Jurors questioned about the opportunity to submit written questions have been strongly supportive. Fully 83% of jurors surveyed by the Seventh Circuit American Jury Project between 2005 and 2008 reported that the opportunity to ask questions of witnesses enhanced their understanding of the facts (Seventh Circuit American Jury Project, 2008). Examining the questions jurors asked and how jurors discussed the answers during deliberations, Arizona Jury Project researchers found that questions helped to clarify conflicting evidence and produce a plausible description of the events in dispute. Discussion of these questions and answers did not dominate jurors' deliberations (Diamond, Rose, Murphy, & Smith, 2006). Allowing jurors to ask question may have the added benefit of reducing their inclination to seek answers online (MacPherson & Bonora, 2010). Finally, although some judges have worried that jurors will be offended by having a question disallowed or will speculate about why a submitted question could not be asked, jurors themselves tend to accept that decision (Diamond, Rose, & Murphy, 2004). Therefore, we see no serious drawbacks to allowing jurors to ask questions. Doing so can clarify their understanding of the evidence, enhance involvement in the trial process, and create an environment more conducive to learning.

The somewhat more controversial reform permits jurors to discuss the evidence during the trial, rather than having to wait until formal deliberations begin. The rules are simple: All jurors must be present in the deliberation room during these discussions, and jurors must keep an open mind and avoid debating verdict options. Psychologists have described a number of potential advantages of such mid-trial discussions based on fundamental principles of cognitive and social psychology. In theory, juror discussions about the evidence can

■ Improve comprehension by permitting jurors to sift through and organize the evidence into a coherent framework over the course of the trial.

■ Improve recollection of the evidence and testimony by emphasizing and clarifying points made during trial.

■ Promote greater cohesion among jurors, thereby reducing the time needed for deliberations (Bregant, 2009).

But there are also several potential drawbacks to jury discussions during trial, and these, too, are based on well-established psychological principles. They include the possibility that jury discussions may

■ Facilitate the formation or expression of premature judgments about the evidence.

■ Diminish the quality of the deliberations as jurors become more familiar with each other's views.

■ Produce more interpersonal conflicts prior to formal deliberations (Bregant, 2009).

The first empirical test of this reform was a field experiment in which researchers randomly assigned approximately 100 civil jury trials to an experimental "trial discussion" condition and an equal number to a control "no discussion" condition (Hannaford, Hans, & Munsterman, 2000). Researchers found that of those who were permitted to discuss the evidence, approximately 70% reported that their jury had at least one such discussion. So even when permitted to talk about the case, a sizeable minority of juries did not. Jurors who reported having discussions were quite positive about them. They said that trial evidence was remembered very accurately during these discussions, that discussions helped them understand the evidence in the case, and that all jurors' points of view were considered during the course of the discussions. The perceived drawbacks were mostly logistical: Jurors said that there were difficulties in getting all members together at the same time. (After all, these short breaks represent the only time in the course of several hours that jurors may use the rest rooms or smoke a cigarette. Some people's desire for these comforts apparently outweighed their interest in talking about the evidence!) Useful data also come from the analysis of videotapes from the Arizona trials (Diamond, Vidmar, Rose, Ellis,

& Murphy, 2003). This study examined all mid-trial jury discussions, as well as the deliberations. These tapes make clear that during discussion jurors seek information from one another, raise questions they intend to ask, and talk about the evidence they would like to hear. Such discussions led to modest enhancements in jurors' understanding of the evidence and did not result in premature judgments.

These findings provide a fascinating and previously unseen picture of the jury at work as it discusses the evidence in the midst of the trial and reaches a final verdict at the end. Pre-deliberation discussion may have the added benefit of reducing reliance on inadmissible evidence and other biases that interfere with jurors' ability to impartially consider evidence. In essence, they function *during* the trial in the same way that deliberations function *after* the trial—as a de-biasing mechanism (Bregant, 2009). We see few negative effects of mid-trial discussion, and believe that allowing jurors to talk about the case simply legitimizes what they are likely to do anyway.

The Jury: Should It Be Venerated or Vilified? Revered or Reviled?

The jury system brings together individuals with diverse backgrounds, experiences, and biases who pool their perceptions of the evidence to reach a verdict (Diamond, 2006). In this way, the trial jury is a remarkable institution and, in important respects, a unique one. The use of average citizens to determine trial outcomes for rich and powerful figures such as Jeff Skilling, the former CEO of Enron, or the growing list of celebrities accused of sexual harassment in late 2017 underscores our country's commitment to egalitarian values. It is no exaggeration to say that the trial jury is sanctified as one of our fundamental democratic institutions. Political scientist Jeffrey Abramson (1994), author of *We, the Jury*, put it eloquently:

> [T]here are all the jurors we never read about, who toil out of the limelight every day, crossing all kinds of racial and ethnic lines to defend a shared sense of justice. These examples convince me that the jury, far from being obsolete, is more crucial than ever in a multiethnic society struggling to articulate a justice common to [all] citizens. Though the jury system is a grand phenomenon—putting justice in the hands of the people—we still have lessons to learn about how to design an institution that gathers persons from different walks of life to discuss and decide upon one justice for all (p. 5).

Although there remains much to learn, psychologists now know a good deal about how juries function. They know that juries don't always get it right; on occasion, jurors are overwhelmed by the sheer volume of evidence, misunderstand their instructions, and use evidence in inappropriate ways. They know that jurors' biases and prejudices can rise to the surface and color their judgments. But by and large, psychologists find little support for the extreme claims that juries perform poorly and irresponsibly. On the contrary, it seems that the institution of the jury is worth defending and worth improving.

Summary

1. *Describe the issue of jury competence.* Some commentators have wondered whether jurors and juries are overly attentive to extralegal information that, in theory, is irrelevant to the guilt decision in criminal cases and to the liability judgment in civil cases. Others have asked whether jurors will misunderstand expert testimony and dismiss it outright. Whether jurors and juries are able to understand and apply their instructions is another question. Finally, some have asked whether jurors can decide the complicated issues that arise in so-called complex cases.

2. *What evidence is most important to jurors when deciding guilt in criminal trials? When deciding liability and damages in civil trials?* In accord with legal expectations, jurors put most weight on the strength of the evidence against a defendant in a criminal trial; convicting when they are convinced beyond a reasonable doubt that the defendant is guilty. When determining liability in a civil trial, jurors focus on the defendant's conduct, although the severity of the plaintiff's losses matter, too. When assessing damage awards, they put most weight on the severity of the plaintiff's injuries.

3. *How can jurors be helped to understand their instructions?* Jurors can be instructed before the trial begins about the relevant elements of the law that they will apply to the facts they hear. Judges can provide written copies of the instructions for all jurors. Unfortunately, judges rarely answer jurors' questions about their instructions.

4. *What is the impact of extralegal information on jurors?* Research studies suggest that occasionally jurors are influenced by evidence of a defendant's prior record or character and propensity to commit crimes. In civil cases, evidence related to an accident victim's injury may influence the judgment of a defendant's liability.

5. *Can jurors disregard inadmissible evidence?* When a question posed or an answer offered during a trial is ruled inadmissible by the judge, jurors are instructed to disregard it. Psychological evidence indicates that it is difficult for jurors to disregard this testimony; in fact, the stronger the judge's admonition, the less effective it may be. Deliberations tend to reduce reliance on inadmissible evidence.

6. *What is meant by the statement "Bias is inevitable in jurors"?* *Bias*, as used here, refers to the human predisposition to make interpretations on the basis of beliefs and past experiences. Bias is inevitable because it is inescapable human nature to make assumptions about human behavior.

7. *What reforms of the jury system do psychologists suggest?* The information-processing demands placed on jurors should be simplified. More clearly worded instructions, in written as well as oral form, delivered at the beginning and at the conclusion of the trial would be helpful. Preinstructions and simplifying complex language may be especially helpful. During the trial, jurors should be able to pose questions that the judge would then ask of the witnesses. Finally, mid-trial discussion of the evidence helps jurors to organize the evidence in a thematic framework and thus improves their memory of the testimony.

KEY TERMS

aversive racism

damages

defensive attribution

dual-process models

evidence-driven
  deliberation

evidentiary strength

extralegal factors

inadmissible evidence

informational social
  influence

juror bias

jury nullification

liable

liberation hypothesis

limiting instruction

normative social
  influence

outcome severity

predecisional distortion

primacy effect

propensity evidence

psycholinguistics

reactance theory

recency effect

schema

story model

sympathy hypothesis

thought suppression

verdict-driven
  deliberation

14 Punishment and Sentencing

ORIENTING QUESTIONS

1. What are the purposes of punishment?

2. How are the values of discretion and fairness reflected in sentencing decisions?

3. What factors influence sentencing decisions?

4. What special factors are considered in the sentencing of juveniles? Of sex offenders?

5. How is the death penalty decided by juries?

6. In what ways has the Supreme Court recently limited the use of capital punishment, and what role have psychologists played in these decisions?

A sentencing decision comes near the end of a criminal prosecution and is typically made by a judge or magistrate. It encapsulates legal, pragmatic, and policy considerations and involves predictions of future criminal conduct (Ruback, 2015). Options include probation, restitution, compensation, fines, community service, imprisonment, and others. The purpose of the sentence—punishment, deterrence, incapacitation, or rehabilitation, for example—depends on the nature of the crime, the characteristics and experiences of the offender, the temperament of the judge, and, in some cases, public sentiment. As you might suspect, judges have considerable latitude or discretion in the sentences they impose in this system, and disparities in sentence length can result. **Sentencing disparities** occur whenever similar offenders who committed similar crimes receive different sentences. Various efforts to reduce disparity, including maximum and minimum sentences, sentencing guidelines, and even revisions in sentencing guidelines have been instituted, with somewhat mixed success.

Great numbers of offenders in the United States are sentenced to prison. One of the most unusual is Sylvester Jiles, who, in 2010, was sentenced to 15 years for attempting to break into the Brevard County (FL) jail one week after he had been released from that very jail! Jiles begged jail officials to take him back into custody because he feared retaliation from his victim's family.

Unusual cases like this aside, for most of the past 40 years, no other industrialized country except Russia has imprisoned its citizens at the rate of the United States. This situation was a result of what Professor Craig Haney, a psychologist and a lawyer, called America's "rage to punish" (Haney, 2006, p. 4). According to Haney, "hundreds of thousands of people have been locked up in American jails and prisons who would not have been incarcerated (for the same misdeeds) in any

other modern Western society" or "if they had committed their crimes at almost any other time in American history" (Haney, 2006, p. 11).

At the end of 2013, there were 6,741,000 adults—1 of every 37 people—under the supervision of correctional systems (i.e., incarceration, probation, or parole) in the United States. Despite the fact that this population has been declining in size for several years (Kaeble & Glaze, 2016), it is still the highest documented incarceration rate in the world (Tsai & Scommegna, 2012). Federal offenders are especially likely to be sentenced to prison (as opposed to probation or community confinement): 77% of federal offenders sentenced in 2012 went to prison. Convictions on two types of offenses— sex offenses and immigration-related offenses—were most likely to result in prison sentences. (Regarding the latter, in 2012, five federal jurisdictions along the U.S.–Mexico border accounted for fully 60% of all federal arrests and 41% of offenders sentenced to prison.) Offenders guilty of drug crimes constitute another sizeable portion of all federal inmates (Motivans, 2015). High rates of incarceration are troubling for many reasons. Incarceration diminishes offenders' ties to their communities, reduces their chances for future employment, and makes their reintegration into society more difficult. It removes offenders from their families, leaving spouses, partners, and children economically and psychologically vulnerable. And it contributes to prison overcrowding.

Racial disparities are also apparent in criminal sentencing. As of 2016, the rate of state prison incarceration was 5 times greater for African Americans and 1.4 times greater for Latinos than for Whites. In 12 states, more than half of the prison population is Black; in Maryland, that figure is 72%. And in Oklahoma, which has the highest overall Black incarceration rate, 1 of every 15 Black men is imprisoned (Nellis,

2016). Some of the disproportion is related to greater involvement in criminal activities by people of color, but analysis of imprisonment data from 2004 suggests that nearly 40% of racial disparity in incarceration *cannot* be explained by that fact alone (Tonry & Melewski, 2008). Structural disadvantages in communities of color, along with biased decision-making by police, prosecutors, and judges, also play a role.

How should a society respond to individual criminals? With an inmate population over 2 million, does it make sense to continue locking up more offenders every year? Incarceration comes at a price; every dollar spent on corrections means one less dollar for public schools, health care, parks, and higher education.

A controversial method to scale back prison populations uses risk assessment measures to apportion sentences. So-called **evidence-based sentencing** aims to reduce incarceration rates by sentencing offenders based on risk factors for recidivism such as criminal history, education, substance abuse, and employment history. Those assessed to be at low risk are given shorter terms than those assessed at higher risk. Critics claim that these plans unfairly target racial minorities, though a recent study comparing risk scores for Blacks and Whites found that regardless of offenders' race, one model of evidence-based sentencing strongly predicted recidivism risk (Skeem & Lowenkamp, 2016). The public has very mixed feelings about this approach, however (Scurich & Monahan, 2016). A somewhat less controversial process for reducing prison populations allows for the release of older and dying inmates prior to the completion of their terms, but is rarely used (Wylie, Knutson, & Greene, 2017).

Philosophical questions about the costs and benefits of punishment and incarceration, as well as the methods for meting out punishment, have been debated for many years. But a convergence of social realities has forced criminal justice officials and legislators to seek new approaches to punishing criminals. One factor has been the significant decline in crime rates since the early 1990s. A second factor driving reforms has been the significant cost of incarceration. Fiscal constraints imposed on federal and state budgets forced policymakers to confront the high cost of imprisonment and examine the cost effectiveness of various sentencing policies. In fact, there has been bipartisan support among federal lawmakers for reforming sentencing, including eliminating mandatory minimum sentences for low-level drug offenders. State legislatures have enacted changes, as well. For example, New Mexico lawmakers repealed the death penalty in 2009

primarily to save money. In other states, legislators reduced the number of probationers sent to prison for violating conditions of their release and the amount of time prisoners must serve before being considered for parole (Mauer, 2011).

As a result of these and other policy changes, state prison populations had been declining for several years, including a nearly 2% decline from 2014 to 2015 (Kaeble, Glaze, Tsoutis, & Minton, 2015). How the landscape will change during the Trump administration is unknown. For several years prior to 2017, crime had decreased in salience as an emotional and political issue, along with a reduction in "tough on crime" rhetoric. There were also modest developments in alternatives to harsh sentencing policies, particularly for drug offenses. But Attorney General Jeff Sessions has called on federal prosecutors to pursue the most serious charges possible against most suspects, including low-level drug offenders. This may lead to reversal of the recent trend toward decreasing federal prison populations.

In this chapter and against this backdrop, we address the issues of punishment and sentencing by describing their multiple goals and purposes, some of which aim to exact retribution from an offender and others that favor practical ends such as deterrence, incapacitation, and rehabilitation. We describe the factors that judges consider in their sentencing decisions, and the specific issues that arise in sentencing of juvenile and sex offenders. Finally, we examine psychological aspects of the ultimate punishment, the death penalty.

The Purposes of Punishment

The crime control model of criminal justice has heavily influenced police, prosecutors, and many judges over the past 40 years. It interprets the primary aim of law enforcement as the apprehension and punishment of criminals so they will not repeat their offenses and others will be deterred from similar acts. But as resources have dwindled, policymakers are increasingly interested in punishments that serve some beneficial function, particularly to the vast majority of offenders who reenter society after spending time behind bars.

These differing viewpoints illustrate the multiple purposes of punishment. Psychologists have identified at least seven different goals (see, e.g., Ruback, 2015).

1. *General deterrence.* The punishment of an offender and the subsequent publicity that comes with it are assumed to discourage other potential lawbreakers. Some advocates of the death penalty,

for example, believe that fear of death may be our strongest motivation; hence, they believe that the death penalty serves as a general deterrent to murder.

2. *Individual deterrence.* Punishment of the offender is presumed to keep that person from committing other crimes in the future. Some theories assume that many criminals lack adequate internal inhibitors; hence, punitive sanctions must be used to teach them that their behavior will be controlled—if not by them, then by society.

3. *Incapacitation.* If a convicted offender is sent to prison, society can feel safe from that felon while he or she is confined. One influential position (Wilson, 1975) sees a major function of incapacitation as simply to age the criminal—an understandable goal, given that the rate of offending declines with age.

4. *Retribution.* Society believes that offenders should not benefit from their crimes; rather, they should receive their "just deserts," or "that which is justly deserved." The moral cornerstone of punishment is that it should be administered to people who deserve it as a consequence of their misdeeds.

5. *Moral outrage.* Punishment can give society a means of catharsis and relief from the feelings of frustration, hurt, loss, and anger that result from being victims of crime; it promotes a sense of satisfaction that offenders have paid for what they have done to others.

6. *Rehabilitation.* One goal in sentencing has always been to help offenders recognize the error of their ways and develop new skills, values, and lifestyles so they can return to normal life and become law abiding. This has been a primary consideration in punishing juveniles.

7. *Restitution.* Wrongdoers should compensate victims for their damages and losses. Typical statutes require that defendants pay for victims' out-of-pocket expenses, property damage, and other monetary losses. Restitution is often a condition of probation.

Utilitarian Approaches

Most of these goals are **utilitarian**: They are intended to accomplish a useful outcome, such as compensating the victim, deterring crime, or incapacitating or rehabilitating the defendant. Utilitarian goals have a practical objective; they right the wrongs of past misconduct and reduce the likelihood of future criminal behavior.

Rehabilitation as a utilitarian goal has been in and out of favor throughout history. The basic notion is that offenders who receive treatment for the underlying causes of criminality will be less likely to reoffend. When it *was* the dominant goal, criminal sentences were expected to accomplish something other than incarceration and punishment.

Though the original purpose of prisons was to rehabilitate (many prisons are still called *correctional* institutions), high **recidivism** rates indicate that prisons have not been very effective at rehabilitating offenders. The extreme version of this view, dubbed the "nothing works" position, is attributed to Robert Martinson. He concluded, after reviewing a large number of outcome studies, that most attempts at offender rehabilitation fail (Martinson, 1974). Martinson's advocacy of another utilitarian approach—deterrence—led to a "get-tough" attitude toward offenders, and to increasingly punitive measures such as the three-strikes laws (laws stating that after a third criminal conviction, offenders go to prison for a very long time) and zero-tolerance policies enacted in the 1980s and 1990s. But after nearly 40 years of this "get-tough" approach with no reduction in recidivism, the pendulum began to swing back slowly in the direction of rehabilitative policies. Psychologists now know that rehabilitation can be effective when it is tailored to an offender's age, race, criminal history, religion, and other personal attributes (Andrews & Bonta, 2010). Unfortunately, many institutions continue to offer only one-size-fits-all interventions. And how rehabilitation efforts will fare amidst recent "tough on crime" rhetoric is, of course, an open question.

Retributive Approaches

Two of the punishment goals we described are **retributive**: they involve looking back at the offense and determining what the criminal "deserves" as a consequence of committing it. These goals are retribution (sometimes called "just deserts") and moral outrage, a close cousin of retribution (Kaplan, 1996). The notion of retribution implies that an offender deserves to be punished and that the punishment should be proportionate to the severity of the wrongdoing.

The stark contrast between utilitarian and retributive approaches raises the question of why we punish people. What are our motives for punishing others? Discovering how ordinary people think about this issue is important because those who draft sentencing laws should know what the public prefers (Carlsmith & Darley, 2008).

Psychologists have taken different approaches to answering this question. Some have simply asked people which philosophy they prefer and have assumed that respondents can report their true beliefs. But in studies that measured people's agreement with various sentencing policies, people tended to agree with all of them (Anderson & MacCoun, 1999)! Furthermore, people are sometimes unaware of the factors that influence their preferences (Wilson, 2002). An alternative research design involves considering the length of sentences that judges actually order and working backward from these sentences to identify the underlying motives (i.e., just deserts/retribution, deterrence, incapacitation). But this method can be fallible, too. Finally, other researchers have presented vignettes to respondents, varying the nature of the crime and details about the offender, and then measuring respondents' sentencing preferences.

Public Preferences for Deterrence and Retribution. In a now-classic study, Carlsmith, Darley, and Robinson (2002) used a **policy capturing** research technique to assess the punishment motives of ordinary people. The specific motives for punishment that they contrasted were deterrence and retribution. Using vignettes that described a variety of harmful actions, the researchers attempted to understand (or "capture") the policies underlying the punishments that people assigned. They varied different elements of the crimes described, elements that should or should not matter to respondents depending on which motive they preferred. For example, the magnitude of the harm should matter to people who are motivated by retribution, and the likelihood of reoffending should matter to those who are concerned with future deterrence. Carlsmith and his colleagues then measured the degree to which each respondent's sentence was influenced by these variables. The data showed a high sensitivity to factors associated with retribution and relative insensitivity to factors associated with deterrence. In fact, people actively seek information relevant to retribution (e.g., the magnitude of the harm and the perpetrator's intent) when they know that a crime has been committed and are asked to assign punishments (Carlsmith, 2006).

But the type of offense and the offender's intentions matter too. People react differently to those who intended to harm than to those

who were simply careless. People respond to the former with a sense of moral outrage and the need for retribution. But their primary reaction to the latter is a desire to seek restitution (Darley & Pittman, 2003). Whether the offense affects one individual or a large group of victims, people's preferences for punishment focus on what an offender deserves.

Interestingly, this is not what people *say* about their punishment beliefs. Responding to opinion polls, people are more likely to indicate support for punishment that deters criminals than punishment that exacts retribution (Carlsmith, 2008). This suggests that people do not have a good sense of their own motivations for punishing others, and may explain why citizens enact legislation one year, then soon reject it as unjust and vote to repeal it shortly thereafter (Carlsmith & Darley, 2008).

Why do people say they support deterrence but act like they favor retribution? One possibility is that people have a limited awareness of their own reasons for their punishment preferences. As social psychologists have pointed out, when it comes to introspecting about why we behave in a particular way, "we are all strangers to ourselves" (Wilson, 2002). It may also be less socially acceptable to say that we favor a penalty based on reprisal and revenge than one based on notions of future good. Or it may be that people favor deterrence for less serious offenses, but move toward retribution when the offender appears to deserve more serious punishment.

These findings appear to support the idea that many people actually favor punitive sanctions, and at least some politicians are happy to respond. Joe Arpaio, the controversial former sheriff of Maricopa County,

An all-female chain gang, instituted by Sheriff Joe Arpaio of Maricopa County in Arizona, is an example of a controversial punitive approach.

Arizona (Phoenix), called himself "America's toughest sheriff." His philosophy, which gained him national notoriety (as well as federal investigations into his management of funds), was to make jail so unpleasant that no one would want to come back—while simultaneously saving money. He sheltered prisoners in "leaky, dilapidated military-surplus tents set on gravel fields surrounded by barbed wire" and fed them "bologna streaked with green and blue packaging dye" (Morrison, 1995). He established the first women's and juveniles' chain gangs. His "air posse" of 30 private planes tracked illegal immigrants and drug smugglers and led to several racial profiling lawsuits against him. But Arpaio's career ended abruptly when he was ousted from office in 2016 and convicted of criminal contempt of court.

Another retributive goal—moral outrage—allows society the satisfaction of knowing that offenders have been made to pay for the harms they caused. Professor Dan Kahan (1996) argued that for a sentence to be acceptable to the public, it must reflect society's outrage. He maintained that the expressive dimension of punishment is not satisfied by "straight" probation, "mere" fines, or direct community service. According to Kahan, probation appears to be no punishment, a fine appears to be a means to "buy one's way out," and community service is something everyone ought to do. Kahan argued that imposing a **shaming penalty** would allow society to express its moral denunciation of criminal wrongdoers.

Shaming was a traditional means by which communities punished offenders. In colonial days, those who committed minor offenses were put in stocks in a public place for several hours for all to see and ridicule. Serious offenders were branded or otherwise marked so they would be "shamed" for life. In Williamsburg, Virginia, thieves were nailed to the stocks by the ear; after a period of time the sheriff would rip the offender from the stocks, thus "ear-marking" the offender for life (Book, 1999). Though shaming has not been used much since the early 1800s, by some accounts it is making a comeback (Porter, 2013).

The modern version of shaming allows low-level offenders—shoplifters, trespassers, and traffic code violators—to avoid all or part of a jail sentence by publicly renouncing their crimes in a humiliating way. The impetus for these alternative sentences is twofold. First, judges have become frustrated with revolving-door justice: a large number of offenders who are released from prison eventually return, suggesting that their punishments had little long-term effectiveness. Second, judges are aware of the longstanding problem of prison overcrowding and the high costs of incarceration. The American Bar Association has urged judges to provide alternatives to incarceration for offenders who might benefit from them. Some judges have been happy to oblige, and some of the sentences they have imposed are truly ingenious. For example, men caught on surveillance cameras in the process of soliciting prostitutes in Oakland, California had their faces plastered on bus stop signs and billboards (Stryker, 2005). Another innovative sentence is described in Box 14.1.

The Case of a Crooked Couple and Their Shaming Penalty

BOX 14.1

Over the course of her 16-year employment as an administrative assistant in the Harris County (Texas) District Attorney's Office, Eloise Mireles discovered a serious weakness in the office's accounting system. But rather than fix it, she and her husband Daniel opted to cheat the county out of more than $255,000. Eloise stole money orders and cashiers' checks intended to compensate crime victims, and Daniel deposited the checks in the couple's account. They spent the money on trips and tickets to concerts and sporting events. After pleading guilty to theft charges, they were ordered to spend six months in jail (one month per year for six years), stand at a busy Houston intersection for five hours at a time (he on Saturdays and she on Sundays) wearing a sign that reads "I am a thief. I stole $255,000 from a crime victims' fund," and display a sign in front of their house that says "The occupants of this residence are convicted thieves." According to Daniel Mireles's attorney, this punishment suited his client just fine because Mireles would rather admit every day that he was wrong than go to prison (Rogers, 2010).

CRITICAL THOUGHT QUESTIONS

Discuss the advantages and disadvantages of shaming as an approach to criminal sentencing in light of the goals of punishment discussed earlier in the chapter.

As you might expect, sentences like these are highly controversial. Some lawyers—defense attorneys and prosecutors alike—applaud them, acknowledging that judges have discretion in sentencing and that incarceration is costly and does not always work. But others worry that the shaming inherent in these sentences is extreme and morally repugnant. Even Dan Kahan, the early proponent of shaming penalties, now shuns them (Kahan, 2006). He asserts that ordinary citizens prefer punishments that affirm, rather than denigrate, their core egalitarian values.

Some recent research suggests that shaming may be effective, though, at least up to a point. The impetus for the study came from a 2004 law mandating that certain DUI offenders in Ohio be issued bright yellow license plates with red lettering and a serial number readily identifiable by law enforcement. Did the restricted license plate punishment have an effect on drinking and driving behaviors? The answer is a qualified yes: there were fewer license suspensions as the "saturation" of restricted plates (that is, the percentage of all plates that were restricted) slowly increased. But the effect leveled off and actually reversed when saturation reached a certain point (Porter, 2013). This suggests that the shaming aspect of the penalty may have some deterrent function because of its novelty. But when the novelty wears off, so does the penalty's effectiveness at changing behavior.

Restorative Approaches

Over the years, many people have become disenchanted with retributive justice. For one thing, punishing offenders in proportion to the severity of their offenses, although cathartic, has apparently done little to curb crime or reduce suffering. For another, inflicting punishment on offenders who "deserve" to be punished provides little opportunity for victims to be involved in the process or to have their own needs met. As a result, victims are often dissatisfied with their experiences in the criminal justice system. Finally, some shamed people become defensive and escape that feeling by denying responsibility altogether (Tangney, Stuewig, & Hafez, 2011).

In recent decades, an approach has emerged that attempts to address the damage caused by criminal offenses and encourage offenders to take responsibility. This approach, **restorative justice**, views crime as a violation of the victim and the community, rather than the state. It uses open dialogue to gain consensus about responsibility-taking and dispute resolution. The goals of restorative justice are to repair the harm and restore the losses caused by offensive activity, reintegrate offenders into society, and empower victims and the community to move from feelings of vulnerability and loss to a sense of understanding and closure (Umbreit, Vos, Coates, & Lightfoot, 2005).

Restorative justice is based on the premise that those who are most affected by crime—victims and offenders—should have a prominent role in resolving the conflict and that the community has a stake in its outcome too. Thus, it expands the circle of participants beyond the offender and the state, and encourages participants to use some combination of apology, remorse, and forgiveness to move beyond the harms caused by crime.

Restorative justice policies are used throughout the world. The Truth and Reconciliation Commissions in South Africa and Rwanda were based on these principles and the entire youth justice system in New Zealand uses a restorative justice model. These practices are becoming more common in the criminal, civil, and juvenile justice systems in the United States, as well. Many jails and prisons now offer victim impact intervention training in which inmates interact with victims in order to understand how victimization has affected them. We provide another example of a restorative procedure in Box 14.2.

How do people feel about achieving justice through a restorative process? Given the public's strong desire to punish offenders, is there support for procedures that focus on other justice goals? People apparently do value its role in repairing harm done to victims and communities. In fact, for less serious crimes, people prefer to respond with restorative measures, and for more serious offenses, people prefer responses that combine restorative procedures and punitive sanctions (i.e., prison sentences), rather than either of these options alone (Gromet & Darley, 2006). Victim satisfaction seems to drive these reactions: When observers believe that victims have achieved satisfaction and closure via a restorative justice process, they are less likely to endorse additional retributive sanctions such as prison sentences for offenders (Gromet, Okimoto, Wenzel, & Darley, 2012). Given the public's preference for both retribution and restoration, it is worthwhile examining how judges assign criminal punishments, to what extent their choices mirror public sentiment, and how psychological factors influence their decisions.

BOX 14.2

The Case for Restorative Justice: Healing a Mother Wounded by Tragedy

On July 19, 2009, Sandy Eversole got the news that all parents fear and dread: her son David Mueller, a star athlete and college student, had been killed in an automobile accident. David was riding in a car driven by his friend Dylan Salazar, travelling nearly 100 mph on a Colorado Springs city street before running off the road. As expected, Sandy and her family were overwhelmed by grief in the first few months after the accident and then angered and frustrated by the claims settlement and criminal justice responses. She wanted to know what had happened that night and why, but after Salazar was sentenced to four years in a youth correctional facility, Sandy had no way to ask questions or seek solace. That changed when the District Attorney's office gave her an opportunity to meet with Salazar in a restorative justice session led by a trained facilitator. Despite initial concerns about whether she would be capable of controlling her rage, Sandy was able to tell Salazar what her family had endured. Also apprehensive, Salazar apologized and took responsibility for the accident. Reflecting on the experience, Sandy recalled, "Right away I could tell that he was full of remorse and sadness. It was hard to find out some of the details but I was glad I did. It was easy to forgive him after I saw his tears" (www.restorativemediationproject.org).

CRITICAL THOUGHT QUESTIONS

Historically, victims have had little say in how criminal offenders are punished. Why? The restorative justice approach seeks to empower victims by giving them a voice in this matter. In your opinion, should victims' perspectives influence the punishment meted out to offenders?

Judicial Discretion in Sentencing

Criminal sentencing lies at the heart of society's efforts to ensure public order. Hoffman and Stone-Meierhoefer (1979) go so far as to state, "Next to the determination of guilt or innocence … the sentencing decision is probably the most important decision made about the criminal defendant in the entire process" (p. 241).

Sentencing is a judicial function, but sentencing decisions are largely controlled by the legislative branch—Congress and state legislatures. The legislative branch dictates the extent of judges' discretion, and many legislators believe that judges should have little or no discretion. They emphasize retribution and argue that the punishment should fit the crime. Mandatory sentences, sentencing guidelines, and the abolition of parole have been the primary ingredients in these "get tough" schemes.

Other legislators maintain that the sentence should also fit the offender—in essence, that judges should have discretion to make the sentence fit both the crime and the criminal. Discretion allows judges to capitalize on their perceptions of an offender's personal and external circumstances so that sentencing decisions can "serve, within limits set by law, that elusive concept of justice which the law in its wisdom refuses to define" (Gaylin, 1974, p. 67). Those who advocate individually tailored sentences note that each offender is different and deserves to be treated as an individual: "Theories [that] place primary emphasis on linking deserved punishments to the severity of crimes, in the interest of treating cases alike … lead to disregard of other ethically relevant differences between offenders—like their personal backgrounds and the effects of punishments on them and their families" (Tonry, 1996, p. 15).

Sentencing Policies

Some states have **indeterminate sentencing** schemes, in which judges exercise their discretion by imposing a variable period of incarceration for a given offense (e.g., 6–20 years), and a parole board determines the actual date of release. Such policies have been both hailed and criticized: hailed because they provide incentives for good behavior and encourage offenders to take advantage of available treatment programs to enhance the chances of earlier release, and criticized because they allow parole boards wide discretion in determining when the conditions of the sentence have been satisfied. When indeterminate sentencing works as it should, offenders are neither released early nor subjected to confinement beyond that necessary to ensure public protection.

In other states, the legislative branch has imposed a **determinate sentencing** system on the judiciary, effectively reducing judges' discretion. In these systems, offenders are sentenced for a fixed length of time determined by statutes and guidelines, and there is no parole. The primary goals of these sentences are retribution and moral outrage. There is little concern for the offender's personal characteristics, apart from his or her criminal record, and less potential for arbitrary or discriminatory decisions about when an offender should be released.

In a further attempt to reduce discretion, some states impose **mandatory minimum sentences** for certain offenses, including drug crimes. These policies require judges to sentence offenders to a minimum number of years in prison regardless of any extenuating circumstances. They, too, have been criticized as unjust. For example, a Utah judge was forced to sentence a first-time offender who had sold marijuana on three occasions to 61.5 years in custody with no parole. The reason: He carried a gun during the marijuana sales. The statute imposed a 5-year minimum term for the first gun count and a minimum of 25 years for each subsequent count in addition to 6.5 years for the sale of the marijuana. The judge noted that on the very day he sentenced the marijuana dealer to 61.5 years, using the same guidelines he sentenced a murderer to a 21-year term (*United States v. Angelos*, 2004).

Review of more than 73,000 cases from 2010 revealed that 75% of offenders subjected to a mandatory minimum penalty were convicted of a drug trafficking offense (U.S. Sentencing Commission, 2011). The American Psychological Association (APA) has spoken out against mandatory minimum sentences: "[T]hey have done nothing to reduce crime or put big-time drug dealers out of business. What they have done … is to fill prisons with young, nonviolent, low-level drug offenders serving long sentences at enormous and growing cost to taxpayers" (Hansen, 1999, p. 14). Consistent with these recommendations, in 2010, President Obama signed into law The Fair Sentencing Act which eliminated mandatory minimum sentences for simple possession of crack cocaine. This trend may be reversing, however. Beginning in 2017 Attorney General Jeff Sessions has prioritized longer sentences for drug offenders.

Current federal sentencing policy is based on the Sentencing Reform Act of 1984, which abolished parole and established a Sentencing Commission to develop mandatory sentencing guidelines. An overriding goal of the Sentencing Commission was to ensure uniformity of sentences. Federal judges were required to sentence offenders within a narrow range prescribed by a complicated analysis of the severity and circumstances of the crime, among other factors. But this scheme also proved to be controversial. In 2005, the U.S. Supreme Court decided that the mandatory nature of the guidelines was unconstitutional (*United States v. Booker*, 2005). Federal sentencing guidelines are now advisory rather than mandatory, meaning that they are among the factors that judges consider. In fact, judges still tend to follow the guidelines, although they are now able to consider more evidence than the guidelines would have permitted. When federal judges do diverge from the sentencing guidelines, though, their sentences are far more likely to be below the guidelines than above them. Meanwhile, the Sentencing Commission is considering alternatives to incarceration for offenders who are amenable to diversion and treatment.

Brian Gall benefited from judges' increased discretion in sentencing. In the late 1990s, while a student at the University of Iowa, Gall, had been involved in a drug ring distributing Ecstasy. But he stopped using drugs, graduated from college, became a master carpenter, and started his own business in Arizona. After being tracked down by federal authorities, he turned himself in and pleaded guilty to conspiracy to distribute a controlled substance. The judge, taking Gall's circumstances into account, departed from the guidelines and imposed a sentence of 36 months of probation and no prison time. In 2007, the Supreme Court upheld the sentence, stating that federal judges have the authority to set any reasonable sentence as long as they explain their reasoning (*Gall v. United States*, 2007).

Sentencing Process

The procedure used in most courts for sentencing has several components. The judge receives a file that contains information about the offender's personal history and prior convictions (if any), and a number of documents describing various procedures (e.g., the date of the arraignment, the formal indictment). The judge reviews the file before the sentencing hearing.

At the hearing, recommendations for a sentence are presented, first by the prosecutor and then by the defense attorney. Statements are arranged in this order to give the defendant the final word before the judge makes a decision. But there may be an unexpected consequence of granting the prosecution the opportunity to make an initial recommendation. A large body of research has shown that initial numeric requests serve as powerful standards or "anchors" on subsequent judgments (Kahneman, 2011). In fact, judges' sentencing decisions are highly influenced by the prosecutor's request for a lengthy sentence (Englich & Mussweiler, 2001), a finding that can be explained by a judgment process called **anchoring**.

Defense attorneys' sentencing recommendations are *also* influenced by the prosecutors' demands. When researchers asked lawyers to assume the role of defense attorneys in a simulated rape case, they found that though defense attorneys requested a lower punishment than prosecutors, they were still influenced by the level of the prosecutors' recommendation, and assimilated their own sentencing demands to those of the prosecutor (Englich, Mussweiler, & Strack, 2005). This behavior, in turn, will affect judges' decisions. So rather than being aided by going last, the defense may be hindered by having to follow, and counter, the prosecution's demand—its "anchor."

In addition to demands from the prosecutor and defense attorney, the sentencing judge has a probation officer's report and recommendation. This report carries a good deal of weight with judges. In one study, the judge agreed with the probation officer's recommendation in 78% of cases that resulted in community sanctions and 62% of cases that resulted in incarceration (Leiber, Beaudry-Cry, Peck, & Mack, 2017). The judge may ask the offender questions and will usually permit the offender to make a statement. In some cases, a forensic mental health professional may provide input on issues such as diminished capacity or coercion and duress (Krauss & Goldstein, 2007), addressing questions such as whether the defendant was able to understand the wrongfulness of the crime, was able to conform his or her conduct to the requirements of the law, and has particular treatment or rehabilitation needs. On the basis of these sources of information and taking sentencing options into account, the judge then sentences the offender.

To this point, we have described a system of **front-end sentencing** by judges that mark the beginning of an offender's punishment. But another sanction, **back-end sentencing**, also merits attention. Back-end sentencing occurs when parolees are arrested for new crimes or violate the conditions of their parole and are returned to prison by state parole boards (Lin, Grattet, & Petersilia, 2010). Back-end sentencing is now responsible for approximately one-third of all prison admissions (Travis, 2007). Examination of these parole revocations shows that parole board officials, eager to protect themselves from public scorn, are especially harsh on sex offenders and serious and violent offenders, regardless of what these offenders did to violate their parole. Parole boards also consider offenders' gender and race when they ratchet penalties up and down (Lin et al., 2010). We discuss these sorts of implicit biases more thoroughly in the next section.

Determinants of Sentencing: Relevant and Irrelevant

Sentencing decisions are based largely on two legally relevant factors: the severity of the offense and the offender's prior record (Ruback, 2015). Even in jurisdictions that grant judges wide latitude in sentencing, more serious crimes earn more severe punishments (Goodman-Delahunty & Sporer, 2010). And across all jurisdictions, offenders with a prior criminal record are sentenced more harshly. "Three strikes laws," also known as habitual offender laws, provide an example. Under these statutes, which exist in more than half the states, a third-time offender with two prior convictions for violent felonies can be sentenced to very lengthy prison terms.

But do judges consider *only* those legally relevant factors or do they also consider seemingly irrelevant factors like race, ethnicity, and gender? Moreover, *should* they consider other factors? For example, should an offender's experiences be taken into account? Should it matter that a convicted offender was deprived as a child, hungry, abused, and denied opportunities to go to school or look for work? Should it matter that an offender is male or female? Black or White? Gay or straight?

To examine whether these extra-legal factors affect judges' decisions, researchers have used a variety of procedures including observational studies, archival analyses of case records and sentencing statistics and interviews. They have conducted experiments in which they manipulate various facts in simulated cases or vignettes and ask sentencers to respond.

What they found is that many of these factors, including the offender's gender and race, influence sentencing decisions, often without conscious awareness of the judge. An archival analysis of cases involving 20,000 male and 3,729 female offenders showed that females received less harsh sentences than males (Steffensmeier & Demuth, 2006). These gender effects vary according to the type of crime. Males are more likely than females to be sentenced to prison and serve longer sentences for property and drug offenses. But women are just as likely as men to be sentenced to prison for committing a violent offense (Rodriguez, Curry, & Lee, 2006).

What accounts for gender disparities? There is some evidence that they arise because judges' presentence reports contain a great deal of detail, which may be difficult to process. To manage the information overload, judges may rely on well-honed stereotypes and attributions about the case and the defendant's characteristics to aid their decisions (Steffensmeier & Demuth, 2006). According to the **focal concerns theory** of judicial decision-making, judges focus on three main concerns in reaching sentencing decisions: (1) the defendant's culpability, (2) protection of the community (emphasizing incapacitation and general deterrence), and (3) practical constraints and consequences of the sentence, including concerns about disrupting ties to children and other family members.

It is not exactly clear how judges evaluate these focal concerns. But evidence from field observations of sentencing hearings (Daly, 1994; Steffensmeier, Ulmer, & Kramer, 1998) suggests that judges may view most women as less likely to reoffend, understand women's crimes in the context of their own victimization (e.g., by coercive men, alcohol or drug problems), and perceive the social costs of detaining women as higher. In fact, judges now consider the social consequences of incarceration—particularly the effects on an offender's family—for both male and female offenders, and those who have familial caretaker roles are less likely to be incarcerated than those who are not caring for others (Freiburger, 2010).

Most of the research on the influence of gender on sentencing has focused on the gender of the *offender*, but crime victims' gender also has an impact on sentencing decisions. For example, among Texas offenders who were convicted of three violent crimes in 1991, offenders who victimized females received substantially longer sentences than those who victimized males (Curry, Lee, and Rodriguez, 2004). Because this analysis controlled for the type and severity of crime, the offenses perpetrated against women were not more serious or more deserving of a longer sentence. Rather, this difference may reflect some subtle form of sexism, paternalism, or an implicit belief that a female crime victim would suffer more than a male victim.

Another important demographic characteristic that influences sentencing decisions is the race of the offender. Determinate sentencing and sentencing guidelines have not been able to eliminate racial disparities. A meta-analysis of the effects of race on sentencing decisions synthesized 71 separate studies and showed that African Americans were sentenced more harshly than Whites who committed comparable crimes (Mitchell, 2005). The disparity is larger for drug offenses (meaning that differences in sentence length for Blacks and Whites are larger for drug crimes than for other crimes). This situation may stem from media and political attention to the "crack epidemic" of the 1980s and 1990s, and public perception that the use and distribution of crack cocaine is associated with serious violent crime.

Other factors may matter, too. Perhaps the effect of race on sentencing is indirect; for example, because race is correlated with socioeconomic status, White offenders in general may be sentenced more leniently because they can more often post bond, afford private lawyers, and seek treatment in the community (Spohn, Gruhl, & Welch, 1981).

Psychologists have also wondered whether attributions and stereotypic beliefs of judges may explain the racial bias in sentencing decisions. According to attribution theory, people make assumptions about whether the cause of crime was something internal to the offender or something in the environment (the internal–external dimension), and whether the behavior is likely to be repeated or was an anomaly (the stable–unstable dimension). Judges impose harsher sentences when they make an internal attribution and believe the cause is stable over time (Bridges & Steen, 1998).

In that light, let's return to the question of the effects of race on sentencing. Judges with stereotypic beliefs might assume, for example, that the deviant behavior of minority offenders is related to their negative dispositions and personality traits, rather than to environmental factors, and that these offenders are more likely to repeat their crimes. As a result, they sentence minority offenders to longer terms. Even judges are not immune from such superficial generalizations.

Another factor that influences judicial sentencing patterns is the way a conviction came about: whether by guilty plea or trial. Defendants who plead guilty are often given a reduced sentence, partly to encourage them to plead guilty and thereby reduce costs for court time and personnel. Using federal sentencing data for the years 2000–2002, Ulmer, Eisenstein, and Johnson (2010) determined that offenders who pled guilty received 15% shorter sentences than those convicted by trial. In addition to costing time and money, trials may also reveal more details pertaining to a defendant's blameworthiness and reduce his moral standing. One defense attorney explained that during trial, "you just sit here and think, 'You [the defendant] really should plead guilty because you're just such a jerk … and you're so arrogant and you're so unappreciative of the fact that you have nobody to blame but yourself, okay? Let's plead guilty, get up, cross your fingers behind your back, tell him [the judge] you're sorry, and cut your losses. Because the more he gets to see into your soul, the darker it's going to look for you" (Ulmer et al., 2010, p. 581).

Obviously, judges are human. When they have latitude in the punishments they can give, their backgrounds and personal characteristics may also influence their decisions (Tiede, Carp, & Manning, 2010). They may be prejudiced for or against certain groups—such as immigrants, antiwar protestors, or homosexuals. They may simply be uninformed. A Dallas judge told a reporter that he was giving a lighter sentence to a murderer because the victims were "queers." He was censured by the Texas State Commission on Judicial Conduct. A Maryland judge acquitted an alleged assailant on domestic violence charges after the victim failed to testify. He stated that one can't simply assume that a woman who is being hit didn't consent to the attack. "Sadomasochists sometimes like to get beat up," he said (Houppert, 2007).

Sentencing Juvenile Offenders

The juvenile justice system differs from the adult system in some crucial ways. First, not all juveniles come into the system via arrests. Some are referred by school officials, social service agencies, and even by parents. Second, there is an emphasis on rehabilitating youthful offenders, rather than simply punishing them. Finally, early in a case, juvenile justice officials must decide whether to send it into the court system or divert the offender to alternative programs such as drug treatment, educational and recreational programs, or individual and group counseling.

If the choice is to involve the courts, then prosecutors may recommend, or juvenile court judges may decide, to transfer cases involving serious charges from juvenile court to criminal court. Sentencing procedures and options vary depending on whether the child is adjudicated in juvenile court or transferred to adult criminal court. Judges' beliefs about the deterrent effects of transfer—the possibility that juveniles will refrain from committing crimes because they fear being tried as adults—affect these decisions (Redding & Hensl, 2011). More experienced judges see greater rehabilitative potential in juveniles and are less likely than inexperienced judges to transfer cases to criminal court.

Juvenile Court Dispositions

The majority of young people whose cases are adjudicated in juvenile court are found to be delinquent (Puzzanchera, Adams, & Sickmund, 2010) and moved to the sentencing or **dispositional phase** of the case. Dispositional hearings typically combine adversarial procedures and attention to the particular needs—social, psychological, physical—of the child. They include recommendations by probation officers and social workers, reports of social and school histories, and discussions with the offender and his or her family, probation staff, and other professionals (Binder, Geis, & Bruce, 2001). Issues of substance abuse, family dysfunction, mental health needs, peer relationships, and school problems may be addressed.

The goals of juvenile court dispositions—ensuring public safety and addressing children's needs—are reflected in the options available to juvenile court judges. These include (1) commitment to a secure facility; (2) probation, sometimes with intensive supervision; (3) referral to a group home or other lower security residential placement; (4) referral to day treatment or a mental health program; or (5) imposition of a fine, community service, or restitution.

When determining the appropriate disposition for a juvenile, judges may consider whether the parents are able to supervise the offender at home, assist in rehabilitation efforts, and insist on school attendance. They may also consider the family's financial resources and the availability of community-based treatment programs and facilities (Campbell & Schmidt, 2000). In 2007, nearly 60% of juvenile offenders were sentenced to probation, and 25% were sentenced to some sort of out-of-home placement (Puzzanchera et al., 2010).

Juvenile court judges are also expected to assess offenders' rehabilitative needs and personal circumstances. Thus, one might expect that they would put considerable weight on offenders' psychosocial functioning, developmental maturity, responsibility taking, and gang involvement. But researchers who examined the effects of these factors on dispositional outcomes (i.e., probation and confinement) in a sample of 1,355 juvenile offenders found that legal factors (e.g., seriousness of the offense, whether the offender had prior court referrals) had the strongest influence on dispositions. Individual factors were not strongly linked to dispositional decisions (Cauffman et al., 2007).

Blended Sentencing

Juveniles who meet the criteria for transfer to adult criminal court may be sentenced under **blended sentencing** statutes that combine the options available in juvenile court with those used in criminal court (Heilbrun, DeMatteo, King, & Filone, 2017). These sentencing laws attempt to simultaneously address rehabilitation concerns and impose a "get tough" accountability (Redding & Mrozoski, 2005). In practice, this means that serious and violent young offenders can stay under juvenile court jurisdiction and receive more lenient sentences than if they were transferred to adult court. But they can also be subjected to harsh sentences if they commit new offenses, violate probation, or fail to respond to rehabilitation efforts (Trulson, Caudill, Belshaw, & DeLisi, 2011). Blended sentencing schemes provide incentives to offenders to avoid the more serious consequences of an adult sentence. Prosecutors often use the threat of transfer to adult criminal court to persuade juvenile offenders to plead guilty and accept a particular blended sentence (Podkopacz & Feld, 2001). But there are troubling questions about the effectiveness of blended sentencing, as roughly 50% of serious delinquents released early without continuing their sentence in adult prison were rearrested for a felony offense (Trulson, Haerle, DeLisi, & Marquart, 2011).

Life Sentences for Juvenile Offenders

Juveniles who commit very serious crimes, such as sexual assault, attempted murder, or murder, are likely to wind up in criminal court and subjected to adult punishments. According to one study, juveniles sentenced to jail or prison actually receive longer sentences than adult offenders (Jordan & McNeal, 2016).

Judges can impose very lengthy prison sentences on offenders who were under 18 when they committed a serious offense. Approximately 2,500 offenders are serving mandatory life without parole sentences for homicides they committed as juveniles (Mills, Dorn, & Hritz, 2016). However, in 2012, the Supreme

Court decided that mandatory life sentences for juvenile offenders are unconstitutional (*Miller v. Alabama*, 2012), though *nonmandatory* life sentences for juveniles remain an option across the United States.

These cases pit human rights and judicial reform advocates on the one hand against prosecutors and victims' rights groups on the other. Human rights groups argue that applying life-without-parole sentences to juveniles constitutes cruel and unusual punishment. Stephen Bright, director of the Southern Center for Human Rights, said, "It goes against human inclinations to give up completely on a young teenager. It's impossible for a court to say that any 14-year-old never has the possibility to live in society." Prosecutors and victims' groups say that such statutes are comforting to victims and make sense in their "adult-crime, adult-time" approach. But public sentiment is generally not supportive of life sentences for juveniles of any age (Greene, Duke, & Woody, 2017). We illustrate the complexity of these issues by describing the case of Jacob Ind, profiled on PBS's *Frontline* episode "When Kids Get Life," in Box 14.3.

Sentencing Sex Offenders

Many people believe that sex offenders are especially likely to reoffend, and therefore require different kinds of punishment than other offenders (Knighton, Murrie, Boccaccini, & Turner, 2014). But the data show otherwise. A meta-analysis of recidivism rates in approximately 4,900 treated and 5,400 untreated sex offenders showed low recidivism rates overall, with just 10.1% of treated and 13.7% of untreated offenders recidivating sexually (Schmucker & Losel, 2015). So the vast majority of convicted sex offenders are *not* rearrested for another sex crime. And when sex offenders *do* commit other crimes, typically they are not sex crimes (Zimring, Piquero, & Jennings, 2007).

But in a number of ways, judges and corrections professionals do treat individuals who offend sexually differently than other (nonsexual) offenders. Upon release from prison, sex offenders in many jurisdictions are required to register with state officials, who then publicly notify the community about the location of the offender's residence. Sex offenders are prohibited from living within certain distances of schools, day-care facilities, parks, and other locations frequented by children, and can be involuntarily committed to a mental health facility following the completion of their sentence. In addition, these individuals can be subjected to

The Case of Jacob Ind: When a Kid Gets Life

BOX 14.3

On the morning of December 17, 1992, 15-year-old Jacob Ind went to school in Woodland Park, Colorado, planning to tell a friend that he had just murdered his mother and stepfather and then to commit suicide. But the friend immediately went to the principal, who called the police, and 18 months later, Jacob was convicted of two counts of first-degree murder and sentenced to life without parole. According to Jacob's older brother, Charles, the murders ended years of physical and sexual abuse of both boys at the hands of their stepfather and of emotional betrayal by their mother. At Jacob's trial, Charles testified that their stepfather would wait for the boys to get home from school, then drag them into the bathroom, tie them with ropes to the toilet, and sexually molest them. Jacob claimed that his mother made it absolutely clear that she hated him (Jacob) and "[to] a child, that is more hurtful than getting hit across the face or getting beaten" (www.pbs.org).

Jacob Ind has now spent more than half his life in prison, including eight years in solitary confinement. (He was sent there shortly after arrival, when prison officials found a rope and a sharpened piece of rebar in his cell. The latter, he alleged, was for self-defense.) He has earned a bachelor's degree in biblical studies and claims to be happier now than he ever imagined being.

That's probably a good thing, because Colorado, like many states, has said that such lengthy sentences are constitutional since inmates will be eligible for parole eventually.

CRITICAL THOUGHT QUESTIONS

Recent research on brain development shows that the adolescent brain is a work in progress, not fully mature with an intact frontal lobe—responsible for reasoning and judgment—until sometime between the ages of 25 and 30. Some psychologists (e.g., Steinberg, 2017) have argued that this means that adolescents are fundamentally different from adults and warrant differential treatment by the law. On the other hand, there is a great deal of variability in brain and behavioral development among same-aged teenagers, and some older adolescents are comparable to young adults in psychological maturity. Should these factors be considered in determining the appropriate punishment for a juvenile offender? For Jacob Ind? Would your decision be affected by learning that psychologists are not particularly good at predicting adult functioning from snapshots of teenage behavior?

extraordinary sanctions, including enhanced sentences and mandatory treatments.

Registration and Notification

Convicted sex offenders are required to register with local law enforcement after they are released from prison and to notify authorities of subsequent changes of address. The period of required registration depends on the classification of the offender, which is a product of a formal risk assessment. In Kentucky, for example, high-risk offenders are required to register for life, whereas moderate- or low-risk offenders are required to register for 10 years after their formal sentence is completed. Unfortunately, many sex offenders do not register and others fail to inform authorities when they move, and a lack of resources within jurisdictions hinders follow-up. One investigation revealed that California authorities lost track of more than 33,000 sex

offenders who were registered at one point (Associated Press, 2003).

In the United States, the federal government and most states also require juveniles, including youth whose sexual offense charges were resolved in juvenile courts, to register as sex offenders, sometimes for life. The intent of these laws is to reduce recidivism among juveniles who committed a sexual crime and prevent other young people from committing their first sexual offense. But the laws seemed to have missed the mark: studies show no changes in recidivism or prevention measures from before to after the registry requirements were implemented (e.g., Sandler, LeTourneau, Vandiver, Shields, & Chaffin, 2017). And offenders subjected to these laws have experienced negative mental health outcomes, school difficulties, harassment, and trouble finding stable housing (Harris, Walfield, Shields, & LeTourneau, 2016). Critics claim that adult criminal justice practices, including

Steve Elwell, left, a registered sex offender in Cape May County, N.J., speaks during a council meeting, opposing local ordinance that bans sex offenders from residing or loitering within 2,500 feet of schools and public areas.

sex offender registration, are simply inappropriate for youthful offenders.

Notification is more controversial than registration. Community notification laws allow states to disseminate information about convicted sex offenders to the public. In some states (New Jersey, for example), police have gone door to door to notify neighbors that a high-risk sex offender has moved into the neighborhood (Witt & Barone, 2004). Now though, states and the federal government rely on the Internet as the primary means of notification. Typically, offenders' names are placed online for the period of their required registration, and law enforcement officials take no further steps to notify the community. But online notification appears to be plagued by the worst of two extremes. On the one hand, it is over-inclusive; the entire world can learn about the offender, even though only one or a few communities really need to know. On the other hand, online notification is under-inclusive; persons who cannot or do not regularly access the sex offender website will not be made aware of a sex offender living in the neighborhood.

Internet posting also raises concerns about invasion of privacy. No matter how minor the offense, states and the federal government post offenders' personal information (including their photos) online for

all to see. A murderer could move to a new community, safe in the knowledge that his or her past, although a matter of public record, is not readily accessible to friends and neighbors. But an individual registered as a sex offender will know that his or her past is available to anyone in the world with the touch of a screen.

When someone learns that an offender is living nearby, the result may be public hysteria. After the community was notified about a released offender in Waterloo, Iowa, children started carrying bats and sticks as they walked to school; the recently released offender was threatened and was ultimately hounded out of the community (VanDuyn, 1999). Community notification has led to harassment and vigilantism directed at sex offenders, and has interfered with offenders' ability to find stable work and housing, important factors in reintegration into the community (Levenson & D' Amora, 2007). Furthermore, registration laws may also be ineffective. Enforcement of sex offender registration tends not to reduce the number of forcible rapes reported (Vasquez, Madden, & Walker, 2008), and as we describe in Box 14.4, does nothing to restrain some sex offenders from committing additional, horrific crimes.

Residency Restrictions

In the best-selling novel *Lost Memory of Skin*, the main character is a young man, recently released from prison and on probation for soliciting an underage female. He is shackled to a GPS device and forbidden from living within 2,500 feet of places where children congregate. Though fictional, the story takes place in the all-too-real community of sex offenders that sprang up under the Julia Tuttle Causeway in Miami.

To manage the risk posed by sex offenders, residency restrictions were enacted by most states and hundreds of communities. They establish a "buffer zone" in which sex offenders may not live around schools, parks, and even bus stops. Though the laws vary with regard to the size of the area, the group of offenders to whom they apply, and whether they also restrict places of employment, all such laws are

BOX 14.4

The Case of John Albert Gardner III: Registered Sex Offender and Confessed Murderer

In 2000, 21-year-old John Albert Gardner III was convicted of luring a 13-year-old neighbor into his mother's home in an upscale community north of San Diego and punching and molesting the child. A psychiatrist who interviewed Gardner recommended a 30-year sentence, noting that Gardner lacked remorse and would continue to pose a danger to young women in the area. But prosecutors wanted to spare the victim from testifying and offered a plea bargain that landed Gardner

John Albert Gardner III is a convicted sex offender.

behind bars for five years. He was released in 2008 and registered as a sex offender.

Registration did little to quell Gardner's urges. Later that year he attempted to rape a jogger in a park near Escondido, California. Two months later, he killed 14-year-old Amber Dubois, who vanished while walking to school, and 17-year-old Chelsea King, whom Gardner admitted to raping and strangling in the same park. To avoid the death penalty, Gardner pleaded guilty to all of these crimes. King's parents championed legislation, fittingly named "Chelsea's Law," that allows life without parole sentences for offenders who kidnap, drug, or use a weapon against a child and requires lifetime parole with GPS tracking for offenders who commit forcible sex crimes against children under age 14. Former Governor Arnold Schwarzenegger signed the law in 2010.

CRITICAL THOUGHT QUESTION

Why, given that Gardner was registered as a sex offender and may have been listed on a sex offender registry website, would residents of surrounding communities have been unlikely to know that he was living nearby?

premised on the idea that sex offenders are opportunistic and seek victims in public places. But an estimated 79–93% of sexual offenses are committed by a person known to the victim (Mercado, 2009), raising questions about the effectiveness of these laws. Residency restrictions result in other problems: they seriously reduce housing options in communities where nearly all residential properties are within the buffer zones (Cha jewski & Mercado, 2009), and result in the clustering of sex offenders in more rural areas, making access to treatment more difficult and destabilizing offenders. Furthermore, they have not been shown to deter recidivism (Socia, 2012).

Although residency restrictions may be a visible way for legislators to attempt to address sexual recidivism, empirical data suggest that they will have little impact. In fact, policies that entail registration, notification, and residency restrictions, though well-intended, exemplify **crime control theater**, because they were enacted

in response to a moral panic and inspired by fear and folk logic about crime, rather than by data about their potential effectiveness (see, e.g., DeVault, Miller, & Griffin, 2016).

Involuntary Commitment

Another form of sanction imposed on repeat sex offenders is involuntary commitment to a mental health facility after the prison term has been completed. Whereas prison sentences are intended to punish an offender for past bad acts, involuntary commitment is intended to protect the public from future harms.

The leading case on this topic is *Kansas v. Hendricks* (1997). Leroy Hendricks was "every parent's nightmare" (Kolebuck, 1998, p. 537). He was in his 60s when, in 1994, he was scheduled to be released from a Kansas prison where he had served 10 years for child molestation, following a long history of sexually abusing children. But he told a Kansas judge that only his death would guarantee that he would never commit another sexual offense on a child. Kansas had recently passed a Sexually Violent Predator (SVP) Act, allowing for the involuntary commitment of offenders suffering from a "mental abnormality" that would make them likely to commit predatory acts of sexual violence. A Kansas judge determined that Hendricks was a SVP and committed him to a psychiatric hospital where he stayed for 10 years prior to release. In *Kansas v. Hendricks*, the U.S. Supreme Court deemed the SVP Act to be constitutional.

Professor Stephen Morse has raised concerns about the role of the *Hendricks* case in striking a balance between the due process and crime control models of criminal justice (Morse, 1998). He asserted that in its quest for public safety, society is now willing to punish people who are merely *at risk for* reoffending, in essence punishing them more severely than they deserve.

Yet, predictably, other states passed statutes similar to the Kansas statute. Nearly half the states and the federal government have enacted some form of civil authorization for the involuntary commitment of sex offenders. Once an individual is committed, release is rare. By 2007, almost 2,700 persons had been committed as SVPs, but only about 250 had been released, half on technical or legal grounds unrelated to treatment (Davey & Goodnough, 2007).

The Supreme Court's rulings on SVP laws make clear that selected individuals must have a "mental abnormality" or personality disorder that predisposes them to sexual violence and makes them oblivious to the prospect of further punishment (Slobogin, 2011). In making assessments of "mental abnormality," evaluators typically use the diagnostic criteria for pedophilia, paraphilia, or antisocial personality disorder set out in the *Diagnostic and Statistical Manual.*

The U.S. Supreme Court has also said that individuals subjected to SVP laws must be unable to control their behavior and thus, likely to commit future sexually violent crimes (*Kansas v. Crane*, 2002). How does one assess the likelihood of some possible event in the future? The risk of sexual reoffending is typically determined via formal risk assessment conducted around the time the offender is scheduled to be released from prison. Risk assessment relies on measures of deviant sexual preferences and persistent antisocial behaviors. These tests compare a given individual to individuals who have similar characteristics and for whom the rates of recidivism are known. Several specialized actuarial measures or structured professional judgment measures

have now been validated on sex offender populations (Otto & Douglas, 2010; van den Berg et al., 2017) and have been shown to be more accurate than clinical judgments (Hanson & Morton-Bourgnon, 2009). Obviously, these instruments cannot predict with certainty that a given individual will behave in any particular way, but especially when combined with individualized clinical risk assessments, they can be quite useful in gauging the likelihood of future behavior (Slobogin, 2011).

Mandated Treatments for Sex Offenders

Unlike other offenders, individuals convicted of sexual offenses are often required to undergo treatment designed to "cure" them of their antisocial tendencies. Offenders sentenced to prison are required to participate in offender treatment programs or give up hope of parole; offenders offered probation are required to participate in counseling sessions. These typically involve cognitive-behavioral interventions that require offenders to acknowledge wrongdoing and that challenge their rationalizations, minimizations (e.g., "no one was hurt"), and other erroneous beliefs that support the commission of the offense. Treatment may also include an assortment of behavior modification techniques, including aversive conditioning that pairs aversive stimuli such as mild electric shock with deviant sexual responses. Over time, the deviant behavior is expected to decrease. Treatment programs that focus on an offender's risk of reoffending and responsiveness to treatment have been successful in reducing recidivism (Hanson, Bourgon, Helmus, & Hodgson, 2009).

Some treatment programs have effectively reduced sexual offending by suppressing offenders' sex drive. This pharmacological approach, sometimes called **chemical castration**, involves administering hormones to reduce testosterone levels and thereby lower sex drive, sexual arousal, and sexual fantasizing. Therapists have also had some success using selective serotonin reuptake inhibitors (SSRIs) to reduce deviant sexual behavior. This class of drugs may reduce intrusive or obsessive thoughts associated with sexual offending (Marshall, Fernandez, Marshall, & Serran, 2006). In the past, judges have sometimes given convicted sex offenders a choice: prison or hormone treatment. It is not surprising that some men have opted for the drugs, even though the possible side effects include lethargy, hot flashes, nightmares, hypertension, and shortness of breath (Keene, 1997).

California was the first state to pass a law requiring repeat child molesters (**pedophiles**) to be treated with hormones as a condition of parole. The California statute requires that clinicians assess offenders to determine whether they suffer from a condition (e.g., pedophilia) that creates a substantial risk of reoffending. If so, the California legislature reasoned, it makes sense to deny parole unless the offender agrees to the treatment. At the time the California Chemical Castration Bill was being considered, Assemblyman Bill Hoge, one of its sponsors, reasoned as follows:

> What we're up against is the kind of criminal who, just as soon as he gets out of jail, will immediately commit this crime again at least 90% of the time. So why not give these people a shot to calm them down and bring them under control? (Ayres, 1996, p. A1)

Although Assemblyman Hoge clearly overstated the probability of reoffending, there may be a certain logic in requiring some sex offenders to take a drug that diminishes their sex drive.

The Death Penalty: The Ultimate Punishment

The ultimate punishment, of course, is death. Citizens of the United States can be executed by the federal government and by the governments of 31 states. But capital punishment has had a controversial and volatile history in this country. Although a majority of Americans historically favored capital punishment, and politicians and appellate judges tended to make decisions that reflect that belief (Ogloff & Chopra, 2004), support for capital punishment is waning. A 2015 poll of 2,700 Americans showed that when offered the choice between capital punishment and life imprisonment without the possibility of parole, only 47% favored the former (Public Religion Research Institute, 2015). The American Bar Association has called for a nationwide moratorium on capital punishment, citing concerns about the way the death penalty is administered. In recent years, several states have abolished the death penalty, and other states have placed a moratorium on executions.

The modern history of capital punishment in the United States began in 1972 when the U.S. Supreme Court effectively abolished the death penalty on the grounds that it constituted "cruel and unusual punishment" (*Furman v. Georgia* , 1972). After the *Furman*

case, state legislatures revised their death penalty laws to address the Court's concern that capital punishment was being applied in an arbitrary and discriminatory fashion as a consequence of the "unbridled discretion" in sentencing given to juries.

To remedy this problem, states passed statutes that guided the sentencing discretion of juries in death penalty cases. (Whereas judges determine most criminal sentences, the choice between life and death in a capital case is made by a jury.) First, legislators made only certain crimes eligible for the death penalty. Second, they changed the structure of capital trials. Now, if a defendant is charged with one of these crimes, the trial is conducted in two phases. The jury decides the guilt or innocence of the defendant in the first phase (the "guilt phase"). If the defendant is found guilty, then the second phase, or "sentencing phase," of the trial is held. During this phase, the jury hears evidence of **aggravating factors** (elements of the crime, such as killing in an especially brutal or heinous manner, that make the defendant more likely to receive a death sentence) and **mitigating factors** (elements of the defendant's background or the crime, such as experiencing mental illness or acting under duress at the time of the offense, that make life imprisonment the more appropriate verdict). Specific aggravating and mitigating factors are listed in the statutes, but a jury is not required to consider only those factors in its deliberations. Before reaching a sentencing decision, jurors hear instructions from the judge on how to weigh the aggravating and mitigating factors. Generally, a jury cannot vote for a death sentence unless it determines that the prosecution has proven at least one aggravating factor. However, even if it decides that one or more aggravating factors were present, it may still, after considering the mitigating factors, return a sentence of life imprisonment.

In 1976, in the case of *Gregg v. Georgia*, and in response to these newly enacted laws and procedures, the Supreme Court reinstituted the possibility of the death penalty. Following the *Gregg* decision, state after state began to execute those convicts who had been sentenced to die. Since the death penalty was reinstated, more than 1,450 people have been executed. The greatest number (98) were executed in 1999, and the rate of executions has declined since then. In 2016, only 20 inmates were executed (Death Penalty Information Center, 2017). More than 80% of executions have occurred in southern states, and Texas alone accounts for more than one-third of them.

Pictured here is a gurney on which prisoners are executed by lethal injection.

Concerns about Innocence

David Protess, a Northwestern University journalism professor, drew attention to the possibility of "executing the innocent" when students under his supervision tracked down and obtained confessions from true killers, thereby exonerating two men on death row. We do not know exactly how many innocent people have been sentenced to death. One estimate is that 2.3% of those sentenced to death may actually be innocent (Gross & O'Brien, 2008). Another estimate puts the figure at 5% (Risinger, 2007). We also do not know exactly how many innocent people have been executed, though some have.

What can account for these errors? A study that analyzed every capital conviction in the United States between 1973 and 1995 revealed that serious mistakes were made in two-thirds of the cases, a startling indictment of the criminal justice system (Liebman, 2000). The most common problems included incompetent defense attorneys (37%), faulty jury instructions (20%), and misconduct on the part of prosecutors (19%). Of those defendants whose capital sentence was overturned because of an error, 82% received a sentence less than death at their retrials, including 7% who were found not guilty of the capital crime with which they had originally been charged.

Since executions resumed after the *Gregg* case, more than 150 people have been freed from death rows upon proof of their innocence (Death Penalty Information Center, 2017). Some of these condemned individuals were cleared when new evidence came to light or when witnesses changed their stories. DNA evidence is credited with proving the innocence of scores of death row inmates (Gross, Jacoby, Matheson, Montgomery, & Patil, 2005). Many of these cases involved defendants who had originally been convicted on the basis of faulty eyewitness identifications or false confessions. As a result of these widely publicized errors, a number of states give death row inmates the right to post-conviction DNA testing, though the Supreme Court has ruled that states are not required to do so (*District Attorney's Office for Third Judicial District v. Osborne*, 2009).

Is the death penalty still justified if we know that innocent people have been executed? Some proponents insist that it is, invoking the analogy that administering a vaccine is justified even though a child might have an adverse—even lethal—reaction to it. Proponents of capital punishment suggest that even though innocent people are occasionally and mistakenly put to death, other compelling reasons justify maintaining this system of punishment.

Justifications for the Death Penalty

Many reasons have been advanced for endorsing the irrevocable penalty of death. While he was the mayor of New York City, Ed Koch contended that the death penalty "affirms life." By failing to execute murderers, he said, we "signal a lessened regard for the value of the victim's life" (quoted by Bruck, 1985, p. 20).

Most justifications for the death penalty reflect retributive beliefs (e.g., "an eye for an eye") and thus extend beyond the capacity of empirical research to prove or disprove. But a testable argument for capital punishment is the expectation that it will act as a deterrent to criminal activity. Proponents of this position suggest that (1) the death penalty accomplishes general, as well as specific, deterrence; (2) highly publicized executions have at least a short-term deterrent effect; and (3) murderers are such dangerous people that allowing them to live increases the risk of injury or death to other inmates and prison guards.

Using a variety of empirical approaches, social scientists have evaluated the deterrent effects of the death penalty, and their studies consistently lead to the conclusion that the death penalty does not affect the rate of crimes of violence (e.g., Zimring, Fagan, & Johnson, 2010). Evidence also contradicts the view that murderers are especially dangerous inmates. A good deal of data indicate that capital murderers tend to commit fewer violent offenses and prison infractions than parole-eligible inmates (Cunningham, 2010).

Equality versus Discretion in Application of the Death Penalty

Does the death penalty further the goal of equal treatment before the law? Nearly 40% of the states, plus the District of Columbia, do not permit it, and vastly different rates of death sentences and executions occur in states that do. For example, the state of New Hampshire has one inmate sentenced to death, whereas Delaware, with a smaller population, has 17. As we have noted, more than a third of all executions in the United States since 1977 have taken place in one state—Texas. So if equal treatment is the goal, it is safe to say that capital punishment has not furthered that goal. The death penalty is administered in only a minority of states and within those states, in only a subset of eligible cases. In the words of former Supreme Court Justice Potter Stewart, receiving the death penalty is like "being struck by lightning for a capriciously selected random handful."

Another concern is the issue of race, particularly of the victim. Although victims of intentional homicide are equally divided between Blacks and Whites, the chance of a death sentence is much greater for offenders who kill Whites than those who kill Blacks (though Devine and Kelly [2015] paint a more complex picture of the relationship). In fact, data from governmental and capital defense organizations show that between the late 1970s and the early 2000s, there was tremendous racial disparity in death sentences. So, for example,

---

The Case of Warren McCleskey: Does Race Matter?

BOX 14.5

Warren McCleskey, a Black man, was convicted in 1978 of armed robbery and the murder of a White police officer who had responded to an alarm while the robbery was in progress. McCleskey was sentenced to die in Georgia's electric chair. He challenged the constitutionality of the death penalty on the ground that it was administered in a racially discriminatory manner in Georgia. In the words of one of his attorneys, "When you kill the organist at the Methodist Church, who is White, you're going to get the death penalty, but if you kill the Black Baptist organist, the likelihood is that it will be plea bargained down to a life sentence" (quoted by Noble, 1987, p. 7).

The foundation for McCleskey's appeal was a comprehensive study of race and capital sentencing in the state of Georgia conducted by David Baldus, a law professor at the University of Iowa, and his colleagues. They analyzed the race of the offender and the race of the victim for about 2,000 murder and manslaughter convictions from 1973 to 1979 and concluded that those who killed Whites were 11 times more likely to receive the death penalty than those who killed Blacks (Baldus, Pulaski, & Woodworth, 1983). Anticipating

the argument that the heinousness of the murders may explain this finding, Baldus and colleagues eliminated cases in which extreme violence or other aggravating circumstances virtually ensured the death penalty and cases in which overwhelming mitigating circumstances almost guaranteed a life sentence. For the remaining cases—which permitted the greatest jury discretion—they found that defendants were about four times more likely to be sentenced to death if their victims were White.

Despite the mass of statistical evidence, the Supreme Court upheld McCleskey's death sentence. Because there was no evidence that individual jurors in his trial were biased, the Court was unwilling to assume that McCleskey's jury valued a White life more than a Black life.

CRITICAL THOUGHT QUESTION

What legally irrelevant factors in McCleskey's case—in addition to the race of the victim—may have increased the likelihood that he would be sentenced to die for his crime?

between 1990 and 1999, California offenders who killed Whites were more than three times more likely to receive the death penalty than offenders who killed Blacks, and more than four times more likely than offenders who killed Latinos (Pierce & Radelet, 2005).

The leading Supreme Court case on the issue of race and application of the death penalty, *McCleskey v. Kemp* (1987), considered this issue. The question was whether the death penalty discriminated against persons who murdered Whites. We describe McCleskey's case in Box 14.5.

Psychologists have determined that not all Black offenders are equally likely to be sentenced to death for killing a White person. Professor Jennifer Eberhardt and her colleagues showed to Stanford undergraduates the photographs of 44 Black offenders whose trials advanced to the penalty phase in Philadelphia between 1979 and 1999, and asked them to rate the stereotypicality of each offender's appearance. Controlling for other factors that influence sentencing, such as the severity of the murder and the defendant's and victim's socioeconomic status, researchers found that offenders whose appearance was rated as more stereotypically Black were more likely to have received the death penalty than offenders whose appearance was less stereotypical (Eberhardt, Davies, Purdie-Vaughns, & Johnson, 2006). Apparently, offenders' appearance can also lead to unequal treatment in the administration of capital punishment.

Capital Jury Decision-Making

The *Furman* and *Gregg* cases, pivotal challenges to the constitutionality of the death penalty, focused on the role of the jury in capital cases. For this reason, it is not surprising that there has been intense public and scientific scrutiny of two aspects of capital jury decision-making: the process of selecting jurors in capital cases, and the ability of those jurors to understand and apply the sentencing instructions they receive from the judge.

How Jurors Are Selected in Capital Cases: "Death Qualification." During jury selection in cases in which the prosecutor seeks a death penalty, prospective jurors are required to answer questions about their attitudes toward capital punishment. This procedure is called **death qualification**. If jurors indicate extreme beliefs about the death penalty, they may be excused "for cause"—that is, dismissed from that case. More precisely, prospective jurors are excluded if their

opposition to capital punishment would "prevent or substantially impair the performance of [their] duties as juror[s] in accordance with [their] instructions and [their] oath" (*Wainwright v. Witt*, 1985, p. 424). Prospective jurors dismissed for this reason are termed *excludables*, and those who remain are termed *death qualified*. (Another group of prospective jurors—those who would automatically impose the death penalty at every opportunity—so-called "automatic death penalty" jurors—are also dismissed for cause, although they are far fewer in number than "excludables.") Death-qualified jurors are qualified to impose the death penalty because they do not hold strong scruples or reservations about it.

Death qualification raises some important questions. Recall that capital cases involve two phases but only one jury to decide both guilt and punishment. Although excludable jurors might be unwilling to impose the death penalty, many could fairly determine the guilt or innocence of the defendant. Yet death qualification procedures deny them the opportunity to make a decision. These procedures also raise concerns about the leanings of jurors who *do* assess guilt, concerns that have grown over the years.

Intuitively, one might expect that death-qualified juries (those made up of people who are not opposed to the death penalty) would be somewhat more conviction prone than the general population. Indeed, research studies have demonstrated the conviction-proneness of death-qualified juries. For example, Cowan, Thompson, and Ellsworth (1984) recruited mock jurors who were either death qualified or excludable and assigned them to juries; some juries were composed entirely of death-qualified jurors and others contained a few excludables. All watched a recorded murder trial. Three-fourths of the death-qualified juries found the defendant guilty, as did only 53% of the juries with excludable jurors. "Mixed" juries took a more serious approach to their deliberations, and were more critical of witnesses and better able to remember the evidence. Death-qualified jurors differ from the general population in other important ways. They interpret evidence in a manner that favors the prosecution and devalue evidence that seems to favor the defense (Thompson, Cowan, Ellsworth, & Harrington, 1994).

Recently, a team of social scientists evaluated whether waning support for the death penalty, apparent in many polls, affects the composition and decision-making of capital juries. Garrett, Krauss, and Scurich (2017) surveyed people reporting for jury duty in Orange County, California, one of the leading U.S. counties in terms of death sentences imposed. Remarkably, given the conservative political leanings of Orange County, 35% of prospective jurors met the criterion for "excludable" and roughly 25% said they would be reluctant to find a person guilty of capital murder if that meant the person might be executed. Compared with numbers from the 1980s, more people today would be dismissed because of their opposition to capital punishment. Who remains? An even narrower swath of the population, even less representative of their communities. As a result, prosecutors may be even more likely to obtain a conviction now than they were in the past.

It is clear that death-qualified juries are more disposed toward conviction than juries that include jurors with scruples against the death penalty. In the mid-1980s, lawyers for Ardia McCree made that argument before the U.S. Supreme Court (*Lockhart v. McCree*, 1986). At McCree's trial in Arkansas, the judge excluded eight prospective jurors who said that they could not, under any circumstances, impose a death sentence. McCree was convicted and sentenced to death. He appealed his conviction by arguing that the process of death qualification produced juries that were likely to be conviction prone and unrepresentative of the larger community.

In spite of the substantial body of empirical support for McCree's position, the Supreme Court held that the jury in McCree's trial was not an improper one. The majority rejected the claim that death-qualified juries were less than neutral in determining guilt and innocence. An impartial jury, Chief Justice William Rehnquist wrote, "consists of nothing more than jurors who will conscientiously apply the law and find the facts." He noted that McCree conceded that each of the jurors who convicted him met that test. Accordingly, the Supreme Court upheld the state's use of a death-qualified jury for the decision at the guilt phase.

How Capital Jurors Use Instructions. Jurors in capital cases receive a set of complex instructions that outline their duties and explain how to evaluate and weigh aggravating and mitigating circumstances to reach a sentencing decision. Several studies indicate that jurors do not adequately comprehend the instructions they receive about mitigating factors because, like other types of judicial instructions, mitigation instructions are couched in legal jargon and are unusually lengthy

and grammatically complex (Lynch & Haney, 2009; Smith & Haney, 2011).

If jurors do not understand a judge's instructions about mitigation, they are more likely to rely on other, more familiar factors to guide their verdicts, such as the heinousness of the crime or extralegal considerations such as racial stereotypes, sympathy for victims, or the expertise of the lawyers. The race of the defendant and victim also appear to affect sentences to a greater extent when comprehension of instructions is low. In a study by Lynch and Haney (2000), jury-eligible participants with poor comprehension of instructions recommended death 68% of the time for Black-defendant/White-victim cases versus 36% of the time for White-defendant/Black-victim cases. Among participants who comprehended the sentencing instructions well, neither the race of the defendant nor that of the victim affected the sentences.

Jurors have particular difficulty understanding how to evaluate mitigating evidence presented during the sentencing phase of a capital case. Professor Margaret Stevenson and colleagues analyzed the content of jury deliberations in a mock capital trial in which there was mitigating evidence that the defendant had been abused as a child. Approximately 40% of jurors relied on evidence of childhood maltreatment to argue for a life sentence, and approximately 60% either ignored it as a mitigating factor or used it as an aggravating factor to argue for a death sentence. They reasoned that being abused as a child increases the likelihood of violent behavior as an adult (Stevenson et al., 2008). Prosecutors may deliberately attempt to convert mitigating evidence about the defendant's life history into aggravating evidence, hoping that jurors will use it to support a death sentence (Vartkessian, 2011). So it is important that jurors understand their instructions.

Would jurors fare better if these all-important instructions were presented in a different format? Professor Richard Wiener and his colleagues posed this question. They tested various methods of improving jurors' **declarative knowledge** (their understanding of legal concepts) and **procedural knowledge** (their ability to know what to do in order to reach a sentencing decision) in a highly realistic trial simulation (Wiener et al., 2004). Their study involved both the guilt and sentencing phases of a capital murder trial based on an actual case, used death-qualified community members as jurors, and included jury deliberations. The modifications to the instructions involved (1) simplifying the language of the instructions, (2) presenting the instructions in a flowchart format so that jurors could understand the progression of decisions they were expected to make, (3) giving jurors the chance to review and practice using the instructions in a mock case so that they would gain some experience prior to the real trial, and (4) offering corrections to common misconceptions that jurors have about aggravating and mitigating circumstances. For example:

> [Some] people believe that an aggravating circumstance is a factor that aggravated or provoked the defendant to kill the victim. This definition is based on the common use of the word aggravation. However, this in an incorrect definition of aggravating circumstance and should not be used in imposing a sentence upon the defendant.

Each of these modifications was helpful in enhancing some aspect of jurors' declarative and procedural knowledge in capital cases.

Limiting Use of the Death Penalty

Another highly controversial aspect of the death penalty has been its use in cases where the defendant, for reasons of youth, intellectual disability, or mental illness, may not be fully culpable. In recent years, the Supreme Court has deemed the death penalty unconstitutional for youthful offenders (*Roper v. Simmons*, 2005), so no one can be executed for crimes committed prior to age 18. But controversies linger regarding intellectual disabilities and mental illness, primarily in terms of their diagnosis and assessment. Psychologists often play a vital role in these cases, evaluating and rendering expert opinions on questions concerning defendants' cognitive abilities and whether they meet diagnostic criteria for various psychiatric disorders.

Intellectual Disability. In 2002, the Supreme Court acknowledged that applying the death penalty to people with intellectual disabilities does not further the legitimate goals of deterrence and retribution and declared that it was cruel and unusual punishment, in violation of the Eighth Amendment, to execute them (*Atkins v. Virginia*, 2002). This landmark ruling reflected awareness that those with limited intellectual abilities often

AP Images/SANGJIB MIN

Daryl Atkins's case led to the Supreme Court ruling the execution of people with intellectual disability is unconstitutional and cruel.

cannot understand the consequences of their actions, the complex and abstract concepts involved in criminal law, or the finality of a death sentence.

But the Court offered only general guidance about how intellectual abilities should be measured, noting that to be spared execution required a showing of subaverage intellectual functioning, a lack of fundamental social and practical skills, and the onset of these conditions before age 18. Interpretation of this ruling was left to the states, which took different approaches (Taylor & Krauss, 2014). Florida, for example, took a "bright line approach," deeming an IQ score of 70 "subaverage." (An IQ score of 100 is considered average.) So, according to Florida law, an offender with an IQ score of 71 is not intellectually disabled.

BOX 14.6

The Case of Dylann Roof: (Lack of) Evidence about Mental Illness

In one of the most vicious mass murders in recent history, White supremacist Dylann Roof walked into Emanual African Methodist Episcopal Church in Charleston, South Carolina during Bible study on June 17, 2015. A Glock semiautomatic handgun was hidden in his clothing. Roof was offered a spot in the prayer circle where he sat for approximately 45 minutes before opening fire, shooting randomly at the 12 congregants and killing 9 of them. Roof confessed immediately, saying that he chose church-goers as his victims to gain notoriety. He stated that he committed the murders as a wake-up call to persecuted Whites, and that he hoped his attack would increase racial tensions and lead to a race war.

Was Roof's thinking delusional? We may never know because he refused to allow evidence of his mental health status to be used during his capital murder trial. (He also opted to represent himself without a lawyer in the penalty phase, which some would argue, is either delusional or reflects extraordinarily poor judgment.) But in court documents unsealed after Roof's conviction and death sentence, a court-appointed psychiatrist who evaluated Roof a few months after the shooting concluded that he "suffers from Social Anxiety Disorder, a Mixed Substance Abuse Disorder, a Schizoid Personality Disorder, depression by history, and a possible Autistic Spectrum Disorder." The document also stated that "the defendant's high IQ is compromised by a significant discrepancy between this ability to comprehend and to process information and a poor working memory." Did these disorders and discrepancies seriously impair Roof's thinking? Do they indicate a deep-seated psychosis or delusion? Since Roof was "steadfastly committed to preventing any public examination of his mental

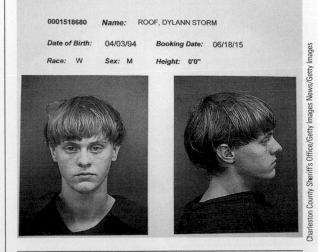

Charleston County Sheriff's Office/Getty Images News/Getty Images

Dylan Roof

state or background" (Sack & Blinder, 2017), no psychiatric or psychological expertise was introduced at his trial. In prominent headlines at the time, "Dylann Roof himself rejects best defense against execution" (Sack & Blinder, 2017).

CRITICAL THOUGHT QUESTION

According to Supreme Court decisions concerning mental illness and the death penalty, what level of understanding must Dylann Roof possess in order to be put to death?

Now consider the case of Freddie Hall, who had been convicted and sentenced to death for murdering a 21-year-old pregnant woman and a deputy sheriff in 1978. After the Supreme Court decided *Atkins v. Virginia*, Hall petitioned to have his death sentence reconsidered, arguing that his intellectual disability exempted him from the death penalty. (Hall had taken multiple intelligence tests and at one point, had scored as low as 60.) But when he was tested in the process of his appeal, his IQ score was (you probably guessed) 71. His appeal to the Supreme Court contended that the 70-point cutoff was overly rigid and that IQ scores should be interpreted as part of a range. (Indeed, the manual that accompanies the IQ test interprets point scores within confidence intervals to account for measurement error, and the 95% **confidence interval**—a range within which we can be 95% sure that the actual score rests—for an IQ score of 70 is between 67.5 and 72.5.) The Supreme Court agreed with Hall, noting that an IQ test has a standard error of measurement that should have been considered in his case (*Hall v. Florida*, 2014).

This decision meant that states with fixed cutoff scores must use a broader range of scores that take measurement error into account. This position squares with psychological research showing that IQ scores change over time (Trahan, Stuebing, Fletcher, & Hiscock, 2014), and can be influenced by literacy skills (Marks, 2011), level of IQ (Spitz, 1989), and who administered the test (McDermott, Watkins, & Rhoad, 2014).

The question of how to diagnose intellectual disability is still not settled, however, and led to another successful appeal to the Supreme Court in 2017. In this case, the Court ruled that Texas erred by using an outdated approach to assessing intellectual disabilities, and should have relied on standards that represent broad professional consensus (*Moore v. Texas*, 2017). Those standards place less emphasis on IQ scores and more emphasis on adaptive functioning.

Mental Illness. Is it cruel and unusual punishment to execute an inmate who, due to mental illness, lacks a rational understanding of why he is being put to death? That was the question posed to the U.S. Supreme Court in the case of *Panetti v. Quarterman* (2007). (Earlier, in *Ford v. Wainwright* [1986], the Supreme Court held that it was unconstitutional to execute those who are incompetent for execution, but did not define the test for competence for execution.) In 1992, Scott Panetti killed his estranged wife's parents, with whom his wife had been living in Fredericksburg, Texas, and held his wife and three-year-old daughter hostage in a lengthy police standoff. Panetti had a history of psychiatric problems prior to his conviction, including 14 hospital stays over 11 years. During earlier stages of the case, four mental health professionals agreed that Panetti suffered from impaired cognitive processes and delusions consistent with schizoaffective disorder. Scott Panetti believed that the government was executing him to prevent him from preaching the Gospel, not because he murdered his in-laws. Thus, the question for the Supreme Court was whether a person with serious mental illness, who may not understand the reason for his execution, still can be put to death.

The American Psychological Association (APA) teamed with the National Alliance on Mental Illness to assist the Court in developing standards for determining what level of mental illness should exempt an offender from execution. In its *amicus curiae* brief to the Supreme Court, the APA distinguished factual understanding from rational understanding. According to one of the authors of this book who consulted on the APA brief (Heilbrun), "factual understanding is about information. Rational understanding allows us to place that information in a meaningful context, without gross interference caused by certain symptoms of severe mental illness, or very serious impairment of intellectual functioning" (Medical News Today, 2007). The APA brief explained that some individuals who suffer from psychotic disorders have bizarre delusions that disrupt their understanding of reality and make it difficult or impossible for them to connect their criminal acts to punishment. The Supreme Court ruled that Panetti's delusions may have prevented him from understanding the reason for his punishment. That decision effectively means that defendants may not be executed if they do not understand *why* they are being put to death.

The question of whether Dylann Roof, the young man who murdered nine Black parishioners in South Carolina in 2016, was also acting under delusional beliefs, may never be answered because Roof refused to allow mental health evidence to be used at his trial. We describe his case, including information about his mental health, in Box 14.6.

Summary

1. ***What are the purposes of punishment?*** Punishment is associated with seven purposes: general deterrence, individual deterrence, incapacitation, retribution, expression of moral outrage, rehabilitation, and restitution. Although many citizens favor the punitive approaches of retribution and incapacitation, recidivism data suggest that they may not be effective. A new perspective on punishment, restorative justice, brings people together to address the damage caused by wrongdoing.

2. ***How are the values of discretion and fairness reflected in sentencing decisions?*** The allocation of punishments is second only to the determination of guilt or innocence in importance to the criminal defendant. The sentencing process reflects many of the conflicts that permeate a psychological approach to the legal system. Historically, judges were given broad discretion in sentencing. Some judges were much more severe than the norm; others were more lenient. In recent years, concern over sentencing disparity led to greater use of determinate sentencing and tighter controls over judicial discretion in sentencing. Now, sentencing guidelines are merely advisory, however.

3. ***What factors influence sentencing decisions?*** Determinants of sentencing can be divided into relevant and irrelevant factors. For example, seriousness of the crime is a relevant factor, and there is a general relationship between it and the severity of the punishment. An offender's criminal history is another relevant determinant of the sentence. But a number of other, less relevant factors also are related to severity of sentence, such as race and gender of the offender and race and gender of the victim.

4. ***What special factors are considered in the sentencing of juveniles? Of sex offenders?*** Sentences for juvenile offenders are influenced by the jurisdiction in which the minor is sentenced (juvenile court, criminal court), the seriousness of the offense, the offender's rehabilitative needs, and professionals' recommendations. Because they are believed to be at high risk for reoffending, sex offenders have been singled out for special punishment including mandatory registration and community notification, residency restrictions, involuntary commitment, and enhanced sentences and treatments such as chemical castration.

5. ***How is the death penalty decided by juries?*** Jurors who oppose the death penalty regardless of the nature of the crime or the circumstances of the case are excluded from both the guilt phase and the sentencing phase of capital trials. Social science research has shown that the remaining so-called death-qualified jurors are conviction prone. But the Supreme Court has not been responsive to these findings. Capital juries tend to misunderstand their instructions, particularly regarding mitigating evidence.

6. ***How has the Supreme Court limited the use of capital punishment, and what role have psychologists played in these decisions?*** The Supreme Court has deemed the death penalty unconstitutional in cases in which the defendant was younger than 18 at the time of the crime, and in which the defendant is intellectually disabled (though assessing intellectual disability has been a challenge). The Supreme Court has also indicated that executing those with mental illness may be limited if such defendants do not understand the reasons for their execution. Psychologists have been involved in these cases to assess offenders' cognitive abilities, diagnose mental illness, and provide data to the court about decision-making and judgment.

Key Terms

aggravating factors
anchoring
back-end sentencing
blended sentencing
chemical castration
confidence interval
crime control theater

death qualification
declarative knowledge
determinate sentencing
dispositional phase
evidence-based
  sentencing
focal concerns theory

front-end sentencing
indeterminate sentencing
mandatory minimum
  sentences
mitigating factors
pedophiles
policy capturing

procedural knowledge
recidivism
restorative justice
retributive
sentencing disparities
shaming penalty
utilitarian

15 Juvenile and Adult Corrections

ORIENTING QUESTIONS

1. What are the important considerations in assessing juveniles prior to placement decisions?

2. What is the evidence for the effectiveness of interventions with juveniles in the community?

3. What are some characteristics of an effective treatment program?

4. How can risk/need/responsivity help to provide effective rehabilitative services for adults?

5. How do specialized problem-solving courts compare to other correctional interventions?

6. What are the differences between jails and prisons and what roles do psychologists play in these settings?

7. What kinds of interventions are delivered in jails and prisons?

8. What are some of the psychological consequences of imprisonment?

9. What are the priorities in preparing individuals for the transition from incarceration to community living (the reentry process)?

At the end of 2014, 1 in 36 Americans was in prison, on probation, or on parole, the highest per capita correctional rate in the world. Despite this high rate, there has been a decrease in the percentage of individuals under correctional supervision in the United States since 2007. The decrease of about 1% annually over this period has been driven by reductions in the number of people under community supervision (parole or probation) (Bureau of Justice Statistics, 2016a, 2016b). But correctional systems disproportionately target young African American males, with more Black men imprisoned or on parole or probation today than were enslaved in 1850, prior to the Civil War (Alexander et al., 2010).

In this final chapter, we discuss the process following a defendant's conviction for a criminal offense. This discussion will include both **adjudication of delinquency** (for juveniles) and **criminal conviction** (for adults). It will address the traditional aspects of corrections—**probation**, commitment to juvenile programs, incarceration in jail and prison for adults, and **parole** following release. But there have been some important innovations in correctional practice during the last 15 years—primarily in response to high rates of incarceration—which we will also discuss. In particular, there is now more emphasis on **diversion** and **reentry** (returning from incarceration to the community) as well as increased specialization in the nature of parole and probation and the rehabilitative services delivered. These efforts have resulted from lawmakers' receptiveness to new models of correctional interventions and from increasingly rigorous analyses by psychologists and others of the effectiveness of these programs.

Four major justifications for correctional intervention have been traditionally cited: incapacitation, deterrence (both general, as it applies to others, and specific to the individual convicted); retribution; and rehabilitation. The role of psychology in addressing these goals is focused largely on deterrence and rehabilitation. The question of whether individuals undergoing juvenile or correctional intervention are deterred from committing further offenses is an important topic that psychological research can help address. Deterrence is also related to the goal of rehabilitation. But the rehabilitative question is broader: Has the individual gained skills, changed patterns of thinking, and decreased deficits? Such changes facilitate a more responsible lifestyle. Much of the discussion in this chapter, as it relates to both juveniles and adults, will address how psychology contributes to the broad goals of deterring future crime, enhancing public safety, and rehabilitation. ●

Juvenile Corrections

Interventions for adjudicated delinquents involve delivering services designed to reduce the risk of future offending, and improve or eliminate deficits that are relevant to such risk. The goal of these interventions is to interrupt the criminal trajectories of young offenders before they become career criminals. This can be done in different settings, ranging from the community to secure residential programs. (In some states, these programs are simply called juvenile prisons.)

It is useful to consider what such interventions might have in common. In 2004, the National Institutes of

Health assembled a "state of the science" conference entitled *Preventing Violence and Related Health-Risking Social Behaviors in Adolescents*. Summarizing the evidence presented at this conference, the organizers concluded that there are certain characteristics shared by programs that are successful in reducing the rates of violence, antisocial behavior, and risky health behavior in adolescents:

- They are derived from sound theoretical rationales.
- They address strong risk factors (such as substance abuse, family problems, and educational problems).
- They involve long-term treatments, often lasting a year and sometimes much longer.
- They work intensively with those targeted for treatment and often use a clinical approach.
- They follow a cognitive behavioral strategy.
- They are multimodal and multicontextual (they use different kinds of interventions and deliver them in different contexts, such as home and school).
- They focus on improving social competency and other skill development strategies for targeted youth and/or their families.
- They are developmentally appropriate.
- They are not delivered in coercive institutional settings.
- They have the capacity for delivery with fidelity (meaning that services are delivered as intended).

Likewise, there are common elements of programs that appear to be ineffective:

- They fail to address strong risk factors.
- They are of limited duration.
- They aggregate high-risk youth in ways that facilitate contagion (i.e., the incarcerated youth are influenced by the antisocial behavior modeled by their peers).
- Their implementation protocols are not clearly articulated.
- Their staff are not well supervised or held accountable for outcomes.
- They are limited to scare tactics (e.g., Scared Straight) or toughness strategies (e.g., classic boot camps).
- They consist largely of adults lecturing at youth (e.g., the classic drug abuse resistance education program D.A.R.E.).

These are elements of interventions, both pro and con, that have a good deal of applicability to juvenile corrections. Consider them as we discuss strategies, procedures, and outcomes, and try to distinguish between what will be effective and what will not.

Assessing Risk and Needs in Juveniles

There are two important considerations that recur in juvenile forensic assessment: public safety and treatment needs/amenability. The former means that courts, the juvenile system, and the larger society are rightly concerned with the question of whether the juvenile will reoffend following completion of the intervention. The second refers to the youth's deficits, problems, and symptoms, particularly those related to reoffense risk—and whether they can be improved or eliminated through intervention and within the time that is available until the youth "ages out" of eligibility for treatment as a juvenile (Grisso, 1998).

Social scientists have recognized that a number of influences are related to the risk of juvenile offending. For example, the Office of Juvenile Justice and Delinquency Prevention (OJJDP), in their 1995 *Guide for Implementing the Comprehensive Strategy for Serious, Violent, and Chronic Juvenile Offenders*, compared the factors used in eight different states to classify the risk for future offending in arrested juveniles. At least four of the states used factors that included age at first justice involvement, number of prior justice involvements, and current offense (taken together, these provide an estimate of how long, how much, and how seriously the juvenile has offended). Other commonly used factors were drug/alcohol problems, school difficulties, negative peers, and family problems. These factors can be either static (with no potential to change through intervention) or dynamic (with the potential to change through intervention).

Focusing on both risk and risk-relevant needs is an approach that was formally conceptualized in the late 1980s. Andrews, Bonta, and Hoge (1990) described three separate considerations, which they termed **risk, need, and responsivity** (RNR). Risk refers to the likelihood of committing future offenses, with those at highest risk receiving the most intensive interventions. Needs are the deficits (such as substance abuse, family problems, educational problems, and procriminal attitudes) that increase the risk of reoffending. These are sometimes called **criminogenic needs**. Responsivity involves the likelihood of a favorable reaction to the interventions, and the influences that may affect such responding. It is easy to see the conceptual relationship between the juvenile priorities of public safety, treatment needs, and treatment amenability on one hand,

and the Andrews, Bonta and Hoge concepts of risk, need, and responsivity on the other. Accordingly, the RNR model is a very useful foundation for the evaluation of juveniles (Andrews & Hoge, 2010).

There are two specialized tools in particular that focus on the measurement of juvenile risk and needs: the Structured Assessment of Violence Risk in Youth (SAVRY) (Borum, Bartels, & Forth, 2005) and the Youth Level of Service/Case Management Inventory (Hoge & Andrews, 2002). Both prompt the user to consider historical factors, such as the nature of current and previous offending, as well as contextual factors (e.g., family, school, peers) and personal factors (e.g., substance abuse, anger, impulsivity, callousness, attitudes toward intervention, offending, and authority). The SAVRY also considers protective influences such as social support, attachment, resilience, and commitment to positive activities. A similar tool, the Risk–Sophistication–Treatment Inventory (Salekin, 2004), also guides the evaluator in appraising influences related to risk and risk-relevant treatment needs. It includes "sophistication" (referring to the youth's adeptness and adult-like attitudes regarding offending), another factor that often appears in the law for decisions on juveniles.

Evaluating youth on the dimensions of risk and needs provides valuable information for several reasons. First, it structures the evaluation to require the psychologist to consider the influences that theory and research indicate are most strongly related to risk and needs. Second, it provides useful information for intervention planning. A specialized risk–needs tool could be used to help the court make a decision about placement, but could also be used by a program once the youth is placed to help determine what interventions should be provided to that individual. Third, it offers one approach to measuring progress and current status. A youth with deficits in certain areas who begins a program should be reevaluated at different times throughout the program to gauge whether he or she is making progress in important areas. This affects the assessment of current risk, as well as the needs for additional interventions following completion of the program. A careful evaluation of youth risk and needs is important for planning and future interventions at various levels in the juvenile system (Borum & Verhaagen, 2006).

Community-Based Interventions

There are a number of approaches to the rehabilitation and management of adjudicated delinquent youth in the community. Youth may be placed on probation, involving a specified set of conditions for which compliance is monitored by the probation officer assigned to the case. A variation on the standard conditions of probation involves **school-based probation**, in which the youth's attendance, performance, and behavior in school are monitored through the probation officer's personal visits to the school. Probation conditions may also include drug use monitoring (through testing blood or urine); substance abuse treatment; mental health treatment; and skills-based training in particular areas (e.g., anger management, decision-making). Probation may also vary in intensity, with **intensive probation** involving more frequent monitoring contact.

Youths who are placed on probation typically live at home. Alternatively, a youth in a community-based placement might participate in a specific program or alternative school during the day but return home at night. Oakland's Evening Reporting Center for juvenile offenders is one such program. In order to remain in the community, adjudicated juveniles must report straight to the Center after school and remain there until 8 P.M. The program provides opportunities to participate in art, music, and sports; a sit-down dinner with caring adults; and a ride home at the end of each evening. Together, these components have contributed to reduced rates of incarceration, particularly for Oakland's minority youths (Porter, 2012).

There is a wide range of specific interventions and broader programs available in the community to youth adjudicated as delinquent. Rather than attempting to describe them all, we focus on three particular community-based interventions for delinquent youth that have been heavily researched: Multisystemic Therapy, Multidimensional Treatment Foster Care, and Functional Family Therapy. On the basis of this research, these interventions can be described as empirically supported, cost-effective, risk-reducing, and amenable to quality assurance monitoring (Henggeler, 2016).

Multisystemic Therapy (MST). As the name implies, **Multisystemic Therapy** (Henggeler, Schoenwald, Borduin, Rowland, & Cunningham, 1998) focuses on multiple "systems": the individual, family, peer, school, and social networks as they relate to identified problems and risk factors for offending. It delivers services based in the home, school, or elsewhere in the community, with three to four therapists working in a team. This increases the frequency of participation well beyond what would be expected from having juveniles and their families come to the program or individual therapist's office. The training of therapists and supervisors in MST is highly standardized (Henggeler & Schoenwald, 1999), and the MST procedures are very clearly specified (Henggeler et al., 1998), so those receiving MST services are likely to receive them as they were intended to be delivered. (Researchers call this "treatment integrity.") Therapists are available 24/7, working to prevent problems or crises in the youth's life from having a major impact. Consequently, the rate of engaging and retaining families in treatment is very high; over the three to six months of direct service usually needed for MST, the retention rates are as high as 98% (Henggeler, Pickrel, Brondino, & Crouch, 1996; Henggeler et al., 1999).

As MST has become more popular, the amount of research on it has grown. The focus on treatment integrity has been important—particularly since studies have supported the link between adherence to MST treatment principles and favorable outcomes (Henggeler, 2016; Schoenwald, Henggeler, Brondino, & Rowland, 2000; Schoenwald, Sheidow, & Letourneau, 2003). In other words, there is a substantial "quality assurance" component built into MST; this intervention was being provided in more than 30 states and 10 nations as of 2009 (Henggeler, Sheidow, & Lee, 2010).

MST is one of the best-validated interventions for juveniles. Henggeler et al. (1986) reported that MST was more effective than usual diversion services in two respects: (1) improving both self-reported and observed family relations and (2) decreasing youth behavior problems and time spent with deviant peers. It has also been shown to reduce recidivism by 43% and decrease placements outside the home by 64% over a 59-week period among juveniles charged with serious offenses (Henggeler, Melton, & Smith, 1992). The percentage of this MST group arrested over a longer outcome period (2.4 years) was about half that of the comparison group (Henggeler, Melton, Smith, Schoenwald, & Hanley, 1993).

A study in which participants were randomly assigned to either MST or individual counseling (the strongest kind of research design, with the random assignment to treatment versus control groups allowing the researcher to draw conclusions about the causal relationship between treatment and outcome) involved 176 chronic juvenile offenders (Borduin et al., 1995). It showed that MST produced better family functioning, better symptom reduction, and a 69% reduction in recidivism over a period of four years. Another randomized assignment study (Henggeler, Melton, Brondino, Scherer, & Hanley, 1997) with juveniles who had chronic histories of offending and were charged with a violent offense (N = 155) yielded similarly favorable results, including a reduction in mental health symptoms, a 26% reduction in recidivism, and a 50% reduction in incarceration over 1.7 years.

A long-term (22-year) follow-up of the differences between those who received MST and those who received another intervention (Sawyer & Borduin, 2011) included criminal and civil court outcomes for 176 serious and violent juvenile offenders who participated an average 21.9 (range = 18.3–23.8) years earlier in a clinical trial of MST, or who, alternatively, received individual therapy. Results showed that felony recidivism rates were significantly lower for MST participants than for individual therapy participants (34.8% vs. 54.8%, respectively) and that the frequency of misdemeanor offending was five times lower for MST participants. Also, the odds of involvement in family-related civil suits during adulthood were twice as high for IT participants as for MST participants.

There is also evidence that MST is effective with delinquent youth in Great Britain (Butler, Baruch, Hickley, & Fonagy, 2011) and Dutch youth with severe and violent antisocial behavior (Asscher, Dekovic, Manders, van der Laan, & Prins, 2013). In the former study, favorable outcomes observed 18 months after MST included reduced offenses (41% decrease), reduced placements (also a 41% decrease), fewer reported signs of delinquency, and improved parenting. The Dutch youth in the latter study showed decreased antisocial behavior and increased association with pro-social peers, with increased parental competence and positive discipline, observed six months after MST was delivered. An important finding in both studies involved the improvements in parenting, and in the relationship between the youth and their parents, reflecting the family as a prioritized aspect of MST.

There is also evidence that MST is effective with juveniles with substance abuse or dependence. Another study using random assignment to MST versus "treatment as usual" for substance-abusing juveniles (N = 118) (Henggeler, Pickrel, & Brondino, 1999) showed a decrease in drug use, a 50% decrease in time in out-of-home placement, and a 26% decrease in recidivism over a one-year period, while a longer follow-up (four years) yielded significantly reduced violent offending and significantly increased drug use abstinence in the MST group (Henggeler, Clingempeel, Brondino, & Pickrel, 2002). Finally, a study conducted by the Washington State Institute for Public Policy (Aos, Phipps, Barnoski, & Lieb, 2001) concluded that the MST intervention costs an average of $4,743 per family. Considering that cost, the evidence of its effectiveness, and the savings from not placing the juvenile outside the home, the study estimated cost savings of nearly $32,000 per youth and about $132,000 in additional savings from decreased costs to victims. We provide a case example in Box 15.1.

The Case of Marcus: A Youth Treated in the Community with Multisystemic Therapy

BOX 15.1

Marcus was 15 years old when he was arrested for stealing a bicycle from a classmate. This was his second arrest. A year earlier he had been arrested for possession of marijuana and received a disposition of six months of school-based probation, which required him to attend school (his probation officer periodically came to his school and checked whether he was there) and undergo urine tests for drug use.

Marcus completed his six-month probation without violating any of his conditions. However, despite this, he continued to have a number of difficulties in his life that increased the risk that he would continue to offend. His father had been absent from the family since Marcus was very young. He and his four siblings lived with his mother and grandmother. Because his mother had serious substance abuse problems herself, she was often unemployed and sometimes absent. The burden for supervising the children and supporting the family financially fell mainly on Marcus's grandmother. As she became older, she began to develop significant medical problems, and could not be as attentive to all the children as she had been previously.

Marcus's grades and behavior in school improved during the first six months of the ninth grade, but after the probation was finished, he began missing a number of school days and falling behind in his work. Marcus was measured in the Average range on a standard IQ test (higher than most juveniles who are arrested), but he found it hard to pay attention to written materials and when his teacher was talking. He tended to avoid doing his homework as a result. He preferred playing basketball with his friends, talking with girls from his neighborhood, and hanging out with older boys who sold drugs.

After he was arrested for his present offense, Marcus was evaluated by a psychologist appointed by the juvenile court judge. The psychologist concluded that Marcus had potentially serious problems with family, school, substance abuse, and negative peers, and diagnosed him with attention deficit disorder (ADD). However, he also had some strengths, including a close relationship with his grandmother who was a strong role model; average intelligence; and an interest in sports. He was recommended for a community disposition that involved treatment with MST.

The judge adjudicated Marcus delinquent on the charge of stealing the bicycle and sentenced him to one year of juvenile probation. One condition of probation involved treatment with MST. Marcus's MST team included a case manager, a family therapist, a substance abuse counselor, and two other staff members responsible for working with Marcus in school and in the neighborhood. The case manager immediately made an appointment with a child psychiatrist, who diagnosed Marcus with attention deficit disorder and prescribed medication for the symptoms. One of his MST team members helped Marcus to join a community basketball league; his team practiced every day after school, and the gym was open for casual play (with adult supervision) after the season ended. His family therapist met with Marcus twice a week in his home to address the issues facing his family, including helping his grandmother schedule her medical appointments more effectively, providing access to job training and substance abuse support for his mother, and arranging for a regular supervision schedule involving Marcus's grandmother, mother, and all the children. During the second week of scheduled appointments, the family therapist and case manager found nobody at home at the time of each appointment. Therefore, they came to the home at 6:00 A.M. on Sunday and held a make-up meeting at that time.

By the end of the six-month MST session, Marcus was doing much better. His school attendance and behavior were consistently improved, his after-school hours were almost always spent playing basketball, his mother and grandmother were much more attentive to him and the other children, and he was able to concentrate on his homework more easily. Much of this improvement resulted because MST was administered in the home, school, and gym rather than the office of a therapist or probation officer. In addition, those administering the MST were careful to do it precisely as intended, and were firm about making sure that appointments were kept.

CRITICAL THOUGHT QUESTION

What are some of the features of MST that make it effective for Marcus?

Oregon Treatment Foster Care (OTFC). Oregon Treatment Foster Care (also called Multisystemic Treatment Foster Care) is another treatment intervention based in the community, developed in the 1980s as an alternative to "treatment as usual" (typically out-of-home placement) for juveniles charged with serious offenses. The procedures for delivering this intervention are described in a treatment manual (Chamberlain & Mihalic, 1998), which increases OTFC's treatment integrity. It involves placing juveniles with specially trained foster parents rather than in residential placement. Like MST, this intervention uses a team approach. The OTFC team includes a case manager and therapists, as well as foster parents who are available 24/7 over the 6–12 months usually needed. OTFC is designed to provide close supervision (including supportive relationships with adult mentors and reduced exposure to negative peers) within consistent limits. A variety of treatment modalities (including individual and group counseling, family therapy, and interventions to improve specific skills such as anger control and decision-making) may be used. These are often conducted with the family, using both the foster parents and the biological parent(s), and in the school.

OTFC has been identified as a model treatment program by the U.S. Surgeon General (U.S. Public Health Service, 1999) and the *Blueprints for Violence Prevention* initiative (Mihalic, Irwin, Elliott, Fagan, & Hansen, 2001). One study involving OTFC (Chamberlain, 1990) treated 13- to 18-year-olds (N = 16) matched with a comparison group of 16 other juveniles treated in community residential treatment. Those in the OTFC group were less likely to be incarcerated and more likely to complete treatment over a two-year follow-up period. A second OTFC study (Chamberlain & Reid, 1998) involved random placement of youth (N = 79) between the ages of 12 and 17 into OTFC or treatment as usual. Youth treated with OTFC were more likely to complete treatment, spent more time with biological relatives and less time in detention over the next year, and were arrested less often during this period. Subsequent analyses using this dataset showed decreased violent recidivism (by 45%; Eddy, Whaley, & Chamberlain, 2004) and decreased substance use (Smith, Chamberlain, & Eddy, 2010).

OTFC is also a relatively cost-effective intervention. An analysis conducted by the Washington State Institute for Public Policy (Aos et al., 2001) estimated the cost per youth of about $2,000 (plus foster placement costs), which represents a savings of about $22,000 per youth relative to placement in group homes, and further savings of more than $87,000 in victim costs for each individual in OTFC.

Functional Family Therapy (FFT). Functional Family Therapy is a third community-based intervention for juvenile offenders. It is somewhat older than either MST or OTFC, having been used for almost 30 years. It is provided by a single therapist, who has a caseload of 12–15 cases, with weekly sessions over an average period of three months. As the name implies, it is family focused and is often delivered in the home (Alexander et al., 1998). Quality assurance/treatment integrity is addressed by careful training of therapists, yearly on-site consultation, ongoing telephone consultation, feedback from families, and weekly supervision. As we have seen, such quality assurance is a component that is common to FFT, MST, and OTFC—each ensures that services are delivered as intended.

The Office of Juvenile Justice and Delinquency Prevention identified FFT as a model treatment program (Mihalic et al., 2001). An early study of FFT (Alexander & Parsons, 1973) involved a randomized trial of FFT delivered to 13- to 16-year-old status offenders (those committing offenses such as truancy or running away from home that would not be illegal if committed by an adult), with 46 families receiving FFT and another 40 receiving family-centered "treatment as usual." The recidivism rate for those receiving FFT was 50% lower than it was in the comparison group. A second study (Gordon, Arbuthnot, Gustafson, & McGreen, 1988) involved 54 youths who had committed more serious offenses. The comparison group was composed of randomly selected youth who had not been referred for family therapy (a *no treatment control group*). The recidivism rate for those receiving FFT (11%) was substantially lower than for those in the group that did not receive treatment (80%).

The effectiveness of FFT depends on adherence to the model, however (Sexton & Turner, 2010). Researchers compared the effectiveness of FFT to that of probation services in a community juvenile justice setting 12 months after treatment. FFT was effective in reducing youth behavioral problems—but only when the therapists adhered to the treatment model. High-adherent therapists delivering FFT had a statistically significant reduction of felony reoffending (35%) and violent reoffending (30%) when compared to the control condition. The low-adherent therapists, however, had significantly higher recidivism rates than either the FFT high-adherent or the control groups.

There is some evidence that FFT is effective in reducing the risk of substance abuse (which itself is a risk factor for criminal offending). Runaway adolescents with alcohol problems receiving FFT showed decreased alcohol use when compared with others provided treatment as usual (Slesnick & Prestopnik, 2009). Other adolescents with substance abuse problems receiving either FFT or a combination of FFT and cognitive behavior therapy showed favorable outcomes for reduced marijuana use three months after treatment (Barrett, Slesnick, Brody, Turner, & Peterson, 2001). While neither of these studies included criminal offending as an outcome, the evidence that they improved problems with substance abuse is encouraging with respect to their potential to reduce reoffense risk by addressing drug and alcohol problems.

These and other studies indicate that FFT is associated with a significant reduction in recidivism when compared with "treatment as usual" and no treatment (Alexander et al., 1998). The same Washington State Institute for Public Policy report (Aos et al., 2001) noted earlier, which described the cost and savings associated with MST and OTFC, indicated that FFT had an average cost of $2,161 per participant, saved an average of $14,149 in costs for intervention compared with standard treatment in the juvenile justice system, and saved another $45,000 in victim costs per participant.

How would Marcus (Box 15.1) have done with OTFC or FFT? Consider the similarities in OTFC, FFT, and MST on the dimensions described earlier in this chapter. All three directly target important influences such as substance abuse, family problems, and educational deficits. All three involve intensive work, including clinical interventions, and protocols to ensure that the planned interventions are actually delivered. (Remember the unscheduled 6:00 A.M. Sunday meeting with Marcus's family after missed appointments? This kind of extreme but effective response is sometimes necessary.) All three approaches use different interventions delivered in more than one setting, such as at home and in the school. These interventions are delivered in the community rather than an institution, and include goals that are developmentally appropriate. Finally, the interventions are carefully planned and monitored for consistency with the plan. Marcus probably would have responded favorably to any of these three empirically supported interventions.

Secure Residential Interventions

The previous section described three interventions that appear effective, both in terms of reducing the risk of reoffending and in saving money. So why not deliver most or all of juvenile interventions in the community, using MST, OTFC, or FFT? There are two answers to this question. First, not all communities offer these interventions. We cannot assume that because an

effective intervention *could* be delivered in the community, it *will* be. Second, many judges would be inclined to place a youth in a secure residential facility as a consequence of a delinquency adjudication for a serious offense, even if that youth could possibly be treated in the community. Why? Community values (which judges represent) may support such a placement. The publicly perceived risk to society is lower when a youth is placed in a secure residential program, even though the actual risk (gauged through outcome research) may not be. Unfortunately, the impact of different placements for juveniles who commit serious offenses is very difficult to judge through research. The ideal study to help understand the impact of a given program or placement involves random assignment to such a program, comparing the outcomes to "treatment as usual." Very few judges, juvenile system leaders, or legislators would support research that randomly placed serious offenders in the community (versus in residential placement) to determine the impact of each on subsequent reoffense risk.

Accordingly, we must describe residential placements and their effectiveness without the best kind of evidence. While this is inconvenient for researchers, it is probably appropriate for those who represent our society and are responsible for promoting its safety. It would be very helpful to have good evidence about program effectiveness, but certainly tragic if citizens were victimized by offending as a result of such research. This is the main reason why research with random assignment is difficult to conduct in the juvenile and criminal justice systems—and why researchers must be satisfied with comparing a given intervention to "treatment as usual" rather than "no treatment." In a study like this, no citizen is put at additional risk, which could occur when "no treatment" is provided to a group of serious offenders.

A meta-analysis of the predictors of general recidivism in juveniles (Cottle, Lee, & Heilbrun, 2001) suggested a number of "treatment targets" that may be addressed at any stage of the intervention process. However, since residential placement is typically longer and more intensive, these targets may be particularly relevant for residential placement. The treatment targets include, in order of their strength, nonsevere pathology (such as conduct disorder); family problems; ineffective use of leisure time; delinquent peers; and substance abuse. A smaller meta-analysis, focusing on predictors of recidivism in violent juvenile offenders (Heilbrun, Lee, & Cottle, 2005), identified cognitive and family therapies as more effective in reducing recidivism rates than usual services (e.g., those with other orientations;

standard case management). This underscores an important weakness in residential interventions: If the juvenile is isolated from his or her family because of the location of the program, it is much more difficult to involve the family in a meaningful way. Conversely, one of the common features of the effective community-based interventions discussed earlier in this chapter is the close involvement of families in the intervention.

One meta-analysis of 32 studies of juvenile and adult treatment programs, many of them residential, found a reduction in recidivism in 75% of the studies (Redondo, Sanchez-Meca, & Garrido, 1999). Behavioral and cognitive-behavioral treatments appear to be most effective in reducing recidivism. Lipsey's (1992) meta-analysis of the impact of intervention on general recidivism risk in juveniles included a large number of studies (443) and estimated a 10% decrease in delinquency rates for juveniles receiving some kind of intervention. More frequent contact and longer periods of treatment were associated with more favorable outcomes—but only to a certain extent. This suggests that there is a "drop-off" in effectiveness of the intervention after a certain time.

In a review of meta-analyses focusing on a broad sample of residential treatment programs for justice-involved youth, the estimated reduction in reoffense risk was from 54.5% (control group) to 45.5% (residential treatment group), a difference of 9% (Grietens & Hellinickx, 2004). More structured and multimodal treatments had a stronger impact. Lipsey and Wilson's (1998) meta-analysis of 83 treatment programs for institutionalized juvenile offenders found that the most effective treatments reduced violent recidivism risk by 15–20%. The most effective of the residential treatments involved interpersonal skills training and family-centered interventions. As with MST, OTFC, and FFT, the most effective treatment programs were attentive to quality assurance, making them consistent with the treatment model. Individual characteristics of the juveniles being treated had little effect on these outcomes.

This research tells us that residential placements for juveniles can be effective, particularly when they focus on skills training (in areas like anger control and decision-making), vocational training, and educational and mental health needs, and also employ a treatment model that is "checked" through quality assurance. They should also be safe. If residents do not feel safe, it is very unlikely that rehabilitation efforts will be effective.

No comprehensive programs in juvenile residential settings have been studied through empirical research regarding their effectiveness. However, there have been studies of specific kinds of facilities, where youth are placed for mental health or substance abuse treatment—sometimes through court order (OJJDP, 2008). The OJJDP identified three residential programs supported by research. Two of the programs focused on the treatment of substance abuse and targeted both juveniles and other youths who were not involved in the juvenile justice system. Participation in either program resulted in reduced levels of drug and alcohol abuse, although one program did not show a reduced rate of offending after one year (Morral, McCaffrey, & Ridgeway, 2004), and the second did not even consider reoffending as an outcome in the study (Morehouse & Tobler, 2000). The third effective residential program combined security with mental health treatment for adolescents who had not responded well to "treatment as usual" in Wisconsin's juvenile justice system (Caldwell & Van Rybroek, 2005). The goal was to interrupt the escalation of defiance and legal consequences. Individualized therapy, behavioral control, and motivational interviewing were among the approaches used in this program. Those treated in this program were significantly less likely to recidivate within two years when compared with other juveniles with similar offenses who had been assessed (but not treated) in this program. This may be a particularly useful approach for serious offenders who also have substantial mental health problems.

A primary goal of residential treatment for juveniles is to reduce the deficits that are associated with reoffending risk. One approach to addressing anger problems (Anger Replacement Training; Goldstein, 2004) can be delivered either in a residential or community setting. It involves meeting with a therapist three times weekly for 10 weeks, and focuses on the development of specific skills such as impulse control, anger control, and thinking ahead, as well as reasoning. Research has demonstrated reductions in anger problems in secure residential settings (Goldstein, 2004), although the impact on recidivism risk has not yet been studied (Heilbrun et al., 2011).

Another anger management program has been developed for girls in residential juvenile facilities. The Juvenile Justice Anger Management (JJAM) Treatment for Girls is an 8-week, 16-session group intervention that is delivered with careful attention to treatment integrity (through manuals and careful training of therapists) and intended to teach self-control, problem-solving, and anger management (Goldstein, Dovidio, Kalbeitzer, Weil, & Strachan, 2007). A randomized controlled trial demonstrated significant reductions in anger, general aggression, verbal aggression, and indirect (relational) aggression for girls who completed the JJAM treatment in addition to treatment as usual, when compared with other girls who received only treatment as usual.

The Case of Thomas Harris: Imprisoned, Violent, and Skeptical

BOX 15.2

In the spring of 2008, 18-year-old Thomas Harris sat in a locked cell in an Ohio juvenile prison, a place he'd been for 2.5 years. (This is longer than most juveniles are incarcerated, even for serious offenses.) In that time, he'd had group therapy approximately twice a month, had been beaten up 12 times, and had sustained a fractured leg and cut lip.

So when the agency that runs Ohio's juvenile prison agreed to improve the conditions for juvenile offenders—including offering better mental health and medical treatment and reducing violence—Harris was understandably skeptical. He said in a telephone interview from prison, "They tell us, 'We're going to hire more staff to make you feel safer and hire more social workers so we can get you on the road to success.' It never happens" (DeMartini, 2008).

Violence in the Ohio juvenile prison system had been escalating around this time. At the Marion County juvenile prison, juveniles attacked one another or a correctional officer 504 times in 2007, up one-third from 2006. Violence may result from incarcerated juveniles' perceptions that they must fight to protect themselves. Violent acts may be used by juveniles to establish themselves in the hierarchy, or to get what they want. Violent behavior may also stem from a feeling of being disrespected. Whatever the reasons why Thomas Harris and others are involved in violence, such behavior must be controlled and minimized for rehabilitation to be effective.

The agreement settled a class-action lawsuit filed against the Ohio prison system by a group of child-advocacy lawyers who claimed that the system was violent and ineffective. The new plan restricted how often and when prison staff can put juvenile offenders in solitary confinement, provided more medical and mental health services, and addressed overcrowding issues by releasing inmates who served their minimum sentence and progressed in therapy.

CRITICAL THOUGHT QUESTION

Why is it particularly important that juveniles be placed in a facility that is rehabilitatively oriented?

The field has increasingly recognized the potential impact of trauma and other adverse experience upon justice involvement and offending risk (Zelechoski, 2016). One program that promotes psychoeducation about trauma response and facilitates better current coping is Trauma Affect Regulation: Guide for Education and Therapy (TARGET; Ford & Russo, 2006). When delivered in a residential facility, this program has been associated with a substantial reduction in disciplinary incidents and related seclusion (Ford & Hawke, 2012). Program participation was not directly related to a reduction in recidivism risk—although overall risk for *all* residents did decline after TARGET was implemented for some.

Residential programs face specific challenges to effective rehabilitation of youth. These include *mental health disorders* (a number of youth may have particular treatment needs for mental health symptoms), *deviancy training* (the process by which deviant peers positively reinforce antisocial communication and behavior), *attitudes toward rehabilitation* (both youth and facility staff may be less than fully committed to rehabilitative goals), and *difficulty of involving families* due to more remote locations (Cruise, Morin, & Affleck, 2016). Residential programs that are more effective must recognize and address these challenges.

When should juveniles be placed in the community, and when should they be assigned to secure residential placements? This decision depends on several considerations. Higher risk juveniles, often with a history of prior offenses, may require more secure placement. A judge may decide that a single offense, if it is very serious, merits a secure placement. Sometimes it can be important to remove a juvenile from extremely problematic circumstances (involving family, peers, gangs, and the like) that would continue with a community placement. However, there are substantial costs (both to the individual adolescent and to society) associated with secure placements. Juveniles very often respond better to correctional interventions when they are delivered in the community and can involve important influences such as family and school. The case described in Box 15.2 highlights some of the complexities of secure placement.

This story raises some important questions about where juvenile correctional interventions should be made. When there are no proper resources and procedures in the community, interventions can be ineffective and put the public at continued risk. When there are no proper resources and procedures in secure settings, interventions are also ineffective and conditions can be brutal and dangerous. How can the necessary resources be obtained? (Lawsuits are one approach, as this story demonstrates.) How can they be most efficiently invested, so that interventions are as effective as possible? Much of the discussion in this chapter centers on the most efficient ways to use resources to provide effective interventions.

Reentry

Behavioral treatments for delinquent youth provided in residential facilities frequently do not generalize to the community after discharge (Quinsey, Harris, Rice, & Cormier, 2006). The process of reentry into the community should include planning for aftercare services (in some states, called juvenile parole) that are important to ensure ongoing treatment in the community and reduced recidivism risk. There are six areas in particular that are important in the reentry planning process: family functioning, housing (if not living with the family), school or job, mental health and/or substance abuse services, monitoring, and social support. Addressing each of these areas can help provide a smoother, safer transition from the youth's placement back to the community. Promising approaches to such relevant aftercare include the intensive aftercare program, wraparound services, and several of the community interventions already discussed (MST, FFT).

Intensive aftercare was developed to address the needs of chronic and serious juvenile offenders who are returning from residential placement. It used a graduated sanctions approach involving three steps: (1) prerelease planning; (2) a structured transition involving institutional and aftercare staff prior to, and following, release; and (3) long-term reintegrative activities to facilitate service delivery and social control (Altschuler & Armstrong, 1997). Studies addressing the impact of intensive aftercare (Altschuler, 1998) have produced mixed results. However, it also appears that many of the intensive aftercare interventions have not been consistent in providing appropriate and adequate treatment services. Accordingly, intensive aftercare remains an approach that appears promising and is consistent with both the emphasis on reentry planning and the "risk"

principle of the RNR model ("treat the highest risk individuals most intensely"). But the empirical evidence about its effectiveness has been limited.

"Wraparound services" involve the delivery of individualized services in the context of collaboration between agencies such as those responsible for mental health care, educational services, and juvenile corrections. In this approach, funding follows the adolescent's treatment, rather than being allocated to particular programs (Brown, Borduin, & Henggeler, 2001). Such services are useful particularly for youths with serious mental or emotional problems.

One example of wraparound services designed to serve emotionally disturbed youths in the juvenile justice system is Wraparound Milwaukee. Families are involved in these services, which use "care coordinators" to assist in obtaining needed services from the available providers. Research on the functioning of Wraparound Milwaukee has indicated that it improves functioning, reduces recidivism, and improves the coordination of service delivery between the juvenile justice, mental health, and child welfare systems (Goldman & Faw, 1999; Kamradt, 2000). It is also less costly than residential treatment (by about $5,000 per month) or inpatient psychiatric care (by about $15,000 per month) (Goldman & Faw, 1999).

Adult Corrections

The justifications for sentencing and intervening with adult offenders are somewhat different than for those with juveniles. Retribution, in particular, has been strongly emphasized during the last 35 years—and particularly since 9/11, when concerns about terrorism were added to societal attention to criminal offending. One commentator has referred to this era of harsh punishment as *the mean season of corrections* (Haney, 2006). We describe some of the psychological consequences to offenders, their families, and their communities in this chapter.

In many respects, though, the role of psychology in adult corrections incorporates the same correctional priorities that were seen with juveniles. Deterrence and rehabilitation as broad goals translate into the need to assess risks and structure interventions to reduce risk-relevant deficits.

Assessing and Diverting Offenders

The risk–need–responsivity (RNR) model, discussed earlier in this chapter, applies as well to adult corrections as it does to juveniles. Offenders who are convicted of criminal offenses (or charged with offenses but diverted from standard prosecution) will be assessed at some time, either as part of the legal proceeding or postsentencing, to gauge their risk and rehabilitation needs. In the prison system, this is called **classification**. Following the offender's commitment to the state department of corrections, he or she typically is evaluated at a classification center before being placed in a particular prison. The "risk" assessed at that stage is typically the risk of escape or misconduct within the prison, as these have direct implications for the security level of the prison to which this individual is assigned.

The risk of reoffending—and the needs related to such risk—is important for the vast majority of offenders who will be released from prison and return to the community following completion of their sentences or on parole. Assessing risk and needs can be facilitated by using a specialized measure. One example of such a measure is the Level of Service/Case Management Inventory (LS/CMI; Andrews, Bonta, & Wormith, 2004).

The LS/CMI is composed of 58 items in the following areas: Criminal History, Education/Employment, Family/Marital, Leisure/Recreation, Companions, Alcohol/Drug Problem, Procriminal Attitude/Orientation, and Antisocial Pattern (Andrews et al., 2004). It has been validated on both males and females. The males (N = 956), drawn from three Canadian correctional facilities, had a mean age of 26.9 years, mean sentence length of 325.6 days, and mean number of convictions of 3.7. The females (N = 1,414) were from the medium-security institution for adult women operated by Ontario Ministry of Correctional Services; they had a mean age of 30.2 years and a mean sentence length of 322 days. LS/CMI total scores have been associated with (1) propensity for rules violations and assigned levels of supervision; (2) outcomes such as program outcome status, recidivism, and self-reported criminal activity in probation settings; (3) parole outcome; (4) the success of halfway house placements; and (5) maladjustment (Andrews & Bonta, 1995). This tool is useful in appraising risk for a variety of outcomes, including prison, various community settings, and under parole supervision.

Community-Based Interventions

Probation for adult offenders remains a frequent form of disposition of criminal charges, with the court placing the convicted offender on community supervision in lieu of incarceration. An estimated 4.65 million adults in the United States were on probation, parole, or some other post-incarceration supervision at the

end of 2015. This was about 62,300 fewer than at the end of 2014, and the lowest number of adults under community supervision since 2000. Those on probation accounted for 81% of the adults under community supervision. A total of 75% of those on probation were male; 55% were non-Hispanic white, 30% were non-Hispanic black, and 13% were Hispanic or Latino. A total of 57% had been convicted of felonies. With respect to those on parole at the end of 2015, 87% were male, 44% were white, 38% were black, and 16% were Hispanic or Latino. Those on parole following a conviction for a crime against persons totaled 32% at the end of 2015 (Bureau of Justice Statistics, 2016a).

Correctional supervision in the community involves monitoring adherence to specified conditions. This is true for both probation and parole. The number of conditions and the nature of the monitoring can vary, depending on the individual's needs. Standard conditions involve specifying how often individuals must meet with a parole or probation officer; where they will live; whether they will work (or receive another kind of financial support, such as Social Security disability); and certain activities that must be avoided (e.g., drinking or drug use, weapon possession). Additional conditions can be added as needed. For example, if the individual had a serious drug abuse problem, he might be required to undergo urine screens and attend substance abuse treatment and Narcotics Anonymous meetings. An individual with a severe mental illness might be required to attend mental health treatment, take prescribed medication, and meet with a case manager.

Requiring adherence to specified conditions, and monitoring whether the individual actually does comply with these conditions, means that some individuals will violate the requirements of their probation or parole. If they do, there may be serious consequences, including the possibility of returning to a correctional facility. These consequences were made clear to offenders who violated the terms of their probation in Hawaii in the mid-2000s, when Judge Steven Alm decided to act swiftly when dealing with transgressors. But rather than sending people to prison, he arranged for offenders who tested positive for drugs or who missed appointments to be arrested within hours, subjected to a hearing within 72 hours, and, if found in violation of the terms of probation, sentenced to a short jail term. Judge Alm called the program HOPE (Hawaii's Opportunity Probation with Enforcement) and planned for a torrent of violation hearings. Happily, they did not materialize, and the rate of positive drug tests dropped by 93% for HOPE probationers, compared with a 14% decline for a comparison group (Rosen, 2010).

The Case of Louise Franklin: A Defendant on Probation

BOX 15.3

Louise Franklin was a 24-year-old mother of three who was arrested for assault following an argument with a neighbor whom she thought was stealing from her. Prior to the disposition of her case, Ms. Franklin was evaluated by a probation officer regarding her criminal history (she had no prior arrests), vocational status and financial circumstances (she was the sole source of support for her children), home and family circumstances, drug and alcohol use here, and medical/mental health history. Based on this evaluation (called a "presentence investigation"), and also using the results of a short actuarial tool to inform the court about reoffense risk level, Ms. Franklin was recommended for probation as a low-risk offender. The judge considered this recommendation and assigned a one-year period of probation following a plea bargain in which Ms. Franklin pled guilty to assault.

There were several "standard" conditions of probation imposed: having monthly meetings with her probation officer, obtaining permission from her probation officer prior to leaving the city, paying $250 in restitution to cover her victim's medical costs, and maintaining continued employment and her current residence. There was one additional condition specific to her probation: completing anger management group therapy. This condition was imposed because the judge observed that Ms. Franklin had been in two arguments (although not physical altercations) with other neighbors during the past year that resulted in police being contacted.

Ms. Franklin was glad that she was not incarcerated. She was also diligent about keeping her scheduled appointments with her probation officer. However, she insisted for the first three months that she had been unfairly treated, that her neighbor had started their dispute, and that she responded by slapping her neighbor (resulting in a fall and a trip to the emergency room) only to protect herself. She also had not paid the $250 in restitution by the six-month mark in her probationary year, when she was required to have done so. Her probation officer indicated to her in their sixth

monthly meeting that she must do so, or he would inform the court that she was in violation of the conditions of her probation. (This would result in a violation hearing and possible incarceration.) After this meeting, Ms. Franklin made arrangements to make this restitution payment within one week.

She attended weekly meetings of her anger management group for a total of 20 sessions, the scheduled duration of the group. She did not miss a meeting, and actively participated in the group. Her contributions reflected her initial feeling that she did not have a temper problem—she felt that others often provoked her, and she was justified in her reactions to such provocations. As the group progressed, however, Ms. Franklin began to see that others with similar perspectives did appear harsh and impulsive in their responses during the group sessions. She learned and practiced alternatives to angry dispute resolution, including identifying her own feelings better, avoiding confrontation when she was already angry, and avoiding "high-risk" situations, but dealing more openly and assertively with conflict, and "pausing and counting" before responding in situations in which unexpected confrontation occurred. She reported a noticeable decrease in the number of times she lost her temper after four months of being involved in this group. She also described the additional benefit of feeling more patient with her children. Her therapist reported to her probation officer that Ms. Franklin had satisfactorily completed anger management group therapy after six months. Ms. Franklin had satisfied all conditions of her probation after one year, so she was discharged from the supervision of the Department of Parole and Probation at that time.

CRITICAL THOUGHT QUESTION

Some research has characterized the approach of probation officers who are particularly effective with clients with mental health problems as "firm but fair." How might this apply to Ms. Franklin's probation officer?

Those who do comply with the conditions of their probation or parole are more likely to be successful in returning, crime-free, to society. We describe a typical defendant on probation in Box 15.3.

Some people are required to undergo mental health treatment as a condition of community supervision. To what extent are probation and parole effective interventions for these individuals? This question was considered in some detail by Skeem and Louden (2006), who reviewed articles published between 1975 and 2005 on adults with mental illness on probation or parole. They concluded that the link between mental illness and supervision failure is complex and indirect (Dauphinot, 1996; Solomon & Draine, 1995; Solomon, Draine, & Marcus, 2002). However, they also noted that specialty agencies, in which offenders are assigned to officers with smaller caseloads, are more effective than traditional agencies. They are also more effective in linking probationers with treatment services and reducing the risk of probation violation, and possibly in reducing the short-term risk of parole violation. The use of specialized probation and parole services for these purposes is consistent with a larger trend, discussed throughout this chapter, of providing specialized rehabilitation services for individuals in particular clinical categories (e.g., severe mental illness, substance abuse). On that note, we now turn to specialized interventions in the community—drug courts, mental health courts, and veterans courts—that are also outside the standard stream of prosecution and incarceration of criminal offenders.

Drug Courts in Corrections. After 1980, in part because of the "War on Drugs" that began in the United States in the 1970s and expanded into the 1980s, the number of those charged with and convicted of drug offenses expanded dramatically. Jail and prison admissions more than tripled during this period (Harrison & Karberg, 2003), with drug offenses involved in about 60% of the federal cases and 30% of the state-level cases that are part of this increase (Harrison & Beck, 2002). Neither punishing drug offenders by incarcerating them for long periods (the *public safety* approach) nor providing treatment while conceptualizing drug addiction as a disease (the *public health* approach) has been particularly effective in reducing the prevalence of drug abuse and drug-related crime. About 70% of drug offenders reoffend within three years of release from prison (Martin, Butzin, Saum, & Inciardi, 1999), while prison drug rehabilitation programs have shown little reoffense risk–reduction impact and even less impact on reducing the rate of drug use relapse (Marlowe, 2002).

A community-based intervention that is both more effective and less costly than incarceration and prison-based rehabilitation would be welcome. Drug courts appear to be such an alternative. They are one form of "problem-solving courts," which have been influenced both by public safety and public health considerations. Consistent with the legal philosophy of therapeutic jurisprudence (Wexler & Winick, 1996), such courts

consider how laws and legal decision makers can improve lives and solve problems and are designed to promote rehabilitation. Like the effective juvenile interventions described earlier in this chapter, drug courts are intended to provide an intensive and specific intervention targeting a very strong risk factor (substance abuse) for reoffending. Theoretically, for offenders with a serious substance abuse problem and a history of offending related directly to this problem, treating this risk factor (and ensuring that the right kind of treatment is delivered) should substantially reduce the risk of criminal reoffending.

Drug courts provide judicially supervised drug abuse treatment and case management services to nonviolent drug-involved offenders, taking them out of the standard "prosecution/conviction/incarceration" process. Participation is voluntary, and whether a defendant is eligible may be at the discretion of the prosecutor. San Francisco's "Back on Track" program is one such service. First-time, nonviolent, non–gang-affiliated drug offenders undergo a mandatory "personal responsibility program" that may include GED classes, community-based job training, parenting workshops and close court supervision to break the revolving door cycle of drug offending. Recidivism rates are less than 10% in a population in which recidivism typically top 50% (Harris, 2009).

Diversion in drug courts comes in two forms. First, those charged with a crime may be diverted entirely from prosecution, with the stipulation that they successfully complete the requirements imposed in drug court or face reinstatement of prosecution. Second, those who are convicted of a crime may be diverted to drug court to avoid prison or modify their probation conditions.

How well do they work? The research conducted during the last 20 years gives reason for optimism about this particular intervention. In essence, drug courts are more effective than virtually any other approach with substance-abusing offenders (Marlowe, DeMatteo, & Festinger, 2003). They seem particularly good at reducing drug use and criminal recidivism (e.g., Belenko, 2001, 2002; Belenko, DeMatteo, & Patapis, 2007; Government Accountability Office, 2005). Belenko (1998, 1999, 2001) described nearly 100 drug courts, concluding that about 60% of drug court clients attended at least one year of treatment, and approximately 50% graduated from the drug court program. These figures compare favorably to probation, where very few individuals (less than 10%) attend one year of treatment (Goldkamp, 2000). Belenko (1999, 2001) also reported that the frequency of positive urine screens for drug court clients (less than 10%) is lower than for those on probation, and that criminal recidivism rates for drug court clients are also lower than for similar offenders under other kinds of supervision in the community.

Three randomized controlled trials (the strongest kind of research design) indicate that drug court effectiveness is greater than standard criminal justice approaches to offenders with substance abuse. Drug court clients in one study (Turner, Greenwood, Fain, & Deschenes, 1999) were rearrested within three years at a rate of 33%, compared with 47% of those with drug problems on probation as usual. A second study using random assignment to drug court (Gottfredson & Exum, 2002) reported that 48% of drug court clients, as compared with 64% of "treatment as usual" adjudicated control clients, were rearrested within one year, although the percentages of those arrested from each group were about the same by the end of the second year (Gottfredson, Najaka, & Kearley, 2003). A third study (Eddy & Bellatty, 2014) focused on mandated post-adjudication intensive drug court services for medium to high risk property offenders using a multisite randomized controlled trial study to evaluate the effectiveness of these drug courts compared with traditional probation. Those in the drug court group had a lower rate of new charges (20.6% lower) than the traditional probation group—and a 30.6% lower rate of new drug charges. All differences were statistically significant, or nearly so.

In addition, one meta-analysis (Wilson, Mitchell, & Mackenzie, 2006) of 50 studies representing 55 drug court program evaluations found that the majority of studies reported lower rates of reoffending among drug court participants, with the average difference being 26% across all studies. A second meta-analysis (Mitchell, Wilson, Eggers, & MacKenzie, 2012) included 154 independent studies (92 of adult drug courts, 34 of juvenile drug courts, and 28 of Driving While Intoxicated courts) and reported that the great majority of adult drug court evaluations report that participants have lower recidivism than nonparticipants. They described the "average effect" of participation as comparable to a drop in recidivism from 50% to 38%, with effects lasting up to three years. DWI drug courts were associated with comparably sized effects, although some rigorous studies did not report these effects. However, juvenile drug courts had much smaller effects on recidivism. The strongest effects were reported in courts with high graduation rates that accepted only nonviolent offenders. Taken together, this research provides strong evidence that drug courts are more effective at reducing the rates of both substance abuse and reoffending over outcome periods of one to three years, compared with more traditional forms of community supervision such as parole and probation.

Mental Health Courts in Corrections. Mental health courts handle both felony and misdemeanor offenders (Redlich, Steadman, Monahan, Petrila, & Griffin, 2005), although some courts exclude those charged with felonies. Juvenile mental health courts have also been developed (Cocozza & Shufelt, 2006). Mental health services that include psychotropic medication, case management, and individual and group therapy are among those delivered through such specialized courts, with progress monitored by the court. Despite local differences, most mental health courts feature (1) a specialized docket for selected offenders, (2) judicial supervision of clients, (3) regularly scheduled hearings, and (4) specific criteria that must be met if an individual is to remain in, and complete, the program (Thompson, Osher, & Tomasini-Joshi, 2007).

Mental health courts provide adjudication and monitoring for a particular group of defendants. In the context of corrections, how well do they work? There is less empirical evidence for the effectiveness of mental health courts than for drug courts. There are also fewer well-designed studies (particularly randomized controlled trials), and the operation of mental health courts varies more widely across different courts. Consequently, it is more difficult to draw conclusions about the operation of mental health courts (Heilbrun et al., 2011).

But there is some relevant research. Boothroyd, Poythress, McGaha, and Petrila (2003) compared mental health court offenders (N = 121) and criminal court offenders (N = 101). They reported that the percentage of individuals under mental health court jurisdiction who received behavioral health services increased from 36% to 53% after coming under mental health court jurisdiction, while only 28% of criminal court offenders received behavioral treatment. Another study compared mental health court clients charged with misdemeanors (N = 368) before and after coming under mental health court jurisdiction. It reported an increase in the hours of case management and medication management, and the days of outpatient service, as well as fewer crisis intervention services and inpatient days (Herinckx, Swart, Ama, Dolezal, & King, 2005).

Several other studies have focused on whether greater access to clinical services actually results in improved clinical functioning. In one study using random assignment of offenders (N = 235) to mental health court versus "treatment as usual" (criminal court), investigators found that participants in both conditions improved in satisfaction and independent functioning, but mental health court individuals reduced their drug use more and developed more independent living skills (Cosden, Ellens, Schnell, Yamini-Diouf, & Wolfe, 2003).

By contrast, another study comparing mental health court offenders (N = 97) with criminal court offenders (N = 77) did not find differences between the mental health functioning of these two groups, or the nature of the mental health services available to both groups (Boothroyd, Mercado, Poythress, Christy, & Petrila, 2005). The investigators suggested that one explanation for these results might be the fact that the mental health court judges did not have much control over whether the mental health services were actually delivered. If their explanation is correct, it underscores the importance of control over service delivery. It would not be particularly useful to develop a specialized mental health court and divert those with particular mental health needs into this court, unless there was some assurance that additional specialized mental health services were available to those under the jurisdiction of this specialized court.

Other research has focused on criminal recidivism as an outcome variable in studying the impact of mental health courts. There is also mixed evidence on this question. One study (Trupin & Richards, 2003) reported that mental health court clients had fewer arrests postdischarge than did criminal court clients, while another study (Christy, Poythress, Boothroyd, Petrila, & Mehra, 2005) reported that the number of arrests decreased for mental health court clients—but not significantly more than it did for those in criminal court. A third study (Cosden et al., 2003) used random assignment of offenders (N = 235) to either assertive community treatment (a particular form of mental health case management involving additional services and small caseloads, sometimes used as part of mental health court) or the standard case management services associated with criminal court. After one year, mental health court clients had significantly fewer arrests and convictions. After two years, however, these differences were much smaller, and both groups showed an increased number of arrests when compared with the first year (Cosden, Ellens, Schnell, & Yamini-Diouf, 2005).

One of the most important considerations in whether mental health court participation reduces criminal recidivism is whether the client actually completes the treatment required by the court; participants completing mental health court in one study were nearly four times less likely to reoffend than were those who did not graduate (Herinckx et al., 2005). Indeed, participants in mental health court who do not complete the program may not differ from those who are processed through traditional criminal court. For instance, Moore and Hiday (2006) reported that those who completed mental health court were rearrested at a rate about one-fourth that of those in criminal court after one year—and those who did *not* complete mental health court were rearrested at about the same rate as the criminal court clients. Other investigators (McNiel & Binder, 2007) also noted both the risk reduction impact of mental health court and the importance of successfully completing mental health court.

One meta-analysis of mental health court outcomes was conducted as part of a doctoral dissertation (Sarteschi, 2009). It was noted that there are over 150 mental health courts operating in the United States, but this was apparently the first meta-analysis (underscoring that there is less relevant research than with drug courts). This meta-analysis reviewed 23 studies conducted through May 2008, with over 11,000 mental health court participants. Aggregate effects included a large effect for recidivism and a medium effect for quality of life, representing the most stable estimate of how mental health courts reduce recidivism and increase quality of life in their participants. But this finding should be replicated, updated, and published to ensure more confidence in these results.

A principle of effective intervention discussed earlier in this chapter is treatment integrity. In order to be effective, interventions need to be delivered the way they were intended, and need to be completed. The data from completers versus noncompleters in mental health courts are consistent with this principle. If a defendant is processed through a mental health court and does not participate in the services required by the court, then we should not expect his or her outcome to be better than it would have been through standard prosecution and disposition.

This research suggests that mental health courts, like drug courts, can have a favorable impact on both symptoms amelioration and reoffense risk reduction—provided that services are delivered and clients participate. Mental health courts vary more than drug courts in how they are administered across sites, however, and the supporting research is not as strong methodologically. Several studies indicate that the value of participation in mental health court is greatly limited when participants do not complete the program required by the court.

Veterans Courts in Corrections. Veterans courts are another kind of problem-solving court, developed using the same approach as drug courts and mental health courts: applying rehabilitative interventions under the jurisdiction of a specialized court (usually but not always on a pre-adjudication basis) for individuals who meet that court's criteria for inclusion. In this case, the veterans court focuses on the problems that are experienced by justice-involved veterans of U.S. military service, including challenges such as substance abuse, PTSD, depression, anxiety, and related difficulties in adjusting to civilian life. The first veterans court opened in Anchorage, Alaska in 2004, followed four years later by the establishment of the Buffalo Veterans Treatment Court (Holbrook & Anderson, 2011). Veterans courts often work closely with Veterans Affairs facilities, particularly VA Veteran Justice Outreach (VJO) Specialists, in providing services to veterans who are VA-eligible.

In telephone surveys conducted in 2012, investigators (McGuire, Clark, Blue-Howells, & Coe, 2013) sought to answer a number of questions about the current operation of veterans courts in the United States. They identified 168 veterans courts, dockets, and tracks in existence at the end of 2012. (The number of these courts has grown rapidly since 2008, but the empirical evidence tracking their operation and effectiveness is very limited—making this survey a welcome contribution to our understanding of veterans courts.) Two-thirds of the courts are specifically considered to be Veteran Treatment Courts; they serve Veterans of all eras. Nearly two-thirds (64%) of the courts provide services to veterans who are not VA-eligible, with these individuals comprising an average of 14% of the caseloads. The inclusion of volunteer veteran mentors is recognized as an important component of the Veterans Treatment Court model, with more than half the courts having mentors. A total of 7,724 Veterans have been part of veterans courts, according to this survey, with court jurisdiction averaging 15–18 months. About two-thirds of veterans who are no longer under court jurisdiction successfully completed court and treatment requirements.

A survey on veterans courts process and outcomes (Holbrook & Anderson, 2011) illustrates both the potential usefulness and the current empirical limitations of our knowledge of veterans courts. They surveyed 53 courts and received responses from 14, so the size of their sample was very small. Of the responding courts, seven indicated that they required a guilty plea as a condition of participation and eight reported that charges would be dismissed upon successful completion, with at least one court reporting that both options are used. Eight of the courts described using veteran peer mentors. Of the 404 court veteran participants tracked by survey responses, there had been 59 graduates, 8 voluntary withdrawals, and 21 early terminations. One of the individuals successfully completing veterans court had been involved in reoffending.

Veterans courts have proliferated rapidly and are clearly a popular and promising kind of problem-solving court. Just as clearly, the field very much needs empirical investigation into how they work and how effective they are.

Institutional Interventions

There are several important differences between jails and prisons, even though both are secure institutional facilities that incarcerate individuals who have been convicted of criminal offenses. A jail is a community-based facility that houses both individuals who are pretrial (those who have been charged with offenses, but not yet convicted) and others who have been convicted of relatively minor offenses, usually with sentences no longer than a year. By contrast, a prison is part of a correctional system that is either operated by the state (usually a state department of corrections will include a number of prisons) or the federal government (which operates the Federal Bureau of Prisons within the Department of Justice). Those who are incarcerated in prison have all been convicted of criminal offenses. They have also received sentences that are longer than the relatively short sentences associated with jail inmates. Prison sentences can range from slightly over one year to life, and prisons also house those who have received a death sentence.

The Federal Bureau of Prisons (2012) provides a range of programs for inmates. These include

- Substance abuse treatment
- Educational and vocational training
- Skills development
- Religious programs
- Work programs

United States Medical Center for Federal Prisoners in Springfield, Missouri.

The nature of this programming reflects the view that the important influences contributing to reoffending risk include deficits in skills, work training, and experience; they also include problems with drugs or alcohol. Religion may serve as a protective factor for some individuals, offering a structure and set of beliefs that are inconsistent with criminal offending. Psychologists may play a role in the delivery of some of these services, particularly substance abuse treatment and skills development. Of course, psychologists may also be involved in the delivery of mental health services to inmates with mental and emotional disorders.

Many of the same kinds of services are provided in prisons operated by the states. For example, the New York Department of Corrections and Community Supervision (2012) has programs and services for inmates that include educational and vocational training, substance abuse treatment, parenting skills, anger management, domestic violence counseling, health education, sex offender treatment, religious services, and others. The substantial overlap between the kinds of rehabilitative services provided by federal and state facilities reflects the common aspects of views about the needs of offenders that would reduce their reoffense risk and promote the possibility that they will live responsible lives without offending, following their return to their communities.

Jails are somewhat different in providing rehabilitative services. While those in prison have been convicted of criminal offenses and are serving sentences, this is true for only a subgroup of individuals in jails. Some have been convicted of offenses that are less serious than those of individuals in state or federal prisons, so they serve shorter sentences in jail rather than prison. Others, however, are awaiting disposition of charges, and will be held in the jail for periods ranging from days (for those who have charges dismissed, for example, or who are able to post bond and are released from incarceration pending disposition of charges) to years (for some with serious charges which, for different reasons, take a longer time to resolve). Since jails cannot anticipate whether their pretrial inmates will remain in the jail, they provide services focusing on immediate needs (e.g., medical and mental health care) rather than longer-term rehabilitation. This may be seen on the website of the nation's largest jail, operated by the Los Angeles County Sheriff's Department (2012). Medical and mental health services are provided, in additional to educational services. Psychologists are involved in delivering such services, but also in assessing inmates' needs and short-term risk for self-harm or violence toward others.

The functions carried out by psychologists also differ between jails and prisons. There are four broad purposes served by mental health professionals, particularly psychologists, in both jails and prisons: classification, consultation/crisis intervention, rehabilitation, and reentry planning. Because the nature of each function varies according to the facility, each will be discussed in terms of whether it is carried out in a jail or a prison.

The Role of Psychologists in Jails. There has been some fluctuation in the number of jail beds in the United States between the years 1999 and 2013. During this period, the number of individuals in local jails increased by 21%, from 605,943 to 731,570. This population was at its highest in 2008 (785,533), subsequently declining to the figure above by the end of 2013. During this period, the inmate population increased by 48%, from approximately 68,100 to 100,940; the male inmate population grew by 17%, from about 537,800 to 630,620. The number of individuals under the age of 18 in local jails at the end of 2013 (4,420) had decreased from its peak in 1999 (9,458) (Kaeble, Glaze, Tsoutsis, & Minton, 2015).

There is a much higher rate of severe mental illness in jail than in the general population (Bureau of Justice Statistics, 2006). For example, using inmate self-report of experiencing symptoms of severe mental illness such as hallucinations or delusions during the last 12 months, 17.5% of jail inmates reported the former and 13.7% the latter. These percentages are substantially higher than the percentage of adults over the age of 18 who report having experienced either symptom (3.1%). Another study (Steadman, Osher, Robbins, Case, & Samuels, 2009) estimated prevalence rates of serious mental illness among adult male and female inmates in five jails during two time periods: 2002–2003 and 2005–2006. A total of 822 admitted inmates at two jails in Maryland and three jails in New York were selected to receive the Structured Clinical Interview for DSM-IV. Serious mental illness (defined as a major mood disorder or a psychotic disorder) was observed in 14.5% of male inmates and 31% of female inmates. (It does not appear that there are more recent empirical studies on the rate of individuals with severe mental illness in jails that would update those conducted between 2010 and 2015.)

Given these numbers, we might expect that many of the psychological services provided to jail inmates would focus on those with mental disorders. Such services, described in a national survey of U.S. jails (Steadman & Veysey, 1997), include

- Screening, evaluation, classification
- Diversion (helping to determine whether a pretrial inmate might meet criteria for a community-based program such as drug court or mental health court)
- Suicide prevention
- Crisis intervention

- Case management services/reentry (liaison with community treatment providers, planning for release, assistance with housing and transportation)
- Coordinating volunteers (teaching, mentoring, tutoring, guiding release)
- Teaching life skills
- Group therapy for inmates and their families

Larger jails with more resources might be able to offer most or all of these services, so a psychologist's role in such jails would be more varied. Smaller jails, by contrast, might be limited to screening, suicide prevention, and crisis intervention.

The Role of Psychologists in Prisons. The contemporary prison can trace its roots to London in the 19th century, when Jeremy Bentham developed the notion that incarceration could be considered part of punishment rather than just a means of holding an individual until trial (as jails do) or execution. Facilities at that time were sometimes called "penitentiaries," reflecting the goal of invoking penance from those who were confined in them.

Imprisoning offenders is not necessarily the most effective approach to reducing the risk of future offending. This is perhaps not a surprise. Among the goals of criminal sentencing and incarceration are retribution, incapacitation, and general deterrence. Although lengthy sentences and punitive prison conditions may be consistent with these goals, such conditions are not necessarily consistent with the goal of rehabilitation. A meta-analysis of over 100 studies (Smith, Goggin, & Gendreau, 2002) indicated that the rate of reoffending following release from prison was 7% higher than following the completion of nonresidential sanctions.

Some approaches to prison-based rehabilitation are more effective than others, however. Bonta (1997) classified rehabilitation programs as either "appropriate" or "inappropriate" by determining their consistency with risk/need/responsivity principles discussed earlier in the chapter. Appropriate (RNR-consistent) treatments reduced criminal reoffending by an average of 50% when compared with inappropriate approaches. Appropriate treatment approaches were those that systematically assessed offender risk and needs with specialized tools (e.g., the Level of Service/Case Management Inventory; Andrews et al., 2004), targeted the criminogenic needs of offenders in treatment, and used cognitive-behavioral approaches to change deficits and increase strengths. By contrast, programs classified as inappropriate provided intensive services for low-risk offenders or targeted noncriminogenic needs such

California Department of Corrections

Pelican Bay prison in Crescent City, California.

as self-esteem. Such interventions were associated with slight *increases* in recidivism. Bonta (1997) concluded that RNR-consistent interventions, whether provided in prison or in the community, reduce recidivism risk and protect the public in the process. The exclusive application of punitive approaches, by contrast, does not reduce reoffending risk and is therefore less useful for public safety—at least via the rehabilitation of offenders.

One other approach that shows promise, particularly in treating drug offenders in prison, is the **therapeutic community** (TC). This is an approach in which the staff, other clients, and physical setting are all part of the therapeutic environment. Group therapy, individual counseling, "community meetings" involving all residents, and specialized interventions to build skills in areas such as anger control, decision-making, and recognizing high-risk situations are all used in the TC. Staff functions are not divided into those responsible for "security" versus those responsible for "treatment" (as is often the case in a secure hospital or correctional setting). Instead, all staff members are considered to be part of the rehabilitation process. All residents are likewise involved in maintaining an environment in which therapeutic goals are clear and important.

In correctional settings, the TC has most often been used to treat those with substance abuse problems. One quasi-experimental study (Welsh, 2007) focused on prison TC drug treatment program participants (N = 217) and comparison group participants (N = 491) for two-year outcomes following release. Prison TC was effective even without mandatory community aftercare, although effects varied somewhat across different outcome measures and sites. TC interventions significantly reduced rearrest and

reincarceration rates, but not drug relapse rates. Postrelease employment predicted a reduction in drug relapse and reincarceration.

One of the questions concerning the impact of rehabilitation in prison concerns "how much is enough?" Criminal sentences are imposed for a specific amount of time, not necessarily with rehabilitation as a primary determinant. But one interesting study (Bourgon & Armstrong, 2005) asked precisely this question: How much treatment is needed to reduce criminal reoffending? Researchers considered the recidivism rates of offenders in a Canadian prison (N = 620) who were followed up for one year after their release. While incarcerated, they had received either (1) no treatment, (2) 100 hours of treatment over 5 weeks, (3) 200 hours of treatment over 10 weeks, or (4) 300 hours of treatment over 15 weeks. Treatment programs were cognitive-behavioral, and focused on substance abuse, criminal attitudes, aggression, and criminal peers. Offenders' risk and needs had also been assessed as part of their incarceration. A total of 31% of offenders who received treatment in any dosage recidivated, compared with 41% who received no treatment. Offenders with different risk–needs levels required different amounts of treatment for an effective "dosage." In high-risk offenders with many criminogenic needs, for example, 300 hours of treatment reduced the observed rate of recidivism from 59% to 38%. By contrast, for medium-risk offenders with few criminogenic needs, 100 hours of treatment was sufficient to reduce recidivism from 28% to 12%—but more treatment was not associated with a further reduction in recidivism. For high- and medium-risk offenders with a moderate number of criminogenic needs, 200 hours of treatment was associated with a recidivism rate of 30%, as compared to 44% for similar offenders who received no treatment.

These results have several implications for rehabilitation in prison. First, just as in correctional interventions with juveniles, it is useful to employ a formal, structured approach to assessing relevant needs and intervening according to those needs. Second, it is possible to identify a "dosage effect" for relevant treatment, and to administer such treatment according to who is likely to receive the most benefit. Third, it is feasible to have a favorable impact over a relatively short period of time. Long sentences are not necessary to rehabilitate many of those who are sentenced to prison—so the justification for keeping inmates in prison for a lengthy period must be drawn from other

The Case of Michael Vick: Was He Rehabilitated in Prison?

BOX 15.4

Michael Vick

Michael Vick was the star quarterback for the Atlanta Falcons until he and his codefendants were arrested and charged with running a dogfighting kennel in Virginia. In September, 2007, while he was awaiting trial, Vick tested positive for marijuana. He was convicted of these charges in federal court, and received a sentence of 23 months in the federal system. He left Virginia in January 2008 to serve his sentence at a U.S. Bureau of Prisons facility in Leavenworth, Kansas.

How would the Bureau of Prisons have attempted to rehabilitate Michael Vick? First, he would have gone through "classification" (a period of assessment and individualized information gathering) to decide where he would be assigned. If he had a long sentence for a very serious charge, presented a substantial risk to harm others, or appeared to be an escape risk, he would probably have been assigned to a high-security facility. Apparently he did not meet these criteria, however, as Leavenworth is a minimum-security prison. Then, prison staff would have needed to decide what

particular deficits contributed to his involvement in the dogfighting charges of which he was convicted.

Another issue was drug use. Given that Vick tested positive for marijuana three months before he was sentenced, he might have been referred for substance abuse treatment by prison staff. Bureau of Prisons policy on treating drug abuse involves having those in treatment (lasting at least 500 hours over a period of 6–12 months) set apart from the general prison population.

Michael Vick was released from federal prison in May 2009. His story is familiar to those who follow professional football, and many who do not. Following his release from prison, he returned to his home in Hampton, Virginia, where he served the two remaining months of his sentence on home confinement. He was subsequently signed by the Philadelphia Eagles as a back-up quarterback. During the 2010–2011 season, he moved from third-string quarterback to starter after the Eagles traded Donovan McNabb and Kevin Kolb suffered a concussion in the season-opening game.

In the previous edition of this book, we asked some important questions about Mr. Vick's transition from prison back into the community—the reentry process. Where would he live? How would he be employed? Was he genuinely remorseful for his offending? Could he live his life without future offending? Could he avoid people and situations that elevate his risk for reoffending?

Those questions have now been answered. For Michael Vick, his return to the community, his family, and his profession seems to have gone well. His professional football career is now over, but there have been no reports of additional problems with the law. How much of this is attributable to his months in prison? That is a difficult question, and certainly not one that can be answered without knowing more about Mr. Vick than can be judged from publicly available information. But his apparently successful return to society and professional football does highlight one important reality: some individuals coming out of prison can (and do) take advantage of the "second chance" they are given to function as law-abiding citizens in our society.

CRITICAL THOUGHT QUESTION

What difference does prior successful functioning make in rehabilitation of an offender?

reasons, such as retribution and deterrence. Box 15.4 concerns the incarceration and possible rehabilitation of a professional athlete.

Psychological Consequences of Imprisonment

The psychological effects of institutional confinement are complex. Vast differences in prison conditions are undoubtedly important: Incarceration in a well-run minimum-security prison with adequate programming and treatment options will have different effects than imprisonment in an overcrowded, mismanaged facility where staff members use highly punitive practices such as excessive surveillance and isolation to control inmates. The psychological vulnerability and resilience of inmates and the length of their confinement matter as well.

For a number of reasons, high-quality empirical studies of the psychological consequences of imprisonment are limited. First, it has been difficult to develop a standard measure to quantify the effects of long-term incarceration because they are so variable and subjective. Second, most studies have assessed the effects of incarceration among inmates still imprisoned (e.g., Bonta & Gendreau, 1990), and because prisoners can adapt and attempt to achieve a tolerable existence *inside* the prison, the full psychological implications of long-term confinement may be apparent only after release (Haney, 2006). It is too simplistic to assert that violent offenders will be more likely to be violent toward others in prison. One study found that although inmates convicted of assault, robbery, and certain other violent offenses were more likely to commit serious rules infractions in prisons, inmates convicted of homicide were not—and those convicted of sexual offenses were even less likely to commit such infractions (Sorenson & Davis, 2011).

But social scientists have learned something about the consequences of long-term incarceration. Many inmates show a particular pattern of coping mechanisms in response to high levels of prison stress. They may become hypervigilant in order to deal with the significant risks to their personal safety, learn to project a "tough-guy veneer," socially isolate themselves and suppress any signs of emotion, and become generally distrustful of others (McCorkle, 1992). None of these characteristics will facilitate their reintegration into society. Indeed, some evidence suggests that assigning an individual to a higher-security prison actually increases that individual's risk for reoffending (Bench & Allen, 2003; Chen & Shapiro, 2007). One study (Gaes & Camp, 2009) even used random

assignment to prison security level to show that inmates with a randomly assigned higher security classification had a rate of returning to prison that was 31% higher than that of their counterparts who were assigned to a prison with a lower security level. There were no differences in the rates of serious institutional misconduct of these participants. These results are consistent with the influence of deviant peers and environmental strain, and inconsistent with specific deterrence theory.

Inmates report that their initial period of confinement is the most difficult (Harding & Zimmerman, 1989). Over time, a gradual process takes place in which prisoners adjust to their environment. Sociologist Donald Clemmer called this process **prisonization** and defined it as "the taking on in greater or less degree of the folkways, mores, customs, and general culture of the penitentiary" (Clemmer, 1958). This tends to happen without conscious awareness in inmates as they gradually learn to give up control of choices and decisions, and to depend on institutional rulemakers to provide structure and routine to their lives. One commentator likened it to a kind of "behavioral deep freeze" (Zamble, 1992) from which it is difficult to emerge, especially into the unstructured and unpredictable world that awaits an inmate upon release.

Contemporary corrections face a number of challenges in working with those who are incarcerated. A recent comprehensive survey (Bureau of Justice Statistics, 2017) describing those in jails and prisons in the United States in 2011–2012 focused on two important indicators of mental health problems: severe psychological distress experienced within the last 30 days, and history of mental health problems. The proportion of incarcerated individuals reporting recent severe psychological distress was 26% in jails and 14% in prisons (for men) and even higher for incarcerated women (32% jails, 20% prisons). Those with a history of mental health problems were estimated at 44% (jails) and 37% (prisons). These figures reflect the substantial proportion of contemporary jail and prison inmates with acute mental health crises, longstanding problems, or both. Treating such individuals in a secure correctional setting, addressing symptoms and adjustment problems, and minimizing the risk of self-harm, victimization by others, or aggression toward others must be high priorities, given these proportions. A comprehensive strategy for developing a strategic framework for addressing the overrepresentation of behavioral health problems among incarcerated populations while prioritizing the correctional goal of reducing reoffense risk has been described (Council for

State Governments Justice Center, 2012). This strategy focuses on addressing mental health and substance abuse problems, particularly when they co-occur, from the perspective of how each contributes to reoffending risk and affects responsiveness to interventions.

One scholar of correctional systems raised the intriguing possibility that prisons themselves serve to further the maladaptive and dysfunctional behavioral patterns that resulted in confinement in the first place:

> [T]he long-term effects of exposure to powerful and destructive situations, contexts, and structures mean that prisons themselves also can act as criminogenic agents—in both their primary effects on prisoners and secondary effects on the lives of the persons who are connected to them.... Programs of prisoner change cannot ignore the situations and social conditions that prisoners encounter after they are released if there is to be any real chance of sustaining whatever positive growth or personal gains were achieved during imprisonment. (Haney, 2006, p. 8)

We discuss the problems associated with reentry into society next.

Reentry

The process of reentry focuses on preparing inmates to move from incarceration back into the community and to face a world that is fundamentally different from the one to which they adapted while in prison. To be successful, they must adjust quickly. Fortunately, and appropriately, there has been more emphasis on this transition during recent years. In this chapter, we have seen the importance of services delivered in the community—and planning so that services are delivered as needed and intended. Partly because of the relatively recent nature of the emphasis on reentry in corrections, there is limited empirical research regarding the effectiveness of reentry programs. Existing research in this area has recently been summarized (Heilbrun et al., 2012).

The priorities for reentry begin with the goal of reducing the risk of reoffending. There are a number of ways to pursue this goal. Just as drug courts and mental health courts target specific constellations of clinical symptoms with the expectation that providing relevant services in these areas will reduce the symptoms, promote better adjustment, *and* reduce recidivism risk, the reentry process aims to target risk-relevant needs as the individual returns to the community. Released inmates account for a large proportion of the population with communicable health problems—for instance, HIV/AIDS and hepatitis B and C (Mellow, Mukamal, LoBuglio, Solomon, Osborne, 2008).

Reentry services can promote the provision of necessary health care services. Reentry services can also yield significant cost savings when provided effectively. This is always an important consideration for local and state governments dealing with crime.

Reentry can actually be considered broadly as including services provided during custody, in preparation for release, and during the period of community supervision and eventual discharge. The custody phase involves measuring offenders' risks, needs, and strengths upon entry to the correctional facility and providing interventions designed to reduce risk, address needs, and build strengths. The release phase includes *inmate release preparation*, with a parole plan for supervision, housing, employment, drug testing, and other considerations, and *release decision-making*, regarding the parole decision. The community supervision/discharge phase involves *supervision and services*, *revocation decision-making* (including graduated sanctions in response to infractions), and *discharge and aftercare*, when community correctional supervision is terminated. This section of the chapter focuses on the community supervision/discharge phase of reentry.

There were over 870,000 individuals on parole in the United States at the end of 2015, a modest increase from the 840,000 on parole at the end of 2010 (Bureau of Justice Statistics, 2016a). (This is a small part of the overall estimated 4.65 million justice-involved adults who were on some form of community supervision during this time, however.) About 20% of those on parole committed some kind of new offense or technical violation in 2015 leading to a revocation of parole, a considerable improvement over this figure (about 33%) in 2005 (Bureau of Justice Statistics, 2016a). An inmate in the California Institute for Men, Dagoberto Noyola, 45, exemplifies both the benefit of reentry programs and the ease with which some inmates slip back into old patterns of behavior upon release. Noyola says that a program that taught him to provide drug counseling to high school students and land a job laying tile for a construction company enabled him to reintegrate into society on his last parole. But the career criminal landed behind bars again after a burglary conviction. Still, he was hoping to return to tiling when released again. Looking over a sea of inmates in the prison's gym, Noyola said "A lot of guys want to go out there and do good. Nobody wants to be in here" (Gould, 2011).

The "community classification center" is part of the trend toward greater structure in reentry. Such facilities accept inmates who are released from prison and returning to the community. However, rather than either placing them directly in the community or sending them home, the community classification centers provide assessment for a limited period of time, and structure the reentry process so that individuals receive housing and services that are consistent with their needs. Some limited evidence suggests that such centers do a good job in both providing treatment services and managing the risk of reoffending during the first 6–12 months in the community following prison (Wilkinson, 2001). Programs that target specific offender needs have also been associated with lower recidivism rates (Seiter & Kadela, 2003).

There have been other changes in practice consistent with contemporary approaches to reentry (Lowenkamp & Latessa, 2005). The Second Chance Act of 2007: Community Safety through Recidivism Prevention, which was signed into law by President Bush in April 2008, provides funding for improving reentry using approaches consistent with evidence-based policy (Burke & Tonry, 2006; Center for Effective Public Policy, 2007). Guidelines to assist in the reentry process have been published (Aos, Miller, & Drake, 2006; International Association of Chiefs of Police, 2006). The interest in using empirical evidence to guide the practice of reentry is strong, as it is in contemporary medicine and mental health under the rubric "evidence-based practice."

There has been a limited amount of empirical research on parole services provided in the reentry process. In the early 1990s, California started a community-based program to facilitate parolee success for reintegration into society (Zhang, Roberts, & Callanan, 2006). The investigators reported that those not participating in this program were 1.4 times more likely to be rearrested within 12 months on parole, and that meeting goals in four specified domains (which this program facilitated) was associated with the lowest risk for reincarceration. A second study (Martin, Lurigio, & Olson, 2003) focused on a community-based supervision facility providing relevant services (e.g., life skills training, violence prevention, literacy classes, job skills training, job placement services, and GED preparation) during the day. The findings of this study reflect the importance of sufficient time in a program. More clients remained arrest-free after a longer period in the program (70+ days) than after a shorter period (less than 10 days). This difference in the recidivism reduction between the two groups (25% reduction for the first versus 10% for the second) provides an estimate of the potential "dosage" impact of this program. A third study (Bouffard & Bergeron, 2006) described a small program targeting serious and violent offenders during reentry; the program provided more referrals

to community-based services and increased drug testing frequency during parole. Participants were less likely to test positive for drug use while on parole, had similar parole revocation rates, and had a 60% lower likelihood of post-parole rearrest.

Research in this area reflects several trends for individuals with severe mental illness returning from prison to the community (Heilbrun et al., 2012). The available evidence does support better criminal justice outcomes (reductions in rates of rearrest or reincarceration) for participants in programs based upon either the Assertive Community Treatment (see, e.g., Lamberti, Deem, Weisman, & LaDuke, 2011) or Intensive Case Management (see, e.g., Steadman & Naples, 2005) models. Evidence on mental health outcomes is also generally favorable, although more mixed; some studies show consistently favorable mental health and community adjustment outcomes, while others suggest that certain health outcomes (e.g., hospital days) may actually be greater for those in specialized programs. The evidence in this area is generally promising, however, subject to the caveat that we clearly need more studies that are well-designed (including comparison/control groups and large samples) to support these conclusions with more confidence.

Reentry as applied to parole is growing in popularity. In fiscal year 2004–2005, for example, nearly 44,000 paroled offenders were required to attend a reentry program (National Offender Management Service, 2005). As yet, however, there is very limited information on the effectiveness of such programs. One study suggested that offenders who "fit" well with the reentry program (in terms of their risk and needs) were more likely to be recommended for placement (McGuire et al., 2008). This is good as far as it goes, but it would be even better if we had more information on the impact of the program on the services delivered, and whether the delivery of such services was related to rearrest.

Somewhat more research has been done on specialized parole services to individuals with mental disorders. A "firm but fair" approach to working with clients seems to distinguish more effective parole officers with this population (Eno Louden, Manchak, O'Connor, & Skeem, 2015; Skeem, Encandela, & Eno Louden, 2003; Skeem & Eno Louden, 2006). Both traditional and specialty parole/probation officers used graduated sanctions, but traditional officers generally responded to noncompliance with more punitive approaches (Eno Louden, Skeem, Camp, & Christensen, 2008). This relates to the differences between specialty agencies and traditional parole services; the former are more likely to focus on monitoring medication and treatment attendance and to use problem-solving strategies, and less likely to use threats of incarceration (Skeem, Emke-Francis, & Eno Louden, 2006). This appears particularly valuable with probationers who have co-occurring mental illness and substance abuse, as these individuals generally have poor relationships with professionals and are more likely to feel coerced into treatment (Skeem, Eno Louden, Manchak, Vidal, & Haddad, 2009).

Several studies have addressed the results of specific programs, although none has been designed with random assignment to the program versus "treatment as usual." Accordingly, we cannot be confident that these reentry programs actually work as intended. One study, focusing on those with a history of violent offending, indicated that participants were less likely to test positive for drugs, and also less likely to be arrested, than were those from a comparison group (Bouffard & Bergeron, 2006). Several other studies noted various problems with noncompliance, however, including difficulty contacting participants following release from prison (Schram & Morash, 2002); having only a small percentage of participants actually receive an aftercare plan, and even fewer actually seek postrelease services (Haas & Hamilton, 2007); and less participation in referred services compared with the comparison group (Bouffard & Bergeron, 2006).

If community reentry programs are to be effective, it is very important that they be committed to the "quality assurance" process described for effective juvenile programs—ensuring that intended services are actually delivered as planned. One consideration is whether such services are voluntary or required as part of parole. One would expect that required participation would increase the overall compliance rate. However, there is some evidence for a self-selection process in which reentry services are voluntary, with the more motivated individuals seeking out and receiving services—and benefiting more. In one California program, for example, services to parolees were provided on a voluntary basis and included employment, substance abuse recovery, math and literacy skills, and housing services. Participants in at least one of these areas had a recidivism rate of 33.6%, compared to a recidivism rate of 52.8% among those not participating in this program (Zhang et al., 2006). These findings raise some complicated questions about whether parolees should be required to avail themselves of reentry services.

Summary

1. **What are the important considerations in assessing juveniles prior to placement decisions?** The considerations that are most often considered by courts with juvenile placements are public safety and offenders' treatment needs and amenability to treatment. These factors, often cited in the law, overlap considerably with components of risk/need/responsivity, a well-supported approach to assessing and treating both juveniles and adults who have committed criminal offenses.

2. **What is the evidence for the effectiveness of interventions with juveniles in the community?** There is strong evidence for the effectiveness of three particular approaches to the community-based treatment of juveniles: Multisystemic Therapy, Oregon Treatment Foster Care, and Functional Family Therapy. These approaches are successful in both providing needed services for offenders, and reducing the risk of reoffending in those who receive them.

3. **What are some characteristics of an effective program?** Research has identified a number of common elements in programs that are effective. They tend to use different treatment modalities, carefully train those who deliver services, use a team approach, monitor service delivery to ensure that services are actually being provided as intended and individuals do not drop out or miss appointments, and deliver services in family and school settings.

4. **How can risk/need/responsivity help to provide effective rehabilitative services for adults?** Assessment of risk helps determine who should be treated at a particular intensity (frequency of service) and dosage (total amount of service received). Assessment of needs helps to target the particular interventions that may be provided to individuals. Assessing responsivity helps a program to decide on the most applicable kinds of interventions—those to which inmates are likely to respond best.

5. *How do specialized problem-solving courts compare to other correctional interventions?* These courts serve specific populations—individuals with particular problems (such as substance abuse or mental illness) or having a particular status (being a veteran, for example), for whom the provision of treatment services would both rehabilitate the individual and reduce the risk of reoffending. Service delivery and treatment participation are monitored by the court, giving participants a strong incentive to complete the planned course of treatment. These courts can either divert defendants from standard prosecution (unlike more conventional correctional dispositions) or function as a specialized form of community corrections similar to probation. In some jurisdictions, if a defendant does not satisfy the required conditions of the specialized problem-solving court, he or she may be returned to the traditional prosecution process.

6. *What are the differences between jails and prisons, and what role do psychologists play in these settings?* A jail is a community-based setting that houses both pretrial defendants and inmates who have been convicted of minor offenses and sentenced to terms of less than two years. A prison is part of a state- or federal-level correctional system, housing only inmates who have been convicted of more serious offenses. There are four particular functions served by pychologists who work in either a jail or a prison: classification, consultation/crisis intervention, rehabilitation, and reentry planning. The nature, scope, and distribution of these tasks vary according to whether the facility is a jail or a prison; they can also vary according to the size and resources of the facility.

7. *What kinds of interventions are delivered in jails and prisons?* Because of heterogeneity in jail populations, jails generally cannot provide rehabilitative services whose delivery requires individuals to remain in the facility for predictable periods of time. Accordingly, they focus on providing present-state services (e.g., medical, mental health, educational, substance abuse). Prisons, by contrast, can offer additional rehabilitative services that include more extensive educational and vocational training, skill building, and specialized interventions (e.g., for sexual offenders). Both kinds of facilities also offer religious services, which may have a protective influence for some individuals at risk of future offending.

8. *What are some of the psychological consequences of imprisonment?* Responses to imprisonment vary significantly as a function of the conditions of incarceration and inmates' psychological resilience and mental health. Many inmates experience adjustment problems early in their imprisonment; they may become hypervigilant, socially isolated, and emotionally suppressed. Exposure to prison violence and sexual offending can have a serious impact on psychological well-being. Individuals who are incarcerated for offenses such as assault and robbery (but not homicide or sexual offenses) may be more likely to behave violently toward others in a jail or prison.

9. *What are the priorities in preparing individuals for the transition from incarceration to community living (the reentry process)?* There are six areas in particular that are important in the reentry planning process. How is the family functioning, and will the individual live within it; if not, where will he or she be housed? Will the individual return to school, have a job, or be actively receiving any kind of job training? What mental health and/or substance abuse services are needed, and how will they be delivered? How will the individual be monitored for adherence to conditions specified in the plan? Will there be particular intensity to this monitoring, or specialized aspects (e.g., case management)? Finally, what kind of social support is available, and what peers will the individual be around?

Key Terms

adjudication of delinquency

classification

criminal conviction

criminogenic needs

diversion

Functional Family Therapy

intensive probation

Multisystemic Therapy

Oregon Treatment Foster Care

parole

prisonization

probation

reentry

risk, needs, and responsivity

school-based probation

therapeutic community

Glossary

A

absolute judgment An eyewitness's process of deciding, when looking at a sequential lineup, whether any of the people shown in the lineup match the description of the perpetrator.

abuse excuse A legal tactic by which a person charged with a crime claims that past victimization justifies his or her present alleged offense.

acute stress disorder The development of anxiety-related, dissociative, and other symptoms that occurs within one month after exposure to an extreme traumatic event and whose duration is between two days and four weeks.

adjudication of delinquency The legal determination that a juvenile is culpable of an offense. When responsible for offending, juveniles are adjudicated delinquent; adults are found guilty.

adjudicative competence The legal capacities necessary for a defendant to stand trial or otherwise resolve criminal charges (see "competence to stand trial" and "competence to plead guilty").

advance medical directives Legal documentation in which an individual indicates the kinds of future medical treatments she will accept should she be incapacitated (and therefore be unable to make treatment decisions) at the time the treatment is needed.

adversarial system A system of resolving disputes in which the parties, usually represented by counsel, argue and present evidence to a neutral fact finder, who makes a decision based on the evidence and arguments presented by the parties; as distinguished from an inquisitorial system, in which the fact finder takes an active part in determining what occurred.

aggravating factors Conditions or components that make a criminal act more serious.

***amicus curiae* brief** A "friend-of-the-court" brief filed by a person or organization not a party to the litigation, but with a strong view on the subject matter in the case.

anchoring A cognitive bias that describes the common human tendency of individuals to rely too heavily, or "anchor," on a suggested piece of information (e.g., a dollar value in the context of damage awards) when making decisions.

anchoring and adjustment bias This occurs when individuals are strongly influenced or "anchored" by an initial starting value and when, in subsequent decisions, they do not sufficiently adjust their judgments away from this starting point.

anomie A sense of alienation or meaninglessness.

antisocial personality disorder A pervasive pattern of disregard for, and violation of, the rights of others that begins in childhood or early adolescence and continues into adulthood.

applied scientist An individual whose research focuses on solving problems rather than acquiring knowledge for the sake of understanding (see basic scientist).

arbitration A form of dispute resolution in which a neutral third party makes a decision that is binding on the two disputants.

archival analysis In psychology and law, a method of data collection that involves examination of previously decided issues and cases.

arraignment A formal statement of charges and an initial plea by the defendant to these charges.

attribution theory A theory in social psychology focusing on people's explanations for the causes of their behavior and the behavior of others.

authoritarianism A set of beliefs and characteristics that includes submissiveness to authority, demands for obedience from subordinates, intolerance of minorities and other outgroups, and endorsement of the use of power and punishment to ensure conformity to conventional norms.

autobiographical memory Memory for one's own life experiences.

aversive racism A description of those who believe in racial equality and view themselves as nonprejudiced, but have unconscious, negative beliefs about people of other races. In situations that elicit these negative beliefs, such individuals try to avoid acting on them or express them in subtle ways.

B

back-end sentencing Sentencing that occurs when parolees are arrested for new crimes or violate the conditions of their parole and are returned to prison by state parole boards as a consequence (as contrasted with front-end sentencing).

basic scientist A scientist who pursues knowledge motivated by scientific curiosity or interest in a scientific question, studying a phenomenon to better understand it rather than to solve a problem.

battered woman syndrome A collection of symptoms described in women who have experienced prolonged and extensive abuse from their partners.

behavioral confirmation An influence in which people's expectations cause them to act in ways that confirm those expectations.

bench trial A trial in which the outcome (verdict) is decided by a judge rather than a jury.

best interests of the child The legal standard by which child custody decisions are made in the United States.

biological theory of crime An explanation for the causes of criminal behavior that uses heredity and constitutional characteristics of the lawbreaker.

bioterrorism A form of terrorism that uses biological "weapons," such as viruses and bacteria, to harm or threaten others.

black-letter law Basic principles of law generally accepted by courts and embodied in statutes.

black-sheep effect The tendency to be more punitive toward those members of one's group who violate the norms of the group.

blended sentencing A sentencing mechanism that allows judges, in sentencing juveniles tried as adults, to combine sanctions available in juvenile court with those used in criminal court.

borderline personality disorder A personality disorder characterized by impulsivity and instability in moods, behavior, self-image, and interpersonal relationships.

brain fingerprinting A procedure that involves the measurement of brain waves in response to a stimulus to assess whether the brain recognizes that stimulus.

Brawner **rule** This rule states that a defendant is not responsible for criminal conduct when, because of a mental disease or defect, he or she lacks substantial capacity either to appreciate the criminality (wrongfulness) of the conduct or to conform his or her conduct to the requirements of the law (also known as the American Law Institute, or ALI, rule).

breached duty The violation, through either negligence or intentional wrongdoing, of a duty that one party legally owes to another party.

burnout A process occurring in response to prolonged stress; manifestations may include detachment from work and personal relationships, exhaustion, cynicism, and reduced productivity.

C

case law The body of previous legal decisions and legal principles developed from these earlier decisions, as contrasted with statutory laws (passed by the legislative branch and approved by the executive branch). Case law develops through the courts over time, based upon precedent, and tends to change slowly because of the legal principle of *stare decisis*.

casuistry Fallacious reasoning in order to justify questionable behavior.

challenges for cause Occurring during jury selection, such challenges can be made by an attorney seeking to excuse a potential juror on grounds of bias. In addition, a judge may excuse a prospective juror for cause without a request to do so from either attorney. There is no limit on the number of challenges for cause that an attorney can make (by contrast, see "peremptory challenges").

change of venue Moving a trial to another locality, usually because extensive pretrial publicity has prevented the assembling of an unbiased jury.

charge bargaining A form of plea bargaining in which a prosecutor reduces the number or severity of charges against a criminal defendant in exchange for a guilty plea.

chemical castration The use of injections of a female hormone into male rapists as a method of reducing their sex drive.

civil commitment The legal process involving the involuntary hospitalization of persons who are mentally ill and dangerous to themselves or others.

civil competencies This term applies to civil (noncriminal) legal contexts in which the question of mental competence for a specific task (e.g., making a will) is raised.

classical conditioning A procedure in which one learns to associate a new response with a stimulus.

classical school of criminology The point of view, which evolved in the 1700s and 1800s, emphasizing the role of free will and cost-benefit analysis in determining criminal behavior.

classification The evaluation of convicted offenders by a correctional facility or parole office to assess the level of risk of criminal recidivism, institutional misconduct, and escape or noncompliance.

closing argument A summation of evidence, made by an attorney at the end of a trial.

cognitive interview A procedure used to assist victims in recalling aspects of a crime or other traumatic event.

cognitive load interviews Interviews that are designed to mentally tax a person through high cognitive demand. In such interviews it becomes difficult to simultaneously answer a question and maintain a lie.

cognizable groups Specific groups of persons, usually defined by demographic characteristics such as race or gender.

commonsense justice Ordinary citizens' basic notions of what is just and fair in contrast to the dictates of formal, statutory law.

community-based policing A policy that increases direct police/citizen contacts within a neighborhood.

compensatory damages The payment or restitution owed to a plaintiff for the damages and harm that have been determined to be caused by a civil defendant.

competence An individual's capacity to understand and behave in a way specified by the particular legal question. There are numerous forms of legal competency.

competence to plead guilty The ability of a defendant to understand the possible consequences of pleading guilty to criminal charges instead of going to trial, and to make a rational choice between the alternatives.

competence to stand trial Sufficient present ability to understand the legal proceedings in which one is involved and to consult with one's attorney with a reasonable degree of rational understanding.

compliant false confessions Confessions elicited when the suspect is induced to comply with the interrogator's demands to make an incriminating statement.

Concealed Information Test An approach to interrogating criminal suspects focusing on relevant concealed knowledge in the suspect's mind, not the truthfulness of his/her statements. Such information is particularly important when only a guilty individual would know it.

concordance rate The extent of similarity in a behavior or characteristic between twins.

confidence interval The amount of uncertainty associated with a population estimate (e.g., the mean plus or minus the margin of error).

confirmation bias A tendency to search for information that confirms one's preconceptions.

confrontation clause Language in the Sixth Amendment of the United States Constitution that guarantees defendants the right to confront their accusers.

containment theory The proposition that societal pressure controls the rate of crime.

Control Question Test A polygraph technique in which the subject is asked a question that elicits an emotional response.

control theory The proposition that people will act in an antisocial way unless they are prevented from doing so.

correctional psychology Application of psychological assessment and intervention to those individuals involved in the correctional system, including those on probation, parole, incarcerated, or involved in alternative community-based dispositions to offending.

counseling Verbal intervention by a trained professional focused on problem-solving, decision-making, and symptomatic improvement.

crime control model The model that emphasizes the reduction of crime rates and vindicating victims' rights by the efficient detection of suspects and the effective prosecution of defendants, to help ensure that criminal activity is being contained or reduced.

crime control theater Legal policies that appear to address crime, but that are reactionary and unsupported by empirical analysis.

criminal conviction The outcome of a criminal prosecution that concludes in a judgment that the adult defendant is guilty of the crime charged.

criminal profiling The use of psychological principles as a crime investigation technique to guide police toward suspects who possess certain personal characteristics as suggested by evidence from the crime scene.

criminalization hypothesis The idea that untreated symptoms of mental illness result in behavior that is criminal, or is treated as criminal.

criminogenic needs The deficits (such as substance abuse, family problems, educational problems, and pro-criminal attitudes) that increase the risk of reoffending.

criminology The study of crime and criminal behavior.

Crisis Intervention Team (CIT) A program designed by the Memphis Police Department (also known as the Memphis Model) to increase officer and public safety while attempting to redirect those with behavioral health problems from the judicial system to treatment-oriented alternatives. It involves training in more effective interactions with those experiencing behavioral health problems.

cycle of violence Behavior involving a pattern of periodic domestic violence, often exhibited by batterers, making their victims fearful of the battering they believe is inevitable.

D

damages Money awarded to a person injured by the unlawful act or negligence of another.

dangerousness A propensity to behavior that involves acts of physical violence or threats by one person against another. In some contexts, it is considered more broadly to include antisocial behavior of other kinds, including property damage, theft, and other illegal acts.

death qualification Questioning of prospective jurors during jury selection in death penalty cases regarding their attitudes toward capital punishment. Jurors endorsing extreme beliefs about the death penalty (such as an unwillingness to impose it under any circumstances) may be dismissed from consideration, leaving the remaining "death-qualified" pool of prospective jurors.

declarative knowledge In the context of jury behavior, jurors' understanding of legal concepts (as contrasted with procedural knowledge).

defensive attribution An explanation for behavior that enables people to deal with perceived inequities in others' lives and to avoid feelings of vulnerability.

deinstitutionalization The long-term trend of closing mental hospitals and transferring care to community-based mental health treatment facilities.

deliberative processes Thought processes that involve mental effort, concentration, motivation, and the application of learned rules.

determinate sentencing A sentence of confinement or probation for a fixed period of time specified by statute, as contrasted with an indeterminate sentence whose duration is determined by the offender's behavior.

diagnostic cues Cues that enable professionals to diagnose or distinguish among available alternatives (e.g., between psychopaths and nonpsychopaths, or between truth-tellers and liars).

diagnosticity A term used to denote the probability of identifying the suspect from a lineup depending on whether the suspect is the culprit or not.

differential association reinforcement theory A learning-theory approach that asserts that criminal behavior is the result of socialization into a system of values that is conducive to violations of the law.

diminished capacity A variation of the insanity defense that is applicable if the defendant (in the words of the law) lacks the ability to "meaningfully premeditate the crime."

discovery A procedure in which the attorney for one side seeks to become aware of the materials used by the other side to form its case.

discretion The ability to act according to one's own judgment and conscience. In judicial decisions, discretion refers to a judge's consideration of factors that may lead to appropriate *variations* in how the system responds to offenses, as opposed to a decision based on predefined legal guidelines or rules.

dispositional attributions Explanations for others' behavior that focus on ability, personality, or even temporary states (such as fatigue or luck) to help understand the behavior.

dispositional phase The sentencing phase of the case in which hearings typically combine adversarial procedures and attention to the particular needs of the defendant.

dissociation The act of "escaping" from a traumatic event by extreme detachment.

distributive justice Concerns about what is right or just with respect to the allocation of goods within a society.

diversion The practice of officially stopping or suspending a case prior to court adjudication (without a formal trial) and referring the defendant to a community education, treatment, or work program in lieu of adjudication or incarceration.

dizygotic twins (DZ) Commonly called fraternal twins, occurring when two eggs are fertilized.

double-blind testing procedures Experimental procedures in which both the participant and experimenter are unaware of the particular conditions being tested.

dual-process models Descriptions of two approaches to human information processing. Typically they propose both a rational, deliberate approach, and a quick, intuitive approach. The former requires motivation, effort, and ability; the latter does not.

due process model A perspective that emphasizes due process or procedural justice (fairness) under the law. In contrast to the crime control model, this model places stronger emphasis on defendants' rights.

duty The obligation that one party legally owes to another party.

E

ecological validity The extent to which the methods, materials, and setting of a research study resemble the real-life phenomena being investigated.

ecphoric experience The process of reviving a memory by relying on one's sense of recognition.

encoding The process of entering a perception into memory.

equality The principle that all who commit the same crime should receive the same consequences.

estimator variable The factors that are beyond the control of the justice system and whose impact on the reliability of the eyewitness can only be estimated (e.g., the lighting conditions at the time of the crime; whether the perpetrator was wearing a disguise).

euthanasia The act of killing an individual for reasons that are considered merciful.

evaluation apprehension Concern about the ways that others evaluate us.

evidence ploys Used in criminal interrogation, these are ruses that involve providing false information to suspects about their guilt, which can apparently cause them to doubt their memories and rely instead on external sources to infer what happened.

evidence-based sentencing The application of findings from risk reduction studies (including offenders' risks, needs, and responsivity) to sentencing practices.

evidence-driven deliberation A form of deliberation in which the jury thoroughly discusses the evidence before taking a vote.

evidentiary strength Refers to the nature of the evidence regarding guilt in a legal proceeding, and is probably the most important determinant of jurors' verdicts.

exculpatory Tending to clear a defendant of fault or guilt.

executive function The cognitive ability to plan and regulate behavior.

experiential inflammatory bias The notion that people who witness the use of virtual environments may be so swept up in the experience and persuaded by the lifelike nature of these scenes that they have difficulty imagining or visualizing a different point of view.

experimental methodology Experimental research studies that involve the manipulation of one or more factors (termed "independent variables"), observation of the effects of these factors on some behavior (termed "dependent variables"), and control of other relevant factors.

experimenter bias An experimenter's influence on the results of a research study.

expert witness A witness who has special knowledge beyond that of the ordinary lay person about a subject enabling him or her to give testimony regarding an issue that requires expertise to understand. Experts are permitted to give opinion testimony, while a nonexpert witness is typically limited to testimony about which he or she has direct knowledge through first-hand observation.

external validity A measure of whether the results of scientific research, conducted with a sample of the population, can be generalized to a larger group or that population.

extralegal factors Influences that are legally irrelevant in that they cannot serve as evidence in a legal proceeding (e.g., age, race, gender, and socioeconomic status).

extrinsic motivation The desire to pursue goals that would please and impress others.

extroversion The personality cluster characterized by outgoing orientation, enthusiasm, and optimism.

F

fabricated evidence False evidence presented by interrogators in order to elicit information from suspects.

false confession An admission of guilt to a crime for which the confessor is not culpable. False confessions occur for different reasons and they can be explained by different situational and dispositional factors.

false denial A guilty suspect's proclamation of innocence and denial of involvement in crimes for which he or she is actually responsible.

field studies Scientific research done in real-world settings, as contrasted with a more artificial environment. Field studies have more ecological validity (a greater resemblance to actual practice) but are more difficult to carefully control.

fitness-for-duty evaluation The psychological assessment of an employee conducted to determine whether that individual is mentally, emotionally, or behaviorally impaired, which might prevent the return to workplace duties. It is often used with those in dangerous occupations, such as police work, firefighters, and the military.

focal concerns perspective A viewpoint in criminology based on focal concerns theory.

focal concerns theory A theory that explains the criminal activities of lower-class adolescent gangs as an attempt to achieve the ends that are most valued in their culture through behaviors that appear best suited to obtain those ends.

forensic evaluator A professional role played by psychologists, psychiatrists, and social workers when providing forensic mental health assessments and expert testimony on a variety of topics related to legal questions involving mental and emotional disorder, intellectual functioning, substance abuse, and other clinical disorders, as well as capacities that are directly related to the legal question.

forensic mental health assessment Evaluations conducted by a variety of professionals including psychiatrists, psychologists, and social workers. The assessments address a wide range of questions in civil, criminal, and family law (e.g., competency to stand trial, child custody, civil commitment, capital sentencing).

forensic psychologists These psychologists apply scientific findings and knowledge to questions and issues related to the legal system. Their work may include conducting forensic mental health assessments for courts and attorneys, providing treatment to those under the supervision of the legal system, offering consultation to law enforcement agencies and personnel, and other related tasks.

framing effects The way decision alternatives are presented (or framed)—as either gains or losses—can have a significant impact on a person's choice. Individuals are more willing to take chances when the decision alternatives are presented in terms of gains than in terms of losses.

front-end sentencing Sentencing imposed following conviction for a crime committed when the offender was not under correctional jurisdiction (as contrasted with back-end sentencing).

Functional Family Therapy A community-based intervention for juvenile offenders. It is provided weekly by a single therapist, over an average period of three months. It is family-focused, and is often delivered in the home.

functional magnetic resonance imaging A type of specialized neuroimaging that registers blood flow related to neural activity in the brain or spinal cord.

fundamental attribution error The belief that behavior is caused by stable factors internal to a person rather than by situational factors external to a person.

G

generic prejudice Prejudice arising from media coverage of issues not specifically related to a particular case but thematically relevant to the issues at hand.

grand jury A group of citizens who hear evidence in closed proceedings and decide whether to issue an indictment.

ground truth A clear and accurate measure of the outcome of interest in a study.

H

harm The losses or adversities suffered by a person who is the victim of wrongdoing.

heuristics A mental shortcut, "rule of thumb," or educated guess used to help solve a problem. These methods typically utilize experimentation and trial-and-error techniques.

hostile workplace harassment A form of workplace harassment that does not involve a specific response (see "*quid pro quo* harassment"), but instead involves gender harassment and unwanted sexual attention, resulting in an intimidating, hostile, or offensive working environment.

I

illusory causation The inaccurate perception that two variables are causally related.

impeachment During a trial, the cross-examination of a witness for the purpose of calling into question his or her credibility or reliability.

implicit bias Unconscious beliefs that influence how people interpret and judge thoughts and actions.

implicit personality theory A person's preconceptions about how certain attributes are related to one another and to behavior.

inadmissible evidence Evidence in a legal proceeding that the court holds cannot be admitted, and therefore cannot be considered by the fact finder.

indeterminate sentencing Sentencing scheme in which the judge imposes an indefinite period of incarceration for a given offense (e.g., 6–20 years) and the actual length of stay depends on the individual's behavior while incarcerated. Such behavior affects whether the individual will be released on parole or will serve the maximum sentence.

indictment An accusation issued by a grand jury charging the defendant with criminal conduct.

informational social influence A process in which people accept evidence provided by others and modify their opinions accordingly.

in-group bias The tendency to favor one's own group.

in-group/out-group differences An in-group shares a common identity and sense of belonging, while an out-group lacks these things.

initial appearance The constitutional right to be brought before a judge within 48 hours of arrest. The primary purpose is for the judge to review the evidence summarized by the prosecutor and determine whether there is sufficient reason to believe that the suspect may have committed the alleged offenses.

inquisitorial system The legal system in which the judge plays a very active role in determining the accuracy of evidence before the court (as contrasted with the adversarial approach, in which the judge is a more passive evaluator of evidence presented in a trial).

insanity The principal legal doctrine permitting consideration of mental abnormality in assessing criminal liability. Those acquitted of criminal charges because they are found not guilty by reason of insanity are typically required to spend an indeterminate period of treatment in a secure mental health facility until they are no longer dangerous to self or others.

intensive probation Probation involving frequent monitoring and contact.

intention The offender's frame of mind in committing a criminal act.

intentional behavior Purposeful conduct in which a person meant the outcome of a given act to occur.

internalized false confessions An inaccurate confession that is genuinely believed. Internalized false confessions can result when, after hours of being questioned, badgered, and told stories about what "must have happened," the suspect begins to develop a profound distrust of his or her own memory.

intrinsic motivation The pursuit of goals that involve internal or personal desires rather than external incentives.

intuitive processes Incidents of spontaneous mental processing that are often acted on but not given careful thought or effort.

J

jail diversion programs Programs attempting to divert certain groups of criminal offenders from jail incarceration into a rehabilitative, community-based alternative.

joint custody A legal outcome in which divorcing parents share or divide various decision-making and control responsibilities for their children.

judicial waiver A judge's decision to transfer a juvenile offender from juvenile court to criminal (adult) court.

juror bias The tendency of any juror to use irrelevant, inadmissible, or extralegal evidence or considerations in the course of legal decision-making.

jury sentiments Beliefs, opinions, and views of jurors that are unrelated to the evidence and the law in a trial.

L

learned helplessness A condition in which people come to believe that they have no personal influence over what happens to them; consequently, they passively endure aversive treatment rather than to try to control it.

learning theory A form of criminological theory that emphasizes how specific criminal behaviors are learned directly from reinforcement and modeling influences.

legal factors Variables related to the offense or the offender's legal history.

legal formalism The model holding (in contrast to legal realism) that legal decision makers dispassionately consider the relevant laws, precedents, and constitutional principles, and that personal bias has no part in decision-making.

legal realism The model holding (in contrast to legal formalism) that judges view the facts of cases in light of their attitudes and values, and make decisions accordingly.

liable Responsible or answerable for some action.

liberation hypothesis The hypothesis that when the strength of the evidence against a defendant is weak, jurors are free to rely on nonlegal information to inform their decisions.

lie bias The assumption that most statements, even truthful statements, are lies and deceptions.

limiting instruction An instruction to the jury placing explicit limitations on how certain evidence can be considered. For example, a judge may limit the consideration of a defendant's prior record to gauging the defendant's credibility only.

M

M'Naghten rule One test for the insanity defense. Under this rule, defendants may be deemed insane by the court if, because of a "disease of the mind," they (1) did not know what they were doing or (2) did not know that what they were doing was wrong.

malingering The deliberate fabrication or exaggeration of physical or psychological symptoms in order to gain an advantage.

mandatory minimum sentences Sentencing schemes in which judges sentence offenders to a minimum number of years in prison following conviction for a given offense regardless of any extenuating circumstances or mitigating behavior while in prison.

mass murderer A person who kills four or more victims in one location during a period of time that lasts anywhere from a few minutes to several hours.

matching heuristic A process in which decision makers search through a subset of available case information and then make a decision based on only a small number of factors (e.g., offense severity and prior record), often ignoring other seemingly relevant information.

mediation A form of alternative dispute resolution in which a neutral third party helps the disputing parties agree on a resolution to their conflict.

mens rea A guilty mind. One of two elements that must be proven by the prosecution (the other being "a guilty act") in order to obtain a criminal conviction.

meta-analysis A statistical technique that combines the results of individual studies using similar variables and addressing similar questions.

Miranda Miranda rights apply to individuals in police custody in the United States. They include, among other things, the right to avoid self-incrimination (Fifth Amendment) and to have a lawyer present and be represented by counsel (Sixth Amendment) that

mitigating factors Factors such as age, mental capacity, motivation, or duress that lessen the degree of guilt in a criminal offense and thus the nature of the punishment.

monozygotic twins (MZ) Commonly called identical twins, multiple births that occur when a single egg is fertilized to form one zygote, which then divides into two embryos.

motion *in limine* A legal request for a judge to make a pretrial ruling on some matter of law expected to arise at the trial.

motivated reasoning A phenomenon in which one's reasoning is directed by the desire to reach a certain conclusion. This may involve seeking out information that confirms a preexisting belief.

Multisystemic Therapy An empirically supported intervention for juvenile offenders implemented in multiple domains (e.g., family, school, structured activity) to reduce serious antisocial behavior and strengthen dysfunctional families.

N

Need for Cognition The inclination to engage in and enjoy effortful cognitive work.

negative incentives In the context of interrogations, tactics (such as accusations, attacks on the suspect's denials, and evidence fabrications) that interrogators use to convey that the suspect has no choice but to confess.

negligence Behavior that falls below a legal standard for protecting others from unreasonable risks; it is often measured by asking whether a "reasonable person" would have acted as the civil defendant acted in similar circumstances.

negotiation The process of conferring with another to attempt to settle a legal matter.

neuroticism A major dimension of personality involving the tendency to experience negative emotions such as anxiety, anger, and depression, often accompanied by distressed thinking and behavior.

normative social influence A process in which people conform to others' expectations, often to gain acceptance.

O

open-ended questions This type of question does not specify or restrict the answers to be given; rather, respondents are prompted to suggest their own ideas for answers.

opening statement Not part of the evidence, these comments made by the lawyers on each side give an overview of the evidence that will be presented.

operant learning A form of learning in which the consequences of a behavior influence the likelihood of its being performed in the future.

Oregon Treatment Foster Care   An empirically supported juvenile intervention that involves placing juveniles with specially trained foster parents rather than in residential placement.

other-race effect   The tendency for people to less accurately recognize faces of other races than faces of their own race.

outcome severity   The severity of an accident or injury.

overconfidence bias   The tendency to hold an unrealistically optimistic view of the likelihood of a favorable outcome in litigation. It applies to defendants who believe (incorrectly) that they have a good chance to win at trial, sometimes leading to rejection of reasonable plea offers from prosecutors.

P

parole   The conditional release from prison of a person convicted of a crime prior to the expiration of that person's term of imprisonment, subject to both the supervision of the correctional authorities during the remainder of the term and a resumption of the imprisonment upon violation of the conditions imposed.

pedophile   A person who derives gratification from sexual contact with children.

peremptory challenges   Opportunities available to each attorney during jury selection to exclude potential jurors without having to give any reason. Their number, determined by the judge, varies from one jurisdiction to another.

perjury   Lying while under oath.

photographic lineup   A display of photographs of potential suspects that police often ask an eyewitness to examine to identify a suspect (also called a photospread).

photospread   A display of photographs of potential suspects that police often ask an eyewitness to examine to identify a suspect (also called a photographic lineup).

physiognomic variability   Perceived differences based on physical features.

plea bargains   In exchange for the defendant's promise to forgo a trial, the government may promise to charge the defendant with a lesser crime or ask the judge for a reduced sentence. When the "bargain" is reached, the defendant pleads guilty and no trial is held.

policy capturing   Research to determine (capture) policy preferences and inclinations (e.g., the punishment motives of ordinary people).

policy evaluator   A role in which psychologists who have methodological skills in assessing policy provide data regarding the impact of such policy (e.g., degree of change, degree of effectiveness, design recommendations, observed outcomes).

polygraph (sometimes called "lie detector")   An instrument for recording variations in several physiological functions that may indicate whether a person is telling the truth.

positive inducements   Tactics used by interrogators to motivate suspects to see that an admission of guilt is in their best interest. It involves conveying that the suspect will receive some benefit in exchange for his confession.

positivist school of criminology   A point of view that emphasized that criminal behavior by a person was determined, rather than a product of free will.

postdiction variable   In the context of eyewitness memory, a variable (such as the speed of an identification) that does not directly affect the reliability of identification, but instead is a measure of some process that correlates with reliability.

post-event information   Details about an event to which an eyewitness is exposed after the event has occurred.

posttraumatic stress disorder (PTSD)   An anxiety disorder in which the victim experiences a pattern of intense fear reactions after being exposed to a highly stressful event.

precedent   A ruling (or opinion) announced in a previous case that provides a framework in which to decide a current case. The expectation that a court should abide by precedent is called *stare decisis*.

predecisional distortion   A phenomenon by which jurors' initial inclinations influence the way they interpret evidence presented during a trial.

predictive validity   One form of psychometric validity, involving the accuracy with which a measure can predict something it should theoretically be able to predict.

preliminary hearing   The step between arrest and trial. At a preliminary hearing, the prosecution must offer some evidence on every element of the crime charged and the judge must decide whether the evidence is sufficient to pursue the case further.

preponderance of evidence   The standard of proof required in civil litigation, in which the evidence for one side must outweigh that on the other side by even a slight margin.

presence   When used in reference to virtual reality, the degree to which a user or observer has the impression of actually "being in another world" due to the presentation in the virtual environment.

preventive detention   The detention of accused persons who pose a risk of flight or dangerousness.

primacy effect   The influence of information that is presented first, or early in a series.

primary deviance   Behavior that violates a law or norm for socially acceptable conduct.

principle of proportionality   The principle that the punishment should be consistently related to the magnitude of the offense.

prisonization   The gradual process in which prisoners adjust to their environment (i.e., assimilate to the customs and culture of the penitentiary).

probabilistic estimates   Predictions about outcomes, made far in advance of the known outcome. Attorneys make probabilistic estimates in deciding whether to accept a case.

probation   The conditional freedom from incarceration following criminal conviction. It involves a specified set of conditions for which compliance is monitored by the probation officer assigned to the case. Probation conditions may include drug use monitoring, substance abuse treatment, mental health treatment, and skills-based training in particular areas (e.g., anger management, decision-making).

probative value   Tending to prove or actually proving.

problem-solving court   A specialized kind of court focusing on the underlying behaviors of criminal defendants and seeking to rehabilitate them, thereby addressing the particular problems causing the offending. Examples include drug courts, mental health courts, domestic violence courts, homeless courts, and veterans' courts.

procedural justice The consideration of the fairness of the methods for resolving a dispute and allocating resources.

procedural knowledge Jurors' awareness of the correct process for reaching a decision (as contrasted with declarative knowledge).

propensity evidence Evidence of a defendant's past wrongdoings that suggest the defendant had the propensity, or inclination, to commit a crime.

proportionality Proportionality in sentencing means that the nature and duration of the sentence should correspond to the seriousness of the offense.

prosecutorial discretion The authority of prosecutors to make decisions about certain aspects of criminal proceedings. In the context of juvenile offenders, it involves deciding whether cases involving serious charges are filed initially in juvenile or adult court.

proximate cause An obvious or substantially supported link between behavior and subsequent harm; a necessary element to establish in personal injury litigation.

psycholinguistics The psychological study of how people use and understand language.

psychological autopsy An attempt to determine the mode of death (whether an accident, suicide, homicide, or natural causes) by an examination of what was known about the behavior of the deceased.

psychological theories (of crime) Scientific principles that are formulated and applied to the analysis and understanding of cognitive and behavioral phenomena. For example, psychological theories of crime emphasize individual differences in behavior and the approaches to thinking, feeling, and decision-making that make some people predisposed to committing criminal acts.

psychopathy A personality disorder characterized by a long-term pattern of antisocial behavior and personal characteristics such as shallow emotion, limited capacities for guilt and empathy, and failure to learn from experience.

psychoticism A major element in the theory of personality, characterized by insensitivity, troublemaking, and lack of empathy.

punitive damages Financial compensation awarded to a prevailing party in civil litigation as a form of punishment for a specific act or omission.

Q

quid pro quo **harassment** An implicit or explicit bargain in which the harasser promises a reward or threatens punishment in exchange for a specific response (often sexual in nature) from a workplace supervisee.

R

racial bias When police officers, prosecutors, jurors, and judges use an individual's race as the primary determinant for discretionary decisions or judgments of his or her behavior.

racial profiling The police practice of using race as a factor in determining actions such as traffic stops, arrests, and questioning of suspects.

randomized controlled trials (RCT) A research methodology in which participants are randomly assigned either to control or treatment conditions and outcomes are compared.

rape trauma syndrome A collection of behaviors or symptoms that are frequent aftereffects of having been raped.

reactance theory A theory proposing that if something is denied or withheld from a person, the person's desire for it will increase.

rebuttal evidence Evidence presented to counter or disprove facts previously introduced by the adverse party.

recency effect The influence on memory and decision-making of information that is presented last or later in a series.

recidivism In the context of criminal behavior, the commission of a new crime resulting in re-arrest, reconviction, or reincarceration.

recross To cross-examine a witness a second time, after redirect examination.

redirect questioning Questioning by the original attorney that follows the opposing counsel's cross-examination.

reentry The process of returning from incarceration to the community.

relative judgment An eyewitness's process of deciding, when looking at a simultaneous lineup, which of the people shown in the lineup most closely resembles the perpetrator.

reminiscence effect When recalling previous experience, people often report (reminisce) new information on each recall attempt, suggesting that recollection is often incomplete on the first telling and that it is normal to produce unrecalled information in later interviews.

repression The process by which unpleasant thoughts or memories are moved outside of conscious awareness.

reservation price In negotiations, a negotiator's bottom line. Defendants in settlement negotiations typically have maximum amounts they are willing to pay and plaintiffs have minimum amounts they are willing to accept.

restorative justice An approach seeking to restore what has been lost through criminal offending. It includes programs designed to reconcile offenders with their victims, helping the offender appreciate the victim's pain and the victim to understand why the offender committed the crime.

retention interval The period of time in which a memory is retained. In eyewitnesses, the retention interval occurs between viewing an event and being questioned about it.

retributive approach The notion that punishment should be exacted on a person who has taken something from another.

retrieval The process by which a memory is returned to consciousness.

reverse waiver Judge's decision to transfer a juvenile offender from criminal (adult) court, where that individual was initially placed, back to juvenile court.

risk assessment The assessment of the probability that a person will behave violently, often accompanied by suggestions for how to reduce the likelihood of violent conduct.

risk averse Seeking to minimize risk.

risk, needs, and responsivity (RNR) A theory that describes three separate considerations (risk, need, and responsivity) involving interventions for criminal offenders. Risk means that the likelihood of committing future offenses should be evaluated; those at highest risk should receive the most intensive interventions. Needs are the deficits (such as substance abuse, family problems, educational problems, and procriminal attitudes) that increase the risk of reoffending. Responsivity involves the likelihood of a favorable response to the interventions, and the influences that may affect such responding.

S

schema An individual's cognitive framework or set of preconceptions that helps that person attend to, organize, and interpret relevant information.

school-based probation A variation on the standard conditions of probation in which the youth's attendance, performance, and behavior in school are monitored through the probation officer's personal visits to the school.

secondary deviance Creating or increasing the deviant identity of a person using official labels or formal legal sanctions.

secondary victimization A process in which post-event negative experiences with legal and medical authorities increase a victim's symptoms.

selection effects A bias that occurs when random assignment is not achieved in a research study and results can be attributed to the selection of respondents.

selective attention People have limited attentional capacity and cannot process all of the stimuli available at a given time, so they unconsciously select the information to which they will attend. The threatening aspect of a weapon is one example of something that would draw attention (see weapon focus effect).

self-defense A legal defense relied upon by criminal defendants typically charged with homicide; it asserts that the defendant's actions were justified by a reasonable belief that he or she was in imminent danger of death or bodily harm from an attacker.

self-determination theory of optimal motivation Theory describing situational and personality factors that cause positive and negative motivation and, eventually, changes in subjective well-being.

self-serving bias The tendency to interpret information or make decisions in ways that are consistent with one's own interests, rather than in an objective fashion.

sentence bargaining A form of plea bargaining in which a prosecutor recommends a reduced sentence in exchange for a guilty plea.

sentencing disparity The differences in the decisions of different judges in sentencing for the same crime.

Sequential Intercept Model The model assesses diversion needs for individuals with serious mental illness. It describes a number of points at which an intervention can be made to prevent further progress along the conventional criminal track. These points are (a) law enforcement and emergency services; (b) initial detention and initial hearings; (c) jail, courts, forensic evaluations, and forensic commitments; (d) reentry from jails, state prisons, and forensic hospitalization; and (e) community corrections and community support.

sequential presentation A lineup presentation in which the choices are shown one at a time.

serial killer A person who kills four or more victims on separate occasions, usually in different locations.

settlement negotiation Process used to resolve (settle) civil disputes without a trial, typically in private negotiations between attorneys representing the disputing parties.

shaming penalty A criminal sanction designed to embarrass an offender by publicizing the offense; shaming penalties are thought to express the community's moral outrage and to deter others from committing this type of crime.

similarity–leniency hypothesis The hypothesis that fact finders treat those similar to themselves more leniently than they treat those they perceive as different from themselves.

simultaneous presentation A lineup presentation in which all choices are shown at the same time.

social cognitive theory The theory that focuses on the role of cognitive processes in social interactions.

social desirability effect People's wishes to present themselves in a socially appropriate and favorable way and the influence of such wishes on their behavior.

social judgments Judgments incorporating information about social categories, such as race and gender.

social labeling theory The theory that the stigma of being branded deviant by society can influence an individual's belief about himself or herself.

social-psychological theory (of crime) A group of theories that propose that crime is learned in a social context; they differ about what is learned and how it is learned.

sociological theories (of crime) A group of theories that maintain that crime results from social or cultural contexts (e.g., family, school/workplace, peer groups, community, and society). The various theories emphasize different social features and differ on the social causes of crime.

sole custody Awarding custody of a child to one parent only (as contrasted with joint custody, in which both parents have custodial involvement).

sophistication-maturity A legal construct often applied to youthful offenders in transfer and reverse transfer proceedings. It encompasses the domains of criminal sophistication and developmental maturity.

source confusion Confusion about the origin of a memory.

source monitoring The ability to accurately identify the source of one's memory.

specialized police responding Police conduct after receiving specialized training in recognizing behavioral health symptoms and interacting with individuals who display such symptoms in a way that deescalates conflict, making treatment alternative more likely and standard criminal prosecution less likely.

specific pretrial publicity Media coverage concerning the details of one specific case prior to trial.

spree killer A person who kills victims at two or more different locations with almost no time between the murders.

stare decisis The legal principle emphasizing the importance of decision-making that is consistent with precedent; literally, "let the decision stand."

statutory exclusion A statute stipulating that certain serious offenses allegedly committed by an adolescent must be filed directly in adult court.

stimulation-seeking theory Theory suggesting that the thrill-seeking and disruptive behaviors of a psychopath serve to increase sensory input and raise arousal to a more tolerable level. As a result, the psychopathic person seems "immune" to many social cues that govern behavior.

stipulate To agree about a fact in a legal proceeding without further argument or examination.

Stockholm syndrome Feelings of dependency and emotional closeness that hostages sometimes develop toward their kidnappers in prolonged hostage situations.

storage That phase of the memory process referring to the retention of information.

story model The notion that people construct a story or narrative summary of the events in a dispute.

structural explanations A key concept of structural approaches is that certain groups of people suffer fundamental inequalities in opportunities that impair their ability to achieve the goals valued by society.

structured interviews Interviews in which the wording, order, and content of the questions are standardized in order to improve the reliability of the information obtained by an interviewer.

subcultural explanations The subcultural version of sociological theory maintains that a conflict of norms held by different groups causes criminal behavior. This conflict arises when various groups endorse subcultural norms, pressuring their members to deviate from the norms underlying the criminal law.

suggestive questions Questions asked in a way that provides cues regarding possible answers.

suicide by cop A crisis situation in which a citizen precipitates his or her own death by behaving in such a fashion that a police officer is forced to use lethal force.

summary jury trial An abbreviated, expedited form of a jury trial that is intended to be helpful in resolving simple, lower-value cases.

sympathy hypothesis The assumption that jurors' decisions will be influenced by feelings of sympathy.

system variable In eyewitness identifications, a variable whose impact on an identification can be controlled by criminal justice system officials. Examples include the way a lineup is presented and the way a witness is questioned.

T

team policing A policy of less centralized decision-making within police organizations.

terrorism The use of threats of violence to achieve certain organizational goals.

testamentary capacity Having the mental capacity to execute a will, including the capacity to resist the pressures or domination of any person who might use undue influence on the distribution of the estate of the person writing the will.

therapeutic community A community-based approach in which all staff and participants are considered to be part of the treatment process. It has generally been used for drug offenders and domestic violence offenders. This approach may include group therapy, individual counseling, and drug testing with the objective of building skills in controlling anger, improving decision-making, and recognizing high-risk situations.

therapeutic jurisprudence An approach to the law emphasizing the favorable mental health impact or otherwise "therapeutic" impact of the legal system upon its participants.

thought suppression The attempt to avoid thinking about something specific.

threat assessment A process that involves carefully considering the nature of the threat, the risk posed by the individual making it, and the indicated response to reduce the risk of harmful action.

tort A private or civil wrong or injury other than breach of contract, subject to civil litigation.

transferred The status of a juvenile charged with committing a serious offense when moved from juvenile court to criminal court.

treatment needs and amenability Rehabilitative needs and the likelihood of favorable response to interventions designed to reduce the risk of future criminal offending. It is an important consideration in decisions involving the transfer of juveniles.

trial consulting The use of professionals trained in the social sciences to assist attorneys in preparing and presenting evidence in a trial.

truth bias The assumption that most statements are honest and truthful. In the context of interrogations, people are better at detecting truthful denials than accurately judging deceptive elaborations.

U

ultimate opinion testimony Testimony that offers a conclusion about the specific defendant or a specific witness, in contrast to testimony about a general phenomenon.

unconscious transference Generation of a memory that is based on the recall of past interactions with a suspect, so that an innocent person may be confused with an offender.

V

validity scales Measures of an individual's approach to a psychological test, typically including the underreporting or overreporting of symptoms, problems, and unusual experiences.

venire A panel of prospective jurors drawn from a large list.

verdict-driven deliberation A form of deliberation in which the jury takes an immediate vote and discussion focuses on reaching agreement on a verdict.

vicarious learning Learning by observing the actions of another person and their outcomes.

victimology The study of the process and consequences of victim's experiences, including recovery.

vividness effect Information has a greater impact on judgments and decisions when it is vivid and attention-grabbing than when it is pallid and bland. Information presented in a highly imaginable way is more persuasive than simple verbal descriptions of the same material.

voir dire The process by which the judge and/or attorneys ask potential jurors questions and attempt to uncover any biases.

voluntary false confessions False confessions that arise because people seek notoriety, desire to cleanse themselves of guilt feelings from previous wrongdoings, want to protect the real criminal, or have difficulty distinguishing fact from fiction.

W

weapon focus effect When confronted by an armed attacker, the victim's tendency to focus attention on the weapon and fail to notice other stimuli.

Z

zero-tolerance An approach to law enforcement in which the police attempt to arrest all lawbreakers, even those who have committed petty or nuisance crimes.

References

Abram, K., Teplin, L. A., Charles, D., Longworth, S., McClelland, G., & Dulcan, M. (2004). Posttraumatic stress disorder and trauma in youth in juvenile detention. *Archives of General Psychiatry, 61*, 403–410. doi:10.1001/archpsych.61.4.403

Abram, K. M., Teplin, L. A., Charles, D. R., Longworth, S. L., McClelland, G. M., & Dulcan, M. K. (2004). Posttraumatic stress disorder and trauma in youth in juvenile detention. *Archives of General Psychiatry, 61*, 403–410.

Abram, K. M., Washburn, J. J., Teplin, L. A., Emanuel, K. M., Romero, E. G., & McClelland, G. M. (2007). Posttraumatic stress disorder and psychiatric comorbidity among detained youths. *Psychiatric Services, 58*, 1311–1316.

Abramson, J. (1994). *We, the jury.* New York, NY: Basic Books.

Acharya, A. P., & Acharya, A. (2017). Cyberterrorism and biotechnology: When ISIS meets CRiSPR. *Snapshot.* Retrieved July 14, 2017, from https://www.foreignaffairs.com/articles/world/2017-06-01/cyberterrorism-and-biotechnology

Ackerman, M. J., & Ackerman, M. C. (1997). Child custody evaluation practices: A survey of experienced professionals (revisited). *Professional Psychology: Research and Practice, 28*, 137–145.

Adams, R. E., Rohe, W. M., & Arcury, T. A. (2005). Awareness of community-oriented policing and neighborhood perceptions in five small to midsize cities. *Journal of Criminal Justice, 33*, 43–54.

Ainsworth, P. (2001). *Offender profiling and crime analysis.* Portland, OR: Willan.

Ake v. Oklahoma, 105 S.Ct. 977 (1985).

Akers, R. L., Krohn, M. D., Lanz-Kaduce, L., & Radosevich, M. (1996). Social learning and deviant behavior: A specific test of a general theory. In D. G. Rojek & G. F. Jensen (Eds.), *Exploring delinquency: Causes and control* (pp. 109–119). Los Angeles, CA: Roxbury.

Alegria, M., Jackson, J., Kessler, R., & Takeuchi, D. (2015). *Collaborative Psychiatric Epidemiology Surveys (CPES), 2001–2003 [United States].* Ann Arbor, MI: Inter-university Consortium for Political and Social Research. doi:10.3886/ICPSR20240.v8

Alexander, J., Barton, C., Gordon, D., Grotpeter, J., Hansson, K., Harrison, R., … Sexton, T. (1998). *Blueprints for violence prevention: Book three. Functional family therapy.* Boulder, CO: Center for the Study and Prevention of Violence.

Alexander, J., & Parsons, B. (1973). Short-term behavioral intervention with delinquent families: Impact on family process and recidivism. *Journal of Abnormal Psychology, 81*, 219–225.

Alexander, K., Quas, J., Goodman, G., Ghetti, S., Edelstein, R., Redlich, A., … Jones, D. (2005). Traumatic impact predicts long-term memory for documented child sexual abuse. *Psychological Science, 16*, 33–40.

Alexander, M. (2012). *The new Jim Crow: Mass incarceration in the age of colorblindness.* New York, NY: New Press.

Alhabib, S., Nur, U., & Jones, R. (2010). Domestic violence against women: Systematic review of prevalence studies. *Journal of Family Violence, 25*, 369–382.

Allison, J. A., & Wrightsman, L. S. (1993). *Rape: The misunderstood crime.* Thousand Oaks, CA: Sage.

Altschuler, D. (1998). Intermediate sanctions and community treatment for serious and violent juvenile offenders. In R. Loeber & D. Farrington (Eds.), *Serious and violent juvenile offenders: Risk factors and successful interventions* (pp. 367–388). Thousand Oaks, CA: Sage.

Altschuler, D., & Armstrong, T. (1997). Aftercare not afterthought: Testing the IAP model. *Juvenile Justice, 3*, 115–122.

Amato, P. (2001). Children of divorce in the 1990s: An update of the Amato and Keith (1991) meta-analysis. *Journal of Family Psychology, 15*, 335–370.

Amato, P., & Booth, A. (2001). The legacy of parents' marital discord: Consequences for children's marital quality. *Journal of Personality and Social Psychology, 81*(4), 627–638.

Amato, P., & Gilbreth, J. (1999). Nonresident fathers and children's well-being: A meta-analysis. *Journal of Marriage and the Family, 61*, 557–573.

Amato, P., & Keith, B. (1991). Parental divorce and the well-being of children: A meta-analysis. *Psychological Bulletin, 110*, 26–46.

Amato, P., Loomis, L., & Booth, A. (1995). Parental divorce, marital conflict, and offspring well-being during early adulthood. *Social Forces, 73*, 895–915.

American Academy of Child and Adolescent Psychiatry (AACAP). (1997). *Practice parameters for child custody evaluation.* Retrieved from http://www.aacap.org/galleries/PracticeParameters/Custody.pdf

American Academy of Pediatrics. (2009). Council on Communications and Media Policy Statement—Media Violence. *Pediatrics, 124*, 1495–1498.

American Bar Association. (1993). *ABA formal opinion 93–379.* Chicago, IL: Author.

American Bar Association. (2015). Lawyer demographics. *Year 2015.* Retrieved from www.americanbar.org/groups/legal_education/resources/statistics.html

American Medical Association. (2007). *Guides to the evaluation of permanent impairment* (6th ed.). Chicago, IL: Author.

American Psychiatric Association. (2000). *Diagnostic and statistical manual* (4th ed., Text Revision). Washington, DC: Author.

American Psychiatric Association. (2013). *Diagnostic and statistical manual of mental disorders* (5th ed.). Arlington, VA: Author.

American Psychological Association. (2009). *Guidelines for child custody evaluations in family law proceedings.* Washington, DC: Author. Retrieved February 15, 2010, from http://www.apa.org/practice/guidelines/child-custody.pdf

American Psychological Association. (2010). Guidelines for child custody evaluations in family law proceedings. *American Psychologist, 65*, 863–867.

American Psychological Association. (2011). *Brief for the American Psychological Association, American Psychiatric Association, and National Association of Social Works as amici curiae in support of petitioners, Miller v. Alabama and Jackson v. Hobbs.* Retrieved July 13, 2012, from http://www.apa.org/about/offices/ogc/amicus/miller-hobbs.pdf

American Psychological Association. (2012). *Miller v. Alabama and Jackson v. Hobbs.* Retrieved from http://www.apa.org/about/offices/ogc/amicus/miller-hobbs.aspx

American Psychological Association. (2013). Specialty guidelines for forensic psychology. *American Psychologist, 68*, 7–19.

American Psychological Association. (2017). *Ethical principles of psychologists and code of conduct.* Retrieved from http://www.apa.org/ethics/code/

American Psychological Association Task Force on Violent Media. (2015). *Technical report on the review of the violent video game literature.* Retrieved October 24, 2016, from www.apa.org/pi/families/review-video-games.pdf

American Society of Trial Consultants. (2017). *The ASTC professional code.* Retrieved from http://www.astcweb.org/astc-bylaws

The Andrea Yates case: Chronology of the Yates case. (2005, January 7). *Houston Chronicle,* p. A10.

Anderson, K. B., Cooper, H., & Okamura, L. (1997). Individual differences and attitudes toward rape: A meta-analytic review. *Personality and Social Psychology Bulletin, 23,* 295–315.

Anderson, M., & MacCoun, R. (1999). Goal conflict in juror assessments of compensatory and punitive damages. *Law and Human Behavior, 23,* 313–330.

Andrews, D. A., & Bonta, J. (1995). *LSI-R: The Level of Service Inventory-Revised.* Toronto, ON: Multi-Health Systems.

Andrews, D. A., & Bonta, J. (2006). *The psychology of criminal conduct* (4th ed.). Newark, NJ: Lexis Nexis/Mathew Bender.

Andrews, D. A., & Bonta, J. (2010). Rehabilitating criminal justice policy and practice. *Psychology, Public Policy, and Law, 16,* 39–55.

Andrews, D. A., & Hoge, R. (2010). *Evaluation for risk of violence in juveniles.* New York, NY: Oxford University Press.

Andrews, D. A., Bonta, J., & Hoge, R. D. (1990). Classification for effective rehabilitation: Rediscovering psychology. *Criminal Justice and Behavior, 17,* 19–52.

Andrews, D. A., Bonta, J., & Wormith, J. (2004). *The Level of Service/Case Management Inventory user's manual.* North Tonawanda, NY: Multi-Health Systems.

Andrews, J. A., Foster, S. L., Capaldi, D., & Hops, H. (2000). Adolescent and family predictors of physical aggression, communication, and satisfaction among young adult couples. *Journal of Consulting and Clinical Psychology, 68,* 195–208.

Antecol, H., & Cobb-Clark, D. (2001). Men, women, and sexual harassment in the U.S. military. *Gender Issues, 19,* 3–18. doi:10.1007/s12147-001-0001-1

Antonio, A., Chang, M., Hakuta, K., Kenny, D., Levin, S., & Milem, J. (2004). Effects of racial diversity on complex thinking in college students. *Psychological Science, 15,* 507–510.

Antrobus, E., McKimmie, B., & Newcombe, P. (2016). Mode of children's testimony and the effect of assumptions about credibility. *Psychiatry, Psychology and Law, 23,* 922–940.

Aos, S., Miller, M., & Drake, E. (2006). *Evidence-based adult corrections programs: What works and what does not.* Olympia, WA: Washington State Institute for Public Policy.

Aos, S., Phipps, P., Barnoski, R., & Lieb, R. (2001). *The comparative costs and benefits of programs to reduce crime.* Olympia, WA: Washington State Institute for Public Policy. (Document No. 01-05-1201).

Appelbaum, P. (2005). Law & psychiatry: Behavioral genetics and the punishment of crime. *Psychiatric Services, 56,* 25–27.

Appelbaum, P. (2007). The new lie detectors: Neuroscience, deception, and the courts. *Psychiatric Services, 58,* 460–462.

Appelbaum, P. S., & Grisso, T. (1995). The MacArthur Treatment Competence Study. I: Mental illness and competence to consent to treatment. *Law and Human Behavior, 19,* 105–126.

Appleby, S., Hasel, L., & Kassin, S. (2013). Police-induced confessions: An empirical analysis of their content and impact. *Psychology, Crime & Law, 19,*111–128.

Appleby, S., & Kassin, S. (2016). When self-report trumps science: Effects of confessions, DNA, and prosecutorial theories on perceptions of guilt. *Psychology, Public Policy, and Law, 22,*127–140.

Arkes, H., & Mellers, B. (2002). Do juries meet our expectations? *Law and Human Behavior, 26,* 625–639.

Aronson, J. (2010). The law's use of brain evidence. *Annual Review of Law and Social Science, 6,* 93–108.

Arrigo, B. (2006). *Criminal behavior: A systems approach.* New York, NY: Pearson.

Arrigo, B., & Claussen, N. (2003). Police corruption and psychological testing: A strategy for preemployment screening. *International Journal of Offender Therapy & Comparative Criminology, 47,* 272–290.

Asendorpf, J. B., Denissen, J. J. A., & van Aken, M. A. G. (2008). Inhibited and aggressive preschool children at 23 years of age: Personality and social transitions into adulthood. *Developmental Psychology, 44,* 997–1011.

Asscher, J., Dekovic, M., Manders, W., van der Laan, P., & Prins, P. (2013). A randomized controlled trial of the effectiveness of multisystemic therapy in the Netherlands: Post-treatment changes and moderator effects. *Journal of Experimental Criminology, 9,* 169–187. doi:10.1007/s11292-012-9165-9

Associated Press. (1988, January 13). Former Kansas woman identifies man in attack. *Kansas City Times,* p. B5.

Associated Press. (2003). State loses track of 33,000 sex offenders. Retrieved from http://articles.latimes.com/2003/jan/08/local/me-offender8

Association of Family and Conciliation Courts. (2000). *Model standards of practice for family and divorce mediation.* Madison, WI: Author. Retrieved December 26, 2016, from www.afccnet.org

Association of Family and Conciliation Courts. (2006). *Model standards of practice for child custody evaluation.* Madison, WI: Author. Retrieved December 26, 2016, from www.afccnet.org

Association of Family and Conciliation Courts. (2016). *Guidelines for examining intimate partner violence: A supplement to the AFCC model standards of practice for child custody evaluation.* Madison, WI: Author. Retrieved December 26, 2016, from www.afccnet.org

Atkins v. Virginia, 536 U.S. 304 (2002).

Axt, J., Ebersole, C., & Nosek, B. (2016). An unintentional, robust, and replicable pro-black bias in social judgment. *Social Cognition, 34,* 1–39.

Ayres, B. D. (1996, August 27). California child molesters face "chemical castration." *The New York Times,* p. A1.

Babcock, B. (1993). A place in the palladium: Women's rights and jury service. *University of Cincinnati Law Review, 61,* 1139–1180.

Badge of Life. (2010). *2010 police suicide statistics from Badge of Life.* Retrieved from http://www.policesuicideprevention.com/id48.html

Badge of Life. (2015). A study of police suicides 2008–2015. Retrieved October 31, 2016, from http://www.policesuicidestudy.com/

Baer, R., Wetter, M., Nichols, J., Greene, R., & Berry, D. (1995). Sensitivity of MMPI-2 validity scales to underreporting of symptoms. *Psychological Assessment, 7,* 419–423.

Bailenson, J., Blascovich, J., Beall, A., & Noveck, B. (2006). Courtroom applications of virtual environments, immersive virtual environments, and collaborative virtual environments. *Law & Policy, 28,* 249–270.

Baker, L. (1983). *Miranda: Crime, law, and politics.* New York, NY: Atheneum.

Baldus, D. C., Pulaski, C., & Woodworth, G. (1983). Comparative review of death sentences: An empirical study of the Georgia experience. *Journal of Criminal Law and Criminology, 74,* 661–753.

Bandura, A. (1973). *Aggression: A social learning analysis.* Englewood Cliffs, NJ: Prentice Hall.

Bandura, A. (1976). Social learning analysis of aggression. In E. Ribes-Inesta & A. Bandura (Eds.), *Analysis of delinquency and aggression* (pp. 203–232). Hillsdale, NJ: Erlbaum.

Bandura, A. (1986). *Social foundations of thought and action: A social cognitive theory.* Englewood Cliffs, NJ: Prentice Hall.

Banks v. Goodfellow, L. R. 5 Q. B. 549 (1870).

Barbaree, H. E., & Marshall, W. L. (1991). The role of male sexual arousal in rape: Six models. *Journal of Consulting and Clinical Psychology, 59,* 621–630.

Barber, L., Grawitch, M., & Trares, S. (2009). Service-oriented and force-oriented emotion regulation strategies in police officers. *Applied Psychology in Criminal Justice, 5,* 182–202.

Bard, M. (1969). Family intervention police teams as a community mental health resource. *Journal of Criminal Law, Criminology, and Police Science, 60,* 24.

Bard, M., & Berkowitz, B. (1967). Training police as specialists in family crisis intervention: A community psychology action program. *Community Mental Health Journal, 3,* 209–215.

Barnett, O., Miller-Perrin, C., & Perrin, R. (2005). *Family violence across the lifespan: An introduction* (2nd ed.). Thousand Oaks, CA: Sage.

Barnow, S., Lucht, M., & Freyberger, H. (2001). Influence of punishment, emotional rejection, child abuse, and broken home on aggression in adolescence: An examination of aggressive adolescents in Germany. *Psychopathology, 34,* 167–173.

Barovick, H. (1998, June). DWB: Driving while black. *Time,* p. 35.

Barr, W. (1992, March). *Comments by the attorney general of the United States.* Speech delivered at the University of Kansas, Lawrence.

Barrett, H., Slesnick, N., Brody, J., Turner, C., & Peterson, T. (2001). Treatment outcomes for adolescent substance abuse at 4- and 7-month assessments. *Journal of Consulting and Clinical Psychology, 69,* 802–813. doi:10.1037/0022-006X.69.5.802

Barth, J., & Huffman, S. (2015). Sentiment toward same-sex divorce. In M. Miller, J. Blumenthal, & J. Chamberlain (Eds.), *Handbook of community sentiment* (pp. 129–141). New York, NY: Springer.

Bartlett, F. C. (1932). *Remembering: A study of experimental and social psychology.* New York, NY: Cambridge University Press.

Bartoi, M. G., & Kinder, B. N. (1998). Effects of child and adult sexual abuse on adult sexuality. *Journal of Sex & Marital Therapy, 24,* 75–90.

Bartol, C. R. (1983). *Psychology and American law.* Belmont, CA: Wadsworth.

Bartol, C. R. (1991). Predictive validation of the MMPI for small-town police officers who fail. *Professional Psychology: Research and Practice, 22,* 127–132.

Bartol, C. R. (1996). Police psychology: Then, now, and beyond. *Criminal Justice and Behavior, 23,* 70–89.

Bartol, C. R., & Bartol, A. (2006). *Current perspectives in forensic psychology and criminal justice.* Thousand Oaks, CA: Sage.

Batson v. Kentucky, 476 U.S. 79 (1986).

Bauserman, R. (1997, October). *Child adjustment in joint custody versus sole custody arrangements: A meta-analytic review.* Paper presented at the 11th Annual Conference of the Children's Rights Council, Arlington, VA.

Bauserman, R. (2002). Child adjustment in joint-custody versus sole-custody arrangements: A meta-analytic review. *Journal of Family Psychology, 16,* 91–102.

Baxter, J., Weston, R., & Qu, L. (2011). Family structure, co-parental relationship quality, post-separation parental involvement and children's emotional wellbeing. *Journal of Family Studies, 17,* 86–109.

Bazelon, D. (1974). Psychiatrists and the adversary process. *Scientific American, 230,* 18–23.

Beattey, R., Matsuura, T., & Jeglic, E. (2014). Judicial bond-setting behavior: The perceived nature of the crime may matter more than how serious it is. *Psychology, Public Policy, and Law, 20,* 411–420.

Bechara, A., Damasio, H., Tranel, D., & Damasio, A. R. (1997). Deciding advantageously before knowing the advantageous strategy. *Science, 275,* 1293–1294.

Beech, A. R., Fisher, D. D., & Thornton, D. (2003). Risk assessment of sex offenders. *Professional Psychology: Research and Practice, 34,* 339–352.

Begam, R. (1977). Voir dire: The attorney's job. *Trial, 13,* 3.

Begany, J. J., & Milburn, M. A. (2002). Psychological predictors of sexual harassment: Authoritarianism, hostile sexism, and rape myths. *Psychology of Men and Masculinity, 3,* 119–126.

Beggs, S., & Grace, R. (2011). Treatment gains for sexual offenders against children predicts reduced recidivism: A comparative validity study. *Journal of Consulting and Clinical Psychology, 79,* 182–192.

Beiser, E. N. (1973). Are juries representative? *Judicature, 57,* 194–199.

Beland, L., & Kim, D. (2016). The effect of high school shootings on schools and student performance. *Educational Evaluation and Policy Analysis, 38,* 113–126. doi:10.3102/0162373715590683

Belanger, H., Curtiss, G., Demery, J., Lebowitz, B., & Vanderploeg, R. (2005). Factors moderating neuropsychological outcomes following mild traumatic brain injury: A meta-analysis. *Journal of the International Neuropsychological Society, 11,* 215–227.

Belenko, S. (1998). Research on drug courts: A critical review. *National Drug Court Institute Review, 1,* 1–42.

Belenko, S. (1999). Research on drug courts: A critical review: 1999 update. *National Drug Court Institute Review, 2,* 1–58.

Belenko, S. (2001). *Research on drug courts: A critical review: 2001 update.* New York, NY: National Center on Addiction and Substance Abuse at Columbia University.

Belenko, S. (2002). Drug courts. In C. Leukefeld, F. Tims, & D. Farabee (Eds.), *Treatment of drug offenders: Policies and issues* (pp. 301–318). New York, NY: Springer.

Belenko, S., DeMatteo, D., & Patapis, N. (2007). Drug courts. In D. Springer & A. Roberts (Eds.), *Handbook of forensic mental health with victims and offenders: Assessment, treatment, and research* (pp. 385–423). New York, NY: Springer.

Bellafante, G. (2017, June 1). Getting rid of bail is only the start. Retrieved from https://www.nytimes.com/2017/06/01/nyregion/getting-rid-of-bail-is-only-the-start.html?smprod=nytcore-iphone&smid=nytcore-iphone-share

Bench, L., & Allen, T. (2003). Investigating the stigma of prison classification: An experimental design. *The Prison Journal, 83,* 307–382.

Bennell, C., Jones, N., Taylor, P., & Snook, B. (2006). Validities and abilities in criminal profiling: A critique of the studies conducted by Richard Kocsis and his colleagues. *International Journal of Offender Therapy and Comparative Criminology, 50,* 344–360.

Benner, A. W. (1986). Psychological screening of police applicants. In J. T. Reese & H. A. Goldstein (Eds.), *Psychological services for law enforcement* (pp. 11–20). Washington, DC: U.S. Government Printing Office.

Berkemer v. McCarty, 468 U.S. 420 (1984).

Berman, M. E. (1997). Biopsychosocial approaches to understanding human aggression: The first 30 years. *Clinical Psychology Review, 15,* 585–588.

Berman, M. E., Tracy, J. I., & Coccaro, E. F. (1997). The serotonin hypothesis of aggression revisited. *Clinical Psychology Review, 17,* 651–665.

Bertman, L., Thompson, J., Waters, W., Estupinan-Kane, L., Martin, J., & Russell, L. (2003). Effect of an individualized treatment protocol on restoration of competency in pretrial forensic inpatients. *Journal of the American Academy of Psychiatry and Law, 31,* 37–35.

Betts v. Brady, 316 U.S. 455 (1942).

Beyer, M. (1997). Experts for juveniles at risk of adult sentences. In P. Puritz, A. Capozello, & W. Shang (Eds.), *More than meets the eye: Rethinking assessment, competency, and sentencing for a harsher era of juvenile justice* (pp. 1–22). Washington, DC: American Bar Association, Juvenile Justice Center.

Bibas, S. (2004). Plea bargaining outside the shadow of trial. *Harvard Law Review, 117,* 2463–2547.

Binder, A. (1988). Juvenile delinquency. In M. R. Rosenzweig & L. W. Porter (Eds.), *Annual review of psychology* (pp. 253–282). Palo Alto, CA: Annual Reviews.

Binder, A., Geis, G., & Bruce, D. D. (2001). *Juvenile delinquency: Historical, cultural & legal perspectives.* Cincinnati, OH: Anderson.

Binder, J. R., Desai, R. H., Graves, W. W., & Conant, L. L. (2009). Where is the semantic system? A critical review and meta-analysis of 120 functional neuroimaging studies. *Cerebral Cortex, 19,* 2767–2796.

Bing, N., Nelson, W., & Wesolowski, K. (2009). Comparing the effects of amount of conflict on children's adjustment following parental divorce. *Journal of Divorce and Remarriage, 50,* 159–171.

Bishop, D. M., Frazier, C. E., Lanza-Kaduce, L., & Winner, L. (1996). The transfer of juveniles to criminal court: Does it make a difference? *Crime and Delinquency, 42,* 171–191.

Black, M., Basile, K., Breiding, M., Smith, S., Walters, M., Merrick, M., … Stevens, M. (2011). *The National Intimate Partner and Sexual Violence Survey (NISVS): 2010 summary report.* Atlanta, GA: National Center for Injury Prevention and Control, Centers for Disease Control and Prevention.

Blair, I., Judd, C., & Chapleau, K. (2004). The influence of Afrocentric facial features in criminal sentencing. *Psychological Science, 15,* 674–679.

Blakely v. Washington, 124 S. Ct. 2348 (2004).

Blanchard, S., Carlson, K., & Meloy, M. (2014). Biased predecisional processing of leading and nonleading alternatives. *Psychological Science, 25,* 812–816.

Blau, T. H. (1986). Deadly force: Psychosocial factors and objective evaluation. A preliminary effort. In J. T. Reese & H. A. Goldstein (Eds.), *Psychological services for law enforcement* (pp. 315–334). Washington, DC: U.S. Government Printing Office.

Bloeser, A., McCurley, C., & Mondak, J. (2012). Jury service as civic engagement: Determinants of jury summons compliance. *American Politics Research, 40,* 179–204.

Blume, J. H., & Helm, R. K. (2014). The unexonerated: Factually innocent defendants who plead guilty. *Cornell Law Review, 100,* 157–191.

Blumenthal, J. A. (1998). The reasonable woman standard: A meta-analytic review of gender differences in perceptions of sexual harassment. *Law and Human Behavior, 22,* 33–58.

Boba, R., Weisburd, D., & Meeker, J. W. (2009). The limits of regional data sharing and regional problem solving: Observations from the East Valley, CA COMPASS Initiative. *Police Quarterly, 12,* 22–41.

Boccaccini, M. T., & Brodsky, S. L. (1999). Diagnostic test usage by forensic psychologists in emotional injury cases. *Professional Psychology: Research and Practice, 30,* 253–259.

Boccaccini, M. T., Murrie, D., Clark, J., & Cornell, D. (2008). Describing, diagnosing, and naming psychopathy: How do youth psychopathy labels influence jurors? *Behavioral Sciences & the Law, 26,* 487–510.

Bock, M., & Schneider, D. (2017). The voice of lived experience: Mobile video narratives in the courtroom. *Information, Communication & Society, 20,* 335–350.

Boehnert, C. (1989). Characteristics of successful and unsuccessful insanity pleas. *Law and Human Behavior, 13,* 31–40.

Boeri, D., & Sobel, Z. (2015, March 3). Judge's quest to find a 'fair and impartial' Tsarnaev jury in Boston finally comes to a close. *WBUR News.* Retrieved from http://www.wbur.org/2015/03/03/tsarnaev-jury-boston-judge-otoole

Boersema, C., Hanson, R., & Keilitz, S. (1991). State court-annexed arbitration: What do attorneys think? *Judicature, 75,* 28–33.

Bond, C., & DePaulo, B. (2006). Accuracy of deception judgments. *Personality and Social Psychology Review, 10,* 214–234.

Bond, C. F., Jr., & DePaulo, B. M. (2008). Individual differences in judging deception: Accuracy and bias. *Psychological Bulletin, 134,* 477–492.

Bonnie, R. J. (1993). The competence of criminal defendants: Beyond *Dusky* and *Drope. University of Miami Law Review, 47,* 539–601.

Bonnie, R. J., & Monahan, J. (1996). *Mental disorder, work disability, and the law.* Chicago, IL: The University of Chicago Press.

Bonta, J. (1997). *Offender rehabilitation: From research to practice.* Ottawa, ON: Department of the Solicitor General of Canada. (User Report No. 1997-01).

Bonta, J., & Gendreau, P. (1990). Reexamining the cruel and unusual punishment of prison life. *Law and Human Behavior, 14,* 347–372.

Booij, L., Tremblay, R. E., Leyton, M., Seguin, J. R., Vitaro, F., Gravel, P., … Benkelfat, C. (2010). Brain serotonin synthesis in adult males characterized by physical aggression during childhood: A 21-year longitudinal study. *PLoS ONE, 5,* ArtID e11255.

Book, A. S. (1999). Shame on you: An analysis of modern shame punishment as an alternative to incarceration. *William and Mary Law Review, 40,* 653–686.

Boothroyd, R., Mercado, C., Poythress, N., Christy, A., & Petrila, J. (2005). Clinical outcomes of defendants in mental health court. *Psychiatric Services, 56,* 829–834.

Boothroyd, R., Poythress, N., McGaha, A., & Petrila, J. (2003). The Broward mental health court: Process, outcomes, and service utilization. *International Journal of Law & Psychiatry, 26,* 55–71.

Borduin, C., Mann, B., Cone, L., Henggeler, S., Fucci, B., & Blaske, D. (1995). Multisystemic treatment of serious juvenile offenders: Long-term prevention of criminality and violence. *Journal of Consulting and Clinical Psychology, 63,* 569–578.

Borgida, E., & Brekke, N. (1985). Psycholegal research on rape trials. In A. Burgess (Ed.), *Research handbook on rape and sexual assault* (pp. 313–342). New York, NY: Garland.

Bornstein, B. (1994). David, Goliath, and Reverend Bayes: Prior beliefs about defendants' status in personal injury cases. *Applied Cognitive Psychology, 8,* 232–258.

Bornstein, B. H. (2004). The impact of different types of expert scientific testimony on mock jurors' liability verdicts. *Psychology, Crime & Law, 10,* 429–446.

Bornstein, B. H., & Greene, E. (2011a). Consulting on damage awards. In R. Wiener & B. Bornstein (Eds.), *Handbook of trial consulting* (pp. 281–296). New York, NY: Springer.

Bornstein, B. H., & Greene, E. (2011b). Jury decision making: Implications for and from psychology. *Current Directions in Psychological Science, 20,* 63–67.

Bornstein, B. H., & Greene, E. (2017). *The jury under fire: Myth, controversy, and reform.* New York, NY: Oxford University Press.

Bornstein, B. H., & Muller, S. (2001). The credibility of recovered memory testimony: Exploring the effects of alleged victim and perpetrator gender. *Child Abuse and Neglect, 25,* 1415–1426.

Bornstein, B. H., & Rajki, M. (1994). Extra-legal factors and product liability: The influence of mock jurors' demographic characteristics and intuitions about the cause of an injury. *Behavioral Sciences & the Law, 12,* 137–147.

Borum, R. (1996). Improving the clinical practice of violence risk assessment: Technology, guidelines, and training. *American Psychologist, 51,* 945–956.

Borum, R., Bartels, P., & Forth, A. (2005). *Structured assessment of violence risk in youth.* Lutz, FL: PAR.

Borum, R., & Fulero, S. M. (1999). Empirical research and the insanity defense and attempted reforms: Evidence toward informed policy. *Law and Human Behavior, 23,* 375–394.

Borum, R., & Verhaagen, D. (2006). *Assessing and managing violence risk in youth.* New York, NY: Guilford.

Borum, R., Williams, M., Deans, M., Steadman, H. J., & Morrissey, J. (1998). Police perspectives on responding to mentally ill people in crisis: Perceptions of program effectiveness. *Behavioral Sciences & the Law, 16,* 393–405.

Bouffard, J., & Bergeron, L. (2006). Reentry works: The implementation and effectiveness of a serious and violent offender reentry initiative. *Journal of Offender Rehabilitation, 44,* 1–29.

Bourgon, G., & Armstrong, B. (2005). Transferring the principles of effective treatment into a "Real World" prison setting. *Criminal Justice and Behavior, 32,* 3–25.

Boyer, P. J. (2000, January 17). DNA on trial. *The New Yorker,* pp. 42–53.

Brandenburg v. Ohio, 395 U.S. 444 (1969).

Brank, E., & Scott, L. (2012). Let's make a deal: The psychology of plea agreements. *APA Monitor, 43*(4), 31.

Brannen, D., Salekin, R., Zapf, P., Salekin, K., Kubak, F., & DeCoster, J. (2006). Transfer to adult court: A national study of how juvenile court judges weight pertinent *Kent* criteria. *Psychology, Public Policy, and Law, 12*, 332–355.

Braun, K., Ellis, R., & Loftus, E. (2002). Make my memory: How advertising can change our memories of the past. *Psychology and Marketing, 19*, 1–23.

Brayer, P. (2015). Hidden racial bias: Why we need to talk with jurors about Ferguson. *Northwestern University Law Review, 109*, 163–170.

Braver, S., Ellman, I., & Fabricius, W. (2003). Relocation of children after divorce and children's best interests: New evidence and legal considerations. *Journal of Family Psychology, 17*, 206–219.

Bregant, J. (2009). Let's give them something to talk about: An empirical evaluation of predeliberation discussions. *University of Illinois Law Review, 2009*(4), 1213–1241.

Brehm, S. S., & Brehm, J. (1981). *Psychological reactance*. New York, NY: Academic Press.

Brennan, P. A., & Raine, A. (1997). Biosocial bases of antisocial behavior: Psychophysiological, neurological, and cognitive factors. *Clinical Psychology Review, 17*, 589–604.

Breslau, N., Chilcoat, H. D., Kessler, R. C., & Davis, G. C. (1999). Previous exposure to trauma and PTSD effects of subsequent trauma: Results from the Detroit Area Survey of Trauma. *American Journal of Psychiatry, 156*, 902–907.

Breslau, N., Kessler, R. C., Chilcoat, H. D., Schultz, L. R., Davis, G. C., & Andreski, P. (1998). Trauma and posttraumatic stress disorder in the community: The 1996 Detroit Area Survey of Trauma. *Archives of General Psychiatry, 55*, 626–632.

Breslau, N., Lucia, V., & Alvarado, G. (2006). Intelligence and other predisposing factors in exposure to trauma and posttraumatic stress disorder: A follow-up study to age 17 years. *Archives of General Psychiatry, 63*, 1238–1245.

Brewer, N., & Burke, A. (2002). Effects of testimonial inconsistencies and eyewitness confidence on mock-juror judgments. *Law and Human Behavior, 26*, 353–364.

Brewer, N., & Wells, G. (2006). The confidence-accuracy relationship in eyewitness identification: Effects of lineup instructions, foil similarity, and target-absent base rates. *Journal of Experimental Psychology: Applied, 12*(1), 11–30.

Brewster, J., & Stoloff, M. (2003). Relationship between IQ and first-year overall performance as a police officer. *Applied H. R. M. Research, 8*, 49–50.

Brey, T. (2009). Child custody evaluation practices: A survey of psychologists. *Dissertation Abstracts International: Section B: The Sciences and Engineering, 69*(7-B), 4410.

Bridges, G., & Steen, S. (1998). Racial disparities in official assessments of juvenile offenders: Attribution stereotypes as mediating mechanisms. *American Sociological Review, 63*, 554–570.

Brigham, J., & Wasserman, A. (1999). The impact of race, racial attitude, and gender on reactions to the criminal trial of O. J. Simpson. *Journal of Applied Social Psychology, 29*, 1333–1370.

Bright, D., & Goodman-Delahunty, J. (2011). Mock juror decision making in a civil negligence trial: The impact of gruesome evidence, injury severity, and information processing route. *Psychiatry, Psychology and Law, 18*, 439–459.

Bright, S. (2014). *Capital punishment: Race, poverty, and disadvantage.* New Haven, CT: Yale University. Retrieved December 2, 2016, www.schr.org/resources/stephen_bright_s_course_capital_punishment_race_poverty_disadvantage_available_online

Broeder, D. W. (1959). The University of Chicago jury project. *Nebraska Law Review, 38*, 744–760.

Broner, N., Lattimore, P., Cowell, A., & Schlenger, W. (2004). Effects of diversion on adults with co-occurring mental illness and substance use: Outcomes from a national multi-site study. *Behavioral Sciences & the Law, 22*, 519–541.

Broner, N., Mayrl, D., & Landsberg, G. (2005). Outcomes of mandated and nonmandated New York City diversion for offenders with alcohol, drug, and mental disorders. *The Prison Journal, 85*, 18–49.

Bronner, G., Peretz, C., & Ehrenfeld, M. (2003). Sexual harassment of nurses and nursing students. *Journal of Advanced Nursing, 42*, 637–644.

Brown, L. T. (2003). Racial discrimination in jury selection: Professional misconduct, not legitimate advocacy. *Review of Litigation, 22*, 209–317.

Brown, T., Borduin, C., & Henggeler, S. (2001). Treating juvenile offenders in community settings. In J. Ashford, B. Sales, & W. Reid (Eds.), *Treating adult and juvenile offenders with special needs* (pp. 445–464). Washington, DC: American Psychological Association.

Brown v. Board of Education, 347 U.S. 483 (1954).

Brown v. Entertainment Merchants Association, Case # 08-1448 U.S. Supreme Court (2011).

Brownmiller, S., & Alexander, D. (1992, January/February). *From Carmita Wood to Anita Hill.* Ms., pp. 70–71.

Brubacher, M. R., Fondacaro, M. R., Brank, E. M., Brown, V. E., & Miller, S. A. (2009). Procedural justice in resolving family disputes: Implications for childhood bullying. *Psychology, Public Policy, and Law, 15*, 149–167.

Brubacher, S., Glisic, U., Roberts, K., & Powell, M. (2011). Children's ability to recall unique aspects of one occurrence of a repeated event. *Applied Cognitive Psychology, 25*, 351–358.

Bruck, D. (1985, May 20). The death penalty: An exchange. *New Republic*, pp. 20–21.

Bruck, M., Ceci, S., & Hembrooke, H. (2002). The nature of children's true and false narratives. *Developmental Review, 22*, 520–554.

Brunner, H., Nelen, M., Breakefield, X., Ropers, H., & van Oost, B. (1993). Abnormal behavior associated with a point mutation in the structural gene for monoamine oxidase A. *Science, 262*, 578–580.

Bryan, P. (2005). *Constructive divorce: Procedural justice and sociolegal reform.* Washington, DC: American Psychological Association.

Bryan, W. J. (1971). *The chosen ones.* New York, NY: Vantage Press.

Buades-Rotger, M., & Gallardo-Pujol, D. (2014). The role of the monoamine oxidase A gene in moderating the response to adversity and associated antisocial behavior: A review. *Psychological Research in Behavior Management, 7*, 185–200.

Buckley, W., & Okrent, C. (2004). *Torts and personal injury law* (3rd ed.). Clifton Park, NY: Thomson Delmar Learning.

Bufkin, J., & Luttrell, V. (2005). Neuroimaging studies of aggressive and violent behavior: Current findings and implications for criminology and criminal justice. *Trauma, Violence, & Abuse, 6*, 176–191.

Bureau of Justice Statistics. (2002). *Rape and sexual assault: Reporting to police and medical attention, 1992–2000.* Washington, DC: U.S. Department of Justice.

Bureau of Justice Statistics. (2005). *Family violence statistics.* Washington, DC: United States Department of Justice. Retrieved October 29, 2016, from https://www.bjs.gov/content/pub/pdf/fvs.pdf

Bureau of Justice Statistics. (2006). *Special report: Mental health problems of prison and jail inmates.* Retrieved January 26, 2009, from http://www.ojp.usdoj.gov/bjs/pub/pdf/mhppji.pdf

Bureau of Justice Statistics. (2010a). *Criminal victimization, 2010.* Retrieved from http://bjs.ojp.usdoj.gov/index.cfm?ty=tp&tid=31

Bureau of Justice Statistics. (2010a). *Press release.* Retrieved July 14, 2011, from http://bjs.ojp.usdoj.gov/content/pub/press/corrections09pr.cfm

Bureau of Justice Statistics. (2011). *Homicides fall to lowest rate in four decades.* Washington, DC: United States Department of Justice. Retrieved November 6, 2016, from http://www.bjs.gov/content/pub/press/htus8008pr.cfm

Bureau of Justice Statistics. (2014). *Rape and sexual assault among college-abge females, 1995–2013.* Washington, DC: United States

Department of Justice. Retrieved November 9, 2016, from http://www.bjs.gov/index.cfm?ty=pbdetail&iid=5176

Bureau of Justice Statistics. (2015a). *Criminal victimization, 2014.* Washington, DC: United States Department of Justice. Retrieved October 29, 2016, from https://www.bjs.gov/content/pub/pdf/cv14.pdf

Bureau of Justice Statistics. (2016a). Prisoners in 2015. Retrieved December 22, 2016, from http://www.bjs.gov/index.cfm?ty=-pbdetail&iid=5519>)

Bureau of Justice Statistics. (2016b). *Probation and parole in the United States, 2015.* Retrieved December 22, 2016, from http://www.bjs.gov/content/pub/pdf/ppus15_sum.pdf

Bureau of Justice Statistics. (2016c). *Criminal victimization, 2015.* Washington, DC: United States Department of Justice. Retrieved April 13, 2017, from https://www.bjs.gov/content/pub/pdf/cv15_sum.pdf

Bureau of Justice Statistics. (2017). *Indicators of mental health problems reported by prisoners and jail inmates, 2011–2012.* Retrieved July 13, 2017, from https://www.bjs.gov/content/pub/pdf/imhprpji1112.pdf

Burger, W. E. (1975). Dissenting opinion in *O'Connor v. Donaldson. U. S. Law Week, 42,* 4929–4936.

Burgess, A. W., & Holmstrom, L. L. (1974). *Rape: Victims of crisis.* Bowie, MA: Robert J. Brady.

Burke, P., & Tonry, M. (2006). *Successful transition and reentry for safer communities: A call to action for parole.* Silver Spring, MD: Center for Effective Public Policy.

Burnet v. Coronado Oil and Gas Co., 52 S.Ct. 443 (1932).

Burt, M. R. (1980). Cultural myths and supports for rape. *Journal of Personality and Social Psychology, 38,* 217–230.

Burt, R., & Morris, N. (1972). A proposal for the abolition of the incompetency plea. *University of Chicago Law Review, 40,* 66–95.

Buss, A. H. (1966). *Psychopathology.* New York, NY: Wiley.

Buss, D. M., & Malamuth, N. M. (Eds.). (1996). *Sex, power, conflict: Evolutionary and feminist perspectives.* New York, NY: Oxford University Press.

Butcher, J., Arbisi, P. A., Atlis, M. M., & McNulty, J. L. (2008). The construct validity of the Lees-Haley Fake Bad Scale: Does this scale measure somatic malingering and feigned emotional distress? *Archives of Clinical Neuropsychology, 23,* 855–864.

Butler, B., & Moran, G. (2007). The impact of death qualification, belief in a just world, legal authoritarianism, and locus of control on venirepersons' evaluations of aggravating and mitigating circumstances in capital trials. *Behavioral Sciences and the Law, 25,* 57–68.

Butler, S., Baruch, G., Hickley, N., & Fonagy, P. (2011). A randomized controlled trial of multisystemic therapy and a statutory therapeutic intervention for young offenders. *Journal of the American Academy of Child and Adolescent Psychiatry, 12,* 1220–1235. doi:10.1016/j.jaac.2011.09.017

Butler, W. M., Leitenberg, H., & Fuselier, D. G. (1993). The use of mental health consultants to police hostage negotiation teams. *Behavioral Sciences & the Law, 11,* 213–221.

Cacioppo, J. T., Petty, R. E., Feinstein, J. A., & Jarvis, W. B. G. (1996). Dispositional differences in cognitive motivation: The life and times of individuals varying in Need for Cognition. *Psychological Bulletin, 119,* 197–253.

Caetano, R., McGrath, C., Ramisetty-Mikler, S., & Field, C. A. (2005). Drinking, alcohol problems and the five-year recurrence and incidence of male-to-female and female-to-male partner violence. *Alcoholism: Clinical & Experimental Research, 29,* 98–106.

Caldwell, M., & Van Rybroek, G. (2005). Reducing violence in serious juvenile offenders using intensive treatment. *International Journal of Psychiatry and Law, 28,* 622–636.

California Civil Jury Instructions. (2011). Retrieved June 12, 2012 from http://www.courts.ca.gov/partners/documents/caci_2012_edition.pdf

Callahan, L., Steadman, H. J., McGreevy, M., & Robbins, P. C. (1991). The volume and characteristics of insanity defense pleas: An eight-state study. *Bulletin of the American Academy of Psychiatry and Law, 19,* 331–338.

Callahan, L. A., & Silver, E. (1998). Factors associated with the conditional release of persons acquitted by reason of insanity: A decision tree approach. *Law and Human Behavior, 22*(2), 147–163.

Campbell, A. (2015). Is there a therapeutic way to balance community sentiment, student mental health, and study safety to address campus-related violence? In M. Miller, J. Blumenthal, & J. Chamberlain (Eds.), *Handbook of community sentiment* (pp. 199–211). New York, NY: Springer.

Campbell, M. A., & Schmidt, F. (2000). Comparison of mental health & legal factors in the disposition outcome of young offenders. *Criminal Justice & Behavior, 27,* 688–715.

Campbell, R., Sefl, T., Barnes, H. E., Ahrens, C. E., Wasco, S. M., & Zaragoza-Diesfeld, Y. (1999). Community services for rape survivors: Enhancing psychological well-being or increasing trauma? *Journal of Consulting and Clinical Psychology, 67,* 847–858.

Canter, D., Alison, L., Alison, E., & Wentink, N. (2004). The organized/disorganized typology of serial murder: Myth or model? *Psychology, Public Policy and Law, 10,* 293–320.

Cara, E. (2014, November 4). The most dangerous idea in mental health. *Pacific Standard.* Retrieved from https://psmag.com/social-justice/dangerous-idea-mental-health-93325

Carlsmith, K. (2006). The roles of retribution and utility in determining punishment. *Journal of Experimental Social Psychology, 42,* 437–451.

Carlsmith, K. (2008). On justifying punishment: The discrepancy between words and actions. *Social Justice Research, 21,* 119–137.

Carlsmith, K., & Darley, J. (2008). Psychological aspects of retributive justice. *Advances in Experimental Social Psychology, 40,* 193–236.

Carlsmith, K., Darley, J., & Robinson, P. (2002). Why do we punish? Deterrence and just deserts as motives for punishment. *Journal of Personality and Social Psychology, 83,* 284–299.

Carnevale, P. (2008). Positive affect and decision frame in negotiation. *Group Decision and Negotiation, 17,* 51–63.

Carroll, J. S., Kerr, N. L., Alfini, J. J., Weaver, F. M., MacCoun, R. J., & Feldman, V. (1986). Free press and fair trial: The role of behavioral research. *Law and Human Behavior, 10,* 187–201.

Carter, T. (2004, June). Red Hook experiment. *American Bar Association Journal, 90,* 37–42.

Casey, P., & Rottman, D. (2005). Problem-solving courts: Models and trends. *The Justice System Journal, 26,* 35–56.

Casey, T. (2004). When good intentions are not enough: Problem-solving courts and the impending crisis of legitimacy. *Southern Methodist University Law Review, 57,* 1459–1519.

Caspi, A., McClay, J., Moffitt, T., Mill, J., Martin, J., Craig, I., … Poulton, R. (2002). Role of genotype in the cycle of violence by maltreated children. *Science, 297,* 851–854.

Castelli, P., Goodman, G., & Ghetti, S. (2005). Effects of interview style and witness age on perceptions of children's credibility in sexual abuse cases. *Journal of Applied Social Psychology, 35,* 297–319.

Catton, B. (1965). *Foreword to Twenty Days by D. Kunhardt & P. Kunhardt.* New York, NY: Harper & Row.

Cauffman, E., Piquero, A., Kimonis, E., Steinberg, L., Chassin, L., & Fagan, J. (2007). Legal, individual, and environmental predictors of court disposition in a sample of serious adolescent offenders. *Law and Human Behavior, 31,* 519–535.

Ceci, S. J., Kulkofsky, S., Klemfuss, J. Z., Sweeney, C. D., & Bruck, M. (2007). Unwarranted assumptions about children's testimonial accuracy. *Annual Review of Clinical Psychology, 3,* 307–324.

Center for Court Innovation. (2012). *Community court.* Retrieved from http://www.courtinnovation.org/topic/community-court

Center for Effective Public Policy. (2007). *Increasing public safety through successful offender reentry: Evidence-based and emerging practices in corrections.* Washington, DC: Author.

Chajewski, M., & Mercado, C. (2009). An evaluation of sex offender residency restriction functioning in town, county, and city-wide jurisdictions. *Criminal Justice Policy Review, 20*, 44–61.

Chamberlain, P. (1990). Comparative evaluation of specialized foster care for seriously delinquent youths: A first step. *Community Alternatives: International Journal of Family Care, 2*, 21–36.

Chamberlain, P., & Mihalic, S. (1998). *Blueprints for violence prevention: Book eight. Multidimensional treatment foster care.* Boulder, CO: Center for the Study and Prevention of Violence.

Chamberlain, P., & Reid, J. (1998). Comparison of two community alternatives to incarceration for chronic juvenile offenders. *Journal of Consulting and Clinical Psychology, 66*, 624–633.

Chan, J., & LaPaglia, J. (2011). The dark side of testing memory: Repeated retrieval can enhance eyewitness suggestibility. *Journal of Experimental Psychology: Applied, 17*, 418–432.

Chappell, A. (2008). Police academy training: Comparing across curricula. *Policing: An International Journal of Police Strategies & Management, 31*, 36–56.

Charman, S., Carlucci, M., Vallano, J., & Gregory, A. (2010). The selective cue integration framework: A theory of postidentification witness confidence assessment. *Journal of Experimental Psychology: Applied, 16*, 204–218.

Charman, S., & Wells, G. (2012). The moderating effect of ecphoric experience on post-identification feedback: A critical test of the cues-based inference conceptualization. *Applied Cognitive Psychology, 26*, 243–250.

Charman, S., & Wells, G. (2006). Applied lineup theory. In R. C. L. Lindsay, D. F. Ross, J. D. Read, & M. P. Toglia (Eds.), *The handbook of eyewitness psychology: Vol. 2. Memory for people* (pp. 219–254). Mahwah, NJ: Erlbaum.

Charman, S. D., & Quiroz, V. (2016). Blind sequential lineup administration reduces both false identifications and confidence in those false identifications. *Law and Human Behavior, 40*, 477–487.

Chen, M. K., & Shapiro, J. (2007). Do harsher prison conditions reduce recidivism? A discontinuity-based approach. *American Law and Economics Review, 9*, 1–29.

Chicago Community Policing Evaluation Consortium. (2004). *Longitudinal evaluation of Chicago's community policing program, 1993–2001.* Chicago, IL: Author.

Chifflet, P. (2015). Questioning the validity of criminal profiling: An evidence-based approach. *Australian & New Zealand Journal of Criminology, 48*, 238–255.

Chlistunoff, M. (2016). Expert testimony and the quest for reliability: The case for a methodology questionnaire. *Texas Law Review, 94*, 1055–1078.

Choi, A., & Edleson, J. L. (1996). Social disapproval of wife assaults: A national survey of Singapore. *Journal of Comparative Family Studies, 27*(1), 73–88.

Christie, R. (1976). Probability v. precedence: The social psychology of jury selection. In G. Bermant, C. Nemeth, & N. Vidmar (Eds.), *Psychology and the law: Research frontiers* (pp. 265–281). Lexington, MA: Lexington Books.

Christy, A., Poythress, N., Boothroyd, R., Petrila, J., & Mehra, S. (2005). Evaluating the efficiency and community safety goals of the Broward County mental health court. *Behavioral Sciences & the Law, 23*, 1–17.

Ciesluk v. Ciesluk, 113 P. 3d 135 (2005).

Cirincione, C., & Jacobs, C. (1999). Identifying insanity acquittals: Is it any easier? *Law and Human Behavior, 23*, 487–497.

CIT National Advisory Board. (2006). *Crisis intervention team core elements.* Memphis, TN: University of Memphis CIT Center.

Clark, J., Boccaccini, M. T., Caillouet, B., & Chaplin, W. F. (2007). Five-factor model personality traits, jury selection, and case outcomes in criminal and civil cases. *Criminal Justice and Behavior, 34*, 641–660.

Clark, S. (2012). Costs and benefits of eyewitness identification reform: Psychological science and public policy. *Perspectives on Psychological Science, 7*, 238–259.

Clark, S., & Davey, S. (2005). The target-to-fillers shift in simultaneous and sequential lineups. *Law and Human Behavior, 29*, 151–172.

Clavet, G. J. (1996, August). *Ironic effects of juror attempts to suppress inadmissible evidence.* Paper presented at the meeting of the American Psychological Association, Toronto, ON, Canada.

Cleary, H. (2014). Police interviewing and interrogation of juvenile suspects: A descriptive examination of actual cases. *Law and Human Behavior, 38*, 271–282.

Cleary, H. D., & Warner, T. C. (2016). Police training in interviewing and interrogation methods: A comparison of techniques used with adult and juvenile suspects. *Law and Human Behavior, 40*, 270–284.

Clemmer, D. (1958). *The prison community.* New York, NY: Rinehart.

Clermont, K., & Eisenberg, T. (1992). Trial by jury or judge: Transcending empiricism. *Cornell Law Review, 77*, 1124–1177.

Clingempeel, W. G., & Reppucci, N. D. (1982). Joint custody after divorce: Major issues and goals for research. *Psychological Bulletin, 92*, 102–127.

Cloninger, C., Dragan, M., & Przybeck, T. (1993). A psychobiological model of temperament and character. *Archives of General Psychiatry, 50*, 975–990.

Cloninger, C., Sigvardsson, S., Bohman, M., & vonKnorring, A. (1982). Predisposition to petty criminality in Swedish adoptees. II: Cross-fostering analysis of gene-environment interaction. *Archives of General Psychiatry, 39*, 1242–1249.

Cloud, J. (1998). Of arms and the boy. *Time,* p. 152.

Clow, K., Leach, A., & Ricciardelli, R. (2012). Life after wrongful conviction. In B. Cutler (Ed.), *Conviction of the innocent: Lessons from psychological research* (pp. 327–341). Washington, DC: American Psychological Association.

Cloward, R. A., & Ohlin, L. E. (1960). *Delinquency and opportunity: A theory of delinquent gangs.* New York, NY: Free Press.

CNN. (2004, June 25). *No charges against man beaten during arrest.* Retrieved June 20, 2005, from http://www.cnn.com/2004/US/West/06/25/lapd.video/index.html

Cochrane, R., Tett, R., & Vandecreek, L. (2003). Psychological testing and the selection of police officers. *Criminal Justice and Behavior, 30*, 511–537.

Cocozza, J., & Shufelt, J. (2006, June). *Juvenile mental health courts: An emerging strategy.* Retrieved July 3, 2008, from http://www.ncmhjj.com/pdfs/publications/JuvenileMentalHealthCourts.pdf

Cogin, J. A., & Fish, A. J. (2009). Gender, work engagement and sexual harassment: An empirical investigation. *Journal of Management and Organisation, 15*, 47–61. doi:10.5172/jmo.837.15.1.47

Cohen, A., Azrael, D., & Miller, M. (2014). Rate of mass shootings has tripled since 2011, Harvard research shows. *Mother Jones.* Retrieved July 16, 2017, from http://www.motherjones.com/politics/2014/10/mass-shootings-increasing-harvard-research/

Cohen, M. I., Spodak, M. K., Silver, S. B., & Williams, K. (1988). Predicting outcome of insanity acquittees released to the community. *Behavioral Sciences & the Law, 6*, 515–530.

Cohen, P., Azrael, D., & Miller, M. (2014). Rate of mass shootings has tripled since 2011, Harvard research shows. Retrieved from www.motherjones.com

Colangelo, J. (2009). The recovered memory controversy: A representative case study. *Journal of Child Sexual Abuse, 18*, 103–121.

Colb, S. (2016, January 15). Bill Cosby and rule against character evidence. *Verdict: Legal analysis and commentary from Justia.* Retrieved from https://verdict.justia.com/2016/01/15/bill-cosby-and-the-rule-against-character-evidence

Cole, D. (2014). The difference prevention makes: Regulating preventive justice. *Criminal Law and Philosophy, 9*, 501–519.

Committee on Ethical Guidelines for Forensic Psychologists. (1991). Specialty guidelines for forensic psychologists. *Law and Human Behavior, 15,* 655–665.

Compton, M., Bahara, M., Watson, A., & Oliva, J. (2008). A comprehensive review of extant research on Crisis Intervention Team (CIT) programs. *Journal of the American Academy of Psychiatry and Law, 36,* 47–55.

Condie, L. O. (2003). *Parenting evaluations for the court: Care and protection matters.* New York, NY: Springer.

Conger, R. (1980). Juvenile delinquency: Behavior restraint or behavior facilitation? In T. Hirschi & M. Gottfredson (Eds.), *Understanding crime: Current theory and research* (pp. 131–142). Newbury Park, CA: Sage.

Connell, A., Klostermann, S., & Dishion, T. (2012). Family Check Up effects on adolescent arrest trajectories: Variation by developmental subtype. *Journal of Research on Adolescence, 22,* 367–380. doi:10.1111/j.1532-7795.2011.00765.x

Connell, N. M., Miggans, K., & McGloin, J. M. (2008). Can a community policing initiative reduce serious crime? A local evaluation. *Police Quarterly, 11,* 127–150.

Connolly, D. A., & Read, J. D. (2006). Delayed prosecutions of historic child sexual abuse: Analyses of 2064 Canadian criminal complaints. *Law and Human Behavior, 30,* 409–434.

Cooper v. Oklahoma, 116 S.Ct. 1373 (1996).

Cooper, J., & Neuhaus, I. M. (2000). The hired gun effect: Assessing the effect of pay, frequency of testifying, and credentials on the perception of expert testimony. *Law and Human Behavior, 24,* 149–172.

Cooper, V., & Zapf, P. (2003). Predictor variables in competency to stand trial decisions. *Law and Human Behavior, 27,* 423–436.

Copson, G., Badcock, R., Boon, J., and Britton, P. (1997). Articulating a systematic approach to clinical crime profiling. *Criminal Behaviour and Mental Health, 7,* 13–17.

Cornell, D. (2003). Guidelines for responding to student threats of violence. *Journal of Educational Administration, 41,* 705–719.

Cornell, D. (2006). *School violence: Fears versus facts.* New York, NY: Routledge.

Cornell, D. G., & Sheras, P. L. (2006). *Guidelines for responding to student threats of violence.* Dallas, TX: Sopris West Educational Services.

Corrado, R. R., Vincent, G. M., Hart, S. D., & Cohen, I. M. (2004). Predictive validity of the Psychopathy Checklist: Youth version for general and violent recidivism. *Behavioral Sciences & the Law, 22,* 5–22.

Cosden, M., Ellens, J., Schnell, J., & Yamini-Diouf, Y. (2005). Efficacy of a mental health treatment court with assertive community treatment. *Behavioral Sciences & the Law, 23,* 199–214.

Cosden, M., Ellens, J., Schnell, J., Yamini-Diouf, Y., & Wolfe, M. (2003). Evaluation of a mental health court with assertive community treatment. *Behavioral Sciences & the Law, 21,* 415–427.

Costanzo, M., Shaked-Schroer, N., & Vinson, K. (2010). Juror beliefs about police interrogations, false confessions, and expert testimony. *Journal of Empirical Legal Studies, 7,* 231–247.

Cottle, C., Lee, R., & Heilbrun, K. (2001). The prediction of criminal recidivism in juveniles: A meta-analysis. *Criminal Justice and Behavior, 28,* 367–394.

Cougle, J., Resnick, H., & Kilpatrick, D. (2009). PTSD, depression, and other comorbidity in relation to suicidality: Cross-sectional and prospective analyses of a national probability sample of women. *Depression and Anxiety, 26,* 1151–1157.

Council for State Governments Justice Center. (2012). Adults with behavioral health needs under correctional supervision: A shared framework for reducing recidivism and promoting recovery. Retrieved July 13, 2017, from https://www.bja.gov/Publications/CSG_Behavioral_Framework.pdf

Cowan, C. L., Thompson, W. C., & Ellsworth, P. C. (1984). The effects of death qualification on jurors' predispositions to convict and on the quality of deliberation. *Law and Human Behavior, 8,* 53–79.

Coy v. Iowa, 487 U.S. 1012 (1988).

Crocker, C., & Kovera, M. (2010). The effects of rehabilitative voir dire on juror bias and decision making. *Law and Human Behavior, 34,* 212–226.

Cruise, K., Morin, S., & Affleck, K. (2016). Residential interventions with justice-involved youths. In K. Heilbrun, D. DeMatteo, & N. Goldstein (Eds.), *APA handbook of psychology and juvenile justice* (pp. 611–639). Washington, DC: American Psychological Association. doi:10.1037/14643-028

Cruzan v. Director, Missouri Department of Health, 497 U.S. 261 (1990).

Cuffe, S. P., Addy, C. L., Garrison, C. Z., Waller, J. L., Jackson, K. L., McKeown, R. E., … Chilappagari, S. (1998). Prevalence of PTSD in a community sample of older adolescents. *Journal of the American Academy of Child & Adolescent Psychiatry, 37,* 147–154.

Culhane, C. E., Hosch, H. M., & Weaver, W. G. (2004). Crime victims serving as jurors: Is there bias present? *Law and Human Behavior, 28,* 649–659.

Cunningham, G., & Benavides-Espinoza, C. (2008). A trend analysis of sexual harassment claims: 1992–2006. *Psychological Reports, 103,* 779–782. doi:10.2466/pr0.103.3.779-782

Cunningham, M. (2010). *Evaluation for capital sentencing.* New York, NY: Oxford University Press.

Curry, T., Lee, G., & Rodriguez, S. (2004). Does victim gender increase sentence severity? Further explorations of gender dynamics and sentencing outcomes. *Crime and Delinquency, 50,* 319–343.

Cutler, B. (2011). *Conviction of the innocent: Lessons from psychological research.* Washington, DC: American Psychological Association.

D'Agostino, C. (1986). Police psychological services: Ethical issues. In J. T. Reese & H. A. Goldstein (Eds.), *Psychological services for law enforcement* (pp. 241–248). Washington, DC: U.S. Government Printing Office.

Daftary-Kapur, T., Dumas, R., & Penrod, S. (2010). Jury decision-making biases and methods to counter them. *Legal and Criminological Psychology, 15,* 133–154.

Daftary-Kapur, T., Penrod, S., O'Connor, M., & Wallace, B. (2014). Examining pretrial publicity in a shadow jury paradigm: Issues of slant, quantity, persistence and generalizability. *Law and Human Behavior, 38,* 462–477.

Daicoff, S. (1999). Making law therapeutic for lawyers: Therapeutic jurisprudence, preventive law, and the psychology of lawyers. *Psychology, Public Policy, and Law, 5,* 811–848.

Dalenberg, C. J., Brand, B. L., Gleaves, D. H., Dorahy, M. J., Loewenstein, R. J., Cardeña, E., … Spiegel, D. (2012). Evaluation of the evidence for the trauma and fantasy models of dissociation. *Psychological Bulletin, 138,* 550–588.

Dalgleish, T. (2004). Cognitive approaches to posttraumatic stress disorder: The evolution of multi-representational theorizing. *Psychological Bulletin, 130,* 228–260.

Daly, K. (1994). *Gender, crime, and punishment.* New Haven, CT: Yale University Press.

Dann, B., & Hans, V. (2004). Recent evaluative research on jury trial innovations. *Court Review, 41,* 12–19.

Dantzker, M. (2010). Differences in pre-employment screening protocols used and reasons for their use between police and clinical psychologists. *Dissertation Abstracts International: Section B: The Sciences and Engineering, 71*(3-B), 2042.

Danziger, S., Levav, J., & Avnaim-Pesso, L. (2011). Extraneous factors in judicial decisions. *Proceedings of the National Academy of Sciences of the United States of America, 108,* 6889–6892.

Darley, J., & Pittman, T. (2003). The psychology of compensatory and retributive justice. *Personality and Social Psychology Review, 7,* 324–336.

Darley, J., Sanderson, C., & LaMantha, P. (1996). Community standards for defining attempt: Inconsistencies with the Model Penal Code. *American Behavioral Scientist, 39,* 405–420.

Daubert v. Merrell Dow Pharmaceuticals, Inc., 113 S.Ct. 2786 (1993).

Dauphinot, L. (1996). *The efficacy of community correctional supervision for offenders with severe mental illness*. Unpublished doctoral dissertation, University of Texas at Austin, Austin, TX.

Davey, M., & Goodnough, A. (2007). *Doubts rise as states hold sex offenders after prison*. Retrieved March 24, 2009, from http://www.nytimes.com/2007/03/04/us/04civil.html

Davis, L. (2011). Rock, powder, sentencing: Making disparate impact evidence relevant in crack cocaine sentencing. *Journal of Gender, Race, and Justice, 14*, 375–404.

Davis v. Monroe County Board of Education (Davis), 526 U.S. 629 (1999).

Day, M., & Ross, M. (2011). The value of remorse: How drivers' responses to police predict fines for speeding. *Law and Human Behavior, 35*, 221–234.

De Tocqueville, A. (1900). *Democracy in America* (Vol. 1) (Henry Reeve, Trans.). New York, NY: Colonial.

Deadman, D., & MacDonald, Z. (2004). Offenders as victims of crime?: An investigation into the relationship between criminal behaviour and victimization. *Journal of the Royal Statistical Society. Series A* (Statistics in Society), *167*, 53–67.

Death Penalty Information Center. (2010). *Facts about the death penalty*. Retrieved March 26, 2010, from http://www.deathpenaltyinfo.org

Death Penalty Information Center. (2017). *Facts about the death penalty*. Washington, DC: Death Penalty Information Center.

Deci, E. L., & Ryan, R. M. (2000). The "what" and "why" of goal pursuits: Human needs and the self-determination of behavior. *Psychological Inquiry, 11*, 227–268.

Deffenbacher, K., Bornstein, B., McGorty, E., & Penrod, S. (2008). Forgetting the once-seen face: Estimating the strength of an eyewitness's memory representation. *Journal of Experimental Psychology: Applied, 14*, 139–150.

Deffenbacher, K., Bornstein, B. H., & Penrod, S. D. (2006). Mugshot exposure effects: Retroactive interference, mugshot commitment, source confusion, and unconscious transference. *Law and Human Behavior, 30*, 287–307.

Deffenbacher, K., Bornstein, B. H., Penrod, S. D., & McGorty, E. (2004). A meta-analytic review of the effects of high stress on eyewitness memory. *Law and Human Behavior, 28*, 687–706.

Degoldi, B. (2008). Lawyers' emerging experiences of interdisciplinary collaborative separation and divorce. *Psychiatry, Psychology and Law, 15*, 396–414.

DeLisi, M., & Scherer, A. (2006). Multiple homicide offenders: Offense characteristics, social correlates, and criminal careers. *Criminal Justice and Behavior, 33*, 367–391.

DeMartini, A. (2008). *Juvenile prisons to make changes*. Retrieved April 15, 2009, from http://www.dispatch.com/live/content/local_news/stories/2008/04/04/Prisons_will_change.ART_ART_04–04–08_A1_579R1G7.html?sid=101

DeMatteo, D., Murrie, D., Anumba, N., & Keesler, M. (2011). *Forensic mental health assessments in death penalty cases*. New York, NY: Oxford University Press.

Dennis, D., & Monahan, J. (Eds.). (1996). *Coercion and aggressive community treatment: A new frontier in mental health law*. New York, NY: Plenum.

Department of Defense. (2004, April). *Task force report on care for victims of sexual assault*. Washington, DC: Author.

Department of Defense Inspector General. (2005). *Report on sexual harassment and assault at the U.S. Air Force Academy*. Washington, DC: Department of Defense.

Department of Justice. (1999). *Postconviction DNA testing: Recommendations for handling requests*. Retrieved December 19, 2001, from http://www.ncjrs.org/pdffiles1/nij/177626.pdf

Department of Veterans Affairs. (2012). *National Center for PTSD*. Retrieved September 2, 2012, from http://www.ptsd.va.gov/index.asp

DePaulo, B. M., Lindsay, J. L., Malone, B. E., Muhlenbruck, L., Charlton, K., & Cooper, H. (2003). Cues to deception. *Psychological Bulletin, 129*, 74–118.

Dershowitz, A. M. (1994). *The abuse excuse*. Boston, MA: Little, Brown.

Detrick, P., & Chibnall, J. T. (2002). Prediction of police officer performance with the Inwald Personality Inventory. *Journal of Police and Criminal Psychology, 17*, 9–17.

Detrick, P., & Chibnall, J. T. (2008). Positive response distortion by police officer applicants: Association of Paulhus Deception Scales with MMPI-2 and Inwald Personality Inventory Validity scales. *Assessment, 15*, 87–96.

Detrick, P., Chibnall, J. T., & Rosso, M. (2001). Minnesota Multiphasic Personality Inventory-2 in police officer selection: Normative data and relation to the Inwald Personality Inventory. *Professional Psychology: Research and Practice, 32*, 484–490.

DeVault, A., Miller, M. K., & Griffin, T. (2016). Crime control theater: Past, present, and future. *Psychology, Public Policy, and Law, 22*, 341–348.

Devenport, J., Stinson, V., Cutler, B., & Kravitz, D. (2002). How effective are the cross-examination and expert testimony safeguards? Jurors' perceptions of the suggestiveness and fairness of biased lineup procedures. *Journal of Applied Psychology, 87*, 1042–1054.

Devine, D. (2012). *Jury decision making: The state of the science*. New York, NY: New York University Press.

Devine, D., Buddenbaum, J., Houp, S., Studebaker, N., & Stolle, D. (2009). Strength of evidence, extraevidentiary influence, and the liberation hypotheses: Data from the field. *Law and Human Behavior, 33*, 136–148.

Devine, D., & Caughlin, D. (2014). Do they matter? A meta-analytic investigation of individual characteristics and guilt judgments. *Psychology, Public Policy, and Law, 20*, 109–134.

Devine, D., Clayton, L., Dunford, B., Seying, R., & Pryce, J. (2001). Jury decision making: 45 years of empirical research on deliberating groups. *Psychology, Public Policy, and Law, 7*, 622–727.

Devine, D., & Kelly, C. (2015). Life or death: An examination of jury sentencing with the capital jury project database. *Psychology, Public Policy, and Law, 21*, 393–406.

Devine, D., Krouse, P., Cavanaugh, C., & Basora, J. (2016). Evidentiary, extraevidentiary, and deliberation process predictors of real jury verdicts. *Law and Human Behavior, 40*, 670–682.

deVries, M., Holland, R., Corneille, O., Rondeel, E., & Whitteman, C. (2012). Mood effects on dominated choices: Positive mood induces departures from logical rules. *Journal of Behavioral Decision Making, 25*, 74–81.

DeWitt, J. S., Richardson, J. T., & Warner, L. G. (1997). Novel scientific evidence and controversial cases: A social psychological examination. *Law & Psychology Review, 21*, 1–28.

Dhami, M. (2003). Psychological models of professional decision making. *Psychological Science, 14*, 175–180.

Dhami, M. (2011). Psychological models of professional decision making. In G. Gigerenzer & T. Pachur (Eds.), *Heuristics: The foundations of adaptive behavior* (pp. 602–610). New York, NY: Oxford University Press.

Dhami, M., & Ayton, P. (2001). Bailing and jailing the fast and frugal way. *Journal of Behavioral Decision Making, 14*, 141–168.

Diamond, S. (2006). Beyond fantasy and nightmare: A portrait of the jury. *Buffalo Law Review, 54*, 717–763.

Diamond, S., Bowman, L., Wong, M., & Patton, M. (2010). Efficiency and cost: The impact of videoconferenced hearings on bail decisions. *Journal of Criminal Law & Criminology, 100*, 869–902.

Diamond, S., Murphy, B., & Rose, M. (2012). The "kettleful of law" in real jury deliberations: Successes, failures, and next steps. *Northwestern University Law Review, 106*, 1537–1608.

Diamond, S., Rose, M., & Murphy, B. (2004). Jurors' unanswered questions. *Court Review, 41*, 20–29.

Diamond, S., Rose, M., Murphy, B., & Meixner, J. (2011). Damage anchors on real juries. *Journal of Empirical Legal Studies, 8*, 148–178.

Diamond, S., Rose, M., Murphy, B., & Smith, S. (2006). Juror questions during trial: A window into juror thinking. *Vanderbilt Law Review, 59*, 1925–1972.

Diamond, S., & Vidmar, N. (2001). Jury room ruminations on forbidden topics. *Virginia Law Review, 87*, 1857–1915.

Diamond, S., Vidmar, N., Rose, M., Ellis, L., & Murphy, B. (2003). *Civil juror discussions during trial: A study of Arizona's rule 39(f) from videotaped discussions and deliberations.* Retrieved October 5, 2005, from http://www.law.northwestern.edu/diamond/papers/arizona_civil_discussions.pdf

Dickerson v. United States, 530 U.S. 428 (2000).

Dickinson, J., Poole, D., & Laimon, R. (2005). Children's recall and testimony. In N. Brewer & K. Williams (Eds.), *Psychology and Law: An empirical perspective* (pp. 151–175). New York, NY: Guilford.

Dierkhising, C., Ko, S., Woods-Jaeger, B., Briggs, E., Lee, R., & Pynoos, R. (2013). Trauma histories among justice-involved youth: Findings from the National Child Traumatic Stress Network. *European Journal of Psychotraumatology, 4*, 1–12. doi:10.3402/ejpt.v4i0.20274

Dirks-Linhorst, A. (2012). Tough on crime or beating the system? *Social Science Space.* Retrieved April 23, 2017, from http://www.socialscience-espace.com/2012/09/tough-on-crime-or-beating-the-system/

District Attorney's Office for the Third Judicial District v. Osborne, U.S. Supreme Court 08-6 (2009).

Ditto, P., Jacobson, J., Smucker, W., Danks, J., & Fagerlin, A. (2006). Context changes choices: A prospective study of the effects of hospitalization on life-sustaining treatment preferences. *Medical Decision Making, 26*, 313–322.

Ditto, P., Smucker, W., Danks, J., Jacobson, J., Houts, R., Fagerlin, A., … Gready, R. M. (2003). Stability of older adults' preferences for life-sustaining medical treatment. *Health Psychology, 22*, 605–615.

Domitrovich, S. (2016). Fulfilling Daubert's gatekeeping mandate through court-appointed experts. *Journal of Criminal Law and Criminology, 106*, 35–48.

Donat, P. L. N., & D'Emilio, J. (1992). A feminist redefinition of rape and sexual assault: Historical foundations and change. *Journal of Social Issues, 48*, 9–22.

Doppelt, J. (1991). Generic prejudice: How drug war fervor threatens the right to a fair trial. *American University Law Review, 40*, 821–836.

Dougall, A. L., Hayward, M. C., & Baum, A. (2005). Media exposure to bioterrorism: Stress and the anthrax attacks. *Psychiatry, 68*, 28–43.

Douglas, J., Burgess, A. W., Burgess, A. G., & Ressler, R. (2006). *Crime classification manual: A standard system for investigating and classifying violent crimes* (2nd ed.). New York, NY: Wiley.

Douglas, J. E., Ressler, R. K., Burgess, A. W., & Hartman, C. R. (1986). Criminal profiling from crime scene analysis. *Behavioral Sciences & The Law, 4*, 401–421.

Douglas, K., Hart, S., Webster, C., & Belfrage, H. (2013). *HCR-20V3.* Simon Fraser University: Mental Health, Law, and Policy Institute.

Dowler, K. (2005). Job satisfaction, burnout, and perception of unfair treatment: The relationship between race and police work. *Police Quarterly, 8*, 476–489. doi:10.1177/1098611104269787

Dragowski, E., Halkitis, P., Grossman, A., & D'Augelli, A. (2011). Sexual orientation victimization and posttraumatic stress symptoms among lesbian, gay, and bisexual youth. *Journal of Gay & Lesbian Social Services: The Quarterly Journal of Community & Clinical Practice, 23*, 226–249.

Driscoll, D. M., Kelly, J. R., & Henderson, W. L. (1998). Can perceivers identify likelihood to sexually harass? *Sex Roles, 38*, 557–588.

Drizin, S., & Colgan, B. (2004). Tales from the juvenile confession front: A guide to how standard police interrogation tactics can produce coerced and false confessions from juvenile suspects. In G. D. Lassiter (Ed.), *Interrogations, confessions, and entrapment* (pp. 127–162). New York, NY: Kluwer Academic/Plenum.

Drizin, S., & Leo, R. (2004). The problem of false confessions in the post-DNA world. *North Carolina Law Review, 82*, 891–1007.

Drizin, S., & Riley, H. (2014, February 12). Knox and Sollecito: Victims of a prosecutor's 'conspiracy theories' to explain away DNA. Retrieved from http://www.huffingtonpost.com/steve-drizin/amanda-knox-and-raffaele-_b_4757435.html

Drummond, M. (2017). Voir dire: Don't let the judge cut you out. *American Bar Association Litigation News.* Retrieved from https://apps.americanbar.org/litigation/litigationnews/articles-print/050412-practice-points-spring12.html

Duncan, G. J., & Hoffman, S. D. (1985). Economic consequences of marital instability. In M. David & T. Smeeding (Eds.), *Horizontal equity, uncertainty, and well-being* (pp. 427–469). Chicago, IL: University of Chicago Press.

Duncan v. Louisiana, 391 U.S. 145 (1968).

Durbin, J., Lin, E., & Zaslavska, N. (2010). Police-citizen encounters that involve mental health concerns: Results of an Ontario police services survey. *Canadian Journal of Community Mental Health, 29*, 53–71.

Durkin, E. (2011). *Kiss our ashes: Many smokers plan to ignore sweeping ban in city parks.* Retrieved June 19, 2012, from http://www.nydaily-news.com/new-york/kiss-ashes-smokers-plan-ignore-sweeping-ban-city-parks-article-1.146021

Dusky v. United States, 362 U.S. 402 (1960).

Dutton, D. G. (1995). Male abusiveness in intimate relationships. *Clinical Psychology Review, 15*, 567–582.

Dutton, D. G. (2000). *The domestic assault of women* (3rd ed.). Vancouver, BC: University of British Columbia Press.

Dutton, M. (2014). Critique of the "battered woman syndrome" model. *American Academy of Experts in Traumatic Stress.* Retrieved November 6, 2016, from http://www.aaets.org/article138.htm

Dvoskin, J., Skeem, J., Novaco, R., & Douglas, K. (Eds.) (2011). *Using social science to reduce violent offending.* New York, NY: Oxford University Press.

Eads, L., Shuman, D., & DeLipsey, J. (2000). Getting it right: The trial of sexual assault and child molestation cases under Federal Rules of Evidence 413–415. *Behavioral Sciences & The Law, 18*, 169–216.

Eagly, I. (2015). Remote adjudication in immigration. *Northwestern University Law Review, 109*, 933–1020.

Earnshaw, V. A., Pitpitan, E. V., & Chaudoir, S. R. (2011). Intended responses to rape as functions of attitudes, attributions of fault, and emotions. *Sex Roles, 64*, 382–393.

Eaton, L. (2004, August 8). Divorced parents move, and custody gets trickier. *The New York Times*, p. 1. Retrieved June 25, 2009, from http://www.nytimes.com/2004/08/08/nyregion/divorced-parents-move-and-custody-gets-trickier.html?pagewanted=all

Eaton, L., & Kaufman, L. (2005, April 26). In problem-solving courts, judges turn therapist. *The New York Times*, p. A1.

Eberhardt, J., Davies, P., Purdie-Vaughns, V., & Johnson, S. (2006). Looking deathworthy: Perceived stereotypicality of Black defendants predicts capital-sentencing outcomes. *Psychological Science, 17*, 383–386.

Ebreo, A., Linn, N., & Vining, J. (1996). The impact of procedural justice on opinions of public policy: Solid waste management as an example. *Journal of Applied Social Psychology, 26*, 1259–1285.

Eckhardt, C. L., Barbour, K. A., & Davison, G. C. (1998). Articulated thoughts of maritally violent and nonviolent men during anger arousal. *Journal of Consulting and Clinical Psychology, 66*, 259–269.

Eckholm, E. (1985, July 4). Stockholm syndrome: Hostages' reactions. *Lawrence Journal-World*, p. 6.

Eckholm, E. (2008, October 14). Courts give addicts a chance to straighten out. *The New York Times*. Retrieved October 15, 2008, from www.nytimes.com/2008/10/15/us/15drugs.html

Eddings v. Oklahoma, 436 U.S. 921 (1982).

Eddy, J., & Bellatty, P. (2014). *Randomized controlled trial of Measure 57 intensive drug court for medium to high risk property offenders*. Oregon Criminal Justic Commission. Retrieved December 22, 2016, from https://www.oregon.gov/cjc/SAC/Documents/M57_Intensive_Drug_Court_Evaluation.pdf

Eddy, J., Whaley, R., & Chamberlain, P. (2004). The prevention of violent behavior by chronic and serious male juvenile offenders: A 2-year follow-up of a randomized clinical trial. *Journal of Emotional and Behavioral Disorders, 12*, 2–8.

Edkins, V. (2011). Defense attorney plea recommendations and client race: Does zealous representation apply equally to all? *Law and Human Behavior, 35*, 413–425.

Ehlers, A., & Clark, D. (2000). A cognitive model of post-traumatic stress disorder. *Behaviour Research and Therapy, 38*, 319–345.

Eigen, Z., & Listokin, Y. (2012). Do lawyers really believe their own hype, and should they? A natural experiment. *Journal of Legal Studies, 41*, 239–267.

Eisele, G. T. (1991). The case against mandatory court-annexed ADR programs. *Judicature, 75*, 34–40.

Eisenberg, T., Hannaford-Agor, P., Hans, V., Waters, N., Munsterman, T., Schwab, S., & Wells, M. T. (2005). Judge-jury agreement in criminal cases: A partial replication of Kalven and Zeisel's *The American Jury*. *Journal of Empirical Legal Studies, 2*, 171–207.

Eisenberg, T., & Hans, V. (2009). Taking a stand on taking the stand: The effect of prior criminal record on the decision to testify and on trial outcomes. *Cornell Law Review, 94*, 1353–1390.

Eisenberg, T., LaFountain, N., Ostrom, B., Rottman, D., & Wells, M. (2002). Juries, judges, and punitive damages: An empirical study. *Cornell Law Review, 87*, 743–782.

Ekman, P., & O'Sullivan, M. (1991). Who can catch a liar? *American Psychologist, 46*, 913–920.

Eldred, L., Gifford, E., McCutchan, S., & Sloan, F. (2016). Factors predicting prosecution in child maltreatment cases. *Child and Youth Services Review, 70*, 201–205.

Eley, T. C. (1997). General genes: A new theme in developmental psychopathology. *Current Directions in Psychological Science, 6*, 90–95.

Ellis, D., Choi, A., & Blaus, C. (1993). Injuries to police officers attending domestic disturbances: An empirical study. *Canadian Journal of Criminology, 35*, 149–168.

Ellis, L. (1989). *Theories of rape: Inquiries into the causes of sexual aggression*. New York, NY: Hemisphere.

Ellis, L. (1991). A synthesized (biosocial) theory of rape. *Journal of Consulting and Clinical Psychology, 59*, 631–642. doi:10.1037/0022-006K.59.5.631

Ellis, L., & Diamond, S. (2003). Race, diversity, and jury composition: Battering and bolstering legitimacy. *Chicago-Kent Law Review, 78*, 1033–1058.

Ellison, K., & Buckhout, R. (1981). *Psychology and criminal justice*. New York, NY: Harper & Row.

Ellsworth, P. C., & Mauro, R. (1998). Psychology and law. In D. Gilbert, S. Fiske, & G. Lindzey (Eds.), *The handbook of social psychology* (Vol. 2, pp. 684–732). Boston, MA: McGraw-Hill.

Ellsworth, P. C., & Reifman, A. (2000). Juror comprehension and public policy: Perceived problems and proposed solutions. *Psychology, Public Policy, and Law, 6*, 788–821.

Elwork, A., Sales, B. D., & Suggs, D. (1981). The trial: A research review. In B. D. Sales (Ed.), *The trial process* (pp. 1–68). New York, NY: Plenum.

Emanuel, E., Onwuteaka-Philipsen, B., Urwin, J., & Cohen, J. (2016). Attitudes and practices of euthanasia and physician-assisted suicide in the United States, Canada, and Europe. *Journal of the American Medical Association, 316*, 79–90.

Emanuel, L., Barry, M., Stoeckle, J., Ettelson, L., & Emanuel, E. (1991). Advance directives for medical care – A case for greater use. *New England Journal of Medicine, 324*, 889–895.

Emery, R., Otto, R., & O'Donohue, W. (2005). A critical assessment of child custody evaluations: Limited science and a flawed system. *Psychological Science in the Public Interest, 6*, 1–29.

Emery, R. E., Laumann-Billings, L., Waldron, M., Sbarra, D., & Dillon, P. (2001). Child custody mediation and litigation: Custody, contact, and coparenting 12 years after initial dispute resolution. *Journal of Consulting and Clinical Psychology, 69*, 323–332.

Englich, B., & Mussweiler, T. (2001). Sentencing under uncertainty: Anchoring effects in the courtroom. *Journal of Applied Social Psychology, 31*, 1535–1551.

Englich, B., Mussweiler, T., & Strack, F. (2005). The last word in court: A hidden disadvantage for the defense. *Law and Human Behavior, 29*, 705–722.

Eno Louden, J., Manchak, S., O'Connor, M., & Skeem, J. (2015). Applying the Sequential Intercept Model to reduce recidivism among probationers and parolees with mental illness. In P. Griffin, K. Heilbrun, E. Mulvey, D. DeMatteo, & C. Schubert, *The Sequential Intercept Model and criminal justice: Promoting community alternatives for individuals with serious mental illness* (pp. 118–136). New York, NY: Oxford.

Eno Louden, J., & Skeem, J. (2007). Constructing insanity: Jurors' prototypes, attitudes, and legal decision-making. *Behavioral Sciences & The Law, 25*, 449–470.

Eno Louden, J., Skeem, J., Camp, J., & Christensen, E. (2008). Supervising probationers with mental disorder: How do agencies respond to violations? *Criminal Justice and Behavior, 35*, 832–847.

Epstein, S. (2003). Cognitive-experiential self-theory of personality. In T. Milton & M. Lerner, (Eds.), *Comprehensive handbook of psychology, Volume 5: Personality and Social Psychology* (pp. 159–184). Hoboken, NJ: Wiley.

Equal Justice Initiative. (2010). *Illegal racial discrimination in jury selection: A continuing legacy*. Retrieved from http://eji.org/reports/illegal-racial-discrimination-in-jury-selection

Erickson, W., Lampinen, J., & Moore, K. (2016). Eyewitness identifications by older and younger adults: A meta-analysis and discussion. *Journal of Police and Criminal Psychology, 31*, 108–121.

Eron, L. (1990). Understanding aggression. *Bulletin of the International Society for Research on Aggression, 12*, 59.

Espelage, D., Aragon, S., & Birkett, M. (2008). Homophobic teasing, psychological outcomes, and sexual orientation among high school students: What influences do parents and schools have? *School Psychology Review, 37*, 202–216.

Evans, J., Michael, S., Meissner, C., & Brandon, S. (2013). Validating a new assessment method for deception detection: Introducing a psychologically based credibility assessment tool. *Journal of Applied Research in Memory and Cognition, 2*, 33–41.

Evans, J., Pimentel, P., Pena, M., & Michael, S. (2017). The ability to detect false statements as a function of the type of statement and the language proficiency of the statement provider. *Psychology, Public Policy, and Law*, Online first publication.

Evans, J. R., Meissner, C. A. Brandon, S. E., Russano, M. B., & Kleinman, S. M. (2010). Criminal versus HUMINT interrogations: The importance of psychological science to improving interrogative practice. *Journal of Psychiatry and Law, 38*, 215–249.

Everington, C. T., & Luckasson, R. (1992). *Competence assessment for standing trial for defendants with mental retardation (CAST-MR) test manual*. Columbus, OH: International Diagnostic Systems.

Ewing, C. (1987). *Battered women who kill: Psychological self-defense as legal justification.* Lexington, MA: Lexington Books.

Ewing, C. (2011). *Justice perverted: Sex offense law, psychology, and public policy.* New York, NY: Oxford University Press.

Eysenck, H. J. (1964). *Crime and personality.* Boston, MA: Houghton Mifflin.

Eysenck, H. J., & Gudjonsson, G. H. (1989). *The causes and cures of criminality.* New York, NY: Plenum.

Fagan, J. (1996). The comparative advantage of juvenile versus criminal court sanctions on recidivism among adolescent felony offenders. *Law & Policy, 18,* 79–113.

Farah, M., Hutchinson, J. Phelps, E., & Wagner, A. (2014). Functional MRI-based lie detection: Scientific and societal challenges. *Nature Reviews: Neuroscience, 15,* 123–151.

Faretta v. California, 422 U.S. 806 (1975).

Farrell, A., Pennington, L., & Cronin, S. (2013). Juror perceptions of the legitimacy of legal authorities and decision making in criminal cases. *Law and Social Inquiry, 38,* 773–802.

Farrington, D. P. (1995). The development of offending and antisocial behavior from childhood: Key findings from the Cambridge Study in Delinquent Development. *Journal of Child Psychology and Psychiatry, 360,* 929–964.

Farwell, L. (2011). Brain fingerprinting: Corrections to *Rosenfeld. The Scientific Review of Mental Health Practice, 8,* 56–68.

Fawcett, J., Peace, K., & Greve, A. (2016). Looking down the barrel of a gun: What do we know about the weapon focus effect? *Journal of Applied Research in Memory and Cognition, 5,* 257–263.

FBI Academy. (2002). *Countering terrorism: Integration of practice and theory.* Retrieved July 22, 2005, from http://www.apa.org/releases/countering_terrorism.pdf

Feder, L., & Dugan, L. (2002). A test of the efficacy of court-mandated counseling for domestic violence offenders: The Broward Experiment. *Justice Quarterly, 19,* 343–375.

Federal Bureau of Investigation. (2011). *Crime in the United States 2010.* Retrieved from http://www.fbi.gov/about-us/cjis/ucr/crime-in-the-u.s/2010/crime-in-the-u.s.-2010/violent-crime/rapemain

Federal Bureau of Investigation. (2013). *A study of active shooter incidents in the United States between 2000 and 2013.* Retrieved July 16, 2017, from https://www.fbi.gov/file-repository/active-shooter-study-2000-2013-1.pdf

Federal Bureau of Investigation. (2014). *Crime in the United States 2013.* Retrieved November 8, 2016, from https://ucr.fbi.gov/crime-in-the-u.s/2013/crime-in-the-u.s.-2013/violent-crime/rape

Federal Bureau of Investigation. (2015a). *2014 law enforcement officers killed and assaulted.* Washington, DC: Department of Justice, Uniform Crime Reports. Retrieved October 31, 2016, from https://ucr.fbi.gov/leoka/2014/officers-feloniously-killed/main

Federal Bureau of Investigation. (2015b). *Crime in the United States.* Washington, DC: Author. Retrieved October 25, 2016, from https://ucr.fbi.gov/crime-in-the-u.s/2015/crime-in-the-u.s.-2015/offenses-known-to-law-enforcement/violent-crime

Federal Bureau of Investigation. (2016). *FBI releases 2015 preliminary statistics for law enforcement officers killed in the line of duty.* Washington, DC: FBI National Press Office. Retrieved October 31, 2016, from https://www.fbi.gov/news/pressrel/press-releases/fbi-releases-2015-preliminary-statistics-for-law-enforcement-officers-killed-in-the-line-of-duty

Federal Bureau of Prisons. (2012). *Inmate matters.* Retrieved from http://www.bop.gov/inmate_programs/

Federal Rules of Evidence. (2009). *Federal Rules of Evidence.* St. Paul, MN: West.

Feige, D. (2006, June 7). *Witnessing guilt, ignoring innocence?* Retrieved July 28, 2008, from http://www.nytimes.com/2006/06/06/opinion/06feige.html?_r=1&scp=11&sq=david%20feige&st=cse&oref=slogin

Feigenson, N., Park, J., & Salovey, P. (2001). The role of emotions in comparative negligence judgments. *Journal of Applied Social Psychology, 31,* 576–603.

Fein, S., McCloskey, A. L., & Tomlinson, T. M. (1997). Can the jury disregard that information? The use of suspicion to reduce the prejudicial effects of pretrial publicity and inadmissible testimony. *Personality and Social Psychology Bulletin, 23,* 1215–1226.

Feinblatt, J., & Berman, G. (2001). *Responding to the community: Principles for planning and creating a community court.* Washington, DC: U.S. Department of Justice.

Feldman, M. P. (1977). *Criminal behavior: A psychological analysis.* New York, NY: Wiley.

Feldmann, T. B. (2001). Characteristics of hostage and barricade incidents: Implications for negotiation strategies and training. *Journal of Police Crisis Negotiations, 1,* 3–33.

Feldman-Summers, S., & Ashworth, C. D. (1981). Factors related to intentions to report rape. *Journal of Social Issues, 37,* 71–92.

Felitti, V. J., Anda, R. F., Nordenberg, D., Williamson, D. F., Spitz, A. M., Edwards, V., … Marks, J. S. (1998). Relationship of childhood abuse and household dysfunction to many of the leading causes of death in adults: The adverse childhood experiences (ACE) study. *American Journal of Preventive Medicine, 14,* 245–258.

Finkel, N. (1989). The Insanity Defense Reform Act of 1984: Much ado about nothing. *Behavioral Sciences & the Law, 7,* 403–419.

Finkel, N. (1995). *Commonsense justice: Jurors' notions of the law.* Cambridge, MA: Harvard University Press.

Finkel, N., & Groscup, J. L. (1997). When mistakes happen: Commonsense rules of culpability. *Psychology, Public Policy, and Law, 3,* 65–125.

Finkel, N., & Slobogin, C. (1995). Insanity, justification, and culpability toward a unifying theme. *Law and Human Behavior, 19,* 447–464.

Finnila, K., Mahlberga, N., Santtilaa, P., Sandnabbaa, K., & Niemib, P. (2003). Validity of a test of children's suggestibility for predicting responses to two interview situations differing in their degree of suggestiveness. *Journal of Experimental Child Psychology, 85,* 32–49.

Fisher, R. P., & Geiselman, R. E. (1992). *Memory enhancing techniques for investigative interviewing: The cognitive interview.* Springfield, IL: Thomas.

Fiske, S., & Taylor, S. (1991). *Social cognition* (2nd ed.). New York, NY: McGraw-Hill.

Fitzgerald, R., & Price, H. (2015). Eyewitness identification across the life span: A meta-analysis of age differences. *Psychological Bulletin, 141,* 1228–1265.

Florence v. Board of Chosen Freeholders, 132 S.Ct. 1510 (2012).

Flynn, C., & Heitzmann, D. (2008). Tragedy at Virginia Tech: Trauma and its aftermath. *The Counseling Psychologist, 36,* 479–489.

Foa, E. B., Hearst-Ikeda, D., & Perry, K. J. (1995). Evaluation of a brief cognitive behavioral program for the prevention of chronic PTSD in recent assault victims. *Journal of Consulting and Clinical Psychology, 63,* 948–955.

Foa, E. B., & Kozak, M. J. (1986). Emotional processing of fear: Exposure to corrective information. *Psychological Bulletin, 99,* 20–35.

Follingstad, D. R. (1994, March 10). *The use of battered woman syndrome in court.* Workshop for the American Academy of Forensic Psychology, Santa Fe, NM.

Ford, J., & Hawke, J. (2012). Trauma affect regulation psychoeducation group and milieu intervention outcomes in juvenile detention facilities. *Journal of Aggression, Maltreatment, and Trauma, 21,* 365–384. doi:10.1080/10926771.2012.673538

Ford, J., & Russo, E. (2006). Trauma-focused, present-centered, emotional self-regulation approach to integrated treatment for posttraumatic stress and addiction: Trauma adaptive recovery group education and therapy (TARGET). *American Journal of Psychotherapy, 60,* 335–355.

Ford Motor Credit Co. v. Sheehan, 373 So. 2d 956 (Fla. App. 1979).

Ford v. Wainwright, 477 U.S. 399 (1986).

Forgas, J. (2011). Affective influences on self-disclosure: Mood effects on the intimacy and reciprocity of disclosing personal information. *Journal of Personality and Social Psychology, 100*, 449–461.

Forst, M., Fagan, J., & Vivona, T. S. (1989). Youth in prisons and training schools: Perceptions and consequences of the treatment-custody dichotomy. *Juvenile and Family Court Journal, 40*, 1–14.

ForsterLee, L., & Horowitz, I. (2003). The effects of jury-aid innovations on juror performance in complex civil trials. *Judicature, 86*, 184–190.

Foster, T. (2011). Adverse life events proximal to adult suicide: A synthesis of findings from psychological autopsy studies. *Archives of Suicide Research, 15*, 1–15.

Foster v. Chatman, 578 U.S. ___ (2016).

Foucha v. Louisiana, 112 S.Ct. 1780 (1992).

Fox, B., & Farrington, D. (2015). An experimental evaluation of the utility of burglary profiles applied in active policy investigations. *Criminal Justice and Behavior, 42*, 156–175.

Fox, D., Gerson, A., & Lees-Haley, P. (1995). Interrelationship of MMPI-2 validity scales in personal injury claims. *Journal of Clinical Psychology, 51*, 42–47.

Fox, J. A., & Levin, J. (1998). Multiple homicide: Patterns of serial and mass murder. *Crime and Justice, 23*, 407–455.

Fox, J. A., & Levin, J. (2005). *Extreme killing: Understanding serial and mass murder.* Beverly Hills, CA: Sage.

Foxnews.com. (2016, June 2). Judge declares Jimmy "Superfly" Snuka incompetent to stand trial in death. Retrieved July 12, 2017, from http://www.foxnews.com/entertainment/2016/06/02/judge-declares-jimmy-superfly-snuka-incompetent-to-stand-trial-in-death.html

Frazer, M. (2006). *The impact of the community court model on defendant perceptions of fairness: A case study at the Red Hook Community Justice Center.* New York, NY: Center for Court Innovation.

Frazier, P. A., & Haney, B. (1996). Sexual assault cases in the legal system: Police, prosecutor, and victim perspectives. *Law and Human Behavior, 20*, 607–628.

Frederick, R. (1997). *Validity Indicator Profile manual.* Minnetonka, MN: NSC Assessments.

Frederick, R. (2000). Mixed group validation: A method to address the limitations of criterion group validation in research on malingering detection. *Behavioral Sciences & the Law, 18*, 693–718.

Frederick, R., & Crosby, R. (2000). Development and validation of the Validity Indicator Profile. *Law and Human Behavior, 24*, 59–82.

Freedman, J., Martin, C., & Mota, V. (1998). Pretrial publicity: Effects of admonition and expression pretrial opinions. *Legal and Criminological Psychology, 3*, 255–270.

Freiburger, T. (2010). The effects of gender, family status, and race on sentencing decisions. *Behavioral Sciences and the Law, 28*, 378–395.

Freiburger, T., Marcum, C., & Pierce, M. (2010). The impact of race on pretrial decision. *American Journal of Criminal Justice, 35*, 76–86.

Frendak v. United States, 408 A. 2d 364 (D.C. 1979).

Friedman, R., Anderson, C., Brett, J., Olekalns, M., Goates, N., & Lisco, C. (2004). The positive and negative effects of anger on dispute resolution: Evidence from electronically mediated disputes. *Journal of Applied Psychology, 89*, 369–376.

Frisell, T., Pawitan, Y., Langstrom, N., & Lichtenstein, P. (2012). Heritability, assortative mating and gender differences in violent crime: Results from a total population sample using twin, adoption, and sibling models. *Behavior Genetics, 42*, 3–18. doi:10.1007/S10519-011-9483-0

Frolik, L. A. (1999). Science, common sense, and the determination of mental capacity. *Psychology, Public Policy, and Law, 5*, 41–58.

Frye v. United States, 293 F. 1013 (D.C. Cir. 1923)

Fuhrmann, G., & Zibbell, R. (2011). *Evaluation for child custody.* New York, NY: Oxford University Press.

Fulero, S. M., & Finkel, N. J. (1991). Barring ultimate issue testimony: An "insane" rule? *Law and Human Behavior, 15*, 495–508.

Funder, D. C. (2004). *The personality puzzle* (3rd ed.). New York, NY: Norton.

Furman v. Georgia, 408 U.S. 238 (1972).

Furstenberg, F., Peterson, J., Nord, C., & Zill, N. (1983). The life course of children of divorce. *American Sociological Review, 48*, 656–668.

Gaes, G., & Camp, S. (2009). Unintended consequences: Experimental evidence for the criminogenic effect of prison security level placement on post-release recidivism. *Journal of Experimental Criminology, 5*(2), 139–162.

Gaines, L. K., & Falkenberg, S. (1998). An evaluation of the written selection test: Effectiveness and alternatives. *Journal of Criminal Justice, 26*, 175–183.

Galanter, M. (2004). The vanishing trial: An examination of trials and related matters in state and federal courts. *Journal of Empirical Legal Studies, 1*, 459–570.

Galanter, M., & Frozena, M. (2014). A grin without a cat: The continuing decline & displacement of trials in American courts. *Daedalus, 143*, 115–128.

Galberson, W. (2011, August 8). By helping a girl testify in a rape trial, a dog ignites a legal debate. *New York Times.* Retrieved June 5, 2012, from http://www.nytimes.com/2011/08/09/nyregion/dog-helps-rape-victim-15-testify.html?pagewanted=all

Galinsky, A., Maddux, W., Gilin, D., & White, J. (2008). Why it pays to get inside the head of your opponent: A differential effects of perspective taking and empathy in negotiations. *Psychological Science, 19*, 378–384.

Gall v. United States, 552 U.S. 38 (2007).

Gallagher, W. (1996). *I.D.: How heredity and experience make you who you are.* New York, NY: Random House.

Gardner, J., Scogin, F., Vipperman, R., & Varela, J. G. (1998). The predictive validity of peer assessment in law enforcement: A 6-year follow-up. *Behavioral Sciences & the Law, 16*, 473–478.

Garofalo, R. (1914). *Criminology* (R. W. Millar, Trans.). Boston, MA: Little, Brown.

Garrett, B. (2008). Judging innocence. *Columbia Law Review, 108*, 55–142.

Garrett, B. (2011). *Convicting the innocent: Where criminal prosecutions go wrong.* Cambridge, MA: Harvard University Press.

Garrett, B., Krauss, D. A., & Scurich, N. (2017). Capital jurors in an era of death penalty decline. *Yale Law Journal Forum, 126*, 417–430.

Garrioch, L., & Brimacombe, C. A. E. (2001) . Lineup administrators' expectations: Their impact on eyewitness confidence. *Law and Human Behavior, 25*, 299–315.

Garvey, S., Hannaford-Agor, P., Hans, V., Mott, N., Munsterman, G. T., & Wells, M. (2004). Juror first votes in criminal trials. *Journal of Empirical Legal Studies, 1*, 371–399.

Gastil, J., Black, L., Deess, E., & Leighter, J. (2008). From group member to democratic citizen: How deliberating with fellow jurors reshapes civic attitudes. *Human Communication Research, 34*, 137–169.

Gatowski, S. I., Dobbin, S. A., Richardson, J. T., Ginsburg, G. P., Merlino, M. L., & Dahir, V. (2001). Asking the gatekeepers: A national survey of judges of judging expert evidence in a post-*Daubert* world. *Law and Human Behavior, 25*, 433–458.

Gau, J. (2016). A jury of whose peers? The impact of selection procedures on racial composition and the prevalence of majority-white juries. *Journal of Crime and Justice, 39*, 75–87.

Gaylin, W. (1974). *Partial justice: A study of bias in sentencing.* New York, NY: Vintage.

Gazal-Ayal, O., & Sulitzeanu-Kenan, R. (2010). Let my people go: Ethnic in-group bias in judicial decisions - Evidence from a randomized natural experiment. *Journal of Empirical Legal Studies, 7*, 403–428.

Gebser v. Lago Vista Independent School District (Gebser), 524 U.S. 274 (1998).

Geiselman, R. E., Fisher, R. P., MacKinnon, D. P., & Holland, H. L. (1985). Eyewitness memory enhancment in the police interview. *Journal of Applied Psychology, 70*, 401–412.

Gelman, A., Fagan, J., & Kiss, A. (2007). An analysis of the New York City Police Department's "stop-and-frisk" police in the context of claims of racial bias. *Journal of the American Statistical Association, 102*, 813–823.

Georges, L., Wiener, R., & Keller, S. (2013). The angry juror: Sentencing decisions in first-degree murder. *Applied Cognitive Psychology, 27*, 156–166.

Geraerts, E. (2012). Cognitive underpinnings of recovered memories of childhood abuse *Nebraska Symposium on Motivation, 58*, 175–191.

Geraerts, E., Bernstein, D., Merckelbach, H., Linders, C., Raymaekers, L., & Loftus, E. (2008). Lasting false beliefs and their behavioral consequences. *Psychological Science, 19*, 749–753.

Geraerts, E., Lindsay, D. S., Merckelbach, H., Jelicic, M., Raymaekers, L., Arnold, M. M., & Schooler, J. W. (2009). Cognitive mechanisms underlying recovered-memory experiences of childhood sexual abuse. *Psychological Science, 20*, 92–98.

Geraerts, E., Schooler, J., Merckelbach, H., Jelicic, M., Hauer, B., & Ambadar, Z. (2007). The reality of recovered memories: Corroborating continuous and discontinuous memories of childhood sexual abuse. *Psychological Science, 18*, 564–568.

Gerber, M. R., Ganz, M. L., Lichter, E., Williams, C. M., & McCloskey, L. A. (2005). Adverse health behaviors and the detection of partner violence by clinicians. *Archives of Internal Medicine, 165*, 1016–1021.

Gergen, K. J. (1994). Exploring the postmodern: Perils or potentials? *American Psychologist, 49*, 412–416.

Giaconia, R. M., Reinherz, H. Z., Silverman, A. B., Pakiz, B., Frost, A. K., & Cohen, E. (1995). Traumas and posttraumatic stress disorder in a community population of older adolescents. *Journal of the American Academy of Child & Adolescent Psychiatry, 34*, 1369–1380.

Gibson, C. (2005, January 7). *Andrea Yates case interview with Andrea Yates's mother* [ABC News Transcript, Good Morning America]. Retrieved August 7, 2005, from http://www.lexisnexis.com/us/lnacademic/results/docview/docview.do?docLinkInd=true&risb=21_T8239962496&format=GNBFI&sort=RELEVANCE&startDocNo=1&resultsUrlKey=29_T8239962499&cisb=22_T8239962498&treeMax=true&treeWidth=0&csi=8277&docNo=7

Gideon v. Wainwright, 372 U.S. 335 (1963).

Gidycz, C., Rich, C., Orchowski, L., King, C., & Miller, A. (2006). The evaluation of a sexual assault self-defense and risk-reduction program for college women: A prospective study. *Psychology of Women Quarterly, 30*, 173–186.

Gilovich, T., Kerr, M., & Medvec, V. H. (1993). Effect of temporal perspective on subjective confidence. *Journal of Personality and Social Psychology, 64*, 552–560.

Givelber, D. (2001). The adversary system and historical accuracy: Can we do better? In S. Westervelt & J. Humphrey (Eds.), *Wrongly convicted: Perspectives on failed justice* (pp. 253–268). New Brunswick, NJ: Rutgers University Press.

Givelber, D., & Farrell, A. (2008). Judges and juries: The defense case and differences in acquittal rates. *Law and Social Inquiry, 33*, 31–52.

Glamser, D. (1997, January 27). Washington State testing therapy for sex felons. *USA Today*, p. 3A.

Glymour, B., Glymour, C., & Glymour, M. (2008). Watching social science: The debate about the effects of exposure to televised violence on aggressive behavior. *American Behavioral Scientist, 51*, 1231–1259.

Glynn, A., & Sen, M. (2015). Identifying judicial empathy: Does having daughters cause judges to rule for women's issues? *American Journal of Political Science, 59*, 37–54.

Godinez v. Moran, 113 S.Ct. 2680 (1993).

Golding, J. M., Bradshaw, G. S., Dunlap, E. E., & Hodell, E. C. (2007). The impact of mock jury gender composition on deliberations and conviction rates in a child sexual assault trial. *Child Maltreatment, 12*, 182–190.

Golding, S. L. (1993). *Interdisciplinary Fitness Interview-Revised: A training manual*. Salt Lake City, UT: State of Utah Division of Mental Health.

Golding, S. L., Roesch, R., & Schreiber, J. (1984). Assessment and conceptualization of competency to stand trial: Preliminary data on the Interdisciplinary Fitness Interview. *Law and Human Behavior, 8*, 321–334.

Goldinger, S., He, Y., & Papesh, M. (2009). Deficits in cross-race face learning: Insights from eye movements and pupillometry. *Journal of Experimental Psychology: Learning, Memory, and Cognition, 35*, 1105–1122.

Goldkamp, J. (2000). The drug court response: Issues and implications for justice change. *Albany Law Review, 63*, 923–961.

Goldman, S., & Faw, L. (1999). Three wraparound models as promising approaches. In B. Burns & S. Goldman (Eds.), *Promising practices in wraparound for children with serious emotional disturbance and their families. Systems of care: Promising practices in children's mental health, 1998 series* (Vol. 4, pp. 35–78). Washington, DC: American Institutes for Research Center for Effective Collaboration and Practice.

Goldstein, A. P. (2004). Evaluations of effectiveness. In A. P. Goldstein, R. Nensen, B. Daleflod, & M. Kalt (Eds.), *New perspectives on aggression replacement training* (pp. 230–244). Chichester, UK: Wiley.

Goldstein, J. (2017, August 17). After backing alt-right in Charlottesville, A.C.L.U. wrestles with its role. *New York Times*. Retrieved from https://www.nytimes.com/2017/08/17/nyregion/aclu-free-speech-rights-charlottesville-skokie-rally.html

Goldstein, N. E. S., Dovidio, A., Kalbeitzer, R., Weil, J., & Strachan, M. (2007). An anger management intervention for female juvenile offenders: Results of a pilot study. *Journal of Forensic Psychology Practice, 7*, 1–28.

Goldstein, R., Grant, B., Ruan, W., Smith, S., & Saha, T. (2006). Antisocial Personality Disorder with childhood- versus adolescence-onset conduct disorder: From the National Epidemiologic Survey on alcohol and related conditions. *Journal of Nervous and Mental Disease, 194*, 667–675.

Gollwitzer, M., & Keller, L. (2010). What you did only matters if you are one of us: Offenders' group membership moderates the effect of criminal history on punishment severity. *Social Psychology, 41*, 20–26.

Gomes, C., Cohen, B., Desai, A., Brainerd, C., & Reyna, V. (2014). Aging and false memory: Fuzzy-trace theory and the elderly eyewitness. In M. Toglia, D. Ross, J. Pozzulo, & E. Pica (Eds.), *The elderly eyewitness in court* (pp. 137–166). New York, NY: Psychology Press.

Goodman, G. S., Pyle-Taub, E., Jones, D., England, P., Port, L., Rudy, L., … Melton, G. B. (1992). Testifying in criminal court: Emotional effects of criminal court testimony on child sexual assault victims. *Monographs of the Society for Research in Child Development, 57* (5, Serial No. 229), i, ii, v, 1–159.

Goodman, G. S., & Quas, J. A. (2008). Repeated interviews and children's memory. It's more than just how many. *Current Directions in Psychological Science, 17*, 386–390.

Goodman, G. S., Tobey, A., Batterman-Faunce, J., Orcutt, H., Thomas, S., & Shapiro, C. (1998). Face-to-face confrontation: Effects of closed-circuit technology on children's eyewitness testimony and jurors' decisions. *Law and Human Behavior, 22*, 265–203.

Goodman-Delahunty, J., & Foote, W. (2011). *Evaluation for workplace discrimination and harassment*. New York, NY: Oxford University Press.

Goodman-Delahunty, J., & Sporer, S. (2010). Unconscious influences in sentencing decisions: A research review of psychological sources of disparity. *Australian Journal of Forensic Sciences, 42*, 19–36.

Goodman-Delahunty, J., Granhag, P. A., Hartwig, M., & Loftus, E. F. (2010). Insightful or wishful: Lawyers' ability to predict case outcomes. *Psychology, Public Policy, and Law, 16*, 133–157.

Goodman-Delahunty, J., Greene, E., & Hsiao, W. (1998). Construing motive in videotaped killings: The role of jurors' attitudes toward the death penalty. *Law and Human Behavior, 22*, 257–271.

Gordon, D., Arbuthnot, J., Gustafson, K., & McGreen, P. (1988). Home-based behavioral-systems family therapy with disadvantaged juvenile delinquents. *American Journal of Family Therapy, 16*, 243–255.

Gordon, R. A. (1986, August). *IQ commensurability of black – white differences in crime and delinquency.* Paper presented at the meeting of the American Psychological Association, Washington, DC.

Gothard, S., Rogers, R., & Sewell, K. W. (1995). Feigning incompetency to stand trial: An investigation of the Georgia Court Competency Test. *Law and Human Behavior, 19*, 363–374.

Gothard, S., Viglione, D. J., Meloy, J. R., & Sherman, M. (1995). Detection of malingering in competency to stand trial evaluations. *Law and Human Behavior, 19*, 493–506.

Gottfredson, D., & Exum, M. (2002). The Baltimore city drug treatment court: One-year results from a randomized study. *Journal of Research in Crime and Delinquency, 39*, 337–356.

Gottfredson, D., Najaka, S., & Kearley, B. (2003). Effectiveness of drug courts: Evidence from a randomized trial. *Criminology & Public Policy, 2*, 171–196.

Gottfredson, L. (1986, August). *IQ versus training: Job performance and black – white occupational inequality.* Paper presented at the meeting of the American Psychological Association, Washington, DC.

Gould, J. (2011). *As California fights prison overcrowding, some see a golden opportunity.* Retrieved June 12, 2012, from http://www.time.com/time/nation/article/0,8599,2094840,00.html

Government Accountability Office. (2005). *Adult drug courts: Evidence indicates recidivism reductions and mixed results for other outcomes.* Washington, DC: Author.

Graham v. Florida, 130 S.Ct. 2011 (2010)

Gray, E. (1993). *Unequal justice: The prosecution of child sexual abuse.* New York, NY: Macmillan.

Gready, R., Ditto, P., Danks, J., Coppola, K., Lockhart, L., & Smucker, W. (2000). Actual and perceived stability of preferences for life-sustaining treatment. *Journal of Clinical Ethics, 11*, 334–346.

Greathouse, S., & Kovera, M. (2009). Instruction bias and lineup presentation moderate the effects of administrator knowledge on eyewitness identification. *Law and Human Behavior, 33*, 70–82.

Greely, H., & Illes, J. (2007). Neuroscience-based lie detection: The urgent need for regulation. *American Journal of Law and Medicine, 33*, 377–421.

Green, A. (2004, August 30). The waiting room: August. *The New Yorker*, pp. 37–38.

Green, S. (2005, January 31). When justice is delayed. *National Law Journal*, p. 22.

Greene, E. (1988). Judge's instructions on eyewitness testimony: Evaluation and revision. *Journal of Applied Social Psychology, 18*, 252–276.

Greene, E. (2002). How effective? Review of *Stack and sway: The new science of jury consulting. Judicature, 85*, 1–3.

Greene, E. (2008). "Can we talk?" Therapeutic jurisprudence, restorative justice, and tort litigation. In B. Bornstein & R. Wiener (Eds.), *Civil juries and civil justice: Empirical perspectives* (pp. 235–258). New York, NY: Springer.

Greene, E. (2009). Psychological issues in the civil trial. In J. Lieberman & D. Krauss (Eds.), *Jury psychology: Social aspects of trial processes. Vol. 1: Psychology of the Courtroom* (pp. 183–206). Burlington, VT: Ashgate.

Greene, E., & Bornstein, B. (2000). Precious little guidance: Jury instructions on damage awards. *Psychology, Public Policy, and Law, 6*, 743–768.

Greene, E., & Bornstein, B. (2003). *Determining damages: The psychology of jury awards.* Washington, DC: American Psychological Association.

Greene, E., Duke, L., & Woody, W. (2017). Stereotypes influence beliefs about transfer and sentencing of juvenile offenders. *Psychology, Crime, & Law*, Advance online publication.

Greene, E., Goodman, J., & Loftus, E. (1991). Jurors' attitudes about civil litigation and the size of damage awards. *American University Law Review, 40*, 805–820.

Greene, E., & Gordon, N. (2016). Can the "hot tub" enhance jurors' understanding and use of expert testimony? *Wyoming Law Review, 16*, 359–385.

Greene, E., Hayman, K., & Motyl, M. (2008). "Shouldn't we consider …?" Jury discussions of forbidden topics and effects on damage awards. *Psychology, Public Policy, and Law, 14*, 194–222.

Greene, E., & Heilbrun, K. (2015). Undergraduate education in psychology and law. In C. Willis-Esqueda & B. H. Bornstein (Eds.), *The witness stand and Lawrence S. Wrightsman, Jr.* (pp. 153–170). New York, NY: Springer.

Greene, E., Johns, M., & Smith, A. (2001). The effects of defendant conduct on jury damage awards. *Journal of Applied Psychology, 86*, 228–237.

Greene, E., & Loftus, E. (1985). When crimes are joined at trial. *Law and Human Behavior, 9*, 193–207.

Greene, J. A. (1999). Zero tolerance: A case study of police policies and practices in New York City. *Crime and Delinquency, 45*, 171–187.

Greenhouse, L. (1994, April 20). High court bars sex as standard of picking jurors. *The New York Times*, pp. A1, A10.

Gregg v. Georgia, 428 U.S. 153 (1976).

Gregory, W. L., Mowen, J. C., & Linder, D. E. (1978). Social psychology and plea bargaining: Applications, methodology, and theory. *Journal of Personality and Social Psychology, 36*, 1521–1530.

Greiner, D. J., & Matthews, A. (2016). Randomized control trials in the United States legal profession. *Annual Review of Law and Social Science, 12*, 295–312.

Grietens, H., & Hellinckx, W. (2004). Evaluating effects of residential treatment for juvenile offenders by statistical meta-analysis: A review. *Aggression and Violent Behavior, 9*, 401–415. doi:10.1016/S1359-1789(03)00043-0

Griffin, M. (2008, March). *Old dogs and new tricks: Demographic variables and interest in technology implementation in the courtroom.* Paper presented at the annual conference of American Psychology-Law Society, Jacksonville, FL.

Griffin, P. (2003). *Trying and sentencing juveniles as adults: An analysis of state transfer and blended sentencing laws.* Pittsburgh, PA: National Center for Juvenile Justice.

Griffin, P., Addie, S., Adams, B., & Firestine, K. (2011). Trying juveniles as adults: An analysis of state transfer laws and reporting. *Juvenile Offenders and Victims: National Report Series Bulletin.* Washington, DC: OJJDP, U.S. Department of Justice. Retrieved April 22, 2017, from https://www.ncjrs.gov/pdffiles1/ojjdp/232434.pdf

Griffin, P., Heilbrun, K., Mulvey, E., DeMatteo, D., & Schubert, C. (Eds.). (2015). *Criminal justice and the Sequential Intercept Model: Promoting community alternatives for people with severe mental illness.* New York, NY: Oxford University Press.

Grills-Taquechel, A., Littleton, H., & Axsom, D. (2011). Social support, world assumptions, and exposure as predictors of anxiety and quality of life following a mass trauma. *Journal of Anxiety Disorders, 25*, 498–506.

Grisso, T. (1986). *Evaluating competencies: Forensic assessments and instruments.* New York, NY: Plenum.

Grisso, T. (1998). *Forensic assessment of juveniles.* Sarasota, FL: Professional Resource Press.

Grisso, T. (2003). *Evaluating competencies: Forensic assessments and instruments* (2nd ed.). New York, NY: Kluwer/Plenum.

Grisso, T., & Appelbaum, P. (1998a). *Assessing competence to consent to treatment: A guide for physicians and other health professionals.* New York, NY: Oxford University Press.

Grisso, T., & Appelbaum, P. (1998b). *MacArthur competence assessment tool for treatment (MacCAT-T).* Sarasota, FL: Professional Resource Press.

Grisso, T., & Appelbaum, P. S. (1995). The MacArthur Treatment Competence Study. III: Abilities of patients to consent to psychiatric and medical treatments. *Law and Human Behavior, 19,* 149–174.

Grisso, T., Appelbaum, P. S., Mulvey, E. P., & Fletcher, K. (1995). The MacArthur Treatment Competence Study. II: Measures of abilities related to competence to consent to treatment. *Law and Human Behavior, 19,* 127–148.

Grisso, T., & Kavanaugh, A. (2016). Prospects for developmental evidence in juvenile sentencing based on Miller v. Alabama. *Psychology, Public Policy, and Law, 22,* 235–249.

Grisso, T., & Saks, M. J. (1991). Psychology's influence on constitutional interpretation: A comment on how to succeed. *Law and Human Behavior, 15,* 205–211.

Grisso, T., Steinberg, L., Woolard, J., Cauffman, E., Scott, E., Graham, S., … Schwartz, R. (2003). Juveniles' competence to stand trial: A comparison of adolescents' and adults' capacities as trial defendants. *Law and Human Behavior, 27,* 333–363.

Gromet, D., & Darley, J. (2006). Restoration and retribution: How including retributive components affects the acceptability of restorative justice procedures. *Social Justice Research, 19,* 395–432.

Gromet, D., Okimoto, T., Wenzel, M., & Darley, J. (2012). A victim-centered approach to justice? Victim satisfaction effects on third-party punishments. *Law and Human Behavior, 36,* 375–389.

Gross, S., Jacoby, K., Matheson, D., Montgomery, N., & Patil, S. (2005). Exonerations in the United States 1989 through 2003. *Journal of Criminal Law and Criminology, 95,* 523–560.

Gross, S., & O'Brien, B. (2008). Frequency and predictors of false conviction: Why we know so little, and new data on capital cases. *Journal of Empirical Legal Studies, 5,* 927–962.

Groth, A. N. (with Birnbaum, H. J.). (1979). *Men who rape.* New York, NY: Plenum.

Grove, W. M., & Barden, R. C. (1999). Protecting the integrity of the legal system: The admissibility of testimony from mental health experts under *Daubert/Kumho* analyses. *Psychology, Public Policy, and Law, 5,* 224–242.

Grych, J. H., & Fincham, F. D. (1992). Interventions for children of divorce: Toward greater integration of research and action. *Psychological Bulletin, 111,* 434–454.

Gudjonsson & Pearse (2011). Suspect interviews and false confessions. *Current Directions in Psychological Science, 20,* 33–37.

Gudjonsson (2010). The psychology of false confessions: A review of the current evidence. In G. D. Lassiter & C. Meissner (Eds.), *Police interrogations and false confessions* (pp. 31–47). Washington, DC: American Psychological Association.

Gudjonsson & Copson (1997). The role of the expert in criminal investigation. In J. L. Jackson & D. A. Bekerian (Eds.), *Offender profiling: Theory, research, and practice* (pp. 61–76). Chichester, UK: Wiley.

Gunnell, J., & Ceci, S. (2010). When emotionality trumps reason: A study of individual processing style and juror bias. *Behavioral Sciences and the Law, 28,* 850–877.

Gunnoe, M. L., & Braver, S. L. (2001). The effects of joint legal custody on mothers, fathers, and children, controlling for factors that predispose a sole maternal vs. joint legal award. *Law and Human Behavior, 25,* 25–43.

Gunter, G. (1985, January 25). Voices across the USA. *USA Today,* p. 12A.

Gutek, B. A., & O'Connor, M. (1995). The empirical basis for the reasonable woman standard. *Journal of Social Issues, 51,* 151–166.

Guthrie, C., Rachlinski, J., & Wistrich, A. (2001). Inside the judicial mind. *Cornell Law Review, 86,* 777–830.

Guthrie, C., Rachlinski, J. J., & Wistrich, A. J. (2009). The "hidden judiciary": An empirical examination of the executive branch of justice. *Duke Law Journal, 58,* 1477–1530.

Haarr, R. N. (2005). Factors affecting the decision of police recruits to "drop out" of police work. *Police Quarterly, 8,* 431–453.

Haas, S., & Hamilton, C. (2007, May). *The use of core correctional practices in offender reentry: The delivery of service delivery and prisoner preparedness for release.* Charleston, WV: Mountain State Criminal Justice Research Services.

Haby, J., & Brank, E. (2013). The role of anchoring in plea bargains. *APA Monitor, 44,* 30.

Hahn, R., & Kleist, D. (2000). Divorce mediation: Research and implications for family and couples counseling. *The Family Journal, 8,* 165–171.

Haj-Yahia, M. M. (2003). Beliefs about wife-beating among Arab men in Israel: The influence of their patriarchal ideology. *Journal of Family Violence, 18,* 193–206.

Hakuta, J., Soroushian, V., & Kralstein. (2008). *Do community courts transform the justice response to misdemeanor crime? Testing the impact of the Midtown Community Court.* New York, NY: Center for Court Innovation.

Hall v. Florida, 134 S. Ct. 1986 (2014).

Hall, G. C., & Hirschman, R. (1991). Toward a theory of sexual aggression: A quadripartite model. *Journal of Consulting and Clinical Psychology, 59,* 662–669.

Halligan, S. L., Michael, T., Clark, D. M., & Ehlers, A. (2003). Posttraumatic stress disorder following assault: The role of cognitive processing, trauma memory, and appraisals. *Journal of Consulting and Clinical Psychology, 71,* 419–431.

Hamilton, A. (2004, December 13). Woof, woof, your honor. *Time,* p. 46.

Haney, C. (2006). *Reforming punishment: Psychological limits to the pains of imprisonment.* Washington, DC: American Psychological Association.

Haney-Caron, E., & Heilbrun, K. (2014). Lesbian and gay parents and determination of child custody: The changing legal landscape and implications for policy and practice. *Psychology of Sexual Orientation and Gender Diversity, 1,* 19–29. doi:10.1037/sgd0000020

Hannaford, P., Hans, V., & Munsterman, G. T. (2000). Permitting jury discussions during trial: Impact of the Arizona reform. *Law and Human Behavior, 24,* 359–382.

Hans, V. P. (1992). Judgments of justice. *Psychological Science, 3,* 218–220.

Hans, V. P. (1996). The contested role of the civil jury in business litigation. *Judicature, 79,* 242–248.

Hans, V. P., Blume, J. H, Eisenberg, T., Hritz, A. C., Johnson, S. L., Royer, C. E., & Wells, M. T. (2015). The death penalty: Should the judge or the jury decide who dies? *Journal of Empirical Legal Studies, 12,* 70–99.

Hans, V. P., Fukurai, H., Ivkovic, S., & Park, J. (2017). Global juries: A plan for research. In M. Kovera (Ed.), *The psychology of juries* (pp. 131–158). Washington, DC: APA.

Hans, V. P., & Reyna, V. F. (2011). To dollars from sense: Qualitative to quantitative translation in jury damage awards. *Journal of Empirical Legal Studies, 8,* 120–147.

Hans, V. P., & Vidmar, N. (1986). *Judging the jury.* New York, NY: Plenum.

Hans, V. P., & Vidmar, N. (1991). The American jury at twenty-five years. *Law and Social Inquiry, 16,* 323–351.

Hansen, C. (2004). Filing a flight plan: Policy and social change to address sexual violence in the military. *Sexual Assault Report, 7,* 60–62.

Hansen, M. (1999, April). Mandatories going, going … going. *American Bar Association Journal, 85,* 14.

Hanson, R., Bourgon, G., Helmus, L., & Hodgson, S. (2009). The principles of effective correctional treatment also apply to sexual offenders: A meta-analysis. *Criminal Justice and Behavior, 36,* 865–891.

Hanson, R. K., & Morton-Bourgon, K. E. (2009). The accuracy of recidivism risk assessment for sexual offenders: A meta-analysis of 188 prediction studies. *Psychological Assessment, 21,* 1–21.

Hanson, S. S. and Doukas, D. J. (2009). Advance directives. In V. Ravitsky, A. Fiester, & A. Caplan (Eds.), *The Penn Center Guide to Bioethics* (pp. 749–760). New York, NY: Springer.

Harding, T., & Zimmerman, E. (1989). Psychiatric symptoms, cognitive stress and vulnerability factors: A study in a remand prison. *British Journal of Psychiatry, 155,* 36–43.

Hare, R. D. (2003). *The Hare Psychopathy Checklist—Revised (PCL-R)* (2nd ed.). Toronto, ON: Multi-Health Systems.

Hare, R. D., & Neumann, C. (2008). Psychopathy as a clinical and empirical construct. *Annual Review of Clinical Psychology, 4,* 217–246.

Hare, T. A., O'Doherty, J., Camerer, C. F., Schultz, W., & Rangel, A. (2008). Dissociating the role of the orbitofrontal cortex and the striatum in the computation of goal values and prediction errors. *Journal of Neuroscience, 28,* 5623–5630.

Harpold, J. A., & Feemster, S. L. (2002). Negative influences of police stress. *FBI Law Enforcement Bulletin, 71*(9), 1–7. Retrieved July 18, 2005, from http://www.fbi.gov/publications/leb/2002/sept2002/sept02leb.htm#page_2

Harrington v. Iowa, 659 NW 2d 509 (Iowa, 2003).

Harris Interactive and GLSEN. (2005). *From teasing to torment: School climate in America, a survey of students and teachers.* New York, NY: GLSEN. Downloaded from http://www.des.emory.edu/mfp/302/302GLSEN2.pdf

Harris v. Forklift Systems, Inc., 510 U.S. 17 (1993).

Harris v. New York, 401 U.S. 222 (1971).

Harris, A., Walfield, S., Shields, R., & LeTourneau, E. (2016). Collateral consequences of juvenile sex offender registration and notification: Results from a survey of treatment providers. *Sexual Abuse: A Journal of Research and Treatment, 38,* 770–790.

Harris, G. T., Rice, M. E., & Quinsey, V. L. (1993). Violent recidivism of mentally disordered offenders: The development of a statistical prediction instrument. *Criminal Justice and Behavior, 20,* 315–335.

Harris, K. (2009, June 26). *San Francisco DA: 'Back on Track' saves money and reduces crime.* Retrieved from http://www.latimes.com/news/opinion/opinionla/la-oew-harris26-2009jun26,0,73758.story

Harris, L., Block, S., Ogle, C., Goodman, G., Augusti, E., Larson, R., … Urquiza, A. (2016). Coping style and memory specificity in adolescents and adults with histories of child sexual abuse. *Memory, 24,* 1078–1090.

Harrison, P., & Beck, A. J. (2002). *Prisoners in 2001. Bureau of Justice Statistics Bulletin.* Washington, DC: U.S. Department of Justice.

Harrison, P. M., & Karberg, J. C. (2003, April). *Prison and jail inmates at midyear 2002. Bureau of Justice Statistics Bulletin.* Washington, DC: U.S. Department of Justice.

Hartley, R. (2008). Dedication for the special issue on problem-solving courts. *Criminal Justice Review, 33,* 289–290.

Hartwig, M. (2011). Methods in deception detection research. In B. Rosenfeld & S. Penrod (Eds.), *Research methods in forensic psychology* (pp. 136–155). Hoboken, NJ: Wiley.

Hartwig, M., & Bond, C. (2014). Lie detection from multiple cues: A meta-analysis. *Applied Cognitive Psychology, 28,* 661–676.

Hartwig, M., Granhag, P., & Luke, T. (2014). Strategic use of evidence during investigative interviews: The state of the science. In D. Raskin,

C. Honts, & J. Kircher (Eds.), *Credibility assessment: Scientific research and applications.* (pp. 1–36). Waltham, MA: Academic Press.

Hasemann, D. (1997). *Practices and findings of mental health professionals conducting workers' compensation evaluations.* Unpublished doctoral dissertation, University of Kentucky, Lexington, KY.

Hassell, K. D., & Brandl, S. G. (2009). An examination of the workplace experiences of police patrol officers: The role of race, sex, and sexual orientation. *Police Quarterly, 12,* 408–430. doi:10.1177/1098611109348473

Hastie, R. (1991). Is attorney-conducted voir dire an effective procedure for the selection of impartial juries? *American University Law Review, 40,* 703–726.

Hastie, R. (2008). What's the story? Explanations and narratives in civil jury decisions. In B. H. Bornstein, R. L. Wiener, R. Schopp, & S. L. Willborn (Eds.), *Civil juries and civil justice: Psychological and legal perspectives* (pp. 23–34). New York, NY: Springer-Verlag.

Hastie, R., & Pennington, N. (1996). The O. J. Simpson stories: Behavioral scientists' reflections on *The People of the State of California v. Orenthal James Simpson. University of Colorado Law Review, 67,* 957–975.

Hastie, R., Penrod, S. D., & Pennington, N. (1983). *Inside the jury.* Cambridge, MA: Harvard University Press.

Hastie, R., Schkade, D. A., & Payne, J. W. (1998). A study of juror and jury judgments in civil cases: Deciding liability for punitive damages. *Law and Human Behavior, 22,* 287–314.

Hatch, D. E. (2002). *Officer-involved shootings and use of force: Practical investigative techniques.* Boca Raton, FL: CRC.

Hatcher, C., Mohandie, K., Turner, J., & Gelles, M. G. (1998). The role of the psychologist in crisis/hostage negotiations. *Behavioral Sciences & the Law, 16,* 455–472.

Hauch, V., Sporer, S., Michael, S., & Meissner, C. (2016). Does training improve the detection of deception? A meta-analysis. *Communication Research, 43,* 283–343.

Haugaard, J. J., & Avery, R. J. (2002). Termination of parental rights to free children for adoption: Conflicts between parents, children, and the state. In B. Bottoms, M. Kovera, & B. McAuliff (Eds.), *Children, social policy, and U.S. Law* (pp. 131–152). Boston: Cambridge University Press.

Haw, R., & Fisher, R. (2004). Effects of administrator—witness contact on eyewitness identification accuracy. *Journal of Applied Psychology, 89,* 1106–1112.

Hawkins, H. C. (2001). Police officer burnout: A partial replication of Maslach's burnout inventory. *Police Quarterly, 4,* 343–360.

Hazelwood, R. R., & Douglas, J. E. (1980). The lust murderer. *FBI Law Enforcement Bulletin, 49,* 18–22.

Hazelwood, R. R., & Michaud, S. (2001). *Dark dreams.* New York, NY: Macmillan.

Hazelwood, R. R., Ressler, R. K., Depue, R. L., & Douglas, J. C. (1995). Criminal investigative analysis: An overview. In A. W. Burgess & R. R. Hazelwood (Eds.), *Practical aspects of rape investigation: A multidisciplinary approach* (2nd ed., pp. 115–126). Boca Raton, FL: CRC.

Heider, F. (1958). *The psychology of interpersonal relations.* New York, NY: Wiley.

Heilbrun, K. (1987). The assessment of competency for execution: An overview. *Behavioral Sciences & the Law, 5,* 383–396.

Heilbrun, K. (2001). *Principles of forensic mental health assessment.* New York, NY: Kluwer Academic/Plenum.

Heilbrun, K. (2009). *Evaluation for risk of violence in adults.* New York, NY: Oxford University Press.

Heilbrun, K., & Brooks, S. (2010). Forensic psychology and forensic science: A proposed agenda for the next decade. *Psychology, Public Policy, and Law, 16,* 219–253.

Heilbrun, K., DeMatteo, D., Brooks-Holliday, S., & LaDuke, C. (Eds.). (2014). *Forensic mental health assessment: A casebook* (2nd ed.). New York, NY: Oxford University Press.

Heilbrun, K., DeMatteo, D., King, C., & Filone, S. (2017). *Evaluating juvenile transfer and disposition: Law, science, and practice.* New York, NY: Routledge.

Heilbrun, K., DeMatteo, D., Yasuhara, K., Brooks Holliday, S., Shah, S., King, C., … Laduke, C. (2012). Community-based alternatives for justice-involved individuals with severe mental illness: Review of the relevant research. *Criminal Justice and Behavior, 39*, 351–419.

Heilbrun, K., Douglas, K., & Yasuhara, K. (2009). Violence risk assessment: Core controversies. In J. Skeem, K. Douglas, & S. Lilienfeld (Eds.), *Psychological science in the courtroom: Controversies and consensus* (pp. 333–357). New York, NY: Guilford.

Heilbrun, K., Dvoskin, J., & Heilbrun, A. (2009). Mass killings on college campuses: Public health, threat/risk assessment, and preventing future tragedies. *Psychological Injury and Law, 2*, 93–99.

Heilbrun, K., Goldstein, N., DeMatteo, D., Hart, A., Riggs Romaine, C., & Shah, S. (2011). Interventions in forensic settings: Juveniles in residential placement, defendants in drug courts or mental health courts, and defendants in forensic hospitals as Incompetent to Stand Trial. In Barlow, D. (Ed.), *Oxford handbook of clinical psychology* (pp. 649–679). New York, NY: Oxford University Press.

Heilbrun, K., Grisso, T., & Goldstein, A. (2009). *Foundations of forensic mental health assessment.* New York, NY: Oxford University Press.

Heilbrun, K., Heilbrun, P., & Griffin, N. (1988). Comparing females acquitted by reason of insanity, convicted, and civilly committed in Florida: 1977–1984. *Law and Human Behavior, 12*, 295–312.

Heilbrun, K., Lee, R., & Cottle, C. (2005). Risk factors and intervention outcomes: Meta-analyses of juvenile offending. In K. Heilbrun, N. Sevin-Goldstein, & R. Redding (Eds.), *Juvenile delinquency: Prevention, assessment, and intervention* (pp. 111–133). New York, NY: Oxford University Press.

Heilbrun, K., & McClaren, H. (1988). Assessment of competency for execution? A guide for mental health professionals. *Bulletin of the American Academy of Psychiatry and the Law, 16*, 206–216.

Heise, M. (2004). Criminal case complexity: An empirical perspective. *Journal of Empirical Legal Studies, 1*, 331–369.

Helm, R. K., & Reyna, V. F. (2017). Logical but incompetent plea decisions: A new approach to plea bargaining grounded in cognitive theory. *Psychology, Public Policy, and Law*, update pagination

Henderson, K., & Levett, L. (2016). Can expert testimony sensitize jurors to variations in confession evidence? *Law and Human Behavior, 40*, 638–649.

Henggeler, S. (2016). Community-based interventions for juvenile offenders. In K. Heilbrun, D. DeMatteo, & N. Goldstein (Eds.), *APA handbook of psychology and juvenile justice* (pp. 575–595). Washington, DC: American Psychological Association.

Henggeler, S., Clingempeel, W., Brondino, M., & Pickrel, S. (2002). Four-year follow-up of multi-systemic therapy with substance-abusing and substance-dependent juvenile offenders. *Journal of the American Academy of Child and Adolescent Psychiatry, 41*, 868–874.

Henggeler, S., Melton, G., Brondino, M., Scherer, D., & Hanley, J. (1997). Multisystemic therapy with violent and chronic juvenile offenders and their families: The role of treatment fidelity in successful dissemination. *Journal of Consulting and Clinical Psychology, 65*, 821–833.

Henggeler, S., Melton, G., & Smith, L. (1992). Family preservation using multisystemic therapy: An effective alternative to incarcerating serious juvenile offenders. *Journal of Consulting and Clinical Psychology, 60*, 953–961.

Henggeler, S., Melton, G., Smith, L., Schoenwald, S., & Hanley, J. (1993). Family preservation using multi-systemic treatment: Long-term follow-up to a clinical trial with serious juvenile offenders. *Journal of Child and Family Studies, 2*, 283–293.

Henggeler, S., Pickrel, S. G., & Brondino, M. J. (1999). Multisystemic treatment of substance abusing and dependent delinquents: Outcomes,

treatment fidelity, and transportability. *Mental Health Services Research, 1*, 171–184.

Henggeler, S., Pickrel, S. G., Brondino, M. J., & Crouch, J. (1996). Eliminating (almost) treatment dropout of substance abusing or dependent delinquents through home-based multisystemic therapy. *American Journal of Psychiatry, 153*, 427–428.

Henggeler, S., Rodick, J., Borduin, C., Hanson, C., Watson, S., & Urey, J. (1986). Multisystemic treatment of juvenile offenders: Effects on adolescent behavior and family interaction. *Developmental Psychology, 22*, 132–141.

Henggeler, S., Rowland, M., Randall, J., Ward, D., Pickrel, S., Cunningham, P., … Santos, A. (1999). Home-based multisystemic therapy as an alternative to the hospitalization of youths in psychiatric crisis: Clinical outcomes. *Journal of the American Academy of Child and Adolescent Psychiatry, 38*, 1331–1339.

Henggeler, S., & Schoenwald, S. K. (1999). The role of quality assurance in achieving outcomes in MST programs. *Journal of Juvenile Justice and Detention Services, 14*, 1–17.

Henggeler, S., Schoenwald, S. K., Borduin, C. M., Rowland, M. D., & Cunningham, P. B. (1998). *Multisystemic treatment of antisocial behavior in children and adolescents.* New York, NY: Guilford.

Henggeler, S., Sheidow, A., & Lee, T. (2010). Multisystem therapy. In J. Bray & M. Stanton (Eds.), *The Wiley-Blackwell handbook of family psychology*. Retrieved January 15, 2010, from http://onlinelibrary.wiley.com/book/10.1002/9781444310238

Henry, M., & Rafilson, F. (1997). The temporal stability of the National Police Officer Selection Test. *Psychological Reports, 81*, 1259–1265.

Herbert, B. (2010, March 2). *Watching certain people.* Retrieved July 13, 2012, from http://www.nytimes.com/2010/03/02/opinion/02herbert.html

Herinckx, H., Swart, S., Ama, S., Dolezal, C., & King, S. (2005). Rearrest and linkage to mental health services among clients of the Clark County Mental Health Court Program. *Psychiatric Services, 56*, 853–857.

Hersch, J., & Viscusi, W. (2004). Punitive damages: How judges and juries perform. *Journal of Legal Studies, 33*, 1–36.

Hershkowitz, I., Lamb, M., Orbach, Y., Katz, C., & Horowitz, D. (2012). The development of communicative and narrative skills among preschoolers: Lessons from forensic interviews about child abuse. *Child Development, 83*, 611–622.

Hetherington, E., & Kelly, J. (2002). *For better or worse: Divorce reconsidered.* New York, NY: Norton.

Hetherington, E. M., Cox, M., & Cox, R. (1982). Effects of divorce on parents and children. In M. Lamb (Ed.), *Non-traditional families* (pp. 223–288). Hillsdale, NJ: Erlbaum.

Hickey, E. (2009). *Serial murderers and their victims.* Belmont, CA: Wadsworth.

Hickman, M. J., & Reaves, B. A. (2001, revised March 27, 2003). *Community policing in local police departments, 1997 and 1999.* Special Report, U.S. Department of Justice, Office of Justice Programs, NCJ 184794, 1–11.

Hiday, V. A., & Goodman, R. R. (1982). The least restrictive alternative to involuntary hospitalization, outpatient commitment: Its use and effectiveness. *Journal of Psychiatry and Law, 10*, 81–96.

Hiday, V. A., & Ray, B. (2010). Arrests two years after a well-established mental health court. *Psychiatric Services, 61*, 463–468.

Higgins, M. (1999, March). Tough luck for the innocent man. *ABA Journal, 85*, 46–52.

Hill, C., Memon, A., & McGeorge, P. (2008). The role of confirmation bias in suspect interviews: A systematic evaluation. *Legal and Criminological Psychology, 13*, 357–371.

Hille, C. A. (2010). Law enforcement-related stress and relationship satisfaction. *Dissertation Abstracts International Section A: Humanities and Social Sciences, 71* (2–A), 729.

Hillebrandt, A., & Barclay, L. (2017). Comparing integral and incidental emotions: Testing insights from emotions as social information theory and attribution theory. *Journal of Applied Psychology*, update pagination

Hilton, N., Harris, G., Rice, M., Lang, C., & Cormier, C. (2004). A brief actuarial assessment for the prediction of wife assault recidivism: The ODARA. *Psychological Assessment, 16*, 267–275.

Ho, B., & Liu, E. (2011). What's an apology worth? Decomposing the effect of apologies on medical malpractice payments using state apology laws. *Journal of Empirical Legal Studies, 8*, 179–199.

Ho, T. (2001). The interrelationships of psychological testing, psychologists' recommendations, and police departments' recruitment decisions. *Police Quarterly, 4*, 318–342.

Hobbs, S., Goodman, G., Block, S., Oran, D., Quas, J., Park, A., … Baumrind, N. (2014). Child maltreatment victims' attitudes about appearing in dependency and criminal courts. *Child and Youth Services Review, 44*, 407–416.

Hoff, R., Baranosky, M., Buchanan, J., Zonana, H., & Rosenheck, R. (1999). The effects of a jail diversion program on incarceration: A retrospective cohort study. *Journal of the American Academy of Psychiatry and the Law, 27*, 377–386.

Hoffberger, C. (2013, August 16). Seale and Balko visit peaceful streets. Police watchers aim to educate public on citizens' rights. *The Austin Chronicle*. Retrieved from http://www.austinchronicle.com/news/2013-08-16/seale-and-balko-visit-peaceful-streets/

Hoffman, D. (2011). Mediation and the art of shuttle diplomacy. *Negotiation Journal, 27*, 263–309.

Hoffman, J. (2014, October 13). In interrogations, teenagers are too young to know better. Retrieved from https://well.blogs.nytimes.com/2014/10/13/in-interrogations-teenagers-are-too-young-to-know-better/

Hoffman, P. B., & Stone-Meierhoefer, B. (1979). Application of guidelines to sentencing. In L. E. Abt & I. R. Stuart (Eds.), *Social psychology and discretionary law* (pp. 241–258). New York, NY: Van Nostrand Reinhold.

Hoge, R. (2016). Risk, need, and responsivity in juveniles. In K. Heilbrun, D. DeMatteo, & N. Goldstein (Eds.), *APA handbook of psychology and juvenile justice* (pp. 179–196). Washington, DC: American Psychological Association. doi:10.1037/14643-009

Hoge, R., & Andrews, D. (2002). *The Youth Level of Service/Case Management Inventory (YLS/CMI) user's manual*. North Tonawanda, NY: Multi-Health Systems.

Hoge, S. K., Bonnie, R. J., Poythress, N., Monahan, J., Eisenberg, M., & Feucht-Haviar, T. (1997). The MacArthur adjudicative competence study: Development and validation of a research instrument. *Law and Human Behavior, 21*, 141–179.

Hoge, S. K., Poythress, N., Bonnie, R., Monahan, J., Eisenberg, M., & Feucht-Haviar, T. (1997). The MacArthur adjudicative competence study: Diagnosis, psychopathology, and competence-related abilities. *Behavioral Sciences & the Law, 15*, 329–345.

Hogg, A., & Wilson, C. (1995). *Is the psychological screening of police applicants a realistic goal? The successes and failures of psychological screening*. Payneham, Australia: National Police Research Unit. (National Police Research Unit Report Series No. 124).

Holbrook, J., & Anderson, S. (2011). *Veterans courts: Early outcomes and key indicators of success*. Widener Law School Legal Series Research Paper. Retrieved December 23, 2016, from http://ssrn.com/abstract=1912655

Hollander-Blumoff, R., & Tyler, T. (2008). Procedural justice in negotiation: Procedural fairness, outcome acceptance, and integrative potential. *Law and Social Inquiry, 33*, 473–500.

Holmes, M. D., & Smith, B. W. (2008). *Race and police brutality*. Albany, NY: SUNY Press.

Holmes, O. (1881). *The common law*. Boston, MA: Little, Brown.

Holmes, R. M., & DeBurger, J. (1988). *Serial murder*. Newbury Park, CA: Sage.

Homant, R. J., & Kennedy, D. B. (1998). Psychological aspects of crime scene profiling. *Criminal Justice and Behavior, 25*, 319–343.

Honegger, L. (2015). Does the evidence support the case for mental health courts? A review of the literature. *Law and Human Behavior, 39*, 478–488.

Honts, C., & Kircher, J. (2011). Research methods for psychophysiological deception detection. In B. Rosenfeld & S. Penrod (Eds.), *Research methods in forensic psychology* (pp. 105–121). Hoboken, NJ: Wiley.

Honts, C. (2004). The psychophysiological detection of deception. In P. Granhag & L. Stromwell (Eds.), *Detection of deception in forensic contexts* (pp. 103–123). London: Cambridge University Press.

Hope, L., & Wright, D. (2007). Beyond unusual? Examining the role of attention in the weapon focus effect. *Applied Cognitive Psychology, 21*, 951–961.

Hopt v. Utah, 110 U.S. 574 (1884).

Horgan, J. (2011). Code rage: The "warrior gene" makes me mad! (Whether I have it or not.) *Scientific American*. Retrieved October 20, 2016, from https://blogs.scientificamerican.com/cross-check/code-rage-the-warrior-gene-makes-me-mad-whether-i-have-it-or-not/

Horan, J., & Maine, S. (2014). Criminal jury trials in 2030: A law odyssey. *Journal of Law and Society, 41*, 551–575.

Horowitz, I. A. (1980). Juror selection: A comparison of two methods in several criminal cases. *Journal of Applied Social Psychology, 10*, 86–99.

Horowitz, M. (1986). *Stress response syndromes* (2nd ed.). New York, NY: Aronson.

Horry, R., Halford, P., Brewer, N., Milne, R., & Bull, R. (2014). Archival analyses of eyewitness identification test outcomes: What can they tell us about eyewitness memory? *Law and Human Behavior, 38*, 94–108.

Horwitz, A., Widom, C. S., McLaughlin, J., & White, H. (2001). The impact of childhood abuse and neglect on adult mental health: A prospective study. *Journal of Health and Social Behavior, 42*, 184–201.

Hotelling, K. (1991). Sexual harassment: A problem shielded by silence. *Journal of Counseling and Development, 69*, 497–501.

Houppert, K. (2007). *Deluded judge suggests domestic violence victim wanted to be hit*. Retrieved February 21, 2009, from http://www.alternet.org/blogs/peek/66153/

Howard, R. C., & Clark, C. R. (1985). When courts and experts disagree: Discordance between insanity recommendations and adjudications. *Law and Human Behavior, 9*, 385–395.

Huber, G., & Gordon, S. (2004). Accountability and coercion: Is justice blind when it runs for office? *American Journal of Political Science, 48*, 247–263.

Huesmann, L. R., Eron, L. D., Lefkowitz, M. M., & Walder, L. O. (1984). Stability of aggression over time and generations. *Developmental Psychology, 20*, 1120–1134.

Huesmann, L. R., Eron, L. D., & Yarmel, P. W. (1987). Intellectual functioning and aggression. *Journal of Personality and Social Psychology, 52*, 232–240.

Huesmann, L. R., Moise-Titus, J., Podolski, C., & Eron, L. D. (2003). Longitudinal relations between children's exposure to TV violence and their aggressive and violent behavior in young adulthood: 1977–1992. *Developmental Psychology, 39*, 201–221.

Hunt, J. (2015). Race, ethnicity, and culture in jury decision making. *Annual Review of Law and Social Science, 11*, 269–288.

Hunt, J. S. (2015). Race in the justice system. In B. L. Cutler & P. A. Zapf (Eds.), *APA Handbook of forensic psychology: Vol. 2. Criminal investigation, adjudication, and sentencing outcomes* (pp. 125–161). Washington, DC: APA.

Hunt, J. S., & Budesheim, T. L. (2004). How jurors use and misuse character evidence. *Journal of Applied Psychology, 89*, 347–361.

Ilies, R., Hauserman, N., Schwochau, S., & Stibal, J. (2003). Reported incidence rates of work-related sexual harassment in the United States: Using meta-analysis to explain reported rate disparities. *Personnel Psychology, 56,* 607–631. doi:10.1111/j.1744-6570.2003. tb00752.x

Imwinkelried, E. J. (1994). The next step after *Daubert*: Developing a similarly epistemological approach to ensuring the reliability of non-scientific expert testimony. *Cardozo Law Review, 15,* 2271–2294.

In re Corrugated Container Antitrust Litigation, 614 F2d 958 (5th Circuit, 1980).

In re Gault, 387 U.S. 1 (1967).

Inbau, F. E., Reid, J. E., Buckley, J. P., & Jayne, B. C. (2013). *Criminal interrogation and confessions* (5th ed.). Burlington, MA: Jones & Bartlett Learning.

Innocence Project. (2015). *Eyewitness misidentification.* Retrieved from http://www.innocenceproject.org/understand/Eyewitness-Misidentification.php

Insabella, G., Williams, T., & Pruett, M. K. (2003). Individual and co-parenting differences between divorcing and unmarried fathers: Implications for court services. *Family Court Review, 41,* 290–306.

International Association of Chiefs of Police. (2006). *Building an offender reentry program: A guide for law enforcement.* Washington, DC: U.S. Bureau of Justice Assistance.

International Association of Chiefs of Police. (2013). *Psychological fitness-for-duty guidelines.* Retrieved March 24, 2017, from http://www.theiacp.org/portals/0/documents/pdfs/psych-fitnessfordutyevaluation.pdf

International Association of Chiefs of Police. (2016). *Discover policing.* Retrieved October 27, 2016, from http://discoverpolicing.org

Inwald, R. (1988). *Hilson personnel profile/success quotient technical manual.* Savoy, IL: Institute for Personality & Ability Testing.

Inwald, R. (1992). *Inwald Personality Inventory technical manual* (Rev. ed.). Kew Gardens, NY: Hilson Research.

Inwald, R. (2008). The Inwald Personality Inventory (IPI) and Hilson Research Inventories: Development and rationale. *Aggression and Violent Behavior, 13,* 298–327.

Inwald, R., Knatz, H., & Shusman, E. (1983). *Inwald Personality Inventory manual.* New York, NY: Hilson Research.

Irwin, J. (1970). *The felon.* Englewood Cliffs, NJ: Prentice Hall.

J.D.B. v. North Carolina, 131 S.Ct. 2394 (2011)

J.E.B. v. Alabama ex rel. T.B., 511 U.S. 127 (1994).

Jackson v. Indiana, 406 U.S. 715 (1972).

Jackson, R. L., Rogers, R., & Sewell, K. W. (2005). Forensic applications of the Miller Forensic Assessment of Symptoms Test (MFAST): Screening for feigned disorders in competency to stand trial evaluations. *Law and Human Behavior, 29,* 199–210.

Jacobson, J., Dobbs-Marsh, J., Liberman, V., & Minson, J. (2011). Predicting civil jury verdicts: How attorneys use (and misuse) a second opinion. *Journal of Empirical Legal Studies, 8,* 99–119.

Jeffers, H. P. (1991). *Who killed Precious?* New York, NY: Pharos.

Johnson v. Zerbst, 304 U.S. 458 (1938).

Johnson, R. (2006). Confounding influences on police detection of suspiciousness. *Journal of Criminal Justice, 34,* 435–442.

Jonakait, R. N. (2003). *The American jury system.* New Haven, CT: Yale University Press.

Jones, A. M., Bergold, A. N., Dillon, M. K., & Penrod, S. D. (2017). Comparing the effectiveness of Henderson instructions and expert testimony: Which safeguard improves jurors' evaluations of eyewitness evidence? *Journal of Experimental Criminology, 13,* 29–52.

Jones, C., Stalker, K., Franklin, A., Fry, D., Cameron, A., & Taylor, J. (2017). Enablers of help-seeking for deaf and disabled children following abuse and barriers to protection: A qualitative study. *Child and Family Social Work, 22,* 762–771.

Jones, J. S., Wynn, B. N., Kroeze, B., Dunnuck, C., & Rossman, L. (2004). Comparison of sexual assaults by strangers versus known assailants in a community-based population. *American Journal of Emergency Medicine, 22,* 454–459.

Jordan, K. L., & McNeal, B. A. (2016). Juvenile penalty or leniency: Sentencing of juveniles in the criminal justice system. *Law and Human Behavior, 40*(4), 387–400.

Judicial Council of California. (2004). *Final report: Task force on jury system improvements.* San Francisco, CA: Author.

Justice Education Center, Inc. (2002). *Evaluation of the Hartford Community Court.* Hartford, CT: Author.

Kadri, S. (2005). *The trial: A history, from Socrates to O. J. Simpson.* New York, NY: Random House.

Kaeble, D., & Glaze, L. (2016). *Correctional populations in the United States, 2015.* Bureau of Justice Statistics. Retrieved from http://www.bjs.gov/index.cfm?ty=pbdetail&iid=5870

Kaeble, D., Glaze, L., Tsoutis, A., & Minton, T. (2015). *Correctional populations in the United States, 2014.* Washington, DC: Bureau of Justice Statistics. Retrieved December 23, 2016, from http://www.bjs.gov/index.cfm?ty=pbdetail&iid=5480

Kahan, D. (1996). What do alternative sanctions mean? *University of Chicago Law Review, 63,* 591–653.

Kahan, D. (2006). What's really wrong with shaming sanctions. *Texas Law Review, 84,* 2075–2095.

Kahan, D., Hoffman, D., Braman, D., Evans, D., & Rachlinski, J. (2012). They saw a protest: Cognitive illiberalism and the speech-conduct distinction. *Stanford Law Review, 64,* 851–906.

Kahneman, D. (2011). *Thinking, fast and slow.* New York, NY: Farrar, Straus, & Giroux.

Kairys, D. (1972). Juror selection: The law, a mathematical method of analysis, and a case study. *American Criminal Law Review, 10,* 771–806.

Kalven, H., & Zeisel, H. (1966). *The American jury.* Boston, MA: Little, Brown.

Kamisar, Y., LaFave, W. R., & Israel, J. (1999). *Basic criminal procedure: Cases, comments and questions.* St. Paul, MN: West.

Kamradt, B. J. (2000). Wraparound Milwaukee: Aiding youth with mental health needs. *Juvenile Justice Journal, 7,* 14–23.

Kane, A., & Dvoskin, J. (2011). *Evaluation for personal injury claims.* New York, NY: Oxford University Press.

Kang, H., Natelson, B., Mahan, C., Lee, K., & Murphy, F. (2003). Post–traumatic stress disorder and chronic fatigue syndrome-like illness among Gulf War veterans: A population-based survey of 30,000 veterans. *American Journal of Epidemiology, 157,* 141–148.

Kang, M., & Shepherd, J. (2011). The partisan price of justice: An empirical analysis of campaign contributions and judicial decisions. *New York University Law Review, 86,* 69–130.

Kansas v. Crane, 534 U.S. 407 (2002).

Kansas v. Hendricks, 117 S. Ct. 2013 (1997).

Kaplan, J. (1996). *Criminal law.* Boston, MA: Little, Brown.

Kaplan, M. F., & Miller, C. E. (1987). Group decision making and normative v. informational influence: Effects of type of issue and decision rule. *Journal of Personality and Social Psychology, 53,* 306–313.

Kaplow, J., & Widom, C. S. (2007). Age of onset of child maltreatment predicts long-term mental health outcomes. *Journal of Abnormal Psychology, 116,* 176–187.

Kar, R., & Mazzone, J. (2016). The Garland affair: What history and the Constitution *really* say about President Obama's powers to appoint a replacement for Justice Scalia. *New York University Law Review, 91,* 53–114.

Karlsen, C. (1989). *The devil in the shape of a woman: Witchcraft in colonial New England.* New York, NY: W.W. Norton & Co.

Kassin, S. (2005). On the psychology of confessions: Does innocence put innocents at risk? *American Psychologist, 60,* 215–228.

Kassin, S. (2012). Why confessions trump innocence. *American Psychologist, 67,* 431–445.

Kassin, S., Drizin, S., Grisso, T., Gudjonsson, G., Leo, R., & Redlich, A. (2009). Police-induced false confessions: Risk factors and recommendations. *Law and Human Behavior.* Published online July 15, 2009. doi:10.1007/s10979.009-9188-6

Kassin, S., Drizin, S., Grisso, T., Gudjonsson, G., Leo, R., & Redlich, A. (2010). Police-induced confessions: Risk factors and recommendations. *Law and Human Behavior, 34,* 3–38.

Kassin, S., Kukucka, J., Lawson, V., & DeCarlo, J. (2014). Does video recording alter the behavior of police during interrogation? A mock crime-and-investigation study. *Law and Human Behavior, 38,* 73–83.

Kassin, S., Leo, R., Meissner, C., Richman, K., Colwell, L., Leach, A., & La Fon, D. (2007). Police interviewing and interrogation: A self-report survey of police practices and beliefs. *Law and Human Behavior, 31,* 381–400.

Kassin, S., & Neumann, K. (1997). On the power of confession evidence: An experimental test of the "fundamental difference" hypothesis. *Law and Human Behavior, 21,* 469–484.

Kassin, S., & Norwick, R. (2004). Why suspects waive their *Miranda* rights: The power of innocence. *Law and Human Behavior, 28,* 211–221.

Kassin, S., & Gudjonsson, G. (2004). The psychology of confessions: A review of the literature and issues. *Psychological Science in the Public Interest, 5,* 33–67.

Kassin, S., Kukucka, J., Lawson, V. Z., & DeCarlo, J. (2017). Police reports of mock suspect interrogations: A test of accuracy and perception. *Law and Human Behavior, 41,* 230–243.

Kassin, S., & Wrightsman, L. S. (1983). The construction and validation of a juror bias scale. *Journal of Research in Personality, 17,* 423–442.

Kassin, S., & Wrightsman, L. S. (1985). Confession evidence. In S. M. Kassin & L. S. Wrightsman (Eds.), *The psychology of evidence and trial procedure* (pp. 67–94). Newbury Park, CA: Sage.

Katz, J. (1988). *Seductions of crime.* New York, NY: Basic Books.

Kebbell, M., & Milne, R. (1998). Police officers' perception of eyewitness factors in forensic investigations. *Journal of Social Psychology, 138,* 323–330.

Keene, B. (1997). Chemical castration: An analysis of Florida's new "cutting-edge" policy towards sex criminals. *Florida Law Review, 49,* 803–820.

Keilin, W. G., & Bloom, L. J. (1986). Child custody evaluation practices: A survey of experienced professionals. *Professional Psychology, Research and Practice, 17,* 338–346.

Keilitz, S. (2004). *Specialization of domestic violence case management in the courts: A national survey.* Washington, DC: United States Department of Justice. Retrieved from https://www.ncjrs.gov/pdffiles1/nij/199724.pdf

Kelly, C., Miller, J., & Redlich, A. (2016). The dynamic nature of interrogation. *Law and Human Behavior, 40,* 295–309.

Kelly, J. (1996). A decade of divorce mediation research. *Family Court Review, 34,* 373–385.

Kelly, J., & Emery, R. (2003). Children's adjustment following divorce: Risk and resilience perspectives. *Family Relations, 52,* 352–362.

Kennard, J. B., Otis, C. C., Austin, J. L., Zimmerman, D. M., & Kovera, M. B. (2014). *Behavioral confirmation in voir dire: Effects on jury selection and verdict choices.* Unpublished manuscript.

Kerr, N., Kramer, G. P., Carroll, J. S., & Alfini, J. J. (1991). On the effectiveness of voir dire in criminal cases with prejudicial pretrial publicity: An empirical study. *American Law Review, 40,* 665–701.

Kerr, N. L., Niedermeier, K. E., & Kaplan, M. F. (1999). Bias in jurors vs. bias in juries: New evidence from the SDS perspective. *Organizational Behavior and Human Decision Processes, 80,* 70–86.

Kessler, R., Berglund, P., Delmer, O., Jin, R., Merikangas, K., & Walters, E. (2005). Lifetime prevalence and age-of-onset distributions of DSM-IV disorders in the National Comorbidity Survey Replication. *Archives of General Psychiatry, 62,* 593–602.

Kiai, J., & Stobo, J. (2010). Prison healthcare in California. *UC Health,* Retrieved January 22, 2010, from http://universityofcalifornia.edu/sites/uchealth/2010/01/22/prison-health-care-in-california/

Kimonis, E., Frick, P., & Barry, C. (2004). Callous-unemotional traits and delinquent peer affiliation. *Journal of Consulting and Clinical Psychology, 72,* 956–966.

Kiser, R. (2010). *Beyond right and wrong.* Berlin, Germany: Springer-Verlag.

Kiser, R., Asher, M., & McShane, B. (2008). Let's not make a deal: An empirical study of decision making in unsuccessful settlement negotiations. *Journal of Empirical Legal Studies, 5,* 551–591.

Klein, D., & Mitchell, G. (Eds.). (2010). *The psychology of judicial decision making.* New York, NY: Oxford University Press.

Kleinberg, H. (1989, January 29). It's tough to have sympathy for Bundy. *Lawrence Journal-World,* p. 5A.

Kleinmuntz, B., & Szucko, J. J. (1984). Lie detection in ancient and modern times: A call for contemporary scientific study. *American Psychologist, 39,* 766–776.

Knighton, J., Murrie, D., Boccaccini, M., & Turner, D. (2014). How likely is "likely to reoffend" in sex offender civil commitment trials? *Law and Human Behavior, 38,* 293–304.

Knudsen, K., & Wigenfeld, S. (2016). A specialized treatment court for veterans with trauma exposure: Implications for the field. *Community Mental Health Journal, 52,* 127–135.

Knutson, A., Gordon, N., & Greene, E. (2015). More than a feelin': Using small group research to inform settlement decisions in civil lawsuits. *Georgia State University Law Review, 31,* 685–714.

Kocsis, R. (2003). Criminal psychological profiling: Validities and abilities. *International Journal of Offender Therapy and Comparative Criminology, 42,* 126–144.

Kocsis, R. (2006). Validities and abilities in criminal profiling: The dilemma for David Canter's investigative psychology. *International Journal of Offender Therapy and Comparative Criminology, 50,* 458–477.

Kocsis, R., & Palermo, G. (2015). Disentangling criminal profiling: Accuracy, homology, and the myth of trait based profiling. *International Journal of Offender Therapy and Comparative Criminology, 59,* 313–332.

Koehler, J., Schweitzer, N., Saks, M., & McQuiston, D. (2016). Science, technology, or the expert witness: What influences jurors' judgments about forensic science testimony? *Psychology, Public Policy, and Law, 22,* 401–413.

Kolebuck, M. D. (1998). *Kansas v. Henricks:* Is it time to lock the door and throw away the key for sexual predators? *Journal of Contemporary Health and Law Policy, 14,* 537–561.

Kopelman, S., Rosette, A. S., & Thompson, L. (2006). The three faces of Eve: An examination of the strategic display of positive, negative, and neutral emotions in negotiations. *Organizational Behavior and Human Decision Processes, 99,* 81–101.

Kopfinger, S. (2007). *PTSD victim tells gripping story.* Retrieved May 15, 2009, from http://lancasteronline.com/article/local/208863_PTSD-victim-tells-gripping-story.html

Korobkin, R., & Doherty, J. (2009). Who wins in settlement negotiations? *American Law and Economics Review, 11,* 162–209.

Kovera, M. (2002). The effects of general pretrial publicity on juror decisions: An examination of moderators and mediating mechanisms. *Law and Human Behavior, 26,* 43–72.

Kovera, M., & Austin, J. (2016). Identifying juror bias: Moving from assessment and prediction to a new generation of jury selection research. In C. W. Esqueda & B. H. Bornstein (Eds.), *The witness* stand and Lawrence S. Wrightsman, Jr. (pp. 75–94). New York, NY: Springer-Verlag.

Kovera, M., Dickinson, J., & Cutler, B. (2002). Voir dire and jury selection. In A. Goldstein (Ed.), *Comprehensive handbook of psychology: Forensic psychology* (Vol. 11, pp. 161–175). New York, NY: Wiley.

Kraemer, G. W., Lord, W. D., & Heilbrun, K. (2004). Comparing single and serial homicide offenses. *Behavioral Sciences & the Law, 22*, 325–343.

Kraemer, H., Kazdin, A., Offord, D., Kessler, R., Jensen, P., & Kupfer, D. (1997). Coming to terms with the terms of risk. *Archives of General Psychiatry, 54*, 337–343.

Kralstein, D. (2005). *Community court research: A literature review.* New York, NY: Center for Court Innovation.

Kramer, G. M., Wolbransky, M., & Heilbrun, K. (2007). Plea bargaining recommendations by criminal defense attorneys: Evidence strength, potential sentence, and defendant preference. *Behavioral Sciences & the Law, 25*, 573–585.

Kramer, G. P., Kerr, N. L., & Carroll, J. S. (1990). Pretrial publicity, judicial remedies, and jury bias. *Law and Human Behavior, 14*, 409–438.

Kraus, L., Thomas, C., & The Committee on Quality Issues (CQI). (2011). Practice parameter for child and adolescent forensic evaluations. *Child & Adolescent Psychiatry, 50*, 1299–1312. doi:10.1016/j.jaac.2011.09.020

Krauss, D., & Goldstein, A. (2007). The role of forensic mental health experts in federal sentencing proceedings. In A. Goldstein (Ed.), *Forensic psychology: Emerging topics and expanding roles* (pp. 359–384). Hoboken, NJ: Wiley.

Krauss, D., McCabe, J., & Lieberman, J. (2012). Dangerously misunderstood: Representative jurors' reactions to expert testimony on future dangerousness in a sexually violent predator trial. *Psychology, Public Policy, and Law, 18*, 18–49.

Kravitz, H. M., & Kelly, J. (1999). An outpatient psychiatry program for offenders with mental disorders found Not Guilty by Reason of Insanity. *Psychiatric Services, 50*, 1597–1605.

Krebs, C., Lindquist, C., Warner, T., Fisher, B., & Martin, S. (2007). *Campus sexual assault study* (final report). Washington, DC: National Institute of Justice. Retrieved March 29, 2017, from https://www.ncjrs.gov/App/abstractdb/AbstractDBDetails.aspx?id=243011

Kreis, M., & Cooke, D. (2013). The manifestation of psychopathic traits in women: An exploration using case examples. *International Journal of Forensic Mental Health, 11*, 267–279.

Kressel, N., & Kressel, D. (2002). *Stack and sway: The new science of jury consulting.* Boulder, CO: Westview.

Krings, F., & Facchin, S. (2009). The moderating role of sexism and personality. *Journal of Applied Psychology, 94*, 501–510.

Kritzer, H., & Drechsel, R. (2012). Local news of civil litigation. All the litigation news that's fit to print or broadcast. *Judicature, 96*, 16–22.

Kropp, R., Hart, S., Webster, C., & Eaves, D. (1994). *Manual for the Spousal Assault Risk Assessment Guide.* Vancouver, BC, Canada: The British Columbia Institute Against Family Violence.

Kropp, R., Hart, S., Webster, C., & Eaves, D. (1999). *Spousal Assault Risk Assessment: User's guide.* Toronto, ON, Canada: Multi-Health Systems, Inc.

Kulik, C., Perry, E., & Pepper, M. (2003). Here comes the judge: The influence of judge personal characteristics on federal sexual harassment case outcomes. *Law and Human Behavior, 27*, 69–86.

Kulka, R., Schlenger, W., Fairbanks, J., Hough, R., Jordan, B., Marmar, C., ... Grady, D. (1990). *Trauma and the Vietnam War generation: Report of findings from the National Vietnam Veterans Readjustment Study.* New York, NY: Brunner/Mazel.

Kumho Tire Co. v. Carmichael, 526 U.S. 137 (1999).

Kunda, Z. (1990). The case for motivated reasoning. *Psychological Bulletin, 108*, 480–498.

Kunen, J. (1983). *"How can you defend those people?" The making of a criminal lawyer.* New York, NY: Random House.

Kurtz, H. (2004, October 29). Bill O'Reilly, producer settle harassment suit: Fox host agrees to drop extortion claim. *The Washington Post.* Retrieved September 1, 2005, from http://www.washingtonpost.com/wp-dyn/articles/A7578–2004Oct28.html

Kutateladze, B., & Andiloro, N. (2014). *Prosecution and racial justice in New York County-Technical Report.* New York, NY: Vera Institute of Justice.

Kwiatkowski, J., & Miller, M. (2015). How attitude functions, attitude change, and beliefs affect community sentiment toward the Facebook law. In M. Miller, J. Blumenthal, & J. Chamberlain (Eds.), *Handbook of community sentiment* (pp. 159–170). New York, NY: Springer.

La Fon, D. (2008). *Psychological autopsies: Science and practice.* Boca Raton, FL: CRC.

La Rooy, D., Katz, C., Malloy, L., & Lamb, M. (2010). Do we need to rethink guidance on repeated interviews? *Psychology, Public Policy, and Law, 16*, 373–392.

Labriola, M., Bradley, S., O'Sullivan, C., Rempel, M., & Moore, S. (2010). *A national portrait of domestic violence courts.* Washington, DC: United States Department of Justice. Retrieved from https://www.ncjrs.gov/pdffiles1/nij/grants/229659.pdf

Lafler v. Cooper, U.S. Supreme Court No. 10–209 (2012).

Lafortune, K. A., & Carpenter, B. N. (1998). Custody evaluations: A survey of mental health professionals. *Behavioral Sciences & the Law, 16*, 207–224.

Lake, D. A. (2002, Spring). Rational extremism: Understanding terrorism in the twenty-first century. *Dialog-IQ, 15*–29.

Lamar, J. V. (1989, February 6). "I deserve punishment." *Time*, p. 34.

Lamb, M. (2016). Difficulties translating research on forensic interview practices to practitioners: Finding water, leading horses, but can we get them to drink? *American Psychologist, 71*, 710–718.

Lamberti, J., Deem, A., Weisman, R., & LaDuke, C. (2011). The role of probation in forensic assertive community treatment. *Psychiatric Services, 62*, 418–421.

Lamberti, J., Weisman, R., Schwarzkopf, S., Price, N., Ashton, R., & Trompeter, J. (2001). The mentally ill in jails and prisons: Towards an integrated model of prevention. *Psychiatric Quarterly, 72*, 63–77.

Lampinen, J., Judges, D., Odegard, T., & Hamilton, S. (2005). The reactions of mock jurors to the department of justice guidelines for the collection and preservation of eyewitness evidence. *Basic and Applied Social Psychology, 27*, 155–162.

Lander, T., & Heilbrun, K. (2009). The content and quality of forensic mental health assessment: Validation of a principles-based approach. *International Journal of Forensic Mental Health, 8*, 115–121.

Landstrom, S., & Granhag, P. (2010). In-court versus out-of-court testimonies: Children's experiences and adults' assessments. *Applied Cognitive Psychology, 24*, 941–955.

Lane, S. (2006). Dividing attention during a witnessed event increases eyewitness suggestibility. *Applied Cognitive Psychology, 20*, 199–212.

Langhout, R., Bergman, M., Cortina, L., Fitzgerald, L., Drasgow, F., & Hunter Williams, J. (2005). Sexual harassment severity: Assessing situational and personal determinants and outcomes. *Journal of Applied Social Psychology, 35*, 975–1007. doi:10.1111/j.1559-1816.2005.tb02156.x

Langleben, D., & Moriarty, J. (2013). Using brain imaging for lie detection: Where science, law, and policy collide. *Psychology, Public Policy, and Law, 19*, 222–234.

Langton, L., & Cohen, T. (2008). *Civil bench and jury trials in state courts, 2005.* Washington, DC: U.S. Department of Justice. (Bureau of Justice Statistics Special Report No. NCJ 223851).

Lapierre, L., Spector, P., & Leck, J. (2005). Sexual versus nonsexual workplace aggression and victims' overall job satisfaction:

A meta-analysis. *Journal of Occupational Health Psychology, 10,* 155–169. doi:10.1037/1076-8998.10.2.155

Larochelle, S., Diguer, L., Laverdiere, O., & Greenman, P. (2011). Predictors of psychological treatment noncompletion among sexual offenders. *Clinical Psychology Review, 31,* 554–562.

Larson, K., & Grisso, T. (2011). *Developing statutes for competence to stand trial in juvenile delinquency proceedings: A guide for lawmakers.* Chicago: National Youth Screening & Assessment Project, Models for Change, John D. and Catherine T. MacArthur Foundation. Retrieved November 29, 2016, from http://www.njjn.org/uploads/digital-library/Developing_Statutes_for_Competence_to_Stand_Trial_in_Juvenile_Delinquency_Proceedings_A_Guide_for_Lawmakers-MfC-3_1.30.12_1.pdf

Lassiter, G. D., Ware, L., Ratcliff, J., & Irvin, C. (2009). Evidence of the camera perspective bias in authentic videotaped interrogations: Implications for emerging reform in the criminal justice system. *Legal and Criminological Psychology, 14,* 157–170.

Laub, C. E., Kimbrough, C. D., & Bornstein, B. H. (2016). Mock juror perceptions of eyewitnesses vs. earwitnesses: Do safeguards help? *American Journal of Forensic Psychology, 34,* 33–56.

Laumann-Billings, L., & Emery, R. (2000). Distress among young adults from divorced families. *Journal of Family Psychology, 14,* 671–87.

Lea, R., & Chambers, G. (2007). Monoamine oxidase, addiction, and the "Warrior" gene hypothesis. *Journal of the New Zealand Medical Association, 120,* U2441.

Lecci, L., & Myers, B. (2009). Predicting guilt judgments and verdict change using a measure of pretrial bias in a videotaped mock trial with deliberating jurors. *Psychology, Crime and Law, 15,* 619–634.

Lees-Haley, P. (1991). A fake bad scale on the MMPI-2 for personal injury claimants. *Psychological Reports, 68,* 203–210.

Lees-Haley, P. (1992). Efficacy of MMPI-2 validity scales and MCMI-2 modifier scales for detecting spurious PTSD claims: F, F-K, Fake Bad Scale, Ego Strength, Subtle-Obvious subscales, DIS, and DEB. *Journal of Clinical Psychology, 48,* 681–689.

Leiber, M., Beaudry-Cry, M., Peck, J., & Mack, K. (2017). Sentencing recommendations by probation officers and judges: An examination of adult offenders across genders. *Women & Criminal Justice,* advance online publication.

Leifman, S., & Coffey, T. (2015). Rethinking mental health legal policy and practice: History and needed reforms. In P. Griffin, K. Heilbrun, E. Mulvey, D. DeMatteo, & C. Schubert (Eds.), *The sequential intercept model and criminal justice: Promoting community alternatives for individuals with serious mental illness* (pp. 217–238). New York, NY: Oxford.

Leipold, A., & Abbasi, H. (2006). The impact of joinder and severance on federal criminal cases: An empirical study. *Vanderbilt Law Review, 59,* 347–404.

Leippe, M. R., Eisenstadt, D., Rauch, S. M., & Stambush, M. A. (2006). Effects of social-comparative memory feedback on eyewitnesses' identification confidence, suggestibility, and retrospective memory reports. *Basic and Applied Social Psychology, 28,* 201–220.

Leistico, A., Salekin, R., DeCoster, J., & Rogers, R. (2008). A large-scale meta-analysis relating the Hare measures of psychopathy to antisocial conduct. *Law and Human Behavior, 32,* 28–45.

Lemert, E. M. (1951). *Social pathology.* New York, NY: McGraw-Hill.

Lemert, E. M. (1972). *Human deviance, social problems, and social control* (2nd ed.). Englewood Cliffs, NJ: Prentice Hall.

Lempert, R. (1993). Civil juries and complex cases: Taking stock after twelve years. In R. E. Litan (Ed.), *Verdict: Assessing the civil jury system* (pp. 181–247). Washington, DC: The Brookings Institution.

Leo, R. (2008). *Police interrogation and American justice.* Cambridge, MA: Harvard University Press.

Leo, R., & Ofshe, R. (1998). The consequences of false confessions: Deprivations of liberty and miscarriages of justice in the age of psychological interrogation. *Journal of Criminal Law and Criminology, 88,* 429–496.

Leonard, K. E., Quigley, B. M., & Collins, R. L. (2002). Physical aggression in the lives of young adults. *Journal of Interpersonal Violence, 17,* 533–550.

Lerner, M. J. (1980). *The belief in a just world.* New York, NY: Plenum.

Levenson, J., & D'Amora, D. (2007). Social policies designed to prevent sexual violence: The emperor's new clothes? *Criminal Justice Policy Review, 18,* 168–199.

Levenson, R., & Dwyer, L. (2003). Peer support in law enforcement: Past, present, and future. *International Journal of Emergency Mental Health, 5,* 147–152.

Levett, L., & Kovera, M. (2008). The effectiveness of opposing expert witnesses for educating jurors about unreliable expert evidence. *Law and Human Behavior, 32,* 363–374.

Lewin, T. (1994, October 21). Outrage over 18 months for a killing. *The New York Times,* p. A18.

Lewis, A. (1964). *Gideon's trumpet.* New York, NY: Knopf.

Lewis, M. (2017). *The undoing project.* New York, NY: W.W. Norton.

Lieberman, J. (2009). The psychology of the jury instruction process. In J. Lieberman & D. Krauss (Eds.), *Jury psychology: Social aspects of trial processes* (pp. 129–156). Burlington, VT: Ashgate.

Lieberman, J. (2011). The utility of scientific jury selection: Still murky after 30 years. *Current Directions in Psychological Science, 20,* 48–52.

Lieberman, J., & Arndt, J. (2000). Understanding the limits of limiting instructions: Social psychological explanations for the failures of instructions to disregard pretrial publicity and other inadmissible evidence. *Psychology, Public Policy, and Law, 6,* 677–711.

Lieberman, J., & Olson, J. (2009). The psychology of jury selection. In J. Lieberman & D. Krauss (Eds.), *Jury psychology: Social aspects of trial processes* (pp. 97–128). Burlington, VT: Ashgate.

Liebman, J. S. (2000). *A broken system: Error rates in capital cases, 1973—1995.* Retrieved October 1, 2005, from http://ccjr.policy.net/cjedfund/jpreport/

Lilly, J. R., Cullen, F. T., & Ball, R. A. (1989). *Criminological theory: Context and consequences.* Newbury Park, CA: Sage.

Lin, J., Gratter, R., & Petersilia, J. (2010). "Back-end sentencing" and reimprisonment: Individual, organizational, and community predictors of parole sanction decisions. *Criminology, 48,* 759–795.

Lind, E. A. (1982). The psychology of courtroom procedure. In N. L. Kerr & R. M. Bray (Eds.), *Psychology in the courtroom* (pp. 13–37). Orlando, FL: Academic Press.

Lind, E. A., Erickson, B. E., Friedland, N., & Dickenberger, M. (1978). Reactions to procedural models for adjudicative conflict resolution. *Journal of Conflict Resolution, 22,* 318–341.

Lindsay, D., Hagen, L., Read, J., Wade, K., & Garry, M. (2004). True photographs and false memories. *Psychological Science, 15,* 149–154.

Lipsey, M. (1992). Juvenile delinquency treatment: A meta-analytic inquiry into the variability of effects. In T. Cook, H. Cooper, S. Cordray, H. Hartmann, L. Hedges, R. Light, et al. (Eds.), *Meta-analysis for explanation: A casebook* (pp. 83–128). New York, NY: Russell Sage Foundation.

Lipsey, M., & Wilson, D. (1998). Effective intervention for serious juvenile offenders: A synthesis of research. In R. Loeber & D. Farrington (Eds.), *Serious and violent juvenile offenders: Risk factors and successful interventions* (pp. 313–345). Thousand Oaks, CA: Sage.

Liptak, A. (2015, November 2). Supreme Court to decide if Georgia went too far in excluding black jurors. Retrieved from http://www.nytimes.com/2015/11/03/us/politics/supreme-court-to-decide-if-georgia-went-too-far-in-excluding-black-jurors.html

Liptak, A. (2016, May 23). Supreme Court finds racial bias in jury selection for death penalty case. Retrieved from https://www.nytimes.com/2016/05/24/supreme-court-black-jurors-death-penalty-georgia.html

Littleton, H., Axsom, D., & Grills-Taquechel, A. (2009). Sexual assault victims' acknowledgment status and revictimization risk. *Psychology of Women Quarterly, 33*, 34–42.

Lockett v. Ohio, 438 U.S. 604 (1978).

Lockhart v. McCree, 476 U.S. 162 (1986).

Loeber, R., & Stouthamer-Loeber, M. (1986). Family factors as correlates and predictors of juvenile conduct problems and delinquency. In M. Tonry & N. Morris (Eds.), *Crime and justice: An annual review of research* (Vol. 7, pp. 29–149). Chicago, IL: University of Chicago Press.

Loftus, E. F. (1974). Reconstructing memory: The incredible witness. *Psychology Today, 8*, 116–119.

Loftus, E. F. (1975). Leading questions and the eyewitness report. *Cognitive Psychology, 7*, 560–572.

Loftus, E. F. (1979). *Eyewitness testimony*. Cambridge, MA: Harvard University Press.

Loftus, E. F. (1984). Expert testimony on the eyewitness. In G. L. Wells & E. F. Loftus (Eds.), *Eyewitness testimony: Psychological perspectives* (pp. 273–282). New York, NY: Cambridge University Press.

Loftus, E. F., & Pickrell, J. E. (1995). The formation of false memories. *Psychiatric Annals, 25*, 720–725.

Lombroso, C. (1876). *L' Uomo delinquente*. Milan: Hoepli.

London, K., Bruck, M., Wright, D. B., & Ceci, S. J. (2008). Review of the contemporary literature on how children report sexual abuse to others: Findings, methodological issues, and implications for forensic interviewers. *Memory, 16*, 29–47.

London, K., & Nunez, N. (2000). The effect of jury deliberations on jurors' propensity to disregard inadmissible evidence. *Journal of Applied Psychology, 85*, 932–939.

Long, B., Rouse, S., Nelsen, R., & Butcher, J. (2004). The MMPI-2 in sexual harassment and discrimination litigants. *Journal of Clinical Psychology, 60*, 643–657.

Los Angeles County Sheriff's Department. (2012). *Home page*. Retrieved June 3, 2012, from http://app4.lasd.org/iic/ajis_search.cfm

Lowenkamp, C., & Latessa, E. (2005, April). Developing successful reentry programs: Lessons learned from the "what works" research. *Corrections Today, 67*, 72–77.

Ludwig, E. (2002). The changing role of the trial judge. *Judicature, 85*, 216–217.

Luna, K., & Migueles, M. (2008). Typicality and misinformation: Two sources of distortion. *Psicologica, 29*, 171–187.

Lurigio, A. A., Watson, A., Luchins, D., & Hanrahan, P. (2001). Therapeutic jurisprudence in action. *Judicature, 84*, 184–189.

Lurigio, A. J., & Skogan, W. G. (1994). Winning the hearts and minds of police officers: An assessment of staff perceptions of community policing in Chicago. *Crime and Delinquency, 40*, 315–330.

Lyall, S. (2017, February 19). Liberals are still angry, but Merrick Garland has reached acceptance. Retrieved from https://www.nytimes.com/2017/02/19/us/politics/merrick-garland-supreme-court-obama-nominee.html

Lynam, D., Moffitt, T., & Stouthamer-Loeber, M. (1993). Explaining the relation between IQ and delinquency: Class, race, test motivation, school failure, and self-control. *Journal of Abnormal Psychology, 102*, 187–196.

Lynch, M., & Haney, C. (2000). Discrimination and instructional comprehension: Guided discretion, racial bias, and the death penalty. *Law and Human Behavior, 24*, 337–358.

Lynch, M., & Haney, C. (2009). Capital jury deliberation: Effects on death sentencing, comprehension, and discrimination. *Law and Human Behavior, 33*, 481–496.

Lynch, T. (2003, Fall). The case against plea bargaining. *Regulation, 26*, 24–27.

MacPherson, S., & Bonora, B. (2010, November). The wired juror, unplugged. *Trial*, 40–45.

Madden-Derdich, D. A., Leonard, S. A., & Gunnell, G. A. (2002). Parents' and children's perceptions of family processes in inner-city families with delinquent youths: A qualitative investigation. *Journal of Marital and Family Therapy, 28*, 355–370.

Madon, S., Guyll, M., Scherr, K., Greathouse, S., & Wells, G. (2011, March). *The differential impact of proximal and distal consequences on the elicitation of criminal confessions*. Paper presented at American Psychology-Law Society, Miami, FL.

Mador, J. (2010, March 22). *New veterans' court aims to help soldiers struggling at home*. Retrieved July 1, 2011, from www.minnesota.public.radio.org/display/web/2010/03/22/veterans-court/

Maeder, E., & Hunt, J. (2011). Talking about a black man: The influence of defendant and character witness race on jurors' use of character evidence. *Behavioral Sciences and the Law, 29*, 608–620.

Magdol, L., Moffitt, T. E., Caspi, A., Newman, D. L., Fagan, J., & Silva, P. A. (1997). Gender differences in rates of partner violence in a birth cohort of 21-year-olds: Bridging the gap between clinical and epidemiological approaches. *Journal of Consulting and Clinical Psychology, 65*, 68–78.

Magdol, L., Moffitt, T. E., Caspi, A., & Silva, P. A. (1998). Developmental antecedents of partner abuse: A prospective-longitudinal study. *Journal of Abnormal Psychology, 107*, 373–389.

Magnussen, S., & Melinder, A. (2012). What psychologists know and believe about memory: A survey of practitioners. *Applied Cognitive Psychology, 26*, 54–60.

Maguigan, H. (1991). Battered women and self-defense: Myths and misconceptions in current reform proposals. *University of Pennsylvania Law Review, 140*, 379–486.

Malpass, R. S., & Devine, P. G. (1981). Eyewitness identification: Lineup instructions and the absence of the offender. *Journal of Applied Psychology, 66*, 482–489.

Mandracchia, J., & Morgan, R. (2011). Understanding criminals' thinking: Further examination of the measure of offender thinking styles-revised. *Assessment, 18*, 442–452.

Mann, S., Vrij, A., & Bull, R. (2004). Detecting true lies: Police officers' ability to detect deceit. *Journal of Applied Psychology, 89*, 137–149.

Marcus, D. R., Lyons, P. M., & Guyton, M. R. (2000). Studying perceptions of juror influence *in vivo*: A social relations analysis. *Law and Human Behavior, 24*, 173–186.

Marder, N. (2012). *Batson* revisited. *Iowa Law Review, 97*, 1585–1612.

Margulies, J. (2011). Deviance, risk, and law: Reflections on the demand for the preventive detention of suspected terrorists. *Journal of Criminal Law and Criminology, 101*, 729–780.

Marks, D. (2011). IQ variations across time, race, and nationality: An artifact of differences in literacy skills. *Counselor Education and Supervision, 50*, 643–664.

Marlowe, D. B. (2002). Effective strategies for intervening with drug abusing offenders. *Villanova Law Review, 47*, 989–1026.

Marlowe, D. B., DeMatteo, D., & Festinger, D. (2003). A sober assessment of drug courts. *Federal Sentencing Reporter, 16*, 113–128.

Marquardt, E. (2006). *Between two worlds: The inner lives of children of divorce*. New York, NY: Three Rivers Press.

Marsee, M., Silverthorn, P., & Frick, P. (2005). The association of psychopathic traits with aggression and delinquency in non-referred boys and girls. *Behavioral Sciences & the Law, 23*, 803–817. doi:10.1002/bsl.662

Marshall, W., Fernandez, Y., & Cortoni, F. (1999). Rape. In V. Van Hasselt & M. Hersen (Eds.), *Handbook of psychological approaches with violent offenders* (pp. 245–266). New York, NY: Kluwer/Plenum.

Marshall, W. L., Fernandez, Y., Marshall, L., & Serran, G. (2006). *Sexual offender treatment: Controversial issues*. West Sussex, UK: Wiley.

Marshall, W. L., Jones, R., Ward, T., Johnston, P., & Barbaree, H. E. (1991). Treatment outcome with sex offenders. *Clinical Psychology Review, 11*, 465–485.

Martin, C., Lurigio, A., & Olson, D. (2003). An examination of rearrests and reincarcerations among discharged day reporting center clients. *Federal Probation, 67*, 24–30.

Martin, S. S., Butzin, C. A., Saum, C. A., & Inciardi, J. A. (1999). Three-year outcomes of therapeutic community treatment for offenders in Delaware. *The Prison Journal, 79*, 294–320.

Martinson, R. (1974). What works? Questions and answers about prison reform. *Public Interest, 35*, 22.

Martire, K. A., & Kemp, R. I. (2011). Can experts help jurors to evaluate eyewitness evidence? A review of eyewitness expert effects. *Legal and Criminological Psychology, 16*, 24–36.

Marvasti, J. (2010). Combat trauma and PTSD in veterans: Forensic aspect and 12-step program. *American Journal of Forensic Psychiatry, 31*, 5–30.

Maryland v. Craig, 110 S.Ct. 3157 (1990).

Maschi, T., Bradley, C., & Morgen, K. (2008). Unraveling the link between trauma and delinquency. *Youth Violence and Juvenile Justice, 6*, 136–157. doi:10.1177/1541204007305527

Maslach, C., & Jackson, S. E. (1984). Burnout in organizational settings. In S. Oskamp (Ed.), *Applied social psychology annual* (pp. 133–154). Newbury Park, CA: Sage.

Mason, C., & Cheng, S. (2001). *Re-arrest rates among youth sentenced in adult court.* Miami, FL: Miami-Dade County Public Defender's Office.

Matal v. Tam, 528 U.S. _____ (2017).

Matsumoto, D., & Hwang, H. (2015). Emotional reactions to crime across cultures. *International Journal of Psychology, 50*, 327–335.

Mauer, M. (2011). Sentencing reform: Amid mass incarcerations–guarded optimism. *Criminal Justice, 26*, 27–36.

Mauer, M., & King, R. S. (2007, July). *Uneven justice: State rates of incarceration by race and ethnicity.* Retrieved October 25, 2008, from http://www.sentencingproject.org

Maxfield, M. G., & Widom, C. S. (1996). The cycle of violence: Revisited 6 years later. *Archives of Pediatrics & Adolescent Medicine, 150*, 390–395.

Maxwell, C. D., Garner, J. H., & Fagan, J. A. (2002). The preventive effects of arrest on intimate partner violence: Research, policy and theory. *Criminology and Public Policy, 2*, 51–80.

Mazzoni, G., & Memon, A. (2003). Imagination can create false autobiographical memories. *Psychological Science, 14*, 186–188.

McAuliff, B., Lapin, J., & Michel, S. (2015). Support person presence and child victim testimony: Believe it or not. *Behavioral Sciences and the Law, 33*, 508–527.

McAuliff, B. D., & Kovera, M. B. (2008). Juror need for cognition and sensitivity to methodological flaws in expert evidence. *Journal of Applied Social Psychology, 38*, 385–408.

McCandless, S. R., & Sullivan, L. P. (1991, May 6). Two courts adopt new standard to determine sexual harassment. *National Law Journal,* pp. 18–20.

McCann, J. (1998). A conceptual framework for identifying various types of confessions. *Behavioral Sciences & the Law, 16*, 441–453.

McCann, T. (2004, August 21). *Jury consultants try to turn voir dire into a science.* Retrieved October 1, 2005, from http://www.zmf.com

McCleskey v. Kemp, 107 S. Ct. 1756 (1987).

McCorkle, R. (1992). Personal precautions to violence in prison. *Criminal Justice and Behavior, 19*, 160–173.

McCrae, R., & Costa, P. (1990). *Personality in adulthood.* New York, NY: Guilford.

McDermott, P., Watkins, M., & Rhoad, A. (2014). Whose IQ is it? Assessor bias variance in high-stakes psychological assessment. *Psychological Assessment, 26*, 207–214.

McDonough, M. (2004, October). Summary time blues. *American Bar Association Journal, 90*, 18.

McGuire, J., Bilby, C., Hatcher, R., Hollin, C., Hounsome, J., & Palmer, E. (2008). Evaluation of structured cognitive-behavioural treatment programmes in reducing criminal recidivism. *Journal of Experimental Criminology, 4*, 21–40.

McGuire, J., Clark, S., Blue-Howells, J., & Coe, C. (2013). *An inventory of VA involvement in Veterans courts, dockets and tracks.* VA Veterans Justice Programs. Retrieved December 23, 2016, from http://www.justiceforvets.org/sites/default/files/files/An%20Inventory%20of%20VA%20involvement%20in%20Veterans%20Courts.pdf

McIntyre, F., & Baradaran, S. (2013). Race, prediction, and pretrial detention. *Journal of Empirical Legal Studies, 10*, 741–770.

McKay v. Ashland Oil Inc., 120 F.R.D. 43 (E.D. Ky. 1988).

McLaurin v. Oklahoma State Regents for Higher Education, 339 U.S. 637 (1950).

McLean, C., & Foa, E. (2011). Prolonged exposure therapy for post-traumatic stress disorder: A review of evidence and dissemination. *Expert Review Neurotherapy, 11*, 1151–1163.

McLoughlin, N., Rucklidge, J. J., Grace, R. C., & McLean, A. P. (2010). Can callous unemotional traits and aggression identify children at high risk of anti-social behavior in a low socioeconomic group? *Journal of Family Violence, 25*, 701–712.

McMurtrie, J. (2015). The unindicated co-ejaculator and necrophilia: Addressing prosecutors' logic-defying responses to exculpatory DNA results. *Journal of Criminal Law and Criminology, 105*, 853–879.

McNatt, D. (2000). Ancient Pygmalion joins contemporary management: A meta-analysis of the result. *Journal of Applied Psychology, 85*, 314–322.

McNiel, D., & Binder, R. (2007). Effectiveness of a mental health court in reducing criminal recidivism and violence. *American Journal of Psychiatry, 164*, 1395–1403.

Meddis, S. S., & Kelley, J. (1985, April 8). Crime drops but fear on rise. *USA Today,* p. A1.

Medical News Today. (2007). *What level of mental illness should preclude execution and how to determine it?* Retrieved April 1, 2009, from www.medicalnewstoday.com

Medina v. California, 112 S.Ct. 2572 (1992).

Meijer, E., Selle, N., Elber, L., & Ben-Shakhar, G. (2014). Memory detection with the Concealed Information Test: A meta-analysis of skin conductance, respiration, heart rate, and P300 data. *Psychophysiology, 51*, 879–904.

Meijer, E., & Verschuere, B. (2010). The polygraph and the detection of deception. *Journal of Forensic Psychology Practice, 10*, 325–338.

Meissner, C., & Brigham, J. (2001). Thirty years of investigating the own-race bias in memory for faces: A meta-analytic review. *Psychology, Public Policy, and Law, 7*, 3–35.

Meissner, C., & Kassin, S. (2002). "He's guilty!": Investigator bias in judgments of truth and deception. *Law and Human Behavior, 5*, 469–480.

Meissner, C., & Kassin, S. (2004). "You're guilty, so just confess!" Cognitive and behavioral confirmation biases in the interrogation room. In G. D. Lassiter (Ed.), *Interrogations, confessions, and entrapment* (pp. 85–106). New York, NY: Kluwer Academic/Plenum.

Meissner, C., Redlich, A., Michael, S., Evans, J., Camilletti, C., Bhatt, S., & Brandon, S. (2014). Accusatorial and information-gathering interrogation methods and their effects on true and false confessions: A meta-analytic review. *Journal of Experimental Criminology, 10*, 459–486.

Meissner, C., Sporer, S., & Susa, K. (2008). A theoretical review and meta-analysis of the description-identification relationship in memory for faces. *European Journal of Cognitive Psychology, 20*, 414–455.

Meissner, C., Tredoux, C., Parker, J., & MacLin, O. (2005). Eyewitness decisions in simultaneous and sequential lineups. *Memory and Cognition, 33*, 783–792.

Melilli, K. (1996). *Batson* in practice: What we have learned about *Batson* and peremptory challenges. *Notre Dame Law Review, 71*, 447–503.

Mellow, J., Mukamal, D. A., LoBuglio, S. F., Solomon, A. L., & Osborne, J. W. L. (2008, May). *The jail administrator's toolkit for reentry.* Washington, DC: Urban Institute.

Meloy, J. R., & Felthous, A. R. (2004). Introduction to this issue: Serial and mass homicide. *Behavioral Sciences & the Law, 22*(3), 289–290.

Meloy, J. R., Hempel, A. G., Gray, B. T., Mohandie, K., Shiva, A., & Richards, T. C. (2004). A comparative analysis of North American adolescent and adult mass murderers. *Behavioral Sciences & the Law, 22*(3), 291–309.

Melton, G., Petrila, J., Poythress, N., & Slobogin, C. (2007). *Psychological evaluations for the courts: A handbook for mental health professionals and lawyers* (3rd ed.). New York, NY: Guilford.

Melton, G., Petrila, J., Poythress, N., Slobogin, C., Otto, R., Mossman, D., & Condie, L. (2018). *Psychological evaluations for the courts: A handbook for mental health professional and lawyers* (4th ed.). New York, NY: Guilford.

Memon, A., Meissner, C., & Fraser, J. (2010). The cognitive interview: A meta-analytic review and study space analysis of the past 25 years. *Psychology, Public Policy, and Law, 16*, 340–372.

Mercado, C. (2009, Summer). Are residence restrictions an effective way to reduce the risk posed by sex offenders? *AP-LS News.* Retrieved from http://www.ap-ls.org/publications/newsletters/aplsnews.sum2009.pdf

Meritor Savings Bank v. Vinson, 106 S.Ct. 2399 (1986).

Merrick, R. A. (1985). The tort of outrage: Recovery for the intentional infliction of mental distress. *Behavioral Sciences & the Law, 3*, 165–175.

Merton, R. K. (1968). *Social theory and social structure.* New York, NY: Free Press.

Migueles, M., Garcia-Bajos, E., & Aizpurua, A. (2016). Initial testing does not necessarily affect eyewitness recall assessed by specific questioning. *Applied Cognitive Psychology, 30*, 294–300.

Mihalic, S., Irwin, K., Elliott, D., Fagan, A., & Hansen, D. (2001). *Blueprints for violence prevention.* Boulder, CO: Center for the Study and Prevention of Violence.

Milchman, M. (2012). From traumatic memory to traumatized remembering: Beyond the memory wars, Part 1: Agreement. *Psychological Injury and Law, 5*, 37–50.

Milgram, S. (1963). Behavioral study of obedience. *Journal of Abnormal and Social Psychology, 67*, 371–378.

Miller v. Alabama, 567 U.S. 460 (2012).

Miller, B., & Curry, B. (2017). Small-group dynamics, ideology, and decision making in the US Courts of Appeal. *Law and Policy, 39*, 48–72.

Miller, G. R., & Boster, F. J. (1977). Three images of a trial: Their implications for psychological research. In B. D. Sales (Ed.), *Psychology in the legal process* (pp. 19–38). New York, NY: Spectrum.

Miller, H. A. (2001). *M-FAST: Miller Forensic Assessment of Symptoms Test professional manual.* Odessa, FL: Psychological Assessment Resources.

Miller, H. A. (2004). Examining the use of the M-FAST with criminal defendants incompetent to stand trial. *International Journal of Offender Therapy and Comparative Criminology, 48*, 268–280.

Miller, J., & Lynam, D. (2001). Structural models of personality and their relation to antisocial behavior: A meta-analytic review. *Criminology, 39*, 765–798.

Miller, L. (2007). *Mettle: Mental toughness training for law enforcement.* Flushing, NY: Looseleaf Law Publications, Inc.

Miller, M., Blumenthal, J., & Chamberlain, J. (2015). *Handbook of community sentiment.* New York, NY: Springer.

Miller, S., Malone, P., Dodge, K., & Conduct Problems Prevention Research Group. (2010). Developmental trajectories of boys' and girls' delinquency: Sex differences and links to later adolescent outcomes. *Journal of Abnormal Child Psychology, 38*, 1021–1032. doi:10.1007/s10802-010-9430-1

Mills, J. R., Dorn, A., & Hritz, A. C. (2016). Juvenile life without parole in law and practice: The end of superpredator era sentencing. *American University Law Review, 65*, 535–605.

Mills, R. B., McDevitt, R. J., & Tonkin, S. (1966). Situational tests in metropolitan police recruit selection. *Journal of Criminal Law, Criminology, and Police Science, 57*, 99–104.

Milstein, V. (1988). EEG topography in patients with aggressive violent behavior. In T. E. Moffitt & S. A. Mednick (Eds.), *Biological contributions to crime causation.* Dordrecht, Netherlands: Martinus Nijhoff.

Minsky, S., Vega, W., Miskimen, T., Gara, M., & Escobar, J. (2003). Diagnostic patterns in Latino, African American, and European American psychiatric patients. *Archives of General Psychiatry, 60*, 637–644.

Miranda v. Arizona, 384 U.S. 486 (1966).

Mitchell, O. (2005). A meta-analysis of race and sentencing research: Explaining the inconsistencies. *Journal of Quantitative Criminology, 21*, 439–466.

Mitchell, O., Wilson, D., Eggers, A., & MacKenzie, D. (2012). Assessing the effectiveness of drug courts on recidivism: A meta-analytic review of traditional and non-traditional drug courts. *Journal of Criminal Justice, 40*, 60–71. doi:10.1016/j.jcrimjus.2011.11.009

Mitchell, P. (1976). *Act of love: The killing of George Zygmanik.* New York, NY: Knopf.

Mize, G. (1999, Spring). On better jury selection: Spotting UFO jurors before they enter the jury room. *Court Review, 36*, 10–15.

Mize, G. E., Hannaford-Agor, P., & Waters, N. L. (2007). *The State-of-the-States Survey of Jury Improvement Efforts: A compendium report.* Williamsburg, VA: National Center for State Courts.

Moffitt, T., & Lynam, D. (1994). The neuropsychology of conduct disorder and delinquency: Implications for understanding antisocial behavior. In D. Fowles, P. Sutker, & S. Goodman (Eds.), *Psychopathy and antisocial behavior: A developmental perspective* (pp. 233–262). New York, NY: Springer-Verlag.

Mohamed, F., Faro, S., Gordon, N., Platek, S., Ahmad, H., & Williams, J. (2006). Brain mapping of deception and truth telling about an ecologically valid situation: Functional MR imaging and polygraph investigation-initial experience. *Radiology, 238*, 679–688.

Monahan, J. (1984). The prediction of violent behavior: Toward a second generation of theory and practice. *American Journal of Psychiatry, 141*, 10–15.

Monahan, J. (2012). The individual risk assessment of terrorism: Conceptual and methodological challenges. *Psychology, Public Policy, and Law, 18*, 167–205. doi:10.10371a0025792

Monahan, J., & Steadman, H. J. (Eds.). (1994). *Violence and mental disorder: Developments in risk assessment.* Chicago, IL: University of Chicago Press.

Monahan, J., & Walker, L. (2014). *Social science in law: Cases and materials* (8th ed.). St. Paul, MN: Foundation Press.

Monahan, K. C., Steinberg, L., & Cauffman, E. (2009). Affiliation with antisocial peers, susceptibility to peer influence, and antisocial behavior during the transition to adulthood. *Developmental Psychology, 45*, 1520–1530.

Montgomery v. Louisiana, 577 U.S. ___ (2016).

Moore v. Texas, 137 S.Ct. 1039 (2017).

Moore, M. (2011). Psychological theories of crime and delinquency. *Journal of Human Behavior in the Social Environment, 21*, 226–239.

Moore, M., & Hiday, V. (2006). Mental health court outcomes: A comparison of re-arrest and re-arrest severity between mental health court and traditional court participants. *Law and Human Behavior, 30*, 659–674.

Moran, G., & Cutler, B. L. (1991). The prejudicial impact of pretrial publicity. *Journal of Applied Social Psychology, 21*, 345–367.

Morehouse, E., & Tobler, N. (2000). Preventing and reducing substance use among institutionalized adolescents. *Adolescence, 35*, 1–28.

Morgan, A. B., & Lilienfeld, S. O. (2000). A meta-analytic review of the relation between antisocial behavior and neuropsychological measures of executive function. *Clinical Psychology Review, 20*, 113–136.

Morgan, C., Hazlett, G., Doran, A., Garrett, S., Hoty, G., Thomas, P., … Southwick, S. M. (2004). Accuracy of eyewitness memory for persons encountered during exposure to highly intense stress. *International Journal of Law and Psychiatry, 27*, 265–279.

Morral, A., McCaffrey, D., & Ridgeway, G. (2004). Effectiveness of community-based treatment for substance abusing adolescents: 12-month outcomes from a case-control evaluation of a Phoenix academy. *Psychology of Addictive Behaviors, 18*, 257–268.

Morris, D., & Parker, G. (2008). Jackson's Indiana: State hospital competence restoration in Indiana. *Journal of the American Academy of Psychiatry and Law, 36*, 522–534.

Morrison, C. (2011). Jury 2.0. *Hastings Law Journal, 62*, 1579–1632.

Morrison, C. (2014). Negotiating peremptory challenges. *Journal of Criminal Law and Criminology, 104*, 1–58.

Morrison, P. (1995, August 21). The new chain gang. *National Law Journal*, pp. A1, A22.

Morse, S. J. (1998). Fear of danger, flight from culpability. *Psychology, Public Policy, and Law, 4*, 250–267.

Morton, R., & Hilts, M. (Eds.) (2008). *Serial murder: Multidisciplinary perspectives for investigators.* Washington, DC: U.S. Department of Justice, Federal Bureau of Investigation.

Mossman, D. (1987). Assessing and restoring competency to be executed: Should psychiatrists participate? *Behavioral Sciences & the Law, 5*, 397–410.

Mossman, D. (2007). Predicting restorability of incompetent criminal defendants. *Journal of the American Academy of Psychiatry and Law, 35*, 34–43.

Motivans, M. (2015). *Federal justice statistics, 2011–2012.* Bureau of Justice Statistics. Washington, DC: U.S. Department of Justice.

Mu'Min v. Virginia, 111 S.Ct 1899 (1991).

Mulford, C. L., Lee, M. Y., & Sapp, S. C. (1996). Victim-blaming and society-blaming scales for social problems. *Journal of Applied Social Psychology, 26*, 1324–1336.

Mullen, P. (2004). The autogenic (self-generated) massacre. *Behavioral Sciences & the Law, 22*, 311–323.

Mulvey, E. (2011). *Highlights from Pathways to Desistance: A longitudinal study of serious adolescent offenders.* Washington, DC: OJJDP. Retrieved April 18, 2017, from http://capcentral.org/juveniles/delinquency/docs/study_of_adoles_offenders.pdf

Mulvey, E., & Cauffman, E. (2001). The inherent limits of predicting school violence. *American Psychologist, 56*, 797–802.

Munetz, M., & Griffin, P. (2006). Use of the sequential intercept model as an approach to decriminalization of people with serious mental illness. *Psychiatric Services, 57*, 544–549.

Munson, L. J., Hulin, C., & Drasgow, F. (2000). Longitudinal analysis of dispositional influences and sexual harassment: Effects on job and psychological outcomes. *Personnel Psychology, 53*, 21–46. doi:10.1111/j.1744-6570.2000.tb00192.x

Murray, J. (2008). Media violence: The effects are both real and strong. *American Behavioral Scientist, 51*, 1212–1230.

Murray, J., & Farrington, D. (2010). Risk factors for conduct disorder and delinquency: Key findings from longitudinal studies. *The Canadian Journal of Psychiatry, 55*, 633–642.

Murrie, D., & Boccaccini, M. (2015). Adversarial allegiance among expert witnesses. *Annual Review of Law and Social Science, 11*, 37–55.

Murrie, D., Boccaccini, M., Guarnera, L., & Rufino, K. (2013). Are forensic experts biased by the side that retained them? *Psychological Science, 24*, 1889–1897.

Murrie, D., Cornell, D., & McCoy, W. (2005). Psychopathy, conduct disorder, and stigma: Does diagnostic labeling influence juvenile probation officer recommendations? *Law and Human Behavior, 25*, 323–342.

Myers, D. L. (2001). *Excluding violent youths from juvenile court: The effectiveness of legislative waiver.* New York, NY: LFB Scholarly.

Myers, M., Stewart, D., & Brown, S. (1998). Progression from conduct disorder to antisocial personality disorder following treatment for adolescent substance abuse. *American Journal of Psychiatry, 155*, 479–486.

Nardulli, P., Eisenstein, J., & Fleming, R. (1988). *The tenor of justice: Criminal courts and the guilty plea process.* Champaign, IL: University of Illinois Press.

Nash, A. R., & Wade, K. A. (2009). Innocent but proven guilty: Eliciting internalized false confessions using doctored-video evidence. *Applied Cognitive Psychology, 23*, 357–371.

Nathanson, R., & Saywitz, K. (2015). Preparing children for court: Effects of a model court education program on children's anticipatory anxiety. *Behavioral Sciences and the Law, 33*, 459–475.

National Archive of Criminal Justice Data. (2010). *National criminal victimization survey, 2010.* Retrieved February 18, 2011, from http://www.icpsr.umich.edu/icpsrweb/NACJD/studies/31202/documentation

National Center for Education Statistics. (2016). *School crime and safety.* Retrieved April 18, 2017, from https://nces.ed.gov/programs/coe/indicator_cld.asp

National Center for State Courts. (2012). *Short, summary & expedited: The evolution of civil jury trials.* Retrieved April 9, 2012, from http://www.ncsc.org/~/media/Files/PDF/Information%20and%20Resources/Civil%20cover%20sheets/Monograph%20FINAL%20Electronic%20Version.ashx

National GAINS Center. (2002). *The Nathaniel Project: An alternative to incarceration program for people with serious mental illness who have committed felony offenses.* Delmar, NY: Author.

National Offender Management Service. (2005). *Annual report for accredited programmes 2004–2005.* London: Author.

National Research Council. (1989). *Improving risk communication.* Washington, DC: National Academy Press.

National Research Council. (2003). *The polygraph and lie detection.* Washington, DC: National Academy of Sciences.

National Research Council. (2009). *Strengthening forensic science in the United States: A path forward.* Washington, DC: Author.

National Research Council. (2014). *Identifying the culprit: Assessing eyewitness identification.* Washington, DC: The National Academies Press.

National Science Board. (2008). *Research and development: National trends and international linkages. Science and Engineering Indicators 2008.* Arlington, VA: National Science Foundation.

National Sexual Violence Resource Center. (2010). *The impact of sexual violence.* Enola, PA: Author. Retrieved November 9, 2016, from http://www.nsvrc.org/sites/default/files/Publications_NSVRC_Factsheet_Impact-of-sexual-violence_0.pdf

National Women's Study. (2000). *National Institute on Drug Abuse.* Retrieved October 1, 2005, from http://data.library.ubc.ca/java/jsp/database/production/detail.jsp?id=528

Neisser, U. (1976). *Cognition and reality: Principles and implications of cognitive psychology.* San Francisco, CA: Freeman.

Nellis, A. (2016). *The color of justice: Racial and ethnic disparity in state prisons.* The Sentencing Project. Retrieved from www.sentencingproject.org

Nelson, N. W., Sweet, J. J., & Demakis, G. J. (2006). Meta-analysis of the MMPI-2 Fake Bad Scale: Utility in forensic practice. *The Clinical Neuropsychologist, 20*, 39–58.

Nettler, G. (1974). *Explaining crime*. New York, NY: McGraw-Hill.

New York ACLU. (2016). Stop-and-frisk data. Retrieved October 31, 2016, from http://www.nyclu.org/content/stop-and-frisk-data

New York Department of Corrections and Community Supervision. (2012). *Home page*. Retrieved from http://www.doccs.ny.gov/

Newton, E. (2009). *Ban on drooping drawers faces legal challenge*. Retrieved April 20, 2009, from http://www.nytimes.com/2009/04/13/us/13pants.html

Nicholls, T., Ogloff, J., Brink, J., & Spidel, A. (2005). Psychopathy in women: A review of its clinical usefulness for assessing risk for aggression and criminality. *Behavioral Sciences & the Law, 23*, 779–802. doi:10.1002/bsl.678

Nicholson, R. A. (1999). Forensic assessment. In R. Roesch, S. D. Hart, & J. R. Ogloff (Eds.), *Psychology and law: The state of the discipline* (pp. 122–173). New York, NY: Kluwer/Plenum.

Nicholson, R. A., & Kugler, K. E. (1991). Competent and incompetent criminal defendants: A quantitative review of comparative research. *Psychological Bulletin, 109*, 355–370.

Nicholson, R. A., & Norwood, S. (2000). The quality of forensic psychological assessments, reports, and testimony: Acknowledging the gap between promise and practice. *Law and Human Behavior, 24*, 9–44.

Nicholson, R. A., Norwood, S., & Enyart, C. (1991). Characteristics and outcomes of insanity acquittees in Oklahoma. *Behavioral Sciences & the Law, 9*, 487–500.

Nielsen, L. (2017). Re-examining the research on parental conflict, coparenting, and custody arrangements. *Psychology, Public Policy, and Law, 23*, 211–231. doi:10.1037/law0000109

Nietzel, M. T. (1979). *Crime and its modification: A social learning perspective*. New York, NY: Pergamon.

Nietzel, M. T., & Dillehay, R. C. (1986). *Psychological consultation in the courtroom*. New York, NY: Pergamon.

Nishith, P., Mechanic, M. B., & Resick, P. A. (2000). Prior interpersonal trauma: The contribution to current PTSD symptoms in female rape victims. *Journal of Abnormal Psychology, 109*, 20–25.

Nix, C. (1987, July 9). 1000 new officers graduate to New York City streets. *New York Times*, p. 15.

Nobile, P. (1989, July). The making of a monster. *Playboy*, 41–45.

Noble, K. B. (1987, March 23). High court to decide whether death penalty discriminates against blacks. *New York Times*, p. 7.

Nord, C. W., Brimhall, D., & West, J. (1997). *Fathers' involvement in their children's schools*. Washington, DC: National Center for Education Statistics.

Nordheimer, J. (1989, January 25). Bundy is put to death in Florida, closing murder cases across U.S. *New York Times*, pp. A1, A11.

Norris, F., Foster, J., & Weishaar, D. (2002). The epidemiology of sex differences in PTSD across developmental, societal, and research contexts. In R. Kimerling, P. Ouimette & J. Wolfe (Eds.), *Gender and PTSD* (pp. 3–42). New York, NY: Guilford Press.

Norton, K., & Ryba, N. L. (2010). An investigation of the ECST-R as a measure of competence and feigning. *Journal of Forensic Psychology Practice, 10*(2), 91–106.

Nunez, N., Kehn, A., & Wright, D. (2011). When children are witnesses: The effects of context, age and gender on adults' perceptions of cognitive ability and honesty. *Applied Cognitive Psychology, 25*, 460–468.

Nunez, N., Myers, B., Wilkowski, B., & Schweitzer, K. (2017). The impact of angry versus sad victim impact statements on mock jurors' sentencing decisions in a capital trial. *Criminal Justice and Behavior, 44*, 862–886.

O'Connor v. Donaldson, 422 U.S. 563 (1975).

Obiakor, F., Merhing, T., & Schwenn, J. (1997). *Disruption, disaster, and death: Helping students deal with crises*. Reston, VA: Council for Exceptional Children.

Odgers, C., Moffitt, T., Broadbent, J., Dickson, N., Hancox, R., Harrington, H., … Caspi, A. (2008). Female and male antisocial trajectories: From childhood origins to adult outcomes. *Development and Psychopathology, 20*, 673–716. doi:10.1017/S0954579408000333

Odgers, C., Reppucci, N. D., & Moretti, M. (2005). Nipping psychopathy in the bud: An examination of the convergent, predictive, and theoretical utility of the PCL-YV among adolescent girls. *Behavioral Sciences & the Law, 23*, 743–763. doi:10.1002/bsl.664

Odinot, G., & Wolters, G. (2006). Repeated recall, retention interval and the accuracy confidence relation in eyewitness memory. *Applied Cognitive Psychology, 20*, 973–985.

Odinot, G., Wolters, G., & Lavender, T. (2009). Repeated partial eyewitness questioning causes confidence inflation but not retrieval-induced forgetting. *Applied Cognitive Psychology, 23*, 90–97.

Offe, H., & Offe, S. (2007). The comparison question test: Does it work and if so how? *Law and Human Behavior, 31*, 291–303.

Office of Juvenile Justice and Delinquency Prevention. (1995). *Guide for implementing the comprehensive strategy for serious, violent, and chronic juvenile offenders*. Washington, DC: Author.

Office of Juvenile Justice and Delinquency Prevention. (2008). *Model programs guide*. Retrieved June 11, 2008, from http://www.dsgonline.com/mpg2.5/mpg_index.htm

Office of Juvenile Justice and Delinquency Prevention. (2015). *Offending by juveniles*. Washington, DC: Author. Retrieved April 13, 2017, from https://www.ojjdp.gov/ojstatbb/offenders/qa03105.asp?qaDate=2014

Office of Juvenile Justice and Delinquency Prevention. (2017a). *Juvenile arrest rate trends*. Washington, DC: Author. Retrieved July 16, 2017, from https://www.ojjdp.gov/ojstatbb/crime/JAR_Display.asp?ID=qa05201

Office of Juvenile Justice and Delinquency Prevention. (2017b). Easy access to FBI arres statistics: 1994–2012. Washington, DC: Author. Retrieved July 16, 2017, from https://www.ojjdp.gov/ojstatbb/ezaucr/asp/ucr_display.asp

Ogloff, J. R. P. (1991). A comparison of insanity defense standards on juror decision making. *Law and Human Behavior, 15*, 509–532.

Ogloff, J. R. P., & Chopra, S. (2004). Stuck in the dark ages: Supreme Court decision making and legal developments. *Psychology, Public Policy, and Law, 10*, 379–416.

Ogloff, J. R. P., & Finkelman, D. (1999). Psychology and law: An overview. In R. Roesch, S. D. Hart, & J. R. Ogloff (Eds.), *Psychology and law: The state of the discipline* (pp. 1–20). New York, NY: Kluwer.

Ogloff, J. R. P., & Otto, R. (1993). Psychological autopsy: Clinical and legal perspectives. *Saint Louis University Law Journal, 37*, 607–646.

Ogloff, J. R. P., & Vidmar, N. (1994). The impact of pretrial publicity on jurors: A study to compare the relative effects of television and print media in a child sex abuse case. *Law and Human Behavior, 18*, 507–525.

Olczak, P. V., Kaplan, M. F., & Penrod, S. (1991). Attorneys' lay psychology and its effectiveness in selecting jurors: Three empirical studies. *Journal of Social Behavior and Personality, 6*, 431–452.

Olson, J., & Zanna, M. (1993). Attitudes and attitude change. *Annual Review of Psychology, 44*, 117–154.

Oppel, R. (2011, September 26). *Sentencing shift gives new leverage to prosecutors*. Retrieved March 22, 2012, from http://www.nytimes.com/2011/09/26/us/tough-sentences-help-prosecutors-push-for-plea-bargains.html?pagewanted=all

Orchowski, L. M., Gidycz, C. A., & Raffle, H. (2008). Evaluation of a sexual assault risk reduction and self-defense program: A prospective analysis of a revised protocol. *Psychology of Women Quarterly, 32*, 204–218.

Osman, S. (2011). Predicting rape empathy based on victim, perpetrator, and participant gender, and history of sexual aggression. *Sex Roles, 64*, 506–515.

Ostrov, E. (1986). Police/law enforcement and psychology. *Behavioral Sciences & the Law, 4*, 353–370.

Otto, R., & Edens, J. (2003). Parenting capacity. In T. Grisso (Ed.), *Evaluating competencies* (2nd ed., pp. 229–308). New York, NY: Springer.

Otto, R., Poythress, N., Starr, K., & Darkes, J. (1993). An empirical study of the reports of APA's peer review panel in the congressional review of the *USS Iowa* incident. *Journal of Personality Assessment, 61*, 425–442.

Owen, D. (2004). *Criminal minds: The science and psychology of profiling.* New York, NY: Barnes & Noble Books.

Packer, H. L. (1964). Two models of the criminal process. *University of Pennsylvania Law Review, 113*, 1–68.

Palmer, M., Brewer, N., & Horry, R. (2013). Understanding gender bias in face recognition: Effects of divided attention at encoding. *Acta Psychologica, 142*, 362–369.

Panetti v. Quarterman, 551 U.S. 930 (2007).

Park, J., & Feigenson, N. (2013). Effects of visual technology on mock juror decision making. *Applied Cognitive Psychology, 27*, 235–246.

Parker, R. (2004). Alcohol and violence: Connections, evidence and possibilities for prevention. *Journal of Psychoactive Drugs, 36* (Suppl. 2), 157–163.

Paterson, H. M., & Kemp, R. I. (2006). Comparing methods of encountering post-event information: The power of co-witness suggestion. *Applied Cognitive Psychology, 20*, 1083–1099.

Patihis, L., Ho L. Y., Tingen, I. W., Lilienfeld, S. O., & Loftus, E. F. (2014). Are the "memory wars" over? A scientist-practitioner gap in beliefs about repressed memory. *Psychological Science, 25*, 519–530.

Patrick, C. (2008). Psychophysiological correlates of aggression and violence: An integrative review. *Philosophical Transactions of the Royal Society B: Biological Sciences, 363*, 2543–2555.

Patton v. Yount, 467 U.S. 1025 (1984).

Payne, B. K., & Button, D. M. (2009). Developing a citywide youth violence prevention plan. *International Journal of Offender Therapy and Comparative Criminology, 53*, 517–534.

Paz-Alonso, P., & Goodman, G. (2016). Developmental differences across middle childhood in memory and suggestibility for negative and positive events. *Behavioral Sciences and the Law, 34*, 30–54.

Peak, K., Bradshaw, R., & Glensor, R. (1992). Improving citizen perceptions of the police: "Back to the basics" with a community policing strategy. *Journal of Criminal Justice, 20*, 24–40.

Pearson, A., Dovidio, J., & Gaertner, S. (2009). The nature of contemporary prejudice: Insights from aversive racism. *Social and Personality Psychology Compass, 3*, 314–338.

Pena-Rodriguez v. Colorado, 137 S. Ct. 855 (2017).

Pennington, N., & Hastie, R. (1986). Evidence evaluation in complex decision making. *Journal of Personality and Social Psychology, 51*, 242–258.

Pennington, N., & Hastie, R. (1988). Explanation-based decision making: Effects of memory structure on judgment. *Journal of Experimental Psychology: Learning, Memory, and Cognition, 14*, 521–533.

Pennington, N., & Hastie, R. (1993). The story model for juror decision making. In R. Hastie (Ed.), *Inside the juror: The psychology of juror decision making* (pp. 192–221). New York, NY: Cambridge University Press.

Penrod, S. D. (1990). Predictors of jury decision making in criminal and civil cases: A field experiment. *Forensic Reports, 3*, 261–278.

Penrod, S. D., Loftus, E. F., & Winkler, J. (1982). The reliability of eyewitness testimony: A psychological perspective. In N. L. Kerr & R. M. Bray (Eds.), *The psychology of the courtroom* (pp. 119–168). Orlando, FL: Academic Press.

People v. Falsetta, 986 P. 2d 182 (1999).

People v. Taylor, 598 N.E.2d 693 (1992).

Perkonigg, A., Kessler, R. C., Storz, S., & Wittchen, H. U. (2000). Traumatic events and post-traumatic stress disorder in the community: Prevalence, risk factors and comorbidity. *Acta Psychiatrica Scandinavica, 101*, 46–59.

Perlin, M. (1996). The insanity defense: Deconstructing the myths and reconstructing the jurisprudence. In B. D. Sales & D. W. Shulman (Eds.), *Law, mental health, and mental disorder* (pp. 341–359). Pacific Grove, CA: Brooks/Cole.

Petherick, W. (2005). *The science of criminal profiling.* New York, NY: Barnes & Noble.

Pew Research Center. (2015). Social and demographic trends. Retrieved December 26, 2016, from http://www.pewsocialtrends.org/2015/12/17/1-the-american-family-today/

Pezdek, K. (2012). Fallible eyewitness memory and identification. In Cutler, B. (Ed.), *Conviction of the innocent: Lessons from psychological research* (pp. 105–124). Washington, DC: American Psychological Association.

Pfohl, S. J. (1984). Predicting dangerousness: A social deconstruction of psychiatric reality. In L. A. Teplin (Ed.), *Mental health and criminal justice* (pp. 201–225). Newbury Park, CA: Sage.

Phillips, A. (2004, February 8). Training to be police officers: What does it take to join the force? These cadets are finding out. *The Austin American Statesman.* Retrieved July 15, 2005, from http://www.statesman.com/opinion/content/editorial/cadets/0208apdcadets.html

Phillips, C. (Producer). (2006, October 1). *Dexter* [Television Series]. Long Beach, CA: Showtime Network.

Phillips, D. A. (1979). *The great Texas murder trials: A compelling account of the sensational T. Cullen Davis case.* New York, NY: Macmillan.

Phillips, M. (2012). *Decade of bail research in New York City.* Bureau of Justice Statistics. Washington, DC: U.S. Department of Justice.

Phillips, M., McAuliff, B., Kovera, M., & Cutler, B. (1999). Double-blind photoarray administration as a safeguard against investigator bias. *Journal of Applied Psychology, 84*, 940–951.

Pickel, K., French, T., & Betts, J. (2003). A cross-modal weapon focus effect: The influence of a weapon's presence on memory for auditory information. *Memory, 11*, 277–292.

Piechowski, L. (2011). *Evaluation of workplace disability.* New York, NY: Oxford University Press.

Pienaar, J., Rothmann, S., & Van de Vijver, F. J. R. (2007). Occupational stress, personality traits, coping strategies, and suicide ideation in the South African Police Service. *Criminal Justice and Behavior, 34*, 246–258. doi:10.1177/0093854806288708

Pierce, G., & Radelet, M. (2005). The impact of legally inappropriate factors on death sentencing for California homicides, 1990–1999. *Santa Clara Law Review, 46*, 1–47.

Pinizzotto, A. J., & Finkel, N. J. (1990). Criminal personality profiling: An outcome and process study. *Law and Human Behavior, 14*, 215–234.

Plessy v. Ferguson, 163 U.S. 537 (1896).

Plumm, K., & Terrance, C. (2009). Battered women who kill: The impact of expert testimony and empathy induction in the courtroom. *Violence Against Women, 15*, 186–205.

Podkopacz, M., & Feld, B. (2001). The back door to prison: Waiver reform, blended sentencing, and the law of unintended consequences. *Journal of Criminal Law & Criminology, 91*, 997–1071.

Police Executive Research Forum. (2013). *A National Survey of Eyewitness Identification Procedures in Law Enforcement Agencies.* Report submitted to the National Institute of Justice, March 8, 2013.

Pollack, D., McFarland, B., Mahler, J., & Kovas, A. (2005). Outcomes of patients in low-intensity, short-duration involuntary outpatient commitment program. *Psychiatric Services, 26*, 863–866.

Poole, D., Brubacher, S., & Dickinson, J. (2015). Children as witnesses. In B. Cutler & P. Zapf (Eds.), *APA Handbook of forensic psychology, Vol. 2. Criminal investigation, adjudication, and sentencing outcome* (pp. 3–31). Washington, DC: APA.

Porter, B. (1983). Mind hunters. *Psychology Today, 17,* 44–52.

Porter, L. (2013). Trying something old: The impact of shame sanctioning on drunk driving and alcohol-related traffic safety. *Law and Social Inquiry, 38,* 863–891.

Porter, R. (2012). *Giving juvenile offenders a second chance at Oakland's Youth UpRising.* Retrieved from http://oaklandlocal.com/posts/2012/03/giving-juvenile-offenders-second-chance-oaklands-youth-uprising-community-voices

Portland State University Criminology and Criminal Justice Senior Capstone. (2011). *Police community partnerships: A review of the literature.* Criminology and Criminal Justice Senior Capstone Project. Paper 7. Retrieved November 1, 2016, from http://pdxscholar.library.pdx.edu/cgi/viewcontent.cgi?article=1005&context=ccj_capstone

Portland State University Criminology and Criminal Justice Senior Capstone. (2014). *Prevention and management of stress in policing: A review of the literature.* Criminology and Criminal Justice Senior Capstone Project. Paper 11. Retrieved from http://pdxscholar.library.pdx.edu/ccj_capstone/11

Posey, A. (2016). From war protestors to corporate litigants: The evolution of the profession of trial consulting. In C. W. Esqueda & B. H. Bornstein (Eds.), *The witness stand and Lawrence S. Wrightsman, Jr.* (pp. 129–151). New York, NY: Springer-Verlag.

Post, C. G. (1963). *An introduction to the law.* Englewood Cliffs, NJ: Prentice Hall.

Post, L. (2004a, June 7). Courts mix justice with social work. *National Law Journal,* p. 1.

Post, L. (2004b, November 8). *Spelling it out in plain English.* Retrieved November 11, 2004, from www.law.com/jsp/nlj

Post, L. (2004c, June 21). Report: Civil trials fall by half. *National Law Journal,* p. 6.

Poulson, R., Wuensch, K., & Brondino, M. (1998). Factors that discriminate among mock juror's verdict selection: Impact of the Guilty But Mentally Ill verdict option. *Criminal Justice and Behavior, 25,* 366–381.

Powers v. Ohio, 499 U.S. 400 (1991).

Poythress, N., Bonnie, R., Monahan, J., Otto, R., & Hoge, S. K. (2002). *Adjudicative competence: The MacArthur Studies.* New York, NY: Kluwer Academic/Plenum.

Poythress, N. G., Bonnie, R. J., Hoge, S. K., Monahan, J., & Oberlander, L. B. (1994). Client abilities to assist counsel and make decisions in criminal cases: Findings from three studies. *Law and Human Behavior, 18,* 437–452.

Poythress, N. G., Nicholson, R., Otto, R. K., Edens, J. F., Bonnie, R. J., Monahan, J., & Hoge, S. K. (1999). *The MacArthur Competence Assessment Tool—Criminal Adjudication: Professional Manual.* Odessa, FL: Psychological Assessment Resources.

Pozzulo, J., & Dempsey, J. (2009). Witness factors and their influence on jurors' perceptions and verdicts. *Criminal Justice and Behavior, 36,* 923–934.

Pozzulo, J. D., Dempsey, J. L., Crescini, C., & Lemieux, J. M. T. (2009). Examining the relation between eyewitness recall and recognition for children and adults. *Psychology, Crime & Law, 15*(5), 409–424.

Prentky, R. A., & Knight, R. A. (1991). Identifying critical dimensions for discriminating among rapists. *Journal of Consulting and Clinical Psychology, 59,* 643–661.

President's Task Force on 21st Century Policing. (2015). *Final report of the President's Task Force on 21st Century Policing.* Washington, DC: Office of Community Oriented Policing Services.

Prettyman, E. B. (1960). Jury instructions—First or last? *American Bar Association Journal, 46,* 10–66.

Price, H., & Fitzgerald, R. (2016). Face-off: A new identification procedure for child eyewitnesses. *Journal of Experimental Psychology: Applied, 22,* 366–380.

Priebe, G., & Svedin, C. G. (2008). Child sexual abuse is largely hidden from the adult society: An epidemiological study of adolescents' disclosures. *Child Abuse & Neglect, 32,* 1095–1108.

Pryor, J. B., Giedd, J. L., & Williams, K. B. (1995). A social psychological model for predicting sexual harassment. *Journal of Social Issues, 51,* 69–84.

Public Religion Research Institute. (2015). Anxiety, nostalgia, and mistrust: Findings from the 2015 American Values Survey. Retrieved from https://www.prri.org/research/survey-anxiety-nostalgia-and-mistrust-findings-from-the-2015-american-values-survey

Purkett v. Elem, 514 U.S. 765 (1995).

Puzzanchera, C., Adams, B., & Sickmund, M. (2010). *Juvenile Court Statistics, 2006–2007.* Pittsburgh, PA: National Center for Juvenile Justice.

Qualters, S. (2010, September 22). Two federal judges offer differing takes on declining trial numbers. *New York Law Journal.* Retrieved from http://www.newyorklawjournal.com/PubArticleNY.jsp?id=1202472305785

Qualters, S. (2012, March 8). *Seventh Circuit gives plaintiff new trial in bias case.* Retrieved June 9, 2012, from http://www.law.com/jsp/law/LawArticleFriendly.jsp?id=1202545092993&slreturn=1

Quas, J., & Goodman, G. (2012). Consequences of criminal court involvement for child victims. *Psychology, Public Policy, and Law, 18,* 392–414.

Quas, J., Goodman, G., Ghetti, S., Alexander, K., Edelstein, R., Redlich, A., … Jones, D. (2005). Childhood sexual assault victims: Long-term outcomes after testifying in criminal court. *Monographs of the Society for Research in Child Development, 70*(2, Serial No. 280), 1–145.

Quas, J., Malloy, L., Melinder, A., Goodman, G., D'Mello, M., & Schaaf, J. (2007). Developmental differences in the effects of repeated interviews and interviewer bias on young children's event memory and false reports. *Developmental Psychology, 43,* 823–837.

Quas, J., & Schaaf, J. (2002). Children's memories of experienced and nonexperienced events following repeated interviews. *Journal of Experimental Child Psychology, 83,* 304–338.

Quay, H. C. (1965). Personality and delinquency. In H. C. Quay (Ed.), *Juvenile delinquency* (pp. 139–169). Princeton, NJ: Van Nostrand.

Quinlivan, D., Neuschatz, J., Cutler, B., Wells, G., McClung, J., & Harker, D. (2012). Do pre-admonition suggestions moderate the effect of unbiased lineup instructions? *Legal and Criminological Psychology, 17,* 165–176.

Quinn, J. (1996). "Attitudinal" decision making in the federal courts: A study of constitutional self-representation claims. *San Diego Law Review, 33,* 701–754.

Quinsey, V., Harris, G., Rice, M., & Cormier, C. (2006). *Violent offenders: Appraising and managing risk* (2nd ed.). Washington, DC: American Psychological Association.

Rabe-Hemp, C., & Schuck, A. (2007). Violence against police officers: Are female officers at greater risk? *Police Quarterly, 10,* 411–428.

Radelet, M., Bedau, H., & Putnam, C. (1992). *In spite of innocence: Erroneous convictions in capital cases.* Boston, MA: Northeastern University Press.

Rafilson, F., & Sison, R. (1996). Seven criterion-related validity studies conducted with the National Police Officer Selection Test. *Psychological Reports, 78,* 163–176.

Raine, A. (2002). Annotation: The role of prefrontal deficits, low autonomic arousal, and early health factors in the development of antisocial and aggressive behavior in children. *Journal of Child Psychology & Psychiatry, 43,* 417–434.

Raine, A., Lencz, T., Bihrle, S., Lacasse, L., & Colletti, P. (2000). Reduced prefrontal gray matter volume and reduced autonomic activity in antisocial personality disorder. *Archives of General Psychiatry, 57,* 119–127.

Raine, A., Meloy, J., & Buchsbaum, M. (1998). Reduced prefrontal and increased subcortical brain functioning using positron emission tomography in predatory and affective murderers. *Behavioral Sciences & the Law, 16,* 319–332.

Raine, A., Venables, P., & Williams, M. (1989). Relationships between N1, P300, and contingent negative variation recorded at age 15 and criminal behavior at age 24. *Psychophysiology, 27,* 567–574.

Rakoff, J. (2014, November 20). Why innocent people plead guilty. *The New York Review of Books.* Retrieved from http://www.nybooks.com/articles/2014/11/20/why-innocent-people-plead-guilty/

Ramirez, G., Zemba, D., & Geiselman, R. E. (1996). Judge's cautionary instructions on eyewitness testimony. *American Journal of Forensic Psychology, 14,* 31–66.

Rassin, E. (2016). Rational thinking promotes suspect-friendly legal decision making. *Applied Cognitive Psychology, 30,* 460–464.

Reaves, B. (2013). *Felony defendants in large urban counties-2009.* Washington, DC: U.S. Department of Justice, Bureau of Justice Statistics.

Reckless, W. C. (1967). *The crime problem* (4th ed.). New York, NY: Meredith.

Redding, R., & Mrozoski, B. (2005). Adjudicatory and dispositional decision making in juvenile justice. In K. Heilbrun, N., Goldstein, & R. Redding (Eds.), *Juvenile delinquency: Prevention, assessment, and intervention* (pp. 232–256). New York, NY: Oxford University Press.

Redding, R. E., Floyd, M. Y., & Hawk, G. L. (2001). What judges and lawyers think about the testimony of mental health experts: A survey of the courts and bar. *Behavioral Sciences & the Law, 19,* 583–594.

Redding, R. E., & Hensl, K. B. (2011). Knowledgeable judges make a difference: Judicial beliefs affect juvenile court transfer decisions. *Juvenile and Family Court Journal, 62,* 15–24.

Reddy, M., Borum, R., Berglund, J., Vossekuil, B., Fein, R., & Modzeleski, W. (2001). Evaluating risk for targeted violence in schools: Comparing risk assessment, threat assessment, and other approaches. *Psychology in the Schools, 38,* 157–172.

Redlich, A., & Shteynberg, R. (2016). To plead or not to plead: A comparison of juvenile and adult true and false plea decisions. *Law and Human Behavior, 40,* 611–625.

Redlich, A., Steadman, H. J., Monahan, J., Petrila, J., & Griffin, P. (2005). The second generation of mental health courts. *Psychology, Public Policy, & Law, 11,* 527–538.

Redlich, A. D., Hoover, S., Summers, A., & Steadman, H. J. (2010). Enrollment in mental health courts: Voluntariness, knowingness, and adjudicative competence. *Law and Human Behavior, 34,* 91–104.

Redondo, S., Sanchez-Meca, J., & Garrido, V. (1999). The influence of treatment programs on the recidivism of juvenile and adult offenders: A European meta-analytic review. *Psychology, Crime and Law, 5,* 251–278.

Reed, K., & Bornstein, B. H. (2013). A stressful profession: The experience of attorneys. In M. K. Miller & B. H. Bornstein (Eds.), *Stress, trauma, and wellbeing in the legal system.* New York, NY: Oxford University Press.

Reed, K., Bornstein, B. H., Jeon, A., & Wylie, L. (2016). Problem signs in law school: Fostering attorney well-being early in professional training. *International Journal of Law and Psychiatry, 47,* 148–156.

Reiber, M., & Weinberg, J. (2010). The complexity of complexity: An empirical study of juror competence in civil cases. *University of Cincinnati Law Review, 78,* 929–968.

Reibstein, L., & Foote, D. (1996, November 4). Playing the victim card. *Newsweek,* pp. 64, 66.

Reisberg, D., & Heuer, F. (2007). The influence of emotion on memory for forensic settings. In M. Toglia, J. Read, D. Ross, & R. Lindsay (Eds.), *The handbook of eyewitness psychology: Memory for events.* Mahwah, NJ: Erlbaum.

Ressler, R. K., Burgess, A. W., & Douglas, J. E. (1988). *Sexual homicide: Patterns and motives.* Lexington, MA: Lexington Books.

Reuland, M., Schwarzfeld, M., & Draper, L. (2009). *Law enforcement responses to people with mental illness: A guide to research-informed policy and practice.* New York, NY: Justice Center, Council of State Governments. Retrieved July 14, 2017, from https://csgjusticecenter.org/wp-content/uploads/2012/12/le-research.pdf

Rhee, N. (2016, April 13). How Chicago police can rebuild trust. *Christian Science Monitor.* Retrieved November 21, 2017 from https://www.csmonitor.com/USA/Justice/2016/0413/How-Chicago-police-can-rebuild-trust

Rhee, S., & Waldman, I. (2002). Genetic and environmental influences on antisocial behavior: A meta-analysis of twin and adoption studies. *Psychological Bulletin, 128,* 490–529. doi:10.1037/0033-2909.128.3.490

Rhode Island v. Innis, 446 U.S. 291 (1980).

Rice, C. (2012). *Power concedes nothing: One woman's quest for social justice in America, from the kill zones to the courtroom.* New York, NY: Scribner.

Richardson, A., & Budd, T. (2003). Young adults, alcohol, crime and disorder. *Criminal Behaviour & Mental Health, 13,* 5–16.

Richey, C. R. (1994). Proposals to eliminate the prejudicial effect of the use of the word "expert" under the federal rules of evidence in civil and criminal jury trials. *Federal Rules Decisions, 154,* 537–562.

Richter, E., & Humke, A. (2011). Demonstrative evidence: Evidence and technology in the courtroom. In R. Wiener & B. Bornstein (Eds.), *Handbook of trial consulting* (pp. 187–202). New York, NY: Springer.

Rickert, J. (2010). Denying defendants the benefit of a reasonable doubt: Federal rule of evidence 609 and past sex crime convictions. *Journal of Criminal Law and Criminology, 100,* 213–242.

Rideau v. Louisiana, 373 U.S. 723 (1963).

Rider, A. O. (1980). The firesetter: A psychological profile. *FBI Law Enforcement Bulletin, 49,* 123.

Ring v. Arizona, 536 U.S. 584 (2002).

Risinger, D., & Loop, J. (2002). Three card monte, Monty Hall, modus operandi, and "offender profiling": Some lessons of modern cognitive science for the law of evidence. *Cardozo Law Review, 24,* 193–253.

Risinger, D. M. (2007). Innocents convicted: An empirically justified factual wrongful conviction rate. *Journal of Criminal Law and Criminology, 97,* 761–806.

Risling, G. (2008). *Jury convicts mother of lesser charges in MySpace suicide case.* Retrieved February 15, 2009, from http://www.law.com

Robbennolt, J. (2000). Outcome severity and judgments of "responsibility": A meta-analytic review. *Journal of Applied Social Psychology, 30,* 2575–2609.

Robbennolt, J. (2002). Punitive damage decision making: The decisions of citizens and trial court judges. *Law and Human Behavior, 26,* 315–342.

Robbennolt, J., & Davidson, S. (2011). Legal research techniques for social scientists. In B. Rosenfeld & S. Penrod (Eds.), *Research methods in forensic psychology* (pp. 3–25). New York, NY: Wiley.

Robbennolt, J. K. (2013). The effects of negotiated and delegated apologies in settlement negotiation. *Law and Human Behavior, 37* (2), 128–135.

Robbennolt, J. K., & Hans, V. P. (2016). *The psychology of tort law.* New York, NY: New York University Press.

Robertiello, G., & Terry, K. (2007). Can we profile sex offenders? A review of sex offender typologies. *Aggression and Violent Behavior, 12*, 508–518.

Roberts, A. L., Gillman, S. E., Breslau, J., Breslau, N., & Koenen, K. C. (2011). Race/ethnic differences in exposure to traumatic events, development of post-traumatic stress disorder, and treatment-seeking for post-traumatic stress disorder in the United States. *Psychological Medicine: A Journal of Research in Psychiatry and the Allied Sciences, 41*, 71–83.

Roberts, C. F., & Golding, S. L. (1991). The social construction of criminal responsibility and insanity. *Law and Human Behavior, 15*, 349–376.

Robertson, C., & Yokum, D. (2011). *Effect of blinded experts on mock jurors' assessments of credibility and verdicts in civil trials.* Arizona Legal Studies Discussion Paper No. 11-30. Retrieved July 17, 2012, from http://papers.ssrn.com/sol3/papers.cfm?abstract_id=1884765

Robertson, C. T. (2010). Blind expertise. *New York University Law Review, 85*, 175–257.

Rodriguez, F., Curry, T., & Lee, G. (2006). Gender differences in criminal sentencing: Do effects vary across violent, property, and drug offenses? *Social Sciences Quarterly, 87*, 318–339.

Roesch, R., Zapf, P., & Eaves, D. (2006). *Fitness Interview Test-Revised (FIT-R): A structured interview for assessing competency to stand trial.* Sarasota, FL: Professional Resource Press.

Rogers, B. (2010, July 8). Couple in theft from DA's victim fund get probation. *Houston Chronicle.* Retrieved from http://www.chron.com/news/houston-texas/article/Couple-in-theft-from-DA-s-victims-fund-get-1535735.php

Rogers, J., Sack, W., Bloom, J., & Manson, S. (1984). Women in Oregon's insanity defense system. *Journal of Psychiatry and Law, 11*, 515–532.

Rogers, R. (1986). *Conducting insanity evaluations.* New York, NY: Van Nostrand.

Rogers, R. (1988). *Clinical assessment of malingering and deception.* New York, NY: Guilford.

Rogers, R. (2001). *Handbook of diagnostic and structured interviewing* (2nd ed.). New York, NY: Guilford.

Rogers, R. (Ed.). (2008). *Clinical assessment of malingering and deception* (3rd ed.). New York, NY: Guilford.

Rogers, R., & Ewing, C. P. (1989). Ultimate opinion proscriptions: A cosmetic fix and a plea for empiricism. *Law and Human Behavior, 13*, 357–374.

Rogers, R., Grandjean, N., Tillbrook, C., Vitacco, M., & Sewell, K. (2001). Recent interview-based measures of competency to stand trial: A critical review augmented with research data. *Behavioral Sciences & the Law, 19*, 503–518.

Rogers, R., Rogstad, J., Gillard, N., Drogin, E., Blackwood, H., & Shuman, D. (2010). "Everyone knows their *Miranda* rights": Implicit assumptions and countervailing evidence. *Psychology, Public Policy, and Law, 16*, 300–318.

Rogers, R., Rogstad, J., Steadham, J., & Drogin, E. (2011). In plain English: Avoiding recognized problems with *Miranda* comprehension. *Psychology, Public Policy, & Law, 17*, 264–285.

Rogers, R., Salekin, R. T., Sewell, K. W., Goldstein, A., & Leonard, K. (1998). A comparison of forensic and nonforensic malingerers: A prototypical analysis of exploratory models. *Law and Human Behavior, 22*, 253–267.

Rogers, R., & Shuman, D. (2000). *Conducting insanity evaluations* (2nd ed.). New York, NY: Guilford.

Rogers, R., Steadham, J. A., Carter, R. M., Henry, S. A., Drogin, E. Y., & Robinson, E. V. (2016). An examination of juveniles' Miranda abilities: Investigating differences in Miranda recall and reasoning. *Behavioral Sciences & the Law, 34*, 515–538.

Rogers, R., Tillbrook, C., & Sewell, K. (2004). *Evaluation of Competence to Stand Trial—Revised: Professional manual.* Lutz, FL: Psychological Assessment Resources.

Rohling, M. L., Binder, L. M., & Langhrinrichsen-Rohling, J. (1995). Money matters: A meta-analytic review of the association between financial compensation and the experience and treatment of chronic pain. *Health Psychology, 14*, 537–547.

Roper v. Simmons, 543 U.S. 551 (2005).

Rose, M., & Diamond, S. (2008). Judging bias: Juror confidence and judicial rulings on challenges for cause. *Law and Society Review, 42*, 513–548.

Rose, M., Ellison, C., & Diamond, S. (2008). Preferences for juries over judges across racial and ethnic groups. *Social Science Quarterly, 89*, 372–391.

Rose, M. R., Diamond, S. S., & Musick, M. A. (2012). Selected to serve: An analysis of lifetime jury participation. *Journal of Empirical Legal Studies, 9*, 33–55.

Rosen, G. M. (1995). The *Aleutian Enterprise* sinking and posttraumatic stress disorder: Misdiagnosis in clinical and forensic settings. *Professional Psychology: Research and Practice, 26*, 82–87.

Rosen, J. (2010, January 10). *Prisoners of parole.* Retrieved July 22, 2011, from http://www.nytimes.com/2010/01/10/magazine/10prisons-t.html?_r=1&pagewanted=all

Rosenbaum, A., & Gearan, P. J. (1999). Relationship aggression between partners. In V. B. Van Hasselt & M. Hersen (Eds.), *Handbook of psychological approaches with violent offenders: Contemporary strategies and issues* (pp. 357–372). New York: Kluver Academic/Plenum.

Rosenbaum, D. P., Graziano, L. M., Stephens, C. D., & Schuck, A. M. (2011). Understanding community policing and legitimacy-seeking behavior in virtual reality: A national study of municipal police websites. *Police Quarterly, 14*, 25–47.

Rosenfeld, J., Soskins, M., Bosh, G., & Ryan, A. (2004). Simple effective countermeasures to P300-based tests of detection of concealed information. *Psychophysiology, 41*, 205–219.

Rosenfeld, J. P. (2005). Brain fingerprinting: A critical analysis. *Scientific Review of Mental Health Practice, 4*, 20–37.

Rosenmerkel, M., Durose, M., & Farole, D. (2009). *Felony sentences in state courts, 2006.* Bureau of Justice Statistics Report NCJ 226846. Washington, DC: Department of Justice.

Rosenthal, R., & Jacobson, L. (1968). *Pygmalion in the classroom: Teacher expectation and pupils' intellectual development.* New York, NY: Holt.

Rotundo, M., Nguyen, D., & Sackett, P. (2001). A meta-analytic review of gender differences in perceptions of sexual harassment. *Journal of Applied Psychology, 86*, 914–922.

Ruback, R. B. (2015). Sentencing. In B. Cutler & P. Zapf (Eds.), *APA handbook of forensic psychology: Vol. 2. Criminal investigation, adjudication, and sentencing outcomes* (pp. 385–414). Washington, DC: APA.

Rubin, D., & Boals, A. (2010). People who expect to enter psychotherapy are prone to believing that they have forgotten memories of childhood trauma and abuse. *Memory, 18*, 556–562.

Runda, J. (1991). *Personal affidavit filed with authors.* Lexington, KY: University of Kentucky Press.

Rusconi, E., & Mitchener-Nissen, T. (2013). Prospects of functional magnetic resonance imaging as lie detector. *Frontiers in Human Neuroscience, 7*, Article 594, 1–12.

Russell, B., & Melillo, L. (2006). Attitudes toward battered women who kill: Defendant typicality and judgments of culpability. *Criminal Justice and Behavior, 33*, 219–241.

Russell, M., & Odgers, C. (2016). Desistance and life-course persistence: Findings from longitudinal studies using group-based trajectory modeling of antisocial behavior. In K. Heilbrun, D. DeMatteo, & N. Goldstein (Eds.), *APA handbook of psychology and juvenile justice* (pp. 159–175). Washington, DC: American Psychological Association. doi:10.1037/14643-015

Ruva, C., & Guenther, C. (2015). From the shadows into the light: How pretrial publicity and deliberation affect mock jurors' decisions, impressions, and memory. *Law and Human Behavior, 39*, 294–310.

Ruva, C., Guenther, C., & Yarbrough, A. (2011). Positive and negative pretrial publicity: The roles of impression formation, emotion, and predecisional distortion. *Criminal Justice and Behavior, 38*, 511–534.

Ruva, C., & McEvoy, C. (2008). Negative and positive pretrial publicity affect juror memory and decision making. *Journal of Experimental Psychology: Applied, 14*, 226–236.

Ruva, C., McEvoy, C., & Bryant, J. (2007). Effects of pretrial publicity and collaboration on juror bias and source monitoring errors. *Applied Cognitive Psychology, 21*, 45–67.

Ryan, W. (1970). *Blaming the victim.* New York, NY: Vintage.

Sabol, W. J., & Couture, H. (2008). *Prison Inmates at Midyear 2007* (NCJ 221944). Retrieved November, 30, 2010, from U.S. Department of Justice, Office of Justice Programs: http://bjs.ojp.usdoj.gov/content/pub/pdf/pim07.pdf

Sack, E. (2002). *Creating a domestic violence court: Guidelines and best practices.* San Francisco, CA: Family Violence Prevention Fund.

Sack, K., & Blinder, A. (2017, January 1). Dylann Roof himself rejects best defense against execution. *New York Times.* Retrieved from https://www.nytimes.com/2017/01/01/us/dylann-roof-execution-defense-charleston-church-shooting.html

Sacks, D., Bushman, B., & Anderson, C. (2011). Do violent video games harm children? Comparing the scientific amicus curiae "experts" in *Brown v. Entertainment Merchants Association. Northwestern University Law Review, 106*, 1–12.

Saks, M. (1997). What do jury experiments tell us about how juries (should) make decisions? *Southern California Interdisciplinary Law Journal, 6*, 1–53.

Salekin, R. (2004). *The Risk-Sophistication-Treatment Inventory.* Lutz, FL: Psychological Assessment Resources.

Salekin, R., Trobst, K., & Krioukova, M. (2001). Construct validity of psychopathy in a community sample: A nomological net approach. *Journal of Personality Disorders, 15*, 425–441.

Salerno, J. (2017). Seeing red: Disgust reactions to gruesome photographs in color (but not in black and white) increase convictions. *Psychology, Public Policy, and Law*, advance online publication.

Salerno, J., & McCauley, M. (2009). Mock jurors' judgments about opposing scientific experts: Do cross-examination, deliberation, and need for cognition matter? *American Journal of Forensic Psychology, 27*, 37–60.

Sales, B. D., & Hafemeister, T. (1984). Empiricism and legal policy on the insanity defense. In L. A. Teplin (Ed.), *Mental health and criminal justice* (pp. 253–278). Newbury Park, CA: Sage.

Sales, B. D., & Shuman, D. W. (1993). Reclaiming the integrity of science in expert witnessing. *Ethics and Behavior, 3*, 223–229.

Salfati, C. G., & Canter, D. V. (1999). Differentiating stranger murders: Profiling offender characteristics from behavioral styles. *Behavioral Sciences & the Law, 17*, 391–406.

Sample, J., Skaggs, A., Blitzer, J., & Casey, L. (2010). The new politics of judicial elections 2000–2009: Decade of change. Retrieved from www.justiceatstake.org/media/cms/JASNPJEDecadeONLINE_EC9663F6F7865.pdf

Sanborn, H. (2002, October). The vanishing trial. *American Bar Association Journal, 87*, 24–27.

Sanders, J. (1993). The jury decision in a complex case: *Havener v. Merrell Dow Pharmaceuticals. The Justice System Journal, 16*, 45.

Sandler, J. C., Letourneau, E. J., Vandiver, D. M., Shields, R. T., & Chaffin, M. (2017). Juvenile sexual crime reporting rates are not influenced by juvenile sex offender registration policies. *Psychology, Public Policy, and Law, 23*(2), 131–140.

Sanschagrin, K., Stevens, T., Bove, A., & Heilbrun, K. (2006, March). *Quality of forensic mental health assessment of juvenile offenders: An empirical investigation.* Paper presented at the annual conference of the American Psychology-Law Society, Tampa, Florida.

Santobello v. New York, 404 U.S. 257 (1971).

Sarteschi, C. (2009). *Assessing the effectiveness of mental health courts: A meta-analysis of clinical and recidivism outcomes.* Doctoral Dissertation, University of Pittsburgh. Retrieved December 22, 2016, from http://d-scholarship.pitt.edu/9275/

Sarteschi, C. M., Vaughn, M. G., & Kim, K. (2011). Assessing the effectiveness of mental health courts: A quantitative review. *Journal of Criminal Justice, 39*, 12–20.

Satterwhite v. Texas, 108 S. Ct. 1792 (1988).

Sawyer, A., & Borduin, C. (2011). Effects of multisystemic therapy through midlife: A 21.9-year follow-up to a randomized clinical trial with serious and violent juvenile offenders. *Journal of Consulting and Clinical Psychology, 79*, 634–652.

Scherr, K., & Madon, S. (2012). You have the right to understand: The deleterious effect of stress on *Miranda* comprehension. *Law and Human Behavior, 36*, 275–282.

Scherr, K., & Madon, S. (2013). "Go ahead and sign": An experimental examination of *Miranda* waivers and comprehension. *Law and Human Behavior, 37*, 208–218.

Schmucker, M., & Losel, F. (2015). The effects of sexual offender treatment on recidivism: An international meta-analysis of sound quality evaluations. *Journal of Experimental Criminology, 11*, 597–630.

Schoenwald, S., Henggeler, S., Brondino, M., & Rowland, M. (2000). Multisystemic therapy: Monitoring treatment fidelity. *Family Process, 39*, 83–103.

Schoenwald, S., Sheidow, A., & Letourneau, E. (2003). Toward effective quality assurance in multisystemic therapy: Links between expert consultation, therapist fidelity, and child outcomes. *Journal of Clinical Child and Adolescent Psychology, 33*, 94–104.

Schram, P. J., & Morash, M. (2002). Evaluation of a life skills program for women inmates in Michigan. *Journal of Offender Rehabilitation, 34*, 47–70.

Schreiber, J., Green, D., Kunz, M., Belfi, B., & Pequeno, G. (2015). Offense characteristics of Incompetent to Stand Trial defendants charged with violent offenses. *Behavioral Sciences & the Law, 33*, 257–278. doi:10.1002/bsl.2174. Epub 2015, March 31.

Schroeder, L. (2014). Cracks in the ivory tower: How the Campus Sexual Violence Elimination Act can protect students from sexual assault. *Loyola University Chicago Law Journal, 45*, 1195–1243.

Schuller, R., McKimmie, B., & Janz, T. (2004). The impact of expert testimony in trials of battered women who kill. *Psychiatry, Psychology and Law, 11*, 1–12.

Science Daily. (2007, June 28). New study shows how often juries get it wrong. *Science Daily.* Retrieved June 5, 2012, from http://www.sciencedaily.com/releases/2007/06/070628161330.htm

Scoboria, A., Wade, K., Lindsay, D., Azad, T., Strange, D., Ost, J., & Hyman, I. (2017). A mega-analysis of memory reports from eight peer-reviewed false memory implantation studies. *Memory, 25*, 146–163.

Scott, Y. M. (2004). Stress among rural and small-town patrol officers: A survey of Pennsylvania municipal agencies. *Police Quarterly, 7*, 237–261. doi:10.1177/1098611103258958

Scurich, N., & Monahan, J. (2016). Evidence-based sentencing: Public openness and opposition to using gender, age, and race as risk factors for recidivism. *Law and Human Behavior, 40*, 36–41.

Seamon, J., Philbin, M., & Harrison, L. (2006). Do you remember proposing marriage to the Pepsi machine? False recollections from a college walk. *Psychonomic Bulletin & Review, 13*, 752–756.

Segal, J., & Spaeth, H. (1993). *The Supreme Court and the attitudinal model.* New York, NY: Cambridge University Press.

Seig, A, Ball, E., & Menninger, J. (1995). A comparison of female versus male insanity acquittees in Colorado. *Bulletin of the American Academy of Psychiatry and Law, 23*, 523–532.

Seiter, R. P., & Kadela, K. R. (2003). Prisoner reentry: What works, what does not, and what is promising. *Crime & Delinquency, 49*, 360–388.

Sell v. U.S., 539 U.S. 166 (2003).

Seltzer, R. (2006). Scientific jury selection: Does it work? *Journal of Applied Social Psychology, 36*, 2417–2435.

Semmler, C., Brewer, N., & Douglass, A. (2012). Jurors believe eyewitnesses. In B. Cutler (Ed.), *Conviction of the innocent: Lessons from psychological research* (pp. 185–209). Washington, DC: American Psychological Association.

The Sentencing Project. (2016). Incarcerated women and girls. Retrieved October 19, 2016, from www.sentencingproject.org/wp/content/uploads/2016/02/Incarcerated-Women-and-Girls.pdf

Settles, I., Buchanan, N., Yap, S., & Harrell, Z. (2014). Sex differences in outcomes and harasser characteristics associated with frightening sexual harassment appraisals. *Journal of Occupational Health Psychology*. Online publication March 17, 2014. doi:10.1037/a0035449

Seventh Circuit American Jury Project. (2008). Retrieved January 30, 2009, from www.7thcircuitbar.org/associations/1507/files/7th%20Circuit%20American%20Jury%20Project%20Final%20Report.pdf

Sevier, J. (2014). The truth-justice tradeoff: Perceptions of decisional accuracy and procedural justice in adversarial and inquisitorial legal system. *Psychology, Public Policy, and Law, 20*, 212–224.

Sexton, T., & Turner, C. (2010). The effectiveness of functional family therapy for youth with behavioral problems in a community practice setting. *Journal of Family Psychology, 24*, 339–348.

Shafer, M., Arthur, B., & Franczak, M. (2004). An analysis of post-booking jail diversion programming for persons with co-occurring disorders. *Behavioral Sciences and the Law, 22*, 771–785.

Shaffer, D. K. (2011). Looking inside the black box of drug courts: A meta-analytic review, *Justice Quarterly, 28*, 493–521.

Shannon v. United States, 114 S.Ct. 2419 (1994).

Shaw, J., Appio, L., Zerr, T., & Pontoski, K. (2007). Public eyewitness confidence can be influenced by the presence of other witnesses. *Law and Human Behavior, 31*, 629–652.

Shaw, J., & Porter, S. (2015). Constructing rich false memories of committing crime. *Psychological Science, 26*, 291–301.

Shaw, L. A. (2010). Divorce mediation outcome research: A meta-analysis. *Conflict Resolution Quarterly, 27*, 447–467.

Sheldon, K., & Krieger, L. (2004). Does legal education have undermining effects on law students? Evaluating changes in motivation, values, and well being. *Behavioral Sciences & the Law, 22*, 261–286.

Sheldon, K., & Krieger, L. (2007). Understanding the negative effects of legal education on law students: A longitudinal test of self-determination theory. *Personality and Social Psychology Bulletin, 33*, 883–897.

Sheley, J. F. (1985). *America's "crime problem": An introduction to criminology.* Belmont, CA: Wadsworth.

Shepherd, J., & Kang, M. (2014). *Citizens United*, television advertising and state supreme court justices' decisions in criminal cases. Retrieved from skewedjustice.org

Sherman, L. W., & Berk, R. A. (1984). *The Minneapolis domestic violence experiment.* Washington, DC: Police Foundation.

Shestowsky, D. (2014). The psychology of procedural preference: How litigants evaluate legal procedures ex ante. *Iowa Law Review, 99*, 637–710.

Shulman, K. I., Cohen, C. A., & Hull, I. (2004). Psychiatric issues in retrospective challenges of testamentary capacity. *International Journal of Geriatric Psychiatry, 20*, 63–69.

Shuman, D. W., & Champagne, A. (1997). Removing the people from the legal process: The rhetoric and research on judicial selection and juries. *Psychology, Public Policy, and Law, 3*, 242–258.

Shusman, E., Inwald, R., & Landa, B. (1984). Correction officer job performance as predicted by the IPI and MMPI. *Criminal Justice and Behavior, 11*, 309–329.

Sickmund, M., & Puzzanchera, C. (Eds.). (2014). *Juvenile offenders and victims: 2014 national report.* Pittsburgh, PA: National Center for Juvenile Justice.

Siegel, A. M., & Elwork, A. (1990). Treating incompetence to stand trial. *Law and Human Behavior, 14*, 57–65.

Sigillo, A. (2015). Promoting positive perceptions of justice by listening to children's sentiment in custody decisions. In M. Miller, J. Blumenthal, & J. Chamberlain (Eds.), *Handbook of community sentiment* (pp. 173–182). New York, NY: Springer.

Silver, E. (1995). Punishment or treatment? Comparing the lengths of confinement of successful and unsuccessful insanity defendants. *Law and Human Behavior, 19*, 375–388.

Silver, E., Cirincione, C., & Steadman, H. J. (1994). Demythologizing inaccurate perceptions of the insanity defense. *Law and Human Behavior, 18*, 63–70.

Silver, R. B., & Silver, D. B. (2009). The Sieve Model: An innovative process for identifying alternatives to custody evaluations. *Conflict Resolution Quarterly, 26*, 333–348.

Singleton, J. V., & Kass, M. (1986). Helping the jury understand complex cases. *Litigation, 12*, 11–13, 59.

Skagerberg, E., & Wright, D. (2008). Co-witness feedback in lineups. *Applied Cognitive Psychology, 21*, 489–497.

Skeem, J., & Bibeau, L. (2008). How does violence potential relate to Crisis Intervention Team responses to emergencies? *Psychiatric Services, 59*, 201–204.

Skeem, J., Emke-Francis, P., & Eno Louden, J. (2006). Probation, mental health, and mandated treatment: A national survey. *Criminal Justice and Behavior, 33*, 158–184.

Skeem, J., Encandela, J., & Eno Louden, J. (2003). Perspectives on probation and mandated mental health treatment in specialized and traditional probation departments. *Behavioral Sciences and the Law, 21*, 429–458.

Skeem, J., & Eno Louden, J. (2006). Toward evidence-based practice for probationers and parolees mandated to mental health treatment. *Psychiatric Services, 57*, 333–342.

Skeem, J., Eno Louden, J., Manchak, S., Vidal, S., & Haddad, E. (2009). Social networks and social control of probationers with co-occurring mental and substance abuse problems. *Law and Human Behavior, 33*, 122–135.

Skeem, J. L., Golding, S. L., Cohn, N. B., & Berge, G. (1998). Logic and reliability of evaluations of competence to stand trial. *Law and Human Behavior, 22*, 519–548.

Skeem, J., & Golding, S. L. (2001). Describing jurors' personal conceptions of insanity and their relationship to case judgments. *Psychology, Public Policy, and Law, 7*, 561–621.

Skeem, J., & Lowenkamp, C. (2016). Risk, race, and recidivism: Predictive bias and disparate impact. *Criminology, 54*, 680–712.

Skogan, W. G., Steiner, L., DuBois, J., Gudell, J. E., & Fagan, A. (2002). *Community policing and "the new immigrants": Latinos in Chicago* (NCJ 189908). Washington, DC: U.S. Department of Justice, Office of Justice Programs, National Institute of Justice.

Slater, D., & Hans, V. P. (1984). Public opinion of forensic psychiatry following the *Hinckley* verdict. *American Journal of Psychiatry, 141*, 675–679.

Slesnick, N., & Prestopnik, J. (2009). Comparison of family therapy outcome with alcohol-abusing, runaway adolescents. *Journal of Marital and Family Therapy, 35*, 255–277. doi:10.1111/j.1752-0606.2009.00121.x

Sloat, L. M., & Frierson, R. L. (2005). Juror knowledge and attitudes regarding mental illness verdicts. *Journal of the American Academy of Psychiatry and Law, 33*, 208–213.

Slobogin, C. (2011). Prevention of sexual violence by those who have been sexually violent. *International Journal of Law and Psychiatry, 34*, 210–216.

Slobogin, C. (2014). Lessons from inquisitorialism. *Southern California Law Review, 87*, 699–731.

Slobogin, C., & Fondacaro, M. (2011). *Juveniles at risk: A plea for preventive justice.* New York, NY: Oxford University Press.

Slobogin, C., Melton, G., & Showalter, S. R. (1984). The feasibility of a brief evaluation of mental state at the time of the offense. *Law and Human Behavior, 8,* 305–321.

Smalarz, L., & Wells, G. (2015). Contamination of eyewitness self-reports and the mistaken-identification problem. *Current Directions in Psychological Science, 24,* 120–124.

Smith, A. (2008). *Case of a lifetime: A criminal defense lawyer's story.* New York, NY: Palgrave Macmillan.

Smith, A., & Haney, C. (2011). Getting to the point: Attempting to improve juror comprehension of capital penalty phase instructions. *Law and Human Behavior, 35,* 339–350.

Smith, C. A., & Farrington, D. C. (2004). Continuities in antisocial behavior and parenting across three generations. *Journal of Child Psychology & Psychiatry, 45,* 230–247.

Smith, D., Chamberlain, P., & Eddy, J. (2010). Preliminary support for multidimensional treatment foster care in reducing substance use in delinquent boys. *Journal of Child and Adolescent Substance Abuse, 19,* 343–358. doi:10.1080/1067828X.2010.511986

Smith, P., Goggin, C., & Gendreau, P. (2002). *The effects of prison sentences and intermediate sanctions on recidivism: General effects and individual differences.* Ottawa, ON: Public Safety Canada. (User Report 2002-01).

Smith, S. (1989). Mental health expert witnesses: Of science and crystal balls. *Behavioral Sciences & the Law, 7,* 145–180.

SmithKline Beecham Corp. v. Abbott Labs., 740 F.3d 471 (9th. Cir. 2014)

Snook, B., Cullen, R., Bennell, C., Taylor, P., & Gendreau, P. (2008). The criminal profiling illusion: What's behind the smoke and mirrors? *Criminal Justice and Behavior, 35,* 1257–1276.

Snook, B., Eastwood, J., Gendreau, P., Goggin, C., & Cullen, R. (2007). Taking stock of criminal profiling: A narrative review and meta-analysis. *Criminal Justice and Behavior, 34,* 437–453.

Snyder, H., & Sickmund, M. (2006). *Juvenile offenders and victims: 2006 national report.* Washington, DC: U.S. Department of Justice, Office of Justice Programs, Office of Juvenile Justice and Delinquency Prevention. (NCJ No. 212906).

Socia, K. M., 2012. The efficacy of county-level sex offender residence restrictions in New York. *Crime & Delinquency, 58,* 612–642.

Solomon, P., & Draine, J. (1995). Jail recidivism in a forensic case management program. *Health and Social Work, 20,* 167–173.

Solomon, P., Draine, J., & Marcus, S. (2002). Predicting incarceration of clients of a psychiatric probation and parole service. *Psychiatric Services, 53,* 50–56.

Solomon, R. C. (1990). *A passion for justice.* Reading, MA: Addison-Wesley.

Sommers, S. (2006). On racial diversity and group decision making: Identifying multiple effects of racial composition on jury deliberations. *Journal of Personality and Social Psychology, 90,* 597–612.

Sommers, S. (2007). Race and decision making of juries. *Legal and Criminological Psychology, 12,* 171–187.

Sommers, S. (2008). Determinants and consequences of jury racial diversity: Empirical findings, implications, and directions for future research. *Social Issues and Policy Review, 2,* 65–102.

Sommers, S., & Kassin, S. (2001). On the many impacts of inadmissible testimony: Selective compliance, need for cognition, and the overcorrection bias. *Personality and Social Psychology Bulletin, 27,* 1368–1377.

Sommers, S., & Norton, M. (2007). Race-based judgments, race-neutral justifications: Experimental examination of peremptory use and the *Batson* challenge procedure. *Law and Human Behavior, 31,* 261–273.

Sommers, S., Warp, L., & Mahoney, C. (2008). Cognitive effects of racial diversity: White individuals information processing in heterogeneous groups. *Journal of Experimental Social Psychology, 44,* 1129–1136.

Sommers, S., & Ellsworth, P. C. (2000). Race in the courtroom: Perceptions of guilt and dispositional attributions. *Personality and Social Psychology Bulletin, 26,* 1367–1379.

Sorenson, J., & Davis, J. (2011). Violent criminals locked up: Examining the effect of incarceration on behavioral continuity. *Journal of Criminal Science, 39,* 151–158.

Sorenson, S. B., & White, J. W. (1992). Adult sexual assault: Overview of research. *Journal of Social Issues, 48,* 1–8.

Soskis, D. A., & Van Zandt, C. R. (1986). Hostage negotiation: Law enforcement's most effective nonlethal weapon. *Behavioral Sciences & the Law, 4,* 423–436.

Sowell v. Walker, 755 A. 2d 438 (2000).

Spano, L., Daftary-Kapur, T., & Penrod, S. (2011). Trial consulting in high-publicity cases. In B. Rosenfeld & S. Penrod (Eds.), *Research methods in forensic psychology* (pp. 215–236). New York, NY: Wiley.

Spence, S. A., Kaylor-Hughes, C., Brook, M., Lankappa, S. T., & Wilkinson, I. D. (2008). "Munchausen's syndrome by proxy" or a "miscarriage of justice"? An initial application of functional neuroimaging to the question of guilt versus innocence. *European Psychiatry, 23,* 309–314.

Spencer, B. (2007). Estimating the accuracy of jury verdicts. *Journal of Empirical Legal Studies, 4,* 305–329.

Spencer, S. (2013, August 30). NFL concussion class-action lawsuit settles for $765 mil. *The Legal Intelligencer.* Retrieved from http://www.thelegalintelligencer.com/id=1202617468396/NFL-Concussion-Class-Action-Lawsuit-Settles-for-$765-Mil

Spilbor, J. M. (2004, October 28). *The sexual harassment case against Fox News's Bill O'Reilly: Why winning may be O'Reilly's costliest option.* Retrieved September 1, 2005, from http://writ.news.findlaw.com/commentary/20041028_spilbor.html

Spitz, H. (1989). Variations in Wechsler interscale IQ disparities at different levels of IQ. *Intelligence, 13,* 157–167.

Spohn, C. (2015). Race, crime, and punishment in the twentieth and twenty-first centuries. *Crime and Justice, 44,* 49–97.

Spohn, C., Gruhl, J., & Welch, S. (1981). The effect of race on sentencing: A re-examination of an unsettled question. *Law and Society Review, 16,* 71–88.

Sporer, S. (2001). Recognizing faces of other ethnic groups: An integration of theories. *Psychology, Public Policy, and Law, 7,* 170–200.

Sprague, J., & Walker, H. (2000). Early identification and intervention for youth with antisocial and violent behavior. *Exceptional Children, 66,* 367–380.

State v. Henderson (No. 062218), (N.J. Supreme Court 2011).

State v. Lawson. 352 Or. 724, 291 P.3d 673 (2012).

State v. Lozano, 616 So. 2d 73 (Fla. App. 1993).

Steadman, H. J., & Naples, M. (2005). Assessing the effectiveness of jail diversion programs for persons with serious mental illness and co-occurring substance use disorders. *Behavioral Sciences & the Law, 23,* 163–170.

Steadman, H. J., & Braff, J. (1983). Defendants not guilty by reason of insanity. In J. Monahan & H. J. Steadman (Eds.), *Mentally disordered offenders: Perspectives from law and social science* (pp. 109–132). New York, NY: Plenum.

Steadman, H. J., Deane, D. W., Borum, R., & Morrissey, J. P. (2000). Comparing outcomes of major models of police responses to mental health emergencies. *Psychiatric Services, 51,* 5, 645–649.

Steadman, H. J., McGreevy, M., Morrissey, J., Callahan, L., Robbin, P., & Cirincione, C. (1993). *Before and after Hinckley: Evaluating insanity defense reform.* New York, NY: Guilford.

Steadman, H. J., Osher, F. C., Robbins, P. C., Case, B., Samuels, S. (2009). Prevalence of serious mental illness among jail inmates. *Psychiatric Services, 60,* 761–765.

Steadman, H. J., & Veysey, B. (1997). *Providing services for jail inmates with mental disorders.* Retrieved February 8, 2009, from http://www.ncjrs.gov./txtfiles/162207.txt

Steblay, N. (2015). Eyewitness memory. In B. Cutler & P. Zapf (Eds.), *APA Handbook of forensic psychology, Vol. 2. Criminal investigation, adjudication, and sentencing outcomes* (pp. 187–224). Washington, DC: APA.

Steblay, N., Besirevic, J., Fulero, S., & Jiminez-Lorente, B. (1999). The effects of pretrial publicity on jury verdicts: A meta-analytic review. *Law and Human Behavior, 23,* 219–235.

Steblay, N., Dysart, J., & Wells, G. (2011). Seventy-two tests of the sequential lineup superiority effect: A meta-analysis and policy discussion. *Psychology, Public Policy, and Law, 17,* 99–139.

Steblay, N., Hosch, H., Culhane, S., & McWerthy, A. (2006). The impact on juror verdicts of judicial instruction to disregard inadmissible evidence: A meta-analysis. *Law and Human Behavior, 30,* 469–492.

Steblay, N. (2013). Lineup instructions. In B. Cutler (Ed.), *Reform of eyewitness identification procedures* (pp. 65–81). Washington, DC: APA.

Steblay, N., Wells, G., & Douglass, A. B. (2014). The eyewitness post-identification feedback effect 15 years later: Theoretical and policy implications. *Psychology, Public Policy, and Law, 20,* 1–18.

Steffensmeier, D., & Demuth, S. (2006). Does gender modify the effects of race-ethnicity on criminal sanctioning? Sentences for male and female White, Black, and Hispanic defendants. *Journal of Quantitative Criminology, 22,* 241–261.

Steffensmeier, D., Ulmer, J., & Kramer, J. (1998). The interaction of race, gender, and age and criminal sentencing: The punishment cost of being young, black, and male. *Criminology, 36,* 763–797.

Steinberg, L. (2017). Adolescent brain science and juvenile justice policymaking. *Psychology, Public Policy, and Law, 23,* 410–420.

Steiner, B., & Wright, E. (2006). Assessing the relative effects of state direct file waiver laws on violent juvenile crime: Deterrence or irrelevance? *The Journal of Criminal Law and Criminology, 96,* 1451–1477.

Stevens, R. (1983). *Law school: Legal education in America from the 1850s to the 1980s.* Chapel Hill, NC: University of North Carolina Press.

Stevenson, M., Bottoms, B., Diamond, S., Stec, I., & Pimentel, P. (2008, March). *How jurors discuss a defendant's childhood maltreatment when they are deliberating on death.* Paper presented at the annual conference of the American Psychology-Law Society, Jacksonville, FL.

Stinchcomb, J. (2004). Searching for stress in all the wrong places: Combating chronic organizational stressors in policing. *Police Practice and Research, 5,* 259–277.

Stinson, V., & Cutler, B. (2011). Training of trial consultants. In R. Wiener & B. Bornstein (Eds.), *Handbook of trial consulting* (pp. 331–350). New York, NY: Springer.

Stipanowich, T. (2010). Arbitration: The "new litigation." *University of Illinois Law Review, 2010,* 1–58.

Stolle, D., & Studebaker, C. (2011). Trial consulting and conflicts of interest: An introduction. In R. Wiener & B. Bornstein (Eds.), *Handbook of trial consulting* (pp. 351–370). New York, NY: Springer.

Storm, J., & Graham, J. (2000). Detection of coached general malingering on the MMPI-2. *Psychological Assessment, 12,* 158–165.

Storm, K., & Rothmann, S. (2003). A psychometric analysis of the Maslach Burnout Inventory-General Survey in the South African Police Service. *South African Journal of Psychology, 33,* 219–226.

Stormo, K. J., Lang, A. R., & Stritzke, W. G. K. (1997). Attributions about acquaintance rape: The role of alcohol and individual differences. *Journal of Applied Social Psychology, 27,* 279–305.

Strauder v. West Virginia, 100 U.S. 303 (1880).

Straus, M. (2011). Gender symmetry and mutuality in perpetration of clinical-level partner violence: Empirical evidence and implications for prevention and treatment. *Aggression and Violent Behavior, 16,* 279–288.

Straus, M. A., & Gelles, R. J. (1988). How violent are American families? Estimates from the National Family Violence Resurvey and other studies. In G. T. Hotaling, D. Finkelhor, J. T. Kirkpatrick, & M. A. Straus (Eds.), *Family abuse and its consequences* (pp. 14–36). Thousand Oaks, CA: Sage.

Strier, F. (1999). Whither trial consulting? Issues and projections. *Law and Human Behavior, 23,* 93–115.

Strier, F. (2011). Reform proposals. In R. Wiener & B. Bornstein (Eds.), *Handbook of trial consulting* (pp. 371–392). New York, NY: Springer.

Strömwall, L., & Granhag, P. (2003). How to detect deception? Arresting the beliefs of police officers, prosecutors and judges. *Psychology, Crime and Law, 9,* 19–36.

Stromwall, L., & Willen, R. (2011). Inside criminal minds: Offenders' strategies when lying. *Journal of Investigative Psychology and Offender Profiling, 8,* 271–281.

Stryker, J. (2005). *Using shame as punishment. Have sex, get infamous.* Retrieved from http://articles.sfgate.com/2005-03-13/opinion/17365359_1_shame-prostitution-legal-system

Studebaker, C., Robbennolt, J., Penrod, S., Pathak-Sharma, M., Groscup, J., & Devenport, J. (2002). Studying pretrial publicity effects: New methods for improving ecological validity and testing external validity. *Law and Human Behavior, 26,* 19–42.

Studebaker, C. A., & Penrod, S. D. (1997). Pretrial publicity: The media, the law and common sense. *Psychology, Public Policy, and Law, 3,* 428–460.

Stukas, A., & Snyder, M. (2002). Targets' awareness of expectations and behavioral confirmation in ongoing interactions. *Journal of Experimental Social Psychology, 38,* 31–40.

Suarez, E., & Gadalla, T. (2010). Stop blaming the victim: A meta-analysis on rape myths. *Journal of Interpersonal Violence, 25,* 2010–2035.

Suchotzki, K., Verschuere, B., Bockstaele, B., Ben-Shakhar, G., & Crombez, G. (2017). Lying takes time: A meta-analysis on reaction time measures of deception. *Psychological Bulletin, 143,* 428–453.

Sullivan, C. M., & Bybee, D. I. (1999). Reducing violence using community-based advocacy for women with abusive partners. *Journal of Consulting and Clinical Psychology, 67,* 43–53.

Sunstein, C., Hastie, R., Payne, J., Schkade, D., & Viscusi, W. (2002). *Punitive damages: How juries decide.* Chicago, IL: University of Chicago Press.

Susman, D. (1992). *Effects of three different legal standards on psychologists' determinations of competency for execution.* Unpublished doctoral dissertation, University of Kentucky, Lexington.

Sutherland, E. H., & Cressey, D. R. (1974). *Principles of criminology* (9th ed.). New York, NY: Lippincott.

Swahn, M. H., Whitaker, D. J., Pippen, C. B., Leeb, R. T., Teplin, L. A., Abram, K. M., & McClelland, G. M. (2006). Concordance between self-reported maltreatment and court records of abuse or neglect among high-risk youths. *American Journal of Public Health: Mental Health for Individuals and Communities, 96,* 1849–1853.

Swain v. Alabama, 380 U.S. 202 (1965).

Sydeman, S. J., Cascardi, M., Poythress, N. G., & Ritterband, L. M. (1997). Procedural justice in the context of civil commitment: A critique of Tyler's analysis. *Psychology, Public Policy, and Law, 3,* 207–221.

Tanay, E. (2010). *American legal injustice: Behind the scenes with an expert witness.* Lanham, MD: Jason Aronson.

Tangney, J. P., Stuewig, J., & Hafez, L. (2011). Shame, guilt, and remorse: Implications for offender populations. *Journal of Forensic Psychiatry & Psychology, 22,* 706–723.

Tanha, M., Beck, C., Figueredo, A., & Raghavan, C. (2010). Sex differences in intimate partner violence and the use of coercive control as a motivational factor for intimate partner violence. *Journal of Interpersonal Violence, 25,* 1836–1854.

Tanielian, T., & Jayco, L., (Eds.) (2008). *Invisible wounds of war: Psychological and cognitive injuries, their consequences, and services to assist recovery*. Santa Monica, CA: RAND Corporation.

Tarasoff v. Regents of the University of California, 529 P. 2d 553 (1974), 551 P. 2d 334 (1976).

Task Force on Community Preventive Services. (2007). Effects on violence of laws and policies facilitating the transfer of youth from the juvenile to the adult justice system. *MMWR: Recommendations and Reports*. Atlanta, GA: Centers for Disease Control. Retrieved April 22, 2011, from https://www.cdc.gov/mmwr/preview/mmwrhtml/rr5609a1.htm?__hstc=26100450.e2973a808d9cc23acf24fb9805991941.1472428800125.1472428800127.1472428800128.2&__hssc=26100450.1.1472428800128&__hsfp=1773666937

Taylor, G. (1992, March 2). Justice overlooked. *National Law Journal*, p. 43.

Taylor, J., & Krauss, D. (2014). Revisiting intellectual disability and the death penalty. *APA Monitor, 45*, 26.

Taylor, S. E., Klein, L. C., Lewis, B. P., Gruenewald, T. L., Gurung, R. A. R., & Updegraff, J. A. (2000). Biobehavioral responses to stress in females: Tend-and-befriend, not fight-or-flight. *Psychological Review, 107*, 411–429.

Tedder-King, A., & Marinakis, C. (2016, October 3). Cut the bull: What can trial consultants really do? Retrieved from http://litigationinsights.com/jury-consulting/bull-cbs-trial-consultants-really-do/

Tehrani, J., & Mednick, S. (2000). Genetic factors and criminality. *Federal Probation, 64*, 24–28.

Teigen, A. (2017, April 17). Juvenile age of jurisdiction and transfer to adult court laws. Retrieved July 12, 2017, from http://www.ncsl.org/research/civil-and-criminal-justice/juvenile-age-of-jurisdiction-and-transfer-to-adult-court-laws.aspx

Teller, J., Munetz, M., Gil, K., & Ritter, C. (2006). Crisis Intervention Team training for police officers responding to mental disturbance calls. *Psychiatric Services, 57*, 232–237.

Temcheff, C. E., Serbin, L. A., Martin-Storey, A. Stack, D. M., Hodgins, S., Ledingham, J., & Schwartzman, A. E. (2008). Continuity and pathways from aggression in childhood to family violence in adulthood: A 30-year longitudinal study. *Journal of Family Violence, 23*(4), 231–242.

Tennessee v. Garner, 471 U.S. 1 (1985).

Teplin, L. A., (2000, July). Keeping the peace: Police discretion and mentally ill persons. *National Institute of Justice Journal*, 8–15.

Teplin, L. A. (1984). The criminalization of the mentally ill: Speculation in search of data. In L. A. Teplin (Ed.), *Mental health and criminal justice* (pp. 63–85). Newbury Park, CA: Sage.

Terman, L. M. (1917). A trial of mental and pedagogical tests in a civil service examination for policemen and firemen. *Journal of Applied Psychology, 1*, 17–29.

Terpstra, D. E., & Baker, D. D. (1988). Outcomes of sexual harassment charges. *Academy of Management Journal, 31*, 185–194.

Terpstra, D. E., & Baker, D. D. (1992). Outcomes of federal court decisions on sexual harassment. *Academy of Management Journal, 35*, 181–190.

Terpstra, J., & Schaap, D. (2013). Police culture, stress conditions, and working styles. *European Journal of Criminology, 10*, 59–73. doi:10.1177/1477370812456343

Terrell, J., & Weaver, C. (2008). Eyewitness testimony in civil litigation: Retention, suggestion, and misinformation in product identification. *North American Journal of Psychology, 10*, 323–346.

Thibaut, J., & Walker, L. (1975). *Procedural justice: A psychological analysis*. Hillsdale, NJ: Erlbaum.

Thibaut, J., & Walker, L. (1978). A theory of procedure. *California Law Review, 66*, 541–566.

Thomas, C. (1996, April 8). *Judging*. Invited address, School of Law, University of Kansas, Lawrence, KS.

Thomas, S. (2017). What happened to the American jury? Proposals for revamping plea bargaining and summary judgment. *Litigation, 43*. Retrieved from https://ssrn.com/abstract=2974069

Thompson, M., Osher, F., & Tomasini-Joshi, D. (2007). *Improving responses to people with mental illnesses: The essential elements of a mental health court*. New York, NY: Council of State Governments Justice Center.

Thompson, W. C., Cowan, C. L., Ellsworth, P. C., & Harrington, J. C. (1984). Death penalty attitudes and conviction proneness: The translation of attitudes into verdicts. *Law and Human Behavior, 8*, 95–113.

Thornton, H. (1995). *Hung jury: The diary of a Menendez juror*. Philadelphia, PA: Temple University Press.

Tiede, L., Carp, R., & Manning, K. L. (2010). Judicial attributes and sentencing-deviation cases: Do sex, race, and politics matter? *Justice System Journal, 31*, 249–272.

Tillbrook, C., Mumley, D., & Grisso, T. (2003). Avoiding expert opinions on the ultimate legal question: The case for integrity. *Journal of Forensic Psychology Practice, 3*, 77–87.

Tjaden, P., & Thoennes, N. (2000). *Full report of the prevalence, incidence, and consequences of violence against women*. Washington, DC: National Institute of Justice, Office of Justice Programs. (NCJ 13781).

Tjaden, P., & Thoennes, N. (2006). *Extent, nature, and consequences of rape victimization: Findings from the National Violence Against Women Survey*. Washington, DC: National Institute of Justice, Office of Justice Programs.

Tolin, D., & Foa, E. (2006). Sex differences in trauma and post-traumatic stress disorder: A quantitative review of 25 years of research. *Psychological Bulletin, 132*, 959–992. doi:10.1037/0033-2909.132.6.959

Tombaugh, T. (1997). *TOMM: Test of Memory Malingering manual*. Toronto, ON: Multi-Health Systems.

Tonry, M. (1996). *Sentencing matters*. New York, NY: Oxford University Press.

Tonry, M., & Melewski, M. (2008). The malign effects of drug and crime control policies on Black Americans. *Crime and Justice, 37*, 1–44.

Toobin, J. (1996, December 9). Asking for it. *New Yorker*, pp. 55–60.

Toot, J., Dunphy, G., Turner, M., & Ely, D. (2004). The SHR Y-chromosome increases testosterone and aggression, but decreases serotonin as compared to the WKY Y-chromosome in the rat model. *Behavioral Genetics, 34*, 515–524.

Torres, A., Boccaccini, M., & Miller, H. (2006). Perceptions of the validity and utility of criminal profiling among forensic psychologists and psychiatrists. *Professional Psychology: Research and Practice, 37*, 51–58.

Trahan, L., Stuebing, K., Fletcher, J., & Hiscock, M. (2014). The Flynn effect: A meta-analysis. *Psychological Bulletin, 140*, 1332–1360.

Travis, J. (2007). Back-end sentencing: A practice in search of a rationale. *Social Research, 74*, 631–44.

Trinkner, R., Tyler, T., & Goff, P. (2016). Justice form within: The relations between a procedurally just organizational climate and police organizational efficiency, endorsement of democratic policing, and officer well-being. *Psychology, Public Policy, and Law, 22*, 158–172.

Trivedi, S. B. (2011). Intellectual differences between violent and nonviolent juveniles: Utilizing the Wechsler Abbreviated Scale of Intelligence: A study of three ethnic groups. *Dissertation Abstracts International: Section B: The Sciences and Engineering, 71*(10-B), 6454.

Trop v. Dulles, 356 U.S. 86 (1958).

Trope, Y., & Liberman, N. (2003). Temporal construal. *Psychological Review, 110*, 403–421.

Trulson, C., Caudill, J., Belshaw, S., & DeLisi, M. (2011). A problem of fit: Extreme delinquents, blended sentencing, and the determinants of continued adult sanctions. *Criminal Justic Policy Review, 22,* 263–284.

Trulson, C., Haerle, D., DeLisi, M., & Marquart, J. (2011). Blended sentencing, early release, and recidivism of violent institutionalized delinquents. *Prison Journal, 92,* 255–278.

Trupin, E., & Richards, H. (2003). Seattle's mental health courts: Early indicators of effectiveness. *International Journal of Law & Psychiatry, 26,* 33–53.

Tsai, T., & Scommegna, P. (2012). U.S. has world's highest incarceration rate. *Population Reference Bureau.* Retrieved from http://www.prb.org/Publications/Articles/2012/us-incarceration.aspx

Tsushima, W. T., Foote, R., Merrill, T. S., & Lehrke, S. A. (1996). How independent are independent psychological examinations? A workers' compensation dilemma. *Professional Psychology: Research and Practice, 27,* 626–628.

Tuohy, A. P., Wrennall, M. J., McQueen, R. A., & Stradling, S. G. (1993). Effect of socialization factors on decisions to prosecute: The organizational adaptation of Scottish police recruits. *Law and Human Behavior, 17,* 167–182.

Turkheimer, E., & Parry, C. D. H. (1992). Why the gap? Practice and policy in civil commitment hearings. *American Psychologist, 47,* 646–655.

Turner, S., Greenwood, P., Fain, T., & Deschenes, E. (1999). Perceptions of drug court: How offenders view ease of program completion, strengths and weaknesses, and the impact on their lives. *National Drug Court Institute Review, 2,* 61–85.

Turvey, B. (2012). *Criminal profiling: An introduction to behavioral evidence analysis* (4th ed.). Burlington, MA: Elsevier.

Tyler, T. (1990). *Why people obey the law.* New Haven, CT: Yale University Press.

Tyler, T., & Huo, Y. (2002). *Trust in the law: Encouraging public cooperation with the police and court.* New York, NY: Russell Sage Foundation.

Tyler, T. R., & Jackson, J. (2014). Popular legitimacy and the exercise of legal authority: Motivating compliance, cooperation and engagement. *Psychology, Public Policy, and Law, 20,* 78–95.

U.S. Department of Education, Office for Civil Rights. (2001). *Revised sexual harassment guidance: Harassment of students by school employees, other students, or third parties.* Washington, DC: Author. Retrieved November 10, 2016, from http://www2.ed.gov/about/offices/list/ocr/docs/shguide.pdf

U.S. Department of Justice. (1999). *Eyewitness evidence: A guide for law enforcement.* Washington, DC: Author.

U.S. Equal Employment Opportunity Commission. (2016). *Select task force on the study of harassment in the workforce: Report of co-chairs.* Washington, DC: Author. Retrieved November 10, 2016, from https://www.eeoc.gov/eeoc/task_force/harassment/upload/report.pdf

U.S. Merit Systems Protection Board. (2016). Issues of merit. Retrieved November 14, 2016, from http://www.mspb.gov/netsearch/viewdocs.aspx?docnumber255805&version256094&application-ACROBATW

U.S. Public Health Service. (1999). *Mental health: A report of the Surgeon General.* Rockville, MD: U.S. Department of Health and Human Services, National Institutes of Health, National Institute of Mental Health.

Uchida, C., & Brooks, L. (1988). *Violence against the police: Assaults on Baltimore County Police, 1984–86, final report.* Washington, DC: U.S. Department of Justice.

Ulmer, J., Eisenstein, J., & Johnson, B. (2010). Trial penalties in federal sentencing: Extra-guidelines factors and district variation. *Justice Quarterly, 27,* 560–592.

Umbreit, M., Vos, G., Coates, R., & Lightfoot, E. (2005). Restorative justice in the 21st century: A social movement full of opportunities and pitfalls. *Marquette Law Review, 89,* 251–304.

United States Department of Justice, Community Oriented Policing Services. (2016). *Grants and funding.* Retrieved December 17, 2016, from http://cops.usdoj.gov

United States Office of Personnel Management. (2008). *Structured interviews: A practical guide.* Washington, DC: Author. Retrieved October 27, 2016, from https://www.opm.gov/policy-data-oversight/assessment-and-selection/structured-interviews/guide.pdf

United States Sentencing Commission. (2011). *Report to Congress: Mandatory minimum penalties in the federal criminal justice system.* Retrieved January 8, 2012, from http://www.ussc.gov/Legislative_and_Public_Affairs/Congressional_Testimony_and_Reports/Mandatory_Minimum_Penalties/20111031_RtC_Mandatory_Minimum.cfm

United States v. Angelos, 345 F. Supp. 2d 1227 (2004).

United States v. Booker, 125 S. Ct. 735 (2005).

United States v. McVeigh, 918 F. Supp. 1467 (1996).

United States v. Salerno, 481 U.S. 739 (1987).

United States v. Telfaire, 469 F. 2d 552 (1972).

United States v. Windsor, 133 S. Ct. 2675 (2013)

US Legal LawDigest. (2016). *Insanity defense.* Retrieved April 21, 2017, from http://lawdigest.uslegal.com/criminal-laws/insanity-defense/7204#CurrentApplicationOfTheInsanityDefense

van den Berg, J. W., Smid, W., Schepers, K., Wever, E., van Beek, D., Janssen, E., & Gijs, L. (2017). The predictive properties of dynamic sex offender risk assessment instruments: A meta-analysis. *Psychological Assessment.* Advance online publication.

VanDuyn, A. L. (1999). The scarlet letter branding: A constitutional analysis of community notification provisions in sex offender statues. *Drake Law Review, 47,* 635–659.

Varela, J. G., Scogin, F. R., & Vipperman, R. K. (1999). Development and preliminary validation of a semi-structured interview for the screening of law enforcement candidates. *Behavioral Sciences & the Law, 17,* 467–481.

Vartkessian, E. S. (2011). Dangerously biased: How the Texas capital sentencing statute encourages jurors to be unreceptive to mitigation evidence. *Quinnipiac Law Review, 29,* 237–288.

Vasquez, B., Maddan, S., & Walker, J. (2008). The influence of sex offender registration and notification laws in the United States: A time-series analysis. *Crime and Delinquency, 54,* 175–192.

Vecchi, G. (2009). Conflict and crisis communication: A methodology for influencing and persuading behavioral change. *Annals of the American Psychotherapy Association, 12,* 34–42.

Vecchi, G., Van Hasselt, V., & Romano, S. (2005). Crisis (hostage) negotiation: Current strategies and issues in high-risk conflict resolution. *Aggression and Violent Behavior, 10,* 533–551.

Verlinden, S., Hersen, M., & Thomas, J. (2000). Risk factors in school shootings. *Clinical Psychology Review, 20,* 3–56.

Victor, T. L., & Abeles, N. (2004). Coaching clients to take psychological and neuropsychological tests: A clash of ethical obligations. *Practice Issues in Forensic Psychology, 35,* 373–379.

Vidmar, N. (1998). The performance of the American civil jury: An empirical perspective. *Arizona Law Review, 40,* 849–899.

Vidmar, N. (2002). Case studies of pre- and midtrial prejudice in criminal and civil litigation. *Law and Human Behavior, 26,* 73–106.

Vidmar, N. (2005). Expert evidence, the adversary system, and the jury. *American Journal of Public Health, 95,* S137–S143.

Vidmar, N. (2011). The psychology of trial judging. *Current Directions in Psychological Science, 20,* 58–62.

Vidmar, N., & Hans, V. P. (2007). *American juries: The verdict.* Amherst, NY: Prometheus.

Vidmar, N., & Wolfe, M. (2009). Punitive damages. *Annual Review of Law and Social Sciences, 5,* 179–199.

Viglione, J., Hannon, L., & DeFina, R. (2011). The impact of light skin on prison time for Black female offenders. *Social Science Journal, 48,* 250–258.

Viljoen, J. L., Roesch, R., Ogloff, J. R. P., & Zapf, P. A. (2003). The role of Canadian psychologists in conducting fitness and criminal responsibility evaluations. *Canadian Psychology, 44*, 369–381.

Viljoen, J., Wingrove, T., & Ryba, N. (2008). Adjudicative competence evaluations of juvenile and adult defendants: Judges' views regarding essential components of competence reports. *The International Journal of Forensic Mental Health, 7*, 107–119.

Vinson, K. V., Costanzo, M. A., & Berger, D. E. (2008). Predictors of verdict and punitive damages in high-stakes civil litigation. *Behavioral Sciences & the Law, 26*, 167–186.

Violanti, J. M., & Aron, F. (1994). Ranking police stressors. *Psychological Reports, 75*, 824–826.

Vitacco, M. J., Rogers, R., & Gabel, J. (2009). An investigation of the ECST-R in male pretrial patients: Evaluating the effects of feigning on competency evaluations. *Assessment, 16*, 249–257.

Vitale, J. E., & Newman, J. P. (2001). Using the Psychopathy Checklist—Revised with female samples: Reliability, validity, and implications for clinical utility. *Clinical Psychology: Science & Practice, 8*, 117–132.

Vossekuil, B., Fein, R., Reddy, M., Borum, R., & Modzeleski, W. (2004). *The final report and findings of the safe school initiative: Implications for the prevention of school attacks in the United States.* Washington, DC: United States Secret Service and United States Department of Education.

Vrij, A. (2015). Deception detection. In B. Cutler & P. Zapf (Eds.), *APA handbook of forensic psychology: Vol 2. Criminal investigation, adjudication, and sentencing outcomes* (pp. 225–244). Washington, DC: APA.

Vrij, A., Fisher, R., & Blank, H. (2015). A cognitive approach to lie detection: A meta-analysis. *Legal and Criminological Psychology, 22*, 1–21.

Vrij, A., Granhag, P., & Porter, S. (2010). Pitfalls and opportunities in nonverbal and verbal lie detection. *Psychological Science in the Public Interest, 11*, 89–121.

Vrij, A., Leal, S., Granhag, P. A., Mann, S., Fisher, R. P., Hillman, J., & Spery, K. (2009). Outsmarting the liars: The benefit of asking unanticipated questions. *Law and Human Behavior, 33*, 159–166.

Vrij, A., Mann, S., Fisher, R., Leal, S., Milne, B., & Bull, R. (2008). Increasing cognitive load to facilitate lie detection: The benefit of recalling an event in reverse order. *Law and Human Behavior, 32*, 253–265.

Wade, K., Garry, M., Read, J., & Lindsay, D. (2002). A picture is worth a thousand lies: Using false photographs to create false childhood memories. *Psychonomic Bulletin & Review, 9*, 597–603.

Wainwright v. Witt, 469 U.S. 412 (1985).

Walker, L., La Tour, S., Lind, E. A., & Thibaut, J. (1974). Reactions of participants and observers to modes of adjudication. *Journal of Applied Social Psychology, 4*, 295–310.

Walker, L. E. (1979). *The battered woman.* New York, NY: Harper & Row.

Walker, L. E. (2009). *The battered woman syndrome* (3rd ed.). New York, NY: Springer.

Wallerstein, J., & Blakeslee, S. (2003). *What about the kids? Raising your children before, during, and after divorce.* New York, NY: Hyperion.

Wallerstein, J., Corbin, S., & Lewis, J. (1988). Children of divorce: A ten-year study. In Hetherington, M., & Arasteh, J. (Eds.), *Impact of divorce, single parenting, and stepparenting on children* (pp. 197–214). Hillsdale, NJ: Erlbaum.

Wallerstein, J., & Kelly, J. (1980). *Surviving the breakup.* New York, NY: Basic Books.

Walsh, B. (2012). *Oil spill: Why the BP settlement is just the beginning of the end.* Retrieved April 3, 2012, from http://ecocentric.blogs.time.com/2012/03/03/oil-spill-why-the-bp-settlement-is-just-the-beginning-of-the-end/

Walters, G. (2002). The Psychological Inventory of Criminal Thinking Styles (PICTS): A review and meta-analysis. *Assessment, 9*, 278–291.

Waltz, J., Babcock, J. C., Jacobson, N. S., & Gottman, J. M. (2000). Testing a typology of batterers. *Journal of Consulting and Clinical Psychology, 68*, 658–669.

Wang, J., Iannotti, R., Luk, J., & Nansel, T. (2010). Co-occurrence of victimization from five subtypes of bullying: Physical, verbal, social exclusion, spreading rumors, and cyber. *Journal of Pediatric Psychology, 35*, 1103–1112.

Ward, S. (2007). Pulse of the legal profession. *American Bar Association Journal.* Retrieved October 11, 2008, from http://www.abajournal.com/magazine/article/pulse_of_the_legal_profession/

Warren, E. (1977). *The memoirs of Earl Warren.* Garden City, NY: Doubleday.

Warren, P., Tomaskovic-Devey, D., Smith, W., Zingraff, M., & Mason, M. (2006). Driving while Black: Bias processes and racial disparity in police stops. *Criminology: An Interdisciplinary Journal, 44*, 709–738.

Wasco, S. M. (2004). An ecological study of repeated sexual victimization among college women. *Dissertation Abstracts International: Section B: The Sciences and Engineering, 65*(3-B), 1565.

Waterhouse, G., Ridley, A., Bull, R., La Rooy, D., & Wilcock, R. (2016). Dynamics of repeated interviews with children. *Applied Cognitive Psychology, 30*, 713–721.

Waterman, A., Blades, M., & Spencer, C. (2001). Interviewing children and adults: The effect of question format on the tendency to speculate. *Applied Cognitive Psychology, 15*, 521–531.

Watson, A., Hanrahan, P., Luchins, D., & Lurigio, A. (2001). Mental health courts and the complex issues of mentally ill offenders. *Psychiatric Services, 52*, 477–481.

Watson, A., Ottati, V., Morabito, M., Draine, J., Kerr, A., & Angell, B. (2010). Outcomes of police contacts with persons with mental illness: The impact of CIT. *Administration and Policy in Mental Health and Mental Health Services Research, 37*, 302–317.

Watson, P. (1996). The search for justice—A case for reform in the civil justice system in Britain. *ILSA Journal of International and Comparative Law, 2*, 453.

Wegner, D. M. (1994). Ironic processes of mental control. *Psychological Review, 101*, 34–52.

Weiss, P., Hitchcock, J., Weiss, W., Rostow, C., & Davis, R. (2008). The Personality Assessment Inventory Borderline, Drug, and Alcohol Scales as predictors of overall performance in police officers: A series of exploratory analyses. *Policing & Society, 18*, 301–310.

Weiss, W., Davis, R., Rostow, C., & Kinsman, S. (2003). The MMPI-2 L scale as a tool in police selection. *Journal of Police and Criminal Psychology, 18*, 57–60.

Wells, G. (1978). Applied eyewitness testimony research: System variables and estimator variables. *Journal of Personality and Social Psychology, 36*, 1546–1557.

Wells, G., & Luus, C. (1990). Police lineups as experiments: Social methodology as a framework for properly conducted lineups. *Personality and Social Psychology Bulletin, 16*, 106–117.

Wells, G., Memon, A., & Penrod, S. (2006). Eyewitness evidence: Improving its probative value. *Psychological Science in the Public Interest, 7*, 45–75.

Wells, G., & Quigley-McBride, A. (2016). Applying eyewitness identification research to the legal system: A glance at where we have been and where we could go. *Journal of Applied Research in Memory and Cognition, 5*, 290–294.

Wells, G., & Quinlivan, D. (2009). Suggestive eyewitness identification procedures and the Supreme Court's reliability test in light of eyewitness science: 30 years later. *Law and Human Behavior, 33*, 1–24.

Wells, G., Small, M., Penrod, S., Malpass, R., Fulero, S., & Brimacombe, C. (1998). Eyewitness identification procedures:

Recommendations for lineups and photospreads. *Law and Human Behavior, 22,* 603–647.

Wells, G., Steblay, N., & Dysart, J. (2015). Double-blind lineup procedures using actual eyewitnesses: An experimental test of the sequential versus simultaneous lineup procedure. *Law and Human Behavior, 39,* 1–14.

Wells, G., Wrightsman, L., & Miene, P. (1985). The timing of the defense opening statement: Don't wait until the evidence is in. *Journal of Applied Social Psychology, 15,* 758–772.

Wells, G. (1993). What do we know about eyewitness identification? *American Psychologist, 48,* 553–571.

Wells, G., Small, M., Penrod, S., Malpass, R. S., Fulero, S. M., & Brimacombe, C. A. E. (1998). Eyewitness identification procedures: Recommendations for lineups and photospreads. *Law and Human Behavior, 22,* 603–647.

Welsh, W. (2007). A multisite evaluation of prison-based therapeutic community drug treatment. *Criminal Justice and Behavior, 34,* 1481–1498.

Wetmore, S., Neuschatz, J., & Gronlund, S. (2014). On the power of secondary confession evidence. *Psychology, Crime, and Law, 20,* 339–357.

Wexler, D., & Winick, B. (Eds.). (1996). *Law in a therapeutic key: Developments in therapeutic jurisprudence.* Durham, NC: Carolina Academic Press.

Wexler, D. (1992). Putting mental health into mental health law: Therapeutic jurisprudence. *Law and Human Behavior, 16,* 27–38.

Whalen v. United States, 346 F. 2d 812 (1965).

Whelan, E. (2016, June 6). Law profs Kar/Mazzone on Senate duty on Supreme Court vacancies-Part 1. Retrieved from http://www.nationalreview.com/bench-memos/436237/kar-mazzone-senate-duty

White, J. W., & Sorenson, S. B. (1992). A sociocultural view of sexual assault: From discrepancy to diversity. *Journal of Social Issues, 48,* 187–195.

Whittemore, K. E., & Ogloff, J. R. P. (1995). Factors that influence jury decision making: Disposition instructions and mental state at the time of the trial. *Law and Human Behavior, 19,* 283–303.

Whren et al. v. United States, 517 U.S. 806 (1996).

Widman, L., & Olson, M. (2013). On the relationship between automatic attitudes and self-reported sexual assault in men. *Archives of Sex Behavior, 42,* 813–823.

Widom, C. S., Schuck, A., & White, H. (2006). An examination of pathways from childhood victimization to violence: The role of early aggression and problematic alcohol use. *Violence and Victims, 21,* 675–690.

Widom, C. S. (1989). Child abuse, neglect, and adult behavior: Research design and findings on criminality, violence, and child abuse. *American Journal of Orthopsychiatry, 59,* 355–367.

Widom, C. S. (1992). *The cycle of violence: National Institute of Justice Research in brief.* Washington, DC: U.S. Department of Justice.

Wiener, R., Arnot, L., Winter, R., & Redmond, B. (2006). Generic prejudice in the law: Sexual assault and homicide. *Basic and Applied Social Psychology, 28,* 145–155.

Wiener, R., Bornstein, B., & Voss, A. (2006). Emotion and the law: A framework for inquiry. *Law and Human Behavior, 30,* 231–248.

Wiener, R., & Gutek, B. (1999). Advances in sexual harassment research, theory, and policy. *Psychology, Public Policy, and Law, 5,* 507–518.

Wiener, R., Hurt, L., Russell, B., Mannen, K., & Gasper, C. (1997). Perceptions of sexual harassment: The effects of gender, legal standard, and ambivalent sexism. *Law and Human Behavior, 21,* 71–94.

Wiener, R., Rogers, M., Winter, R., Hurt, L., Hackney, A., Kadela, K., … Morasco, B. (2004). Guided jury discretion in capital murder cases: The role of declarative and procedural knowledge. *Psychology, Public Policy, and Law, 10,* 516–576.

Wiener, R., Winick, B., Georges, L., & Castro, A. (2010). A testable theory of problem-solving courts: Avoiding past empirical and legal failures. *International Journal of Law and Psychiatry, 33,* 417–427.

Wikstrom, P., Ceccato, V., Hardie, B., & Treiber, K. (2010). Activity fields and the dynamics of crime: Advancing knowledge about the role of the environment in crime causation. *Journal of Quantitative Criminology, 26,* 55–87.

Wilcox, P., Sullivan, L., Jones, S., & van Gelder, J. (2014). Personality and opportunity: An integrated approach to offending and victimization. *Criminal Justice and Behavior, 41,* 880–901.

Wilkenfeld, J. (2004). Newly compelling: Reexamining judicial construction of juries in the aftermath of *Grutter v. Bollinger. Columbia Law Review, 104,* 2291–2327.

Wilkinson, R. (2001). Offender reentry: A storm overdue. *Corrections Management Quarterly, 5,* 46–51.

Will, G. (1984, January 22). Fitting laws to dynamic society likened to trousers on 10-year-old. *Lawrence Journal-World,* p. 6.

Williams, C. W., Lees-Haley, P. R., & Djanogly, S. E. (1999). Clinical scrutiny of litigants' self-reports. *Professional Psychology: Research and Practice, 30,* 361–367.

Williams, K., & Houghton, A. (2004). Assessing the risk of domestic violence reoffending: A validation study. *Law and Human Behavior, 24,* 437–455.

Williams, L. M. (1994). Recall of childhood trauma: A prospective study of women's memories of child sexual abuse. *Journal of Consulting and Clinical Psychology, 62,* 1167–1176.

Williams, M. (2016). From bail to jail: The effect of jail capacity on bail decisions. *American Journal of Criminal Justice, 41,* 484–497.

Willness, C. R., Steel, P., & Lee, K. (2007). A meta-analysis of the antecedents and consequences of workplace sexual harassment. *Personnel Psychology, 60,* 127–162. doi:10.1111/j.1744-6570.2007.00067.x

Wilson, A. E., Calhoun, K. S., & Bernat, J. A. (1999). Risk recognition and trauma-related symptoms among sexually revictimized women. *Journal of Consulting and Clinical Psychology, 67,* 705–710.

Wilson, C., Desmarais, S., Nicholls, T., Hart, S., & Brink, J. (2013). Predictive validity of dynamic factors: Assessing violence risk in forensic psychiatric inpatients. *Law and Human Behavior, 37,* 377–388.

Wilson, D., Mitchell, O., & Mackenzie, D. (2006). A systematic review of drug court effects on recidivism. *Journal of Experimental Criminology, 2,* 459–487.

Wilson, J. Q. (1975). *Thinking about crime.* New York, NY: Basic Books.

Wilson, J. Q., & Herrnstein, R. (1985). *Crime and human nature.* New York, NY: Simon & Schuster.

Wilson, T. (2002). *Strangers to ourselves: Discovering the adaptive unconscious.* Cambridge, MA: Harvard University Press.

Winick, B. (1996). Incompetency to proceed in the criminal process: Past, present, and future. In B. D. Sales & D. W. Shulman (Eds.), *Law, mental health, and mental disorder* (pp. 310–340). Pacific Grove, CA: Brooks/Cole.

Winick, B., Wiener, R., Castro, A., Emmert, A., & Georges, L. (2010). Dealing with mentally ill domestic violence perpetrators: A therapeutic jurisprudence judicial model. *International Journal of Law and Psychiatry 33,* 428–439.

Winslade, W. J., & Ross, J. W. (1983). *The insanity plea.* New York, NY: Scribners.

Wissler, R., & Dauber, B. (2007). Court-connected arbitration in the Superior Court of Arizona: A study of its performance and proposed rule changes. *Journal of Dispute Resolution, 2007,* 65–99.

Wistrich, A., Guthrie, C., & Rachlinski, J. (2005). Can judges ignore inadmissible information? The difficulty of deliberately disregarding. *University of Pennsylvania Law Review, 153,* 1251–1345.

Wistrich, A., & Rachlinski, J. (2013). How lawyers' intuitions prolong litigation. *Southern California Law Review, 86,* 571–636.

Wistrich, A., Rachlinski, J., & Guthrie, C. (2015). Heart versus head: Do judges follow the law or follow their feelings? *Texas Law Review, 93*, 855–923.

Witt, P., & Barone, N. (2004). Assessing sex offender risk: New Jersey's methods. *Federal Sentencing Reporter, 16*, 170.

Wixted, J. T., & Wells, G. (2017). The relationship between eyewitness confidence and identification accuracy: A new synthesis. *Psychological Science in the Public Interest, 18*, 10–65.

Woestehoff, S. A., & Meissner, C. A. (2016). Juror sensitivity to false confession risk factors: Dispositional vs. situational attributions for a confession. *Law and Human Behavior, 40*, 564–579.

Wogalter, M., Malpass, R., & McQuiston, D. (2004). A national survey of U.S. police on preparation and conduct of identification lineups. *Psychology, Crime, and Law, 10*, 69–82.

Wolf, S. M. (2009). A study of the differences in trauma related symptoms in adult female rape victims across levels of support systems. *Dissertation Abstracts International: Section B: The Sciences and Engineering, 69*(12-B), 7828.

Wolff, N., Fabrikant, N., & Belenko, S. (2011). Mental health courts and their selection processes: Modeling variation for consistency. *Law and Human Behavior, 35*, 402–412.

Woodrell, D. (1996). *Give us a kiss.* New York, NY: Henry Holt.

Woodworth, M., & Porter, S. (2000). Historical foundations and current applications of criminal profiling in violent crime investigations. *Expert Evidence, 7*, 241–264.

Woolard, J., & Fountain, E. (2016). Serious questions about serious juvenile offenders: Patterns of offending and offenses. In K. Heilbrun, D. DeMatteo, & N. Goldstein (Eds.), *APA handbook of psychology and juvenile justice* (pp. 141–157). Washington, DC: American Psychological Association. doi:10.1037/14643-015

Worden, A., & Carlson, B. (2005). Attitudes and beliefs about domestic violence: Results of a public opinion survey. *Journal of Interpersonal Violence, 20*, 1219–1243.

Wordsworth, A. (2005, January 7). Child-killer unfairly convicted, court rules: Expert witness misled jury in Andrea Yates trial. *National Post, Toronto Edition*, p. A13.

Wrightsman, L. (1999). *Judicial decision making: Is psychology relevant?* New York, NY: Kluwer Academic/Plenum Publishers.

Wrightsman, L. (2006). *The psychology of the Supreme Court.* New York, NY: Oxford University Press.

Wrightsman, L. (2010). The Supreme Court on Miranda rights and interrogations: The past, the present, and the future. In G. D. Lassiter & C. Meissner (Eds.), *Police interrogations and false confessions* (pp. 161–178). Washington, DC: American Psychological Association.

Wrightsman, L., & Kassin, S. (1993). *Confessions in the courtroom.* Thousand Oaks, CA: Sage.

Wyatt, G. E., Guthrie, D., & Notgrass, C. M. (1992). Differential effects of women's child sexual abuse and subsequent sexual revictimization. *Journal of Consulting and Clinical Psychology, 60*, 167–173.

Wylie, L., Knutson, A., & Greene, E. (2017). Extraordinary and compelling: The use of compassionate release laws in the United States. *Psychology, Public Policy, and Law.*

Yip, J., & Schweitzer, M. (2016). Mad and misleading: Incidental anger promotes deception. *Organizational Behavior and Human Decision Processes, 137*, 207–217.

York, E., & Cornwell, B. (2006). Status on trial: Social characteristics and influence in the jury room. *Social Forces, 85*, 455–477.

Young, C. (2014). Employing virtual reality technology at trial: New issues posed by rapid technological advances and their effects on jurors' search for "the truth". *Texas Law Review, 93*, 257–274.

Youngjohn, J. (1995). Confirmed attorney coaching prior to neuropsychological evaluation. *Assessment, 2*, 279–283.

Zamble, E. (1992). Behavior and adaptation in long-term prison inmates. *Criminal Justice and Behavior, 19*, 409–425.

Zapf, P., Boccaccini, M., & Brodsky, S. (2003). Assessment of competency for execution: Professional guidelines and an evaluation checklist. *Behavioral Sciences & the Law, 21*, 102–120.

Zapf, P., & Roesch, R. (1997). Assessing fitness to stand trial: Institution-based evaluations and brief screening interview. *Canadian Journal of Community Mental Health, 16*, 53–66.

Zapf, P., & Roesch, R. (1998). Fitness to stand trial: Characteristics of remands since the 1992 Criminal Code amendments. *Canadian Journal of Psychiatry, 43*, 287–293.

Zapf, P., & Roesch, R. (2009). *Evaluation of competence to stand trial.* New York, NY: Oxford University Press.

Zapf, P., & Roesch, R. (2011). *Evaluation of competence to stand trial.* New York, NY: Oxford.

Zelechoski, A. (2016). Trauma, adverse experience, and offending. In K. Heilbrun, D. DeMatteo, & N. Goldstein (Eds.), *APA handbook of psychology and juvenile justice* (pp. 325–342). Washington, DC: American Psychological Association. doi:10.1037/14643-007

Zelle, H., Romaine, C., & Goldstein, N. (2015). Juveniles' *Miranda* comprehension: Understanding, appreciation, and totality of circumstances factors. *Law and Human Behavior, 30*, 281–293.

Zhang, A., Musu-Gillette, L., & Oudekerk, B. A. (2016). Indicators of school crime and safety: 2015 (NCES 2016-079/NCJ 249758). National Center for Education Statistics, U.S. Department of Education, and Bureau of Justice Statistics, Office of Justice Programs. Washington, DC: U.S. Department of Justice.

Zhang, S., Roberts, R., & Callanan, V. (2006). Preventing parolees from returning to prison through community-based reintegration. *Crime & Delinquency, 52*, 551–571.

Zhao, J., Lovrich, N., & Thurman, Q. (1999). The status of community policing in American cities: Facilitators and impediments revisited. *Policing: An International Journal of Police Strategies and Management, 22*, 74–92.

Zill, N., Morrison, D., & Coiro, M. (1993). Long-term effects of parental divorce on parent-child relationship, adjustment, and achievement in young adulthood. *Journal of Family Psychology, 7*, 91–103.

Zimring, F., Fagan, J., & Johnson, D. (2010). Executions, deterrence, and homicide: A tale of two cities. *Journal of Empirical Legal Studies, 7*, 1–29.

Zimring, F. E., Piquero, A. R., & Jennings, W. G. (2007). Sexual delinquency in Racine: Does early sex offending predict later sex offending in youth and young adulthood? *Criminology & Public Policy, 6*, 507–534.

Zinger, I., & Forth, A. E. (1998). Psychopathy and Canadian criminal proceedings: The potential for human rights abuses. *Canadian Journal of Criminology, 40*, 237–277.

Zonana, H., Bartel, R., Wells, J., Buchanan, J., & Getz, M. (1990). Part II: Sex differences in persons found not guilty by reason of insanity: Analysis of data from the Connecticut NGRI registry. *Bulletin of the American Academy of Psychiatry and Law, 18*, 129–142.

Zora, M. (2012). The real social network: How jurors' use of social media and smart phones affects a defendant's Sixth Amendment rights. *University of Illinois Law Review, 2012*, 577–610.

Zottoli, T., Daftary-Kapur, T., Winters, G., & Hogan, C. (2016). Plea discounts, time pressures, and false-guilty pleas in youth and adults who pleaded guilty to felonies in New York City. *Psychology, Public Policy, and Law, 22*, 250–259.

Zukov, I., Ptacek, R., & Fischer, S. (2008). EEG abnormalities in different types of criminal behavior. *Activitas Nervosa Superior, 50*, 110–113.

Zulawski, D. E., & Wicklander, D. E. (2001). *Practical aspects of interview and interrogation.* Boca Raton, FL: CRC Press.

Name Index

A

Abbasi, H., 183
Abeles, N., 257
Abram, K., 150
Abram, K. M., 132
Abramson, J., 303, 310, 323
Acharya, A. P., 85
Ackerman, M. C., 267, 268
Ackerman, M. J., 267, 268
Adams, B., 245, 337
Adams, R. E., 93
Addie, S., 245
Affleck, K., 362
Ainsworth, P., 156
Ake v. Oklahoma, 241
Akers, R. L., 61
Alegria, M., 130, 131
Alexander, D., 146
Alexander, J., 360
Alexander, K., 115
Alexander, M., 354
Alfini, J. J., 290
Alhabib, S., 132
Alison, E., 161
Alison, L., 161
Allen, T., 374
Allison, J. A., 136
Altschuler, D., 363
Alvarado, G., 131
Ama, S., 367
Amato, P., 266
American Academy of Child and Adolescent Psychiatry, 267
American Academy of Pediatrics, 35
American Bar Association, 38, 191
American Medical Association, 258
American Psychiatric Association, 57, 140
American Psychological Association, 11, 18, 22, 62, 68, 221, 264, 267
American Society of Trial Consultants, 23
Anderson, C., 35
Anderson, K. B., 137
Anderson, M., 330
Anderson, S., 369
Andiloro, N., 185, 191
Andrews, D. A., 69, 244, 329, 355, 356, 364, 371
Andrews, J. A., 82
Antecol, H., 148
Antonio, A., 280
Antrobus, E., 117
Anumba, N., 244
Aos, S., 357, 359, 360, 376
Appelbaum, P., 54, 166, 261, 262
Appio, L., 111
Appleby, S., 172, 175
Aragon, S., 125

Arbisi, P. A., 259
Arbuthnot, J., 359
Arcury, T. A., 93
Arkes, H., 305
Armstrong, B., 372
Arndt, J., 317
Arnot, L., 295
Aron, F., 88
Aronson, J., 168
Arrigo, B. A., 52, 75
Arthur, B., 210
Asendorpf, J. B., 67
Asher, M., 194
Ashworth, C. D., 138
Asscher, J., 357
Associated Press, 104, 339
Association of Family and Conciliation Courts, 267, 269
Atkins v. Virginia, 244, 348, 350
Atlis, M. M., 259
Austin, J., 290, 291
Avery, R. J., 269
Avnaim-Pesso, L., 36
Axsom, D., 131, 142
Axt, J., 284
Ayres, B. D., 343
Ayton, P., 187
Azrael, D., 49, 157

B

Babcock, B., 286
Babcock, J. C., 134
Badcock, R., 155
Badge of Life, 89
Baer, R., 78
Bahara, M., 81, 209
Bailenson, J., 201
Baker, D., 150
Baker, L., 170
Baldus, D. C., 345
Ball, E., 238
Ball, R. A., 53
Bandura, A., 61, 62
Banks v. Goodfellow, 263
Baradaran, S., 187
Baranosky, M., 210
Barbaree, H. E., 138, 144
Barber, L., 75
Barbour, K. A., 135
Barclay, L., 194
Bard, M., 83
Barden, R. C., 250
Barnett, O., 82
Barnoski, R., 357
Barnow, S., 67
Barone, N., 340
Barovick, H., 10

Barr, W. P., 8
Barrett, H., 360
Barry, C., 68
Barry, M., 261
Bartel, R., 238
Bartels, P., 244, 356
Barth, J., 33
Bartlett, F. C., 309
Bartoi, M. G., 141
Bartol, A., 75, 86
Bartol, C. R., 75, 77, 86, 161
Baruch, G., 357
Basora, J., 288, 306
Batson v. Kentucky, 284
Baum, A., 85
Bauserman, R., 265
Baxter, J., 206
Bazelon, D. T., 250
Beall, A., 201
Beattey, R., 185
Beaudry-Cry, M., 335
Bechara, A., 55
Beck, C., 133
Bedau, H., 177
Beech, A. R., 136
Begam, R., 290
Begany, J. J., 150
Beggs, S., 144
Beiser, E. N., 279
Beland, L., 47
Belanger, H., 257
Belenko, S., 214, 366
Belfi, B., 228
Belfrage, H., 272
Bellafante, G., 185
Bellshaw, S., 338
Bench, L., 374
Bennell, C., 161
Benner, A. W., 75
Ben-Shakhar, G., 165, 168
Berge, G., 226
Berger, D. E., 288
Bergeron, L., 376, 377
Bergold, A. N., 112
Berk, R. A., 83
Berkemer v. McCarty, 171
Berkowitz, B., 83
Berman, G., 218
Berman, M. E., 56
Bernat, J. A., 141
Bertman, L., 229
Betts, J., 101
Betts v. Brady, 40
Beyer, M., 245
Bibas, S., 190
Bibeau, L., 80, 210
Bihrle, S., 56

Wong, M., 201
Woodrell, D., 49
Woods-Jaegar, B., 132
Woodworth, G., 345
Woodworth, M., 155, 161
Woody, W., 338
Woolard, J., 67
Worden, A., 133
Wordsworth, A., 222
Wormith, J., 364
Wrennall, M. J., 79
Wright, D., 101, 102, 115, 117
Wright, E., 245
Wrightsman, L. S., 37, 136, 176, 178, 197, 199, 290
Wuensch, K., 242
Wyatt, G. E., 141
Wylie, L., 41, 328
Wynn, B. N., 136

Y
Yamini-Diouf, Y., 368
Yap, S., 146
Yarbrough, A., 295
Yarmel, P. W., 67
Yasuhara, K., 81, 272
Yip, J., 194
Yokum, D., 20
York, E., 288
Young, C., 201
Youngjohn, J., 257

Z
Zamble, E., 374
Zanna, M., 289
Zapf, P., 223, 226, 228, 229, 232, 241
Zaslavska, N., 209
Zeisel, H., 276, 277, 278, 305, 313
Zelechoski, A., 67, 128, 129, 150, 362

Zemba, D., 112
Zerr, T., 111
Zhang, A., 47
Zhang, S., 376, 377
Zhao, J., 92
Zibbell, R., 264, 266, 267
Zill, N., 266
Zimmerman, D. M., 290
Zimmerman, E., 374
Zimring, F., 338
Zinger, I., 60
Zingraff, M., 90
Zonana, H., 210, 238
Zora, M., 312
Zottoli, T., 191
Zukov, I., 55
Zulawski, D. E., 173

Subject Index